International Applied Computational Electromagnetics Society Symposium (ACES 2017)

Firenze, Italy
26 - 30 March 2017

ISBN: 978-1-5108-4285-4

Printed from e-media with permission by:

Curran Associates, Inc.
57 Morehouse Lane
Red Hook, NY 12571

Some format issues inherent in the e-media version may also appear in this print version.

Printed by Curran Associates, Inc. (2017)

The Applied Computational Electromagnetics Society (ACES)
www.aces-society.org

Additional copies of this publication are available from:

Curran Associates, Inc.
57 Morehouse Lane
Red Hook, NY 12571 USA
Phone: 845-758-0400
Fax: 845-758-2633
Email: curran@proceedings.com
Web: www.proceedings.com

2017 International Applied Computational Electromagnetics Society (ACES) Symposium

Firenze, Italy, March 26-30, 2017

ACES 2017 Conference Program

2017 International Applied Computational Electromagnetics Society (ACES) Symposium
Firenze, Italy, March 26-30, 2017

General Chair:	**Sami Barmada**
General Co-Chair:	**Rocco Rizzo**
Technical Program Chairs:	**Mauro Tucci and Atef Elsherbeni**
International Advisory Committee Chairs:	**Ulrich Jakobus, Ozlem Kilic, and Giacomo Oliveri**
Registration and Finance Chair:	**Osama Mohammed**
Awards Committee Chair:	**Andrew Peterson**
Short Course/Tutorials Chair:	**Randy Haupt**
Publication Chair:	**Emanuele Crisostomi**
Sponsorship/Exhibition Chair:	**Sami Barmada**
Publicity Chair:	**C. J. Reddy**
Local Arrangements Chair:	**Zaira Lombardo**
Student Paper Contest Chair:	**Daniel Weile**
Web Masters:	**Kyle Patel and Matthew Inman**
Administrative Assistant:	**Shanell Lopez**

Welcome Message

Welcome to the 2017 International ACES Conference in Firenze!

On behalf of the Applied Computational Electromagnetics Society and the entire conference organization committee, it is with great pleasure to welcome you to the 2017 ACES Conference in Firenze, Italy, the "Cradle of the Renaissance".

I'd like to start this welcome message by thanking you for choosing to participate to our conference; I'd also like to express my gratitude to the session organizers who voluntarily did a great job to raise up the technical level of the event.

We received more than 250 papers and the conference attendees come from more than 20 different countries around the world, renewing once again the success of the ACES annual symposium. The conference is organized in stimulating parallel sessions, seven outstanding plenary presentations by distinguished speakers of our community, exhibits and a great series of tutorials offered for free to the attendees. The usual friendly, but also highly technical atmosphere that you always find at ACES conferences finds a perfect match here in Firenze: you will find yourself immersed in culture, social life, and you will constantly have the feeling of being in an enchanting international gathering place. I definitely hope that you will find your experience fruitful from any point of view.

A few words about Firenze: it originated as a Roman city, and later, after a long period as a flourishing trading and banking medieval commune, it was the birthplace of the Renaissance. It was politically, economically, and culturally one of the most important cities in Europe and the world from the 14th to 16th centuries. The Etruscans first built in 200 BC the small settlement of Fiesole, whereas the present city of Firenze was established by Julius Caesar in 59 BC as a settlement for his veteran soldiers and was named originally Fluentia, owing to the fact that it was built close to a river.

Firenze is now the capital city of the Italian region of Tuscany; it is the most populous city in Tuscany, with almost 400,000 inhabitants, expanding to over 1.5 million in the metropolitan area.

It was declared a World Heritage Site by UNESCO in 1982. The city is noted for its culture, Renaissance art and architecture and monuments. The city also contains numerous museums and art galleries, such as the Uffizi Gallery (make your reservation on the internet before your trip to avoid long lines) and the Palazzo Pitti, exerts an influence in the fields of art, culture and politics, it is a major national economic centre, as well as a tourist and industrial hub.

Due to Florence's artistic and architectural heritage, it has been ranked by Forbes as one of the most beautiful cities in the world, in addition it is ranked in the top 15 fashion capitals of the world.

Welcome to Firenze!

Sami Barmada
ACES President and General Chairman – ACES 2017

2017 International Applied Computational Electromagnetics Society (ACES) Symposium
Firenze, Italy, March 26-30, 2017

Conference Sponsors and Exhibitors

PLANTINUM LEVEL SPONSOR

Altair

EXHIBITORS

CST

Altair

TECHNICAL CO-SPONSORS

IEEE MAGNETICS SOCIETY
- ITALY CHAPTER -

IEEE
MTT-S
- NORTH ITALY CHAPTER-

IEEE
ITALY SECTION

Session Organizers

Peter Aaen
Hakan Bagci
Sami Barmada
Bruno Bisceglia
Lorenzo Codecasa
James B. Cole
Alessandra Costanzo
Vijay Devabhaktuni
Luca Di Rienzo
Ozgur Ergul
Sunday Cookey Expo
Alessandro Fanti
Alessandro Formisano
Simone Genovesi
D'Assunção Levent Gurel
Taha Imeci
Ulrich Jakobus
Li Jiang
Ozlem Kilic
Slawomir Koziel
Antonio Maffucci
Sergey Maksimenko
Salucci Marco
Osama Mohammed
Agostino Monorchio
Paolo Nepa
Salah Obayya
Lara Pajewski
Zhen Peng
Lorenzo Poli
Shishir Punjala
C.J. Reddy
Mohamed Swillam
Antonello Tamburrino
Huseyin Arda Ulku
Lalita Upda

Session Chairs

Hakan Bagci
Salvatore Campione
Victor Chechetkin
William O'Keefe Coburn
James B. Cole
Alessandra Costanzo
Adaildo G. D'Assunção
Vijay Devabhaktuni
Luca Di Rienzo
Achim Dreher
Ozgur Ergul
Alessandro Fanti
Alessandro Formisano
Luca Giaccone
Levent Gurel
Taha Imeci
Ulrich Jakobus
Ozlem Kilic
Slawomir Koziel
Antonio Maffucci
Sergey Maksimenko
Salucci Marco
Osama Mohammed
Agostino Monorchio
Paolo Nepa
Salah Obayya
Lara Pajewski
Lorenzo Poli
Shishir Punjala
Markus Schick
Antonello Tamburrino
Huseyin Arda Ulku
Daniel Weile

2017 International Applied Computational Electromagnetics Society (ACES) Symposium
Firenze, Italy, March 26-30, 2017

Conference Reviewers

Peter Aaen
Abd Arkadan
Ercument Arvas
Sami Barmada
Bruno Bisceglia
Aldo Canova
William Coburn
Lorenzo Codecasa
James Cole
Alessandra Costanzo
María Elena de Cos
Veysel Demir
Vijay Devabhaktuni
Luca Di Rienzo
Alistair Duffy
Sunday Cookey Ekpo
Khaled ElMahgoub
Ozgur Ergul
Alessandro Fanti
Alessandro Formisano
Simone Genovesi
Luca Giaccone
Levent Gurel
Randy Haupt
Nathan Ida
Jamie Infantolino
Ulrich Jakobus
Li Jun Jiang
Yasushi Kanai
Ozlem Kilic
Slawomir Koziel
Rudresh Kumar
Giovanni Leone
Antonio Maffucci
Sergey Maksimenko
Paolo Mezzanotte
Osama Mohammed
Antonino Musolino
Paolo Nepa
Quang Nguyen
Branislav Notaros
Salah Obayya
Lara Pajewski
Zhen Peng
Andrew Peterson
Shishir Punjala
C.J. Reddy
Rocco Rizzo
Vince Rodriguez
Marco Salucci
Kubilay Sertel
Raffaele Solimene
Jiming Song
Jason Soric
Jeyali Subbiah
Mohamed Swillam
Antonio Topa
Mauro Tucci
Huseyin Arda Ulku
Daniel Weile
Douglas Werner
Aihua Wood
Amir Zaghloul

2017 International Applied Computational Electromagnetics Society (ACES) Symposium
Firenze, Italy, March 26-30, 2017

Plenary Speaker

Levent Gurel

ABAKUS Computing Technologies, Turkey
University of Illinois at Urbana-Champaign, USA

(Heterogeneous) Parallel Solutions of Billion-Unknown Problems: Applications and Big-Data Aspects

While tackling some of the largest problems in computational electromagnetics, we have to deal with various aspects of big-data issues routinely. Recently, we have been solving larger than 1,000,000,000x1,000,000,000 (one billion!) dense matrix equations. This effort involves physical understanding of electromagnetics problems, novel parallelization strategies (computer science), constructing parallel clusters (computer architecture), advanced mathematical methods for integral equations, fast solvers, iterative methods, preconditioners, linear algebra, and big data. Furthermore, solving such large problems on a regular basis requires the generation, representation, storage, processing, analysis, transfer and communication, visualization and interpretation of extremely large data sets in the order of multiple terabytes.

Accurate formulations of real-life electromagnetics problems with integral equations necessitate

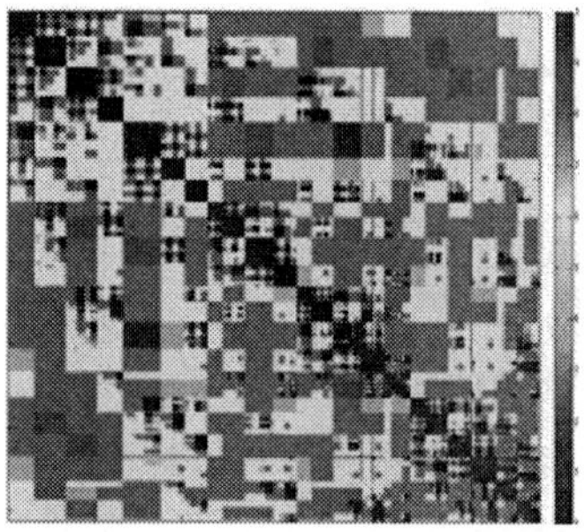

the solution of extremely large dense matrix equations. Solutions of such tremendously challenging problems cannot be achieved with a brute-force approach, even when using the most powerful computers with state-of-the-art petascale computing capabilities. Instead, we have been employing fast algorithms implemented on parallel computers. In the case of heterogeneous architectures, we carefully control the data traffic to/from GPUs. Furthermore, we use MPI and OpenMP simultaneously in a parallelization strategy designed to reduce data duplications among processes so that vast numbers of cores can be efficiently utilized without requiring extra memory.

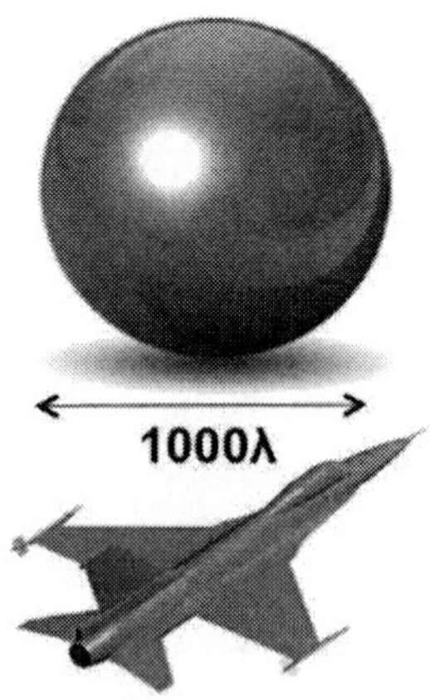

In this talk, I will present fast and accurate solutions of large-scale electromagnetic modeling problems involving three-dimensional geometries that are larger than 1000 wavelengths using the multilevel fast multipole algorithm (MLFMA) and parallel MLFMA. I will mention various applications, including inverse problems. Solving the world's largest computational electromagnetics problems has important implications in terms of obtaining the solutions of future grand-challenge problems in various areas of science, such as imaging, (subsurface) scattering, optics, bioelectromagnetics, metamaterials, nanotechnology, remote sensing, etc. For more information: www.abakus.computing.technology.

Levent Gürel (Fellow of IEEE, ACES, and EMA) received the M.S. and Ph.D. degrees from the University of Illinois at Urbana-Champaign (UIUC) in 1988 and 1991, respectively, in Electrical and Computer Engineering. He worked at the IBM Thomas J. Watson Research Center, Yorktown Heights, New York, in 1991-94. During his 20 years with Bilkent University, he served as the Founding Director of the Computational Electromagnetics Research Center (BiLCEM) and a Professor of Electrical Engineering. He is an Adjunct Professor at UIUC. Prof. Gürel is the Founder and CEO of ABAKUS Computing Technologies, a company that is geared towards advancing the use of cutting-edge computing technologies for solving difficult scientific problems with important real-life applications and societal benefits. Among the recognitions of Prof. Gürel's accomplishments, the two prestigious awards from the Turkish Academy of Sciences (TUBA) in 2002 and the Scientific and Technological Research Council of Turkey (TUBITAK) in 2003 are the most notable. He is conferred the UIUC ECE Distinguished Alumni Award in 2013. He was named an IEEE Distinguished Lecturer for 2011-2014. Prof. Gürel has served as a plenary speaker in various meetings, such as the ACES Conference, the Mediterranean Microwave Symposium, and the TEDx Conference. He has been organizing and serving as the General Chairman and Editor of the biennial Computational Electromagnetics International Workshops held in 2007-2017. He is the coauthor of a monograph titled "The Multilevel Fast Multipole Algorithm (MLFMA) for Solving Large-Scale Computational Electromagnetics Problems" published by Wiley-IEEE Press. In 2015, Prof. Gürel received the IEEE Harrington-Mittra Award in Computational Electromagnetics.

Plenary Speaker

Apostolos Georgiadis

**Heriot-Watt University School of Engineering and Physical Sciences
Scotland, UK**

Wireless Power Transfer and Energy Harvesting for RFID and Wireless Sensors

RFID technology provides a foundation, an enabling technology towards the realization of 'zeropower' wireless sensors and implementing the Internet-of-Things (IoT) and machine-to-machine (M2M) communication. Interest in RFID technology is further enhanced by its fundamental capability for wireless powering of devices, allowing for battery-less operation. The presentation begins with an overview of ambient energy availability and energy harvesting technology challenges for low power circuits and sensors. Design challenges and novel technologies and materials, such as paper, textiles, and inkjet/3D printing are highlighted. Special focus is placed on electromagnetic energy transfer and harvesting for range maximization of passive RFID systems. Rectenna design and optimization under different operating conditions and in different operating frequencies from HF to millimeter waves is addressed. Multiple technology harvesters leading to the development of energy harvesting assisted RFIDs are discussed. Low profile and conformal solar antennas and solar–electromagnetic harvesters including examples implemented on paper and textile substrates are presented. The integration of an antenna with a thermoelectric generator is demonstrated. Finally, waveform optimization in wireless power transfer is addressed, and the ability to improve the RF-DC power conversion efficiency of electromagnetic energy harvesting devices by tailoring the characteristics of the transmitted signals is discussed.

Apostolos Georgiadis was born in Thessaloniki, Greece. He received the Ph.D. degree in Electrical Engineering from the University of Massachusetts at Amherst, in 2002. In 2007, he joined Centre Tecnologic de Telecomunicacions de Catalunya (CTTC), Barcelona, Spain, as a Senior Researcher. In 2013 - 2016 he coordinated the Microwave Systems and Nanotechnology Department at CTTC. In 2016 he joined Heriot-Watt University, Edinburgh, as an Associate Professor. His research interests are energy harvesting, wireless power transfer, RFID technology and active antennas and antenna arrays. He serves as an Associate Editor of the IEEE Microwave Wireless Components Letters and IEEE Journal of RFID. He is Founder and Editor in Chief of Cambridge Wireless Power Transfer journal. He is past Chair of the IEEE MTT-S Technical Committee MTT-24 on RFID Technologies and member of IEEE MTT-26 on wireless energy transfer and conversion. He received the 2014 IEEE RFID-TA Best Paper Award and the 2015 Premium Award for Best Paper in the IET Microwaves, Antennas and Propagation journal. He is Vice-Chair of URSI Commission D Electronics and Photonics. He is Distinguished Lecturer of IEEE Council on RFID. He has contributed to over 150 publications: books, book chapters, technical journals and conferences.

2017 International Applied Computational Electromagnetics Society (ACES) Symposium
Firenze, Italy, March 26-30, 2017

Plenary Speaker

Prof. Giuliano Manara

Dipartimento di Ingegneria dell'Informazione
University of Pisa, Italy

Near-Field Focused Antennas for Short-Range Wireless Systems

Short-range wireless systems often require focusing electromagnetic power in a size-limited spot volume, lying in the antenna radiative near-field region. To cite some applications, we can make reference to non-destructive microwave sensing technologies, objects detection inside lossy media, plasma heating, high data-rate Near Field Communication (NFC) systems, radio frequency and microwave identification and localization, wireless power transfer. As a consequence, antennas must be designed by following unconventional procedures, in particular when electrically large antennas have to be considered. The basic working principles and design criteria of near-field focused microwave antennas will be reviewed in this talk, with specific attention to the main parameters used to characterize such radiating systems. An overview will be provided of several antenna implementations based on different technologies, as for instance: microstrip arrays, leaky wave antennas, planar lens antennas, slotted waveguide antennas, dielectric resonator antennas, reflectarrays and transmitarrays. Some design ideas and prototypes will be also presented.

Giuliano Manara received the Laurea (Doctor) degree in Electronics Engineering (*summa cum laude*) from the University of Florence, Italy, in 1979. Currently, he is a Professor at the School of Engineering of the University of Pisa, Italy. Since 1980, he has been collaborating with the Department of Electrical Engineering of the Ohio State University, Columbus, Ohio, USA, where, in the summer and fall of 1987, he was involved in research at the ElectroScience Laboratory.

His research interests have centered mainly on the asymptotic solution of radiation and scattering problems to improve and extend the uniform geometrical theory of diffraction. In this framework, he has analyzed electromagnetic wave scattering from material bodies, with emphasis on both isotropic and anisotropic impedance wedges. He has also been engaged in research on numerical, analytical and hybrid techniques (both in frequency and time domain), scattering from rough surfaces, frequency selective surfaces (FSS), and electromagnetic compatibility. More recently, his research has also been focused on the design of microwave antennas with application to broadband wireless networks, on the development and testing of new microwave materials (metamaterials), and on the analysis of antennas and propagation problems for Radio Frequency Identification (RFID) systems, including characterization of chipless RFID tags.

Prof. Manara was elected an IEEE (Institute of Electrical and Electronic Engineers) Fellow in 2004 for "contributions to the uniform geometrical theory of diffraction and its applications."

Since 2002 to 2008, he served as the Secretary/Treasurer of the Italian Society on Electromagnetics (Società Italiana di Elettromagnetismo, SIEm). Then, since 2009 to 2015, he served as the Treasurer of SIEm. In May 2004, Prof. Manara was the Chairman of the Organizing Committee for the International Symposium on Electromagnetic Theory of Commission B of the International Union of Radio Science (URSI), which was held in Pisa. He also served as a Special Session Organizer, member of the Technical Pogram Committee and Session Chair of several international conferences organized in the framework of the activities of both IEEE and URSI. In August 2008, he was elected the Vice-Chair of the International Commission B "Fields and Waves" of URSI. He served as the International Chair of URSI Commission B for the triennium 2011-2014. In this context, Prof. Manara was the General Chair of the International Symposium on Electromagnetic Theory (EMTS 2013) of URSI Commission B, held in Hiroshima, Japan, May 20-24, 2013.

2017 International Applied Computational Electromagnetics Society (ACES) Symposium
Firenze, Italy, March 26-30, 2017

Plenary Speaker

Prof. Salah Obayya
Zewail City of Science and Technology
Giza, Egypt

Analysis of Plasmonic and Nano-Photonic Devices

Computational photonics employs numerical methods to study characteristics and propagation of light in optical waveguides. Within this field, numerous techniques had been presented to study the behavior of light and light-matter interactions using analytical and computational models. This emerging field of computational science is playing a critically important role in designing new generations of integrated optical devices. Generally, computational photonics is understood as the alternative of the experimental methods, where the performance of the optical device can be tested on computer. Computational photonics approach reduces development cost and speeds-up development of novel devices. On the other hand, plasmonics recently started to gain increased interest as it is expected to play a vital role in achieving high density integrated photonic circuits. However, the efficient analysis of plasmonic devices is still a challenge facing numerical modeling techniques. There are three categories of problems in computational photonics: frequency-domain eigen solvers, frequency-domain solvers and time-domain simulations. Unfortunately, modeling techniques such as finite difference time domain (FDTD), finite difference frequency domain (FDFD), finite element method (FEM) and complex mode matching methods (CMMM) require huge computational efforts in terms of time and memory and become extremely complicated in dealing with nano-photonic devices and especially plasmonics. In this talk, the recent developments in the field of creation and use of novel, numerically-efficient and yet accurate for analysing plasmonic and nano-photonic devices.

Salah S. A. Obayya received the B.Sc. (first class honors) and M.Sc. degrees in Electronics and Communications Engineering from Mansoura University, Egypt, in 1991 and 1994, respectively. In 1999, and under joint supervision between City University of London and Mansoura University he gained his Ph.D. in Photonics. He joined Zewail City of Science and Technology in 2012 where he is currently the Vice Chairman, Zewail City of Science and Technology, Egypt and previously he was The Director-General of Research Institutes at the same institution. Prior to Zewail City, he took up several academic posts at Brunel University UK (Associate Professor, 2002), University of Leeds, UK (Reader, 2006) and University of South Wales, UK (Chair Professor, 2008) where he was the Founding Director of Photonics Research Center, and recently he was the Founding Director of Center for Photonics and Smart Materials (CPSM) at Zewail City of Science and Technology.

He has built an outstanding international reputation in the area of green nano-photonics with focus on the intelligent computational modeling of modern nano-photonic devices enabling technologies needed to realise low-carbon green society. He has published **160** journal publications, mostly in OSA, IEEE and IET/IEE, authored **2** books (Computational Photonics, Wiley 2010 and Computational Liquid Crystal Photonics, Wiley 2016) both are adopted references for Graduate Programs in Photonics at international Universities, and **210** conference papers in international conference in photonics, many of these are invited talks, and keynote lectures, attracted external funding, from both industry and Research Councils, in the region of **$3M**, and supervised to successful completion **25** Ph.D. students, over **50** M.Sc./M.Res. students and **15** postdoctoral research fellows. He led the team that developed one of the world's best comprehensive numerical packages for the analysis, design and optimization of nano-photonic devices, and subsystems, where a number of "world-first" numerical approaches have been developed. His numerical package has been widely adopted by the Photonics community to analyse, design and optimise the performance of a wide range of nano-photonic devices employed for applications in solar cells, optical telecoms, sensing, optical imaging and other applications.

He has served the International Photonics Society through active contribution to the organization and technical committees of a number of international conferences. Since 2007, he has been an Associate Editor-in-Chief of the IEEE Photonics Technology Letters, and Associate Editor-in-Chief of the Journal of Optical and Quantum Electronics, and served as Guest Editor-in-Chief of J Optical and Quantum Electronics (2010), and acted as Reviewer for many international Photonics Journals such as IEEE J. Lightwave Technology, IEEE Photonics Journal IEEE J. Quantum Electronics, IEEE J. Selected Topics in Quantum Electronics, IET Optoelectronics, OSA Optics Express, OSA Optics Letters, and many others. Moreover, he acted as Technical expert and Reviewer for a number of research funding councils and learnt societies such as Engineering and Physical Sciences Research Council (EPSRC), UK, Royal Society, UK, Royal Academy of Engineering, UK, National Academy of Arts and Sciences, Holland, Science and Technology Development Fund, Egypt, National Telecom Regulatory Authority (NTRA), Egypt and others. He was elected Fellow of the Institute of Engineering and Technology, IET (formerly FIEE), UK, 2010, elected Fellow of The Institute of Physics (IoP), UK, 2010, elected Fellow of The Higher Education Academy, UK, and Senior Member of IEEE, USA, 2005, Member of Board of Academy of Scientific Research and Technology (Egypt's National Academy of Science), Member of Wales Institute of Mathematical and Computational Sciences (WIMCS), UK, Member of Optical Society of America (OSA), Member of International Society for Optical Engineering (SPIE), USA and Member of Applied Computational Electromagnetic Society (ACES).

As remarkable recognition of his research achievements, he was the recipient of many national and international awards and recognitions such as D.Sc. degree in Photonics from City University of London in Jan 2016; a degree awarded only to those who gained international distinction in their own fields, Arab Thought Foundation Award in Scientific Creativity (Lebanon), Dec. 2015; only one award in all fields of Science and Engineering is granted each year for one Arab Scientist, Egyptian Academy of Scientific Research and Technology (ASRT) Award in Engineering Sciences Creativity, Sept. 2014; only one award is granted each year for an Egyptian Scientist in Engineering Sciences, Abdul Hameed Shoman Foundation (Jordan) Award for Arab Scientists in Engineering Sciences, Oct. 2014; only one award is granted each year for one Arab Scientists in Engineering Sciences, State Award of Excellence for Engineering Sciences from the Egyptian State, Sept. 2013; only one scientist is awarded this prestigious award every year, Incentive State Award for Engineering Sciences from the Egyptian State, Sept. 2005, and many others.

2017 International Applied Computational Electromagnetics Society (ACES) Symposium
Firenze, Italy, March 26-30, 2017

Plenary Speaker

Prof. Nathan Ida
Department of Electrical and Computer Engineering
University of Akron, Ohio, USA

Models for AC Induced Corrosion - A New Challenge in Computational Electromagnetics

Corrosion is a major problem with significant economic and safety consequences. The classical model for corrosion is based on electrochemical processes in which exchange of ions in an electrolytic cell lead to formation of corrosion products. This has led to simple resistive-capacitive models to take into account the resistance of the electrolytic cell, the resistance of the media involved and the capacitive effect of the surface potential at the interface between conductors and the electrolyte. Nonlinear elements are sometimes added to the model to explain more complex observed phenomena. To counteract the corrosion process, an opposite flow of ions is employed in what is called passive or active cathodic protection. For some time now it has been ascertained that AC currents not only contribute to corrosion but can actually accelerate the process, whereas existing models and understanding do not allow for these effects. The corrosion that takes place at low and at high frequencies in the presence of existing cathodic protection cannot be predicted by existing models. New models that can take into account both electrical and electrochemical quantities are needed if we are to understand the process of corrosion in the presence of AC. This talk presents some of the existing models including an FEM model that confirms some of the effects observed. However, the main purpose is to challenge the community to take up this new area of activity in computational electromagnetics.

Nathan Ida is currently Distinguished Professor of Electrical and Computer Engineering at the University of Akron, Akron, OH. He teaches electromagnetics, antenna theory, electromagnetic compatibility, sensing and actuation, and computational methods and algorithms. His current research interests include numerical modeling of electromagnetic fields, especially in relation to sensors, electromagnetic wave propagation, theoretical issues in computation, nondestructive testing of materials at low and microwave frequencies as well as in communications, especially in low-power remote control and wireless sensing. He has published extensively on electromagnetic field computation, nondestructive testing of materials, surface impedance boundary conditions, sensing and actuation and others. He is the author or coauthor of six books including a textbook on sensing and actuation and one on engineering electromagnetics and currently serves as editor in chief for Sensing and Imaging (Springer). Dr. Ida is a Life Fellow of the IEEE, Fellow of the IET, Fellow of the American Society of Nondestructive Testing and Fellow of the Applied Computational Electromagnetics Society.

2017 International Applied Computational Electromagnetics Society (ACES) Symposium
Firenze, Italy, March 26-30, 2017

Plenary Speaker

Dr. Sergey Yuferev
Infineon Technologies
Austria

Electromagnetic Modeling of Integrated Power Stages

Modeling of traditional DC-DC or AC-DC power converters, consisting of discrete components, is usually performed by circuit simulation methods. Situation is changing with development of integrated power stages, incorporating power transistors and a driver in one package of a larger size and complex shape. Current density distribution in such packages is strictly non-uniform that increases resistance and may even lead to local overheating in the areas of current "hot spots". Growth of the driver frequencies requires skin and proximity effects being taken into consideration. Therefore, early design stage optimization and reduction of DC and eddy current losses in integrated power stages cannot be done without the electromagnetic field simulations. Analyses of losses using 3-D electromagnetic simulators (employing Maxwell's equations) are obviously performed without semiconductor objects. In integrated systems, it may result in smoother simulated distribution of the current density and, consequently, provides lower loss estimation than it may happen in a real system, especially in the package parts nearest to the chips. In this talk we discuss the use of 3-D electromagnetic models of chips to provide continuous current flow in the system. Elements of the chip, critical from electromagnetic point of view, are included in 3-D model and properties of semiconductor material are approximated for different states in accordance with the reference data. Another topic to be discussed in the talk is application of the surface impedance concept to simulate the skin effect and eddy current losses in the power stage package under condition of non-harmonic excitation. It enables to separate spatial and temporal problems. As a first step, numerical solution in the perfect electrical conductor limit is obtained using a commercial 3-D simulator. Then power losses in key parts of the power stage package are calculated in the time domain at post-processing stage using the analytical technique. Special attention is given to calculation of losses for the case of practically important case of weak skin effect ("grey zone" of the surface impedance concept). Application by the simulation methodologies is illustrated by numerous examples.

Sergey Yuferev was born in St. Petersburg, Russia, in 1964. He received his M.Sc. in Computational Fluid Mechanics from St. Petersburg Technical University, St. Petersburg, in 1987, and his Ph.D. in Computational Electromagnetics from Ioffe Institute, St. Petersburg, in 1992. From 1987 to 1998, he worked in Ioffe Institute. From 1999 to 2000, he was a Visiting Associate Professor at the University of Akron, Akron, Ohio. From 2000 to 2011, he was with Nokia Corp. Since 2011, he has been with Infineon Technologies, Villach, Austria. His current research interests include numerical and analytical methods of computational electromagnetics and their application to semiconductor and electronic devices and products. He is author of 40+ papers and monograph "Surface Impedance Boundary Conditions: A Comprehensive Approach".

ACES 2017 Conference Program at a Glance - March 26-30, 2017

Date	Time	Continenti	Americhe	Pacifico	Atlantico
SUNDAY					
26-Mar	02:00PM - 05:00PM	Conference Registration			
	01:30PM - 05:00PM	ACES Board of Directors Meeting			
MONDAY					
27-Mar	08:00AM - 05:00PM	Conference Registration			
	02:00PM - 05:30PM	Exhibitors			
	08:30AM - 08:35AM	Welcome Message			
	08:35AM - 08:40AM	ACES Business Meeting			
	08:40AM - 09:30AM	(1) Plenary Talk - 1: Sergey Yuferev			
	09:40AM - 10:30AM	(2) Plenary Talk - 2: Nathan Ida			
	10:30AM - 11:00AM	Break			
	11:00AM - 01:20PM	(3) Algorithms for Unique Applications - I	(4) Metamaterials	(5) Novel Photonic Material and Devices - I	(6) Sensors and Imaging Applications
	01:20PM - 02:30PM	Lunch			
	02:30PM - 04:30PM	(7) Novel Antennas for Upstream and Downstream Satellite Applications	(8) Student Paper Competition - I	(9) Advances in EM Modeling and Optimization: From Theory to Applications - I	(10) EM Simulations using Sonnet - I
	04:30PM - 04:50PM	Break			
	04:50PM - 06:30PM	(11) Antenna Design - I	(12) Student Paper Competition - II	(13) Advances in EM Modeling and Optimization: From Theory to Applications - II	(14) EM Simulations using Sonnet - II
	07:00PM - 08:30PM	Welcome Cocktail			
TUESDAY					
28-Mar	08:00AM - 05:00PM	Conference Registration			
	02:00PM - 05:30PM	Exhibitors			
	08:40AM - 09:30AM	(15) Keynote Talk: Yahya Rahmat-Samii			
	09:40AM - 10:30AM	(16) Plenary Talk - 3: Giuliano Manara			
	10:30AM - 11:00AM	Break			
	11:00AM - 01:20PM	(17) Uncertainty Quantification in CEM	(18) Computational Electromagnetics, Advanced Algorithms and Emerging Applications - I	(19) Modeling with FEKO	(20) Integration Equation Techniques & Applications
	01:20PM - 02:30PM	Lunch			
	02:30PM - 04:30PM	(21) Low Frequency Electromagnetics	(22) Computational Electromagnetics, Advanced Algorithms and Emerging Applications - II	(23) Vendor Tutorial - 1: CST (24) Tutorial - 1: James B. Cole	(25) Frequency and Time Domain Integral Equation Solvers - I
	04:30PM - 04:50PM	Break			
	04:50PM - 06:30PM	(26) Big-Data Aspects of Computational Electromagnetics	(27) Computational Electromagnetics, Advanced Algorithms and Emerging Applications - III	(28) Optimization and Modeling Methods for EM-Driven Design	(29) Human Exposure to Electromagnetic Fields: EMF Dosimetry, Applications, Compliance Methods
	06:10PM - 07:00PM	(30) Plenary Talk - 4: IDS			
WEDNESDAY					
29-Mar	08:00AM - 05:00PM	Conference Registration			
	02:00PM - 05:30PM	Exhibitors			
	08:40AM - 09:30AM	(31) Plenary Talk - 5: Apostolos Georgiadis			
	09:40AM - 10:30AM	(32) Plenary Talk - 6: Levent Gurel			
	10:30AM - 11:00AM	Break			
	11:00AM - 01:20PM	(33) Electromagnetic Techniques for the Internet of Things - I	(34) Computational Electromagnetics, Advanced Algorithms and Emerging Applications - IV	(35) Nanoelectronics and Nanoelectromagnetics: Modeling and Applications	(36) Antenna Design - II
	01:20PM - 02:30PM	Lunch			
	02:30PM - 04:30PM	(37) Electromagnetic Techniques for the Internet of Things - II	(38) Low-Frequency Electromagnetic Inverse Problems - I	(39) Tutorial - 2: Roberto D. Graglia, Andrew F. Peterson (40) Tutorial - 3: Andrew F. Peterson, Roberto D. Graglia	(41) Antenna Design - III
	04:30PM - 04:50PM	Break			
	04:50PM - 06:30PM		(42) Wireless Power Transfer	(43) Advanced Applications - I	(44) Advanced Applications - II
	08:00PM - 10:30PM	Banquet			
THURSDAY					
30-Mar	08:00AM - 05:00PM	Conference Registration			
	02:00PM - 05:30PM	Exhibitors			
	08:40AM - 09:30AM	(45) Plenary Talk - 7: Salah Obayya			
	09:50AM - 10:30AM	(46) Algorithms for Unique Applications - II	(47) Computational Electromagnetics, Advanced Algorithms and Emerging Applications - V	(48) Electromagnetic Non Destructive Evaluation	(49) Antenna Design - IV
	10:30AM - 11:00AM	Break			
	11:00AM - 01:20AM	(50) Novel Computational Methodologies for Electromagnetics, Optics and Photonics	(51) Inverse Scattering Techniques for GPR and Subsurface Imaging	(52) Novel Photonic Material and Devices - II	(53) Biological Effects of Electric, Magnetic and Electromagnetic Fields: Innovative Applications in Daily Life - I
	01:20PM - 02:30PM	Lunch			
	02:30PM - 04:30PM	(54) Applications of Antennas and Arrays	(55) Low-Frequency Electromagnetic Inverse Problems - II	(56) Tutorial - 4: Paolo Rocca	(57) Biological Effects of Electric, Magnetic and Electromagnetic Fields: Innovative Applications in Daily Life - II
	04:30PM - 04:50PM	Break			
	04:50PM - 06:30PM	(58) Recent Advances on Characteristic Mode Analysis and Applications			(59) Frequency and Time Domain Integral Equation Solvers - II

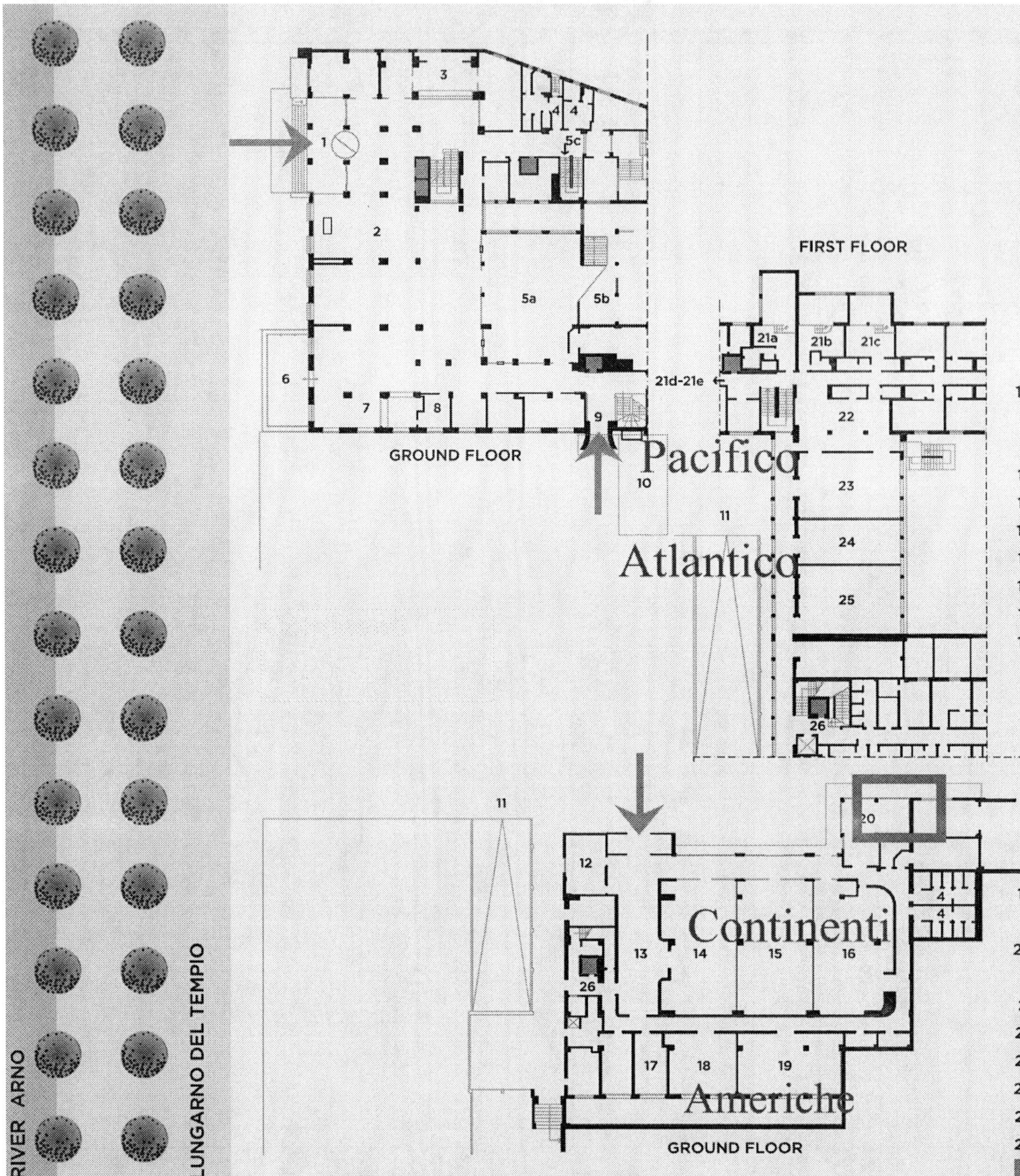

Legenda

1 Main entrance
2 Hall
3 Reception
4 Toilets
5 Restaurants (a, b, c)
6 Bar terrace
7 American bar
8 Internet point
9 Second entry
10 Covered connection to the congress center
11 Ramp access to the garage
12 Meeting and congress office
13 Foyer
14 Meeting room Europa
15 Meeting room Asia
16 Meeting room Africa
17 Meeting room Australia
18 Meeting room America del Sud
19 Meeting room America del Nord
20 Meeting room Giardino d'Inverno
21 Business rooms (a,b,c,d,e)
22 Foyer
23 Meeting room Pacifico
24 Meeting room Indiano
25 Meeting room Atlantico
26 Floor connection
■ Elevator

Certifications: ISO 9001, ISO 14001, EMAS

ACES 2017 Tutorials

Title and Presenter **Room Pacifico**

Tuesday, March 28, 2017

(02:30PM - 03:30PM) Vendor Tutorial
"How to Simulate Electrically Large Platforms for RF and EMC Applications"
CST

(03:30PM - 04:30PM) Tutorial - 1
"Introduction to the Nonstandard Finite Difference Time Domain Methodology - The Devils in the Details"
James B. Cole

Wednesday, March 29, 2017

(02:30PM - 03:30PM) Tutorial - 2
"Higher-Order Hierarchical Vector Polynomial Bases for CEM"
Roberto D. Graglia, Andrew F. Peterson

(03:30PM - 04:30PM) Tutorial - 3
"Developing Singular Vector Bases for CEM"
Andrew F. Peterson, Roberto D. Graglia

Thursday, March 30, 2017

(02:30PM - 03:30PM) Tutorial – 4
"Tolerance Analysis and Robust Design in Engineering Electromagnetics - An Interval Analysis Perspective"
Paolo Rocca

ACES 2017 Plenary Talks

Title and Presenter **Room Continenti**

Monday, March 27, 2017

(08:40AM - 09:30AM) Plenary - 1
"Electromagnetic Modeling of Integrated Power Stages"
Sergey Yuferev

(09:40AM - 10:30AM) Plenary - 2
"Models for AC Induced Corrosion - A New Challenge in Computational Electromagnetics"
Nathan Ida

Tuesday, March 28, 2017

(08:40AM - 09:30AM) Keynote
"The Marvels of Periodic Structures in Modern Electromagnetics and Antennas: A New Look at FSS, EBG, Reflectarrays and Nano-Pillars"
Yahya Rahmat-Samii

(09:40AM - 10:30AM) Plenary - 3
"Near-Field Focused Antennas for Short-Range Wireless Systems"
Giuliano Manara

(06:10PM - 07:00PM) Plenary - 4
"Using Different Techniques for Electromagnetic Design and Verification of Large and Complex Structures: Industrial Cases of Interest"
IDS

Wednesday, March 29, 2017

(08:40AM - 09:30AM) Plenary - 5
"Wireless Power Transfer and Energy Harvesting for RFID and Wireless Sensors"
Apostolos Georgiadis

(09:40AM - 10:30AM) Plenary - 6
"(Heterogeneous) Parallel Solutions of Billion-Unknown Problems: Applications and Big-Data Aspects"
Levent Gürel

Thursday, March 30, 2017

(08:40AM - 09:30AM) Plenary - 7
"Analysis of Plasmonic and Nano-Photonic Devices"
Salah Obayya

ACES 2017 Sessions Overview

Monday, March 27, 2017 (Sessions 1-14)

Session Title	Room
1- Plenary Talk – 1: Electromagnetic Modeling of Integrated Power Stages	Continenti
2- Plenary Talk – 2: Models for AC Induced Corrosion - A New Challenge in Computational Electromagnetics	Continenti
3- Algorithms for Unique Applications – 1	Continenti
4- Metamaterials	Americhe
5- Novel Photonic Material and Devices – 1	Pacifico
6- Sensors and Imaging Applications	Atlantico
7- Novel Antennas for Upstream and Downstream Satellite Applications	Continenti
8- Student Paper Competition – 1	Americhe
9- Advances in EM Modeling and Optimization: From Theory to Applications – 1	Pacifico
10- EM Simulations using Sonnet – 1	Atlantico
11- Antenna Design – 1	Continenti
12- Student Paper Competition – 2	Americhe
13- Advances in EM Modeling and Optimization: From Theory to Applications – 2	Pacifico
14- EM Simulations using Sonnet – 2	Atlantico

ACES 2017 Sessions Overview

Tuesday, March 28, 2017 (Sessions 15-30)

Session Title	Room
15- Keynote Talk: The Marvels of Periodic Structures in Modern Electromagnetics and Antennas: A New Look at FSS, EBG, Reflectarrays and Nano-Pillars	Continenti
16- Plenary Talk – 3: Near-Field Focused Antennas for Short-Range	Continenti
17- Uncertainty Quantification in CEM	Continenti
18- Computational Electromagnetics, Advanced Algorithms and Emerging Applications – 1	Americhe
19- Modeling with FEKO	Pacifico
20- Integration Equation Techniques & Applications	Atlantico
21- Low Frequency Electromagnetics	Continenti
22- Computational Electromagnetics, Advanced Algorithms and Emerging Applications – 2	Americhe
23- Vendor Tutorial: How to Simulate Electrically Large Platforms for RF and EMC Applications	Pacifico
24- Tutorial – 1: Introduction to the Nonstandard Finite Difference Time Domain Methodology - The Devils in the Details	Pacifico
25- Frequency and Time Domain Integral Equation Solvers – 1	Atlantico
26- Big-Data Aspects of Computational Electromagnetics	Continenti
27- Computational Electromagnetics, Advanced Algorithms and Emerging Applications – 3	Americhe
28- Optimization and Modeling Methods for EM-Driven Design	Pacifico
29- Human Exposure to Electromagnetic Fields: EMF Dosimetry, Applications, Compliance Methods	Atlantico
30- Plenary Talk – 4: Using Different Techniques for Electromagnetic Design and Verification of Large and Complex Structures: Industrial Cases of Interest	Continenti

ACES 2017 Sessions Overview

Wednesday, March 29, 2017 (Sessions 31-44)

Session Title	Room
31- Plenary Talk – 5: Wireless Power Transfer and Energy Harvesting for RFID and Wireless Sensors	Continenti
32- Plenary Talk – 6: (Heterogeneous) Parallel Solutions of Billion-Unknown Problems: Applications and Big-Data Aspects	Continenti
33- Electromagnetic Techniques for the Internet of Things – 1	Continenti
34- Computational Electromagnetics, Advanced Algorithms and Emerging Applications – 4	Americhe
35- Nanoelectronics and Nanoelectromagnetics: Modeling and Applications	Pacifico
36- Antenna Design – 2	Atlantico
37- Electromagnetic Techniques for the Internet of Things – 2	Continenti
38- Low-Frequency Electromagnetic Inverse Problems – 1	Americhe
39- Tutorial – 2: Higher-Order Hierarchical Vector Polynomial Bases for CEM	Pacifico
40- Tutorial – 3: Developing Singular Vector Bases for CEM	Pacifico
41- Antenna Design – 3	Atlantico
42- Wireless Power Transfer	Americhe
43- Advanced Applications – 1	Pacifico
44- Advanced Applications – 2	Atlantico

ACES 2017 Sessions Overview

Thursday, March 30, 2017 (Sessions 45-59)

Session Title	Room
45- Plenary Talk – 7: Analysis of Plasmonic and Nano-Photonic Devices	Continenti
46- Algorithms for Unique Applications – 2	Continenti
47- Computational Electromagnetics, Advanced Algorithms and Emerging Applications – 5	Americhe
48- Electromagnetic Non Destructive Evaluation	Pacifico
49- Antenna Design – 4	Atlantico
50- Novel Computational Methodologies for Electromagnetics, Optics and Photonics	Continenti
51- Inverse Scattering Techniques for GPR and Subsurface Imaging	Americhe
52- Novel Photonic Material and Devices – 2	Pacifico
53- Biological Effects of Electric, Magnetic and Electromagnetic Fields: Innovative Applications in Daily Life – 1	Atlantico
54- Applications of Antennas and Arrays	Continenti
55- Low-Frequency Electromagnetic Inverse Problems – 2	Americhe
56- Tutorial – 4: Tolerance Analysis and Robust Design in Engineering Electromagnetics - An Interval Analysis Perspective	Pacifico
57- Biological Effects of Electric, Magnetic and Electromagnetic Fields: Innovative Applications in Daily Life – 2	Atlantico
58- Recent Advances on Characteristic Mode Analysis and Applications	Continenti
59- Frequency and Time Domain Integral Equation Solvers – 2	Atlantico

ACES 2017 Technical Program

Sunday, March 26

02:00PM-05:00PM	**Conference Registration**	**Business Center**
03:00PM-06:30PM	**ACES Board of Directors Meeting**	**America del Nord**

Monday, March 27

08:00AM-05:00PM	**Conference Registration**	**Business Center**
08:30PM-05:30PM	**Exhibitors**	**Main Hall**
07:00PM-08:30PM	**Welcome Cocktail**	**Main Hall**
08:30AM-08:35AM	**Welcome Message** **Sami Barmada, Conference General Chair**	**Room Continenti**
08:35AM-08:40AM	**ACES Business Meeting** **Sami Barmada, ACES President**	**Room Continenti**
Session 1 **08:40AM-09:30AM**	**Plenary Talk – 1** "Electromagnetic Modeling of Integrated Power Stages" **Sergey Yuferev**	**Room Continenti**
Session 2 **09:40AM-10:30AM**	**Plenary Talk – 2** "Models for AC Induced Corrosion - A New Challenge in Computational Electromagnetics" **Nathan Ida**	**Room Continenti**
10:30AM-11:00AM	**Break**	

	Room Continenti
Session 3 **11:00AM-01:20PM**	**Algorithms for Unique Applications – 1** **Session Chair: Andrew Peterson**
11:00AM-11:20AM	"Algorithm of Bispectral Video Signal Recovery under Conditions of Industrial Noise" 1 Rostislav I. Sokolov and Renat R. Abdullin
11:20AM-11:40AM	"High Frequency RCS Characterization of a Unique Two-Way Field Probe" 3 Andrew Knisely, Peter Collins, and Andrew Terzouli
11:40AM-12:00PM	"A Double Green Function Method for an Inverse Source Problem Related to a Hemisphere" 5 Sevda Vatansever, Ali Alkumru, Hakan Sertlek, H. Arda Ülkü, and Gokhan Çınar
12:00PM-12:20PM	"TF/SF Separation Characteristics in the 3D NS-FDTD Technique Using Rectangular Cells" 7 Tadao Ohtani, Yasushi Kanai, and Nikolaos V. Kantartzis
12:20PM-12:40PM	"Nonredundant NF–FF Transformation with Spherical Spiral Scan for an Offset Mounted Volumetric AUT" 9 Francesco D'Agostino, Flaminio Ferrara, Claudio Gennarelli, Rocco Guerriero, and Massimo Migliozzi
12:40PM-01:00PM	"TD-UAPO Solutions for the Diffraction by Co-Planar Adjacent Blocks" 11 Marcello Frongillo, Giovanni Riccio, and Gianluca Gennarelli
01:00PM-01:20PM	"Assessment of AC Interference Caused by Transmission Lines on Buried Metallic Pipelines Using F.E.M." 13 Arturo Popoli, Andrea Cristofolini, Leonardo Sandrolini, Bolanle T. Abe, and Adisa Jimoh
01:20PM-02:30PM	**Lunch** — **Hotel Restaurant**

	Room Americhe
Session 4 **11:00AM-01:20PM**	**Metamaterials** **Session Chairs: Salvatore Campione, James L. Vedral**
11:00AM-11:20AM	"A Tunable Dual-band Left-Handed Metamaterial Implementation" 15 Si Li, Wenxing Li, Yunlong Mao, Wenhua Yu, and Atef Z. Elsherbeni
11:20AM-11:40AM	"Novel Complementary Metasurfaces for the Orbital Angular Momentum Generation" 17 Menglin L. N. Chen, Li Jun Jiang, and Wei E. I. Sha
11:40AM-12:00PM	"Simulations of Realistic Multifunctional Nanoantenna Enabled Detectors" 19 Salvatore Campione, Larry K. Warne, Roy E. Jorgenson, Paul S. Davids, and David W. Peters
12:00PM-12:20PM	"Size Reduction of Patch Elements for Homogeneous Perfect Absorbing Material" 21 James L. Vedral and Randall L. Musselman
12:20PM-12:40PM	"Refraction at Metamaterial Interface in Terms of Induced Phase at Resonant Frequency" 23 Quang Nguyen, Amir I. Zaghloul, and Steven Weiss
01:20PM-02:30PM	**Lunch** — **Hotel Restaurant**

	Room Pacifico
Session 5 **11:00AM-01:20PM**	**Novel Photonic Material and Devices – 1** **Session Organizers: Salah Obayya, Mohamed Swillam** **Session Chair: Salah Obayya**
11:00AM-11:20AM	"Time Delay Signature of Chaotic Nanolasers and its Concealment" 25 Amr Elsonbaty, Salem F. Hegazy, and Salah S. A. Obayya
11:20AM-11:40AM	"Subwavelength Focusing in the Infrared Range Using a Meta Surface" 27 Manar Abdel-Galil, Yehea Ismail, and Mohamed Swillam
11:40AM-12:00PM	"Hybrid Plasmonic Conductor-gap-silicon Microring-on-disks Electro-optic Modulator" 29 N. H. Fouad, A. O. Zaki, D. C. Zografopoulos, L. A. Shahada, R. Beccherelli, and M. A. Swillam
12:00PM-12:20PM	"Full 3D Electromagnetic Wave Analysis Using 2D Simulation" 31 Raghi S. El Shamy, Mohamed Swillam, and Salah Obayya
12:20PM-12:40PM	"High Performance Silicon Mach-Zehnder Interferometer Based Photonic Modulator" 33 Ahmad B. Ayoub and Mohamed A. Swillam
12:40PM-01:00PM	"Effective Modelling of Silicon Nanowire Solar Cells" 35 Mohamed Hussein, M. F. O. Hameed, S. S. A. Obayya, and Mohamed A. Swillam
01:20PM-02:30PM	**Lunch** — **Hotel Restaurant**

	Room Atlantico
Session 6 **11:00AM-01:20PM**	**Sensors and Imaging Applications** **Session Organizer: Sunday Cookey Expo** **Session Chair: Hongfan Zhu**
11:00AM-11:20AM	"A Novel Subspace Partition Method for Fourth-Order Statistics Based MUSIC Algorithm" 37 Wenxing Li and Yu Zhao
11:20AM-11:40AM	"Multiple Model Multi-Object Particle PHD Filter" 39 Hongfan Zhu, Liwei Wang, and Zhiyu Qu
11:40AM-12:00PM	"A Real-valued MUSIC Algorithm with Forward/Backward Technique" 41 Yan Wang, Weijian Si, and Kun Wang

12:00PM-12:20PM	"Extract Pulse Clustering in Radar Signal Sorting" 43 Yang Sheng, Changbo Hou, and Weijian Si	
12:20PM-12:40PM	"An Improved Null Broadening Beamforming Method based on Covariance Matrix Reconstruction" 45 Wenxing Li and Bin Yang	
12:40PM-01:00PM	"A New Interference Rejection Algorithm for Direction-of-Arrival Estimation" 47 Wenxing Li and Mengjun Chen	
01:20PM-02:30PM	**Lunch**	**Hotel Restaurant**

	Room Continenti
Session 7 **02:30PM-04:30PM**	**Novel Antennas for Upstream and Downstream Satellite Applications** **Session Organizer: Sunday Cookey Ekpo** **Session Chair: Osama Mohammed**
02:30PM-02:50PM	"High Isolation Design of a Two-Element Planar UWB-MIMO Monopole Antenna" 49 Yue Dong, Yingsong Li, Kai Yu, and Yanyan Wang
02:50PM-03:10PM	"Low-Profile Dual-Band Emulated GPS Constellation Antenna" 51 Emanuel J. Merulla
03:10PM-03:30PM	"20/30 GHz Circularly Polarized Antenna Arrays with Pairs of Slots on Substrate Integrated Waveguide" 53 Christos Kalialakis, Fermin Mira, and Apostolos Georgiadis
03:30PM-03:50PM	"Multi-Band Metamaterial-Based Microstrip Antenna for WLAN and WiMAX Applications" 55 Kai Yu, Yingsong Li, and Yanyan Wang
04:30PM-04:50PM	**Break**

	Room Americhe
Session 8 **02:30PM-04:30PM**	**Student Paper Competition – 1** **Session Organizer: Sami Barmada** **Session Chair: Daniel Weile**
02:30PM-02:50PM	"Electromagnetic Material Parameter Extraction of Ferrites up to the GHz Range via Measurements and Simulations" 57 Christian Reinhold, Peter Scholz, and Ulrich Jumar
02:50PM-03:10PM	"A Modified CoSaMP Algorithm for Electromagnetic Imaging of Two Dimensional Domains" 59 Ali Imran Sandhu and Hakan Bagci
03:10PM-03:30PM	"A Comparison of Numerical Mode-Matching Techniques for the Analysis of Well-Logging Tools" 61 Guilherme S. Rosa, Maiquel S. Canabarro, José R. Bergmann, and Fernando L. Teixeira
03:30PM-03:50PM	"Novel Complementary Metasurfaces for the Orbital Angular Momentum Generation" 63 Menglin L. N. Chen, Li Jun Jiang, and Wei E. I. Sha
03:50PM-04:10PM	"A Square Slot Circularly Polarized Microstrip Antenna with Enhanced Bandwidth" 65 Obeng Kwakye Kingsford Sarkodie, Kang Kai, and Mujeeb Abdullah
04:10PM-04:30PM	"Boundary Integral Equation Study of the Influence of Finite Conductivity on Antenna Radiation Using a 3-D Differential Surface Admittance Operator" 67 Martijn Huynen, Daniel De Zutter, and Dries Vande Ginste
04:30PM-04:50PM	**Break**

	Room Pacifico
Session 9 02:30PM-04:30PM	**Advances in EM Modeling and Optimization: From Theory to Applications – 1** **Session Organizers: Vijay Devabhaktuni, Peter Aaen** **Session Chair: Vijay Devabhaktuni**
02:30PM-02:50PM	"Fast Multi-Criterial Statistical Analysis and Design Optimization of Compact Microwave Couplers" 69 Slawomir Koziel and Adrian Bekasiewicz
02:50PM-03:10PM	"A New Coplanar EBG Power Supply Layer Based on Zigzag Line for Adjacent Inductance Enhancing" 71 Qiannan Xue, Ziyuan Wang, Yi Tian, Peng Wang, and Ziyuan Wang
03:10PM-03:30PM	"The Branch-Line Couplers Miniaturization Method with Microstrip Filters" 73 Denis A. Letavin, Victor A. Chechetkin, and Yury E. Mitelman
03:30PM-03:50PM	"Compact Microstrip Three-Loop Coupler" 75 Denis A. Letavin
03:50PM-04:10PM	"Online Failure Detection in Large Massive MIMO Linear Arrays" 77 Daniele Pinchera, Marco Donald Migliore, Mario Lucido, Fulvio Schettino, and Gaetano Panariello
04:10PM-04:30PM	"Feed Horn Optimization using Feed+Reflector Co-Simulation for Advanced Reflector Antennas" 79 Joshua M. Kovitz, Vignesh Manohar, and Yahya Rahmat-Samii
04:30PM-04:50PM	**Break**

	Room Atlantico
Session 10 02:30PM-04:30PM	**EM Simulations using Sonnet – 1** **Session Organizer: Taha Imeci** **Session Chair: Taha Imeci**
02:30PM-02:50PM	"L, U, T and F-Shaped Slots in Patch Antenna" 81 Buket Kul, Gamze Kirman, Pakize Ergül, Zeynep Banaz Kartal, and Taha Imeci
02:50PM-03:10PM	"High Gain Perturbed Pentagonal Shaped Diamond Slotted Patch Antenna at 17.1 GHz" 83 Şakir Kandönmez, Orhan Kolancıoğlu, Dilara H. Boyacı, Melis E. Koca, and Taha İmeci
03:10PM-03:30PM	"E-Shaped Patch Antenna with Five Resonances" 85 Ayse Kansız, Salih Yılmaz, and Taha Imeci
03:30PM-03:50PM	"Square Shape Patch Antenna with Triangular Slot" 87 Ahmet Burcakbas, Selman Soylu, Burak Bektas, and S. Taha Imeci
03:50PM-04:10PM	"F-Shaped Monopole Antenna" 89 Hakan İncesulu, Gül Ulutaş, Hakan Bilge, Ş. Taha Imeci, and Tahsin Durak
04:10PM-04:30PM	"Spiral Patch Antenna at 12 GHz" 91 Yunus Emre Ozmen and Taha Imeci
04:30PM-04:50PM	**Break**

	Room Continenti
Session 11 04:50PM-06:30PM	**Antenna Design – 1** **Session Chair: Paolo Nepa**
04:50PM-05:10PM	"Compact 4-Port MIMO Antenna System for 5G Mobile Terminal" 93 Mujeeb Abdullah, Yong-Ling Ban, Kai Kang, Obeng Kwakye Kingsford Sarkodie, and Ming-Yang Li
05:10PM-05:30PM	"A Novel Reflecarray Antenna Backed with Double Layer FSS for RCS Reduction" 95

	Hande Bodur, Sibel Çimen, Gonca Çakır, and Sibel Ünaldı
05:30PM-05:50PM	"Patch Antenna Size-Reduction Parametric Study" 97 James L. Vedral and Randall L. Musselman
05:50PM-06:10PM	"Design of a Low-Profile 2 to 6 GHz Circular Polarized Single Arm Hexagonal Spiral Array Antenna" 99 Yongduk Oh and Sangwook Nam
06:10PM-06:30PM	"Sidelobe Reduction in Linear Microstrip Arrays Driven through Microstrip Corporate Feeds" 101 Stanislav Ogurtsov and Slawomir Koziel
06:30PM-06:50PM	"Compact Meander Printed Dipole Antenna" 103 Chongyi Yue, Wenxing Li, Atef Elsherbeni, and Veysel Demir

	Room Americhe
Session 12 **04:50PM-06:30PM**	**Student Paper Competition – 2** **Session Organizer: Sami Barmada** **Session Chair: Daniel Weile**
04:50PM-05:10PM	"Sodium Imaging of the Human Knee Cartilage with Magnetic Resonance at Ultra High Field: Development of a Double Frequency ($^{1}H/^{23}Na$) RF Coil" 105 Francesca Maggiorelli, Joshua D. Kaggie, Martin J. Graves, Guido Buonincontri, Alessandra Retico, Laura Biagi, Gianluigi Tiberi, and Michela Tosetti
05:10PM-05:30PM	"Artificial Ionospheric Scintillation Effects on Communication Signals in the V and W Bands" 107 David Smith, Peter Collins, James Fee, James C. Petrosky, Andrew Terzuoli, and Caglar Yardim

	Room Pacifico
Session 13 **04:50PM-06:30PM**	**Advances in EM Modeling and Optimization: From Theory to Applications – 2** **Session Organizers: Vijay Devabhaktuni, Peter Aaen** **Session Chair: Vijay Devabhaktuni**
04:50PM-05:10PM	"Realization of Dual Notch Bands in UWB Bandpass Filter Using Two T-shaped Resonators" 109 Xuemei Zheng and Tao Jiang
05:10PM-05:30PM	"Design of Modified Pythagorean Fractal Antenna for Multiband Application" 111 Henrique Adler M. Silva, Adaildo G. D'Assunção, and José P. Silva
05:30PM-05:50PM	"Critical Parameters Affecting the Design of High Frequency Transmission Lines in Standard CMOS Technology" 113 Talal Al-Attar, Abdullah Alshehri, Abdullah Almansouri, and Abdullah Alturki
05:50PM-06:10PM	"A Dual-Band Metamaterial Absorber with Polarization Insensitive and Tunable Characteristics" 115 Kai Yu, Yingsong Li, and Yanyan Wang
06:10PM-06:30PM	"Simple and Efficient Design of Reconfigurable FSS with Triangular Patch Elements" 117 André N. Silva, Rafaela G. G. Carvalho, Adaildo G. D'Assunção, and José P. Silva

	Room Atlantico
Session 14 **04:50PM-06:50PM**	**EM Simulations using Sonnet – 2** **Session Organizer: Taha Imeci** **Session Chair: Taha Imeci**
04:50PM-05:10PM	"Floating Crescent Star in a Slot Patch Antenna" 119 Mustafa E. Yılmaz, Ömer F. Alperen, Muhammet Ali Akyıldız, and Taha Imeci

05:10PM-05:30PM	"A Compact Size Circular Sector Patch Antenna for Ku-band Applications" 121 G. Kemal Oğuz and Ş. Taha İmeci
05:30PM-05:50PM	"E Shaped Antenna Surrounded with U Shape" 123 D. Delikanli, S. Keskiner, and S. T. Imeci
05:50PM-06:10PM	"Dual-Band Gemini-Shaped Microstrip Patch Antenna for C-Band and X-Band Applications" 125 Gerard Djengomemgoto, Reha Altunok, Cem Karabacak, Ş. Taha˙Imeci, and Tahsin Durak
06:10PM-06:30PM	"An Antenna for Implanted Device Systems" 127 Emircan Zincircioğlu, İsmail Pekdemir,Rafiq Rzayew, Emre Ilıksu, Merve Dede, Ş. Taha Imeci, and Tahsin Durak
06:30PM-06:50PM	"Rectangular Slotted Square Patch Antenna with a Floating Ring" 129 Yasin Anıl Öztürk, Uğur Sarı, Ş. Taha Imeci, and Tahsin Durak

ACES 2017 Technical Program

Tuesday, March 28

08:00AM-05:00PM	**Conference Registration**	**Business Center**
08:30PM-05:30PM	**Exhibitors**	**Main Hall**
Session 15 08:40AM-09:30AM	**Keynote Talk** "The Marvels of Periodic Structures in Modern Electromagnetics and Antennas: A New Look at FSS, EBG, Reflectarrays and Nano-Pillars" **Yahya Rahmat-Samii**	**Room Continenti**
Session 16 09:40AM-10:30AM	**Plenary Talk – 3** "Near-Field Focused Antennas for Short-Range Wireless Systems" **Giuliano Manara**	**Room Continenti**
10:30AM-11:00AM	**Break**	

		Room Continenti
Session 17 11:00AM-01:20PM	**Uncertainty Quantification in CEM** **Session Organizers: Luca Di Rienzo, Lorenzo Codecasa** **Session Chair: Luca Di Rienzo**	
11:00AM-11:20AM	"Multilevel Monte Carlo Simulation of the Eddy Current Problem with Random Parameters" 131 Armin Galetzka, Zeger Bontinck, Ulrich Römer, and Sebastian Schöps	
11:20AM-11:40AM	"Model Order Reduction Approach to Uncertainty Quantification in Eddy Current Problems" 133 Lorenzo Codecasa and Luca Di Rienzo	
11:40AM-12:00PM	"Reduced-Order Stochastic Macro-Models in FDTD, for Characterizing Uncertainty in Aperture Antennas" 135 Ata Zadehgol	
12:00PM-12:20PM	"Uncertainty Quantification in Transcranial Magnetic Stimulation with Correlation Between Tissue Conductivities" 137 Lorenzo Codecasa, Luca Di Rienzo, Konstantin Weise, and Jens Haueisen	
12:20PM-12:40PM	"Uncertainty Analysis on Band-Stop Filter Using Data-Driven Arbitrary Polynomial Chaos" 139 Osama Alkhateeb and Nathan Ida	
12:40PM-01:00PM	"Stochastic Collocation for Uncertainty Quantification of Systems Described by Neutral Delayed Differential Equations" 141 F. Ferranti, D. Romano, G. Antonini, and L. De Camillis	
01:00PM-01:20PM	"Research on Workflow of Improving Electromagnetic Compatibility of Search and Rescue Helicopter" 143 Ping Xu, Fanping Shi, Xiaowei Zhang, Tao Jiang, and Sanjun Dong	
01:20PM-02:30PM	**Lunch**	**Hotel Restaurant**

	Room Americhe
Session 18 11:00AM-01:20PM	**Computational Electromagnetics, Advanced Algorithms and Emerging Applications – 1** **Session Organizers: Zhen Peng, Li Jiang** **Session Chairs: Achim Dreher, Guilherme S. Rosa**
11:00AM-11:20AM	"A MoM-PO Hybrid Solution for TM Plane Wave Scattering by a Buried Conducting Cylinder" 145

	Cengiz Ozzaim and Inci Umakoglu	
11:20AM-11:40AM	"Discrete Mode Matching Method for the Analysis of Microstrip Lines on Uniaxial Anisotropic Substrates" 147 Veenu Kamra and Achim Dreher	
11:40AM-12:00PM	"An Efficient Boundary Condition Based on Surface Impedance Concept in FDTD Simulations" 149 Yunlong Mao, Tao Jiang, and Atef Z. Elsherbeni	
12:00PM-12:20PM	"Local Mesh Morphing Technique for Parametrized Macromodels in the Finite Element Method" 151 Martyna Czarniewska, Grzegorz Fotyga, and Michał Mrozowski	
12:20PM-12:40PM	"Robust and Efficient Model-Order Reduction for Lossless Microwave Structures Using the Impedance Formulation of the Finite Element Method" 153 Rolf Baltes and Romanus Dyczij-Edlinger	
12:40PM-01:00PM	"An Efficient 2D/3D Hybrid DGTD Transient Analysis for Arbitrarily Shaped Anti-Pads in Power-ground Plate-Pair" 155 Wending Mai and Jun Hu	
01:00PM-01:20PM	"A Comparison of Numerical Mode-Matching Techniques for the Analysis of Well-Logging Tools" 157 Guilherme S. Rosa, Maiquel S. Canabarro and José R. Bergmann, and Fernando L. Teixeira	
01:20PM-02:30PM	**Lunch**	**Hotel Restaurant**

		Room Pacifico
Session 19 **11:00AM-01:20PM**	**Modeling with FEKO** **Session Organizer: C.J. Reddy** **Session Chair: Markus Schick**	
11:00AM-11:20AM	"Summary of the Latest Extensions to the Electromagnetic Field Solver Package FEKO" 159 Andrés G. Aguilar, Ulrich Jakobus, Mary Longtin, Marlize Schoeman, Wilco Strydom, and Johann J. van Tonder	
11:20AM-11:40AM	"Wave Propagation and Radio Network Planning Software WinProp added to the Electromagnetic Solver Package FEKO" 161 Reiner Hoppe, Gerd Wölfle, and Ulrich Jakobus	
11:40AM-12:00PM	"The Effect of Fabrication Tolerances on a Suspended Plate Antenna" 163 William O. Coburn and Seth A. McCormick	
01:20PM-02:30PM	**Lunch**	**Hotel Restaurant**

	Room Atlantico
Session 20 **11:00AM-01:20PM**	**Integration Equation Techniques & Applications** **Session Organizer: Ulrich Jakobus** **Session Chair: Ulrich Jakobus**
11:00AM-11:20AM	"An Accurate and Efficient Analysis of Very Large but Narrow Zero-Thickness PEC Annular Rings" 165 M. Lucido, M. D. Migliore, G. Panariello, D. Pinchera, C. Santomassimo, and F. Schettino
11:20AM-11:40AM	"An Effective Method for the Analysis of Propagation in Polygonal Cross-Section Dielectric Waveguides" 167 M. Lucido, G. Panariello, and C. Santomassimo
11:40AM-12:00PM	"Conversion of Singular Surface Integrals for to Line Integrals with Nonsingular Integrands for Non-planar Configurations of RWG Basis Functions" 169 Elizabeth Bleszynski, Marek Bleszynski, and Thomas Jaroszewicz

12:00PM-12:20PM	"Efficient Use of Singular Hierarchical Vector Functions for the FEM Solution of Multiscale Problems" 171 Roberto D. Graglia, Paolo Petrini, and Andrew F. Peterson
12:20PM-12:40PM	"Integral Operators Formulation for Transient Radiation from Parabolic Antennas Using Modified Raised Cosine Feeder" 173 Stefania de Sousa Faria, Cassio Goncalves do Rego, and Fernando Jose da Silva Moreira
12:40PM-01:00PM	"MoM-SIE Scattering Models of Snow and Ice Hydrometeors Based on 3D Shape Reconstructions from MASC Images" 175 Branislav M. Notaroš, V. N. Bringi, Cameron Kleinkort, Sanja B. Manić, Elene Chobanyan, Gwo-Jong Huang, Patrick Kennedy, and Merhala Thurai
01:00PM-01:20PM	"Resolution of 2D Time Domain Electric Field Integral Equation: Novel Formulation of RWG Associated to Laguerre Polynomials" 177 Auns Khaled, Dorsaf Omri, and Taoufik Aguili
01:20PM-02:30PM	**Lunch** — **Hotel Restaurant**

	Room Continenti
Session 21 **02:30PM-04:30PM**	**Low Frequency Electromagnetics** **Session Organizer: Osama Mohammed** **Session Chairs: Luca Di Rienzo, Abd A. Arkadan**
02:30PM-02:50PM	"2D BEM for Processing Magnetic Field Maps of Accelerator Magnets" 179 Alberto Cosmai, Luca Di Rienzo, and Stephan Russenschuck
02:50PM-03:10PM	"Reconstruction of PWM Signal Based on Double Fourier Transform and Minimum Phase System" 181 Yaxiu Sun, Yida Lai, Junpeng Fang, and Meng Lin
03:10PM-03:30PM	"EM-AI Model of Microgrids in Islanding Mode" 183 A. A. Arkadan
03:30PM-03:50PM	"Electromechanical Analysis of an Electrodynamic Bearing" 185 Antonino Musolino, Rocco Rizzo, Mauro Tucci, Sami Barmada, Emanuele Crisostomi, Fabrizio Impinna, Joaquim Girardello Detoni, Nicola Amati, and Andrea Tonoli
03:50PM-04:10PM	"Breakdown Voltage Assessment of GaN HEMT Devices through Physics-Based Modeling" 187 Christopher R. Lashway, Alberto Berzoy, Nour Elsayad, and Osama Mohammed
04:10PM-04:30PM	"Predictions of the Power Quality of AC Electric Arc Furnace Connected to Power Grids" 189 Hailong Zhang, Liang Wang, Gang Ma, Wei Yan, and Enrong Wang
04:30PM-04:50PM	**Break**

	Room Americhe
Session 22 **02:30PM-04:30PM**	**Computational Electromagnetics, Advanced Algorithms and Emerging Applications – 2** **Session Organizers: Zhen Peng, Li Jiang** **Session Chairs: Giovanni Angiulli, Kirill Zeyde**
02:30PM-02:50PM	"Computation of Nonlinear Eigenvalues Related to Parameters of Microwave Structures by using Group Theory" 191 Giovanni Angiulli, Mario Versaci, and Francesco Carlo Morabito
02:50PM-03:10PM	"Numerical Study of a Family of IMEX-DGTD Methods for the 3D Time-Domain Maxwell's Equations" 193 Hao Wang, Li Xu, and Bin Li
03:10PM-03:30PM	"Analysis of Transmission-Line Equation Based on LOD-FDTD" 195 Yaxiu Sun, Ming Zhang, Junzhu Qian, and Jianli Wang

03:30PM-03:50PM	"A General Model for Pattern Synthesis of Linear Antenna Arrays by Metaheuristic Algorithms" 197 Suad Basbug
03:50PM-04:10PM	"Discernibility of Metallic Sphere in Rectangular Waveguide" 199 Kirill Zeyde
04:10PM-04:30PM	"An Efficient Numerical Method to Analyze Discontinuity of Coaxial Cable" 201 Jingyi Wang, Junwu Tao, and Fayçal Benmohamed
04:30PM-04:50PM	**Break**

Session 23 **02:30PM-03:30PM**	**Vendor Tutorial**	**Room Pacifico**
	"How to Simulate Electrically Large Platforms for RF and EMC Applications" N/A **CST Workshop**	
Session 24 **03:30PM-04:30PM**	**Tutorial – 1**	**Room Pacifico**
	"Introduction to the Nonstandard Finite Difference Time Domain Methodology - The Devils in the Details" 461 **James B. Cole**	
04:30PM-04:50PM	**Break**	

	Room Atlantico
Session 25 **02:30PM-04:30PM**	**Frequency and Time Domain Integral Equation Solvers – 1** **Session Organizers: Huseyin Arda Ulku, Hakan Bagci, Ozgur Ergul** **Session Chairs: Huseyin Arda Ulku, Hakan Bagci, Ozgur Ergul**
02:30PM-02:50PM	"Radon Transform Interpretation of Retarded-Time Potentials for SWG Bases" 203 Mahmut Akkuş, Fatih Dikmen, H. Arda Ülkü, and A. Arif Ergin
02:50PM-03:10PM	"Integration Rules and Experimental Evidence for the Stability of Time Domain Integral Equations" 205 Daniel S. Weile, Ismail Uluer, Jielin Li, and David A. Hopkins
03:10PM-03:30PM	"A Novel Preconditioner for the EFIE Discretised with the H_{div} Inner Product" 207 Kazuki Niino and Naoshi Nishimura
03:30PM-03:50PM	"Modified Combined Tangential Formulation for Stable and Accurate Analysis of Plasmonic Structures" 209 Barıscan Karaosmanoglu and Ozgur Ergul
03:50PM-04:10PM	"Boundary Integral Equation Study of the Influence of Finite Conductivity on Antenna Radiation Using a 3-D Differential Surface Admittance Operator" 211 Martijn Huynen, Daniel De Zutter, and Dries Vande Ginste
04:10PM-04:30PM	"On the Initial Condition Problem of the Time Domain PMCHWT Surface Integral Equation" 213 Ismail E. Uysal, Hakan Bagci, A. Arif Ergin, and H. Arda Ulku
04:30PM-04:50PM	**Break**

	Room Continenti
Session 26 **04:50PM-06:30PM**	**Big-Data Aspects of Computational Electromagnetics** **Session Organizers: Ozlem Kilic, Levent Gurel** **Session Chairs: Ozlem Kilic, Levent Gurel**
04:50PM-05:10PM	"Successes and Frustrations in the Solution of Large Electromagnetic Problems in Supercomputers" 215 Luis Landesa, José M. Taboada, Juan Luis Campon, Alberto Serna, Fernando Obelleiro, Jose L. Rodríguez, Diego M. Solis, and Marta Araujo
05:10PM-05:30PM	"Electromagnetic Optimization of MIMO Channels using GPUs" 217 Alfonso Breglia, Amedeo Capozzoli, Claudio Curcio, Salvatore Di Donna, and Angelo Liseno

05:30PM-05:50PM	"Accelerating Fast Marching for Geometrical Optics" 219 Amedeo Capozzoli, Claudio Curcio, Angelo Liseno, and Salvatore Savarese
05:50PM-06:10PM	"Large Inverse-Scattering Solutions with DBIM on GPU-Enabled Supercomputers" 221 Mert Hidayetoglu, Carl Pearson, Weng Cho Chew, Levent Gurel, and Wen-Mei Hwu

	Room Americhe
Session 27 **04:50PM-06:30PM**	**Computational Electromagnetics, Advanced Algorithms and Emerging Applications – 3** **Session Organizers: Zhen Peng, Li Jiang** **Session Chairs: Shunichi Futatsumori, Adaildo G. D'Assunção**
04:50PM-05:10PM	"Aircraft Electromagnetic Field Estimation for Wireless Avionics Intra-Communication Band Using Large-Scale FDTD Analysis" 223 Shunichi Futatsumori, Kazuyuki Morioka, Akiko Kohmura, Naruto Yonemoto, Takashi Hikage, Kanji Yahagi, Masami Shirafune, Manabu Yamamoto, Toshio Nojima, and Shoichi Narahashi
05:10PM-05:30PM	"A Uniform Geometrical Theory of Diffraction Formulation for the Diffraction by a Perfect Electric Conductor and Impedance Finite Width Strip" 225 Mohammad Rashedi and Abdorreza Torabi
05:30PM-05:50PM	"Design of Rotatable Metasurface Microstrip Antenna with Reconfigurable Polarization" 227 Felipe F. Araújo, Adaildo G. D'Assunção, Luis F. V. T. Costa, and William S. Alves
05:50PM-06:10PM	"A Speeding up Technique for Lossy Anisotropic Algorithm in FDTD Method" 229 Fatih Kaburcuk and Atef Z. Elsherbeni

	Room Pacifico
Session 28 **04:50PM-06:30PM**	**Optimization and Modeling Methods for EM-Driven Design** **Session Organizer: Slawomir Koziel** **Session Chair: Slawomir Koziel**
04:50PM-05:10PM	"Rapid Design Optimization of Compact Couplers Using Response Features and Adjoint Sensitivities" 231 Slawomir Koziel and Adrian Bekasiewicz
05:10PM-05:30PM	"Multi-Objective EM-Driven Design of Integrated Spiral Inductors by Pareto Front Exploration" 233 Slawomir Koziel and Piotr Kurgan
05:30PM-05:50PM	"Surrogate-assisted Transformation Optics Inspired GRIN Lens Design and Optimization" 235 Sawyer D. Campbell, Jogender Nagar, John A. Easum, Douglas H. Werner, and Pingjuan L. Werner
05:50PM-06:10PM	"Research on EM Characteristics Modeling of Sea Surface by Ship EDF" 237 Gao Shuang, Mei Jiahe, Guo Lingfei, Jiang Tao, and Zhang Yachen

	Room Atlantico
Session 29 **04:50PM-06:30PM**	**Human Exposure to Electromagnetic Fields: EMF Dosimetry, Applications, Compliance Methods** **Session Organizers: Luca Giaccone, Aldo Canova** **Session Chair: Luca Giaccone**
04:50PM-05:10PM	"The Role of the Skin Modeling in LF Dosimetry" 239 Valerio De Santis, Tommaso Campi, Silvano Cruciani, and Mauro Feliziani

05:10PM-05:30PM	"Assessment of the Uncertainty in 50 Hz Foetal Exposure due to Tissues Conductivity Variation" 241 Serena Fiocchi, Paolo Ravazzani, and Marta Parazzini
05:30PM-05:50PM	"Assessment of Fetal Exposure to 4G LTE Tablet in Realistic Scenarios using Stochastic Dosimetry" 243 E. Chiaramello, M. Parazzini, P. Ravazzani, and J. Wiart
05:50PM-06:10PM	"Exposure to Electric and Magnetic Fields at Intermediate Frequencies of Household Appliances" 245 Sam Aerts, Carolina Calderon, Blaz Valic, Matthias Van den Bossche, Leen Verloock, Myron Maslanyj, Darren Addison, Peter Gajsek, Luc Martens, Martin Roosli, Elisabeth Cardis, and Wout Joseph

Session 30 **06:10PM-07:00PM**	**Plenary Talk – 4**	**Room Continenti**
	"Using Different Techniques for Electromagnetic Design and Verification of Large and Complex Structures: Industrial Cases of Interest" **IDS Ingegneria dei Sistemi**	

ACES 2017 Technical Program

Wednesday, March 29

08:00AM-05:00PM	**Conference Registration**	**Business Center**
08:30PM-05:30PM	**Exhibitors**	**Main Hall**
08:00PM-10:30PM	**Banquet**	**Room Continenti**
Session 31 **08:40AM-09:30AM**	**Plenary Talk – 5**	**Room Continenti**
	"Wireless Power Transfer and Energy Harvesting for RFID and Wireless Sensors" **Apostolos Georgiadis**	
Session 32 **09:40AM-10:30AM**	**Plenary Talk – 6**	**Room Continenti**
	"(Heterogeneous) Parallel Solutions of Billion-Unknown Problems: Applications and Big-Data Aspects" **Levent Gürel**	
10:30AM-11:00AM	**Break**	

		Room Continenti
Session 33 **11:00AM-01:20PM**	**Electromagnetic Techniques for the Internet of Things – 1** **Session Organizers: Paolo Nepa, Alessandra Costanzo** **Session Chairs: Paolo Nepa, Alessandra Costanzo**	
11:00AM-11:20AM	"Phase-Only Synthesis of Convex Metallic Reflectarray Antennas for Multi-beam Radiations via Steepest Descent Method" 247 Jen-Wei Liu and Hsi-Tseng Chou	
11:20AM-11:40AM	"Energy Paradigms of Augmented Tags for the Internet of Things Deployment" 249 Smail Tedjini, Gianfranco Andia Vera, and Yvan Duroc	
11:40AM-12:00PM	"Principal Component Analysis of CSI for the Robust Wireless Detection of Passive Targets" 251 F. Viani, A. Polo, E. Giarola, M. Salucci, and A. Massa	
12:00PM-12:20PM	"Miniature Rectenna Design" 253 Hubregt J. Visser	
12:20PM-12:40PM	"A Portable RFID Reader Augmented with Tracking Capabilities for Indoor Monitoring of People" 255 Giacomo Paolini, Diego Masotti, and Alessandra Costanzo	
12:40PM-01:00PM	"3D Antenna for Wireless Power Transmission" 257 Gonçalo Dias, Pedro Pinho, Ricardo Gonçalves, and Nuno Carvalho	
01:00PM-01:20PM	"RFID Sensing Breadboard for Industrial IoT" 259 Cecilia Occhiuzzi, Sabina Manzari, Stefano Caizzone, Sara Amendola, and Gaetano Marrocco	
01:20PM-02:30PM	**Lunch**	**Hotel Restaurant**

	Room Americhe
Session 34 **11:00AM-01:20PM**	**Computational Electromagnetics, Advanced Algorithms and Emerging Applications – 4** **Session Organizers: Zhen Peng, Li Jiang** **Session Chairs: Fayçal Benmohamed**
11:00AM-11:20AM	"Numerical Simulation of Wave Propagation in Microstrip Line Containing Magnetic Layer" 261 Fayçal Benmohamed, Didier Vincent, Jingyi Wang, and Junwu Tao

11:20AM-11:40AM	"Wave Concept in MoM-GEC Formalism" 263 Ahmed Nouainia, Mohamed Hajji, and Taoufik Aguili
11:40AM-12:00PM	"Determined Factor Parameter Analysis for System of Information Recovery from USB-Keyboard Compromising Emanations" 265 Rostislav I. Sokolov and Renat R. Abdullin
12:00AM-12:20PM	"Radar Big Data Reduction Using Hardware and Software Solutions" 267 Sabikun Nahar, Lingyun Ren, Aly E. Fathy, Nghia Tran, and Ozlem Kilic
01:20PM-02:30PM	**Lunch** — **Hotel Restaurant**

	Room Pacifico
Session 35 **11:00AM-01:20PM**	**Nanoelectronics and Nanoelectromagnetics: Modeling and Applications** **Session Organizers: Antonio Maffucci, Sergey Maksimenko** **Session Chairs: Antonio Maffucci, Sergey Maksimenko**
11:00AM-11:20AM	"Can a Degenerate Electron Gas Stabilize Excitons in Semiconductors?" N/A Axel Hoffmann, C. Nenstiel, G. Callsen, F. Nippert, and M. R. Wagner
11:20AM-11:40AM	"Electron Beam Induced Terahertz Čerenkov Radiation from Multilayer Graphene Sandwiches" 271 Konstantin Batrakov and Sergey Maksimenko
11:40AM-12:00PM	"Tunable Electromagnetic Response of Free-standing 3D Carbon Nanotube Network in the Ka-band" 273 M. V. Shuba, D. Yuko, P. P. Kuzhir, S. A. Maksimenko, and M. Scarselli
12:00PM-12:20PM	"Carbon Thin Films as Effective Absorbers of Microwave Radiation: Experiment and EMC Applications" 275 Polina Kuzhir, Alesia Padabskaya, Nadezhda Volynets, Konstantin Batrakov, Sergey Maksimenko, Tommi Kaplas, Yuri Svirko, and Philippe Lambin
12:20PM-12:40PM	"Carbon Nanotube Interconnects with Negative Temperature Coefficient of the Resistance" 277 A. Maffucci, G. Miano, F. Micciulla, A. Cataldo, and S. Bellucci
01:20PM-02:30PM	**Lunch** — **Hotel Restaurant**

	Room Atlantico
Session 36 **11:00AM-01:20PM**	**Antenna Design – 2** **Session Chair: Michael Johnson**
11:00AM-11:20AM	"A System-by-Design Approach for Efficient Multiband Patch Antennas Design" 279 M. Salucci, G. Oliveri, P. Rocca, and A. Massa
11:20AM-11:40AM	"On the Comparison and Evaluation of Sparse Array Synthesis Methods" 281 Daniele Pinchera, Marco Donald Migliore, Mario Lucido, and Fulvio Schettino
11:40AM-12:00PM	"Uniform Theory of Diffraction Approximation for Large Antenna Array Fields" 283 Michael R. Johnson and Omar W. Ali
12:00PM-12:20PM	"Optimal Synthesis of Monopulse Beamforming Weights for Airborne Radars through Convex Optimization" 285 G. Gottardi, N. Ebrahimi, P. Rocca, and A. Massa
12:20PM-12:40PM	"Optimization-based Design of Innovative Grating-lobe Free Radar UWB Architectures" 287 L. Tenuti, P. Rocca, and A. Massa
12:40PM-01:00PM	"Circular Slotted Reconfigurable Multiband Patch Antenna for Wireless Applications" 289 Rashid Saleem and Asim Quddus
01:20PM-02:30PM	**Lunch** — **Hotel Restaurant**

	Room Continenti
Session 37 02:30PM-04:30PM	**Electromagnetic Techniques for the Internet of Things – 2** **Session Organizers: Paolo Nepa, Alessandra Costanzo** **Session Chairs: Paolo Nepa, Alessandra Costanzo**
02:30PM-02:50PM	"Autonomous Wearable RFID-Based Sensing Platform for the Internet-of-Things" 291 Sam Lemey, Sam Agneessens, Patrick Van Torre, Kristof Baes, Hendrik Rogier, and Jan Vanfleteren
02:50PM-03:10PM	"Synthesis of Near Field Focused Arrays Including Far Field Constrains" 293 Rafael G. Ayestaran, Marcos R. Pino, and Paolo Nepa
03:10PM-03:30PM	"Resonant Inductive WPT Link Operating in a Coupling-independent Regime" 295 Alessio De Angelis, Marco Dionigi, Paolo Carbone, Mauro Mongiardo, Qinghua Wang, Wenquan Che, Franco Mastri, Alessandra Costanzo, Giuseppina Monti, and Luciano Tarricone
03:30PM-03:50PM	"The SARFID Technique in Handling Systems Applications" 297 Alice Buffi, Paolo Nepa, and Marcos R. Pino
03:50PM-04:10PM	"A Proximity Wireless Sensor Based on Backscatter Communication" 299 Angel Servent, Spyros Daskalakis. Ana Collado, and Apostolos Georgiadis
04:10PM-04:30PM	"Experimental Assessment of a Design Criterion for RFID Wearable Antennas" 301 P. Nepa, A. Michel, G. Manara, R. Colella, L. Catarinucci, L. Tarricone, G. A. Casula, G. Mazzarella, and G. Montisci
04:30PM-04:50PM	Break

	Room Americhe
Session 38 02:30PM-04:30PM	**Low-Frequency Electromagnetic Inverse Problems – 1** **Session Organizer: Alessandro Formisano** **Session Chair: Alessandro Formisano**
02:30PM-02:50PM	"Sensor Selection via Convex Optimization in Remote Contact-free Measurement of Currents" 303 Fatemeh Ghasemifard and Martin Norgren
02:50PM-03:10PM	"Magnetic Polarizability Tensors for Low Frequency Object Classification and Detection" 305 P. D. Ledger and W. R. B. Lionheart
03:10PM-03:30PM	"Lorentz Force Evaluation with an Extended Area Approach" 307 E.-M. Dölker, R. Schmidt, K. Weise, B. Petković, M. Ziolkowski, H. Brauer, and J. Haueisen
03:30PM-03:50PM	"Calculation of Eddy Currents in Moving Conductors Using the Meshfree Charge Simulation Method" 309 B. Petković and J. Haueisen
03:50PM-04:10PM	"Spatial Harmonic Current Density Basis for Faults Identification in Fuel Cell Stack from External Magnetic Field Measurements" 311 Lyes Ifrek, Olivier Chadebec, Gilles Cauffet, Yann Bultel, Sébastien Rosini, and Luc Rouveyre
04:10PM-04:30PM	"Generalization of the Vector Hysteron Model through the Dependence of Moving Functions on Frequency" 313 Antonino Laudani, Gabriele-Maria Lozito, Francesco Riganti-Fulginei, Alessandro Salvini, Ermanno Cardelli, Antonio Faba, and Simone Quondam
04:30PM-04:50PM	Break

Session 39 02:30PM-03:30PM	**Tutorial – 2**	**Room Pacifico**
	"Higher-Order Hierarchical Vector Polynomial Bases for CEM" 490 **Roberto D. Graglia, Andrew F. Peterson**	

Session 40 03:30PM-04:30PM	**Tutorial – 3**	**Room Pacifico**
	"Developing Singular Vector Bases for CEM" 515 **Andrew F. Peterson, Roberto D. Graglia**	
04:30PM-04:50PM	**Break**	

	Room Atlantico
Session 41 02:30PM-04:30PM	**Antenna Design – 3** **Session Chairs: Lorenzo Poli, Victor Chechetkin**
02:30PM-02:50PM	"Power Pattern Sensitivity Analysis of Reflectarray Antennas to Substrate Uncertainties through the Minkowski Interval Analysis" 315 N. Ebrahimi, P. Rocca, and A. Massa
02:50PM-03:10PM	"Equivalent Circuit Model of a Triple Frequency Rejection Band UWB Antenna" 317 Yanyan Wang, Tao Jiang, and Yingsong Li
03:10PM-03:30PM	"Innovative Simplified Array Design for Wireless Power Transmission" 319 G. Oliveri, P. Rocca, L. Poli, and A. Massa
03:30PM-03:50PM	"An Integer Genetic Algorithm for Optimal Clustering in Phased Array Antenna" 321 L. Poli, G. Oliveri, and A. Massa
03:50PM-04:10PM	"Reconfigurable Electrically Small Split Ring Resonator Antenna" 323 A. Bakhmutov, N. Knyazev, and V. Chechetkin
04:10PM-04:30PM	"A Square Slot Circularly Polarized Microstrip Antenna with Enhanced Bandwidth" 325 Obeng Kwakye Kingsford Sarkodie, Kang Kai, and Mujeeb Abdullah
04:30PM-04:50PM	**Break**

	Room Americhe
Session 42 04:50PM-06:30PM	**Wireless Power Transfer** **Session Organizer: Shishir Punjala** **Session Chair: Shishir Punjala**
04:50PM-05:10PM	"Wireless Power Transfer via Negative Permittivity Metamaterials as Resonating Elements" 327 Antonios G. Pelekanidis, Antonios X. Lalas, Nikolaos V. Kantartzis, Tadao Ohtani, and Yasushi Kanai
05:10PM-05:30PM	"A Multiantenna Approach to Maximize Wireless Power Transfered to Implantable Devices" 329 H. Dinis, I. Colmiais, and P. M. Mendes
05:30PM-05:50PM	"Coil Designs that Enable Wireless Powering by Cancelling Flux Leakage" 331 Shishir Punjala

	Room Pacifico
Session 43 04:50PM-06:30PM	**Advanced Applications – 1** **Session Chair: Paolo Petrini**
04:50PM-05:10PM	"Microwave Measurement Technique for Evaluating the Polarization of the Electromagnetic Field within a Reverberating Chamber" 333 Antonio Sorrentino, José. J. Gil, Maurizio Migliaccio, Giuseppe Ferrara, and Sergio Cappa
05:10PM-05:30PM	"Artificial Ionospheric Scintillation Effects on Communication Signals in the V and W Bands" 335 David Smith, Peter Collins, James Fee, James C. Petrosky, Andrew Terzuoli, and Caglar Yardim
05:30PM-05:50PM	"Variational Analysis of Substrate-Integrated Waveguides with Longitudinal Slot" 337 Nghia Nguyen-Trong, Leonard Thomas Hall, and Christophe Fumeaux

05:50PM-06:10PM	"Proposal of EMTP Analysis Model for a Surge Phenomenon Arising on a Power Cable Assembled in a Transmission Tower" 339 Ryoji Oshiro, Yuto Hachiman, Taishi Shiozuka, and Eiji Kaneko
06:10PM-06:30PM	"Propagation Modelling and Channel Estimation: A Comparison among Different Channel Indicators in Severe Multipath Environments" 341 Antonio Sorrentino, Giuseppe Ferrara, Maurizio Migliaccio, Sergio Cappa, and Lorenzo Mucchi

	Room Atlantico
Session 44 **04:50PM-06:30PM**	**Advanced Applications – 2** **Session Chairs: Meng Lin, Tao Jiang**
04:50PM-05:10PM	"Analysis of New Discrete-Rotary Crosstalk Model Based on FDTD" 343 Yaxiu Sun, Meng Lin, Yida Lai, and Junpeng Fang
05:10PM-05:30PM	"Frequency Domain Analysis of New Differential-mode Twisted Wire Crosstalk Model" 345 Yaxiu Sun, Jianli Wang, Junzhu Qian, and Ming Zhang
05:30PM-05:50PM	"Analysis and Evaluation of One-dimensional Sea Surface Features Based on FSV" 347 Nan Bi, Xiaojun Wang, Tao Jiang, and Yachen Zhang
05:50PM-06:10PM	"Groundwave Propagation in a Nonhomogeneous Atmosphere: Prediction Using 3D Parabolic Equation" 349 Zeina El Ahdab and Funda Akleman
06:10PM-06:30PM	"The Calculation of Equivalent Electromagnetic Parameters in Multilayer Composite Materials" 351 Yaxiu Sun, Junzhu Qian, Jianli Wang, and Ming Zhang

ACES 2017 Technical Program

Thursday, March 30

08:00AM-05:00PM	**Conference Registration**	**Business Center**
08:30PM-05:30PM	**Exhibitors**	**Main Hall**
Session 45 **08:40AM-09:30AM**	**Plenary Talk – 6**	**Room Continenti**
	"Analysis of Plasmonic and Nano-Photonic Devices" **Salah Obayya**	

	Room Continenti
Session 46 **09:50AM-10:30AM**	**Algorithms for Unique Applications – 2** **Session Chair: Paolo Petrini**
09:50AM-10:10AM	"Portable High-Performance Software Design Using Templated Meta-Programming for EM Calculations" 353 Jamie Infantolino, James Ross, and David Richie
10:10AM-10:30AM	"Modeling of Stability of Electrostatic and Magnetostatic Systems" 355 Michael Grinfeld and Pavel Grinfeld
10:30AM-11:00AM	**Break**

	Room Americhe
Session 47 **09:50AM-10:30AM**	**Computational Electromagnetics, Advanced Algorithms and Emerging Applications – 5** **Session Organizers: Zhen Peng, Li Jiang** **Session Chair: Fatih Kaburcuk**
09:50AM-10:10AM	"Fast Wideband Solution Using MBPE with MOM" 357 Fatih Kaburcuk and Mehmet Onur Kok
10:10AM-10:30AM	"Modelling of Electromagnetic Scattering from Large and General Intakes on Complex Platforms" 359 A. Mori, S. Bertini, M. Bercigli, P. de Vita, and S. Sensani
10:30AM-11:00AM	**Break**

	Room Pacifico
Session 48 **09:50AM-10:30AM**	**Electromagnetic Non Destructive Evaluation** **Session Organizers: Lalita Upda, Antonello Tamburrino** **Session Chair: Antonello Tamburrino**
09:50AM-10:10AM	"Electromagnetic Material Parameter Extraction of Ferrites up to the GHz Range via Measurements and Simulations" 361 Christian Reinhold, Peter Scholz, and Ulrich Jumar
10:10AM-10:30AM	"Monotonicity Principle in Pulsed Eddy Current Testing and Its Application to Defect Sizing" 363 Zhiyi Su, Lalita Udpa, Gaspare Giovinco, Salvatore Ventre, and Antonello Tamburrino
10:30AM-11:00AM	**Break**

	Room Atlantico
Session 49 **09:50AM-10:30AM**	**Antenna Design – 4** **Session Chair: William O'Keefe Coburn**
09:50AM-10:10AM	"Concentric Substrate Geometry for a Multi-Mode and Dual-Band Rectangular Array" 365 Gregory Mitchell and Amir Zaghloul
10:10AM-10:30AM	"Suspended Plate Antenna Array for High Power" 367 Seth A. McCormick and William O. Coburn
10:30AM-11:00AM	**Break**

	Room Continenti	
Session 50 **11:00AM-01:20PM**	**Novel Computational Methodologies for Electromagnetics, Optics and Photonics** **Session Organizer: James B. Cole** **Session Chair: James B. Cole**	
11:00AM-11:20AM	"A One-dimensional Randomly Rough Interface that Produces a Specified Angular Distribution of the Intensity of the Light Transmitted Through it" 369 Ingve Simonsen and Alexei A. Maradudin	
11:20AM-11:40AM	"Control of the Coherence of Light Transmitted through a One-dimensional Randomly Rough Interface that acts as a Schell-model Source" 371 Alexei A. Maradudin and Ingve Simonsen	
11:40AM-12:00PM	"Complete Families in Inverse Obstacle Scattering" 373 Giovanni Franco Crosta	
12:00PM-12:20PM	"An Improved Subspace Projection Method of Underdetermined Direction of Arrival Estimation for Frequency Hopping Signals" 375 Chaozhu Zhang and Yu Wang	
12:20PM-12:40PM	"A Hybrid LVD-HAF Method of Quadratic Frequency-Modulated Signals" 377 Fulong Jing, Weijian Si, and Shuhong Jiao	
12:40PM-01:00PM	"Equilibrium Shape of Ferrofluid in the Uniform External Field" 379 Michael Grinfeld and Pavel Grinfeld	
01:00PM-01:20PM	"Scattering by a Chiral Elliptic Cylinder Placed in Another Infinite Chiral Medium" 381 A.-K. Hamid	
01:20PM-02:30PM	**Lunch**	**Hotel Restaurant**

	Room Americhe
Session 51 **11:00AM-01:20PM**	**Inverse Scattering Techniques for GPR and Subsurface Imaging** **Session Organizers: Lorenzo Poli, Salucci Marco, Lara Pajewski** **Session Chairs: Lorenzo Poli, Salucci Marco, Lara Pajewski**
11:00AM-11:20AM	"Frequency-Hopping GPR Prospecting of Sparse Scatterers through Bayesian Compressive Sensing" 383 M. Salucci, L. Tenuti, G. Oliveri, and A. Massa
11:20AM-11:40AM	"Pros and Cons of Microwave Imaging Techniques for the Reconstruction of Velocity Profiles of Cylindrical Targets in Axial Motion" 385 Massimo Brignone, Matteo Pastorino, Mirco Raffetto, and Andrea Randazzo
11:40AM-12:00PM	"On Time-Domain Use of the Cylindrical Wave Approach" 387 Cristina Ponti and Giuseppe Schettini
12:00PM-12:20PM	"Development of Electromagnetic Simulators for Ground Penetrating Radar" 389 Lara Pajewski, Sinisa Antonijevic, Vicko Doric, Dragan Poljak, Antonios Giannopoulos, Craig Warren, and Daniele Pirrone

12:20PM-12:40PM	"Short-Term Scientific Missions on Forward and Inverse Electromagnetic-Scattering Techniques for Ground Penetrating Radar" 391 Lara Pajewski, Antonios Giannopoulos, Marian Marciniak, Simone Meschino, Alexei Popov, Igor Prokopovich, Alessio Ventura, and Craig Warren
12:40PM-01:00PM	"Ground Penetrating Radar Data Imaging via Kirchhoff Migration Method" 393 X. Liu, M. Serhir, A. Kameni, M. Lambert, and L. Pichon
01:00PM-01:20PM	"Advanced Imaging for Down-Looking Contactless GPR Systems" 395 Davide Comite, Alessandro Galli, Ilaria Catapano, and Francesco Soldovieri
01:20PM-02:30PM	**Lunch** — **Hotel Restaurant**

	Room Pacifico
Session 52 **11:00AM-01:20PM**	**Novel Photonic Material and Devices – 2** **Session Organizers: Salah Obayya, Mohamed Swillam** **Session Chair: Salah Obayya**
11:00AM-11:20AM	"Intersecting Silicon Nano-Walls with Planar Nano-Gold Layers for Solar Energy Harvesting" 397 Nihal F. F. Areed, Sami Zenad, and Salah S. A. Obayya
11:20AM-11:40AM	"Padé Boundary Conditions for Finite Element Time Domain Beam Propagation Method" 399 Khaled S. R. Atia, A. M. Heikal, and S. S. A. Obayya
11:40AM-12:00PM	"Modified BPM for Plasmonic Modeling" 401 Adel Shaaban, M. F. O. Hameed, S. S. A. Obayya, Lotfi R. Gomaa, and M. A. Swillam
12:00PM-12:20PM	"Light Absorption Enhancement in Thin Film Hydrogenated Amorphus Si Solar Cells" 403 C. Mennucci, M. C. Giordano, C. Martella, D. Repetto, F. Buatier De Mongeot, M. H. Muhammad, A. H. K. Mahmoud, M. F. O. Hameed, and S. S. A. Obayya
12:20PM-12:40PM	"Surface Plasmon Photonic Crystal Fiber Biosensor for Glucose Monitoring" 405 Mohammad Y. Azab, M. F. O. Hameed, A. M. Heikal, S. S. A. Obayya, and M. A. Swillam
01:20PM-02:30PM	**Lunch** — **Hotel Restaurant**

	Room Atlantico
Session 53 **11:00AM-01:20PM**	**Biological Effects of Electric, Magnetic and Electromagnetic Fields: Innovative Applications in Daily Life – 1** **Session Organizers: Alessandro Fanti, Bruno Bisceglia** **Session Chair: Alessandro Fanti**
11:00AM-11:20AM	"Electromagnetic Stimuli in Therapeutics and Resuscitation" 407 Oana Mihaela Drosu
11:20AM-11:40AM	"Sodium Imaging of the Human Knee Cartilage with Magnetic Resonance at Ultra High Field: Development of a Double Frequency ($^{1}H/^{23}Na$) RF Coil" 409 Francesca Maggiorelli, Joshua D. Kaggie, Martin J. Graves, Guido Buonincontri, Alessandra Retico, Laura Biagi, Gianluigi Tiberi, and Michela Tosetti
11:40AM-12:00PM	"Robustness of Flexible 7T-MRI Coil Behaviour" 411 Andrea Melis, Sergio Casu, Alessandro Fanti, Giuseppe Mazzarella, Claudio Puddu, and Patrizia Boccacci
12:00PM-12:20PM	"Application of EMFs at Microwave Frequencies for Brain Stroke Detection: Preliminary Results" 413 I. Bisio, A. Fedeli, F. Lavagetto, G. Luzzati, M. Pastorino, M. Raffetto, A. Randazzo, and E. Tavanti
12:20PM-12:40PM	"Antenna for Contact Microwave Radiometers for Monitoring of the Brain Microwave Radiation" 415

	B. A. Panchenko, V. S. Kublanov, S. A. Baranov, V. I. Borisov, and Y. E. Sedelnikov	
01:20PM-02:30PM	**Lunch**	**Hotel Restaurant**

	Room Continenti
Session 54 **02:30PM-04:30PM**	**Applications of Antennas and Arrays** **Session Chair: Randy Haupt**
02:30PM-02:50PM	"A Ku band Circularly Polarized 2x2 Microstrip Antenna Array for Remote Sensing Applications" 417 Roger Ferré, Fermín Mira, Guido Luzi, Jordi Mateu, and Christos Kalialakis
02:50PM-03:10PM	"Investigation of Efficient Simulation Methods for Finite Large X-Band Arrays in HFSS" 419 Elicia Harper, Carolyn Reistad, and Alkim Akyurtlu
03:10PM-03:30PM	"Genetic Algorithm Optimization of a Dual Polarized Concentric Ring Array" 421 Pedro Mendes Ruiz, Israel D. Hinostroza Sáenz, Régis Guinvarc'h, and Randy L. Haupt
03:30PM-03:50PM	"Mutual Coupling Reduction in Array Elements Using EBG Structures" 423 Hassan Sajjad, Sana Khan, and Ercument Arvas
03:50PM-04:10PM	"Design of Compact Dual-Element Antenna Array for LTE700 and WWAN Applications" 425 Hari Shankar Singh and Manoj Kumar Meshram
04:30PM-04:50PM	**Break**

	Room Americhe
Session 55 **02:30PM-04:30PM**	**Low-Frequency Electromagnetic Inverse Problems – 2** **Session Organizer: Alessandro Formisano** **Session Chair: Alessandro Formisano**
02:30PM-02:50PM	"A Modified CoSaMP Algorithm for Electromagnetic Imaging of Two Dimensional Domains" 427 Ali Imran Sandhu and Hakan Bagci
02:50AM-03:10AM	"Optimal Design of Closed Multilayer Magnetic Shields" 429 Aldo Canova, Fabio Freschi, Luca Giaccone, and Maurizio Repetto
03:10AM-03:30AM	"Mitigation of Background Field Effects on Coils Characterization from Magnetic Measurements" 431 Andrea Gaetano Chiariello, Alessandro Formisano, Francesco Ledda, Raffaele Martone, and Francesco Pizzo
04:30PM-04:50PM	**Break**

Session 56 **02:30PM-03:30PM**	**Tutorial – 4**	**Room Pacifico**
	"Tolerance Analysis and Robust Design in Engineering Electromagnetics - An Interval Analysis Perspective" 541 **Paolo Rocca**	
04:30PM-04:50PM	**Break**	

	Room Atlantico
Session 57 **02:30PM-04:30PM**	**Biological Effects of Electric, Magnetic and Electromagnetic Fields: Innovative Applications in Daily Life – 2** **Session Organizers: Alessandro Fanti, Bruno Bisceglia** **Session Chair: Alessandro Fanti**
02:30PM-02:50PM	"ELF Fields in Agriculture: New Techniques for a Sustainable Development" 433 Bruno Bisceglia and Simona Valbonesi

02:50PM-03:10PM	"Directive 2013/35/EU: A Critical Analysis" 435 Bruno Bisceglia, Claudia Carciofi, and Simona Valbonesi
03:10PM-03:30PM	"Evaluation of Temperature Increase During Magnetic Resonance Examinations by Combining Electromagnetic/Thermal Simulations and B1 Maps" 437 Nunzia Fontana, Gianluigi Tiberi, Mauro Costagli, M. R. Symms, Michela Tosetti, and Agostino Monorchio
03:30PM-03:50PM	"Electromagnetic Fields: Scientific Basis of Regulatory Frameworks" 439 Bruno Bisceglia and Simona Valbonesi
03:50PM-04:10PM	"In Silico Analysis of Farmlands Disinfection using Microwave" 441 Michele Spanu and Matteo Bruno Lodi
04:30PM-04:50PM	**Break**

	Room Continenti
Session 58 **04:50PM-06:30PM**	**Recent Advances on Characteristic Mode Analysis and Applications** **Session Organizers: Agostino Monorchio, Simone Genovesi** **Session Chair: Agostino Monorchio**
04:50PM-05:10PM	"Analysis of Dielectric Coated Conducting Bodies Using Characteristic Mode Theory" 443 Liwen Guo, Yikai Chen, and Shiwen Yang
05:10PM-05:30PM	"An Enhanced Algorithm in Tracking Characteristic Modes of Dielectric Objects" 445 H. Alroughani
05:30PM-05:50PM	"Pattern Control for Portable Devices by Exploiting Phase-Shifted Characteristic Modes" 447 Francesco Alessio Dicandia, Simone Genovesi, and Agostino Monorchio
05:50PM-06:10PM	"Reverse Operation Self-consistent Evaluation Applied to IE-DDM with Phase Extracted Basis Function" 449 Jun Hu, Ming Jiang, Lin Lei, and Zaiping Nie

	Room Atlantico
Session 59 **04:50PM-06:30PM**	**Frequency and Time Domain Integral Equation Solvers – 2** **Session Organizers: Huseyin Arda Ulku, Hakan Bagci, Ozgur Ergul** **Session Chairs: Huseyin Arda Ulku, Hakan Bagci, Ozgur Ergul**
04:50PM-05:10PM	"Progress in Developing Custom Cubature Rules for Computational Electromagnetics" 451 Malcolm M. Bibby and Andrew F. Peterson
05:10PM-05:30PM	"Fast Monostatic Scattering Analysis Based on Bayesian Compressive Sensing" 453 Huan Huan Zhang, Wei E. I. Sha, and Li Jun Jiang
05:30PM-05:50PM	"Small Incident Angle Transient Scattering from Shallow Cavities in a Ground Plane" 455 Richard Uber and Aihua Wood
05:50PM-06:10PM	"Distributed Macrobasis Decomposition for the Electromagnetic Solution of Large Periodic Structures" 457 Alberto Serna, Luis Landesa, Jose Manuel Taboada, and Mario F. Manzano
06:10PM-06:30PM	"Multi-trace Boundary Integral Formulations with Eddy Current Models" 459 Xavier Claeys and Edouard Demaldent

Additional Paper:

"Complex Permittivity Measurements of Dielectrics for Space Antenna Radome and Substrates in X-Band" 269
F. Ozturk, V. Akan, K. Topalli, E. Kiraz, L. Kuzu, M. Gokten

Algorithm of Bispectral Video Signal Recovery under Conditions of Industrial Noise

Rostislav I. Sokolov, Renat R. Abdullin
Institute of Radioelectronics and Informational Technologies,
Ural Federal University named after the first President of Russia B.N.Yeltsin,
19 Mira str, Yekaterinburg, Russian Federation

***Abstract*—A binary communication channel under the action of additive Gaussian and non-Gaussian broadband and narrow-band interferences is considered in order to identify the possibilities of using the method of bispectral analysis for the detection and recovery of the useful signal. The discrete random process with SL Johnson distribution is taken as non-Gaussian noise. The estimation of periodic signal detection and recovery effectiveness has been held by means of bispectral processing the mixture of noise and a priori unknown signal. The digital simulation was implemented in MatLab software. It has been shown the method of bispectral analysis allows recovering the signal more qualitative in comparison with the ordinary spectral analysis when SNR is close to unity. The use of developed algorithm allows detecting the periodic pulse packets at large SNR values.**

***Keywords*—bispectral analysis; signal recovery; industrial noise; Gaussian noise.**

I. Introduction

One of the most perspective approaches ensuring the good results in the solution of signal recovery tasks under the presence of intensive noises is the approach based on the use of third order correlation functions and a bispectrum [1]. The bispectrum means a two-dimensional Fourier transform of the third order correlation function [2].

It is possible to use the indirect method to estimate the bispectrum message density [3]. Based on this method the algorithm of signal recovery assessment has been developed and implemented in MatLab software. The signal is recovered from the spectrum vector of averaged bispectrum values obtained by a recursive method.

II. Algorithm of Bispectral Analysis

The indirect method of spectral density estimation contains the following sequence of procedures [1]:

1. Calculation of the aggregate M of sample estimates of tertiary autocorrelation function (TACF) (sampling third order moments) $R^{(m)}(k,l)$ for each of the m = 1, 2 ... M implementations of a time sequence of real samples $\{x^{(m)}(0), x^{(m)}(1), x^{(m)}(2), ..., x^{(m)}(I-1)\}$ as:

$$R^{(m)}(k,l)=\sum_{i=0}^{I-1}x^{(m)}(i)x^{(m)}(i+k)x^{(m)}(i+l). \quad (1)$$

It is supposed the considered process $\{x^{(m)}(i)\}$ in (1) has zero mean $E = 0$.

2. The statistical averaging of sample estimates over the ensemble of M realizations, the result of which is the sample estimate of TACF:

$$R_m(k,l)=\frac{1}{M}\sum_{m=1}^{M}R^{(m)}(k,l). \quad (2)$$

It is necessary to note that for ergodic process the procedure of statistical realizations ensemble averaging (2) can be replaced by an averaging procedure in the time domain, for example, by M segments of temporal sequence $\{x^{(m)}(i)\}$.

3. Formation of the spectral density estimate in a two-dimensional array of complex samples $\dot{B}_{xind}(p,q)=\left|\dot{B}_{xind}(p,q)\right|e^{j\dot{\gamma}_{xind}(p,q)}$ using the procedure of direct two-dimensional discrete Fourier transform of assessment $R_m(k,l)$, which can be written as

$$\left|\hat{S}(2)\right|=\left|\dot{B}_s(1,1)\right|/\left(\left|\hat{S}(1)\right|\left|\hat{S}(1)\right|\right), \quad (3)$$

where $\left|\dot{B}_{xind}(p,q)\right|$ and $\dot{\gamma}_{xind}(p,q)$ are the two-dimensional assessment of the bispectrum amplitude and phase, respectively; $W(k,l)$ is two-dimensional weighting window function, which can be used for stability improvement and providing the consistency of assessment of the spectral density.

Let's consider the digital method of bispectral analysis in tasks of signal filtering and recovery.

The accuracy and the limits of applicability of traditional signal filtering and recovery methods are dependent highly on SNR at the measuring system input. In practice required accuracy of signal parameters estimating can be realized often only for large (much greater than one) values of SNR.

The advantage of bispectral analysis annexed to tasks of signal filtering and recovery is the possibility of recovery and evaluation of non-Gaussian random processes forms in conditions of almost complete a priori uncertainty about the statistical properties of the original signal and noise at low SNR.

The work was supported by Act 211 Government of the Russian Federation, contract № 02.A03.21.0006.

Supposedly the finite set of M realizations of additive mixture of useful signal and noise with unknown characteristics is registered at the digital filtration system input. Here m-th observed realization $x^{(m)}(i)$ (m = 1, 2, ... M) going at the measurement system input is the sum of useful signal $s(i)$ and noise $n_G(i)$. Along with the noise influence the useful signal can be distorted by time shifts, whose value varies between realizations randomly. The original information signal s(i) is given by one-dimensional set of real time samples, the number of which i = 1, 2, ..., I-1 is limited by observation interval in the measurement system. Thus TACF of original information signal is different from zero.

In considered model m-th realization $x^{(m)}(i)$ can be presented as a real discrete sequence:

$$x_m(i) = s\left(i-\tau^{(m)}\right) + n_G^m(i),\; i = 1,2,...,I;\; m = 1,2,...,M, \qquad (4)$$

where n^m_G is m-th realization of additive stationary noise with zero mean $\langle n^m_G \rangle = 0$ and sample variance, which value σ^2_{nmG} is considered to be unknown *a priori*; $\tau^{(m)}$ is an integer random shift of the original useful signal $s(i)$. The maximum shift deviation is less than I. Component n^m_G noise is uncorrelated with the useful signal $s(i)$.

According to (4) *a priori* unknown signal $s(i)$ form is subject to evaluation.

Since the bispectrum is symmetric, to restore the Fourier spectrum of the signal it is enough to perform the calculations at frequencies, which are inside the main triangular area $0 < p < q$ and $p + q < I - 1$. This feature, in practice, allows reducing significantly the memory capacity and machine time required to restore the signal.

III. Digital Simulation

The discrete random process with normal or S_L Johnson distribution is considered as the noise [4]. The task of forming the detection and recovery algorithm for video signal mixed with noise is solved by bispectral analysis method with the next main assumptions:

1. The signal is a sequence of 1,000 video pulses of positive polarity (squarewave), with the following parameters: amplitude is 1 V; single pulse duration is 1 microsecond; the first pulse arrival time coincides with the initial point of observation.

2. The noise is the discrete random process with Gaussian or S_L Johnson distribution. The digital simulation has been held with the given distribution parameters $\gamma = 0$ and $\eta = 1$.

3. The noise is uncorrelated process ($R = 0$).

Bispectrum of video pulse packet mixed with S_L noise, when SNR = 0 dB, obtained during the digital experiment is shown in Fig. 1.

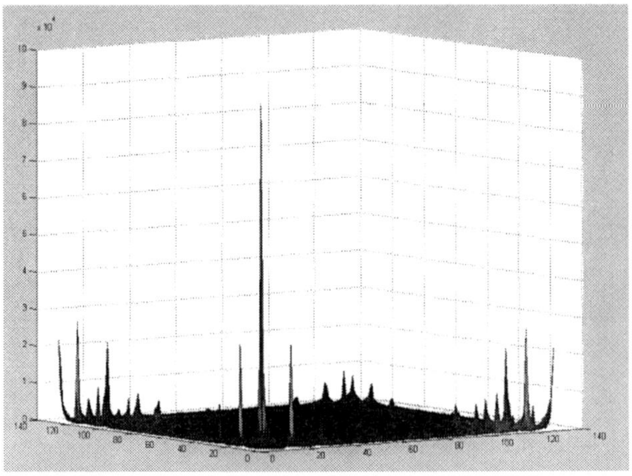

Fig. 1. Bispectrum of uncompromising emanations and S_L Johnson noise at SNR = 0 dB.

IV. Conclusion

1. The developed algorithm of applying the bispectral analysis allows detecting the periodical signal in a mixture with noise by the amplitude-frequency response characteristic of averaged bispectrum estimation with small values of SNR when it is impossible for method of ordinary spectral analysis.

2. When using the chosen simulation parameters, the use of S_L noise leads to quality loss in detection of periodic signal compared with WGN.

3. The method of bispectral analysis allows recovery the signal more qualitative in comparison with ordinary spectral analysis when SNR is closed to unity.

4. The use of bispectral analysis allows reducing significantly the impact of pulse interference on periodic signal recovery quality for almost any SNR.

References

[1] V. N. Vazhinskiy, V.V. Teterin, "Third order correlation function and bispectrum in tasks of signal processing [Korrelatsionnaya funktsiya tret'yego poryadka i bispectr v zadachakh obrabotki signalov]", OMP, no 4, pp. 4-14, 1991.

[2] Fackrell, J.W.A., Bispectral Analysis of Speech Signals. PhD thesis, The University of Edinburgh, UK, 1996.

[3] *Digital signal and image processing in radio physical applications [Tsifrovaya obrabotka signalov i izobrazheniy v radiofizicheskikh prilozheniyakh]*. Moscow: Fizmatlit, 2007, 544 p.

[4] M.G. Kendall, A. Stuart. The Advanced Theory of Statistics: Distribution theory. Macmillan, 1977.

High Frequency RCS Characterization of a Unique Two-Way Field Probe

Andrew Knisely, Peter Collins, and Andrew Terzouli

Institute of Electrical and Electronucs Engineers (IEEE), USA

Abstract—**This research explores the use of a shielded octocopter to function as a two-way field probe for conducting electromagnetic (EM) field measurements at a radar cross section (RCS) range. A high frequency (2-18 GHz) Global RCS assessment of an aluminum shield is conducted to determine the effective cut-off frequency, where the shield no longer provides a consistent RCS profile across each aspect. Upon examining the sector averaging of the targets' RCS, it was determined that the shield's cut-off frequency is approximately 2.8 GHz.**

Keywords—Electromagnetic (EM), RCS, Scattering, Octocopter

I. Introduction

RCS measurement accuracy is largely dependent on the quality of the RCS range where the measurement is conducted. The use of indoor or outdoor RCS ranges to conduct these measurements is largely dependent on the size of the target and the far-field requirements to measure the target. The commonalities between these ranges are the deviations exhibited in the EM waves incident upon the target. Uncertainty in the RCS measurement is a byproduct of these deviations experienced within the test volume or the region between the radar and target. Field probes are used to quantify this uncertainty.

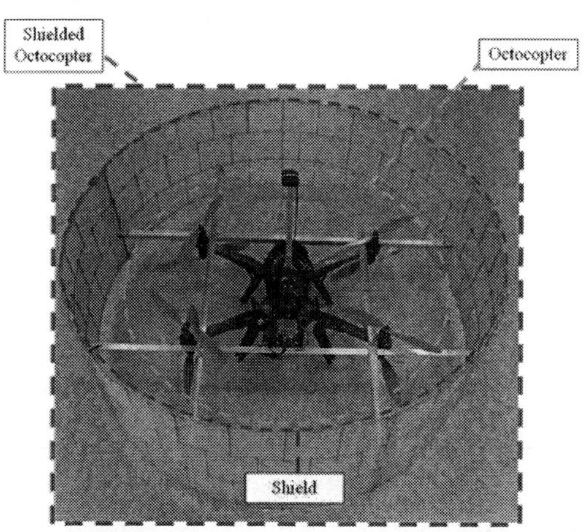

Figure 1.1: Shielded X8 Octocopter

The unique two-way field probe concept introduced in this research involves utilizing a drone configured as a probe to traverse a test volume, allowing for a continuous probe measurment. The particular drone examined in this research is the X8 octocopter. Configuring the X8 as a field probe requires a canonical shield to encapsulate the drone. The canonical shield provides a predictable RCS scattering profile that is compared to a calibrated or analytic RCS solution. The difference in the actual and calibrated RCS measurements determines the deviation in the incident EM waves. The canonical design of the shield involves a squat cylinder shaped comprised of aluminum 14 gauge fencing and aluminum wire mesh. Integration of the shield involves fixing 4 aluminum L-channels to the frame of the drone, providing 8 attach points (see Figure 1.1).

II. Methodology

The objective of the high frequency testing is to determine the limiting frequency threshold of the shield before its RCS conforms to an inconsistent scattering profile. The shield and octocopter are used to establish baseline measurements for comparison against the shielded octocopter. Utilizing high frequency radar, each target is oriented at a varied elevation angle to examine the variations in the scattering profile. This is of particular interest for the shielded X8, where the shield may no longer inhibit the octocopter's RCS at a particular elevation angle. The test matrix is shown in Table I:

TABLE I: RCS Measurement Matrix

Target	Freq./Polarization	Azimuth	Elevation
750 Cal Cyl	2.0:0.1:18.0GHz/HH	0^0	0^0
900 Cal Cyl	2.0:0.1:18.0GHz/HH	0^0	0^0
Cal Mount	2.0:0.1:18.0GHz/HH	0^0	0^0
Target Mount	2.0:0.1:18.0GHz/HH	0^0	0^0
Shield	2.0:0.1:18.0GHz/HH	$0.0:1.0:360.0^0$	$0^0, 5^0, 10^0, 15^0$
Octocopter	2.0:0.1:18.0GHz/HH	$0.0:1.0:360.0^0$	$0^0, 5^0, 10^0, 15^0$
Shielded Octocopter	2.0:0.1:18.0GHz/HH	$0.0:1.0:360.0^0$	$0^0, 5^0, 10^0, 15^0$
750 Cal Cyl	2.0:0.1:18.0GHz/HH	0^0	0^0
900 Cal Cyl	2.0:0.1:18.0GHz/HH	0^0	0^0

The 750 and 900 cylinders are used to establish a calibration function comprised of quadrature components that are dependent on the polarization and frequency of the incident electromagnetic wave. The calibration mount and target mounts are measured to establish the background function of the facility where the RCS measurements are conducted. The calibration and target mount measurements are subtracted from the final series of target measurements (shield, octocopter, and shielded octocopter), enabling the global RCS assessment of each target without background interference. The expected result is the measurment of the shield and shielded octocopter should correlate as the shield will dominate the RCS detected on the radar up to certain frequency value. Beyond this value, the RCS of the shielded octocopter will correlate more towards the octocopter's unique RCS measurement. Sector averaging of each target will be used to compare their respective RCS measurements over a notional frequency range of 2 - 18 GHz.

III. Results and Analysis

The global RCS of the unshielded and shielded octocopter is shown in Figure 1.2. It is observed that the aluminum L-channels of the unshielded octocopter contribute to specular reflections when broadside to the radar. The composite ISAR reveals the most prominently illuminated features of the X8 which include the motor casings and the legs of the drone. Encapsulating the drone in the shield, the exposed portion of the drone are the legs. Examining the global RCS, a definitive scattering response is seen at approximately 10°-40°, 140°, 235°, and 310°.

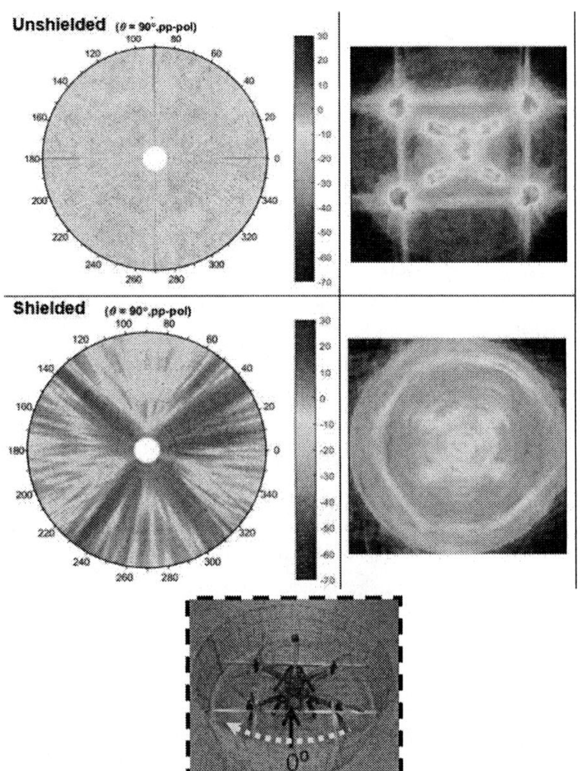

Figure 1.2: Global RCS (left) and Composite ISAR (right)

It is believed that the specular response is not a result of the EM waves directly penetrating the shield but rather the waves are traveling above and below the shield, creeping over the edges. This is more prominent above 2.8 GHz. Figure 1.3 shows the sector partitions, in which each cut represents a cumulative percentile average of the RCS compared over the 2-18 GHz frequency range.

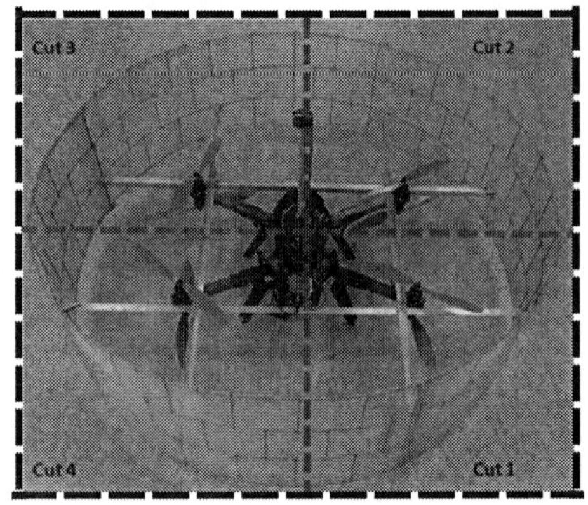

Figure 1.3: Target Sector Partitions (4 Cuts)

The averaged values for each target are shown in Figure 1.4 for the 50th (median RCS) and 100th (maximum RCS) cumulative percentiles. The RCS response of the shielded octocopter correlates with the shield only measurment. Beyond 2.8 GHz, the shielded octocopter's RCS response diverges away from the shield only response. The deviation is gradual over the remaining frequencies, indicating that the shield still dominates the RCS response in comparison to the octocopter-only response.

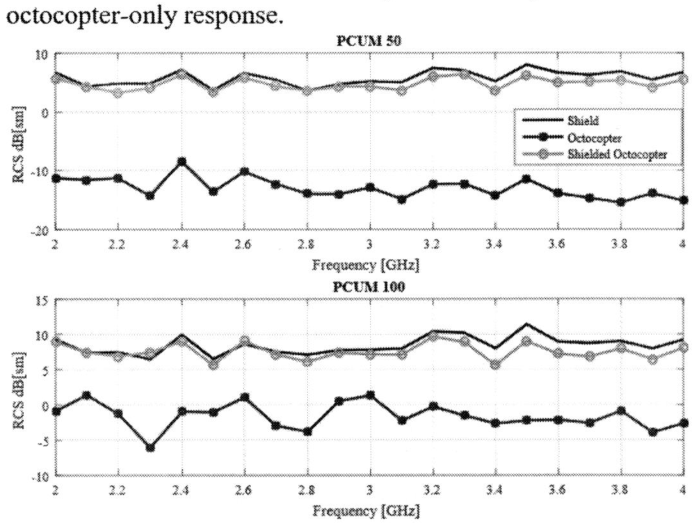

Figure 1.4: Sector Average of all targets, Cut 1, Elevation: 0° "waterline"

IV. Conclusion

The expected performance of the shielded octocopter for the high frequency testing was supported by the sector averaging results, in which each target is compared to determine if the shield's RCS is prominent across the testable frequency band (2-18 GHz). The cut-off frequency is determined to be approximately 2.8 GHz. This indicates that this field probe configuration is operable for ultra-high frequency (UHF) in which the band is 300MHz to 3GHz. Further research will examine the use of this field probe with a noise radar that operates at the 300 to 700MHz band.

A Double Green Function Method for an Inverse Source Problem Related to a Hemisphere

Sevda Vatansever, Ali Alkumru, Hakan Sertlek, H. Arda Ülkü
Department of Electronics Engineering
Gebze Technical University
41400, Kocaeli, Turkey
{svatansever, alkumru, hsertlek, haulku}@gtu.edu.tr

Gokhan Çınar
Electrical and Electronics Engineering Department
Osmangazi University
26480, Eskişehir, Turkey
gcinar@ogu.edu.tr

***Abstract*—In this study, a novel estimation method to determine the electromagnetic or acoustic sources located in a hemisphere using two different Green functions is developed. The inverse source problem is formulated for a scalar function which can be considered as an electromagnetic scalar potential or an acoustic pressure field. Using the explicit expressions of the Green functions obtained for two different boundary conditions satisfied by the corresponding scalar function on the surface of the hemisphere, the inverse source problem is first reduced into an integral equation and then its solution is obtained by discretizing the resulting integral equation.**

***Keywords*—Green function, inverse source problem, integral equation.**

I. Introduction

Inverse scattering problems can be mainly considered in two different groups: The first of these is the determination of the material properties and the geometry of the scatterer from the measurements realized on the scattered waves. This kind of problems has a huge number of applications in many basic engineering areas such as bio-medical imaging, determination of underground resources, Radar, Sonar, undamaged test for buried objects and astronomy [1]-[2]. The second and important type of inverse scattering problems is to determine the source with the help of the radiated fields. This kind of inverse scattering problem is called as the inverse source problem. Inverse source problems, have great importance in many engineering applications, e.g. detection of high-voltage-direct-current (HV-DC) power cables, antenna synthesis applications, determination of the electrical currents, charges or heat sources which cause some damages and irregularities in the human brain can be cited among these applications [3]-[4].

In this study, a method to determine the position and density of the sources existing in a hemisphere using two different Green functions is proposed. By considering the well-known Green identities, an integral equation satisfied by the Green function whose explicit expression is obtained from the measurements effectuated on the hemisphere's surface is presented for the main problem [5]. Diversely from the existing literature, arbitrary boundary conditions which are slightly different than the main problem are considered to obtain an auxiliary second Green function and consequently, another integral equation satisfied by this Green function. The appropriate combination of the above mentioned integral equations (for main and auxiliary problems) reveals a new regular integral equation which can be easily solved numerically by a discretization method to determine the location and density of the source.

The main reason of using two different Green functions in this study is to eliminate the singularity problem that arises in the single Green function method. In this case, it is also expected that ill-posedness which is a basic feature of such problems will disappear. To the best of our knowledge any work devoted to this approach does not exist in the open literature.

II. Formulation and Solution of The Problem

Let the volume D denotes a hemispherical region bounded by the surfaces Σ_1 and Σ_2 as shown in Fig. 1. The Helmholtz equation

$$\Delta u(x) + k^2 u(x) = f(x) \quad , \quad x \in \mathrm{D} \tag{1}$$

with the homogeneous boundary conditions

$$\alpha \frac{\partial u(x)}{\partial n} + \beta u(x) = 0 \quad , \quad x \in \Sigma_1 \tag{2}$$

and

$$\frac{\partial u(x)}{\partial n} = 0 \quad , \quad x \in \Sigma_2 \tag{3}$$

is considered. In the above relations, α and β are known constants while k is the wavenumber related to the region D. In (1)-(3), $x = x(x_1, x_2, x_3)$ denotes the coordinates of a point in D as well as on Σ_1 and Σ_2, $u(x)$ and $f(x)$ represent the scalar function and the source expression which will be determined, respectively. Here, the parameter n expresses the unit normal vectors of the surfaces Σ_1 and Σ_2 being directed towards the outside of the hemispherical region.

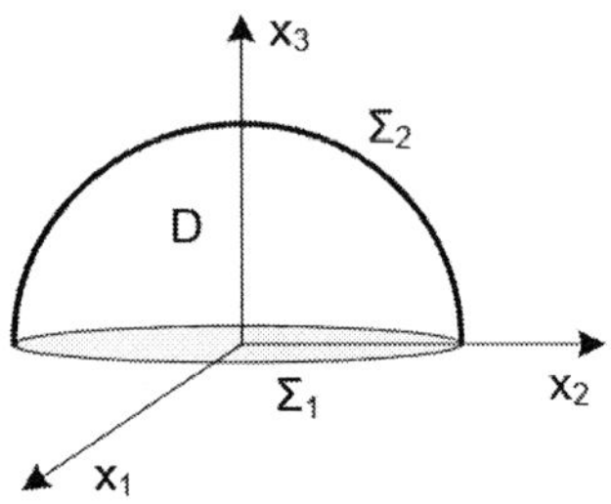

Fig. 1. Geometry of the problem.

Now let us consider that the Green function related to boundary-value problem given by (1)-(3) (main problem) is denoted by G_1. It is obvious that when the boundary condition in (3) is replaced by $u(x) = 0$ while (1) and (2) are remaining the same, a new boundary-value problem (auxiliary problem) having the Green function G_2 occurs. By subtracting the two different solutions written in integral forms of the functions G_1 and G_2 related to the above mentioned boundary-value problems, the following new integral equation given by

$$\int_{\Sigma_2} u(x)\frac{\partial G_2(x,y)}{\partial n}d\Sigma_x = \int_D \{G_1(x,y) - G_2(x,y)\} f(x)dx \quad (4)$$

is obtained to determine the source function $f(x)$.

From (4) it is evident that by considering the measurements realized on Σ_2 for the scalar function $u(x)$, the solution of $f(x)$ can easily be obtained in terms of discrete values from the set of linear algebraic equations as follows:

$$\sum_{i=1}^{N} u(\Sigma_2^i)\int_{\Sigma_2^i}\frac{\partial G_2(x,y_j)}{\partial n_x}d\Sigma_x \approx$$
$$\sum_{i=1}^{N} f(x_i)\int_{D_i}\{G_1(x,y_j)-G_2(x,y_j)\}dx, \quad j=1,2,...,N. \quad (5)$$

In (5) $y_j = (y_1^j, y_2^j, y_3^j) \in D$ and $f(x_i)$ show the selected arbitrary points in D and the discrete values of the source function $f(x)$ at the points $x_i = (x_1^i, x_2^i, x_3^i) \in D_i$, respectively. Additionally, $u(\Sigma_2^i)$ appearing here represents the values of $u(x)$ obtained by measurements on the surface Σ_2. Due to the geometry of the problem the explicit expressions related to the Green functions which stand in (5) are also given in the spherical coordinates by

$$G_{1,2}(r,\theta,\phi,y_j) = \begin{cases} \sum_{m=-\infty}^{\infty}\sum_{n=1}^{\infty}\Psi_n(kr)\begin{Bmatrix} B_{mn}^{1,2}P_{\nu_n}^{(m)}(\cos\theta) \\ +C_{mn}^{1,2}Q_{\nu_n}^{(m)}(\cos\theta)\end{Bmatrix}e^{im\phi} \\ \text{for } 0<\theta_j'\le\theta\le\pi/2, \\ \sum_{m=-\infty}^{\infty}\sum_{n=1}^{\infty}A_{mn}^{1,2}\Psi_n(kr)P_{\nu_n}^{(m)}(\cos\theta)e^{im\phi} \\ \text{for } 0\le\theta\le\theta_j'\le\pi/2. \end{cases} \quad (6)$$

In this last expression $\Psi_n(kr)$, $P_{\nu_n}^{(m)}(\cos\theta)$ and $Q_{\nu_n}^{(m)}(\cos\theta)$ are the spherical Bessel function, regular associated Legendre polynomial and associated Legendre polynomial having the logarithmic singularities at $\theta = \{0, \pi\}$, respectively. In (6) $A_{mn}^{1,2}$, $B_{mn}^{1,2}$ and $C_{mn}^{1,2}$ are known constant coefficients that are determined from the boundary conditions satisfied by the corresponding Green functions while θ_j' is the spherical coordinate component related to the point $y_j = (r_j', \theta_j', \phi_j')$.

III. Conclusion and Forthcoming Studies

In this work, an efficient and accurate method to determine the characteristics such as position and density of the sources which are located in a hemispherical region has been established. The proposed method, which can be also called as *double Green function technique,* is based on the solution of an integral equation containing two different Green functions. The main reason to consider this method is to expect that the solutions for this kind of inverse source problems will not be affected by the well-known property *ill-posedness*, if the singularities in the structure of Green functions vanish. In order to demonstrate the effectiveness as well as the accuracy of the method some numerical applications are still in process of computation. In order to verify the validity of the results that will be obtained by the method described here, the solution of this inverse source problem will also be considered by a separate alternative numerical technique which is based on the finite element method.

Acknowledgment

This work is supported by the Scientific and Technical Research Council of Turkey (TUBITAK) under Grant No. EEEAG-116E007.

References

[1] D. Colton and R. Kress, Inverse Acoustic and Electromagnetic Scattering Theory. Springer,2013.

[2] H. Ammari, An Introduction to Mathematics of Emerging Biomedical Imaging. Springer, 2008.

[3] S. Norberdo, S. Gustafsson, and B. Nilsson, "Fault localization for HVDC power cables," in Proc. 6th International Conference on Inverse Problems: Modelling and Simulation, Fethiye, Turkey, p. 208, 2012.

[4] M. Hamalainen, R. Hari, R. J. Ilmoniemi, J. Knuutila, and O.V. Lounasmaa, "Magnetoencephalographytheory, instrumentation, and applications to noninvasive studies of the working human brain," Reviews of Modern Physics, vol. 65, no.2, pp. 413-497, 1993.

[5] D. G. Dudley, Mathematical Foundations for Electromagnetic Theory. IEEE Press, 1994.

TF/SF Separation Characteristics in the 3D NS-FDTD Technique Using Rectangular Cells

Tadao Ohtani
1-17-134 Omachi
Asahikawa 070-0841, Japan
bytcg100@ybb.ne.jp

Yasushi Kanai
IEE Department
Niigata Institute of Technology
Kashiwazaki, 945-1195, Japan
kanai@iee.niit.ac.jp

Nikolaos V. Kantartzis
ECE Department
Aristotle University of Thessaloniki
Thessaloniki 54124, Greece
kant@auth.gr

***Abstract* — The separation ability of the total-field/scattered-field (TF/SF) model, tailored for the 3D non-standard finite-difference time-domain (NS-FDTD) technique via rectangular cells, is presented in this paper. Applying the method to the radar cross section (RCS) analysis of electrically large regions, the new TF/SF model exhibits almost the same separation performance compared to the cubic cell case. Finally, the proposed scheme is applied to a complicated realistic structure to reveal its merits.**

Keywords—FDTD methods; electrically large structures; non-standard schemes; radar cross section; total-/scattered-field model.

I. INTRODUCTION

The total-field/scattered-field (TF/SF) separation scheme is an instructive algorithm for the radar cross section (RCS) analysis through the FDTD method [1]. Recently, this scheme has been applied to electrically large areas, considering a trait of the NS-FDTD operators [2]-[4], for the case of cubic cells. However, for modern aircrafts, with components much thinner than their span, the use of rectangular cells in the TF/SF separation model can drastically improve the performance of the NS-FDTD technique, as well as in other RCS applications.

In this paper, we develop the TF/SF separation model [4] for the rectangular-cell NS-FDTD algorithm [5]. The RCS values of the SF components are derived in order to validate the TF/SF separation behavior. As a practical application, a B2 Spirit stealth aircraft is investigated and the computed RCS for rectangular- and cubic-cell NS-FDTD implementations are compared.

II. TF/SF SEPARATION SCHEME FOR THE NS-FDTD METHOD

Our assumed-known incident fields [1] are calculated in accordance with the flowchart of Fig. 1. In the involved time-update equations, E_0 and H_0 are the amplitudes, $j^2 = -1$, ω the angular frequency, n the time step, Δt the time increment, $\boldsymbol{k}_{num}$ the numerical wave-number given by the dispersion equation [5], $\boldsymbol{r}$ the position vector, $S_\omega(\Delta t) = 2\sin(\omega\Delta t/2)/\omega$, and $\nu, \bar{\nu}$ tuning parameters for the matching of numerical fields. In [4], $\nu = 0, 0.2$ and $\bar{\nu} = 0.1$, while $\nabla^{(0),(1)}$ are the Hamilton operators in the NS-FDTD method [2]. Furthermore, $(\boldsymbol{E}, \boldsymbol{H})_{sub}$ components are computed separately from the main NS-FDTD calculation area, as comprehensively depicted in Fig. 2.

Finally, the SF and TF calculation formulas in the main NS-FDTD area, adjacent to the TF/SF separation, surface are

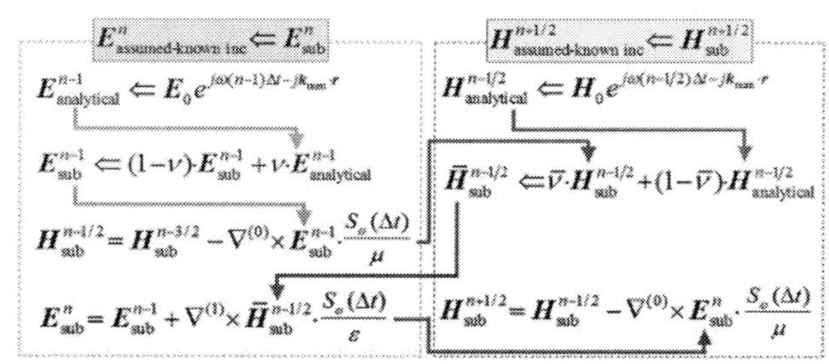

Fig. 1. Flowchart for the $(\boldsymbol{E}, \boldsymbol{H})_{assumed\text{-}known\ inc}$ calculation.

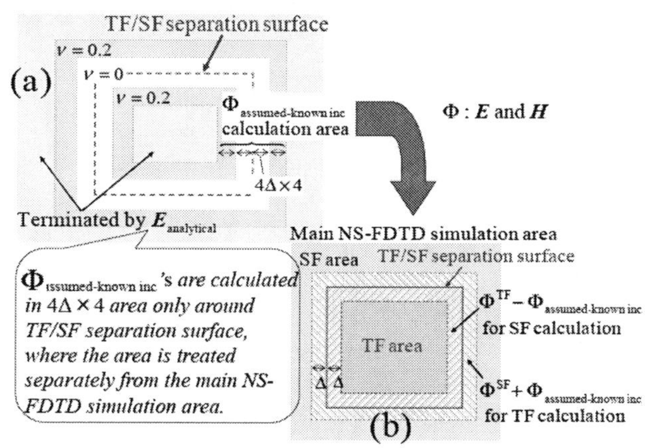

Fig. 2. (a) Multi-layered area structure for the $(\boldsymbol{E}, \boldsymbol{H})_{sub}$ calculation and (b) its connection model in the main NS-FDTD simulation area.

$$\mu\partial \boldsymbol{H}^{SF/TF}/\partial t = -\nabla^{(0)}\times(\boldsymbol{E}^{TF/SF} \mp \boldsymbol{E}_{assumed\text{-}known\ inc}), \quad (1)$$

$$\varepsilon\partial_t \boldsymbol{E}^{SF/TF}/\partial t = \nabla^{(1)}\times(\boldsymbol{H}^{TF/SF} \mp \boldsymbol{H}_{assumed\text{-}known\ inc}). \quad (2)$$

III. NUMERICAL VERIFICATION

To validate our method, Fig. 3 shows a verification model for the novel TF/SF scheme. Firstly, we calculate the unphysical waves generated from the TF/SF separation surface toward the outer space and evaluate the separation ability of our TF/SF model via the RCS values. Note that the TF area is free space, while the SF region is truncated by a perfectly matched layer (PML), where SF terms are converted to RCS through the near-to-far-field transformation [1]. Figure 4 provides the RCS, with the "Div *L*-*M*-*N*" notation standing for $\Delta x = \lambda/L$, $\Delta y = \lambda/M$, and

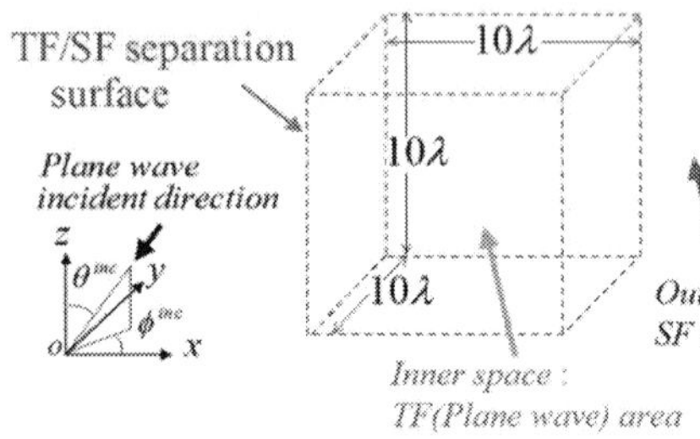

Fig. 3. Geometry of the verification model for the investigation of the TF/SF separation ability in the 3D NS-FDTD method with rectangular cells.

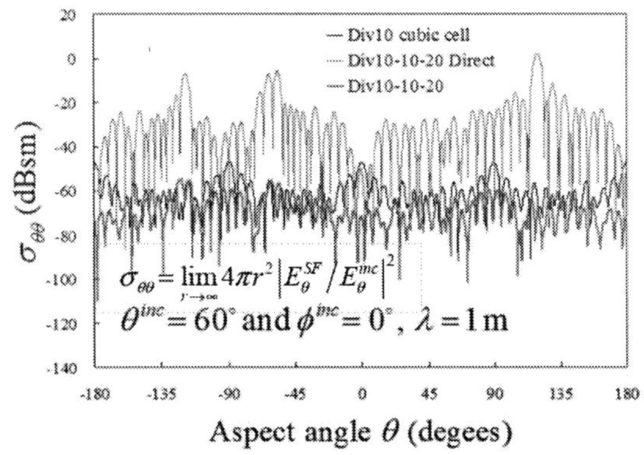

(a)

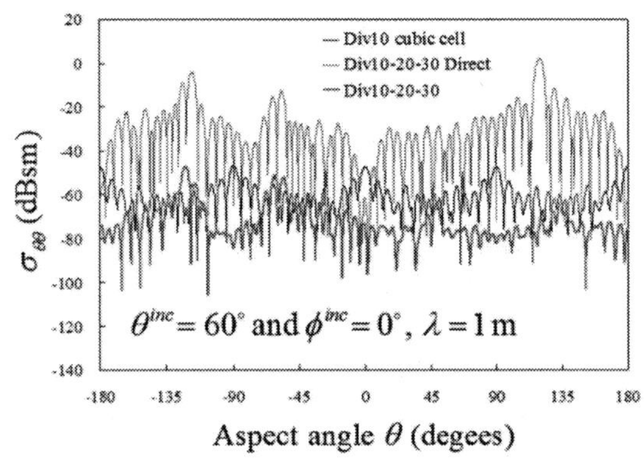

(b)

Fig. 4. Computed RCS values in the SF region of the featured TF/SF scheme. (a) Comparison among the: Div 10 cubic-cell, Div 10-10-20 Direct, and Div 10-10-20 (proposed) implementation and (b) comparison among the: Div 10 cubic-cell, Div 10-20-30 Direct, and Div 10-20-30 (proposed) implementation.

$\Delta z = \lambda/N$. On the other hand, the extra "Direct" characterization denotes that the specific RCS values are obtained by using the $(\boldsymbol{E}, \boldsymbol{H})_{\text{analytical}}$ terms for the $(\boldsymbol{E}, \boldsymbol{H})_{\text{assumed-known inc}}$ ones in Fig. 1, which corresponds to the standard FDTD TF/SF separation model [1]. As observed, both cubic- and rectangular-cell cases have the same low spurious SF level and guarantee a very high TF/SF separation ability, compared to the "Direct" scheme.

Moving to a more realistic application, Fig. 5(a) presents the discretized model of a B2 Spirit aircraft [6], with a much thinner shape than its span. Notice that detailed structures, like the air intake or the cockpit window, are not considered, while the cockpit region is modeled by an ellipsoid and the wing by a flat plate. The aircraft is discretized in orthogonal cells of perfect electric conductor (PEC), while the overall model is checked via the cdview software package [7]. Also, the incident wave is E_θ^{inc}. As detected from Fig. 5(b), both cell cases have almost the same satisfactory separation ability. In conclusion, it can be safely confirmed that our TF/SF model is valid not only for cubic cells, but for rectangular ones, as well.

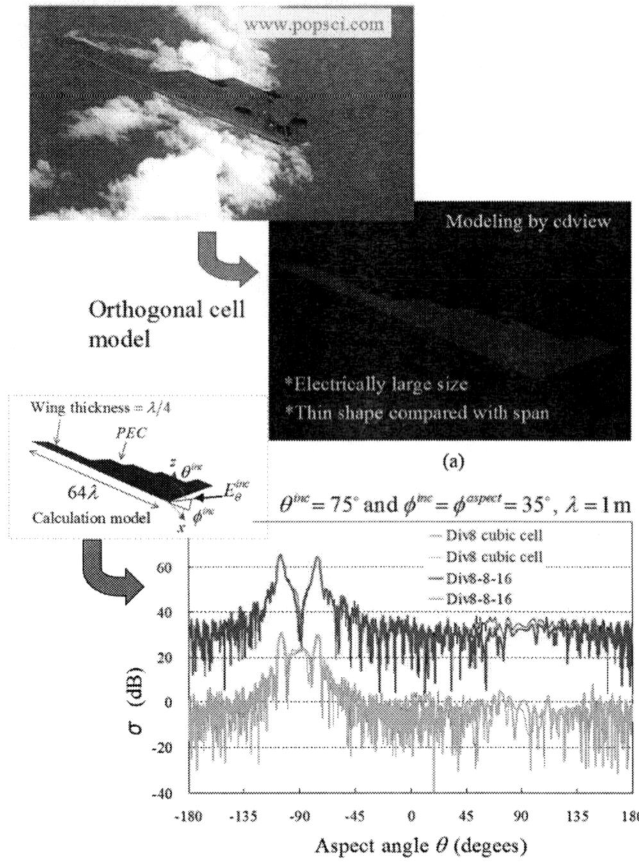

(b)

Fig. 5. (a) The B2 Spirit model and (b) comparison of the RCS with cubic and rectangular cells. The model size is shown in [6] and normalized by λ.

REFERENCES

[1] A. Taflove and S. Hagness, *Computational Electrodynamics: The Finite-Difference Time-Domain Method.* Norwood, MA: Artech House, 2005.

[2] J. B. Cole, "A high-accuracy realization of the Yee algorithm using non-standard finite-differences," *IEEE Trans. Microw. Theory Tech.*, vol. 45, no. 6, pp. 991-996, Jun. 1997.

[3] T. Ohtani, Y. Kanai, and N. V. Kantartzis, "An enhanced total-field/scattered-field scheme for the 3-D nonstandard finite-difference time-domain method," *IEEE Trans. Magn.*, vol. 52, no. 3, art. 7204705, 2016.

[4] T. Ohtani, Y. Kanai, and N. V. Kantartzis, "Wide-angle elimination of TF/SF-generated spurious waves in the nonstandard FDTD method," *IEEE Trans. on Magn.* 2016. (submitted)

[5] T. Ohtani and Y. Kanai, "Coefficients of finite difference operator for rectangular cell NS-FDTD method," *IEEE Trans. Antennas Propag.*, vol. 59, no. 1, pp. 206-213, Jan. 2011.

[6] https://en.wikipedia.org/wiki/Northrop_Grumman_B-2_Spirit.

[7] cdview ver. 3.13, *Visualization software for molecular simulation*, http://cdview.sourceforge.net/

Nonredundant NF–FF Transformation with Spherical Spiral Scan for an Offset Mounted Volumetric AUT

Francesco D'Agostino, Flaminio Ferrara, Claudio Gennarelli, Rocco Guerriero, Massimo Migliozzi
D.I.In. - Università di Salerno, via Giovanni Paolo II, 132 - 84084 Fisciano (Italy)
{fdagostino, flferrara, cgennarelli, rguerriero, mmigliozzi}@unisa.it

***Abstract*—An effective probe compensated near-field – far-field (NF – FF) transformation with spherical spiral scanning for an offset mounted antenna, which uses a number of NF data minimum and practically coincident with that needed in the centered configuration, is developed in this work.**

Keywords — antenna measurements; NF–FF transformations; spherical spiral scan; nonredundant representations of EM fields

I. Introduction

The near-field – far-field (NF – FF) transformation technique with spherical scanning [1] is the most attractive one, owing to its unique features to allow the full antenna pattern reconstruction and to avoid the error related to scanning area truncation. As well-known, one of the hottest issue concerning the NF–FF transformations is the measurement time reduction, which is nowadays very much greater than the computer time to perform the transformation. To this end, spherical NF–FF transformations for antennas with one or two predominant dimensions, requiring a minimum number of NF data, have been developed in [2], by properly exploiting the nonredundant sampling representations of the electromagnetic (EM) fields [3] and adopting very flexible models to shape the antenna under test (AUT). Another effective possibility to save the measurement time is, as suggested in [4], to make faster the scanning by acquiring on fly the NF data through continuous and synchronized movements of the probe and AUT. To this end, NF–FF transformations with spherical spiral scan have been recently proposed. They rely on the nonredundant representations of EM fields and use optimal sampling interpolation (OSI) formulas [3] to efficiently recover the NF data required by the classical spherical NF–FF transformation [1], as modified in [2], from the acquired ones. In particular, the nonredundant sampling representation on the sphere from spiral samples and the related OSI expansion have been developed in [5-7] by adopting a spherical AUT model and choosing the spiral pitch equal to the sample spacing needed for interpolating along a meridian. Then, NF–FF transformations with spherical spiral scan for long or quasi-planar antennas (see [8]) have been obtained by properly applying the unified theory of spiral scans for nonspherical antennas [9].

A nonredundant NF–FF transformation with spherical spiral scan, requiring practically the same number of NF data both in the centered and offset mountings of the AUT, is here developed. This is worthy since, sometimes, due to practical constraints, the AUT cannot be mounted in a centered configuration. Note that, in such a case, the NF data number needed by the classical spherical NF–FF transformation [1] can remarkably increase, being related to the radius of the minimum sphere able to contain the AUT and having the center coincident with scanning sphere one.

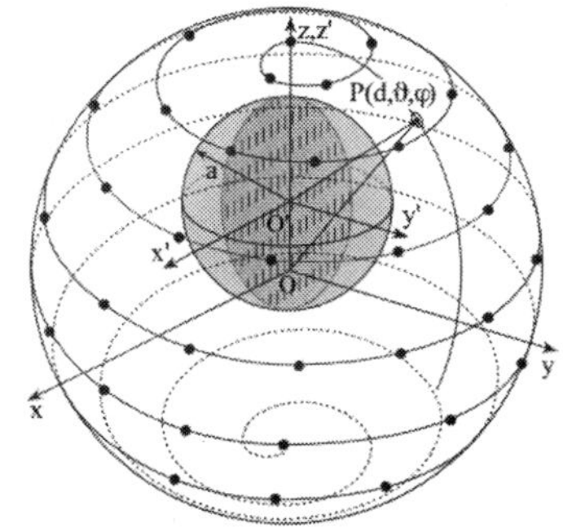

Fig. 1. Spherical spiral scanning for an offset mounted antenna.

II. Nonredundant Sampling Representation

Let us consider an AUT enclosed in the smallest sphere Σ of radius a and a nondirective probe scanning a spiral that wraps a sphere of radius d in the antenna NF region. The spherical coordinate system $S(r,\vartheta,\varphi)$, with the origin on the scanning sphere center at O, is adopted to denote an observation point P. The AUT center O' is on the axis z at distance d_S from O. A spherical coordinate system $S'(r',\vartheta',\varphi')$ with the origin at O' and the axis z' coincident with z is also introduced (Fig. 1). According to [3, 7], an effective nonredundant voltage representation in S' along a curve C on the scanning surface is got by using a proper parameter ξ to describe C and introducing the "reduced voltage" $\tilde{V}(\xi)=V(\xi)\,e^{j\psi(\xi)}$, $\psi(\xi)$ being a proper phase function and $V(\xi)$ the voltage V_p or V_r measured by the probe or by the rotated probe. The error, occurring when $\tilde{V}(\xi)$ is approximated by a bandlimited function, is negligible as the bandwidth exceeds a critical value W_ξ [3] and can be effectively controlled by considering an enlarged bandwidth $\chi' W_\xi$. According to [7], the spiral pitch must be equal to the sample spacing needed for interpolating along a meridian curve. The corresponding bandwidth, optimal parameter and phase function are:

$$W_\xi=\beta a\;;\quad \xi=\vartheta'\;;\quad \psi=\beta\sqrt{r'^2-a^2}-\beta a\cos^{-1}(a/r') \qquad (1)$$

where β is the wavenumber. Therefore, the spiral pitch is $\Delta\vartheta'=2\pi/(2N''+1)$ where $N''=\lfloor\chi N'\rfloor+1$, $\lfloor x\rfloor$ is the integer part of x, $N'=\lfloor\chi'\beta a\rfloor+1$, and $\chi>1$ an oversampling factor [3]. Thus, the spiral equations are: $x'=r'\sin\theta'\cos\phi'$, $y'=r'\sin\theta'\sin\phi'$, $z'=r'\cos\theta'$, where ϕ' is the parameter describing it and $\theta'=k\phi'=\phi'/(2N''+1)$. Note that the spiral angle θ', unlike the zenithal angle ϑ', can assume negative values [7]. The expressions of the phase function γ and of the parameter η relevant to the nonredundant sampling representation along the spiral are [7]:

$$\gamma=\psi\;;\quad \eta=(\beta a/W_\eta)\int_0^{\phi'}\sqrt{k^2+\sin^2 k\delta}\,\mathrm{d}\delta \qquad (2)$$

Hence, η is β/W_η times the arclength of the projecting point on the spiral wrapping Σ. The bandwidth W_η is got in such a way that η covers a 2π range when describing the whole projecting spiral. Thus, W_η is β/π times the length of the spiral wrapping from pole to pole the modeling sphere [7]. The voltages V_p, V_r at the points $P(\vartheta', \varphi')$ needed by the NF–FF transformation [1], as modified in [2], can be recovered by the OSI expansion [7]

$$V(\vartheta', \varphi') = e^{-j\psi(\vartheta')} \sum_{n=n_0-q+1}^{n_0+q} \tilde{V}(\vartheta'_n)\, \Omega_N(\vartheta' - \vartheta'_n, \bar{\vartheta})\, D_{N''}(\vartheta' - \vartheta'_n) \quad (3)$$

where $\vartheta'_n = \vartheta'_n(\varphi') = k\varphi' + n\Delta\vartheta' = \vartheta'_0 + n\Delta\vartheta'$, $D_{N''}(\cdot)$ and $\Omega_N(\cdot,\cdot)$ are the Dirichlet and Tschebyscheff sampling functions [3], $\bar{\vartheta} = q\Delta\vartheta'$ $n_0 = \lfloor(\vartheta' - \vartheta'_0)/\Delta\vartheta'\rfloor$, $N = N'' - N'$, and $2q$ is the number of the retained reduced voltage samples $\tilde{V}(\vartheta'_n)$, at the intersections between the spiral and the meridian curve through P. These last can be evaluated via the OSI expansion along the spiral

$$\tilde{V}(\eta(\vartheta'_n)) = \sum_{m=m_0-p+1}^{m_0+p} \tilde{V}(\eta_m)\, \Omega_M(\eta - \eta_m, \bar{\eta}) D_{M''}(\eta - \eta_m) \quad (4)$$

where $\eta_m = m\Delta\eta = 2\pi m/(2M''+1)$, $m_0 = \lfloor\eta(\vartheta'_n)/\Delta\eta\rfloor$, $2p$ is the number of the retained samples, $\bar{\eta} = p\Delta\eta$, $M'' = \lfloor\chi M'\rfloor + 1$, $M' = \lfloor\chi' W_\eta\rfloor + 1$, and $M = M'' - M'$. Note that χ' must be properly increased nearby the poles to avoid a significant growth of the bandlimitation error [7]. To apply the described procedure, in the measurement step, the coordinates of the sampling points (known in the reference system S') must be expressed in the S one, whereas, in the post-processing step, the coordinates of the points needed by the NF–FF transformation (given in S) must be determined in S'. The formulas relating the coordinates in S and S' are straightforward and are omitted for space saving.

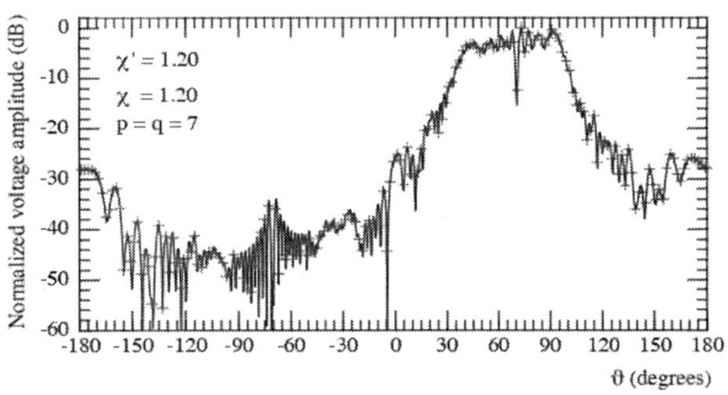

Fig. 2. Amplitude of V_r on the cut plane at φ = 90°. Solid line: exact. Red crosses: interpolated from the nonredundant NF spherical spiral samples.

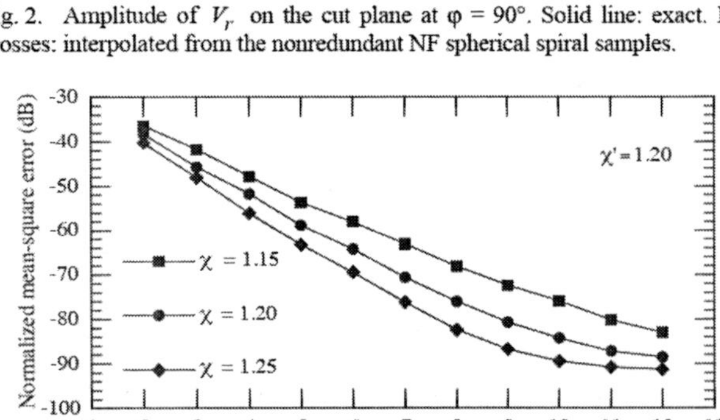

Fig. 3. Normalized mean-square errors relevant to the reconstruction of V_r versus the number of the retained samples.

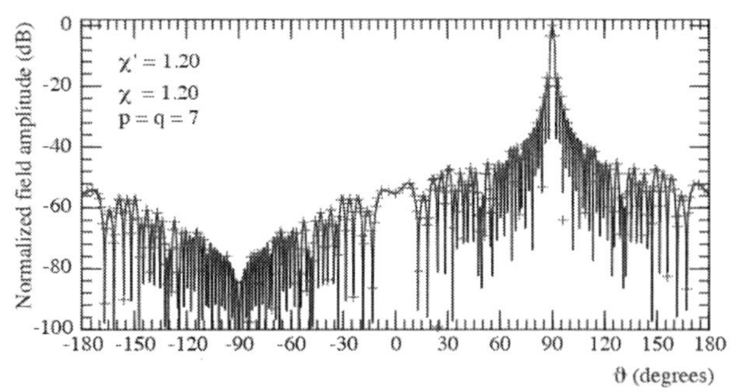

Fig. 4. E-plane pattern. Solid line: exact. Red crosses: reconstructed from the nonredundant NF spherical spiral samples.

The reported simulations refer to a scanning sphere of radius $d = 30\,\lambda$ (λ being the wavelength) and to a uniform planar circular array with diameter $2a = 31.2\,\lambda$, lying in the plane $y = 0$ and with its center O' on the z axis at distance $d_s = 10\,\lambda$ from O. The array elements, symmetrically placed with respect to the plane $z' = 0$, are elementary Huygens sources linearly polarized along z and spaced of $0.52\,\lambda$ along the radial and azimuthal lines. The AUT has been considered as enclosed in a sphere with radius $a = 15.6\,\lambda$, centered in O'. An open-ended WR90 rectangular waveguide is used as probe. Figure 2 shows the reconstruction of the amplitude of V_r on the meridian at $\varphi = 90°$. As can be seen, the reconstruction is very good. The normalized mean-square errors, reported in Fig. 3, assess quantitatively the validity of the technique. At last, its overall efficacy is assessed by the E-plane pattern reconstruction shown in Fig. 4. The number of used NF samples is 26810 (including 880 extra samples around the poles) instead of that 65160 required by the NF–FF transformation [1].

References

[1] J. Hald, J.E. Hansen, F. Jensen, and F.H. Larsen, Spherical near-field antenna measurements, J.E. Hansen, (ed.), London, Peter Peregrinus, 1998.

[2] F. D'Agostino, F. Ferrara, C. Gennarelli, R. Guerriero, and M. Migliozzi, "Effective antenna modellings for NF–FF transformations with spherical scanning using the minimum number of data," Int. Jour. Antennas Prop., vol. 2011, ID 936781, 11 pages, 2011.

[3] O.M. Bucci, C. Gennarelli, and C. Savarese, "Representation of electromagnetic fields over arbitrary surfaces by a finite and nonredundant number of samples," IEEE Trans. Antennas Prop., vol. 46, pp. 351-359, Mar. 1998.

[4] R.G. Yaccarino, L.I. Williams, and Y. Rahmat-Samii, "Linear spiral sampling for the bipolar planar antenna measurement technique," IEEE Trans. Antennas Prop., vol. 44, pp. 1049-1051, 1996.

[5] O.M. Bucci, F. D'Agostino, C. Gennarelli, G. Riccio, and C. Savarese, "NF–FF transformation with spherical spiral scanning," IEEE Antennas Wireless Prop. Lett., vol. 2, pp. 263-266, 2003.

[6] F. D'Agostino, F. Ferrara, J.A. Fordham, C. Gennarelli, R. Guerriero, and M. Migliozzi, "An experimental validation of the near-field - far-field transformation with spherical spiral scan," IEEE Antennas Prop. Magaz., vol. 55, pp. 228-235, 2013.

[7] F. D'Agostino, C. Gennarelli, G. Riccio, and C. Savarese, "Theoretical foundations of near-field–far-field transformations with spiral scannings," Prog. in Electr. Res., vol. 61, pp. 193-214, 2006.

[8] R. Cicchetti, F. D'Agostino, F. Ferrara, C. Gennarelli, R. Guerriero, and M. Migliozzi, "Near-field to far-field transformation techniques with spiral scannings: a comprehensive review," Int. Jour. Antennas Prop., vol. 2014, ID 143084, 11 pages, 2014.

[9] F. D'Agostino, F. Ferrara, C. Gennarelli, R. Guerriero, and M. Migliozzi, "The unified theory of near-field–far-field transformations with spiral scannings for nonspherical antennas," Prog. in Electr. Res. B, vol. 14, pp. 449-477, 2009.

TD-UAPO Solutions for the Diffraction by Co-Planar Adjacent Blocks

Marcello Frongillo, Giovanni Riccio
D.I.E.M.
University of Salerno
Via Giovanni Paolo II 132, 84084 Fisciano (SA), Italy
griccio@unisa.it

Gianluca Gennarelli
Institute for Electromagnetic Sensing of the Environment
National Research Council
Via Diocleziano 328, 80124 Naples, Italy
gennarelli.g@irea.cnr.it

***Abstract*—Efficient closed form solutions are proposed for computing the time domain diffraction coefficients related to plane waves impacting a structure consisting of two co-planar adjacent blocks formed by metallic and dielectric materials. They are determined by applying the inverse Laplace transform to the corresponding Uniform Asymptotic Physical Optics diffraction coefficients in the frequency domain. No closed form solutions exist for the considered time domain problem.**

Keywords—propagation; diffraction; time domain solutions

I. Introduction

Analytical techniques exist for solving scattering problems concerning a limited number of perfect electrically conducting (PEC) structures excited by an electromagnetic pulse (see [1]-[5] as reference). In this framework, the time domain (TD) version of the uniform geometrical theory of diffraction (UTD) [3]-[5] furnishes a simple physical representation for radiation and scattering phenomena since it uses the same rays (incident, reflected and diffracted contributions) as the frequency domain (FD-UTD) one [6]. The TD expressions are obtained by applying analytical transformations to the FD-UTD solutions.

The approach presented in [3] has been recently applied by the authors to obtain the TD versions [7]-[9] of the frequency domain Uniform Asymptotic Physical Optics (FD-UAPO) diffraction coefficients for plane wave diffraction problems involving dielectric wedges. The TD-UAPO formulation uses the same physical representation of the TD-UTD one.

This paper provides closed form expressions of the TD-UAPO diffraction coefficients to be used for evaluating the transient diffracted field due to an arbitrary function plane wave impacting a structure consisting of two co-planar adjacent 90° wedges filled by metallic and dielectric materials (see Fig. 1). The metallic wedge is considered as a PEC block. The structure is excited by *E*-polarized plane waves impinging at normal incidence with respect to the common edge along the *z*-axis. The TD-UAPO solutions are attained by applying the inverse Laplace transform to the FD-UAPO diffraction coefficients determined by the authors in [10], where two separate diffraction problems relevant to the dielectric (internal) region and the space surrounding the structure (external region) have been solved. The approach can be applied to available UTD-like solutions.

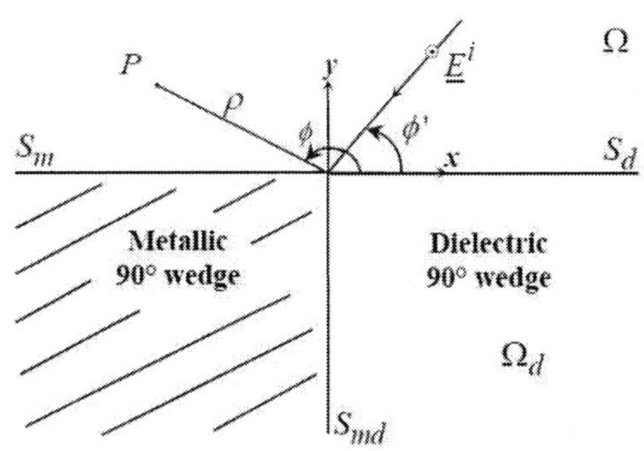

Fig. 1. *E*-polarized plane wave incident on a structure formed by two co-planar adjacent 90° wedges consisting of metallic and dielectric materials.

II. TD-UAPO Diffraction Coefficients

The following expressions are obtained by applying the inverse Laplace transform to the corresponding FD-UAPO diffraction coefficients [10] in the free-space region Ω and the 90° dielectric region Ω_d.

A. Free-space region Ω

$$d_\Omega = -\frac{1}{2\sqrt{2\pi}}(1+R)\frac{\sin\phi+\sin\phi'}{\cos\phi+\cos\phi'}\, G\left(2\rho\cos^2\left(\frac{\phi+\phi'}{2}\right),t\right) \quad (1)$$

where the angle ϕ' controls the direction of impinging plane waves ($\phi'=0$ corresponds to the grazing incidence), the polar coordinates (ρ,ϕ) define the observation point *P*, the Fresnel reflection coefficient *R* accounts for the reflection from the dielectric surface S_d, and

$$G(X,t) = \frac{X}{\sqrt{\pi ct}\,(t+X/c)} \quad (2)$$

if *c* is the light velocity in the considered region.

B. Dielectric region Ω_d

1) $0<\phi'<\pi/2$

$$d_{\Omega_d}=\frac{T}{2\sqrt{2\pi}}\times\left[\frac{\sin\phi-\cos\theta_t}{\cos\phi+\sin\theta_t}G\left(2\rho\cos^2\left(\frac{\phi-(\pi/2-\theta_t)}{2}\right),t\right)+\right.$$
$$\left.-\frac{2\sin\theta_t}{\sin\phi+\cos\theta_t}G\left(2\rho\cos^2\left(\frac{\phi-(\pi/2+\theta_t)}{2}\right),t\right)\right] \tag{3}$$

2) $\pi/2<\phi'<\pi$

$$d_{\Omega_d}=\frac{T}{2\sqrt{2\pi}}\frac{\sin\phi-\cos\theta_t}{\cos\phi-\sin\theta_t}G\left(2\rho\cos^2\left(\frac{\phi-(\pi/2+\theta_t)}{2}\right),t\right) \tag{4}$$

where T is the Fresnel transmission coefficient associated to S_d and $\theta_t=\sin^{-1}(|\cos\phi|/\sqrt{\varepsilon_r})$ if ε_r is the relative permittivity of the dielectric.

The above expressions can be used for calculating the TD electric field diffracted in each observation region by means of the following integral:

$$e^d(P,t)=\frac{1}{\sqrt{\rho}}\int_{t_0}^{t-\rho/c}d\left(t-\frac{\rho}{c}-\tau\right)e^i(Q,\tau)\mathrm{d}\tau \tag{5}$$

with $t-\rho/c>t_0$. The forcing function is the incident field e^i at the diffraction point Q.

III. Numerical Tests

The 90° dielectric wedge considered in this section is characterized by $\varepsilon_r=3$ and the incidence direction is $\phi'=60°$. Figure 2 shows the electric field arriving at $P(5\text{m},286°)$. The observation point is very close to the shadow boundary ($\phi=286.7°$) for the field transmitted through S_d and reflected by S_{md}. In order of arrival, it is possible to identify the Geometrical Optics contributions (solid line), i.e., transmission and transmission-reflection waveforms, and the diffraction one (dashed line). The diffraction and transmission-reflection waveforms arrive together at *P*, but they possess opposite positivity. The transmission-reflection contribution vanishes when crossing the boundary and the positivity of the diffraction contribution changes (see Fig. 3).

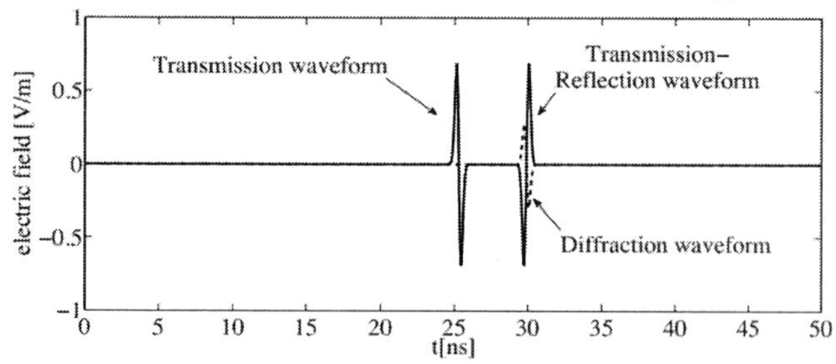

Fig. 2. Electric field when $\phi'=60°$ and $P(5m,286°)$.

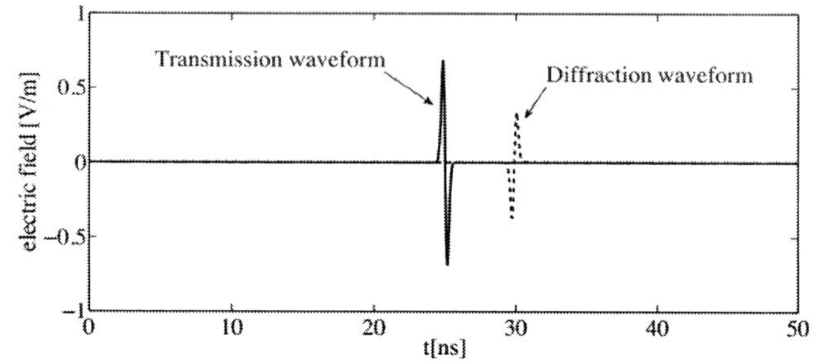

Fig. 3. Electric field when $\phi'=60°$ and $P(5m,287°)$.

References

[1] P.M. Johansen, "Time-domain version of the physical theory of diffraction," *IEEE Trans. Antennas Propag.*, vol. 47, pp. 261–270, 1999.

[2] C.G. Rego and F.J.V. Hasselmann, "A Time-domain uniform asymptotic theory applied to the analysis of pulse-excited PEC wedges," *IEEE Antennas Wireless Propag. Lett.*, vol. 10, pp. 955–958, 2011.

[3] T.W. Veruttipong, "Time domain version of the uniform GTD," *IEEE Trans. Antennas Propag.*, vol. 38, pp. 1757–1764, 1990.

[4] P.R. Rousseau and P.H. Pathak, "Time domain uniform geometrical theory of diffraction for a curved wedge," *IEEE Trans. Antennas Propag.*, vol. 43, pp. 1375–1382, 1995.

[5] P.R. Rousseau and P.H. Pathak, "A time domain uniform geometrical theory of slope diffraction for a curved wedge," *Turk. J. Elec. Engin.*, vol. 2, pp. 385–398, 2002.

[6] R.G. Kouyoumjian and P.H. Pathak, "A uniform geometrical theory of diffraction for an edge in a perfectly conducting surface," *Proc. IEEE*, vol. 62, pp. 1448-1461, 1974.

[7] G. Gennarelli and G. Riccio, "Time domain diffraction by a right-angled penetrable wedge," *IEEE Trans. Antennas Propag.*, vol. 60, pp. 2829–2833, 2012.

[8] G. Gennarelli and G. Riccio, "Obtuse-angled penetrable wedges: a time domain solution for the diffraction coefficients," *J. Electromagn. Waves Appl.*, vol. 27, pp. 2020–2028, 2013.

[9] M. Frongillo, G. Gennarelli and G. Riccio, "TD-UAPO diffracted field evaluation for penetrable wedges with acute apex angle," *J. Opt. Soc. Am. A*, vol. 32, pp. 1271–1275, 2015.

[10] M. Frongillo, G. Gennarelli and G. Riccio, "Plane wave diffraction by co-planar adjacent blocks," *Proc. LAPC 2016*.

Assessment of AC Interference Caused by Transmission Lines on Buried Metallic Pipelines Using F.E.M.

Arturo Popoli, Andrea Cristofolini, Leonardo Sandrolini
Department of Electrical, Electronic, and Information Engineering, University of Bologna
Bologna, Italy I-40136

Bolanle T. Abe, Adisa Jimoh
Department of Electrical Engineering, Faculty of Engineering and the Built Environment
Tshwane University of Technology, Pretoria, South Africa

***Abstract*—The focus of this paper is on the implementation and subsequent improvement of a technique for computing AC interference on buried metallic pipelines due to nearby power transmission lines. In order to perform this task, the finite element method (F.E.M.) is employed. After performing a description of the implementation of the classic F.E.M. approach, a hybrid technique designed to reduce the size of the mesh and therefore the computational time is presented. The results obtained with the two approaches are finally compared.**

***Index Terms*—AC interference, electromagnetic compatibility, finite element method, mesh, pipelines, AC corrosion**

I. Introduction

The issue of AC interference on metallic pipelines is a matter of concern in many industrialized countries, in which for geographical and economic reasons power transmission lines often end up sharing the same corridors with pipelines designated to water or gas transportation. In such circumstances, the currents induced on the pipelines may compromise the physical integrity of the structure, create corrosion effects and be harmful to human personnel. In the event of faults, the induced voltages can reach several kV [1]. The aforementioned interference can be caused by inductive, conductive and/or capacitive coupling. However, as the conductive coupling can be only caused by currents flowing from the line into the soil, and as the capacitive coupling does not affect buried pipelines [2], these are not taken into account in this work.

II. Field theory analysis

This approach is based on solving the diffusion equation of the magnetic potential vector $\boldsymbol{A}$ over the whole physical domain:

$$\nabla \times \left(\frac{1}{\mu}\nabla \times \boldsymbol{A}\right) = \boldsymbol{J_0} - \sigma\frac{\partial \boldsymbol{A}}{\partial t} \qquad (1)$$

where J_o is the current density. Equation (1) reprisents 3 scalar equations, one for each axis $(x,\ y,\ z)$. These are obtained if the quasi-stationary approximation is performed, thus assuming $\boldsymbol{J} \gg \partial \boldsymbol{D}/\partial t$ in the considered domain, where $\boldsymbol{D}$ is the displacement current. In a 2D problem, assuming that $\boldsymbol{A} = \boldsymbol{A_z}(x,\ y)$, $\boldsymbol{J} = \boldsymbol{J_z}(x,\ y)$ and that all the derivatives along z are null, then $\boldsymbol{A}$ satisfies the equation $\nabla \cdot \boldsymbol{A} = 0$. The problem formulation can be therefore rewritten as:

$$-\nabla \cdot \left(\frac{1}{\mu}\nabla \boldsymbol{A_z}\right) = \boldsymbol{J_0} - \sigma\frac{\partial \boldsymbol{A_z}}{\partial t}. \qquad (2)$$

Then, for sinusoidal quantities, (2) becomes:

$$-\nabla \cdot \left(\frac{1}{\mu}\nabla \boldsymbol{A_z}\right) = \boldsymbol{J_0} - j\omega\sigma \boldsymbol{A_z}. \qquad (3)$$

Due to the usual complexity of this kind of geometries, the analytical solution of (3) is not an option. Therefore, an approximated solution is obtained using the F.E.M., subdividing the whole domain into many sub-domains, called elements. The unknown function $\boldsymbol{A_z}$ is therefore approximated on the nodes of the mesh by making use of some kind of interpolation. An element matrix $[\boldsymbol{K_{el}}+j\omega S_{el}]$ is written for each element, and a coefficient matrix $[\boldsymbol{M}]$ is then constructed by assembling the element matrices. The same approach is then applied to the sources, thus writing a source-term matrix $[\boldsymbol{t_{el}}]$ for each element and finally constructing the matrix $[\boldsymbol{t}]$. Consequently, a problem described by partial differential equations is now described by a linear system:

$$[\boldsymbol{M}][\tilde{\boldsymbol{A}}_{\boldsymbol{z}}] = [\boldsymbol{t}]. \qquad (4)$$

Once the distribution of $\boldsymbol{A_z}$ has been calculated, the magnetic flux density can be obtained as $B(x,y) = \nabla \times \boldsymbol{A_z}$, and the current density over the whole domain can then be expressed as:

$$\boldsymbol{J_z} = \boldsymbol{J_0} - j\omega\sigma \boldsymbol{A_z}. \qquad (5)$$

$\boldsymbol{J_0}$ is non-zero only on the conductors of the line conductors, whereas $j\omega\sigma\boldsymbol{A_z}$ is responsible for currents flowing through the earth and the pipeline[3]. The $\boldsymbol{J_z}$ distribution on a conductor and the spatial distribution of $\boldsymbol{A_z}$ produced by the three phase conductors are depicted in Fig. 1.

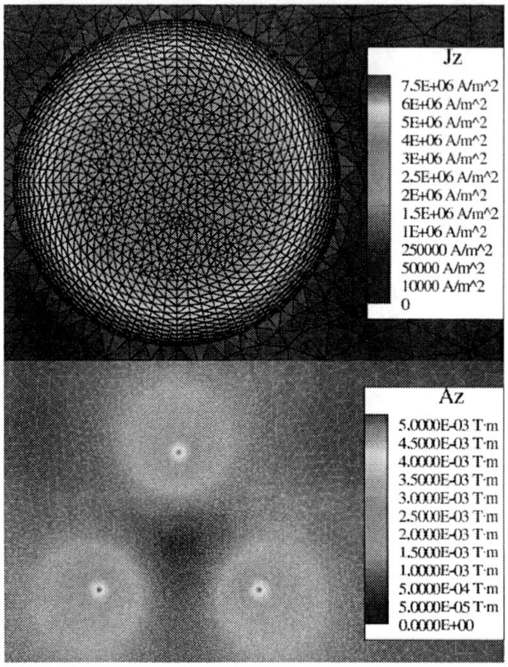

Figure 1. Distribution of $|\boldsymbol{J_z}|$ and $|\boldsymbol{A_z}|$.

III. Analytical calculation of $\mathbf{A_z}$

The computational time, which is the main drawback of the field theory approach, is related to the number of nodes of the mesh. For the type of problems considered in this paper, often a large nonhomogenous domain needs to be discretised, involving different media (e.g., air and ground with a multilayered structure). The aim of this work is thus to implement a technique that enables a reduction of the mesh size without affecting the quality of the results. $\boldsymbol{A_z}$ can be expressed by $\boldsymbol{A_z} = \boldsymbol{A_0} + \boldsymbol{A_r}$, where $\boldsymbol{A_0}$ is produced by the three phases of the power transmission line, and $\boldsymbol{A_r}$ is produced by all the other conductors as a *reaction* to $\boldsymbol{A_0}$. Unlike $\boldsymbol{A_r}$, $\boldsymbol{A_0}$ can be calculated analytically [3] with:

$$\boldsymbol{A_0} = \sum_{k=1}^{n} \hat{i}_z \frac{\mu \boldsymbol{I_k}}{2\pi} ln \left(\frac{R_0}{R} \right) \tag{6}$$

where n is the number of phase conductors, I_k is the current of the kth phase conductor, R is the distance between the given node and the center of the kth phase conductor and R_0 is the reference radius.

Therefore, as $\nabla \times \left(\frac{1}{\mu} \nabla \times \boldsymbol{A_0} \right) = \boldsymbol{J_0}$, (1) becomes:

$$\nabla \times \left(\frac{1}{\mu} \nabla \times \boldsymbol{A_r} \right) = -j\omega\sigma \left(\boldsymbol{A_0} + \boldsymbol{A_r} \right) \tag{7}$$

and, as now $[\boldsymbol{t}] = -j\omega[S][\boldsymbol{A_0}]$, the linear system becomes:

$$[\boldsymbol{M}][\tilde{\boldsymbol{A_r}}] = -j\omega\sigma[S][\boldsymbol{A_0}]. \tag{8}$$

The advantage of this technique is that the effects of the line currents are now at the right hand side of (8). Therefore the mesh will be used only for calculating $\boldsymbol{A_r}$. As a consequence of this, there is no reason for representing the power transmission line conductors, with an evident advantage in terms of the mesh size. As an example, using the traditional F.E.M. method for a three phase configuration with no overhead ground wires and one pipeline buried 2m deep in the ground, the number of mesh nodes m_1 is 35854, and the computed current I_{p1} flowing through the pipeline has an amplitude of 65.464A. If the proposed methodology is used instead, the number of mesh nodes becomes $m_2 = 20648$, and the computed current I_{p2} has now an amplitude of 65.507A, with a 40% reduction of the mesh size. The two simulations have been run using the same physical conditions, summarized in Fig. 2. The discretized region has the shape of a circle, whose radius is set to 80m. The boundary condition $A_z = 0$ is enforced on the edge of the discretized region. This leads to the field lines of $B_{x,y}$ being tangential to the edge itself.

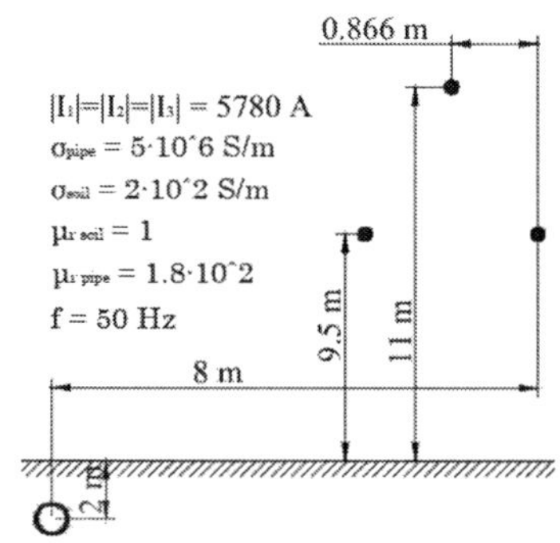

Figure 2. Geometry (section).

The computational time using the traditional F.E.M. is 120s, whereas the hybrid algorithm runs in 44s.

IV. Conclusions

A technique for combining F.E.M. and analytical calculations was presented, which can be used for reducing the size of the mesh employed to solve those kind of problems where the domain is large and nonhomogeneous without loosing accuracy. It is worth highlighting that for this example the number of line conductors was limited to three. In case of an higher number of phases, the resulting beneficial effects of the application of this concept would be proportionally increased, as the mesh has indeed the most dense areas around the conductors.

References

[1] C. W. G. 36.02, "Guide on the influence of high voltage ac power systems on metallic pipelines," *CIGRE*, 1995.

[2] F. P. Dawalibi and R. D. Southey, "Analysis of electrical interference from power lines to gas pipelines. i. computation methods," *IEEE Transactions on Power Delivery*, vol. 4, pp. 1840–1846, Jul 1989.

[3] F. B. F. Gasparini, *Fondamenti di elettrotecnica*. UTET, 1989.

A Tunable Dual-band Left-Handed Metamaterial Implementation

Si Li, Wenxing Li, Yunlong Mao
College of Communication and Information Engineering,
Harbin Engineering University,
Harbin, 150001, China
liwenxing@hrbeu.edu.cn

Wenhua Yu
2COMU, INC. Fairfax,
VA, 22030, USA
Wenyu@2comu.com

Atef Z Elsherbeni
Department of Electrical and Computer Engineering
Colorado School of Mines,
Golden, CO, 80401, USA
aelsherb@mines.edu

***Abstract* — In this paper, we propose a tunable dual-band left-handed metamaterial (LHM) implemented by embedding a variable capacitor to a single-band LHM. The proposed LHM is analyzed with equivalent circuits from both the aspects of magnetic and electric resonators. From the simulated results and the retrieved effective parameters, it is figured out that double negative characteristics are achieved at two frequency ranges, one is stable while the other one sweeps most of the desired frequencies with the change of the capacitor. Hence, this LHM is able to adjust its negative index frequency ranges according to different requirements.**

Keywords — Metamaterials, dual-band, LHM, variable capacitance.

I. Introduction

Recently, Some researchers focused their studies on multi-band metamaterials (MTMs). In [1-4], multi-band MTM was proposed. All these multi-band MTMs are implemented with well-designed shapes, hence, they can't change the negative index frequency ranges according to different requirements. In [5], a tunable multi-band single negative MTM (SNG) is proposed. While in [6], the proposed tunable MTM is available to sweep the resonant frequency from 2.67 GHz to 3.52 GHz.

This paper propose a tunable dual-band double negative MTM (DNG). The geometry of this MTM is the same as the single-band LHM that Xin and his team published in 'Nature Communications' [7] while the loaded diode is replaced with a variable capacitor. This dual-band LHM is analyzed with equivalent circuits from the aspects of electric and magnetic resonators, and is simulated using HFSS. The effective parameters are retrieved using 'S-parameter retrieval method' [8].

II. MODEL AND EQUIVALENT CIRCUIT

The geometry and equivalent circuit of the LHM proposed in [7]is displayed in Fig. 1, where L_s and C_s denote the inductance and capacitance of the split ring, L_0denotes the inductance of the metallic wires. In our study, we embed a variable capacitor, C_e, to port P. Therefore, a second resonant frequency is introduced. The equivalent circuit of magnetic resonator and the electric resonator are illustrated in Fig. 2, where $L_1 = 2L_0$, and the L_s'-C_s' branch is equivalent to the paralleled L_s-C_s branch in Fig.1.

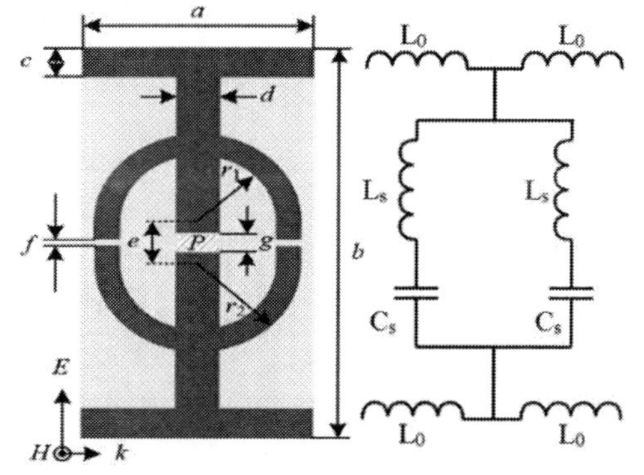

Fig. 1. One cell of the single-band LHM (a) geometry illustration (b) its equivalent circuit.

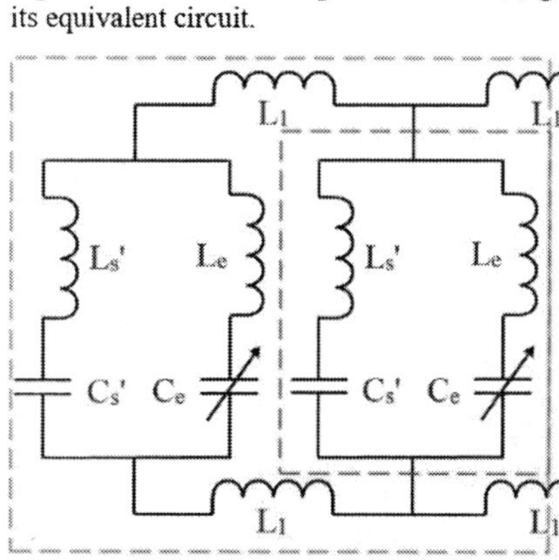

Fig. 2. Equivalent circuits of the electric resonator and the magnetic resonator. The red dashed area refers to the electric resonator circuit, while the blue dashed area refers to the magnetic resonator circuit.

At the resonant frequencies, Im(Z)=0. Therefore, the resonant frequencies of this magnetic resonator are:

$$\begin{cases} f_{m1} = \frac{1}{2\pi}\sqrt{\frac{L_1+L_e}{aC_s} \pm \frac{kL_1}{2a\sqrt{C_eC_s}}}, ('+' if \frac{L_1+L_e}{C_s} > \frac{2L_1+L_s}{C_e}) \\ f_{m2} = \frac{1}{2\pi}\sqrt{\frac{2L_1+L_s}{aC_e} \pm \frac{kL_1}{2a\sqrt{C_eC_s}}}. ('+' if \frac{L_1+L_e}{C_s} < \frac{2L_1+L_s}{C_e}) \end{cases} \quad (2)$$

Where k is a constant. The relationship of $(L_1+L_e)/C_s$ and $(2L_1+L_s)/C_e$ is determined with a certain C_e. Hence, there are two resonant frequencies in (5). One of the resonant frequencies is mainly decided by C_s, while the other one is mainly decided by C_e.

Accordingly, the resonant frequency of the electric resonator is calculated as:

$$f_e = \frac{1}{2\pi}\sqrt{\frac{C_e+2C_s}{(L_s+2L_e)C_sC_e}}. \quad (3)$$

If C_e is much larger than C_s, then from (3), the resonant frequency is mainly decided by C_s.

III. SMULATIONS AND ANALYSIS

In the simulations, the variable capacitor is changing from 7 pf to 25 pf linearly with a step size of 3 pf. For capacitance smaller than 7 pf or larger than 25 pf, the real part of the retrieved permittivity will be positive. The simulated S parameters is displayed in Fig.3, and the retrieved effective parameters is displayed in Fig.4.

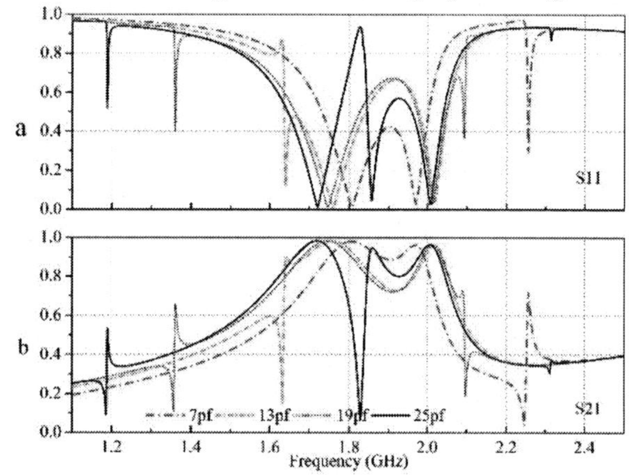

Fig. 3. Magnitude of (a) S11 and (b) S21 of the LHM embedded with a variable capacitor. C_e = 7 pf, 13 pf, 19 pf, and 25 pf, respectively.

When C_e is small, there is only one right-handed (RH) passing band. With the increase of C_e, another RH passing band appears and moves from higher frequencies to lower frequencies. There are two left-handed (LH) passing bands, of whom one is approximately from 1.98 GHz to 2.11 GHz despite the change of C_e, while the other one sweeps the desired frequencies with the change of C_e, except for the RH passing band.

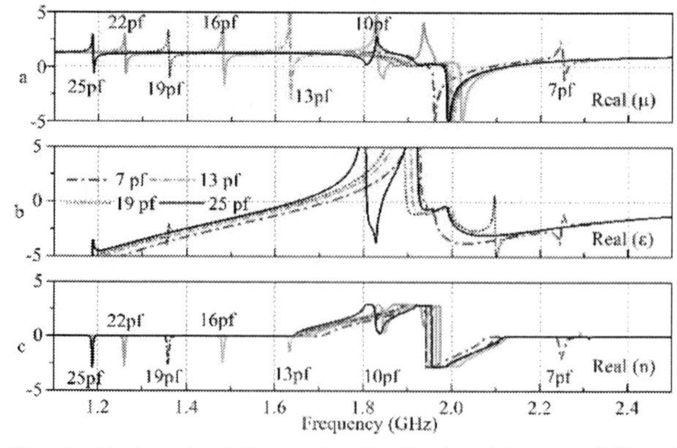

Fig. 4. Real part of the retrieved effective (a) permeability, (b) permittivity and (c) refractive index with C_e ranging from 7pf to 25 pf.

IV. CONCLUSION

A tunable dual-band LHM is proposed in this paper. From the simulations and retrieved effective parameters, it is identified that one of the LH passing band is approximately from 1.98 GHz to 2.11 GH, while the other one experiences a shift from 1.18 GHz to 2.26GHz, except for a right-hand passing band from around 1.7 GHz to 1.95 GHz. Generally speaking, this LHM is able to adjust its negative index frequency ranges according to different requirements.

ACKNOWLEDGEMENT

This paper is funded by the International Exchange Program of Harbin Engineering University for Innovation-oriented Talents Cultivation.

REFERENCES

[1] A. Sarkhel, D. Mitra, and S. R. B. Chaudhuri, "A compact metamaterial with multi-band negative-index characteristics," *Applied Physics A*, vol. 122, pp. 1-10, 2016.

[2] S. Islam, M. Faruque, and M. Islam, "The Design and Analysis of a Novel Split-H-Shaped Metamaterial for Multi-Band Microwave Applications," *Materials*, vol. 7, pp. 4994-5011, 2014.

[3] H. X. Xu, G. M. Wang, C. X. Zhang, Q. Liu, Z. M. Xu, X. Chen, *et al.*, "Multi-band left-handed metamaterial inspired by tree-shaped fractal geometry," *Photonics and Nanostructures - Fundamentals and Applications*, vol. 11, pp. 15-28, 2013.

[4] O. Turkmen, E. Ekmekci, and G. Turhan-Sayan, "Nested U-ring resonators: a novel multi-band metamaterial design in microwave region," *Iet Microwaves Antennas & Propagation*, vol. 6, pp. 1102-1108, 2012.

[5] E. Ekmekci, K. Topalli, T. Akin, and G. Turhansayan, "A tunable multi-band metamaterial design using micro-split SRR structures," *Optics Express*, vol. 17, pp. 16046-58, 2009.

[6] W. Withayachumnankul, C. Fumeaux, and D. Abbott, "Planar Array of Electric- LC Resonators With Broadband Tunability," *IEEE Antennas & Wireless Propagation Letters*, vol. 10, pp. 577-580, 2011.

[7] D. Ye, K. Chang, L. Ran, and H. Xin, "Microwave gain medium with negative refractive index," *Nat Commun*, vol. 5, p. 5841, 2014.

[8] X. Chen, T. M. Grzegorczyk, B. I. Wu, P. J. Jr, and J. A. Kong, "Robust method to retrieve the constitutive effective parameters of metamaterials," *Physical Review E*, vol. 70, pp. 811-811, 2004.

Novel Complementary Metasurfaces for the Orbital Angular Momentum Generation

Menglin L.N. Chen, Li Jun Jiang, and Wei E.I. Sha
Electrical and Electronic Engineering Department
The University of Hong Kong, Hong Kong
menglin@connect.hku.hk

***Abstract*—Besides amplitude, phase and polarization, wavefront is an important property of electromagnetic (EM) waves. EM waves with twisted wavefronts are known to carry orbital angular momentum (OAM). In this paper, a complementary-type metasurface is proposed to generate an OAM beam at microwave regime. Two metasurfaces that can produce OAM of order 2 and 4 are designed. By using our novel design methods,which are based on circuit model and dyadic Green's function, a high conversion efficiency has been achieved with a very low profile.**

I. Introduction

In 1992, Allen proved that the Laguerre-Gaussian beam, which has the azimuthal phase dependence carries orbital angular momentum (OAM) [1]. OAM offers a new degree of freedom extending beyond the existing wave feature and allows for promising applications in communications [2].

Recently, the metasurface concept is developed and various metasurfaces have been proposed to achieve low-profile designs to manipulate the electromagnetic (EM) waves in various aspects, including the OAM generation. However, the conversion efficiencies of these metasurfaces are usually low. At microwave frequencies, apart from the efficiency issue, simulation of the whole designed aperture with the complicated fine structures and large simulation domain result in a long simulation time.

In this paper, we propose an ultrathin complementary metasurface composed of sub-wavelength scatterers to produce OAM with high efficiency. On one hand, the design of the scatterers is based on equivalent circuit model. On the other hand, according to equivalence principle, these scatterers are replaced by equivalent magnetic dipoles and their EM response is calculated with the help of magnetic dyadic Green's function. The simplified model is validated by comparing to the full-wave simulation results.

II. Methodology

We consider an EM wave propagating along the z direction. To model the EM response of a scatterer, a transmission matrix is constructed to connect the transmitted field ($E^t_{x,y}$) to the incident field ($E^i_{x,y}$):

$$\begin{pmatrix} E^t_x \\ E^t_y \end{pmatrix} = \begin{pmatrix} T_{xx} & T_{xy} \\ T_{yx} & T_{yy} \end{pmatrix} \begin{pmatrix} E^i_x \\ E^i_y \end{pmatrix} = \mathbf{T} \begin{pmatrix} E^i_x \\ E^i_y \end{pmatrix} \tag{1}$$

If $T_{yy} = -T_{xx}$ and $T_{yx} = T_{xy} = 0$, a new $\mathbf{T}$ for an axially rotated scatterer with an angle of α is written as,

$$\mathbf{T}(\alpha) = T_{xx} \begin{pmatrix} \cos(2\alpha) & \sin(2\alpha) \\ \sin(2\alpha) & -\cos(2\alpha) \end{pmatrix} \text{(linear basis)} \tag{2a}$$

$$\mathbf{T}_{circ}(\alpha) = T_{xx} \begin{pmatrix} 0 & e^{-2i\alpha} \\ e^{2i\alpha} & 0 \end{pmatrix} \text{(circular basis)} \tag{2b}$$

Obviously, the EM wave will be changed from left (right) to right (left) circular polarization after its interaction with the scatterer. Additionally, an extra phase term $e^{\pm 2i\alpha}$ is introduced. By arranging the scatterers with spatially varying rotation angle α, $e^{\pm 2i\alpha}$ can be designed to coincide with the azimuthal phase dependence $e^{\pm il\phi}$ of an OAM mode. The order of the induced OAM is determined by $l = 2\alpha/\phi$.

III. Design

We propose a complementary scatterer as shown in Fig. 1. It consists of two types of complementary split-ring resonators (CSRRs) with different size and orientation. The fundamental resonances of the CSRRs in Fig. 1 (a) and (b) are excited by the y and x polarized waves, respectively.

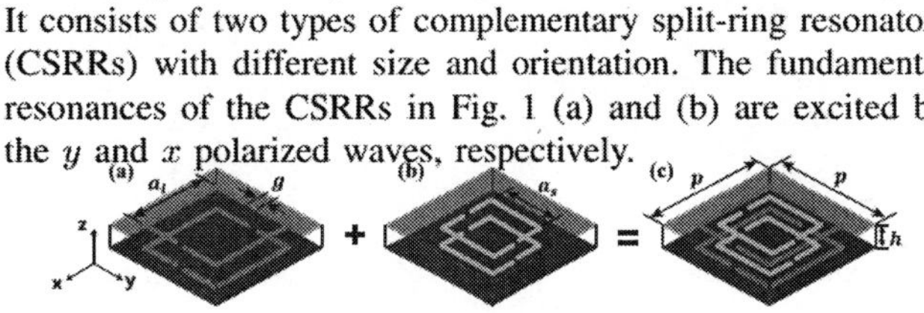

Figure 1. Schematic of the proposed scatterer. (a) the larger bi-layer CSRR; (b) the smaller bi-layer CSRR; (c) composite CSRRs.

The two types of CSRRs share the same equivalent circuit. Considering their bi-layer feature, two parallel inductor-capacitor (LC) circuits are used [3]. Fig. 2(b) shows the simulated S parameter based on the circuit model. At the frequency band of interest, the phase changes from 90° to −260°, which is much larger than the 180° phase change for a single resonator. In other words, the two LC circuits offer a sufficient phase coverage for design optimization.

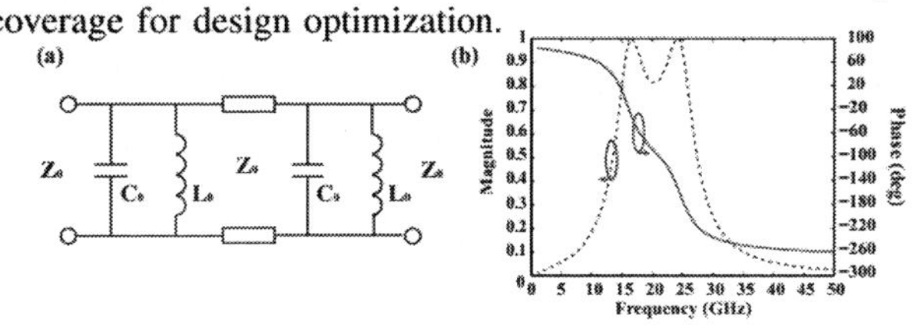

Figure 2. Equivalent circuit model of the scatterer in Fig. 1(a) and (b). (a) equivalent circuit; (b) simulated S_{21}.

Full-wave simulation is done in MWS CST. The results are shown in Fig. 3. The divergence between the curve shape and that from that in Fig. 2(b) is due to the high-order resonant mode of the CSRRs. Except for the fundamental half-wavelength mode, i.e. the one being considered in the equivalent circuit, the most significant mode is the full-wavelength resonant mode. The sharp phase shift in the phase curve imply the full-wavelength resonance. The periodicity of the unit cell isapproximated to be $0.4\lambda_0 \times 0.4\lambda_0$ at 17.85 GHz and the thickness is 0.048 λ_0. The proposed design has very low profile.

The metasurface is built by placing the designed scatterers with different rotation angle α. According to equivalent principle, the scattered field from CSRRs can be calculated by the equivalent magnetic currents distributed at the slots. We

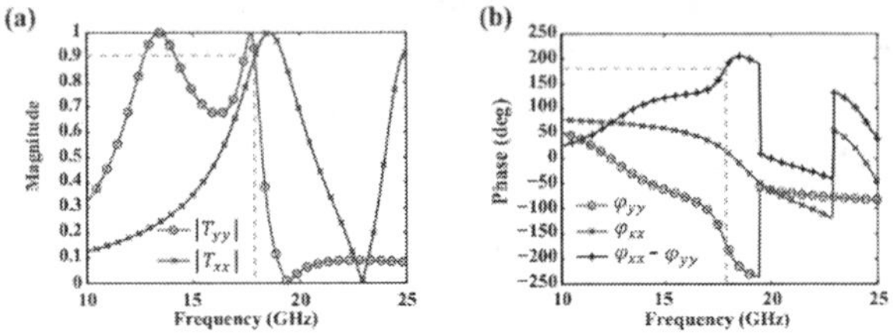

Figure 3. Simulated co-transmission coefficients of the proposed scatterer. (a) magnitude; (b) phase. The period of the unit cell is 7×7 mm^2. Side lengths of the two types of square CSRRs are $a_l = 5.2$ mm and $a_s = 3.9$ mm. The length of the gap is $g = 0.2$ mm. F4B220 is chosen as the dielectric substrate. The relative permittivity and thickness are $\epsilon_r = 2.2$ and $h = 0.8$ mm. The loss tangent is 0.003.

represent each scatterer as two orthogonal magnetic dipoles as shown by the arrows in Fig. 4. The EM response from the whole metasurface is then equivalent to that from magnetic dipoles with varying location, orientation and strength.

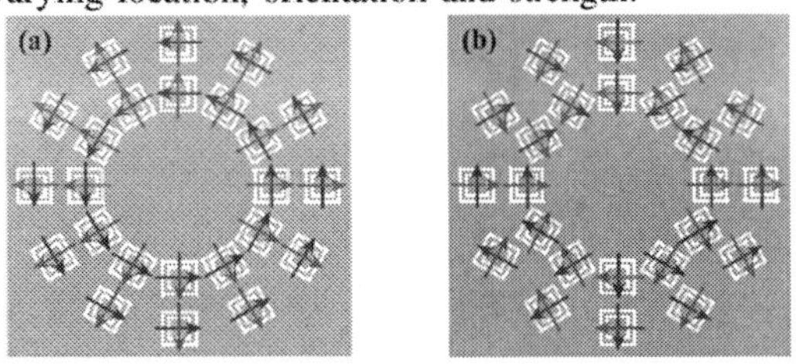

Figure 4. Top view of the metasurfaces and the equivalent magnetic dipoles for generating OAM of order (a) 2; (b) 4.

To start with, we write $\mathbf{T}$ for the CSRRs,

$$\mathbf{T}_l = \begin{pmatrix} -1 & 0 \\ 0 & 0 \end{pmatrix}, \quad \mathbf{T}_s = \begin{pmatrix} 0 & 0 \\ 0 & 1 \end{pmatrix} \tag{3}$$

where l and s stand for the larger and smaller CSRRs. The minus sign of the non-zero element in $\mathbf{T}_l$ is introduced based on the designed 180° phase difference between T_{xx} and T_{yy}.

The $\mathbf{T}$ for rotated CSRRs is written as,

$$\mathbf{T}_l(\alpha) = \begin{pmatrix} -\cos^2\alpha & -\sin\alpha\cos\alpha \\ -\sin\alpha\cos\alpha & -\sin^2\alpha \end{pmatrix} \tag{4a}$$

$$\mathbf{T}_s(\alpha) = \begin{pmatrix} \sin^2\alpha & -\sin\alpha\cos\alpha \\ -\sin\alpha\cos\alpha & \cos^2\alpha \end{pmatrix} \tag{4b}$$

At the incidence of circularly polarized wave, i.e., $\mathbf{E}_i = [1 \; -i]^T$, we obtain the expression of the equivalent magnetic dipoles, having both x and y components,

$$\mathbf{M}_l(\alpha) = \mathbf{T}_l(\alpha)\mathbf{E}_i = \begin{pmatrix} M_{l,x} \\ M_{l,y} \end{pmatrix} = -e^{-i\alpha}\begin{pmatrix} \cos\alpha \\ \sin\alpha \end{pmatrix} \tag{5a}$$

$$\mathbf{M}_s(\alpha) = \mathbf{T}_s(\alpha)\mathbf{E}_i = \begin{pmatrix} M_{s,x} \\ M_{s,y} \end{pmatrix} = ie^{-i\alpha}\begin{pmatrix} \sin\alpha \\ -\cos\alpha \end{pmatrix} \tag{5b}$$

Then, the scattered electric field from the equivalent magnetic dipoles $\mathbf{M}(\mathbf{r}')$ is calculated by,

$$\mathbf{E}(\mathbf{r}) = 2\int_V \overline{\mathbf{G}}_m(\mathbf{r},\mathbf{r}') \cdot \mathbf{M}(\mathbf{r}')d\mathbf{r}' \tag{6}$$

where $\overline{\mathbf{G}}_m(\mathbf{r},\mathbf{r}')$ is the magnetic dyadic Green's function.

In Fig. 5, we show the analytical and simulated phase patterns. As expected, phase changes 4π and 8π over a circle around the center for $l = 2$ and $l = 4$, respectively. The shift in the rotation ((c) vs (a); (d) vs (b)) comes from the different distance between the effective aperture and the plane for plotting. Compared to pattern with $l = 2$, the pattern with $l = 4$ shows a more significant difference from the analytical one. It is caused by the stronger high-order diffraction from each scatterer, resulting from the periodicity breaking in the azimuthal direction.

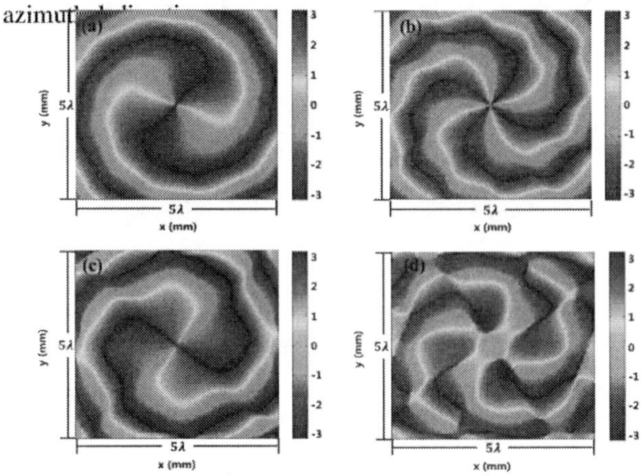

Figure 5. Phase patterns (in radian) of the cross-circularly polarized component of the electric field at a transverse plane of $z = 0.6\lambda_0$. (a,b) analytical results; (c,d) simulation results; (a,c) $l = 2$; (b,d) $l = 4$.

The EM energy is calculated by $U = \oint_A \mathbf{S} \cdot d\mathbf{A}$, where A is a closed surface and $\mathbf{S}$ is the Poynting vector. The conversion efficiency defined as the ratio of the OAM-wave energy to the total transmitted-wave energy is 81.8% for $l = 2$. But the ratio of the OAM-wave energy to the incident-wave energy is 15.2% and it is predicted to be 81% by the simulation results of the periodic unit cells in Fig. 3. This is because the periodicity along the x and y directions cannot be conserved and the truncation effect exists for the metasurface. By extending the two-circle metasurface in Fig. 4 to six-circle configuration, the efficiency is increased from 15.2% to 45%. For the case of $l = 4$, same trend can be observed. Therefore, it is reasonable to conclude that by increasing the number of scatterers, the conversion efficiency can be improved.

IV. Conclusion

In summary, an ultrathin complementary metasurface is proposed for OAM generation. The circuit model was established during the design process to reveal the working physics. The whole metasurface was modelled by the equivalent magnetic dipoles. Thanks to the complementary design, a high transmission efficiency can be potentially achieved for arbitrary-order OAM generation.

Acknowledgment

This work was supported in part by the Research Grants Council of Hong Kong (GRF 716713, GRF 17207114, and GRF 17210815), NSFC 61271158, Hong Kong ITP/045/14LP, and Hong Kong UGC AoE/PC04/08.

References

[1] L. Allen, M. W. Beijersbergen, R. Spreeuw, and J. Woerdman, "Orbital angular momentum of light and the transformation of laguerre-gaussian laser modes," *Phys. Rev. A*, vol. 45, no. 11, p. 8185, Jun. 1992.
[2] J. Wang, J. Y. Yang, I. M. Fazal, N. Ahmed, Y. Yan, H. Huang, Y. Ren, Y. Yue, S. Dolinar, M. Tur, and A. E. Willner, "Terabit free-space data transmission employing orbital angular momentum multiplexing," *Nat. Photonics*, vol. 6, no. 7, pp. 488–496, Jun 2012.
[3] J. Bonache, I. Gil, J. García-García, and F. Martín, "Artificial perfect electric conductor-perfect magnetic conductor anisotropic metasurface for generating orbital angular momentum of microwave with nearly perfect conversion efficiency," *J. Appl. Phys.*, vol. 119, no. 6, p. 064506, 2016.

Simulations of Realistic Multifunctional Nanoantenna Enabled Detectors

Salvatore Campione, Larry K. Warne, Roy E. Jorgenson
Electromagnetic Theory Department
Sandia National Laboratories
Albuquerque, NM, USA
sncampi@sandia.gov, lkwarne@sandia.gov, rejorge@sandia.gov

Paul S. Davids, David W. Peters
Applied Photonic Microsystems Department
Sandia National Laboratories
Albuquerque, NM, USA
pdavids@sandia.gov, dwpeter@sandia.gov

***Abstract*—The goal of this paper is to investigate full-wave simulations of realistic implementations of multifunctional nanoantenna enabled detectors (NEDs). We realize a 2x2 pixelated array structure that supports two wavelengths of operation. After designing each resonating structure independently using full-wave simulations with periodic boundary conditions mimicking the whole infinite array, we construct a supercell made of a 2x2 pixelated array with periodic boundary conditions mimicking the full NED. In the NED, each pixel comprises 10-20 nanoantennas. Our simulations account for the cross-talk between contiguous pixels. We observe that, even though there are finite extent effects, the pixels work as designed, each responding at the respective wavelength of operation. We want to stress that realistic simulations of multifunctional NEDs need to be performed to verify the design functionality by taking into account finite extent and cross-talk effects.**

Keywords—multifunctional detectors; nanoantenna enabled detectors; finite extent; cross-talk.

I. Introduction

Tremendous progress has been made in the last decade on infrared detector arrays based on narrow bandgap, III-V semiconductors [1]. Semiconductors containing antimony have enabled certain heterostructures to exhibit a broken gap that is advantageous in some newer detector designs [2, 3]. These narrow bandgap semiconductors show good promise in electronic applications such as high-frequency, low-noise high-electron-mobility-transistors [4]. Highly doped semiconductor materials have also been explored as alternative plasmonic materials [5-7].

Infrared detection has recently been enhanced through the use of plasmonic nanoantenna arrays on top of semiconductor heterostructures that contain the active material of a photodetector [8-10] [see schematic in Fig. 1(a)]. We define these detectors as *nanoantenna enabled detectors* (NEDs). Enhanced fields are generated by the nanoantenna arrays, which in turn induce enhanced absorption within the active material of a photodetector, enhancing its overall performance. Such a nanoantenna array is usually designed by using full-wave simulations of a single resonator employing periodic boundary conditions: this kind of simulation mimics an infinitely extended array.

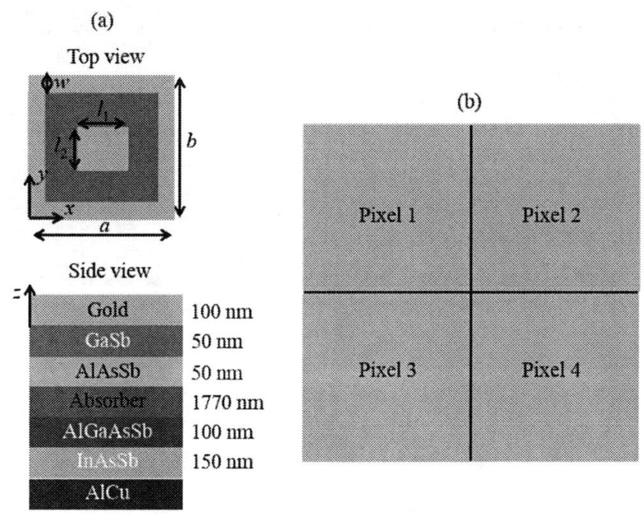

Fig. 1. (a) Illustration of a unit cell of a gold nanoantenna array, together with the semiconductor heterostructure. Periods a and b, patch sides l_1 and l_2, and width w. (b) Illustration of a multifunctional nanoantenna enabled detector made of a 2x2 pixel array, where each pixel is composed of a different, finite nanoantenna array and may perform a different functionality.

In general, there is the need to have multifunctional detectors, and this can be potentially realized using NEDs. Two alternative options exist: (1) one NED that can change its performance via external stimuli, such as a bias voltage; and (2) multiple NEDs interleaved in space [see schematic in Fig. 1(b), also referred to as pixelated arrays], where each pixel is designed to perform different functionalities. While the former is a very attractive platform, the difficulties that are inherent to such a tunable design make the use of pixelated arrays the most viable present solution for multifunctional NEDs. Functionalities may include different polarization properties, different spectral properties, etc. In this paper, we focus on modeling dual-band NEDs made of pixelated arrays. While each resonating structure can be independently designed using full-wave simulations with periodic boundary conditions, there is no guarantee that a pixelated array would perform as desired. This is because the extent of each pixel is finite and thus comprises a finite number of unit cells and may not fulfill the infinite condition imposed by the periodic boundary conditions; and the cross-talk between contiguous pixels may dramatically affect the NED performance. It is our intent to stress that realistic simulations of multifunctional NEDs need to be performed to verify the design functionality and improve their performance [11].

II. Realistic dual-band nanoantenna enabled detectors

We aim to design an NED structure that contains subpixels that work at different wavelengths. For simplicity of discussion, we focus on 4 pixels, displaced in a 2x2 pixelated array in a checker pattern as in Fig. 1(b) and Fig. 2(a), where each diagonal pair works at two different wavelengths: 1) pixel 2 and pixel 3 contain 10 unit cells and work at ~10 µm, with $a = b = 1500$ nm, $l_1 = l_2 = 900$ nm and $w = 50$ nm; and 2) pixel 1 and pixel 4 contain 18 unit cells and work at ~8 µm with $a = b = 800$ nm, $l_1 = l_2 = 150$ nm and $w = 50$ nm.

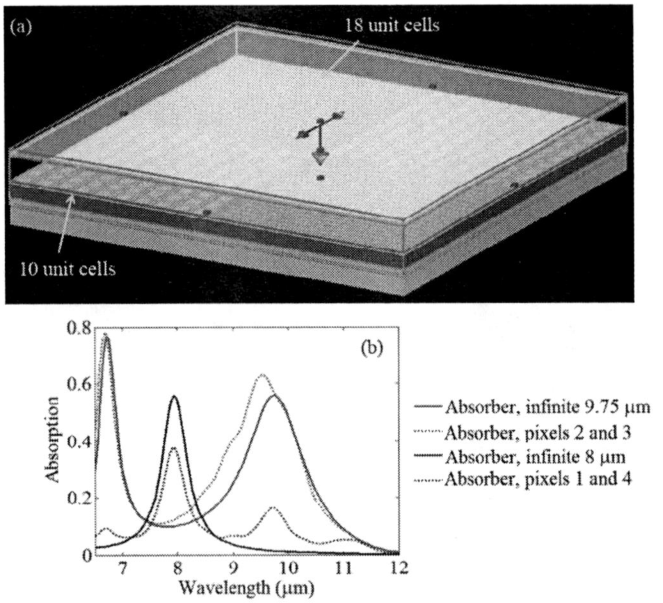

Fig. 2. (a) Illustration of the 2x2 pixelated array NED in checker pattern. Note the finite extent of each pixel. (b) Absorption spectrum of the dual-band detector, highlighting the contributions of main-diagonal and anti-diagonal pixels separately (dotted lines). The results are compared to the infinite arrays (solid lines).

Because of the finite extent of each pixel, it is of interest to determine if the detector will behave as designed, or rather if the optical properties would be dramatically affected by cross-talk between the different pixels. We thus plot in Fig. 2(b) the absorption spectrum of the dual-band detector in Fig. 2(a), restricting the contributions to the main-diagonal (pixels 1 and 4) and anti-diagonal pixels (pixels 2 and 3) separately. One can see that the pixels supporting the resonance at ~10 µm behave better than designed, given that the absorber receives more power (see solid versus dotted red curves). Some minor finite extent and cross-talk effects are observed as a shoulder at ~9 µm. When looking at the result relative to the pixels supporting the resonance at ~8 µm, we see that they behave worse than designed. In particular, we see that the absorber receives less power, and absorbs in frequency bands where it shouldn't, due to evident finite extent and cross-talk effects. Nonetheless, the overall behavior of the NED array is satisfactory, and these realistic simulations can be used to assess (and possibly improve) NED performance.

III. Conclusion

In this paper we have investigated full-wave simulations of realistic implementations of multifunctional nanoantenna enabled detectors. It is pivotal to simulate the entire detector comprising finite extent pixels to correctly account for the cross-talk between contiguous pixels. Even though there are finite extent and cross-talk effects affecting the performance of the dual-band NED under analysis, the pixels work as designed, each responding at the respective wavelength of operation. However, realistic simulations of multifunctional detectors need to be performed to verify the design functionality by taking into account finite extent and cross-talk effects.

Acknowledgment

This work was supported by the Laboratory Directed Research and Development program at Sandia National Laboratories. Sandia National Laboratories is a multi-mission laboratory managed and operated by Sandia Corporation, a wholly owned subsidiary of Lockheed Martin Corporation, for the U.S. Department of Energy's National Nuclear Security Administration under contract DE-AC04-94AL85000.

References

[1] N. K. Dhar, R. Dat, and A. K. Sood, "Advances in Infrared Detector Array Technology," in Optoelectronics - Advanced Materials and Devices, S. L. Pyshkin and J. M. Ballato, Eds., ed: InTech, 2013.

[2] P. Martyniuk, M. Kopytko, and A. Rogalski, "Barrier infrared detectors," Opto Electron. Rev., vol. 22, pp. 127-146, 2014.

[3] E. A. Plis, "InAs/GaSb Type-II Superlattice Detectors," Adv. Electron., vol. 2014, p. 12, 2014.

[4] C. Liu, Y. Li, and Y. Zeng, "Progress in Antimonide Based III-V Compound Semiconductors and Devices," Engineering, vol. 2, pp. 617-624, 2010.

[5] S. Law, R. Liu, and D. Wasserman, "Doped semiconductors with band-edge plasma frequencies," J. Vac. Sci. Technol. B, vol. 32, p. 052601, 2014.

[6] D. Wei, C. Harris, C. C. Bomberger, J. Zhang, J. Zide, and S. Law, "Single-material semiconductor hyperbolic metamaterials," Opt. Express, vol. 24, pp. 8735-8745, 2016.

[7] S. Law, D. C. Adams, A. M. Taylor, and D. Wasserman, "Mid-infrared designer metals," Opt. Express, vol. 20, pp. 12155-12165, 2012.

[8] D. W. Peters, C. M. Reinke, P. S. Davids, J. F. Klem, D. Leonhardt, J. R. Wendt, et al., "Nanoantenna-enabled midwave infrared focal plane arrays," 2012, pp. 83533B-6.

[9] S. Choi and K. Sarabandi, "Bowtie nanoantenna integrated with indium gallium arsenide antimonide for uncooled infrared detector with enhanced sensitivity," Appl. Opt., vol. 52, pp. 8432-8438, 2013.

[10] D. W. Peters, P. S. Davids, J. K. Kim, D. Leonhardt, T. E. Beechem, S. W. Howell, et al., "Application of plasmonic subwavelength structuring to enhance infrared detection," 2014, pp. 899419-6.

[11] S. Campione, L. K. Warne, R. E. Jorgenson, P. S. Davids, and D. W. Peters, "Towards simulations of realistic multifunctional nanoantenna enabled detectors," unpublished.

Size Reduction of Patch Elements for Homogeneous Perfect Absorbing Material

James L. Vedral and Randall L. Musselman
Department of Electrical and Computer Engineering
United States Air Force Academy
Colorado Springs, CO, USA
james.vedral@usafa.edu; randall.musselman@usafa.edu

Abstract—**Size-reduction of circular patch absorbing elements are analyzed by introducing slits, holes, and cut-out rings. Parametric variation results are presented for slit depth, hole size, and concentric rings to reduce the size of absorbing elements. ANSYS Electronics Desktop, a finite-element method (FEM) solver, was used to simulate the absorption from an array of circular patches, while analyzing parametric studies of the slit depth, hole radius, and ring radius, each of which increases absorption and reduces element size.**

Keywords—Absorbers; metamaterials; frequency selective surfaces;

I. Introduction

Radar cross section (RCS) reduction has been an interest to aerospace researchers for nearly half of a century. In the past, RCS reduction materials were constructed from magnetic or metallic materials [1]. However, these absorbers can add significant weight. Recently, the emergence of ultra-thin absorbers has been shown to provide near perfect absorption without adding significant weight [2]. Many of these perfect absorbers are based on patch elements, which are shown to be very efficient and predictable [2]. The patch elements absorb by electromagnetic mutual coupling between elements, in order to form either capacitive or inductive frequency-selective surfaces [4]. These types of absorbing elements are typically on the order of one-half wavelength or greater in diameter [2]. The large element size can be problematic when reducing the RCS of an object that has small features or surfaces. The inability to cover a small surface with a sufficient number of half-wavelength elements could result in inhomogeneous coverage. Furthermore, placing these patch elements too closely can cause undesirable coupling, significantly reducing the level of RCS reduction [2]. This paper introduces absorber size-reduction techniques based on similar techniques applied to patch antennas [5,6]. Additionally, we introduce a new size-reduction technique that explores the use of concentric-ring cutouts.

II. Patch

A circular patch was used as the absorbing element cell. The mode that drives a circular patch antenna is the same mode that provides absorption, using the exact same dimensions. Therefore, the absorption resonance can be analytically estimated from the antenna's dominate resonant mode, TM_{110}

$$f = \frac{1.8412c}{2\pi R\sqrt{\varepsilon_r}} \tag{1}$$

where f is the resonant frequency, c is the speed of light, R is the effective radius of the circular patch, and ε_r is the relative permittivity of the dielectric material on which it is printed [7].

The patch was designed and analyzed as an element in an infinite array, using the finite element solver in ANSYS Electronics Desktop, formerly known as "HFSS". Periodic *master* and *slave* boundaries were used to simulate the infinite array of the absorbing patches. Each unmodified patch was designed using (1) to have an estimated absorption at 8.95 GHz, a dielectric relative permittivity, ε_r of 4.4, and radius, R of 4.69mm. The loss tangent of the dielectric was 0.2, and the thickness of the dielectric was kept at a constant 0.2mm. Simulations revealed resonance at 9.05GHz absorbing 94% of the incident radiation, as seen in Fig 1.

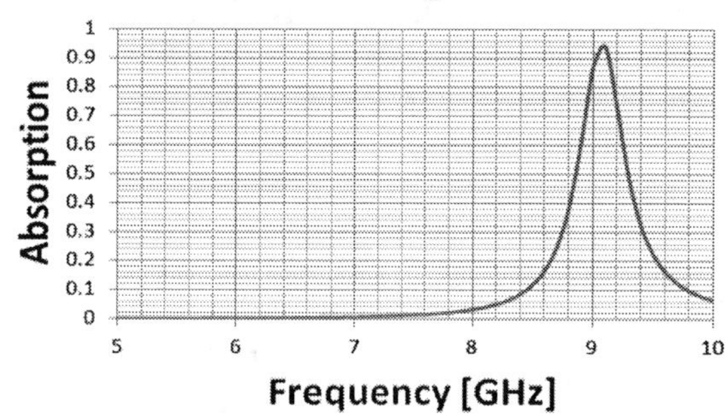

Fig 1. Graph of absorption vs frequency of a base patch element without modifications for size reduction.

III. Size Reduction: Slits

Of the abundance of size-reduction techniques that are available for patch antennas, slits offer favorable results [5]. This same slit technique has also shown significant size reduction for absorbing patches [6]. The slit lengths, L in Fig. 2 were varied from 0.525mm to 4.55mm, while keeping the slit width, W at a constant 0.14mm. These slits were shown to reduce the effective element diameter by 22%.

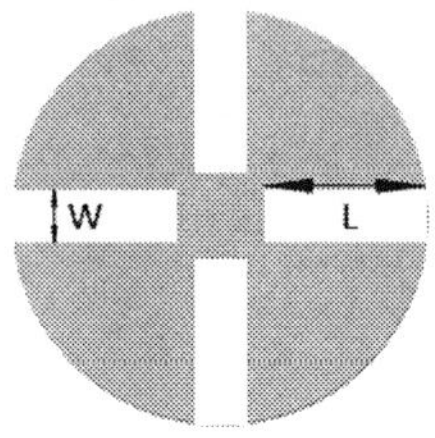

Fig 2. Patch absorbing element with slits for size reduction.

IV. Size Reduction: Ring

Figure 3 shows a circular hole cut out of the patch absorber in an attempt to reduce the size of each element. The inner radius, *R*, was varied as a percentage of the constant outer radius, ranging from 5% to 90%. This technique provided even better absorption than the slits, reaching 100% at 7.7GHz and 90% as low 6.3 GHz, as shown in Fig. 4. Since the resonance was reduced by 30% while still achieving 90% absorption, the diameter of the patch at resonance was effectively reduced by that same 30%, compared to an unmodified circular patch absorber. Even greater size reduction can be achieved with this technique; however, the absorption rate drops below 90%.

V. Size Reduction: Inner Disk

The third method for unit-cell size reduction was the geometry depicted in Fig 5, showing a concentric ring cut out of the patch. The radius of the inner patch, *R* was varied as a percentage of the constant outer radius. The gap spacing, *G*, was kept constant at 0.4mm simply to reduce the degrees of freedom. Figure 6 shows absorption greater than 90% for frequency reduction down to 6.48GHz, indicating that the effective diameter of the patch can be reduced by over 28%, compared to an unmodified patch. This method provided slightly less size reduction than was demonstrated in Section IV, however different values for *G* could potentially yield more favorable results.

VI. Conclusion

Three methods were presented to reduce the area of circular patches used as absorbing elements. Two of these methods reduced the diameter of a circular patch by nearly 30%, compared to the unmodified absorbing patch. Additionally, each method produced greater maximum absorption than the unmodified patch element.

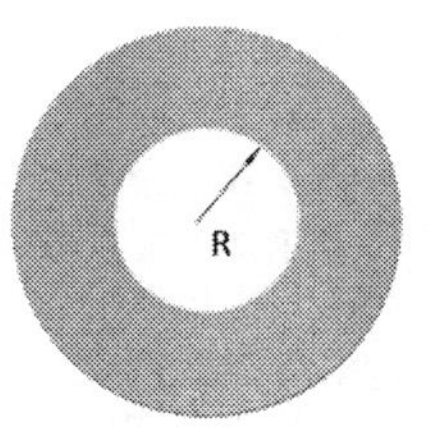

Fig 3. Patch absorbing elements with inner radius cut out. R is the inner radius removed from the element.

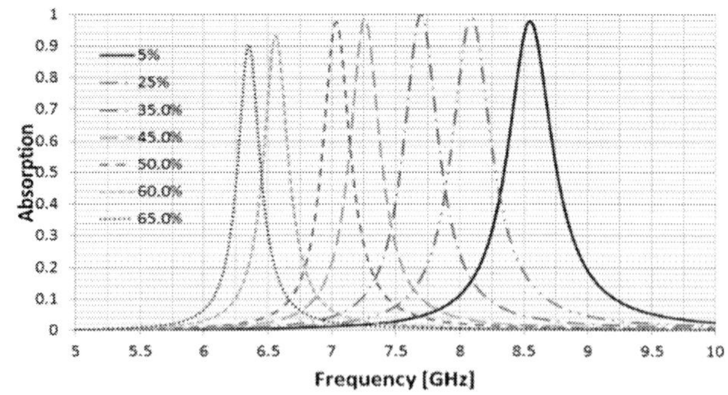

Fig 4. Graph of absorption versus frequency for the unit cell in Fig 3. Each curve denotes a change in inner radius, as a percentage of the outer radius.

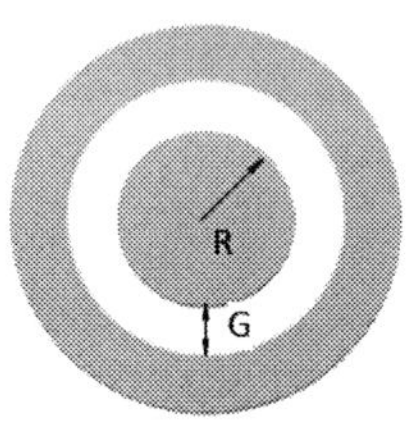

Fig 5. Patch absorbing elements with cut-out ring. *R* is the radius of the inner conductive patch and *G* is the gap separating the inner and outer conducting elements.

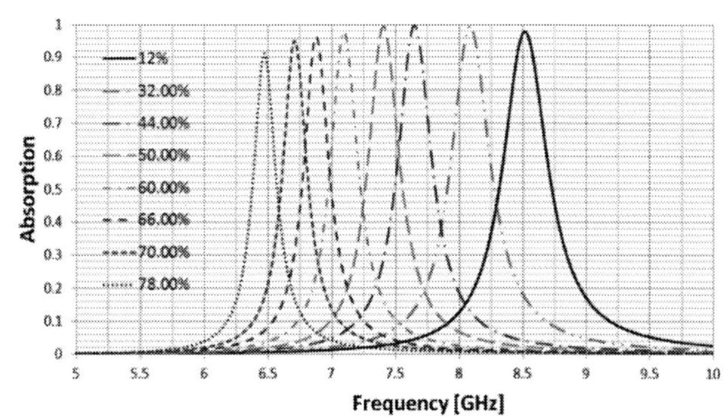

Fig 6. Graph of absorption versus frequency of the unit cell in Fig 5. Each curve represents a different in inner radius, *R*, as a percentage of the total radius. Gap width, *G* was held constant at 0.4mm.

References

[1] Saville, Paul. Review of radar absorbing materials. No. DRDC-TM-2005-003. DEFENCE RESEARCH AND DEVELOPMENT ATLANTIC DARTMOUTH (CANADA), 2005.

[2] *Propagation*, 58.5 (2010): 1551-1558.

[3] Zhu, Jianfei, et al. "Ultra-broadband terahertz metamaterial absorber." *Applied Physics Letters*, 105.2 (2014): 021102.

[4] Sievenpiper, Dan, et al. "High-impedance electromagnetic surfaces with a forbidden frequency band." *IEEE Transactions on Microwave Theory and techniques*, 47.11 (1999): 2059-2074.

[5] Musselman, Randall, et al. "Circular array for Satcom Interference Rejection." Wireless Information Technology and Systems (ICWITS), 2012.

[6] Vedral, James; Musselman, Randall "Analysis of Slits in a Perfect Absorber Element" Digests of the 2016 17th Biennial IEEE Conference on Electromagnetic Field Computation. 2016.

[7] Balanis, Constantine A., *Antenna Theory - Analysis and Design* (3rd ed.), John Wiley & Sons, Hiboken, New Jersey, 2016.

Refraction at metamaterial interface in terms of induced phase at resonant frequency

Quang Nguyen, Amir I. Zaghloul, and Steven Weiss
US Army Research Laboratory, Adelphi, MD, 20783, USA
93nguyen@cua.edu; amir.i.zaghloul.civ@mail.mil; steven.j.weiss14.civ@mail.mil

***Abstract*—Phase shift in reflection and transmission coefficients is critical to understand the constitutive effective parameters of metamaterial. In this paper, we study the phase of S_{11} (reflection coefficients) and S_{21} (transmission coefficients) for a plane wave incident normally on a slab of metamaterial. This study can help to predict the resonant frequency band and whether the permittivity, ε_r, is negative or the permeability, μ_r, is negative.**

***Index Terms*—Metamaterial, negative permittivity, negative permeability, phase shift, transmission, reflection.**

I. Introduction

METAMATERIALS have received considerable attention in electromagentic community over the last two decades due to their unique properties, such as negative refrative index, which can't be found in the conventional materials and composites. They were first theorized by Veselago in 1968 [1], then they have been developed to the point that they are ready to be used to design perfect lens or cloaking [2], [3].

The effective constitutive parameteres have proved sucessful in descrbing and predicting the properties of waves travel in metamaterials. These parameters are obtained through the retrieval process which uses the scattering (*S*) parameters as the input.

In this paper, we analyze the phase shift in S parameters to study the resonant frequency and the effective permititvity, ε_r, and permeability, μ_r, in metamaterials. First, we study in the fictitious slab which we know in advance ε_r and μ_r values. Then we study split-ring resonator (SRR) and the electric-LC resonator (ELC) which yield negative permeability and negative permitivity respectively.

II. Simulation of the Fictitious Slab

In this section, we analyze the phase of S-parameters of the fictitious slab whose ε_r and μ_r, is negative one at a time. The unit cell of the slab $(2.2mm \times 2.5mm \times 0.25\,\text{mm})$ is placed at the origin and excited by a y-polarized electric field in a plane wave traveling along x axis, as shown in figure 1.

The S parameters for the unit cell of figure 1 are obtained using FEKO, as shown in figure 2, for both amplitude and phase. The solid line shows S_{11} and the dotted line shows S_{21}. The red and the blue color indicate that the slab has negative permittivity $(\varepsilon_r = -4.4 - 0.1j, \mu_r = 1)$ and the negative permeability $(\varepsilon_r = 1, \mu_r = -4.4 - 0.1j)$ respectively.

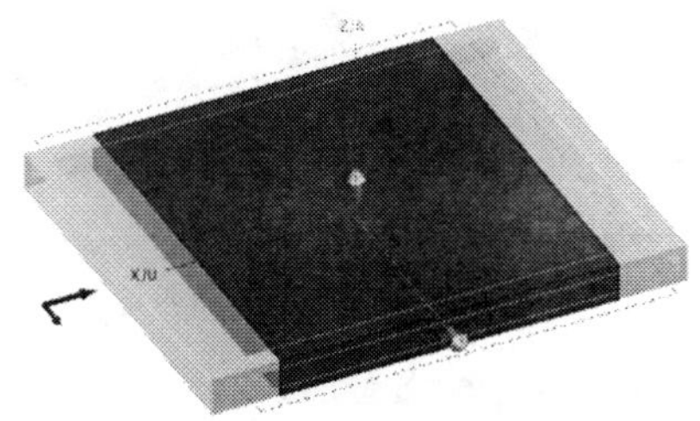

Figure 1. Unit cell of the slab.

As we can see, the case of negative ε_r has the same S parameters – magnitude as the case of negative μ_r (see figure 2a). Furthermore, they also have the same phase of S_{21} (see figure 2b). This is implying that the refractive index can be determined from just S_{21} only [4]. However, to indicate whether the material has negative ε_r or μ_r, the phase of S_{11} is needed. From the figure 2b, there is 180^0 phase shift between negative ε_r and negative μ_r. This can be verified by using the equivalent transmission line (TL) circuits to represent the slab. In a TL circuit, ε_r is represented by the distributed series shunt admittance (Y') and μ_r is represented by impedance (Z') as discussed in [5]. Obtaining S-parameters from two port TL circuit, one can easily prove 180^0 phase shift between negative ε_r and negative μ_r as shown in Figure 2b.

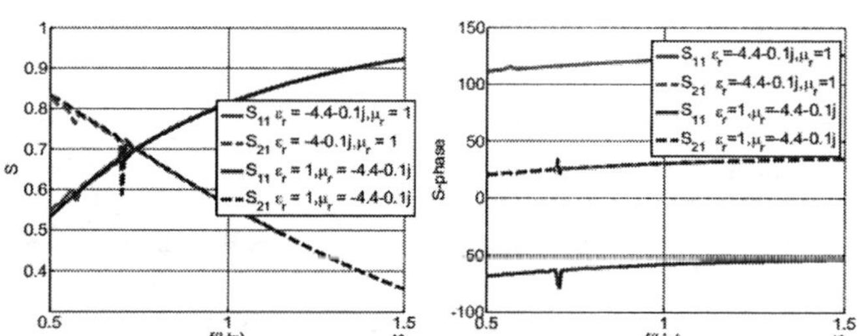

(a) (b)

Figure 2. (a) Magnitude and (b) phase of simulated S-parameters for the unit cell in Figure 1.

III. SIMULATION OF SRR AND ELC CONFIGURATIONS

In this section, we continue analyze the phase of S-parameters of two typical metamaterial structure: the spit-ring resonator, which yields the negative permeability; the electric-LC resonator, which yields the negative permittivity. The geometry and dimension of the SRR and ELC used in this study (see figure 3) are chosen to be the same as in [6].

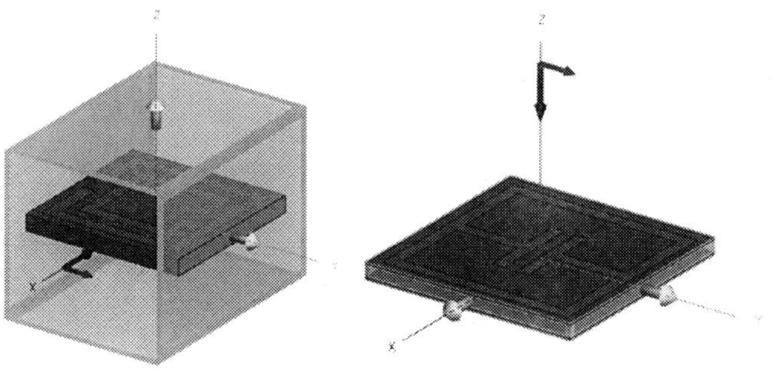

(a) (b)

Figure 3. Two typical metamaterial structure: (a) SRR, and (b) ELC.

The S parameters for SRR and ELC are computed using FEKO, as shown in Figure 4 and Figure 5, for both amplitude and phase respectively. The phase of S_{21} yields a useful information. The flip in the phase of S_{21} can indicate the resonant frequency band in which the permittivity, the permeability, or the refractive index can be negative. To determine μ_r or ε_r is negative, the phase of S_{11} is needed.

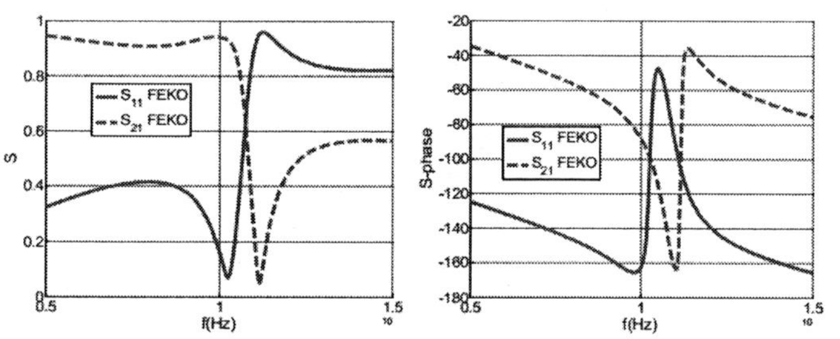

(a) (b)

Figure 4. (a) Magnitude and (b) phase of simulated S-parameters for the SRR.

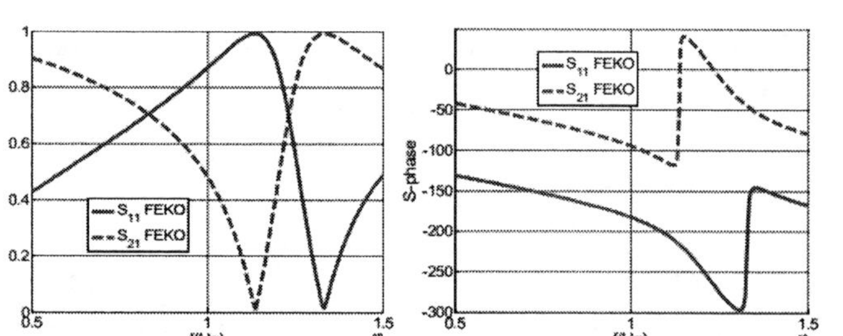

(a) (b)

Figure 5. (a) Magnitude and (b) phase of simulated S-parameters for the ELC.

As we can see, at the resonant frequency band of SRR (10.8GHz-12.6GHz), the phase values of S_{11} varies from -70^0 to -147^0. At the resonant frequency band of ELC (10.75GHz-12.7GHz), the phase values of S_{11} varies from -198^0 to -284^0. There is approximately 130^0 phase shift between two cases. Ideally, it should be 180^0 phase shift between the region where μ_r is negative, ε_r is positive and the region where μ_r is positive, ε_r is negative as discussed in previous section.

Figure 6 and 7 show the constitutive parameter of SRR and ELC to confirm the region where μ_r is negative and ε_r is negative respectively.

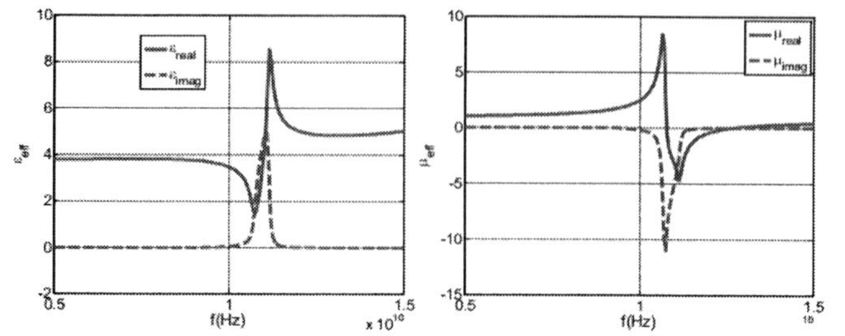

(a) (b)

Figure 6. Constitutive permittivity (a) and permeability (b) of SRR in figure 3a using the retrieval approach.

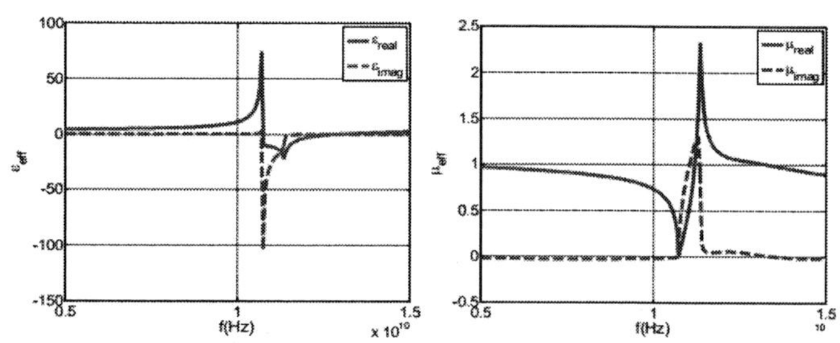

(a) (b)

Figure 7. Constitutive permittivity (a) and permeability (b) of ELC in figure 3b using the retrieval approach.

IV. CONCLUSION

In this work, we stud the phase shift in S parameters for metamaterial structure. The flip in the phase of S_{21} can indicate the resonant frequency band in which ε_r or μ_r can be negative. The phase of S_{11} can be used to determine whether ε_r is negative or μ_r is negative.

REFERENCES

[1] Veselago, Viktor G. "The electrodynamics of substances with simultaneously negative values of and?." *Soviet physics uspekhi.*, vol. 10, no. 4, pp. 509, 1968.

[2] Pendry, John Brian. "Negative refraction makes a perfect lens." *Physical review letters.*, vol. 85, no. 18, pp. 3966, 2000.

[3] Pendry, John B., David Schurig, and David R. Smith. "Controlling electromagnetic fields." *Science.*, vol. 312, no. 5781, pp. 1780-1782, 2006.

[4] Starr, A. F., P. M. Rye, D. R. Smith, and S. Nemat-Nasser. "Fabrication and characterization of a negative-refractive-index composite metamaterial." *Physical Review B.*, vol. 70, no. 11, pp. 113102, 2004.

[5] Eleftheriades, George V., and K. G. Balmain, *Negative refraction metamaterials: Fundamentals properties and applications*, 15, John Wiley & Sons, New York, 2005.

[6] Liu, Ruopeng, Tie Jun Cui, Da Huang, Bo Zhao, and David R. Smith. "Description and explanation of electromagnetic behaviors in artificial metamaterials based on effective medium theory." *Physical Review E* vol. 76, no. 2, pp. 026606, 2007.

Time Delay Signature of Chaotic Nanolasers and its Concealment

Amr Elsonbaty, Salem F. Hegazy and Salah S. A. Obayya*
Center for Photonics and Smart Materials,
Zewail City of Science and Technology
6th of October City, Giza, Egypt
sobayya@zewailcity.edu.eg*

***Abstract*— In this paper, we investigate the presence of time delay (TD) signature in chaotic intensity outputs of nanolasers subject to different optical feedbacks (OFs). Simulation results reveal the occurrence of obvious TD feature for the cases where conventional, phase conjugate and grating mirror feedbacks are employed. So, a proposed scheme for generating optical chaos with concealed TD signature is proposed to overcome the drawbacks of previously mentioned OFs and render the system more appropriate for applications of secure communications and fast physical random number generators.**

Keywords*— *Nanolasers; Optical chaos; Time delay signature; Optical feedback.

I. Introduction

Nanolaser systems provide variety of promising applications in system-on-a-chip technologies, photonic integrated circuits, optical communications and information processing. Also, the generation of optical chaos has witnessed a great interest due to its broadband spectrum, extreme sensitivity to initial conditions, and ability to establish chaos synchronization between two remote systems [1]. It can be employed in many interesting applications including chaos- based secure communications, chaotic radar, chaotic lidar and ultra-fast physical random bits generations [1,2]. Optical chaos can be generated in nanolasers by optical injection or introducing time delay (TD) terms into the rate equations describing the system via conventional or phase conjugate optical feedbacks [3,4]. In an attempt to increase further the security and enhance statistical performance of optical chaos, recently, we have proposed hybrid scheme for suppression of TD feature in the chaotic output of a single VCSEL [5]. However, theoretical and experimental studies of TD signature presence in chaotic nanolasers, along with the possible techniques to conceal it, are still unexplored. In this paper, we first investigate the occurrence of TD feature in chaotic nanolasers when different types of OFs are implemented, from which the grating mirror OF are analyzed for first time. Second, a proposed technique capable to effectively suppress the TD feature is presented. Numerical results reveal the efficiency of the hybrid (all optical/electro-optic) scheme and its role in achieving the ultimate security of chaotic nano-lasers.

II. System Description and Numerical Results

The rate equations describe the nanolasers system for different OFs can be written in general as [1,3]

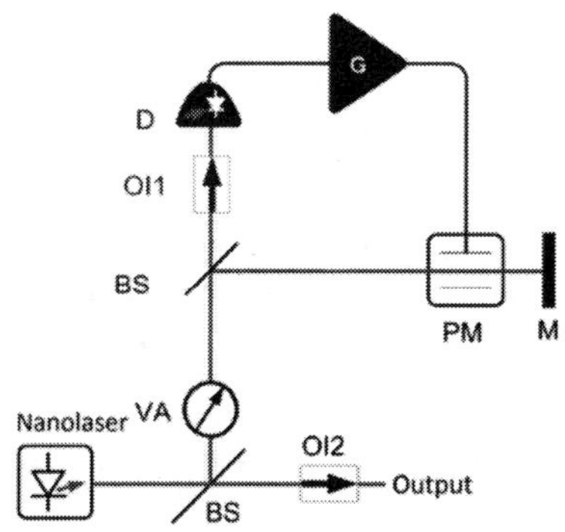

Fig.1. Schematic of the proposed optical-chaos setup.

$$\begin{aligned}\frac{dI(t)}{dt} &= \gamma\left(\frac{F\beta N(t)}{\tau_n} + \frac{g_n(N(t)-N_0)}{1+\epsilon I(t)} I(t)\right) - \frac{1}{\tau_p} I(t) \\ &\quad + 2k\sqrt{I(t)I(t-\tau)}\cos(\theta(t)), \\ \frac{d\varphi(t)}{dt} &= \frac{\alpha}{2}\gamma g_n(N(t)-N_{th}) - k\sqrt{I(t-\tau)/I(t)}\sin(\theta(t)), \\ \frac{dN(t)}{dt} &= \frac{J_{dc}}{eV_a} - \frac{N(t)}{\tau_n}(F\beta + 1 - \beta) - \frac{g_n(N(t)-N_0)}{1+\epsilon I(t)} I(t).\end{aligned} \tag{1}$$

where the parameters are described in [1,3] while $\theta(t)$ is set as $\omega_0\tau + \varphi(t) - \varphi(t-\tau)$, $\varphi(t) + \varphi(t-\tau)$ and $\omega_g\tau + \varphi(t) - \varphi(t-\tau) + \Delta\omega t$ for the cases of conventional mirror OF, phase conjugate mirror OF and grating mirror OF, respectively.

On the other hand, the recent scheme introduced for optical chaos generation incorporates both optical and electro-optic TDs into the rate equations of the nano-lasers. As sketched in Fig. 1, the two feedbacks reinject a sample of the nano-laser output phase-modulated by a previous sample of the output. The mathematical model takes into account the dynamics of the polarization interferometer embedded in the system such that $\theta(t) = \omega_0\tau + \varphi(t) - \varphi(t-\tau_o) - I(t - 2\tau_{o1} - \tau_{o2} - \tau_e)$ in this case.

The fourth order Runge-Kutta method is used to obtain the time series of chaotic output. In order to identify the TD signature from these time series, the highly efficient autocorrelation function (ACF) is utilized. The parameters' values of (1) are given in [3] except for values of k, ω_g, $\Delta\omega$ and TDs which will be provided below.

The values of TDs employed in the system can be retrieved from locations of peaks in ACF plots that represent a landmark for presence of TD signature. Our analysis is organized as follows. First, we consider the case of conventional mirror OF. We track locations of peaks in ACF plots for different values of τ and k which produce chaotic output. Fig. 2 illustrates the results obtained for $\tau = 0.1$ ns while $k = 65.4$ GHz (i.e. $f = 0.013$) in (a) and $k = 100$ GHz ($f = 0.020$) in (b). The obvious peaks at the value of TD and its multiple can be easily identified which means that the system is vulnerable to any eavesdropper's attack.

Next, we continue this study by taking the phase conjugate OF. It is known that larger value of k is needed, relative to conventional mirror OF, in order to induce instabilities and chaotic behavior in laser output [3]. However, clear TD signature can be observed in ACF graph corresponding to chaotic time series as illustrated in Fig. 3 which gives two examples for $k = 452$ GHz ($f = 0.09$) in (a) and $k = 654$ GHz ($f = 0.13$) in (b). These results verify the occurrence of TD signature for this type of OF. Now, we study the feedback from a grating mirror. Although, grating optical feedback is originally applied for stabilizing laser oscillations, it can sometimes induce instabilities in lasers [1], that is the state we consider. We set the values of grating wavelength and nano-laser wavelength as 1593 nm and 1591 nm, respectively, while keeping $\tau = 0.1$ ns as done previously. The presence of TD feature is still confirmed from monitoring simulation results in Fig. 4.

Finally, the proposed scheme is applied at $\tau = 2(\tau_{o1} + \tau_{o2}) = 1\,ns$ and $\tau_e = 1.6\,ns$ where Fig. 5 illustrates the ACF plots for $k = 452$ GHz ($f = 0.09$) in (a) and $k = 654$ GHz ($f = 0.13$) in (b). It is obvious that TD signature is effectively concealed in the case where the hybrid technique is employed compared with the other mentioned technique. The obvious large value of ACF at small time lag exist at the value of relaxation oscillation of nanolasers and does not contain any critical information about TDs employed in optical setup. However, for large values of k, a small indistinguishable peak, marked by brown arrow, is observed at time lag of $2\tau_{o1} + \tau_{o2} + \tau_e$. This clarifies the need for further investigation of ACF values in pane of $TDs - k$ parameters.

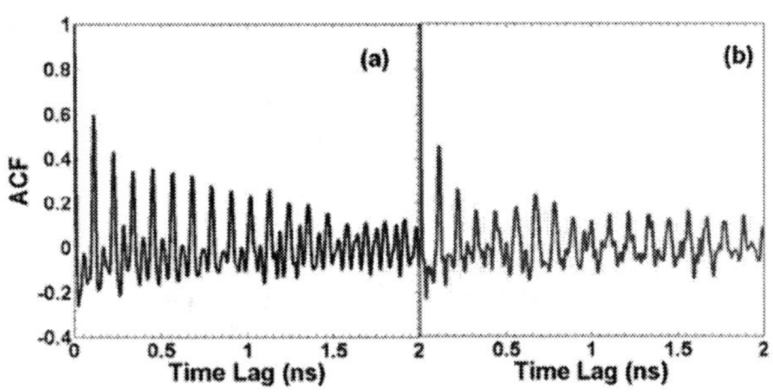

Fig. 2. The ACF obtained for conventional mirror OF.

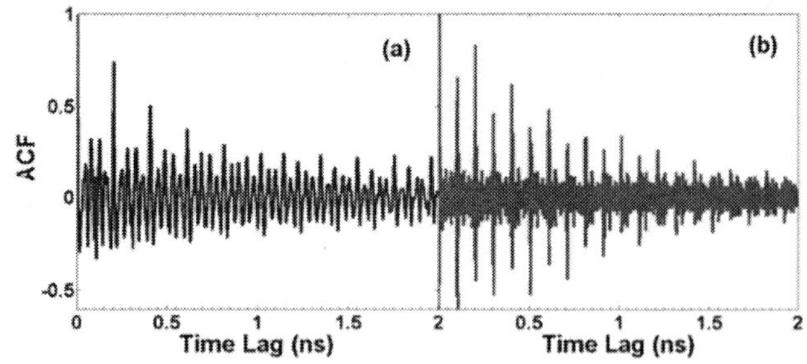

Fig. 3. The ACF obtained for phase conjugate mirror OF.

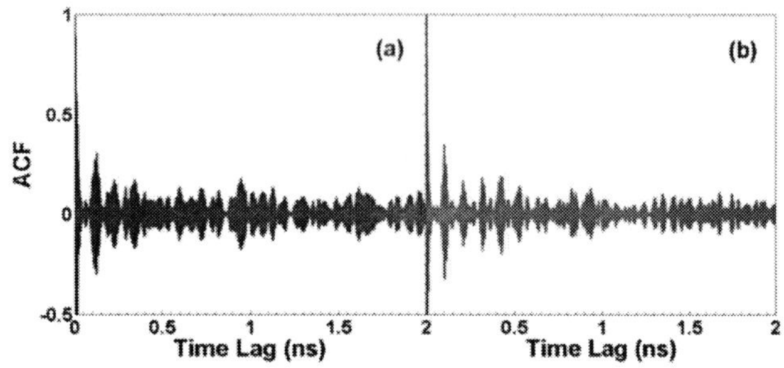

Fig. 4. The ACF obtained for grating mirror OF.

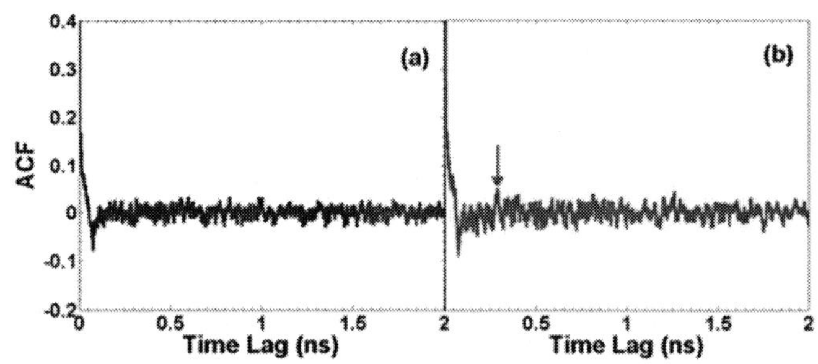

Fig. 5. The ACF obtained for the proposed setup.

III. Conclusion

In this paper, the TD signature in chaotic nanolasers has been analyzed for three different types of OFs. Also, a proposed technique for effective concealment of TD feature is presented.

References

[1] J. Ohtsubo, Semiconductor Lasers Stability, Instability and Chaos, Springer, 2013.

[2] A. Elsonbaty, S. F. Hegazy, and S. S. A. Obayya, "Numerical analysis of ultrafast physical random number generator using dual-channel optical chaos," Optical Engineering, vol. 55, no. 9, 094105, Sep. 2016.

[3] Z. A. Sattar and K. A. Shore, "Phase Conjugate Feedback Effects in Nano-Lasers," IEEE Journal of Quantum Electronics, vol. 52, no.4, 1100108, 2016.

[4] Z. A. Sattar, N. A. Kamel, and K. A. Shore, "Optical Injection Effects in Nano-Lasers," IEEE Journal of Quantum Electronics, vol. 52, no.2, 1200108, 2016.

[5] A. Elsonbaty, S. F. Hegazy, and S. S. Obayya, "Simultaneous Suppression of Time-Delay Signature in Intensity and Phase of Dual-Channel Chaos Communication," IEEE Journal of Quantum Electronics, vol. 51, no.9, pp. 1-9, 2015.

Subwavelength Focusing In The Infrared Range Using A Meta Surface

Manar Abdel-Galil , Yehea Ismail
Center for Nanoelectronics and Devices (CND),
Zewail City of Science and Technology/American University in Cairo (AUC),
New Cairo, Egypt.

Email:manar.mansour@aucegypt.edu

Mohamed Swillam
Department of Physics, School of Science and Engineering, American University in Cairo (AUC),
New Cairo, Egypt.

Email:m.swillam@aucegypt.edu

***Abstract*—This paper shows how a structure of a single subwavelength aperture surrounded by a finite number of gratings can be used to achieve subwavelength focusing of the infrared electromagnetic radiation. We use copper as a material which is CMOS compatible. The structure focuses the infrared incident radiation into a hot-spot of full width at half maximum (FWHM) smaller than the wavelength of the incident wave. This work opens up the possibility of many potential applications in the infrared range such as infrared miniaturized spectrometers, biosensors and the analysis of material properties and their chemical composition.**

***Keywords*—subwavelength focusing; infrared; plasmonic lens**

I. Introduction

According to the diffraction theory, when light passes through a subwavelength aperture, it diffracts uniformly in all directions and has a very weak transmission [1]. This puts a limitation on the smallest feature size that can be realized in photonics. In order to manipulate light on a very small scale, we should be able to control both the transmission and diffraction of the incident light.

In 1998, it was found that an opaque screen containing subwavelength holes transmits more light than what was expected according to the total area of the individual holes, a phenomenon that was referred to as extraordinary optical transmission (EOT) [2]. This enhanced transmission of light through subwavelength apertures in metal films was attributed to the excitation of surface plasmon polaritons (SPPs) which are charge density waves in essence [3, 4].

In 2002, researchers reported enhanced light transmission and beaming from a subwavelength aperture surrounded by periodic gratings on a metallic film [5]. Those results were of specific importance as they opened the way to manipulate light in the subwavelength regime. Since then, there have been many works trying to focus the visible radiation in the subwavelength scale using different structures and materials [6-8].

In this paper, we present a structure made of copper to focus the infrared radiation in the subwavelength scale.

II. The Importance of the IR wavelength range

The IR wavelength range finds its importance in many biological, physical and chemical applications. It can be used in communications and thermal imaging. It's useful, for example, in medical diagnosis, health tests and spectroscopy because many molecules have unique absorption spectra or signature in this range. This facilitates the study and analysis of different materials and biological structures. Plasmonics in the IR range will specifically be important for chemical sensors, thermal photovoltaic cells and heat harvesting. Other potential applications include infrared integrated camera, environmental monitoring and control [9, 10]. With all these important applications in mind, it's very necessary to be able to manipulate and control the infrared electromagnetic radiation at a very small scale. The structure presented in this paper focuses the infrared radiation in the subwavelength regime.

III. The structure

The presented structure consists of an aperture of width w and a number of gratings N on each side of the aperture as shown in Fig. 1. Each groove has a depth h and a width w. The gratings are periodic with period p.

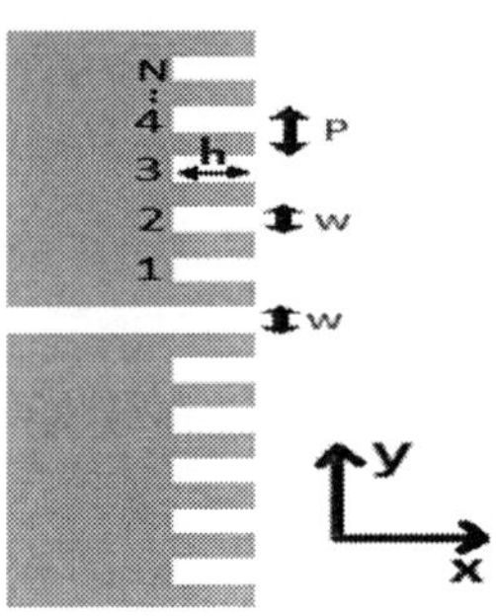

Figure 1. The structure used for focusing infrared radiation: a single subwavelength aperture of width w surrounded by N gratings on each side in the output surface. The gratings are periodic with period p and each grating has a depth h and a width w. The structure is symmetrical about the x-axis (i.e. $y = 0$ lies on the axis of symmetry). An EM plane wave is incident from the left along the x-axis.

Focusing results were achieved at a wavelength of $\lambda = 8.47$ μm for the following structure parameter values:
$w = 0.8$ μm, $p = 2$ μm, $h = 1.336$ μm and $N = 8$. The material of the structure is copper.

IV. Focusing results

Fig.2. shows the electric field intensity profile. The radiation emerging from the structure is concentrated into a hot-spot that has the coordinates $(x, y) = (33.79, 0)$ in microns. i.e. the focal length of the hot-spot is 33.79 μm. The full width at half maximum (FWHM) is 7.42 μm which is less than the wavelength of the incident radiation ($\lambda = 8.47$ μm).

Fig. 3. depicts the electric field intensity versus x at y=0. It's obvious that along the middle of the structure (y=0 line), the electric field intensity is high near the slit then it drops at some point and rises to its maximum value again at the focal length (x=33.79 μm). Fig.4. shows the electric field intensity versus y at the focal length position. We notice that the electric field intensity has its peak value at the middle of the structure (at y=0).

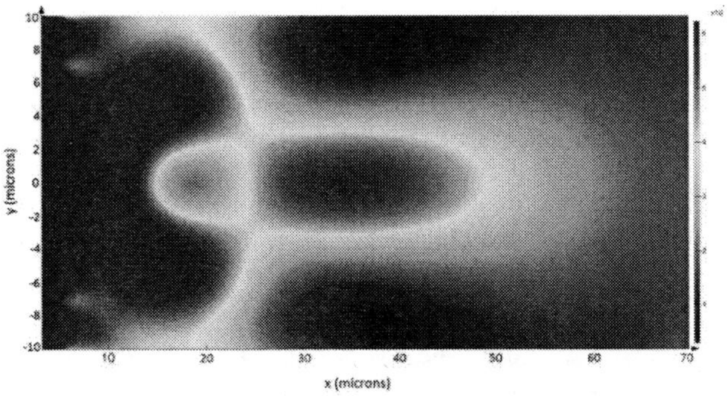

Figure 2. Electric field intensity profile as a function of x and y (in microns) for the case of $w = 0.8$ μm, $p = 2$ μm, $h = 1.336$ μm, $N = 8$ and for incident plane wave of wavelength $\lambda = 8.47$ μm (in the infrared range).

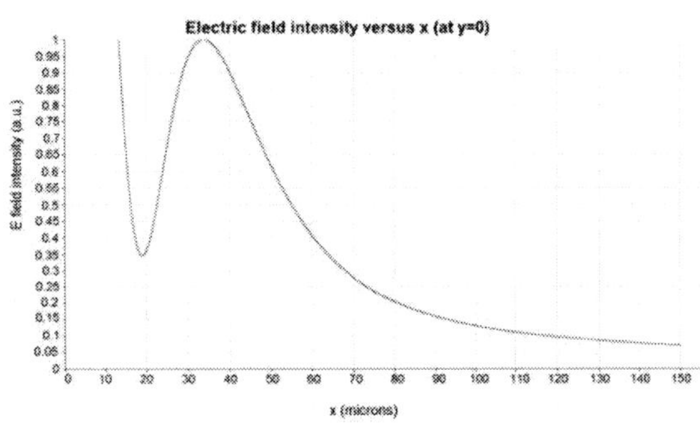

Figure 3. The electric field intensity versus x (at y=0) where x and y are in microns and the electric field intensity has arbitrary units.

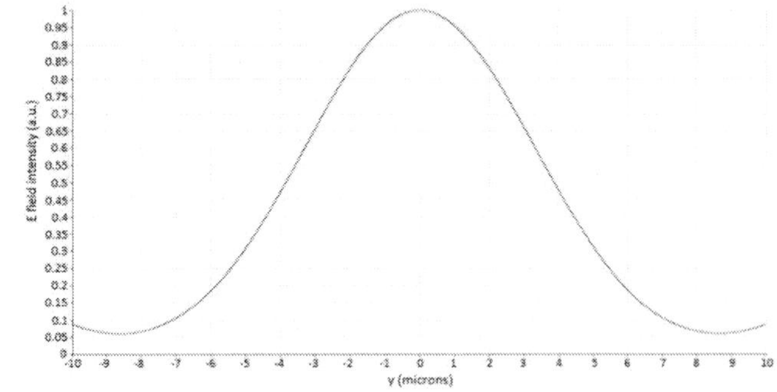

Figure 4. The electric field intensity versus y (at x= 33.79) where x and y are in microns and the electric field intensity has arbitrary units.

V. Conclusion

We showed how we can use a copper structure consisting of a single subwavelength aperture surrounded by a number of gratings to achieve focusing of the IR radiation in the subwavelength scale. A hot-spot of FWHM = 7.42 μm and focal length= 33.79 μm was achieved for an incident plane wave of wavelength $\lambda = 8.47$ μm.

Acknowledgement

This work has been partially supported by the fund received from Egyptian academy of scientific research and technology (ASRT), under the grant titled "Innovation Management cluster for local manufacturing of industrial electronic components (DLMEI)".

References

[1] H. A. Bethe, "Theory of diffraction by small holes," Phys. Rev. **66**, 163-182 (1944).

[2] Ebbesen T W, Lezec H J, Ghaemi H F, Thio T and Wolff P A 1998 "Extraordinary optical transmission through subwavelength hole arrays" Nature 391 667–9

[3] L. B. Yu, D. Z. Lin, Y. C. Chen, Y. C. Chang, K. T. Huang, J. W. Liaw, J. T. Yeh, J. M. Liu, C. S. Yeh, and C. K. Lee, "Physical origin of directional beaming emitted from a subwavelength slit," Phys. Rev. B 71, 041405 (2005).

[4] T. Thio, K. Pellerin, R. Linke, H. Lezec, and T. Ebbesen, "Enhanced light transmission through a single subwavelength aperture," Opt. Lett. 26, 1972-1974 (2001).

[5] Lezec H J, Degiron A, Devaux E, Linke R A, Martin-Moreno L, Garcia-Vidal F J and Ebbesen T W 2002 "Beaming light from a subwavelength aperture" Science 297820–2.

[6] F. J. Garcia-Vidal, L. Martin-Moreno, H. J. Lezec, and T. W. Ebbesen, "Focusing light with a single subwavelength aperture flanked by surface corrugations," Appl. Phys. Lett. 83, 4500-4502 (2003).

[7] Fu, Y. and Zhou, X. 2010 Plasmonic lenses: a review Plasmonics 5 287–310.

[8] M. El Maklizi, M. Hendawi, and M. A. Swillam, "Super-focusing in visible and UV using a meta surface, " J. Opt. 16, p. 105007, 2014.

[9] R. Soref, "Mid-infrared photonics," *Optical Fiber Communications Conference and Exhibition (OFC), 2015*, Los Angeles, CA, 2015, pp. 1-3.

[10] R. Stanley, "Plasmonics in the mid-infrared, " Nature Photonics. 6, 409 (2012)

Hybrid Plamonic Conductor-gap-silicon Microring-on-disks Electro-optic Modulator

N. H. Fouad[1], A. O. Zaki[1,2], D. C. Zografopoulos[3], L. A. Shahada[4], R. Beccherelli[3], and M. A. Swillam[1]*
[1]Department of Physics, School of Sciences and Engineering, The American University in Cairo, Cairo, Egypt
[2]Engineering Physics Department, Faculty of Engineering, Ain Shams University, Cairo, Egypt
[3]Consiglio Nazionale delle Ricerche, Istituto per la Microelettronica e Microsistemi (CNR-IMM), Roma, Italy
[4]Department of Chemistry and Earth Sciences, College of Arts and Science, Qatar University, Doha
* m.swillam@aucegypt.edu

***Abstract*—In this work, we propose a novel design of a double microring-on-disk electro-optic modulator based on hybrid plasmonic conductor-gap-silicon platform utilizing the electromagnetic induced transparency response. The modulator can be realized using relatively simple fabrication processes and has a very low power consumption of about 2.12 fJ/bit.**

***Keywords*—conductor-gap-silicon; electromagnetic induced transperancy; electro-optic modulator; low power consumption.**

I. Introduction

Recently, surface plasmon polaritons (SPPs) have been utilized in many applications in the optical communication field. They have the ability to highly confine the light at the interface between a metal and a dielectric beyond the diffraction limit [1]. This field is often known as "plasmonics", and it eases the integration between the optical and electrical components on the same chip through overcoming the size mismatch [2] challenge. In the past years, many plasmonic waveguide-based applications, such as metal-insulator-metal (MIM) waveguides [3][4], tunable waveguides [5], periodic metal waveguides [6] and resonators [7], were investigated. However, they suffer from high propagation losses, which limit the waveguide lengths to few microns.

Contrarily, silicon waveguides offer low power attenuation but also low confinement factor [7]. Many Si-based optical components were studied. Some of which employ the electro-optic effect [8], where the refractive index is changed according to the applied electrical potential. This effect allows high modulation frequencies compared to the thermo-optic [9][10] effect-based modulators , which operate at low modulation frequencies around 1MHz [10][11]. However, silicon photonics platform cannot be solely reliable for producing efficient optical components due to low confinement.

A new platform is recently proposed and it aims to combine the advantages of both the plasmonic and pure silicon waveguides. This platform is called silicon hybrid plasmonic waveguide (HPW), and it offers high energy confinement in the nanoscale, which is significantly superior to that of pure silicon. Furthermore, it has low propagation losses relative to other plasmonic waveguides. These key characteristics have drawn the attention of many researchers to HPW-based optical components. Yet, only few applications have emerged.

We have previously utilized the HPW platform in designing a double microdisk [12] and a double microring [13] resonator modulators as well as directional coupler switches [14]. In general, conductor-gap-silicon (CGS) [12][13] can be used to realize microrings and microdisks. This can lead to very interesting features such as low power consumption, high Q factor, strong modulation depth, small capacitance and miniature footprint. For the same fabrication process, microdisks are easier to fabricate as they require etching at the outer radius border only. This reduces the surface roughness, hence a more controlled operation frequency. On the other hand, microrings offer lower capacitance, resulting in lower power consumption. In this paper, we propose a novel CGS microring-on-disks electro-optic modulator based on electromagnetic induced transparency (EIT) response. The next section examines the design parameters and structure of the proposed modulator. It will be followed by the key results and a brief discussion. Finally, the concluding remarks are provided in the last section.

II. Modulator Design

Our novel modulator design is shown in Fig. 1. The main aim of the design is to combine the advantages of both microdisk and microring modulators. This is achieved by employing microring-on-disks cavities. The device consists of two electro-optic polymer (EOP) disks inserted between silicon disks and silver rings on a silica substrate. These two cavities are separated by a coupling distance from the input CGS waveguide, in which a TM plasmonic mode is excited. The modulating potential is applied as in [12] between the silver rings and the silicon disks in a push-pull configuration. All the CGS waveguide widths are set to be 220 nm with a separation distance of 140 nm between the input waveguide and the cavities. The layer thicknesses of the silicon, EOP and silver are 300 nm, 30 nm and 100 nm, respectively, which rely on a substrate of SiO_2 with thickness 500 nm at $\lambda = 1550$ nm. The outer radius of the cavities is 805 nm.

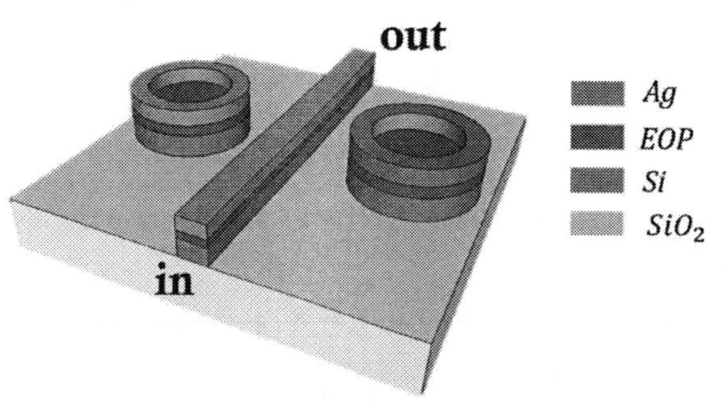

Fig. 1 HPW microring-on-disks modulator with CGS waveguide widths of 220 nm, separation distance of 140 nm and outer radius of 805 nm.

The refractive indices of silicon and silica are 3.45 and 1.45, respectively. A Dispersive Red 1 – poly-methyl-methacrylate (DR1 – MMA) EOP [15] with a 1.6 refractive index is used. It has an electro-optic coefficient of 300 pm/V. A John and Christy [16] Drude model is used to describe the dispersive characteristics of silver.

All the transmission spectra and the resonant wavelengths are obtained by the means of Lumerical FDTD software with Perfect Matched Layer (PML) boundary condition on all boundaries, meshing accuracy of order 7, a simulation time of 2ps and a background index of unity. The total capacitance of the device is calculated through the electrostatic model in COMSOL Multiphysics.

III. Results and Discussion

Our novel proposed design yields a very good compromise between good performance and easy fabrication method. The reactive ion etching is eliminated at the inner walls of the silicon and EOP layers. This provides more frequency accuracy and less optical scattering. The device has a total equivalent capacitance of 2.12 fF, which is very close to that of the double microring modulator in [13]. Thus, we can conclude that both the silicon and EOP disks have not affected the total capacitance of the device. Furthermore, the same resonance quality is achieved. The EIT response of the device operating in the "off" and "on" states at 0 V and 2 V, respectively, are shown in Fig. 2. The key advantage of this design lies in the relatively easy fabrication process while maintaining a low power consumption of about 2.12 fJ/bit.

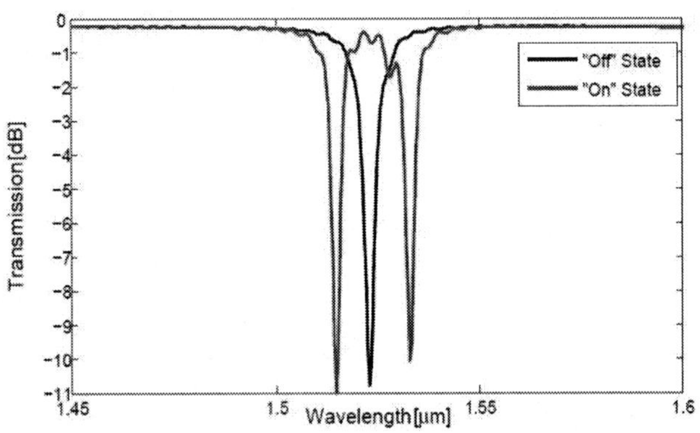

Fig. 2 The transmission spectra of the microring-on-disks modulator operating at the "off" and "on" states at 0 V and 2 V, respectively.

IV. Conclusion

In this work, we have designed a novel CGS microring-on-disks EOP modulator based on EIT. An easier fabrication process is used while maintaining superior optical properties: low insertion loss (0.52 dB), high extinction ratio (10.34 dB), ultra-small capacitance (2.12 fF) leading to very low power consumption (2.12 fJ/bit). This modulator have a Full Width at Half Maximum (FWHM) bandwidth of 0.65 THz, which is believed to potentially operate at very high speed (> 100 Gb/s) applications.

Acknowledgment

This report was made possible by an NPRP award [NPRP 7-456-1-085] from the Qatar National Research Fund (a member of The Qatar Foundation). The statements made herein are solely the responsibility of the authors.

References

[1] D. K. Gramotnev and S. I. Bozhevolnyi, "Plasmonics beyond the diffraction limit," Nature Photonics, vol. 4, no. 2, pp. 83–91, Jan. 2010.

[2] D. C. Zografopoulos, R. Beccherelli, A. C. Tasolamprou, and E. E. Kriezis, "Liquid–crystal tunable waveguides for integrated plasmonic components," Photonics and Nanostructures - Fundamentals and Applications, vol. 11, no. 1, pp. 73–84, Feb. 2013.

[3] L. Liu, Z. Han, and S. He, "Novel surface plasmon waveguide for high integration," Optics Express, vol. 13, no. 17, p. 6645, 2005.

[4] L. Liu, Z. Han, and S. He, "Novel surface plasmon waveguide for high integration," Optics Express, vol. 13, no. 17, p. 6645, 2005.

[5] D. C. Zografopoulos, R. Beccherelli, A. C. Tasolamprou, and E. E. Kriezis, "Liquid–crystal tunable waveguides for integrated plasmonic components," Photonics and Nanostructures - Fundamentals and Applications, vol. 11, no. 1, pp. 73–84, Feb. 2013.

[6] P. Holmström, L. Thylén, and A. Bratkovsky, "Composite metal/quantum-dot nanoparticle-array waveguides with compensated loss," Applied Physics Letters, vol. 97, no. 7, p. 073110, 2010.M. Young, The Technical Writer's Handbook. Mill Valley, CA: University Science, 1989.

[7] R. A. Soref, "Silicon-based optoelectronics," Proceedings of the IEEE, vol. 81, no. 12, pp. 1687–1706, 1993.

[8] J. P. Lorenzo and R. A. Soref, "1.3 µm electro-optic silicon switch," Applied Physics Letters, vol. 51, no. 1, p. 6, 1987.

[9] G. Cocorullo and I. Rendina, "Thermo-optical modulation at 1.5µm in silicon etalon," Electronics Letters, vol. 28, no. 1, pp. 83–85, Jan. 1992.

[10] G. Cocorullo, M. Iodice, I. Rendina, and P. M. Sarro, "Silicon thermooptical micromodulator with 700-kHz -3-dB bandwidth," IEEE Photonics Technology Letters, vol. 7, no. 4, pp. 363–365, Apr. 1995.

[11] S. Papaioannou et al., "Active plasmonics in WDM traffic switching applications," Scientific Reports, vol. 2, Sep. 2012.

[12] D. C. Zografopoulos, M. Swillam, and R. Beccherelli, "Hybrid Plasmonic Modulators and filters based on Electromagnetically induced transparency," IEEE Photonics Technology Letters, vol. 28, no. 7, pp. 818–821, Apr. 2016.

[13] Zaki, Aya O., et al. "Low-power compact hybrid plasmonic double-microring electro-optical modulator." SPIE OPTO. International Society for Optics and Photonics, 2016.

[14] D. C. Zografopoulos, M. A. Swillam, L. A. Shahada, and R. Beccherelli, "Hybrid electro-optic plasmonic modulators based on directional coupler switches," *Applied Physics A*, vol. 122, no. 4, Mar. 2016.

[15] Michel, Sébastien, et al. "High-performance electro-optic modulators realized with a commercial side-chain DR1-PMMA electro-optic copolymer." *OPTO*. International Society for Optics and Photonics, 2010.

[16] P. B. Johnson and R. W. Christy, "Optical constants of the Noble Metals," *Physical Review B*, vol. 6, no. 12, pp. 4370–4379, Dec. 1972.

Full 3D Electromagnetic Wave Analysis Using 2D Simulation

Raghi S. El Shamy and Mohamed Swillam
Department of Physics
The American University in Cairo
New Cairo, Egypt
raghisamir@aucegypr.edu and m.swillam@aucegypt.edu

Salah Obayya
Department of Physics
Zewail City of Science and Technology
6th of October, Egypt
sobayya@zewailcity.edu.eg

***Abstract*— A promising technique that reduce significantly the simulation time of 3D finite difference time domain (FDTD) electromagnetic (EM) simulation is proposed. The technique uses the well-known effective index method (EIM) to reduce the 2D index profile waveguide to an equivalent 1D slab waveguide which then can be simulated significantly faster using 2D FDTD simulation. We examined our technique by simulating ring resonator using standard silicon-on-insulator (SOI) waveguide. The 2D FDTD simulation results show very good agreement compared with the 3D FDTD simulation.**

Keywords—electromagnetic wave analysis, effective index method (EIM).

I. Introduction

The analysis of real 3D photonic devices need solving the complex Maxwell equations in three dimensions, which in many cases can't lead to closed-form expressions. Hence, numerical techniques are essential for the analysis and design of the photonic devices such as directional couplers, ring resonators and other. The simulation of real optical waveguides with 2D index profile waveguides requires a 3D simulation. 3D electromagnetic (EM) simulations consume very large amount of time, especially finite difference time domain (FDTD) method which solves Maxwell equation rigorously without any approximations. This large simulation time of the 3D EM simulation can be reduce significantly if we can replace the 2D index profile waveguide with an equivalent 1D index profile (slab waveguide).

Several techniques have been proposed to solve 2D waveguides. Analytical methods proposed by Marcatili [1] and Kumar [2] and the effective index method (EIM) [3-4]. Also, numerical methods like finite element method (FEM) and finite difference method (FDM).

In this paper we replace the time-consuming 3D EM simulation with 2D simulation by using EIM. This method was applied to ring resonators and shows very good matching with the 3D FDTD [5] simulation.

II. Methods

Here we use the standard SOI strip waveguide with h=220nm, width 400nm and air clad. Using EIM the 2D index profile (Figure 1-a) of the strip waveguide is reduced to equivalent 1D index profile (slab waveguide, Figure 1-c) by solving the slab waveguide in Figure 1-b. The slab waveguide in Figure 1-b is solved using the eigenvalue equation (2) at different wavelengths using MATLAB to get neffg(λ). Next we make 2D FDTD simulation of our photonic device (directional coupler, ring resonator, etc.) using the slab waveguide in Figure 1-c after defining new material in the FDTD tool with n(λ) = neffg(λ) and assign this material to the slab core index.

$$n_{effg} = \frac{\beta}{k_0} = n_1 \sin\theta_1 \quad (1)$$

$$k_0 n_1 h \cos\theta_1 - m\pi = \tan^{-1}\left[\frac{\sqrt{\sin^2\theta_1 - (n_2/n_1)^2}}{\cos\theta_1}\right] + \tan^{-1}\left[\frac{\sqrt{\sin^2\theta_1 - (n_3/n_1)^2}}{\cos\theta_1}\right] \quad (2)$$

where k_0 is the propagation constant of free space, β the propagation constant in the direction of light propagation (z-direction in our case) of the 1st slab waveguide with effective index neffg, n1,n2 and n3 the refractive index of the core clad and substrate respectively. Also, w and h the width and thickness respectively of our waveguide.

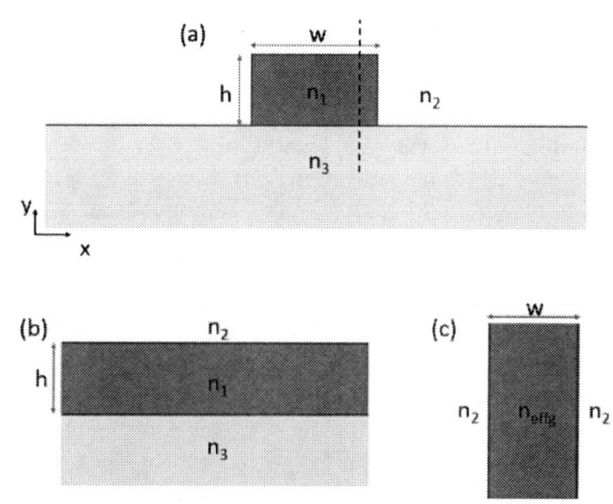

Fig. 1. Effective index method steps: (a) 2D strip waveguide, (b) 1st slab waveguide and (c) 2nd slab waveguide

Note that if we seek an electric field polarized in the x direction (TE mode) then we use the TE eigenvalue equation (2) when solving the 1st slab waveguide (Figure 1-b) to get neffg(λ). However, for the next step when simulating the 2nd slab in 2D FDTD simulation we solve for TM polarization, because with respect to the 2nd slab waveguide (Figure 1-c), the field is polarized in the TM direction. We also assume that the effective clad index of the 2nd slab is n_2 which is air in our case. Using our technique we simulated ring resonator by 2D FDTD and compared it with 3D FDTD.

III. Results and Discussions

In this part we present the results of our technique for a ring resonator (Figure 2) with width w=400nm, thickness h=220nm and radius R=1.8μm compared with 3D FDTD simulation (of a TE_0 mode) at wavelength around 1.55μm.

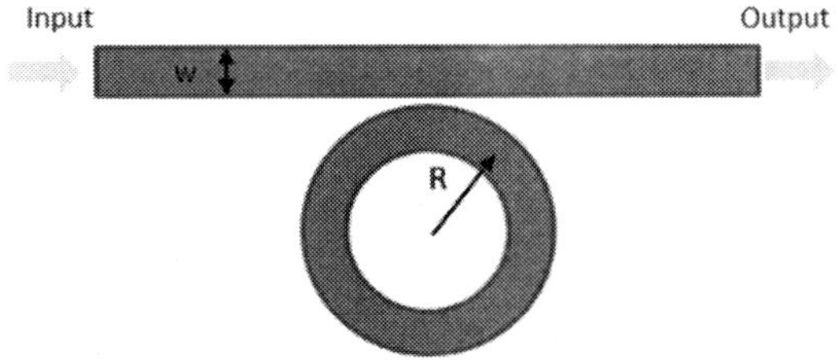

Fig. 2. Ring resonator

We first assume that the effective clad index of the 2nd slab is n_2 which is air in our case. The results show FSR of 46nm around 1.5μm for the 3D simulation and FSR of 48nm for our 2D simulation. The FSR value are very close but the exact resonance wavelength are shifted. Also, the losses due to bend in the ring is underestimated in the 2D simulation by about 1dB/90°bend in the case of 1.8μm radius.

The most important characteristic in the ring resonator is the resonant wavelengths, so we need to match the resonant wavelengths of the 2D simulation (using our technique) and the 3D simulation. The clad index of the effective slab waveguide (2nd slab) was assumed to be equal with the clad refractive index of the SOI strip waveguide, which is air. This is an approximation because the effective clad index should be between the clad (air) and substrate (SiO_2) index (1 and 1.45 respectively). We have tried different clad indices and each index was matching certain resonant wavelength. Hence, to match all the resonant wavelengths in the range of interest a linear wavelength dependent model was used for the clad index, to match the resonance of the 3D simulation.

Figure 3 shows the normalized reflection of the ring resonator using both 3D FDTD simulation and 2D FDTD simulation using EIM and the clad index model. As shown, the resonant wavelengths of the 2D simulation are in very good agreement with that of 3D simulation. Exact agreement in the resonant wavelengths can be reached if we use nonlinear wavelength dependent model for the clad index. Moreover, the difference in the power levels (especially nulls) is due to waveguide bend loss which is underestimated in the case of 2D simulation.

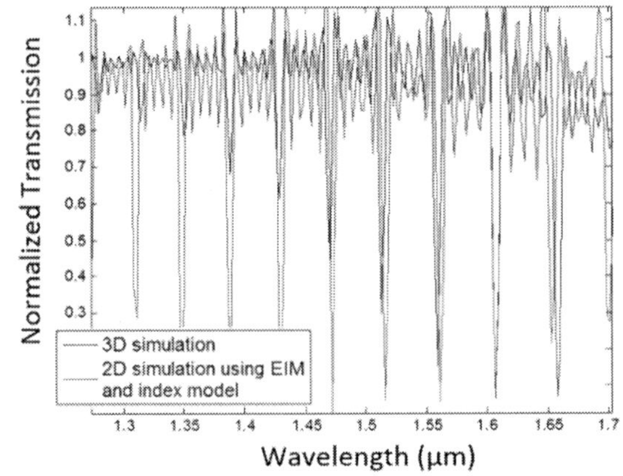

Fig. 3. Comparison of 3D FDTD simulation and 2D FDTD simulation using EIM and the clad index model of a ring resonator with w=400nm, h=220nm and R=1.8μm

The 3D FDTD simulation of the ring resonator takes 27min and 260MB memory in 4 cores, 2.5GHz processor, 64GB RAM and 64bit machine. While the 2D FDTD simulation takes 30sec (54 times less than 3D FDTD) and 27MB memory (9.6 times less than 3D FDTD) on the same machine. Hence, our derived model saves a very large amount of time and memory.

Conclusion

The EIM technique used to reduce the 3D FDTD simulation to 2D FDTD simulation is very promising. This technique reduces significantly the time of the 3D FDTD simulation. We tested this technique using ring resonator and the results was in very good agreement with the 3D FDTD simulation.

Acknowledgment

This work was supported by Information Technology Industry Development Agency (ITIDA) under the ITAC Program CFP#70.

References

[1] Marcatili, Enrique AJ. "Dielectric rectangular waveguide and directional coupler for integrated optics." *Bell System Technical Journal* 48, no. 7 (1969): 2071-2102.

[2] Kumar, Arun, K. Thyagarajan, and Ajoy K. Ghatak. "Analysis of rectangular-core dielectric waveguides: an accurate perturbation approach." *Optics letters* 8, no. 1 (1983): 63-65.

[3] Knox, R. M., and P. P. Toulios. "Integrated circuits for the millimeter through optical frequency range." In *Proc. Symp. Submillimeter Waves*, vol. 20, pp. 497-515. Brooklyn, NY, 1970.

[4] Tamir, T. 1975. *Integrated Optics*. Chap. 2, Berlin: Springer-Verlag.

[5] Lumerical Solutions, Inc. 2016 [7 July 2016]; Available from: https://www.lumerical.com/tcad-products/fdtd/.

High Performance Silicon Mach-Zehnder Interferometer Based Photonic Modulator

Ahmad B. Ayoub, Mohamed A. Swillam
Department of Physics, School of Sciences and Engineering
American University in Cairo
Cairo, Egypt
ahmad.ayoub@aucegypt.edu, m.swillam@aucegypt.edu

Abstract— **A new design for silicon Mach-Zehnder photonic interferometer with a different cross-sectional area than that for conventional silicon waveguide is proposed. The structure has the potential to be used as a modulator with extremely large extinction ratio as compared to conventional silicon waveguides based MZI modulators. This enabled using our design in different micro-scale applications including optical sensing and modulation using photonic structures.**

Keywords— interference, modulation, photonics

I. INTRODUCTION

Silicon Photonics is considered the optimum solution for applications requiring high bandwidth, low power consumption, low cost, and compatibility with complementary metal oxide semiconductor (CMOS) fabrication techniques [1]. In the last few years, the need for electronic-optical integration has been increasing and the need for higher bandwidth in the intra- and inter-core communication as well as data centers make this integration a necessity [1], opening the door for what is called "More-than-Moore" [2]. Optical modulators represent the main cornerstone in such type of optoelectronic chips by modulating the electronic data into its counterpart optical signal to be transmitted through the optical interconnect.

Different types of optical modulators exist; electro-refraction modulation, electro-absorption modulation, thermo-optic modulation. Electro-optic modulation is based on having a polymer whose real part of the refractive index changes as a result of applying an external voltage or electric field on the polymer. Pockels and Kerr effects are the most common two effects for electro-refraction modulation in which the change in the refractive index is directly proportional with the field and its square, respectively [1]. Unfortunately, silicon lacks each of these effects at typical wavelengths for telecommunications in range between 1300 nm and 1600 nm. A lot of optical modulators have been proposed and demonstrated in the last decade. Alloatti et al. [3] proposed a silicon organic hybrid modulator that is operating at frequencies up to 100 GHz and beyond. Despite it long length of 500 μm, the device offered a capacitance per length of about 100ff/mm. High-speed silicon MZM with low insertion loss, based on the carrier depletion effect was demonstrated in [4]. A 1.9 dB on-chip insertion loss and a figure of merit less than 2 V•cm were achieved in an MZM with a 750 μm-long phase shifter.

From the previous examples it can be shown that achieving a high extinction ration implies large modulation length and hence this affect both the capacitance of the modulator as well as the total energy consumption per bit. In this paper, a new design for MZI based modulator is proposed with optimized dimensions other than the conventional dimensions for silicon waveguide which will in turn enhance the extinction ratio with reasonable sizes.

II. STRUCTURE DESIGN

Figure 1 shows a schematic for the optical modulator. An EO polymer with refractive index of 1.6 is used [5]. The polymer used has an electro-optic coefficient equals 310 pm/V. The change in the refractive index (Dn) is given by

$$Dn = -0.5 * n_0^3 * r_{33} * V/t \quad (1)$$

Where n_0 is the original refractive index = 1.6, r_{33} is the electro-optic coefficient, V is the applied voltage, while t is the thickness of the dielectric between the two metal layers. The use of the EO polymer with high electro-optic coefficient will permit a noticeable change in the refractive index of the polymer with low applied voltage. A DC voltage of 2V is applied on the left metal layer while the driving voltage will be applied on the upper side resulting in "On" and "Off" states. Applying the voltage in push-pull configuration (+/- 1V) can help in having the same effect with less driving voltage and hence the reduction of the power consumption. To allow for better interaction between the optical mode and the surroundings, a shallow waveguide with lateral side of 50 nm thickness is designed with the width chosen to be 2 μm to sustain the fundamental TM optical mode. This structure results in having a mode profile as shown in figure 2.a. As can be seen from the mode profiles, the mode is highly affected by the surrounding media yielding a small effective index since a considerable portion of the field is outside the waveguide and hence high extinction ratio can be achieved with much lower arm lengths which result in small size low power consumption optical modulator, making it a promising solution for many of optical modulation applications in photonic integrated circuits.

Fig. 1. Schematic of the proposed MZI modulator

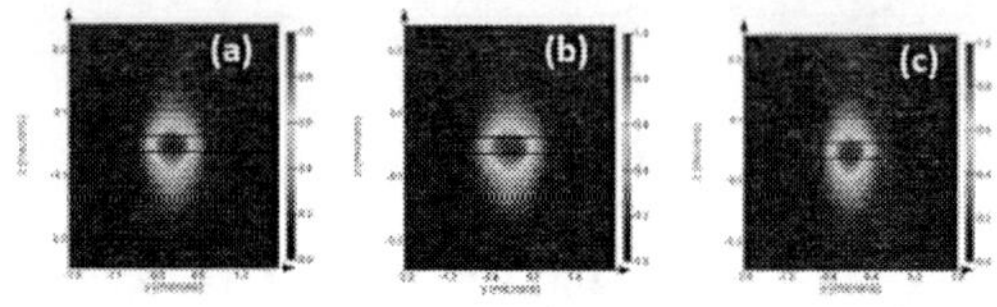

Fig. 2. Mode Profiles for different dimensions. a, 2000 nm * 50 nm waveguide and neff=1.57. b, 1500 nm * 50 nm waveguide and neff=1.53. c, 1250 nm * 50 nm waveguide and neff=1.50.

III. RESULTS

Using opti-beam propagation method (BPM) commercial tool of Opti-FDTD simulator [6], the modulator schematic is designed and simulated.

The MZI arms are designed to have slight curvature to satisfy the conditions of the BPM technique. The arm length is designed to be 215 μm with a polymer cross sectional area equals 2 μm*200 nm yielding a capacitance of 48.7 fF. For an operating frequency of 100GHz, the power consumption can be calculated by

$$P = 0.5 * f * C * V^2 \quad (2)$$

Therefore, at an applied voltage of 1V in a push pull configuration, the power consumption equals 2.435 mW. The energy per bit equals 24.35 fJ/bit. Figure 3 shows the transmission as a function of wavelength in the on and off states. To validate the high performance of this design, an MZI based modulator is designed with the same arm length but using the conventional single mode waveguide with cross section of 220 nm * 400 nm and the results of both modulators are compared. The proposed MZI have much higher extinction ratio of 23.15 dB compared to a maximum extinction ratio of 14 dB at operating wavelength 1.64 μm for the conventional MZI. Such large extinction ratio is owing to the fact of having an optical mode that is highly altered by the surrounding due to small lateral thickness of 50nm.

Compared to previous work proposed in [3], this work has relatively shorter arm length with lower capacitance and thus it highly fits to on-chip applications that require small size and low energy per bit consumption. In addition, the design outperforms the modulator proposed in [4] with respect to the modulator length. Further investigations on the insertion loss and the figure of merit shall be made.

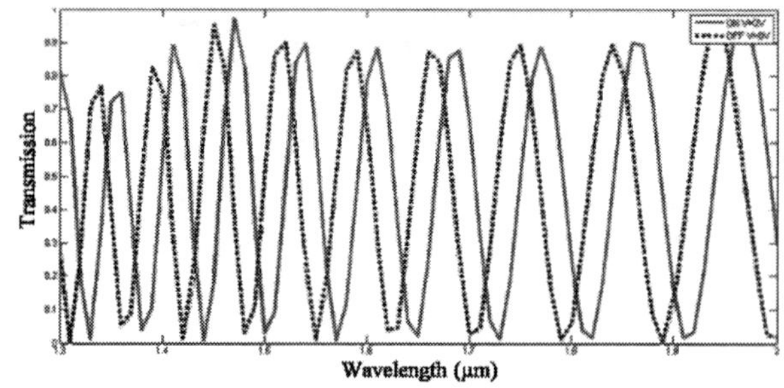

Fig. 3. Transmission versus wavelength in the 'on' and 'off' states

IV. CONCLUSION

New architecture of photonic MZI–based modulator is proposed. The modulator can help in having a high extinction ratio with small arm lengths as compared to conventional MZI-based modulators. The use of an EO polymer with high electro-optic coefficients permits having a high-extinction ratio photonic modulator. An ultimately high extinction ratio equals 23.15 dB is reported at 1550 nm with arm length of 215 μm. By applying a 1V in a push pull configuration, power consumption and energy per bit of 2.435 mw and 24.25 fJ/bit are achieved respectively. The reported extinction ratio is twice the maximum extinction ratio value reported for conventional waveguide based MZI. Such value will help in designing high performance modulators while keeping the ease of fabrication processes exploited in the conventional waveguides. The proposed device can help in minimizing the size of photonic integrated circuits while keeping the high performance in terms of extinction ratio, power consumption, and energy per bit. This structure has the potential to be used in other optical applications including optical sensing, and optical integrated circuits.

ACKNOWLEDGMENT

This work was made possible by a NPRP award [NPRP7-456- 1- 085] from the Qatar National Research Fund (member of the Qatar Foundation). The statements made herein are solely the responsibility of the authors.

REFERENCES

[1] Reed, G.T., et al., "Silicon optical modulators," Nature Photonics *4*, p. 518-526 (2010).

[2] Ozbay, E., "Plasmonics: Merging Photonics and Electronics at Nanoscale Dimensions," Science *311*. p. 5 (2006).

[3] Luca Alloatti, et al., "100 GHz silicon–organic hybrid modulator," Light: Science & Applications *3*. p. 4 (2014).

[4] Xi Xiao, et al., "High-speed, low-loss silicon Mach–Zehnder modulators with doping optimization," OPTICS EXPRESS *21*, p. 10 (2013).

[5] Anna L. Pyayt, " Guiding Light in Electro-Optic Polymers," Polymers *3*, p.p. 1591-1599 (2011).

[6] Opti-FDTD, Opti-wave, Inc. (http://www. optiwave.com).

Effective Modelling of Silicon Nanowire Solar Cells

Mohamed Hussein, M.F.O. Hameed, S.S.A. Obayya*
Center for Photonics and Smart Materials,
Zewail City of Science and Technology
6th of October City, Giza, Egypt
sobayya@zewailcity.edu.eg*

Mohamed A. Swillam
Department of Physics,
The American University in Cairo,
New Cairo, Egypt

***Abstract*— In this paper, the 3D finite difference time domain method (FDTD) has been used to investigate the effects of the surface roughness of the silicon nanowires (SiNWs) on their optical characteristics for solar cell applications. The ultimate efficiency (η) is used as a figure of merit to measure the absorption capabilities of the SiNWs. The numerical results show that the absorption of the SiNWs with surface roughness is higher than their smoothed cylindrical counterpart. This enhancement is attributed to the surface roughness which allows multiple scattering between nanowire sides. Therefore, the light trapping and the absorption through SiNWs are enhanced.**

Keywords*— *Silicon nanowire; Surface roughness; Ultimate efficiency; Solar cells.

I. Introduction

Recently, semiconductor nanowires (NWs) are attracting broad attention as important building blocks for the next-generation optoelectronic devices. Various devices based on NWs have been designed and fabricated such as: NWs solar cells, light-emitting diodes (LED) and photodetectors [1]. In particular, for solar cell applications, silicon NWs show unique antireflection, superior absorption and efficient carrier transport and hence low-cost high-efficiency solar cells can be achieved. Several experimental and theoretical studies prove that the silicon nanowire (SiNWs) can achieve higher conversion efficiency than thin-film devices counterpart with reduced cost and materials [1-6]. Numerous studies concerned with increasing the efficiency of the NWs have been established through controlling the physical shape of the nanowire such as, cylindrical, elliptically, conical and funnel shapes. Other studies have enhanced the light trapping by changing the nanowire distributions in a square lattice, hexagonal lattice and decagonal lattice [2]. However, the previous studies didn't take into consideration the surface roughness of the studied shapes. Different techniques can be used to fabricate SiNWs such as vapor liquid solid (VLS) or molecular beam epitaxy (MBE). The electron beam lithography (EBL) or nano imprint can be used to create pattern masks that are responsible for tuning the nanowire radius or pitch [7]. Due to the deficiency in the fabrication process, it is difficult to fabricate nanowire with smoothed surfaces. Therefore, the effect of surface roughness in SiNWs is crucial for realizing highly efficient solar cells. Consequently, this work is dedicated to investigate the effect of the surface roughness on the optical absorption and the efficiency of SiNWs using 3D FDTD method [8] via lumerical software package. From this study, we numerically show that the SiNWs with rough surfaces have higher absorption and consequently higher ultimate efficiency than smoothed counterpart by 5.9 %. This enhancement is due to the surface roughness which creates continuous scattering between nanowires sides. Therefore, the light confinement and hence the absorption have been enhanced.

II. Design Considerations

Figure 1. (a) and (b) show schematic diagrams in x-y and x-z planes for the cylindrical SiNWs with and without surface roughness. In order to achieve a fair comparison, the SiNWs diameters and height for both designs are fixed to 400 nm and 2330 nm, respectively. In this study the roughness is calculated by built-in function in the FDTD software package with percentage of 10%. These values are chosen according to optimum parameters in the previous studies [4].

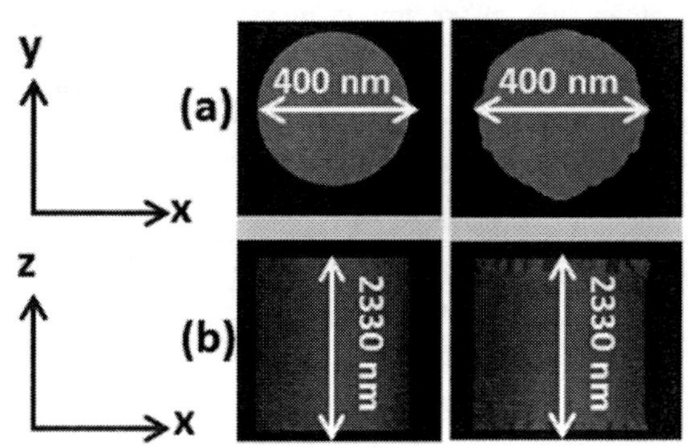

Fig. 1. Schematic diagram of cylindrical SiNWs with smoothed and with surface roughness in (a) x-y plan and (b) x-z plan.

III. Simulation Methodology

In this study, the 3D FDTD method via lumerical software package [8] is used to investigate the effect of the surface roughness on the optical characteristics of SiNWs solar cells. The SiNWs are illuminated from the Z direction by plane wave with the wavelength range from 300 nm to 1100 nm. The SiNWs are surrounded by periodic boundary condition in x and y planes while perfect matched layers is applied in z direction. The width and length of the unit cell are fixed to 500 nm while the computational domain height is taken as 4000 nm.

In this study, a fine mesh of Δx= Δy= Δz = 5 nm is used in order to achieve high accuracy, which is less than 1/60 of the shortest wavelength. The absorption in SiNWs is calculated by

$$A(\lambda) = 1 - T(\lambda) - R(\lambda) \quad (1)$$

where $T(\lambda)$ and $R(\lambda)$ are wavelength dependent of the reflection and transmission, respectively. The wavelength-dependent transmission and reflection are calculated by using two frequency domain monitors placed below and above the unit cell, respectively. The ultimate efficiency (η) is used as a figure of merit to quantify the overall absorption capabilities of the SiNWs [4]. The ultimate efficiency is calculated over the standard air mass 1.5 (A.M. 1.5) direct normal and circumsolar by the following equation

$$\eta = \frac{\int_{310\,\mathrm{nm}}^{\lambda_g} I(\lambda)A(\lambda)\frac{\lambda}{\lambda_g}\,d\lambda}{\int_{310\,\mathrm{nm}}^{4000} I(\lambda)A(\lambda)\,d\lambda} \quad (2)$$

where $I(\lambda)$ is the intensity of the solar spectrum, λ is the incident photon wavelength, $A(\lambda)$ is the absorption of the silicon nanowire design and λ_g is the wavelength related to the silicon bandgap. The ultimate efficiency represents the upper bound for achievable optical efficiency of solar cells, assuming that each absorbed photon with energy greater than the bandgap produce one electron-hole pair.

IV. Numerical Results

Figure 2(a) shows the absorption spectra of the cylindrical SiNWs with and without surface roughness. It is found that the SiNWs with surface roughness show higher absorption than smoothed cylindrical counterpart. The SiNWs with surface roughness show an ultimate efficiency of 28.6 % which is higher than 27% of the smoothed SiNW counterpart by 5.9%. The surface roughness offers continues scattering between SiNWs surfaces resulting in high light trapping which increases the absorption. The field profiles shown in Fig. 2 (b) and (c) in x-y plane are plotted to further confirm the underlying mechanism of the absorption enhancement at λ = 600 nm for cylindrical nanowire without and with surface roughness, respectively. It is worth to mention that the rough surfaces on the sides of the SiNWs allow more light confinement and penetration than smoothed cylindrical SiNWs counterpart.

V. Conclusion

In this paper, we numerically investigate the effect of surface roughness using 3D-FDTD method on the optical absorption of SiNWs solar cells. The cylindrical SiNWs with surface roughness shows an ultimate efficiency of 29.6% with an enhancement of 5.9 % over the smoothed cylindrical counterpart. This improvement is due to light scattering at rough surfaces which enhances the light absorption and hence the ultimate efficiency.

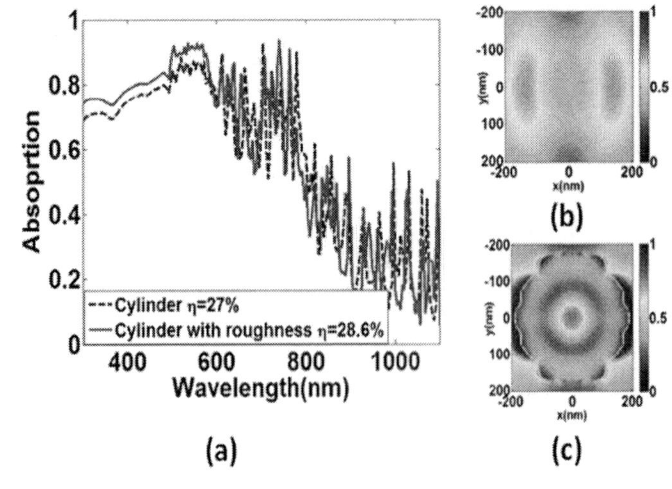

Fig. 2. (a) Variation of the absorption spectra of smoothed cylindrical SiNWs and cylindrical SiNWs with surface roughness. The field profiles in x-y plane of (b) smoothed cylindrical SiNWs and (c) cylindrical SiNWs with surface roughness at λ= 600 nm.

References

[1] Z. Li, Y. C. Wenas, L. Fu, S. Mokkapati, H. H. Tan and C. Jagadish, "Influence of electrical design on core–shell GaAs nanowire array solar cells," IEEE Journal of Photovoltaics, vol. 5, no. 3, pp. 854-864, 2015

[2] M Hussein, M F. O. Hameed, N. F. F. Areed, S. S. Obayya, "Ultra-high efficient solar cell based on decagonal arrays of silicon nanowires," Opt. Eng. vol.53, no. 11, 2014.

[3] S. Obayya, N. F. Areed, M. F. O Hameed, M. Hussein, "Optical nano-antennas for energy harvesting," IGI Global, 2015.

[4] M. Hussein, M. F. O. Hameed, N. F. F. Areed, A. Yahia, and S. S. A. Obayya, "Funnel-shaped silicon nanowire for highly efficient light trapping," Optics Letters, vol. 41, no. 5, pp.1010-1013, 2016.

[5] M. H. Muhammad, M. F. O. Hameed, S. S. A. Obayya, "Broad band Absorption Enhancement in periodic structure solar cells," Optical Quantum Electronics, vol. 47, pp. 1487-1494, 2015.

[6] D. M. A. Rahman, M. F. O. Hameed, S. S. A. Obayya, "Light harvesting improvement of polymer solar cell through nanohole photoactive layer," Optical Quantum Electronics, vol. 47, pp. 1443–1449, 2015.

[7] K. T. Fountaine, C. G. Kendall and Harry A. Atwater, "Near-unity broadband absorption designs for semiconducting nanowire arrays via localized radial mode excitation," Opt. Express22, pp. A930-A940, 2014.

[8] www.lumerical.com/tcad-products/fdtd/

A Novel Subspace Partition Method for Fourth-Order Statistics Based MUSIC Algorithm

Wenxing Li
College of Information and Communications Engineering
Harbin Engineering University
Harbin, China, 150001
liwenxing@hrbeu.edu.cn

Yu Zhao
College of Information and Communications Engineering
Harbin Engineering University
Harbin, China, 150001
zhaoyu0816@hrbeu.edu.cn

***Abstract*—It is known that accurate partition of subspaces is important to fourth-order statistics based multiple signal classification (FO-MUSIC) algorithm. However, when the number of signals exceeds the number of array elements, the error of conventional subspace partition method will increase, and the performance of FO-MUSIC algorithm will decrease. A novel subspace partition method for FO-MUSIC algorithm is proposed in this paper. Subspaces can be divided properly by the proposed method according to the way of array expansion. Good performance of FO-MUSIC algorithm can be obtained. The validity of the proposed method is verified by simulation results.**

Keywords*—*multiple signal classification; direction of arrival estimation; subspace partition;virtual array

I. INTRODUCTION

Direction-of-arrival (DOA) estimation is widely used in sonar, radar, wireless communications and many other fields. Multiple signal classification (MUSIC) [1] algorithm is one of the most popular DOA estimation algorithms for its high resolution. MUSIC is a subspace based algorithm [2], that is to say, sample covariance matrix should be accurately divided into the signal and noise subspaces according to the prior knowledge of signals number. If the subspaces are wrongly divided, the performance of DOA estimation will decrease.

High-order statistics are used to improve the performance of MUSIC algorithm [3], and fourth-order statistics based MUSIC (FO-MUSIC) algorithm is proposed. Compared with MUSIC, better performance can be obtained and more sources can be estimated by FO-MUSIC algorithm [4]. The covariance matrix of FO-MUSIC is expanded compared with MUSIC algorithm. However, the eigenvector number of signal subspace was thought to be the same as MUSIC algorithm [5-7]. When the number of signals exceeds the number of array elements, the error of subspace partition (SP) will increase, and the performance of FO-MUSIC algorithm will decrease. A novel SP method for FO-MUSIC algorithm is proposed in this paper, which is more suitable for application when the number of signals exceeds the number of a uniform linear array (ULA).

II. FO-MUSIC ALGORITHM

Assume that M far-field narrowband signals impinging on a ULA of N sensors with one-half wavelength element spacing. The received data of array $\boldsymbol{X}(t)$ can be expressed as:

$$\boldsymbol{X}(t)=\boldsymbol{A}\boldsymbol{S}(t)+\boldsymbol{N}(t) \tag{1}$$

where $\boldsymbol{A}=\left[\boldsymbol{a}(\theta_1),\boldsymbol{a}(\theta_2),\cdots,\boldsymbol{a}(\theta_M)\right]$ is the matrix of steering vector, $\boldsymbol{S}(t)$ is the complex signal envelope, and $\boldsymbol{N}(t)$ is the noise of array.

The fourth-order covariance matrix $\boldsymbol{R}_{\mathrm{x}}$ can be expressed as follows [5]:

$$\begin{aligned}\boldsymbol{R}_{\mathrm{x}}=&\mathrm{E}\left\{\boldsymbol{x}_{\mathrm{k}_1}(t)\boldsymbol{x}^*_{\mathrm{k}_2}(t)\boldsymbol{x}^*_{\mathrm{k}_3}(t)\boldsymbol{x}_{\mathrm{k}_4}(t)\right\}\\&-\mathrm{E}\left\{\boldsymbol{x}_{\mathrm{k}_1}(t)\boldsymbol{x}^*_{\mathrm{k}_2}(t)\right\}\mathrm{E}\left\{\boldsymbol{x}^*_{\mathrm{k}_3}(t)\boldsymbol{x}_{\mathrm{k}_4}(t)\right\}\\&-\mathrm{E}\left\{\boldsymbol{x}_{\mathrm{k}_1}(t)\boldsymbol{x}^*_{\mathrm{k}_3}(t)\right\}\mathrm{E}\left\{\boldsymbol{x}^*_{\mathrm{k}_2}(t)\boldsymbol{x}_{\mathrm{k}_4}(t)\right\},\end{aligned} \tag{2}$$

where $(\cdot)^*$ denotes conjugate, $\mathrm{E}\{\cdot\}$ denotes the expectation, and $\boldsymbol{x}_{\mathrm{k}}$ is the stochastic process.

According to Schmidt's orthogonal subspace resolution theory, $\boldsymbol{R}_{\mathrm{x}}$ can be express as:

$$\boldsymbol{R}_{\mathrm{x}}=\boldsymbol{U}\boldsymbol{\Sigma}\boldsymbol{U}^{\mathrm{H}} \tag{3}$$

where $\boldsymbol{U}$ is a matrix containing the eigenvectors of $\boldsymbol{R}_{\mathrm{x}}$, and $\boldsymbol{\Sigma}$ is a diagonal matrix containing the eigenvalues of $\boldsymbol{R}_{\mathrm{x}}$ in a decreasing order.

$\boldsymbol{R}_{\mathrm{x}}$ can be divided into the signal and noise subspaces as follows:

$$\boldsymbol{R}_{\mathrm{x}}=\boldsymbol{U}_{\mathrm{s}}\boldsymbol{\Sigma}_{\mathrm{s}}\boldsymbol{U}_{\mathrm{s}}^{\mathrm{H}}+\boldsymbol{U}_{\mathrm{n}}\boldsymbol{\Sigma}_{\mathrm{n}}\boldsymbol{U}_{\mathrm{n}}^{\mathrm{H}} \tag{4}$$

where the $N^2\times(N^2-M)$ matrix $\boldsymbol{U}_{\mathrm{n}}$ denotes noise subspace. $\boldsymbol{U}_{\mathrm{n}}$ is composed of N^2-M eigenvectors that corresponding to the small eigenvalues [5-7]. $\boldsymbol{U}_{\mathrm{s}}$ denotes signal subspace.

Virtual array elements are formed and the steering vector of array is expanded as follows:

$$\boldsymbol{b}(\theta)=\boldsymbol{a}(\theta)\otimes\boldsymbol{a}^*(\theta) \tag{5}$$

where $\otimes$ denotes the Kronecker product.

The spatial spectrum is defined as:

$$P_{\text{FO-MUSIC}} = \frac{1}{\boldsymbol{b}(\theta)^{\mathrm{H}} \boldsymbol{U}_{\mathrm{n}} \boldsymbol{U}_{\mathrm{n}}^{\mathrm{H}} \boldsymbol{b}(\theta)} \quad (6)$$

The SP method of FO-MUSIC is similar to that of MUSIC algorithm, that is to say, the eigenvector number of signal subspace is considered to be M. When the number of signals is less than that of array, it will work. However, if the number of signals exceeds that of array, the error will increase and the performance of FO-MUSIC will decrease. A novel SP method is proposed in this paper, which is more suitable to be applied when the number of signals exceeds that of array.

III. The Proposed Method

The novel SP method is proposed basing on the consideration that the eigenvector number of signal subspace changes with the expansion of steering vectors of array. The theory of the proposed SP method is easy to be understood without formula derivation, which can be explained as the way of array expansion.

According to formula (5), the steering vector of array is expanded through translation for $N-1$ times. The number of non-repetitive array elements increases from N to $2N-1$. It is shown in Fig. 1 as follows:

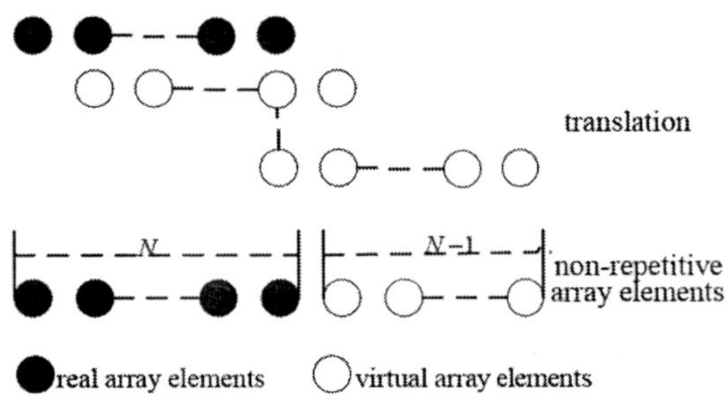

Fig. 1. Schematic diagram of array expansion.

As is shown in Fig. 1 that virtual array elements are formed through the translation of array, and repetitive array elements are formed too. The repetitive array elements number of each non-repetitive array elements changes regularly. We consider that the N^2 array elements stand for the N^2 eigenvectors. There should be $M+1$ non-repetitive array elements to deal with M signals. When the number of signals exceeds the number of real array elements, all the eigenvectors (repetitive items included) corresponding to the $M+1$ non-repetitive array elements should be involved in the signal subspace. The number of eigenvectors can be expressed as:

$$L = \frac{4N^2 - 2N + M + M^2 - 4MN}{2} \qquad (M \geq N) \quad (7)$$

where L is the eigenvectors number of the noise subspace.

IV. Simulation Results

Assume that three far-field narrowband signals impinging on a ULA of three sensors with one-half wavelength element spacing. The three independent signals illumine in the directions -40°, 0° and 30°. The number of snapshots is 200. Fig. 2 shows the root mean square error (RMSE) versus the input signal to noise ratio (SNR) of FO-MUSIC algorithm using different values of L.

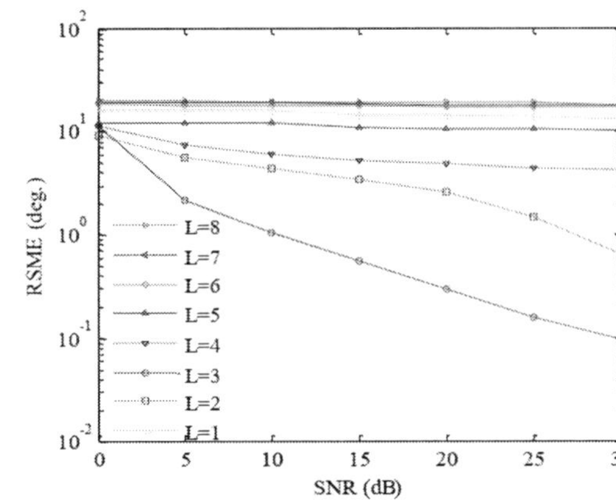

Fig. 2. RMSE versus SNR using different values of L.

It can be observed from Fig. 2 that the RMSE of the proposed SP method, where L is equal to 3, is smaller than the others. The proposed SP method is effective.

V. Conclusion

A subspace partition method for FO-MUSIC algorithm is proposed, by which the subspaces can be divided accurately when the number of signals exceeds the number of array elements. Simulation results shows that the proposed subspace partition method is effective for the FO-MUSIC algorithm.

Acknowledgment

This paper is funded by the International Exchange Program of Harbin Engineering University for Innovation-oriented Talents Cultivation.

References

[1] R.O. Schmidt, "Multiple emitter location and signal parameter estimation," IEEE Transactions on Antennas and Propagation, vol. 34, pp. 276 – 280, 1986.

[2] W.J. Zen, X.L. Li and X.D. Zhang, "Direction-of-arrival estimation based on the Joint diagonalization structure of multiple fourth-order cumulant matrices," IEEE Signal Processing Letters, vol. 16, pp. 164 – 167, 2009.

[3] B. Porat and B. Friedlander, """ Direction finding algorithms based on high-order statistics," IEEE Transactions on Signal Processing, vol. 39, pp. 2016 – 2024, 1991.

[4] S. Lie, A.R. Leyman and Y.H. Chew, "Fourth-order and weighted mixed order direction-of-arrival estimators," IEEE Signal Processing Letters, vol. 13, pp. 691 – 694, 2006.

[5] Q. Wang, H. Chen, G.H. Zhao, et al, "An improved direction finding algorithm based on toeplitz approximation," Sensors, vol. 13, pp. 746 757, 2013.

[6] B. Liao and S.C. Chan, "A cumulant-based method for direction finding in uniform linear arrays with mutual coupling," IEEE Antennas and Wireless Propagation Letters, vol. 13, pp. 1717 – 1720, 2014.

[7] X. Zhang, X.M Liu, H.X. Yu and C. Liu, "Improved MUSIC algorithm for DOA estimation of coherent signals via toeplitz and fourth-order-cumulants," International Journal of Control and Automation, vol. 8, pp. 261 – 272, 2015.

Multiple Model Multi-Object Particle PHD Filter

Hongfan Zhu, Liwei Wang, Zhiyu Qu
College of Information and Communication Engineering
Harbin Engineering University
Harbin, China
quzhiyu@hrbeu.edu.cn

***Abstract*—Recently, multi-object particle PHD (MOP-PHD) filter was proposed and has been shown to outperform conventional GM-PHD filter. In this paper, we extend this filter for tracking maneuvering targets based on multiple model (MM) method. The performance of proposed filter shows a significant improvement in performance compared to multiple model Gaussian mixture PHD (MM-GM-PHD) filter.**

Keywords—maneuvering targets; probabilitiy hypothesis density; multiple model

I. Introduction

Multi-target tracking (MTT) is an important topic with wide applications in radar surveillance systems. The probability hypothesis density (PHD) filter [1] approximates the multi-object posterior by its first moment, which makes it free of data association. Due to its computational efficiency, it is widely researched.

A novel algorithm called multi-object particle PHD (MOP-PHD) filter proposed in [2] constructs a particle approximation of the predicted multi-object density and update it by multi-object measurement likelihood. Moreover, the PHD intensity is approximated by a Gaussian mixture (GM), which relaxes the Poisson assumption for the cardinality. It improves the performance of the standard PHD filter significantly.

When targets perform maneuver, the motion mode is uncertain. Since targets might switch between different modes of operation, it is inefficient to use single model to represent the motion. Hence, multiple model (MM) method is the mainstream approach to maneuvering target tracking under motion mode uncertainty.

In this paper, a MM-MOP-PHD filter is proposed for multiple maneuvering targets tracking.

II. MM-MOP PHD Filter

In this section, the MOP-PHD filter is reviewed at first. Then we present the calculation method of model probability and derive the MM-MOP-PHD filter.

A. Original MOP-PHD Filter

Approximate the predicted multi-object density by P randomly sampled multi-object particles $X^{p}_{k|k-1}$

$$f\left(X_k \mid Z^{k-1}\right) \approx \sum_{p=1}^{P} P^{-1}\delta\left(X_k, X^{p}_{k|k-1}\right) \tag{1}$$

The posterior multi-object density is given by the Bayes update

$$f\left(X_k \mid Z^{k}\right) = \frac{\sum_{p=1}^{P} f\left(Z_k \mid X_k\right)\delta\left(X_k, X^{p}_{k|k-1}\right)}{\sum_{p=1}^{P}\int f\left(Z_k \mid X_k\right)\delta\left(X_k, X^{p}_{k|k-1}\right)\delta X_k} \tag{2}$$

For each multi-object particle we have

$$f\left(Z_k \mid X_k\right)\delta\left(X_k, X^{p}_{k|k-1}\right) = \sum_{\theta\in\Theta}\mathcal{L}^{p,\theta}_{k|k-1}\prod_{i\in I_p}\mathcal{N}\left(x_i; m^{i,\sigma_i}_{k|k}, P^{i,\sigma_i}_{k|k}\right) \tag{3}$$

where I_p denotes each sample set, $\theta = \{\sigma_i\}$ denotes a set of associations. More details can be found in [3].

Use the JPDA measurement update algorithm, the natural logarithm of $\tilde{\mathcal{L}}^{p}_{k|k-1}$ can be obtained [3].

With $W^{p}_{k|k} = \frac{\tilde{\mathcal{L}}^{p}_{k|k}}{\sum_{p=1}^{P}\tilde{\mathcal{L}}^{p}_{k|k}}$, the multi-object particle approximation of the posterior multi-object density is given by

$$f\left(X_k \mid Z^{k}\right) = \sum_{p=1}^{P} W^{p}_{k|k}\tilde{\mathcal{L}}^{p}_{k|k}\delta\left(X_k, \tilde{X}^{p}_{k|k}\right) \tag{4}$$

B. Posterior Model Probability

For each measurement $z \in Z_k$, the model likelihood of i th target is computed using the PDA "likelihood" function

$$p^{i}_{k}\left(z \mid r\right) = \left(V^{i}_{k}\right)^{-N^{z}_{k}}\left(1 - P_D P_G\right) + \left(V^{i}_{k}\right)^{-N^{z}_{k}+1}\frac{P_D}{N^{z}_{k}}\sum_{j=1}^{N^{z}_{k}}\mathcal{N}\left(z^{j}_{k}; \hat{z}^{i}_{k}, S^{i}_{k}\right) \tag{5}$$

where P_D is the detection probability, P_G is the gate probability, N^{z}_{k} is the number of measurements. The centralized gating techniques is adopted in this paper to calculate V^{i}_{k} [4]. The posterior model probability is given by

$$p^{i}_{k}\left(r \mid z\right) = \frac{p\left(r\right)p^{i}_{k}\left(z \mid r\right)}{\sum_{r} p\left(r\right)p^{i}_{k}\left(z \mid r\right)} \tag{6}$$

This work is supported by the International Exchange Program of Harbin Engineering University for Innovation-oriented Talents Cultivation., the Aeronautical Science Foundation of China (Grant No. 201401P6001) and the Natural Science Foundation of Heilongjiang Province of China (No. QC2016085).

where $p(r)$ is the prior model probability.

C. Implementation method

A motion mode parameter r is imported to represent PHD intensity conditioned on different models. We summarize the algorithm as

Prediction:

$$D_{k|k-1}(x \mid r)=\sum_{j=1}^{J_{k|k-1}} \omega_{k|k-1}^{j,r}\mathcal{N}\left(x;m_{k|k-1}^{j,r},P_{k|k-1}^{j,r}\right) \quad (7)$$

Multi-object density approximation:

$$f\left(X_k \mid Z^{k-1},r\right)\approx\sum_{p=1}^{P}P^{-1}\prod_{i\in I_p}\mathcal{N}\left(x_i;m_{k|k-1}^{i,r},P_{k|k-1}^{i,r}\right) \quad (8)$$

Update:

$$D_{k|k}(x \mid r)=\sum_{p=1}^{P}W_{k|k}^{p,r}\sum_{i\in I_p}\mathcal{N}\left(x;\tilde{m}_{k|k}^{p,i,r},\tilde{P}_{k|k}^{p,i,r}\right) \quad (9)$$

compute the model probability (6), for output purpose only, the fusion posterior density of the MM-MOP-PHD filter is given by

$$D_{k|k}(x)=\sum_{r}\sum_{p=1}^{P}W_{k|k}^{p,r}\sum_{i\in I_p}\mathcal{N}\left(x;\tilde{m}_{k|k}^{p,i,r},\tilde{P}_{k|k}^{p,i,r}\right)p_k^{p,i}(r \mid z) \quad (10)$$

Note that the conditioned posterior density of the MM-MOP-PHD filter are used in prediction step at next time step.

III. SIMULATION

In this section, we demonstrate the performance of the MM-MOP-PHD filter and compare it with MM-GM-PHD filter proposed in [3]. There are four maneuvering targets appearing in surveillance region successively.

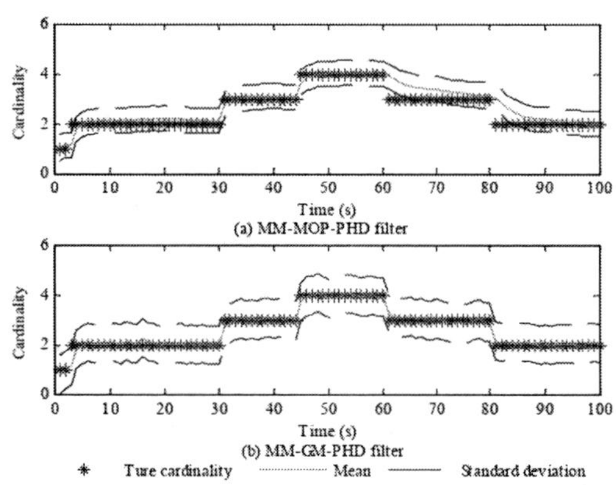

Fig.1. Average cardinality estimates ($p_D = 0.75$)

Clutters follow Poisson distribution and Poisson rate is $\lambda_c = 20$ .Cardinality estimation and optimal subpattern assignment metric (OSPA) distances [5] of them are simulated with 200 of Monte Carlo (MC) runs. Fig.1 shows the means and standard deviation of the target number. It is obvious that the MM-MOP-PHD filter outperforms MM-GM-PHD filter in cardinality estimation.

The OSPA distance of the MM-MOP-PHD filter is significantly smaller than MM-GM-PHD filter as shown in Fig.2. It is obvious that the proposed MM-MOP-PHD filter is robust to missed detections. The side-effect of this feature is that the MM-MOP-PHD filter is slow at "killing" target estimates after the true targets have disappeared from the surveillance region.

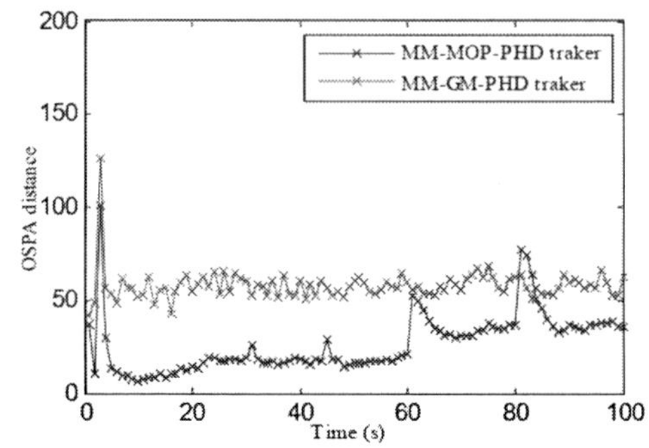

Fig.2. Average OSPA distance ($p_D = 0.75$)

IV. CONCLUSION

In this paper, we propose the MM-MOP-PHD filter for multiple maneuvering targets tracking based on MM method and MOP-PHD filter. Simulation results show that the proposed filter can track maneuvering targets reliably in low-detection environment.

ACKNOWLEDGMENT

This paper is funded by the International Exchange Program of Harbin Engineering University for Innovation-oriented Talents Cultivation. This work was also partially supported by the Aeronautical Science Foundation of China (Grant No. 201401P6001) and the Natural Science Foundation of Heilongjiang Province of China (No. QC2016085).

REFERENCES

[1] R. Mahler, "Multitarget Bayes filtering via first-order multitarget moments," IEEE Trans. AES, vol. 39, no. 4, pp. 1152-1178, 2003.

[2] Granstrom K, Willett P, and Bar-Shalom Y, "PHD filter with approximate multiobject density measurement update," Int. Conf. on Information Fusion, pp. 1802-1809, 2015.

[3] Wang X, Han CZ, "An improved multiple model GM-PHD filter for maneuvering target tracking," Chin J Aeronaut, vol. 26, no. 1, pp. 179–85, 2013.

[4] Wang, Xuezhi, S. Challa, and R. Evans, "Gating techniques for maneuvering target tracking in clutter," IEEE Trans. AES, vol. 38, no. 3, pp. 1087-1097, 2002.

[5] Schuhmacher D, Vo B T, Vo B N, "A Consistent Metric for Performance Evaluation of Multi-Object Filters," IEEE Trans. SP, vol. 56, no. 8, pp. 3447-3457, 2008.

A Real-valued MUSIC Algorithm with Forward/Backward Technique

Yan Wang*, Weijian Si and Kun Wang
College of Information and Communication Engineering,
Harbin Engineering University ,
Harbin, 150001, China
*wangyan17855@hrbeu.edu.cn

***Abstract*—This paper presents a novel real-valued multiple signal classification (RV-MUSIC) algorithm, which tremendously reduces the computation complexity than the complex one by a factor of four. The covariance matrix of the sensor output is firstly transformed into a real-valued covariance matrix via unitary forward/backward (FB) technique. Then the MUSIC algorithm in real domain is used to estimate the direction of arrival (DOA) by utilizing the symmetry properties of array structure. The proposed algorithm can solve problem with multiple incident signals in one- or two-dimensional scenarios. Simulation results show the effectiveness of the proposed methods.**

Keywords—signal processing; direction finding; real-valued MUSIC algorithm; forward/backward technique

I. INTRODUCTION

Direction of arrival estimation based on sensor arrays has been a hot topic in signal processing for decades, and it is widely applied to radar, sonar, seism, and wireless communication [1, 2]. The forward/backward technique is a well-known approach that has been utilized in various direction of arrival estimations in [3-5]. In this paper, by using FB technique we propose a real-valued MUSIC algorithm transforms the process of direction finding into real domain to reduce computation cost observably.

II. ARRAY SINGAL MODEL

Let a uniform linear array (ULA) be composed of N sensors. Assume that there are M uncorrelated narrowband signals, having traveled through a homogeneous isotropic medium, impinge on the arrays from the directions $\phi_1, \phi_2, \ldots, \phi_M$. The sensor output is modeled as

$$\boldsymbol{x}(t) = \boldsymbol{A}\boldsymbol{s}(t) + \boldsymbol{n}(t) \tag{1}$$

where $\boldsymbol{A} = [\boldsymbol{a}(\phi_1), \boldsymbol{a}(\phi_2), \cdots, \boldsymbol{a}(\phi_M)]$ is array manifold matrix, $\boldsymbol{s}(t)$ is signal vector, $\boldsymbol{n}(t)$ symbolizes the zero-mean additive complex Gaussian noise, and superscript $(\bullet)^T$ denotes transpose. The estimation of the covariance matrix shows as

$$\hat{\boldsymbol{R}} = \frac{1}{L}\sum_{l=1}^{L} \boldsymbol{x}_l(t)\boldsymbol{x}_l^H(t) = \boldsymbol{X}(t)\boldsymbol{X}^H(t) \tag{2}$$

where $\boldsymbol{X}(t) = 1/\sqrt{L}\left[\boldsymbol{x}_1(t), \ldots, \boldsymbol{x}_L(t)\right]$ is array observation matrix, and superscript $(\bullet)^H$ denotes Hermitian transpose.

III. REAL-VALUED MUSIC ALGORITHM WITH FB TECHNIQUE

A. Real-valued Covariance Matrix

The estimated FB covariance matrix can be defined by

$$\hat{\boldsymbol{R}}_{FB} = \boldsymbol{X}_{FB}(t)\boldsymbol{X}_{FB}^H(t) = \tfrac{1}{2}\left(\hat{\boldsymbol{R}} + \boldsymbol{J}\hat{\boldsymbol{R}}^*\boldsymbol{J}\right) \tag{3}$$

where $\boldsymbol{X}_{FB}(t) = 1/\sqrt{2}\left[\boldsymbol{X}(t) \quad \boldsymbol{J}\boldsymbol{X}^*(t)\right]$ is FB observation matrix. In addition, $\boldsymbol{J}$ is the exchange matrix with ones on its anti-diagonal and zeros elsewhere, and superscript $(\bullet)^*$ denotes conjugate. The eigendecomposition of matrix (3) can be readily written that

$$\hat{\boldsymbol{R}}_{FB} = \sum_{i=1}^{2N} \lambda_i \boldsymbol{u}_i \boldsymbol{u}_i^H \tag{4}$$

where λ_i denotes the eigenvalues, and $\boldsymbol{U} = [\boldsymbol{u}_1, \boldsymbol{u}_2, \ldots \boldsymbol{u}_N]$ are the corresponding orthonormal eigenvectors. Thus the signal subspace $\boldsymbol{U}_S$ and noise subspace $\boldsymbol{U}_N$ are defined as

$$\boldsymbol{U}_S = [\boldsymbol{u}_1, \boldsymbol{u}_2, \ldots \boldsymbol{u}_M],\ \boldsymbol{U}_N = [\boldsymbol{u}_{M+1}, \ldots \boldsymbol{u}_N] \tag{5}$$

Let the real-valued covariance matrix as

$$\boldsymbol{B}_{rv} = \boldsymbol{Q}^H \hat{\boldsymbol{R}}_{FB} \boldsymbol{Q} \tag{6}$$

where

$$\boldsymbol{Q} = \frac{1}{\sqrt{2}}\begin{bmatrix} \boldsymbol{I} & j\boldsymbol{I} \\ \boldsymbol{J} & -j\boldsymbol{J} \end{bmatrix} (N \text{ is even}), \text{and} \frac{1}{\sqrt{2}}\begin{bmatrix} \boldsymbol{I} & \boldsymbol{0} & j\boldsymbol{I} \\ \boldsymbol{0} & \sqrt{2} & \boldsymbol{0} \\ \boldsymbol{J} & \boldsymbol{0} & -j\boldsymbol{J} \end{bmatrix} (N \text{ is odd}) \tag{7}$$

is an unitary column conjugate symmetric matrix. The eigendecomposition of real-valued covariance matrix, the signal subspace $\boldsymbol{V}_S$ and noise subspace $\boldsymbol{V}_N$ are shown as

$$\boldsymbol{B}_{rv} = \sum_{i=1}^{2N} \delta_i \boldsymbol{v}_i \boldsymbol{v}_i^H,\ \boldsymbol{V}_S = [\boldsymbol{v}_1, \boldsymbol{v}_2, \ldots \boldsymbol{v}_M],\ \boldsymbol{V}_N = [\boldsymbol{v}_{M+1}, \ldots \boldsymbol{v}_N] \tag{8}$$

Therefore, we can obtain the relationships between the eigenvectors and eigenvalues of the matrices (3) and (6)

$$\boldsymbol{U}_N = \boldsymbol{Q}\boldsymbol{V}_N,\ \lambda_i = \delta_i \tag{9}$$

Let $\boldsymbol{Z}_{FB}$ is defined according to

$$\boldsymbol{Z}_{FB} = \boldsymbol{Q}^H \boldsymbol{X}_{FB} \boldsymbol{P} \tag{10}$$

where $\boldsymbol{P}$ is a unitary transformation defined by

$$\boldsymbol{P} = \frac{1}{\sqrt{2}}\begin{bmatrix} \boldsymbol{I}_L & j\boldsymbol{I}_L \\ \boldsymbol{I}_L & -j\boldsymbol{I}_L \end{bmatrix} \tag{11}$$

then

$$\boldsymbol{B}_{rv} = \boldsymbol{Q}^H \boldsymbol{R}_{FB} \boldsymbol{Q} = \boldsymbol{Q}^H \boldsymbol{X}_{FB} \boldsymbol{P} \cdot \boldsymbol{P}^H \boldsymbol{X}_{FB}^H \boldsymbol{Q} = \boldsymbol{Z}_{FB} \boldsymbol{Z}_{FB}^T \tag{12}$$

and it can be proven that $\boldsymbol{Z}_{FB}$ is a real-valued matrix.

This paper is supported by the International Exchange Program of Harbin Engineering University for Innovation-oriented Talents Cultivation, the Aeronautical Science Foundation of China (Grant No. 201401P6001) and Fundamental Research Funds for the Central Universities (Grant No. HEUCF160807).

Consider the case that the number of arrays is odd. Partition matrix $X = \left[X_1^T, x_{(N+1)/2}^T, X_2^T\right]^T$, then

$$Z_{FB} = Q^H X_{FB} P = \frac{1}{\sqrt{2}} \begin{bmatrix} \mathrm{Re}(X_1 + JX_2) & -\mathrm{Im}(X_1 + JX_2) \\ \sqrt{2}\,\mathrm{Re}(x_{(N+1)/2}) & -\sqrt{2}\,\mathrm{Im}(x_{(N+1)/2}) \\ \mathrm{Im}(X_1 - JX_2) & \mathrm{Re}(X_1 - JX_2) \end{bmatrix} \quad (13)$$

From the above, the whole process of obtaining noise subspace from array observation matrix can be easily calculated with real-valued matrices, and the real-valued eigendecomposition has reduced computational complexity than the complex one by as much as 75% [2].

B. Direction Finding in Real Domain

The real-valued MUSIC spectrum estimation formula is

$$P_{RV\text{-}MUSIC}(\phi) = \frac{1}{a^H(\phi) U_N U_N^H a(\phi)} \quad (14)$$

For odd N, the steering vector can be partition according to

$$a(\phi) = \begin{bmatrix} a_1(\phi) \\ 1 \\ (Ja_1(\phi))^* \end{bmatrix} \quad (15)$$

then real-valued steering vector is obtained as

$$h(\phi) = K^H a(\phi) = \sqrt{2} \begin{bmatrix} \mathrm{Re}(a_1(\phi)) \\ \sqrt{2} \\ \mathrm{Im}(a_1(\phi)) \end{bmatrix} \quad (16)$$

Substitute equation (9) and (16) into equation (14), The real-valued MUSIC spectrum estimation formula is expressed as

$$P_{RV\text{-}MUSIC}(\phi) = \frac{1}{2h^T(\phi) V_N V_N^T h(\phi)} \quad (17)$$

For even N, we can also obtain the similar formulas to equations (15), (16) and (17). According to equation (17), we can get DOA estimation

$$\hat{\phi} = \arg\max P_{RV\text{-}MUSIC}(\phi) \quad (18)$$

IV. Simulations

First assume that a ULA with nine omnidirectional sensors is placed with inter-element spacing of half-wavelength. And four equally powered narrowband sources are impinging on the sensors with the directions of arrival $(\phi_1, \phi_2, \phi_3, \phi_4) = (-40^\circ, 0^\circ, 20^\circ, 30^\circ)$, where the snapshot number is 100 and the signal-to-noise ratio (SNR) is 10dB. From the simulation results in Fig.1, we can see there are four spectrum peaks evidently corresponding to each DOA. It proves the multiple-signal-resolution capability of the proposed algorithm.

In the second simulation, we set DOAs of incident signals $(\phi_1, \phi_2) = (15^\circ, 25^\circ)$, then change the SNR from -20dB to 30dB with step of 5dB in Fig.2(a), and the snapshot from 10 to 900 in Fig.2(b). The simulation results in Fig.2 investigate the proposed algorithm outperforms the conventional MUSIC (C-MUSIC) algorithm, especially in the lower SNR. All the following results about root mean square error (RMSE) are obtained by 200 Monte Carlo trails.

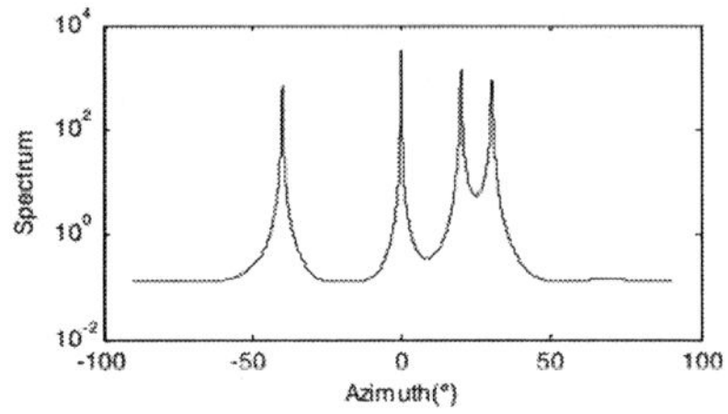

Fig.1. four signals with DOAs $(\phi_1, \phi_2, \phi_3, \phi_4) = (-40^\circ, 0^\circ, 20^\circ, 30^\circ)$

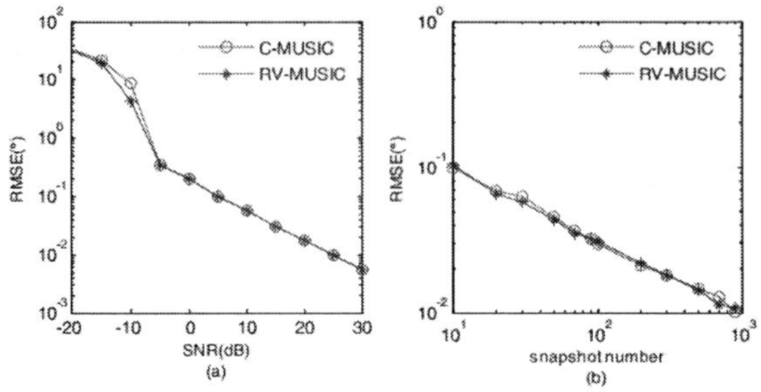

Fig.2. (a) RMSE of DOA versus SNR; (b) RMSE of DOA versus snapshot number.

V. Conclusion

To reduce the computational cost of the conventional MUSIC algorithm, the real-valued MUSIC algorithm utilizing FB technique is proposed in this paper. The covariance matrix of the sensor output is firstly transformed into a real-valued covariance matrix. Then the real-valued spectrum estimation formula is presented. The simulation results demonstrate that the real-valued MUSIC algorithm yields higher resolution capabilities, especially in lower SNR situations.

Acknowledgment

This paper is funded by the International Exchange Program of Harbin Engineering University for Innovation-oriented Talents Cultivation. This work is also partially supported by the Aeronautical Science Foundation of China (Grant No. 201401P6001) and Fundamental Research Funds for the Central Universities (Grant No. HEUCF160807).

References

[1] R. Schmidt, "Multiple emitter location and signal parameter estimation," *IEEE Transactions on Antennas and Propagation*, vol. 34, pp. 276-280, 1986.

[2] Y. Song, Y. L. Li, and K. T. Wong, "Acoustic direction finding using a pressure sensor and a uniaxial particle velocity sensor," *IEEE Transactions on Aerospace and Electronic Systems*, vol. 51, pp. 2560-2569, 2015.

[3] M. Pesavento, A. B. Gershman, and M. Haardt, "Unitary root-MUSIC with a real-valued eigendecomposition: a theoretical and experimental performance study," *IEEE Transactions on Signal Processing*, vol. 48, pp. 1306-1314, 2000.

[4] Y. Wang, M. Yang, B. Chen, and Z. Xiang, "Improved DOA estimation based on real-valued array covariance using sparse Bayesian learning," *Signal Processing*, vol. 129, pp. 183-189, 12, 2016.

[5] Y. Song, Y. L. Li, and K. T. Wong, "Acoustic direction finding using a pressure sensor and a uniaxial particle velocity sensor," *IEEE Transactions on Aerospace and Electronic Systems*, vol. 51, pp. 2560-2569, 2015.

Extract Pulse Clustering in Radar Signal Sorting

Yang Sheng, Changbo Hou* and Weijian Si
College of Information and Communication Engineering,
Harbin Engineering University,
Harbin, 150001, China
*houchangbo@hrbeu.edu.cn

***Abstract*—Radar signal sorting is a process of detecting and identifying the target radar emitter. This paper presents an extract pulse clustering algorithm based on support vector clustering, which tremendously reduces the CPU run time without loss of accuracy. The basic idea of the algorithm is to extract part of the radar signal pulses randomly and analyze the extracted pulses. Simulation results show the effectiveness of the proposed method.**

Keywords—Radar signal sorting; Support vector clustering; Extract pulse clustering;

I. INTRODUCTION

Radar signal sorting plays an important role in radar reconnaissance system. At present, there are two broad kinds of algorithms to be used in radar signal sorting. One is single parameter algorithm based on the time of arrival (TOA), such as cumulative difference histogram (CDIF) [1] and sequential difference histogram (SDIF) [2]. The other one is multi-parameter algorithm, such as support vector clustering(SVC) [3] and singular value decomposition (SVD) [4]. Compared with the single parameter sorting algorithm, the multi-parameter algorithm makes full use of the difference of parameters among the pulses from different radar emitters, which can complete the radar signal sorting far more effectively. This paper presents extract pulse clustering algorithm based on SVC. Compared with SVC, the main advantage of the proposed method is reducing the CPU run time.

II. SIGNAL MODEL

The pulse received from the radar emitter includes many parameters, such as the direction of arrival (DOA), frequency (RF), pulse width (PW), pulse repetition interval (PRI), and TOA, as shown in Fig.1.

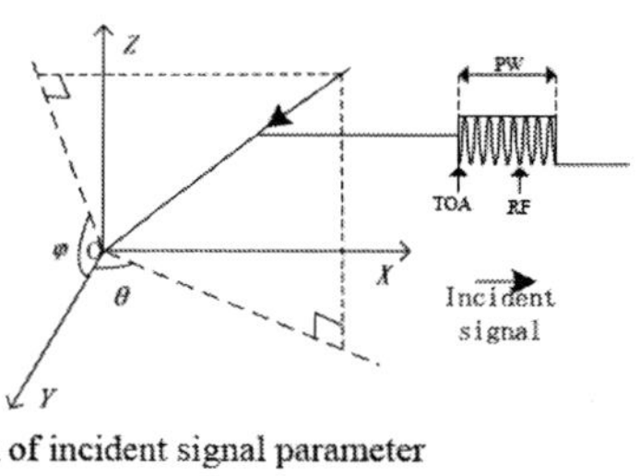

Fig.1.The definition of incident signal parameter

The radar signals consist of modulated pulses. For two pulses from two different radar emitters, at least one of the parameters among the DOA, RF and PW is different from others. This is the foundation we recognize the difference between pulses and extract the target radar emitter.

This paper is funded by the International Exchange Program of Harbin Engineering University for Innovation-oriented Talents Cultivation. This work is also supported by the Aeronautical Science Foundation of China (Grant No.201401P6001)

III. EXTRACT PULSE CLUSTERING BASED ON SVC

In this paper we use two-dimensional parameters, PW and CF of the pulse. Radar pulse can be described by two-dimensional vector $v_i = \{RF, PW\}$, all of the v_i form the set $V = \{v_i\}$, $i = 1,2,\cdots,N$ (N is the total number of samples).

A. Support Vector Clustering

The main point of SVC is to use a non-linear transformation Φ from V to some high dimensional space. In the dimensional space, we look for the smallest enclosing sphere of radius R, we can use the constraints to describe the sphere:

$$\left\|\Phi(v_i)-a\right\|^2 \le R^2+\xi_i \tag{1}$$

where $\|\cdot\|$ is the Euclidean norm and a is the center of the sphere. Slack variable $\xi_i \ge 0$ is the soft constraints. The Lagrangian formulation plays an important role in solving the problem :

$$L = R^2 - \sum_i\left(R^2+\xi_i-\left\|\Phi(v_i)-a\right\|^2\right)\beta_i - \sum \xi_i\mu_i + C\sum\xi_i \tag{2}$$

where $\beta_i \ge 0$ and $\mu_j \ge 0$ are Lagrange multipliers, C is a constant, and $C\sum\xi_i$ is a penalty term.

According to the Karush-Kuhn-Tucker:

1. If $\beta_i = C$, the point $\Phi(v_i)$ lies outside of the feature space sphere .
2. If $0<\beta_i<C$,the point $\Phi(v_i)$ is mapped to the surface of the feature space sphere.
3. All the other points lie inside of the feature space sphere.

We can get the Wolfe dual form with further transformation:

$$W = \sum_i \Phi(v_i)^2\beta_i - \sum_{i,j}\beta_i\beta_j\Phi(v_i)\Phi(v_j) \tag{3}$$

B. Extract Pulse Clustering

If all the sample data $V=\{v_i\}, i=1,2,\cdots,N$ are analyzed by SVC, it will cost lots of time. According to the computing architectures, the running time of the SVC can be described by $e^{\tau N}$, where $\tau(\tau>0)$ is a constant. Pulse sequence can be described by:

$$g(t) = \sum_{n=1}^{N} \delta(t - t_n) \quad (4)$$

That is to say, the parameters of any radar emitter will spread the whole timeline. So it is viable to use part of the total sample data to complete the clustering process. Extract pulse clustering algorithm is proposed to pre-process the sample data .The detailed steps are as follows:

1. Input the samples data $V = \{v_i\}$, $i = 1, 2, \cdots, N$ (N is the total number of samples).
2. Divide V into m subsets $G_j\{g_{ji}\}$ randomly, m is extraction coefficient, $j = 1, 2, \cdots, m$, $i = 1, 2, \cdots, N/m$. In other words, each of the v_i will be assigned to one of the subsets equiprobably, so the probability is $1/m$ and the size of the subset $G_j\{g_{ji}\}$ approximately equals N/m .
3. Analyze each of the subset by SVC respectively and get the cluster centers.
4. Merge the cluster centers and get the final result.

The V is divided into 2 parts, as shown in Fig.2. The running-time of V is $e^{\tau N}$, while the run time of X and Y is $e^{\tau k_1}$, $e^{\tau k_2}$. We know that:

$$e^{\tau N} > e^{\tau k_1} + e^{\tau k_2} + \cdots + e^{\tau k_n} \quad (4)$$

$$k_1 + k_2 + \cdots + k_n = N \quad (5)$$

So the run time can be reduced by the improved method.

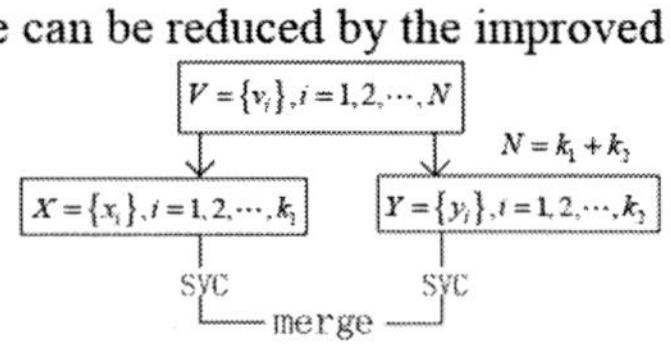

Fig.2. Implementation diagram of extract pulse clustering algorithm

IV. SIMULATION

In this section, the performance of the proposed algorithm is validated via two examples. The radar parameters are shown in Table I.

TABLE I. The radar parameters information

Radars	PRI (us)	PW (us)	RF (MHz)
radar1	5	0.5	1100
radar2	27	1	1000
radar3	10	1	900
radar4	9	0.8	1240~1555

In the first example, we set the extraction coefficient of the proposed algorithm $m = 2$ and get the sorting result, as shown in Fig.3. The result shows 4 cluster centers of radars, so the accuracy is verified.

In the second example, we change the number of the radar pulses and record the running time of SVC and the proposed algorithm, as shown in the Fig.4. The time complexity of proposed method is $m\left(O\left(N/m\right)^2\right)$.

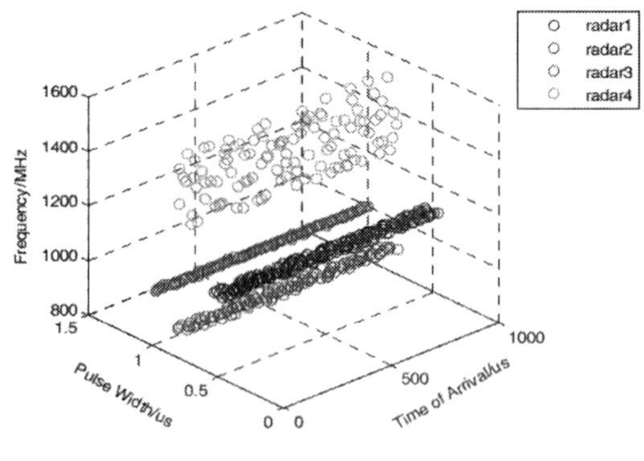

Fig.3. The sorting result by extract pulse clustering algorithm.

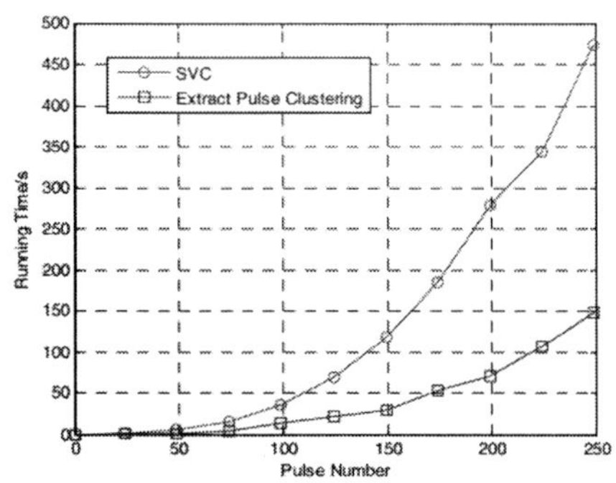

Fig.4. CPU run time comparison between SVC and extract pulse clustering algorithm

V. CONCLUSION

The extract pulse clustering algorithm is proposed to pre-process the original sample pulses based on the SVC. Through the theory analysis and simulation, the improved method tremendously reduces the CPU run time without loss of accuracy.

ACKNOWLEDGMENT

This paper is funded by the International Exchange Program of Harbin Engineering University for Innovation-oriented Talents Cultivation. This work is also supported by the Aeronautical Science Foundation of China (Grant No.201401P6001).

REFERENCES

[1] Mardia H K. New techniques for the deinterleaving of repetitive sequences[C]//Radar and Signal Processing, IEE Proceedings F. IET, 1989, 136(4): 149-154.

[2] Milojević D J, Popović B M. Improved algorithm for the deinterleaving of radar pulses[C]//Radar and Signal Processing, IEE Proceedings F. IET, 1992, 139(1): 98-104.

[3] Ben-Hur A, Horn D, Siegelmann H T, et al. Support vector clustering[J]. Journal of machine learning research, 2001, 2(Dec): 125-137.

[4] Guo Q, Nan P, Zhang X, et al. Recognition of radar emitter signals based on SVD and AF main ridge slice[J]. Journal of Communications and Networks, 2015, 17(5): 491-498.

An Improved Null Broadening Beamforming Method based on Covariance Matrix Reconstruction

Wenxing Li
College of Information and Communications Engineering
Harbin Engineering University
Harbin, China, 150001
liwenxing@hrbeu.edu.cn

Bin Yang
College of Information and Communications Engineering
Harbin Engineering University
Harbin, China, 150001
s315080101@hrbeu.edu.cn

Abstract—**The performance of adaptive beamformer will degrade in the case of jammer motion and shaking platform. In order to improve the performance of adaptive beamformer, an improved null broadening adaptive beamforming method is proposed. The proposed method is realized by the reconstruction of interference-plus-noise covariance matrix. Null broadening can be obtained by the proposed method and the null depth is deeper. The proposed method which can against jammer motion and shaking platform efficiently is demonstrated by simulation results.**

Keywords—adaptive beamformer; performance; reconstruction ; covariance matrix; null

I. INTRODUCTION

Adaptive beamforming techniques have been widely studied during the past decades [1]. Minimum variance distortionless response (MVDR) beamformer is popular now. However, the performance of the MVDR will degrade in the case of jammer motion and shaking platform.

Null broadening techniques can be realized by producing broad trough at the incident angle of interference to against jammer motion and shaking platform. Mailloux and Zatman have proposed null broadening methods respectively [2-3]. Guerci proposed the concept of "covariance matrix taper" (CMT) [4], which unified both of two methods mentioned above and verified that the CMT make nulls depth shallower because of the reduction of output power. Yang Kai proposed an adaptive beamforming algorithm with wide nulls which based on covariance matrix reconstruction (ABA-CMR) [5]. The algorithm can broaden the null and make null depth deeper successfully. On the basis of ABA-CMR, this paper propose an improved null broadening beamforming method to further improve the performance of array.

II. INTERFERENCE-PLUS-NOISE COVARIANCE MATRIX RECONSTRUCTION ALGORITHM

Assume that a uniform linear array (ULA) of N sensors with one-half wavelength element spacing receives signals from multiple narrowband sources. The received data of array $\boldsymbol{X}(t)$ at time t can be expressed as:

$$\boldsymbol{X}(t) = \boldsymbol{A}\boldsymbol{S}(t) + \boldsymbol{N}(t) \tag{1}$$

where $\boldsymbol{A} = [a(\theta_1), a(\theta_2), \cdots, a(\theta_N)]$ is the matrix of steering vector, $\boldsymbol{S}(t)$ is an envelope vector of the signal and interferences, and $N(t)$ is the noise of array.

The standard MVDR beamformer can be implemented as follows:

$$\min_{w} w^{\mathrm{H}} \boldsymbol{R}_{i+n} w \ \ subject\ to\ \ w^{\mathrm{H}} a(\theta_1) = 1 \tag{2}$$

where $(\cdot)^{\mathrm{H}}$ denotes the Hermitian transpose, $\boldsymbol{R}_{i+n}$ is the inference-plus-noise covariance matrix, θ_1 is the incident angle of desired signal. Since $\boldsymbol{R}_{i+n}$ is unavailable even in signal-free applications, it is usually replaced by the sample covariance matrix with K snapshots $\hat{\boldsymbol{R}}$. Then, the optimal solution of (2) is

$$w = \frac{\hat{\boldsymbol{R}}^{-1} a(\theta_1)}{a^H(\theta_1) \hat{\boldsymbol{R}}^{-1} a(\theta_1)} \tag{3}$$

where $\hat{\boldsymbol{R}} = (1/K)\sum_{i=1}^{k} X(k) X^H(k)$.

Adaptive beamformers are sensitive to mismatch caused by various reasons when $\boldsymbol{R}_{i+n}$ is replaced with $\hat{\boldsymbol{R}}$. Gu Y proposed a new adaptive beamforming algorithm which reconstructed the interference-plus-noise covariance matrix [6]. The $\boldsymbol{R}_{i+n}$ can be reconstructed as:

$$\hat{\boldsymbol{R}}_{i+n} = \int_{\bar{\Theta}} \frac{a^H(\theta) a(\theta)}{a^H(\theta) \hat{R}^{-1} a(\theta)} d\theta \tag{4}$$

where $\bar{\Theta}$ is the complement sector of Θ. Θ is angular sector in which the desired signal is located. Hence, the reconstructed covariance matrix removes the effect of the desired signal and collects information on interference and noise in the $\bar{\Theta}$ [6].

III. THE PROPOSED METHOD

An improved method is proposed based on the method of ABA-CMR. In fact, according to the formula (4), the denominator is the Capon spatial spectrum estimator as follows:

$$P(\theta) = \frac{1}{a^{H}(\theta)\hat{R}^{-1}a(\theta)} \quad (5)$$

The incident angles of interferences can be estimated accurately. The method of ABA-CMR inserts some virtual interferences around the incident angle of interference and defines it as follows:

$$Q(\theta) = \frac{1}{M1+M2+1}\sum_{m=-M1}^{M2} P(\theta + m\Delta\theta) \quad (6)$$

where $[-M1\times\Delta\theta, M2\times\Delta\theta]$ is the width of null, $\Delta\theta$ is the spacing between every virtual interference. The virtual interferences can be estimated by Capon spatial spectrum estimator to broaden nulls.

Instead, Capon spatial spectrum estimator can't be changed by the method proposed in this paper so that it can get accurate incident angles of interferences. Reconstruct correlation matrix of steering vector by inserting virtual interferences. Then the reconstructed matrix Z which contains the width information of nulls can be defined as follow:

$$Z = \int_{-\Delta\theta}^{\Delta\theta} a(u(\theta))a^{H}(u(\theta))d\theta \quad (7)$$

where $[-\Delta\theta, \Delta\theta]$ is the width of nulls we hope to get. Use Z of formula (7) to broaden nulls around the accurate incident angles of interferences. So the improved interference-plus-noise covariance matrix $\hat{R}_v$ can be defined as:

$$\hat{R}_V = \int_{\bar{\Theta}} ZP^{b}(u)du = \int_{\bar{\Theta}} \frac{Z}{[a^{H}(u)\hat{R}^{-1}a(u)]^{b}}du \quad (8)$$

where b is a control parameter which can control the depth of nulls [5]. INR can be improved by increasing the value of b to make nulls deeper. Replace the $\hat{R}$ in the formula (3) with $\hat{R}_v$ from formula (8), the weight vector can be defined as:

$$w = \frac{\hat{R}_v^{-1}a(\theta_1)}{a^{H}(\theta_1)\hat{R}_v^{-1}a(\theta_1)} \quad (9)$$

Because the method proposed in this paper doesn't change Capon spatial spectrum estimator, it can get accurate incident angles of interferences. Broaden nulls in the accurate incident angles by reconstructing correlation matrix of steering vector, so it can get better performance.

IV. SIMULATION RESULTS

Assume that a ULA with N=16 omnidirectional sensors spaced a half-wavelength apart is used. Additive noise is modeled as independent complex Gaussian noise with zero mean and unit variance. A signal with the signal-to-noise ratio is equal to $0dB$. The incident angle of desired signal θ_1 is 0°. Two independent interferences illumine in the directions -30° and 40° respectively. The interference-to-noise ratio (INR) of interferences are both $30dB$. Assume that Θ from -5° to 5° and the width of null is 6° which means that $\Delta\theta = 3^{\circ}$. The number of snapshots $K = 300$ and the control parameter $b = 1.5$. The performance of several algorithms are compared in Fig. 1.

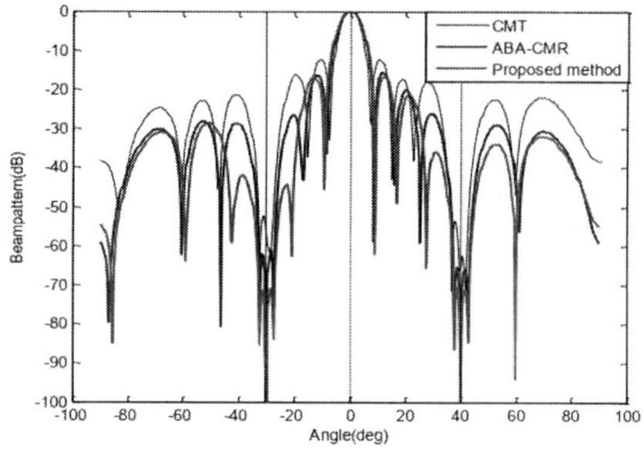

Fig. 1. Beampatterns of several null broadening beamforming methods

It can be observed form Fig. 1 that the method proposed in this paper can produce wide and deep nulls in incident angles of interferences effectively. The depth of nulls are about $5dB$ deeper than method of ABA-CMR and much deeper than method of CMT. In summary, method proposed in this paper can produce a better performance to against jammer motion and shaking platform.

V. CONCLUSION

An improved null broadening beamforming method based on covariance matrix reconstruction is proposed in this paper. Simulation results shows that the improved method proposed in this paper can broaden nulls and make nulls depth deeper effectively to against jammer motion and shaking platform.

ACKNOWLEDGMENT

This paper is funded by the International Exchange Program of Harbin Engineering University for Innovation-oriented Talents Cultivation.

REFERENCES

[1] S. A. Vorobyov, "Principles of minimum variance robust adaptive beamforming design," Signal Process, vol. 93, no. 12, pp. 3264-3277, 2013.

[2] R.J. Mailloux, "Covariance matrix augmentation to produce adaptive array pattern troughs," Electronics Letters, vol. 31, no.10, pp. 771–772, 1995.

[3] M. Zatman, "Production of adaptive array troughs by dispersion synthesis," Electronics Letters, vol. 31, no. 25, pp. 2141–2142, 1995.

[4] J. R. Guerci, "Theory and application of covariance matrix tapers for robust adaptive beamforming," IEEE Transactions on Signal Processing, vol. 47, no. 4, pp. 977–985, 1999.

[5] Yang Kai and Yang Shanguo, "An adaptive beamforming algorithm with wide nulls" Electronic Information Warfare Technology, vol. 30, no. 2, pp. 57-61, 2015. (in Chinese)

[6] Gu Y, Leshem A. Robust Adaptive Beamforming Based on Interference Covariance Matrix Reconstruction and Steering Vector Estimation[J]. IEEE Transactions on Signal Processing, vol. 60, no. 7, pp. 3881-3885, 2012.

A New Interference Rejection Algorithm for Direction-of-Arrival Estimation

Wenxing Li
College of Information and Communications Engineering
Harbin Engineering University
Harbin, China, 150001
liwenxing@hrbeu.edu.cn

Mengjun Chen
College of Information and Communications Engineering
Harbin Engineering University
Harbin, China, 150001
1654464543@qq.com

***Abstract*—In this paper, a new algorithm to suppress the interferences for Direction-of-Arrival(DOA) estimation is presented. The method is based on the property of the noise subspace invariant to power of emitters. With theoretical analysis and computer simulations, it is shown that the proposed method has a good performance on signal DOA estimation under disturbances.**

Keywords—DOA estimation; restrain interference; signal subspace; noise subspace

I. INTRODUCTION

Signal detection and parameter estimation has been widely used in many fields such as radar, communications, seismic and geophysical seismology. However, in the presence of interference source condition, the successful probability of the signals DOA estimation will be greatly reduced. Solutions to the problem are mostly based on strong interferences and weak signals and can be summed up in two categories of the general: either using beamforming method by forming on the incident direction of zero trapped to detect the targets, or using super-resolution method to handle interferences and signals simultaneously.

At the present time, a lot of researches have been performed on blocking pretreatment methods, such as [3] presents an interference blocking algorithm, which can simultaneously restrain the interferences and estimate the signals' DOA information effectively, but the incident direction of interferences is required precisely known. The interference jamming method is presented in the literature [2], and this article analyzes the relation between the transfer matrix and the interference suppression matrix.

In this paper, a new algorithm to suppress the interferences for DOA estimation is presented, which is based on the noise subspace invariant to power of emitters. This method needs to know the number of interference-to-noise ratio and signals, but it has lower computational cost without spectral peak searching. With computer simulations, it is shown that the proposed algorithm is not limited to strong interferences, and when the interference power is greater than 5dB signal power, the method just can accurately estimate the azimuth of signals and restrain the interferences at the same time.

II. PROPOSED METHOD

An array is composed of M elements and spacing for half a wavelength, and let $\mathbf{R}$ denotes the theoretical covariance matrix of the array output data. When I ($I < M$) narrowband plane waves incident to the array, $\mathbf{R} > 0$ has the following form:

$$\mathbf{R}=E\{\mathbf{x}(t)\mathbf{x}(t)^H\}=\sum_{i=1}^{I}\eta_i^2 a(\theta_i)a(\theta_i)^H+\sigma_n^2\mathbf{I}, \tag{1}$$

where η_k^2 and σ_n^2 respectively represent the power of kth wave signal and each array noise and $a(\theta)$ is the array steering vector in direction θ. In practical applications, $\mathbf{R}$ is replaced by the sample covariance matrix $\hat{\mathbf{R}}$, where

$$\hat{\mathbf{R}}=\frac{1}{N}\sum_{n=1}^{N}\mathrm{x}_n\mathrm{x}_n^*, \tag{2}$$

with N representing snapshots and x_n denoting the nth snapshot. The eigen-decomposition of the sample covariance matrix is

$$\hat{\mathbf{R}}=\sum_{i=1}^{I}\lambda_i\mathbf{e}_i\mathbf{e}_i^H+\sum_{i=I+1}^{I+S}\lambda_i\mathbf{e}_i\mathbf{e}_i^H+\sum_{i=I+S+1}^{M}\lambda_i\mathbf{e}_i\mathbf{e}_i^H, \tag{3}$$

Where I and S are respectively the number of interference-to-noise ratio and signals, and λ_i is eigenvalue, $\lambda_1\ge\cdots\ge\lambda_I\ge\lambda_{I+1}\ge\cdots\ge\lambda_{I+S}\ge\cdots\ge\lambda_M$, and $\mathbf{e}_i$ is the eigenvector corresponding to λ_i. In view of the orthogonality between the eigenvectors and subspace theory, $\mathbf{E}_I=span(\mathbf{e}_1,\cdots,\mathbf{e}_I)$, $\mathbf{E}_S=span(\mathbf{e}_{I+1},\cdots,\mathbf{e}_{I+S})$ and $\mathbf{E}_N=span(\mathbf{e}_{I+S+1},\cdots,\mathbf{e}_M)$ are respectively the interference subspace, the signal subspace and the noise subspace.

If we keep the incidence angle of the signal fixed and change their powers, then the last $(M-I)$ eigenvalues and their corresponding eigenvectors of new covariance matrix are invariant. According to this, we can define a new matrix $\mathbf{D}^\theta$ as

$$\mathbf{D}^\theta=\mathbf{R}+\varepsilon\mathbf{a}(\theta)\mathbf{a}(\theta)^H, \tag{4}$$

where $\mathbf{R}$ is given in (1), $a(\theta)$ is $M\times 1$ array steering vector for direction θ and ε is a positive constant. If setting the direction θ for a specific one, say $\theta=\theta_1$, then we have

$$\mathbf{D}^{\theta_1} = \mathbf{R} + \varepsilon \mathbf{a}(\theta_1)\mathbf{a}(\theta_1)^H$$
$$= (\eta_1^2 + \varepsilon)\mathbf{a}(\theta_1)\mathbf{a}(\theta_1)^H + \sum_{i=2}^{I} \eta_i^2 \mathbf{a}(\theta_i)\mathbf{a}(\theta_i)^H + \sigma_n^2 \mathbf{I} \tag{5}$$

Compare the formulas (1) and (5), note that $\mathbf{D}^{\theta_1}$ actually increase the energy of direction θ_1. When the direction θ_1 belongs to the interference subspace or the noise subspace, it is equivalent to introduce a new interference, namely increasing the number of interference-to-noise ratio one. Now, the sample covariance matrix $\hat{\mathbf{D}}^{\theta_1}$ is decomposed into

$$\hat{\mathbf{D}}^{\theta_1} = \hat{\mathbf{R}} + \varepsilon \mathbf{a}(\theta_1)\mathbf{a}(\theta_1)^H$$
$$= \sum_{k=1}^{I+1} \mu_k \mathbf{v}_k \mathbf{v}_k^H + \sum_{k=I+2}^{I+S+1} \mu_k \mathbf{v}_k \mathbf{v}_k^H + \sum_{k=I+S+2}^{M} \mu_k \mathbf{v}_k \mathbf{v}_k^H, \tag{6}$$

where μ_k is eigenvalue,

$\mu_1 \geq \cdots \geq \mu_{I+1} \geq \mu_{I+2} \geq \cdots \geq \mu_{I+S+1} \geq \mu_{I+S+2} \geq \cdots \geq \mu_M$, and $\mathbf{v}_k$ is the eigenvector corresponding to μ_k. Due to the power of the signal remains the same, now we can get

$$\mu_{I+2} = \lambda_{I+1}. \tag{7}$$

However, when the direction θ_1 belongs to the signal subspace, it corresponds to increase the power of this direction, and the eigen-decomposition of the matrix $\hat{\mathbf{D}}^{\theta_1}$ is

$$\hat{\mathbf{D}}^{\theta_1} = \sum_{k=1}^{I} \mu_k \mathbf{v}_k \mathbf{v}_k^H + \sum_{k=I+1}^{I+S} \mu_k \mathbf{v}_k \mathbf{v}_k^H + \sum_{k=I+S+1}^{M} \mu_k \mathbf{v}_k \mathbf{v}_k^H, \tag{8}$$

then compare the formulas (3) and (8), now we can get

$$\mu_k > \lambda_i, k, i = I+1. \tag{9}$$

Comprehensive two cases of direction θ_1, we have new space spectrum function to estimate the DOA of the targets and suppress the interferences

$$F(\theta) = (\lambda_{I+1} - \mu_{I+1})(\lambda_{I+1} - \mu_{I+2}). \tag{10}$$

Due to the performance of the proposed method greatly affected by parameter ε in (4), in order to better application of the proposed algorithm, we give ε take a proper value. The most appropriate value obtained by simulation experiments is

$$\varepsilon = \frac{tr(\hat{\mathbf{R}})}{M}, \tag{11}$$

where $tr(\hat{\mathbf{R}})$ denotes trace of $\hat{\mathbf{R}}$. The value of ε in (11) has the property that $tr(\hat{\mathbf{R}}) = tr(\varepsilon \mathbf{a}(\theta)\mathbf{a}(\theta)^H)$.

III. Simulation Results

In order to verify the proposed method, we do the following simulation experiments. Assume that wave signals are coherence and narrowband and antenna array is the ULA of 16 sensors with half wavelength spacing. The signal direction is 0° and 20°. The snapshot is 100 and the signal-to-noise ratio is 0dB. -50° and 60° direction interference power is 30dB and -30° direction interference power is 40dB. Three hundred independent repeats for every experiment. Fig.1 shows the spectrum of the proposed method. Fig.2 shows the relation of successful probability and signal SNR. Fig.3 shows the relation of the root mean squared error and signal SNR. The simulation results indicate the proposed method has a good performance on signal DOA estimation under disturbances.

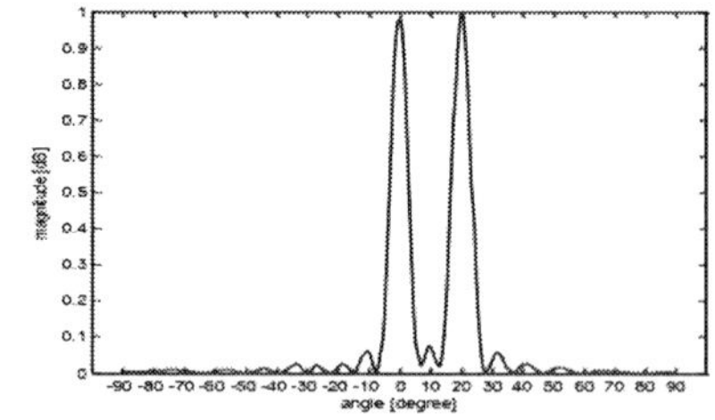

Fig. 1. Spectrum of the proposed method with two signals and three interferences.

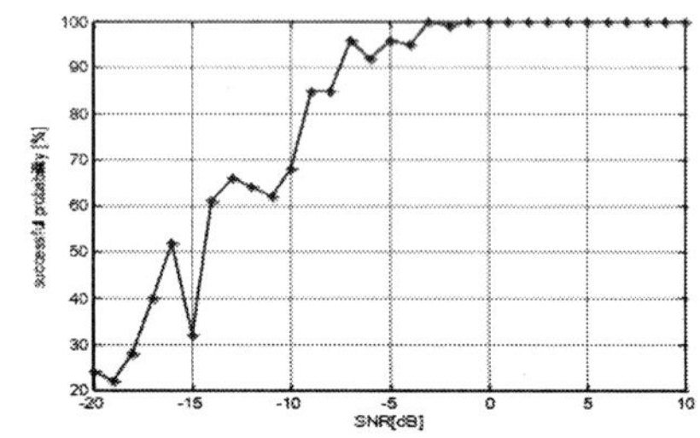

Fig. 2. The successful probability versus signal SNR.

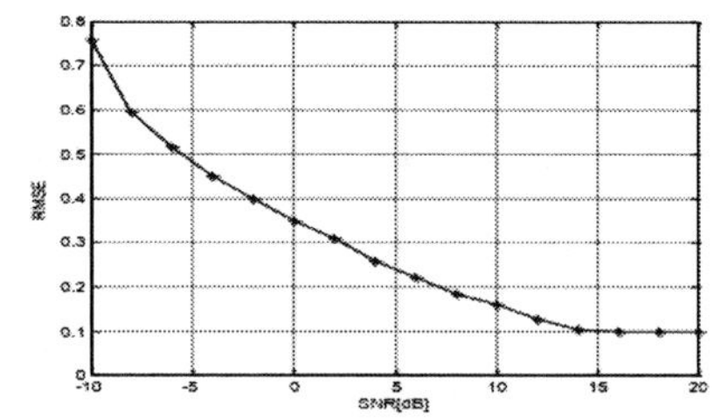

Fig. 3. The RMSE versus signal SNR.

IV. Conclusion

A new algorithm to suppress the interferences for DOA estimation is presented. The simulation results show that the proposed method has a good performance on signal DOA estimation under disturbances.

Acknowledgment

This paper is funded by the International Exchange Program of Harbin Engineering University for Innovation-oriented Talents Cultivation.

References

[1] Ali Olfat. A new signal subspace processing for DOA estimation[J]. Signal Processing: IEEE, 2004, vol:84, 721-728.

[2] Wang Yongliang. Interference jamming DOA estimation algorithm[A]. 2005 IEEE Antennas and Propagation Society International Symposium APS-05, 2005.

[3] Qu jinyou, xun Li, and yijun Wen. A new method for weak signals' DOA estimation in the presence of strong interferences[A]. 2012 IEEE 11th International Conference on Signal Processing, 2012.

[4] Qian Ma, Chao Sun, Xionghou Liu, et al. Passive direction-of-arrival estimation under high noise and strong interference condition for volumetric array [A]. 2013 IEEE Region 10 Conference [C]:1-5.

[5] Zili Xu, Matthew Trinkle, Douglas A. Gray. Week interference direction of arrival estimation in the GPS L1 frequency band [A]. 2015 IEEE International Conference on Acoustics, Speech and Signal Processing [C]:2649 - 2653.

High Isolation Design of a Two-Element Planar UWB-MIMO Monopole Antenna

Yue Dong, Yingsong Li*, Kai Yu, Yanyan Wang
College of Information and Communications Engineering,
Harbin Engineering University,
Harbin 150001, China
*liyingsong@ieee.org

***Abstract*— Two-element ultra-wideband (UWB) multiple input and multiple output (MIMO) antennas are presented to obtain high isolation. The designed UWB-MIMO antennas are composed of two identical orthogonal antenna elements, and a defected ground structure with I-shaped slot and a pair of L-shaped stub are employed to get better isolation. Bandwidth of the proposed antennas range from 3.28 GHz-12 GHz. Also, the proposed antennas have isolations better than -18.6 dB. Moreover, an isolation of -20 dB is obtained within 3.73 GHz-10.26 GHz. The results show that the proposed UWB-MIMO antennas have wide bandwidth and high isolation performance.**

Keywords— high isolation; microstrip feed; orthogonal antenna elements; UWB-MIMO antenna

I. Introduction

Wideband and high speed communication techniques have been extensively researched and used in our daily life in recent decades. In particular, the ultra-wideband (UWB) system released by Federal Communication Commission (FCC) in 2002 has become an attractive topic, which is to provide a covering band-width of 3.1-10.6GHz for commercial UWB communications [1]. For constructing such a wideband communication system, UWB antenna is important to transmit and receive the desired signal. Moreover, the UWB system occupies a wide bandwidth to cover the FCC standard. After that, a great deal of UWB antennas have been developed to meet the requirements released by FCC [1-7]. Among these existing UWB antenna designs, the printed UWB antennas have attracted much more attention in recent decades owing to its simple structures and easy to fabricate, which includes monopole antennas and dipole antennas. Also, different feeding structures have been presented in detail [1-7]. Judging from the complexity of the antenna geometry, microstrip fed monopole antenna has simple structure and can provide a wide bandwidth for serving the indoor UWB communication systems. However, the UWB system has low radiation power.

On other hand, multi-input multi-output (MIMO) can improve the channel capacities and has been used for solving the problem of how to improve the channel capacity and how to increase the transmission rate. To enhance the performance of the UWB communication system, UWB technique and MIMO technique have been combined to create an amazing technique named as UWB-MIMO communication system [2-7]. Then, UWB-MIMO antennas have been becoming a hot topic in recent years. Moreover, several UWB-MIMO antennas have been presented to provide a desired communication requirements [3-7]. However, the coupling between the MIMO antenna elements is always high because of the compact antenna design and the space limitation of the modern portable communication terminals. Then, many UWB-MIMO antennas with high isolation have been exploited to reduce the coupling between the used antenna elements [3-7]. Unfortunately, some of the UWB antennas are complexity in structure, others are large in size.

In this paper, we present UWB-MIMO antennas to reduce the coupling between the antenna elements. The designed UWB-MIMO antennas consist of two identical microstrip feeding circular patch antennas which are set orthogonally. Decoupling structures comprised of stub and slots are employed to give rise to a coupling reduction of the proposed UWB-MIMO antennas. The antennas were optimized by using the HFSS. The simulation results given by the HFSS demonstrate that the designed UWB-MIMO antennas can provide a good service for covering the UWB bandwidth from 3.28-12 GHz, which almost covers the UWB frequency band. Furthermore, within the scope of the UWB band, its isolation is less than -18.6 dB by considering the transmission coefficients between the two antenna elements. It is worth noting that the proposed UWB-MIMO antenna achieves a high isolation that is better than -20dB in most of the UWB band. The results indicate that the proposed UWB-MIMO antenna can not only provide a wide bandwidth and a high isolation, but also has a good impedance matching characteristic.

II. Antenna Geometry

The design process and configuration of the proposed UWB-MIMO antennas are shown in Fig.1. The proposed UWB-MIMO antennas are printed on a substrate with its relative permittivity of ε_r =4.4, loss tangent of δ =0.02, and the thickness of h =1.6mm. The proposed UWB-MIMO antennas are comprised of two identical microstrip feeding circular patch antennas which are set orthogonally. The feeding and the circular patch are printed on the top layer of the substrate, while the ground is installed at the bottom layer. Also, the design procedure of the proposed UWB-MIMO antenna can be divided into three stages, which are denoted as UWB-MIMO antenna-1, UWB-MIMO antenna-2, UWB-MIMO antenna-3. As for the UWB-MIMO antenna-1, a slot is etched in the ground plane. For the UWB-antenna-2, two inverted L-shaped stubs are integrated into the UWB-MIMO antenna-1. UWB-MIMO antenna-3, combining the antenna-1 and antenna-2, is the proposed final design. The dimensions of the proposed antenna are: l=35mm, W=52mm, W1=3.1mm, W2=4mm, l1=14mm, l2=2mm, l3=3mm, l4=7mm, l5=0.7mm, l6=2mm, w3=4mm, w5=6mm, lg=13.2mm, lr=7mm, wf=0.5mm.

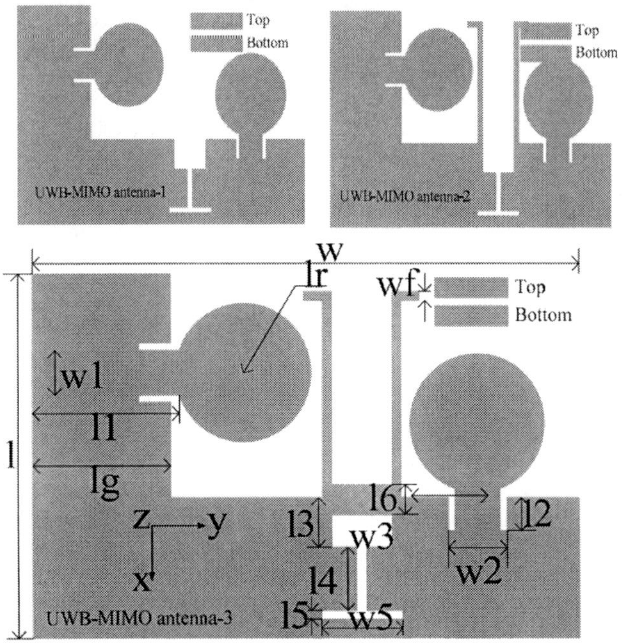

Fig.1 Procedure of the proposed UWB-MIMO antenna

III. Performance of the proposed UWB-MIMO antenna

The performance of the proposed UWB-MIMO antenna is done by using HFSS. The S-parameter of the proposed antenna is shown in Fig.2. It can be found that the proposed UWB-MIMO antenna still has a wide bandwidth ranging from 3.28 GHz to 12 GHz. By using the stubs, the bandwidth of the UBW-MIMO antenna is narrowed from antenna-1 to antenna-2. The proposed UWB-MIMO antenna-2 and UWB-MIMO antenna-3 have the same bandwidth and both of them can provide a high isolation. The isolation is less than -18.6 dB and it is better than -20dB in some bands. The radiation patterns are shown in Fig.3. We can see that the proposed

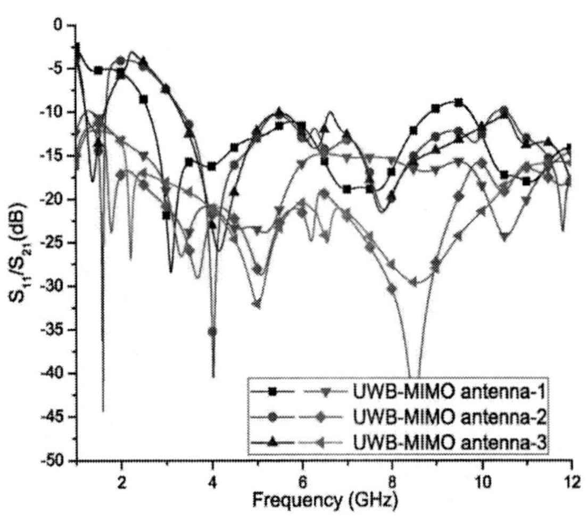

Fig.2 S11 and S12 of the proposed UWB-MIMO antennas

UWB-MIMO antenna has nearly omnidirectional radiation patterns in both XOZ and YOZ plane, which is useful for diversity applications.

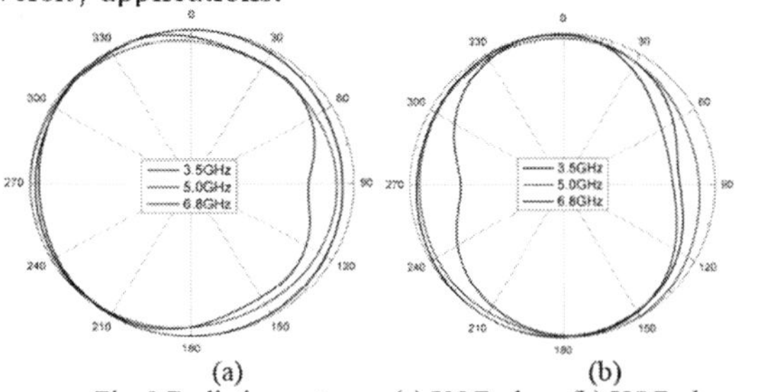

Fig. 3 Radiation patterns: (a) XOZ-plane (b) YOZ-plane

IV. Conclusion

In this paper, three UWB-MIMO antennas have been proposed and their performance has been investigated by using HFSS. The coupling has been reduced by using slots and stubs. The proposed antenna achieved a -18.6dB isolation in the operating UWB bands. Also, the proposed UWB-MIMO antenna has wide bandwidth and good matching, which is suitable for UWB communication applications.

Acknowledgment

This paper is funded by the International Exchange Program of Harbin Engineering University for Innovation-oriented Talents Cultivation. This work was also partially supported by the National Key Research and Development Program of China-Government Corporation Special Program (2016YFE0111100), the Science and Technology innovative Talents Foundation of Harbin (2016RAXXJ044), Projects for the Selected Returned Overseas Chinese Scholars of Heilongjiang Province and MOHRSS of China, and the Foundational Research Funds for the Central Universities (HEUCFD1433, HEUCF160815).

References

[1] Y. Li, W. Li, W. Yu, "A switchable UWB slot antenna using SIS-HSIR and SIS-SIR for multi-mode wireless communications applications," Applied Computational Electromagnetics Society Journal, vol.27, no.4, pp.340-351, 2012. 23.

[2] T. Jiang, T. Jiao, Y. Li, "Array mutual coupling reduction using L-loading E-shaped electromagnetic band gap structures," International Journal of Antennas and Propagation, vol.2016, Article ID:6731014, pp.1-9, 2016.

[3] Y. Li, W. LI, C. Liu, T. Jiang, "Two UWB-MIMO antennas with high isolation using sleeve coupled stepped impedance resonators," 2012 Asia-Pacific Conference on Antennas and Propagation (APCAP 2012), August 27-29, Singapore, 2012.

[4] X. Yang, L. Zhang, L. zhou, R. Wang, "Planar two-element UWB MIMO antennas with high isolations," IEEE International Conference on Computational Electromagnetics (ICCEM), Hong Kong, pp. 363-365, 2015.

[5] Y. Li, W. Li, C. Liu, T. Jiang, "Two UWB-MIMO Antennas with High Isolation Using Sleeve Coupled Stepped Impedance Resonators," IEEE Asia-Pacific Conference on Antennas and Propagation, Singapore, pp. 21-22, 2012.

[6] J. Ren, W. Hu, Y. Yin, R. Fan, "Compact Printed MIMO Antenna for UWB Applications," IEEE Antennas and Wireless Propagation Letters, vol. 13, pp. 1517-1520, 2014.

[7] Y. Li, W. Li, W. Yu, "A multi-band/UWB MIMO/diversity antenna with an enhance isolation using radial stub loaded resonator," Applied Computational Electromagnetics Society Journal, vol.28, no.1, pp.8-20.

Low-Profile Dual-Band Emulated GPS Constellation Antenna

Emanuel J. Merulla
US Army CERDEC
Aberdeen Proving Grounds, MD USA

***Abstract*— a novel low-profile dual-band emulated GPS constellation antenna design is proposed. The antenna consists of a cube with four square spirals printed on a Rogers's 4003C circuit board. The antenna is fed with a 4:1 transmission line splitter with a quadrature output for right hand circular polarization. The antenna presented has a cosecant-squared antenna radiation pattern.**

Keywords—Emulated Constellation Antenna, L1, L2, GPS

I. Introduction

The US Army has shown interest in antennas with cosecant-squared radiation patterns due to their ability to emulate GPS constellations. These types of antennas can be used to evaluate the performance of GPS antennas in different environments.

II. Desired Antenna Pattern

This section assumes the emulated GPS constellation antenna is either mounted on an airborne structure or a large tower to simulate a satellite in the sky. These antennas typically need a special radiation pattern called a cosecant-squared pattern. This type of radiation pattern, when transmitted from an emulated GPS constellation, allows GPS receivers to receive at relatively constant signal levels to prevent front end receiver saturation. This is especially critical when the GPS receiver is directly under the GPS constellation transmitter. The radiation pattern would ideally fit (1) below, however this is impractical in practice. A realistic cosecant-squared radiation pattern is shown in Fig. 1, which would give an approximate constant received signal strength.

$$G(\varphi,\theta),\text{dBi}=\begin{cases} G_0,\text{ dBic}+20\log_{10}\csc\left(\frac{\pi\cdot(90-|\theta|)}{180}\right), & \text{for } \begin{cases} 0^\circ\leq|\theta|\leq\theta_1 \\ 0^\circ\leq\varphi\leq360^\circ \end{cases} \\ G_2,\text{ dBic},\ 70^\circ\leq|\theta|\leq100^\circ \end{cases}$$

Where G_0= -8 dBic, and G_2= 0 dBic (1)

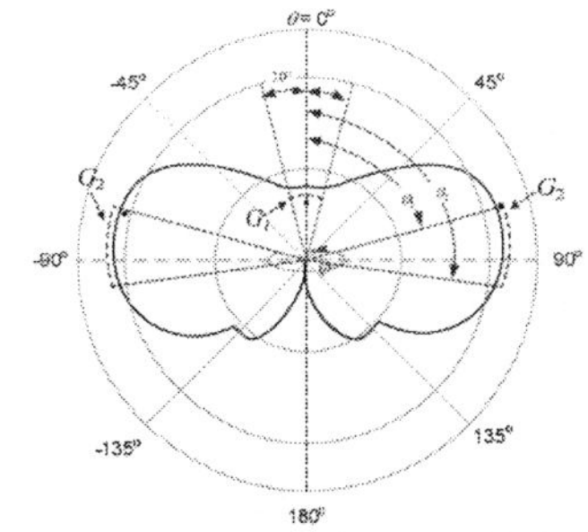

Figure 1. Ideal Cosecant-Squared Radiation Pattern

III. Element Design

To create an antenna with a cosecant-squared radiation pattern, it was necessary to optimize the radiating elements using the trust region routine in CST Microwave Studio. The elements were designed on 60 mil Rogers 4003C laminate 73.3 mm x 73.3 mm with a strip width of 0.7 mm. The optimization points are shown in Fig. 2, where points P1-P12 were optimized for the ideal cosecant-squared radiation pattern at both 1575.5 MHz and 1227.6 MHz. The entire length of the square spiral is optimized for resonant operation at the lower frequency band while achieving the cosecant-squared radiation pattern. To provide resonant operation at the higher frequency band, a trap circuit is placed at point 7 in Fig. 2. The trap consists of a parallel LC circuit (lumped components) that has infinite impedance (e.g., open circuit) at its resonant frequency. At the lower frequency, the trap circuit acts similar to a short with a low reactive impedance. This allowed the antenna to achieve the correct pattern at both L1 and L2 bands. The trap circuit values are L = 6.8 nh and C = 1.5 pf [1]. In order to match the antenna at the lower frequency, a shorted matching leg was required, shown in red in Fig. 2. This section also contained the same trap discussed above. The dimensions of the leg were also optimized to achieve a good impedance match at the lower frequency. The optimized values are shown in Table 1. During the optimization, it was found that matching both bands while maintaining the correct radiation pattern was very difficult, therefore requiring a separate matching network to obtain a good match at the higher frequency. The matching network consisted of an inductor in series with the feed and capacitor to ground with the values of L = 9.6 nh and C= .83 pf.

$$f=\frac{1}{2\pi\sqrt{LC}}=\frac{1}{2\pi\sqrt{6.8e-9*1.51e-12}}=1575.5\text{ MHz} \quad (2)$$

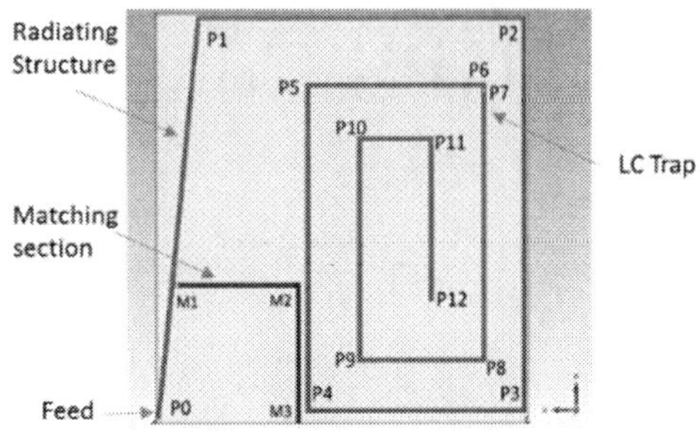

Figure 2. Antenna Element Layout

Table 1. Optimized Antenna Dimensions (mm)

	X	Z		X	Z
P0	36.3	1.0	P8	-27.5	11.4
P1	28.3	72.5	P9	-3.2	11.4
P2	-35.8	72.5	P10	-3.2	51
P3	-35.8	2.4	P11	-17.1	51
P4	7.0	2.4	P12	-17.1	22
P5	7.0	60.5	M1	32.2	24.7
P6	-27.5	60.5	M2	8.8	24.7
P7	-27.5	59.5	M3	8.8	0

IV. GPS CONSTELLATION ANTENNA

The antenna was assembled as shown in Fig. 3 by creating a cube using four of the optimized elements from the previous section. The cube is placed on a 75 mm x 75 mm ground plane. The four square spiral arms are excited with sequential phase variation, 0°, 90°, 180°, 270° to obtain circular polarization [2]. Each of the feeds are placed at point 0 shown in Fig. 2.

Figure 3. Assembled GPS Constellation Antenna

V. ANTENNA PERFORMANCE

The optimized antenna had a return loss of greater than 10 dB at both L1 and L2 frequency bands as shown in Fig. 4. The antenna achieved a good Right Hand Circular Polarized (RHCP) radiation pattern as shown in Figure 5. Polar Plots for both L1 and L2 frequency bands are shown in Fig. 6, which show that the cosecant-squared radiation pattern was achieved.

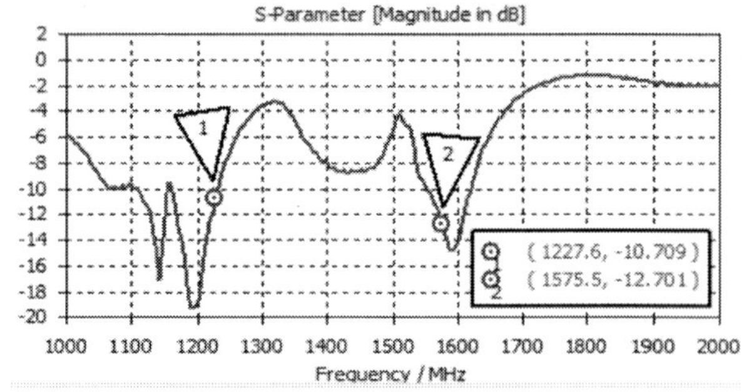

Figure 4. Return Loss (S11)

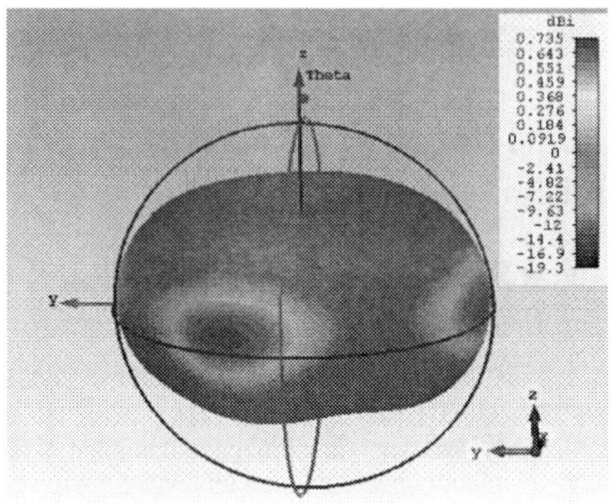

Figure 5. 3-D RHCP Radiation Pattern at 1227.6 MHz

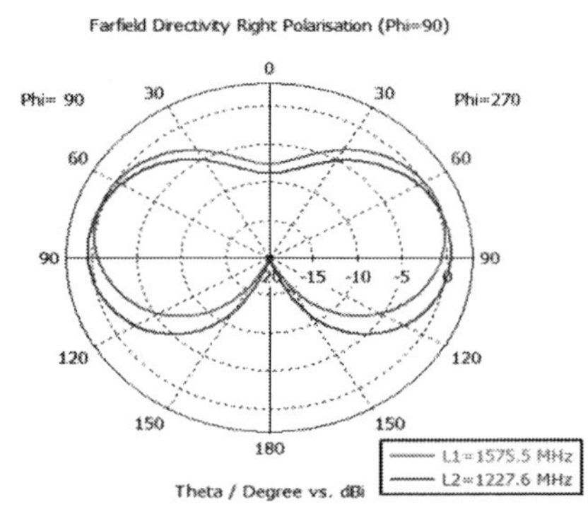

Figure 6. 2-D Radiation Patterns

VI. CONCLUSION

An Antenna was designed to resonate with a return loss of greater than 10 dB in both L1 and L2 frequency bands while achieving a cosecant-squared radiation pattern for use in emulated GPS constellation applications. The antenna is low-profile compared to typical quadrifilar helical designs. This design also included a 4:1 transmission line quadrature splitter that is necessary to build the antenna. The details of this splitter were omitted from this paper.

REFERENCES

[1] D. Lamensdorf, M.A. Smolinski, "Dual band Quadrifilar Helix Antenna", Antennas and Propagation Society International Symposium, 2002. IEEE, Vol. 3 April, 2002 pp 488-491

[2] W. Son, W. Lim, M. Lee, S. Min, J. Yu, "Printed Square Quadrifilar Helix Antenna (QHA) for GPS Receiver", Proceedings of the 38th European Microwave Conference, IEEE, Oct. 2008, PP 1292-1295

20/30 GHz Circularly Polarized Antenna Arrays with Pairs of Slots on Substrate Integrated Waveguide

Christos Kalialakis, Fermin Mira
Microwave Systems and Nanotechnology Department,
Centre Tecnològic de Telecomunicacions de Catalunya
(CTTC/CERCA)
08860 Castelldefels, Spain
christos.kalialakis@cttc.es, fermin.mira@cttc.es

Apostolos Georgiadis
School of Engineering and Physical Sciences
Institute of Sensors, Signals and Systems
Edinburgh, EH14 4AS, UK
apostolos.georgiadis@ieee.org

***Abstract*—Designs of four element travelling wave antenna arrays based on Substrate Integrated Waveguide (SIW) technology are presented. The antenna element is comprised by a pair of orthogonal slots that generates circular polarization. The frequencies of operation are chosen to be compatible with emerging High Throughput Satellite Systems terminals; namely the K band(20GHz) and the Ka Band (30 GHz).**

***Index Terms*—SIW, Circular Polarization, Satellite communications, antenna arrays.**

I. Introduction

There are several satellite systems in development, such as Xpress by Inmarsat, that aim to deliver broadband communications on mobile platforms using the K-band for downlink and the Ka band for uplink.

Earth stations on Mobile Platforms (ESOMPs) can be used in a harmonized way in terms of spectrum regulatory constraints [1]. Planar antennas can an offer an attractive alternative to the widely used reflector antennas. Some antenna designs operating in K-Ka bands have been presented in the literature, mostly as reflectarrays [2].

In this work, customized slots on SIW technology are proposed to combine the benefits of waveguide technology along with the integration capability of planar technology [3]. The pair of slots introduced in [4]-[5] for waveguides, is adapted here for SIW. A travelling wave array configuration is utilized.

Section II presents the details of the antenna elements and the array geometry. Section III presents preliminary results including axial ratio(AR) measurements of the antenna elements. Conclusions and future work directions are given in Section IV.

II. ANTENNA GEOMETRY AND DESIGN

A. Antenna Element Geometry

The antenna is composed by two slots of the same dimensions (L, W), orthogonal to each other [5]. The geometry (Fig.1) is governed by three additional parameters; the distance d_s between the centers of the slots, the offset by x in the lateral dimension and the angle of rotation φ_s.

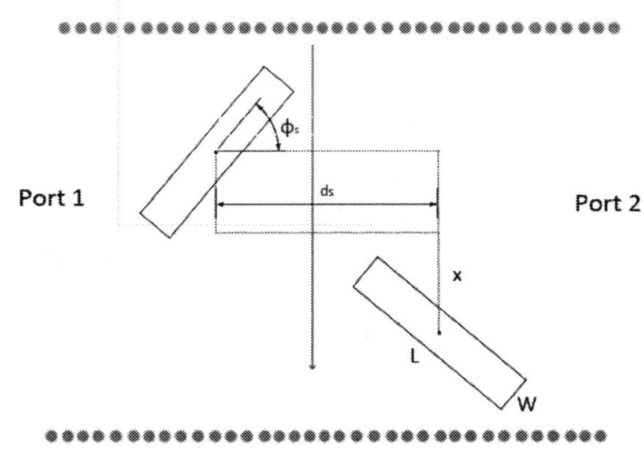

Fig. 1. Geometrical parameters for the pair of slots.

The antenna can generate circular polarization either by excitation from Port 1 (RHCP) or Port 2(LHCP).

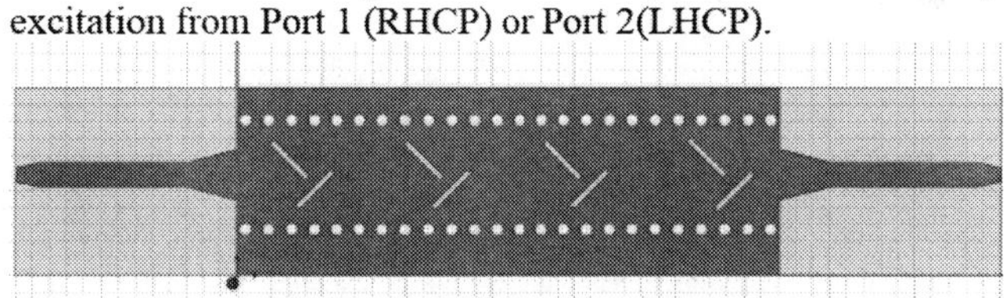

Fig. 2. The geometry of a four element travelling wave SIW array for the Ka Band. Microstrip transitions are used for each excitation port.

Each band is designed separately (Fig.2). When one port is excited the other port is terminated with 50Ω. This is done in order to show the RH and LH capabilities of the design. Versions with open end or shorted ends are readily feasible for improved matching.

B. Design approach

The design procedure for the determination of the slot dimensions follows [5] by utilizing the SIW-waveguide equivalence [3]. The simulations were carried out using a widely used simulator (ANSYS HFSS). The center frequency of each band is used as the design frequency. For several combinations of the geometry parameters, the magnitudes of S_{11}, S_{21} and AR are recorded. Each slot length corresponds to a different value of S_{21}. These S_{21} values are then utilized in the synthesis of the traveling wave array such as the Taylor current distribution [8].

The dimensions of the slots pair for each band are given in Table I with reference to Fig.2. The substrate used is Arlon (ε_r=3.38, h=0.51mm, tanδ=0.0025). The SIW width is 6.382mm with vias of diameter of 0.7 mm and spacing 0.9mm.

TABLE I. SLOT PAIR ANTENNA DIMENSIONS

No	Parameter	20 GHz	30 GHz
1	L(mm)	2.95	2
2	W(mm)	0.3	0.3
3	x(mm)	0.85	1
4	d_S(mm)	2.5	1.7
5	φ_S(°)	42	56

III. PRELIMINARY PERFORMANCE RESULTS

Prototypes were fabricated on an Arlon 25N substrate (εr=3.38, h=0.508 mm) A K-band slotted pair was fabricated with microstrip to SIW transitions that allow excitation from both sides of the SIW. Measured Axial Ratio results are shown in Fig.3 under excitation of Port 1. Good AR results were also obtained with excitation from Port 2.

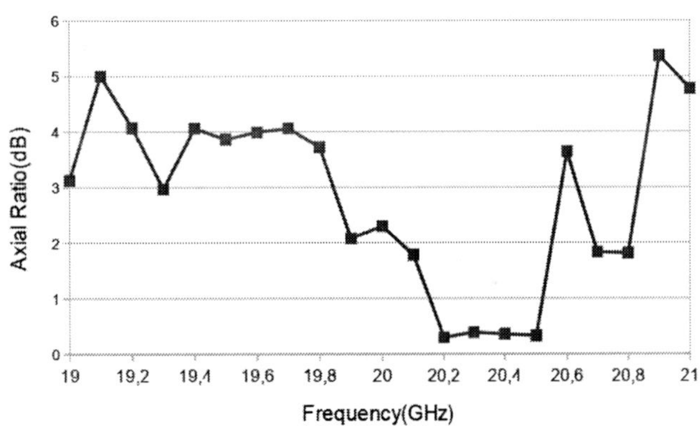

Fig. 3. MeasuredAxial Ratio for the slotted pairs at K Band (Port 1 excited)

The simulated radiation patterns of the two arrays in K and Ka bands are shown in Fig.4 and Fig. 5 respectively.

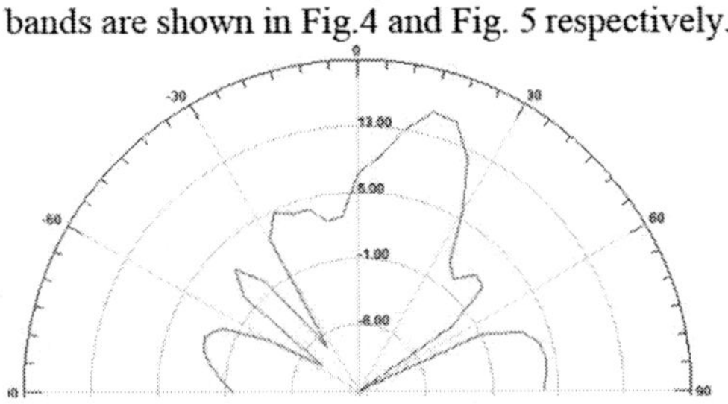

Fig. 4. Simulated RHCP Radiation Pattern for the K Band array

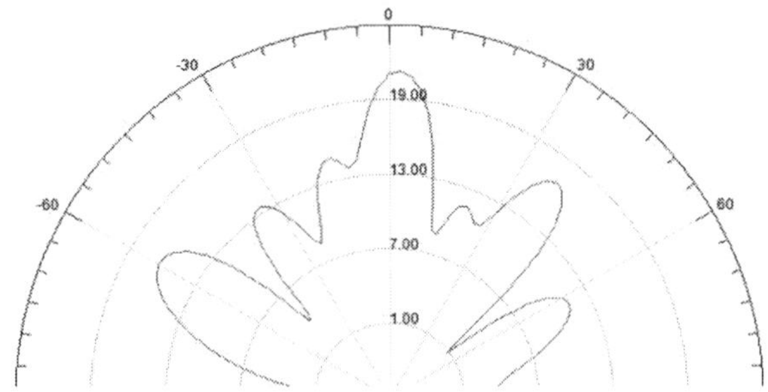

Fig. 5. Simulated RHCP Radiation Pattern for the Ka Band array

IV. CONCLUSIONS

Traveling wave antenna arrays composed of orthogonal slots on SIW that operate in the K and Ka bands have been presented. The Axial Ratio is dictated by the relative positioning of the slots and can be controlled through five geometry parameters. The proposed antenna arrays can easily generate RHCP or LHCP. More results will be presented in the conference.

ACKNOWLEDGMENT

The work of C. Kalialakis was supported under EU H2020 Marie Sklodowska-Curie Grant Agreement 654734. The work of F.Mira has been supported by the Catalan Government under Grant 2014 SGR 1551.

REFERENCES

[1] European Communications Committee, "The Use of Earth Stations on Mobile Platforms Operating with GSO Satellite Networks in the Frequency Range 17.3-20.2 GHz and 27.5-30.0 GHz", Report 184, February 2013.

[2] R.Deng, Y.Mao; S.Xu, and F.Yang, "A Single-Layer Dual-Band Circularly Polarized Reflectarray With High Aperture Efficiency," IEEE Transactions on Antennas and Propagation, vol.63, no.7, pp.3317-3320, July 2015.

[3] M Bozzi,, A Georgiadis, and Ke Wu. "Review of substrate-integrated waveguide circuits and antennas," IET Microwaves, Antennas & Propagation, 5.8 (2011), 909-920.

[4] G. Montisci, "Design of circularly polarized waveguide slot linear arrays." IEEE Transactions on Antennas and Propagation,54(10), 2006, 3025-3029.

[5] Montisci, Giorgio, Michela Musa, and Giuseppe Mazzarella. "Waveguide slot antennas for circularly polarized radiated field." IEEE Transactions on Antennas and Propagation, 52.2 (2004): 619-623.

[6] F.Hyjazie, P.Watson, H.Boutayeb. "Dual Band Interleaved Base Station Phased Array Antenna With Optimized Cross-Dipole and EBG/AMC Structure". IEEE APS 2014, Jul 2014, United States.

[7] Guo, Hua, C. J. Guo, and Jun Ding. "Pattern Synthesis of Dual-band Shared Aperture Interleaved Linear Antenna Arrays." Radioengineering 23.3 (2014).

[8] H.Boutayeb, and K.Wu. "Analysis and Design of Millimeter-Wave Circularly Polarized Substrate Integrated Travelling-Wave Antennas." Progress In Electromagnetics Research C, 49 (2014): 67-77.

Multi-Band Metamaterial-Based Microstrip Antenna for WLAN and WiMAX Applications

Kai Yu, Yingsong Li*, Yanyan Wang
College of Information and Communications Engineering,
Harbin Engineering University, Harbin 150001, China
*liyingsong@ieee.org

***Abstract*- Two multi-band metamaterial based microstrip antennas are designed for WLAN and WiMAX applications. Antenna 1 consists of a simple rectangle monopole radiator with a 2×3 complementary split ring resonator (CSRR) printed on its back ground. By using CSRR technique, two frequency bands operating at 3.2-3.9 GHz and 5.65-5.8 GHz are achieved. Antenna 2 is composed of a rectangle patch with a CSRR slot and a conventional ground plane, which can provide a triple-band characteristic covering 2.4-2.48 GHz, 3.3-3.9 GHz and 5.15-5.7 GHz. The operational bands of these two antennas can be used for WiMAX at 2.5/3.5/5.5 GHz and WLAN at 2.4/5.2/5.8 GHz, and it has omnidirectional radiation patterns, which can be the good candidate for WiMAX and WLAN applications.**

Keywords—*metamaterial antenna; multi-band antenna; split ring structure (SRS); WiMAX/WLAN applications*

I. Introduction

In recent years, microstrip antennas have got more and more attentions due to the rapid development of wireless communications and their advantages of low cost, easy of fabrication. Moreover, wireless device requires a single antenna to satisfy the multi-band communication applications. Then, multi-band antenna techniques are popular and amazing in the last decades. Many methods have been developed to obtain a good multi-band performance, including etching slots on the patch [1] and loading shorted pins and walls [2]. The emergence of metamaterial technology provides a new choice for the multi-band antenna designs. As we know, the split ring resonator (SRR) and complementary split ring resonator (CSRR) are the most used basic metamaterial unit-cells. By etching these unit-cells on the radiation patch or loading them on the substrate, ground plane and setting them around the patch, multi-band characteristics can be realized [3-4]. Meanwhile, as wireless technology rapidly develops, smartphone, laptop and other personal terminal devices are being popular in our everyday life. Thus, both the wireless local area network (WLAN) and worldwide interoperability for microwave access (WiMAX) are in great demand for our portable terminals, which leads to the design of multi-band antennas for WLAN and WiMAX [5-6].

In this paper, we propose two multi-band metamaterial antennas. With 2×3 CSRRs printed on the back of the microstrip antenna, a dual-band antenna can be achieved, which can operate at two bands at 3.5/5.7 GHz for WiMAX 3.5GHz and WLAN 5.8 GHz bands. Also, this antenna is denoted as antenna 1. The second antenna is carried out by the means of integrating a CSRR unit-cell into the radiation patch, resulting in a triple-band functions operating at 2.4/3.5/5.3 GHz and 3.5/5.5GHz for covering the WLAN and WiMAX bands. The results indicate that the proposed antennas can not only be used for WLAN/WiMAX applications, but also have omnidirectional radiation patterns.

II. Antenna Design

A. *Antenna 1 with 2×3 CSRRs*

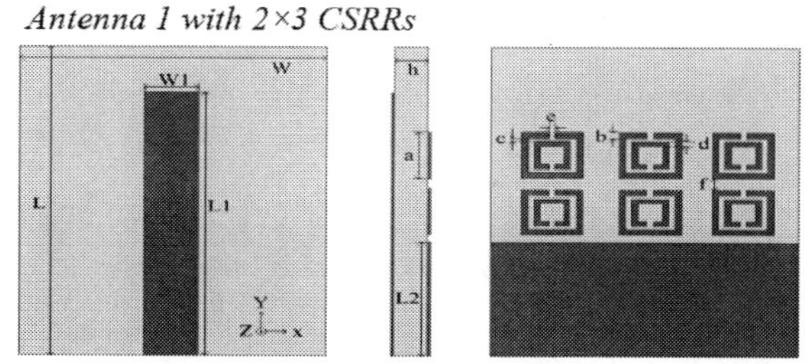

Fig. 1 Geometry of proposed dual-band metamaterial monopole Antenna 1

The configuration of the proposed dual-band metamaterial monopole antenna is depicted in Fig. 1, which is composed of a simple rectangle radiation patch, a conventional rectangle ground plane and a 2×3 CSRR array printed on the back of the antenna. Here, the 2×3 CSRRs act as a metamaterial structure to realize the multi-band performance. The antenna is printed on a FR4 substrate with a thickness of h=1.6 mm and a relative permittivity of ε_r=4.4. The antenna has a total size of 20mm×30mm. The optimized parameters obtained from HFSS are L= 30, L1= 27.5, L2= 10, W1= 3, a= 4.5, b= 0.4. c= 0.75, d= 0.4, e= 0.4, h= 1.6 (unit: mm).

B. *Antenna 2 with a CSRR slot*

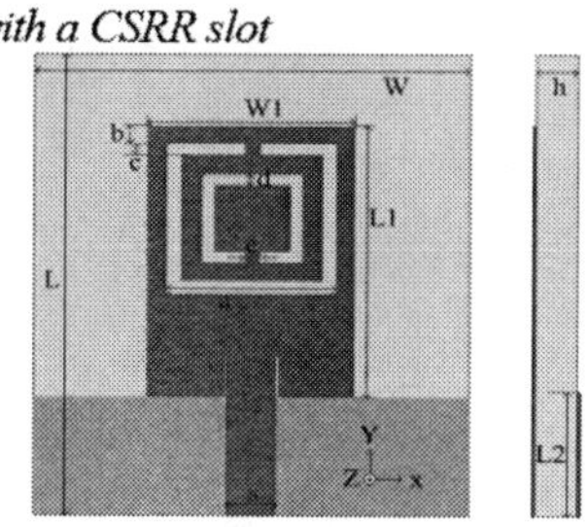

Fig. 2 Geometry of proposed triple-band metamaterial patch Antenna 2

The geometry of the tri-band antenna consists of a rectangular patch that is printed on a substrate with relative permittivity of 2.65 and thickness of 0.9 mm. By etching a CSRR unit on the patch of this antenna, a triple-band characteristic is created. The overall dimension of the antenna is 35×35mm^2 as shown in Fig. 2 and the optimized parameters are L= 35, L1= 22, L2= 10, W= 35, W1= 14, a= 11.5, b= 0.6, c= 1.6, d= 0.6, e= 1.6, s=2.8, h=0.9 (unit: mm).

III. Performance of the Antennas

A. *Antenna 1*

The return losses of a monopole antenna without the metamaterial loading and our proposed metamaterial Antenna

1 are shown in Fig. 3. From fig. 3, we can observe that the original monopole antenna has only one operating band at 3.5 GHz, and our proposed antenna 1 can provide two frequency bands at 3.2 to 3.9 GHz for WiMAX and from 5.75 to 5.85 GHz for WLAN. Thus, we can say that the 3.5 GHz band is produced by the radiation patch, while the second resonance band is gotten by the loading CSRR units.

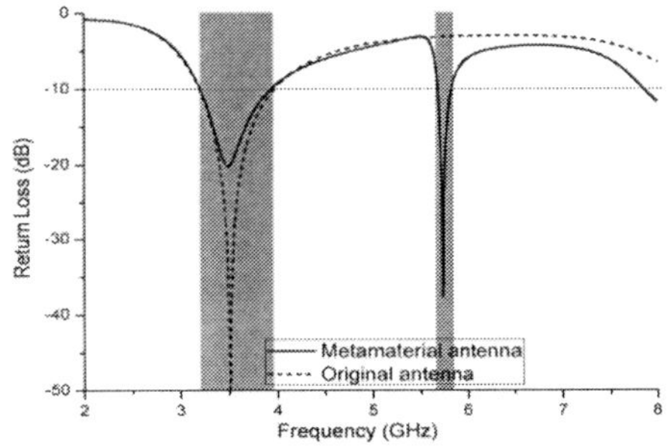

Fig. 3 Return losses of original antenna and proposed metamaterial antenna 1

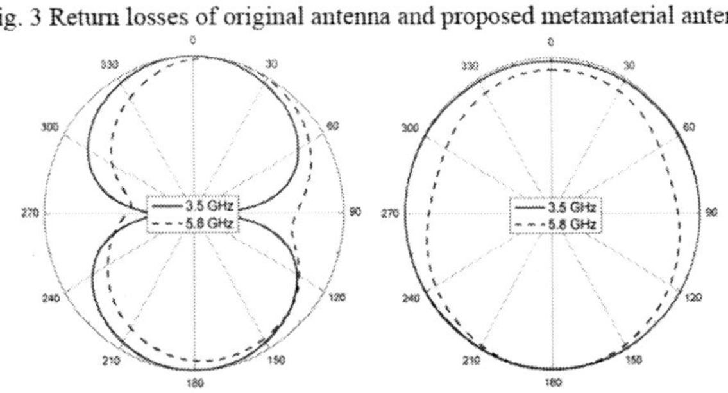

(a) (b)

Fig. 4 Radiation patterns: (a) XOY plane, (b) XOZ plane.

The radiation patterns of the proposed metamaterial monopole antenna 1 at 3.5 GHz and 5.8 GHz are shown in Fig. 4. It can be seen that the radiation patterns of antenna 1 are nearly omnidirectional in XOZ plane and a figure-of-eight radiation patterns in XOY plane, indicating that the antenna 1 is very suitable for wireless communication applications.

B. Antenna 2

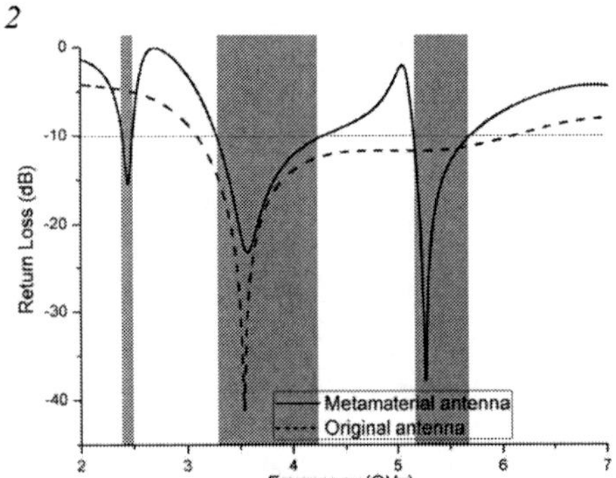

Fig. 5 Return loss of original antenna and proposed metamaterial Antenna 2

The return losses of the proposed metamaterial Antenna 2 are shown in Figure. 5. It can be found that the original antenna has a band at 3.5 GHz. By etching the CSRR unit-cell on the patch, the Antenna 2 can give three operating bands at 2.35-2.48 GHz for 2.4 GHz WLAN, 3.3-4.2 GHz for 3.5 GHz WiMAX and 5.15-5.65 GHz for 5.2 GHz WLAN and 5.5 GHz WiMAX.

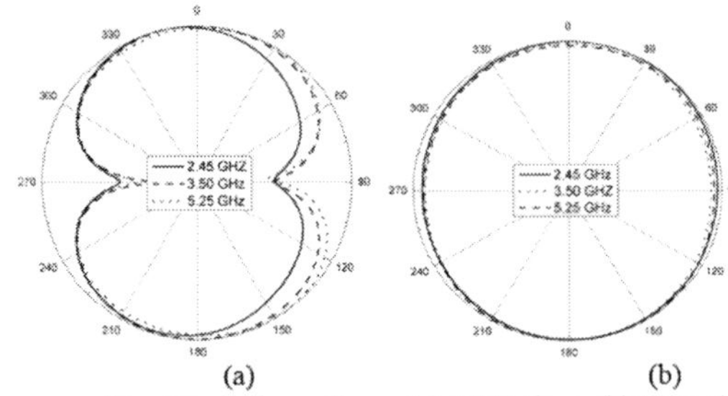

(a) (b)

Fig. 6 Radiation patterns: (a) XOY plane, (b) XOZ plane.

The radiation patterns of the proposed metamaterial patch antenna 2 at 2.45 GHz, 3.5 GHz and 5.25 GHz are shown in Fig. 6. From the results, we can find that the radiation patterns are nearly omnidirectional in XOZ plane and a "8"-like radiation patterns in XOY plane, which indicate that the antenna 2 is a good candidate to meet the requirement of multi-band wireless transmission applications.

IV. CONCLUSIONS

In this paper, two multi-band metamaterial antennas have been designed. By integrating a 2×3 CSRR metamaterial structure on the back of a monopole antenna, the metamaterial Antenna 1 can give two bands at 3.5 GHz for WiMAX and 5.8 GHz for WLAN applications. By etching a CSRR unit on the radiation patch, the metamaterial Antenna 2 can provide three operating bands operating at 2.35-2.48 GHz, 3.3-4.2 GHz and 5.15-5.65 GHz, which can be used for 2.4 GHz WLAN, 3.5GHz WiMAX and 5.2GHz WLAN/5.5 GHz WiMAX.

ACKNOWLEDGMENT

This paper is funded by the International Exchange Program of Harbin Engineering University for Innovation-oriented Talents Cultivation. This work was also partially supported by the National Key Research and Development Program of China-Government Corporation Special Program (2016YFE0111100), the Science and Technology innovative Talents Foundation of Harbin (2016RAXXJ044), Projects for the Selected Returned Overseas Chinese Scholars of Heilongjiang Province and MOHRSS of China, and the Foundational Research Funds for the Central Universities (HEUCFD1433, HEUCF160815).

REFERENCES

[1] Garima, A. Kaur, R. Khanna, "Dual- and Triple- Band U-slot Microstrip Patch Antenna for WLAN Applications," International Journal of Advanced Research in Computer and Communication Engineering, vol. 2, pp. 2201-2204, 2013.

[2] Y. Cheol, S. H. Choi, H. C. Lee and H. D. Park, "Small Microstrip Patch Antennas with Short-Pin Using A Dual-Band Operation," Microwave and Optical Technology Letters, vol. 50, pp. 367–371, 2008.

[3] Y. H. Xie, C. Zhu, L. Li, and C. H. Liang, "A Novel Dual-Band Metamaterial Antenna Based on Complementary Split Ring Resonators," Microwave and Optical Technology Letters, vol. 54, pp. 1007-1009, 2012.

[4] H. Cheribi, F. Ghanem and H. Kimouche, "Metamaterial-Based Frequency Reconfigurable Antenna," Electronics Letters, vol. 49, no. 5, pp. 315-316, 2013.

[5] Y. S. Li and W. H. Yu, "A Miniaturized Triple Band Monopole Antenna for WLAN and WiMAX Applications," International Journal of Antennas and Propagation, vol. 2015, pp.1-12, 2015.

[6] Y. S. Li, W. X. Li and Q. B. Ye, "A Compact Asymmetric Coplanar Strip-Fed Dual-Band Antenna for 2.4/5.8 GHz WLAN Applications," Microwave and Optical Technology Letters, vol.55, pp.2066-2070, 2015.

Electromagnetic Material Parameter Extraction of Ferrites up to the GHz Range via Measurements and Simulations

Christian Reinhold and Peter Scholz
PHOENIX CONTACT Electronics GmbH
Bad Pyrmont, Germany
Email: {creinhold,pscholz}@phoenixcontact.com

Ulrich Jumar
ifak - Institut f. Automation u. Kommunikation e.V.
Magdeburg, Germany
Email: ulrich.jumar@ifak.eu

Abstract—**A new methodology is presented for determination of electromagnetic material parameters $\underline{\mu}$ and $\underline{\varepsilon}$ for typical ferrite core geometries used in electronic and power electronic systems. The material parameters of a measurement sample are determined in such a way that measurements and simulations of the impedance have a maximum match in a broad frequency range. The extracted material parameters show that at high frequencies in the GHz range dielectric properties of the investigated MnZn ferrite core are significant. The simulated impedance parameters of a structure containing the ferrite are in good agreement with simulation showing the usability of the method.**

I. Introduction

Materials with a high permeability like ferrites are widely used in electronic systems. Power electronic systems components like inductive elements or transformers are typically operating in a low frequency range up to a few MHz. In order to design the system as well as forecast the electromagnetic behavior of electronic systems containing ferrites, the material parameters e.g. the complex permeability $\underline{\mu} = \mu_0(\mu_r' - j\mu_r'')$ need to be known in the operational frequency range. For some investigations like a combined wireless power and data transmission [1], [2], [3], the knowledge of the dielectric permittivity $\underline{\varepsilon} = \varepsilon_0(\varepsilon_r' - j\varepsilon_r'')$ in a broad frequency range is essential as well.

In this contribution a method is presented allowing for the extraction of material parameters via a coupling of measurement and simulation. In contrast to known techniques [4], [5], [6], [7] this method can be applied for typical core geometries used in electronic systems. This new approach does not require machining or preparation of the samples and it covers a wide frequency range extending from low frequencies in the kHz range up to the microwave region.

II. Material Parameter Extraction Technique

The proposed method is based on measurement of a transmission line containing the port $a-b$ and $c-d$ able of accepting a sample as presented in Fig. 1. The network parameters e.g. the impedance matrix $\underline{Z}$ of the transmission line can be measured. The network parameters of the transmission line change when a material sample is inserted.

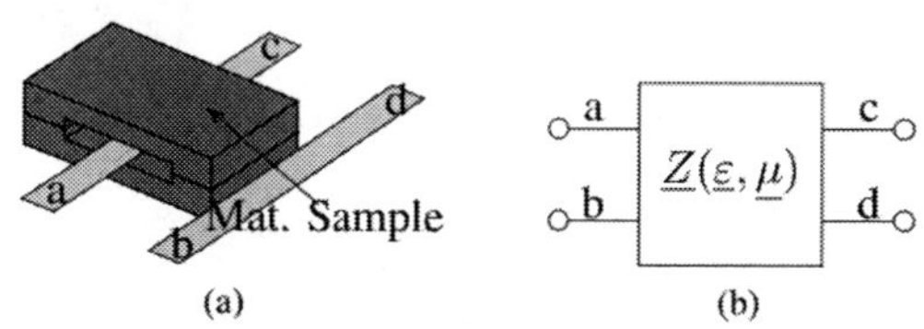

Fig. 1. Conceptual setup for determination of material parameters (a) and the network representation of the setup (b).

With the aid of EM-simulation techniques like the finite element method the network parameters can be calculated if the material parameters are known. However if the material parameters are sought based on the knowledge of the measured network parameters an inverse problem has to be solved. This is carried out via an iterative procedure sketched in Fig. 2.

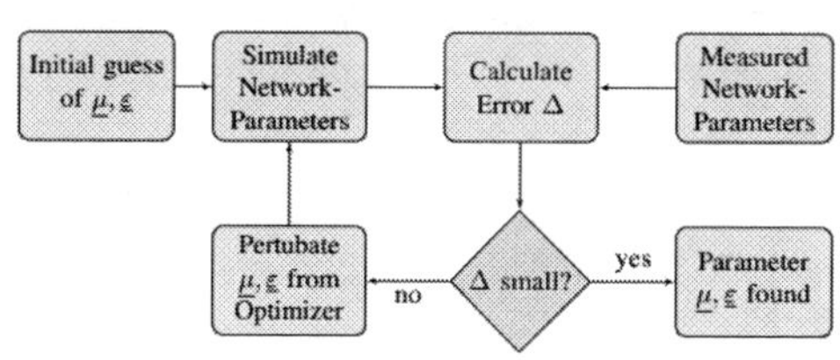

Fig. 2. Sketch of the iterative search procedure.

The iterative search procedure is carried out as follows: The network parameters are calculated with an initial guess of the material parameters. After this an error Δ is calculated quantifying the difference between the measured and calculated parameters. If the error is below a certain limit, the optimization is terminated, otherwise the material parameters are disturbed by means of an optimization algorithm and the new network parameters and the deviation from the measurement is calculated. The last steps are repeated until the desired accuracy is reached.

III. Measurement Results

A transformer core consisting of two U-shaped profiles as persented in Fig. 1 was used as the material under test. The core samples materials is a MnZn ferrite. An ungrounded coplanar line as presented in Fig. 3 was used as a transmission line allowing for guiding a wave in a broad frequency range. The two cores present a closed magnetic circuit enclosing the center conductor $a - c$ giving rise to a high sensitivity related to the magnetic material properties of the sample. In order to enhance the sensitivity of the structure with respect to dielectric properties, a metallic bridge was added in the center of the line.

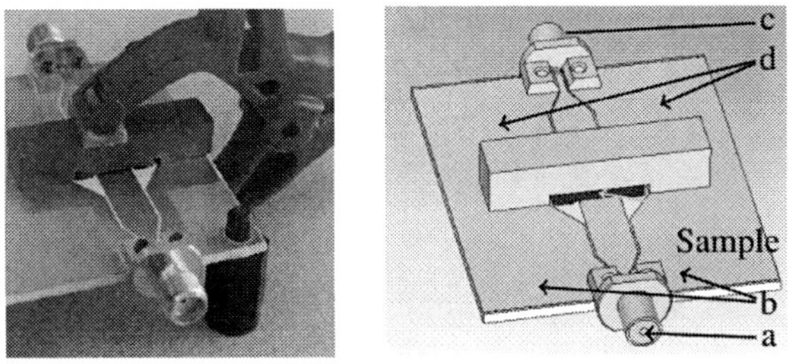

(a) Measurement setup (b) 3D Simulation Model

Fig. 3. Utilized measurement setup for the material parameter extraction.

Measurements were carried out with the aid of an impedance analyzer as well as a two-port vector network analyzer. All four material parameter $\mu_r', \mu_r'', \varepsilon_r', \varepsilon_r''$ are retrieved with a single optimization for discrete frequency samples. EM-Field simulations were carried out with CST® Microwave-Studio and the frequency domain solver. A Nelder-Mead simplex method was applied for optimization.

The relative permeability and relative permittivity as a function of frequency is shown in Fig. 4. A broadband fit allows for interpolation in the investigated frequency range. The real part of the relative permeability μ_r' approaches unity for frequencies above approximately 400 MHz. Magnetic losses represented by the imaginary part of the permeability μ_r'' are present in the entire investigated frequency band.

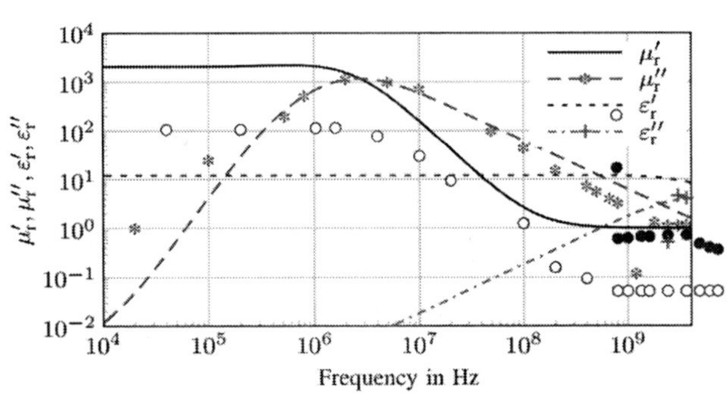

Fig. 4. The permittivity and permeability extracted from measurements. Markers: Gained data via the iterative scheme, solid lines: causal broadband material model fit fulfilling the Kramers-Kronig relations.

The dielectric parameters show a considerable value up to the microwave region. At 3 GHz a drop in the real part of the dielectric constant and an increase in the imaginary part seem to reveal an electronic relaxation.

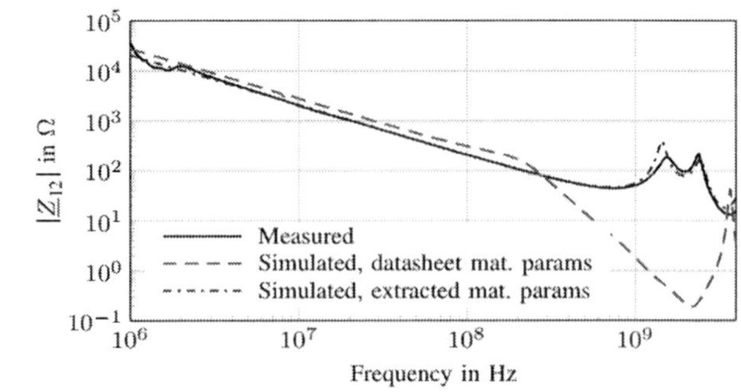

Fig. 5. Comparison between measurement and simulation of the impedance of a line with the investigated core.

In Fig. 5 a comparison between the measured and simulated magnitude of the impedance parameter $|\underline{Z}_{12}|$ is shown. If the material parameters given by the manufacturers data sheet are inserted into the simulation model i.e. only permeability data at low frequencies, a big deviation from the measured values is noticeable especially at high frequencies. However taking into account all material parameters from Fig. 4 strongly reduces the deviation proving the usability of the material model. Factors like the band limited causal fit and measurement imperfections give rise to slight deviations.

IV. Conclusion

The presented method allows for determination of the EM-material parameter for typical core geometries. The results show that the real part of the permeability of the investigated MnZn ferrite is significant in the low frequency range but at frequencies in the GHz range they can be neglected. However the dielectric parameters as well as magnetic losses cannot be neglected at high frequencies. Forecasting the impedance parameters via simulation shows good agreement if the deduced material parameters are included in the simulation model.

References

[1] R. Bosshard and J. Mhlethaler and J. W. Kolar and I. Stevanovi *Optimized magnetic design for inductive power transfer coils*, Applied Power Electronics Conference and Exposition (APEC), 2013 Twenty-Eighth Annual IEEE, 2013

[2] A. Abdolkhani *Fundamentals of Inductively Coupled Wireless Power Transfer Systems, Wireless Power Transfer - Fundamentals and Technologies*, InTech 2016

[3] R. Trevisan and A. Costanzo *A UHF Near-Field Link for Passive Sensing in Industrial Wireless Power Transfer Systems*, IEEE TRANSACTIONS ON MICROWAVE THEORY AND TECHNIQUES, VOL. 64, NO. 5, MAY 2016

[4] V. Radonić N. Blaž and Lj. Živanov *Measurement of Complex Permeability Using Short Coaxial Line Reection Method*, ACTA PHYSICA POLONICA A Vol. 117, No. 5, pp 820-824, 2010

[5] J. Xu and M. Y. Koledintseva and Y. He and R. E. DuBroff and J. L. Drewniak and B. Matlin and A. Orlando *Measurement of electromagnetic parameters and FDTD modeling of ferrite cores*, 2009 IEEE International Symposium on Electromagnetic Compatibility, pp 83-88, Aug 2009

[6] S. Takeda and T. Hotchi and S. Motomura and H. Suzuki *Permeability Measurements of Magnetic Thin Films using Shielded Short-Circuited Microstrip Lines* Journal of the Magnetics Society of Japan, 2015, Vol. 39, No. 6, pp 227-231

[7] C. Vollinger and F. Caspers and E. Jensen *Permittivity and permeability measurements methods for particle accelerator related materials*, Proceedings of IPAC2014, Dresden, Germany, 2014

A Modified CoSaMP Algorithm For Electromagnetic Imaging of Two Dimensional Domains

Ali Imran Sandhu and Hakan Bagci
Division of Computer, Electrical, and Mathematical, Sciences and Engineering
King Abdullah University of Science and Technology (KAUST)
Thuwal 23955-6900, Saudi Arabia
{aliimran.sandhu, hakan.bagci}@kaust.edu.sa

***Abstract*— The compressive sampling matching pursuit (CoSaMP) algorithm is used for solving the electromagnetic inverse scattering problem on two-dimensional sparse domains. Since the scattering matrix, which is computed by sampling the Green function, does not satisfy the restricted isometry property, a damping parameter is added to the diagonal entries of the matrix to make the CoSaMP work. The damping factor can be selected based on the level of noise in the measurements. Numerical experiments, which demonstrate the accuracy and applicability of the proposed algorithm, are presented.**

***Keywords*— Compressive sensing, inverse scattering, greedy pursuits, CoSaMP, microwave imaging**

I. Introduction

Various compressed sensing (CS) techniques [1-2], which have originally been developed for efficient reconstruction of sparse signals in image processing applications, have recently been applied to solving electromagnetic inverse scattering problems [3-6]. The resulting inversion algorithms have promising applications in nondestructive testing, crack detection and hydrocarbon reservoir exploration, which are naturally sparse domains.

Greedy heuristic algorithms including orthogonal matching pursuit (OMP) [7] and compressive sampling matching pursuit (CoSaMP) [8] have been developed as fast alternatives to techniques making use of convex relaxation. Even though they have gained popularity in signal and image processing communities, their application to solving inverse problems has been very limited [9-11]. This is simply due to the fact that scattering matrix, which is obtained by sampling the Green function between investigation domain and receiver locations, does not satisfy restricted isometry property [9].

In this work, for the first time, the CoSaMP algorithm is applied to solving the electromagnetic inverse scattering problem on two-dimensional (2D) domains where the dielectric permittivity profile is sparse. First, samples of the current induced in the investigation domain (under individual excitations from each transmitter) are recovered from the scattered field samples measured away from the investigation domain using the CoSaMP algorithm. The scattering matrix between the samples of the current and scattered field is "damped" by adding a constant parameter to its diagonal entries to make the CoSaMP work. Then, the recovered currents are used to estimate the total field samples in the investigation domain. At the final step, dielectric profile samples are obtained by solving a least squares problem involving the samples of the current and total field. Numerical results, which demonstrate the accuracy of the dielectric profile recovered using this approach, are provided.

II. Formulation

A. 2D Electromagnetic Scattering Equations

Let S represent the support of a 2D (z-invariant) investigation domain residing in an unbounded background medium. The permittivity and permeability on lossless S and in the lossless background medium are $\{\varepsilon(\mathbf{r}),\mu_0\}$ and $\{\varepsilon_0,\mu_0\}$. S is surrounded by N^T line-source transmitters. Let $E_i^{inc}(\mathbf{r})$ represent the transverse (to z direction) magnetic (TM^z) incident field generated by the ith transmitter. Upon excitation by $E_i^{inc}(\mathbf{r})$, electric current density $J_i(\mathbf{r})$ is induced on S and $J_i(\mathbf{r})$ generates the scattered field $E_i^{sca}(\mathbf{r})$:

$$E_i^{sca}(\mathbf{r}) = j\omega\mu_0 \int_S J_i(\mathbf{r}')G(\mathbf{r},\mathbf{r}')ds'. \quad (1)$$

where $G(\mathbf{r},\mathbf{r}') = H_0^{(2)}(k_0|\mathbf{r}-\mathbf{r}'|)/(4j)$ is the Green function in the background medium and $H_0^{(2)}(.)$ is the zeroth order Hankel function of the second kind. Additionally, $J_i(\mathbf{r})$ satisfies

$$J_i(\mathbf{r}) = j\omega\varepsilon_0\tau(\mathbf{r})E_i(\mathbf{r}) \quad (2)$$

$$E_i(\mathbf{r}) = E_i^{sca}(\mathbf{r}) + E_i^{inc}(\mathbf{r}). \quad (3)$$

Here, $\tau(\mathbf{r}) = \varepsilon(\mathbf{r})/\varepsilon_0 - 1$ is the contrast and $E_i(\mathbf{r})$ is total field. Investigation domain S is discretized by N square cells with dimension Δd. Let $p_k(\mathbf{r})$ denote a pulse basis function defined on cell k with support S_k and center $\mathbf{r}_k$. $J_i(\mathbf{r})$ is approximated using

$$J_i(\mathbf{r}) = \sum_{k=1}^{N} J_{i,k}p_k(\mathbf{r}) \quad (4)$$

where $J_{i,k} = J_i(\mathbf{r}_k)$. It is assumed that S is surrounded by N^R receivers located at $\mathbf{r}_m^R$, $m = 1,\ldots,N^R$. Inserting (4) into (1) and sampling the resulting equation at $\mathbf{r}_m^R$, $m = 1,\ldots,N^R$ yield

$$\bar{E}^{sca} = \bar{G}^s\bar{J} \quad (5)$$

where $\{\bar{E}^{sca}\}_{m,i} = E_i^{sca}(\mathbf{r}_m^R)$, $\{\bar{J}\}_{k,i} = J_{k,i}$, and $\{\bar{G}^s\}_{m,k} = j\omega\mu_0\int_{S_k} G(\mathbf{r}_m^R,\mathbf{r}')ds'$.

B. Modified CoSaMP Algorithm

Since the support of $J_i(\mathbf{r})$ is assumed to be sparse, the electromagnetic inverse problem is constructed in the form

$$\bar{J} = \min_{\bar{J}} \|\bar{J}\|_0, \quad \text{s.t. } \bar{E}^{mea} = \bar{G}^s\bar{J}. \tag{6}$$

It is clear that (6) is a L_0 − minimization problem and it cannot be solved directly. One can use the CoSaMP algorithm directly on (6) to obtain the solution, however, it may not converge since $\bar{G}^s$ does not satisfy the restricted isometric property [9]. To address this problem and also to increase the robustness of the solution to noise in $\bar{E}^{mea}$, the minimization problem (6) is modified as

$$\bar{J} = \min_{\bar{J}} \|\bar{J}\|_0, \quad \text{s.t. } \bar{E}^{mea} = (\bar{G}^s + \lambda\bar{I})\bar{J} \tag{7}$$

where $\bar{I}$ is the identity matrix and λ is a damping factor which can be selected based on the priori knowledge of the noise level. Then the CoSaMP algorithm [8] is applied to (7).

C. Computation of Contrast Samples

Once $\bar{J}$ is computed using the modified CoSaMP algorithm described in Section II-B, samples of contrast $\tau_k = \tau(\mathbf{r}_k)$, $k = 1,\ldots,N$ are obtained as explained next. Inserting (1) and (4) into (3) and sampling the resulting equation at $\mathbf{r}_k$, $k = 1,\ldots,N$ yield

$$\bar{E} = \bar{E}^{inc} + \bar{G}\bar{J} \tag{8}$$

where $\{\bar{E}\}_{k,i} = E_i(\mathbf{r}_k)$, $\{\bar{E}^{inc}\}_{k,i} = E_i^{inc}(\mathbf{r}_k)$, and $\{\bar{G}\}_{k,k'} = j\omega\mu_0 \int_{S_{k'}} G(\mathbf{r}_k, \mathbf{r}')ds'$. Once $\bar{E}$ is estimated using (8), (2) is sampled at $k = 1,\ldots,N$ and the resulting equations is solved using least squares to yield [11]

$$\tau(\mathbf{r}_k) = \tau_k = \sum_{i=1}^{N^T}\left(\{\bar{E}\}_{k,i}^{*}\{\bar{J}\}_{k,i}\right) \Big/ \sum_{i=1}^{N^T}\left|\{\bar{E}\}_{k,i}\right|^2. \tag{9}$$

III. Numerical Results

The investigation domain includes four point-like targets [9]. The transmitter-receiver configuration is same as the one described in [9] with frequency 300 MHz, number of transmitter $N^T = 30$, and number of receivers $N^R = 50$. The domain is discretized with square cells of dimension $\Delta d = 0.1$m resulting in $N = 1369$ elements. Reconstruction of the dielectric profile is done using the modified CoSaMP proposed in this work and the flexible-tree-search based orthogonal matching pursuit (FTB-OMP) proposed in [9] for different levels of measurement noise changing between 5dB to 50dB. Damping parameter of the CoSaMP, $\lambda = 0.01$ for the first simulation with 5dB noise and $\lambda = 0.001$ for the rest. Relative error in the reconstructed dielectric profile is plotted against noise level in Fig. 1(a). Clearly, CoSaMP is more accurate for all noise levels. Fig. 1(b) plots the profile reconstructed by the CoSaMP under 30dB noise and demonstrates its accuracy.

IV. Conclusions

The CoSaMP algorithm is used to solve the 2D electromagnetic inverse scattering problem on sparse domains.

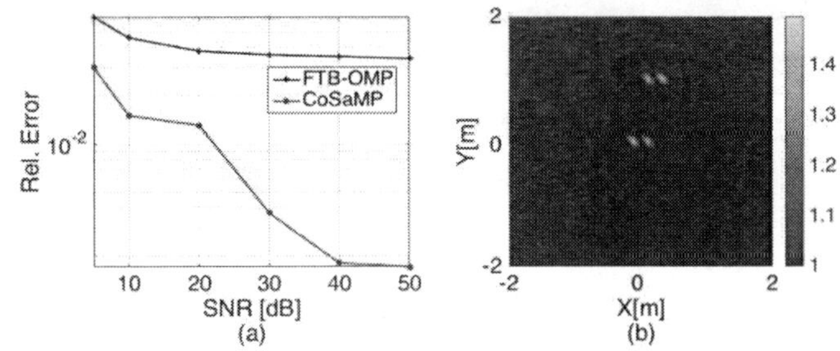

Fig. 1. (a) Relative mean square error in the dielectric profile reconstructed by the FTB-OMP and CoSaMP vs. the level of measurement noise. (b) The profile reconstructed by the CoSaMP under 30dB noise.

To make the CoSaMP work, a damping parameter is added to the diagonal entries of the scattering matrix. Numerical results demonstrate the potential of the proposed algorithm.

One limitation of the CoSaMP algorithm is that it requires the knowledge of the number of non-sparse samples in the domain (i.e., sparsity level). Integration of methods, which can adaptively estimate the sparsity level during the execution of the CoSaMP, is underway.

References

[1] E. J Candes, and M. B. Wakin, "An introduction to compressive sampling," *IEEE Signal Process. Mag*, vol. 25, no. 2, pp. 21-30, 2008.

[2] I. Daubechies, M. Defrise, and C. De Mol, "An iterative thresholding algorithm for linear inverse problems with a sparsity constraint," *Commun. Pure Appl. Math*., vol. 57, no. 11, pp. 1413–1457, 2004.

[3] A. Massa, P. Rocca, and G. Oliveri, "Compressive sensing in electromagnetics - A review." *IEEE Antennas Propag. Mag.*, vol. 57, no. 1, pp. 224-238, 2015.

[4] A. Desmal, and H. Bagci, "Shrinkage-thresholding enhanced Born iterative method for solving 2D inverse electromagnetic scattering problem," *IEEE Trans. Antennas Propag.*, vol. 62, no. 7, pp. 3878-3884, 2014.

[5] A. Desmal and H. Bagci, "A preconditioned inexact Newton method for nonlinear sparse electromagnetic imaging," *IEEE Geosci. Remote Sens. Lett.*, vol. 12, no. 3, pp. 532-536, 2015.

[6] A. Desmal, and H. Bagci, "Sparse electromagnetic imaging using nonlinear Landweber iterations," *Progress in Electromagnetics*, vol. 152, pp. 77-93, 2015.

[7] A. J. Tropp and A. C. Gilbert, "Signal recovery from random measurements via orthogonal matching pursuit," *IEEE Trans. Inf. Theory*, vol. 53, no. 12 ,pp. 4655-4666, 2007

[8] D. Needell and J. A. Tropp, "CoSaMP: Iterative signal recovery from incomplete and inaccurate samples," *Appl. Comput. Harmon. Anal.*, vol. 26, no. 3, pp. 301–321, May 2009.

[9] R. V. Senyuva, O. Ozdemir, G. K. Kurt, and E. Anarım,, "Electromagnetic imaging of closely spaced objects using matching pursuit based approaches," *IEEE Antennas Wireless Propag. Lett.*, vol. 15, pp.1179-1182, 2016.

[10] L. Pan, X. Chen and S. P. Yeo, "A compressive-sensing-based phaseless imaging method for point-like dielectric objects," *IEEE Trans. Antennas Propag.*, vol. 60, no. 11, pp. 5472-5475, Nov. 2012.

[11] T. C. Ye, and S. Y. Lee, and S. Y. March, "Non-iterative exact inverse scattering using simultaneous orthogonal matching pursuit (S-OMP)," in Proc. *IEEE Int. Conf. Acoustics, Speech and Signal* Process., pp. 2457-2460, 2008.

A Comparison of Numerical Mode-Matching Techniques for the Analysis of Well-Logging Tools

Guilherme S. Rosa, Maiquel S. Canabarro and José R. Bergmann
Center for Telecommunications Studies
Pontifical Catholic University of Rio de Janeiro
Rio de Janeiro, RJ 22451-900, Brazil
guilhermesimondarosa@cetuc.puc-rio.br,
canabarro@cetuc.puc-rio.br, bergmann@cetuc.puc-rio.br

Fernando L. Teixeira
ElectroScience Laboratory
The Ohio State University
Columbus, OH 43212, USA
teixeira.5@osu.edu

***Abstract*—Two numerical mode-matching (NMM) techniques are compared for the analysis of logging-while-drilling (LWD) tools within borehole crossing in geophysical formations. The logging tools as well as the borehole and the surrounding geophysical formation are modeled as a stratified medium in cylindrical coordinates. One NMM technique perform a vertical expansion of the fields and a mode-matching is used to incorporate the radial stratifications. In the second NMM formulation, the fields are first expanded in radial direction and subsequently matched along each axial boundary. We present validation results and a preliminary analysis of the accuracy of these two NMM approaches to model typical well-logging tools used for hydrocarbon exploration.**

Keywords*—*well logging; numerical mode-matching; logging-while-drilling

I. Introduction

The numerical mode-matching (NMM) technique [1]-[5] can efficiently model three-dimensional (3-D) structures by means of a one-dimensional (1-D) modal expansion (typically found by means of a numerical method such as finite-differences (FD) or finite elements (FE)) in combination with an analytical boundary matching.

Logging-while-drilling (LWD) tools, as those illustrated in Fig. 1, are commonly modeled using a NMM formulation [1], [2], [6], whereby a FE discretization is used along each horizontal layer of a cylindrical stratified medium. In the vertical directions, an analytical mode-matching procedure is then used to match the fields between each horizontal layer. This approach will be denoted here as axial NMM (A-NMM). This approach is computationally much more efficient than 3-D brute-force techniques such as FD, FE and finite volumes [7]-[11], and, as such, it is more suited for integration into reconstruction (inversion) algorithms.

A typical LWD tool moves with the downhole drilling so that, at each new tool position along the well, it is necessary to recalculate several matrices incorporating the reflections from the horizontal layers above and below the source and the receiving antennas. This is a drawback of the A-NMM, as pointed out in [12]. In [12]-[15], an alternative NMM approach was proposed to circumvent this issue in LWD applications. As both transmitting and receiving LWD antennas are placed around a metallic mandrel inside the borehole and typically have the same radius, they are located in the same radial layer regardless of the the axial position of the tool in the logging well. Therefore, it becomes more efficient to first perform a mode expansion of the fields along vertical direction and then a mode-matching along each radial layer. This approach will be denoted here as R-NMM. Although the R-NMM presents a series of advantages to model smooth holes, in this paper we shown that the presence of roughness in the borehole wall (see Fig. 1b) can significantly affect the efficiency of this NMM approach.

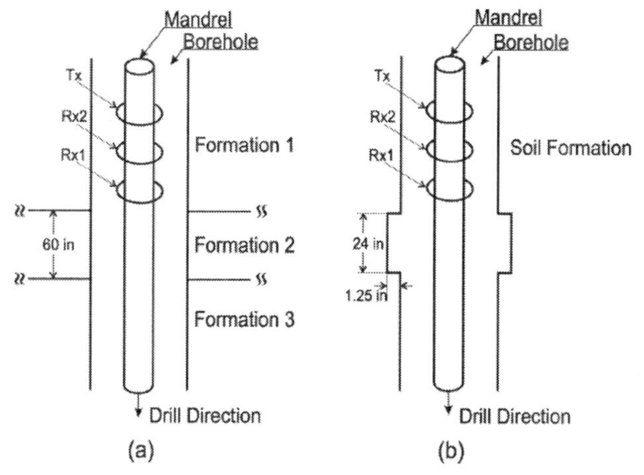

Fig. 1. Geometry of a triaxial LWD tool placed around a metalic mandrel. A three-vertical-layer formation with a smooth borehole is illustrated in (a) while a logging well with hole rugosity is depicted in (b).

II. Formulation Overview

In our R-NMM algorithm we employ a methodology similar to that presented in [8], [15], but using instead cubic B-splines functions to expand the fields in the axial direction, with multiple knots to improve the fields representation near the axial interfaces. In this way, a coarser mesh can be used while maintaining the same accuracy. The A-NMM implementation employed here follows [1], [4], [5] but instead of expanding the fields along the radial direction using local basis function, it uses a judicious choice of cylindrical eigenfunctions.

III. RESULTS AND DISCUSSION

We first consider a smooth borehole traversing an Earth formation with three horizontal layers, as shown in Fig. 1a. The LWD tool consist of one transmitter operating at 500 kHz and two receiver coil antennas. The axial positions of the transmitter, and receivers RX2 and RX1 are z_T, z_T+24 [in] and z_T +30 [in], respectively, where 1 [in] = 2.54 x 10^{-2} m. The conductivity of formations 1, 2 and 3 are 1 S/m, 0.01 S/m and 1 S/m, respectively. The borehole is filled with a lossy mud with conductivity equal to 2 S/m. For more details on this geometry, see [7], [8]. Fig. 2 shows the ratio of the RX2 and RX1 voltages (e.m.f.). Good agreement is observed among the R-NMM and A-NMM results and those from [7]. Since there is no variation on the borehole diameter, the R-NMM is a more natural choice to solve this problem.

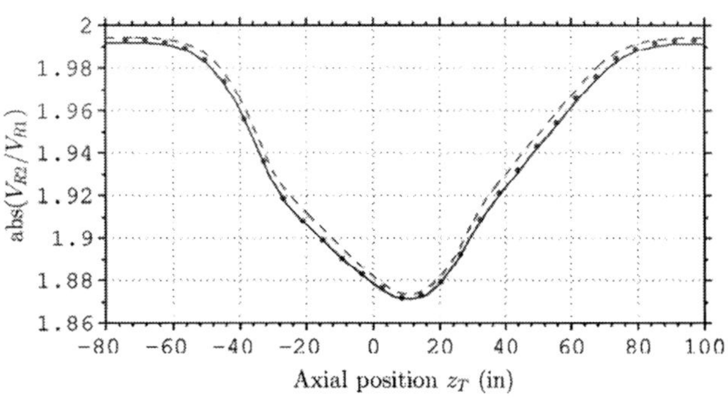

Fig. 2. Voltage amplitude ratio for a triaxial LWD logging tool operating at 500 kHz inside a smoth borehole. The results from the R-NMM and A-NMM are indicated by solid and dashed lines, respectively. The small dots are results from [7].

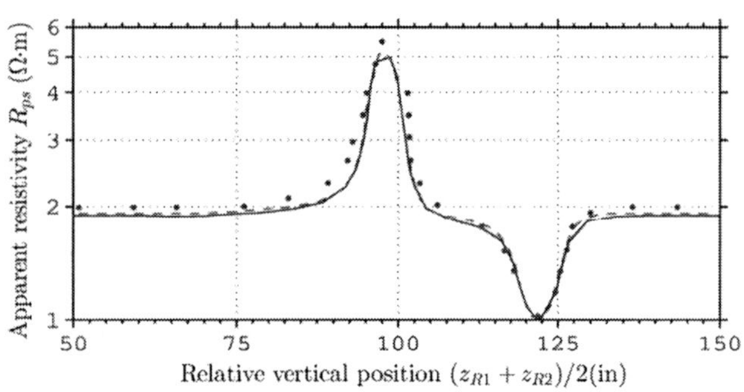

Fig. 3. Voltage amplitude ratio for a triaxial LWD logging tool operating at 2 MHz inside a rugose borehole. The results from the R-NMM and A-NMM are indicated by solid and dashed lines, respectively. The small dots are results from [16].

Next, we consider the effects of roughness on the borehole wall, as depicted in Fig. 1b. The LWD tool operates at 2 MHz, and again we consider one transmitter and two receiving coil antennas axially placed at z_T, z_T+28 in and z_T+34 in, respectively, inside a borehole with resistivity 0.1 Ω.m, surrounded by a soil formation with resistivity 2 Ω.m. For more details on this geometry, see [16]. Again, good agreement are observed between both R-NMM and A-NMM approaches versus those in [16], but differently to the smooth borehole wall case, the A-NMM appears more suitable to model rough borehole problems. By incorporated multiple knots at discontinuities in the R-MMM, better agreement is obtained with less overall number of knots.

ACKNOWLEDGMENT

G. S. R. and M. S. C. thank support from the Brazilian Agencies CNPq and CAPES through the doctoral fellowships 140236/2013-9, 141847/2016-6, 000316/2015-06, 2444/2011-9 and 150454/2016-3.

REFERENCES

[1] W. C. Chew *et al.*, "Diffraction of axisymmetric waves in a borehole by bed boundary discontinuities," *Geophys.*, vol. 49, pp. 1586–1595, 1984.

[2] W. C. Chew and B. Anderson, "Propagation of electromagnetic waves through geological beds in a geophysical probing environment," *Radio Sci.*, vol. 20, pp. 611–621, 1985.

[3] W. C. Chew, *Waves and Fields in Inhomogeneous Media*. New York, NY, USA: Van Nostrand Reinhold, 1990.

[4] Q. H. Liu and W. C. Chew, "Diffraction of nonaxisymmetric waves in cylindrically layered media by horizontal discontinuities," *Radio Sci.*, vol. 27, no. 5, pp. 569–581, 1992.

[5] Q.-H. Liu, "Electromagnetic field generated by an off-axis source in a cylindrically layered medium with an arbitrary number of horizontal discontinuities," *Geophys.*, vol. 58, pp. 616–625, 1993.

[6] H. Wang, H. Tao, J. Yao, and Y. Zhang, "Efficient and reliable simulation of multicomponent induction logging response in horizontally stratified inhomogeneous ti formations by numerical mode matching method," *IEEE Trans. Geosci. Remote Sens.*, vol. 50, no. 9, pp. 3383--3395, Sep. 2012.

[7] Y.-K. Hue and F. L. Teixeira, "FDTD simulation of MWD electromagnetic tools in large-contrast geophysical formations," *IEEE Trans. Magn.*, vol. 40, pp. 1456–1459, Mar. 2004.

[8] Y.-K. Hue, F. L. Teixeira, L. San Martin, and M. Bittar, 'Three-dimensional simulation of eccentric LWD tool response in boreholes through dipping formations,' *IEEE Trans. Geosci. Remote Sens.*, vol. 43, no. 2, pp. 257-268, 2005.

[9] H. O. Lee and F. L. Teixeira, "Cylindrical FDTD analysis of LWD tools through anisotropic dipping-layered earth media," *IEEE Trans. Geosci. Remote Sens.*, vol. 45, pp. 383–388, 2007.

[10] L. Hui, S. Y. Ze, and Z. X. Fang, "Numerical simulation of resistivity LWD tool based on higher-order vector finite element," *Journal of Petroleum Exploration and Production Technology*, pp.1–11, 2015.

[11] M. S. Novo, L. C. da Silva, and F. L. Teixeira, "Three-dimensional finite-volume analysis of directional resistivity logging sensors," *IEEE Trans. Geosci. Remote Sens.*, vol. 48, no. 3, pp. 1151–1158, Mar. 2010.

[12] D. M. Pai, "Induction log modeling using vertical eigenstates," *IEEE Trans. Geosci. Remote Sens.*, vol. 29, no. 2, pp. 209–213, Mar. 1991.

[13] D. M. Pai, J. Ahmad, and W. D. Kennedy, "Two-dimensional induction log modeling using a coupled-mode, multiple-reflection series method," *Geophysics*, vol. 58, no. 4, pp. 466–474, Apr. 1993.

[14] J. Li and L. C. Shen, "Vertical eigenstate method for simulation of induction and MWD resistivity tools," *IEEE Trans. Geosci. Remote Sens.*, vol. 31, no. 2, pp. 399–406, Mar. 1993.

[15] Y.-K. Hue and F. L. Teixeira, "Numerical mode-matching method for tilted-coil antennas in cylindrically layered anisotropic media with multiple horizontal beds," *IEEE Trans. Geosci. Remote Sens.*, vol. 45, pp. 2451–2462, 2007.

[16] B. Clark et al., "A Dual Depth resistivity measurement for FEWD," in *SPWLA Twenty-Ninth Annual Logging Symposium*, June 5–8, 1988.

Novel Complementary Metasurfaces for the Orbital Angular Momentum Generation

Menglin L.N. Chen, Li Jun Jiang, and Wei E.I. Sha
Electrical and Electronic Engineering Department
The University of Hong Kong, Hong Kong
menglin@connect.hku.hk

Abstract—**Besides amplitude, phase and polarization, wavefront is an important property of electromagnetic (EM) waves. EM waves with twisted wavefronts are known to carry orbital angular momentum (OAM). In this paper, a complementary-type metasurface is proposed to generate an OAM beam at microwave regime. Two metasurfaces that can produce OAM of order 2 and 4 are designed. By using our novel design methods,which are based on circuit model and dyadic Green's function, a high conversion efficiency has been achieved with a very low profile.**

I. Introduction

In 1992, Allen proved that the Laguerre-Gaussian beam, which has the azimuthal phase dependence carries orbital angular momentum (OAM) [1]. OAM offers a new degree of freedom extending beyond the existing wave feature and allows for promising applications in communications [2].

Recently, the metasurface concept is developed and various metasurfaces have been proposed to achieve low-profile designs to manipulate the electromagnetic (EM) waves in various aspects, including the OAM generation. However, the conversion efficiencies of these metasurfaces are usually low. At microwave frequencies, apart from the efficiency issue, simulation of the whole designed aperture with the complicated fine structures and large simulation domain result in a long simulation time.

In this paper, we propose an ultrathin complementary metasurface composed of sub-wavelength scatterers to produce OAM with high efficiency. On one hand, the design of the scatterers is based on equivalent circuit model. On the other hand, according to equivalence principle, these scatterers are replaced by equivalent magnetic dipoles and their EM response is calculated with the help of magnetic dyadic Green's function. The simplified model is validated by comparing to the full-wave simulation results.

II. Methodology

We consider an EM wave propagating along the z direction. To model the EM response of a scatterer, a transmission matrix is constructed to connect the transmitted field ($E^t_{x,y}$) to the incident field ($E^i_{x,y}$):

$$\begin{pmatrix} E^t_x \\ E^t_y \end{pmatrix} = \begin{pmatrix} T_{xx} & T_{xy} \\ T_{yx} & T_{yy} \end{pmatrix} \begin{pmatrix} E^i_x \\ E^i_y \end{pmatrix} = \mathbf{T} \begin{pmatrix} E^i_x \\ E^i_y \end{pmatrix} \quad (1)$$

If $T_{yy} = -T_{xx}$ and $T_{yx} = T_{xy} = 0$, a new $\mathbf{T}$ for an axially rotated scatterer with an angle of α is written as,

$$\mathbf{T}(\alpha) = T_{xx} \begin{pmatrix} \cos(2\alpha) & \sin(2\alpha) \\ \sin(2\alpha) & -\cos(2\alpha) \end{pmatrix} \text{(linear basis)} \quad (2a)$$

$$\mathbf{T}_{circ}(\alpha) = T_{xx} \begin{pmatrix} 0 & e^{-2i\alpha} \\ e^{2i\alpha} & 0 \end{pmatrix} \text{(circular basis)} \quad (2b)$$

Obviously, the EM wave will be changed from left (right) to right (left) circular polarization after its interaction with the scatterer. Additionally, an extra phase term $e^{\pm 2i\alpha}$ is introduced. By arranging the scatterers with spatially varying rotation angle α, $e^{\pm 2i\alpha}$ can be designed to coincide with the azimuthal phase dependence $e^{\pm il\phi}$ of an OAM mode. The order of the induced OAM is determined by $l = 2\alpha/\phi$.

III. Design

We propose a complementary scatterer as shown in Fig. 1. It consists of two types of complementary split-ring resonators (CSRRs) with different size and orientation. The fundamental resonances of the CSRRs in Fig. 1 (a) and (b) are excited by the y and x polarized waves, respectively.

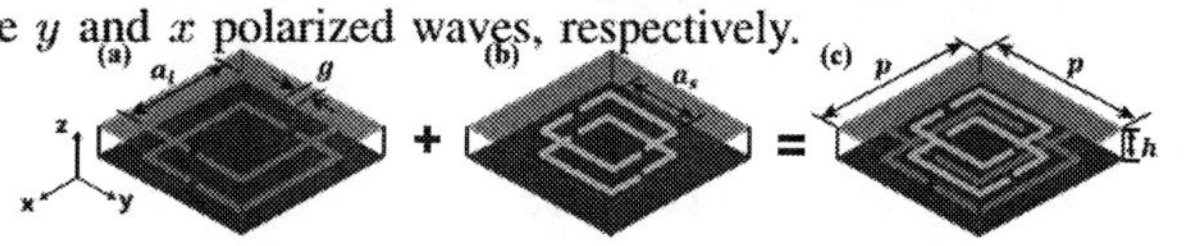

Figure 1. Schematic of the proposed scatterer. (a) the larger bi-layer CSRR; (b) the smaller bi-layer CSRR; (c) composite CSRRs.

The two types of CSRRs share the same equivalent circuit. Considering their bi-layer feature, two parallel inductor-capacitor (LC) circuits are used [3]. Fig. 2(b) shows the simulated S parameter based on the circuit model. At the frequency band of interest, the phase changes from 90° to −260°, which is much larger than the 180° phase change for a single resonator. In other words, the two LC circuits offer a sufficient phase coverage for design optimization.

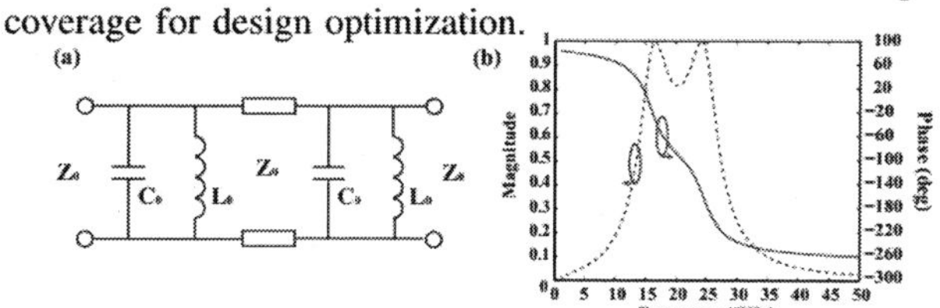

Figure 2. Equivalent circuit model of the scatterer in Fig. 1(a) and (b). (a) equivalent circuit; (b) simulated S_{21}.

Full-wave simulation is done in MWS CST. The results are shown in Fig. 3. The divergence between the curve shape and that from that in Fig. 2(b) is due to the high-order resonant mode of the CSRRs. Except for the fundamental half-wavelength mode, i.e. the one being considered in the equivalent circuit, the most significant mode is the full-wavelength resonant mode. The sharp phase shift in the phase curve imply the full-wavelength resonance. The periodicity of the unit cell isapproximated to be $0.4\lambda_0 \times 0.4\lambda_0$ at 17.85 GHz and the thickness is $0.048\ \lambda_0$. The proposed design has very low profile.

The metasurface is built by placing the designed scatterers with different rotation angle α. According to equivalent principle, the scattered field from CSRRs can be calculated by the equivalent magnetic currents distributed at the slots. We

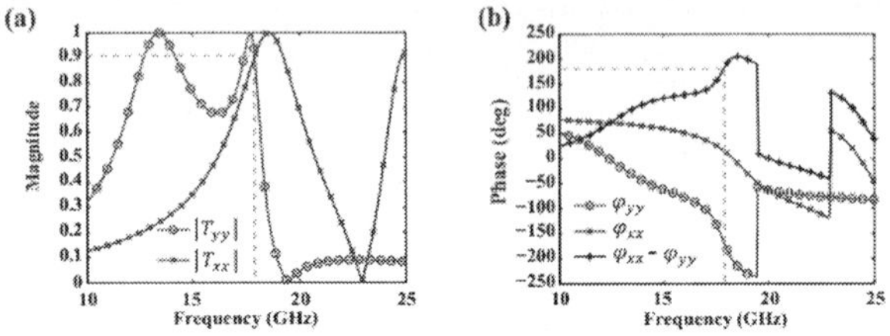

Figure 3. Simulated co-transmission coefficients of the proposed scatterer. (a) magnitude; (b) phase. The period of the unit cell is 7×7 mm^2. Side lengths of the two types of square CSRRs are $a_l = 5.2$ mm and $a_s = 3.9$ mm. The length of the gap is $g = 0.2$ mm. F4B220 is chosen as the dielectric substrate. The relative permittivity and thickness are $\epsilon_r = 2.2$ and $h = 0.8$ mm. The loss tangent is 0.003.

represent each scatterer as two orthogonal magnetic dipoles as shown by the arrows in Fig. 4. The EM response from the whole metasurface is then equivalent to that from magnetic dipoles with varying location, orientation and strength.

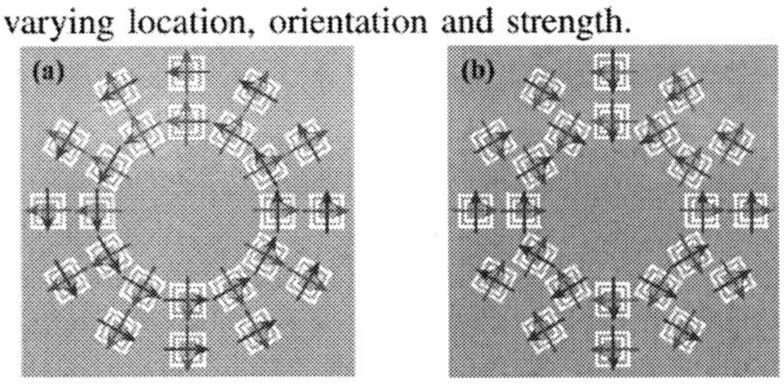

Figure 4. Top view of the metasurfaces and the equivalent magnetic dipoles for generating OAM of order (a) 2; (b) 4.

To start with, we write $\mathbf{T}$ for the CSRRs,

$$\mathbf{T}_l = \begin{pmatrix} -1 & 0 \\ 0 & 0 \end{pmatrix}, \quad \mathbf{T}_s = \begin{pmatrix} 0 & 0 \\ 0 & 1 \end{pmatrix} \tag{3}$$

where l and s stand for the larger and smaller CSRRs. The minus sign of the non-zero element in $\mathbf{T}_l$ is introduced based on the designed 180° phase difference between T_{xx} and T_{yy}.

The $\mathbf{T}$ for rotated CSRRs is written as,

$$\mathbf{T}_l(\alpha) = \begin{pmatrix} -\cos^2\alpha & -\sin\alpha\cos\alpha \\ -\sin\alpha\cos\alpha & -\sin^2\alpha \end{pmatrix} \tag{4a}$$

$$\mathbf{T}_s(\alpha) = \begin{pmatrix} \sin^2\alpha & -\sin\alpha\cos\alpha \\ -\sin\alpha\cos\alpha & \cos^2\alpha \end{pmatrix} \tag{4b}$$

At the incidence of circularly polarized wave, i.e., $\mathbf{E}_i = [1 - i]^T$, we obtain the expression of the equivalent magnetic dipoles, having both x and y components,

$$\mathbf{M}_l(\alpha) = \mathbf{T}_l(\alpha)\mathbf{E}_i = \begin{pmatrix} M_{l,x} \\ M_{l,y} \end{pmatrix} = -e^{-i\alpha}\begin{pmatrix} \cos\alpha \\ \sin\alpha \end{pmatrix} \tag{5a}$$

$$\mathbf{M}_s(\alpha) = \mathbf{T}_s(\alpha)\mathbf{E}_i = \begin{pmatrix} M_{s,x} \\ M_{s,y} \end{pmatrix} = ie^{-i\alpha}\begin{pmatrix} \sin\alpha \\ -\cos\alpha \end{pmatrix} \tag{5b}$$

Then, the scattered electric field from the equivalent magnetic dipoles $\mathbf{M}(\mathbf{r}')$ is calculated by,

$$\mathbf{E}(\mathbf{r}) = 2\int_V \overline{\mathbf{G}}_m(\mathbf{r},\mathbf{r}') \cdot \mathbf{M}(\mathbf{r}')d\mathbf{r}' \tag{6}$$

where $\overline{\mathbf{G}}_m(\mathbf{r},\mathbf{r}')$ is the magnetic dyadic Green's function.

In Fig. 5, we show the analytical and simulated phase patterns. As expected, phase changes 4π and 8π over a circle around the center for $l = 2$ and $l = 4$, respectively. The shift in the rotation ((c) vs (a); (d) vs (b)) comes from the different distance between the effective aperture and the plane for plotting. Compared to pattern with $l = 2$, the pattern with $l = 4$ shows a more significant difference from the analytical one. It is caused by the stronger high-order diffraction from each scatterer, resulting from the periodicity breaking in the azimuthal direction.

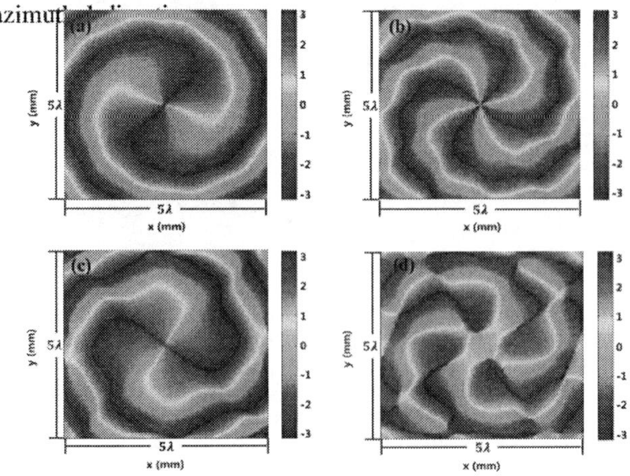

Figure 5. Phase patterns (in radian) of the cross-circularly polarized component of the electric field at a transverse plane of $z = 0.6\lambda_0$. (a,b) analytical results; (c,d) simulation results; (a,c) $l = 2$; (b,d) $l = 4$.

The EM energy is calculated by $U = \oint_A \mathbf{S} \cdot d\mathbf{A}$, where A is a closed surface and $\mathbf{S}$ is the Poynting vector. The conversion efficiency defined as the ratio of the OAM-wave energy to the total transmitted-wave energy is 81.8% for $l = 2$. But the ratio of the OAM-wave energy to the incident-wave energy is 15.2% and it is predicted to be 81% by the simulation results of the periodic unit cells in Fig. 3. This is because the periodicity along the x and y directions cannot be conserved and the truncation effect exists for the metasurface. By extending the two-circle metasurface in Fig. 4 to six-circle configuration, the efficiency is increased from 15.2% to 45%. For the case of $l = 4$, same trend can be observed. Therefore, it is reasonable to conclude that by increasing the number of scatterers, the conversion efficiency can be improved.

IV. Conclusion

In summary, an ultrathin complementary metasurface is proposed for OAM generation. The circuit model was established during the design process to reveal the working physics. The whole metasurface was modelled by the equivalent magnetic dipoles. Thanks to the complementary design, a high transmission efficiency can be potentially achieved for arbitrary-order OAM generation.

Acknowledgment

This work was supported in part by the Research Grants Council of Hong Kong (GRF 716713, GRF 17207114, and GRF 17210815), NSFC 61271158, Hong Kong ITP/045/14LP, and Hong Kong UGC AoE/PC04/08.

References

[1] L. Allen, M. W. Beijersbergen, R. Spreeuw, and J. Woerdman, "Orbital angular momentum of light and the transformation of laguerre-gaussian laser modes," *Phys. Rev. A*, vol. 45, no. 11, p. 8185, Jun. 1992.

[2] J. Wang, J. Y. Yang, I. M. Fazal, N. Ahmed, Y. Yan, H. Huang, Y. Ren, Y. Yue, S. Dolinar, M. Tur, and A. E. Willner, "Terabit free-space data transmission employing orbital angular momentum multiplexing," *Nat. Photonics*, vol. 6, no. 7, pp. 488–496, Jun 2012.

[3] J. Bonache, I. Gil, J. García-García, and F. Martín, "Artificial perfect electric conductor-perfect magnetic conductor anisotropic metasurface for generating orbital angular momentum of microwave with nearly perfect conversion efficiency," *J. Appl. Phys.*, vol. 119, no. 6, p. 064506, 2016.

A square slot circularly polarized microstrip antenna with enhanced bandwidth

Obeng Kwakye Kingsford Sarkodie
School of Electronic Engineering
Univ. of Electronic Science and Technology of china
Chengdu, China

Kang Kai, Mujeeb Abdullah
School of Electronic Engineering
Univ. of Electronic Science and Technology of China
Chengdu, China

***Abstract*—A square slot circularly polarized (CP) microstrip antenna with enhanced bandwidth is presented. The proposed antenna consists of a C-shape patch and four rectangular strips around the four corners on the lower ground, and is excited by a microstrip feedline. A broadband CP antenna can be achieved by adjusting the size of the strips. The measured results of -10 db impedance bandwidth is 157.2% (2-16.7 GHz) and the measured 3 dB axial ratio(AR) bandwidth is 62.2% (8.2-15.7 GHz). Measured and simulated results show good agreement.**

Keywords—antenna, axial ratio, circular polarization, square slot.

I. Introduction

In recent modern communication systems such as global positioning system, radio-frequency identification and wireless local area network, particular attention has been given to printed slot antennas due to their low cost, light weight and wider bandwidth. In [1], a lot of printed slot antennas are analyzed to give broadband circularly polarized characteristics. More than 38.2% wide-band axial ratio bandwidth (ARBW) can be attained in [2], where two inverted L strips around two opposite corners is employed to achieve circular polarization radiation. In [3], a series microstrip-line-feed configuration coupling to two orthogonal sides of the square-ring slot is deployed to excite a circular polarization wave. The reported axial ratio bandwidth is more than 6%. A protruding T-shaped metallic strip from the ground plane is found to produce a circular polarization radiation in [4]. The axial-ratio bandwidths can reach as large as 18%. An inverted-L tuning stub protruded from the signal line of the CPW is employed by [5] to radiate a CP wave. Axial ratio bandwidth greater than 30% is reported. A CP wave is found to radiate in [6] by employing a branched microstrip feed line to excite the monopole and the slot in parallel, with a 46.8% axial ratio bandwidth.

In this letter, a new simple structure is proposed, where a microstrip-line-feed with a C-shape radiation patch square slot antenna radiates a circular polarization wave at 10.5 GHz. The measured -10 dB impedance bandwidth is 157.2% (2-16.7 GHz)and the 3 dB axial ratio bandwidth is 62.2% (8.2-15.7 GHz). With simplicity in the antenna structure, it is suitable for easy integration in a wide varieties of wireless systems

A. Antenna Design

The structure of the proposed bandwidth enhancement CP antenna is shown in Fig. 1. The antenna consists of three parts, namely; an upper C-shape radiation patch, an FR4 substrate material where ($\varepsilon_r = 4.4, \tan\delta = 0.02$) with dimensions $50 \times 50 \times 0.8\ \text{mm}^3$, and a lower ground. The C-shape radiation patch is fed by a $50\ \Omega$ microstrip line ($L_1 \times W$) which is etched on the upper surface of the substrate. There

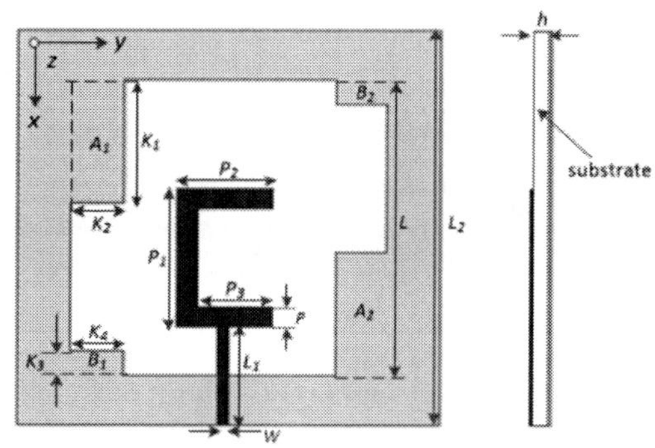

Fig. 1 Antenna structure
a. Top view
b. Side view

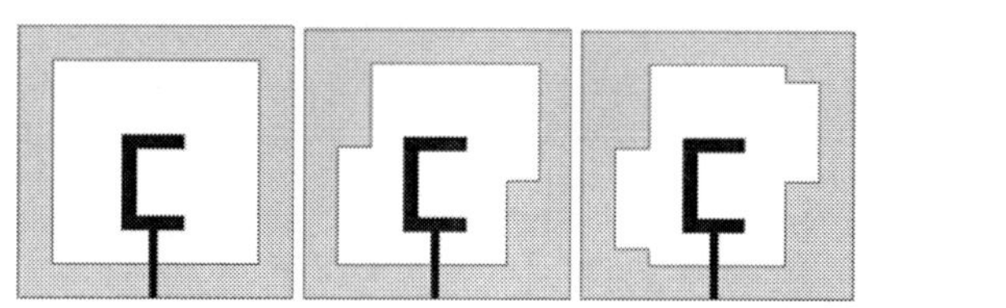

Fig. 2 Design steps to realize the proposed antenna (Ant. 1 - 3)

are four rectangular strips (A_1, A_2, B_1, B_2), where dimensions of $A_1 = A_2$, ($K_2 \times K_1$) and $B_1 = B_2$, ($K_4 \times K_3$), one at each corner of the lower ground. Fig. 2. depicts how the final structure of the proposed square slot CP antenna is achieved. Ant. 1 includes only the C-shape radiation patch. Ant. 2 includes two opposite but similar rectangle strips (A_1, A_2). Ant. 3 further includes two similar rectangular strips, (B_1, B_2) at the other opposite corners of the lower ground. Fig. 3 depicts the S_{11} and axial ratio bandwidths of the three antennas. All three antennas are circularly polarized. Ant. 1 has a poor S_{11}. After adding two opposite but equal rectangular strips (A_1, A_2), the impedance and axial ratio bandwidths are improved in Ant. 2. Two additional rectangular strips at the other opposite corners of the lower ground (B_1, B_2) greatly improves the impedance

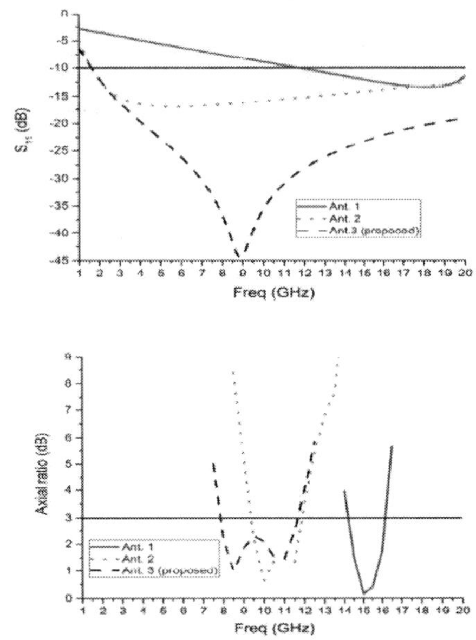

Fig. 3 S_{11} and axial ratio of the three antennas

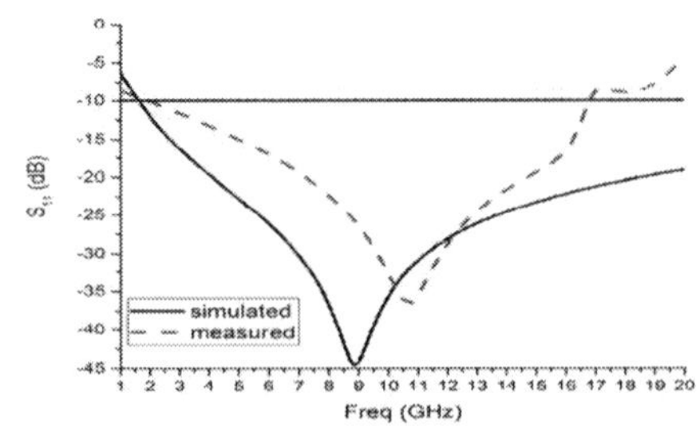

Fig. 4 Simulated and measured S_{11}

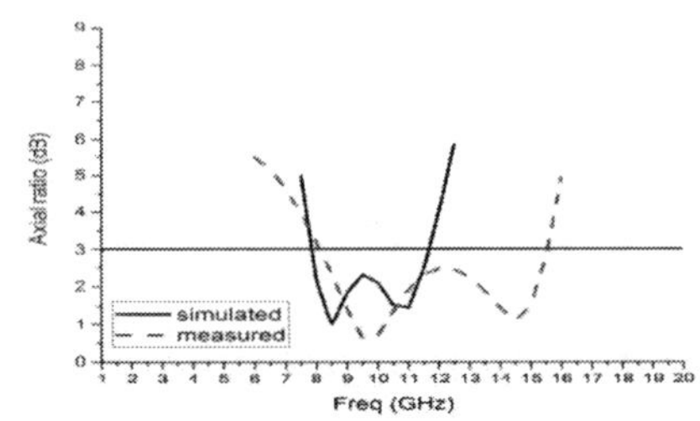

Fig. 5 Simulated and measured AR

and axial ratio bandwidths of Ant. 3.

B. Antenna Performance

The parameters of the proposed antenna are as follows: $L=38$, $L_1=12.5$, $L_2=50$, $P=3$, $P_1=18$, $P_2=11$, $P_3=8$, $K_1=15$, $K_2=6$, $K_3=3$, $K_4=6$, $W=2, h=0.8$; all units in mm. The performance comparison of simulated and measured return loss is shown in Fig. 4. The measured impedance bandwidth for $S_{11} < -10$ dB is 157.2% (2-16.7 GHz), whereas the simulated result is very wide, from 2 GHz to more than 40 GHz. Fig. 5 illustrates both the simulated and measured axial ratio bandwidth. The measured 3 dB AR bandwidth is 62.2% (8.2 - 15.7 GHz), whereas the simulated 3 dB AR bandwidth is 35.9% (8 - 11.5 GHz). Fig. 5 suggests that the measured 3 dB AR bandwidth is much greater than the simulated. The measured peak gain is 3.6 dBic at 10.5 GHz. The far-field pattern of the proposed antenna is shown in Fig. 6 (a) and (b). The figure depicts the normalized radiation patterns at 10.5 GHz in the *xoz*- and *yoz*-planes, which shows low side lobe levels and a -19 dB cross-polarization discrimination at beam peak. The simulated and measured results are in good agreement.

C. Conclusion

A square slot circularly polarized antenna with enhanced bandwidth is presented in this letter. Good agreements have been achieved between the measured and simulated results. The measured -10 dB impedance bandwidth is 157.2% (2 - 16.7 dB) and the 3 dB axial ratio bandwidth is 62.2% (8.2 - 15.7 GHz). Low side lobe levels and a -19 dB cross polarization levels at beam peak has been achieved. Due to the simple structure of the proposed antenna, it is suitable for easy integration in a wide varieties of wireless systems.

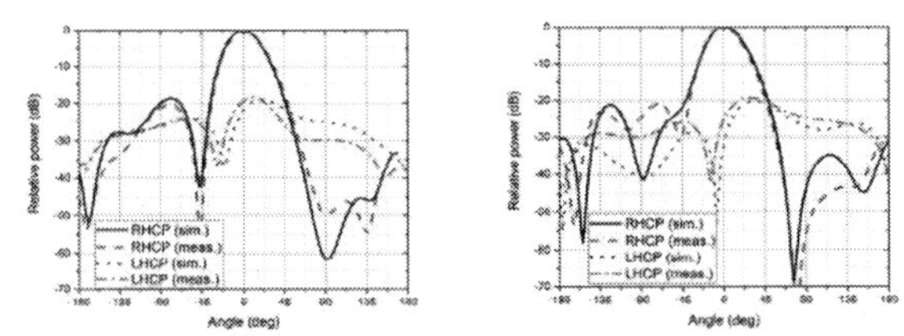

(a) *xz-plane* (b) *yz-plane*

Fig. 6 Measured and simulated radiation pattern of the proposed antenna at 10.5 GHz

REFERENCES

[1] Gao, S., Luo, Q., and Zhu, F.: "Antenna theory-analysis and design" (John Wiley & Sons, Ltd, 2014).

[2] Pourahmadazar, J., and Mohammadi, S.: "Compact circularly-polarized slot antenna for UWB applications," Electronics Lett., 2011, 47, (15), pp. 837-838.

[3] Row, J.-S.: "The design of a squarer-ring slot antenna for circular polarization," IEEE Trans. Antennas Propag., 2005, 53, (6), pp. 1967-1972.

[4] Sze, J.-Y., Wong, K.-L., and Huang, C.-C.: "Coplanar waveguide-fed square slot antenna for broadband circularly polarized radiation," IEEE Trans. Antennas Propag., 2003, 51, (8), pp. 2141-2144.

[5] Sze, J.-Y., Wang J.-C., and Chang C.-C.: "Axial ratio enhancement of asymmetric-CWP-fed circularly-polarized square slot antenna," Electronics Lett., 2008, 44, (18) pp. 1048-1049.

[6] Cai Yuan-Ming, Li Ke, Yin Ying-Zeng, Hu Wei, "Broadband circualrly polarized printed antenna with branched microstrip feed," Antenna and Wireless Propag., Lett., 2014, 13, pp. 674-677.

Boundary Integral Equation Study of the Influence of Finite Conductivity on Antenna Radiation Using a 3-D Differential Surface Admittance Operator

Martijn Huynen, Daniël De Zutter, Dries Vande Ginste
Department of Information Technology
Ghent University, Belgium
Email: martijn.huynen@UGent.be

***Abstract*—A novel method to simulate scattering and radiation from arbitrary materials, including good conductors, in a boundary integral equation (BIE) framework, is described in this contribution. The utilized technique relies on the differential surface admittance operator, which introduces an equivalent surface current density, effectively changing the antenna's material to that of the background medium. Constructed out of the volume's eigenmodes, the operator is employed to assess the radiation properties of a lossy Yagi-Uda antenna.**

I. Introduction

The impact of the finite conductivity on scattering and antennas has been a research topic for over half a century. Initially, approximate current distributions were utilized to include the imperfect conductors' effect for thin-wire antennas [1]. This method has since been replaced by employing a surface impedance boundary condition, such as the Leontovich boundary condition, to couple the exterior electric and magnetic field without solving the interior problem [2]. This technique is, however, not applicable in all situations due to fundamental limitations and assumptions [3]. The differential surface admittance operator can circumvent these shortcomings [4]. This operator defines a fictitious surface current density that replaces the material by the background medium. Subsequently applying adequate numerical techniques such as the method of moments (MoM), yields the surface current density. This approach has been applied to 2-D scattering problems [5] and was recently proposed in 3-D for scattering at relatively simple geometries in [6]. In this contribution, the Dirichlet-to-Neumann operator [4] is applied in 3-D to assess the impact of conductivity on the characteristics of a realistic antenna structure. In Section II, the differential surface admittance operator concept is introduced for 3-D problems and an expression composed of the eigenvectors of the volume is presented. Section III features the validation of the novel method by means of a lossy Yagi-Uda antenna's analysis.

II. Theory

We study the geometries in Fig. 1 assuming time-harmonic ($e^{j\omega t}$ dependence) electromagnetic fields. In Fig. 1(a) a homogeneous, non-magnetic material with wavenumber k is confined to the volume $\mathcal{V}$ with boundary surface $\mathcal{S}$ while the remaining, surrounding space is denoted $\mathcal{V}_0$ and defined by the

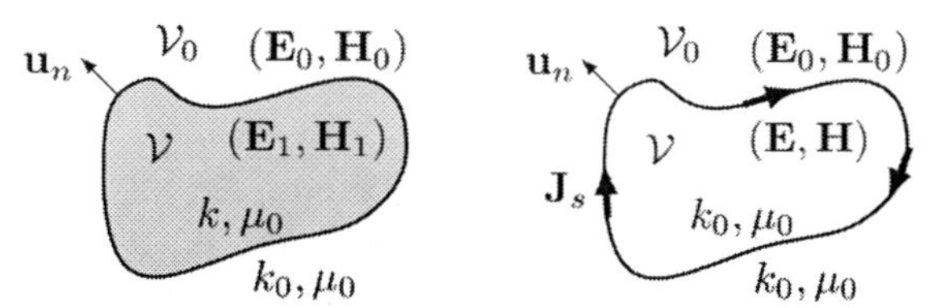

(a) Original situation. (b) Equivalent situation.

Fig. 1. (a) A homogeneous volume $\mathcal{V}$ with boundary $\mathcal{S}$ is embedded in another homogeneous volume $\mathcal{V}_0$. In (b), the inner material is replaced by the background medium and a surface current density $\mathbf{J}_s$ is introduced on $\mathcal{S}$.

wavenumber k_0. This outside region is governed by the fields $(\mathbf{E}_0, \mathbf{H}_0)$ while the inner region's fields are $(\mathbf{E}_1, \mathbf{H}_1)$. On $\mathcal{S}$, these quantities are related through the Dirichlet-to-Neumann (DtN) operator $\mathcal{D}_k$ as follows:

$$\mathbf{u}_n \times \mathbf{H}_1 = \mathcal{D}_k \mathbf{E}_1^t, \tag{1}$$

with $\mathbf{u}_n$ the outward pointing normal to $\mathcal{S}$ and the superscript t indicating the tangential component of a field. In the different, but similar case of Fig. 1(b), the inner material is replaced by the background material. The field quantities inside $\mathcal{V}$ are now given by $(\mathbf{E}, \mathbf{H})$. As before, a DtN operator on the boundary surface links these fields:

$$\mathbf{u}_n \times \mathbf{H} = \mathcal{D}_{k_0} \mathbf{E}^t. \tag{2}$$

In order to retain the same field distribution in $\mathcal{V}_0$, a surface current density $\mathbf{J}_s$ is introduced. Given the boundary condition

$$\mathbf{u}_n \times (\mathbf{H}_1 - \mathbf{H}) = \mathbf{u}_n \times (\mathbf{H}_0 - \mathbf{H}) = \mathbf{J}_s \tag{3}$$

and (1)–(2), we introduce the differential surface admittance operator $\mathcal{Y}$ in the following expression for the surface current density:

$$\mathbf{J}_s = \mathcal{Y}\mathbf{E}_1^t = \left(\mathcal{D}_k - \mathcal{D}_{k_0}\right)\mathbf{E}_1^t, \tag{4}$$

where the tangential continuity of the electric field at $\mathcal{S}$ is exploited. An expression based on the eigenfunctions of the volume $\mathcal{V}$ is derived in [6] and is given by

$$\mathbf{J}_s = \mathcal{Y}\mathbf{E}_1^t = \eta \sum_l \left[\frac{|k_l|^2 \int_{\mathcal{S}} (\mathbf{u}_n \times \mathbf{E}_1^t) \cdot \mathbf{h}_l^* \, \mathrm{d}S}{(k_l^2 - k^2)(k_l^2 - k_0^2)\mathcal{N}_l^2} \right] (\mathbf{u}_n \times \mathbf{h}_l). \tag{5}$$

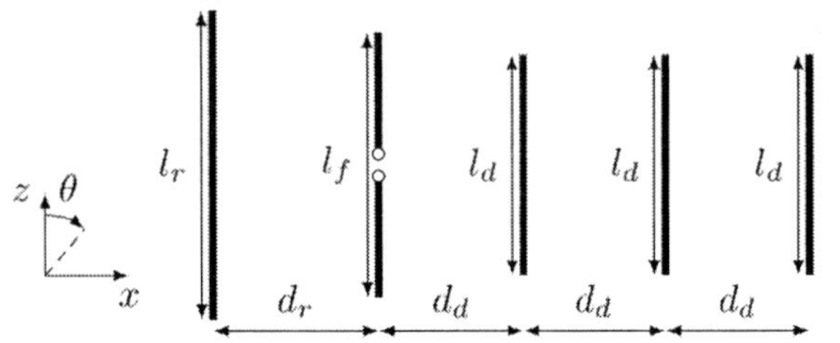

Fig. 2. Yagi-Uda wire antenna with dipole feed, one reflector and three directors. Dimensions for operation at 110 MHz can be found in Table I.

TABLE I
DIMENSIONS (IN m) OF THE ANTENNA IN FIG. 2.

Parameter	Value	Parameter	Value
l_f	1.332	r	0.001
l_r	1.348	d_r	0.8
l_d	1.12	d_d	0.637

The contrast parameter η is defined as $\left(k^2 - k_0^2\right)/j\omega\mu_0$, k_l is the wavenumber of the l-th eigenmode $\mathbf{h}_l$, the solenoidal magnetic eigenmodes of the volume $\mathcal{V}$ with normalization constant $\mathcal{N}_l^2$. These eigenvectors satisfy equations (10.13) and (10.14) in [7]. For general shapes, the eigenmodes have to be calculated numerically but for some simple, omnipresent shapes such as the cuboid or the circular cylinder, closed expressions can readily be found in literature. In order to solve for $\mathbf{J}_s$, the exterior problem has to be solved as well. A boundary integral equation method (BIE) such as MoM is ideally suited for this type of situation. Employing a standard discretization scheme to both the selected BIE and (5) results in a set of matrix equations that can be solved using regular techniques. A more detailed description of this procedure can be found in [6].

III. EXAMPLE

Consider the Yagi-Uda antenna displayed in Fig. 2. The driving component of this structure is a dipole antenna with length l_f. The remaining elements are of parasitic nature: one reflector with length l_r at a distance d_r behind the central dipole and three directors with length l_d which are placed in front with a spacing of d_d. All wires have the same radius r. Values for these parameters can be found in Table I for the Yagi-Uda operating at 110 MHz, i.e., the center frequency of the localizer in an instrument landing system (ILS). The gain of this configuration is calculated numerically by means of the differential surface admittance operator for circular cylinders for varying inclination angles θ in the vertical plane (xz-plane). This gain pattern is plotted in Fig. 3 for decreasing values of the skin depth $\delta = \sqrt{2/(\omega\mu\sigma)}$, i.e., for increasing conductivity σ. A reference solution for a perfectly electrically conducting (PEC) Yagi-Uda is obtained through 4nec2 [8], a free NEC based antenna modeler. Due to the inherent symmetry of the structure under study, only half the range of θ is shown. It is apparent that the antenna response evolves towards that of the PEC solution for decreasing skin

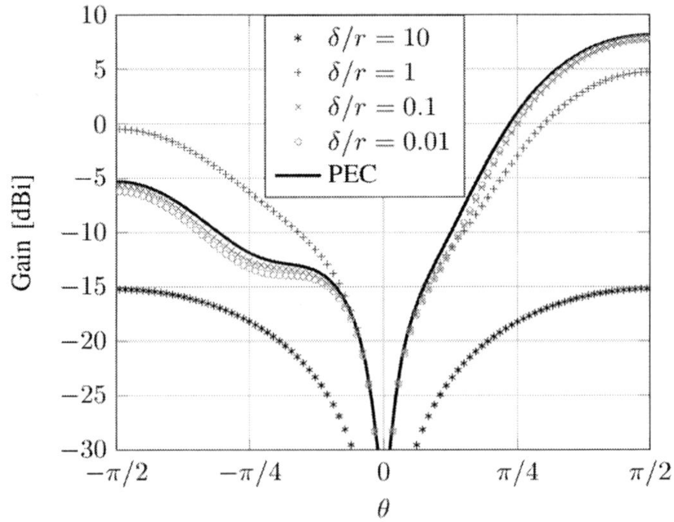

Fig. 3. Gain of the Yagi-Uda antenna at 110 MHz for various values of the skin depth. The reference PEC solution is obtained through 4nec2 [8].

depths. Moreover, it is shown that an insufficient conductivity detrimentally affects the antenna's characteristics. The remaining discrepancy between the solution for $\delta/r = 0.01$ and the PEC reference can be attributed to both the fundamental approximations of the reference solution, viz., thin-wire MoM, and the finite mesh of the employed method.

IV. CONCLUSION

In this paper, we have presented a 3-D differential surface admittance operator for the analysis of a realistic antenna configuration, i.e., a Yagi-Uda antenna used in ILS systems. Through incorporation into a BIE-MoM structure, the 3-D operator's appositeness to the assessment of material properties on antenna performance is demonstrated.

REFERENCES

[1] R. King and T. Wu, "The imperfectly conducting cylindrical transmitting antenna," *IEEE Trans. Antennas Propag.*, vol. 14, no. 5, pp. 524–534, Sep. 1966.

[2] L. Medgyesi-Mitschang and J. Putnam, "Integral equation formulations for imperfectly conducting scatterers," *IEEE Trans. Antennas Propag.*, vol. 33, no. 2, pp. 206–214, Feb. 1985.

[3] D.-S. Wang, "Limits and validity of the impedance boundary condition on penetrable surfaces," *IEEE Trans. Antennas Propag.*, vol. 35, no. 4, pp. 453–457, Apr. 1987.

[4] D. De Zutter and L. Knockaert, "Skin effect modeling based on a differential surface admittance operator," *IEEE Trans. Microw. Theory Techn.*, vol. 53, no. 8, pp. 2526–2538, Aug. 2005.

[5] H. Rogier, D. De Zutter, and L. Knockaert, "Two-dimensional transverse magnetic scattering using an exact surface admittance operator," *Radio Science*, vol. 42, no. 3, Jun. 2007.

[6] M. Huynen, M. Gossye, D. De Zutter, and D. Vande Ginste, "A 3-D differential surface admittance operator for lossy dipole antenna analysis," *IEEE Antennas Wireless Propag. Lett.*, 2016, Early Access. [Online]. Available: http://dx.doi.org/10.1109/LAWP.2016.2619558

[7] J. Van Bladel, *Electromagnetic Fields*. John Wiley & Sons, 2007.

[8] A. Voors, "4nec2: Antenna modeler," http://www.qsl.net/4nec2/, 2015.

Fast Multi-Criterial Statistical Analysis and Design Optimization of Compact Microwave Couplers

Slawomir Koziel[1,2] and Adrian Bekasiewicz[1,2]

[1] School of Science and Engineering
Reykjavik University, Reykjavik, Iceland
koziel@ru.is, bekasiewicz@ru.is

[2] Faculty of Electronics, Telecommunications and Informatics
Gdansk University of Technology, Gdansk, Poland

***Abstract*—A rapid statistical analysis and yield estimation of compact microwave couplers involving multiple performance parameters has been presented. The analysis is realized using a fast surrogate model representing appropriate characteristic points of the coupler response. Because of less nonlinear dependence of the characteristic points on the structure geometry (compared to the original response, i.e., *S*-parameters vs. frequency), a small number of training points is necessary to setup a reliable surrogate. Our approach is demonstrated using a compact rat-race coupler and validated using direct EM-based Monte Carlo analysis. Accelerated yield optimization is also presented.**

Keywords—Statistical analysis, uncertainty quantification, compact circuits, surrogate modeling, yield optimization.

I. INTRODUCTION

Nominal design of microwave structures assumes errorless fabrication and no uncertainty concerning material parameters. In practice, manufacturing tolerances have to be taken into account so as to increase the probability of satisfying given performance specifications under the assumed deviations of the design variables from their nominal values. This is referred to as robust or tolerance-aware design [1]. In order to enable computationally feasible design processes, fast statistical analysis methods are indispensable [2].

For the sake of reliability, performance evaluation of microwave structures has to be realized using full-wave EM simulation which is computationally expensive. Therefore, direct EM-based statistical analysis (e.g., Monte Carlo) is normally computationally prohibitive. The costs can be reduced by using surrogate modeling techniques [3], [4], polynomial chaos expansion [5], or principal component analysis [6].

Feature-based modeling and optimization (FBO) is an alternative approach to fast statistical analysis that has been proposed in [7]. It allows for reformulating the design problem in terms of suitably-defined response features which leads to simplifying the functional landscapes handled in the design process. Here, FBO is adopted for fast statistical analysis of microwave couplers. We take into account several performance parameters such as bandwidth, power split error and the phase response. FBO is also utilized for fast yield optimization. Our approach is demonstrated using a compact microstrip rat-race coupler and validated by direct EM-based Monte Carlo analysis.

II. UNCERTAINTY QUANTIFICATION AND YIELD OPTIMIZATION USING RESPONSE FEATURES

A. Yield Estimation Using Response Features

We denote by $\boldsymbol{R}(\boldsymbol{x})$ a response of an EM model of the structure of interest; $\boldsymbol{x}$ is a vector of designable parameters. We denote by $\boldsymbol{x}^0 = [x_1^0\ x_2^0\ \ldots\ x_n^0]^T$ a nominal design. Due to manufacturing tolerances, the actual parameters of the fabricated structure are $\boldsymbol{x}^0 + \boldsymbol{dx}$, where $\boldsymbol{dx} = [dx_1\ \ldots\ dx_2\ dx_n]^T$ is a random (e.g., Gaussian) deviation. We define a function [7]

$$H(\boldsymbol{x}) = \begin{cases} 1 & \text{if } \boldsymbol{R}(\boldsymbol{x}) \text{ satisfies the design specifications} \\ 0 & \text{otherwise} \end{cases} \quad (1)$$

The probability of satisfying the specs (referred to as yield) at the nominal design $\boldsymbol{x}^0$ can be calculated as [7]

$$Y(\boldsymbol{x}^0) = N^{-1}\sum_{j=1}^{N} H(\boldsymbol{x}^0 + \boldsymbol{dx}^j) \quad (2)$$

where the vectors $\boldsymbol{dx}^j$, $j = 1, \ldots, N$, are random samples as discussed above.

The major bottleneck of evaluating (2) is high computational cost as reliable yield estimation requires a large number of samples. Here, yield estimation is performed using using response features [7]. The coupler responses are highly nonlinear and narrowband so that building a reliable replacement model (surrogate) is difficult. However, dependence of coordinates of critical points extracted from S-parameter characteristics (such as those corresponding to –20 dB level, or $|S_{21}|/|S_{31}|$ at the operating frequency) on geometry parameters of the coupler is normally much less nonlinear, which permits construction of reliable local surrogate using just a handful of samples [8]. These points are sufficient to verify satisfaction/violation of the specs.

The feature-based surrogate is a second-order polynomial constructed for all relevant feature points and based on a so-called star-distributed training set containing $2n + 1$ points [8], including the nominal design, $\boldsymbol{R}(\boldsymbol{x}^0) = \boldsymbol{R}([x_{0.1}\ x_{0.2}\ \ldots\ x_{0.n}]^T)$, and at the perturbed designs $\boldsymbol{x}^k = [x_{0.1}\ \ldots\ x_{0.k} + \text{sign}(k)\cdot d_k\ \ldots\ x_{0.n}]^T$, $k = -n, \ldots, -1, 1, \ldots, n$. The size parameters $\boldsymbol{d} = [d_1\ \ldots\ d_n]^T$ correspond to the maximum assumed deviation of the design variables.

Let $\boldsymbol{p}_k^j = [f_k^j\ r_k^j]^T$, $j = 1, \ldots, K$, be feature points of the response vector $\boldsymbol{R}(\boldsymbol{x}^k)$, where f and r are their frequency and magnitude components; K is the total number of the relevant feature points. The feature-based surrogate is constructed as

$$\boldsymbol{s}^j(\boldsymbol{x}) = [s_f^j(\boldsymbol{x})\ \ s_r^j(\boldsymbol{x})]^T \quad (3)$$

where s^j is the model of the jth feature point p^j; $s_f^{\,j}$ and $s_r^{\,j}$ are models of its frequency and level coordinates.

The yield can be quickly estimated using (1), (2) with the surrogate (3) replacing the original EM model $\boldsymbol{R}$.

B. Yield Optimization

Feature-based surrogate can be used for accelerated yield optimization. Let $Y_s(\boldsymbol{x})$ be the yield estimated, at the design $\boldsymbol{x}$, using the surrogate model (3), and $Y_s(\boldsymbol{x};\boldsymbol{x}^0)$ be the yield estimated at the design $\boldsymbol{x}$ using the feature-based surrogate established at a design $\boldsymbol{x}^0$. Yield optimization works as follows ($\boldsymbol{x}^{(0)}$ is the initial design; $\boldsymbol{d}$ is the size vector):

1. Set $i = 0$;
2. Set up the surrogate model at $\boldsymbol{x}^{(i)}$;
3. Solve $\boldsymbol{x}^{(i+1)} = \arg \min_{\boldsymbol{x}^{(i)}-\boldsymbol{d}/2\le \boldsymbol{x}\le \boldsymbol{x}^{(i)}+\boldsymbol{d}/2} \{-Y_s(\boldsymbol{x};\boldsymbol{x}^{(i)})\}$;
4. Set up the surrogate model at the design $\boldsymbol{x}^{(i+1)}$;
5. If $Y_s(\boldsymbol{x}^{(i+1)};\boldsymbol{x}^{(i+1)}) > Y_s(\boldsymbol{x}^{(i)};\boldsymbol{x}^{(i)})$ then set $i = i + 1$ and go to 3; else END.

The cost of each iteration is $2n + 1$ EM simulations. Up to three iterations are sufficient in practice to converge to the optimum yield. The optimization process in Step 3 is constrained to the box of the size $\boldsymbol{d}/2$ around $\boldsymbol{x}^{(i)}$ to ensure reliability of the yield estimation.

III. Case Study

Consider the compact rat-race coupler (RRC) shown in Fig. 1 [9]. It is implemented on RF-35 substrate ($\varepsilon_r = 3.5$, $h = 0.762$ mm) and it is supposed to operate at 1 GHz. The designable parameters are given by: $\boldsymbol{x} = [l_1\ l_2\ l_3\ d_1\ d_2\ d_3\ w_1\ w_2]^T$, with relative variable $d_1 = d + |w - w_1|$ and dimensions $w_0 = 1.7$, $l_0 = 15$ fixed (all in mm). The EM model is implemented in CST Microwave Studio (~220,000 mesh cells, simulation time 15 minutes).

The nominal design of the coupler is $\boldsymbol{x}^0$ = [3.63 10.52 20.10 1.06 1.01 1.01 0.88 0.82]^T (optimized for maximum bandwidth, equal power split and zero-degree phase response at 1 GHz). Manufacturing tolerances are modeled using independent Gaussian distributions with zero mean and variance σ (Case I $\sigma = 0.017$ mm, Case II $\sigma = 0.033$ mm). The design specifications are: (i) –20 dB bandwidth ≥ 200 MHz (symmetric w.r.t. f_0), (ii) power split error ≤ 0.2 dB, (iii) phase error ≤ 0.5 degree. Table I shows the results of yield estimation obtained using feature-based surrogate and conventional EM-based Monte Carlo analysis (see also Fig. 2). The agreement between the two methods is very good. Table II shows the results of yield optimization using feature-based surrogate.

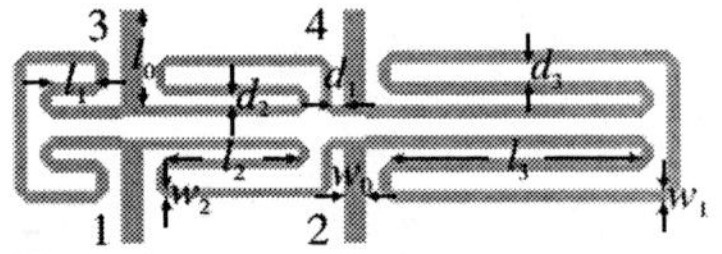

Fig. 1. Layout of the compact folded RRC.

TABLE I: YIELD ESTIMATION FOR COMPACT RRC

Case	Geometry Parameter Deviations	Yield Estimation Method	Estimated Yield	CPU Cost[1]
I	Gaussian $\sigma = 0.017$ mm	Feature-based (this work)	0.81	17
		EM-based Monte Carlo	0.77	500
II	Gaussian $\sigma = 0.033$ mm	Feature-based (this work)	0.46	17
		EM-based Monte Carlo	0.47	500

[1] Estimation cost in number of EM analyses. Feature-based yield estimation utilizes $N = 5000$ random samples.

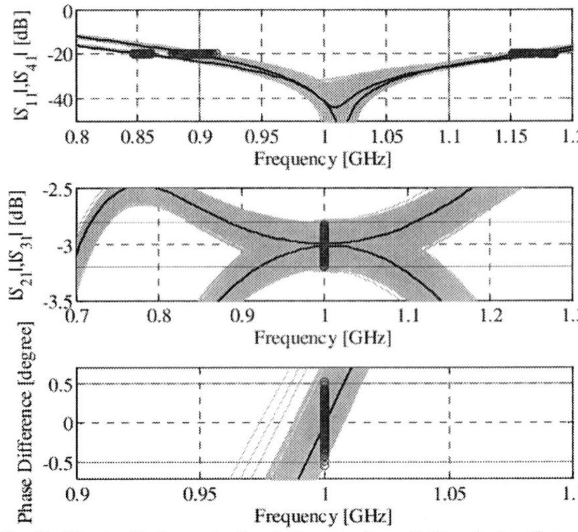

Fig. 2. Monte Carlo analysis of the coupler of Fig. 1 for Case I: EM simulations (gray plots) and feature-based surrogate (circles); nominal design shown in black. Design specifications marked with think lines.

TABLE II: YIELD OPTIMIZATION OF COMPACT RRC

Case	Parameter Deviations	Yield Estimation	Estimated Yield	Optimization cost (Number of EM antenna simulations)
I	Gaussian $\sigma = 0.017$ mm	Initial	0.81	51
		Optimized	0.97	
II	Gaussian $\sigma = 0.033$ mm	Initial	0.46	51
		Optimized	0.64	

Acknowledgment

This work is partially supported by the Icelandic Centre for Research (RANNIS) Grant 141272051 and by National Science Centre of Poland Grant 2014/15/B/ST7/04683.

References

[1] G. Scotti, P. Tommasino, and A. Trifiletti, "MMIC yield optimization by design centering and off-chip controllers," *IET Proceedings - Circuits, Devices and Systems*, vol. 152, no. 1, pp. 54-60, 2005.

[2] R. Biernacki, S. Chen, G. Estep, J. Rousset, J. Sifri, "Statistical analysis and yield optimization in practical RF and microwave systems," *IEEE MTT-S Int. Microw. Symp. Dig.*, Montreal, Canada, pp. 1-3, 2012.

[3] S. Koziel, J. Bandler, A. Mohamed, and K. Madsen, "Enhanced surrogate models for statistical design exploiting space mapping technology," *IEEE MTT-S Int. Microw. Symp. Dig.*, pp. 1-4, 2005.

[4] H.L. Abdel-Malek, A.S.O. Hassan, E.A. Soliman, S.A. Dakroury, "The ellipsoidal technique for design centering of microwave circuits exploiting space-mapping interpolating surrogates," *IEEE Trans. Microwave Theory Tech.*, vol. 54, no. 10, pp. 3731-3738, 2006.

[5] I.S. Stievano, P. Manfredi, and F.G. Canavero, "Parameters variability effects on multiconductor interconnects via hermite polynomial chaos," *IEEE Trans. Components, Packaging and Manufacturing Technology*, vol. 1, no. 8, pp. 1234-1239, 2011.

[6] J.S. Ochoa, and A.C. Cangellaris, "Random-space dimensionality reduction for expedient yield estimation of passive microwave structures," *IEEE Trans. Microwave Theory Techn.*, vol. 61, no. 12, pp. 4313-4321, 2013.

[7] S. Koziel and J.W. Bandler, "Rapid yield estimation and optimization of microwave structures exploiting feature-based statistical analysis," *IEEE Trans. Microwave Theory Tech.*, vol. 63, no., 1, pp. 107-114, 2015.

[8] S. Koziel and A. Bekasiewicz, "Rapid surrogate-assisted statistical analysis of compact microstrip couplers," *Int. Conf. Radar and Wireless Communications*, Krakow, Poland, May 9-11, 2016.

[9] S. Koziel, A. Bekasiewicz, P. Kurgan, and J.W. Bandler, "Expedited multi-objective design optimization of miniaturized microwave structures using physics-based surrogates," *IEEE Int. Microwave Symp.*, 2015.

A New Coplanar EBG Power Supply Layer Based on Zigzag Line for Adjacent Inductance Enhancing

Qiannan Xue, Ziyuan Wang, Yi Tian, Peng Wang
Tianjin Key Laboratory for Civil Aircraft Airworthiness and Maintenance, Civil Aviation University of China, Tianjin 300300, China

Ziyuan Wang
College of Economics and Manage, Civil Aviation University of China, Tianjin 300300, China

***Abstract*—Synchronous switching noise generated between the power supply and the ground plane of a high-speed digital circuit is considered to be one of the most important factors affecting the signal integrity of a circuit system. In order to suppress the synchronous switching noise (SSN), a new coplanar electromagnetic band-gap structure is proposed in this paper. Based on the zigzag line and square patch bridge, the inductance between the neighboring units can be enhanced. The results showed that the bandwidth of the band-gap is 0.1 ~ 12.6GHz when the depth of the NW-EBG structure is -30 dB. The relative bandwidth is about 48.7% and the cut-off frequency of the stop-band lower limit is reduced by 600MHz, compared to the same parameter of the L-bridge structure. The SSN on the power supply plane can be suppressed in all directions.**

Keywords—electromagnetic band-gap structure; high-speed digital circuits; synchronous switching noise; coplanar EBG

I. Introduction

With the rapid development of modern high-speed digital circuits, the operating frequency of the system clock is getting higher and higher. And according to the requirements of high power and low supply voltage, how to provide a clean power for the circuit system has become a major challenge in high-speed digital circuit system design. High-speed signal transmission on the interconnection, the signal transmission will be unstable caused by some noise, affecting the signal integrity (SI) and resulting in electromagnetic interference (EMI). Simultaneous switching noise (SSN) problem [1] not only reduces the noise tolerance of digital circuits, but also reduces the performance of analog circuits in mixed-signal systems. Conventional methods commonly used in the suppression of SSN circuit were that increasing the decoupling capacitors, power supply segmentation or designing through-hole location. Because of limited scope of application or the method too complex, these methods have not been widely used. In recent years, people gradually pay attention to use EBG structure for SSN suppression.

EBG structure was first proposed to be used in the antenna to suppress the surface wave. The EBG structure could better inhibit the spread of electromagnetic waves in a certain frequency range. So it has been used in high-speed printed circuit board (PCB) for SSN suppression. Several structures of the electromagnetic band-gap [2] were designed, such as mushroom-liked electromagnetic band-gap structure [3], Fork-like EBG, FTS-EBG and so on. The structure of the mushroom-liked electromagnetic band-gap has prominent advantages in suppressing synchronous switching noise. However, it makes the PCB board three-layer structure, the processing is difficult, the cost increased, and the frequency of suppressing synchronous switching noise is narrow, which limits the application in high-speed digital circuits. Therefore, there are more and more researches on coplanar electromagnetic band-gap structures.

This paper reported a novel coplanar EBG structure which is based on zigzag line for adjacent inductance enhancing. The zigzag line and the square patch bridge are used to construct the unit lattice to realize the new electromagnetic band-gap structure, which make the inductance between the neighboring units lattices enhanced. It could be expected to achieve better suppression characteristics for synchronous switching noise in a high-speed digital circuit.

II. Structure Design of New Coplanar EBG Power

A. Unit structure

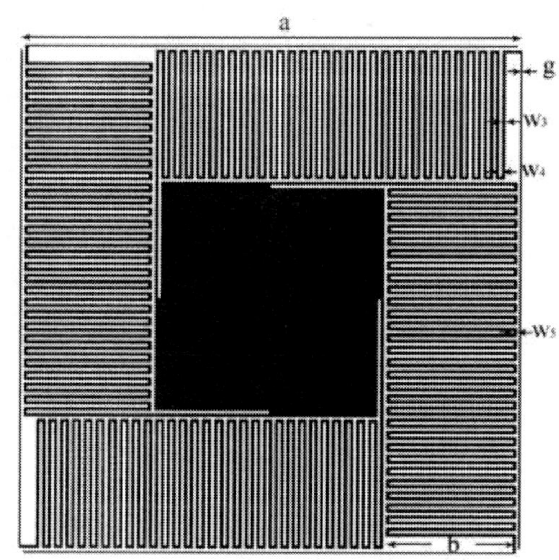

Fig. 1. The new structure design

The planar electromagnetic band-gap structure proposed in this paper is designed based on local resonance principle. Local resonant electromagnetic band-gap structure of the principle, mainly through the electromagnetic band-gap itself to form a periodic structure of local resonance band-gap, inhibit the propagation of electromagnetic waves nearby, which can inhibit the synchronous switching noise. The new coplanar EBG structure (NW-EBG) mainly increases the equivalent inductance L by increasing the bridge wire on the EBG structure, thus reducing the stop-band center frequency of the EBG structure, increasing the stop-band width of the EBG structure, and finally improving the suppression effect of the EBG structure on the SSN.

NW-EBG structure design size shown in Figure 1, where a = 30mm, b = 5.2mm, w1 = w2 = w3 = 0.2mm, g = 0.1mm, line spacing are 0.2mm. A double-layer PCB with 3 × 3 cell array was designed, and the EBG structure was embedded in the plane of the power plane. The new coplanar EBG structure was simulated by the Ansoft HFSS, and three lumped ports were set up as shown in the Figure 2(a). Port 2 and port 3 were set as output ports and port 1 was set as the input port. Figure 2(b) is the physical photo.

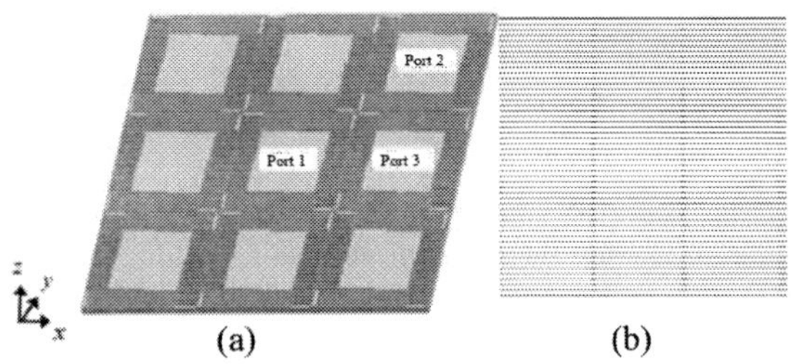

Fig. 2. (a), the 3D view and (b), PCB circuit physical photos

III. DATA ANALYSIS AND SIMULATION VERIFICATION

A. Comparison with typical L-bridge type EBG structure characteristics

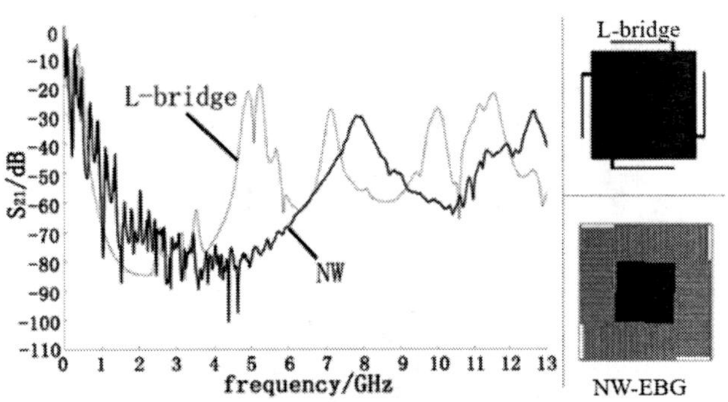

Fig. 3. Comparison of EBG and L-bridge EBG Characteristic Curve of NW Type Planar.

The L-bridge EBG structure is a typical electromagnetic band-gap structure. We compared the band-gap characteristics of NW-EBG and L-bridge-EBG. From Fig.3, it can be seen that the suppression frequency of NW-EBG is 0.1-12.6GHz, the band-stop bandwidth is 12.5GHz and the relative band-stop bandwidth is 196.9% when the suppression depth is -30dB, . Compared with L-bridge-EBG, the lower cut-off frequency of NW-EBG structure decreases from 700MHz to 100MHz, and the relative stop-band bandwidth increases from 148.1% to 196.9%, and the bandwidth is 48.8% of the 4GHz expanded to 12.5GHz. It can be seen that the NW-EBG structure can suppress the SSN at a lower operating frequency, and the inhibition range is wider than the L-bridge-EBG. That may because the longer bridge wire and the Zigzag structure make a bigger the equivalent inductance L of NW-EBG structure, and the suppression effect was suppressed.

B. Omnidirectional suppression performance of a new planar EBG structure

By comparing the basic trend of the S21 and S31 characteristic curves, it is proved that the electromagnetic band-gap structure can suppress the synchronous flip noise (SSN) between the power supply layer and the ground. Figure 4 shows the loss characteristics of port 2 and port 3 in the NW-EBG structure under different port outputs. It can be seen that the curves of S21 and S31 are basically consistent when the suppression depth is -30dB, which indicates that the NW-EBG structure can suppress the SSN in all directions.

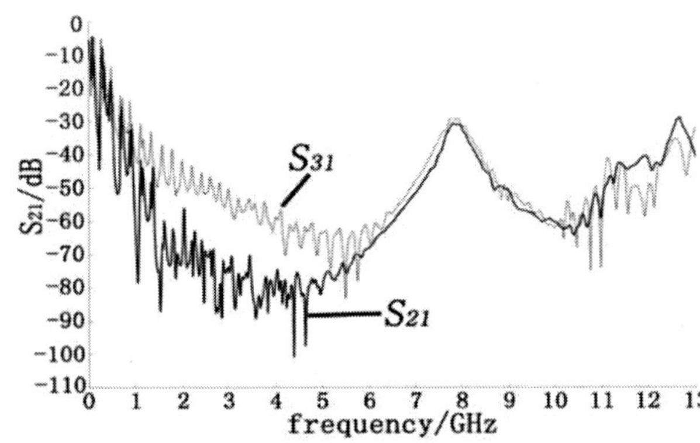

Fig. 4. Comparison of S21 and S31 Characteristic Curve of NW-EBG.

IV. CONCLUSION

In this paper, a novel coplanar EBG structure is proposed, which is applied to the plane of PCB power supply. The unit cell is composed of a combination of zigzag line and square patch, which could enhance the inductance between the neighboring units. Compared with the traditional L-bridge structure, the band-stop bandwidth is increased by 48.7% as shown from the simulation results. The novel coplanar EBG power supply layer structure has a lower suppression frequency, a wider suppression bandwidth, and can effectively suppress synchronous switching noise on the high-speed circuit all-directionally.

REFERENCES

[1] M.M. Bait-Suailam and O.M. Ramahi, "Ultrawideband Mitigation of simultaneous switching noise and EMI reduction in high-speed PCBs using complementary split-ring resonators," IEEE T. Electromagn. C., vol. 54, pp. 389-396, April 2012.

[2] M. A. Alshargabi, Z. Z. Abidin and M. Z. M. Jenu , "High speed PCB & spiral with patch EBG planar integration for EMI reduction," 2015 International Conference on Computer, Communications, and Control Technology (I4CT), 21-23 April 2015 .

[3] M. Zhang, J. Mao and Y. Long, "Power noise suppression using power-and-ground via pairs in multilayered printed circuit boards," IEEE T. Adv. Packaging., vol .1 , pp. 374-385, March 2011.

The Branch-Line Couplers Miniaturization Method with Microstrip Filters

Denis A. Letavin, Victor A. Chechetkin, Yury E. Mitelman
Institute of Radioelectronics and Information Technologies
Ural Federal University
Yekaterinburg, Russian Federation
v.a.chechetkin@urfu.ru

***Abstract*—the original layout of the microstrip branch-line 3-dB coupler with considerably smaller dimensions, compared to the conventional one, due to the use of a sequence of high- and low-impedance lines representing a lowpass filter is presented in this paper. Such filters have smaller longitudinal size than conventional microstrip line. The proposed design with a central frequency of 2000 MHz was simulated to obtain its frequency-dependent characteristics. The measured parameters of the manufactured prototype showed good agreement with simulation results. The proposed method allowed reduction of the occupied area by 68.5 % comparing to the conventional design.**

Keywords—miniaturization, microstrip line, lowpass filter, 3-dB coupler.

I. Introduction

3-dB coupler is a device with four ports, intended to divide power equally between two outputs, though the remaining output is decoupled (isolated). Such devices are one of the most important functional elements of variety of microwave devices, such as power dividers and combiners, balanced amplifiers, mixers, modulators, phase shifters. Interest in miniaturization of such devices is primarily due to the tendency of including microwave devices into integrated circuits, while maintaining their characteristics. For miniaturization of couplers the following well-known approaches are presented, e.g. quasi-lumped elements [1], periodic capacitive loads [2], asymmetrical T-structures [3], slow-wave structures [4], fractal lines [5], and high-impedance lines [6]. Typically, these methods do not allow preserving the characteristics of the device on the same level as for the conventional ones. The developed method allows keeping the miniaturized device characteristics in a wide bandwidth and has a relatively simple design procedure. The method is based on the replacement of the transmission line segment with a low pass filter (LPF) having the same phase response at the central frequency as the replaced segment. Recent authors' researches are also dedicated to the miniaturization of various power splitting devices [7]–[8].

II. The Proposed Procedure

Widely used microstrip 3-dB couplers have various design solutions. One of the most common designs of the branch-line coupler is a two-segment 50-ohm transmission line interconnected by 35-Ohm quarter-wave stubs.

The research was executed by the grant of the Russian Science Foundation (project № 14-19-01396).

In this paper, compact design of the microstrip coupler is investigated. The layout of the proposed coupler is designed for a central frequency of 2000 MHz. The proposed method of creating a compact coupler is based on the assumption that replacement of a quarter-wavelength transmission line with equivalent lowpass filter having a phase response of 90° at a desired frequency will reduce the device size. The substrate material was chosen to be FR-4 with dielectric constant $\varepsilon = 4.4$, $tg\delta = 0.02$ and thickness $h = 1$ mm.

The development consists of the following stages:

- Selection of the order and cut-off frequency of the microstrip lowpass filter with 50-Ohm ports so that the phase response of 90° is at the operating frequency of the device. This step includes synthesis of lowpass filter using AWR Design Environment software. Fig. 1 shows comparison of the electrical lengths of quarter-wavelength microstrip line and the corresponding LPF.
- A similar calculation for the 35-Ohm transmission line is performed. The comparison with conventional microstrip transmission lines is presented in Table 1.

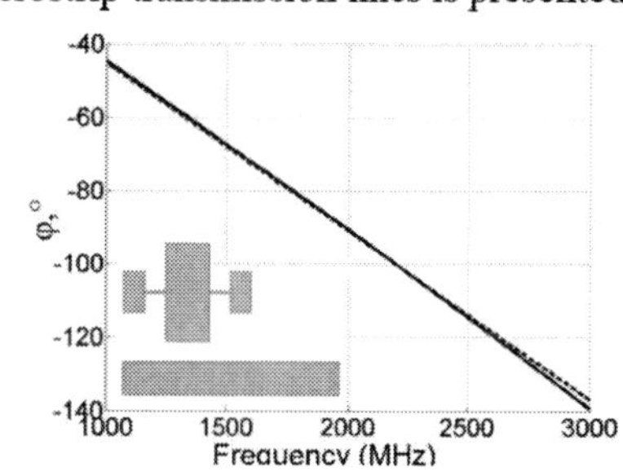

Fig. 1. Electrical lengths of microstrip line (continous) and the LPF (dashed)

TABLE I. Comparison of Lengths of Microstrip Transmission Lines and LPFs

		L, mm	W, mm
50 Ohm	Conventional line	24.7	1.86
	LPF	13.6	5.3
35 Ohm	Conventional line	24.1	3.2
	LPF	11.6	8.5

- Uniting filters into one circuit. For the further miniaturization, it is essential to make filters layouts asymmetric by moving the low-impedance segments to the inner area (Fig. 2). The resulting design consists of two pairs of identical filters of the 5th order.

Additional size reduction is provided by the usage of common end capacitors by the adjacent filters. The process of the design is complicated by the appearance of parasitic capacitances in the areas of close proximity of various elements of the LPFs. This makes it necessary to optimize the sizes of these elements, but only with a few iterations.

The simulation results of the proposed and conventional devices are shown in Fig. 3. Similarity in characteristics in the operating frequency band is obvious (at the isolation level of at least 20 dB).

The prototype based on the simulated layout with occupied area of 13.5 mm × 14.5 mm = 195.75 mm^2 (Fig. 4) was fabricated. The measured characteristics are presented in Fig. 5. The obtained parameters are in good agreement with the simulation results. Table 2 shows the comparison between the couplers designs.

It should be noted that the effectiveness of miniaturization depends on the chosen substrate, because LPF microstrip capacitors have capacity proportional to their area, and the thickness of the substrate, and inversely proportional to the dielectric constant of the substrate.

The area of the coupler is reduced by 68.5% and the bandwidth based on the isolation level of -20 dB is 196 MHz. The simulation results show the return loss (S_{11}) -14.5 dB on the central frequency of 2 GHz.

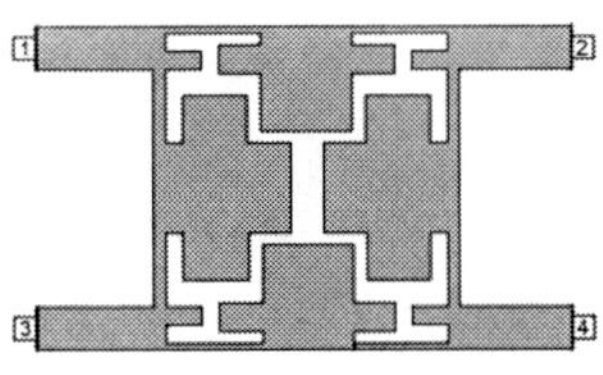

Fig. 2. The layout of the compact 3 dB coupler

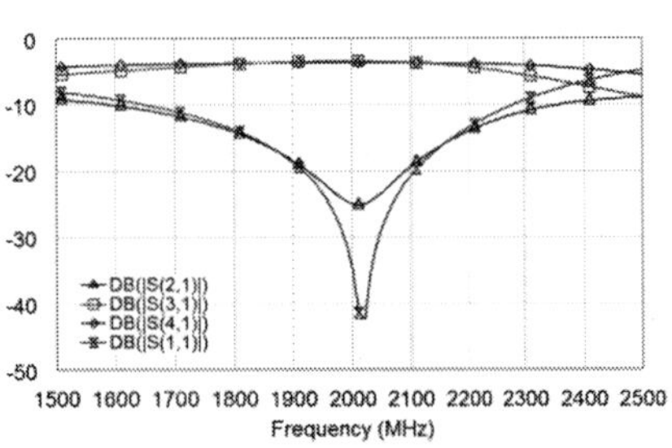

Fig. 3. The simulated S-parameters

TABLE II. COMPARISON OF THE DESINGS

Design	Isolation bandwidth, MHz@-20 dB	Area, mm^2
Conventional	220	622
Proposed	196	195.75

Fig. 4. Compact and conventional couplers

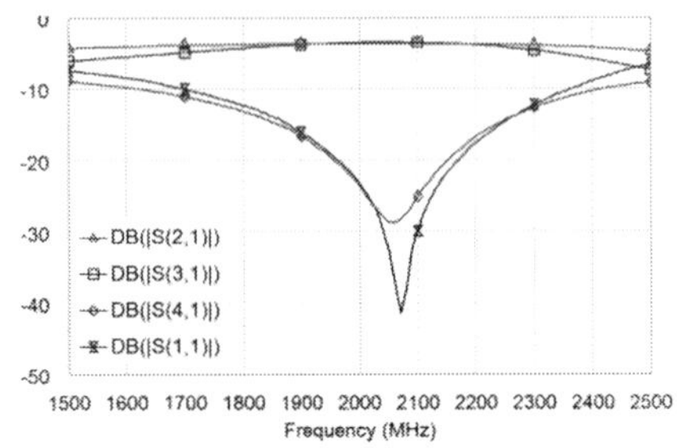

Fig. 5. The measured S-parameters of the compact coupler

III. CONCLUSION

The usage of lowpass filter instead of transmission line makes it possible to implement effectively miniaturized designs of microwave devices. The resulting layout of the compact microstrip coupler operating at a central frequency of 2 GHz is 68.5% smaller than the conventional one. The operating frequency band at the level of -20 dB isolation is reduced by 15%.

REFERENCES

[1] S.-S. Liao and J.-T. Peng, "Compact planar microstrip branch-line couplers using the quasi-lumped elements approach with nonsymmetrical and symmetrical T-shaped structure," IEEE Trans. Microw. TheoryTech.,vol. 54, pp. 3508-3514, Sep. 2006.

[2] K. W. Eccleston and S. H. M. Ong, "Compact planar microstripline branch-line and rat-race coupler," IEEE Trans. Microw. Theory Tech., vol. 51, pp. 2119-2125, Oct. 2003.

[3] S.-S. Liao, P.-T.Sun, N.-C.Chin and J.-T.Peng, "A novel compact-size branch-line coupler," IEEE Microw.WirelessCompon.Lett. vol. 15, pp. 588-590, Sep. 2005.

[4] J. Wang, B. Z. Wang, Y.-X.Guo, L.-C.Ong, and S. Xiao "A compact slow-wave microstrip branch-line coupler with high performance," IEEE Microw.WirelessCompon.Lett. vol. 17, pp. 501-503, Jul. 2007.

[5] H.Ghali, and T. A. Moselhy, "Miniaturized fractal rat-race, branch-line, and coupler-line hybrids," IEEE Trans. Microw. Theory Tech., vol. 52, pp. 2513-2520, Nov. 2004.

[6] C. W. Tang and M.-G.Chen, "Synthesizing microstrip branch-line coupler with predetermined compact size and bandwidth," IEEE Trans. Microw. Theory Tech., vol. 55, pp. 1926-1934, Sep. 2007.

[7] Letavin, D.A., Mitelman, Y.E., Chechetkin, V.A., "Investigation of the frequency influence on the miniaturization efficiency of microstrip devices using LPFs", 2016 10th European Conference on Antennas and Propagation, EuCAP 2016, DOI: 10.1109/EuCAP.2016.7481614.

[8] Letavin, D.A., Mitelman, Y.E., Chechetkin, V.A., "Realization of miniaturized branch-line coupler using lowpass microstrip filters", 2015 Loughborough Antennas and Propagation Conference, LAPC 2015, DOI: 10.1109/LAPC.2015.7366013.

Compact microstrip three-loop coupler

Denis A. Letavin
Institute of Radioelectronics and Information Technologies
Ural Federal University
Yekaterinburg, Russian Federation
d.a.letavin@urfu.ru

***Abstract*— In this work we have studied a design of a miniature three-loop quadrature coupler. Miniaturization of this device is performed by using artificial transmission lines providing the same functions as quaterwave sections. Numerical modeling has been carried out by using 3D electrodynamic modeling software, which allowed to take into consideration a great number of factors that can affect the performance of the device. The center frequency for the design process was set to 1,800 MHz. The operating frequency band begins at 1,605 MHz and ends at 2,012 MHz. The coupler proposed has a size 67.5% smaller than that of a standard design.**

Keywords—miniaturization, microstrip line, coupler.

I. Introduction

A coupler is a device with four inputs designed for coupling a half of the power from the main channel to the auxiliary channel. A loop coupler consists of two sections of microstrip transmission lines connected to each other with the help of two or more loop lines. The lengths and distances between those are equal to a quarter of the wavelength determined in the strip transmission line. It should be noted that with an increase of the number of loop lines the operating frequency range increases, but the longitudinal size of the coupler increases as well. Therefore, such devices occupy a lot of space, especially at low frequencies, which is why miniaturization of such couplers represents a matter of great interest. Scientific literature currently covers a wide variety of microwave coupler miniaturization methods, such as quasi-lumped elements [1], periodic capacitive loads [2], asymmetrical T-structures [3], slow-wave structures [4], fractal lines [5], high-impedance lines [6], low-pass filter [7-9], retarding structures [10,11]. However, it should be said that not all the methods listed are characterized by simplicity of compact design development, compactness and maintaining the device performance at the level of a regular design. This work is devoted to three-loop coupler miniaturization that allows to maintain the device performance within a broad enough frequency band and at the same time has a technologically realizable size.

II. The Proposed Procedure

First, before the miniaturization process, we developed a standard design of a three-loop coupler. The most widespread design of such coupler consists of two 35-Ohm transmission lines connected with a 35-Ohm loop line in the middle and with two 120-Ohm loop lines on the sides. All the distances and sections are equal to a quarter of the wavelength in the line and have a phase shift of 90 degrees. The whole procedure of the coupler designing was performed using AWR DE software. FR-4 with dielectric permittivity $\varepsilon = 4.4$, dielectric loss angle tangent $tg\delta = 0.02$ and thickness h=1 mm was chosen as the substrate material. Modeling of electrodynamic structures is performed using AWR DE 12. Standard three-loop coupler are shown in Fig. 1The results of numerical modeling of a standard three-loop coupler are shown in Fig. 2.

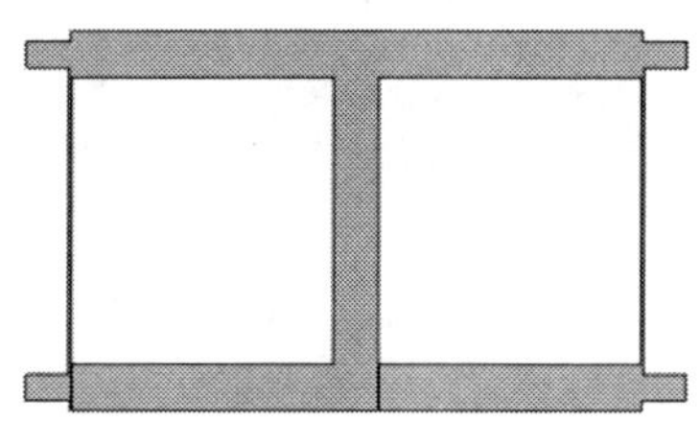

Fig. 1. The layout of the standard 3 dB coupler

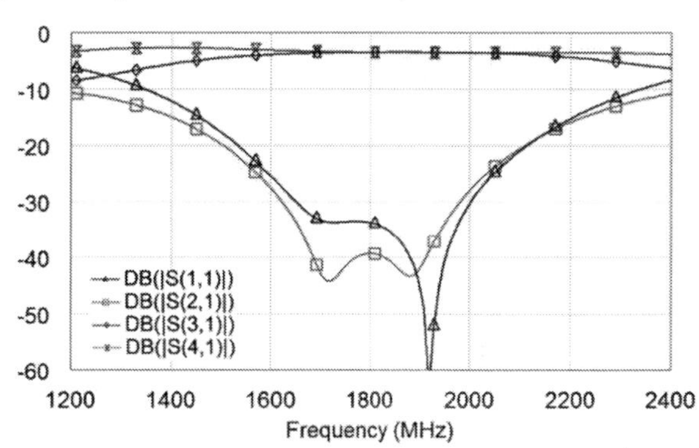

Fig. 2. Simulated S-parameters of the standard three-loop

The characteristics obtained demonstrate that the center frequency of the device is 1800 MHz, the transmission band (evaluated at the decoupling level of -20 dB) is 595 MHz. The coordination of input, S_{11} coefficient does not exceed -20 dB within the entire operating frequency band S_{21} and S_{31} transmission ratios are both equal to -3.7 dB.

Having developed a traditional design, we can begin developing miniature coupler designing according to the

The research was executed by the grant of the Russian Science Foundation (project № 14-19-01396).

following procedure: We synthesize equivalent structures for quarterwave sections of microstrip transmission lines.

Replacement of 35-Ohm microstrip transmission lines with artificial transmission lines allowed to reduce the size of the device by 35% in comparison to a standard design. Artificial transmission line - a line consisting of a microstrip line is connected to the open-circuit shunt stubs. However, inside the coupler there is still a lot of free space, which is not put to use. Therefore, for further reduction we should first replace the central loop line and then bend the high-ohmic loop lines into the shape of a meander, maintaining the previous length. The Central loop line model using microstrip lines and is connected with two sides of the transmission lines. Two transmission lines is used to efficiently use the space inside the coupler. It is bending that should be used in this case, since if synthesis of an equivalent line is performed, its dimensions will be too small and it will not be easy to manufacture. It should be taken into consideration that in case of any change in the dimensions of the device it is necessary to monitor its characteristics so that they remain the same. In Fig. 3 you can see the final configuration of a compact three-loop coupler, which can be easily manufactured using standard methods of microstrip devices manufacturing, and Fig. 4 shows the results of numerical modeling. The final configuration has a size 67.5% smaller than a standard design.

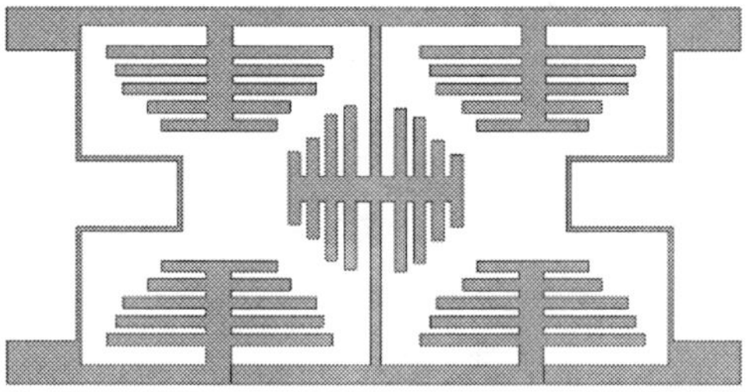

Fig. 3. The layout of the compact 3 dB coupler

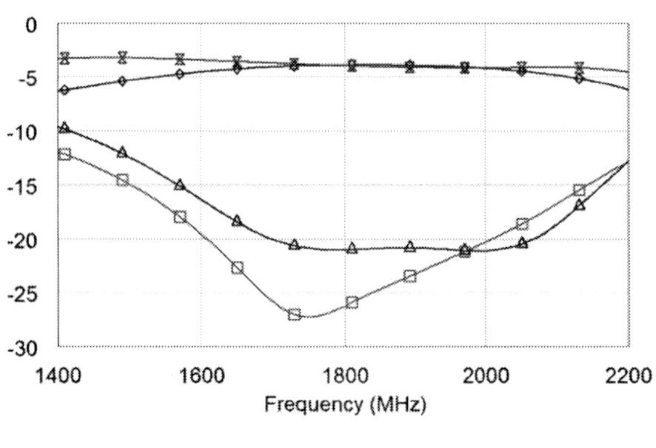

Fig. 4. "Simulated S-parameters of the proposed compact coupler

From the numerical modeling results obtained we can deduce the center frequency of the coupler, which is 1,807 MHz. There is a 7 MHz (0.4%) shift, the operating frequency band (evaluated at the decoupling level of -20 dB) begins at 1605 MHz and ends at 2012 MHz, which is 22.6% of the relative frequency band. S11 parameter in the transmission band does not exceed -15 dB. S_{21} and S_{31} transmission ratios equal -3.85 and -3.95 dB respectively. A 0.1 dB disbalance is insignificant and acceptable. Table 1 shows the comparison between the couplers designs.

TABLE I. COMPARISON OF THE DESINGS

Design	Isolation bandwidth, MHz@-20 dB	Area, mm²
Conventional	595	1315
Proposed	407	427

III. CONCLUSION

In this work we have studied a miniaturized design of a three-loop coupler. Miniaturization was carried out by using artificial transmission lines, which perform the same functions as the section replaced, but have a significantly smaller size. This method is distinguished by its simplicity, because it does not require heavy and complex mathematical calculations. The sample manufactured has a 427 mm^2 area, which is 67.5% smaller in comparison to a regular design. In spite of this degree of miniaturization, the coupler maintains the same performance within a wide enough frequency band.

REFERENCES

[1] S.-S. Liao and J.-T. Peng, "Compact planar microstrip branch-line couplers using the quasi-lumped elements approach with nonsymmetrical and symmetrical T-shaped structure," IEEE Trans. Microw. TheoryTech.,vol. 54, pp. 3508-3514, Sep. 2006.

[2] K. W. Eccleston and S. H. M. Ong, "Compact planar microstripline branch-line and rat-race coupler," IEEE Trans. Microw. Theory Tech., vol. 51, pp. 2119-2125, Oct. 2003.

[3] S.-S. Liao, P.-T.Sun, N.-C.Chin and J.-T.Peng, "A novel compact-size branch-line coupler," IEEE Microw.WirelessCompon.Lett. vol. 15, pp. 588-590, Sep. 2005.

[4] J. Wang, B. Z. Wang, Y.-X.Guo, L.-C.Ong, and S. Xiao "A compact slow-wave microstrip branch-line coupler with high performance," IEEE Microw.WirelessCompon.Lett. vol. 17, pp. 501-503, Jul. 2007.

[5] H.Ghali, and T. A. Moselhy, "Miniaturized fractal rat-race, branch-line, and coupler-line hybrids," IEEE Trans. Microw. Theory Tech., vol. 52, pp. 2513-2520, Nov. 2004.

[6] C. W. Tang and M.-G.Chen, "Synthesizing microstrip branch-line coupler with predetermined compact size and bandwidth," IEEE Trans. Microw. Theory Tech., vol. 55, pp. 1926-1934, Sep. 2007.

[7] Letavin, D.A., Mitelman, Y.E., Chechetkin, V.A., "Investigation of the frequency influence on the miniaturization efficiency of microstrip devices using LPFs", 2016 10th European Conference on Antennas and Propagation, EuCAP 2016, DOI: 10.1109/EuCAP.2016.7481614.

[8] Letavin, D.A., Mitelman, Y.E., Chechetkin, V.A., "Realization of miniaturized branch-line coupler using lowpass microstrip filters", 2015 Loughborough Antennas and Propagation Conference, LAPC 2015, DOI: 10.1109/LAPC.2015.7366013.

[9] Letavin, D.A., Mitelman, Y.E., Chechetkin, V.A., "A novel method of design of miniaturized microstrip microwave devices using filters", 2015 IEEE International Conference on Microwaves, Communications, Antennas and Electronic Systems, COMCAS 2015, DOI: 10.1109/COMCAS.2015.7360482.

[10] J. Wang, B. Z. Wang, Y.-X.Guo, L.-C.Ong, and S. Xiao "A compact slow-wave microstrip branch-line coupler with high performance," IEEE Microw.WirelessCompon.Lett. vol. 17, pp. 501-503, Jul. 2007.

[11] Wei-Shin Chang and Chi-Yang Chang, "A High Slow-Wave Factor Microstrip Structure With Simple Design Formulas and Its Application to Microewave Circuit Design,"IEEE Trans. Microw. Theory Tech., vol. 60, no. 11, pp. 3376-3383, Nov. 2012.

Online failure detection in large massive MIMO linear arrays

Daniele Pinchera, Marco Donald Migliore, Mario Lucido, Fulvio Schettino, Gaetano Panariello
DIEI - University of Cassino and Southern Lazio
Cassino, FR, Italy
pinchera@unicas.it, mdmiglio@unicas.it, lucido@unicas.it, schettino@unicas.it, panariello@unicas.it

***Abstract*—In this paper we discuss the feasibility of an online failure detection algorithm for large linear arrays for massive MIMO applications. By means of a numerical optimization of the position of few near field probes, a good failure detection performance has been verified.**

I. Introduction

One of the most promising technology to meet the challenging goals of the forthcoming 5G personal communication systems is the massive MIMO. The key point of this technology is the use of arrays of hundreds of elements [1], [2]. While there is a large literature on the use of large arrays in 5G in the communication community, research on the technological problems is much more limited. In particular, one of the issues when a large number of elements are involved is the increased probability of failures. Ideally, the presence of failures should be detected and possibly compensated [3]–[10].

Compressed sensing represents an interesting approach to identify the failures in arrays [11], [12].

More recently, the technique has been applied to correct the effects of the fault elements during the normal operation of the communication system adding a preliminarily redundancy in the array [13].

In the aforementioned paper a square array with a number of probes creating a frame around was taken as test case. The position of the probes' frame was determined by means of an optimal field sampling approach. The same approach can not be directly employed in the large linear arrays that are expected to be used in massive MIMO systems, in particular the ones employing the "Grid of Beam" technique. In this contribution we use a simple numerical optimization of the position of the probes to achieve a good detection performance with a limited number of near field probes. Furthermore, thanks to the very large number of elements, a satisfactory degree of compensation of the errors can be achieved also without the use of a preliminary added redundancy. The proposed technique could be also used in other large linear arrays, like the ones used in [14]

II. System description and probe locations

With reference to [13], let us briefly recall the main rationale of the approach: a number of probes measures the near field around the antenna during normal operation. The field

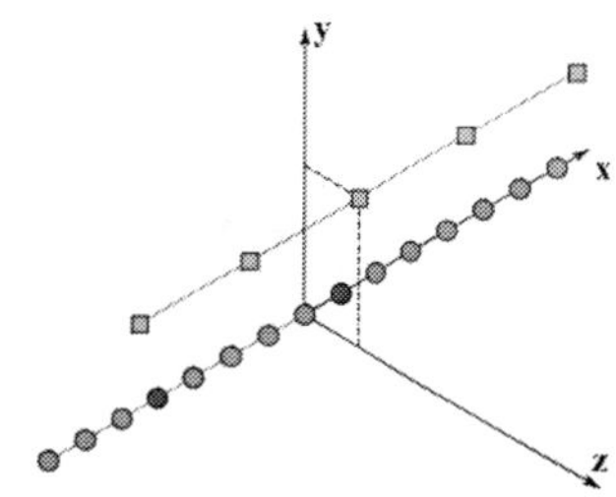

Fig. 1. Scheme of the array with probes. Green: working elements; red: defective elements; cyan: probes.

measured by the probes can be compared with a reference (without defects) field:

$$\mathbf{A}\tilde{\mathbf{x}} = \tilde{\mathbf{y}} \tag{1}$$

where $\tilde{\mathbf{y}}$ is the difference between the measured field and reference field, $\tilde{\mathbf{x}}$ is the difference of the reference excitation and the excitation with defects and $\mathbf{A}$ is a matrix modelling the linear relationship of the excitations and the field detected by the probes. When one or more elements present failures we would have a sparse $\tilde{\mathbf{x}}$ vector, so it could be possible to use an ℓ_1 minimization approach to recover the position of the defective elements:

$$\arg\min \|\tilde{\mathbf{x}}\|_1 \quad \text{subject to} \quad \|\mathbf{A}\tilde{\mathbf{x}} - \tilde{\mathbf{y}}\|_2 \leq \epsilon \tag{2}$$

wherein $||\cdot||_1$ stands for ℓ_1 norm and ϵ takes into account the unavoidable presence of errors in the measured data.

It is easy to understand that the number and position of the probes with respect to the array pays a fundamental role on the performances of the detection algorithm. While in previous works the position of the probes was determined by means of a optimum field sampling approach (that is non necessarily optimal for the failure detection problem), for large linear arrays we would like to use an array of probes like the one depicted in Fig.1. If the linear array is aligned along the x axis, also the array of probes could be aligned along the same axis, but slightly translated with respect to y and z in order to measure the field without interfering with the normal operation of the array.

The choice of this positioning is twofold. First, it is very simple, and it has a small impact on the complexity of

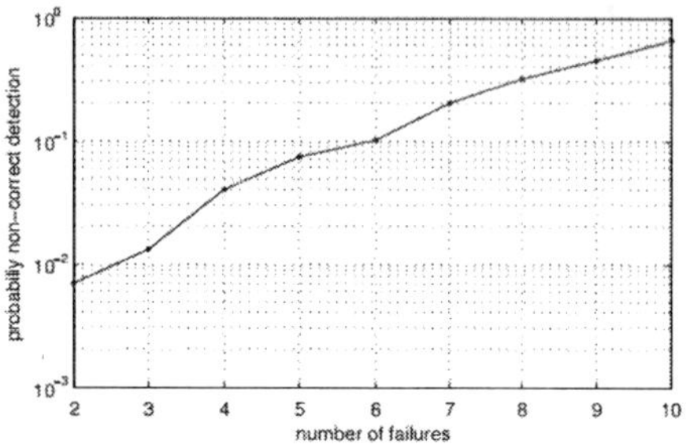

Fig. 2. Probability of error in failure detection.

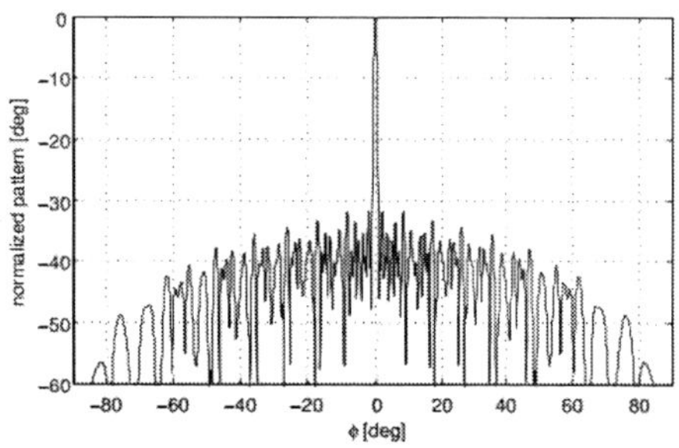

Fig. 3. Pattern of the 200 element array with 4 failures

the overall communication system; second, we have just 3 parameters to optimize (the y_P and z_P coordinates of the probes and their number N_P), making the choice of the probes position easier.

III. Numerical Examples

Let us consider, for instance, a linear array of 200 elements, $\lambda/2$ equispaced along the x axis as in Fig.1, with λ the free space wavelength. For sake of simplicity we suppose that the array feeds are $\lambda/2$ diameter circularly polarized circular apertures. We want to use a small number of probes, say $N_P = 20$, and we can put them 5λ equispaced in order to have a length similar to that of the array. By means of a parametric optimization we have found that good values for the coordinates of the probes are $y_P = 3.5044\lambda$ and $z_P = 5.8199\lambda$.

In Fig.2 we provide the results of the detection of the failures achieved by means of the aforementioned probes and the elaboration in (2), with a measurement noise of -40dB; for sake of simplicity the failures simply "turn off" the defective radiating elements. The probability of a wrong detection of the failures is lower that 4% for up to 4 failures, and is lower that 1% for two failures.

Once the failures are detected is desirable to compensate for those errors; as an example, in Fig.3 it is possible to see the pattern of the 200 elements array, with the excitations chosen to radiate a -40dB Taylor pattern: because of 4 failures, the pattern deviates with respect to the specification very much, in particular the sidelobes increase up to -32dB. By means of convex programming it is instead possible to achieve a pattern showing sidelobes lower than -40dB with the same beamwith

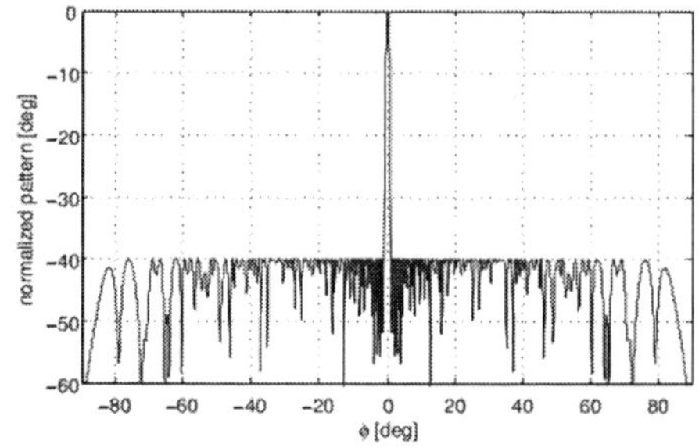

Fig. 4. Pattern of the 196 non defective element after correction

using only the 196 non-defective elements (Fig.4), with a decrease of the directivity of only 0.2dB. More examples will be discussed during the presentation.

References

[1] E. G. Larsson, O. Edfors, F. Tufvesson, and T. L. Marzetta, "Massive mimo for next generation wireless systems," *IEEE Communications Magazine*, vol. 52, no. 2, pp. 186–195, 2014.

[2] L. Lu, G. Y. Li, A. L. Swindlehurst, A. Ashikhmin, and R. Zhang, "An overview of massive mimo: Benefits and challenges," *IEEE Journal of Selected Topics in Signal Processing*, vol. 8, no. 5, pp. 742–758, 2014.

[3] J. Lee, E. M. Ferren, D. P. Woollen, and K. M. Lee, "Near-field probe used as a diagnostic tool to locate defective elements in an array antenna," *IEEE Transactions on Antennas and Propagation*, vol. 36, no. 6, pp. 884–889, 1988.

[4] J. Lord, G. Cook, and A. Anderson, "Reconstruction of the excitation of an array antenna from the measured near-field intensity using phase retrieval," in *IEE Proceedings H-Microwaves, Antennas and Propagation*, vol. 139, no. 4. IET, 1992, pp. 392–396.

[5] D. Rochblatt, P. Richter, and T. Otoshi, "A microwave performance calibration system for nasa's deep space network antennas. 2. holography, alignment, and frequency stability," in *Antennas and Propagation, Tenth International Conference on (Conf. Publ. No. 436)*, vol. 1. IET, 1997, pp. 150–155.

[6] O. M. Bucci, M. D. Migliore, G. Panariello, and D. Pinchera, "An effective algorithm for the synthesis of a plane wave generator for linear array testing," in *2012 IEEE APS International Symposium*, 2012, pp. 1–2.

[7] G. Oliveri, P. Rocca, and A. Massa, "Reliable diagnosis of large linear arraysa bayesian compressive sensing approach," *IEEE Transactions on Antennas and Propagation*, vol. 60, no. 10, pp. 4627–4636, 2012.

[8] O. M. Bucci, M. D. Migliore, G. Panariello, and D. Pinchera, "Plane-wave generators: Design guidelines, achievable performances and effective synthesis," *IEEE Transactions on Antennas and Propagation*, vol. 61, no. 4, pp. 2005–2018, 2013.

[9] M. D. Migliore, "Array diagnosis from far-field data using the theory of random partial fourier matrices," *IEEE Antennas and Wireless Propagation Letters*, no. 12, pp. 745–748, 2013.

[10] B. Fuchs, L. Le Coq, and M. D. Migliore, "Fast antenna array diagnosis from a small number of far-field measurements," *IEEE Transactions on Antennas and Propagation*, vol. 64, no. 6, pp. 2227–2235, 2016.

[11] M. D. Migliore, "A simple introduction to compressed sensing/sparse recovery with applications in antenna measurements," *IEEE Antennas and Propagation Magazine*, vol. 2, no. 56, pp. 14–26, 2014.

[12] S. Costanzo, A. Borgia, G. Di Massa, D. Pinchera, and M. D. Migliore, "Radar array diagnosis from undersampled data using a compressed sensing/sparse recovery technique," *Journal of Electrical and Computer Engineering*, vol. 2013, p. 8, 2013.

[13] M. D. Migliore, D. Pinchera, M. Lucido, F. Schettino, and G. Panariello, "A sparse recovery approach for pattern correction of active arrays in presence of element failures," *IEEE Antennas and Wireless Propagation Letters*, vol. 14, pp. 1027–1030, 2015.

[14] D. Pinchera, M. D. Migliore, and G. Panariello, "A virtual subarray architecture for imaging radar," *IEEE Transactions on Antennas and Propagation*, vol. 62, no. 10, pp. 5171–5179, 2014.

Feed Horn Optimization using Feed+Reflector Co-Simulation for Advanced Reflector Antennas

Joshua M. Kovitz, Vignesh Manohar, and Yahya Rahmat-Samii
Electrical Engineering Department
University of California Los Angeles
Los Angeles, CA, USA
Email: jmkovitz@ucla.edu, vignesh04@ucla.edu, rahmat@ee.ucla.edu

***Abstract*—Optimal illumination of a reflector is essential to maximize a reflector antenna's gain. In practice, this has been accomplished by specifying certain feed horn pattern characteristics, e.g. 10 dB BW, and independently optimizing the feed antenna to meet these requirements. In this investigation, we consider the possibility of optimizing the reflector antenna system through a co-simulation of the feed horn and reflector. Each test design is evaluated by first computing the feed horn pattern, followed by a physical optics reflector analysis using the simulated far-field feed pattern. Such a platform enables the fine-tuning of important pattern features within the feed+reflector system, such as cross-polarization, aperture efficiency, or sidelobes. As an example, the application of this reflector-feed co-simulation to a 1 meter Ka-Band offset reflector is compared to the conventional feed optimization approach, where the feed is optimized independently.**

I. Introduction

The conventional approach to optimize feed horn antennas draws on the knowledge and observations made from the fundamental research investigations on reflector antennas [1]. Typically, feed horn antenna requirements are derived from rules-of-thumb and guidelines given from these previous investigations. Examples of such requirements include 10 dB feed taper beamwidths, sidelobe levels, cross-polarization level, or even a pattern mask. These requirements are then utilized in an optimization routine that attempts to achieve these goals for the horn pattern. The resulting horn design is then integrated into the reflector to realize a high gain antenna. Reflecting on this approach naturally leads to our primary question: can we do better by directly optimizing the *reflector system* performance, rather than independently optimizing the feed?

In this paper, an alternative approach that optimizes the entire reflector system is investigated. Referring to Fig. 1, the feed horn optimization routine co-simulates the feed horn antenna performance using FEM and the reflector antenna using physical optics based on the resulting feed pattern. The potential advantage of such an approach is that subtle changes in the feed pattern can help further improve the design performance. Not only is this co-simulation approach intuitive; it simplifies the fitness function by directly relating the relevant reflector performance metrics to the optimizer. As a first demonstration, a spline-profiled feed horn antenna is optimized to maximize the directivity of a 1 meter Ka-band offset reflector antenna system. We also compare this to a design found using the conventional approach.

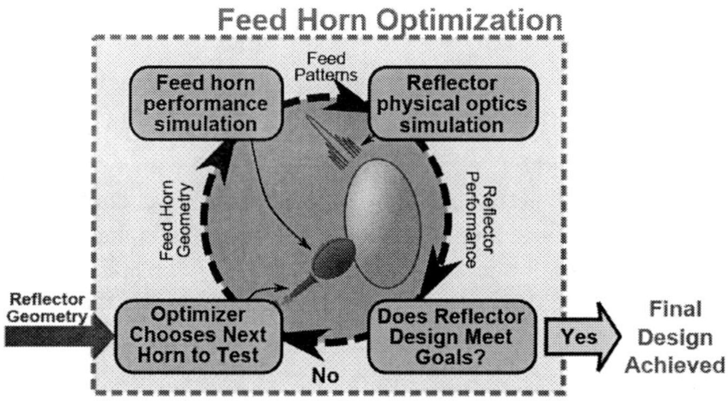

Fig. 1. Illustration of the co-simulation optimization approach, where the reflector is directly optimized by co-simulating the feed horn and reflector system in each evaluation.

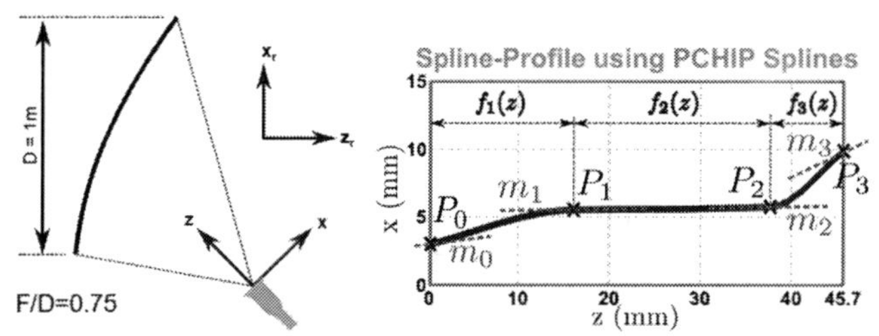

(a) (b)

Fig. 2. (a) Offset reflector system geometry. The feed size in this figure is not to scale. (b) Spline profile used to shape the feed horn.

II. Reflector Geometry and Feed Horn Design

As an example, we chose an offset reflector geometry with a 1 meter aperture diameter because there has been recent interest in developing such a design for emerging CubeSat applications [2]. The reflector geometry is illustrated in Fig. 2a. The offset reflector geometry used an $F/D = 0.75$ as illustrated in Fig. 2a, providing subtended angles of 64° and 62° in the XZ and YZ planes respectively. The clearance height for this reflector was 0.1312 meters.

For the feed horn antenna, we employed a spline-profiled horn design. The horn antenna is created by applying a body of revolution to a smooth curve created from splines. This is illustrated in Fig. 2b, where an example of a set of points P_0, P_1, P_2, and P_3 uniquely define the spline shown. Ultimately, the spline profile is shaped by adjusting the (z, x) positions of the spline points $\{P_0, ..., P_3\}$ similar to the approach used in [3]. To make fabrication easier, we forced the spline to be monotonic, which placed constraints on the slopes $\{m_0, ..., m_k\}$ at each of the points. The input waveguide diameter is set to 6mm.

For the optimization problem, this means that we are optimizing a total of 6 parameters. The restriction on the slopes and the waveguide entrance allows the optimizer to focus on optimizing the positions (z_1, x_1), (z_2, x_2), and (z_3, x_3). Our simulations are done at 35.75 GHz.

A. Conventional Approach using Specified Feed Requirements

The conventional approach attempts to optimize the feed horn antenna based on a set of prescribed requirements. For this particular reflector antenna design problem, we quantified the performance using the fitness function

$$f(\mathbf{x}) = (BW_{E,10} - 64^\circ)^2 + (BW_{H,10} - 62^\circ)^2 + S_{11} + 0.2X_p + 0.2B_L + 0.5L_t \quad (1)$$

where x is the vector of optimization variables, $BW_{E,10}$ and $BW_{H,10}$ are the E-plane and H-plane 10dB beamwidths of the horn design in degrees, S_{11} is the impedance matching, X_p is the cross-polarization level in the D-plane, B_L is the backlobe level, and L_t is the total length of the horn antenna assembly in mm. The horn is linearly-polarized along x. Further details of each term and coefficients has been divulged in [2].

B. Co-Simulation Approach

The co-simulation approach attempts to optimize the reflector system as a whole. The hope is that a more direct link between the optimizer and the total reflector performance would provide more control to the optimizer to fine-tune the system. As a first test, we created the following fitness function

$$f(\mathbf{x}) = S_{11} - 10D_0 \quad (2)$$

where x represents the optimization variables (same parameters as in the conventional approach), S_{11} is the horn impedance matching in dB, and D_0 is the reflector broadside ($\theta_r = 0$) directivity in dB when illuminated by a given feed horn design. This directivity is calculated based on the total radiated power P_{rad} from the feed horn and a far-field radiation intensity U_0 calculation based on physical optics. The coefficient 10 for D_0 places more emphasis on D_0 than S_{11}.

III. Results and Discussion

The spline-profiled horn antenna was optimized using both approaches. The final design geometries are shown in Fig. 3. Interestingly, the conventional approach produced a longer horn despite having the length as a goal in the fitness function. The aperture of the conventional horn is also larger, most likely to compensate for the quadratic phase error near aperture edge (caused by the steep slope near the aperture). Our investigations showed that the aperture distributions appeared to primarily consist of the $TE_{11} + TM_{11}$ modes. Both horns had $S_{11} < -30$ dB when connected to circular waveguide.

The big question in this investigation is whether any boost in reflector performance is achieved through the co-simulation approach. The horn patterns shown in Fig. 4 reveal some

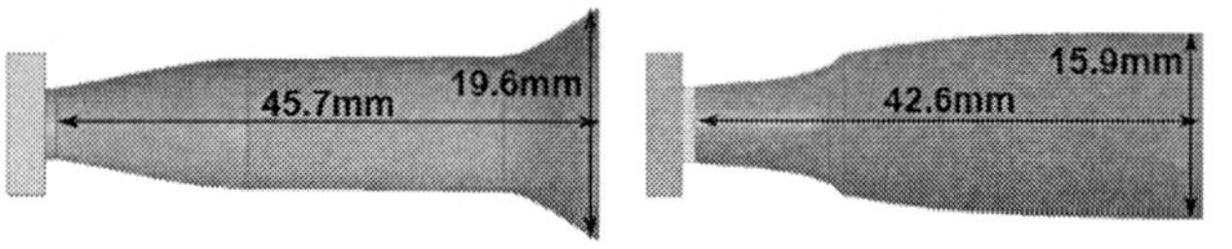

(a) (b)

Fig. 3. Final horn geometries from each approach. (a) Conventional approach. (b) Co-simulation approach. Both designs are shown at the same scale.

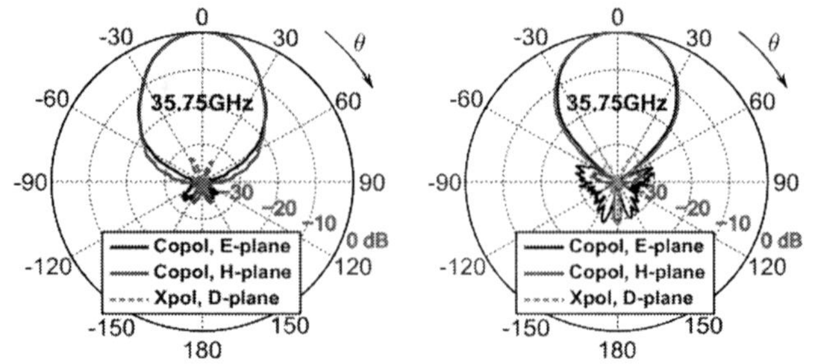

(a) (b)

Fig. 4. Simulated pattern performance for the final optimized horn antennas. (a) Conventional approach. (b) Co-simulation approach.

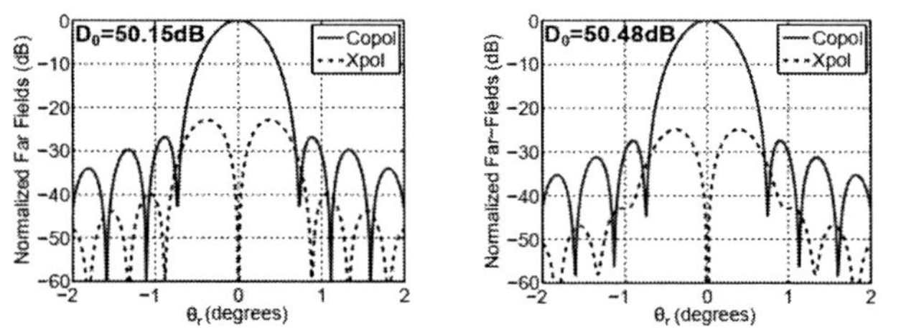

(a) (b)

Fig. 5. Simulated H-plane (y_r-z_r plane) reflector patterns with the final optimized horns. (a) Conventional approach. (b) Co-simulation approach.

interesting features. First, the conventional design provides an almost perfect 10 dB feed taper at the desired subtended angles. The co-simulated design has higher feed taper at these subtended angles. The rapid taper of the co-simulated design's pattern beyond $\theta = 31^\circ$, however, is extremely advantageous to minimize spillover. The ultimate result is that a noticeable boost in directivity is achieved. The final design from the conventional approach provided $D_0 = 50.15$ dB, while that from the co-simulated approach produced $D_0 = 50.48$ dB. This 0.33 dB difference is substantial for many applications.

In summary, the optimization of horn antennas has been revisited for the application of high-performance feeds in reflectors. In particular, the direct optimization of the full reflector and feed was explored, where the feed and reflector are co-simulated to evaluate the performance. As one might expect, the co-simulation approach is able to achieve a boost in performance. The co-simulation fitness function also more directly relates to the system goals. In the end, one can extend this approach to optimize other important system aspects.

References

[1] Y. Rahmat-Samii, "Reflector antennas," in *Antenna Handbook*, Y. T. Lo and S. W. Lee, Eds. Springer, 1988, pp. 949–1072.

[2] J. M. Kovitz, V. Manohar, and Y. Rahmat-Samii, "Spline-Profiled Horn Antenna Assembly Optimized for Deployable Ka-Band Offset Reflector Antennas in CubeSats," in *IEEE Int. Symp. Antennas and Prop.*, 2016.

[3] P. S. Simon, P. Kung, and B. W. Hollenstein, "Electrically large spline profile smooth-wall horns for spot beam applications," in *IEEE Int. Symp. Antennas and Prop.*, 2011.

L, U, T and F-Shaped Slots in Patch Antenna

Buket Kul, Gamze Kirman,
Pakize Ergül, Zeynep Banaz Kartal
Electrical &Electronic Engineering Departmant
Istanbul Commerce University
Istanbul, Turkey
{kulbuket, gamze.kirmann, pakizeegul,
zeynepbanazkartal}@gmail.com

Taha Imeci
Electrical &Electronic Engineering Departmant
Istanbul Commerce University
Istanbul, Turkey
timeci@ticaret.edu.tr

***Abstract*— In this work, different shaped slots such as L, U, T and F-shaped were used to design a microstrip patch antenna. The radiating elements of the proposed antenna was designed to be a symmetrical rectangular shape with respect to horizontal axis which have geometrical slots inside of it. Feed type of the designed antenna is circular shape via with 0.55mm. radius. The antenna was fed from center for the purpose to keep the symmetric form of the antenna. This patch antenna have all kind of slots combined thereby achieving more design degrees of freedom comparing similar antennas found in literature.**

Keywords — Microstrip patch antenna, slot antenna with rectangular shape, L, U, T and F-shaped.

I. INTRODUCTION

Microstrip patch antenna is a key building in wireless communication and Global Positioning system [1]. Microstrip patch antennas offer an attractive solution to compact and ease-low-cost design of modern wireless communication systems due to their many advantages as light weight and low volume, low profile, planar configuration which can be easily made conformal to host surface, low fabrication cost, and the capability of obtaining dual and triple frequency operations [2]. However, patch antennas have a main disadvantage: narrow bandwidth [3]. Typically about 5% bandwidth with respect to center frequency [4]. One of the techniques to design a compact microstrip antenna is cutting slots or slits on the radiating patch to increase the length of the patch of the surface current [5]. By cutting the slots from a patch, gain, return loss and bandwidth of microstrip antennas can be improved [6]. In [7], which was inspired for design of our antenna, the gain was increased by 2 dB by cutting slots in rectangular patch antenna. In our design we achieved maximum gain 7.27 dB by increasing area of the slots and changing the shape of the slots. Air thickness alters the effective permittivity of the microstrip geometry that, in turn, tunes the resonance frequency of the antenna [8]. That is the reason why we increased the air thickness from 10mm to 50mm in our antenna design. Furthermore, we reviewed variety of papers such as E-shaped microstrip patch antenna [4] and performance analysis of FR-4 substrate [9] that were found in the literature.

II. DESIGN AND SIMULATION RESULTS

Beginning step of the antenna design was double-fed but, the pattern of the antenna was not symmetrical. In order to eliminate this, for the other four design steps, size of the antennas remained constant, and slots had been changed for each step, and they had been fed by the center. In Table 1 and Table 2 those results were shown for S11 (dB), Resonance Frequency (GHz) and Gain (dB) with using FR4 and RogerRT6002. These values have been determined for each of the 5 different antennas. Fig.1 has fabricated antenna.

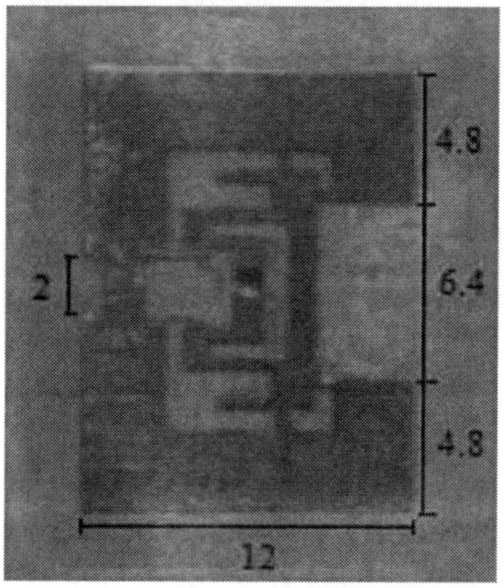

Fig. 1. Top view of the Final Antenna

Input match (-23.8 dB) and radiation pattern (7.27dB) are shown in Figures 2 and 3.

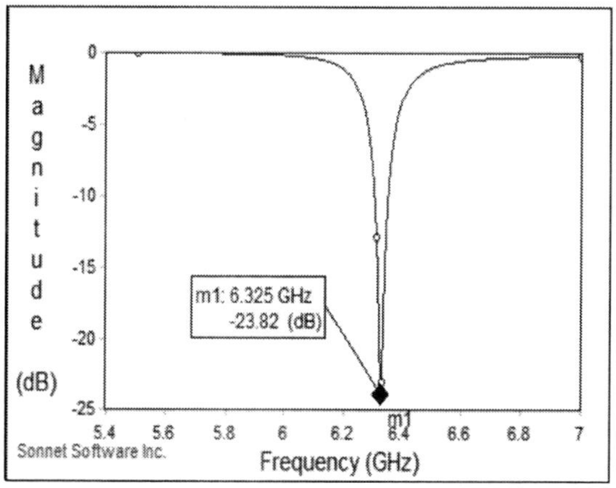

Fig. 2. Input match, S11.

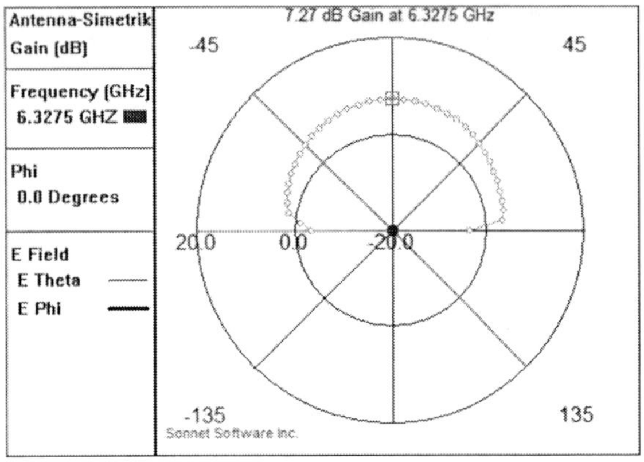

Fig. 3. Gain Value

As shown in Table 1 and Table 2, the thickness of RogerRT6002 was 0.762 mm, the thickness of FR4 was 1.6 mm and thickness of both of the substrates air thickness were 10 mm chosen to find the results with different values. However, as a result of changes in air thickness, which were shown in Table 3, by using 0.762 mm thickness of RogerRT6002 substrate and 50 mm air thickness gave the final result.

TABLE I. RESULTS FOR FR4

Antenna	Reflection Coefficient S11(dB)	Resonance Frequency (GHz)	Gain (dB)
1	-22.47	6.55	0.62
2	-25.98	4.4	1.97
3	-4.43	4.92	3.13
4	-1.06	4.94	2.57
5(Final)	-.041	6.14	-0.2

TABLE II. RESULTS FOR ROGER RT6002

Antenna	Reflection Coefficient S11(dB)	Resonance Frequency (GHz)	Gain (dB)
1	-43.74	7.3	5.37
2	-2.55	5.12	5.73
3	-11.32	5.78	6.26
4	-17.14	6.1	6.43
5(Final)	-14.08	6.34	6.56

While designing the antenna, the chosen air thickness and substrate thickness has been changed for different possibilities of Input match S11 (dB), Resonance Frequency (GHz), and Gain (dB) values. Calculation with different values is shown in Table 3. In first step, air thickness was constant at 10 mm, RogerRT6002 substrate thickness had different values and the results of these values have been listed. After that, the insulator thickness remained constant at 0.762 mm, which is used in the antennas final design to calculate air thickness with different values. Final result of 7.27dB gain were obtained when using RogerRT6002 dielectric with thickness of 0.762 mm and the air thickness with 50mm.

TABLE III. CHANGING OF S11, FREQUENCY AND GAIN VALUES DEPENDING ON AIR THICKNESS AND DIELECTRIC THICKNESS

Air Thickness (mm)	Dielectric Thickness (mm)	Reflection Coefficient S11(dB)	Resonance Frequency (Ghz)	Gain (dB)
10	0,127	-3,93	5,8	3,69
10	0,508	-12,03	6,24	6,33
10	0,762	-14,08	6,34	6,56
10	3,048	-0,57	6,24	3,02
25	0,762	-14,24	6,34	6,14
35	0,762	-20,11	6,34	7,11
50	0,762	-24,53	6,32	7,27
60	0,762	-15,96	6,32	6,72

III. CONCLUSION

This paper presents a parametric study of design process of a microstrip patch antenna which have conventional slots inside of it. The simulation results were compared for different types of dielectric materials and same material of different thicknesses which used in the proposed antenna design. Final simulation results were found by using Roger RT6002 substrate which has thickness of 0.762 mm with air thickness of 50 mm. Design specifications were met with S11 of -23.8 dB, gain of 7.27 dB at frequency of 6.32 GHz. We are about to add measured results of the S11 and radiation pattern of the antenna.

REFERENCES

[1] B. Akhilesh Babu, G. Karthikeya, G. Sharmila, G. Rajkumar, M. Sujatha, "Design of E-Shape Microstrip Patch Antenna for UltraWideband Applications" IOSR Journal of Electronics and Communication Engineering (IOSR-JECE), vol. 9, pp. 14-18, March-April 2014.

[2] R.C. Hadarig, M. E. de Cos, F. Las-Heras, "Microstrip Patch Antenna Bandwidth Enhancement Using AMC/EBG Structures" International Journal of Antennas and Propagation, vol. 2012, pp. 6, 2012.

[3] F. Yang, X. X. Zhang, X. Ye, Y. Rahmat-Samii, "Wide band E-shaped patch antennas for wireless communications" IEEE Trans. Antennas Propagat., vol. 49, pp. 1094-1100, July 2001.

[4] M. T. Islam, M. N. Shakib, N. Misran,"Multi-Slotted Microstrip Patch Antenna For Wireless Communication" Progress In Electromagnetics Research Letters, vol. 10, pp. 11-18, 2009.

[5] B. Mazumdar, U. Chakraborty, A. Bhowmik, S.K. Chowdhury, A.K. Bhattacharjee" A Compact Microstrip Patch Antenna for Wireless Communication" Global Journal of researches in engineering Electrical and electronics engineering, vol. 12, pp. 12-16, April 2012.

[6] A. Yadav, B. Chauhan, A. Jain, "Microstrip Symmetrical E-Shape Patch Antenna for the Wireless Communication Systems" International Journal of Emerging Technology and Advanced Engineering, vol. 2, pp. 241-244, December 2012.

[7] S.C. Basaran, "Compact dual-band split-ring antenna for 2.4/5.2 GHz WLAN applications" Turk J Elec Eng & Comp Sci, vol. 20, pp. 347-352, 2012.

[8] V. K. Tiwari, A. Kimothi, D. Bhatnagar, J. S. Saini, V. K. Saxena, "Effect of On The Performance Circular Sector Antennas" Indian Journal of Radio & Space Physics, vol. 34, pp. 417-423, December 2005.

[9] A. A. Qureshi, M. U. Afzal, T. Taqueer, M. A. Tarar, "Performance Analysis of FR-4Substrate for High Frequency Microstrip Antennas" Proceedings of the China-Japan Microwave Conference (CJMW), pp. 1-4, April 2011.

High gain perturbed pentagonal shaped diamond slotted patch antenna at 17.1 GHz

Şakir Kandönmez, Orhan Kolancıoğlu
Electrical and Electronics Engineering
Istanbul Commerce University
Istanbul, Turkey
sakirkandonmez@gmail.com
orhankolancioglu@gmail.com

Dilara H. Boyacı, Melis E. Koca, Taha İmeci
Electrical and Electronics Engineering
Istanbul Commerce University, Turkey
dilarahilalboyaci@gmail.com
melis.koca@hotmail.com
timeci@ticaret.edu.tr

Abstract—**This paper proposes a compact sized, high frequency microstrip patch antenna with probe feeding. The patch of the antenna is pentagonal shaped which has a t-slot in the upper-center. Main contribution of the paper is to perturbe the side edges of the patch and to add a dimond slot. Parametric study of those two-geometrical change was investigated. The proposed structures were simulated by using the Sonnet Suites, a planar 3D electromagnetic simulation software which gave S11 value of -12.77 dB and Gain value of 9.97 dB at 17.1 GHz. This proposed antenna is suitable for singleband wireless communication systems and mobile equipment.**

Keywords—Single band; T slot; Pentagonal antenna; wireless communication; mobile equipment.

I. Introduction

Recent advancements in compact mobile and wireless handsets leads demand of multi-frequency and multiband compact size antennas with broadband and high gain performance. For placing these antennas in communication systems, modifications in patch geometries are desired [1]. With the growing interest in compact wireless communication systems microstrip antennas are modified to work satisfactorily on these systems. Several patch antennas have been proposed in recent times for broadband operation [2]. Pentagonal geometry is one of the various shapes for microstrip antennas capable of circular polarization operation that has been reported in literature but it can be also used for linear polarization [3]. Here, it will be designed pentagonal antenna using thick substrate for enhancing bandwidth of antenna with a simple configuration. The other shape of pentagonal like a kite has been proposed by Weinschel which shows the characteristic of antenna parameter similarly with pentagonal antenna [4]. The results of characteristic performance, especially bandwidth of axial ratio of the pentagonal antenna is good, caused by a new shape of pentagonal antenna using air-gap and good choosing of a feed position [4]. The Microstrip Patch is the most demanding antenna based on their applications [5]. Changing some parameters of designed antenna (the angles of σ and θ) affected the values of S11, gain and also changed the shape of the antenna. Both parameters; return loss and gain, make pentagonal patch antenna suitable for the Rectanna application [6].

II. Design Steps

The size of the antenna is 14.0 X 16.6 mm. Substrate material is FR- 4 and the thickness of it is 1 mm. (ε_r= 4.01, dielectric losstangent = 0.0018). The thickness of air is taken as 3 times of the thickness of the FR-4, (3 mm). Figure 1 shows the picture of the fabricated antenna.

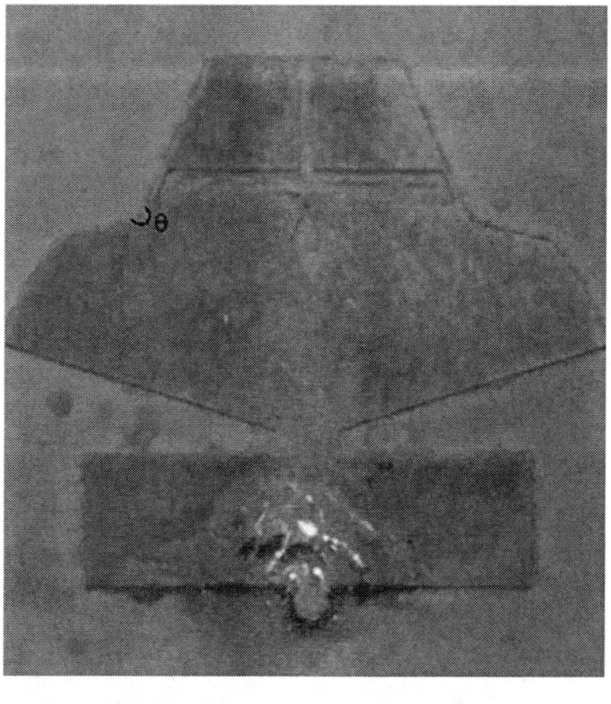

Fig. 1. Picture of the fabricated antenna

III. SIMULATION RESULTS

Analyses were performed in the Sonnet software program. The frequency range is between 14 - 20 GHz. In two different frequency values; magnitude values were obtained below -10dB. When the magnitude of S11 is -14.1 dB, gain is +5.99 dB. At 19.7 GHz. In second analysis, frequency was 17.1 GHz and S11 was -12.35 dB and the antenna functions at its highest level, so does the current. When compared with the first antenna, the size of the antenna is changed from 13.6 X 16.9mm to 14.0 X 16.4mm. Also, two new polygons added near to the input made gain higher. However, the frequency value got affected reversely. In figure 2, S11 Graph is shown and at 17.1 GHz, -12.35 dB magnitude was found.

In figure 3, Gain-Frequency Graph is shown and +9.97 gain is found at 17.1 GHz

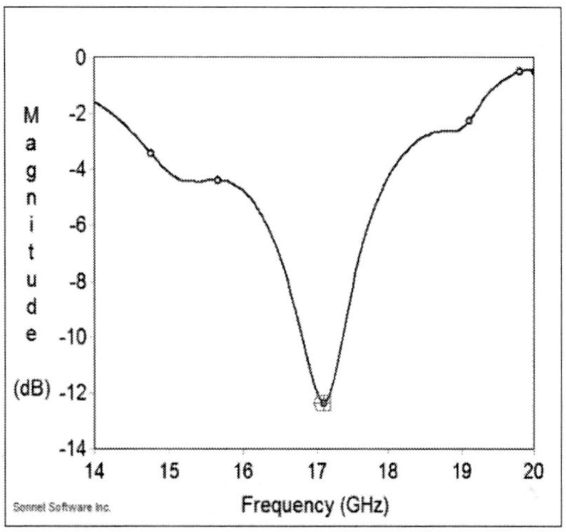

Fig. 2. S11 Graph

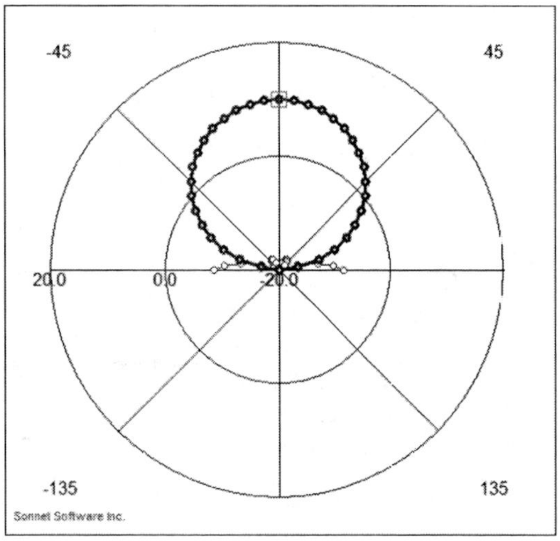

Fig. 3. Radiation pattern (Gain) Graph

Table 1 shows the results and comparisons due to the change of θ which makes the pentagonal shaped antenna "perturbed". Theta is shown in figure 1.

TABLE I. RESULTS AND COMPORISONS

Theta (θ)	*Frequency*	*S11*	*Gain*
210°	17.15 GHz	-11.12 dB	8.20 dB
212°	17.15 GHz	-10.81 dB	8.31 dB
216°	17.1 GHz	-12.35 dB	9.97 dB
219°	17.1 GHz	-10.08 dB	8.50 dB

IV. CONCLUSION

In this work, perturbed pentagonal cross-slotted patch antenna was designed, simulated and fabricated. Compared to the first analysis, in the second analysis there was an increase in the gain value. So, when the frequency is at 19.9 GHz, S11 is -14.1 dB and the gain value is found as + 5.99 dB. In the second analysis when the frequency is at 17.1 GHz, S11 is -12.35 dB and the gain is found as +9.97 dB. Two different analyses were compared in this article. We are also in the process of measuring the fabricated antenna for further studies on single band operations.

REFERENCES

[1] B. Sharma,V. Sharma ,K.B. Sharma , K. G. Jangid and D. Bhatnagar "Compact Dual Band Microstrip Patch Antenna for Wi - Max Communication Systems" 2014 International Conference on Signal Propagation and Computer Technology (ICSPCT), pp 741.

[2] B. Sharma, V. Sharma, D. Bharadwaj, K.B. Sharma,V. K. Saxena, J. S. Saini and D. Bhatnagar "Broadbanddual frequency pentagonal microstrip antenna for wireless communication systems" International Conference on Microwave- 08, pp 904.

[3] M. Tecpoyotl-Torres and J. G. Vera-Dimas "Dual band Pentagonal Microstrip Antenna for Wi-Fi Applications" 2010 Electronics, Robotics and Automotive Mechanics Conference, pp 255.

[4] M. Fauzan, E. Purnomo , E. Supriana "Circularly Polarized Array Pentagonal Microstrip Antenna for Mobile Satellite Applications" QiR (Quality in Research), 2013 International Conference, pp244.

[5] B. Garg, N. Agrawal, V. Sharma, A. Tomar, P. Dubey "Rectangular Microstrip Patch Antenna with "Pentagonal Rings" Shaped Metamaterial Cover" 2012 International Conference on Communication Systems and Network Technologies", pp 40.

[6] Anuroop, D. Gangwar, R. L. Yadava "Design and Analysis of a Pentagonal Rectenna" 2014 International Conference on Signal Processing and Integrated Networks (SPIN), pp 656.

E-Shaped Patch Antenna with Five Resonances

Ayse Kansız, Salih Yılmaz
Department of Electrical and Electronics Engineering
Ozyegin University
Istanbul, Turkey
ayse.kansiz@ozu.edu.tr,
salih.yilmaz@ozu.edu.tr

Taha Imeci
Department of Electrical and Electronics Engineering
Istanbul Commerce University
Istanbul, Turkey
timeci@ticaret.edu.tr

Abstract — In this paper, we designed, simulated, built and test 'E- shaped patch antenna with five resonances' that gives 9 dB radiation pattern gain. Our simulation and experimental investigation aimed to understand the behavior of the two slits. The first frequency is 4.64GHz with 8.5dB gain the second frequency is 5.3GHz with 7.10dB gain, the third frequency is 10.1GHz with 9dB, the fourth is 12.9GHz with 9.62dB gain and the last frequency is 15.0 GHz with 8.63dB gain.

Keywords— Antenna; Microstrip patch antenna; E shape patch

I. Introduction

Slot antennas are known very good radiators and have been widely used in wireless communication devices planar constructions and array syntheses, MMICs. The substrate is a microwave substrate backed by a foam material, and for ease of fabrication. The microstrip line is laid symmetrically on the substrate strip. E shape patch antenna made up and experimentally ascertained for operation in AWS, GSM and WLAN [1]. Microstrip antenna arrays are widely used in many applications, such as satellite and wireless communications, radar, missiles, ISM BAND etc. [2]. Microstrip antennas also suffer from narrow impedance bandwidth, which can be improved significantly by employing coupled resonator structures such as stacked microstrip antennas or U- and E-slots-Loaded patches [1], [2]. Different patch structures such as E shaped are used for improved bandwidth of the antenna. [3]. Both E-shape and U-slot-Loaded single-layer rectangular microstrip patch antennas have shown the potential to provide 2:1 VSWR impedance bandwidths of 30%-35% on electrically thick substrate materials [1]-[4]. Wideband directed dipole antennas cannot easily maintain a stable radiation pattern over the operating frequency range [5]. There are several techniques in order to get maximum gain in spite of narrow bandwidth and difficulty of operating frequency range. Modifying the shape or by inserting a single or double shorting wall to the antenna are efficient at receiving good gain. The main goals of the research work and literature related to the patch antenna are focusing on achieving bands, improving the impedance bandwidth performance and stable gain [6]. The simulation program used in this paper is Sonnet Suites [7].

II. Design Parameters

Top view of the E shape microstrip patch antenna is seen in figure 1.The feeding line is close to the top of the antenna. As it can be seen in the figure, the length of the H1 is 19mm, H2 is 17.5mm, H3 is 6mm and H4 is 1.5mm. The width of the antenna, W1 is 49mm, W2 is 16.5mm W3 is 5mm, and separation width, W4 is 5.5mm. Air thickness is 10mm and air Er is 1.0. Substrate thickness is 0.76m, Er is 2.94. Box is 495- 255. The total size of the antenna is 49x25. Table 1 demonstrates a parametric study in order to increase the gain. The distance between the top point of the antenna and the top point of the feeding line is varying. It provides good impedance matching and higher bandwidth.

III. Simulation and Measurement Results

According to millimeter changes in antenna size, we have observed parametric changes in the antenna's S11 in used frequencies. The results of these observations, we can observe a decrease and increases according to margin of error in the production stage in the frequency of 5. For instance, when the value of the h1 is decreased 1mm, antenna is not work in the values of 4.64 and 12.9 GHz but we observe that the gain of antenna is increased in the 10.1 GHz. in 15.0 GHz it cannot seen evident changes. When the dimension of the h1 is increased, the gain is decreased in 4.64, 10.1, 12.9GHz and antennas are unavailable. In 4.64, 5.3 GHz, the 1mm decline in the h2, the gain decreased slightly. It is seen that in 10.1, S11 is decreased. In 12.9, antenna does not work but in15.0ghz, the value of the s11 is increased. The 1mm increasing of the h2 does not affect 4.64, 5.3 and 10.1 GHz but the antenna is unavailable in the 12.9 and 15.0 GHz. The reduction of h3 does not affect any frequency negatively. The increase h3 affects only S11 in the 10.1 GHz a little bit negatively. The 1mm increase in h4 has no effect in 4.64GHz and 15.0 GHz but it affects other frequencies negatively. The reduction in the h4 value caused of decrease in all of frequencies. The 1mm reduction and increase in w1 value affected all frequencies negatively. The decrease in w2 affected to 4.64, 12.9 and 5.3 GHz negatively but the frequency in 10.1 does not change. The increase in w2 does not affect 4.64 and 5.3 GHz but it decreases the other frequencies' values. The reduction in w3 decrease the S11 of 4.64 and it affects 5.3 and 12.9 values dramatically. The increase of w3 value affected only 15.0 and 4.64 GHz but it decreased the values of other frequencies. The 2mm decreasing on the air affected to S11 positively but it affected gain a little bit negatively. The 2mm increase on the air cause of S11 and gain losses in all values. The air to 10 gives us maximum result. As it is shown in figure 2 and figure 3, simulated gain and input match (S11) agree well with measurement. Measured gains other than 12.9 GHz were not plotted because of their lower measurement values. That might be a fabrication error of some substrate etching problems as seen in Figure 1.

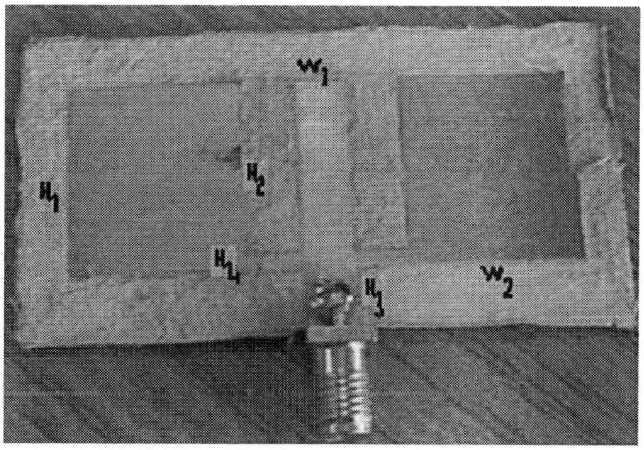

Fig 1.Top view of the antenna.

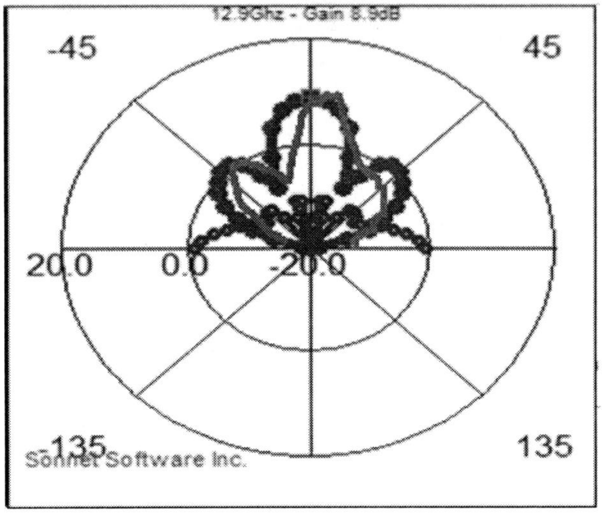

Fig. 2. Gain of the antenna at 12.9 GHz.

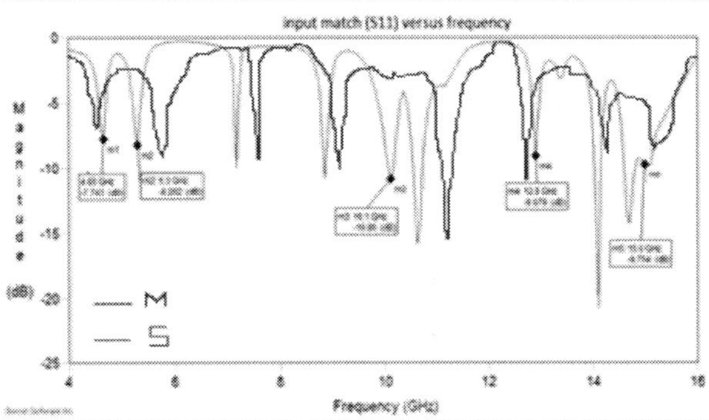

Fig. 3. S11 of the antenna

IV. Conclusion

In this work, E--shaped patch antenna with five resonances (4.64 Ghz, 5.3Ghz, 10.1 Ghz, 12.9 Ghz, 15.0 Ghz), edge-fed, E shape microstrip patch antenna was designed, simulated built and tested in order to meet the design specifications. As seen in parametric studies, it can be achieved better results by playing with the size in the desired frequency range. A distinctive feature of the E shape microstrip antenna is working of many frequencies. Measurement results agree well with simulation results for most frequencies of S11, but the only significant measured gain was obtained at 12.9 GHz. The reason might be the problem of the milling machine used to etch the antenna as seen in Figure 1.

References

[1] R. Garg, P. Bhartia, 1. Bahl, and A. ittipiboon, Microstrip Antenna Design Handbook. Boston, MA: Artech House, 2001.

[2] F. Yang and Y. Rahmat-Samii, "Wide-band E-shaped patch antennas for wireless communications," IEEE Trans. Antennas Propag., vol. 49, no. 7, pp. 1094-1100, Jul. 2001

[3] A.Gupta, R.K.Prasad, D.K.Srivastava, "Design and Analysis of Dual-Band C-Shaped Microstrip Patch Atenna" in International Journal of Advances in Engineering & Technology, Sept 2012. pp. 311-312.

[4] J.A Ansari, N.P.Yadar, P.Singh and A.Mishra, "Broadband Rectangular Microstrip Antenna Loaded With Double U-Shaped Slot" in International Journal of Microwave and Optical Technology, pp 1011-1016, July 2011,

[5] H.T.Hui and Edward K.N.Yung "Study of a dielectric-loaded slot antenna fed by a finite- width substrate microstrip line" in Radio Science, pp 1389-1400, November-December 1999

[6] H.F.Abutarbaoush, D.Budimur, R.Nilavolan and H.S.Al-Raweshidy, "Connected U-Slots Patch Antenna for Wimax Applications" in International Journal of RF & Microwave CAE, pp. 1-2, London,England.

[7] Sonnet Suites, version 16.52, www.sonnetsoftware.com.

TABLE 1. PARAMETRIC CHANGES

		4.64 Ghz		5.3Ghz		10.1 Ghz		12.9 Ghz		15.0 Ghz	
	mm	S11	Gain	S11	Gain	S11	Gain	S11	Gain	S11	Gain
H1	18	-1.41	8.5	-5.87	6.67	-27.3	9	-1.61	5.24	-9.33	7.1
H1	20	-1.17	3.9	-8.41	7.06	-1.96	2.5	-2.61	9.15	-8.64	8.26
H2	16.5	-6.91	7.65	-7.32	6.94	-17.9	8.75	-0.38	5.9	-14.2	7.94
H2	18.5	-9.39	7.7	-9.31	6.95	-7	8.69	-2.98	8.24	-4.24	7.83
H3	5	-6.60	7.71	-6.93	6.93	-11.7	8.66	-9.40	8.89	-13.5	8.02
H3	7	-8.78	7.65	-7.87	6.97	-6.36	8.79	-10.0	8.92	-7.90	7.80
H4	0.5	-4.73	7.55	-2.88	7.03	-5.21	8.20	-4.56	9.62	-4.29	7.65
H4	1.4	-7.5	7.46	-7.76	6.93	-11.6	8.42	-9.76	9.35	-8.96	7.88
H4	1.6	-7.63	7.47	-7.17	6.90	-11.1	8.50	-7.98	9.23	-10.1	7.91
H4	2.5	-7.79	7.64	-4.68	6.92	-4.20	9.16	-1.34	8.39	-13.1	7.85
W1	15.5	-5.49	8.02	-1.12	6.87	-1.92	6.94	-2.49	8.29	-3.44	5.58
W1	16.2	-6.91	7.67	-5.85	7.01	-5.35	8.98	-6.87	9.25	-5.72	7.71
W1	16.8	-7.97	7.12	-3.88	6.79	-6.98	6.64	-5.76	9.13	-5.79	6.67
W1	17.5	-5.37	5.67	-0.91	6.37	-1.96	0.48	-1.45	6.88	-28.7	2.42
W2	4	-5.82	7.70	-5.22	6.89	-8.92	8.88	-6.15	9.10	-11.2	8.08
W2	4.6	-6.75	7.48	-6.41	6.90	-10.5	8.51	-8.53	9.35	-10.2	7.93
W2	5.2	-8.02	7.45	-8.12	6.94	-11.8	8.44	-8.62	9.25	-9.26	7.88
W2	6	-10.7	7.63	-9.07	7.03	-6.19	8.62	-5.73	8.74	-6.00	7.76
W3	4.5	-7.24	7.71	-6.11	6.81	-10.1	8.77	-1.60	9.33	-8.73	8.04
W3	6.5	-7.55	7.60	-6.16	7.10	-4.69	8.78	-0.84	5.09	-9.76	7.87
Air	8	-9.39	7.1	-9.04	6.62	-10.7	9.41	-9.74	9.15	-10.3	8.63
Air	**10**	**-8.07**	**7.7**	**-8.21**	**6.9**	**-10.8**	**8.7**	**-9.1**	**8.9**	**-9.74**	**7.5**
Air	12	-7.41	7.98	-7.85	7.07	-9.99	8.18	-8.89	8.70	-9.18	7.59

Square Shape Patch Antenna with Triangular Slot

Ahmet Burcakbas, Selman Soylu, Burak Bektas
Electrical and Electronics Engineering
Istanbul Commerce University
Istanbul, Turkey
{aburcakbas.32, selmansoylu1994, bektasburak94}@gmail.com

S. Taha Imeci
Department of Electrical and Electronics Engineering
Istanbul Commerce University,
Istanbul, Turkey
timeci@ticaret.edu.tr

***Abstract*— This paper presents the effect of the triangular slot square shape microstrip patch antenna. The antenna has 9.37 dB gain at 8.1 GHz and input match of antenna -17.5 dB. This work emphasis that size of the slot on the antenna effect the performance. The simulation results are given and parametic studies were presented in detail. The system will be used in SHF bands where radar systems are the main applications.**

Keywords*— *Microstrip Antenna; Patch Antenna; Triangular; Slot; Sonnet Software; SHF Bands

I. Introduction

The paper presents a square shape microstrip patch antenna with equilateral triangular slot design supported by simulation. The proposed antenna have equilateral triangular slot and the slot might considered as a rectengular slot also in other papers [1]. In [2], there are 4 triangular slots fed by 2 vias. Our study has one equilateral triangular slot and fed by one via. Square shape microstrip antennas without triangular slot have large inductive reactance in input impedance of the patch, due to thick substrate. So, triangular slot introduces a capacitive component in the input impedance that compensates for the inductive component of the coaxial probe [3]. The work to be presented in another paper is also a compact microstrip antenna design obtained by cutting a equilateral triangular slot on the patch. [4]. In [5], they have a rectangular shape microstrip patch antenna with a larger triangular slot located at the left hand side of the antenna at 2.15 GHz and 5.43 GHz. We have square shape patch with smaller triangular slot located at the bottom and working at higher frequency. The better characteristics of the microstrip-fed slot antenna over the patch antenna has wider bandwidth, less conductor loss, and better isolation between the radiating element and feeding network [2]. The slot antennas are type of antennas which have many configurations and geometry shapes. In [6], it concentrates on the effect of antenna resonant frequency and other antenna parameters due to slots in patch and ground plane to design the compact antenna with improved bandwidth and efficiency.

II. Design and Simulation Results

A. Design

The proposed antenna design is depicted in Fig. 1. In this work, a patch antenna was designed by probe-feeding it from right-center of the patch. The main material of antenna is Rogers RT5880LZ with thickness of the substrate 1.6 mm and dielectric constant is 1.96 mm. The side length of the antenna is 37.8 mm.

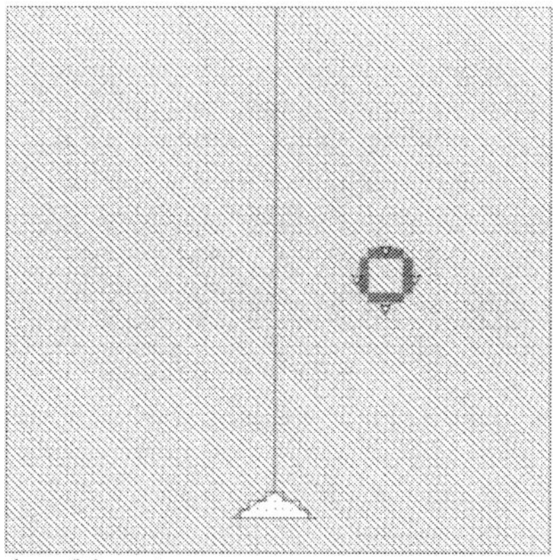

Fig.1. Final design of the antenna.

For the efficient antenna the width and length of the patch can be calculated by

$$W = c/2f\,[(\epsilon_r + 1)/2]-1/2 \text{ and } L = c/2f\sqrt{\epsilon_e} - 2\Delta l \qquad (1)$$

where, ϵ_ε Δl can be calculated from [7]. The antenna has been designed using Sonnet Suites [8].

B. Simulation Results

In order to analyze the effect of the triangular shape slot, a parametric study was conducted by changing the area of the slot. The parametric study results of square shape microstrip antenna with triangular slot is shown in Table I and Table II in terms of frequency, gain, input match. In addition to all of these, Table II presents the final results that meet the design specifications.

TABLE I. Parameter Changes With Triangular Size

Dimensions of triangular slot (mm)	*Frequency (GHz)*	*S11 (dB)*	*Gain (dB)*
[1.69 - 1.69 - 2.40]	8.20	-13.95	9.44
[3.50 – 3.50 – 6.00]	8.10	-17.5	9.37
[4.30 - 4.30 – 7.20]	8.225	-11.45	9.48
[5.60 – 5.60 – 9.60]	8.15	-17.65	9.36

Dimensions of triangular slot (mm)	Frequency (GHz)	S11 (dB)	Gain (dB)
[1.69 - 1.69 - 2.40]	8.20	-13.95	9.44
[6.99 - 6.99 - 12.00]	8.225	-10	9.35
[7.30 - 7.30 - 12.00]	8.175	-13.47	9.34

TABLE II. FINAL RESULTS

Length [3.50 – 3.50 – 6.00]				
Gain (dB)			Frequency (GHz)	S11 (dB)
e-theta (-60°)	e-theta (0°)	e-theta (60°)		
5.61	6.03	6.13	7.40	-1.71
5.35	6.54	6.78	7.775	-4.75
8.15	9.37	8.84	8.1	-17.5
8.16	9.46	8.76	8.2	-13.69

The graph of S11 and simulated gain are shown in Figure 2 and Figure 3 according to analysis of square shape microstrip antenna with triangular slot. Note that, some frequencies have lower resonances in terms of input match, compared to operating frequency of 8.1 GHz in Figure 2, but they do not have enough gain. As seen in Figure 3, electric field theta polarized (co-pol) gain have radiation in three different locations such as $\theta = 0°$ and $\pm 60°$ respectively. Note that, maximum radiation is achieved at $\theta = 0°$ as 9.46 dB. Electric field phi-polarization (cross-pol) level is well below than -9 dB.

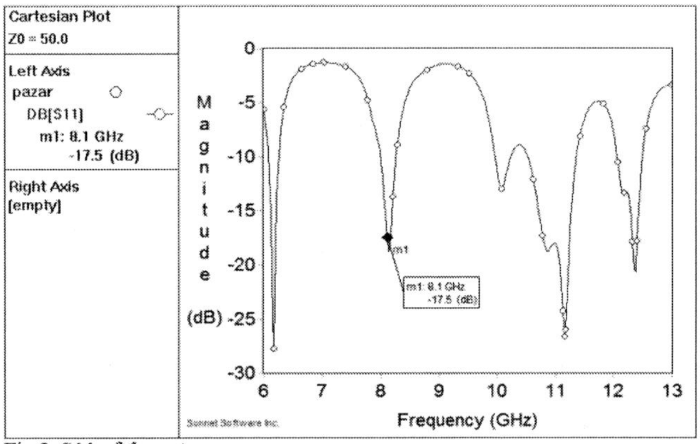

Fig.2. S11 of the antenna.

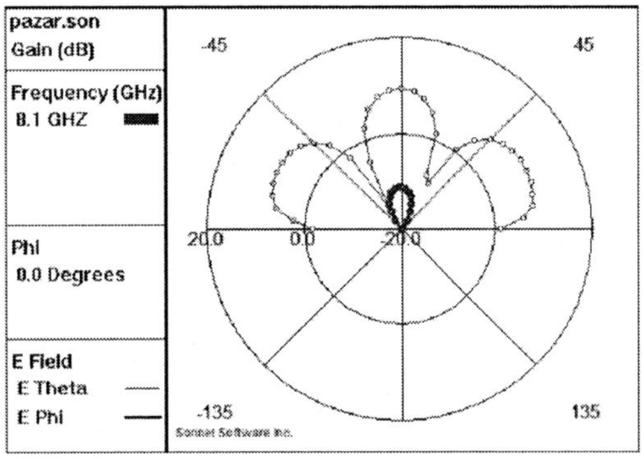

Fig.3. Simulated Gain.

III. CONCLUSION

In this work main target is to design and simulate a microstrip patch antenna with triangular slot for using in radar system which works between 8 and 10 GHz. In order to see the effect of the triangular slot on square shape microstrip patch antenna some parametric studies performed. In additional to those parametric study; geometry, dielectric layers and air thickness are optimized in order to meet the design specifications. As a result of planar 3-D electromagnetic simulation software, -17.5 dB input match and 9.37 dB gain, was obtained in 8.1 GHz. Cross polarization level is less than -11 dB. Due to the effect of triangular slot on square shape microstrip antenna for the patch surface current path as compared to the reference antenna without slot, surface current paths of the resonant modes can be lengthened, resulting in the decrease of corresponding resonant frequencies [9]. This antenna suits well for X-band frequency spectrum in radar communications area. For future works, implementation and measurement are planned.

ACKNOWLEDGMENT

Authors would like to thank the support of all staffs of the Department of Electrical and Electronics Engineering, Istanbul Commerce University. We would also like to thank Mr. Jason Rudick from Sonnet Software for their continuing technical and licensing support.

REFERENCES

[1] M. Malek, et al. "Equilateral triangular microstrip patch antenna with spur lines embedded," Antennas and Propagation Conference (LAPC), Loughborough, 2013, pp. 303-306.

[2] S.Y. Lin, K.L. Wong, "A dual-frequency microstrip-line-fed printed slot antenna," Microwave and Optical Technology Letters, vol. 28, no. 6, March 2001.

[3] C.S.Patil, P.S. Patil, M.U. Birare, "Dual Feed Triangular Slotted Microstrip Patch Antenna," International Journal of Advanced Research in Electrical, Electronics and Instrumentation Engineering, vol. 2, no. 10, October 2013.

[4] I.J. Bahl, P. Bhartia, "Microstrip Antennas," Artech House, 1980.

[5] S.S. Sran, J.S. Sivia, "Rectangular Microstrip Patch Antenna with Triangular Slot," International Conference on Advancements in Engineering and Technology (ICAET), 2015.

[6] R. Kumar, J.P. Shinde, M.D. Uplane, "Effect of Slots in Ground Plane and Patch on Microstrip Antenna Performance," International Journal of Recent Trends in Engineering, vol. 2, no. 6, November 2009.

[7] M. Kirchning, R.H. Jansen, N.H.L. Koster, "Accurate Model for open end effect of Microstrip line," Electronic Letter 17, February 1981, pp. 123-125.

[8] Sonnet Suites, version16.52, www.sonnetsoftware.com.

[9] S. Bhunia, "Effects of Slot Loading on Microstrip Patch Antennas," International Journal of Wired and Wireless Communications, vol. 1, no. 1, October 2012.

F-Shaped Monopole Antenna

Hakan İncesulu[1], Gül Ulutaş[1], Hakan Bilge[1]
[1]Department of Electrical & Electronics Engineering,
Özyeğin University, Istanbul, Turkey
hakan.incesulu@ozu.edu.tr gul.ulutas@ozu.edu.tr
hakan.bilge@ozu.edu.tr

Ş. Taha İmeci[2] and Tahsin Durak[3]
[2]Department of Electrical & Electronics Engineering,
Istanbul Commerce University, Istanbul, Turkey
[3] Department of Technology, NSU, Norfolk, VA
timeci@ticaret.edu.tr tahsind@gmail.com

Abstract— **In this paper, effects of F antenna arm length on the frequency, gain and s11 values are studied. The arms and the total length of the F determine the resonance frequency of the antenna. The inverted F shaped antennas are used in the cell phones. The outcome showed that the middle length of the antenna determines the input match and gain of the antenna. We achieved the highest gain of 6.32 dBi at 4.21 GHz frequency with input match of -16.91 dB.**

Keywords— F-shaped, antenna, radiation, monopole, patch antenna.

I. Introduction

Micro-strip patch antenna (MPA) consists of a conducting patch of any planar or nonplanar geometry on one side of a dielectric substrate with a ground plane on other side. MPAs became increasingly useful because of many advantages they offer such as low cost, light weight and low profile. The electronics industry requires smaller, more efficient and more mobile antennas in order to use them [1]. Due to these reasons, F shaped antennas, compared to other types of antennas, have been widely used in industrial, scientific and medical (ISM) band applications. F shaped antenna is one of the good candidates to meet up most of the mentioned requirements, within the micro-strip printed antennas [2].

The F shaped antenna in cell phones are designed to minimize radiated power when a cell phone is placed against the ear of the user, while maximize radiation in the opposite direction [3]. This nice feature of F-shaped antenna makes it more popular in other applications as well. It's applications are not limited to cellular phones [4]. The inverted-F antenna is well known for its ability to provide flexibility in impedance matching and to provide both vertically and horizontally polarized electric fields [5].

The rest of this paper is organized as follows; the design parameters are described in Section II, Section III presents simulation and parametric study and Section IV concludes the paper.

II. Design Parameters

Theoretical resonance frequency formula of the F shaped monopole antenna was provided in [2].

Based on initial calculations, and starting with an ideal antenna model, we had some idea about what the outcomes of our antenna should be. Later we ran so many simulations using "Sonnet Suites" [6] and simulations increased our understanding of the antenna behavior based on the changes, and the characteristics of the antenna.

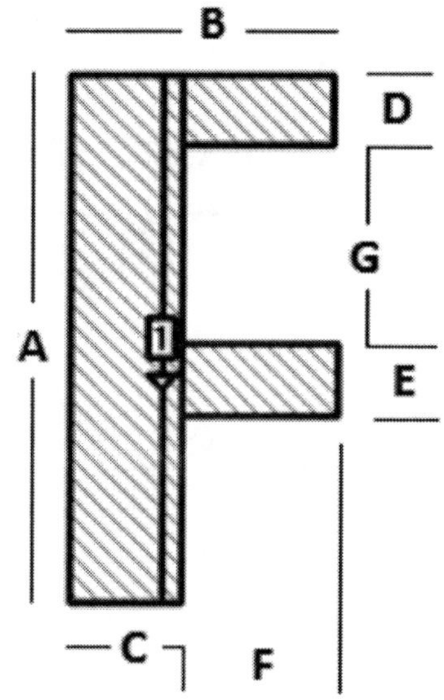

Fig. 1. Top view of the F-shaped antenna.

The proposed F-shaped monopole patch antenna is designed using RT/duroit 6002 substrate with dielectric constant of 2.94, thickness $h=0.76mm$ and loss tangent of 0.0012. Substrate dimensions are 35mm x 20mm. Fig. 1 shows the top view of the designed antenna. Optimized antenna dimensions are as follows; height (A) is 30.7 mm, width (B) is 15.27 mm, bottom width (C) is 6.4 mm, top arm width (D) is 4.35 mm, middle arm width (E) is 3.85mm, middle arm length (F) is 9.57 mm and spacing between top and middle arm (G) is 11.6 mm.

We decreased and increased the length (F) of the middle arm. The minimum length was 8.875 mm, and the longest length was 15.27mm. Also, theoretical calculations for these new designs were carried out.

The variations in the length of the middle arm of the antenna resulted with the variations in resonance frequency, return loss and gain of the antenna. Based on the application, antenna can be tuned by adjusting the length of the middle arm (F).

TABLE I. FREQUENCY, S11 AND GAIN

Air Thickness	Frequency	S11 (dB)	Gain (dBi)	Middle Arm (F)
18 mm	4,21 GHz	-16,91	6,32	9,57 mm
18 mm	4,58 GHz	-7,18	5,87	8,875 mm
18 mm	3,59 GHz	-12,99	6,127	15,27 mm

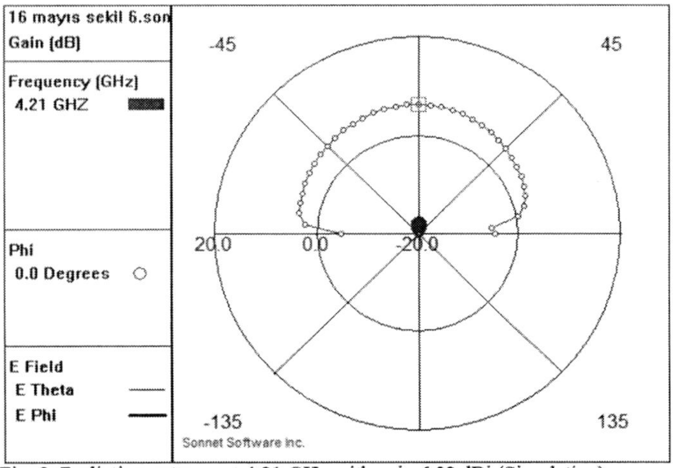

Fig. 2. Radiation patterns at 4.21 GHz with gain 6.32 dBi (Simulation).

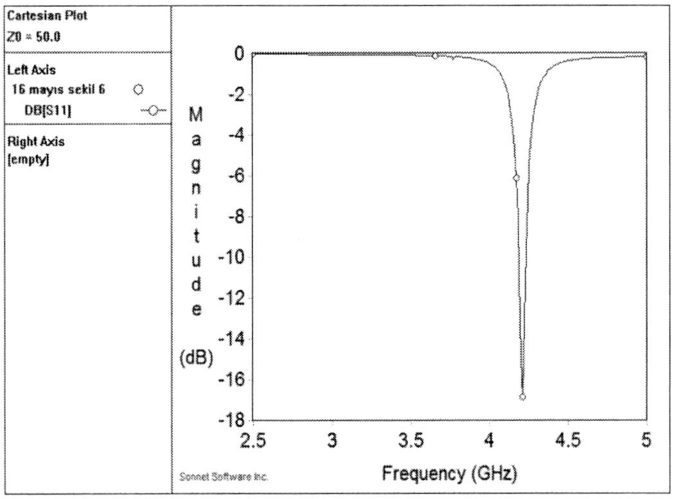

Fig. 3. Input match (|S11|) of the proposed F-shaped patch antenna

III. SIMULATION AND PARAMETRIC STUDY

This section presents the simulation results of the proposed F-shaped monopole patch antenna. Table I shows the simulation results of the three antennas. During simulations, we kept the air thickness same, but changed middle arm (F) lengths of the antenna.

The first simulation achieved the highest gain (6.32dBi) and lowest return loss (-16.91dB). As mentioned before, all simulations were done using Sonnet Suite. Fig 2 shows radiation pattern and Fig. 3 shows the return loss of the F shaped simulated antenna.

The second simulation is with shorter middle arm (F). We observed an increase in the resonance frequency of the antenna (4.58 GHz), also increased s11 to -7.18 dB but decreased in the gain to 5.87 dBi. As for the last simulation we increased the length of the middle arm (F) of the antenna, as a result we observed lower resonance frequency (3.59 GHz), increased return loss -12.99dB and decreased gain of 6.12 dBi.

Based on these simulations results, first antenna simulation achieved the highest gain and lowest return loss.

As seen in the graphs, simulated antenna has a nice vertical propogation pattern and acceptable gain and return loss for a patch antenna. F-shaped antenna is an ideal candidate for cellphone applications. It offers minimum radiated power when a cell phone is placed against the ear of the user, while maximum radiation is in the opposite direction.

IV. CONCLUSION

We managed to estimate resonance frequencies of the antennas using theoretical formula provided above. When compared to inverted-F shaped antennas, our antenna has higher resonance frequencies than inverted-F shaped antennas. F shaped antennas have a vertical radiation pattern; it is an ideal antenna type for cell phone and medical device applications. Our highest gain of 6.32dBi is slightly less than inverted-F antenna version. This antenna can be easily incorporated into systems for cellphones and medical devices. As a feature work, we would like to build, measure the return loss and determine propagation pattern of the antenna. We would like to compare measures results to simulated ones.

ACKNOWLEDGMENT

We would like to thank to Sonnet Software for their services.

REFERENCES

[1] Butler, C., Koeber, R., & Allred, R., Dual Band Antenna Design for 2.45 & 5.50 GHz, Journal of Electrical Engineering The Institution of Engineers, 13-17 (2005)

[2] Karmokar, K. D., & Morshed, K. M., Analysis of Inverted-F and Loaded Inverted-F Antennas for 2.4 GHz ISM Band Applications. Journal of Electrical Engineering The Institution of Engineers, 4-9 (2009)

[3] Manrique, S., Loero, L., & Xu, Y., Design, Build, and Test of Dual-Band PIFA Journal of Electrical Engineering, 13-17 (1997)

[4] Nagel, J. R., Hammer, D. B., & Smith, J., A Dual Band PIFA with Branch Line Slit, Planar Antennas for Wireless Communication, 21-24 (2008)

[5] Soras, C., Karaboikis, M., Tsachtsiris, G., & Makios, V., Anaylsis and Design of an Inverted-F Antenna Printed on a PCMCIA Card for the 2.4 GHz ISM Band

[6] Sonnet Suites, version 16.52, www.SONNETSOFTWARE.com

Spiral Patch Antenna at 12 GHz

Yunus Emre Ozmen
Department of Electrical and Electronics Engineering
Istanbul Commerce University
Istanbul, Turkey
y.emreozmen92@gmail.com

Taha Imeci
Department of Electrical and Electronics Engineering
Istanbul Commerce University
Istanbul, Turkey
simeci@gmail.com

***Abstract*— In this project, a microstrip square spiral patch antenna is presented. Our design has probe feed. The square-shaped microstrip patch antenna indicates a theta polarized radiation pattern with gain of 4.31 dB at 12.04 GHz. The measurement of the fabricated antenna confirms the simulation results obtained in an electromagnetic simulation program, called Sonnet Suites. This antenna can be easily integrated into systems for satellite communications. We designed, simulated, built and tested the antenna.**

Keywords—Square Shaped; high frequency; microstrip patch antenna; Spiral

I. INTRODUCTION

In the recent years, there has been rapid growth in wireless communication. Day by day users are increasing, but limited bandwidth is available and operators are trying hard to optimize their network for larger capacity and improved quality coverage. This surge has led the field of antenna engineering to accommodate the need for broadband, low cost miniaturized and easily integrated antennas [1-2-4]. Microstrip patch antennas are commonly used in wireless communications like Bluetooth, applications owing to their attractive features such as small size and hence conformal nature, easy to feed and design, low fabrication cost, robust nature, light in weight, and easily combined with monolithic microwave integrated circuits [2-9-14]. For microstrip patch antenna, three types of methods of analysis are determined such as; transmission line model, cavity model, and full wave model. In this spiral antenna design, transmission line model is used thickness of 8.28 mm total and 1.28 mm as dielectric thickness [3-5-15]. It's dielectric constant is 6.5 (ε_r) and air layer on top of it has ε_r =1. It has very compact size with (edge length 65mm lower length 104 mm middle slot length 50 mm) spiral slot microstrip patch antenna fed from the middle center [7-8-10]. The simulation results show that this antenna can be applied to serve in WLAN applications [5-6-13].

II. DESIGN AND SIMULATION RESULTS

The design and simulation of proposed square spiral microstrip patch antennas was conducted using Sonnet Suites planar-3D software with the resonant frequency of the antenna at 12.04GHz. The parametric study of the substrate properties are shown in Table I and Table II, respectively. The layout of the antenna demonstrate in milimeters with dimension of 8.28mm (h), 27mm (w), 9 mm(inner radius), 3mm (gap) and 2 turns of spiral. Simulation results compared each other changing different parameters of thickness, dielectric constant, frequency range etc. After the desired results were maintained, the design was manufactured and measured.

TABLE I. S11 AND GAIN RESULTS WITH DIFFERENT DIELECTRICS

Dielectric Constant	S11 (dB)	Gain (dB)
6.4 (ε_r)	-19.42	2.54
6.45 (ε_r)	-20.3	3.6
6.5 (ε_r)	**-25.01**	**4.31**
6.55 (ε_r)	-22.3	3.9
6.6 (ε_r)	-18.47	4.2

TABLE II. S11 AND GAIN RESULTS WITH DIFFERENT THICKNESS

Thickness	S11 (dB)	Gain (dB)
1.1 (mm)	-18.66	2.47
1.25(mm)	-19.46	3.2
1.28 (mm)	**-25.01**	**4.31**
1.4 (mm)	-21.6	2.89
1.48(mm)	-19.51	4.25

Inner radius is that the length from feeding point to end of the substrate. The size of the inner radius was changed and simulated in case of the fabrication errors. These changes can not be massive because, it would change the main characteristic of the design. Milimetric changes of the inner radius are listed in Table III and fabricated antenna is shown in Figure 1.

TABLE III. S11 AND GAIN WITH DIFFERENTINNER RADIUS

Inner radius	S11 (dB)	Gain (dB)
8.7(mm)	-20.44	3.02
8.9(mm)	-22.55	4.2
9(mm)	**-25.01**	**4.31**
9.2(mm)	-24.89	4.22
9.5(mm)	-23.45	3.45

Fig. 1. Top View of the Design

The input match simulation and measured results are shown in Figure 2. The minimum value of the resonance is seen ad -25.01 dB at 12.04 GHz.

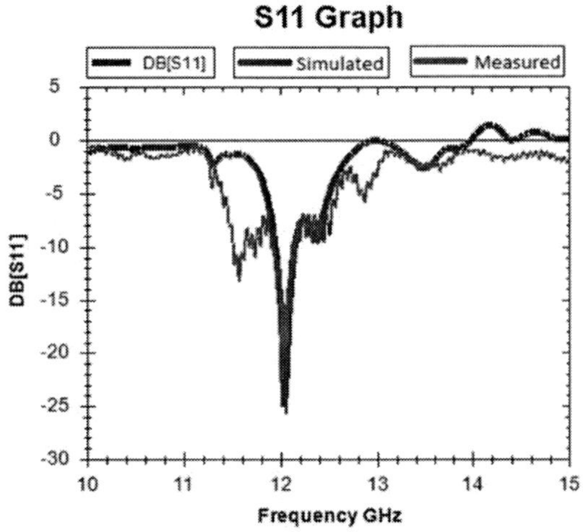

Fig. 2. Simulated and Measured Input match (S11) of the Design

We can see the simulation and measured results of the Electric field Theta polarization as (4.31 dB) in Figure 3. It could be seen that both results agrees well.

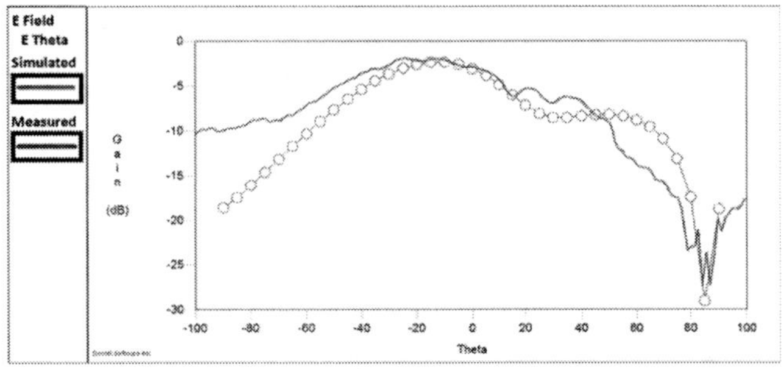

Fig. 3. Gain graph of the design normalized to zero dB.

III. Conclusion

In this project, single resonance, spiral microstrip patch antenna designed, simulated, manufactured and tested. Simulation and measurement results of the input match and radiation pattern were presented in graphs and they are matching with each other. This antenna preferable for low profile when compared to similar designs found in literature [10-11-16]. This antenna can be easily applicable into systems for satellite communication applications. The design, simulation, manufacture and examination of the antenna is made by using a 3D planar electromagnetic simulator, called Sonnet Suites [12-14-17].

REFERENCES

[1] Churng-Jou Tsai, Chia-Hsn Lin, Wei-Chih Chen, Chen-Lin Lu and Jinn-KweiGuo, "A CPW-Feed Printed Antenna for Dual-band WLAN operations", IEEE, 2011.

[2] K.-L. Wong, "Compact and Broadband Microstrip Antennas", Wiley and Sons, Inc., New York, vol. 1, (2002), pp. 12-15.

[3] C. A. Balanis, "Antenna Theory, Analysis and Design," ISBN 978-81-265-2422-8, John Wiley & Sons, Inc., U.K., 2013.

[4] A. A. Deshmukh and G. Kumar, "Compact broadband gap-coupled shorted L-shaped microstrip antennas," in IEEE Antennas and Propagation International Symposium, vol 1, (Baltimore, Maryland), pp. 106–109, IEEE, July 2001

[5] Balanis, C. A., Antenna Theory Analysis and Design, John Wiley & Sons, Inc., 1997.

[6] Huang, C. Y., J. Y Wu, and K. L. Wong, "Cross-slot coupled microstrip antenna and dielectric resonator antenna for circular polarization," IEEE Trans. Antennas Propagat., Vol. 47, 605–609, Apr. design 1999.

[7] Iwasaki, H., "A circularly polarized small-size microstrip antenna with a cross slot," IEEE Trans. Antennas Propagat., Vol. 44, 1399–1401, Oct. 1996.

[8] Ravindra Kumar Yadav, Jugul Kishor and Ram Lal Yadava, "Design of Hexagonal Patch Antenna for Mobile Wireless System," IEEE IJSTM, Vol. 2 Issue 4,IEEE Trans. Antennas Propag., vol.978, no. 1, pp.174-December 2011.

[9] Xian-Ling Liang, Tayeb A. Denidni, Li-Na Zhang, Rong-Hong Jin, JunPing Geng and Quan Yu , " Printed binomial curved slot antennas for wideband applications," IEEE Trans. Microwave theory and techniques, vol. 59, no. 4, pp. 1058-1065, 2011.

[10] Ge, Y., K. P. Esselle, and T. S. Bird, "Acompact E-shaped patch antenna with corrugated wings," IEEE Trans. Antennas Propagat., Vol. 54, No. 8, 2411–2413, Aug. 2006.

[11] R.Garg, P.Shartia, I. Bahl, A.Ittipiboon, "Microstrip Antenna Design Handbook" pp:2, Artech House, 978-0890065136, 2001.

[12] Sonnet Suites, version 13.52, www.sonnetsoftware.com.

[13] Y.Ozmen, T.Imeci, S.H. Ozkul, K. Calıskan, H.C. Sarıgül, "Ku Band Microstrip Patch Antenna" SIU 2015 23th, pp. 2165-0608, 2015.

[14] Ronald Edward Jackson, Jr., "Mems Based Tunable Microstrip Patch Antenna Fabricated Using Printed Circuit Processing Techniques," pp:1, Auburn, Alabama, August 7, 2006.

[15] Abdullah Çerkezi, Ş. Taha İmeci, Ylli Rama, "Double E-Shaped Multi-Resonance High-Gain Patch Antenna", pp.4, 2015 Texas Symposium on Wireless and Microwave Circuits and Systems Baylor University April 23-24, 2015.

[16] Dinisio Raony Ribeiro, Leonardo Augusto de Santana, Marlen Carneiro Alves and Jose Felipe Almeida, Carlos Leonidas da S.S. Sobrinho,"Spiral Microstrip Antenna", IEEE MTT-S International Microwave & Optoelectronics Conference (IMOC 2007), pp. 104-106,2007.

[17] Y.X.Du, L.Qin, X.L.Xi, "The Analysis and Simulation of Microstrip Spiral Antenna for Microwave Hyperthermia" IEEE Bioinformatics and Biomedical Engineering 3rd International Conference, pp. 1-4, 2009

Compact 4-Port MIMO Antenna System for 5G Mobile Terminal

Mujeeb Abdullah, Yong-Ling Ban, Kai Kang, Obeng Kwakye Kings ford Sarkodie, Ming-Yang Li
School of Electronic Engineering, University of Electronic Science and Technology of China
Chengdu, Sichuan, P. R. China, 611731
E-mail: mujeeb.abdullah@gmail.com, byl@uestc.edu.cn, kangkai@uestc.edu.cn, obengsark@yahoo.com

***Abstract*—A compact four-port multiple input multiple output (MIMO) antenna system is proposed operating in C-band at 3.5 GHz (3400 ~ 3600) for future fifth generation 5G technology mobile broadband services. The four-port MIMO antenna system consist of an Inverted-L(IL)shape monopole on the edges of non-ground portion of 9×9 mm² with substrate FR-4 and ground plane of dimensions of 136×68 mm². The compact size of the MIMO antenna system is realized by using IL-shape shorted stripe and IL-shape slot etched in the ground plane to increase the electrical length of the IL-shape monopole for achieving the desired resonating frequency of 3.5 GHz.The antennas are placed orthogonally to each other results in reduce mutual coupling (less than -15 dB) with impendence bandwidth of 200 MHz for ($S_{11} \leq -6$ dB) and polarization and pattern diversity is also achieved.**

Keywords—Multiple-input multiple-output (MIMO), mutual coupling, printed antennas, pattern and polarization diversity.

I. Introduction

The multiple-input multiple output(MIMO) operation is promising method to enhance data throughput using multi-path for transmission and reception of data with different channels[1].To realize MIMO operation for mobile phone handset multi-antenna structure can be used for having polarization and pattern diversity for reliable communication with minimum mutual coupling.At WRC-15 (World Radio communication Conference 2015) in Nov 2015 major decision was made allocating 3.5 GHz C-band (3400~3600 MHz) for future broadband mobile services, implementing beamforming techniques required for 5G mobile terminal and implementing multi-antenna structure for massive MIMO antenna array as reported in [2]-[3].In this paper compact four port MIMO antenna system is presented with potential application for 5G mobile terminal.

II. Antenna Design

In this study the MIMO antenna system is designed on the FR4 substrate with thickness of 0.8-mm and relative permittivity of 4.4 with length of 136 mm and width of 68 mm. The system ground plane has same dimensions as of the substrate leaving two non-ground portion of size 9×9 mm² at the corner edges as shown in Fig.1.The IL-Shape monopole antenna is fed by coaxial cable with impendence of 50 Ω. The radiating IL-shape monopole is of compact size of 6.3×5 mm². Antenna dimensions are as follow: L_1= 1.8 mm, S_1=5.3 mm, L_2=3 mm, S_2=6.3 mm, W_1=1.6 mm, W_{sh} = 0.4 mm, W_2=2 mm, L_{S1}=5, L_{S2}=3.5 mm, W_{S1}=0.37 mm, WS_2=0.25 mm. The profile of the IL-monopole antenna is reduced by adding the shorted IL-shorted stripe and IL-slot etched in the ground plane to lower resonating frequency length of guided wavelength in the FR-4 substrate is also helpful in the impendence matching.

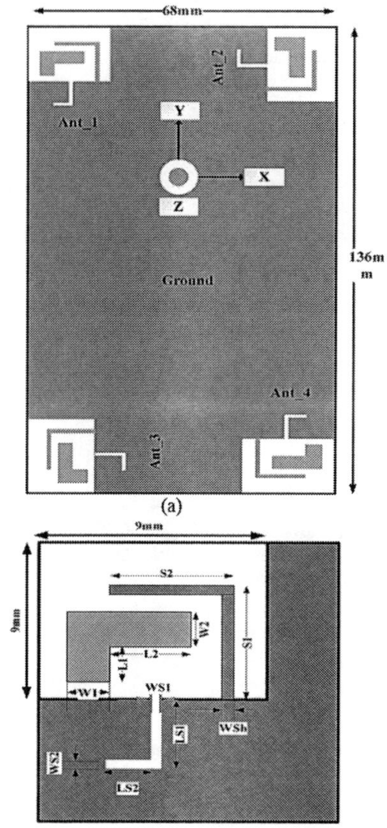

(b)
Fig.1 (a) Full Structure view for proposed MIMO antenna system (b) Detail dimensions of the unit single IL-shape monopole antenna with IL-shorted stripes and IL-shape slot in groud plane.

III. Result & Discussion

A. S-Parameters Results For Four Port MIMO Antenna System

The proposed four-port MIMO antenna system is carried out with CST microwave studio. Due to symmetry of the proposed structure and for the clarity only four characteristic curves are considered for this study (S_{11},S_{12},S_{13},S_{14}) as shown Fig.2.The proposed four port MIMO antenna systemincorporates IL-short stripe and IL-slot for each four inverted L-shape monopole antenna.The shorting stripe reduce the inductive behavior of the IL-monopole and thus it resonate at lower frequency whereas inserting the slot in the ground plane reroute the path of current launched by radiating element.
The parameter of interest for the proposed four port MIMO antenna system is L_{S1} with simulated S-parameter is shown in Fig.3. As the value of L_{S1} increased from 4 mm to 5 mm the resonating frequency shift from 3.8 to 3.6 GHz due to fact that the current at the edge of slot is taking long path to travel to the shorted IL stripe.The mutual coupling among antennas is well below the required standard of below -15 dB without using any decoupling network.

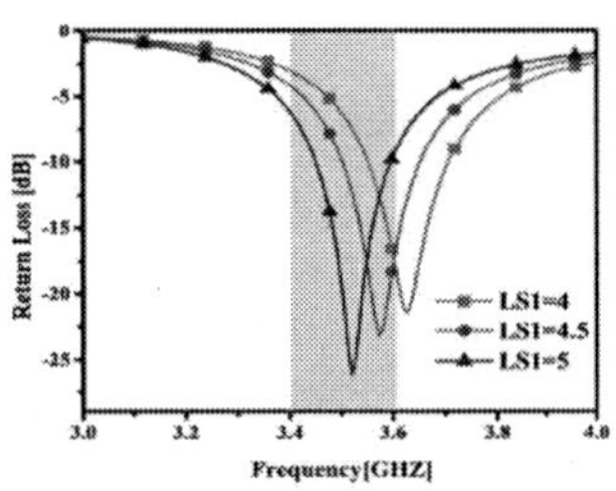

Fig.2 Simulated S-Parameter result for the parametric study of the proposed MIMO antenna system (Ant_1).

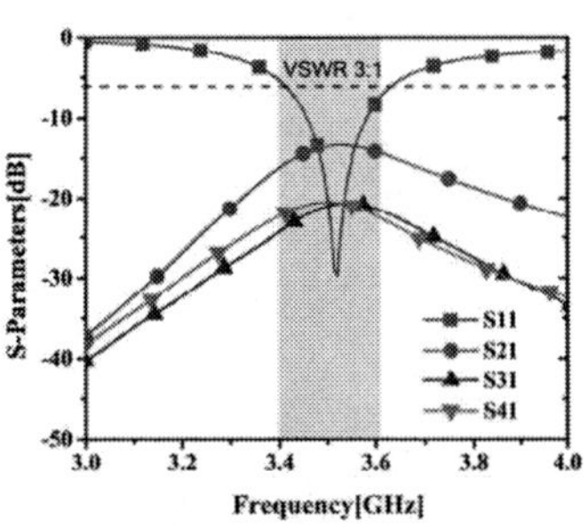

Fig.3 Simulated S-Parameters result for the optimized MIMO antenna system (Ant1).

B. Fairfield Radiation Pattern, Diversity Performance, Specific Absorption Rate

The radiation characteristic for the simulated for the proposed MIMO antenna system is plotted for 3.5 GHz in the x-y, x-z planes.The radiation is directive in some direction due to short stripes surrounding the IL-Shaped monopole antenna. The simulation results are carried with the corresponding port terminated in 50 Ω impedance.The pattern diversity can be noted in x-y and x-z plane depicted in Fig.4 and Fig.5 respectively. The MIMO antenna system performance metrics of interest for are Envelope correlation coefficient (ECC less than 0.5), Diversity gain (DG) and Mean effective gain (MEG) with $|MEG_i\text{-}MEG_j|$ less than 3 dB for the operating band where (i,j) are the number of antenna element and the proposed MIMO antenna system did satisfy this criteria. The simulated value for Specific Absorption Rate(SAR) at for head the propose MIMO antenna system at 3.5GHz for 1-g is 0.8 and 10-g at 0.5 meet the required standard as reported as [3].

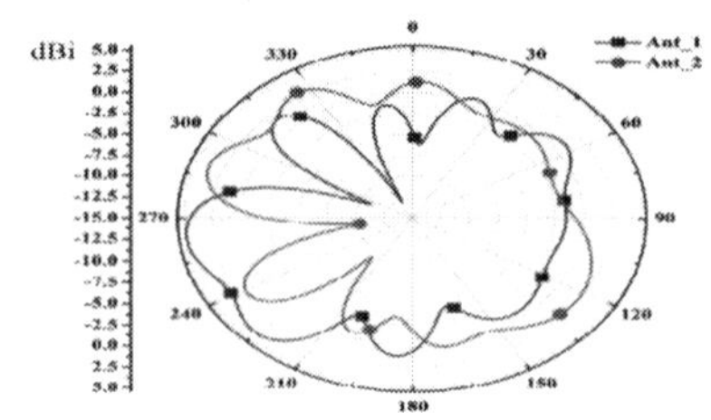

Fig. 4 Simulated 2-D radiation pattern x-y plane at 3.5 GHz.

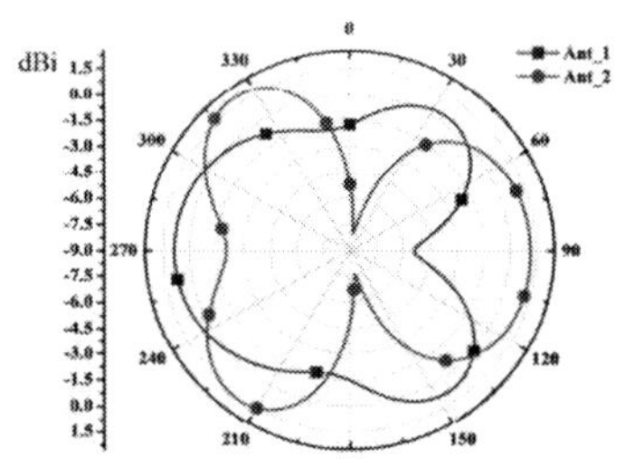

Fig. 5 Simulated 2-D radiation pattern x-z plane at 3.5 GHz.

Table II.

S.NO	MEG1 (XPR=0 dBi)	MEG2 (XPR=6 dBi)	ECC ρ_{12}= ρ_{21}	Diversity Gain
Ant_1	-3	-4.33	0.027	9.93
Ant_2	-2.99	-4.36		9.91

IV. Conclusion

A four port MMIO antenna system for future 5G technology covering the 3.5GHz C-band (3400~3600) GHz band for mobile broadband service has been presented. The significance of this paper,as compared to the reported worked on 8 and 16 antenna array, the proposed MIMO antenna system explore the additional capability of polarization and pattern diversity without using antenna decoupling network with impedance bandwidth of 200 MHz.The diversity performance parameters consist of ECC and MEG is numerically calculated from the far field radiation pattern considering multi-path environment..

References

[1] A. Lozano, F. R. Farrokhi and R. A. Valenzuela, "Lifting the limits on high speed wireless data access using antenna arrays," in *IEEE Communications Magazine*, vol. 39, no. 9, pp. 156-162, Sep.2001

[2] M. Y. Li; Y. L. Ban; Z. Q. Xu; G. Wu; C. Y. D. Sim; K. Kang; Z. F. Yu, "8-Port Orthogonally Dual-Polarized Antenna Array for 5G Smartphone Applications," in *IEEE Transactions on Antennas and Propagation*, vol.64, no.9, pp.3820-3830,Sep.2016

[3] Wong, K.-L., Lu, J.-Y., Chen, L.-Y., Li, W.-Y. and Ban, Y.-L. (2016), "8-antenna and 16-antenna arrays using the quad-antenna linear array as a building block for the 3.5-GHz LTE MIMO operation in the smartphone" *Microw. Opt. Technol. Lett.*, vol. 58, no. 1, pp. 174-181, Nov.2015

A Novel Reflecarray Antenna Backed With Double Layer FSS for RCS Reduction

Hande Bodur, Sibel Çimen, Gonca Çakır
Electronics and Communication Engineering
Kocaeli University
Kocaeli, Turkey
hande.bodur@kocaeli.edu.tr, sibelgunduz@kocaeli.edu.tr,
gonca@kocaeli.edu.tr

Sibel Ünaldı
Electrical and Electronics Engineering
Bilecik Şeyh Edabali University
Bilecik, Turkey
sibel.unaldi@bilecik.edu.tr

***Abstract*—In this paper, a novel frequency selective surface (FSS) is designed for reduction of radar cross section (RCS) level in the reflectarray antenna. A 9x9 variable size FSS structure is constructed on double opposite side geometry. The reduction of RCS performance is compared with ground plane backed and designed FSS backed reflectarray antenna. The simulation results demonstrate that the FSS backed reflectarray antenna can achieve the reduction of RCS level in-band and out-of-band. Also gain and radiation performance of FSS backed reflectarray antenna is nearly same with ground plane backed reflectarray antenna.**

Keywords*— *radar cross section; reflectarray antenna; frequency selective surface.

I. INTRODUCTION

Reflectarray antennas are classed at high gain antennas which are used in communication systems and radar applications. They have many advantages when compared with traditional parabolic reflector as low cost, low profile, small antenna mass, easy production, no feeding networks and electronically beam direction ability. [1]

It is widely known that high gain antennas increase the RCS level and this case play an essential role on stealth performance of antennas in military applications (aircraft, ships and so on) about reducing detectability.

There are several methods for reduction of RCS, including radar absorbing material (RAM) coating [2], passive or active cancellations [3], ferrite substrate [4] and using FSS [5]. In this work, FSS is investigated for RCS reduction.

This work has two important goals. First goal is reduction of RCS level with FSS both in-band and out-of-band. Second is preserve gain and radiation performance of original reflectarray antenna. A 9x9 elements reflectarray antenna backed with opposite side double layer FSS structure are designed and simulated. The simulation results show that FSS backed is reduced the RCS level when compared the ground plane backed. On the other hand gain and radiation results are in a good agreement with original reflectarray antenna.

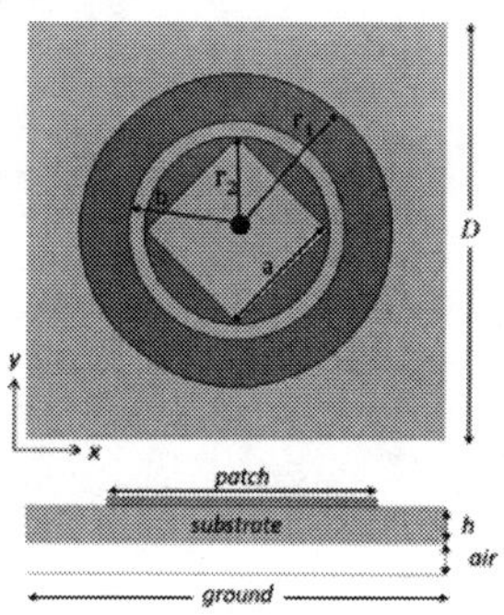

Fig. 1. The view of the reflect array unit cell.

II. DESIGN PROCEDURE

A. Reflectarray Antenna Structure

The reflectarray antenna which used for the reduction of RCS level consists of 9 x 9 elements and each element has 16 x 16 mm dimensions in xy plane. The geometry of unit cell of the reflectarray antenna is shown in Figure 1. The used design parameters of the unit cell are r_1 =variable, $r_2=t_* r_1$, $a=s_* 2r_2$, $b=s_* 2r_1$, s=1.4, t=0.6, air=5.5 mm and r_1 is changing from 3.5 mm to 5.9 mm. The reflectarray antenna is presented for X-band applications and the unit cell dimension is chosen as D=16 mm. The prosposed unit cell is designed on a dielectric substrate Arlon AR 600 ($\varepsilon_0 = 6.15$) with thickness h =0.508 mm. Figure 2 shows phase shifts versus r_1 of designed geometry at 10 GHz. By using variable size of elements, approximately 430° phase range is obtained.

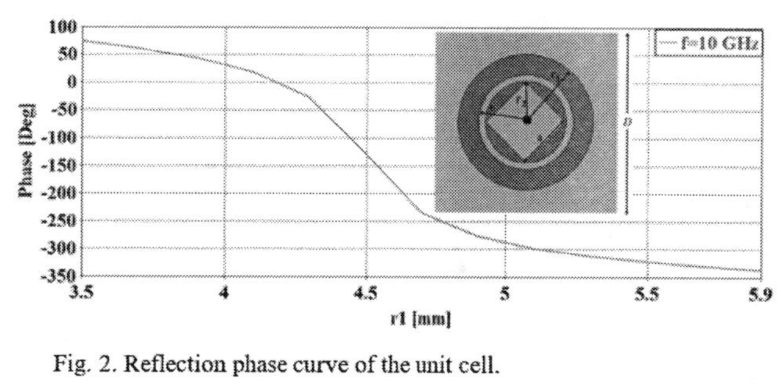

Fig. 2. Reflection phase curve of the unit cell.

B. *FSS Backed Reflectarray Antenna*

Instead of a single layer of FSS, double layer FSS arranged on the back side of the reflectarray to obtain RCS reduction. The same reflectarray arrangement is used as a FSS ground plane. Two layers settlement with an opposite sides arrangement in back plane of reflectarray is shown in Figure 3. While making RCS simulations with FSS backed reflectarray antenna 5mm thick air layer is used between reflectarray and each FSS planes demonstrated in Figure 3.

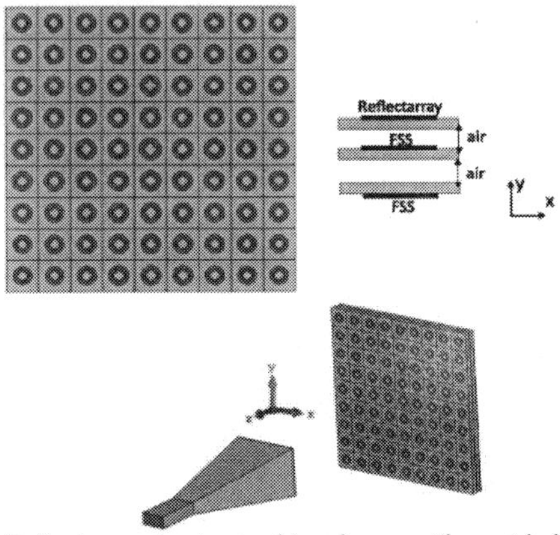

Fig. 3. Reflectarray structure and two layers settlement in back plane of reflectarray used for FSS ground layer.

III. SIMULATION RESULTS

In Figure 4 simulation results of the monostatic RCS of the ground plane backed reflectarray antenna and FSS backed reflectarray antenna designs are compared. The two opposite layers FSS backed on the reflectarray reduced the RCS level obviously.

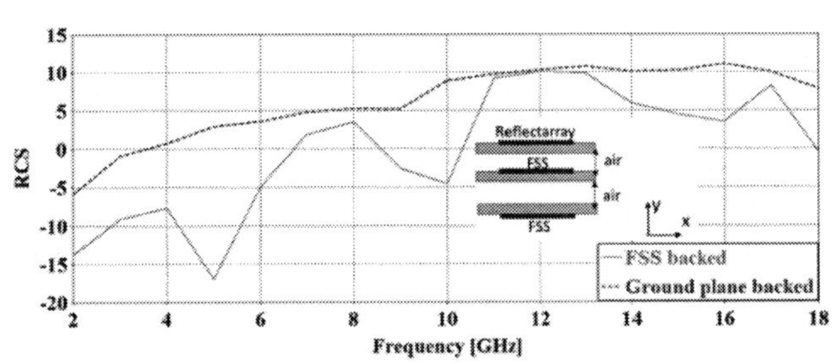

Fig. 4. Simulation Results of monostatic RCS of the ground plane backed and FSS backed reflectarray antennas.

Good agreement between gain results for ground plane backed and FSS backed reflectarray antennas are obtained as seen in Figure 5.

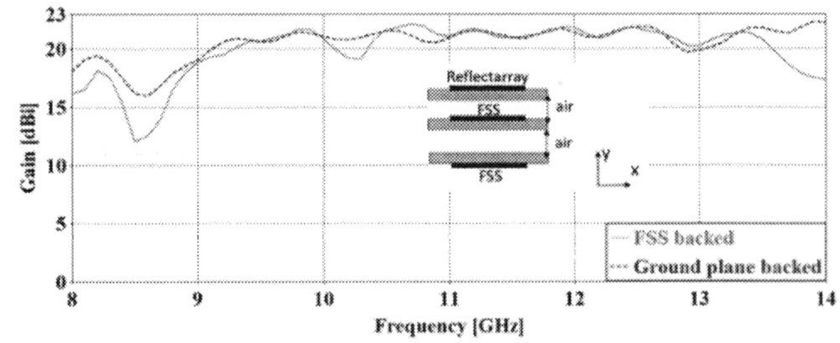

Fig. 5. Gain curves for the ground plane backed reflectarray antenna and FSS backed reflectarray antenna.

Reduced RCS level is the main research for the reflect array without changing the radiation performance of the antenna. Thus the effects of the FSS backed reflectarray design, are examined on performance of the reflectarray. For this reason gain curves are compared in ground plane backed and FSS backed cases. Obtained results given in Figure 5 show that gain curves of the reflectarray antennas in each case are not different from the each other.

IV. CONCLUSION

A novel opposite side double layer FSS structure is entegreted to reflectarray antenna as a ground for RCS reduction. The conventional reflectarray with ground plane backed and new configuration of reflectarray is simulated by using CST Microwave Studio. The simulation results demonstrate that the RCS level of designed reflectarray with FSS ground is reduced in-band and out-of-band. Gain and radiation performance of original reflectarray antenna is preserved.

ACKNOWLEDGMENT

The authors wish to acknowledge the assistance and support of The Scientific and Technological Research Council of Turkey (TUBITAK) for supporting this work (Project No: 114E500).

REFERENCES

[1] J. Huang and J. A. Encinar, Reflectarray Antennas. Piscataway, NJ, USA:IEEE Press/Wiley, 2008.

[2] G. G. Peixoto, A. L. de Paula, L. A. Andrade, C. M. A. Lopes and M. C. Rezende, "Radar absorbing material (RAM) and shaping on radar cross section reduction of dihedral corners," SBMO/IEEE MTT-S International Conference on Microwave and Optoelectronics, 2005.

[3] E. F. Knott, J. F. Shaeffer, and M. T. Tuley, Radar Cross Section. Raleigh, NC, USA: SciTech, 2004

[4] D. M. Pozar, "Radiation and scattering characteristics of microstrip antennas on normally biased ferrite substrates," IEEE Trans. Antennas Propag., vol. 40, pp. 1084–1092, 1992.

[5] S. Genovesi, F. Costa, and A. Monorchio, "Low-profile arraywith reduced radar cross section by using hybrid frequency selective surfaces," IEEE Trans. Antennas Propag., vol. 60, no. 5, pp. 2327–2335, May 2012.

Patch Antenna Size-Reduction Parametric Study

James L. Vedral and Randall L. Musselman
Department of Electrical and Computer Engineering
United States Air Force Academy
Colorado Springs, CO, USA
james.vedral@usafa.edu; randall.musselman@usafa.edu

Abstract— **Size-reduction techniques are applied to a circular UHF patch antenna, by varying parameters to better predict its desired resonant frequency. Specifically, slits are introduced into the patch, which are parametrically varied to determine the optimum slit dimensions for maximum size reduction.**

Keywords – patch, UHF antenna, antenna size reduction

I. Introduction

Patch antennas typically resonate with dimensions that are near one-half wavelength, $\lambda/2$ [1], which can be cumbersomely large at UHF frequencies. This large size is reduced by a factor of approximately $1/\sqrt{\varepsilon_r}$ by using higher permittivity ($\varepsilon = \varepsilon_o\varepsilon_r$) material; although, the decreased bandwidth caused by higher permittivity can make this approach unattractive. In order to focus on size-reduction techniques rather than exotic materials, we chose to use common FR4 printed circuit-board material for our UHF patch-antenna size-reduction analysis. FR4 has relative permittivity, ε_r of approximately 4.5 at UHF, which should reduce patch dimensions nearly 50%, if no other size-reduction techniques were used.

The addition of slits in the circular patch antenna has proven to reduce the patch radius by nearly an additional 50%, beyond the effects of permittivity alone [2,3,4]. However, the choice of slit dimensions has so far been an iterative approach. In this paper, we present the results of a parametric study of the slit dimensions in Fig. 1, in order to aid in the optimum design of size-reduced circular patch antennas.

II. Slotted Patch Antenna Design

To compare the results of the parametric study, an ordinary circular patch, without slits, was simulated in ANSYS Electromagnetic Desktop, a commercial finite element solver. The patch was simulated with radius, R, of 4.5*cm*, dielectric thickness of 1.7*mm*, dielectric constant of $\varepsilon_r = 4.5$, and probe fed at a distance of 0.45cm from the center of the patch. The theoretical resonant frequency can be calculated by

$$f = \frac{1.8412c}{2\pi R\sqrt{\varepsilon_r}} \qquad (1)$$

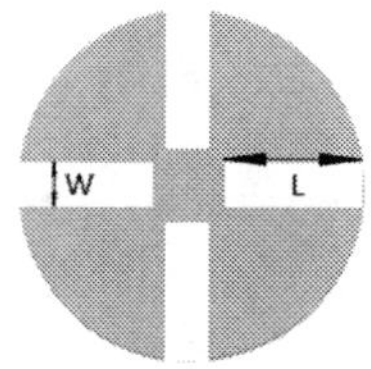

Fig. 1. Mask of the slotted circular patch antenna. *L* is the slot depth from the outer edge, *W* is the width of the slot. Both parameters were varied in this paper as a way to reduce patch size.

The length, L and width, W of the slots in Fig. 1 were incrementally changed in an attempt to estimate their effects on the resonant frequency. These two parameters were considered independently to take into account that each can be fine-tuned for different purposes, in spite of the fact that their combined dimensions add to the increased effective circumference of the circular patch. As expected, increasing both L and W decreases the resonance frequency. However, the standing-wave ratio (*SWR*) of the feed tended to change unpredictably as W and L increased. By increasing the slot length, L while fixing the width, W at a constant 1*mm*, the resonant frequency monotonically decreased. The input impedance can be fine-tuned as the parameters are varied, by changing the feed location; however, we chose to leave it fixed at 49% of R at 45° from an arbitrary slit to avoid introducing too many degrees of freedom at once. The corresponding reduction in the patch radius, as L is increased, can be seen in Fig. 2, indicating that the only limit to the size-reducing benefit of increasing L is the physical radius itself, i.e., L nearly equal to R. The data in Fig. 2 suggests that the original patch radius, which resulted in resonance at 914*MHz*, can be made resonant at 471*MHz* by the addition of slits that almost meet in the center of the patch. Without these slits, the circular patch antenna would require a radius of 8.8cm in order to be resonant at 471*MHz*, instead of 4.5cm (51% of 8.8*cm*).

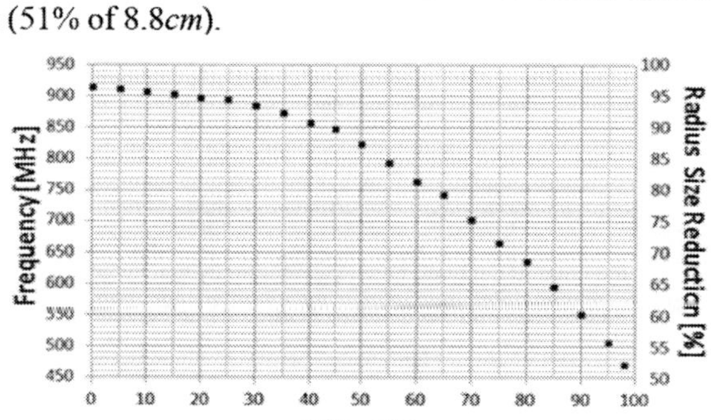

Fig 2. Top: The change in resonant frequency/Size reduction vs the change in slot length, L.

As previously suggested, the slit width, *W* can also be increased, in order to decrease the patch radius for a desired resonant frequency. To explore the effects of changing *W, L* was kept at a constant 98% of *R*. Two of the slits were removed, shown in Fig. 3 to allow the width to increase without intersecting one another, and thus cutting the patch into two halves. The symmetric slits at 90^0 depicted in Fig 1 are only necessary for circularly polarized. Decreased resonant frequency with increased *W* is evident in Fig 4. However, this is not without some design limitations. As previously discussed, four orthogonally oriented slits shown in Fig. 1 are required for circularly polarized transmission, which limit the relationship between *L* and *W* to prevent the slits from touching one another. Also, the SWR changes significantly with changes in *W*, while keeping the feed point constant. Due to this SWR variation one would need to find the optimal feed point for each *L-W* combination, in order to achieve a desired input impedance. Although time consuming, finding the optimal feed point can be done using known methods [5,6]. These methods are constrained only by the available area to place the feed point.

We explored various combinations of *W* and *L* with the geometry depicted in Fig 1, in order to find a predictable pattern. The results shown in Fig 5 indicate that as *W* was varied for several different values of *L*, a linear relationship emerged for small values of *W/L*, i.e., $W < 0.02L$. As $W > 0.02L$, further increasing *W* yields diminishing returns.

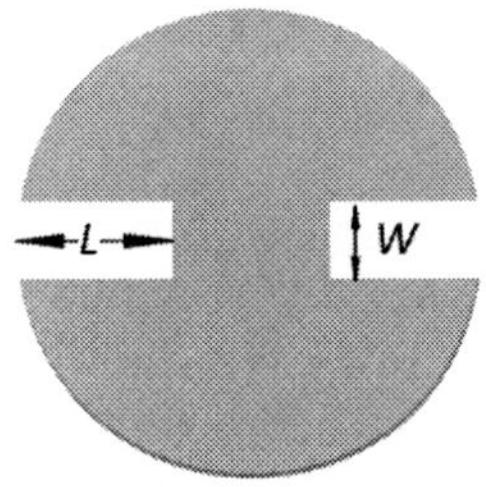

Fig. 3. Mask of the slotted circular patch antenna. *L* is the slot depth from the outer edge, w is the width of the slot. The two slotted design was made to vary *W* with fewer restrictions.

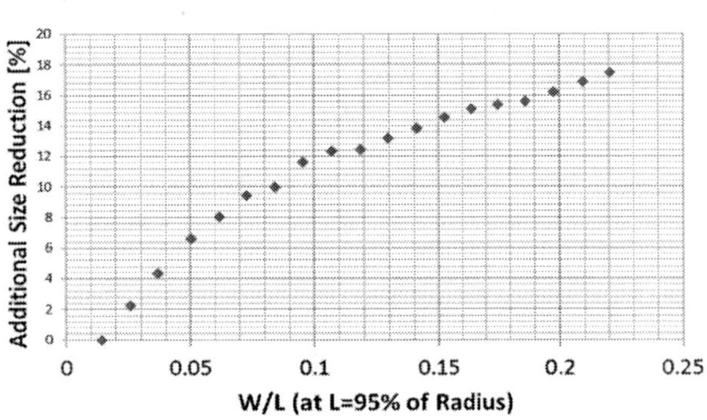

Fig 4. The change in resonant frequency vs the change in *W/L* from the geometry in Fig 3, *W* while *L=95% of R*.

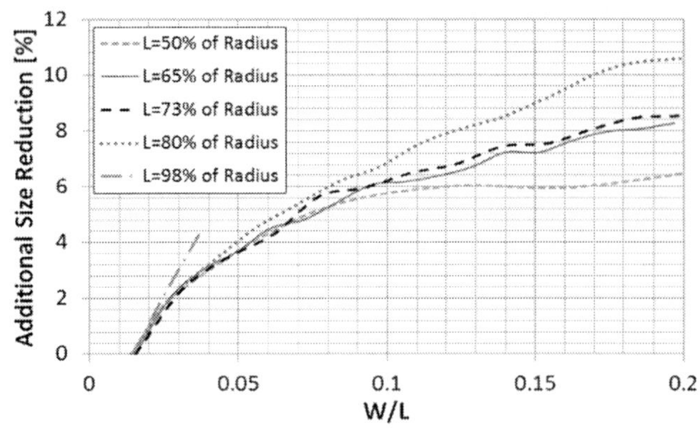

Fig 5. The change in resonant frequency vs the change in *W/L* using the geometry in Fig 1.

III. CONCLUSION

A parametric study of slit dimensions in a circular patch antenna was performed in order to characterize the size-reduction benefits of these slits. It was shown that as the slit length and width increase the resonant frequency of the patch decreases. However, size reduction is much more sensitive to L than W. The *W/L* relationship is linear for *W/L*<2%. As *W/L* > 2%, further increasing *W* yields diminishing returns. Maximum size reduction can be achieved when L is just shy of touching the opposite slit. When *L* is 98% of the radius the maximum achievable *W/L* before the orthogonal slits touch is 3.6%. This optimum slit design will maximize size reduction and the available patch area, in order to locate the feed point for minimum *SWR*.

REFERENCES

[1] Constantine A. Balanis, *Antenna Theory Analysis and Design*, New York, Harper & Row, 1982.
[2] Randall L. Musselman, Shawn Killpack, et al., "Adaptive null-steered interference-rejection for a mobile satellite receiver", IEEE Int'l Symp. on Phased Array Syst. and Tech., Boston, October 2010.
[3] Randall L. Musselman, Daniel Parker, et al., "Circular Array for Satcom Interference Rejection", IEEE Int'l Conf. on Wireless Inf. Tech. and Syst., Maui, November 2012.
[4] Randall L. Musselman, James Vedral, "Circular Patch Antenna Size-Reduction Technique" Digests of the 2016 17th Biennial IEEE Conference on Electromagnetic Field Computation. 2016.
[5] Sharma, P. C., and K. C. Gupta. "Analysis and optimized design of single feed circularly polarized microstrip antennas." IEEE Transactions on Antennas and Propagation 31.6 (1983): 949-955.
[6] Raval, Falguni, and Jagruti Makwana. "optimization of resonance frequency of circular patch antenna at 5 GHz using particle swarm optimization." (2011).

Design of a low-profile 2 to 6 GHz circular polarized single arm hexagonal spiral array antenna

Yongduk Oh, Sangwook Nam
School of Electrical and Computer Engineering and INMC, Seoul National University
Seoul, 151-742, Korea
domybest24@ael.snu.ac.kr

***Abstract*— We introduce a low-profile circular polarized, single-arm hexagonal spiral array antenna having a 30° beam scan without grating lobe operating 3:1(2 to 6 GHz) bandwidth placed on a ground plane. The array is composed of regular hexagonal spirals fed by 50 Ohm coaxial cable without Balun. A spurious resonance occurs in the feeding structure due to the periodic structure when the element antennas are arranged, and the resonance can be suppressed by using ferrite. A prototype 8 × 8 array is fabricated and measured. As a result, we implemented a circularly polarized antenna with an axial ratio of 3.5 or less that enables 30° beam steering of 2~6GHz(3:1)**

Keywords*— *low-profile Spiral antenna arrays, Circular polarization, Wideband

I. Introduction

In this paper, we design and manufacture a jammer antenna for electronic warfare. Antennas for jammers need to have special characteristics such as broadband, circular polarization, high gain, and beam steering capability. A method for implementing a high gain antenna is to increase the antenna aperture area by arranging the element antenna according to the purpose. Antennas for jammers should be able to control the antenna radiation pattern to quickly respond to ground and airborne threats and prevent anti-jamming. It is difficult to satisfy these conditions with a single-element antenna, and a good method is to use an antenna array. Although array antennas have advantages of high gain and beam steering, it is difficult to realize broadband because electrical distances are different for each frequency when element antennas are arranged [1]. To overcome this difficulty, WAVES [2] and WIPA methods are proposed, but gain in low frequency band is a problem [3]. In this paper, we propose a miniaturized hexagonal spiral antenna and array them by triangular lattice arrangement to improve element antenna density and increase gain in low frequency band. Recently, Tzanidis [4] proposed ISPA which use Balun for feeding, which complicates the feed network. In the proposed array, all the element antennas having the same structure are arranged periodically. We used coaxial feeding structure for easiness of feeding and low-profile array structure, however, it was found that there is a spurious resonance in the array at the frequency where the total length from a matching disk to the neighboring matching disk including the feeding cable and ground becomes one wavelength. At the frequency, the efficiency of the spiral antenna is lowered by radiation in the feed structure. In order to suppress the resonance, the outer conductor of coaxial feed line was wrapped around by the ferrite to prevent the current from flowing to the outer surface of the outer conductor by the large resistance of the ferrite, thereby suppressing the resonance. The spiral antenna is basically a traveling wave antenna. However, in the low frequency band, the reflection occurs at the arm end and it shows standing wave and the axial ratio is deteriorated. In our design, small resistors are distributed in the outer part of the spiral arm to improve the axial ratio at low frequency band.

II. Element Design Configuration

The element antenna is depicted in Fig. 1. Two arm spiral antenna needs a Balun for feeding balanced structure. Unlike the conventional two arm spiral antenna, the single-arm spiral antenna is fed by 50 Ohm coaxial cable. Inner conductor of the coaxial cable is connected to center of the spiral arm and outer conductor of the coaxial cable is connected to the disk[5]. Coaxial cable is wrapped around the ferrite. The spiral arm is placed on 1mm thick dielectric substrate (ε_r=4.3), where an antenna height (H_{ant}) is 10mm (0.07 wave length at the lowest frequency of 2 GHz). The shape of unit element is regular hexagon with side length(L) of 20.8mm, dx of 36mm, dy of 41.6mm, arm width (w) and spacing (s) of 1mm as shown in Fig. 1. Small resistors are distributed to reduce reflection wave at the arm end [6].

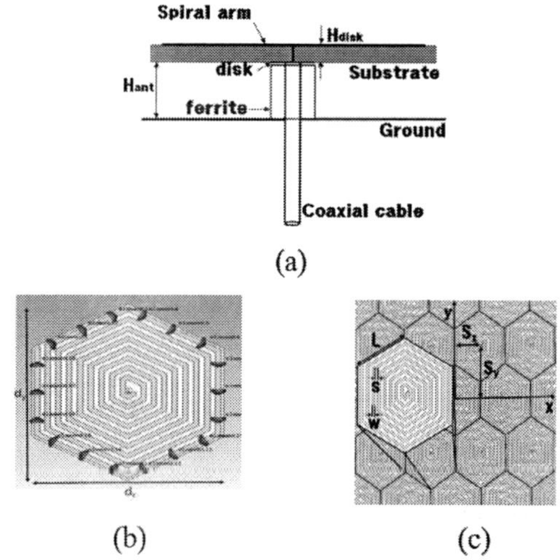

Fig. 1. (a) side view of element. (b) top view of element. (c) top view of array.

III. ARRAY ANTENNA

An array antenna has inherently narrow bandwidth, since electrical distances are different for each frequency. Therefore, it is important to reduce inter-element spacing to implement broad bandwidth. A scan angle 30° at 6 GHz is investigated to determine a longest (electrical) inter-element spacing without any grating lobe. The condition for avoidance of grating lobe is given by

$$\frac{d}{\lambda} < \frac{1}{1+\sin|\theta|} \quad (1)$$

Where d is the inter-element spacing, θ is the scan angle. Hence, For scan angle 30° at 6 GHz without grating lobe, d < 33.3mm is required. The inter-element spacing, S_x and S_y have different value each other ($S_x = \sqrt{3}L/2$, S_y = 1.5L, L=20.8mm), but they satisfy the aforementioned condition. By using the resistor, the element antenna can be miniaturized and the element antenna can be arranged in a triangular lattice to prevent the occurrence of grating lobe.

When the element antennas were arranged, VSWR has a high value at 3.96 GHz as shown in Fig. 2. In the feed structure, the current flowing out of the outer conductor of the coaxial cable, disk and ground plane is as shown in the Fig. 2. No current flows at the boundary of the element antenna. Resonance occurs when the current flowing length becomes one wavelength. When all the lengths of disk, cable and ground are combined, it is similar to the wavelength at 3.96. The efficiency of the spiral antenna is lowered at the frequency while the radiation structure radiates by resonance.

In order to suppress the resonance, a ferrite having a large resistance was used. The ferrite has a large resistance to prevent currents from flowing outside the outer conductor of the coaxial cable. As a result, it is possible to suppress the resonance and prevent the decrease in efficiency. VSWR is less than 2 as shown in Fig. 2.

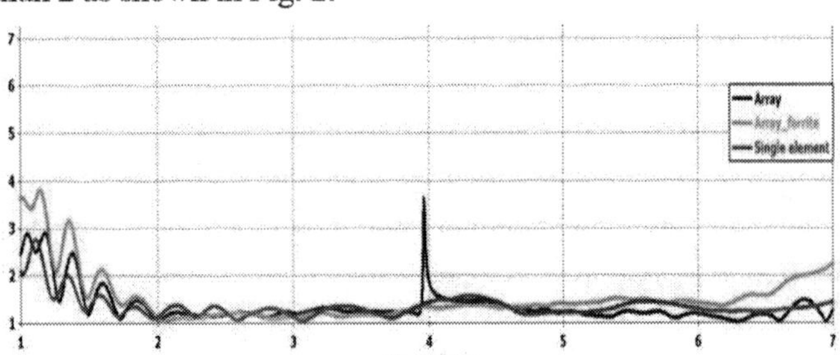

(a)

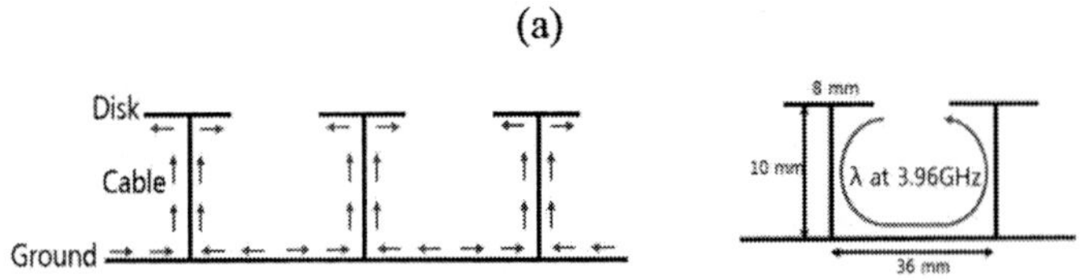

(b) (c)

Fig. 2. (a) VSWR of single element and array. (b) currents distribution. (c) resonance at 3.96GHz

IV. MANUFACTURE AND MEASUREMENT

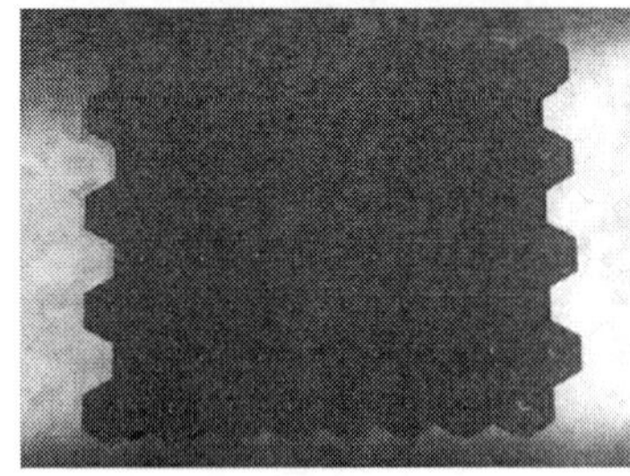

(a)

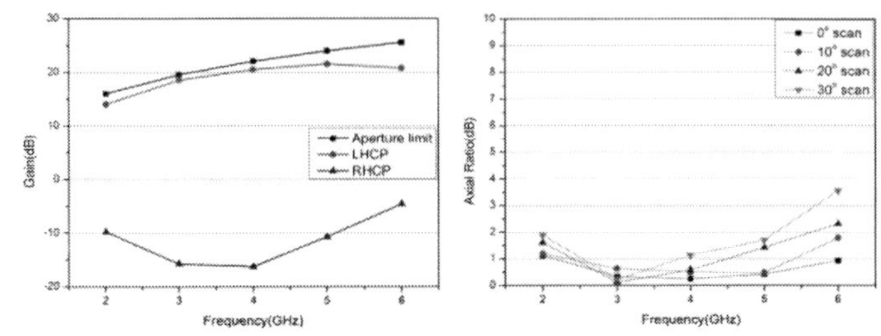

(b) (c)

Fig. 3. (a) Top view of manufactured antenna. (b) Gain. (c) Axial ratio.

A prototype 8 × 8 array was fabricated and measured. The gain shows a high gain of 14dB from 21dB. As a result of reducing the reflected wave effectively using the resistors distributed on the outside of the antenna, the array shows a good axial ratio less than 3.5dB at 30° beam scan.

V. CONCLUSION

A low-profile wideband, simple feeding, single arm hexagonal spiral antenna array is proposed. By arranging the resistors in a distributed manner, it was possible to achieve miniaturization of the antenna and circularly polarized wave of 3.5 dB or less in 3:1 bandwidth. Because the element antenna is designed as hexagonal shape and arrayed triangular lattice, the element spacing is reduced and the side lobe level is set to -10dB or less when the beam is steered up to +/- 30°. The spurious resonance generated by arranging the element antennas in array was suppressed by using ferrite.

REFERENCES

[1] Yi Huang, Kevin Boyle, Antennas:from Theory to Practice, John Wiley & Sons, 2008.

[2] E. Caswel, "Design and analysis of star spiral with applications to wideband arrays with variable element sizes," Ph.D. Dissertation, 2001.

[3] Hongzhao Ray Fang, Ramanan Balakrishnan, Regis Guinvarc'h, Koen Mouthaan, "Comparison of phased array configurations of spiral antenns", IEEE Conference publication :EuCAP, pp.1-5, 2015

[4] Ioannis Tzanidis, Kubilay sertel, John L. Volakis, "Interwoven spiral array (ISPA) with a 10:1 bandwidth on a ground plane", IEEE antenna and wireless propag. Letters, vol. 10, 2011.

[5] H. Nakno, R. Satake, and J. Yamauchi, "Extremely low-profile, single-arm, wideband spiral antenna radiating a circularly polarized wave," IEEE Trans. Antennas Propag., vol. 58, No. 5, May 2010.

[6] Meng Zou, Jin Pan, Pengcheng Li, Le Zuo, "Design and performance of a lumped resistively loaded spiral antenna" , 2012 IEEE international symposium on antennas and progag, pp. 1-2, 2012.

Sidelobe Reduction in Linear Microstrip Arrays Driven through Microstrip Corporate Feeds

Stanislav Ogurtsov and Slawomir Koziel
School of Science and Engineering
Reykjavik University
Reykjavik, Iceland
stanislav@ru.is, koziel@ru.is

***Abstract*— Simulation-based optimization is demonstrated for design of broadside linear microstrip antenna arrays energized through corporate feeds. Corporate feeds that are of interest here implement non-uniform amplitude excitation while include only equal-power split T-junctions as power distributing elements. A corporate feed designed and simulated as stand-alone microstrip circuit provides required complex wave amplitude at the outputs and is well matched at the input. Embedded elements of the linear microstrip array also well matched. On the other hand, a circuit comprising the antenna array connected to the feed exhibits increased sidelobes and degraded reflection coefficient. This results from deviations of the incident wave amplitudes from their expected values at the inputs of the array elements. To reduce sidelobes and keep the reflection coefficient at an acceptable level, the entire antenna-feed circuit is optimized and validated using numerical optimization and discrete electromagnetic simulations at the high-fidelity level of description. Surrogate-based methodology is exploited to speed up the optimization process. Our approach does not introduce extra hardware complications. A case study of two twelve-element microstrip array-feed circuits explains and demonstrates our approach.**

Keywords*— *linear antenna array; microstrip antenna array; corporate feed; simulation-based optimization

I. Introduction

Corporate feeds (CFs) with unequal power-split T-junctions and/or multi-port power splitters can implement required non-uniform excitation of linear antenna arrays, e.g., for microstrip/stripline [1,2] and waveguide [3] feeds. Non-decoupling of outputs and increased reflection (from the higher-impedance output) of such components needs to be addressed. Wilkinson power dividers improve the feed performance at the expense of increased complexity.

In this work, we consider microstrip CFs providing non-uniform amplitude excitation for linear antenna array. These CFs, however, are configured with equal power split T-junctions (matched only at the input), uniform straight microstrips, and mitered 90-degree microstrip bends. Despite structural simplicity, a circuit comprising the designed linear microstrip antenna array connected to the designed CF can exhibit increased sidelobes and degraded reflection coefficient. According to our studies and numerical experiments, these issues are caused by deviations (from values expected for a particular corporate feed) of the incident wave amplitudes at the inputs of the array elements and non-decoupled and not well-matched outputs of the T-junctions. To reduce sidelobes and keep the reflection coefficient at an acceptable level, the entire antenna-feed circuit is adjusted and validated using numerical optimization and discrete electromagnetic simulations. A case study for a twelve-element linear array of microstrip patch antennas (MPAs) is described.

II. Candidate Corporate Feed Architectures

For a 12-element linear array, outlined in Fig. 1(a), we detected two candidate CF architectures, outlined in Fig 1(b) and (c), with reduced sidelobe level (SLL). The search has been executed using the array factor over all possible sets of array factor amplitudes $a_n = 2^{-k_n/2}$ subject to conservation of power within the CF (input power = output power), assuming that the minimum incident power per array element is 1/64 of the input power, and for SLL defined over different sectors of angles (beyond the main lobe of the uniform amplitude half wavelength spaced 12 element array). Notice that k_n, referred to as the element level, e.g., in Fig. 2, stands for the number of T-junctions within a half CF the signal passes to reach element n. Cases of uniform half-wavelength and nonuniform spacings (with different constrains) have been checked using numerical optimization. For instance, the CF of Fig. 1(b) provide the array factor (AF) SLL = –16.5dB with half-wavelength spacings for SLL defined beyond sector [–9.6°, 9.6°]; the CF of Fig. 1(c) provide SLL = –23.8 dB for SLL defined beyond sector [–10°, 10°], spacings constrained within [0.41, 0.60], and the array aperture constrained by 5.5 wavelength.

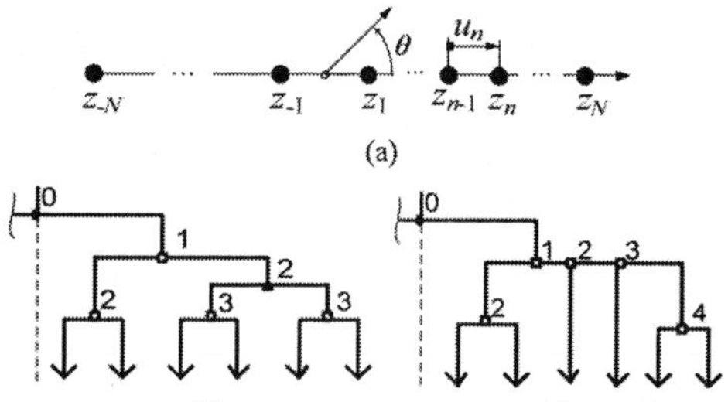

Fig. 1. A linear symmetrical array and CFs architectures: (a) array with an even number of elements; (b) CF with element levels [2 2 3 3 3 3]; (c) CF with element levels [2 2 2 3 4 4].

III. Array and Feed Implementation

The 12-element array with the two CFs is implemented as microstrip antenna-feed circuit with the bandwidth centered at 5.8 GHz. The array of twelve MPAs resides on a 1.574 mm TLP-5 substrate. Each MPA patch is 14.85 mm by 14.85 mm, and energized through a ground plane slot as shown in Fig. 2(b), where s_n stands for the length of the open-end microstrip of element n. Dimensions and location of the slots are parametrized and the same for all MPAs. The CFs resides on a 0.762 mm RF-35 substrate on the back side of the circuit as shown in Fig. 2 (c) and (d). The feeds are parametrized in such a way that regardless of the spacings, the path lengths to all elements are the same. The array-feed circuit is modelled and simulated in CST MWS [4]. The initial designs of the microstrip array-feed circuits exhibit poor SLLs, e.g., as illustrated in Fig. 3. (about −13 dB at 5.8 GHz). According to our analysis and numerical study, the high SLL of the initial design is a result of deviation (from the expected values with a particular CF) of the incident wave amplitudes at the inputs of the embedded elements. Reflection coefficient of the initial design with the CF of Fig. 2(c) is also quite high, e.g., -12dB at 5.8GHz. These issues are addressed using simulation-based optimization.

IV. Simulation-Based Optimization

There are twenty four design variables in the array-feed circuit with the CF of Fig. 2(c) for uniformly spaced MPAs and thirty design variables for non-uniformly spaced MPAs. With the CF of Fig. 2(d) there are, respectively, twenty six design variables thirty two design variables. In order to conduct simultaneous adjustment of all variables (necessary to find an optimum design) computationally feasible, surrogate-assisted optimization with variable-fidelity EM models has been executed [5]. More specifically, the array sidelobes have been minimized using a gradient-based algorithm embedded in the trust-region framework [5] with linear expansion model of the array responses obtained by estimating the gradients at the coarse-discretization EM model level [6]. A penalty function has been added to the primary objective in order to control the reflection response.

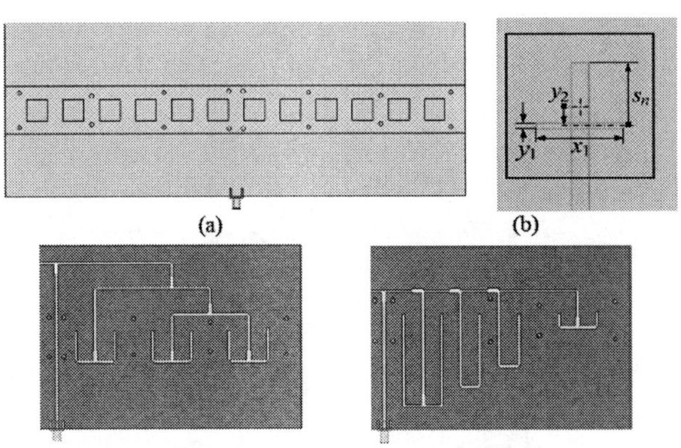

Fig. 2. Array-feed circuit: (a) linear array aperture; (b) MPA elemen shown transparentt; (c) back view, a half of a microstrip CF shown, a realization of an architecture with the elements' levels [2 2 3 3 3 3]; (d) back view, a half of a CF, a realization of an architecture with the elements' levels [2 2 2 3 4 4].

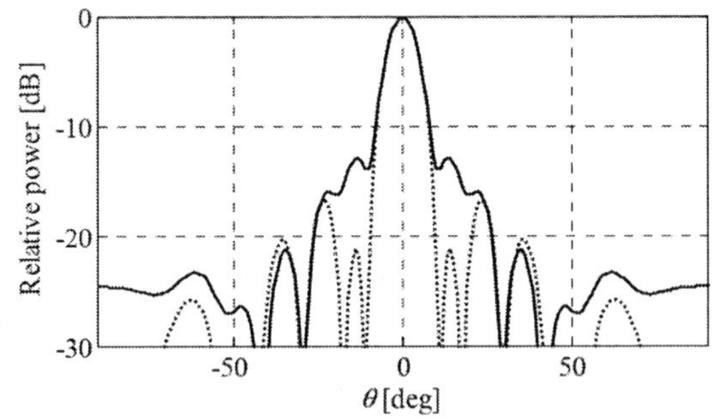

Fig. 3. Simulated power pattern of the array-feed circuit with the CF elements' levels [2 2 3 3 3 3] at 5.8 GHz: array of MPAs driven by the required incident wave amplitudes (···), there is no CF; the array-feed circuit (with the CF) at the initial design (—). MPAs are half-wavelength spaced.

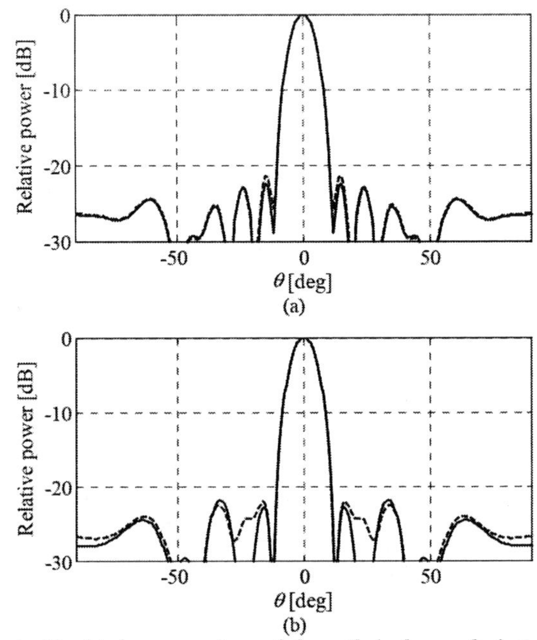

Fig. 4. Simulated power pattern of the optimized array-feed at 5.8 GHz circuit: (a) with the CF of Fig. 2(c), half-wavelength spacings (—), SLL = -22dB, $|S_{11}|$= −23dB at 5.8 GHz, non-uniform spacings (- - -) constrained within [0.41, 0.6] wavelength, SLL = -21dB, $|S_{11}|$= −26dB at 5.8 GHz; (b) with the CF of Fig. 2(d), half-wavelength spacings (—), SLL = -22dB, $|S_{11}|$= −20 dB at 5.8 GHz, non-uniform spacings (- - -) constrained within [0.41, 0.6] wavelength, SLL = -22dB, $|S_{11}|$= −20dB at 5.8 GHz

References

[1] P.S. Hall, J.R. James, "Design of microstrip antenna feeds. Part 2: Design and performance limitations of triplate corporate feeds," *IEE Proc. H - Microwaves, Optics and Ant.*, vol. 128, iss. 1, pp. 26-34, 1981.

[2] T.-S. Horng, N.G. Alexopoulos, "Corporate feed design for microstrip arrays," *IEEE Trans. Ant. Propag.*, vol. 41, iss. 12, pp. 1615-1624, 1993.

[3] T.K. Anthony, A.I. Zaghloul, "Designing a 32 element array at 76GHz with a 33dB taylor distribution in waveguide for a radar system," *Proc. IEEE APS Int. Sym.*, North Charleston, SC, USA, June 2009, pp. 1-4.

[4] CST Microwave Studio, ver. 2015, CST AG, Darmstadt, Germany.

[5] S. Koziel, S. Ogurtsov, Antenna design by simulation-driven optimization. Surrogate-based approach, Springer, 2014.

[6] S. Koziel, "Fast simulation-driven antenna design using response-feature surrogates," *Int. J. RF & Microwave CAE*, vol. 25, no. 5, pp. 394-402, 2015.

Compact Meander Printed Dipole Antenna

Chongyi Yue, Wenxing Li
Department of Information and Communication Engineering
Harbin Engineering University,
Harbin, China
yuechongyi@hrbeu.edu.cn,
liwenxing@hrbeu.edu.cn

Atef Elsherbeni
Department of Electrical Engineering and Computer Science
Colorado School of Mines,
Golden, CO, USA
aelsherb@mines.edu

Veysel Demir
Department of Electrical Engineering
Northern Illinois University
DeKalb, IL 60115, USA
vdemir@niu.edu

***Abstract*—Three antennas including a printed dipole, a meander antenna and a loop meander antenna operating at 2.46 GHz are presented. They are simulated, fabricated and measured. The results show that the design of meaner antenna and meander loop antenna do expand the bandwidth without increasing the antenna size.**

Keywords—meander antenna; wideband dipole antenna

I. Introduction

The meander antennas have been widely used and studied since they are proposed by Rashed and Tai [1-3]. The meander antennas are suitably placed in a very limited space, however, they generally have narrow bandwidth and perform at the first resonant mode [4]. The narrow bandwidth limits the application of the meander antennas because many applications require flat shaped antenna with a sufficient bandwidth and compact size.

In this study, a printed dipole antenna is presented first. Then, a novel design of a meander antenna is introduced. Although the meander antenna has the same operating frequency as the dipole, the size of the meander arm is reduced by 30.6%. To improve the bandwidth of the antenna, another meander loop antenna is designed. Compared to the dipole antenna, the bandwidth of this meander loop antenna increases by 43.5% while there is no increase in the arm size.

The designs of all the antennas are simulated by HFSS and verified by home-made software package CEMS [5], which is a 3D electromagnetic simulation tool based on the finite-difference time- domain method (FDTD) and is developed to run on both CPU and GPU. Fabrications and measurements of all the antennas are performed and S_{11} measurements are compared with the simulation results.

II. Printed Dipole Antenna

Firstly, a printed dipole operating at 2.46 GHz is modeled. The front and back side of the printed dipole is shown in Fig. 1. The thickness of the substrate is 0.75 mm and the relative permittivity is ε_r=2.2. These two parameters are also used to the designs of following antennas. The simulation of this printed dipole is conducted using HFSS and CEMS. The S_{11} parameter of this printed dipole from these two simulation tools match well, as is shown in Fig. 2 (a).

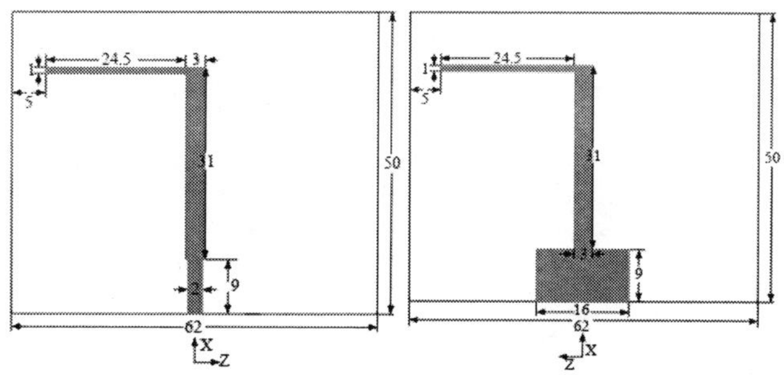

(a) (b)

Fig. 1. Front view (a) and back view of the printed dipole. The unit is mm.

III. Meander and Meander Loop Antenna

Then, a meander antenna is designed in order to expand the bandwidth, and the model is shown in Fig. 3. Two parameters including the strip width L and gap width G are optimized for the meander dipole. The bandwidth varies slightly with the strip width L and gap width associates with the gap width and 1.5 mm and 1.8 mm are finally chosen as the value of L and G after the optimizations. The S_{11} parameters of the meander antenna from HFSS and CEMS have a good agreement, which is shown in Fig. 2 (b).

Although the design of the meander antenna reduces the size of the antenna and improves its bandwidth, a better bandwidth of the antenna is desired. The geometry model of the meander loop antenna has a larger bandwidth is shown in Fig. 4. The parameter BG which denotes the distance between the two meander part and gap width G are optimized for the meander loop antenna.

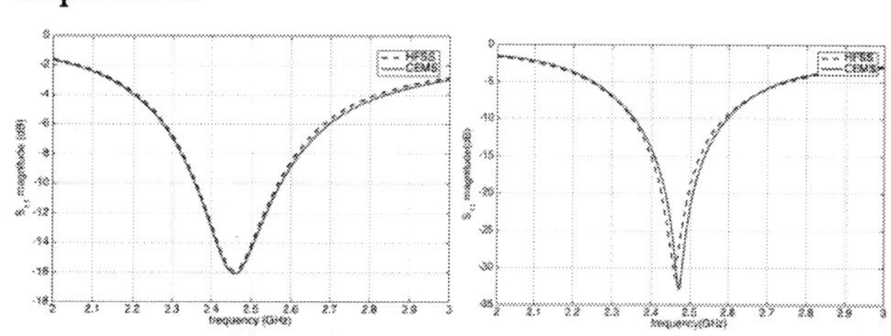

(a) (b)

Fig. 2. The S_{11} parameter of (a) the printed antenna and (b) the meander antenna.

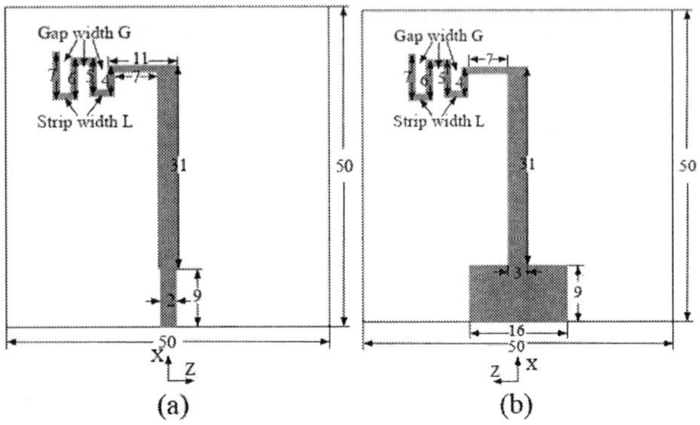

Fig. 3. Front view (a) and back view of the meander antenna. The unit is mm.

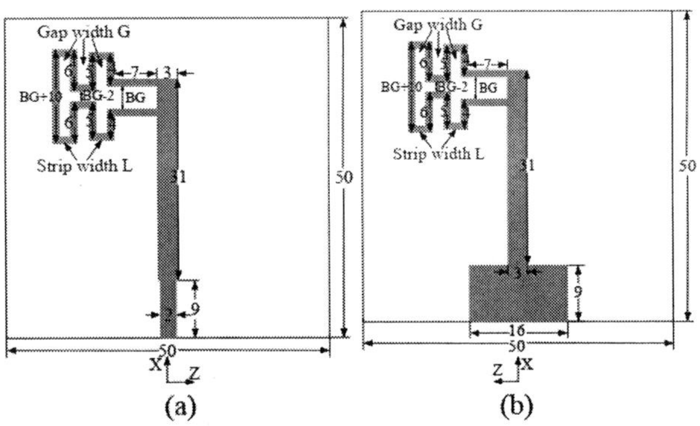

Fig. 4. Front view (a) and back view of the meander antenna. The unit is mm.

The S_{11} curves of the optimized meander loop antenna from HFSS and CEMS are shown in Fig. 5 (a). The operating frequency and arm length of three antennas are shown in Table 1. These three antennas are fabricated and the picture of them are shown in Fig. 6. The S11 measurements of the three antennas are shown in Fig. 5 (b).

The S_{11} simulated results and measurements show a good agreement, as is listed in the Table 1. It is shown from the measurements that both antennas with meandered arms improve the bandwidth. Compared to the printed dipole, the bandwidth of the meander antenna increases by 21.1%, as well as the arm length reduces by 24.8%. In addition, the bandwidth increase of the meander loop antenna is 54.5% with the 18.7% reduction of the arm length compared to the printed dipole.

TABLE I. MEASURED AND SIMULATED S_{11} OF THE THREE ANTENNAS

	Dipole Antenna		**Meander Antenna**		**Meander Loop Antenna**	
	Simu. [a]	***Mean.*** [b]	***Simu.***	***Mean.***	***Simu.***	***Mean.***
f_{lower} (GHz)	2.36	2.36	2.35	2.34	2.315	2.30
f_0 (GHz)	2.46	2.46	2.46	2.46	2.46	2.43
f_{upper} (GHz)	2.57	2.55	2.585	2.57	2.625	2.59
Band-Width	8.53%	7.72%	9.59%	9.35%	12.6%	11.93%
Arm (mm)	24.5	24.5	18.4	18.4	19.9	19.9

[a] Simu. means simulation results; [b] Mean. means measurements.

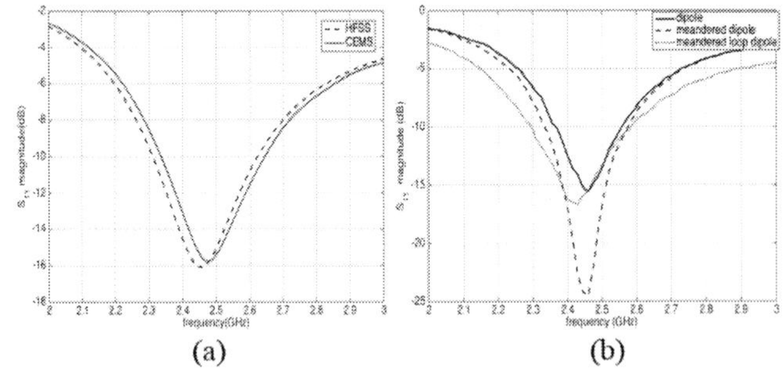

Fig. 5. (a) The S_{11} curves of optimized meander loop antenna; (b) The comparison of measured S_{11} of dipole, meander antenna and meander loop antenna.

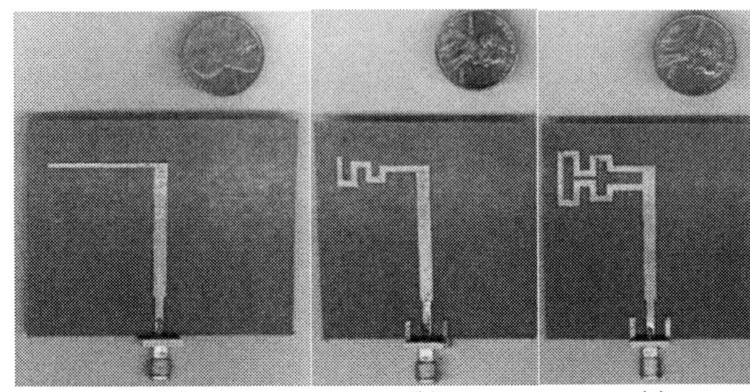

(a) (b) (c)

Fig. 6. The picture of (a) printed dipole, (b) meander antenna and (c) loop meander antenna.

IV. Conclusion

This paper presents designs of a printed dipole, a meander antenna, and a meander loop antenna all working at a center frequency of 2.46 GHz. The models of these antennas are simulated, fabricated and measured. Simulation results and measurements have a good agreement, which shows that compared to printed dipole, the meander antenna and meander loop antenna both have approximately 19% reduction in the arm length. In addition, both designs of meander antenna and meander loop antenna allow the antenna bandwidth to increase. Especially the meander loop antenna has an approximately 50% increase in bandwidth with comparison to the traditional printed dipole.

References

[1] J. Rashed and C.-T. Tai, "A new class of resonant antennas," IEEE Trans. on Antennas and Propag., vol. 39, no. 9, pp. 1428–1430, Sep. 1991.

[2] Olusola O. Olaode, W. Devereus Palmer and William T. Joines, "Characterization of meander dipole antennas with a geometry-based, frequency-independent lumped element model," IEEE Antennas Wireless Propag. Lett., vol. 11, pp. 346-349, Mar. 2012.

[3] Cuthbert M. Allen, Atef Z. Elsherbeni, Charles E. Smith, Chun-Wen P. Huang and Kai-Fong Lee, "Tapered meander slot antenna for dual band personal wireless communication systems," Microwave Opt. Technol. Lett., vol. 36, no. 5, pp. 381-385, Mar, 2003.

[4] K.L. Wong, Compact and Broadband Microstrip Antennas. New York, NY: John Wiley and Sons, 2002.

[5] CEMS, a software package based on the book "The Finite Difference Time Domain Method for Electromagnetics: With MATLAB Simulations, second edition" by A. Elsherbeni and V. Demir, SciTech Publishing, an Imprint of the IET, Edison, NJ, 2016.

Sodium imaging of the human knee cartilage with Magnetic Resonance at Ultra High Field: development of a double frequency ($^{1}H/^{23}Na$) RF coil

Francesca Maggiorelli
Dip. di Scienze Fisiche della Terra e dell'Ambiente
Università degli Studi di Siena e INFN (Sez. Pisa)
Pisa, Italy

Joshua D. Kaggie, Martin J. Graves
Dep. of Radiology, University of Cambridge
Cambrige, UK

Guido Buonincontri, Alessandra Retico
Istituto Nazionale di Fisica Nucleare (INFN, Sez. Pisa)
Pisa, Italy

Laura Biagi, Gianluigi Tiberi, Michela Tosetti
IRCCS Stella Maris e Fondazione IMAGO7
Pisa, Italy

***Abstract*—Sodium Magnetic Resonance Imaging (MRI) is an attractive imaging technique for early detection of osteoarthritis, as sodium concentrations correlate with proteoglycan content. However sodium yields much less signal in human tissues compared to hydrogen: it has a very rapid transverse signal decay (T2) and rapid longitudinal relaxation (T1), low gyromagnetic ratio and much smaller concentration than hydrogen. Ultra High Field (UHF) 7T MRI systems play an essential role to enhance the SNR, to achieve sufficient spatial resolution and to obtain images with diagnostically relevant contrast. This work shows how to design, develop and test a dual-tuned proton/sodium surface radio-frequency coil for 7T UHF MRI systems.**

Keywords—Magnetic Resonance Imaging (MRI); ultra-high field MRI; dual tuned radio-frequency coils; sodium imaging

I. Introduction

A clinical application of Ultra High Field (UHF) 7T Magnetic Resonance Imaging (MRI) that could relevantly impact the daily life is in the early detection and assessment of osteoarthritis (OA). It is the most common chronic condition of the joints, affecting approximately 15% of the population. OA occurs when the cartilage between joints degrades leading to pain, stiffness and swelling. Negatively charged proteoglycans, which are significantly reduced in the cartilage affected by OA, attract positive sodium ions. Therefore, sodium MRI is an interesting technique for early detection of osteoarthritis (OA) [1]. MRI with nuclei different from ^{1}H, for which the available signal is limited, benefits from the improved SNR obtainable with ultra-high magnetic fields. However, imaging at high field comes with several limitations such as inhomogeneous RF fields, a higher Specific Absorption Rate (SAR), and a relative lack of specialized and commercially available RF coils compared to lower field systems. This research shows how to design, simulate, prototype and validate a dual-tuned ^{1}H-^{23}Na surface RF coil for knee MR imaging (see Fig. 1).

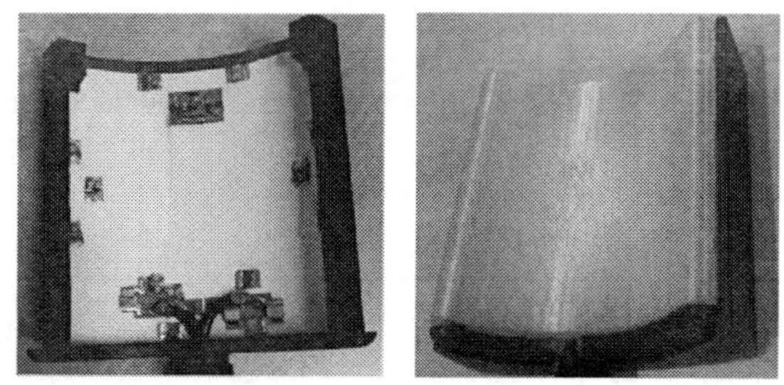

a) b)

Fig. 1. a) Double tuned $^{1}H/^{23}Na$ coil. b) Double tuned $^{1}H/^{23}Na$ coil showing holder & covers.

II. Materials and Methods

The coil consists of two concentric loops: the inner is tuned to sodium Larmor frequency (78.89MHz @ 7T), the outer is tuned to proton Larmor frequency (298.03MHz @ 7T).

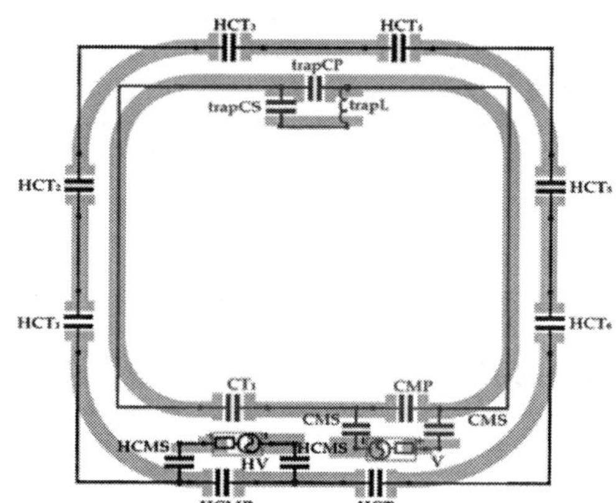

Fig. 2. Circuit of the dual-tuned ^{1}H and ^{23}Na RF coil. The trap circuit and the matching circuits are also visible.

The ^{1}H transmit and receive (Tx/Rx) loop is realized by etching an external square loop having side length of 110 mm. The ^{23}Na loop is realized by etching a rectangular loop of 95 mm × 85 mm (see Fig. 2). The corners of the coils are

rounded: the curvature radius is 30 mm for the main loops and 2 mm for the end point of the strip. To minimize antenna effect the number of tuning capacitors is chosen so that the length of the conductors for both loop is less than $\lambda/10$, where λ is the wavelength at the two resonant frequencies (298.03MHz for proton and 78.89MHz for sodium). The matching for both loops is obtained with a series capacitive matching network and matching capacitors were determined by using a Smith Chart procedure [3]. The ^{23}Na channel is decoupled from the ^{1}H channel by the insertion in the ^{23}Na loop of a series second-order trap circuit [2]. The trap circuit is basically a parallel LC resonant circuit and acts as a high impedance (ideally an open circuit) at proton Larmor frequency at which coupling occurs [4]. The resonant circuits of the RF coil consist of a PCB in FR4 (board thickness 200 µm, copper thickness 35 µm). The other materials used in the design are Non-magnetic chip capacitors (100B, 800B, 800A from ATC ceramics), RG-58 cables (Micro-coax, Belden). The support holding, which is visible in Fig. 1, is designed in AutoCAD, and 3D printed, using a polylactide (PLA) thermoplastic as printing material.
Components' values are chosen in agreement with preliminary simulations. Referring to Fig. 2, the list of components used for assembling the coil is given in Table. 1.

Table 1. RF components of the dual-tuned coil.

$HCT_{1,4}$	8.2 pF	CMP	(33+10) pF
$HCT_{2,3,6}$	6.8 pF	CMS	22 pF
CT_{1}	33 pF	trapCP	(33+4.7) pF
HCMP	4.7 pF	trapCS	(33+2.1) pF
HCMS	33 pF	trapL	10 nH

Simulations performed with *CST Microwave Studio®*, are also used for evaluating B_1^+ - and E - fields maps.
The load used in the electromagnetic model is a cylinder equivalent to the human knee (radius 60 mm, height 200 mm, $\varepsilon_r = 80$ and $\sigma = 0.60$ S/m), placed 15 mm away from the coil circuit. The simulated B_1^+ - and E - fields maps obtained for unitary input power of 1 W for both the ^{1}H and the ^{23}Na channels are shown in Fig. 3. The ^{1}H and ^{23}Na B_1^+ field maps are in agreement with literature [5].

III. RESULTS

The workbench measurements for the ^{1}H and the ^{23}Na loops provided the performance values reported in Table 2.

Table 2. Workbench measurements for the dual-tuned coil.

	^{1}H loop	^{23}Na loop
Q unloaded	88	217
Q loaded (human knee)	23	37
Matching (S_{11}, S_{22})	-16dB	-20dB
Coupling (S_{12}, S_{21})	-19dB	-14dB

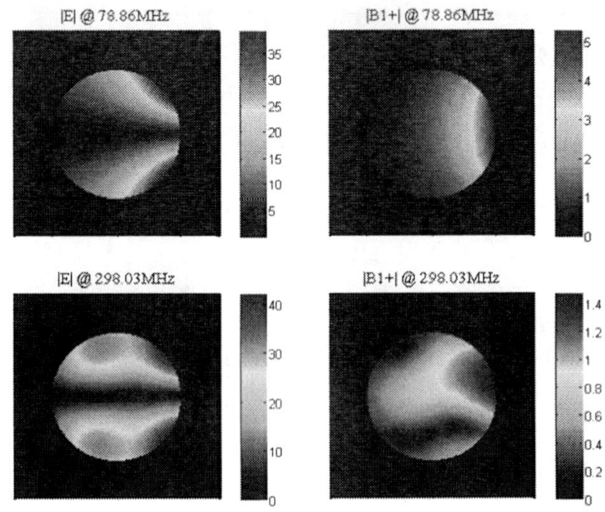

Fig. 3 Simulated B_1^+ (µT) and E (V/m) field maps for unitary input power of 1W for both the ^{1}H and the ^{23}Na channels of the dual-tuned surface RF coil.

Workbench measurements showed a satisfying agreement with simulated result (S_{11}=-23dB, S_{22}=-34dB, coupling <-14dB).

IV. CONCLUSIONS

We designed and developed dedicated RF surface coils for ^{1}H-^{23}Na imaging. Excellent agreement was obtained between workbench measurements and simulations. The RF coil prototype has been validated *in vivo* on healthy volunteers, showing that the knee cartilage imaging can take great advantage from the UHF MRI [6].

REFERENCES

[1] Schmitt B., Zbyn S., Stelzeneder D., et al, "Cartilage Quality Assessment by Using Glycosaminoglycan Chemical Exchange Saturation Transfer and 23Na RM Imaging at 7T", Radiology, Volume 260, No. 1, 2011.

[2] A. Retico, R. Stara, M. E. Fantacci, et al, "Non-Invasive Assessment of Neuromuscular Disorders by 7 Tesla Magnetic Resonance Imaging and Spectroscopy", IEEE-MeMeA 2015 CR 7145175, pp 74-78.

[3] J. Mispelter, M. Lupu and A. Briguet, "NMR Probeheads for Biophysical and Biomedical Experiments: Theorical Principles Pratical Guidilines," Imperial College Press, 2006.

[4] M. Alecci, S. Romanzetti, J. Kaffanke, et al "Practical design of a 4 Tesla double-tuned RF surface coil for interleaved 1H and 23Na MRI of rat brain," J. Magn. Reson., vol 181(2), pp. 203-211, Aug 2006.

[5] Tiberi, G., Fontana, N., Costagli, M., et al, "Investigation of maximum local specific absorption rate in 7 T magnetic resonance with respect to load size by use of electromagnetic simulations" Bioelectromagnetics, 36: 358–366, 2015.

[6] JD. Kaggie, F Maggiorelli, F Riemer et al, "7 T Sodium/Proton Knee Imaging: First Results", UHF ISMRM Symposium, 2016.

Artificial Ionospheric Scintillation Effects on Communication Signals in the V and W Bands

David Smith, Peter Collins, James Fee, James C. Petrosky, Anderw Terzuoli, and Caglar Yardim

Institute of Electrical & Electronics Engineers (IEEE), USA

***Abstract*—Secure communications are critical for many applications. While natural ionospheric effects will be negligible on frequencies above 30 GHz, amplitude scintillation caused by a high altitude nuclear event (HANE) could degrade communication links. Amplitude scintillation is modeled using the multiple phase screen method. The results show that after a HANE, amplitude scintillation will degrade signals at frequencies below 60 GHz but the duration of the effect is only for a few minutes after the event.**

Keywords—propagation; scintillation; artificial ionosphere; V band; W band; HANE

I. INTRODUCTION

Secure communication is of critical importance for many commercial and government applications. The increased reliance on global communications and real-time information has driven the need for continuous access to celestial communication. Currently, the radio frequency bands for celestial communication are cluttered with many commercial users making priority of use a concern. One solution is to take advantage of the unused V and W radio bands, 40 – 75 GHz and 75 – 110 GHz respectively. Currently, no commercial entities are using the V and W bands, leaving two entire bands free for exclusive use. Therefore, an investigation into the reliability of these bands during extreme conditions is warranted.

Under normal conditions the troposphere dominates celestial communication signal propagation with little to no effect from the ionosphere. However, the ionosphere can become an important factor for a period of time following a high altitude nuclear event (HANE); a nuclear event occurring is above 100 km [1]. Generally, a HANE is expected to occur between 100 – 300 km when the purpose of the detonation is to maximize EMP effects. Early time (E1-E2) EMP are phenomena that are related to the Compton current effect due to gamma propagation. Instead, this paper focuses on what is typically referred to as "other atmospheric effects" which includes EMP, but also includes Argus effect, Red Out and Blackout. After a HANE, a portion of the electrons and detonation debris, primarily in the form if ionized particles, travels downward into the Earth's denser atmosphere where it further ionizes the air molecules. The electrons and resultant ionized debris expand and rise along the earth's geomagnetic lines, Figure 1. As a result, the electron density in the ionosphere can rise to values of 10^9 electrons/cm^3. (The natural ionosphere is 10^6 electrons/cm^3 at its peak.) The elevated electron density can last for periods of 60 s or longer [1].

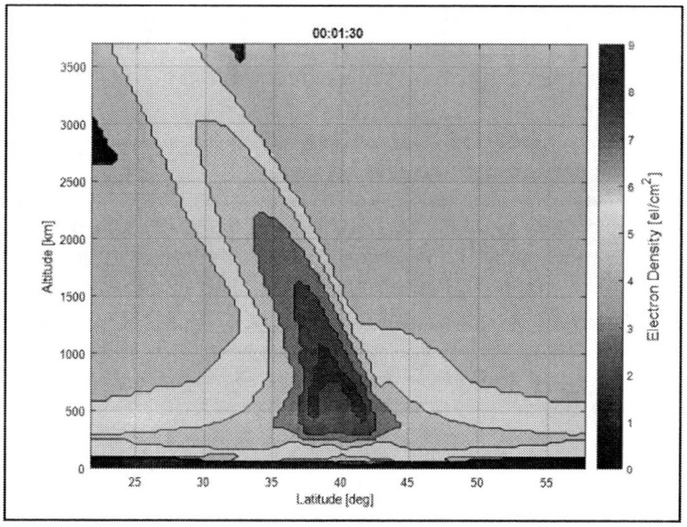

Fig. 1. Snapshot 90 s after a 5 MT detonation at 200 km. The electron structures rise in altitude along the Earth's geomagnetic lines. The numbers on the right of the bar graph represent powers of 10 (i.e. 10^4 through 10^9).

Based upon [2], a 1 MT HANE at an altitude of 600 km will increase the ion and electron density sufficient to interfere with SATCOM crosslinks up to 200 GHz. This paper will focus on the effects of a 5 MT detonation at 200 km, specifically examining the effects on an electromagnetic wave propagation from the ground to a location at 4,800 km above the earth's surface. The primary effect of interest is the amplitude scintillation caused by the increases in electron density. Ion debris absorption is not considered.

II. PROPAGATION EFFECT

As an electromagnetic (EM) wave traverses through a plasma various effects can be observed. Some of these effects include Faraday rotation, group delay, phase advance, dispersion, and scintillation. Calculations can show that since frequency of the EM wave (40 – 110 GHz) is much greater that the resulting plasma frequency most of the effects will be negligible, with the exception of scintillation.[2]

Scintillation is defined as amplitude changes on an EM wave. Scintillation is caused by forward scattering of the propagating wave as it travels through the plasma. One approach to EM modeling of plane wave propagation through a plasma, naturally occurring (ionosphere), or artificial (e.g. HANE), is the multiple phase screen (MPS) method [3]. The MPS method is described by equations (1) and (2).

$$E(x,z,\omega) = U(x,z,\omega)e^{-jkz}$$
$$U(x,z_2,\omega) = e^{-jk\Delta z}\mathcal{F}^{-1}\left[\mathcal{F}[U(x,z_1,\omega)]e^{j(z_1-z_2)\sqrt{k^2K_x}-k}\right] \quad (1)$$

$$U(x,z_2,\omega) = U\left(x,-\frac{\Delta z}{2},\omega\right)e^{-jk\int_{-\Delta z/2}^{\Delta z/2}\Delta n(x,z',\omega)dz'} \quad (2)$$

Here $\mathcal{F}$ is a Fourier transform, z is the direction of propagation, x is transverse direction, K_x is the spatial wavenumber in the x direction, E is the electric field, U is the electric field in the parabolic approximation, ω is the radian frequency of the EM wave, k is the EM wavenumber, and n is the index of refraction. Equation (1) describes the wave propagation to the phase screen and equation (2) describes the wave propagation through the phase screen. Both equations (1) and (2) are used in an iterative manner until the wave has propagated through the entire plasma.

Phase screens are generated from the power-law phase power spectral density (PSD). The PSD method is useful as it represents many observations and allows control over inner and outer-scales of the ion turbulence. This PSD is defined in equation (3).

$$S_\phi(K_x) = \frac{\sigma_\phi^2\left(1/\sqrt{2\pi}\right)l_i\left(l_i/L_o\right)^{m-1/2}H_{m/2}\left(l_i\sqrt{K_x+1/L_o^2}\right)}{H_{m-1/2}\left(l_i/L_0\right)\left(l_i\sqrt{K_x+1/L_o^2}\right)^{m/2}} \quad (3)$$

$$\sigma_\phi^2 = 2(r_e\lambda)^2 L_o\Delta z\sigma_{N_e}^2$$

Here H is a Bessel function of the third kind, L_o and l_i are outer and inner scales, m is the power law slope, r_e is the classic electron radius, λ is wavelength, and σ_{Ne}^2 is the plasma electron variance. The effect of plasma scintillation can be calculated with the MPS method. The S_4 scintillation index can then be determined from (4).

$$S_4 = \sqrt{\frac{\left\langle \left(A-\langle A\rangle\right)^2\right\rangle}{\langle A^2\rangle}} \quad (4)$$

In (4) < > indicates averaging and A is the amplitude of the received wave. An S_4 index of 0.3 indicates signal fading with 0.6 indicating a strong scatter.

III. Results

Tables 1 and 2 list the scintillation effects and signal loss at the receiver for a given channel. The data in these tables show that the scintillation effects will only impact signals below frequencies of 60 GHz with the majority of the scintillation happening at 1 to 4 minutes after the HANE event. Significant signal loss can occur for frequencies between 40 and 50 GHz (up to 4 db). Comparably, an ionosphere naturally disturbed from solar radiation will produce scintillation loss up to 0.025 db at 40 GHz (determined using the MPS method).

The scintillation effects grow until they peak at about 1.5 minutes after the blast and then begin to drop off. After five minutes, the effects from the charged particle debris cloud dissipate as the electrons begin to spread along the magnetic field lines reducing the electron density. The resultant data suggest that the lower part of the V band will be unavailable for approximately 3 minutes after the HANE due to amplitude scintillation effects.

TABLE I. S_4 INDEX

Freq[a]	S4 Scintillation Index						
	0 sec	*3 sec*	*10 sec*	*1 min*	*1.25 min*	*1.5 min*	*5 min*
40	0.2	0.2	0.1	0.4	0.3	0.2	0.0
50	0.1	0.1	0.1	0.1	0.2	0.2	0.0
60	0.0	0.0	0.0	0.1	0.1	0.1	0.0
70	0.0	0.0	0.0	0.1	0.1	0.0	0.0
110	0.0	0.0	0.0	0.0	0.0	0.0	0.0

a. Frequency is in GHz

TABLE II. SIGNAL LOSS FROM HANE

Freq[b]	Signal Loss [db]						
	0 sec	*3 sec*	*10 sec*	*1 min*	*1.25 min*	*1.5 min*	*5min*
40	-1.52	-2.77	-1.20	-3.89	-3.64	-4.00	-0.06
50	-0.96	-1.52	-0.87	-2.23	-2.29	-2.70	-0.04
60	-0.63	-1.30	-0.55	-1.67	-1.76	-1.71	-0.03
70	-0.45	-0.89	-0.40	-1.23	-1.37	-1.37	-0.02
110	-0.20	-0.39	-0.16	-0.50	-0.52	-0.56	-0.01

b. Frequency is in GHz

IV. Conclusion

Although the natural ionosphere will have negligible effects on EM wave propagation from 40 – 110 GHz, an artificially disturbed ionosphere from a HANE will significantly reduce signals below 60 GHz. This research shows that the lower part of the V band will be limited for approximately 3 minutes after the HANE due to amplitude scintillation. Thus, the impact of amplitude scintillation is minimal, due to its short period after a HANE.

References

[1] S. Glasstone and P. J. Dolan, "The Effects of Nuclear Weapons," *United States Department of Defense*, 1977. [Online]. Available: https://www.fourmilab.ch/etexts/www/effects/. [Accessed: 15-Aug-2016].

[2] R. Middlestead, R. LeLevier, and M. Smith, "Satellite Crosslink Communications Vulnerability in a Nuclear Environment," *IEEE J. Sel. Areas Commun.*, vol. 5, no. 2, pp. 138–145, Feb. 1987.

[3] D. L. Knepp, "Multiple Phase-Screen Calculation of the Temporal Behavior of Stochastic Waves," *Proc. IEEE*, vol. 71, no. 6, pp. 722–737, 1983.

Realization of Dual Notch Bands in UWB Bandpass Filter Using Two T-shaped Resonators

Xuemei ZHENG [1,2]
[1]College of Information and Communications Engineering
Harbin Engineering University, Harbin, China
[2]College of Information Engineering,
Northeast Dianli University, Jilin, China
zhengxuemei@hrbeu.edu.cn

Tao JIANG[1,*]
College of Information and Communications Engineering
Harbin Engineering University
Harbin, China
jiangtao@hrbeu.edu.cn

***Abstract*—An ultra-wideband (UWB) bandpass filter with dual notch bands using a short-circuited T-shaped resonator and an inner T-shaped resonator is proposed. It is based on the filter of microstrip lines and rectangular patch multiple mode resonator with inner rectangular slot. The proposed filter using a short-circuited T-shaped resonator coupled to the main transmission line of the basic BSF to achieve the low-frequency resonance at 3.3 GHz and using an inner T-shaped resonator to achieve the high-frequency resonance at 5.2 GHz. The proposed BSF has passband from 2.9 to 10.6 GHz with sharp rejection skirts outside the passband and its insertion loss is less than 0.8 dB over the entire frequency band. The design parameters is optimized by 3D EM commercial software HFSS 13.0, and the simulation results indicated that the proposed filter can generate two notch bands at 3.3 GHz and 5.2 GHz. The proposed filter can efficiently reduce the interference from undesired signals at 3.3 GHz in WiMAX and at 5.2 GHz in WLAN with certain application prospects.**

Keywords—bandstop filter (BSF); ultra-wideband (UWB); short-circuited T-shaped resonator, inner T-shaped resonator

I. INTRODUCTION

With the development of wireless communication technology, ultra-wideband (UWB) filters have been widely applied in microwave circuits[1]. Dual-band UWB bandstop filters as a key component for WiMAX and WLAN applications have become attractive due to their low passband insertion loss, low group delay, which can achieve such as by using a multiple-mode resonator structure [2], a E-shaped resonator [3], a defected ground structure [4], a defected microstrip slot [5], or a defected microstrip structure [6]. In this paper, a new dual-band UWB bandstop filter using a short-circuited T-shaped resonator and an inner T-shaped resonator is proposed, which can generate independently controlled two notch bands at 3.3 GHz and 5.2 GHz for WiMAX and WLAN applications.

II. FILTER DESIGN

The proposed filter using short-circuited T-shaped resonator and inner T-shaped resonator has designed on the basis of BPF [3]. In order to reduce the size of the filter, the proposed filter with a rectangular slot on the microstrip lines, which can obtain good passband property in range from 2.8 GHz to 10.9 GHz. Fig. 1 shows the improved circuit of basic bandpass filter (BPF) without T-shaped resonator. Fig.2 shows the S-parameters of UWB BPF without T-shaped resonator. Fig. 3 shows the circuit configuration of the proposed BSF based on short-circuited T-shaped resonator and inner T-shaped resonator placed in the middle of the microstrip lines. Fig.4 shows the S-parameters of the proposed BSF.

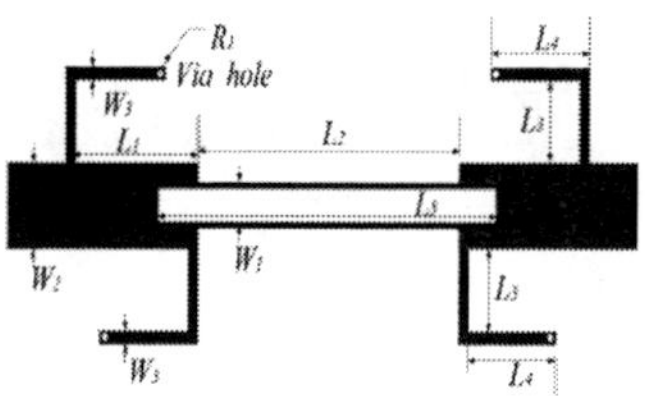

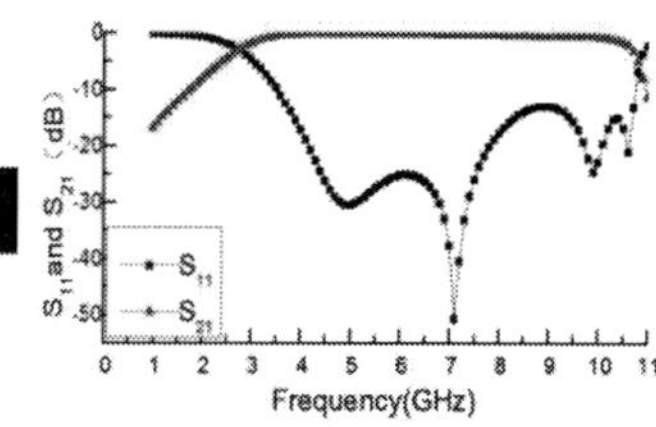

Fig. 1. Configuration of improved BPF Fig. 2. S-parameters of improved BPF

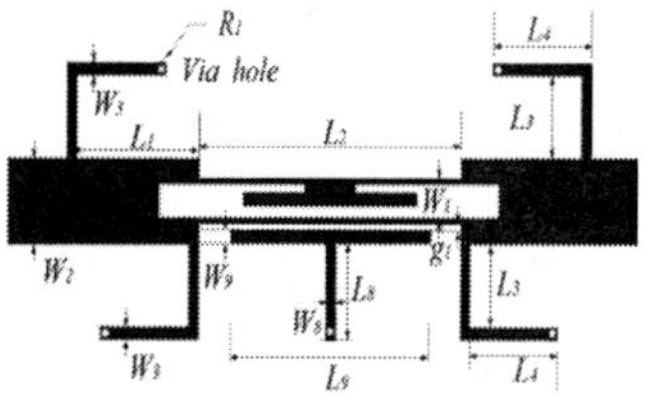

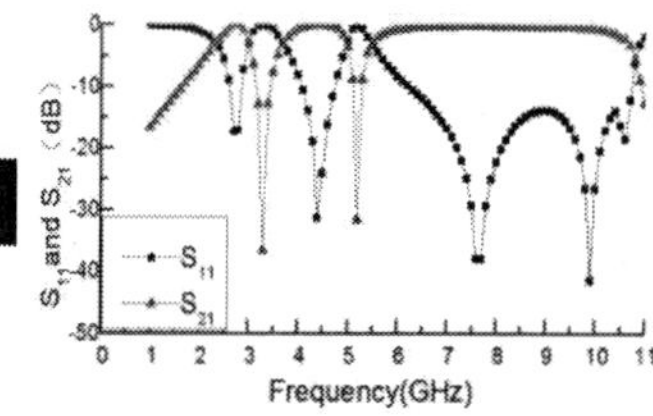

Fig. 3. Configuration of proposed BSF Fig. 4. S-parameters of proposed BSF

III. SIMULATION RESULTS AND DISCUSSIONS

The S parameters of the proposed UWB BSF is optimized by 3D EM commercial software HFSS 13.0. The structure of the proposed UWB BSF is selected as follows: L_1=5 mm, L_2= 15 mm, L_3=4 mm, L_4=5.3 mm, L_5=18 mm, L_6=2 mm, L_7=9.2 mm, L_8=5.3 mm, L_9=10.6 mm, R_1=0.1 mm, W_1=1.7 mm, W_2=3 mm, W_3=0.3 mm, W_4=1.4 mm, W_5=0.45 mm, W_6=0.4 mm, W_7=0.2 mm, W_8=0.3 mm, W_9=0.3 mm. The substrate is RT/Duorid5880 with the thickness of 1.0 mm and the dielectric constant of 2.2. The configuration of the proposed inner T-shaped resonator is shown in Fig. 5(a), an equivalent circuit model of inner T-shaped resonator, as is shown in Fig. 5(b). Rough equivalent transmission line model [6] of the inner T-shaped resonator is plotted in Fig. 6. The equivalent capacitance C and inductance L can be expressed as [7], where f_u and f_l are upper and lower cutoff frequency at 10 dB, respectively.

$$C=\frac{1}{2\pi Z_0(f_u-f_l)},L=\frac{1}{4\pi^2 f_0^2 C} \quad (1)$$

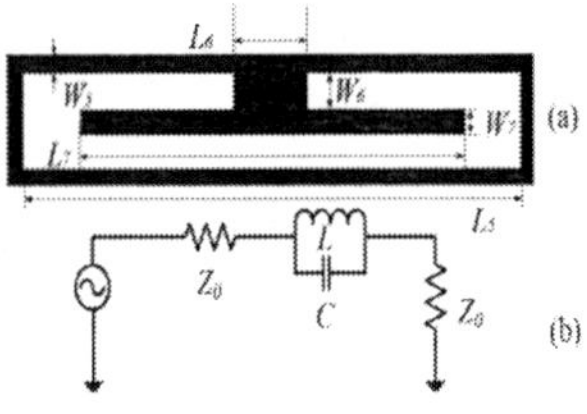

Fig. 5(a) Inner T-shaped resonator. (b) Equivalent circuit model.

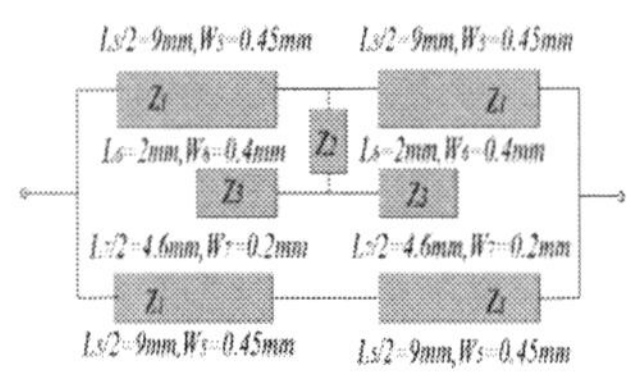

Fig. 6. Equivalent transmission line model of inner T-shaped resonator.

Simulated frequency responses of BPF only using short-circuited T-shaped resonator is plotted in Fig. 7 and Fig. 8. It shows that the low-frequency resonance frequency (f_1) increase along with parameter g_1 increasing and parameter L_9 decreasing, which generated by short-circuited T-shaped resonator. When g1 is increased from 0.1 mm to 0.3 mm, f_1 increased from the 3.2 to 3.8 GHz. When L_9 is decreased from 12 mm to 10 mm and $L_8=L_9/2$, f_1 increases from the 2.7 to 3.4 GHz. Simulated frequency responses of BPF only using inner T-shaped resonator is plotted in Fig. 9 and Fig. 10. It shows that the high-frequency resonance frequency (f_2) increase along with parameter L_7 decreasing and parameter W_7 decreasing, which generated by inner T-shaped resonator. When L_7 is decreased from 9.4 to 5.2 mm, f_2 increases from the 4.6 to 5.3 GHz. When W_7 is decreased from 0.2 to 0.05 mm, f_2 increases from the 4.7 to 5.3 GHz. It can be seen that f_1 decreases with L_9 and increases with g_1, and f_2 decreases with L_7 and increases with W_7. Therefore, by appropriately adjusting the two resonators dimensions, dual notched bands can be respectively achieved at desired frequencies in WiMAX and WLAN bands.

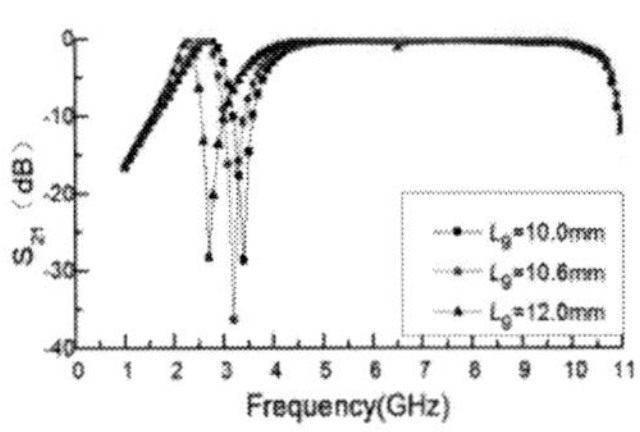

Fig.7. S_{21} of BPF only using short-circuited T-shaped resonator

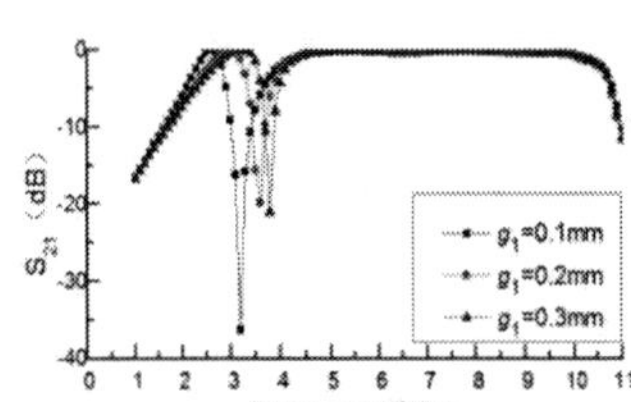

Fig. 8. S_{21} of BPF only using short-circuited T-shaped resonator

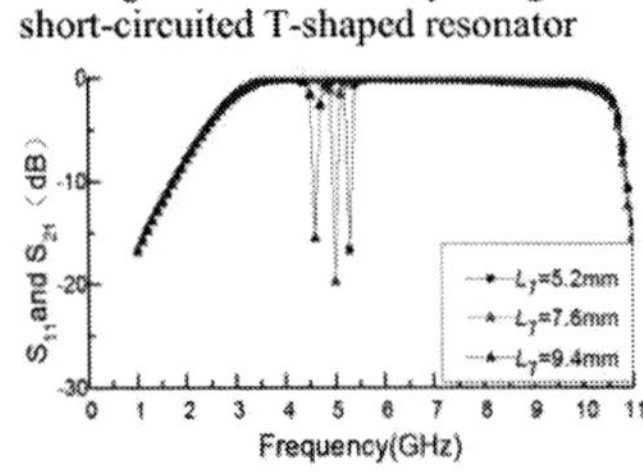

Fig. 9. S_{21} of BPF only using inner T-shaped resonator.

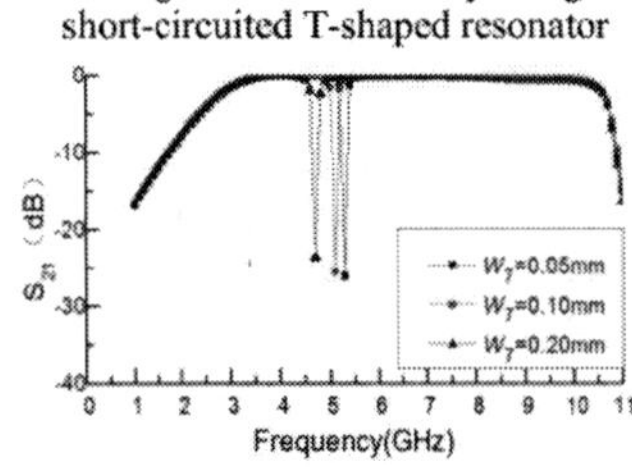

Fig. 10. S_{21} of BPF only using inner T-shaped resonator.

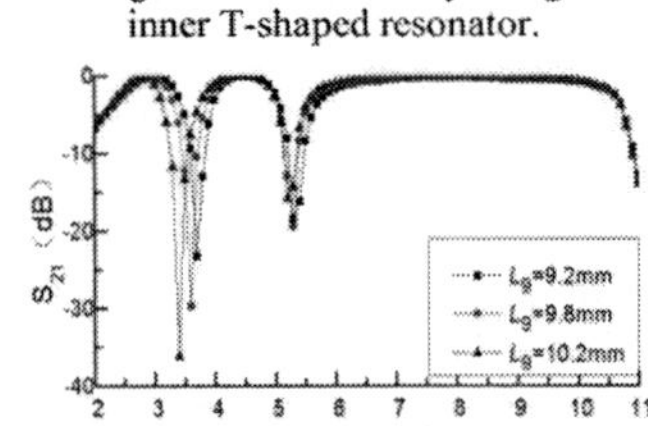

Fig.11. S_{21} of BPF with different L_9.

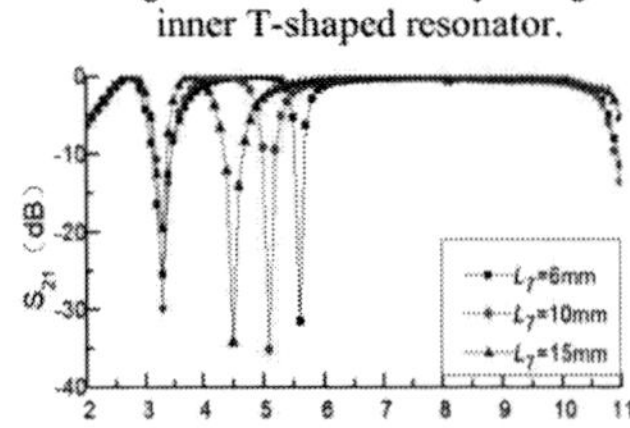

Fig.12. S_{21} of BPF with different L_7.

Fig.11 shows that S_{21} of the proposed BSF with different L_9. When L_7=9.2 mm, W_5=0.8 mm and other parameters are unaltered, with the increasing L_9 from 9.2 to 10.2 mm, the f_1 decreases from the 3.8 to 3.3 GHz and the S_{21} decreases from the -24.7 to -37.5 dB, and 3-dB bandwidth increases from 6.58% (5.43~5.8 GHz) to 17.39% (4.2~5.0 GHz), and the high-frequency resonance frequency (f_2) is almost unchanged at 5.3 GHz. Fig.12 shows that S21 of the proposed UWB BSF with different L_7. When W_5=0.8 mm and other parameters are unaltered and, with the increasing the length of L_7 from 6 to 10 mm, f_2 decreases from the 5.6 GHz to 4.5 GHz and 3-dB bandwidth increases from 6.58% (5.43~5.8 GHz) to 17.39% (4.2~5.0 GHz), and f_1 is almost unchanged at 3.3 GHz.

IV. CONCLUSION

In this paper, a new ultra-wideband (UWB) bandpass filter with dual notch bands using two T-shaped resonators is proposed. Compared with the bandstop filter[3], the proposed filter with the bandwidth from 2.8~10.7 GHz which covers the UWB band of 3.1~ 10.6 GHz allocated by FCC. The filter features dual stop bands at 3.3 GHz and 5.2 GHz with higher selectivity and more less insertion loss response of -36.6 dB and -32.1 dB at the respective stop bands than the bandstop filter[3]. The HFSS simulation results show that the proposed filter is individually controllable dual-band filter with the magnitude of insertion loss less than 0.8 dB in UWB pass bands and more than 30 dB in stop bands. By changing the parameters (g_1, L_9) of the resonator, the low-frequency resonance frequency (f_1) is adjusted to 3.3 GHz. By changing the parameters (L_7, W_7) of the inner T-shaped resonator, the high-frequency resonance frequency (f_2) is adjusted to 5.2 GHz. This filter can enhance the interference immunity of WIMAX and WLAN with sharp roll-off characteristic.

ACKNOWLEDGMENT

This paper is funded by the International Exchange Program of Harbin Engineering University for Innovation-oriented Talents Cultivation. This work is also partially supported by the Science and Technology innovative Talents Foundation of Harbin (2013RFXXJ083, 2016AXXJ044) and the Foundational Research Funds for the Center Universities (HEUCFD1433, HEUCF160815).

REFERENCES

[1] Yang Y., Zhang W., Hu Y.. " Research on Algorithm of Joint Location Based on Ultra-Wideband," Journal of Northeast Dianli University, vol. (1), pp. 83-87, 2015.

[2] Peng Y, Zhang L, Fu J, et al. "Compact Dual-band Bandpass Filter Using Coupled Lines Multimode Resonator," IEEE Microwave & Wireless Components Letters, vol. 25(4), pp. 1-1, 2015.

[3] Zheng, X., & Jiang, T. "Compact Band Notched UWB Filter Based on Open-load Stub," IEEE/PIERS Progress in Electromagnetics Research Symposium, 2015.

[4] Sung YJ, Kim YS. "An improved design of microstrip patch antennas using photonic bandgap structure," IEEE Trans Antennas Propag, vol. 53(5), pp. 1799–804, 2005.

[5] D. Cheng, H.C. Yin, H.X. Zheng." A compact dual-band bandstop filter with defected microstrip slot," Journal of Electromagnetic Waves & Applications, vol. 26(10), pp. 1-7, 2012.

[6] Xiao J K, Zhu Y F. "Multi-band bandstop filter using inner T-shaped defected microstrip structure (DMS),"AEU - International Journal of Electronics and Communications, vol. 68(2), pp. 90-96, 2014.

[7] Pramod K, Jugul K, Shrivastav AK. "Formulation of size reduction technique in microstrip circuits by using DGS and DMS," In: Proceedings of the International Conference on Microwave. pp. 861–4.2008.

Design of Modified Pythagorean Fractal Antenna for Multiband Application

Henrique Adler M. Silva, Adaildo G. D'Assunção, and José P. Silva
Department of Communication Engineering
Federal University of Rio Grande do Norte
Natal, Brazil
henriqueadler@hotmail.com, adaildo@ct.ufrn.br, patroc@ct.ufrn.br

***Abstract*—This paper presents the design of a Pythagorean tree fractal patch antenna, where the squares made on the base of the conducting patch are scaled down by different factors. The antenna is designed to achieve multiband characteristics. The proposed antenna design is developed for the second iteration geometry. The antenna is simulated using *Ansoft Designer* software. A prototype is fabricated for comparison purpose. The prototype measurement results are found in good agreement with the simulated ones.**

***Keywords*—fractal; multiband antenna; Pythagorean fractal tree**

I. Introduction

Multiband antenna systems that provide a variety of applications in a single portable and compact device are in great demand, reducing infrastructure costs for communications. In this sense, the fractal antennas, due to their space filling properties, show many advantages like miniaturization, multiband operation, and impedance matching. Thus, they are widely used in current trends of communication systems [1]-[3].

A promising fractal geometry that ensures a successful design of a multiband antenna is known as the Pythagoras tree. In recent years, numerous studies for fractal patch antenna using Pythagorean tree shape as the fractal geometry, operating at arbitrary frequencies, have been reported. Aggarwal and Kartikeyan proposed a Pythagorean tree antenna dual band with coplanar waveguide (CPW) feeding [4]. Kumar et al. proposed a traditional Pythagorean tree geometry antenna with coaxial line fed using SMA connector [5]. Sharma and Kokane implemented an antenna with holes in the Pythagorean tree geometry and microstrip line (MSL) feeding [6]. Kumar et al. suggested Pythagorean tree antenna design with impedance steps and finite ground plane [7]. Throughout these studies there is a common aspect, related to the fact that each square is further scaled down by the same factor, and specifically, the angle between consecutive patches is kept constant and equal to 45°.

In contrast to earlier approaches, this paper presents a novel modified fractal Pythagorean tree antenna design, where the squares made on the base of the conducting patch are scaled down by different factors. The angles between one bigger and one smaller consecutive patch are adjusted to control resonant frequencies. As a low-profile antenna, the proposed fractal is useful for mobile systems, fixed or portable communications operating in 1.3 GHz, 2.5 GHz, 3.0 GHz, 3.7 GHz, and 4.5 GHz, bands with -10 dB return loss criterion, which includes the applications in WLAN, Wi-Max, and satellite mobile communication. The design of the antenna is performed using the method of moments (MoM), implemented in the *Ansoft Designer* software package. The following sections describe the design, implementation, and performance of the proposed antenna.

II. Antenna Design

Fig. 1 shows a modified Pythagorean tree fractal antenna. A Pythagorean tree fractal patch is printed on a FR-4 substrate with thickness h = 1.57 mm, relative permittivity ε_r = 4.4, and loss tangent $tan\delta$ = 0.02. The antenna is fed by a microstrip line. As shown in Fig. 2, a modified two-iteration Pythagorean tree fractal patch is generated by changing the scale factor at each iteration step to control the resonant frequencies. In this work, the sizes of the bigger and smaller patches are calculated for the nth iteration using the formation rules $[1/2^{0.5}]^n$ and $[1/2]^n$, respectively. Fig. 2 illustrates the recursive method for a modified Pythagorean tree antenna.

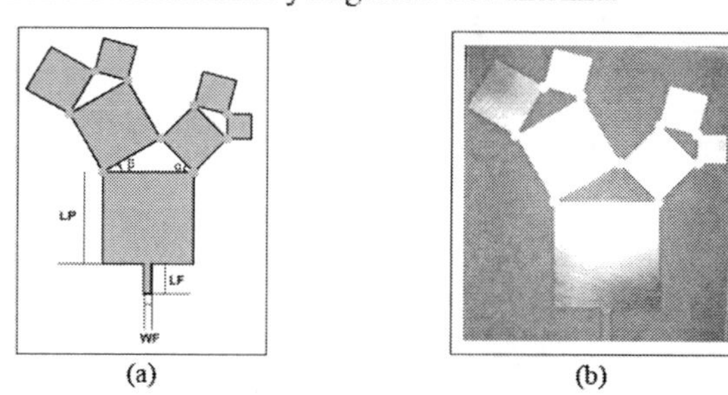

(a) (b)

Fig. 1. The proposed Pythagorean tree multiband fractal antenna. (a) Configuration of the antenna patch. (b) Photograph of the antenna prototype.

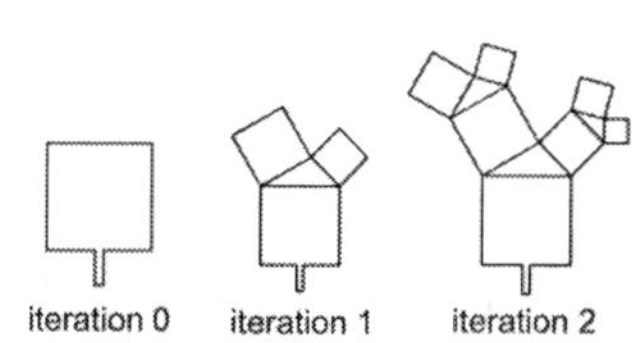

(a) (b) (c)

Fig. 2. Pythagoras tree modified generation process: (a) Initiator, (b) first iteration, and (c) second iteration.

The first iteration produces two new squares. The new bigger square is scaled down by $[1/2^{0.5}]$ while the new smaller square is scaled down by [1/2]. The process is repeated for the second iteration. Fig. 1 shows the design of the proposed Pythagorean tree fractal antenna after two iterations.

The aim of this configuration is that the proposed antenna can operate in most of the wireless communication bands, which may include WLAN, WiMax, and mobile satellite communications. To achieve a good performance for the antenna, the traditional Pythagorean tree fractal patch is modified (Fig. 1). In addition, small connective circular conducting patches of 3 mm radius are used to tune the impedance matching for better signal transmission.

Furthermore, instead of keeping α and β (Fig. 1) constant and equal to 45°, as in the traditional Pythagorean tree patch design, it is simulated and fabricated a modified Pythagorean tree geometry with $\alpha = 45°$ and $\beta = 30°$ (Fig. 1). In this way, the basic patch is scaled down by two different factors. This technique is used to control the resonant frequencies. The proposed antenna is simulated and optimized using *Ansoft Designer*. The optimum parameters are LP = 58.38 mm, LF = 18.95 mm, WF = 4.58 mm, $\alpha = 45°$, and $\beta = 30°$, for a FR-4 microstrip substrate with $\varepsilon_r = 4.4$, $h = 1.57$ mm, and $\tan\delta = 0.02$. Fig. 1(b) shows a photograph of the antenna prototype. A microstrip line is used to feed the antenna.

III. Simulation and Measurements

The proposed antenna is simulated using *Ansoft Designer*. The return loss of the antenna is simulated and measured in the frequency range from 1 GHz to 4.5 GHz. The antenna is simulated and fabricated for the second iteration depth. Multiband behavior is achieved where the first band is at 1.3 GHz, with return loss (RL) = -16.43 dB. The second band is at 2.5 GHz frequency, with (RL) = -10.64 dB, the third band is obtained at 3.0 GHz with (RL) = -19.17dB, the fourth band is at 3.7 GHz with (RL) = -13.45 dB, and the fifth band is at 4.5 GHz, having minimum value of (RL) = -10.38 dB. Fig. 3 shows simulation and measurements return loss results for the proposed antenna (Fig. 1) with the optimized parameters described in Section II.

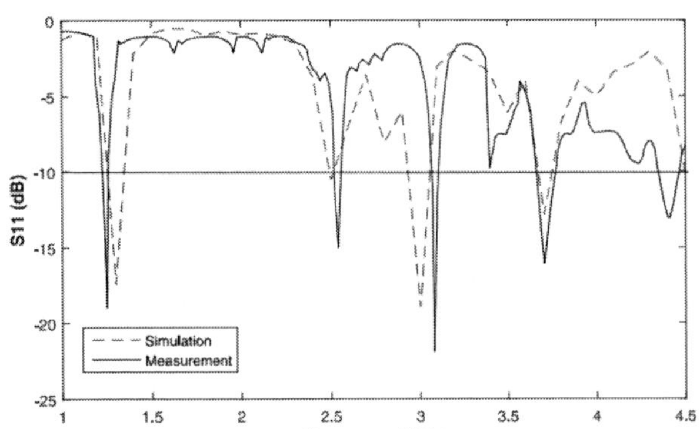

Fig. 3. Simulated and measured return loss results of the multiband Pythagorean tree fractal antenna.

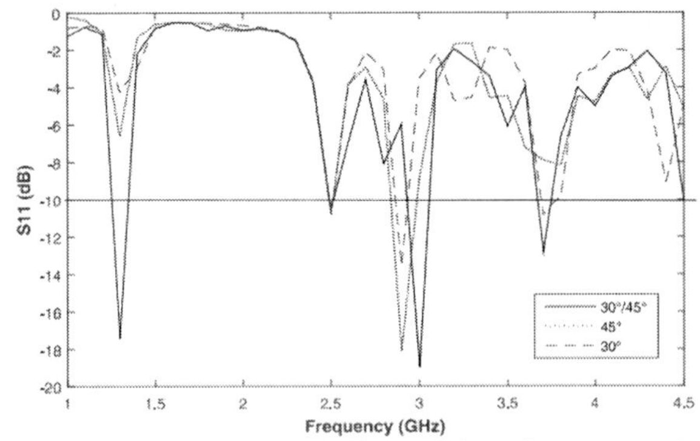

Fig. 4. Effects of changing the scale factor of the Pythagorean tree fractal antenna.

Fig. 4 shows simulation results for the proposed antenna when the scale factor is changed. It is observed that instead of keeping a constant scale factor $\alpha = \beta = 30°$ or even $\alpha = \beta = 45°$, the frequency response is improved when two different scales of iteration for the same structure are used ($\alpha = 45°$ and $\beta = 30°$).

IV. Conclusion

This paper described the design of a modified planar Pythagorean tree fractal antenna for multiband communication systems. It is presented how the modified fractal structure affected the antenna performance, with respect to the generation of several frequency bands and good impedance matching, according to changes in the scale factor. Small circular conducting patches are used to connect the squares in the Pythagorean tree fractal design and to enhance the antenna impedance matching performance. The proposed antenna is fabricated and measured. The antenna exhibits operational bands at 1.3, 2.5, 3.0, 3.7, and 4.5 (GHz), and is capable to operate in WLAN, WiMax, and satellite mobile communication systems.

References

[1] D.H. Werner and R. Mittra, Frontiers in Electromagnetics, IEEE Press, New York, 2000.

[2] J.P. Gianvittorrio and Y. Rahmat-Samii, "Fractal antennas: A novel antenna miniaturization technique and applications," IEEE Antennas Propag. Mag., vol. 44, pp. 20-36, 2002.

[3] A. Aggarwal and M.V. Kartikeyan, "Design of Sierpinski carpet antenna using two different feeding mechanisms for WLAN applications," 35th Int. Conf. Infrared, Millimeter, THz Waves, Rome, Italy, pp. 1-3, 2010.

[4] A. Aggarwal and M.V. Kartikeyan, "Pythagoras tree: a fractal patch antenna for multi-frequency and ultra-wide bandwidth operations," Progress Electromagnetics Research C, vol.16, pp. 25-35, 2010.

[5] D. Kumar, A. Kumar, and A. K. Singh, "Design analysis of Pythagoras tree shaped multiband fractal antenna," Int. Conf. Comput. Intelligence Commun. Networks (CICN), Bhopal, pp.41-45, 2014.

[6] R. Sharma and D.N. Kokane, "Pythagorean tree multiband fractal antenna," Int. Journal Eng. Res. Gen. Science, vol. 3, pp. 1031-1035, 2015.

[7] A. Kumar, B.R. Dutta, and S. Budhauliya, "Iterated Pythagorean fractal tree multiband antenna," Int. Journal Scientific Res. Pub., Vol. 3, No. 9, pp. 1-3, 2013.

[8] D.H. Werner and S. Ganguly, An overview of fractal antenna engineering research," IEEE Antennas Propag. Mag., vol. 45, pp. 38-57, 2003.

Critical parameters affecting the design of high frequency transmission lines in standard CMOS technology

Talal Al-Attar*, Abdullah Alshehri, Abdullah Almansouri and Abdullah Alturki
Department of Electrical Engineering
King Abdullah University of Science and Technology
Thuwal, Saudi Arabia
* Talal.Attar@kaust.edu.sa

***Abstract*— Different structures of transmission lines were designed and fabricated in standard CMOS technology to estimate some critical parameters including the RMS value of the surface roughness and the loss tangent. The input impedances for frequencies up to 50 GHz were modeled and compared with measurements. The results demonstrated a strong correlation between the used model with the proposed coefficients and the measured results, attesting the robustness of the model and the reliability of the incorporated coefficients values.**

Keywords—component; surface roughness; high frequency; tangent loss; coplanar waveguide; transmission line; skin depth.

I. Introduction

There is high demand for designing high frequency on-chip connectors, antennas and transmission lines that operate in the tens of GHz range. Such components are essential for many applications like monolithic millimeter-wave circuits, and SerDes design. In order to predict the behavior of the transmission line, we use one of the available commercial EM field solvers. However and in many cases; theses solvers don't provide or include parameters such as the loss tangent and surface roughness, especially at high frequencies.

When the desired operating frequency is high, the skin depth significantly affects the signal propagation especially when the conductor's surface is rough [1]. With the wavelength (λ) less than or equal to the height of the surface roughness, the attenuation becomes more critical and increases as a function of the frequency [2]. Once fabricated and measured, the roughness of the conductor's surface should be considered in the models [2] for its impact on the degradation of the propagation velocity and on the increase of the conduction and dielectric losses [3].

In the last decade, multiple researchers were investigating the properties of the transmission lines and the losses caused by the surface roughness [4-7]. Hammerstad and Jensen presented a simple equation for single and couple microstrip line parameters including the losses posed by the surface roughness. But, their equation is valid only for rectangular profile [8]. Scogna and Schaure enhanced the equation of Hammerstad and Jensen by including the triangular and cylindrical profiles [2].

In this study, we are recommending some values for the critical parameters extracted from analyzing the existing models [4-7]. The adaptability of these factors enhances the accuracy of the used models [8] for the different fabricated samples. They mainly impact the RMS value of the surface roughness and the loss tangent and extracted from microstrip transmission lines (TRL) and Coplanar Waveguide transmission lines (CPW) fabricated in standard CMOS technology.

II. Proposed Coefficients

In general, the total losses are a combination of the dielectric and conduction losses ($\alpha_{dielectric} + \alpha_{condution\ total}$). Equation (1) presents the conduction losses including the surface roughness (Δ), proposed by Hammerstad and Jensen [8].

$$\alpha_{\text{condution total}} = \alpha_c \left[1 + \frac{2}{\pi} \tan^{-1}\left(1.4 \left(\frac{\Delta}{\delta} \right)^2 \right) \right] \quad (1)$$

where δ is the skin depth. After testing multiple samples with widths ranging from 2 µm up to 100 µm with a fixed length of roughly 1mm, two main findings for accurate modeling of the total losses were proposed. First, the RMS value of the surface roughness (Δ) has a frequency dependent component, described by:

$$\Delta = A \times f \quad (2)$$

where A is a correction factor found to be varying depending on the dimensions of the transmission line and f is the frequency. Also, the measurements revealed the fact that A increases almost linearly when reducing the width of the transmission line. Moreover, the CPW has experienced twice the A value compared to a TRL having the same dimensions.

Second, for $\alpha_{dielectric}$ there is a frequency dependent component for the loss tangent, and it is modeled as follows:

$$\tan(\delta) = B + C \times f \quad (3)$$

where B and C are correction factors found to be varying with the structure and the width of the TRL. The models consistently revealed the use of 0.006 as the value of the B factor for the TRL. This B value is about thirty times smaller for the CPW case. In addition, the C factor increases almost linearly by reducing the width of the TRL, while it vanishes completely for CPW.

III. RESULTS AND DISCUSSION

Multiple transmission lines with different structures (Microstrip and CPW) and dimensions were designed and fabricated in five metal layers standard CMOS technology in order to extract the previously mentioned critical parameters. Fig. 1 demonstrates one microstrip transmission line (Fig. 1A) and one CPW (Fig. 1B). Fig. 2 shows a compression for the real and imaginary parts of the input impedance between the existing model shown in equation (1) including the correction factors and the measured results up to 50 GHz. The strong correlation between the proposed coefficient and the measured results proves the robustness of the model and the reliability of the used coefficients.

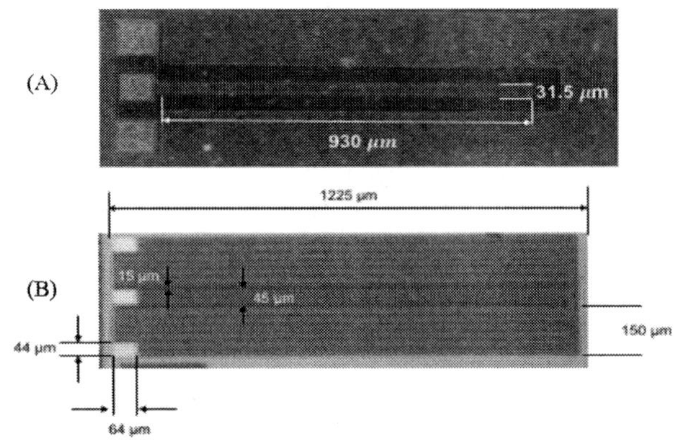

Fig. 1. (A) the microstrip line (TRL) and (B) Coplanar waveguide (CPW).

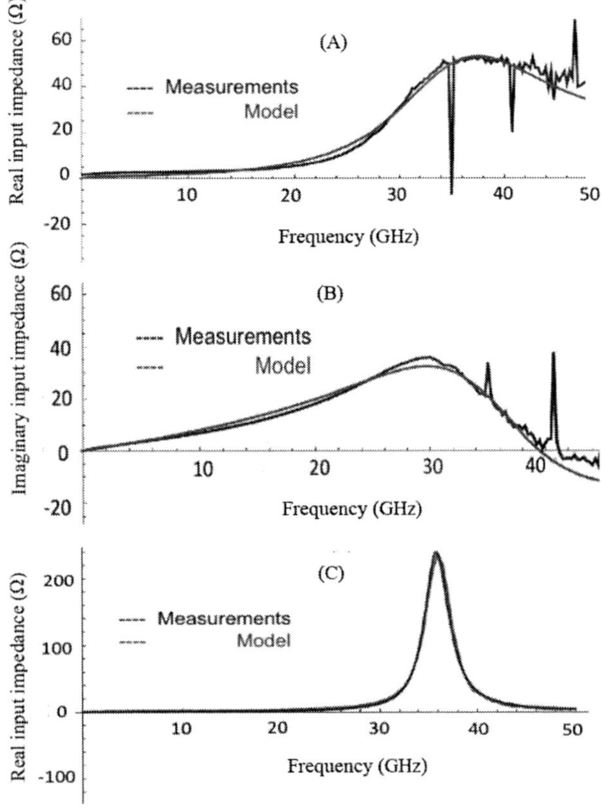

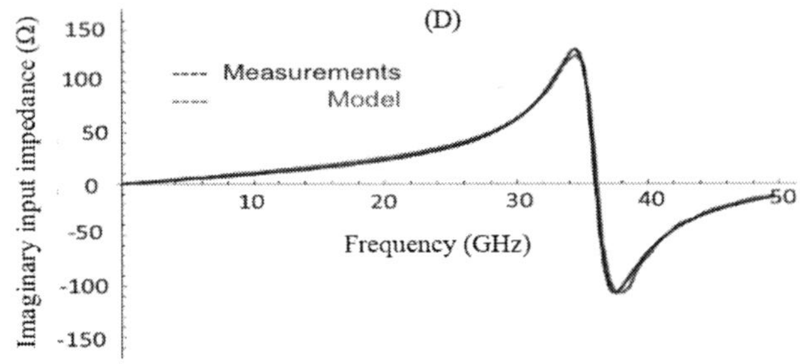

Fig. 2. (A) and (B) are the modeled and measured input impedance of TRL for real and imaginary parts, (C) and (D) are the modeled and measured input impedance of CPW for the real and imaginary parts

IV. CONCLUSION

This paper provided a guideline for the designers to include some critical values that affect the surface roughness and the loss tangent when it was difficult to find them in many of the references. Different structures of transmission lines were designed and fabricated in standard CMOS technology to estimate and extract the RMS value of the surface roughness and the loss tangent. We confirmed the dependency of the RMS value of the surface roughness on the frequency and revealed the relationship between the surface roughness and the width of the transmission line. Furthermore, we discussed the coefficients of the loss tangent including the constant factor and the frequency dependent factor and presented its relationship with the width of the transmission line as well.

REFERENCES

[1] A. C. Scogna and M. Schauer, "Performance analysis of stripline surface roughness models," 2008 International Symposium on Electromagnetic Compatibility (Emc Europe), pp. 572-577, 2008.

[2] A. F. Horn, J. W. Reynolds, and J. C. Rautio, "Conductor profile effects on the propagation constant of microstrip transmission lines," in 2010 IEEE MTT-S International Microwave Symposium, 2010, pp. 868-871.

[3] Q. Chen and N. Wong, "A Stochastic Integral Equation Method for Resistance Extraction of Conductors with Random Rough Surfaces," in 2006 International Symposium on Intelligent Signal Processing and Communications, 2006, pp. 411-414.

[4] T. Liang, S. Hall, H. Heck, and G. Brist, "A Practical Method for Modeling PCB Transmission Lines with Conductor Surface Roughness and Wideband Dielectric Properties," in 2006 IEEE MTT-S International Microwave Symposium Digest, 2006, pp. 1780-1783.

[5] T. Al-Attar and T. H. Lee, "Monolithic integrated millimeter-wave IMPATT transmitter in standard CMOS technology," IEEE Transactions on Microwave Theory and Techniques, vol. 53, pp. 3557-3561, 2005.

[6] C. D. Morcillo, S. K. Bhattacharya, A. Horn, and J. Papapolymerou, "Conductor surface-roughness effect in the loss tangent measurement of low-loss organic substrates from 30 GHz to 70 GHz," in 2010 Proceedings 60th Electronic Components and Technology Conference (ECTC), 2010, pp. 727-734.

[7] J. E. Chan, K. Sivaprasad, and K. A. Chamberlin, "High-Frequency Modeling of Frequency-Dependent Dielectric and Conductor Losses in Transmission Lines," IEEE Transactions on Components and Packaging Technologies, vol. 30, pp. 86-91, 2007.

[8] E. Hammerstad and O. Jensen, "Accurate Models for Microstrip Computer-Aided Design," in 1980 IEEE MTT-S International Microwave symposium Digest, 1980, pp. 407-409.

A Dual-Band Metamaterial Absorber with Polarization Insensitive and Tunable Characteristics

Kai Yu, Yingsong Li* and Yanyan Wang
College of Information and Communications Engineering
Harbin Engineering University, Harbin 150001, China
*liyingsong@ieee.org

Abstract- **In this paper, we propose a metamaterial absorber for dual-band applications. The unit cell of the proposed absorber consists of a cross H-like structure within a metal square ring and a ground plane, which are printed on both sides of the substrate. The results show that our designed absorber gives two absorption bands at 5.6 GHz and 13 GHz, and the absorption peaks are both higher than 99%. The proposed dual-band absorber has a polarization insensitive characteristic and the absorption performance is almost invariable with different polarization angles. Furthermore, the resonance centers of the two absorption bands can be adjusted by changing the related parameters. The dual-band absorber can be used in practical applications due to its excellent absorption characteristics and simple structure.**

Keywords—*Dual-band performances; Perfect metamaterial absorber; Polarization Insensitive; Tunable characteristic*

I. Introduction

In recent years, metamaterials have received considerable interests due to their unique characteristics such as negative refraction, superlensing and reversed Doppler Effect [1]. Because of these properties, metamaterials have been used in designing many electromagnetic devices, and the emergence of metamaterial technology provides a new choice for the perfect absorber design. Due to the advantage of its ultra-thin thickness, lighter weight and increased effectiveness, these reported metamaterial absorbers are created to replace the conventional absorbers [2-3]. As we all know, the absorption bandwidth and polarization sensitivity are the most important indicators for the absorber. Wide absorption bandwidth and multi-band absorption features are the hot spot for the current researchers [4-5]. Also, polarization insensitivity and wide-angle absorption are also essential aspects for the perfect absorbers [6-7]. An absorber with a quite wide absorption bandwidth, multi-band and polarization insensitivity will have broad prospects.

In this paper, we propose an absorber for dual-band applications, which has polarization insensitive and can be tunable. To obtain dual-band performance, a cross H-shaped structure is integrated into a square ring. Also, a metal ground is printed on the other sides of the substrate. The results show that the proposed absorber can provide two absorption bands operating at 5.6 GHz and 13 GHz, and the absorption peaks are higher than 99%. Moreover, our proposed absorber has a polarization insensitive and tunable characteristic, rendering it suitable for using in many absorbing fields.

II. Absorber Design

The configuration of the proposed dual-band absorber unit cell is depicted in Fig. 1, which is fabricated on a FR-4 substrate with a relative permittivity of 4.4, a loss tangent of 0.02, a thickness of 0.8 mm, and the total size is 10 mm × 10 mm. A metal square ring is printed on the top of the substrate. In the interior of the square ring, there is a crossed H-like structure with a square patch at the center of the structure. At the bottom, a ground plane is installed, which has the same size as the substrate. The optimization dimensions are obtained by using HFSS and are listed as L= 10, a= 3, b= 6, c= 0.5, d= 0.5, e= 0.5, h= 0.5 (unit: mm).

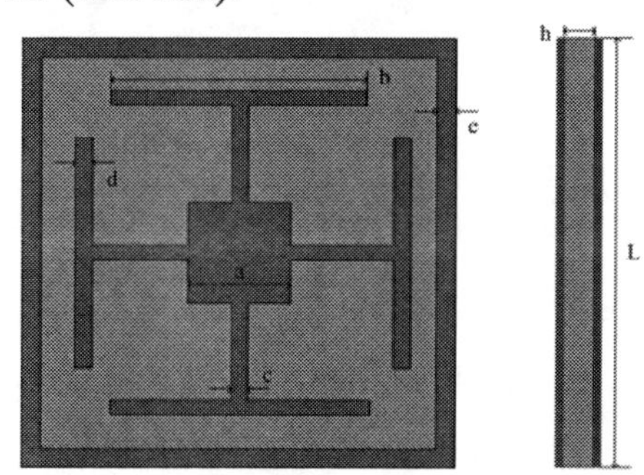

Fig. 1: Geometry structure of the proposed dual-band metamaterial absorber.

III. Performance Analysis

The performance is gotten by the HFSS, where we use periodic boundary conditions and floquet port excitation. The boundary condition and direction of excitation are shown in Fig. 2.

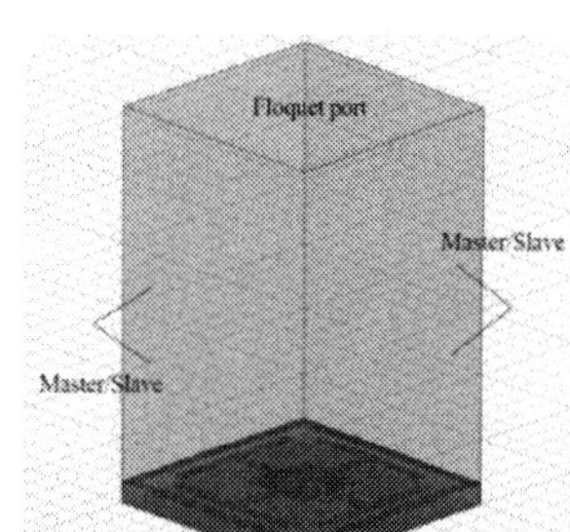

Fig. 2: 3-D view along with the boundary conditions and excitation

Assuming that the absorption, reflectance and transmittance are A (ω), R (ω), and T (ω). And T (ω) = $S21^2$ and reflectance R (ω) = $S11^2$, respectively. The absorption A (ω) can be obtained by A (ω) = 1 – R (ω) – T (ω). Due to the metal ground plane, the transmission is zero. Then, we can get the absorptivity A (ω) = 1 - R (ω) [8].

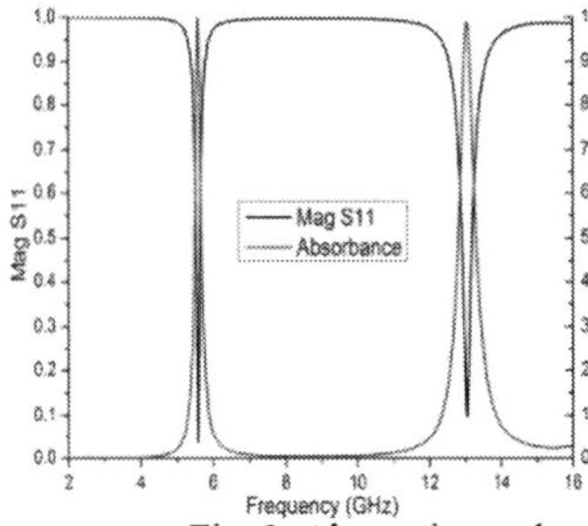

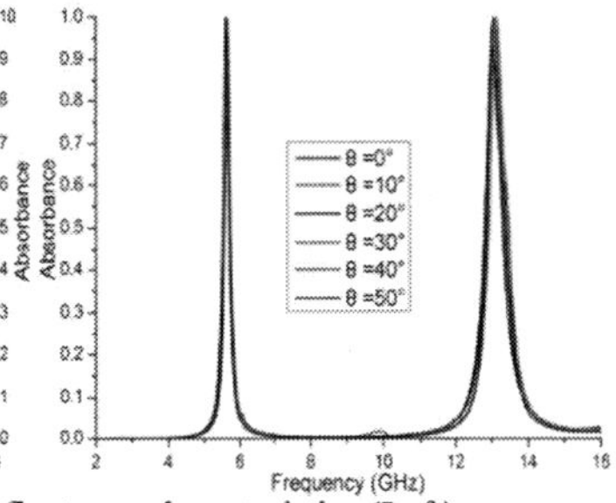

Fig. 3: Absorption and reflectance characteristics (Left).

Fig. 4: Absorption rate with different polarization angles (Right).

Figure 3 shows the absorbance and reflectivity of the unit cell of proposed absorber operating from 2GHz to 16GHz. From Fig.3, we can see that the reflectance is 0.002 and 0.008 at 5.6 GHz and 13 GHz, respectively. Thus, we can get that the peak absorptions at both bands are higher than 99%. Absorption rate of our absorber with different polarization angle are depicted in Fig. 4. It can be found that the absorption rate has a little change when the polarization angle ranges from 0° to 50°, which is to say that our designed dual-band metamaterial absorber has a polarization insensitive characteristic.

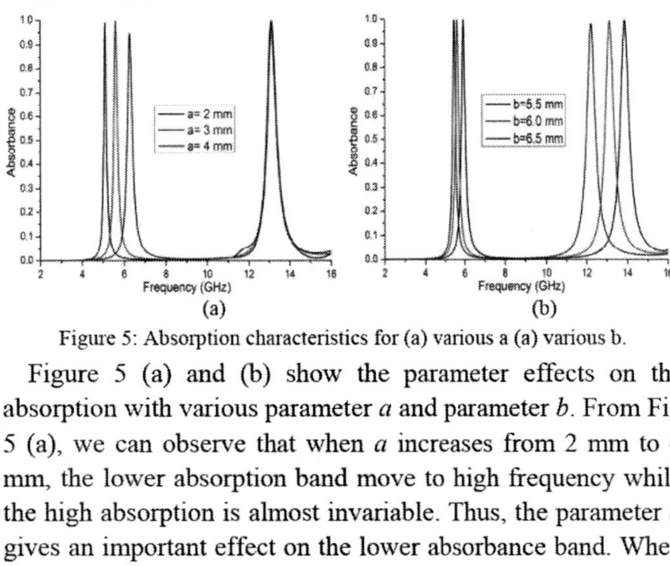

(a) (b)

Figure 5: Absorption characteristics for (a) various a (a) various b.

Figure 5 (a) and (b) show the parameter effects on the absorption with various parameter *a* and parameter *b*. From Fig. 5 (a), we can observe that when *a* increases from 2 mm to 4 mm, the lower absorption band move to high frequency while the high absorption is almost invariable. Thus, the parameter *a* gives an important effect on the lower absorbance band. When parameter *b* increases from 5.5 mm to 6.5 mm, the high absorption band rapidly shifts toward to low frequency, which is given in Fig. 5 (b). Thereby, the upper absorbance band can be adjusted by selecting parameter *b*.

To further understand the principle of the proposed dual-band absorber, current distributions at 5.6 GHz and 13 GHz are investigated and given in Fig. 6. It is obvious that the current at low frequency band is concentrated in the cross H-like structure and the middle square structure, which means that the lower absorption is generated by these structures. Similarly, the upper band absorption function is generated by both sides of the H-like structure.

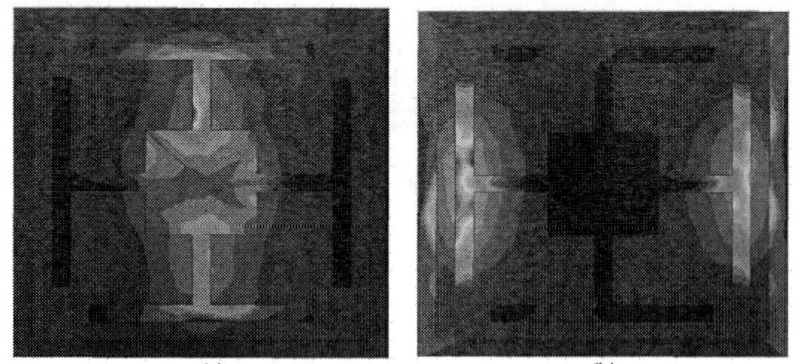

(a) (b)

Figure 6: Current distributions of the absorber at (a) 5.6 GHz, (b) 13 GHz.

IV. Conclusion

In this paper, a dual-band metamaterial absorber cell unit is designed and discussed. The designed absorber has two absorption bands at 5.6 GHz and 13 GHz, and the peak absorbance rates is better than 99 %. Additionally, the center frequencies of two absorption bands can be adjusted by properly selecting the parameters. Also, the designed absorber has a polarization insensitive characteristic and wide-angle absorption.

Acknowledgment

This paper is funded by the International Exchange Program of Harbin Engineering University for Innovation-oriented Talents Cultivation. This work was also partially supported by the National Key Research and Development Program of China-Government Corporation Special Program (2016YFE0111100), the Science and Technology innovative Talents Foundation of Harbin (2016RAXXJ044), Projects for the Selected Returned Overseas Chinese Scholars of Heilongjiang Province and MOHRSS of China, and the Foundational Research Funds for the Central Universities (HEUCFD1433, HEUCF160815).

References

[1] X. Liu, X. Zhao, "Perfect absorber metamaterial for designing low-RCS patch antenna," IEEE Antennas and Wireless Propagation Letters, vol. 13, pp. 1473-1476, 2014.

[2] H. Zhai, C. Zhan, Z. Li, C. Liang, "A triple-band ultrathin metamaterial absorber with wide-angle and polarization stability," IEEE Antennas and Wireless Propagation Letters, vol. 14, pp. 241-244, 2014.

[3] F. Costa, S. Genovesi, A. Monorchio, G. Manara, "A circuit-based model for the interpretation of perfect metamaterial absorbers," IEEE Transactions on Antennas and Propagation, vol. 61, pp. 1201-1209, 2012.

[4] Y. Zhong, S. Fu, M. Tu, B. Chen, A. Lin, "A multimetal broadband metamaterial perfect absorber with compact dimension," IEEE Photonics Journal, vol. 8, pp. 1943-0655, 2016.

[5] G. Wang, B. Wang, "Five-band terahertz metamaterial absorber based on a four-gap comb resonator," Journal of Lightwave Technology, vol. 33, pp. 5151-5156, 2015.

[6] H. Jiang, Z. Xue, W. Li, W. Ren, "Multiband polarisation insensitive metamaterial absorber based on circular fractal structure," IET Microwaves, Antennas & Propagation, vol. 10, pp.1141-1145, 2016.

[7] M. Agarwal, A. K. Behera, M. K. Meshram, "Wide-angle quad-band polarisation-insensitive metamaterial absorber," Electronics Letters, vol. 52, pp. 340-342, 2016.

[8] W. Ma, Y. Wen, X. Yu, "theoretical and experimental demonstrations of a dual-band metamaterial absorber at mid-infrared," IEEE Photonics Technology Letters, vol. 26, no. 19, pp. 1940-1943, 2014.

Simple and Efficient Design of Reconfigurable FSS with Triangular Patch Elements

André N. Silva, Rafaela G. G. Carvalho, Adaildo G. D'Assunção, and José P. Silva
Department of Communication Engineering
Federal University of Rio Grande do Norte
Natal, Brazil
eng.andrensilva@gmail.com, rafaelaggc@gmail.com, adaildo@ct.ufrn.br, patroc@ct.ufrn.br

***Abstract*—This paper proposes a reconfigurable frequency selective surface (FSS) operating in the X band composed of triangular elements periodically placed on a single FR-4 dielectric layer. The reconfiguration of the proposed FSS allows a quasi-linear variation of the rejecting resonant frequency as function of the incident wave angle. The variation of the incident wave angle is provided by rotation of the FSS structure from 0° to 40°, for the TE mode, and can be used in cognitive radio technology through a micro-controlled interface.**

Keywords—Frequency selective surface; FSS; reconfigurable FSS; X-band

I. Introduction

A frequency selective surface (FSS) is usually defined as a periodic array of conductive patch or aperture elements, arranged in a dielectric substrate, capable of behaving as a transparent interface or not, at certain frequency bands. Such frequency selective behavior depends on the polarization of the incident wave and several structural parameters such as dimensions and shape of the patch or aperture elements, array periodicity, and substrate thickness and permittivity [1], [2].

These structures can be used, for example, in military applications such as reduction of radar cross section (RCS) of targets, radomes, electromagnetic shielding (protection of indoor propagation environments from unwanted interference), and absorbers [1]-[3].

For some of these applications the FSS operating frequencies should be independent of the wave incident angle and polarization at the resonance bands. Recent research in the area discuss various proposals to improve the angular stability of FSS through mechanisms such as miniaturization of the cell element, cell skewing, use of metamaterials, use of dissimilar cell elements, and different configurations of fractals [1]-[3]. However, the FSS angular non-stability can be used in the development of reconfigurable structures, through its rotation, providing operation at different frequencies.

Microwave circuits reconfigurability is a very important feature in modern communication systems, because it allows a same structure to adapt to different scenarios of a particular application, such as radomes and adaptive screens, used to reject unwanted wireless transmissions. This feature can be achieved by traditional methods such as the use of active semiconductor devices (PIN and Schottky diodes) or variable capacitors coupled to the FSS cell elements, requiring the use of a separate circuit to power on these devices. However, these methods require a large number of active elements, which increases the complexity and cost of manufacture [4], suggesting the use of simpler and more robust techniques for frequency selectivity as the mechanical reconfigurability [5].

This paper describes the development of a simple reconfigurable FSS structure, with triangular patch elements on a single dielectric layer, to be used as a FSS reject filter for applications in the X-band (8.2 GHz to 12.4 GHz). Reconfigurability is provided by mechanical rotation of the proposed FSS structure, and the operating frequency varies with the angle of the incident wave.

II. FSS Geometry and Results

The proposed FSS structure is composed of triangular patch elements in a square array configuration. The FSS unit cell dimensions are $T_x = T_y = 20$ mm and consists of a triangular patch element with dimensions $D_b = D_h = 10$ mm, as illustrated in Fig. 1. The triangular patch is printed on a FR-4 substrate with relative permittivity $\varepsilon_r = 4.4$, loss tangent $tan\delta = 0.02$, and thickness h = 1.5 mm.

A parametric analysis has been performed using Ansoft Designer to investigate the frequency response effect of rotating the proposed FSS structure. The rotation angle, θ, has been varied from 0° to 40° (with a step of 5°) for both TE and TM polarization.

Simulation results of the frequency behavior of the FSS transmission coefficient for particular values of the rotation angle, θ, are shown in Figs. 2 and 3, for TE and TM polarizations, respectively.

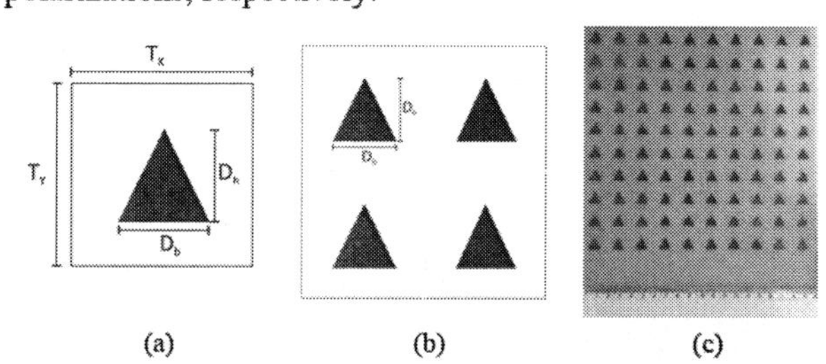

Fig. 1. FSS structure with triangular patch elements: (a) unit cell, (b) array, and (c) prototype photo.

Results are obtained for the FSS geometry shown in Fig. 1, with $T_x = T_y = 20$ mm and $D_b = D_h = 10$ mm. For TE polarization, a significant deviation in the FSS resonant frequency value is obtained as the rotation angle is varied, indicating that the FSS is angularly unstable (Fig. 2). In addition, it is observed the existence of an approximately linear relationship between the resonant frequency and rotation angle values. For TM polarization, no significant deviation in the FSS resonant frequency is obtained as the rotation angle is varied, indicating that the FSS is relatively stable, with a deviation of about 200 MHz, for a variation of the rotation angle θ from 0° to 40° (Fig. 3).

Table I presents simulation results of the FSS resonance bands and bandwidths for different values of the rotation angle θ and for TE and TM polarizations. For TE polarization, when the rotation angle θ varies from 0° to 40°, the FSS rejection band limits and corresponding bandwidths decreases. In fact, a 50 % reduction is observed for the FSS bandwidth, in the worst case. However, a bandwidth minimum of 200 MHz is available in the worst cases ($\theta \geq 30°$). For TM polarization, the FSS exhibits band rejection performance for $0° \leq \theta \leq 20°$. In the range $25° \leq \theta \leq 40°$, the lower transmission coefficient value does not reach the threshold of -10 dB, and the proposed structure does not act like a band stop filter.

Fig. 4 shows the effect of the rotation angle on the proposed FSS resonant frequency, resulting in a quasi-linear dependence, emphasizing its reconfigurability potential. Thus, the proposed FSS is easily integrated with a micro-controlled interface to allow the choice of particular operating frequencies according to specific angular rotation values. The FSS resonant frequency measurement results show 5.4 % deviation from simulation results.

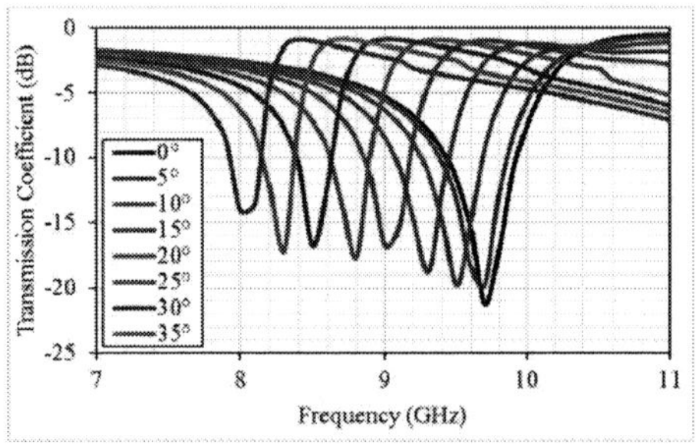

Fig. 2. Simulation transmission coefficient results for TE polarization.

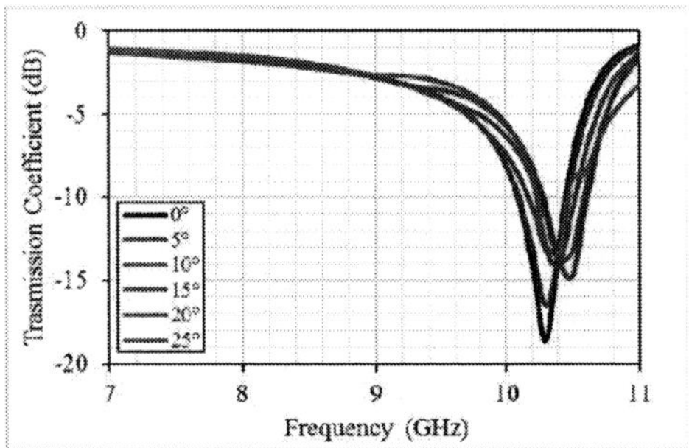

Fig. 3. Simulation transmission coefficient results for TM polarization.

TABLE I. SIMULATED FSS RESONANCE BAND AND BANDWIDTH FOR TE AND TM POLARIZATIONS

	TE polarization		TM polarization	
θ (°)	*Frequency Band (GHz)*	*Bandwidth (GHz)*	*Frequency Band (GHz)*	*Bandwidth (GHz)*
0	9.5 – 9.9	0.4	10.1 – 10.4	0.3
5	9.4 – 9.8	0.4	10.1 – 10.4	0.3
10	9.3 – 9.7	0.4	10.2 – 10.5	0.3
15	9.1 – 9.4	0.3	10.3 – 10.5	0.2
20	8.9 – 9.2	0.3	10.3 – 10.6	0.3
25	8.6 – 8.9	0.3	–	–
30	8.4 – 8.6	0.2	–	–
35	8.2 – 8.4	0.2	–	–
40	7.9 – 8.1	0.2	–	–

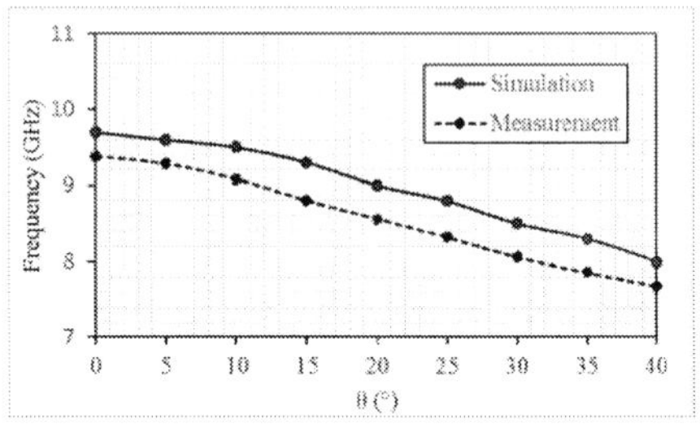

Fig. 4. FSS simulation and measurement resonant frequency results as function of the rotation angle (θ).

III. CONCLUSION

A simple and efficient reconfigurable FSS structure has been proposed to operate at X band. The FSS geometry is composed of triangular patch elements printed on a FR-4 dielectric substrate. Transmission coefficient results are presented for both TE and TM polarizations. Reconfigurability is provided rotating the main axis of the FSS and occurs for TE polarization, exhibiting a quasi-linear relationship between the FSS transmission coefficient and rotating angle, allowing the implementation of a microcontroller system to be used in communications systems. For TM polarization, the proposed FSS transmission coefficient results showed angular stability performance for small variation of the rotation angle (lower than 20°). Unit cell skewing effect is investigated as well.

REFERENCES

[1] A. Newblold, "Designing buildings for the wireless-age," IEE Commun. Eng., vol. 2, pp. 18-21, 2004.

[2] X. Liu, Q. Wang, W. Zhan, M. Jin, and M. Bai, "On the improvement of angular stability of the 2nd-Order miniaturized FSS structure," IEEE Antennas Wireless Propag. Lett., vol. 15, pp. 826-829, 2016.

[3] M.R. Silva, C.L. Nóbrega, P.H.F. Silva, and A.G. D'Assunção, "Stable and compact multiband frequency selective surfaces with Peano pre-fractal configurations," IET Microwaves, Antennas & Propag., vol. 7, pp. 543-551, 2013.

[4] C. Mias, "Varactor-tunable frequency selective surface with the resistive lumped element biasing grids," IEEE Microw. Wireless Comp. Lett., vol. 15, pp. 570-572, 2005.

[5] S.N. Azemi, K. Ghorbani, and W.S.T. Rowe, "A reconfigurable FSS using a spring resonator element," IEEE Antennas Wireless Propag. Lett., vol. 12, pp. 781-784, 2013.

Floating Crescent Star in a Slot Patch Antenna

Mustafa E. Yılmaz, Ömer F. Alperen
Dep. of Electrical-Electronics Engineering
Istanbul Commerce University
Maltepe, Istanbul
memrey@outlook.com, ofalperen@gmail.com

Muhammet Ali Akyıldız, Taha Imeci
Dep. of Electrical-Electronics Engineering
Istanbul Commerce University
Maltepe, Istanbul
a.akyildiz7@gmail.com, timeci@ticaret.edu.tr

***Abstract*—This article introduces a rectangular single-band planar crescent-star figured patch antenna simulated for wireless communication systems. The introduced antenna is designed for Wlan and Wimax applications. Significant parametric study was conducted in terms of dielectric constant, dielectric thichness, slot dimensions. The designed patch antenna has an input match resonance of -30 dB at 4.46 GHz, and 5.4 dB gain.**

Keywords—Planar Antenna, Patch Antenna, Single-Band Antenna, Sonnet Software, Wlan, Wimax.

I. INTRODUCTION

At the present time, the demand of antennas introduced by different wireless technology applications increases, which provides data, voice, image and video transmission [1]. The WiMAX standard specifies among other things the transmission layer (modulation, channel access etc.). The useable frequency range is given a 2 to 11 GHz. [2] The antenna which designed for GPS technology operates in L1 frequency with a microstrip structure of E-shaped. In comparison with this antenna, the antenna introduced here designed for Wimax and Wlan technologies and operates in higher bandwidth. The parameters like length, thickness, shape, slot size and shapes, feeding point position and method have their own roles on operating needed bands. In [3- 4] it is mentioned that cutting slots or notching to the edges can provide adjusting dual frequency operations. In [5-6], four different patch antennas are obtained by cutting different slots in a way that change resonance frequency.

In [7], patch antennas can be analysed by three modeling. These are transmission-line modeling, cavity modeling and full-wave modeling. In this design, Method of Moment was used. The design is simulated by using 3D-planar electromagnetic software, called Sonnet Suites [8].

II. STRUCTURE OF THE ANTENNA

For the bottom layer of design, Rogers RT/duroid 5880™ which has ε_r =2.2 and for the top layer, air which has ε_r= 1 were used as dielectric matterial. The antenna's dimensions were set as H=36.5 mm, W=43 mm, thickness=1.588 mm as it seen in Figure1.

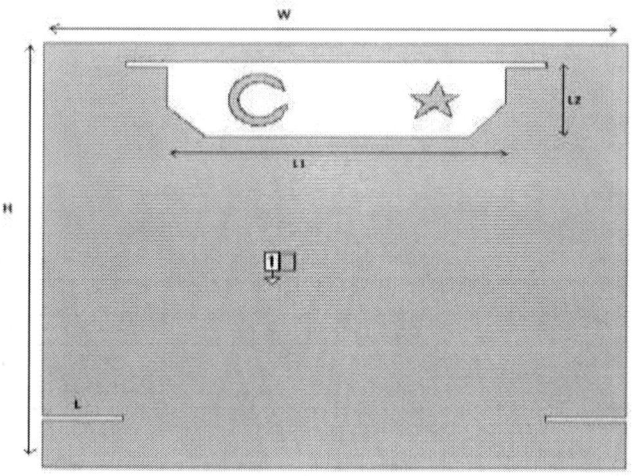

Fig. 1. Top view of the antenna.

The big slot's dimensions are L1=25 mm, L2=6.5 mm. Additionally two (3.0x0.5 mm) little slots to the edges of big slot and two (3.62 mm) right triangles to the bottom corners of big slot were placed to increase the gain. Two (6.0x0.5 mm) little slots were added to the edges of antenna.

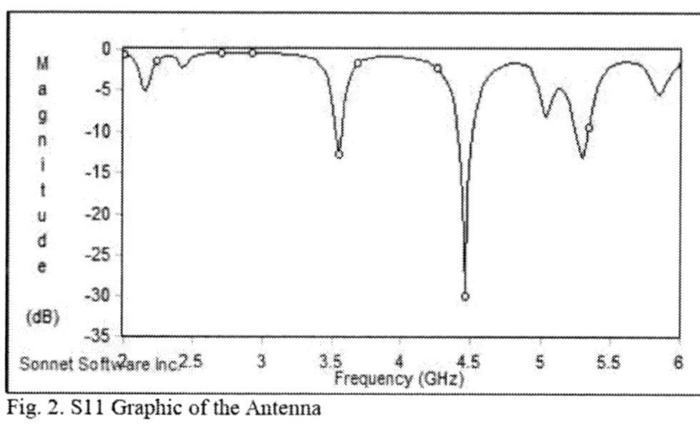

Fig. 2. S11 Graphic of the Antenna

We located the port autoground type 50 Ω that feeds the antenna at 25.09 mm from top left corner. We placed a 18.48 mm^2 crescent 4.59 mm from left edge of big slot and a 11.16 mm^2 star on a 1 mm length-bar 3.4 mm from right edge of big slot for an optimum gain. It is shown that S11 graphic is in Figure 2, gain graphic is in Figure 3. Parametric study of changing ε_r is in Table I, distance between crescent and star is in Table II, dimensions of L slot change is in Table III and thickness is in Table IV.

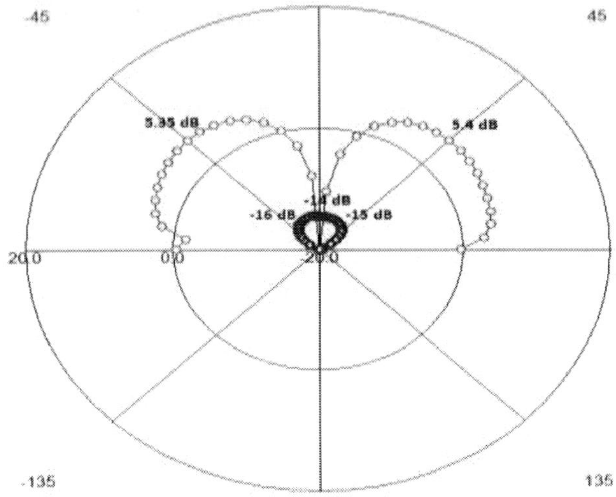

Fig. 3. Gain graphic of antenna at 4.46 GHz.

TABLE I. ε_R-GAIN – S11

ε_r	S11(dB)	Gain(dB)	
		e-theta(-45°)	e-theta(45°)
1.99	-20.27	5.05	5.13
2	-29.33	5.57	5.67
2.1	-31.95	5.46	5.54
2.2	-30,002	5.35	5.4
2.3	-21.32	5.17	5.21
2.4	-24.83	5.12	5.13

As seen in Table I, by increasing εr with 0.1, S11 was effected massively even though it doesn't make the same change with gain.

TABLE II. DISTANCE–GAIN – S11

Distance (mm)	S11 (dB)	Gain (dB)	
		e-theta(-45°)	e-theta(45°)
15.8	-11.78	0	0
12.4	-18.19	5.73	5.8
9.3	30.002	5.35	5.4
4.4	-13.69	-5.97	-5.57
0.4	-13.3	-6.60	-2.41

Table II shows that changing the distance 4 mm, caused big changes in S11, but gain is not changing when the distance between crescent and star was around 10 mm.

TABLE III. SLOT DIMENSION-GAIN-S11

Slot (mmxmm)	S11(dB)	Gain (dB)	
		e-theta(-45°)	e-theta(45°)
6x0.3	-29.12	5.37	5.42
6x0.4	-29.34	5.35	5.4
6x0.5	-30	5.35	5.4
5.7x0.5	-28.92	5.36	5.41
5.8x0.5	28.99	5.36	5.41
5.9x0.5	-29.07	5.36	5.41

Table III shows that keeping one slot edge constant and, increasing other edge 0.1 mm and then keeping the other slot edge same and increasing the other one 0.1 mm does not change S11 and gain much.

TABLE IV. THICKNESS-GAIN –S11

Thickness (mm)	S11 (dB)	Gain (dB)	
		e-theta(-45°)	e-theta(45°)
1.55	-29.38	5.34	5.39
1.56	-29.55	5.34	5.39
1.57	-29.77	5.34	5.39
1.58	30	5.35	5.4
1.59	-30.16	5.35	5.4
1.6	-30.39	5.35	5.4

Table IV states that, by changing dielectric thickness, S11 and gain don't change much, which is good in terms of fabrication tolerances.

III. CONCLUSION

In this article, a planar slot patch antenna that is used in wireless communication systems, operating in single frequency band is presented. The antenna has a floating crescent star shaped patch in a large slot. A detailed parametric study was performed on the geometry and results shown in Tables and discussed. Next work is fabrication.

REFERENCES

[1] http://www.wimo.com/wimax-antennas_e.html
[2] S. Erdemir, A.E. Yılmaz, "L1 frekansında çalışan E şekilli mikroşerit GPS anteni tasarımı," Uludağ Üniversitesi Mühendislik Mimarlık Fakültesi Dergisi vol. 19, pp. 1, 2014.
[3] D.D. Krishna, M. Gopikrina, C.K. Aanandan, P. Mohanan, K. Vasudevan, "Compact dual band slot loaded circular microstrip antenna with superstrate," Progress In Electromagnetics Research, PIER 83, pp. 245-255, 2008.
[4] A. Mishra, P. Singh, N.P. Yadav, A.J. Ansari, "Compact shorted microstrip patch antenna for dual band operation," Progress in Electromagnetic Research vol. 9, pp. 171–182, 2009.
[5] A. Cap, Z. Raida, H.Z. Palmero, R. Lamadrid, "Multi- band planar antennas: a comparative study," Radioengineering vol. 14 pp. 4 December 2005.
[6] G. Sami, M. Mohanna, M.L. Rabeh, "Tri-band microstrip antenna design for wireless communication applications," In: NRIAG Journal of Astronomy and Geophysics vol. 2, pp. 39-44, 2013.
[7] T.M. Hsueh, H.T. Hsu, H.T. Chou, K.L. Hung, "Dual Band omnidirectional planar antenna for WiMAX applications," In: Antennas and Propagation Society International Symposium, pp. 1–4. 2008.
[8] Sonnet Suites, version 13.52 www.sonnetsoftware.com.

A Compact Size Circular Sector Patch Antenna For Ku-band Applications

G. Kemal Oğuz
Department of Electrical and Electronics Engineering
Istanbul Commerce University
Istanbul, Turkey

Ş. Taha İmeci
Department of Electrical and Electronics Engineering
Istanbul Commerce University
Istanbul, Turkey

Abstract—**In this paper, a circular sector microstrip patch antenna has been designed, simulated and fabricated. The operating frequency of the antenna is 14.5 GHz with -14.25 dB input match and 6.57 dB gain. Other designs given in the literature are generally in C-band. However, our circular sector shape antenna has higher frequency in Ku-Band providing a compact size.**

Keywords—Circular sector shaped; high frequency, microstrip patch antenna; co-axial feed.

I. INTRODUCTION

We have focused on designing a patch antenna having a resonance frequency in Ku-band in this study, In order to obtain higher frequencies, we have chosen a circular sector shape for the patch to design the proposed antenna. Circular patches were reported to lose less energy by radiation and thus provide larger quality factors than other configurations such as rectangular patches [1]. The circular patch has only one degree of freedom to control, i.e. radius of the patch [2]. However, by using notch cutting method, we have added another control parameter, an angle of the circular sector. There is another circular sector shaped antenna in [3]. Because of its small size compared to other shapes such as rectangular and circular patch antennas, they provide circular polarization desired in wireless communication. For circular sector patch antenna, the expression of the radius "a" of the patch is:

$$a = \frac{k_{mn} c}{2\pi f_r \sqrt{\varepsilon_r}}$$

k_{mn} is the zero of the equation J '(k_{mn}) = 0, J is the Bessel function [3], f_r is resonant frequency, c is velocity of light in free space, ε_r is dielectric constant. Figure 1 shows the geometry of the circular shape.

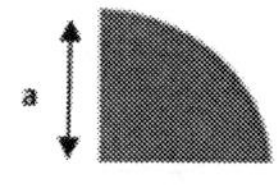

Fig. 1. Geometry of the circular sector patch antenna [3].

In this work, notch cutting technique was used and the angle of the sector was modified multiple times to optimize the shape of the antenna based on the resonance frequency. Antenna was designed and simulated by using Sonnet Suites [4].

II. DESIGN AND SIMULATION RESULTS

The design of Ku-Band circular sector microstrip patch antenna with dielectric substrate Rogers RT/Duroid 6002 where the dielectric constant of ε_r = 2.94 and the thickness of 50 mils for 14.5 GHz is proposed in this paper. There is a 200 mils air thickness on top of the dielectric. Circular diameter is 7.62 mm. The proposed antenna comprises of a ground plane, Rogers RT/Duroid 6002 substrate material, circular patch and a microstrip co–axial feeding. The main advantage of this type of feeding scheme is that the feed can be placed at any desired position inside the patch in order to obtain impedance matching [5]. The basic shape of the antenna is shown in Figure 2. There is a single resonance frequency showing the input reflection coefficient, S11 in Figure 3. Gain and cross polarization graph is shown in Figure 4. By changing the angle of the sector, the simulated S11 and the desired thicknesses, the gain is determined for 14.5 GHz frequency. This work is shown in Table I. Larger return loss indicates higher power being radiated by the antenna which eventually increases the gain [6]. Following optimized results were determined after the simulations: gain, S11, cross polarization are 6.57 dB, -14.25 dB and -5 dB respectively.

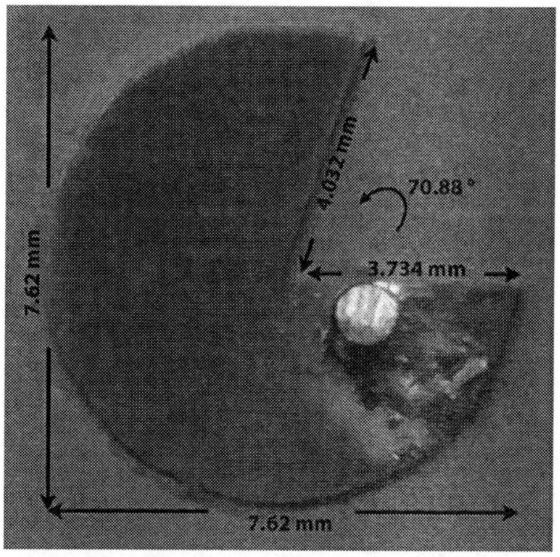

Fig. 2. Picture of the fabricated antenna (Top view).

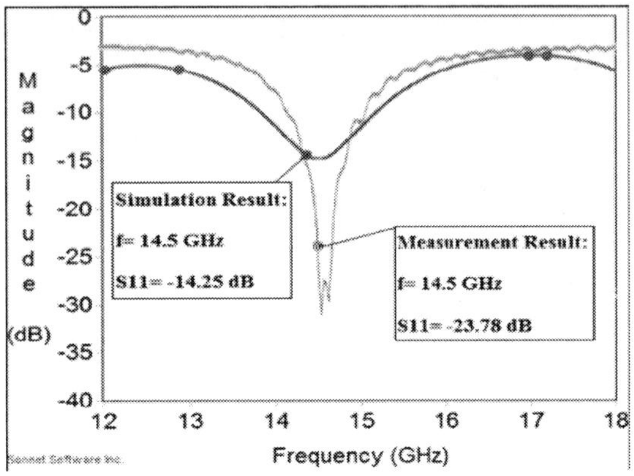

Fig. 3. Simulated and measured S11 of the fabricated antenna.

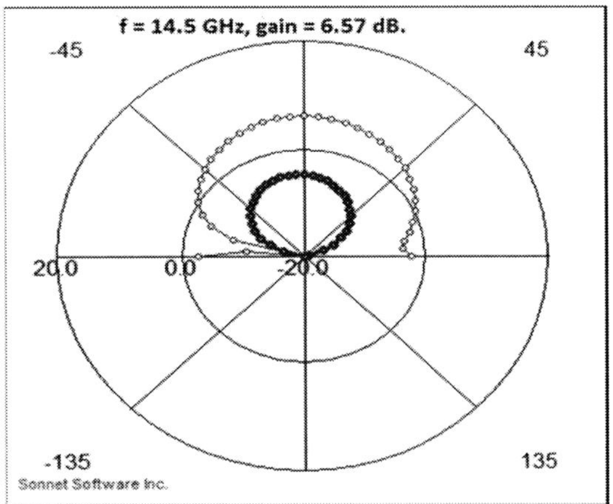

Fig. 4. Simulated gain graph of the fabricated antenna.

TABLE I. FREQUENCY-GAIN-INPUT MATCH WITH DIFFERENT THICKNESSES

Thicknes s [mils]	*Frequency [GHz]*	*Angle [Degree]*	*Gain [dB]*	*S11 [dB]*
30	14.5	80.88	6.62	-7.51
30	14.5	75.88	6.63	-6.65
30	14.5	70.88	6.63	-6.07
30	14.5	65.88	6.63	-5.70
30	14.5	60.88	6.63	-5.63
40	14.5	80.88	6.61	-9.61
40	14.5	75.88	6.61	-9.15
40	14.5	70.88	6.61	-8.86
40	14.5	65.88	6.61	-8.81
50	14.5	80.88	6.57	-11.54
50	14.5	75.88	6.58	-12.89
50	14.5	70.88	6.57	-14.25
50	14.5	65.88	6.55	-15.80
60	14.5	80.88	6.50	-10.53
60	14.5	75.88	6.50	-12.51
60	14.5	70.88	6.48	-15.08
60	14.5	65.88	6.46	-16.42

III. CONCLUSION

The proposed antenna has been designed, simulated, analyzed, fabricated and measured successfully. The antenna which was simulated and analyzed by using Sonnet Suites was optimized to resonate in Ku-band using circular sector shape. The simulations give the following results; the operating frequency is 14.5 GHz, S11 is −14.25 dB, cross polarization is about −5 dB and antenna gain is 6.57 dB, also measured S11 is -23.78 dB. The angle of notched sector and thickness of the substrate are primary design parameters for adjusting the gain, S11 and the cross polarization. The design was optimized after multiple modifications of the sector angle between 60.88° and 80.88° and the substrate thicknesses between 30 mils and 60 mils. Figure 2. has prototype of the designed antenna. S11 parameter was measured meticulously. Figure 3. compares both simulation and measurement results of S11 for circular sector patch antenna. It is shown that the S11 value is changed about -9 dB. The differences between these two results are due to losses in equipment such as SMA connector and non-ideal fabrication process. There are similar works for Ku-Band in literature but the antenna in these works have conventional E-shape with larger dimensions [7]. A compact sized antenna using circular sector shape and providing operation at high frequencies such as Ku-Band is produced successfully in this work.

REFERENCES

[1] N. M. Thaker, V. Ramamoorthy, "A Review on Circular Microstrip Patch Antenna with Slots for C Band Applications," International Journal of Scientific & Engineering Research, vol. 5, Issue 12, ISSN 2229-5518, December 2014.

[2] C. A. Balanis, "Antenna Theory, Analysis and Design", Third Edition, John Wiley & Sons, Inc. April 4 2005.

[3] A. Dalli, L. Zenkouar, and S. Bri, "Comparison of Circular Sector and Rectangular Patch Antenna Arrays in C-Band," Journal of Electromagnetic Analysis and Applications, vol. 4, No. 11 pp. 457-467, 2012.

[4] Sonnet Suites, version 14.52, http://www.sonnetsoftware.com/

[5] Tejal B Tandel, "Rectangular Microstrip Patch Antenna UsingCoaxial Probe Feeding Technique for 5.2 GHz WLAN Application," International Journal of Scientific & Engineering Research, vol. 6, Issue 7, ISSN 2229-5518, July 2015.

[6] F. Lee, Ed , Advances in Microstrip and Printed Antennas, John Wiley, 2012.

[7] S. Malisuwan, J. Sivaraks, N. Madan, and N. Suriyakrai, "Design of Microstrip Patch Antenna for Ku-Band Satellite Communication Applications," International Journal of Computer and Communication Engineering, vol. 3, No. 6, November 2014.

E shaped antenna surrounded with u shape

D. Delikanlı, S. Keskiner
Department of Electrical and Electronics Engineering
Ozyegin University
Istanbul, Turkey
demet.delikanli@ozu.edu.tr
selim.keskiner@ozu.edu.tr

Ş.T. Imeci
Department of Electrical and Electronics Engineering
Istanbul Commerce University
Istanbul, Turkey
timeci@ticaret.edu.tr

***Abstract*— In this work we designed, simulated, fabricated and measured E-shape microstrip patch antenna. In the process of design, we surrounded E-shape patch antenna with "U" figure. As a result of this work, resonance frequency is 4.27 GHz and S11 is -9.69 dB and gain is 7.22 dB. Parametric study on different gap lengths between E and U shaped metals was studied. This antenna design is an improvement from last years research published in Aces conference 2016.**

Keywords*— *E-shape patch antenna, gain, Surrounding U-shape, probe-feed, .

I. Introduction

E-shape microstrip patch antennas have been used in different areas such as GSM, digital enhanced cordless telephone, WIMAX (worldwide interoperability for microwave access), Wireless Local Area Network, GPS (Global Positioning System) [1]. Microstrip patch antennas are from the class of resonant type antennas that offers a low profile, i.e. thin and easily manufacture ability, which provides great advantages over traditional antennas [2]. Different techniques are used to overcome this narrow bandwidth limitation. These techniques include increasing the thickness of the dielectric substrate, decreasing dielectric constant and using parasitic in E-Shaped patches [3-4].

II. ANTENNA DESIGN, SIMULATION AND MEASUREMENT RESULTS

The operating frequencies of the antenna is 4.27 GHz, the substrate is used with dielectric constant of 4.3 and thickness of 1.6mm. Figure 1 shows the top view of the measured antenna and designed antenna shows some parameters that examined, respectively.

After some successive iteration of simulations, the optimized dimensions shown in Table I was obtained. When we changed the values of W2, W3 and W4, results was not quite sufficient.

Looking at the reference papers [5-6]; we thought that if a floating "U" shape is surrounded the E-shape antenna, the gain of the antenna could increase. Moreover, we observed negative effect of increasing thickness of "U" shape on the gain of antenna during this application. We can see how this distance between U shape and E shape affects S11 and the gain in Table II.

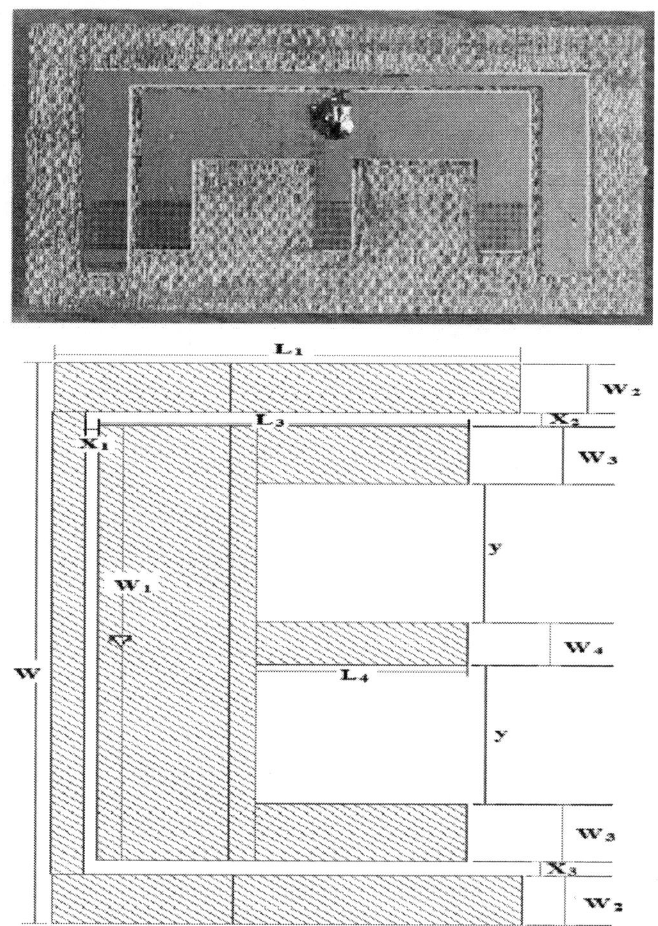

Fig. 1. Designed and produced antenna

Figure 2 has the simulated and measured S11. Figure 3 shows the simulated and measured gain of the proposed microstrip patch antenna. Both figures show good agreement with simulation and measurement results. Note that, highest Phi-polarized electric field gain is 7.22 dB at 4.27 GHz.

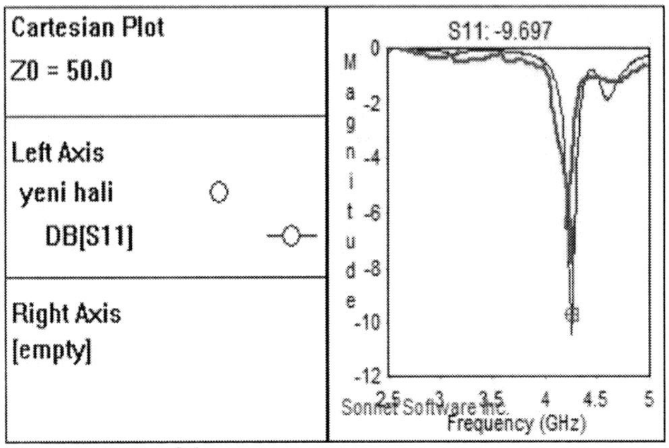

Figure 2: S11 of the antenna

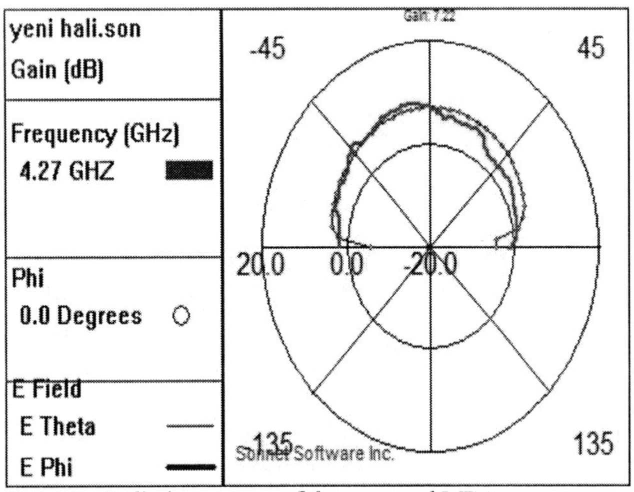

Figure 3: Radiation pattern of the proposed MPA

TABLE I: PARAMETER OF THE E-SHAPED ANTENNA

Air Thickness	F (GHz)	S11 (dB)	Gain(dB)	
14	4.27	-9.697	7.22	
L_1 (mm)	L_2 (mm)	L_3 (mm)	L_4(mm)	
18.7	18.9	14.9	8.5	
X_1 (mm)	X_2 (mm)	X_3 (mm)	Y (mm)	
0.5	1	1	9.9	
W (mm)	W_1 (mm)	W_2 (mm)	W_3 (mm)	W_4 (mm)
40	31	3.5	4.1	3

TABLE II: EFFECT OF PARAMETER CHANGES ON S11 AND GAIN

X_1	X_2	X_3	F(dB)	S11(dB)	Gain(dB)
2.5	1.2	1.2	4.49	-4.096	5.26
0.5	0.5	0.5	4.27	-13.359	7.096
1	1	1	2.4	-6.006	4.68
0.5	1	1	4.27	-9.697	7.22

III. CONCLUSION

In this work, an E-shaped (surrounded with floating U-shaped) microstrip patch antenna has been designed, simulated, fabricated and tested. E-shaped microstrip antenna has gain of 7.22dB and S11 of -9.697dB at frequency 4.27GHz. When we extend the supply via, the gain started to decrease. In addition, when we increase the distance between U-shape and E-shape, the gain result was not quite sufficient.

It has also been observed that position of via point has a critical effect on the performance of the designed antenna. When we change position and size of via, the gain fell significantly. Simulation and measured results were founded satisfactory. Proposed antenna can be used in different applications such as in wireless communication.

REFERENCES

[1] Toktaş, Abdurrahim; Akdağlı, Ali; "E Şekilli Kompact Microşerit Antenlerin Rezonans Frekansının Hesaplanması"; *Journal of the Faculty of Engineering and Architecture of Gazi University;* Vol: 27; No: 04; Page: 847; 2012.

[2] S. K. Tripathi and V. Kumar, "E-Shaped Slotted Micro strip Antenna with Enhanced Gain for Wireless Communication", *IEEE Transactions on Antenna & Propagation*, July to August 2011.

[3] M.K.verma, Sapna Verma, and D.C.Dhubkarya, "Analysis and designing of E-shape microstrip patch antenna for wireless communication system", *IEEE Transactions on Emerging Trends in Electronic and Photonic Devices & Systems*, 2009

[4] G. Kumar and K.P. Ray, "Broadband Microstrip Antennas", *Artech House Boston* · London, 2003.

[5] I.B.Pauria, S.Kumar, S.Sharma, "Design and Simulation of E-Shape Microstrip Patch Antenna for Wideband Applications" ISSN: 2231-2307, Volume-2, Issue-3, July 2012

[6] A. Yadav, B. Chauhan, and A. Jain, "Microstrip Symmetrical E-Shape Patch Antenna for the Wireless Communication Systems", *International Journal of Emerging Technology and Advanced Engineering,* ISSN:2250-2459, Volume-2, Issue-12, December 2012

[7] Sonnet Software, Version:16, www.sonnetsoftware.com

Dual-Band Gemini-Shaped Microstrip Patch Antenna for C-Band and X-Band Applications

Gerard Djengomemgoto [1], Reha Altunok [1], Cem Karabacak [1]

[1] Department of Electrical & Electronics Engineering, Özyeğin University, Istanbul, Turkey

Ş. Taha İmeci [2] and Tahsin Durak [3]

[2] Department of Electrical & Electronics Engineering, Istanbul Commerce University, Istanbul, Turkey

[3] Department of Technology, NSU, Norfolk, VA

***Abstract*— In this paper, a novel single-layer Gemini-shaped patch antenna with dual-band characteristics is presented. The proposed patch antenna, with design operating frequencies of 6.53 GHz and 8.62 GHz, is targeted for applications in C-band and X-band. More importantly, the Gemini-shaped microstrip patch antenna exhibits a theta polarized radiation pattern with gains of 6.036 dBi and 9.556 dBi with corresponding reflection coefficients of -18.69 dB (VSWR = 1.263) and -24.31 dB (VSWR = 1.129) at 6.53 GHz and 8.62 GHz, respectively. The measurements of the fabricated patch antenna corroborate the simulation results obtained in Sonnet Suites version 16.52. This dual-resonance antenna, with comparatively high gain performance, can be easily integrated into systems for satellite and radar communications.**

Keywords—Gemini-shaped, patch antenna, C-band, X-band, high gain, dual-band.

I. Introduction

For over six decades since their first introduction, Microstrip patch antennas (MPAs) have sparked tremendous research efforts with great prospects and they have been widely integrated into many wireless applications. The salient features of MPAs have made them the ultimate candidates for applications, such as spaceborn systems, radar or satellite systems, where lightweight and cost-effective antennas with low-profile and simple geometrical structure for ease of fabrication and installation are required [1]. In line with these research efforts, different MPAs have been proposed for applications in the C-band and X-band in the literature [2], [3]. As an illustration, according to [8], C-band covers frequencies between 4 GHz to 8 GHz and X-band lies between 8 GHz to 12 GHz.

In [2], the author made use of E-shaped slot on the fractal patch for bandwidth improvement. The ground plane of the antenna is also slotted with L- and H-shaped geometries in order to obtain a multiband response while achieving the optimum gains of 4.05 dBi and 5.32 dBi in the S-band and C-band, respectively. Similarly, reference [3] presents an inverted S-shaped tri-band MPA for X-band applications. An elliptical-shaped slots on the ground plane were used in order to optimize the gain up to about 5.1 dBi with good bandwidth performance.

Moreover, MPAs with dual-band operations and good bandwidth characteristics for both C-band and X-band applications have been suggested in [4] and [5]. The former presents a dual-resonant coplanar waveguide (CPW) fed square patch antenna with peak gain below 5 dBi while the latter proposes a dual-band U-slotted MPA with/without Defected Ground Structure (DGS) with gains of 1.2 dBi at 5.39 GHz and 4.4 dBi at 8.8 GHz for the case of DGS. This paper proposes a R-shaped patch antenna, with comparatively superior gains, for C-band and X-band applications.

The rest of this paper is organized as follows. The design parameters and parametric study are described in Section II, Section III presents the simulation and parametric study and Section IV concludes the paper.

II. Design Parameters

The proposed Gemini-shaped patch antenna is designed using RT/duroit 6002 substrate with dielectric constant of 2.94, thickness $h=0.76mm$ and loss tangent of 0.0012. Fig. 1 presents the geometries of the proposed antenna in going from the initial design (*A*) to the optimized structure (*D*) through a parametric study. The antenna structure in Fig. 1 (*A*) was designed using the fundamental equations (14 – 1), (14 – 2), (14 – 6) and (14 – 7) described in [1]. The dimensions of ground plane of the patch, width (*Wg*) and length (*Lg*), are set by extending the width (*W*) and length (*L*) of the patch antenna by *6h*, respectively. In addition, the method described in section *4.3.7* of reference [6] has been used to find the feed point location for geometry *A*. The coaxial probe feeding technique is adopted in this antenna design. This will allow us to easily move the feed point to any desired location on the patch as a way to better achieve input impedance matching as stated in [7].

The initial antenna geometry (*A*) is then optimized through a meticulous parametric study, as shown in Fig. 1, in order to get the dual-band response in the C-band and X-band with high gains. The patch antenna has an area of $25m \times 25mm$. The optimized Gemini-shaped patch antenna in Fig. 1 (*D*) is selected for fabrication and analysis presented in Section III.

Figure		Resonant Frequency (GHz)	Gain (dBi)	S11 (dB)
A		3.897	6.33	-12.21
B	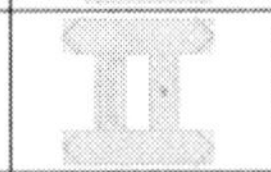	6.13	4.92	-23.99
		7.91	3.087	-10.29
C		6.53	5.479	-21.587
		8.63	8.995	-18.74
D		**6.53**	**6.032**	**-18.69**
		8.62	**9.556**	**-24.31**

Fig. 1. Antenna Geometries: Initial antenna design (A), optimized patch antenna (*D*)

Fig. 2. Top view of the fabricated Gemini-shaped antenna.

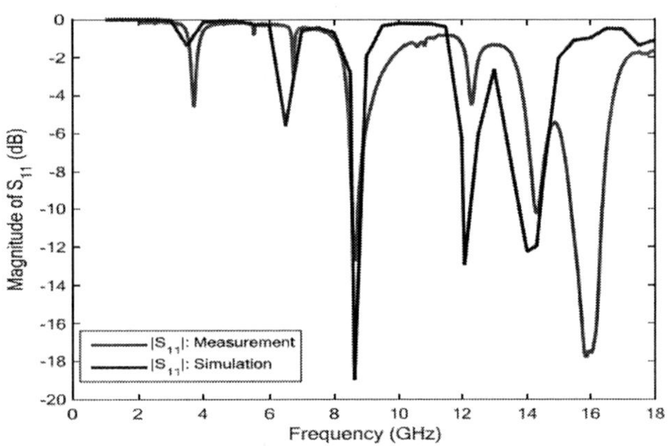

Fig. 3. Input match (|S11|) of the proposed Gemini-shaped patch antenna with resonant frequencies of 6.53 GHz (C-band) and 8.62 GHz (X-band).

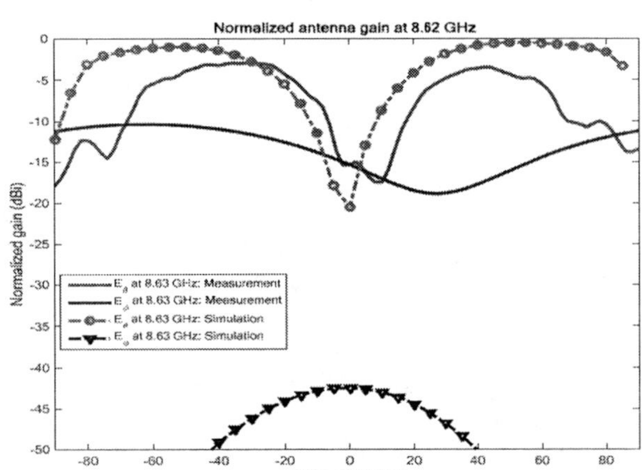

Fig. 4. Radiation patterns at 8.62 GHz with gains 9.536 dBi (Simulation), 7.796 dBi (Measurement)

III. Simulation And Parametric Study

This section presents the simulation results of the proposed Gemini-shaped patch antenna. In addition, the measurement results for the prototyped patch antenna are also shown for validation purposes. Fig. 2 depicts the simulated response for input match of the dual-band Gemini-shaped patch antenna. Input matches (|S11|) of -18.62 dB (with VSWR=1.263) and -24.31 dB (with VSWR=1.129) are achieved at resonant frequencies of 6.53 GHz (C-band) and 8.62 GHz (X-band), respectively. These results show how best the antenna is matched. Fig. 2 presents the top view of the fabricated Gemini-shaped patch antenna. Moreover, the Gemini-shaped patch antenna exhibits a theta polarized radiation patterns for both frequency bands as shown in Fig. 3. The radiated electric field (E - theta) presents gains of 7.79 dBi in measurement and 9.536 dBi in simulation. However, the gain of phi (cross) polarization (E-Phi) falls below -20 dBi in the C-band and it is less than -40 dBi in the X-band.

IV. Conclusion

A dual-band Gemini-shaped patch antenna, of size $25mm \times 25mm \times 0.76mm$ and fabricated on RT/duroit 6002 substrate, is presented and analyzed. The newly proposed patch antenna presents a good impedance matching with input match (|S11| < -10dB) for operating frequencies in the C-band and X-band, respectively. In addition, the MPA exhibits a theta polarized radiation pattern with high gain performance compare to the previous works presented in the literature. This antenna can be easily incorporated into systems for radar and satellite communications.

Acknowledgment

We would like to thank to Sonnet Software for their services.

References

[1] C. A. Balanis, Antenna Theory: Analysis and Design, John Wiley, 2005.
[2] Mehr-e-Munir and K. Mahmood, "Miniaturized microstrip patch antenna using stack configuration for S-band, C-band & mobile applications", International Conference on Emerging Technologies (ICET), Peshawar,2015, pp. 1-5.
[3] M. Samsuzzaman, N. Misran, J. S. Mandeep and M. T. Islam, "An inverted S-shaped multi-frequency patch antenna for X band applications", International Conference on Informatics, Electronics & Vision (ICIEV),Dhaka, 2013, pp. 1-4.
[4] R. Rajkumar, P. Thiruvalarselvan, C. Elavarasi and R. J. Banu, "CPWFED square patch compact antenna for C and X band applications," International Conference on Information Communication and Embedded Systems (ICICES), Chennai, 2014, pp. 1-4.
[5] S. Gupta, S. S. Dhillon, P. Khera and A. Marwaha, "Dual Band U-Slotted Microstrip Patch Antenna for C Band and X Band Radar Applications," 5th International Conference on Computational Intelligence and Communication Networks (CICN), Mathura, 2013, pp. 41-45.
[6] R. Garg, P. Bhartia, I. Bahl, and A. Ittipiboon, Microstrip Antenna Design Handbook, Artech House, 2001.
[7] A. Kumar, J. Kaur and R. Singh, "Performance Analysis of Different Feeding Techniques", International Journal of Emerging Technology and Advanced Engineering, Volume 3, Issue 3, March 2013, pp 884-890
[8] IEEE Standard Letter Designations for Radar-Frequency Bands," in IEEE Std 521-2002 (Revision of IEEE Std 521-1984) , vol., no., pp.0 1-3, 2003

An Antenna for Implanted Device Systems

Emircan Zincircioğlu[1], İsmail Pekdemir[1],Rafiq Rzayew[1], Emre Ilıksu[1], Merve Dede[1]
[1]Department of Electrical and Electronics Engineering
Özyeğin University
Istanbul, Turkey
emircan.zincircioglu@ozu.edu,tr

Ş. Taha ˙Imeci [2] and Tahsin Durak[3]
[2] Department of Electrical & Electronics Engineering,
Istanbul Commerce University,
Istanbul, Turkey
[3] Department of Technology, NSU, Norfolk, VA
timeci@ticaret.edu.tr tahsind@gmail.com

Abstract—**In this study, we designed and simulated an embedded spiral-shaped microstrip patch antenna for medical biotelemetry applications. Important design parameters were studied to understand their effect on the antenna performance. The antenna is able to download patient's health information from the implanted devices. Sonnet Suite, a 3-D Planar Electromagnetic simulation tool is used for simulations. Simulated antenna has maximum gain of 6.6 dB with -13 dB input match at 8.87 GHz. The antenna impedance is easily adjusted by controlling the inner stub length.**

Keywords—Antenna, Implanted devices, Sonnet, microstrip, wireless biotelemetry, medical implant Communications Services, MICS.

I. INTRODUCTION

Recently, biomedical implants became a topic of big interest for health monitoring purposes. Implanted devices are inserted into a human or animal body, and communicate physiological information such as glucose level, blood pressure, and temperature to external equipment. An implantable antenna ensures wireless biotelemetry, and is therefore a key and crucial part of the implanted components, which also include a transceiver, chips with circuits, and biosensors [1]. Biomedical sensor networks mounted on or implanted within the human body have drawn greater attention for healthcare monitoring. Due to increased health care expenses, many governments are looking for remote health care solutions. Wearable and implanted monitoring systems have the capability to monitor medical data [2]. So, the development of this field will result in real-time access for the patient's condition what in its turn will lead to growth in disease prevention. Appropriate antennas must be miniaturized and must have a good gain to reduce transmit power and save energy [3].

Embedded microstrip antennas have been used therapeutically for a number of applications including cardiac ablation, balloon angioplasty and cancer treatment using hyperthermia. Designers of antennas for sensing or therapy capitalize on some of the problems that plague embedded antennas for communication antennas are inherently sensitive to their environment and inherently deposit large amounts of power in the near field of the antenna, particularly when it is embedded in a lossy material, thus becoming good therapeutic tools [4].

In [5], Spiral shaped proposed antenna along with proper RF transceiver, DSP system integrated together in a microchip & with micro camera can be used in retinal prosthesis for vision improvement of patient suffering with AMD & RP.

One of main design factors for implant antennas is the size of the antenna. The length of antenna and the wavelength are proportional; thus, in order to maximize the length without exceeding acceptable implant size, spiral antennas are preferred. The limitation on the transmit power is due to the amount of battery power available as well as due to concerns about the exposure of the human body to electromagnetic radiation. Typically these devices are allowed to have a peak power of 25 uW (-16dBm), which is quite insufficient at higher frequencies especially when embedded deep into the tissue [6].

II. DESIGN PARAMETERS

The proposed Spiral-shaped patch antenna is designed using Rogers RT 6010 substrate with dielectric constant of 2.94, thickness $h=1.28mm$ and loss tangent of 0.0012. At the top level, the air thickness is 7.6 mm. Fig. 1 shows the top view of optimized antenna. Antenna size is 26 x 17 mm. The coaxial probe feeding technique is adopted in this antenna design. This will allow us to easily move the feed point to any desired location on the patch as a way to better achieve input impedance matching as stated in [7]. Additionally, the box size is 300mm x 300mm.

III. SIMULATION AND PARAMETRIC STUDY

This section presents the simulation results of the proposed Gemini-shaped patch antenna. During our study, we simulated our design within the frequency band between 1 GHz and 12 GHz with cell size as 0.1 mm. Rogers RT6010 was used as a dielectric material. Fig. 2 depicts the simulated response for input match of the proposed antenna. Input matches (|S11|) of -13 dB is achieved at resonant frequency of 8.87 GHz with Electric field phi polarized gain of 6.59dB. As seen in Figures 2 and 3, design specifications were found to be satisfactory. Note that cross polarization, which is E_{theta}, under -7 dB.

In order to see the effect of the inner stub length, L1, a parametric study was made as shown in the table 1. It turns out that, the radiation gets worse at mid lengths but the antenna radiates better at shorter and longer lengths. If geometry could be enlarged, antenna could give much more gain but we stick with this geometry due to its smaller size.

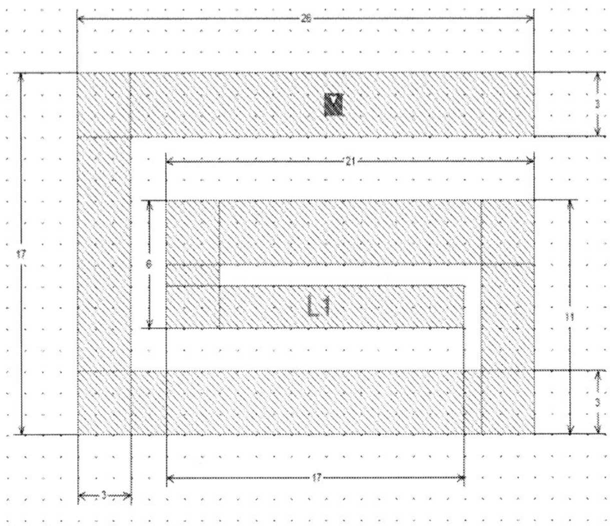

Fig. 1. Top view of the antenna

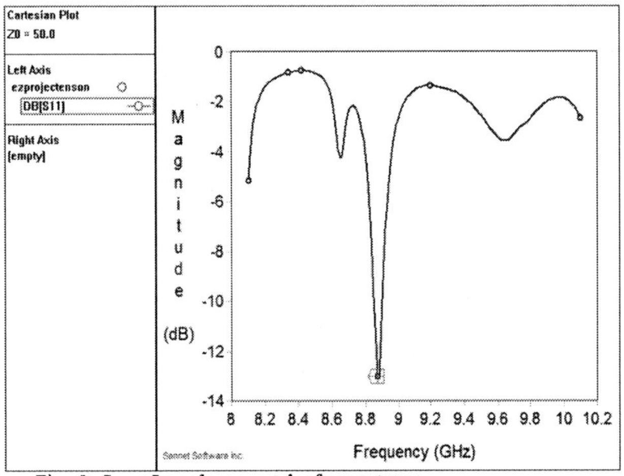

Fig. 2. Input Impedance match of our antenna

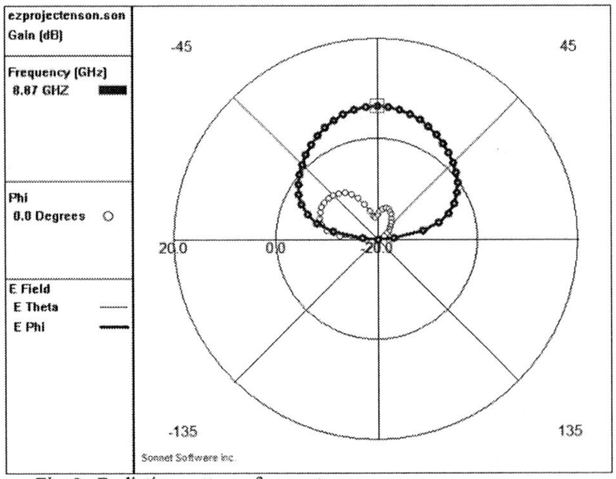

Fig. 3. Radiation pattern of our antenna

TABLE I. PARAMETER CHANGES WITH L1

	(mm)	Frequency (GHz)	S11 (dB)	Gain (dB)
L1	10	8.94	-24.95	6.02
L1	11	8.88	-13.29	6.33
L1	12	8.82	-12.15	5.69
L1	13	8.8	-12.44	4
L1	14	8.76	-21	3.2
L1	15	8.72	-13	2.43
L1	16	8.79	-13.49	6.45
L1	17	8.87	-13	6.59

IV. CONCLUSION

In this work, an embedded spiral-shaped microstrip antenna is designed, simulated and tested with different geometries. Due to its small geometry it can use implanted in human body safely. The simulation results are satisfactory with 6.59 dB gain with low cross polarization levels and -13 dB input match at 8.87 GHz. Our goal is to manufacture the proposed antenna and compare simulation results with the measured values.

ACKNOWLEDGMENT

We would like to thank to Sonnet Software for their services.

REFERENCES

[1] Jae-Ho Lee, Dong-Wook Seo,and Hyung Soo Lee "*Design of Implantable Rectangular Spiral* Antenna for Wireless Biotelemetry in the MICS Band " ETRI Journal, Volume 37, Number 2, April 2015.

[2] Gareth A. Conway, William G. Scanlon, Member, IEEE and D. Linton, Senior Member, IEEE "*Low-Profile Microstrip Patch Antenna for Over-Body Surface Communication at 2.45 GHz*" in Vehicular Technology Conference, 2007. VTC2007-Spring. IEEE 65th, 22-25 April 2007, pp. 392 – 396.

[3] Kamya Yekeh Yazdandoost, Ryuji Kohno "*An Antenna for Medical Implant Communications System*" in Microwave Conference, 2007. European,9-12Oct.2007,pp.968–971

[4] Pichitpong Soontornpipit, Cynthia M. Furse, Senior, Member, and You Chung Chung, Senior, Member " *Design of Implantable Microstrip Antenna for Communication With Medical Implants* " in IEEE transactions on microwave theory and techniques, vol. 52, no. 8, august 2004.

[5] Chandra Prakash & RPS Gangwar "*Spiral Shaped, Multilayered, Microstrip Antenna Implanted in Vitreous Humor in Med-Radio Band*" in International Journal of Electronic and Electrical Engineering. ISSN 0974-2174, Volume 7, Number 2 (2014), pp. 143-148.

[6] Yasir Ahmed,Yang Hao, Clive Parini "*A 31.5 GHz Patch Antenna Design for Medical Implants*" in International Journal of Antennas and PropagationVolume 2008, Article ID 167980.

[7] A. Kumar, J. Kaur and R. Singh, "Performance Analysis of Different Feeding Techniques", International Journal of Emerging Technology and Advanced Engineering, Volume 3, Issue 3, March 2013, pp 884-890

Rectangular Slotted Square Patch Antenna with a Floating Ring

Yasin Anıl Öztürk[1], Uğur Sarı[1]
[1]Department of Electrical & Electronics Engineering,
Özyeğin University, Istanbul, Turkey
yasin.ozturk@ozu.edu.tr
ugur.sari@ozu.edu.tr

Ş. Taha İmeci[2] and Tahsin Durak[3]
[2]Department of Electrical & Electronics Engineering,
Istanbul Commerce University, Istanbul, Turkey
[3] Department of Technology, NSU, Norfolk, VA
timeci@ticaret.edu.tr tahsind@gmail.com

***Abstract*— In this paper, a rectangular slotted square patch antenna with a floating ring and single point feed is presented. The proposed patch antenna, when optimized, achieved the highest gain of 7.17 dB at 7.12 GHz with -6.97 dB input match. Which presented theta polarized radiation pattern. Simulations conducted by changing the size of inner ring shape and high gains were observed between the frequencies of 7.08 and 7.13 GHz.**

Keywords*— *Antenna, Microstrip, Patch, Rectangular Slotted, Floating Ring.

I. Introduction

Slot antennas are generally used for communication devices and array syntheses because of their radiation patterns, low costs, low weights and low volumes. Simply by inserting a pair of wide slits at one of the radiating edges of the rectangular patch, good impedance matching over a wide bandwidth can easily be achieved for the proposed antenna [1]. Microstrip antenna arrays are widely used in many applications, such as satellite and wireless communications, radar, missiles, ISM BAND etc. Microstrip patch antennas are similar to parallel plane capacitors. Both have parallel plates of metal layer and a sandwiched dielectric substrate between them. But in microstrip antenna, one of these metal plates is infinitely extended than the other, to form the ground plane; whereas the smaller metal plate is described as radiating patch [2]. Patch antennas play a very significant role in today's world of wireless communication systems [3]. A Microstrip patch antenna is relatively simple in construction and makes use of a conventional microstrip fabrication technique which comprises of the etching of the antenna element pattern in a metal trace which is bonded to an insulating dielectric substrate [4]. Modifying the shape of the antenna affects the efficiency and the gain of the antenna. The main goals of the research work and literature related to the patch antenna are focusing on achieving bands, improving the impedance bandwidth performance and stable gain [5]. Sonnet Suite, a 3-D Planar Electromagnetic simulation software is used for simulations [6].

The rest of this paper is organized as follows. The antenna design parameters are described in Section II, Section III presents the simulation and parametric study and Section IV concludes the paper.

II. Design Parameters

Fig 1. is the top view of the proposed rectangular slotted square patch antenna with a floating ring. The feeding line is at the center of the left slot, it is marked as 1 in the figure. The substrate is Rogers RT 6002 with dielectric constant of 2.94, thickness $h=0.76mm$ and loss tangent of 0.00120. Outer dimensions of rectangular patch is 22,4 mm x 22,4 mm. Inner slot lengths are shown as X and Y. Small floating ring inside the square patch has the lengths C and D. The width of the floating ring is shown with Z. The space between the square patch and the inner floating ring is shown as B. Table 1 demonstrates the parametric study in order to higher gain and lower input match.

III. Simulation And Parametric Study

To obtain Table I, we changed A, B, C, D, X and Y variables and simulated the antenna. While keeping Y variable the same, the inner slot length X was varied from 12.4 mm to 12.8 mm. While Y value was varied, X value was kept the same. As a result, different S11 and gain values were observed. When inner slot length X was 12.8 mm and lengths of the floating ring C and D were 9.2 mm and 6.8 mm the antenna has the maximum gain of 7.17 dB at 7.12 GHz as shown in Fig 2. and Fig 3. When C and D values were smaller, the antenna gain was slightly higher. Width of the floating ring kept the same during simulations. We simulated three B values 0.2 mm, 0.4 mm and 0.6 mm, B value had so minimal effect on gain and input match. Antenna had slightly higher gain when B increased.

IV. Conclusion

In this project, a rectangular slotted micro strip patch antenna with a floating ring was designed and simulated. The width of the antenna was 22.4 mm, other parameters C and D were designated as 9.2mm and 6.8mm. 7.17 dB the gain and -6.77 dB S11 were maintained at 7.12 GHz. Thickening of slot slightly increased the gain. As a future work, we would like to manufacture the proposed antenna and compare the measured results against simulation results.

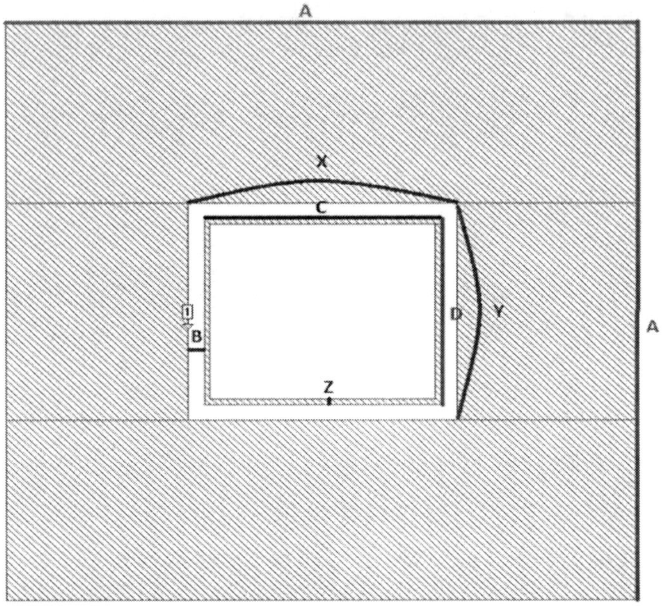

Fig. 1. Top view of the proposed antenna.

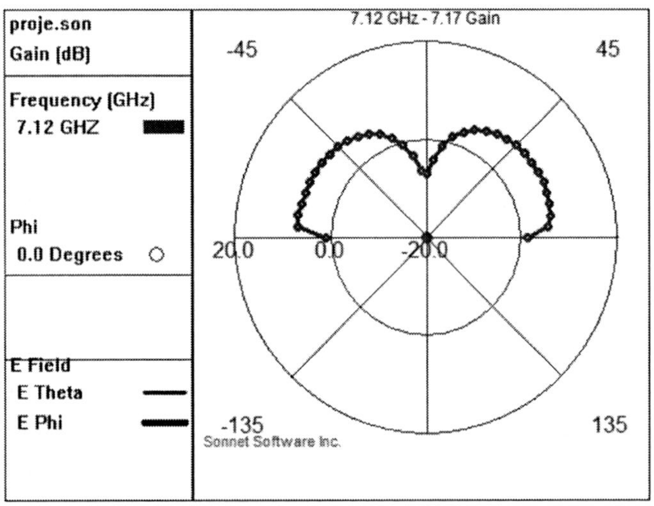

Fig. 2. Radiation pattern and gain of the proposed anteanna.

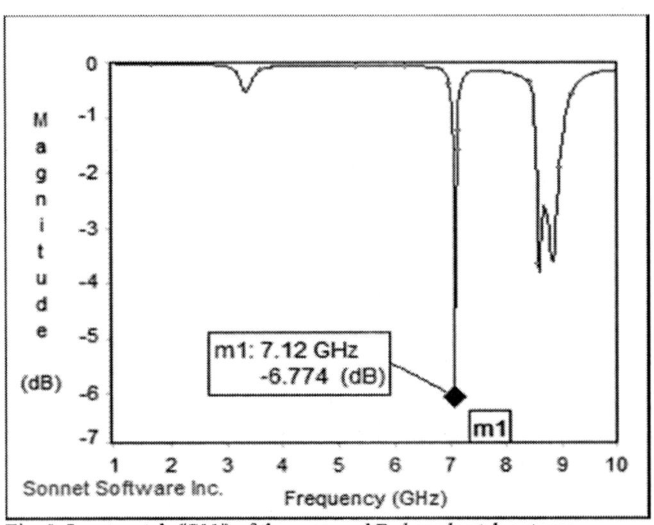

Fig. 3. Input match (|S11|) of the proposed F-shaped patch antenna.

TABLE I. SIMULATION RESULTS

	A	B	C	D	S11	Gain
	Reference X - Y values					
1	22,4	0,2	9,6	7,6	-17,9	6,44
2	22,4	0,4	9,2	7,2	-12,5	6,55
3	22,4	0,6	8,8	6,8	-17,3	6,45
	X 0.4mm smaller, Y same					
1	22,4	0,2	9,2	7,6	8,61	5,96
2	22,4	0,4	8,8	7,2	8,6	5,96
3	22,4	0,6	8,4	6,8	-6,46	5,82
	X 0.4mm bigger, Y same					
1	22,4	0,2	10	7,6	6,95	7,16
2	22,4	0,4	9,6	7,2	6,96	7,16
3	22,4	0,6	9,2	6,8	6,97	7,17
	X same, Y 0.4mm smaller					
1	22,4	0,2	9,6	7,2	9,71	6,13
2	22,4	0,4	9,2	6,8	9,68	5,95
3	22,4	0,6	8,8	6,4	9,82	6,2
	X same, Y 0.4mm bigger					
1	22,4	0,2	9,6	8	18,2	6,28
2	22,4	0,4	9,2	7,6	18,2	6,27
3	22,4	0,6	8,8	7,2	18,2	6,27
	X 0.4mm smaller, Y 0.4mm smaller					
1	22,4	0,2	9,2	7,2	12,5	6,32
2	22,4	0,4	8,8	6,8	12,5	6,32
3	22,4	0,6	8,4	6,4	12,4	6,34
	X 0.4mm bigger, Y 0.4mm bigger					
1	22,4	0,2	8,8	8	12,5	6,25
2	22,4	0,4	8,8	7,6	12,5	6,3
3	22,4	0,6	8,4	7,2	12,6	6,31

ACKNOWLEDGMENT

We would like to thank to Sonnet Software for their services.

REFERENCES

[1] S. Satthamsakul, N. Anantrasirichai1, C. Benjangkaprasert and T. Wakabayashi , Rectangular Patch Antenna with Inset Feed and Modified Ground-Plane for Wideband Antenna , 1ReCCIT, Faculty of Engineering, King Mongkut's Institute of Technology Ladkrabang (KMITL), pp.2-3, 2008

[2] Soumyojit Sinha and Anjumanara Begam, Design of Probe Feed Microstrip Patch Antenna in S-Band, International Journal of Electronics and Communication Engineering, pp.417-423, 2012.

[3] Prasanna Ramachandran, and T.S.Keshav, Antenna Design, Simulation and Fabrication, Deemed University, pp. 26-27, 2007.

[4] Devan Bhalla, and Krishan Bansal, design of a Microstrip Patch Antenna Using Inset Feet Technique, IOSR Journal of Electronics and Communication Engineering, pp. 8, 2013.

[5] H.F.Abutarbaoush, D.Budimur, R.Nilavolan and H.S.Al-Raweshidy, "Connected U-Slots Patch Antenna for WiMAX Applications" in International Journal of RF & Microwave CAE, pp. 1-2, London, England.

[6] Sonnet Suites, version 16.52, www.sonnetsoftware.com

Multilevel Monte Carlo Simulation of the Eddy Current Problem With Random Parameters

Armin Galetzka*, Zeger Bontinck*†, Ulrich Römer*† and Sebastian Schöps*†

*Institut für Theorie Elektromagnetischer Felder
Technische Universität Darmstadt, Darmstadt, Germany
Email: armin_herbert.galetzka@stud.tu-darmstadt.de, roemer@temf.tu-darmstadt.de

†Graduate School of Computational Engineering
Technische Universität Darmstadt, Darmstadt, Germany
Email: {bontinck, schoeps}@gsc.tu-darmstadt.de

***Abstract*—The multilevel Monte Carlo method is applied to an academic example in the field of electromagnetism. The method exhibits a reduced variance by assigning the samples to multiple models with a varying spatial resolution. For the given example it is found that the main costs of the method are spent on the coarsest level.**

I. Introduction

The two most known approaches to propagate uncertainties in the field of uncertainty quantification rely on generalized Polynomial Chaos (gPC) expansions [1] or use the classical Monte Carlo (MC) method. When the number of random parameters is small and the solution depends in a smooth way on these parameters, a gPC approach is known to have a superior convergence rate [1]. However, as the number of uncertain parameters d increases, the method becomes inefficient. This is often called the curse of dimensionality (see e.g. [2]). For a large number of random variables and a lack of regularity one has to rely on MC methods, since their convergence doesn't depend on d. However, the error of classical MC converges slowly with $\mathcal{O}(N^{-1/2})$, with N the necessary number of samples. Many efforts have been undertaken to overcome the slow convergence rate. One way is to use quasi-MC methods e.g. [3]. Another way out is using multilevel Monte Carlo (MLMC) [4]. In this paper every level refers to a spatial discretization level. The gain in the cost of MLMC with respect to MC originates from the fact that a big part of the uncertainty can be captured by using models with coarse spatial discretization. This means that the number of evaluations on the finest grid can be reduced drastically. The idea of this paper is to apply the MLMC method to an academic example in the field of electromagnetism. Also a study of the computational costs is done. More details on MLMC in the context of (elliptic) partial differential equations, can be found in [5].

II. Application

Let us consider a conducting wire centered in a steel tube, Fig. 1. The region between the wire and the tube is filled with air. The steel pipe has a relative permeability μ_{III} and conductivity σ. The wire and the air region are modeled by vacuum permeability $\mu_0 = \mu_{\text{I}} = \mu_{\text{II}}$ but without conductivity.

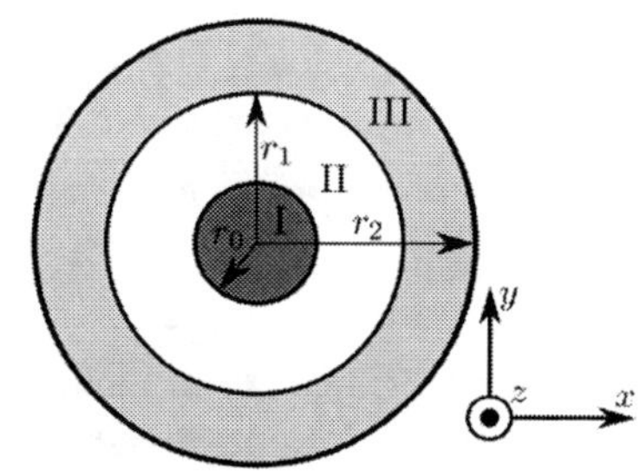

Figure 1: Cross-sectional view of the conducting wire (region I) in a steel tube (region III). Region II is filled with air.

The wire has a source current density $J_s = I_0 \sin(\omega t)/\pi r_0^2$, with I_0 the magnitude of the current, r_0 the radius of the wire and ω the angular frequency. As a test case we consider three ($d = 3$) random variables: r_1, which is the inner radius of the steel tube, μ_{III} and I_0. They are uniformly distributed

$$r_1(\theta) = \bar{r}_1 + X(\theta), \qquad X(\theta) \sim \mathcal{U}(-0.1\,\text{m}, 0.1\,\text{m}), \tag{1}$$

$$I_0(\theta) = \bar{I}_0 + Y(\theta), \qquad Y(\theta) \sim \mathcal{U}(-10\,\text{A}, 10\,\text{A}), \tag{2}$$

$$\mu_{\text{III}}(\theta) = \bar{\mu}_{\text{III}} + Z(\theta), \qquad Z(\theta) \sim \mathcal{U}(-400, 400), \tag{3}$$

where θ depicts the random outcome of a quantity. The nominal values are defined by

$$\bar{r}_1 = \mathbb{E}[r_1(\theta)] = 0.5\,\text{m}, \tag{4}$$

$$\bar{I}_0 = \mathbb{E}[I_0(\theta)] = 100\,\text{A}, \tag{5}$$

$$\bar{\mu}_{\text{III}} = \mathbb{E}[\mu_{\text{III}}(\theta)] = 1000, \tag{6}$$

where $\mathbb{E}[\,\cdot\,]$ denotes the expectation value. The problem can be treated by the magnetoquasistatic approximation of Maxwell's equations. Modeling the source current density as a time harmonic function one retrieves

$$\nabla \times \left(\frac{1}{\mu(\theta)} \nabla \times \vec{A}(\theta) \right) + j\omega\sigma\vec{A}(\theta) = \vec{J}_s(\theta), \tag{7}$$

where $\vec{A}$ is the magnetic vector potential. Imposing Dirichlet boundary conditions on the outer radius of the pipe one can solve (7) for $\vec{A}$. This allows the calculation of the energy

$$W(\theta) = \sum_{i \in \{\text{I,II,III}\}} \int_{V^{(i)}} \frac{\mu_i \vec{H}^{(i)}(\theta) \cdot \underline{\vec{H}}^{(i)}(\theta)}{2} \text{d}V, \tag{8}$$

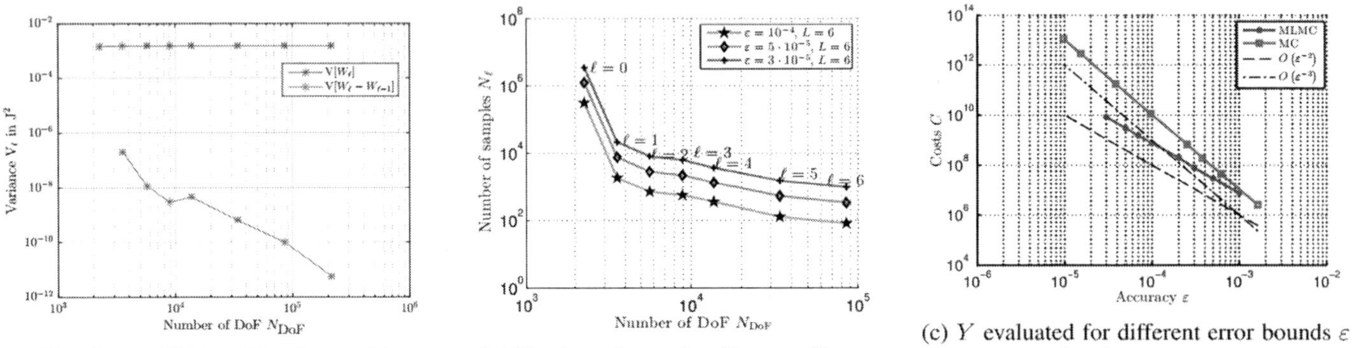

(a) $\mathbb{V}[W_\ell]$ and $\mathbb{V}[W_\ell - W_{\ell-1}]$ over N_{DoF}.

(b) Number of samples N_ℓ over N_{DoF}.

(c) Y evaluated for different error bounds ε over computational costs.

Figure 2: Variance, number of samples in dependence of DoFs and Cost per Accuracy

where $\vec{H}^{(i)}(\theta) = \frac{1}{\mu_i(\theta)} \nabla \times \vec{A}^{(i)}(\theta)$ is the magnetic field and $i \in \{\text{I}, \text{II}, \text{III}\}$ refers to the regions.

Since it assumed that $\vec{A} = (0, 0, A_z)$, (7) is solved in 2D and lowest order finite elements are used. The discretization is done by a triangular grid [6].

III. Multilevel Monte Carlo

The main principles of MLMC are recalled from [4] in the following. Let $\mathbb{E}[W]$ be the quantity of interest and W_ℓ be the energy on level $\ell = 0, \dots, L$, with 0 and L referring to the coarsest and finest level, respectively. Also, let Y denote an approximation to $\mathbb{E}[W]$, i.e. the MC or MLMC estimator. For the mean square error (MSE) there holds

$$\text{MSE} = \mathbb{V}[Y] + (\mathbb{E}[Y - W])^2 . \tag{9}$$

Hence, an overall MSE of ε^2 can be achieved, by reducing both the weak error $(\mathbb{E}[Y - W])^2$ and the variance $\mathbb{V}[Y]$ below $\varepsilon^2/2$. In MLMC, the weak error is dominated by the spatial resolution of the finest level and can be controlled accordingly. The variance is reduced by adding more and more samples to the different levels. More precisely, by decomposing Y as

$$Y = \mathbb{E}[W_0] + \sum_{\ell=1}^{L} \mathbb{E}\left[W_\ell - W_{\ell-1}\right], \tag{10}$$

the conventional MC method is used with N_ℓ samples for each term on the rhs in (10). The associated variance reads

$$\mathbb{V}[Y] = N_0^{-1}\mathbb{V}[W_0] + \sum_{\ell=1}^{L} N_\ell^{-1}\mathbb{V}[W_\ell - W_{\ell-1}]. \tag{11}$$

For a fixed computational budget, there exists an optimal choice of N_ℓ minimizing the variance given by (11), see [4]. This optimum is readily computable if asymptotic bounds on $\mathbb{V}[W_\ell - W_{\ell-1}]$ and the cost per level can be determined. The coefficients in these bounds are problem dependent and determined numerically in this work.

IV. Results

The variance $\mathbb{V}[W_\ell]$ is nearly constant over all levels as shown in Figure 2a and thus independent of the number of degrees of freedom (DoF) N_{DoF}. This observation confirms the fact that the MSE can be divided into an error determined by the variance of the estimator and an error determined by the FEM approximation. In Figure 2b the number of samples is plotted. Different error bounds are used. As anticipated, the lower the bounds the more samples are needed. Taking more samples also implies an increase in the overall computational cost for every level. It is found that the biggest computational cost is spent on the coarsest level. The reason can be seen by looking to Figure 2a. More samples are needed on the coarsest level for the convergence of the variance, however less samples are needed on the finer levels since $\mathbb{V}[W_\ell - W_{\ell-1}]$ is small. In Figure 2c the costs $C = N_{\text{DoF}} N_{\text{MC}}$ of MLMC and MC are compared in dependence of the demanded accuracy. The number of MC samples is depicted by N_{MC}. One clearly sees that for $\varepsilon < 10^{-3}$ the costs of MLMC are lower than the ones using MC.

V. Conclusion

The cost of MLMC is determined by the costs on the coarsest level since the reduction of the variance is dominating. Adding more levels does not alter the variance much, but helps reducing the weak error. Comparing the costs of MLMC with classical MC, one sees that for an accuracy $\varepsilon < 10^{-3}$ the costs of MLMC are lower than the ones of MC.

Acknowledgment

This work is supported by the German BMBF in the context of the SIMUROM project, by the 'Excellence Initiative' of the German Federal and State Governments and the Graduate School of CE at TU Darmstadt.

References

[1] D. Xiu and G.E. Karniadakis, "The Wiener–Askey Polynomial Chaos for Stochastic Differential Equations," *SIAM J. Sci. Comput.*, vol. 24, no. 2, pp. 619–644, 2002.

[2] F.Y. Kuo and I. H. Sloan, "Lifting the curse of dimensionality," *Notices Amer. Math. Soc.*, vol 52., no. 11, pp. 1320–1328, 2005.

[3] J. Dick, F. Y. Kuo and I.H. Sloan, "High-dimensional integration: the quasi-Monte Carlo way," *Acta. Num.*, vol. 22, pp. 133–288, 2013.

[4] M.B. Giles, "Multilevel Monte Carlo," *Acta. Num.*, vol. 24, pp. 259–328, 2015.

[5] A. L. Teckentrup, R. Scheichl, M. B. Giles and E. Ullmann, "Further analysis of multilevel Monte Carlo methods for elliptic PDEs with random coefficients," *Numer. Math.*, vol. 125, no. 3, pp. 569–600, 2013.

[6] S.J. Salon, *Finite Element Analysis of Electrical Machines*, Kluwer, 1995.

Model Order Reduction Approach to Uncertainty Quantification in Eddy Current Problems

Lorenzo Codecasa
Politecnico di Milano,
Dipartimento di Elettronica, Informazione e Bioingegneria
Milano, Italy
lorenzo.codecasa@polimi.it

Luca Di Rienzo
Politecnico di Milano,
Dipartimento di Elettronica, Informazione e Bioingegneria
Milano, Italy
luca.dirienzo@polimi.it

***Abstract*—An approach based on Model Order Reduction and Polynomial Chaos Expansion is proposed for uncertainty quantification in eddy current problems due to randomness in material parameters. Corresponding deterministic problems are solved with the Finite Integration Technique. As a test case, the method is applied to a simplified geometry of a typical system for resistance welding in ac conditions.**

***Keywords*—model order reduction, uncertainty quantification, finite integration technique.**

I. Introduction

A Model Order Reduction (MOR) approach to Uncertainty Quantification (UQ) was already proposed by the authors for an electrokinetic problem [1] and for transcranial magnetic stimulation [2]. The starting point of the method is the non-intrusive Polynomial Chaos Expansion (PCE) approach [3], in which the PCEs of the variables are estimated from the solutions of the deterministic problems for all values of the random material parameters in a sparse grid. Instead of solving all the deterministic problems, a parametric reduced order model is constructed and used to approximate the solution of the deterministic problems. Such reduced model is tailored to approximate with a chosen accuracy the deterministic problems for the values of the random material parameters in the chosen sparse grid. Finally, an intrusive stochastic approach is applied to the obtained reduced order model. The proposed MOR approach is applied here to an eddy current problem and is validated by modeling a simplified geometry of a typical system for resistance welding in ac conditions [4]. In this situation the MOR approach allows to reduce the computational time by about two orders of magnitude with respect to that of a standard non-intrusive PCE approach, maintaining the same level of accuracy. A similar approach is presented in [5] to a waveguide with uncertain material parameters, using FEM and MOR based on the proper orthogonal decomposition.

II. Test Case

The geometry of the test problem under analysis is shown in Fig. 1. It includes three aluminum electrodes over a conductive aluminum substrate, immersed in air. Three contact resistances are modeled by three layers of three uniformly distributed and statistically independent conductivities σ_1, σ_2, σ_3, in the range $\sigma_i^{\min}$ - $\sigma_i^{\max}$, i=1,...,3. The deterministic problem is formulated at a frequency of 50 Hz, using scalar and vector potentials.

Boundary conditions are fixed by setting to zero the tangent components of the vector potential and assigning the values of the scalar potential over the part of the boundary belonging to the electrodes, as indicated in Fig. 1. The energetic approach to FIT is applied to tetrahedral grids and barycentric dual grids. A set of primal tetrahedral grids is generated. Among these a tetrahedral grid with about 15,000 volumes is chosen whose further refining introduces variations in the solution of the deterministic discrete eddy current problems lesser that 1 % in the energy norm.

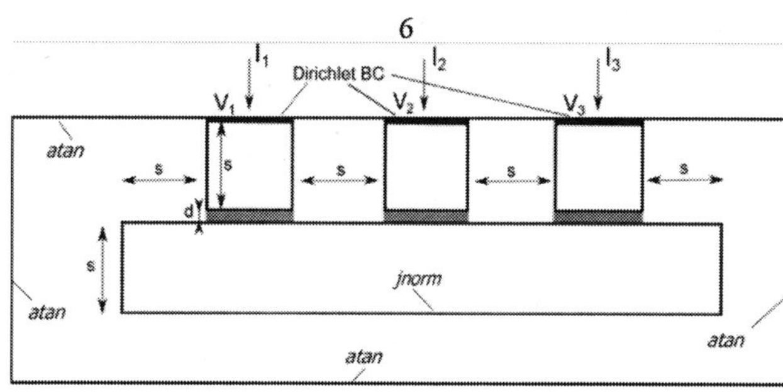

Fig. 1. 2D section of the considered example, the depth being equal to s =10 mm and d=1 mm.

III. Model Order Reduction and Stochastic Formulation

Let us consider the deterministic linear system of equations obtained by the Finite Integration Technique (FIT) discretization of a magnetic vector potential-electric scalar potential formulation, according to the formulation introduced in [3]:

$$\begin{bmatrix} \mathbf{A}_{11} & \mathbf{A}_{12} \\ \mathbf{A}_{21} & \mathbf{A}_{22} \end{bmatrix} \begin{bmatrix} \boldsymbol{\varphi}_{\bar{b}} \\ \boldsymbol{a}_{\bar{b}} \end{bmatrix} = \begin{bmatrix} \mathbf{B}_1 \\ \mathbf{B}_2 \end{bmatrix} \boldsymbol{\varphi}_b \quad (1)$$

in which

$$\mathbf{A}_{11} = \tilde{\mathbf{C}}_{\bar{b}}^T \mathbf{C}^T \mathbf{M}_\nu \mathbf{C} \tilde{\mathbf{C}}_{\bar{b}} + i\omega \tilde{\mathbf{C}}_{\bar{b}}^T \mathbf{M}_\sigma \tilde{\mathbf{C}}_{\bar{b}},$$

$$\mathbf{A}_{12} = \mathbf{A}_{21}^T = i\omega \tilde{\mathbf{C}}_{\bar{b}}^T \mathbf{M}_\sigma \mathbf{G} \tilde{\mathbf{D}}_{\bar{b}},$$

$$\mathbf{A}_{22} = i\omega \tilde{\mathbf{D}}_{\bar{b}}^T \mathbf{G}^T \mathbf{M}_\sigma \mathbf{G} \tilde{\mathbf{D}}_{\bar{b}},$$

while

$$\mathbf{B}_1 = -\widetilde{\mathbf{C}}_b^T \mathbf{M}_\sigma \mathbf{G} \widetilde{\mathbf{D}}_b, \qquad \mathbf{B}_2 = -\mathbf{D}_b^T \mathbf{G}^T \mathbf{M}_\sigma \mathbf{G} \widetilde{\mathbf{D}}_b.$$

Please note that in the angular frequency ω is assigned. Writing (1) as

$$Ax(\boldsymbol{p}) = \boldsymbol{b}(\boldsymbol{p}), \tag{2}$$

where $\boldsymbol{p}$ is the vector of the material parameters and x is the vector of the uknowns, a reduced order model can be derived assuming

$$\boldsymbol{x} = V\widehat{\boldsymbol{x}} \tag{3}$$

and projecting (1) onto the reduced space, so that

$$\hat{A}\widehat{\boldsymbol{x}}(\boldsymbol{p}) = \widehat{\boldsymbol{b}}(\boldsymbol{p}), \tag{4}$$

with $\boldsymbol{x}(\boldsymbol{p}) = V\widehat{\boldsymbol{x}}(\boldsymbol{p})$ and $\hat{A} = V^{*}AV$, indicating with V^{*} the conjugate transpose of V. Matrix V is obtained by means of an algorithm similar to [1], with the difference that complex quantities are managed instead of real quantities. The material parameters, entries of vector $\boldsymbol{p}$, are now considered as indipendent random variables. Either an intrusive or a non-intrusive PCE can then be applied to (4):

$$\widehat{\boldsymbol{x}}(\boldsymbol{p}) = \sum_{|\beta| \le M} \widehat{\boldsymbol{x}}_\beta \psi_\beta(\boldsymbol{p}), \tag{5}$$

in which $\psi_\beta(\boldsymbol{p})$ are polynomials forming an orthonormal basis with respect to the inner product weighted by the probability density function (PDF) of the random variables [3, 4]. From (3)-(5) the PCE of $\boldsymbol{x}(\boldsymbol{p})$ is determined.

IV. Numerical Results

In order to compare the results obtained by the MOR approach with previous results reported in [3], the case $\sigma_i^{\min}$ =1.41 MS/m and $\sigma_i^{\max}$ =11.3 MS/m is considered. Each conductivity is modeled as a uniform random variable. The PCE of the electric currents I_1, I_2, and I_3 is estimated in the situation in which V_1=V_3=j V and V_2=0. A PCE order M=7 is assumed and a Gauss-Legendre sparse grid of dimension 681 is used. With these choices, a non-intrusive PCE approach requires the solution of 681 systems of equations, each one requiring about 2 s on a 2.3 GHz Intel Core i7 for a total of about 20 min. From the PCE the Probability Density Functions (PDFs) are obtained and a very good agreement with those obtained applying the intrusive FIT as in [4] is observed (Fig. 2).

Fig 3 represents the norm of the residual when the approximate solution obtained with a reduced model of order k is substituted in (1), normalized to the norm of the residual in the case of k=1. A reduced model of dimension k = 20 is obtained in about 14 s using the above computer. The PCE expansion of the reduced-order model requires a fraction of a second of these 14 s. Precisely, the non-intrusive PCE approach requires 0.33 s. The more robust intrusive PCE approach, performed as suggested in [6], is more efficient and requires about 0.17 s. Both approaches practically are of the same accuracy. The PDF of real and imaginary components of I_1, I_2, and I_3 are computed and the same results reported in [4] are obtained.

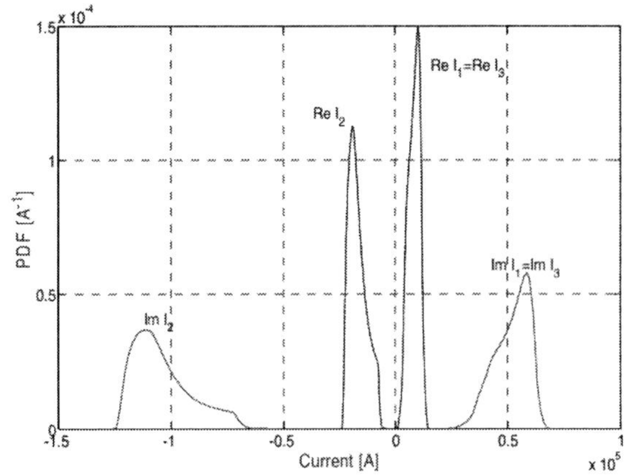

Fig. 2. PDF of currents I_1, I_2, and I_3. Dashed line: instrusive PCE as in [3]; continuos line: MOR.

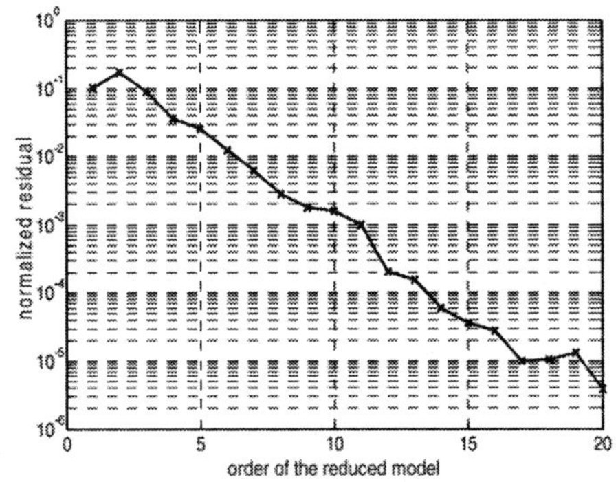

Fig. 3. Relative error in the energy norm of the PCE of the solution as a function of the dimension of the reduced basis.

References

[1] L. Codecasa and L. Di Rienzo, "Fast model order reduction approach to uncertainty quantification in electrokinetics," in *Proc. of Progress in Electromagnetics Research Symposium* (PIERS) 2015, Prague, Czech Republic, 06-09 July, 2015, pp. 369-373, ISBN: 978-1-934142-30-1.

[2] L. Codecasa, L. Di Rienzo, K. Weise, S. Gross, and J. Haueisen, "Fast MOR-based approach to transcranial magnetic stimulation", *IEEE Transactions on Magnetics*, vol. 52, no. 3, Article #: 7200904, pp.1-4, March 2016.

[3] D. Xiu, *Numerical methods for stochastic computations: a spectral method approach*, Princeton University Press, 2010.

[4] L. Codecasa and L. Di Rienzo, "Stochastic finite integration technique for eddy current problems," *IEEE Trans. Magn.*, vol. 15, no. 3, Article #: 7200204, pp.1-4, March 2015.

[5] P. Benner and J. Schneider, "Uncertainty quantification for Maxwell's equations using stochastic collocation and model order reduction," *International Journal for Uncertainty Quantification*, vol. 5, no. 3, pp. 195-208, 2015.

[6] L. Codecasa and L. Di Rienzo, "Stochastic finite integration technique for magnetostatic problems," *International Journal of Numerical Modelling*, DOI 10.1002/jnm.2209, *in press*.

Reduced-Order Stochastic Macro-Models in FDTD, for Characterizing Uncertainty in Aperture Antennas

Ata Zadehgol, Senior Member IEEE
Department of Electrical and Computer Engineering
University of Idaho
Moscow, Idaho 83844-10203
Email: azadehgol@uidaho.edu
Website: http://www.webpages.uidaho.edu/azadehgol/

***Abstract*—Recently, a reduced-order stochastic electromagnetic macro-model in finite-difference-time-domain (FDTD) was developed, based on stochastic collocation on the sparse Smoljak grid. Here, we apply the technique to quantify the uncertainty in electromagnetic response of an aperture antenna whose conductivity and permittivity vary randomly according to Gaussian distributions. The results are correlated against standard Monte Carlo simulations, and show excellent agreement.**

I. Introduction

The recent work by [1], [2], [3] develops a reduced-order stochastic electromagnetic macro-model in FDTD, based on the stochastic collocation (SC) method [4] in the sparse Smoljak grid [5]. Here, we apply the technique to computation of the electromagnetic fields of an aperture antenna whose conductivity and permittivity exhibit random variations according to Gaussian probability distribution function (PDF).

The standard Monte Carlo (MC) method is used to correlate the results obtained from SC. For K experiments in random space, MC simulations converge as $1/\sqrt{K}$; thus, we choose $K = 10,000$ sample points in random space for each independent variable, to obtain a solution accuracy of within 1%. Model order reduction is performed using the ENOR algorithm [6] with the expansion frequency $s_0 = f_{max}/2$, relative tolerance $tol_{rel} = 10^{-3}$, and maximum iteration $k_{iter} = 3$. The numerical examples are carried out with plane-wave excitation implemented with the total-field/scattered-field (TF/SF) method [7]. For each SC simulation on the Smoljak grid, and MC simulation on the regular grid, the FDTD simulation may be performed on parallel computational nodes to significantly reduce the total CPU time. The perfectly matched layer (PML) is used as the absorbing boundary condition, where the number of PML cells on each side is 20 cells, with a grading polynomial of order 3.0; details about the PML formulation this may be found in [7].

It's been reported [8] that under sufficiently smooth conditions in random space, the convergence rate of the SC solution may be almost exponential; this, significantly reduces the computational cost of the SC technique compared to the standard MC. Using Gaussian PDF to represent the uncertainty of the random variables, we find that a relatively small number of sample points is sufficient for the SC solution to converge to the MC solution.

II. Aperture Antenna under Uncertainty

The aperture antenna is placed at the center of the grid, as shown in Figure 1. Let $\mathbb{V}_1$ designate a certain portion of the fine-featured aperture region represented by the stochastic macro-model at the center of the grid, labeled as MM. The macro-model is of dimension 9×9 grid cells, and it is placed at the center of the FDTD grid of size 200×200 cells, terminated at PML boundaries.

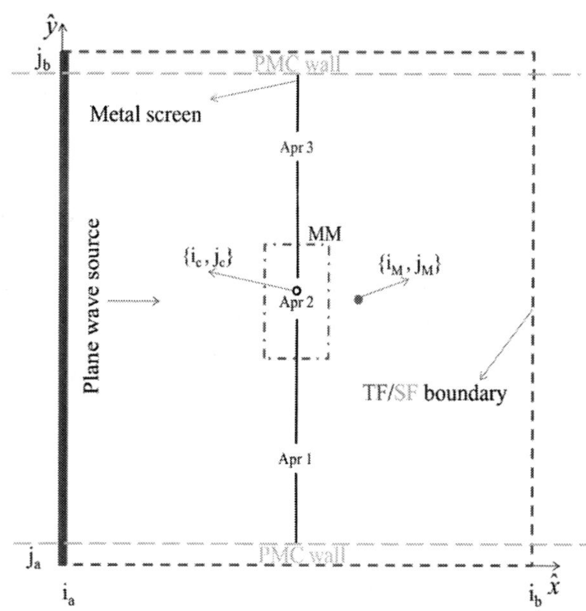

Fig. 1. The macro-model over aperture.

Assume that uncertainty is according to the Gaussian (normal) probability density function

$$\rho[x] = \frac{1}{\sigma\sqrt{2\pi}} e^{\frac{-(x-\mu)^2}{2\sigma^2}} \tag{1}$$

where the mean is μ, and the standard deviation is σ.

The assumed PDF and distributions of the random variable $\mathbb{V}_1$ for relative permittivity, and $\mathbb{V}_2$ for conductivity, are shown in Figure 2.

We run the MC simulations using the pseudo-random distributions shown in Figure 2. Next, we use the Smoljak sparse

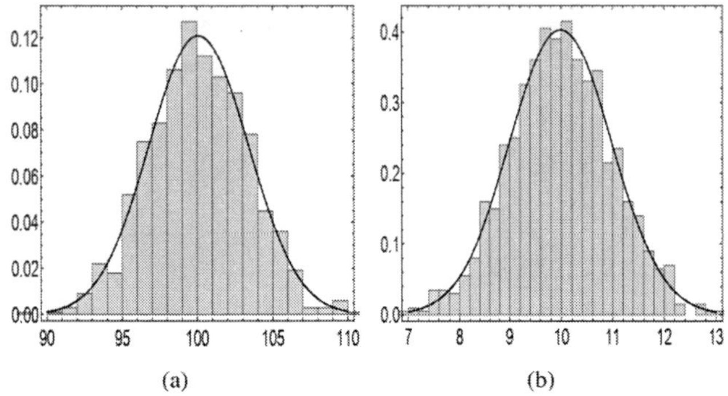

Fig. 2. Histogram of pseudo-random numbers used in Monte Carlo simulations for (a) relative permittivity in $\mathbb{V}_1$, and (b) conductivity in $\mathbb{V}_2$. The overlapping black line shows the desired PDF.

grid with level $k = 5$ containing 145 nodes, corresponding to Smoljak parameters $d = 2, q = 7$. The exponential rate of convergence of the SC method together with interpolation in random space makes it possible to obtain the stochastic electromagnetic response using a smaller number of sample points in random space.

The electric field E_z along the z-axis vs. time-step, at point $\{i_M, j_M\}$ outside the macro-model, is computed using the SC method and results are compared against the standard MC method, as shown in Figure 3.

III. Conclusion

We applied the recently developed reduced-order stochastic electromagnetic macro-model developed in FDTD, to the problem of uncertainty in aperture antenna. The permittivity and conductivity of regions within the aperture were designated as two independent variables in random space, subject to the Gaussian probability distribution function. The mean and standard deviation of the electric field E_z in time-domain were computed using the macro-model on the sparse Smoljak grid, and compared against results from the standard Monte Carlo method. The comparison shows very good agreement, while the macro-model required integration over a significantly smaller number of nodes (145 SC nodes vs. 10,000 MC nodes).

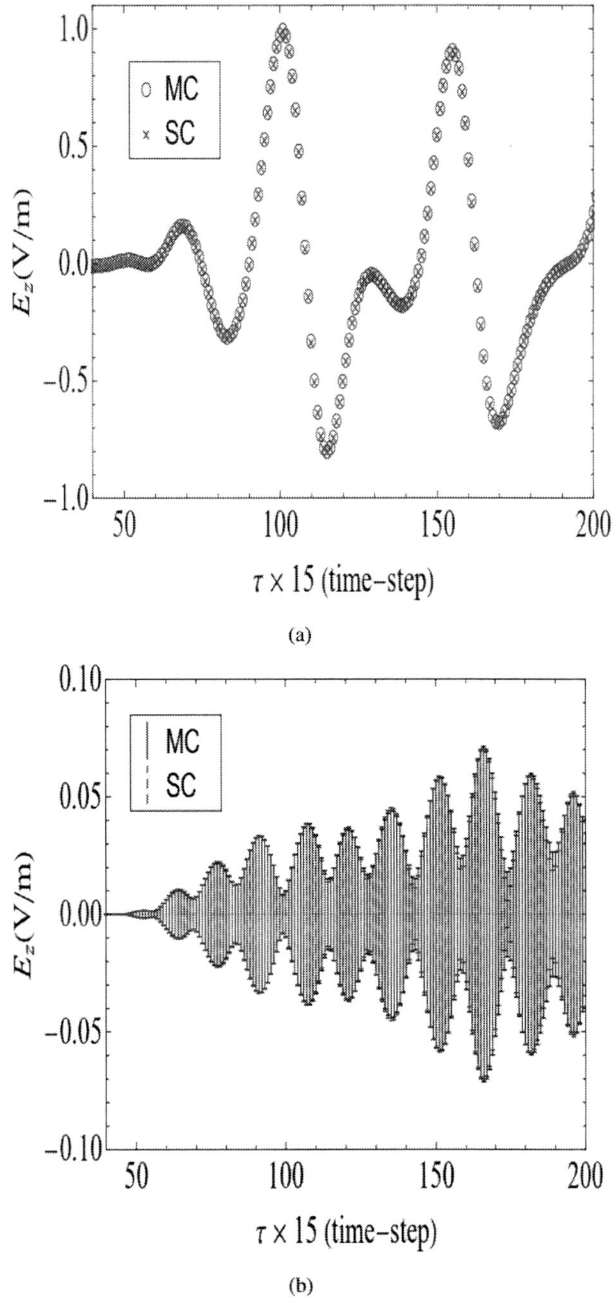

Fig. 3. Comparison of Monte Carlo (MC) shown with circle or solid line vs. stochastic collocation (SC) shown with cross or dashed line, for a point outside the macro-model. Results of uncertainty in relative permittivity and conductivity. (a) Mean, (b) standard deviation.

Acknowledgment

I'd like to acknowledge Professor Andreas C. Cangellaris, at the University of Illinois at Urbana-Champaign, for his invaluable guidance.

References

[1] Ata Zadehgol. Stochastic reduced-order electromagnetic macro-models in FDTD. *IEEE Transactions on Antennas and Propagation*, 46(8):3496 – 3508, 2016.

[2] Ata Zadehgol. Deterministic reduced-order macromodels for computing the broadband radiation-field pattern of antenna arrays in FDTD. *IEEE Transactions on Antennas and Propagation*, 64(6):2418–2430, 2016.

[3] Ata Zadehgol. An impedance transfer function formulation for reduced-order macro-models of sub-gridded regions in FDTD. *IEEE Transactions on Antennas and Propagation*, TBD(TBD):1–4, 2016.

[4] Ivo Babuška, Fabio Nobile, and Raúl Tempone. A stochastic collocation method for elliptic partial differential equations with random input data. *SIAM Review*, 52(2):317–355, 2010.

[5] S. A. Smoljak. Quadrature and interpolation formulas for tensor products of certain function classes. *Doklady Akademii Nauk SSSR; English Transl. in Soviet Math. Dokl. 4 (1963)*, 148(4):1042–1045, 1963.

[6] B.N. Sheehan. ENOR model order reduction of RLC circuits using nodal equations for efficient factorization. In *Design Automation Conference, 1999. Proceedings. 36th*, pages 17–21, 1999.

[7] Allen Taflove and Susan C. Hagness. *Computational Electrodynamics: The Finite-Difference Time-Domain Method.* Boston, London: Artech House Publishers, 3rd edition, 2005.

[8] Dongbin Xiu. Fast numerical methods for stochastic computations: A review. *Communications in Computational Physics*, 5(2-4):242–272, February 2009.

Uncertainty quantification in transcranial magnetic stimulation with correlation between tissue conductivities

Lorenzo Codecasa, Luca Di Rienzo
Politecnico di Milano
Milan, Italy
luca.dirienzo@polimi.it

Konstantin Weise, Jens Haueisen
Technische Universität Ilmenau
Ilmenau, Germany
konstantin.weise@tu-ilmenau.de

***Abstract*—The uncertainty quantification problem in Transcranial Magnetic Stimulation is solved by means of a realistic head model and considering the statistical correlation between grey matter and white matter electrical conductivities. The fast model order reduction approach, introduced by the authors, is extended here to the general case of correlated random parameters. Numerical results prove that correlations between tissue conductivities must be taken into account since their impact on the probability density function of the induced electric field is relevant.**

***Keywords*— uncertainy quantification, transcranial magnetic stimulation, model order reduction**

I. Introduction

Transcranial magnetic stimulation (TMS) targets the non-invasive stimulation of the human brain using strong time-dependent magnetic fields. As a consequence, electric fields are induced inside the head, leading to excitatory or inhibitory behavior of the afflicted neuronal populations. The distribution of the induced electric field strongly depends on the complex geometry of the human brain as well as on the electrical conductivities assigned to grey and white matter (GM, WM) and cerebrospinal fluid (CSF). Furthermore, measurement data show variations among individuals, so that the complex field problem at hand necessitates an efficient methodology to analyze the impact of those uncertainties on the induced electric field.

Former studies in [1] address this problem considering a simplified model of a gyrus/sulcus structure. The non-intrusive generalized polynomial chaos method (gPC) is used, to provide first insights into TMS related sensitivity analysis. In [2], the study is extended to a realistic head model and a parametric model order reduction approach (MOR) is proposed, which makes it possible to significantly reduce the computational cost to solve the underlying stochastic field problem. In [1-2] it is assumed that the electrical conductivities of the different brain tissues are independent of each other. This assumption does not hold when considering water content and ion concentration as influencing factors. Several studies [3, 4] show a dependency between the electrical conductivity and the water content of brain tissue. In this case, the electrical conductivities are correlated and cannot be treated as independent anymore. Furthermore, water content is only one out of many factors of inter-subject variability of conductivities.

For correlated random variables, techniques based on polynomial chaos expansion (PCE) become cumbersome and are generally not applied in practice [5, 6]. Hence, in the present contribution the following more straightforward approach to uncertainty quantification (UQ) is proposed for dealing with correlated random conductivities: a parametric reduced-order model is extracted by means of a Model Order Reduction (MOR) technique from the deterministic problem, as in [2]; the deterministic relationship between the material parameters and the solution of the electromagnetic problem is represented by a polynomial spectral approximation; this approximation is used for estimating any statistics of the solution by means of Monte-Carlo analysis, assuming the actual multivariate probability density function of the tissue conductivities. High levels of accuracy and efficiency are observed. Since a reduced-order model is used, the strategy typically requires negligible computational time.

II. Numerical Results

A. TMS Modeling and Uncertainty Quantification

As in [2], in the deterministic modeling phase we use a realistic head model, which is shown in Fig. 1, discretized using approximately $N = 2.8 \cdot 10^6$ linear tetrahedral finite elements. The source of the magnetic field is a double coil with 9 windings and is approximated by 2712 magnetic dipoles constituted in three layers. The electromagnetic problem at hand is simplified due to the low electrical conductivities and moderate excitation frequencies which are in the range of 2-3 kHz so that the secondary magnetic field from the induced eddy currents can be neglected.

The electrical conductivities of scalp and skin are modelled as deterministic since they hardly affect the induced electric field inside the human brain. On the other hand, the conductivities of CSF, GM, and WM are modelled as uniform distributed random variables, with the ranges reported in [2]. In order to model the correlation between GM and WM, the corresponding conductivities are modeled as two correlated

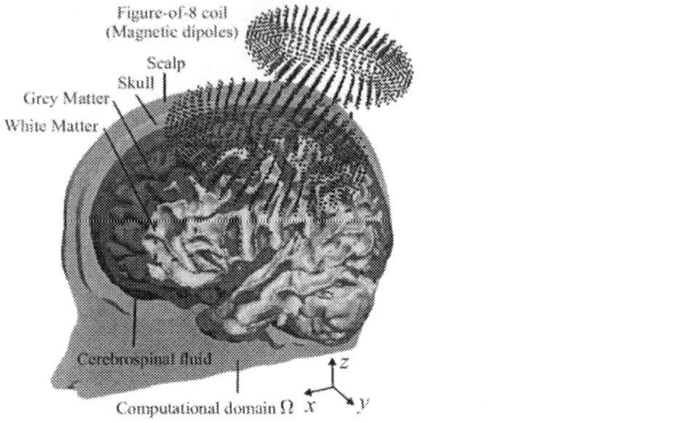

Fig. 1. FEM model of the human head used for uncertainty quantification. The red rectangle indicates the view displayed in Fig. 2.

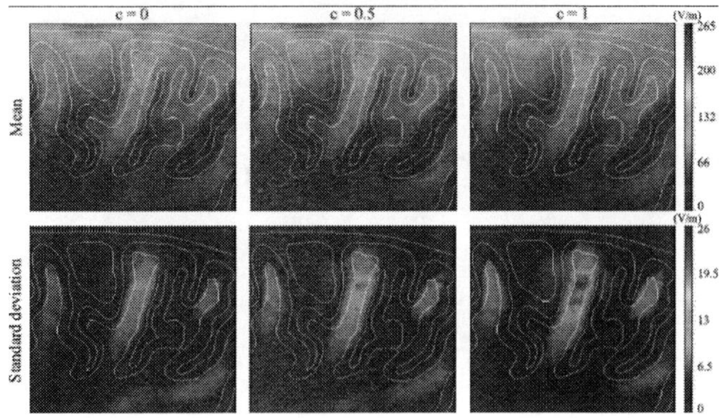

Fig. 2. Mean and standard deviation of the electric field in the sagittal plane under the excitation coil for three values of the correlation coefficient c.

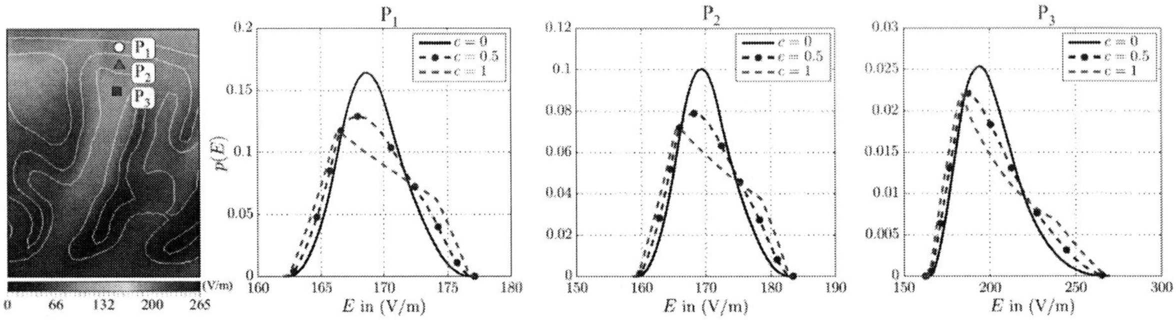

Fig. 3. PDFs of the electric field in three points located right under the excitation coil, for different values of the correlation coefficient c.

random variables, with uniform marginal PDFs considered in [2] but with a Gaussian copula with covariance equal to c [7].

B. Statistical Characterization of the Induced Electric Field

Once the spectral polynomial expansion of the reduced model is obtained, the statistical quantities of interest can be computed by means of a Monte-Carlo analysis applied to the spectral expansion of the reduced model, here using 10^6 samples.

Fig. 2 shows the mean and the standard deviation of the electric field in the sagittal plane under the excitation coil, for three values of the correlation coefficient c. Recent measurements reported in [8] indicate a value of about $c = 0.5$. It can be observed that the correlation degree has a low impact on the mean but a relevant impact on the standard deviation. The higher c the higher the standard deviation. The effect is most prominent in white matter.

Fig. 3 shows the computed PDFs of the magnitude of the electric field in three points (of special interest for TMS). It can be seen that the correlation between GM and WM conductivities has a strong impact on the shape of the PDFs, which suggests that the correlation coefficient primarily influences the statistical moments of higher order.

REFERENCES

[1] K. Weise, L. Di Rienzo, H. Brauer, J. Haueisen, and H. Toepfer, "Uncertainty analysis in transcranial magnetic stimulation using non-intrusive polynomial chaos expansion," IEEE Trans. Magn., vol. 51, p. 5000408, July 2015.

[2] L. Codecasa, L. Di Rienzo, K. Weise, S. Gross, and J. Haueisen, "Fast MOR-based approach to uncertainty quantification in transcranial magnetic stimulation," IEEE Trans. Magn., vol. 52, p. 7200904, March 2015.

[3] J. L. Schepps, and K. R. Foster, "The UHF and microwave dielectric properties of normal and tumour tissues: variation in dielectric properties with tissue water content," Phys. Med. Biol., vol. 25, pp. 1149-1159, November 1980.

[4] E. Michel, D. Hernandez, and S. Y. Lee, "Electrical conductivity and permittivity maps of brain tissues derived from water content based on T1-weighted acquisition," Magn. Reson. Med., in press.

[5] J. Feinberga and H. P. Langtangen, "Chaospy: an open source tool for designing methods of uncertainty quantification, " J. Comput. Sci., vol. 11, pp. 46-57, 2015.

[6] C. Soize and R. Ghanem, "Physical systems with random uncertainties: chaos representations with arbitrary probability measures", J. Sci. Comput., vol. 26, No. 2, pp. 395-410, 2004.

[7] Roger B. Nelsen, An introduction to copulas, Springer-Verlag, New York, 1998.

[8] L. Koessler, S. Colnat-Coulbois, T. Cecchin, J. Hofmanis, J.P. Dmochowski, A.M. Norcia, L.G. Maillard, "In-vivo measurements of human brain tissue conductivity using focal electrical current injection through intracerebral multicontact electrodes," Hum. Brain Mapp., 2016, in press.

Uncertainty Analysis on Band-Stop Filter Using Data-Driven Arbitrary Polynomial Chaos

Osama Alkhateeb and Nathan Ida
Department of Electrical and Computer Engineering
The University of Akron
Akron, Ohio OH 44325-3904 Email: ida@uakron.edu

***Abstract*—A non-intrusive arbitrary polynomial chaos (APC) method is applied to a problem of a band-stop filter with geometrical imperfections. The construction of APC scheme only requires to evaluate a finite number of moments, and does not involve assigning analytical probability density functions for the uncertain parameters of a stochastic model. Therefore, APC is well suited for applications where the uncertain parameters are represented by raw data samples, as with the case of experimental measurements. The numerical examples show that the APC approach is accurate even with a limited number of input samples.**

***Keywords*—Uncertainty Quantification, Data-Driven Arbitrary Polynomial Chaos, Generalized Polynomial Chaos, Monte Carlo Sampling.**

I. Introduction

Methods of uncertainty quantification (UQ) have been widely used with computational electromagnetics (CEM) to address real-world problems that have probabilistic interpretation. Classically, the well-known Monte Carlo (MC) method is used to estimate the influence of the uncertain parameters on the output metrics of a stochastic model [1]. However, the MC method is a sampling method that requires large number of realizations to obtain accurate results. Therefore, in many cases applying the MC method is challenging, especially when incorporated with full-wave solvers. Alternatively, the generalized polynomial chaos (GPC) method [2] overcomes this drawback for a modest number of input parameters. In the GPC approach, the probability density function (PDF) of the output is interpolated by orthogonal polynomials defined uniquely for a given probability distribution. In [2], recursive relations of polynomial bases are provided for various types of parametric distributions.

Recently, Oladyshkin and Nowak [3] introduced a moment-based polynomial chaos approach referred to as arbitrary polynomial chaos (APC). The construction of the polynomial bases in APC does not require an exact knowledge of the input distributions and depends solely on the input moments. This allows APC to be used with a broad range of applications, including applications with known input distributions (as in GPC), and with data-driven applications where only limited data samples are available (usually through measurements). Another advantage of APC, is that since the input data are processed directly in the algorithm through the input moments, undesirable errors related to distribution fitting are avoided.

The objective of this paper is to utilize the non-intrusive APC method [3] in uncertainty analysis of a CEM application. A band-stop filter based on an electromagnetic band gap (EBG) unit cell is considered as a model problem. The case studies address geometrical imperfections induced during the manufacturing process. This includes imperfections in the size and the corners of the EBG cell. To emphasize the data-driven concept, part of the work considers the treatment of limited input data sets.

II. Model Problem

The notch filter considered in this paper consists of microstrip line suspended over a mushroom-type electromagnetic band gap (MSEBG) unit cell. The filter configuration is shown in Figure 1. The resonance frequency (f_r) and bandwidth (BW) of the filter are determined based on the transmission coefficient (S_{12}). For a filter operating at $f_r = 94$GHz and BW $= 7.62$GHz, the input parameters (see Figure 1b) are set as: $w = 0.21$mm, $t = 0.05$mm, $r = 0.075$mm, $h_1 = h_2 = 1$mm, and $\epsilon_1 = \epsilon_2 = 3.78$. Figure 2 shows the transmission coefficient of the filter with respect to frequency. BW is defined where S_{12} falls below -20dB.

III. Statistical Framework

A. Non-intrusive Polynomial Chaos

Consider a vector of independent random variables $\boldsymbol{x} = \{x_1, x_2, ..., x_N\}$, defined on a sample space Ω , with a joint probability density function (PDF) $f_{\boldsymbol{X}}(\boldsymbol{x}) = \prod_{i=1}^{N} f_{X_i}(x_i)$. N is the dimension of $\boldsymbol{x}$ and f_{X_i} is the marginal PDF of x_i. The kth moment of x_i is defined as

$$\mu_{k,i} = \int_{\Omega_i} x_i^k f_{X_i}(x_i) \partial x \tag{1}$$

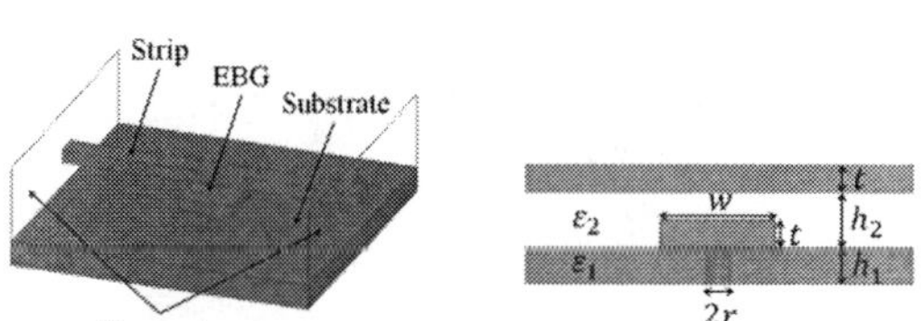

(a) Filter configuration (b) Input parameters

Fig. 1: Notch filter.

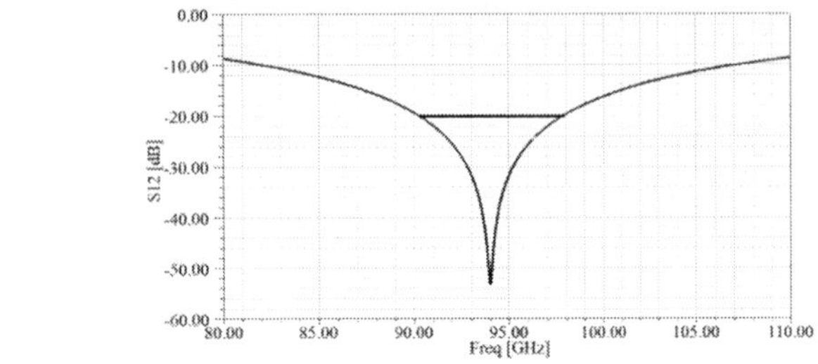

Fig. 2: S_{12} parameter.

However, in some problems $f_{X_i}(x_i)$ is not known and only M number of x_i samples is available. In this case the moments are given by

$$\mu_{k,i} = \frac{1}{M}\sum_{j=1}^{M} x_{i,j}^{k} \tag{2}$$

Let $y = g(\boldsymbol{x})$ be the model under consideration. x_i represents an input under uncertainty such as the geometrical sizes and the electrical parameters of the filter, while y represents an output of interest. I.e., the resonance frequency or the bandwidth. y can be approximated by the expansion

$$y(\boldsymbol{x}) = y(x_1, x_2, ..., x_N) = \sum_{i=1}^{\mathrm{P_{out}}} \alpha_i \Phi_i(x_1, x_2, ..., x_N) \tag{3}$$

α_i are unknown coefficients, and $\mathrm{P_{out}}$ is the order of the expansion. Φ_i forms a set of multidimensional orthogonal polynomials with respect to $f_{\boldsymbol{X}}(\boldsymbol{x})$

$$\langle \Phi_i, \Phi_j \rangle = \int_{\Omega} \Phi_i(\boldsymbol{x})\Phi_j(\boldsymbol{x}) f_{\boldsymbol{X}}(\boldsymbol{x})\partial \boldsymbol{x} = ||\Phi_i^2||\delta_{ij} \tag{4}$$

Based on the orthogonality condition in Equation 4, the coefficients α_i are determined by the spectral projection method

$$\alpha_i = \frac{\langle y, \Phi_i \rangle}{||\Phi_i^2||} \tag{5}$$

The mean and the variance of y satisfy:

$$\mu_y = \alpha_1 ||\Phi_1||, \quad \sigma_y^2 = \sum_{i=2}^{\mathrm{P_{out}}} \alpha_i^2 ||\Phi_i^2|| \tag{6}$$

B. Construction of Orthogonal Polynomials for an Arbitrary Distribution

As already mentioned APC is a moment-based method. Therefore, the next step is to express the polynomial basis Φ_i in terms of the statistical moments of $\boldsymbol{x}$. To do so we first write Φ_i in terms of univariate orthogonal polynomials using a multi-index I_j^i as

$$\Phi_i(x_1, x_2, ..., x_N) = \prod_{j=1}^{N} P_j^{(I_j^i)}(x_j) \tag{7}$$

$P_j^{(k)}$ refers to the jth univariate polynomial of degree k. It has the form

$$P_j^{(k)}(x_j) = \sum_{i=0}^{k} p_{i,j}^{(k)} {x_j}^i \tag{8}$$

with $p_{i,j}^{(k)}$ being the polynomial coefficients. In [3], it is shown that with straight forward algebra Equations 1, 2, and 4 can be used to find the coefficients $p_{i,j}^{(k)}$ in terms of the input moments. This relation is given by the matrix

$$\begin{bmatrix} \mu_{0,j} & \mu_{1,j} & \cdots & \mu_{k,j} \\ \mu_{1,j} & \mu_{2,j} & \cdots & \mu_{k+1,j} \\ \vdots & \vdots & \vdots & \vdots \\ \mu_{k-1,j} & \mu_{k,j} & \cdots & \mu_{2k-1,j} \\ 0 & 0 & \cdots & 1 \end{bmatrix} \begin{bmatrix} p_{0,j}^{(k)} \\ p_{1,j}^{(k)} \\ \vdots \\ p_{k-1,j}^{(k)} \\ p_{k,j}^{(k)} \end{bmatrix} = \begin{bmatrix} 0 \\ 0 \\ \vdots \\ 0 \\ 1 \end{bmatrix} \tag{9}$$

The moment matrix in Equation 9 may become ill-conditioned when high order polynomials are required. One way to reduce the order of the polynomials without affecting the accuracy of the solutions is by using the multi-element approach [4].

IV. Preliminary Results

First we consider variations in the patch size w (see Figure 1b). In this case w follows a normal distribution truncated at $3\sigma_w$. I.e $\Delta w = \pm 3\sigma_w$. μ_w and the other parameters of the filter are fixed at the values provided in Section II. Figure 3 shows the maximum relative error obtained for the expected value and the standard deviation of the model outputs vs. number of input samples, computed at $\mathrm{P_{out}} = 5$ and $\Delta w = \pm 0.1t$ (t is the patch thickness). The relative error follows the formula $\max\{||\mathrm{Z_{Approx}}(n) - \mathrm{Z_{Exact}}||/||\mathrm{Z_{Exact}}||\}$, where $\mathrm{Z_{Approx}}(n)$ and $\mathrm{Z_{Exact}}$ refer to a statistical measure computed by the nth sample set and the exact distribution, respectively. As the convergence rate in both cases is of order ~ 0.5, it is clear that the error is due to the statistical sampling used to generate the input sets. However, The results show that acceptable accuracies are achievable with relatively small input sets ($100 \leq M \leq 1000$).

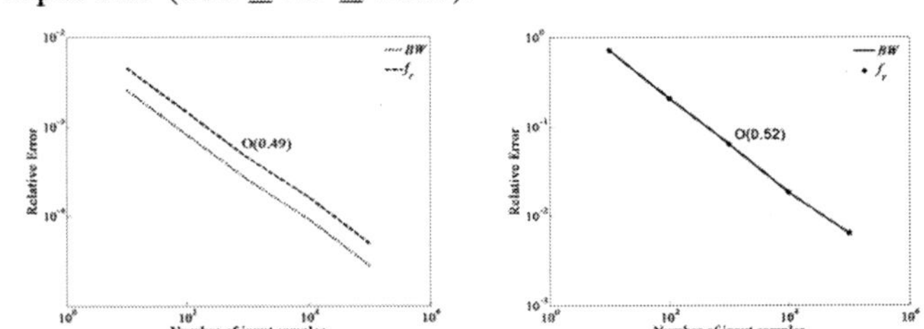

(a) Expected value (b) Standard deviation

Fig. 3: Convergence rate of expected value and standard deviation vs. number of w samples, with $\Delta w = \pm 0.1t$.

References

[1] C. Chauvière, J. S. Hesthaven, and L. Lurati, "Computational modeling of uncertainty in time-domain electromagnetics," *SIAM Journal on Scientific Computing*, vol. 28, no. 2, pp. 751–775, Feb. 2006.

[2] D. Xiu and G. E. Karniadakis, "The wiener–askey polynomial chaos for stochastic differential equations," *SIAM Journal on Scientific Computing*, vol. 24, no. 2, pp. 619–644, 2002.

[3] S. Oladyshkin and W. Nowak, "Data-driven uncertainty quantification using the arbitrary polynomial chaos expansion," *Reliability Engineering & System Safety*, vol. 106, pp. 179 – 190, 2012.

[4] X. Wan and G. E. Karniadakis, "An adaptive multi-element generalized polynomial chaos method for stochastic differential equations," *Journal of Computational Physics*, vol. 209, no. 2, pp. 617 – 642, 2005.

Stochastic Collocation for Uncertainty Quantification of Systems Described by Neutral Delayed Differential Equations

F. Ferranti[1], D. Romano[2], G. Antonini[2] and L. De Camillis[2]

[1] Institut Mines-Télécom Atlantique, CNRS UMR 6285 Lab-STICC, 29238 Brest CEDEX 3, France

[2] Università degli Studi dell'Aquila, Via G. Gronchi 18, 67100, L'Aquila, Italy

Email: [1]francesco.ferranti@telecom-bretagne.eu, [2]daniele.romano.vis@gmail.com, [2]giulio.antonini@univaq.it, [2]lucadecamillis@gmail.com

***Abstract*—A technique is presented for variability analysis of large circuits described by neutral delayed differential equations. It is based on a delayed formulation of the partial equivalent element method coupled with stochastic collocation schemes. Pertinent numerical results validate the proposed technique.**

I. Introduction

Among all electromagnetic (EM) methods, the Partial Element Equivalent Circuit (PEEC) method [1] has been found particularly useful for modeling PCBs, interconnects, and problems involving both electromagnetic fields and circuits. A PEEC formulation that includes delay elements becomes necessary for electrically long/large structures and leads to systems of neutral delayed differential equations [2], [3]. A comprehensive introduction to the subject of delayed differential equations and related solvers can be found in [4].

Predicting the effect of the variability of design parameters on the performance of high-speed systems is of paramount importance for a successful design. Monte Carlo (MC) analysis gives accurate results and it is easy to implement, but it requires a large number of simulations and it results to be computationally expensive. Alternative approaches have been proposed in the literature, such as Stochastic Collocation (SC) methods [5].

SC schemes approximate the unknown stochastic solution by a polynomial interpolation function in the multidimensional space of the stochastic variables. The interpolation is constructed by repeatedly solving (sampling) the deterministic problem at a predetermined set of nodes (samples). This approach offers high accuracy, fast convergence rate and easy implementation. The computational effort required for a stochastic collocation approach depends on the number of support nodes used for constructing the interpolation.

In this paper, we propose a method for efficient variability analysis of large circuits described by neutral delayed differential equations. It is based on a delayed formulation of the PEEC method coupled with stochastic collocation schemes.

II. Proposed Variability Analysis Technique

The basic idea of SC schemes is to approximate the unknown stochastic solution by a polynomial interpolation function in the multidimensional space of the stochastic parameters. A stochastic solution $\mathbf{Y}(s,\boldsymbol{\xi})$ using tensor product grids [6], [7] can be expressed as

$$\mathbf{Y}(s,\xi^{(1)},\cdots,\xi^{(d)}) \approx \mathcal{F}_{\boldsymbol{i}}(\mathbf{Y}) = \sum_{j_1=1}^{N_1}\cdots\sum_{j_d=1}^{N_d}\mathbf{Y}(s,\xi_{j_1}^{(1)},\cdots,\xi_{j_d}^{(d)})L_{j_1}(\xi^{(1)})\cdots L_{j_d}(\xi^{(d)}) \quad (1)$$

where s represents the Laplace variable, $\boldsymbol{\xi} = (\xi^{(1)},\ldots,\xi^{(d)})$ denotes the vector of stochastic parameters and $\{L_{j_k}(\xi^{(k)})\}$ represents the interpolation basis functions. The polynomial interpolation can be expressed by using the Lagrange interpolation polynomials [5], [6]. The nodes can be chosen according to quadrature rules in tensor product grids.

The m-th stochastic moment of $\mathbf{Y}(s,\boldsymbol{\xi})$ can be expressed as

$$\mathbb{E}[\mathbf{Y}^m(s,\xi^{(1)},\ldots,\xi^{(d)})] = \int_{\Gamma_1}\cdots\int_{\Gamma_d}\mathbf{Y}^m(s,\xi^{(1)},\ldots,\xi^{(d)})W(\xi^{(1)},\ldots,\xi^{(d)})d\xi^{(1)}\ldots d\xi^{(d)} \approx \sum_{j_1=1}^{N_1}\ldots\sum_{j_d=1}^{N_d}\mathbf{Y}^m(s,\xi_{j_1}^{(1)},\ldots,\xi_{j_d}^{(d)})w_{j_1}^{(1)},\ldots,w_{j_d}^{(d)} = \mathcal{Q}_{\boldsymbol{i}}(\mathbf{Y}^m) \quad (2)$$

$$w_p^{(r)} = \int_{\Gamma_r} L_p(\xi^{(r)})W(\xi^{(r)})d\xi^{(r)} \quad (3)$$

where $\boldsymbol{W}(\boldsymbol{\xi}) = W(\xi^{(1)})\cdots W(\xi^{(d)})$ is a joint probability density function with support $\Gamma_1\times\cdots\times\Gamma_d$. By using sparse grids constructed by the Smolyak algorithm, the curse of dimensionality associated with full tensor product grids is reduced. Sparse grids are constructed from a linear combination of tensor product grids with a relatively small numbers of grid points, while preserving a high level of accuracy. Using sparse grids, (1) and (2) can be rewritten as [6], [7]:

$$\mathbf{Y}(s,\xi^{(1)},\ldots,\xi^{(d)}) \approx \mathcal{A}_{q,d}(\mathbf{Y}) = \sum_{q-d+1\le|\boldsymbol{i}|\le q}(-1)^{q-|\boldsymbol{i}|}\binom{d-1}{q-|\boldsymbol{i}|}\mathcal{F}_{\boldsymbol{i}}(\mathbf{Y}) \quad (4)$$

$$\mathbb{E}[\mathbf{Y}^m(s,\xi^{(1)},\ldots,\xi^{(d)})] \approx \sum_{q-d+1\le|\boldsymbol{i}|\le q}(-1)^{q-|\boldsymbol{i}|}\binom{d-1}{q-|\boldsymbol{i}|}\mathcal{Q}_{\boldsymbol{i}}(\mathbf{Y}^m) \quad (5)$$

where $|\boldsymbol{i}| = i_1 + i_2 + ... + i_d$ and q is denoted as the accuracy level of the sparse grid.

The response of a system described by the delayed PEEC method with a set of stochastic parameters (e.g., layout parameters) $\boldsymbol{\xi}$ can be expressed by the mathematical representation

$$s\mathbf{C}(s,\boldsymbol{\xi})\mathbf{X}(s,\boldsymbol{\xi}) = -\mathbf{G}(s,\boldsymbol{\xi})\mathbf{X}(s,\boldsymbol{\xi}) + \mathbf{B}\mathbf{V}_p(s) \quad (6)$$

$$\mathbf{I}_p(s,\boldsymbol{\xi}) = \mathbf{L}\mathbf{X}(s,\boldsymbol{\xi}) \quad (7)$$

$$\mathbf{C}(s,\boldsymbol{\xi}) = \mathbf{C}_0(\boldsymbol{\xi}) + \sum_{k=1}^{n_\tau(\boldsymbol{\xi})} \mathbf{C}_k(\boldsymbol{\xi})e^{-s\tau_k(\boldsymbol{\xi})} \quad (8)$$

$$\mathbf{G}(s,\boldsymbol{\xi}) = \mathbf{G}_0(\boldsymbol{\xi}) + \sum_{k=1}^{n_\tau(\boldsymbol{\xi})} \mathbf{G}_k(\boldsymbol{\xi})e^{-s\tau_k(\boldsymbol{\xi})} \quad (9)$$

where $\mathbf{C}, \mathbf{G}$ are parameter-dependent EM matrices, $\mathbf{X}$ is the vector of state variables, $\mathbf{V}_p$ is the vector of input voltages, $\mathbf{I}_p$ is the parameter-dependent current (output) response, $\mathbf{B}$ and $\mathbf{L}$ are constant input and output selection matrices, respectively, and n_τ denotes the number of delays. The delayed nature of the EM equations is described by the exponential functions in the Laplace domain. This is an admittance representation.

Once the location of the nodes in the sparse grid is selected, the admittance frequency response of the system at these nodes $\mathbf{Y}(s, \xi_{j_1}^{(1)}, \cdots, \xi_{j_d}^{(d)})$ can be computed. In our example, the admittance representation is transformed into a scattering parameters (S) representation, which is very often used to analyze high-frequency systems. Finally, stochastic quantities (e.g., mean and standard deviation) of these responses are evaluated based on the previously discussed SC formulas. Each node corresponds to a set of EM PEEC equations for the system under study.

III. Numerical Example

A three-port microstrip power-divider circuit (see Fig. 1) has been modeled in this example. The blue lines represent the ports. The relative permittivity of the dielectric is $\varepsilon_r = 2.2$. The stochastic physical parameters are ℓ_x, ℓ_y, w_c and t_c with a uniform distribution with mean values $\ell_{x,\mu} = 9$ mm, $\ell_{y,\mu} = 7.2$ mm, $w_{c,\mu} = 0.8$ mm, $t_{c,\mu} = 0.05$ mm and lower and upper bounds equal to 90% and 110% of the mean values. Smolyak grids based on the Gauss-Patterson quadrature rules have been used leading to an isotropic sparse grid of 49 points. The frequency range of interest is $freq \in [0.01 - 8]$ GHz.

Fig. 2 compares the mean and standard deviation for the real part of S_{22} over the frequency range of interest obtained by the proposed approach (49 samples) and a standard Monte Carlo approach (2000 samples). A good agreement between the two approaches is achieved. Similar results are obtained for the other entries of the scattering parameters matrix.

The computation of the system response at one frequency sample takes in average 10 s on a PC platform with 16GB RAM and 2.4GHz Intel processor using Matlab® (R2016b). Therefore, a significant speedup can be obtained by using the proposed variability analysis technique.

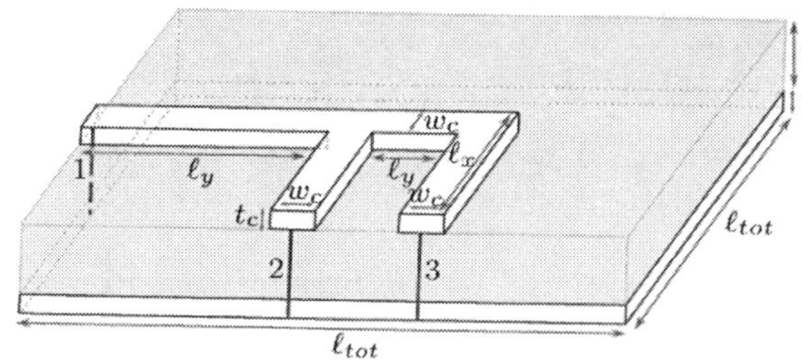

Fig. 1. Structure of the three-port microstrip power-divider circuit, $\ell_{tot} = 20$ mm and $t_d = 0.5$ mm.

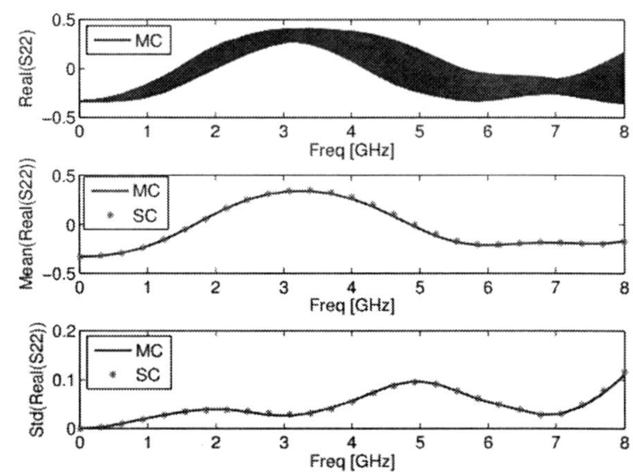

Fig. 2. Statistical analysis for the real part of S_{22}.

IV. Conclusion

An efficient method has been presented for variability analysis of large circuits described by neutral delayed differential equations. Stochastic collocation schemes are used to estimate stochastic quantities of the response of systems modeled by a delayed PEEC formulation. Numerical results have confirmed the efficiency and accuracy of the proposed technique in comparison with a standard Monte Carlo approach.

References

[1] A. E. Ruehli, "Equivalent circuit models for three dimensional multiconductor systems," *IEEE Transactions on Microwave Theory and Techniques*, vol. 22, no. 3, pp. 216–221, Mar. 1974.

[2] P. J. Restle, A. Ruehli, S. G. Walker, G. Papadopoulos, "Full-wave PEEC time-domain for the modeling of on-chip interconnects," *IEEE Transactions on Computer-Aided Design*, vol. 20, no. 7, pp. 877–887, July 2001.

[3] F. Ferranti, M. S. Nakhla, G. Antonini, T. Dhaene, L. Knockaert, and A. E. Ruehli, "Multipoint full-wave model order reduction for delayed peec models with large delays," *IEEE Transactions on Electromagnetic Compatibility*, vol. 53, no. 4, pp. 959–967, Nov 2011.

[4] C. T. H. Baker, C. A. H. Paul, and D. R. Willé, "Issues in the numerical solution of evolutionary delay differential equations," *Advances in Computational Mathematics*, vol. 3, no. 1, pp. 171–196, 1995.

[5] D. Xiu and J. S. Hesthaven, "High-order collocation methods for differential equations with random inputs," *SIAM Journal on Scientific Computing*, vol. 27, no. 3, pp. 1118–1139, 2005.

[6] L. W.-T. Ng and M. Eldred, "Multifidelity uncertainty quantification using non-intrusive polynomial chaos and stochastic collocation," in *53rd Structures, Structural Dynamics and Materials Conference*, 2012.

[7] N. Agarwal and N. R. Aluru, "Weighted smolyak algorithm for solution of stochastic differential equations on non-uniform probability measures," *Int. J. Numer. Meth. Eng.*, vol. 85, no. 11, pp. 1365–1389, 2011.

Research on Workflow of Improving Electromagnetic Compatibility of Search and Rescue Helicopter

Ping Xu, Fanping Shi, Xiaowei Zhang, Tao Jiang
College of Information and Communications Engineering,
Harbin Engineering University,
Harbin 150001, China
{xuping808, shifanping, zhangxiaowei, jiangtao}@hrbeu.edu.cn

Sanjun Dong
School of Electronics and Information
Northwestern Polytechnical University
Xi'an, China
sanjundong@mail.nwpu.edu.cn

***Abstract*—In this paper, it is discussed the problem of electromagnetic compatibility after the installation of rescue system which broaden the usage of modern helicopter and it is proposed some technical measures to improve the electro-magnetic compatibility. It is presented a deep research on the performance of the search and rescue helicopters' electro-magnetic compatibility evaluation workflow including the simulation, prediction, test and evaluation of performance. The research has important guiding significance to carry out the work of the helicopter installation electromagnetic compatibility.**

Keywords—helicopter; electromagnetic compatibility; technical measure; system simulation; test

I. INTRODUCTION

Rescue helicopter is based on the common helicopter platform, and achieves the special purpose of aviation rescue and emergency relief through the installation of the corresponding search radar, digital cameras, life-saving radio, rescue pods and information processing equipment consisting of search and rescue system. Due to the small space inside the helicopter, installation of search and rescue system makes airborne equipment and the layout of the external antenna more intensive [1], and the helicopter's own electromagnetic environment even worse. In addition, for search and rescue system installation space and location is limited, there will inevitably be new electromagnetic compatibility problems in the installation process. Therefore, to give full play to design function of the search and rescue system, it is necessary to take corresponding technical measures to improve the electromagnetic compatibility of search and rescue helicopters.

II. ISSUE OF ELECTROMAGNETIC COMPATIBILITY CAUSED BY INSTALLATION OF SEARCH AND RESCUE SYSTEM

Airborne search and rescue systems include search radar, digital cameras, life-saving radio, life-saving pods and information processing equipment, etc. Installation of airborne search and rescue system on helicopters may bring electromagnetic compatibility problems [2], which is shown in Figure 1.

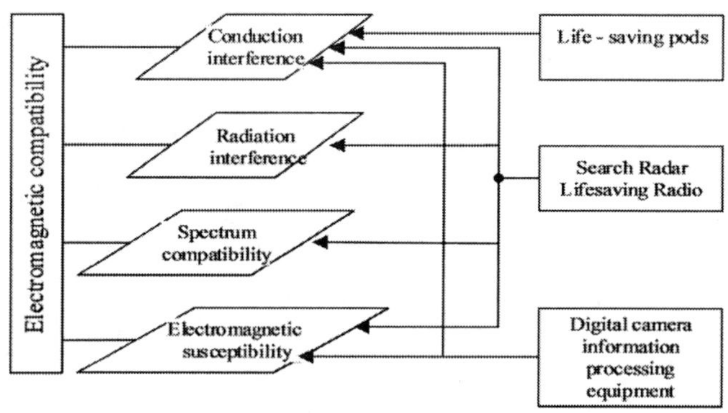

Fig. 1. Issue of electromagnetic compatibility caused by installation of search and rescue system

III. TECHNICAL MEASURES ON IMPROVING ELECTROMAGNETIC COMPATIBILITY

From the above analysis, we can see the major electromagnetic compatibility problems of that the helicopter with installed search and rescue system are electromagnetic interference problems and high sensitivity of the electromagnetic sensitivity of equipment problems. On the one hand, conduction and radiation interference signals, which are into the airborne equipment through the cable connector, antenna port and metal gap, make airborne equipment can not work or reduce performance; on the other hand, radiation interference signals will lead to the spectrum of conflict between helicopter communications, radar and data transmission systems. To improve its electromagnetic compatibility performance, common technical measures are shown as following.

A. The Whole Design

The overall layout of the search and rescue system is very important to effectively control of the electromagnetic interference, and the unreasonable placement and routing will induce the mutual interference between systems [3].

B. The treatment of installing technical

- The power line cable of the search and rescue system must pass through the powered filter to access main powered network of the helicopter; import and export cables of filter should be isolated as far as possible, and shortened laying distance.

- For the search and rescue system in the equipment shell ground, it should be set up to separate the chassis, the signal ground, AC ground terminal, and then connected to the body main grounding system through the ground wire.

C. *Spectrum Compatibility Management*

Spectrum planning and the use of frequency optimization is the main technical means to avoid conflict and incompatibility issues of frequency for installed search radar, life-saving radio and other frequency equipment in the course of the use of frequency.

IV. Test Evaluation of Electromagnetic Compatibility

In order to evaluate the effectiveness of the above electromagnetic compatibility improvement measures, we must carry out electromagnetic compatibility test and evaluation work, the specific work flow is shown in Figure 2.

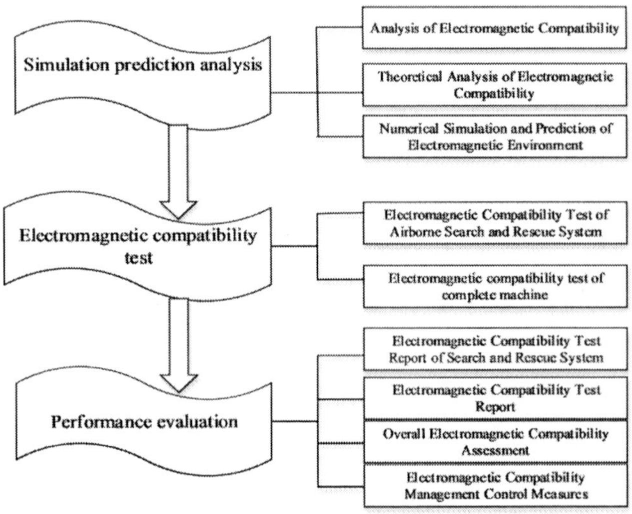

Fig. 2. Workflow of Electromagnetic Compatibility Test Evaluation

A. *Simulation and Prediction of Electromagnetic Compatibility*

The main purpose of electromagnetic compatibility simulation analysis is to use electromagnetic compatibility theory analysis method and computer numerical simulation method. Currently, applicable electromagnetic simulation softwares of electromagnetic compatibility analysis are HFSS, CST, FEKO, etc. Some commonly used simulation algorithms are moments, finite difference time domain method, physical optics, etc [6, 7].

B. *Electromagnetic Compatibility Test*

Doing installed electromagnetic compatibility test is the most direct technical means to measure the effectiveness of improvement techniques of evaluation of helicopter electromagnetic compatibility. Test of Helicopter' electromagnetic compatibility with installed search and rescue system includes test the installation of camera system' related components, and the installation of the machine [4, 5].

C. *Evaluation of Electromagnetic Compatibility*

Combined with the results of electromagnetic compatibility prediction analysis, carry out the work of the whole electromagnetic compatibility assessment, make sure the search and rescue helicopter's overall electromagnetic compatibility and the actual use of the need to take the electromagnetic compatibility management control measures.

V. Conclusion

Helicopter internal space is narrow, airborne equipment installation is intensive and electromagnetic environment is complex, so the installation of search and rescue system on the carrier platform will inevitably bring about a new problem of electromagnetic compatibility. Based on the background, this paper analyzes the electromagnetic compatibility issues that may be brought after the installation of the system, and the technical measures for improving electromagnetic compatibility are put forward. On this basis, we are in-depth study the search and rescue helicopter electromagnetic compatibility test assessment work flow. The study of these aspects of helicopter equipped with engineering electromagnetic compatibility has important guiding significance.

Acknowledgment

This paper is funded by the International Exchange Program of Harbin Engineering University for Innovation-oriented Talents Cultivation. This work was also partially supp orted by the Science and Technology innovative Talents Foun dation of Harbin (2013RFXXJ083), the Foundational Researc h Funds for the Central Universities (HEUCF131602, HEUCF D1433).

References

[1] Policy for Management and Use of the Electromagnetic Spectrum. Department of Defense Directive. 2004 .07.08.

[2] Electromagnetic Environmental Effects Requirements For Systems. Department of Defense Interface Standard. December 2002.

[3] Electromagnetic Environmental Effects and Spectrum Supportability Guidance For The Acquisition Process. Department of Defense Handbook. May 2005.

[4] Hongpeng Sun. System level electromagnetic compatibility test [J]. Ship Electronic Engineering, 2004 (24):176-180.

[5] Zheng Wang, Xingdong Zhu ect. Research on electromagnetic compatibility of aircraft and aircraft equipment [J]. Proceedings of the Symposium on automatic detection and measurement assurance of aviation equipment2004:150-153.

[6] Tianshun Wang, Hong Lei. Aircraft electromagnetic compatibility analysis [J]. Aircraft design 2004 (12) : 39-44.

[7] Yougang Gao.General electromagnetic compatibility [M]. Beijing University of Posts and Telecommunications Press 2001.

A MoM-PO Hybrid Solution for TM Plane Wave Scattering by a Buried Conducting Cylinder

Cengiz Ozzaim
Dept. of Electrical & Electronics Eng.
Anadolu University
Eskisehir, Turkey
cozzaim@anadolu.edu.tr

Inci Umakoglu
Dept. of Electrical & Electronics Eng.
Dumlupinar University
Kutahya, Turkey
inci.umakoglu@dpu.edu.tr

***Abstract*—A method is presented for scattering of a plane wave by a perfectly conducting cylinder (PEC) buried near a two-media interface. Surface equivalence principle is employed to form a set of coupled integral equations. The unknown perturbed equivalent electric currents over the infinite interface are expressed in terms of the difference in current with cylinder present case and the exact physical optics (PO) solution with cylinder removed. Data for the induced current on a buried strip and the perturbed currents are presented for verification.**

Keywords— Buried-object detection, electromagnetic scattering.

I. INTRODUCTION

The problem of electromagnetic scattering by a conducting cylinder of arbitrary cross-section below an infinite dielectric interface has been studied by many authors because the scattered fields can be used in various applications such as detecting buried mines and pipes, geophysical exploration, etc. Since the exact analytical solution of the problem is not available, various analytical and numerical techniques have been employed to obtain approximate solutions for the induced current on the cylinder and the scattered field [1]-[4]. In this paper, we consider the problem of scattering of a plane wave by a PEC cylinder located below an infinite planar dielectric interface by employing a particular formulation of the surface equivalence principle for dielectric materials to form a set of coupled integral equations [5].

II. INTEGRAL EQUATIONS

Consider an infinite dielectric interface at y=0. The interface separates two homogeneous and lossless dielectric half-spaces as illustrated in Fig. 1(a). The medium above and below the interface is characterized as seen in the figure. A PEC cylinder of arbitrary cross section is buried in the lower medium. A transverse magnetic (TM) plane wave ($\mathbf{E}^{inc}, \mathbf{H}^{inc}$) is incident and induces a surface current **J** on the surface C of the cylinder. The fields are time harmonic with $e^{j\omega t}$, which is suppressed. A model which is equivalent to the original structure and source in the upper half-space is shown in Fig. 1(b). In this model all space is filled with the homogeneous material (μ_a, ε_a) and an equivalent electric current $\mathbf{J}_1$ is impressed on the infinite flat surface S. The total fields in region a can be written as

$$\mathbf{E}^a = \mathbf{E}^{inc} + \mathbf{E}^a(\mathbf{J}_1) \quad (1)$$

$$\mathbf{H}^a = \mathbf{H}^{inc} + \mathbf{H}^a(\mathbf{J}_1). \quad (2)$$

In the model constructed to be equivalent to the original structure in the lower half-space, the entire space is filled with the material (μ_b, ε_b). On the imaginary planar surface S an electric surface current $\mathbf{J}_2$ is introduced as seen in Fig. 1(c). An induced current **J** is also introduced on C. The total fields in this model is due to $\mathbf{J}_2$ and **J**:

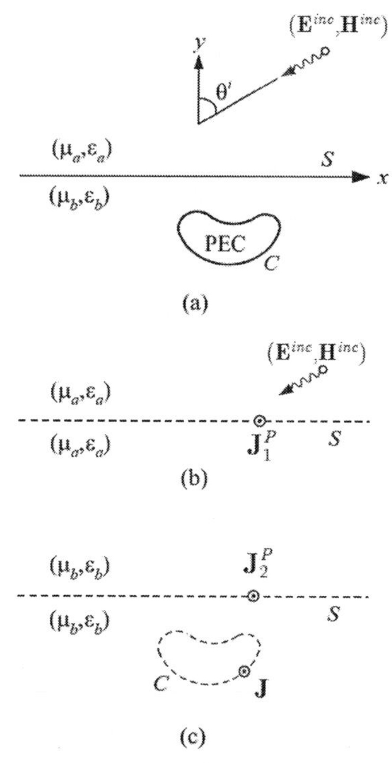

Fig. 1. (a) Original problem, (b) Upper half-space equivalence, (c) Lower half-space equivalence.

$$\mathbf{E}^b = \mathbf{E}^b(\mathbf{J}_2) + \mathbf{E}^b(\mathbf{J}) \quad (3)$$

$$\mathbf{H}^b = \mathbf{H}^b(\mathbf{J}_2) + \mathbf{H}^b(\mathbf{J}). \quad (4)$$

Enforcing continuity of tangential components of the total electric and magnetic field at S, and forcing the tangential component of electric field to be zero on C, lead to the following coupled integral equations in terms of equivalent electric currents on dielectric bodies [5]:

$$[\mathbf{E}^a(\mathbf{J}_1) - \mathbf{E}^b(\mathbf{J}_2) - \mathbf{E}^b(\mathbf{J})]_{\tan} = -\mathbf{E}^{inc}_{\tan}\,, \text{ on } S \quad (5)$$

$$[\mathbf{H}^{a\downarrow}(\mathbf{J}_1) - \mathbf{H}^{b\uparrow}(\mathbf{J}_2) - \mathbf{H}^b(\mathbf{J})]_{\tan} = -\mathbf{H}^{inc}_{\tan}\,, \text{ on } S \quad (6)$$

$$[\mathbf{E}^b(\mathbf{J}_2) + \mathbf{E}^b(\mathbf{J})]_{\tan} = 0, \text{ on } C. \quad (7)$$

Because the tangential magnetic field is discontinuous at a surface electric current, the superscript arrows "↓" and "↑" are used in (6) to indicate that the surface S is approached from above and below, respectively. Note that equations (5) to (7) are justified by considering the semi-infinite lower half-space as a finite dielectric body which contains a conductor [5]. The above integral equations cannot be solved by the Method of Moments (MoM) since the field exists in the infinite surface S. Those equations can be solved if we compare them with the integral equations of the same problem without the conductor. To this end, we remove the conductor and define the equivalent currents $\mathbf{J}_1^{\mathrm{PO}}$ and $\mathbf{J}_2^{\mathrm{PO}}$ to replace $\mathbf{J}_1$ and $\mathbf{J}_2$ of Fig. 1, respectively. The integral equations for the dielectric half-space in the absence of the conductor become

$$[\mathbf{E}^a(\mathbf{J}_1^{\mathrm{PO}}) - \mathbf{E}^b(\mathbf{J}_2^{\mathrm{PO}})]_{\tan} = -\mathbf{E}^{inc}_{\tan}\,, \text{ on } S \quad (8)$$

$$[\mathbf{H}^{a\downarrow}(\mathbf{J}_1^{\mathrm{PO}}) - \mathbf{H}^{b\uparrow}(\mathbf{J}_2^{\mathrm{PO}})]_{\tan} = -\mathbf{H}^{inc}_{\tan}\,, \text{ on } S. \quad (9)$$

Now we take the difference of the total fields on common surface S between the two problems. Subtracting (8) from (5) and (9) from (6), defining perturbed currents as $\mathbf{J}_1^{\mathrm{P}} = \mathbf{J}_1 - \mathbf{J}_1^{\mathrm{PO}}$ and $\mathbf{J}_2^{\mathrm{P}} = \mathbf{J}_2 - \mathbf{J}_2^{\mathrm{PO}}$, and using the linearity of operators we get the following integral equations

$$[\mathbf{E}^a(\mathbf{J}_1^P) - \mathbf{E}^b(\mathbf{J}_2^P) - \mathbf{E}^b(\mathbf{J})]_{\tan} = 0\,, \text{ on } S \quad (10)$$

$$[\mathbf{H}^{a\downarrow}(\mathbf{J}_1^P) - \mathbf{H}^{b\uparrow}(\mathbf{J}_2^P) - \mathbf{H}^b(\mathbf{J})]_{\tan} = 0\,, \text{ on } S \quad (11)$$

$$[\mathbf{E}^b(\mathbf{J}_2^P) + \mathbf{E}^b(\mathbf{J})]_{\tan} = -[\mathbf{E}^b(\mathbf{J}_2^{PO})]_{\tan}\,, \text{ on } C. \quad (12)$$

Right hand side of (12) is the electric field in the lower half-space with the conducting cylinder removed. This field is analytically obtained using the principles of PO. Equations (10) to (12) can now be solved by the MoM since the perturbed currents exist in a finite portion of S near the cylinder.

III. Results and Conclusion

In order to validate the results of this work, the data of Fig. 2(a) is reproduced from an earlier work [1]. Fig. 2(a) and (b) show the normalized current magnitude on the buried horizontal strip and the corresponding perturbed equivalent electric currents on the interface, respectively, for two different angles of the incident field for $h=-0.2\lambda_b$, $2w=1.0\lambda_b$. The perturbed electric currents over the interface and the induced current on the cylinder are normalized with respect to $\mathbf{H}^i$ where $\mathbf{H}^i$, is the total magnetic field with the cylinder removed [1]. The material parameters of the two media are selected as $\mu_a=\mu_b=\mu_0$, and $\varepsilon_a=\varepsilon_0\,, \varepsilon_b=4\varepsilon_0$. The currents are non symmetric when the angle of incidence is 30°, and the perturbed currents are localized near the strip as expected. Because the proposed method contains only free space integral operators, it is far simpler than the methods containing half space Green's functions. The convergence of the method depends on the size and depth of the conductor in terms of the wavelength.

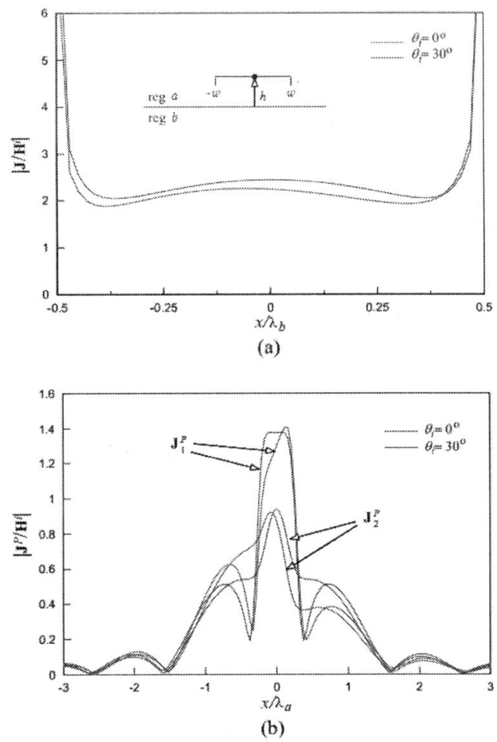

Fig. 2. Results for a buried strip. (a) Induced current magnitude. (b) Perturbed equivalent electric currents.

References

[1] C. M. Butler, X. B. Xu, and A. W. Glisson, "Current induced on a conducting cylinder located near the planar interface between two semi-infinite half-spaces," *IEEE Trans. Antennas Propag.*, vol. AP-33, no. 6, pp. 616–624, Jun. 1985.

[2] X. B. Xu and C. M. Butler, "Current induced by TE excitation on a conducting cylinder located near the planar interface between two semi-infinite half-spaces," *IEEE Trans. Antennas Propagat.*, vol. AP-34, pp. 880–890, 1986.

[3] M. Di Vico, F. Frezza, L. Pajewski, and G. Schettini, "Scattering by a finite set of perfectly conducting cylinders buried in a dielectric halfspace: A spectral-domain solution," *IEEE Trans. Antennas Propag.*, vol. 53, no. 2, pp. 719–727, Feb. 2005.

[4] M. Lucido, "Scattering by a tilted strip buried in a lossy half-space at oblique incidence," *PIER M*, vol. 37, pp. 51-62, 2014.

[5] R. F. Harrington, "Boundary integral formulations for homogeneous material bodies," *JEMWA*, vol. 3, no. 1, pp. 1-15, 1989.

Discrete Mode Matching Method for the Analysis of Microstrip Lines on Uniaxial Anisotropic Substrates

Veenu Kamra and Achim Dreher
German Aerospace Center (DLR)
Institute of Communications and Navigation, Oberpfaffenhofen
D-82234 Wessling, Germany
E-mail: veenu.kamra@dlr.de, achim.dreher@dlr.de

***Abstract*—This paper presents the extension of the discrete mode-matching (DMM) method for the analysis of microstrip multilayered structures filled with anisotropic material. The work contributes the theory behind this method for the analysis of microstrip lines. The validation of the results has been done with open literature and the commercial software HFSS. A very good agreement has been found between the results.**

***Index Terms*—Discrete mode matching, multilayered microwave structures, anisotropic media.**

I. Introduction

The discrete mode-matching (DMM) is an efficient space-/spectral-domain numerical method for the full-wave analysis, which has successfully been applied to planar and cylindrical multilayered microwave structures with isotropic material, such as transmission lines and microstrip antennas [1], [2]. It uses a sampling of the wave equation in one or two dimensions and the analytical solutions in the remaining direction perpendicular to the layers. For this reason only two or four lateral boundaries are required. The formulation employs a full-wave equivalent circuit (FWEC) for the determination of the system equations in spectral domain.

In [3] the FWEC for the analysis of multilayered structures with anisotropic material has been introduced, whereby waveguides were analysed. In the present paper, DMM is applied for structures with metallisations in the interfaces. First, the expressions needed to set up the system equations are presented, then they are applied for the analysis of microstrip lines to demonstrate the method. The results are compared with open literature and also with the commercially available software, i.e. Ansys HFSS.

II. Theory

Consider a stratified dielectric structure as shown in Fig. 1. The analysis starts from Helmholtz's wave equation, normalized by free space wave number k_0, which is set up for the two independent field components $\psi = E_y, H_y$ in layer k

$$\left(\frac{\partial^2}{\partial x^2} + \frac{\partial}{\partial z^2} + \varepsilon_d\right)\psi_k = 0, \qquad \varepsilon_d = K^2 - k_y^2, \quad (1)$$

where K is the propagation constant for anisotropic media. We assume the structure is infinite in propagation direction, i.e. y, so just 1D discretization is used for the analysis of multilayered microstrip line (Fig. 2). The field components

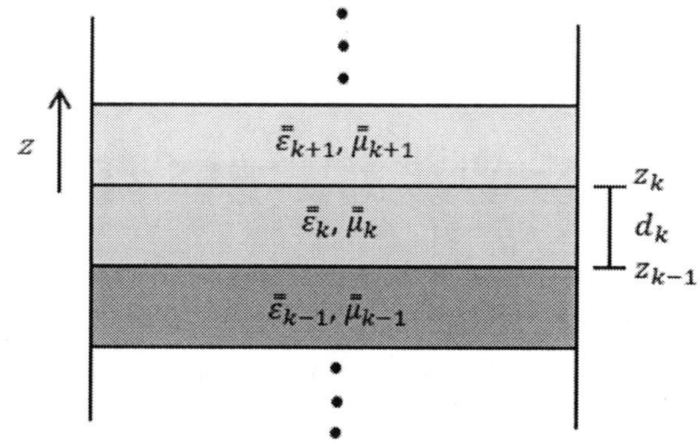

Fig. 1. Stratified dielectric.

are sampled at N equidistant points x_j between the lateral walls. Transformation equation of field components having N modes discretized by N samples is given by

$$\psi_j(x_j, z) = \sum_{i=1}^{N} \tau(k_{xi}x_j) \cdot \tilde{\psi_i}(z) \qquad \text{or} \qquad \boldsymbol{\psi} = \boldsymbol{T}\tilde{\boldsymbol{\psi}}, \quad (2)$$

where $\boldsymbol{T}$ is the transformation matrix using the exact eigen solutions $\tau(k_{xi}x_j)$ of the wave equation which are dependent on the lateral boundary conditions.

By using the dyadic Green's function $(\widetilde{\boldsymbol{G}})$ in the spectral domain as discussed in [4], one can set up the system equation that has to be solved to determine the current densities on the metallisation. There is a simple network analysis technique to obtain a relation between the currents on the strip and the tangential electric field components on the interfaces by means of

$$\widetilde{\boldsymbol{G}} \cdot \widetilde{\boldsymbol{J}} = \widetilde{\boldsymbol{E}} \quad (3)$$

or in space domain

$$\eta_0 \begin{bmatrix} G_{xx} & G_{xy} \\ G_{yx} & G_{yy} \end{bmatrix} \begin{bmatrix} J_x \\ J_y \end{bmatrix} = j \begin{bmatrix} E_x \\ E_y \end{bmatrix} \quad (4)$$

where

$$\begin{bmatrix} G_{xx} & G_{xy} \\ G_{yx} & G_{yy} \end{bmatrix} = \begin{bmatrix} T_h & 0 \\ 0 & T_e \end{bmatrix} \begin{bmatrix} \tilde{G}_{xx} & \tilde{G}_{xy} \\ \tilde{G}_{yx} & \tilde{G}_{yy} \end{bmatrix} \begin{bmatrix} T_h^{-1} & 0 \\ 0 & T_e^{-1} \end{bmatrix} \quad (5)$$

with T_e and T_h representing transformations matrices for e- and h-lines. The boundary conditions now require that

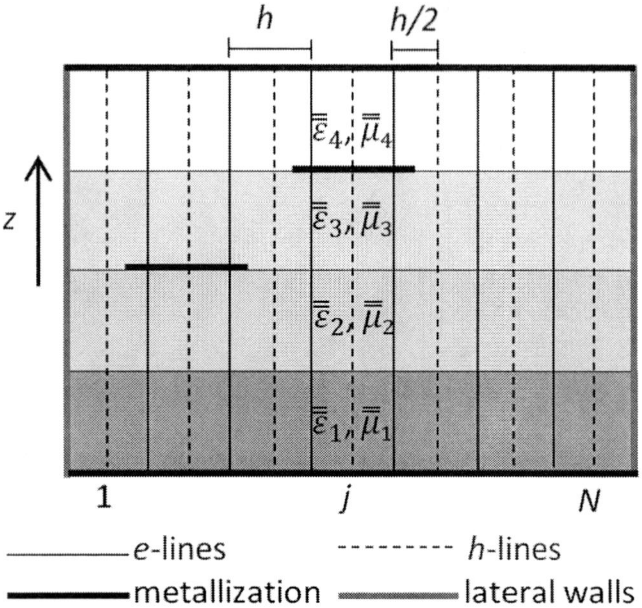

Fig. 2. Multilayered microstrip line with discretization.

the tangential electric field components must vanish on the metallisations and the electric currents outside that region. This results in a reduced matrix as

$$\boldsymbol{G}_{\text{red}} \cdot \boldsymbol{J}_{\text{red}} = 0 \qquad \text{or} \qquad \boldsymbol{Y}_{\text{red}} \cdot \boldsymbol{E}_{\text{red}} = 0, \tag{6}$$

which can be solved as indirect eigenvalue problem to find the propagation constants for the microstrip line.

III. Application

To verify this approach, an enclosed microstrip line is analysed. Here, the uniaxial electric anisotropy in the dielectric layers with optic axis in the z direction is considered, or $\bar{\bar{\varepsilon}} = (\varepsilon_t, \varepsilon_t, \varepsilon_z)$. According to the theory suggested by Lindell [5], electromagnetic waves can be decomposed into TE and TM modes in uniaxial anisotropic media. Using dispersion relation, it has been found that the propagation constant, K, has two roots representing ordinary waves (TE mode) and extraordinary waves (TM mode) as [6]

$$K_1^2 = \varepsilon_t \qquad \text{and} \qquad K_2^2 = \frac{\varepsilon_t \varepsilon_z}{\varepsilon_t \sin^2\theta + \varepsilon_z \cos^2\theta}, \tag{7}$$

where θ is the angle between optic axis and the direction of wave propagation. The basic geometry and the results are given in the Fig. 3, which shows the propagation constant k_y for the two lowest-order modes with respect to a wide frequency range. The FWEC used for the analysis is presented in Fig. 4. The system equation can thus be obtained from

$$\left(\widetilde{\boldsymbol{Z}}_1^{-1}\widetilde{\boldsymbol{V}}_1 + \widetilde{\boldsymbol{B}}_2\widetilde{\boldsymbol{Z}}_2^{-1}\right)\widetilde{\boldsymbol{E}}_1 = \widetilde{\boldsymbol{J}}_1 \quad \text{using} \quad \widetilde{\boldsymbol{K}}_i = \begin{bmatrix} \widetilde{\boldsymbol{V}}_i & \widetilde{\boldsymbol{Z}}_i \\ \widetilde{\boldsymbol{Y}}_i & \widetilde{\boldsymbol{B}}_i \end{bmatrix}. \tag{8}$$

The propagation constant for the TM mode is taken into consideration. From Fig. 3, it can be realised that the results

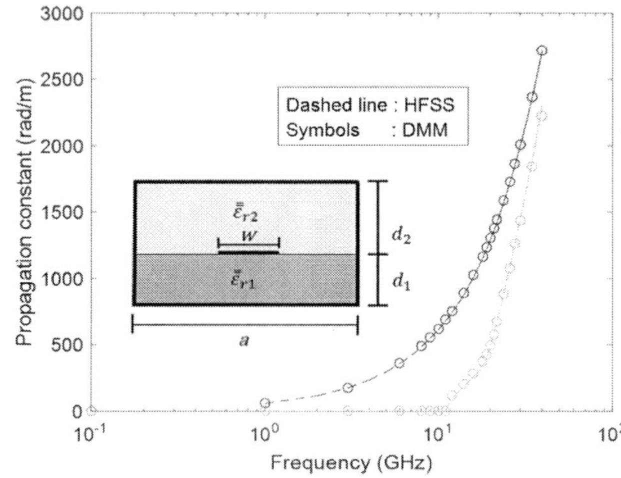

Fig. 3. Dispersion curve for the lowest 2 modes of a shielded microstrip line filled with anisotropic material. (w = 1.27 mm, a = $10w$, $d_1 = w$, $d_2 = a\text{-}d_1$, $\bar{\bar{\varepsilon}}_{r1}$ = (9.4,9.4,11.6), $\bar{\bar{\varepsilon}}_{r2}$ = (1,1,1))

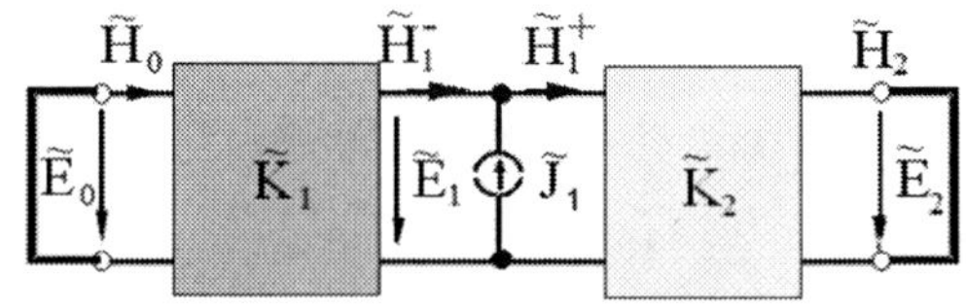

Fig. 4. Full-wave equivalent circuit for a shielded microstrip line.

obtained from DMM and Ansys HFSS agree very well. They are also in good agreement with the open literature [7].

IV. Conclusion

In this paper, the application of the discrete mode matching method to analyse microstrip line filled with anisotropic dielectric material is presented. Numerical results are validated with the finite-element based software Ansys HFSS and the open literature. It has been concluded that the proposed method can provide convincible results in a shorter computing time with few lines on the strip.

References

[1] A. Dreher, "Discrete mode matching for the full-wave analysis of planar waveguide structures," *Microwave Symposium Digest, 1990., IEEE MTT-S International*, San Francisco, CA, USA, 1996, pp. 193-196 vol.1.

[2] M. V. T. Heckler and A. Dreher, "Analysis of cylindrical microstrip lines using the discrete mode matching method," *IEEE Microw. Compon. Lett.*, vol. 16, no. 7, pp. 392-394, July 2006.

[3] V. Kamra and A. Dreher, "Full-wave equivalent circuit for the analysis of waveguides with multiple anisotropic layers," submitted in *IEEE Microw. Compon. Lett.*

[4] A. Dreher, "A new approach to dyadic Green's function in spectral domain," *IEEE Trans. Antennas Propag.*, vol. 43, no. 11, pp. 1297 - 1302, Nov. 1995.

[5] I. V. Lindell, "TE/TM decomposition of electromagnetic sources in uniaxial anisotropic media," *Microw. Opt. Technol. Lett.*, vol. 9, pp. 108111, 1995.

[6] K. Zhang and D. Li, *Electromagnetic Theory for Microwaves and Optoelectronics (2nd ed.).* Heidelberg, Germany: Springer, 2008.

[7] K. Mao, *Finite element analysis of multilayer transmission line and circuit components,* Ph.D. dissertation, University of Illinois, Urbana-Champaign, 2007.

An Efficient Boundary Condition Based On Surface Impedance Concept in FDTD Simulations

Yunlong Mao, Tao Jiang
College of Information
and Communication Engineering
Harbin Engineering University
Harbin, 150001, China
maoyunlong@hrbeu.edu.cn, jiangtao@hrbeu.edu.cn

Atef Z. Elsherbeni
Department of Electrical
Engineering and Computer Science
Colorado School of Mines
Golden, 80401, USA
aelsherb@mines.edu

***Abstract*—Surface impedance boundary condition (SIBC) is a potential way to improve the efficiency of finite difference time domain (FDTD) method. In this paper, we propose an efficient SIBC, the PEC backed SIBC (PEC-SIBC). We first derived the updating equations of PEC-SIBC for 1D. The updating equations for 2D and 3D can be derived following the same procedure. Later, we verified the accuracy of PEC-SIBC and analyzed its calculation complexity with a 2D examples. Even though the calculation amount for PEC-SIBC is a little larger than the traditional SIBC, it is better for improving the efficiency of implementing the FDTD method.**

***Index Terms*—FDTD, PEC, SIBC.**

I. Introduction

FDTD method is one of the main full-wave simulation methods for electromagnetic analysis. One big problem of FDTD that confronts the researchers in the past decades is that the FDTD method requires a lot of memory storage for the simulation domain. A potential solution is SIBC, which is introduced by Leontovich[1]. SIBC reveals the inherent relationship of tangential electric field and magnetic field on the interface of two different materials. Therefore, the electromagnetic field beyond SIBC boundary can be ignored, thus reducing the computational domain and the calculation amount. It was until 1992 that the researchers were able to implement SIBC with FDTD. The method proposed by Beggs et al [2] is specified for good conductors. Maloney and Smith [3] proposed a more general method which requires a pre-processing. In 1995, Oh and Schutt-Aine proposed another general method in [4]. In [5], Santis et al. made an improvement by using vector fitting rational function instead of Chebyshev rational function.

However, all those proposed methods require specified updating equations. The main updating procedure was concluded in [6] such that:

1. Divide the whole domain into SIBC and non-SIBC regions.
2. Update E and H components of the non-SIBC region;
3. Update E and H components of the SIBC region with specified SIBC updating equations;

Following the procedure above, we may need to divide the non-SIBC region into a few smaller regions, which is annoying and error-prone, and varies with the changing of problem geometrical parameters.

Therefore, we propose the PEC backed SIBC (PEC-SIBC) in this paper. PEC-SIBC is characterized by PEC and SIBC together, and the PEC character makes it available for being integrated with the conventional FDTD updating equations. Thus, there is no need for the multi-region division, and the updating procedure is simplified.

II. Formulation

Consider a one dimensional problem with E_z and H_y. A gaussian pulse travels from free space towards an infinite planar surface of a lossy dielectric medium located at the positive end of the x direction. PEC-SIBC is made of two parts: SIBC surface and PEC area, as illustrated in Fig. 1. Assuming there is a artificial E component, $E_z(i+1/2)$, located at the same point of H component on the SIBC surface.

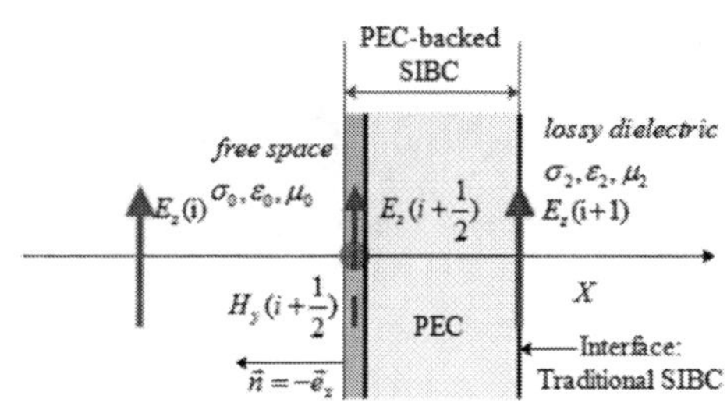

Fig. 1. Geometry of PEC-backed SIBC in 1D configuration.

Following the procedure proposed in [4], and applying the collocation technology proposed in [6], we can obtain that:

$$H_y^{n+\frac{1}{2}}(i+\frac{1}{2}) = \frac{1-Z_1Z_0}{1+Z_1Z_0}H_y^{n-\frac{1}{2}}(i+\frac{1}{2}) + \frac{Z_1}{1+Z_1Z_0}\sum_{p=1}^{8}\Psi_p^n - \frac{2dt}{\mu dx\,(1+Z_1Z_0)}E_z^n(i), \tag{1}$$

where dt is the time step, $a=\sigma_2/\varepsilon_2$, $\eta_2=\sqrt{\mu_2/\varepsilon_2}$, $k_p = (1-e^{-a\omega_p dt})C_p/\omega_p$, $Z_0 = 1-\sum_{p=1}^{8} k_p$, $Z_1 = dt\eta_2/(\mu_0 dx)$, and $\Psi_p^n = k_p e^{-a\omega_p dt}[H_y^{n-1/2}(i+1/2)+H_y^{n-3/2}(i+1/2)] + e^{-a\omega_p dt}\Psi_p^{n-1}$, $C_p and \omega_p$ are listed in [4].

Considering the fact that the half spatial area (light yellowed in Fig. 1) is defined as PEC, we can come up with:

$$H_y^{n+\frac{1}{2}}(i+\frac{1}{2}) = \frac{1-Z_1Z_0}{1+Z_1Z_0}H_y^{n-\frac{1}{2}}(i+\frac{1}{2}) + \frac{Z_1}{1+Z_1Z_0} \times \sum_{p=1}^{8}\Psi_p^n + \frac{2dt}{\mu dx\,(1+Z_1Z_0)}[E_z^n(i+1) - E_z^n(i)], \quad (2)$$

where $E_z^n(i+1) = 0$. Equation (2) is the final updating euqation for PEC-SIBC. It can be figured out that (2) has a same format as the corresponding equation of conventional FDTD listed in [7]. If we regard $\sum_{p=1}^{8}\Psi_p^n$ as a magnetic source and assign $Chyh = (1-Z_1Z_0)/(1+Z_1Z_0)$, $Chyez = 2dt/(\mu dx(1+Z_1Z_0))$, $Chym = Z_1/(1+Z_1Z_0)$, we can successfully integrated PEC-SIBC with conventional FDTD method, and the updating procedure can be simplified as below:

1. Update all the H components in the FDTD domain ;
2. Update $\sum_{p=1}^{8}\Psi_p^n$ during the updating for the sources.

Compared to the traditional updating procedure for SIBC, there is no need for multi-region division.

III. Verification and Complexity Analysis

The geometry of the verification example is illustrated in Fig. 2. Same example was also discussed in [4] and [5].

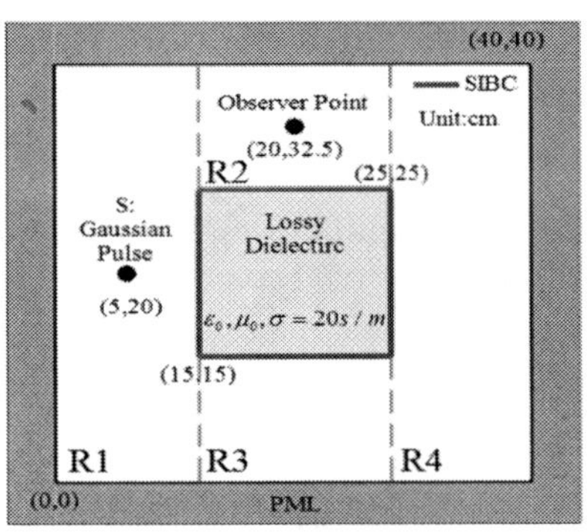

Fig. 2. Geometry of a 2D example and its multi-region division.

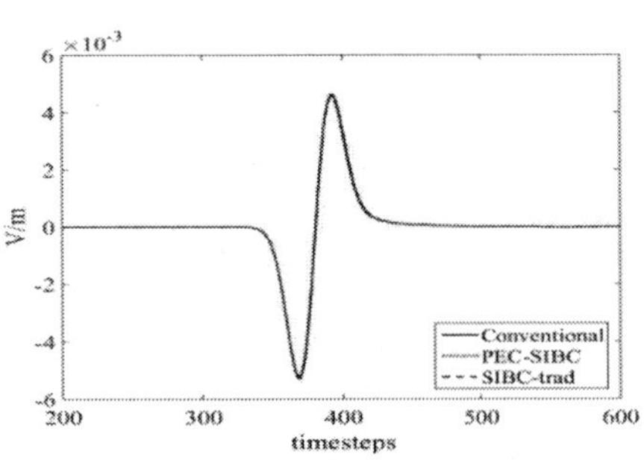

Fig. 3. Observed waveform at the observer point.

From Fig. 3, PEC-SIBC, traditional SIBC and conventional FDTD method have a comparable performance. For the traditional SIBC method, the whole problem domain is divided into 4 regions, $R1 - R4$, as illustrated in Fig. 2.

TABLE I
Calculation amount comparison for the configuration in Fig. 2

Methods	Addition	Multiplication
Conventional	480000	480000
SIBC-trad	456800	457600
PEC-SIBC	486000	486400

we also made a complexity analyze of calculating Hy based on the updating equations of these 3 methods in Table I.

Note that the calculation amount requires another 6000 addition and 6400 multiplication operations specialized for updating the assumed source, $\sum_{p=1}^{8}\Psi_p^n$, compared to conventional FDTD method.

Among the presented methods, the calculation amount of traditional SIBC is the smallest. That's because the electromagnetic fields inside the lossy dielectric are not calculated.

Considering the multi-region division and calculation amount together, the proposed PEC-SIBC is better than the traditional SIBC method especially for complex problems because it avoids the multi-region division processing utilized the conventional updating equation form.

IV. Conclusion

In this paper, we propose an efficient surface impedance boundary condition, PEC-SIBC. It can be easily integrated with conventional FDTD methods, thus avoiding the necessity of multi-region division. The accuracy and calculation complexity of PEC-SIBC is verified and analyzed via a 2D example. The results indicate that PEC-SIBC is easiest to implement with no significant overhead in memory usage or cpu time.

Acknowledgment

This paper is funded by the International Exchange Program of Harbin Engineering University for Innovation-oriented Talents Cultivation.

References

[1] M. Leontovich, "Approximate boundary conditions for the electromagnetic field on the surface of a good conductor," *Investigations on radiowave propagation*, vol. 2, pp. 5–12, 1948.
[2] J. H. Beggs, R. J. Luebbers, K. S. Yee, and K. S. Kunz, "Finite-difference time-domain implementation of surface impedance boundary conditions," *Antennas and Propagation, IEEE Transactions on*, vol. 40, no. 1, pp. 49–56, 1992.
[3] J. G. Maloney and G. S. Smith, "The use of surface impedance concepts in the finite-difference time-domain method," *Antennas and Propagation, IEEE Transactions on*, vol. 40, no. 1, pp. 38–48, 1992.
[4] K. S. Oh and J. E. Schutt-Aine, "An efficient implementation of surface impedance boundary conditions for the finite-difference time-domain method," *Antennas and Propagation, IEEE Transactions on*, vol. 43, no. 7, pp. 660–666, 1995.
[5] V. De Santis, S. Cruciani, M. Feliziani, and M. Okoniewski, "Efficient low order approximation for surface impedance boundary conditions in finite-difference time-domain method," *Magnetics, IEEE Transactions on*, vol. 48, no. 2, pp. 271–274, 2012.
[6] G. Kobidze, "Implementation of collocated surface impedance boundary conditions in fdtd," *Antennas and Propagation, IEEE Transactions on*, vol. 58, no. 7, pp. 2394–2403, 2010.
[7] A. Z. Elsherbeni and V. Demir, *The finite-difference time-domain method for electromagnetics with MATLAB simulations*. Raleigh, NC: SciTech Publishing Inc., 2009.

Local Mesh Morphing Technique for Parametrized Macromodels in the Finite Element Method

Martyna Czarniewska, Grzegorz Fotyga and Michał Mrozowski
Faculty of Electronics, Telecommunications and Informatics
Gdansk University of Technology
Gdansk, Poland

***Abstract*—This paper presents a novel approach for enhancing the efficiency of the design process of microwave devices by means of the finite element method. It combines mesh morphing with local model order reduction (MOR) and yields parametrized macromodels that can be used to significantly reduce the number of variables in the FEM system of equations and acceleration of computer simulation. A projection basis for local reduction is generated only once, for the original geometry and the associated mesh. The projection basis generated for the nominal design is subsequently used for updated geometries and morphed meshes thereby allowing for reducing the numerical cost and the computational time of parametric studies or the optimization process. The performance of the proposed approach is demonstrated on a two dimensional example.**

I. Introduction

Numerical simulations are commonly used in the process of designing modern devices that are intended to be used in high-frequency electronic systems. One of the most popular simulation techniques is the finite element method (FEM). The basic steps of FEM are as follows: discretizing the geometry to be analysed by means of small elements (typically triangular in 2D and tetrahedral in 3D), selecting interpolating basis functions, formulation of the global system of equations and finally, the solution of the resulting sparse system. Since achieving high accuracy of computations requires fine mesh, simulations by means of FEM tend to be time and memory consuming. This problem exacerbates in the process of optimization or even parametric studies as multiple solves are performed for modified geometries. One of the methods to speed up the computations by means of FEM is to apply local model order reduction (MOR) [1], [2]. However, this approach does not allow for effective optimization of the geometry of the designed structures. Every change in the geometry within the subdomain requires generating a new mesh, FEM matrices, as well as a new projection basis.

This paper shows the novel approach, which combines macromodeling with mesh morphing [3]–[5]. The most time consuming process which is projection basis (denoted by $\mathbf{V}$) generation, is performed only once - for the original mesh. Subsequently, this basis is reused for the new geometry, that is obtained by shifting the mesh nodes. This is possible because the topology of the mesh remains the same as the mesh undergoes deformation. The only numerical cost of this operation is associated with the generation of the new FEM matrices (however this process is not time consuming, since it is very well parallelized [6]) and the projection onto the subspace spanned by the basis $\mathbf{V}$.

II. Theory

Let us consider a cross section of a simple waveguide structure with a fin (Fig.1). Suppose, that the goal of the analysis is to optimize the length of the fin in order to obtain the desired value of cutoff frequency, associated with the dominant mode. To this end the scalar 2D FEM formulation can be applied, which leads to the generalized eigenvalue problem (1):

$$(\mathbf{\Gamma} - k^2\mathbf{C})E = 0. \tag{1}$$

$\mathbf{C}$ and $\mathbf{\Gamma}$ are mass and stiffness matrices, while eigenvector E and eigenvalue k are the solution of the equation (1). E is a column vector of order N, which contains the values of transverse electric field in all nodes of the mesh, while the eigenvalue k represents the cutoff wavenumber of the waveguide [7].

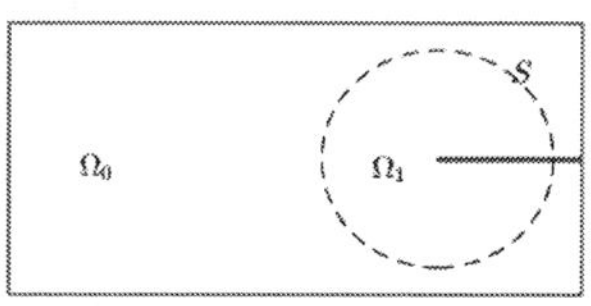

Fig. 1. Cross-section of the analysed waveguide.

In the optimization process the only part of the structure to be modified is the length of the fin. Therefore we have separated the tip of the fin and its vicinity (denoted by Ω_1) from the rest of the computational domain (Ω_0) by means of the boundary S. Due to the consistent numbering of the unknowns, the system of equations is split into the following blocks [8]:

$$\mathbf{\Gamma} = \begin{bmatrix} \Gamma_0 & G_0^T & 0 \\ G_0 & \Gamma_S & G_1^T \\ 0 & G_1 & \Gamma_1 \end{bmatrix}, \qquad \mathbf{C} = \begin{bmatrix} C_0 & S_0^T & 0 \\ S_0 & C_S & S_1^T \\ 0 & S_1 & C_1 \end{bmatrix}. \tag{2}$$

Since the region that is affected by the geometry changes is isolated from the rest of the computational domain, varying the length of the fin requires shifting the nodes of the mesh only inside Ω_1, without introducing any changes in Ω_0 and S.

Therefore, local MOR can be applied to the blocks of matrices $\mathbf{\Gamma}$ and $\mathbf{C}$ associated with the subregion Ω_1.

The orthogonal projection basis $\mathbf{V}$ used in the local MOR approach is obtained by means of the macromodeling algorithm presented in [2]. The efficiency of this method depends on the reduction order q and the number of nodes on the boundary S. In order to improve the efficiency of macromodeling, the compression of the number of variables at S is applied, which means that the field at S is projected onto the subspace spanned by discretized trigonometrical functions [2].

The projection basis $\mathbf{V}$ is generated only once - for the initial geometry. If the geometry is modified (the fin length changes), new FEM matrices are generated and reduced by means of the same basis $\mathbf{V}$. In this preliminary studies a simple mesh morphing algorithm was applied in which the degree each node within Ω_1 moves decreased exponentially with respect to the distance from the tip.

III. Numerical results

The simulation was carried out for the waveguide structure shown in Fig. 1. The height of the waveguide and the width is 10 mm and 20 mm, respectively, while the initial length of the fin was set to 5 mm. The radius of the subregion Ω_1 is 4 mm. The triangle mesh consisted of almost 15000 elements, which gave 7194 variables in the whole computational domain and 3312 variables within Ω_1. The number of functions in the projection at the boundary S is 20. For the initial geometry of Ω_1 the orthogonal projection basis $\mathbf{V}$ was generated, using $q = 15$, which reduced the number of variables to 4313.

The goal of the numerical experiment was to construct a local parametrized macromodel, that can be then used for optimization, and to investigate the error caused by the proposed methodology as the parameter changes. The length of the fin was varied in the range of 3 mm - from 3.5 mm to 6.5 mm in 0.1 mm steps. For each geometry, the mesh within Ω_1 was deformed, new FEM matrices were generated, compression at the boundary was applied and a new set of eigenvalues of the problem defined by (1) was computed - these results were used as reference values. Note, that in this case, the projection basis was generated anew for each new geometry. Subsequently, the reduction was carried out for the same sequence of deformed meshes but this using the same projection basis $\mathbf{V}$, obtained for the original mesh and a new set of eigenvalues was computed. Relative errors for the three lowest cutoff frequencies as a function of a fin length are shown in Fig. 2. The relative error increases as the shift of the nodes grows, but it remains below $5 \cdot 10^{-6}$ in a relatively wide range (with respect to the dimensions of the waveguide). The comparison of computation time for the standard FEM, FEM with macromodels and the proposed method is presented in Table I. The results show, that the proposed method speeds up the computations while the accuracy is deteriorated only marginally.

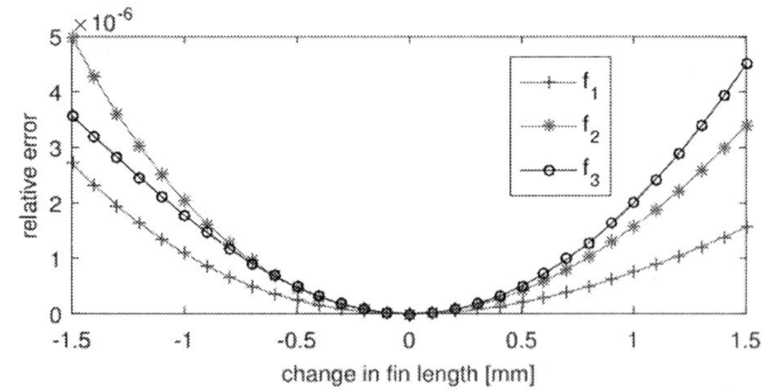

Fig. 2. Error in cutoff frequency caused by the reduction using morphed mesh.

TABLE I
Comparison of computation time

	FEM	FEM_{MM}	The proposed method
Runtime for a single mesh-shift [s]	17.03	13.26	6.95
Total runtime for 31 mesh-shifts [s]	527.93	411.06	219.8

IV. Conclusion

In this paper the new approach for enhancing the efficiency of optimization-oriented finite element method analysis is presented. The method combines mesh morphing with macromodeling technique and brings about the reduction of the computational cost, without comprising the accuracy. The proposed technique can be applied in many subregions of the computational domain, also in a 3D analysis.

Acknowledgment

This work was supported by the Polish National Science Centre under Agreement 2012/07/B/ST7/01241 and 2013/09/B/ST7/04202.

References

[1] Y. Zhu and A. C. Cangellaris, "Macro-elements for efficient FEM simulation of small geometric features in waveguide components," *IEEE Transactions on Microwave Theory and Techniques*, vol. 48, no. 12, pp. 2254–2260, 2000.

[2] G. Fotyga, K. Nyka, and M. Mrozowski, "Efficient model order reduction for FEM analysis of waveguide structures and resonators," *Progress In Electromagnetics Research*, vol. 127, pp. 277–295, 2012.

[3] A. Lamecki, "A Mesh Deformation Technique Based on Solid Mechanics for Parametric Analysis of High-Frequency Devices With 3-D FEM," *IEEE Transactions on Microwave Theory and Techniques*.

[4] S. Burgard, O. Farle, P. Loew, and R. Dyczij-Edlinger, "Fast Shape Optimization of Microwave Devices Based on Parametric Reduced-Order Models," *IEEE Transactions on Magnetics*, vol. 50, no. 2, pp. 629–632, Feb 2014.

[5] W. Wang and M. N. Vouvakis, "Mesh morphing strategies for robust geometric parameter model reduction," in *Proceedings of the 2012 IEEE International Symposium on Antennas and Propagation*. IEEE, 2012, pp. 1–2.

[6] A. Dziekonski, P. Sypek, A. Lamecki, and M. Mrozowski, "Generation of large finite-element matrices on multiple graphics processors," *International Journal for Numerical Methods in Engineering*, vol. 94, no. 2, pp. 204–220, 2013.

[7] J.-M. Jin, *The finite element method in electromagnetics*. John Wiley & Sons, 2014.

[8] G. Fotyga and K. Nyka, "Efficient analysis of structures with rotatable elements using model order reduction," *Radioengineering*, 2016.

Robust and Efficient Model-Order Reduction for Lossless Microwave Structures Using the Impedance Formulation of the Finite Element Method

Rolf Baltes and Romanus Dyczij-Edlinger
Chair of Electromagnetic Theory,
Saarland University, D-66123 Saarbrcken, Germany
Email: r.baltes@lte.uni-saarland.de

***Abstract*—In the lossless case, immittance formulations of the finite element method lead to real-valued system matrices. This reduces memory consumption and solution times. However, their solutions may get corrupted by interior resonances. The scattering formulation, in contrast, is inherently stable, but the resulting matrices are always complex-valued. This article presents a model-order reduction technique for lossless microwave structures that combines the low computational costs of the impedance formulation with the high robustness of the scattering approach. It extends the authors' previous work to structures fed by inhomogeneous waveguides.**

I. Introduction

Thanks to its flexibility in modeling geometry and adjusting approximation order, the finite element (FE) method is a very powerful tool for the numerical simulation of linear microwave structures. In the lossless case, the widely used impedance (Z) formulation [1] is particularly efficient, because it then leads to real-valued system matrices. However, it suffers from the occurrence of interior resonances [2]. In contrast, the scattering (S) formulation [3] is inherently stable, but the system matrices are always complex-valued, even in the lossless case. All FE formulations have in common that the resulting systems of linear equations are of large scale and parameterized in terms of the operating frequency. Thus, computing the frequency response of a system becomes computationally expensive, because it requires assembling and factorizing the FE matrix at a large number of frequency points. In such multi-query settings, methods of model-order reduction (MOR) may greatly accelerate computations, by constructing reduced-order models (ROM) of low dimension, which are evaluated at little cost.

In the multi-point approach of [4], the FE system is solved at a small number of expansion frequencies, which are adaptively selected by an error indicator, and the solutions serve as entire-domain basis functions for building a projection matrix $\mathbf{V}$ of low column rank. The ROM is obtained by applying a Galerkin process to the parameterized FE system, using $\mathbf{V}$. For structures fed by homogeneous waveguides (WG), it was observed in [2] that a ROM for the S formulation may be generated from the projection matrix produced by the Z-based FE model. The method thus combines low FE solution cost and a robust ROM formulation. The present paper generalizes this approach to the transversally inhomogeneous case. The key difficulty is that the transversal WG mode patterns are no longer constant, so that there are contributions to the system matrix and right-hand sides (RHS) whose frequency-dependence is not explicitly known.

II. Problem Statement

Consider a source-free domain Ω, with isotropic and lossless material. Let the boundary of Ω consist of electric walls Γ_E and of the cross-section Γ_P of one feeding WG, whose material properties may be inhomogeneous in the transversal direction. For clarity, only one WG mode is considered.

III. Finite Element Formulations

A. *Impedance Formulation*

Let k_0 denote the free-space wavenumber, η_0 the free-space characteristic impedance, i the modal current, and u the modal voltage, respectively. Then the Z formulation is given by

$$\left(\mathbf{S} - k_0^2\mathbf{T}\right)\mathbf{x}_Z = -\mathrm{j}k_0\eta_0\mathbf{b}i, \tag{1a}$$

$$u = -\mathbf{b}^T\mathbf{x}_Z, \tag{1b}$$

where $\mathbf{S}$ and $\mathbf{T}$ are real-valued FE matrices. The excitation $\mathbf{b}$ is computed from the propagation coefficient γ and field pattern $\mathbf{v}$ of the WG mode, which are obtained by FE analysis, too.

B. *Scattering formulation*

The amplitudes of the incident and reflected waves, a and b, are given by

$$a = \tfrac{1}{2}(u+i), \qquad b = \tfrac{1}{2}(u-i). \tag{2}$$

They yield a formulation that is free of interior resonances [2], but the system is complex-valued even in the lossless case:

$$\left(\mathbf{S} - k_0^2\mathbf{T} + \mathrm{j}k_0\eta_0\mathbf{b}\mathbf{b}^T\right)\mathbf{x} = -2\mathrm{j}k_0\eta_0\mathbf{b}a \tag{3a}$$

$$b = -\mathbf{b}^T\mathbf{x} - 1. \tag{3b}$$

IV. Reduced Order Model

In the following, ROM quantities are denoted by $\tilde{}$. The first step is to construct a ROM for the WG modes after [5] [4]. It is parameterized in terms of k_0 and takes the form

$$\left(\sum\nolimits_{n=0}^{4} k_0^n\tilde{\mathbf{A}}_n Big\right)\tilde{\mathbf{v}} = \tilde{\gamma}^2\left(\sum\nolimits_{n=0}^{2} k_0^n\tilde{\mathbf{B}}_n\right)\tilde{\mathbf{v}}, \tag{4}$$

with constant matrices $\tilde{\mathbf{A}}_n$ and $\tilde{\mathbf{B}}_n$. Eq. (4) leads to an affine representation of the RHS vector $\mathbf{b}(k_0)$,

TABLE I

COMPUTATIONAL DATA*, EVALUATION AT 368 FREQUNECY SAMPLES.

Fromulation	C	Z	S
Dimension FE	-	441124	441126
Evaluation time FE (s)	-	9 274	23 988
Nonzeros in factors	-	261 820 569	268 252 453
Generation time ROM (s)	353	354	906
Evaluation time ROM (s)	0.31	0.30	0.35

* Implemented in Matlab®-R2014a on Intel®Core i5-3570K, 3.4 GHz, 32 GB RAM. FE systems solved with PARDISO of the Intel®MKL version 10.2.6.037.

$$\mathbf{b}(k_0) = \sum g_n(k_0, \tilde{\gamma}(k_0))\mathbf{G}_n\tilde{\mathbf{v}}(k_0), \quad (5)$$

with constant matrices $\mathbf{G}_n$ and functions g_n. The matrix $\mathbf{V}$ is constructed from the solutions of the Z formulation at a set of adaptively chosen expansion wavenumbers $\{k_{0,1}, \ldots, k_{0,N}\}$, by Modified Gram-Schmidt orthogonalization. Thus

$$\text{span}\{\mathbf{V}\} = \text{span}\{\mathbf{x}_Z(k_{0,1}), \ldots, \mathbf{x}_Z(k_{0,N})\}. \quad (6)$$

Applying a Galerkin approach to (3) leads to the ROM

$$\left(\tilde{\mathbf{S}} + \mathrm{j}k_0\eta_0\tilde{\mathbf{b}}\tilde{\mathbf{b}}^T - k_0^2\tilde{\mathbf{T}}\right)\tilde{\mathbf{x}}_S = -2\mathrm{j}k_0\eta_0\tilde{\mathbf{b}}a, \quad (7a)$$

$$\tilde{b} = -\tilde{\mathbf{b}}^T\mathbf{x}_S - 1, \quad (7b)$$

with

$$\mathbf{x}_S \approx \mathbf{V}\tilde{\mathbf{x}}_S, \quad b \approx \tilde{b}, \quad \tilde{\mathbf{S}} = \mathbf{V}^T\mathbf{S}\mathbf{V}, \quad \tilde{\mathbf{T}} = \mathbf{V}^T\mathbf{T}\mathbf{V}, \quad (8a)$$

$$\tilde{\mathbf{b}}(k_0) = \sum g_n(k_0, \tilde{\gamma}(k_0))\mathbf{V}^T\mathbf{G}_n\tilde{\mathbf{v}}(k_0). \quad (8b)$$

While the matrices $\tilde{\mathbf{S}}$, $\tilde{\mathbf{T}}$, and $\mathbf{V}^T\mathbf{G}_n$ are pre-computed during the offline phase of the algorithm, $\tilde{\mathbf{b}}(k_0)$ needs to be calculated at every solution wavenumber. For this purpose, the WG-ROM (4) is solved, and the eigenpair $(\tilde{\gamma}, \tilde{\mathbf{v}})$ is plugged into (8b). Since the matrices $\mathbf{V}^T\mathbf{G}_n$ are of reduced order (mapping from the WG-ROM to the driven ROM), the procedure is cheap.

V. NUMERICAL EXAMPLE

To validate the proposed method, a section of shielded dielectric image guide [6] is analyzed in the range [1, 17] GHz; see Fig. 1a. The adaptive scheme of [4], with a residual threshold of 10^{-4}, results in WG-ROMs of order 7. For the driven structure, two ROMs of dimension 20 are built, using equidistant expansion frequencies. The one is for the combined (C) approach of this work, whereas the other uses the Z formulation for the ROM, as in [7], and converts $\mathbf{Z}$ to $\mathbf{S}$ afterwards. Table I gives computational data, including a memory-efficient FE implementation of the S formulation (3): Computational costs for the C-ROM and the Z-ROM are equal; for both, ROM generation is over 2.5 times faster than when the underlying FE solutions are computed by the S formulation. The amplitude response of the S parameters is given in Fig. 2, and the error $e_{\max}$ in S_{ik}, defined by

$$e_{\max} = \max(|S_{11}^{ROM} - S_{11}^{FE(S)}|, |S_{12}^{ROM} - S_{12}^{FE(S)}|), \quad (9)$$

is shown in Fig. 1b. In all plots, a non-physical resonance is visible for the Z formulation. It occurs in the vicinity of 12 GHz, where the length of the structure corresponds to a quarter wavelength of the guided mode. Away from that interior resonance, both ROMs are in excellent agreement with reference data, with error levels below 10^{-8}.

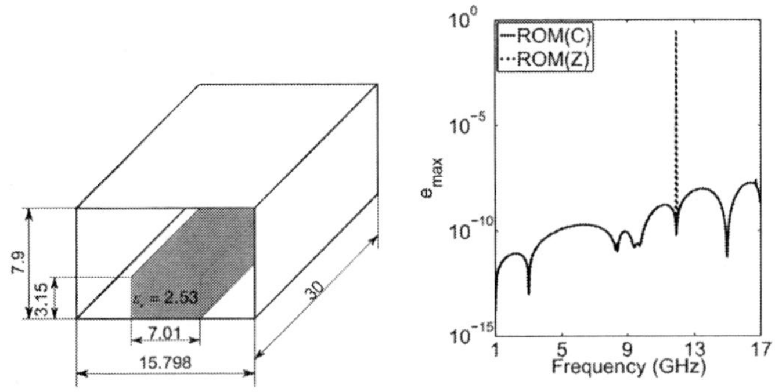

(a) Geometry. Dimensions are in mm. (b) Error in scattering parameters.

Fig. 1. Shielded dielectric image guide.

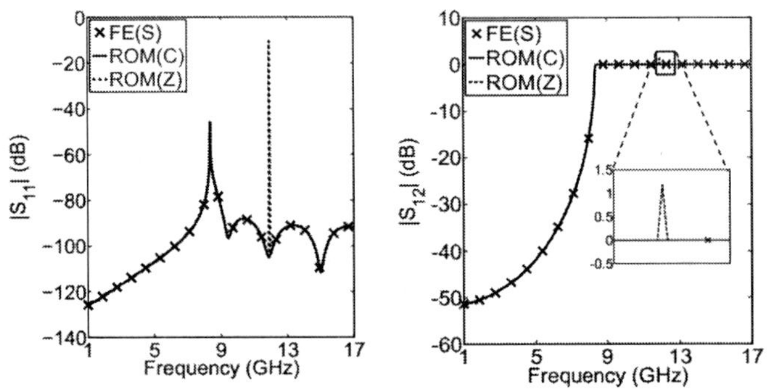

(a) $|S_{11}|$ versus frequency. (b) $|S_{12}|$ versus frequency.

Fig. 2. Amplitude response of S parameters for different formulations.

REFERENCES

[1] M. De Pourcq, "Field and power-density calculations by three-dimensional finite elements," *Microwaves, Optics and Antennas, IEE Proceedings H*, vol. 130, no. 6, pp. 377–384, October 1983.

[2] O. Farle, M. Lösch, and R. Dyczij-Edlinger, "Efficient fast frequency sweep without nonphysical resonances," *Electromagnetics*, vol. 30, pp. 51–68, 2010.

[3] Z. J. Cendes and J.-F. Lee, "The transfinite element method for modeling MMIC devices," *IEEE Trans. Microwave Theory Tech.*, vol. 36, no. 12, pp. 1639–1649, Dec. 1988.

[4] Y. Konkel, O. Farle, A. Köhler, A. Schultschik, and R. Dyczij-Edlinger, "Adaptive strategies for fast frequency sweeps," *COMPEL-The international journal for computation and mathematics in electrical and electronic engineering*, vol. 30, no. 6, pp. 1855–1869, 2011.

[5] A. Schultschik, O. Farle, and R. Dyczij-Edlinger, "A model order reduction method for the finite element simulation of inhomogeneous waveguides," *IEEE Trans. Magn.*, vol. 44, no. 6, pp. 1394–1397, Jun. 2008.

[6] J. Strube and F. Arndt, "Rigorous hybrid-mode analysis of the transition from rectangular waveguide to shielded dielectric image guide," *IEEE Trans. Microwave Theory Tech.*, vol. 33, no. 5, pp. 391–401, May 1985.

[7] R. Baltes, A. Sommer, O. Farle, and R. Dyczij-Edlinger, "Adaptive model order reduction for structures fed by dispersive waveguide modes," in *Electromagnetics in Advanced Applications (ICEAA), 2015 International Conference on*, Sept 2015, pp. 1072–1075.

An Efficient 2D/3D Hybrid DGTD Transient Analysis for Arbitrarily Shaped Anti-Pads in Power-ground Plate-Pair

Wending Mai, Jun Hu
School of Electronic Engineering
University of Electronic Science and Technology of China
Chengdu, China
Email: hujun@uestc.edu.cn

***Abstract*—An efficient hybrid 3D and 2D discontinuous Garlerkin time-domain (DGTD) methods is proposed for signal/power integrity analysis of multiple arbitrarily shaped anti-pads in power-ground. The entire structure is decomposed into anti-pad-domain (3D) and plate-domain (2D). Complicated fields exist around anti-pad, yet, in plate domain, only zeroth-order parallel-plate mode exists. Therefore, triangular prism element (3D) could be simplified as triangle element (2D), which has fewer unknowns. The accuracy of the hybrid method has been validated by comparison with commercial software. Its flexibility, and enhancement of efficiency, are also demonstrated.**

***Keywords*—Domain decomposition, discontinuous Galerkin time domain method (DGTD), hybrid method, power-ground plate-pair, via-modeling**

I. INTRODUCTION

As the clock frequency of systems increase, proper via structure design is essential to ensure signal integrity.

DGTD method [1]–[4], can be regarded as an element-level decomposition method. A 2D DGTD method was proposed in [5] to study via structure, but such 2D method requires consistency in z-axis, not suitable for anti-pad structures. Only very recently in [6], a 3D DGTD method using triangular prism element, was proposed to analyze multi arbitrary shape anti-pad. Yet, it fails to give efficiency consideration.

In this paper, the whole via structure is divide into anti-pad-domains and plate-domains, like in [7]. Different with DDM method in [8], domains in this work are separated with each other naturally because of DGTD's element level decomposition property, and connect with each other by numerical flux. Moreover, the dispersion effect is considered by introducing Debye-model, in the auxiliary differential equation (ADE) way [9]. The algorithm is parallelized to fully exploit the DGTD advantage and enhance the efficiency.

II. BASIC FUNCTIONS AND HYBRID DGTD FORMATION

Fig. 1 illustrates an example of via-structure with anti-pads.

This work is supported partly by the National Natural Science Foundation of China under Grant No. 61271033, National Excellent Youth Fund by NSFC under Grant No.61425010, and the Changjiang Scholar Program of Chinese Ministry of Education.

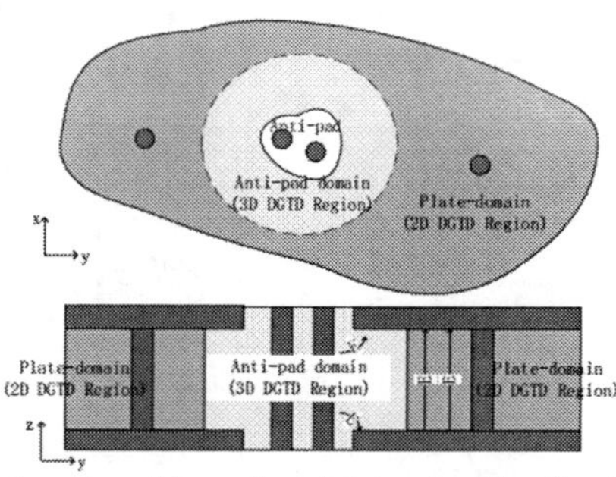

Fig. 1. Illustration of an arbitrary shaped plate pair with anti-pad structure.

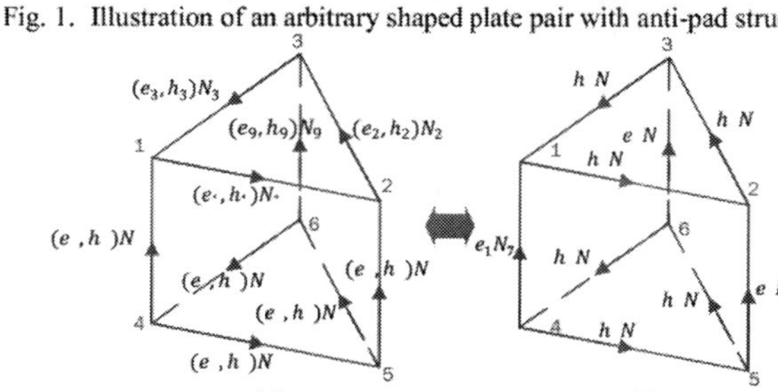

(a) (b)

Fig. 2. Geometrical illustration of (a) 3D and (b) 2D element.

Since triangular prism elements are simply extruding of triangle 2D elements, they share some similarities with each other, thus the coupling between them becomes easier. As show in Fig. 2, each triangular prism has nine edges and corresponding vector basis function N_i are defined as the same in [6]. As a whole, 18 unknowns for one single 3D triangular prism element, while 6 unknowns for 2D one.

To decrease unknowns and enhance efficiency, 2D triangle elements are introduced as equivalence in parallel-plate region, where the E and H field has only vertical and horizontal directions, respectively. That is, in 2D parallel-plate region:

$$\begin{cases} e_{1:6} = 0 \\ h_{1:3} = h_{4:6} \\ h_{7:9} = 0 \end{cases} \quad (1)$$

By conducting Galerkin testing method over the two first-order time-derivative Maxwell functions, using ADE method, it forms the DGTD semi-discrete matrix equations:

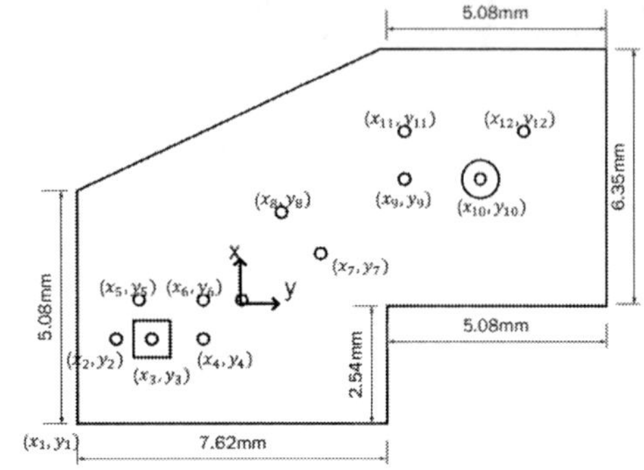

Fig. 3. Geometrical illustration the irregular plate pair with two antipads. The separation distance of the plates is 0.381mm, the radius of via barrel is 0.127mm, the radius of the sphere antipad (Port 1/2) is 0.381mm, the length and width of the rectangular antipad (Port 3/4) are both 0.762mm.

TABLE I

GEOMETRY PARAMETERS OF POWER GROUND IN FIG.3 (UNIT: MILLIMETER)

x_1	x_2	x_3	x_4	x_5	x_6	x_7	x_8	x_9	x_{10}	x_{11}	x_{12}
-3.81	-3	-2	-1	-2.5	-1	2	1	4	6	4	7
y_1	y_2	y_3	y_4	y_5	y_6	y_7	y_8	y_9	y_{10}	y_{11}	y_{12}
-2.54	-1	-1	-1	0	0	1	2	3	3	4	4

$$\bar{M}_e^i \frac{\partial e^i}{\partial t} = \bar{S}_e^i h^i + \sum_{f=1}^{n_i^f} \left(\bar{F}_{ee}^{ii,f} e_f^i + \bar{F}_{ee}^{ij,f} e_f^j + \bar{F}_{eh}^{ii,f} h_f^i + \bar{F}_{eh}^{ij,f} h_f^j \right) + \beta \cdot \bar{F}_e^{i,M_s} \quad (2)$$

$$\bar{M}_h^i \frac{\partial h^i}{\partial t} = -\bar{S}_h^i e^i + \sum_{f=1}^{n_i^f} \left(\bar{F}_{hh}^{ii,f} h_f^i + \bar{F}_{hh}^{ij,f} h_f^j + \bar{F}_{he}^{ii,f} e_f^i + \bar{F}_{he}^{ij,f} e_f^j \right) + \beta \cdot \bar{F}_h^{i,M_s} \quad (3)$$

$$\bar{M}_q^i \frac{\partial \gamma^i}{\partial t} + \frac{1}{\tau_q} \bar{M}_q^i \gamma^i = \frac{\epsilon_0 \Delta\epsilon_q}{\tau_q} \bar{M}_{c,q}^i \frac{\partial e^i}{\partial t} \quad (4)$$

Detail matrices expressions in above equations and the time iteration can be referred in [6].

It is crucial to determine which elements can be equalized to 2D ones while others cannot. Like in [7], a distance, d_{min}, is selected as criterion, considering high order modes decay exponentially, away from anti-pads.

I. NUMERICAL RESULTS

In this section, an irregular plate pair with two antipads (Fig. 3) is used to demonstrate the accuracy and efficiency.

The Debye-like dispersive material is calculated with $\epsilon_\infty = 2.2, \Delta\epsilon_1 = 2.0$, and $\tau_1 = 2.5 \times 10^{-10}$. For comparison, the results from the HFSS are shown in Fig. 4. As can be seen, very good agreements are achieved.

The efficiency of the hybrid method is then demonstrated. The total CPU time with different parameters are compared in Table II. As the number of mesh layer increases, the efficient improvement becomes manifest. Corresponding HFSS solution consumes 1108s. All experiment is done on a laptop with Intel i6700HQ CPU of 2.6 GHz, 8 threads, and 16 GB of memory.

II. CONCLUSION

In this paper, a 2D/3D hybrid DGTD algorithm is proposed for studying via structure in power-ground plate-pair. This hybrid algorithm is efficient because of simpler element, fewer unknowns and highly parallelizability. Numerical example demonstrating the accuracy and efficiency is presented.

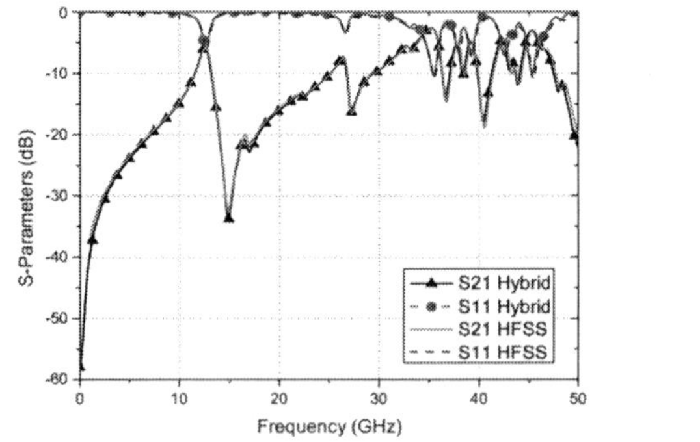

Fig. 4. Comparison of the S-Parameters by HFSS and present hybrid method with 1 mesh layer, distance criterion of 0.381mm

TABLE II

COMPARISON OF CPU TIME IN SECONDS UNDER DIFFERENT PARAMETERS

Mesh Layer Number	Hybrid method		3D DGTD
	d_{min} =0.381 mm	d_{min} =1.27 mm	d_{min} =8 mm
	number of 3D elements/total number of all elements *ratio*		
	7.82%	19.16%	100%
1	212s	306s	438s
3	615s	813s	2109s
5	908s	1317s	3464s

REFERENCES

[1] J. S. Hesthaven and T. Warburton, *Nodal discontinuous Galerkin methods: algorithms, analysis, and applications*. New York: Springer, 2008.

[2] P. Li and L. J. Jiang, "Integration of Arbitrary Lumped Multiport Circuit Networks Into the Discontinuous Galerkin Time-Domain Analysis," *IEEE Trans. Microw. Theory Tech.*, vol. 61, no. 7, pp. 2525–2534, Jul. 2013.

[3] P. Li, Y. Shi, L. J. Jiang, and H. Bağcı, "A Hybrid Time-Domain Discontinuous Galerkin-Boundary Integral Method for Electromagnetic Scattering Analysis," *IEEE Trans. Antennas Propag.*, vol. 62, no. 5, pp. 2841–2846, May 2014.

[4] P. Li, Y. Shi, L. J. Jiang, and H. Bağcı, "DGTD Analysis of Electromagnetic Scattering From Penetrable Conductive Objects With IBC," *IEEE Trans. Antennas Propag.*, vol. 63, no. 12, pp. 5686–5697, Dec. 2015.

[5] H. M. Lee, S. Gao, E. X. Liu, G. S. Samudra, and E. P. Li, "Two-Dimensional Discontinuous Galerkin Time-Domain Method for Modeling of Arbitrarily Shaped Power-Ground Planes," *IEEE Trans. Electromagn. Compat.*, vol. 57, no. 6, pp. 1744–1747, Dec. 2015.

[6] P. Li, L. J. Jiang, and H. Bağci, "Transient Analysis of Dispersive Power-Ground Plate Pairs With Arbitrarily Shaped Antipads by the DGTD Method With Wave Port Excitation," *IEEE Trans. Electromagn. Compat.*, vol. 59, no. 1, pp. 172–183, Feb. 2017.

[7] Y. J. Zhang *et al.*, "An Efficient Hybrid Finite-Element Analysis of Multiple Vias Sharing the Same Anti-Pad in an Arbitrarily Shaped Parallel-Plate Pair," *IEEE Trans. Microw. Theory Tech.*, vol. 63, no. 3, pp. 883–890, Mar. 2015.

[8] J. Hu *et al.*, "Domain Decomposition Method Based on Integral Equation for Solution of Scattering From Very Thin, Conducting Cavity," *IEEE Trans. Antennas Propag.*, vol. 62, no. 10, pp. 5344–5348, Oct. 2014.

[9] P. Li and L. J. Jiang, "Modeling of Magnetized Graphene From Microwave to THz Range by DGTD With a Scalar RBC and an ADE," *IEEE Trans. Antennas Propag.*, vol. 63, no. 10, pp. 4458–4467, Oct. 2015.

A Comparison of Numerical Mode-Matching Techniques for the Analysis of Well-Logging Tools

Guilherme S. Rosa, Maiquel S. Canabarro and José R. Bergmann
Center for Telecommunications Studies
Pontifical Catholic University of Rio de Janeiro
Rio de Janeiro, RJ 22451-900, Brazil
guilhermesimondarosa@cetuc.puc-rio.br,
canabarro@cetuc.puc-rio.br, bergmann@cetuc.puc-rio.br

Fernando L. Teixeira
ElectroScience Laboratory
The Ohio State University
Columbus, OH 43212, USA
teixeira.5@osu.edu

***Abstract*—Two numerical mode-matching (NMM) techniques are compared for the analysis of logging-while-drilling (LWD) tools within borehole crossing in geophysical formations. The logging tools as well as the borehole and the surrounding geophysical formation are modeled as a stratified medium in cylindrical coordinates. One NMM technique perform a vertical expansion of the fields and a mode-matching is used to incorporate the radial stratifications. In the second NMM formulation, the fields are first expanded in radial direction and subsequently matched along each axial boundary. We present validation results and a preliminary analysis of the accuracy of these two NMM approaches to model typical well-logging tools used for hydrocarbon exploration.**

***Keywords*—well logging; numerical mode-matching; logging-while-drilling**

I. Introduction

The numerical mode-matching (NMM) technique [1]-[5] can efficiently model three-dimensional (3-D) structures by means of a one-dimensional (1-D) modal expansion (typically found by means of a numerical method such as finite-differences (FD) or finite elements (FE)) in combination with an analytical boundary matching.

Logging-while-drilling (LWD) tools, as those illustrated in Fig. 1, are commonly modeled using a NMM formulation [1], [2], [6], whereby a FE discretization is used along each horizontal layer of a cylindrical stratified medium. In the vertical directions, an analytical mode-matching procedure is then used to match the fields between each horizontal layer. This approach will be denoted here as axial NMM (A-NMM). This approach is computationally much more efficient than 3-D brute-force techniques such as FD, FE and finite volumes [7]-[11], and, as such, it is more suited for integration into reconstruction (inversion) algorithms.

A typical LWD tool moves with the downhole drilling so that, at each new tool position along the well, it is necessary to recalculate several matrices incorporating the reflections from the horizontal layers above and below the source and the receiving antennas. This is a drawback of the A-NMM, as pointed out in [12]. In [12]-[15], an alternative NMM approach was proposed to circumvent this issue in LWD applications. As both transmitting and receiving LWD antennas are placed around a metallic mandrel inside the borehole and typically have the same radius, they are located in the same radial layer regardless of the the axial position of the tool in the logging well. Therefore, it becomes more efficient to first perform a mode expansion of the fields along vertical direction and then a mode-matching along each radial layer. This approach will be denoted here as R-NMM. Although the R-NMM presents a series of advantages to model smooth holes, in this paper we shown that the presence of roughness in the borehole wall (see Fig. 1b) can significantly affect the efficiency of this NMM approach.

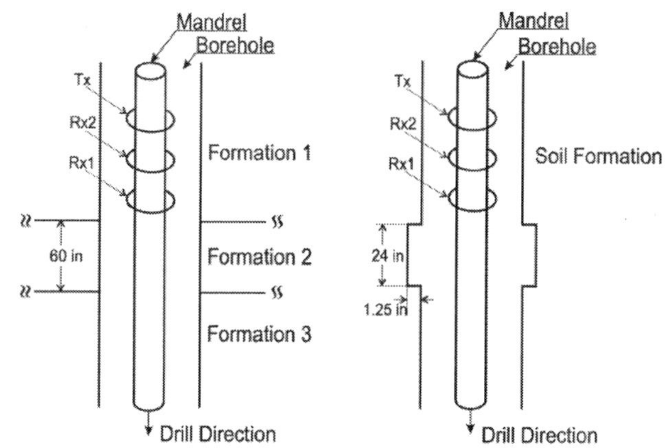

(a) (b)

Fig. 1. Geometry of a triaxial LWD tool placed around a metalic mandrel. A three-vertical-layer formation with a smooth borehole is illustrated in (a) while a logging well with hole rugosity is depicted in (b).

II. Formulation Overview

In our R-NMM algorithm we employ a methodology similar to that presented in [8], [15], but using instead cubic B-splines functions to expand the fields in the axial direction, with multiple knots to improve the fields representation near the axial interfaces. In this way, a coarser mesh can be used while maintaining the same accuracy. The A-NMM implementation employed here follows [1], [4], [5] but instead of expanding the fields along the radial direction using local basis function, it uses a judicious choice of cylindrical eigenfunctions.

III. Results and Discussion

We first consider a smooth borehole traversing an Earth formation with three horizontal layers, as shown in Fig. 1a. The LWD tool consist of one transmitter operating at 500 kHz and two receiver coil antennas. The axial positions of the transmitter, and receivers RX2 and RX1 are z_T, z_T+24 [in] and z_T +30 [in], respectively, where 1 [in] = 2.54 x 10^{-2} m. The conductivity of formations 1, 2 and 3 are 1 S/m, 0.01 S/m and 1 S/m, respectively. The borehole is filled with a lossy mud with conductivity equal to 2 S/m. For more details on this geometry, see [7], [8]. Fig. 2 shows the ratio of the RX2 and RX1 voltages (e.m.f.). Good agreement is observed among the R-NMM and A-NMM results and those from [7]. Since there is no variation on the borehole diameter, the R-NMM is a more natural choice to solve this problem.

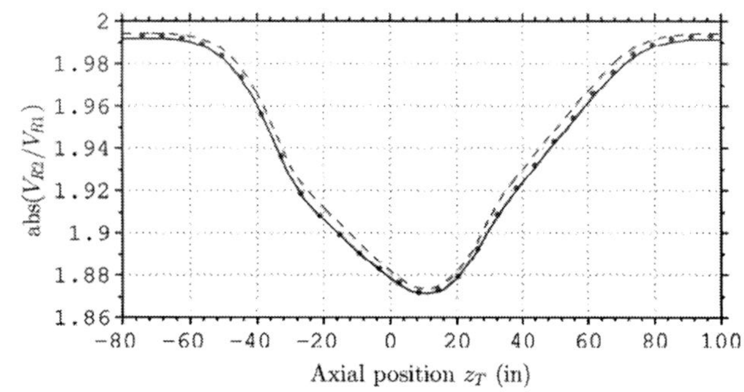

Fig. 2. Voltage amplitude ratio for a triaxial LWD logging tool operating at 500 kHz inside a smoth borehole. The results from the R-NMM and A-NMM are indicated by solid and dashed lines, respectively. The small dots are results from [7].

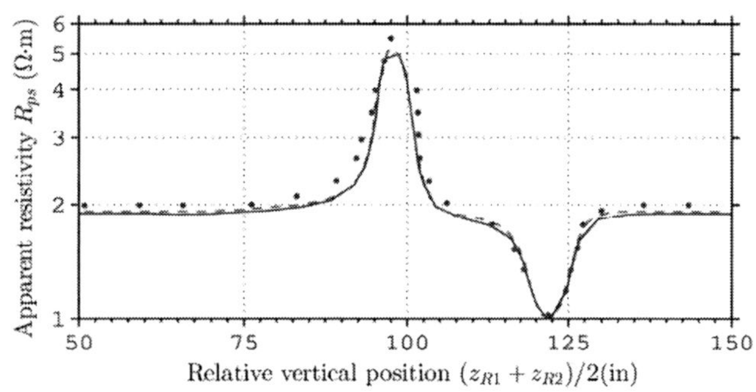

Fig. 3. Voltage amplitude ratio for a triaxial LWD logging tool operating at 2 MHz inside a rugose borehole. The results from the R-NMM and A-NMM are indicated by solid and dashed lines, respectively. The small dots are results from [16].

Next, we consider the effects of roughness on the borehole wall, as depicted in Fig. 1b. The LWD tool operates at 2 MHz, and again we consider one transmitter and two receiving coil antennas axially placed at z_T, z_T+28 in and z_T+34 in, respectively, inside a borehole with resistivity 0.1 Ω.m, surrounded by a soil formation with resistivity 2 Ω.m. For more details on this geometry, see [16]. Again, good agreement are observed between both R-NMM and A-NMM approaches versus those in [16], but differently to the smooth borehole wall case, the A-NMM appears more suitable to model rough borehole problems. By incorporated multiple knots at discontinuities in the R-MMM, better agreement is obtained with less overall number of knots.

Acknowledgment

G. S. R. and M. S. C. thank support from the Brazilian Agencies CNPq and CAPES through the doctoral fellowships 140236/2013-9, 141847/2016-6, 000316/2015-06, 2444/2011-9 and 150454/2016-3.

References

[1] W. C. Chew *et al.*, "Diffraction of axisymmetric waves in a borehole by bed boundary discontinuities," *Geophys.*, vol. 49, pp. 1586–1595, 1984.

[2] W. C. Chew and B. Anderson, "Propagation of electromagnetic waves through geological beds in a geophysical probing environment," *Radio Sci.*, vol. 20, pp. 611–621, 1985.

[3] W. C. Chew, *Waves and Fields in Inhomogeneous Media*. New York, NY, USA: Van Nostrand Reinhold, 1990.

[4] Q. H. Liu and W. C. Chew, "Diffraction of nonaxisymmetric waves in cylindrically layered media by horizontal discontinuities," *Radio Sci.*, vol. 27, no. 5, pp. 569–581, 1992.

[5] Q.-H. Liu, "Electromagnetic field generated by an off-axis source in a cylindrically layered medium with an arbitrary number of horizontal discontinuities," *Geophys.*, vol. 58, pp. 616–625, 1993.

[6] H. Wang, H. Tao, J. Yao, and Y. Zhang, "Efficient and reliable simulation of multicomponent induction logging response in horizontally stratified inhomogeneous ti formations by numerical mode matching method," *IEEE Trans. Geosci. Remote Sens.*, vol. 50, no. 9, pp. 3383--3395, Sep. 2012.

[7] Y.-K. Hue and F. L. Teixeira, "FDTD simulation of MWD electromagnetic tools in large-contrast geophysical formations," *IEEE Trans. Magn.*, vol. 40, pp. 1456–1459, Mar. 2004.

[8] Y.-K. Hue, F. L. Teixeira, L. San Martin, and M. Bittar, 'Three-dimensional simulation of eccentric LWD tool response in boreholes through dipping formations,' *IEEE Trans. Geosci. Remote Sens.*, vol. 43, no. 2, pp. 257-268, 2005.

[9] H. O. Lee and F. L. Teixeira, "Cylindrical FDTD analysis of LWD tools through anisotropic dipping-layered earth media," *IEEE Trans. Geosci. Remote Sens.*, vol. 45, pp. 383–388, 2007.

[10] L. Hui, S. Y. Ze, and Z. X. Fang, "Numerical simulation of resistivity LWD tool based on higher-order vector finite element," *Journal of Petroleum Exploration and Production Technology*, pp.1–11, 2015.

[11] M. S. Novo, L. C. da Silva, and F. L. Teixeira, "Three-dimensional finite-volume analysis of directional resistivity logging sensors," *IEEE Trans. Geosci. Remote Sens.*, vol. 48, no. 3, pp. 1151–1158, Mar. 2010.

[12] D. M. Pai, "Induction log modeling using vertical eigenstates," *IEEE Trans. Geosci. Remote Sens.*, vol. 29, no. 2, pp. 209–213, Mar. 1991.

[13] D. M. Pai, J. Ahmad, and W. D. Kennedy, "Two-dimensional induction log modeling using a coupled-mode, multiple-reflection series method," *Geophysics*, vol. 58, no. 4, pp. 466–474, Apr. 1993.

[14] J. Li and L. C. Shen, "Vertical eigenstate method for simulation of induction and MWD resistivity tools," *IEEE Trans. Geosci. Remote Sens.*, vol. 31, no. 2, pp. 399–406, Mar. 1993.

[15] Y.-K. Hue and F. L. Teixeira, "Numerical mode-matching method for tilted-coil antennas in cylindrically layered anisotropic media with multiple horizontal beds," *IEEE Trans. Geosci. Remote Sens.*, vol. 45, pp. 2451–2462, 2007.

[16] B. Clark et al., "A Dual Depth resistivity measurement for FEWD," in *SPWLA Twenty-Ninth Annual Logging Symposium*, June 5–8, 1988.

Summary of the Latest Extensions to the Electromagnetic Field Solver Package FEKO

Andrés G. Aguilar, Ulrich Jakobus, Mary Longtin, Marlize Schoeman,
Wilco Strydom, and Johann J. van Tonder
Altair Engineering, Inc.
Troy, MI, USA
jakobus@altair.com

***Abstract*—This paper summarises the latest extensions to the electromagnetic field solver package FEKO. Advanced parallelisation options for full wave methods (MLFMM, FDTD), speed improvements for cable harness modelling, extensions to the asymptotic RL-GO solver, and improved mode tracking for CMA are discussed.**

Keywords—MLFMM; FDTD; cable harness modelling; RL-GO; mode tracking; CMA

I. Introduction

In order to respond to the ever increasing demands and challenges in the area of computational electromagnetics (CEM) when applied to complex and large scale, real world problems, available algorithms must be refined and improved in terms of applicability, run-time and memory footprint. In this paper we introduce a few such extensions that were recently added to the CEM code FEKO.

II. Specific Improvements of FEKO

A. Parallel MLFMM memory scaling

The parallel MLFMM in FEKO is based on a distributed memory scheme using MPI, so that it also works on clusters. It is well known [1] that for many processors the MLFMM memory scaling efficiency is reduced. For a typical MLFMM example with 8 million unknowns executed on 144 cores, the total memory required for the transfer functions can be as much as 10 times larger than the memory required for the near-field matrix. An elegant solution to this problem is to use MPI-3 shared memory (SHM) programming. The MPI-SHM formulation was designed to be compatible with existing MPI codes, as compared to the more difficult hybrid MPI/OpenMP implementations. Using MPI-SHM only a single copy of the transfer function tables is stored which can be accessed by all processors. In addition, the computation of these tables can now be done in parallel, with every processor filling only its own unique part of the tables. As example, for a 6000 λ long structure, when executed in parallel using 20 cores, the total memory requirement (sum of the memory for all processes/nodes) can be reduced from 617 GByte to 387 GByte by using this MPI-SHM technique. The saving is even higher when using more cores / CPUs on one cluster node.

B. MPI Parallisation of FDTD

The FDTD solver in FEKO supported already GPU acceleration and shared memory parallel systems. Support for MPI based distributed memory systems (clusters) has been added. The voxel grid is divided in blocks among the available processes, and each process is responsible for the time-domain update of the electric and magnetic fields in its block.

Fig. 1 shows an example of the performance improvement from the FDTD solver using up to 20 parallel processes.

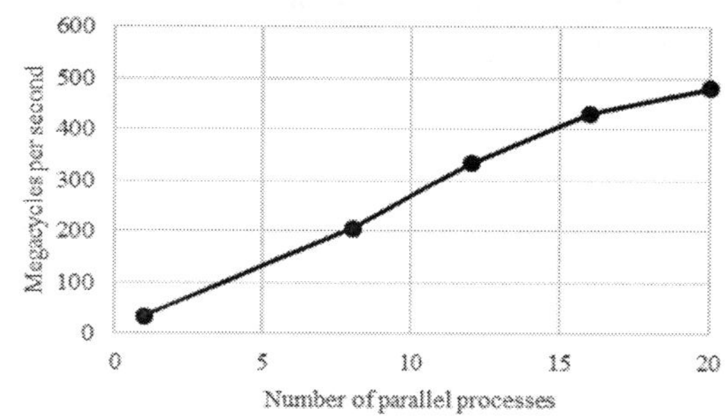

Fig. 1. Performance of the MPI based parallel FDTD solver.

C. Speed improvements for cable harness modelling

FEKO supports the solution of coupled EM field / cable harness problems. Several phases in the cable harness calculation have been optimized. Significant speedup factors are observed depending on the cable problem (harness details and cross section), the solution request (radiation or irradiation coupling) and the frequency range. Table I illustrates the speedup obtained for three typical cable cross sections.

TABLE I. Speedup Factor Obtained for Typical Cross Sesctions

	Examples		
	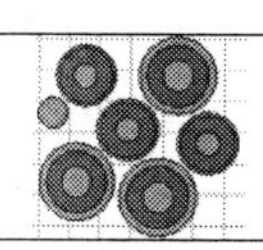	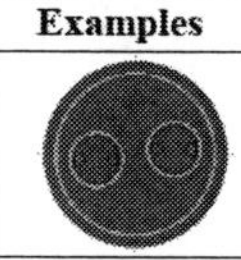	
No. of segments	500	800	600
No. of nodes	52027	73619	14403
No. of components	152535	113624	33613
Speedup factor	2.1	15.3	34.4

D. Extensions to RL-GO

The Ray-Launching Geometrical Optics (RL-GO) method [2] is an asymptotic high frequency technique very suitable for electrically large objects. With RL-GO rays are shot from every source on an adaptive grid in all directions [3], and are reflected and/or transmitted. In FEKO in the past, equivalent Huygens sources resulting from the ray tracing were stored in memory for later use during the field computation phase. A feature was added to compute the fields on the fly avoiding the storage of the Huygens sources resulting in drastic memory savings.

For RL-GO the computation time grows linearly with the number of sources. This makes the use of aperture near field sources with RL-GO rather time consuming, as typically the aperture may need hundreds or thousands of field samples. Thus, in order to accelerate the ray-tracing, an automatic grouping and transformation of an aperture near field source into one or more equivalent spherical mode sources has been implemented.

As an example, a near field aperture is surrounded by a dielectric radome. Fig. 2 compares the computed far field pattern using RL-GO in FEKO 14.0.411 (all near field samples acting as source) and the equivalent source transformation into one spherical source with RL-GO in FEKO 14.0.430. Also the reference solution with MLFMM is indicated. Table II shows how the runtime and memory is greatly improved.

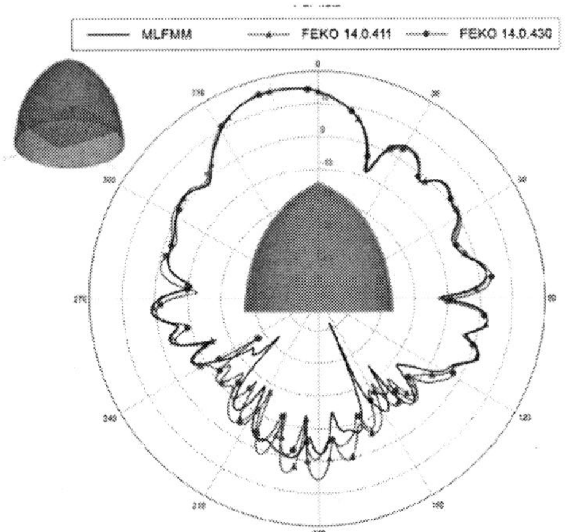

Fig. 2. Far field of a near field aperture covered by a dielectric radome.

TABLE II. RUNTIME AND MEMORY OF AN APERTURE NEAR FIELD COVERED BY A RADOME AT 9.5GHZ

FEKO 14.411		**FEKO 14.430**	
Runtime	**Memory**	**Runtime**	**Memory**
2.6 hours	11.8 GByte	29.3 sec	60.9 MByte

E. Characteristic mode tracking

Characteristic Mode Analysis (CMA) was pioneered by Garbacz, Harrington, and Mautz in the early 1970s and is experiencing a revived and growing interest. The analysis requires resolving a set of frequency dependent eigenvalue problems, with solutions at different frequency steps being independent of one another, and having no inherent correlation. Modal tracking is then applied, whereby one attempts to define a measure of similarity between modal eigenvectors and eigenvalues. In FEKO a bounded linear correlation of eigenvectors at adjacent frequencies is used to perform tracking [4]. This tracking approach often requires a much finer frequency discretization than that of the MoM to accurately capture higher order mode behaviour. Furthermore, it is often observed that two eigenvalue traces approaching each other may have a period of coupling where modal current distributions briefly morph before the modes experience a *cross avoidance* [5]. Continuous development within FEKO has resulted in stabilized higher order mode tracking, better tracking over larger frequency increments, and increased tracking robustness at points of modal interaction. Fig. 1 shows an example where the new tracking correctly resolves both cross avoidances.

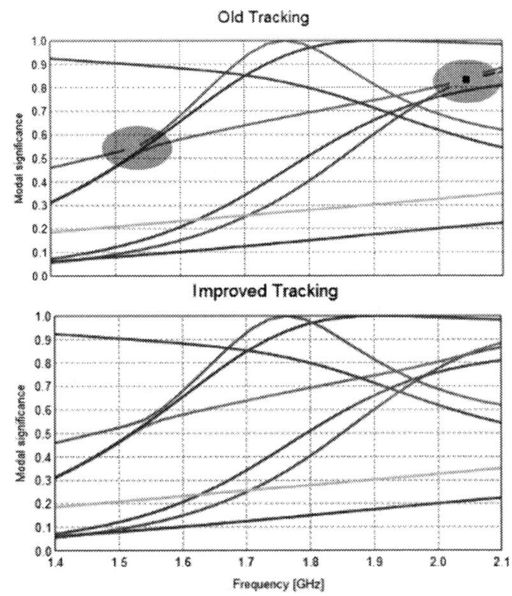

Fig. 3. FEKO tracking algorithm correctly resolving two modal interaction points where tracking previously failed.

References

[1] S. Velamparambil, W.C. Chew and J. Song, “10 million unknowns: Is it that big?”, IEEE Antennas and Propagation Magazine, vol. 45, no. 2, pp. 43-58, April 2003.

[2] H. Ling, R. C. Chou, and S. W. Lee, “Shooting and Bouncing Rays: calculating the RCS of an arbitrarily shaped cavity,” IEEE Trans. on Antennas and Propagation, vol. 37, no. 2, pp. 194–205, Feb. 1989

[3] A.G. Aguilar, J. van Tonder, U. Jakobus and F. Illenseer, “Overview of recent advances in the electromagnetic field solver FEKO,” 9th European Conference on Antennas and Propagation (EuCAP), Lisbon, Aug. 2015.

[4] D. J. Ludick, U. Jakobus and M. Vogel, "A tracking algorithm for the eigenvectors calculated with characteristic mode analysis," 8th European Conference on Antennas and Propagation (EuCAP), pp. 569-572, 2014.

[5] K. R. Schab, J. M. Outwater, M. W. Young and J. T. Bernhard, "Eigenvalue crossing avoidance in characteristic modes," IEEE Trans. Antennas Propagation, vol. 64, no. 7, pp. 2617-2627, July 2016.

Wave Propagation and Radio Network Planning Software WinProp added to the Electromagnetic Solver Package FEKO

Reiner Hoppe, Gerd Wölfle, Ulrich Jakobus
Altair Engineering GmbH
Böblingen, Germany
reiner.hoppe@altair.de

***Abstract*—The WinProp software has been added to the Electromagnetic Solver FEKO. WinProp includes sophisticated ray-optical and empirical wave propagation models for computing the radio coverage as well as for the radio channel analysis. The supported scenarios range from large rural or suburban areas to dense urban city centers, and even complex indoor scenarios can be predicted. For the detailed network planning modules for almost all air interfaces (incl. LTE, WLAN) are available, which compute the overall signal and interference situation by superposing the contributions from multiple transmitting sites.**

Keywords—radio channel; radio network planning; ray tracing; wave propagation modeling

I. INTRODUCTION

The future information society will rely on mobile communications to provide a wide variety of applications including completely new industrial and professional services with diverse requirements. In order to meet these challenges significantly higher mobile data throughputs, much higher number of connected devices, and reduced end-to-end latencies shall be supported as feasible today, at a similar cost and power consumption level.

For the installation of (mobile) radio systems, wave propagation models are necessary to determine propagation characteristics for any arbitrary configuration. The predictions are required for a proper coverage planning, the determination of multipath effects as well as for interference and cell calculations, which are the basis for the high-level network planning process. In a cellular network this planning process includes e.g. the prediction of the received power for each transmitting antenna. With the evolution of wireless broadband services in 4G and 5G systems or in Wireless Local Area Networks (WLAN) the wideband properties (e.g. delay spread, angular spread and impulse response) of the mobile radio channel become more and more important for system design and the site-specific planning process.

A specific challenge is to provide realistic and high quality wave propagation models that are required for a successful development and optimization of the evolving radio access networks. In order to cope with the expected exceptional growth of wireless communications traffic, both more efficient transmission schemes and additional spectrum allocations are needed. In this context various scenarios are of interest which range from indoor office over dense urban areas to new applications for the device-to-device communication as e.g. in the vehicular domain to avoid traffic accidents and improve traffic efficiency. Hence wave propagation prediction methods are required covering the full range of potential scenarios and special environments like tunnels, stadiums or along highways.

II. SIMULATION METHODOLOGY

A. Wave Propagation Models

The mobile radio channel in urban and indoor areas is characterized by multi-path propagation as shown in Fig. 1. Dominant propagation phenomena in these scenarios are the shadowing behind obstacles, the reflection at the walls of buildings, the wave guiding effects (due to multiple reflections) in street canyons or corridors, and the diffractions at vertical and horizontal wedges. The ray tracing models used for the deterministic modeling of the multi-path situation are based on the evaluation of 3D building data representing the given environment [1].

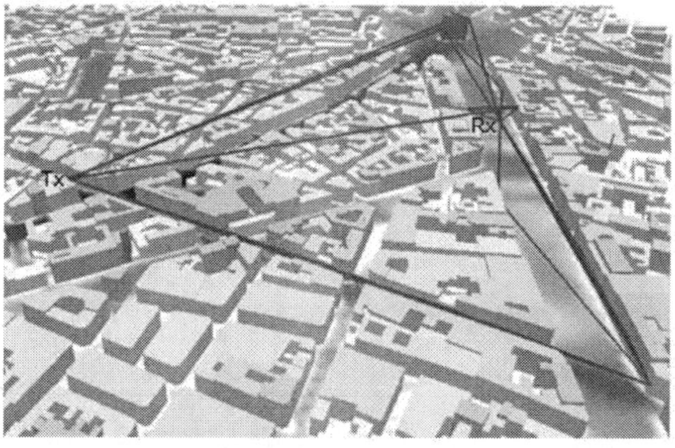

Fig. 1. 3D vector database with propagation paths between transmitter and receiver in an urban environment.

The WinProp propagation models are fully three dimensional, i.e. consider 3D object data and compute all rays in 3D. The prediction of the path loss along the ray is computed either with the uniform theory of diffraction (UTD) and with the Fresnel coefficients for the reflections or with an empirical interaction model. In order to accelerate the time-consuming path determination the Intelligent Ray Tracing (IRT) model [2] can be utilized, which is based on a single pre-processing of the building data. For pure predictions of the radio coverage the unique dominant path model (DPM) can be applied which combines high accuracy with short computation time [3].

B. 3D Antenna Patterns

Besides the obstacles present in the corresponding environment (e.g. buildings in an urban scenario) the performance of the wireless transmission is also significantly impacted by the performance of the transmitting and receiving antennas. Therefore it is important to consider 3D antenna patterns describing the antenna characteristic in all directions and furthermore to combine these antenna patterns with the above mentioned wave propagation models.

Electromagnetic simulation can be used to design the antennas themselves, and also to compute the radiation characteristic in terms of a 3D antenna pattern. For this purpose the various solvers included in FEKO can be applied. The resulting 3D antenna patterns describe the antenna characteristic in the far field and can then be considered within the WinProp wave propagation models.

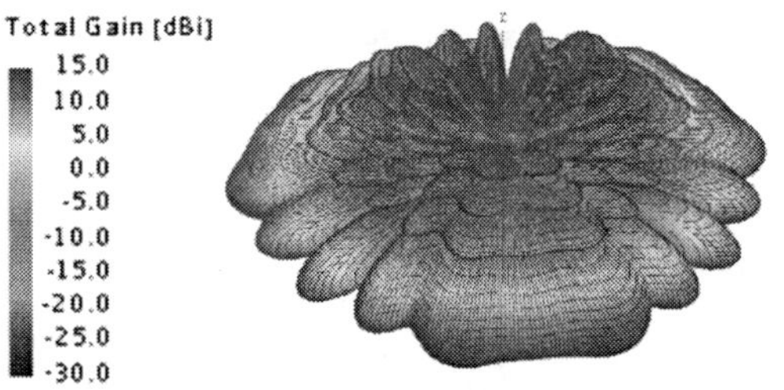

Fig. 2. 3D pattern of an outdoor 3-sector antenna at 1.8 GHz.

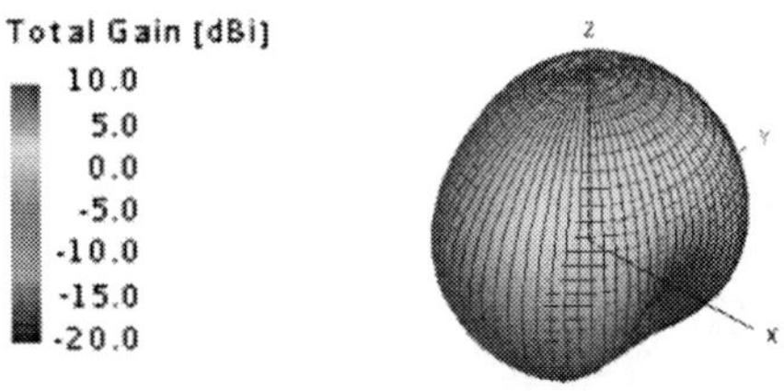

Fig. 3. 3D pattern of an indoor WLAN antenna at 5.8 GHz.

C. Test Cases and Results

Two test cases have been selected in order to show the link between FEKO and WinProp. This paper focuses on two classic scenarios of interest – an outdoor 3-sector antenna mounted on a mast, and an indoor WLAN antenna.

The type of antenna selected for the outdoor analysis is the high gain bi-quad array antenna [4] for a 3-sector LTE base station, operating at 1.8 GHz. The radiation pattern for this antenna as computed with FEKO is shown in Fig. 2. For the indoor scenario a printed monopole antenna [5] on high impedance surface is used as designed and optimized in FEKO, in order to achieve a low-profile antenna with high gain at 5.8 GHz. The corresponding antenna pattern is shown in Fig 3.

The Fig. 4 shows the urban radio coverage in S band computed in WinProp with a ray-optical wave propagation model considering the shown outdoor 3-sector antenna, and Fig. 5 shows the indoor radio coverage for the mentioned WLAN antenna. Verifications against measurement data confirm the high accuracy of the WinProp propagation models.

Fig. 4. Urban coverage for outdoor antenna at 1.8 GHz computed in WinProp with ray-optical model.

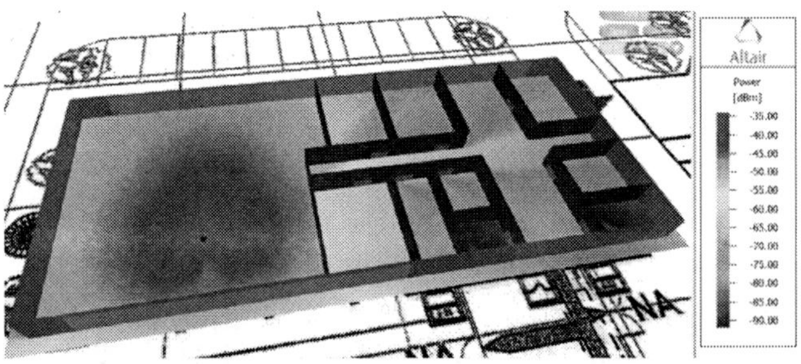

Fig. 5. Indoor coverage for WLAN antenna at 5.8 GHz computed in WinProp evaluating 3D building data with different materials and subdivisions.

REFERENCES

[1] R. Hoppe, G. Wölfle, P. Wertz, F. M. Landstorfer, "Advanced Ray-Optical Wave Propagation Modelling for Urban and Indoor Environments Including Wideband Properties", European Transactions on Telecommunications (ETT), January/February 2003 (Number 01/2003), January 2003.

[2] T. Rautiainen, G. Wölfle, and R. Hoppe: "Verifying Path Loss and Delay Spread Predictions of a 3D Ray Tracing Propagation Model in Urban Environments", 56th IEEE Vehicular Technology Conference (VTC) 2002 - Fall, Vancouver, Canada, September 2002.

[3] R. Wahl, G. Wölfle: "Combined Urban and Indoor Network Planning Using the Dominant Path Propagation Model", 1st European Conference on Antennas and Propagation (EuCAP 2006), Nice, France, November 2006.

[4] D. Campbell and C.J. Reddy: "Antenna Design Considerations for LTE Enabled Base Stations", 2015 IEEE International Symposium on Antennas and Propagation, Vancouver, July 2015.

[5] G. Gampala, R. Sammeta and C.J. Reddy: "A thin, low-profile antenna using a novel high impedance ground plane", Microwave Journal, July 2010,

The Effect of Fabrication Tolerances on a Suspended Plate Antenna

William O. Coburn and Seth A. McCormick
US Army Research Laboratory
Adelphi, MD. USA
william.o.coburn.civ@mail.mil; seth.a.mccormick.civ@mail.mil

***Abstract*—A suspended plate antenna (SPA) with L-probe feed is of interest as an efficient non-contacting feed method. It maintains high efficiency even when the plate is constructed of poorly conducting materials such as conductive inks. An SPA is designed at 10 GHz where fabrication tolerances can have an impact on performance. The SPA as designed has 36 percent impedance bandwidth and 8 to 9 dBi of gain. The prototype has a somewhat different impedance bandwidth indicating that the as-built plate is slightly tilted and different in size owing to fabrication errors. A tolerance analysis is shown to confirm the sensitivity of this design to fabrication accuracy at high frequency. The CEM model is adjusted to better represent the prototype antenna for a simple metal plate on foam support and also for a microstrip version on a thin substrate.**

Keywords—suspended plate antenna; L-probe feed; tolerance analysis; characteristic modes

I. Introduction

This paper presents the design, modeling, and measurement of a suspended plate antenna (SPA) at 10 GHz. The design has an impedance bandwidth (IBW) of 36 percent and up to 9 dBi of gain over the frequency band of 8.4 to 10.6 GHz. The prototype has somewhat different input impedance so a tolerance analysis was conducted with the computational model. The results indicate the sensitivity of the SPA impedance to fabrication errors at this frequency.

Two different antenna geometries were considered: the SPA using a 6061 aluminum plate on foam support and a microstrip version using 0.5 mm Duroid R3003 substrate. Both were simple to construct, but at these frequencies the measured impedance was different than predicted. By adjusting the model for up to ±10% fabrication error the difference could be explored to better determine the best fabrication method.

The next section details the background and design of the SPA where the radiation mechanism over the IBW is not well described in the literature. The following section details the modeling and measurement comparisons for the reflection coefficient and radiation pattern. Modeling was performed using the Method of Moments (MoM) solver in the commercial computational electromagnetics (CEM) code FEKO (www.feko.info), and measurements were taken in a Near Field Range. The final section concludes the paper with a tolerance analysis and a model for the as-built prototypes.

II. Antenna Design

The SPA can be designed similar to the theory for a typical microstrip patch antenna in the case where the substrate relative permittivity approaches unity and the thickness becomes large. Having smaller relative permittivity and larger ground separation than a patch antenna, gives the SPA the potential to have a larger IBW and gain than a conventional patch antenna. Also, not needing a substrate can make the SPA simpler and cheaper to build [1]. Variations of the slotted patch can be designed to have similar performance.

There are several different ways to feed an SPA such as with a microstrip, vertical probe, and aperture coupled much like a patch [1]. The feeding method with the broadest impedance bandwidth is one using a non-connecting method like the aperture coupled, but a simpler method using an L-probe has been reported in the literature [1, 2]. The L-probe fed SPA can have 36 percent impedance bandwidth and 8 – 9 dBi of gain. Its disadvantage is poor cross-polarization isolation in the H-plane pattern owing to probe radiation in addition to exciting higher order modes [3, 4]. The field and current distributions show the TM10 mode but using the patch antenna design equations provides only the high frequency edge of the IBW not the center frequency. The theory and design for the center frequency and lower edge of the IBW are not well described in the literature but will be discussed in the presentation with a characteristic mode analysis (CMA). The CMA indicates two dominant modes for the SPA compared to a single mode for a patch antenna.

The SPA in this paper is a model from Antenna Magus (www.antennamagus.com) shown in Fig. 1. The as-designed antenna is L-probe fed with dimensions 11.25 mm x 13.5 mm (W x L) and is constructed from 6061 aluminum with thickness 1.575 mm. The ground plane is four times the plate size being a 54 mm x 45 mm sheet of 6061 with the same thickness. The L-probe is centered on the ground plane and is constructed from #26 AWG wire (0.45 mm diameter) inserted in a panel mount SMA. The height of the L-probe is 2.3 mm with a length after the bend of 5.175 mm. The plate edge is offset 1.35 mm from the feed point and vertically spaced 2.97 mm from the ground. These dimensions are used to construct a 6061 plate adhesive mounted on foam support and also for a 0.5 mm Duroid R3003 substrate bolted to a Duroid 5870 support shown in Fig. 2. In both prototypes the measured reflection coefficient is somewhat different than predicted with a different frequency response. Using the model to explore fabrication variations shows the sensitivity of this design at 10 GHz to fabrication tolerances.

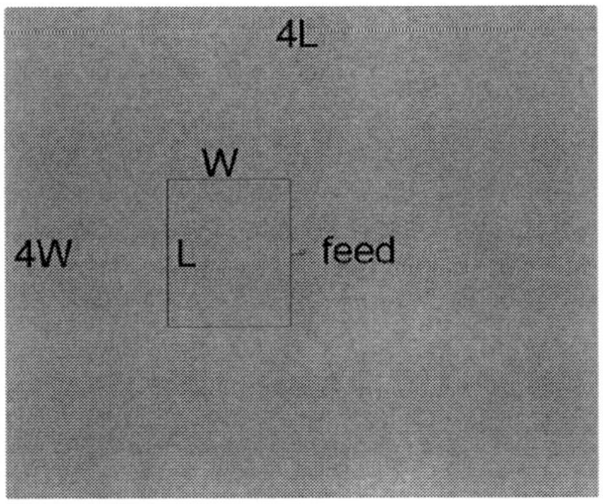

Fig. 1. SPA top view showing feed centered on ground plane.

Fig. 2. Thick plate (left) and thin substrate (right) SPAs as-built.

III. Simulation and Measurement Results

The simulated and measured reflection coefficient comparison is shown in Fig. 3 for the thick plate SPA. Based on a tolerance analysis by simulation the model was modified to obtain good agreement between simulation and measurement. The probe height and length were increased 8.7% while the plate dimensions were reduced 2% and tilted up 2° to better represent the foam supported plate (see Fig. 2). The ground plane is four times the plate size so it was also reduced 2%. The measured impedance bandwidth is 3.75 GHz (39%) being somewhat larger than predicted.

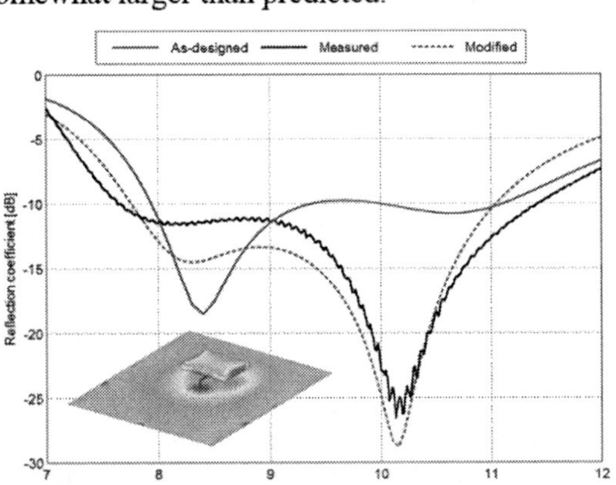

Fig. 3. Simulated and measured reflection coefficient for the thick SPA.

The simulated and measured reflection coefficient comparison is shown in Fig. 4 for the thin substrate SPA. Based on a tolerance analysis by simulation the model was modified to obtain better agreement between simulation and measurement. The probe height and length were increased 8.7% and 6.3%, respectively. The plate width was reduced 6% while the length was increased 6% and tilted up 2° to better represent the thin substrate SPA. The result for a 10% error in the plate dimension is included but reduces the IBW to less than measured. The measured impedance bandwidth is 3.13 GHz (31.9%) being less than the as-designed result but similar to the revised model with 6% error. The radiation patterns are not shown here, but will be shown in the conference briefing. There was found to be fair agreement between simulation and measurement in a Near Field Range.

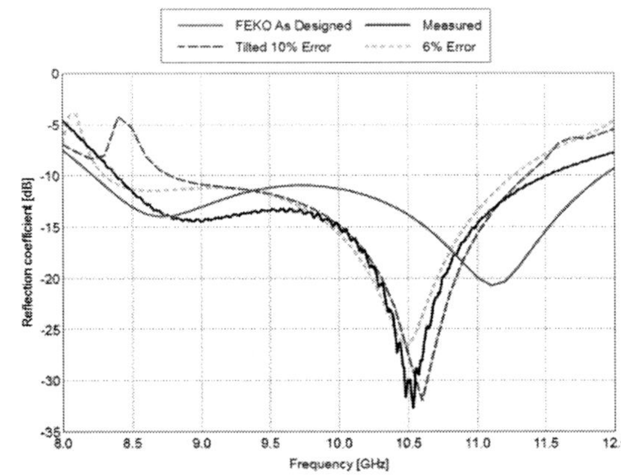

Fig. 4. Simulated with dimensional errors and measured reflection coefficient for the thin substrate SPA.

IV. Conclusion

The SPA is a simple, lightweight antenna with high gain (8 – 9 dBi) and good impedance bandwidth (~32 percent). The approach has the potential to efficiently excite even poorly conducting plates. The results indicate that the small antenna size makes it sensitive to fabrication tolerances. Although not shown in this paper, additional simulations with a thin carbon nanotube patch on R3003 and a Germanium Telluride (GeTe) patch on glass substrate will be shown in the conference briefing. Alternative designs such as slotted or stacked patches require additional machining which can be problematic for these type materials. The results of such simulations showed only a small adverse impact on the antenna performance. But at X-band and above tight fabrication tolerances will be required.

References

[1] J. L. Volakis, Antenna Engineering Handbook, 4th ed., New York: McGraw-Hill, 2007, pp. 37.2-37.10.

[2] C. L. Mak, K. M. Luk, K. F. Lee, and Y. L. Chow, "Experimental Study of a Microstrip Patch Antenna with an L-Shaped Probe," IEEE Trans. On Ant. and Prop., vol. 48, no. 5, May 2000.

[3] Z. N. Chen and M. Y. W. Chia, "Experimental Study on Radiation Performance of Probe-Fed Suspended Plate Antennas," IEEE Trans. On Ant. and Prop., vol. 51, no. 8, Aug. 2003.

[4] Z. N. Chen and M. Y. W. Chia, "Design of Broadband Probe-Fed Plate Antenna with Stub," IEEE Proc. Microw. Ant. Prop. Vol. 148, no. 4, Aug. 2001.

An Accurate and Efficient Analysis of Very Large but Narrow Zero-Thickness PEC Annular Rings

M. Lucido, M.D. Migliore, G. Panariello, D. Pinchera, C. Santomassimo, and F. Schettino
Department of Electrical and Information Engineering (D.I.E.I.)
University of Cassino and Southern Lazio
03043 Cassino, Italy

***Abstract*—In the analysis of the scattering by very large but narrow perfectly electrically conducting (PEC) annular rings, high frequency methods suffer due to the multiple diffraction by the edges and full-wave methods usually require an enormous number of mesh-cells to reconstruct the solution. In order to overcome this problem, in this paper a novel guaranteed and fast convergent full-wave method is proposed.**

Keywords—annular ring, electromagnetic scattering, guaranteed convergence.

I. Introduction

The analysis of the electromagnetic scattering by very large but narrow PEC annular rings is a very difficult task. As a matter of fact, high frequency methods, which would seem to be the most appropriate to deal with the problem at hand, suffer due to the multiple diffraction by the edges of the annular ring [1]. On the other hand, full-wave methods are in general inefficient in terms of computation time and storage requirement when large objects are considered. Moreover, for techniques for which it is not possible to apply Fredholm theory, the convergence cannot be generally guaranteed [2].

Guaranteed convergence is achieved in the papers [3]-[13] devoting to the analysis of propagation, radiation and scattering by PEC and dielectric polygonal cross-section cylinders and canonical shape PEC surfaces. In these papers the obtained integral equation is recast as an infinite matrix equation at which Fredholm alternative can be applied by means of Galerkin method with a complete set of expansion functions reconstructing the expected physical behaviour of the unknowns that makes the most singular part of the integral operator invertible with a continuous two-side inverse [14].

The same line of reasoning are followed in this paper to analyze the scattering by a zero-thickness PEC annular ring. As will be shown to follow, the proposed method is accurate and efficient in analyzing very large but narrow annular rings.

II. Formulation and Solution of the Problem

Let us consider a zero-thickness PEC annular ring in free space of internal radius ρ_1, external radius ρ_2, whose axis coincides with the z axis of a cylindrical coordinate system (ρ,ϕ,z) with the origin at the centre of the ring. An incident field induces a surface current on the scatterer surface. The revolution symmetry of the scatterer with respect to the z axis suggests to expand the surface current in cylindrical harmonics. By imposing the tangential components of the electric field to be vanishing on the scatterer surface, an integral equation in the vector Hankel transform (VHT) domain is obtained [13]

$$\frac{1}{2\pi}\sum_{n=-\infty}^{+\infty} e^{jn\phi}\int_0^{+\infty}\underline{\underline{\mathbf{H}}}^{(n)}(w\rho)\underline{\underline{\mathbf{G}}}(w)\underline{\tilde{\mathbf{J}}}^{(n)}(w)w\,dw=-\underline{\mathbf{E}}^{inc}(\rho,\phi,z=0) \quad (1)$$

for $\rho_1\leq\rho\leq\rho_2$, where $\underline{\mathbf{E}}^{inc}(\rho,\phi,z)$ is the incident field,

$$\underline{\tilde{\mathbf{J}}}^{(n)}(w)=\begin{pmatrix} d/dw \\ n/w \end{pmatrix}\int_0^{+\infty}J_n(w\rho)J_\rho^{(n)}(\rho)d\rho_0+ \\ -j\begin{pmatrix} n/w \\ d/dw \end{pmatrix}\int_0^{+\infty}J_n(w\rho)J_\phi^{(n)}(\rho)d\rho_0 \quad (2)$$

is the VHT of the n-th harmonic of the surface current density $\underline{J}^{(n)}(\rho)$, while $\underline{\underline{\mathbf{H}}}^{(n)}(w\rho)$ and $\underline{\underline{\mathbf{G}}}(w)$ are defined in [13].

Equation (1) is discretized by using Galerkin method. The physical behaviour at the edges of the annular ring of the n-th harmonic of the surface current density components is reconstructed by choosing the following expansion functions

$$f_t^{(n,h)}(\rho)= \\ =\frac{4\rho\left[\left(\rho^2-\rho_1^2\right)\left(\rho_2^2-\rho^2\right)\right]^{\alpha_t}}{\pi(ab)^{2\alpha_t+1}}T_n\left(\frac{\rho^2+\rho_1\rho_2}{2\rho a}\right)T_h\left(1-\frac{\rho^2-\rho_1^2}{2ab}\right), \quad (3)$$

with $t\in\{\rho,\phi\}$, where $\alpha_\rho=1/2$, $\alpha_\phi=-1/2$, $a=(\rho_1+\rho_2)/2$, $b=(\rho_2-\rho_1)/2$, $T_l(\cdot)$ is the Chebyshev polynomial of first kind and order l [15]. With such a choice, $\underline{\tilde{\mathbf{J}}}^{(n)}(w)$ can be expressed in closed form being

$$\int_0^{+\infty}J_n(w\rho)f_\phi^{(n,h)}(\rho)d\rho_0=\left[J_{n+h}(aw)+(-1)^h J_{n-h}(aw)\right]J_h(bw), \quad (4)$$

$$\int_{0}^{+\infty} J_n(w\rho) f_{\rho}^{(n,h)}(\rho) d\rho_0 = 2\bar{f}_{\phi}^{(n,h)}(w) - \bar{f}_{\phi}^{(n,h+2)}(w) - \bar{f}_{\phi}^{(n,h-2)}(w), \quad (5)$$

and $J_n(\cdot)$ is the Bessel functions of first kind and order n [15].

III. Numerical Results

The following normalized truncation error is introduced in order to appreciate that few cylindrical harmonics and expansion functions are needed to achieve accurate results

$$\mathrm{err}(N,M,Q,P) = \left\| \boldsymbol{j}_{N,M} - \boldsymbol{j}_{Q,P} \right\| / \left\| \boldsymbol{j}_{N,M} \right\|, \quad (6)$$

where $\|\cdot\|$ is the usual Euclidean norm and $\boldsymbol{j}_{N,M}$ is the vector of the expansion coefficients evaluated by using $2N-1$ cylindrical harmonics and M expansion functions for each component of each harmonic.

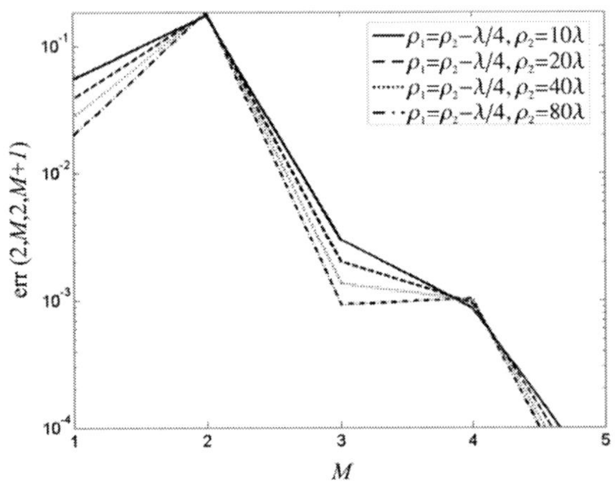

Fig. 1. Normalized truncation error for an annular ring with varying the radii. $\underline{E}_0=\hat{\rho}\cos\phi-\hat{\phi}\sin\phi$ V/m.

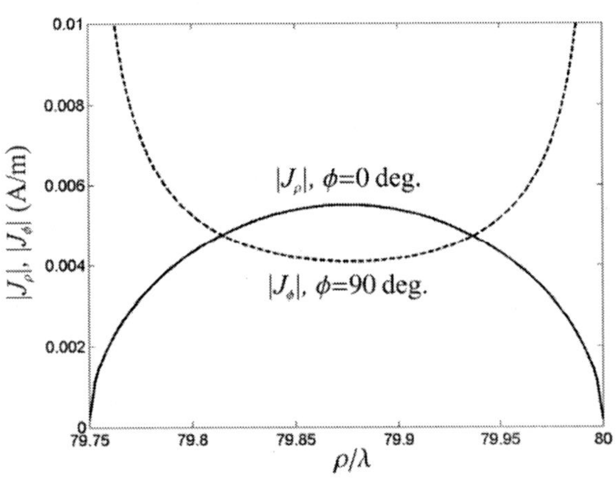

Fig. 2. Components of the surface current density on an annular ring. $\rho_1=\rho_2-\lambda/4$, $\rho_2=80\lambda$, $\underline{E}_0=\hat{\rho}\cos\phi-\hat{\phi}\sin\phi$ V/m.

In figure 1 the normalized truncation error for very large but narrow annular rings is plotted with varying the radii, when a plane wave of amplitude $\underline{E}_0 = \hat{\rho}\cos\phi - \hat{\phi}\sin\phi$ V/m orthogonally impinges onto the scatterer surface. In such a case, only the cylindrical harmonics for $n=\pm 1$ contribute to reconstruct the surface current density. As can be observed, the convergence is very fast (of exponential type), i.e., the number of expansion functions needed to achieve highly accurate solutions is very low (an error less than 10^{-2} is achieved for $M=3$, while $M=5$ allows us to obtain an error less than 10^{-4}). Moreover, the convergence rate strictly depends on $(\rho_2-\rho_1)/\lambda$ independently of the largeness of the ring. For the sake of completeness, in figure 2 the components of the obtained surface current densities are sketched.

References

[1] Y. Chunfei and Z. Wenxun, "New approach to electromagnetic scattering from a conductive disc-ring structure," Journal of Electronics (China), vol. 12 no. 2, pp. 168–176, 1995.

[2] A. I. Nosich, "Method of analytical regularization in computational photonics," Radio Science, vol. 8, pp. 1421–1430, 2016.

[3] K. Hongo and H. Serizawa, "Diffraction of electromagnetic plane wave by rectangular plate and rectangular hole in the conducting plate," IEEE Trans. Antennas Propag., vol. 47, no. 6, pp. 1029–1041, June 1999.

[4] J. L. Tsalamengas, "Rapidly converging direct singular integral-equation techniques in the analysis of open microstrip lines on layered substrates," IEEE Trans. Microw. Theory Tech., vol. 49, no. 3, pp. 555–559, March 2001.

[5] V. Losada, R. R. Boix, and F. Medina, "Fast and accurate algorithm for the short-pulse electromagnetic scattering from conducting circular plates buried inside a lossy dispersive half-space," IEEE Trans. Geosci. Remote Sensing, vol. 41, pp. 988–997, May 2003.

[6] M. Lucido, G. Panariello, and F. Schettino, "Accurate and efficient analysis of stripline structures," Microwave and Optical Technology Letters, vol. 43, pp. 14–21, 2004.

[7] K. Hongo and Q. A. Naqvi, "Diffraction of electromagnetic wave by disk and circular hole in a perfectly conducting plane," Progress In Electromagnetics Research (PIER), vol. 68, pp. 113-150, 2007.

[8] G. Coluccini, M. Lucido, and G. Panariello, "TM scattering by perfectly conducting polygonal cross-section cylinders: a new surface current density expansion retaining up to the second-order edge behavior," IEEE Trans. Antennas Propag., vol. 60, no. 1, pp. 407-412, January 2012.

[9] M. Lucido, "An analytical technique to fast evaluate mutual coupling integrals in spectral domain analysis of multilayered coplanar coupled striplines," Microwave and Optical Technology Letters, Vol. 54, No. 4, pp. 1035-1039, Apr. 2012.

[10] G. Coluccini, M. Lucido, and G. Panariello, "Spectral domain analysis of open single and coupled microstrip lines with polygonal cross-section in bound and leaky regimes," IEEE Trans. Microw. Theory Tech., vol. 61, no. 2, pp. 736-745, February 2013.

[11] M. Lucido, "An efficient evaluation of the self-contribution integrals in the spectral-domain analysis of multilayered striplines," IEEE Antennas and Wireless Propagation Letters, Vol. 12, pp. 360-363, (Mar.) 2013.

[12] G. Coluccini and M. Lucido, "A new high efficient analysis of the scattering by a perfectly conducting rectangular plate," IEEE Trans. Antennas Propag., vol. 61, no. 5, pp. 2615-2622, May 2013.

[13] F. Di Murro, M. Lucido, G. Panariello, and F. Schettino, "Guaranteed-convergence method of analysis of the scattering by an arbitrarily oriented zero-thickness PEC disk buried in a lossy half-space", IEEE Trans. Antennas Propag., Vol. 63, No. 8, pp. 3610-3620, Aug. 2015.

[14] L. V. Kantorovich and G. P. Akilov, Functional Analysis, 2nd ed., Pergamon Press, Oxford-Elmsford, N.Y., 1982.

[15] M. Abramowitz, I.A. Stegun, Handbook of Mathematical Functions, Verlag Harri Deutsch, 1984.

An Effective Method for the Analysis of Propagation in Polygonal Cross-Section Dielectric Waveguides

M. Lucido, G. Panariello, and C. Santomassimo
Department of Electrical and Information Engineering (D.I.E.I.)
University of Cassino and Southern Lazio
03043 Cassino, Italy

***Abstract*—In this paper, a fast (and) convergent method to analyze propagation in polygonal cross-section dielectric waveguides is presented. The problem formulated as an homogeneous surface integral equation in the spectral domain is discretized by means of Galerkin method with analytically Fourier transformable expansion functions reconstructing the behavior of the fields on the wedges. Moreover, the elements of the obtained coefficients' matrix are efficiently evaluated by means of a suitable analytical asymptotic acceleration technique and an optimized C++ code implementation.**

Keywords—Dielectric waveguides, edge behavior, Galerkin method, surface integral equation.

I. INTRODUCTION

Dielectric waveguides are important building blocks in modern optical communication systems and integrated optical circuits [1]. Recently, dielectric waveguides with complicated structures, such as photonic crystal fibers and plasmonic waveguides, have been proposed due to properties which are not available in traditional waveguides [2], [3]. Despite the number of methods developed in the last decades for studying dielectric waveguides, the accurate analysis of some recently developed optical waveguides remains a difficult task. This is particularly true for waveguides with high index-contrast, wedges and complex micro-structures, for which scalar or semi-vectorial models are no longer valid, and a rigorous full-vectorial analysis is needed to achieve accurate results.

The aim of this paper is to present a fast (and) convergent method, already applied to investigate propagation, radiation and scattering problems (see [4] and the references therein for an overview), for the analysis of the propagation in polygonal cross-section dielectric waveguides. An homogeneous surface integral equation in the spectral domain, opportunely devised to be valid for objects with wedges, is discretized by using Galerkin method with analytically Fourier transformable expansion basis reconstructing the edge behavior and the continuity conditions of the fields on the wedges. A suitable analytical asymptotic acceleration technique and an optimized C++ code implementation allow to the efficient evaluation of the elements of the coefficients' matrix.

II. FORMULATION AND SOLUTION OF THE PROBLEM

Let us consider an polygonal cross-section homogeneous and isotropic lossless dielectric waveguide in a homogeneous and isotropic lossless medium. A coordinate system with the z axis parallel to the cylinder axis is introduced and a behavior of the fields with z of the kind $e^{-jk_z z}$ is assumed, where k_z is the propagation constant of the generic mode.

The L sides of the polygonal cross-section are progressively numbered. On the i-th side, of length $2a_i$, a local coordinate system (x_i, y_i, z) is introduced with the origin at the centre of the side itself and y_i oriented in the outward direction. By means of equivalence principle, the fields in both media are readily expressed as integral-differential operators in the spectral domain involving the following fictitious electric and magnetic surface current densities [5]

$$\underline{J}_i(x_i)e^{-jk_z z} = \begin{cases} \hat{y}_i \times \underline{H}(x,y,z)\big|_{y_i=0} & |x_i| \le a_i \\ 0 & |x_i| > a_i \end{cases}, \tag{1}$$

$$\underline{J}_{mi}(x_i)e^{-jk_z z} = \begin{cases} -\hat{y}_i \times \underline{E}(x,y,z)\big|_{y_i=0} & |x_i| \le a_i \\ 0 & |x_i| > a_i \end{cases}, \tag{2}$$

for $i=1,2,...,L$, where the $(\underline{E},\underline{H})$ denotes the electromagnetic field in the external medium.

Following the same line of reasoning presented in [6], the obtained integral-differential operators are reduced to integral operators. Hence, by imposing the continuity of the tangential components of the fields on the waveguide surface, a homogeneous surface integral equation governing the propagation in the considered structure is obtained.

In general, no closed form solutions exist for the nonstandard eigenvalue problem at hand. However, the obtained integral equation can be recast as an infinite matrix equation at which Steinberg's theorems [7] can be applied by means of Galerkin method with a complete set of expansion functions that makes the most singular part of the integral operator invertible with a continuous two-side inverse [8]. This goal is fully reached in this paper by expanding the longitudinal components and the derivative of the transverse components of the surface current densities on each side by means of the following expansion functions

$$\varphi_n^{(\alpha_i,\beta_i)}(x_i/a_i)=(1-x_i/a_i)^{\alpha_i}(1+x_i/a_i)^{\beta_i}\frac{P_n^{(\alpha_i,\beta_i)}(x_i/a_i)}{\xi_n^{(\alpha_i,\beta_i)}}\Pi(x_i/a_i) \quad (3)$$

for $i=1,2,...,L$ and $n\geq 0$, where $P_n^{(\alpha,\beta)}(\cdot)$ is the Jacobi polynomial of order n [9] and the parameters α,β are chosen in order to factorize the edge behavior of the fields on the wedges [10], $\xi_n^{(\alpha,\beta)}$ is a normalization quantity and $\Pi(\cdot)$ is the unitary rectangular window. Moreover, the continuity of the transverse components of the currents on the wedges is imposed. Besides ensuring the convergence of the proposed method, such expansion bases allow to obtain accurate solutions quickly.

The Fourier transform of (3) is analytical and can be expressed in terms of confluent hypergeometric function of first kind [9]

$$\begin{aligned}\tilde{\varphi}_n^{(\alpha_i,\beta_i)}(a_i u)&=\frac{a_i \mathrm{B}(n+\alpha_i+1,n+\beta_i+1)}{\pi n!2^{-\alpha_i-\beta_i}\xi_n^{(\alpha_i,\beta_i)}}\cdot \\ &\cdot(2jua_i)^n e^{-jua_i}\,{}_1F_1(n+\beta_i+1;2n+\alpha_i+\beta_i+2;2jua_i)\end{aligned} \quad (4)$$

where $\mathrm{B}(a,b)$ is the complete Beta function [9]. Hence, the elements of the coefficients' matrix are reduced to improper single integrals of oscillating and slowly decaying functions involving product of confluent hypergeometric functions of first kind. The symmetries of the coefficients' matrix lead to a significant reduction of the number of the elements to be numerically evaluated. Anyway, such kind of integrals are efficiently evaluated by means of an effective C++ code implementation, in which particular attention is devoted to the accurate and efficient evaluation of the confluent hypergeometric functions of first kind, and by using the analytical asymptotic acceleration technique detailed in [11].

III. Numerical Results

In order to appreciate the accuracy and efficiency of the presented technique, in Tables I and II the propagation constants (normalized to the wavenumber of the vacuum $k_0=2\pi/\lambda$ where λ is the wavelength) for the fundamental mode propagating in the square and trapezoidal cross-section waveguides sketched in the top figures are reported as a function of the number of expansion functions used. It can be seen that an accuracy for the solution of 4 significant figures is achieved in both the examined cases by using only 3 expansion functions for each component of the surface current densities on each side of the waveguides. Moreover, at most 5 expansion functions are needed to achieve an accuracy for the solution of 7 significant figures. Comparisons with the literature and the commercial software CST Microwave Studio (CST-MWS) are also shown. The agreement with the results reported in [12], obtained formulating the problem in terms of a boundary integral equation discretized by means of Nyström method, is perfect while CST-MWS achieves an accuracy within 5 significant figures by using more than 300K meshcell to discretize the transverse cross-section.

Table I. Normalized Propagation Constant for the Fundamental Mode in a Square Waveguide for Different Number of Expansion Functions Used (N). $a=2\lambda/3$, $n=\sqrt{8}$.

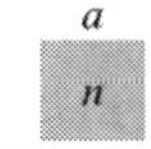

N	k_z/k_0
3	2.657039
4	2.656789
5	2.656796
15	2.656796
[12]	2.656796
CST-MWS	2.656750

Table II. Normalized Propagation Constant for the Fundamental Mode in a Trapezoidal Waveguide for Different Number of Expansion Functions Used (N). $a=2\lambda/3$, $b/a=1/\sin(5\pi/9)$, $c/a=1+2\tan(\pi/18)$, $n=\sqrt{8}$.

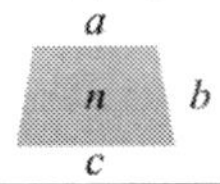

N	k_z/k_0
3	2.683908
4	2.683610
5	2.683643
15	2.683643
[12]	2.683643
CST-MWS	2.683608

References

[1] A. W. Snyder and J. D. Love, Optical Waveguide Theory, Chapman and Hall, London, 1983.

[2] J. C. Knight, T. A. Birks, P. St. J. Russell, and J. P. de Sandro, "Properties of photonic crystal fiber and the effective index model," J. Opt. Soc. Am. A, vol. 15, pp. 748-752, 1998.

[3] W. Xue, Y. Guo, P. Li, and W. Zhang, "Propagation properties of a surface plasmonic waveguide with double elliptical air cores," Opt. Express, vol. 16, pp. 10710-10720, 2008.

[4] F. Di Murro, M. Lucido, G. Panariello, and F. Schettino, "Guaranteed-convergence method of analysis of the scattering by an arbitrarily oriented zero-thickness PEC disk buried in a lossy half-space", IEEE Trans. Antennas Propag., Vol. 63, No. 8, pp. 3610-3620, Aug. 2015.

[5] M. Lucido, G. Panariello, and F. Schettino, "Scattering by polygonal cross-section dielectric cylinders at oblique incidence," IEEE Trans. Antennas Propag., vol. 58, pp. 540–551, Feb. 2010.

[6] M. Lucido, G. Panariello, and F. Schettino, "TE scattering by arbitrarily connected conducting strips," IEEE Trans. Antennas Propag., vol. 57, pp. 2212–2216, Jul. 2009.

[7] S. Steinberg, "Meromorphic families of compact operators," Archive for Rational Mechanics and Analysis, vol. 31, no. 5, pp. 372-379, 1968.

[8] L. V. Kantorovich and G. P. Akilov, Functional Analysis, 2nd ed., Pergamon Press, Oxford-Elmsford, N.Y., 1982.

[9] M. Abramowitz, I.A. Stegun, Handbook of Mathematical Functions, Verlag Harri Deutsch, 1984.

[10] J. Meixner, "The behavior of electromagnetic fields at edges," IEEE Trans. Antennas Propag., vol. 20, pp. 442–446, Jul. 1972.

[11] M. Lucido, G. Panariello and F. Schettino, "Electromagnetic scattering by multiple perfectly conducting arbitrary polygonal cylinders," IEEE Trans. Antennas Propag., vol. 56, pp. 425-436, Feb. 2008.

[12] W. Lu , Y.Y. Lu, "Waveguide mode solver based on Neumann-to-Dirichlet operators and boundary integral equation", Journal of Computational Physics, vol. 231, n° 4, pp. 1360-1371, Feb. 2012.

Conversion of Singular Surface Integrals for to Line Integrals with Nonsingular Integrands for Non-planar Configurations of RWG Basis Functions

Elizabeth Bleszynski[1]*, Marek Bleszynski[1], Thomas Jaroszewicz[1],
[1]Monopole Research, Thousand Oaks, Ca 91360
* email address: elizabeth@monopoleresearch.com

***Abstract*—A novel procedure is presented for the evaluation of integrals involving singular Green function and Rao-Wilton-Glisson basis functions with arbitrary mutual non-planar geometrical configuration which appear in surface integral equations representation of Maxwell equations. The proposed procedure constitutes a generalization of our previously reported result valid for planar geometries. The method employs a suitably constructed representation of the Helmholtz equation Green function in terms of an differential operator acting on an auxiliary function which allows one to reduce four-dimensional surface integrals with singular integrands to line integrals over triangle edges with regular integrands. Advantages of our approach include simplicity and high accuracy at a computational cost considerably lower than for previously considered methods, such as the singularity subtraction technique.**

***Index Terms*—Integral equations, Moment methods, Numerical analysis**

I. Introduction

In our recent paper [1] we presented a procedure for the evaluation of matrix elements of the kernels of surface integral equation operators – the tensor and the vector Green functions – sandwiched between the surface Rao-Wilton-Glisson (RWG) [2] basis functions defined on triangular supports located on either a plane and on a pair of parallel planes. Our procedure consisted of converting four-dimensional surface integrals with singular integrands to two-dimensional line integrals involving auxiliary non-singular functions. The most essential element of the procedure consisted of employing a representation of the Green function of the scalar Helmholtz equation, $g(R) = \frac{e^{ikR}}{4\pi R}$ in terms of an auxiliary, non-singular function $m(\xi)$ of a single scalar argument $\xi \equiv ik|\boldsymbol{R}|$, $\boldsymbol{R} = \boldsymbol{R}_1 - \boldsymbol{R}_2$

$$g(|\boldsymbol{R}|) = -\frac{1}{4\pi\kappa}\nabla^{(2)}_{\boldsymbol{R}} \cdot \nabla^{(2)}_{\boldsymbol{R}}\, m(\xi), \qquad (1)$$

where $\nabla^{(2)}_{\boldsymbol{R}}$ represents the two-dimensional gradient.

The function $m(\xi)$ was found by solving the differential equation

$$m''(\xi) + \frac{m'(\xi)}{\xi} = \frac{e^{\xi}}{\xi}, \qquad (2)$$

The representation (1) allowed us to convert, by making use of the Gauss divergence theorem, the integral over the surfaces of two triangular facets (or more general polygonal shapes) to line integrals with regular integrands over triangle edges.

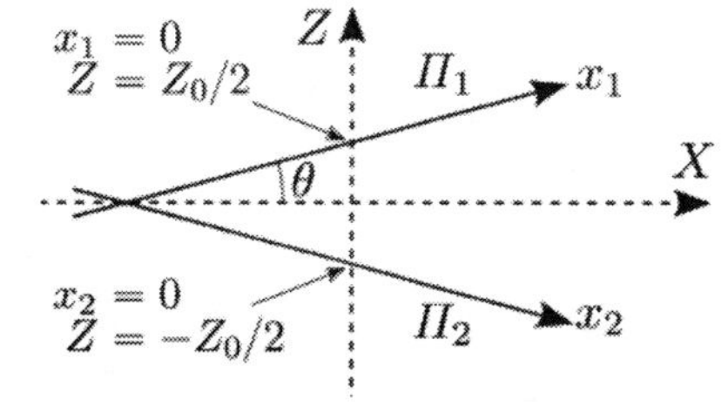

Fig. 1: Geometry of two intersecting planes, Π_1 and Π_2. The coordinates x_i are measured relative to the plane $X = 0$.

Here we consider an extension of our method to problems involving non-planar geometries. The essence of the proposed approach is to generalize the representation (1) of the Green function to non-parallel geometry elements: the new representation involves a bilinear form of two gradient operators ***acting in two different planes***, Π_1 and Π_2, containing the triangles T_1 and T_2. Specifically, we find a function Φ such that

$$g(|\boldsymbol{R}_1 - \boldsymbol{R}_2|) = \{\nabla_1 \cdot [\hat{M}\,\nabla_2]\}\,\Phi(\boldsymbol{R}_1 - \boldsymbol{R}_2), \qquad (3)$$

where

$$\nabla_1 = \hat{\boldsymbol{n}}_1 \times [\nabla_{\boldsymbol{R}_1} \times \hat{\boldsymbol{n}}_1],$$

$$\nabla_2 = \hat{\boldsymbol{n}}_2 \times [\nabla_{\boldsymbol{R}_2} \times \hat{\boldsymbol{n}}_2],$$

and

$$\hat{\boldsymbol{n}}_1 \neq \hat{\boldsymbol{n}}_2$$

represent unit vectors perpendicular to the planes Π_1 and Π_2.

$$\hat{M} = \begin{pmatrix} 1 & 0 \\ 0 & \cos^2(\theta) \end{pmatrix} \qquad (4)$$

is a suitably chosen diagonal non-singular matrix with position-independent elements.

In order to obtain the solution for the function Φ we have written the representation (3) in a suitably chosen coordinate system

$$S: \quad (\hat{\boldsymbol{X}}, \hat{\boldsymbol{Y}}, \hat{\boldsymbol{Z}}),$$

whose $\hat{\boldsymbol{Y}}$ axis coincides with the line of intersection of the two planes Π_1 and Π_2, as illustrated, schematically, in Fig. 1.

The triangles, $T_1 : (\boldsymbol{v}_1, \boldsymbol{v}_2, \boldsymbol{v}_3) \in \Pi_1$ and $T_2 : (\boldsymbol{w}_1, \boldsymbol{w}_2, \boldsymbol{w}_3) \in \Pi_2$. define the normals to the planes,

$$\hat{\boldsymbol{n}}_1 = \frac{(\boldsymbol{v}_2 - \boldsymbol{v}_1) \times (\boldsymbol{v}_3 - \boldsymbol{v}_2)}{|(\boldsymbol{v}_2 - \boldsymbol{v}_1) \times (\boldsymbol{v}_3 - \boldsymbol{v}_2)|},$$

and similarly for $\hat{\boldsymbol{n}}_2$, in agreement with the right-hand screw convention. The angle between the planes (and between the normals) is denoted by 2θ.

The axes of the coordinate system (X, Y, Z) can be then obtained from

$$\begin{aligned} \hat{\boldsymbol{X}} &= \frac{-\hat{\boldsymbol{n}}_1 + \varepsilon_{12}\hat{\boldsymbol{n}}_2}{|-\hat{\boldsymbol{n}}_1 + \varepsilon_{12}\hat{\boldsymbol{n}}_2|}, \\ \hat{\boldsymbol{Y}} &= \frac{\hat{\boldsymbol{n}}_1 \times \hat{\boldsymbol{n}}_2}{|\hat{\boldsymbol{n}}_1 \times \hat{\boldsymbol{n}}_2|}, \\ \hat{\boldsymbol{Z}} &= \hat{\boldsymbol{X}} \times \hat{\boldsymbol{Y}} = \frac{\varepsilon_{12}\hat{\boldsymbol{n}}_1 + \hat{\boldsymbol{n}}_2}{|\varepsilon_{12}\hat{\boldsymbol{n}}_1 + \hat{\boldsymbol{n}}_2|}, \end{aligned} \tag{5}$$

where

$$\varepsilon_{12} = \operatorname{sign} \hat{\boldsymbol{n}}_1 \cdot \hat{\boldsymbol{n}}_2 . \tag{6}$$

By rewriting the equation (3) in the variables $s = \hat{\boldsymbol{Z}} \cdot \boldsymbol{R}$, $t = \hat{\boldsymbol{Y}} \cdot \boldsymbol{R}$, $y = \hat{\boldsymbol{Y}} \cdot \boldsymbol{R}$ and $\rho = \sqrt{t^2 + y^2}$ We obtained a second order differential equation for the function $\Phi(s, \rho)$

$$(1-a), \left(-\frac{a}{1-a}\frac{\partial^2}{\partial s^2} + \frac{\partial}{\rho \partial \rho}\frac{\rho \partial}{\partial \rho} \right) \Phi(s, \rho) = g(\sqrt{\rho^2 + s^2}) . \tag{7}$$

where $a = \sin^2(\theta)$

Applying the above differential operator to the function $g(\boldsymbol{R}_1 - \boldsymbol{R}_2)$ and using the Stokes theorem allows us to convert the integral of g over two flat surfaces $\Sigma_1 \subset \Pi_1$ and $\Sigma_2 \subset \Pi_2$ (e.g., triangles T_1 and T_2) to the integral over surfaces' perimeters,

$$\begin{aligned} &\int_{\Sigma_1} \mathrm{d}S_1 \int_{\Sigma_2} \mathrm{d}S_2 \{ \boldsymbol{\nabla}_1 \cdot [\hat{M}\, \boldsymbol{\nabla}_2] \} \Phi(\boldsymbol{R}_1 - \boldsymbol{R}_2) \\ &= \oint_{\partial\Sigma_1} \mathrm{d}l_1 \oint_{\partial\Sigma_2} \mathrm{d}l_2 \{ \hat{\boldsymbol{u}}_1 \cdot [\hat{M}\, \boldsymbol{u}_2] \} \Phi(\boldsymbol{R}_1 - \boldsymbol{R}_2) , \end{aligned} \tag{8}$$

with $\hat{\boldsymbol{u}}_1$ and $\hat{\boldsymbol{u}}_2$ representing unit vectors perpendicular to the perimeter lines, lying in the planes Π_1 and Π_2.

We obtained an analytical solution for the function $\Phi(s, \rho)$ In particular the solution

The simplest problem is evaluation of the first-order expansion, i.e., the the function Φ for $k = 0$,

$$\begin{aligned} \Phi(\rho, s) &= \frac{\sqrt{\rho^2 + s^2}}{8\,\pi} \Psi_a(x) , \\ x &= \frac{s}{\sqrt{\rho^2 + s^2}}, \end{aligned} \tag{9}$$

The function $\Psi_a(x)$ appearing in the above expression is expressible in terms of elementary functions

$$\begin{aligned} \Psi_a(x) &= 2 - \sqrt{x}\Big(L(x) - \mathrm{H}(x-a)[L(w) - 2w] \Big) + \\ &+ \mathrm{i}\sqrt{x}\Big\{ 2\mathrm{H}(a-x)[w - \tan^{-1} w] + \pi \Big\} \end{aligned} \tag{10}$$

with $L(x) = \ln \frac{1+\sqrt{x}}{1-\sqrt{x}}$ and $w = \sqrt{\frac{|x-a|}{x(1-a)}}$.

The **nonsingular function** $\Psi_a(x)$, plotted in Fig. 2, is continuous and bounded by

$$0 \le \Psi_a(x) \le 2 \quad \text{for all } x \in [0, 1],\ a \in [0, \tfrac{1}{2}] , \tag{11}$$

including the value $a = 0$, corresponding to parallel planes Π_1 and Π_2. In the latter case we have

$$\Psi_0(x) = 2 \left[1 - \sqrt{x} - \sqrt{x} \ln \frac{1 + \sqrt{x}}{2\sqrt{x}} \right] . \tag{12}$$

i

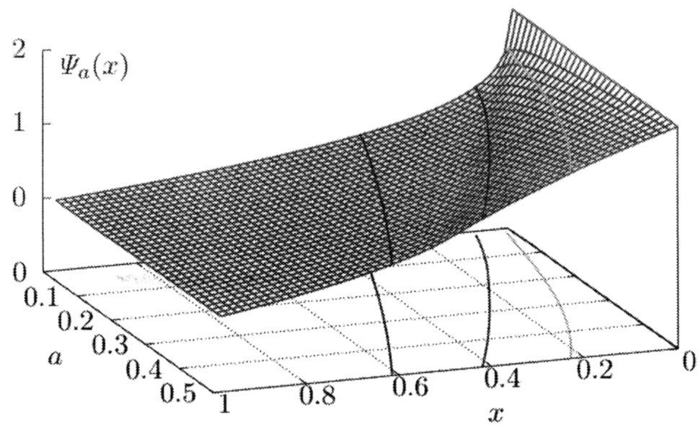

Fig. 2: The function $\Psi_a(x)$, Eq. (**??**), plotted in the full range of its arguments.

Results for terms of higher-order in k can also be expressed in terms of elementary functions and will be reported in a subsequent publication

ACKNOWLEDGMENTS

This work was partly supported by the Air Force Office of Scientific Research under the grant number FA9550-12-1-0121.

REFERENCES

[1] E. H. Bleszynski, M. K. Bleszynski, and T. Jaroszewicz, "Reduction of singular surface integrals to non-singular line integrals in integral equations for planar geometries," *IEEE Transactions on Antennas and Propagation*, vol. 64, pp. 4760–4769, 2016.

[2] S. M. Rao, D. R. Wilton, and A. W. Glisson, "Electromagnetic scattering by surfaces of arbitrary shape," *IEEE Transactions on Antennas and Propagation*, vol. AP-30, pp. 409–418, 1982.

Efficient Use of Singular Hierarchical Vector Functions for the FEM Solution of Multiscale Problems

Roberto D. Graglia, Paolo Petrini
DET - Politecnico di Torino,
Corso Duca degli Abruzzi 24,
10129 Torino, Italy
roberto.graglia@polito.it; paolo.petrini@polito.it

Andrew F. Peterson
School of Electrical and Computer Engineering
Georgia Institute of Technology,
Atlanta GA 30332 USA
peterson@ece.gatech.edu

***Abstract*—A number of new hierarchical and singular (scalar and vector) basis functions for field representation in two- and three-dimensional cells have been recently developed and discussed in a series of papers, and in a new book. The hierarchical functions are designed for adaptive *p*-refinement on domains meshed with differently shaped cells. The polynomial order of the functions may vary from cell to cell to facilitate application to multiscale problems, and to permit one to use large cells. Additive singular basis function sets are needed to efficiently handle corner and wedge singularities. In this paper we take advantage of the fact that (1) each singular basis function can be computed on the fly and (2) that the FEM integrals involving these functions can also be analytically determined provided that the singular cells are rectilinear. It is here proven that this results in (1) a noticeable reduction of the computation time since there is no need to use sophisticated integration routines, (2) an augmented accuracy of the numerical results, and (3) the possibility to include in the model a very high number of singularity coefficients. For sake of brevity the reported results consider the two-dimensional test case of the L-shaped waveguide.**

Keywords—Basis functions, Finite element methods, Hierarchical basis functions, Singular basis functions

I. Introduction

Recently, the authors have developed a number of new singular hierarchical basis functions of the additive kind for field representation in two- and three-dimensional cells. Scalar and vector basis functions of both interpolatory and hierarchical types together with singular functions of the additive kind are discussed in detail, with results, in a recent book [1], as well as in several other publications by the same authors. The hierarchical *scalar* bases for the most common (triangular and quadrilateral) 2D and 3D (tetrahedral, hexahedral and prism) cells are reported in [1]. The hierarchical vector functions are of the Nedelec kind [5], [6] to minimize the number of nullspace Degrees of Freedoms (DoF) associated with a curl (or divergence) operator.

The philosophy behind additive singular bases is that the singular functions are combined with the entire regular basis set of some order, to provide additional degrees of freedom to represent the corner or edge singularities without removing any of the polynomial degrees. One difficulty with this process is the possible lack of linear independence between the singular functions and the members of the existing set. To reduce the growth of the matrix condition numbers associated with the augmented set of functions, some orthogonalization is necessary. Thus, in previous works, we developed mutually orthogonal singular functions that have the sufficient flexibility to be made orthogonal to the polynomial bases in the original set. In addition, for generality, it is desirable to work with singular functions having arbitrary fractional exponents chosen in a list of possible exponents $\nu=\{\nu_1, \nu_2, \ldots, \nu_N\}$, so that a single set of functions can be used with a singularity of any order. For sake of brevity, below we discuss only singular (rectilinear) triangular elements. On a triangular element, each singular basis function

$$\varphi_{n\ell}(\nu,\chi,\sigma) = R_n(\nu,\chi)\Theta_\ell(\sigma) = \frac{1}{c_n}\sum_{p=1}^{n+1} b_{np}(\chi^{\nu_n} - \chi^p) \quad (1)$$

is constructed in a triangular-polar coordinate frame (depicted in Fig. 1) as the product of a radial singular function

$$R_n(\nu,\chi) = \frac{1}{c_n}\sum_{p=1}^{n+1} b_{np}(\chi^{\nu_n} - \chi^p) \quad (2)$$

with an azimuthal function $\Theta_\ell(\sigma)$ expressed in terms of orthogonal Jacobi polynomials [1]. Singular vector functions are easily constructed from the gradient of (1). The exponent

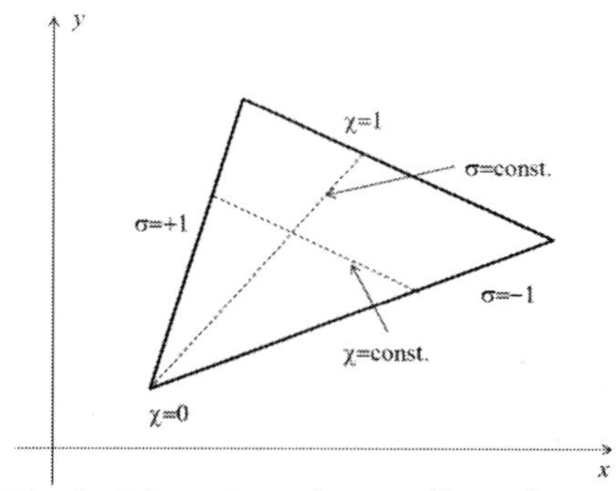

Fig. 1. Triangular-polar coordinate frame.

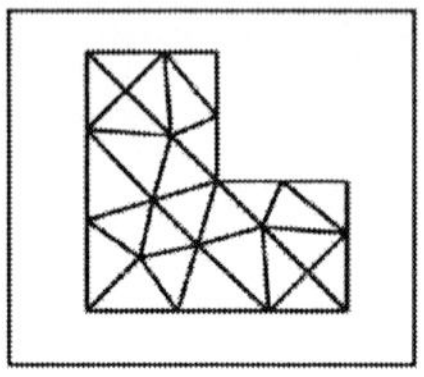

Fig.2. Test case - cross section.

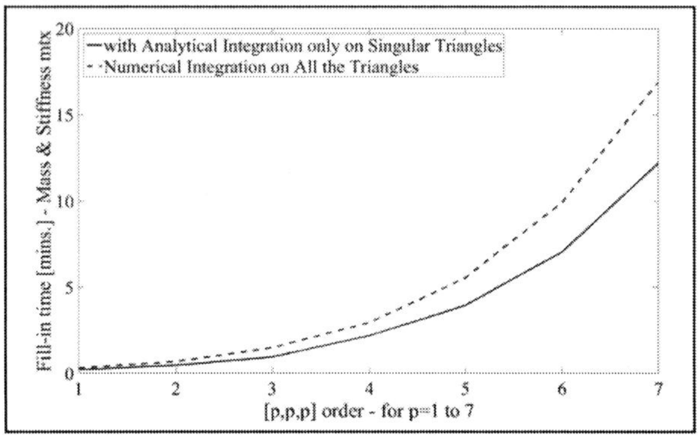

Fig. 3. CPU time comparison.

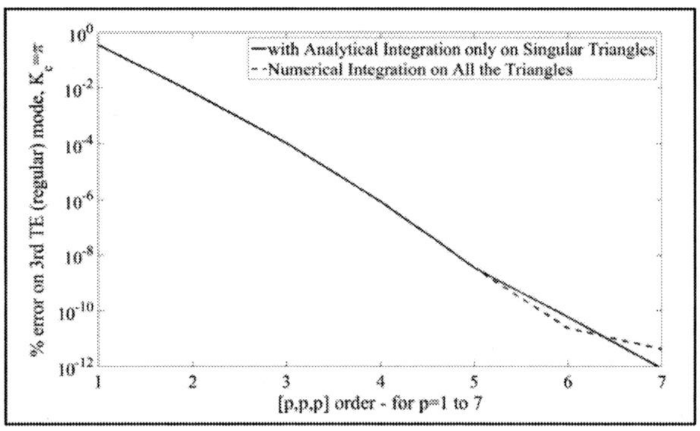

Fig. 4. Error comparison for regular mode.

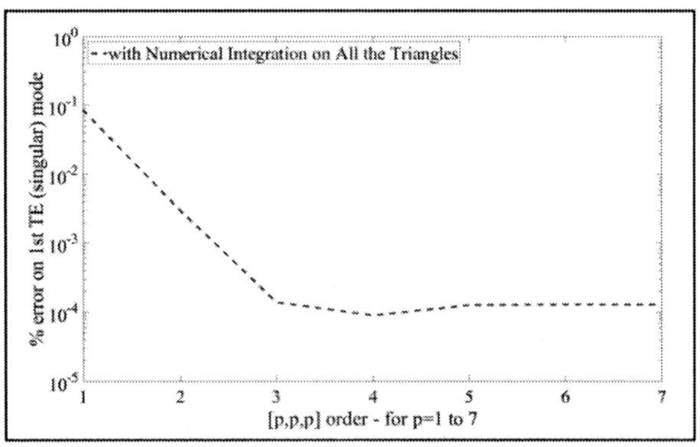

Fig. 5. Error for singular mode.

in (1) for n = 1 is expected to be in the range $0<v_n<1$; this is therefore a bounded function but usually has an unbounded derivative. Functions of this form may be used to represent the longitudinal electric or magnetic fields parallel to corners, while their derivatives contribute to the vector fields transverse to the edge in question.

The coefficients that define the radial functions $R_n(v, \chi)$ (for n=1 to N) can be obtained numerically by a recursive algorithm that requires, at the n-th step, the solution of a linear system plus the evaluation of the square root of a quadratic form [1]. The most difficult FEM integrals are performed analytically in the triangular-polar reference-frame and, for rectilinear triangles, they are computed only once. After lengthy manipulations, the radial integrals are obtained in the form of double summations that involve only the c_n and b_{np} coefficients of the radial functions and all the singularity exponents. Since the azimuthal integrals only involve polynomials, they are conveniently stored in arrays and matrices. (Tables to report these results will be published in a future paper since, for sake of brevity, they cannot be reported here.)

II. Results

The reported results are relative to the L-shaped waveguide depicted in Fig. 2 (26 triangular cells including five singular cells).

An FEM code to obtain the eigenmodes of the structure has been developed [1, 3]. Fig. 3 compares the CPU time to fill-in the stiffness and mass matrices by using pure numerical integration on all elements (dashed line) against the time using the analytical precomputed singular integrals (solid line). The machine used is a laptop computer (3 GHz multicore CPU). The numerical integrals were obtained using a Kronrod-Patterson rule for complex integrand on a rectangular domain; that is, in the triangular-polar frame σ=[-1,+1]; χ=[0,1]. Figure 4 shows the percentage error on k_c for the third regular TE mode (exact $k_c= \pi$). Figure 5 shows the percentage error on k_c for the first singular mode obtained by using pure numerical integration on all elements and by assuming as reference value the k_c computed by using the analytical integration and the basis set of order [7,7,7].

References

[1] R.D. Graglia, A.F. Peterson, *Higher-order Techniques in Computational Electromagnetics*, 392 pages, Edison, NJ, SciTech Publishing (an imprint of the IET), 2015 - ISBN:978-1-61353-016-0

[2] R.D. Graglia, A.F. Peterson, L. Matekovits, P. Petrini, "Hierarchical additive basis functions for the finite-element treatment of corner singularities," special issue on "Finite Elements for Microwave Engineering," *Electromagnetics*, vol. 34, pp. 171-198, 2014.

[3] R.D. Graglia, P. Petrini, A.F. Peterson, L. Matekovits, "Full-wave analysis of inhomogeneous waveguiding structures containing corners with singular hierarchical curl-conforming vector bases," *IEEE Antennas and Wireless Propagation Letters*, vol. 13, pp. 1701-1704, 2014.

[4] R.D. Graglia, G. Lombardi, "Singular Higher-Order Complete Vector Bases for Finite Methods," *IEEE Trans. Antennas Propagat.*, vol. 52, pp. 1672-1685, 2004.

[5] J. C. Nedelec, "Mixed finite elements in R3," *Num. Math.*, vol. 35, pp. 315-341, 1980.

[6] J. C. Nedelec, "A new family of mixed finite elements in R3," *Num. Math.*, vol. 50, pp. 57-81, 1986.

Integral Operators Formulation for Transient Radiation from Parabolic Antennas Using Modified Raised Cosine Feeder

Stefânia de Sousa Faria
Federal Universtity of Minas Gerais
Belo Horizonte, Minas Gerais, Brazil
Email: stefaniadesousa@hotmail.com

Cássio Gonçalves do Rego
Department of Electronic Engineering
Federal Universtity of Minas Gerais
Belo Horizonte, Minas Gerais, Brazil
Email: cassio@cpdee.ufmg.br

Fernando José da Silva Moreira
Department of Electronic Engineering
Federal Universtity of Minas Gerais
Belo Horizonte, Minas Gerais, Brazil
Email: fernandomoreira@ufmg.br

***Abstract*—A closed-form solution in time-domain for integral operators associated to a modified raised cosine feeder is developed and analytical results have been generated and compared to the original raised cosine model.**

I. Introduction

The temporal characterization of parabolic reflector antennas is a technique highly used when the transmitted pulse via the antenna is ultra-short or when high data rates are employed [1]. The analysis of these problems in frequency-domain becomes impractical due to the large operation bandwidths, so this way, the scattered field from conducting surfaces has been approached directly in time domain [2]. In the present work, integral operators are developed to obtain the transient response of reflector antennas using the aperture method. Such operators are valid near and far from the reflector and by means of a temporal convolution, can be applied to define the antenna radiated field with arbitrary sources.

Initially, the integral operators are found in frequency-domain and then converted into time-domain using Inverse Laplace Transform. The formulation developed here is based on [1] and [3]. In [1], the transient field generated by a parabolic reflector antenna uses an elemental Huygen's source at the focus while in [3], the feeder utilized is the raised cosine model. This paper intends to investigate the same transient field developed in those previous works but this time, considering a modified raised cosine model feeder.

One of the advantages of using a modified raised cosine model as a feeder is due to the simpler closed-form solution for integral operators obtained when compared to the original raised cosine model. Analytical results were obtained and compared to the results found for the raised cosine model introduced in [3] using the same parameters.

II. Formulation

A. Frequency-Domain Field

The electric field radiated in free space can be expressed as equation 16 of [1] where s is the complex frequency, c is the free-space velocity of light, Z_0 is the free-space impedance, Y_0 is the free-space admittance, R is the distance between the source and the observer and $\bar{E}_a$ and $\bar{H}_a$ are the electric and magnetic aperture fields respectively.

Applying the parameters associated to the paraboloid in equation 16 of [1], the integral operator in frequency-domain can be written as [1]

$$\tilde{\vec{E}}_r^{\delta}(\vec{r},s)=\frac{FV_0}{\pi c}\iint_{S_a}\frac{\vec{g}\left(\vec{\rho}',\phi'\right)}{R\left(\rho'^2+4F^2\right)}e^{\frac{-s}{c}\left(R+F+\frac{D^2}{16F}\right)}\mathrm{d}S' \quad (1)$$

where V_0 is a constant, D is the surface diameter, F is the focal distance and $g\left(\vec{\rho}',\phi'\right)$ is a generalized function related to the feeder.

B. Time-Domain Field

In order to obtain the radiated field in time-domain, the Inverse Laplace Transform was applied and the equation 1 becomes [1]

$$\vec{E}_r^u(\vec{r},t)=\frac{FV_0}{\pi c}\iint_{S_a}\frac{\vec{g}\left(\vec{\rho}',\phi'\right)}{R\left(\rho'^2+4F^2\right)}\delta\left(t-\frac{R+F+\frac{D^2}{16F}}{c}\right)\mathrm{d}S' \quad (2)$$

In this paper, it was used a modified raised cosine feeder with $n=1$ and the argument equal to $\frac{\theta_F}{2}$. Hence, after some extensive mathematical manipulations, the integral operator can be written as

$$\vec{E}_r^u(\vec{r},t)=E_{r_x}^u(\vec{r},t)\hat{x}+E_{r_y}^u(\vec{r},t)\hat{y}+E_{r_z}^u(\vec{r},t)\hat{z} \quad (3)$$

where

$$\vec{E}_x^u(\vec{r},t)=-\frac{FV_0}{\pi}\Pi(t)\left\{\int_{\alpha_1}^{\alpha_2}\left[\frac{\delta_3\cos^2(\theta_P)\sin^2(\psi+\phi)}{(\delta_1+\delta_2\cos(\psi))^{\frac{3}{2}}}\right]\mathrm{d}\psi+\int_{\alpha_1}^{\alpha_2}\left[\frac{\delta_3\sin^2(\theta_P)}{(\delta_1+\delta_2\cos(\psi))^{\frac{3}{2}}}\right]\mathrm{d}\psi\right\} \quad (4)$$

$$\vec{E}_y^u(\vec{r},t)=\frac{FV_0}{\pi}\Pi(t)\left\{\int_{\alpha_1}^{\alpha_2}\left[\frac{\delta_3\cos^2(\theta_P)\cos(\psi+\phi)\sin(\psi+\phi)}{(\delta_1+\delta_2\cos(\psi))^{\frac{3}{2}}}\right]\mathrm{d}\psi+\int_{\alpha_1}^{\alpha_2}\left[\frac{\delta_3}{(\delta_1+\delta_2\cos(\psi))^{\frac{3}{2}}}\right]\mathrm{d}\psi\right\} \quad (5)$$

$$\vec{E}_z^u(\vec{r},t) = -\frac{FV_0}{\pi}\Pi(t)\left\{\int_{\alpha_1}^{\alpha_2}\left[\frac{\delta_3\cos(\theta_P)\sin(\theta_P)}{(\delta_1+\delta_2\cos(\psi))^{\frac{3}{2}}}\right]d\psi\right\} \quad (6)$$

where $\Pi(t)$ collects the time duration of the operator $\vec{E}_r^u(\vec{r},t)$, δ_1, δ_2 and δ_3 are parameters associated to the parabolic antenna and ρ, ξ', α_1 and α_2 are defined according to [1].

III. Case studies

The results obtained here show the magnitude of the integral operators in near and far field regions. It was considered a parabolic reflector antenna with $D = 7.5$ m and $F = 0.4D$ at the plane $\phi = 0$. Figure 1 presents the magnitude of the operator considering the $cos\left(\frac{\theta_F}{2}\right)$ feeder and a radial distance equal to 50 m while Figure 2 shows the same operator, however the computed feeder now is $\cos(\theta_F)$ [3]. In Figures 3 and 4, the magnitude of the integral operators are obtained in the far field region, considering a radial distance equal to 5000 m and the $\cos(\theta_F)$ and $cos\left(\frac{\theta_F}{2}\right)$ feeders, respectively.

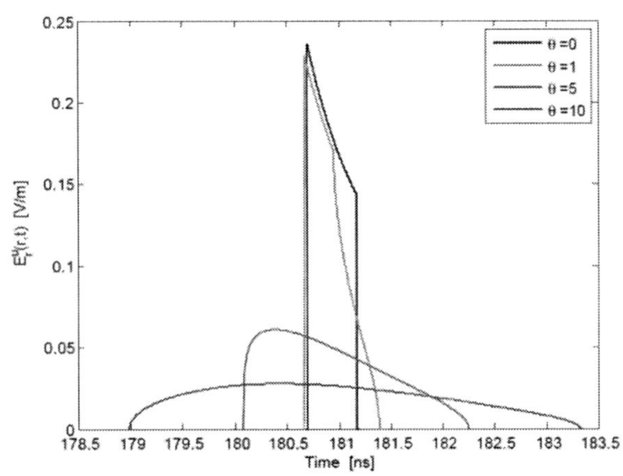

Fig. 1. Magnitude of the integral operator at $r = 50$ m generated by a parabolic antenna using the $\cos\left(\frac{\theta_F}{2}\right)$ feeder.

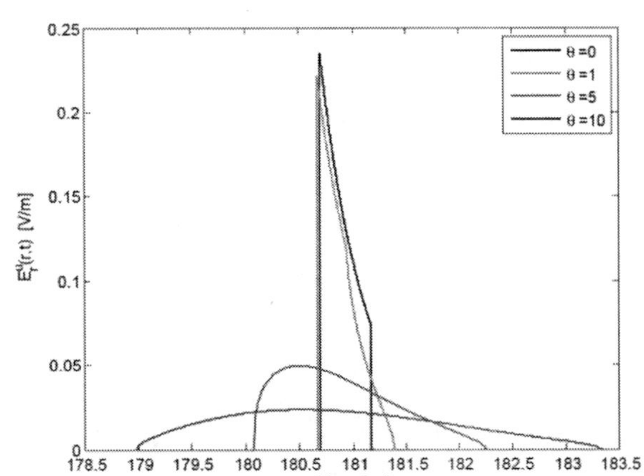

Fig. 2. Magnitude of the integral operator at $r = 50$ m generated by a parabolic antenna using the $\cos(\theta)$ feeder.

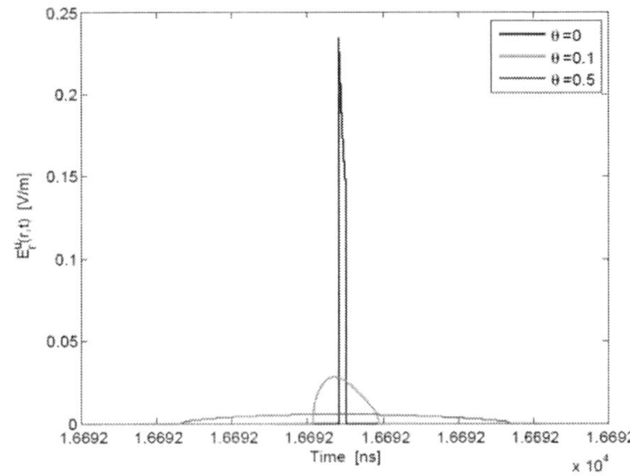

Fig. 3. Magnitude of the integral operator at $r = 5000$ m generated by a parabolic antenna using the $\cos\left(\frac{\theta_F}{2}\right)$ feeder.

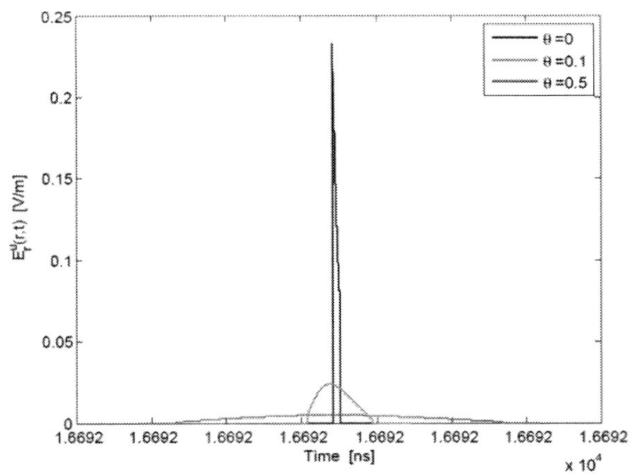

Fig. 4. Magnitude of the integral operator at $r = 5000$ m generated by a parabolic antenna using the $\cos(\theta)$ feeder.

IV. Conclusion

The time-domain formulation developed in this paper can be applied to generalized feeders and once the integral operators are known, the radiated field from the parabolic reflector antenna can be easily found by means of a temporal convolution. The huge advantage of this technique is the low time consumption to generate radiated fields from parabolic antennas using generic sources. Analytical results were obtained for two different feeders in the near and far field regions.

Acknowledgment

This work was partially supported by CAPES and CNPq.

References

[1] H.-T. Chou, P. H. Pathak, and P. R. Rousseau, "Analytical solution for early-time transient radiation from pulse-excited parabolic reflector antennas," *IEEE Transactions on Antennas and Propagation*, vol. 45, no. 5, May 1997.

[2] C. G. Rego, S. T. M. Gonçalves, and F. J. S. Moreira, "High-frequency asymptotic formulation for prompt response of parabolic reflector atennas," *International Journal of Electronicsand Communications*, 2008.

[3] C. G. Rego, "Closed-form solution for integral operators applied to the calculation of radiated fields from paraolic reflector antennas," *IEEE MTT-S International Mricrowave & Optoelectronics Conference (IMOC)*, 2009.

MoM-SIE Scattering Models of Snow and Ice Hydrometeors Based on 3D Shape Reconstructions from MASC Images

Branislav M. Notaroš, V. N. Bringi, Cameron Kleinkort, Sanja B. Manić, Elene Chobanyan, Gwo-Jong Huang, Patrick Kennedy, Merhala Thurai
Electrical and Computer Engineering Department
Colorado State University
Fort Collins, CO, USA
notaros@colostate.edu

***Abstract*—We present scattering models of snow and ice hydrometeors and computation of full polarimetric radar variables for winter precipitation using a higher order method of moments (MoM) in the surface integral equation (SIE) formulation. The studies of winter precipitation are based primarily on measurements by a multi-angle snowflake camera (MASC), reconstruction of 3D hydrometeor shapes by means of the visual hull method, MoM-SIE scattering computations, and measured polarimetric observables by CSU-CHILL Radar.**

Keywords—scattering; surface integral equation; method of moments; snow observations; polarimetric radar; winter precipitation; shape reconstruction.

I. Introduction

Computation of polarimetric radar measurables in winter precipitation cannot be done solely based on spheroidal shape models. Even for Rayleigh scattering, where the spherical or spheroidal shape assumption is reasonable for evaluation of the reflectivity [1], *Z*, such an assumption is not sufficient for computing the full scattering matrix and related radar observables, required, for example, for radar-based hydrometeor classification. So, even at the S-band, the frequency band for the network of WSR-88D weather radars, some radar observables significantly depend on the shape and composition of particles.

This summary paper addresses scattering models of snow and ice hydrometeors and computation of full polarimetric variables for winter precipitation, focusing only on single particle scattering. It presents our continued studies of winter precipitation within the MASCRAD (MASC + Radar) project, tied with snow observations as part of MASCRAD winter campaigns near Greeley, Colorado, USA [2]. The studies are based primarily on measurements by a multi-angle snowflake camera (MASC), reconstruction of three-dimensional (3D) hydrometeor shapes using the visual hull method, scattering computations by a higher order method of moments (MoM) in the surface integral equation (SIE) formulation [3], and measured polarimetric observables by CSU-CHILL Radar.

This work was supported by the National Science Foundation under grant AGS-1344862.

II. Realisctic MoM-SIE Scattering Modeling of Snow and Ice Particles Based on MASC Measurements

The MASC, shown in Fig. 1, is an instrument for capturing high-resolution photographs of snow and ice particles in freefall from three views, while simultaneously measuring their fall speed [4]. Shown in Fig. 1 is also the Colorado State University's version of the MASC, where, in order to improve reconstruction of 3D shapes of particles, two additional cameras were added to the MASC, "externally," to provide additional views. Fig. 1 also shows an example of snowflake reconstruction using the visual hull method [2]. The reconstructed mesh of the particle is used as input to the MoM-SIE technique, for scattering analysis [5]. The fall-speed measured by the MASC is used to estimate the particle mass (Böhm's method), and then, using the volume of 3D reconstructions, estimate the permittivity of the particles, based on a Maxwell-Garnet formula [2].

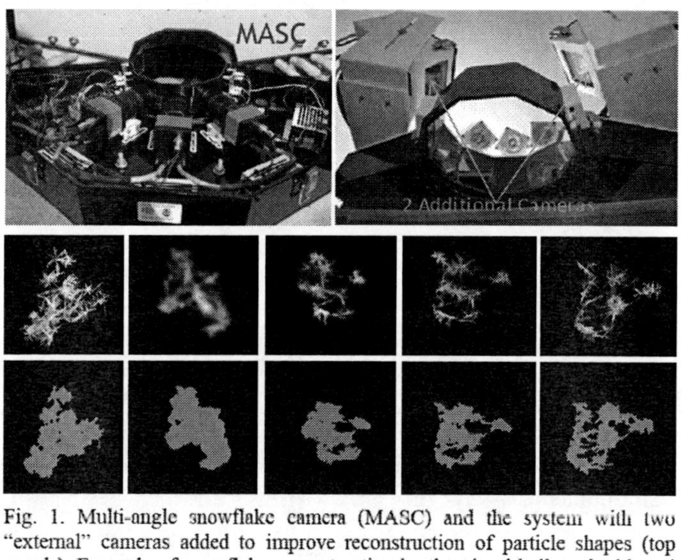

Fig. 1. Multi-angle snowflake camera (MASC) and the system with two "external" cameras added to improve reconstruction of particle shapes (top panels). Example of snowflake reconstruction by the visual hull method based on five photographs of a snowflake collected by the 5-camera MASC system: MASC images (middle panels) and corresponding projections of the visual hull generated 3D mesh to camera image planes (bottom panels).

III. Results and Discussion

Fig. 2 shows bistatic scattering results for a dielectric spherical scatterer 4 mm in diameter at 10 GHz, modeling a rain drop with relative permittivity $\varepsilon_r = 80 - j20$. This simple case is an excellent evaluation example because of the analytical solution in the form of Mie's series. The results are obtained using the higher order MoM-SIE technique, the discrete dipole approximation (DDA) method [6], and the Mie solution. Note that the DDA method along with the T-matrix method [5] are the two most frequently used tools in atmospheric particle scattering analysis. The plane wave is incident from the negative z direction, and we compute the Mueller-matrix element M_{11} [1] in the plane $\phi = 0$. The MoM-SIE model is constructed from 24 curved quadrilateral patches of second orders in both geometry and current approximation (for electric and magnetic equivalent surface currents), which results in a total of only 384 unknown current-distribution coefficients. The DDA model consists of 60 dipoles in each dimension of the scatterer, namely, a total of 216,000 dipoles. We observe a higher accuracy of the MoM results when compared to the DDA results, with the higher order MoM-SIE code being about 573 times faster than the DDA.

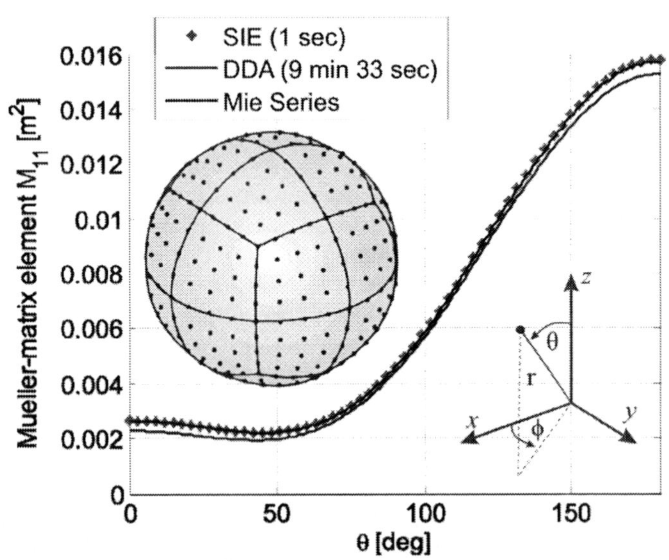

Fig. 2. Bistatic Mueller-matrix element M_{11} for a spherical rain drop: higher order MoM-SIE (model in the inset), DDA, and exact (Mie's series) solutions.

Fig. 3 shows illustrative results of the MASC/visual-hull/scattering observation/analysis methodology for an individual snowflake captured during a snow storm on February 21st, 2015 at the MASCRAD instrumentation site. As can be seen, the computed linear depolarization ratio, LDR, and differential reflectivity, Z_{dr} [1], single-particle values (given just for illustration) agree well with those measured simultaneously by the CSU-CHILL Radar. These results illustrate one of the end goals of using the visual hull method for 3D shape reconstructions of snow and ice particles based on MASC images.

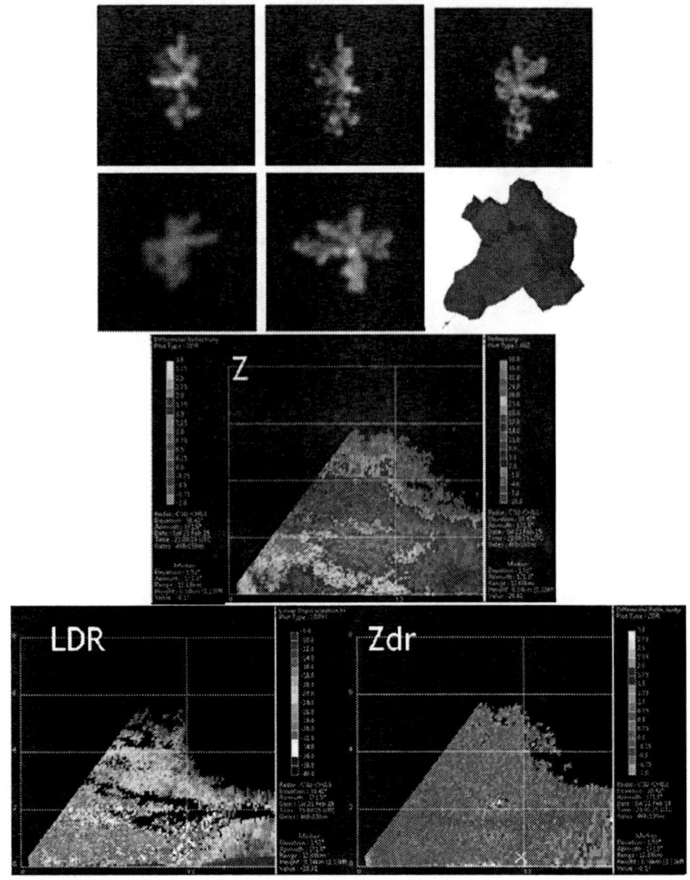

Fig. 3. Illustrative results of MoM-SIE scattering calculations based on the MASC (Fig. 1) images of a snowflake captured at the MASCRAD instrumentation site during a snow event on February 21st, 2015 and the resulting visual hull 3D shape reconstruction, in comparison with the corresponding CSU-CHILL radar range height indicator (RHI) plots of LDR and Z_{dr} at the same time. The site is at the 12.92-km range from the radar (white "×" marker in the plots). Radar: LDR = −29 dB; $Z_{dr} = -0.17$ dB; $Z = 20$ dBz; Scattering: LDR = −31 dB, $Z_{dr} = -0.1$ dB, Dielectric Constant: 1.216 − j0.0002.

References

[1] V. N. Bringi, and V. Chandrasekar, "Polarisation Doppler Weather Radar", *Cambridge University Press*, August 2001.

[2] B. M. Notaroš, V. N. Bringi, C. Kleinkort, P. Kennedy, G.-J. Huang, M. Thurai, A. J. Newman, W. Bang, and G. Lee, "Accurate Characterization of Winter Precipitation Using Multi-Angle Snowflake Camera, Visual Hull, Advanced Scattering Methods and Polarimetric Radar," invited paper, Special Issue "Advances in Clouds and Precipitation," *Atmosphere*, vol. 7, no. 6, pp. 81–111, June 2016.

[3] M. Djordjevic and B. M. Notaros, "Double Higher Order Method of Moments for Surface Integral Equation Modeling of Metallic and Dielectric Antennas and Scatterers," *IEEE Transactions on Antennas and Propagation*, Vol. 52, No. 8, August 2004, pp. 2118-2129.

[4] T. J. Garrett, C. Fallgatter, K. Shkurko, and D. Howlett, "Fallspeed measurement and high-resolution multi-angle photography of hydrometeors in freefall," *Atmos. Meas. Tech. Discuss.*, vol. 5, 2012, pp. 4827–4850.

[5] E. Chobanyan, N. J. Sekeljic, A. B. Manic, M. M. Ilic, V. N. Bringi, and B. M. Notaros, "Efficient and Accurate Computational Electromagnetics Approach to Precipitation Particle Scattering Analysis Based on Higher-Order Method of Moments Integral Equation Modeling," *J. Atmos. Oceanic Technol.*, Vol. 32, October 2015, pp. 1745–1758.

[6] B. T. Draine and P. J. Flatau, DDSCAT 7.2 code, 2012, http://arxiv.org/abs/1202.3424.

Resolution of 2D Time Domain Electric Field Integral Equation:Novel formulation of RWG associated to Laguerre Polynomials

Auns Khaled,Dorsaf Omri and Taoufik Aguili
LR99ES21 Laboratoire de Systèmes de Communications
Université de Tunis El Manar, Ecole Nationale d'Ingénieurs de Tunis
Tunis, Tunisie
Auns.Khaled@enit.rnu.tn

Abstract—This paper presents a novel algorithm for analyzing transient radiation from square plate illuminated by an incident electromagnetic wave. The algorithm is based on spatio-temporal Integral Equation (Electric Field Integral Equation) to predict the transient response of the plate. The Laguerre functions are used as temporal basis. In order to simplify the space modeling, we reformulate the space basis RWG. This basis is expressed in polar coordinate that defines by pairs of adjacent triangular. The later presents the analyzed sub-domain characterized by their triangle's centroid. Numerical results that validate and demonstrate the efficacy of the proposed algorithm are presented.

Keywords—Laguerre functions; Method of Moments;RWG functions; Time Domain Integral Equation; trensient current.

I. INTRODUCTION

The electromagnetic pollution is increasing in our daily environment. Hence, predict the electromagnetic environment is important to protect some derogatory components in the system in the presence of the electric and magnetic fields, which is computed as a description of electromagnetic compatibility.

In most of the aforementioned studies, TD-IE has been adopted to treat the scattering problems. In fact, the marching-on time MOT is usually employed to solve it, but a serious drawback of the algorithm is the instability of the solution for late time. In order to avoid this instability, we apply the TD-MoM [1]. Therefore, we can lead the desired result by solving a matrix equation recursively with a finite number of basis functions.

In this paper, we will address the mesh of the adopted structure, so that, it is mandatory to choose the appropriate space basic functions for the structure's meshing because it has a direct impact on the final result. The surface modeling approach has been adequately successful in treating many problems, particularly in those requiring the prediction of transient radiation from illuminated complex surface.

The present approach follows the strategy outlined in [1] which is based on triangular mesh. We keep the geometric flexibility of the triangular 2-D mesh related to RWG basis.

Indeed, the goal of this paper is developed a 2-D formulation of TD-MoM [1] using the RWG functions as a spatial basis for an arbitrary structure's meshing [2]. As is well known, we have to subdivide the structure's surface into triangle elements generated of an RWG space basis, to analyze the inducted current on it. So, that an alternative space formulation is proposed to solve the TD-EFIE. With the aim of simplify the advanced algorithm, RWG functions are expressed in polar coordinate. This coordinate system has been used to facilitate the calculation of the scalar product. It's intended to employ them to model a square plate and pointed out the possibility of extending this approach to model arbitrary surfaces.

In this work, we analyze the scattering problems related to arbitrary shape illuminated by a transient incident field. We firstly proceed by establishing an Integral Equation. Then we apply the TD-MoM to solve it.

This paper is organized as follows. Section II introduces a general formulation of the problem. Section III gives numerical results for scattering by a plane transient wave including a comparison with using another basis function. Section IV summarizes the contents of our paper.

II. FORMULATION

In order to model a 2-D problem, we consider an arbitrary surface S excited by a transient electromagnetic wave $E^{inc}(t)$. The surface of the shape is a perfect conductor. For that purpose, we apply the boundary conditions at the conductor's surface, as following:

$$\vec{n} \times \overrightarrow{E^{inc}} + \vec{n} \times \overrightarrow{E^{sca}} = \vec{0} \quad (1)$$

Where $\overrightarrow{E^{inc}}$, $\overrightarrow{E^{sca}}$ are the incident and the scattered field respectively and $\vec{n}$ is the normal to the surface S.

The scattered field is expressed in terms of the scalar and the vector potentials [1]:

$$\boldsymbol{E}^{sca}(\boldsymbol{r},\mathrm{t}) = -\frac{\partial}{\partial t}\boldsymbol{A}(\boldsymbol{r},\mathrm{t}) - \nabla\varphi(\boldsymbol{r},t)\,;\forall\,\mathbf{r}\in \mathrm{S} \quad (2)$$

A. Space resolution: RWG functions

To solve the TD-EFIE formed by (1) and (2), we apply a 2-D formulation of the MoM method [1]. Indeed, we start by the definition of the space basis functions RWG, expressed by:

$$f_n^{\pm}(\mathbf{r}) = \begin{cases} \dfrac{l_n}{2A_n^{\pm}} \rho_n^{\pm}, & r \epsilon T_n^{\pm} \\ 0, & otherwise \end{cases} \quad (3)$$

The unknown induced current at the surface of the patch is approximated in terms of the spatial basis functions (3), as following:

$$C(r,t) = \sum_{n=1}^{N} C_n(t) f_n(r) \quad (4)$$

Where N is the number of space domains.

B. Polar coordinate

To simplify the expression of the TD-EFIE, we use the polar coordinate. Let note that the polar coordinates of the observation point are p (ρ, θ) and of the source point is p' (ρ', θ') designed either by the position vector **r** and **r**' respectively, and defined with respect to O (Fig.1). Thus, the distance rr' is expressed by:

$$rr' = \sqrt{\rho^2 + \rho'^2 - 2\rho\rho'\cos(\theta - \theta')} \quad (5)$$

Hence, the expression of the vector $\rho_n^{\pm}$ in the definition of the RWG function will be expressed also on polar coordinate. The Hertz vector is expressed with the basis function $f_n(\boldsymbol{r})$. Then, we proceed by applying the Galerkin's method. Consequently, we project the TD-EFIE on the space basis.

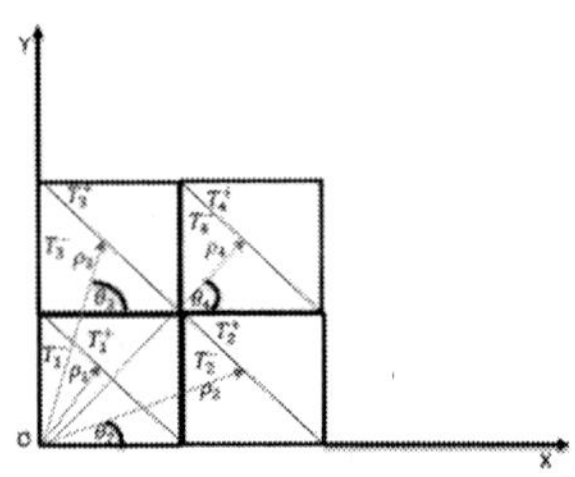

Fig.1. The structure's meshing.

C. Temporal resolution

For the temporal resolution of the TD-EFIE, we start by expressing the Hertz vector (4) in terms of Laguerre functions [1] used as temporal basis.

$$c_n(t) = \sum_{i=0}^{M} c_{n,i} \varphi_i(st) \quad (6)$$

We note that « s » is the scaling factor. The determination of « s » is very important and it can influence on the stability of the result [3].

we apply Galerkin's Method in the Methods of Moments context, we obtain the following matrix system:

$$[\boldsymbol{A}] * [\boldsymbol{C}]^a = [\boldsymbol{B}]^a \quad (7)$$

The spatial matrix A is independent of the order of the Laguerre polynomial. The spatial distribution of the Hertz vector is calculated by inversion of the matrix A and by raising the Laguerre order "a": 0, 1……M.

III. NUMERICAL RESULTS

We present below some representative numerical results obtained using our developed algorithm. Hence, we consider a conducting patch of length L=1m and radius a=0.001 m. The patch is excited by a transient wave in free space expressed by:

$$E^{inc}(t) = \begin{cases} 1, 10^{-9}s \leq t \leq 10^{-8}s \\ 0, otherwire \end{cases} \quad (8)$$

We set the observation interval I$[0, 1.4 * 10^{-7}\ s]$ subdivides on under domains of length $\Delta t = 0.7 * 10^{-9}$s. The Laguerre's parameters are defined by the number of the Laguerre's function M and the scaling factor « s », with M=80 and s=7.068*10^8.

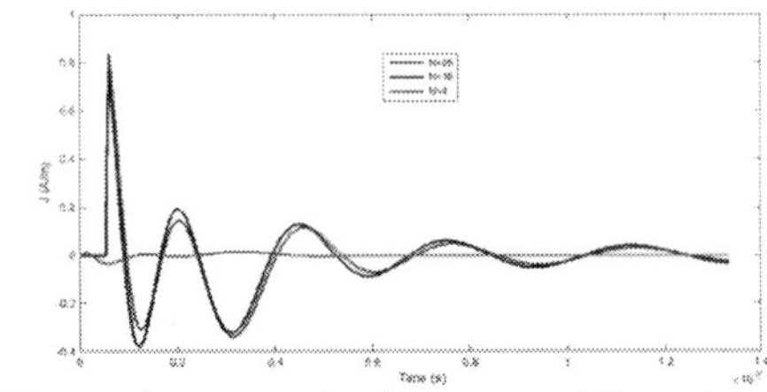

Fig.2. The transient current density response at the center of the patch.

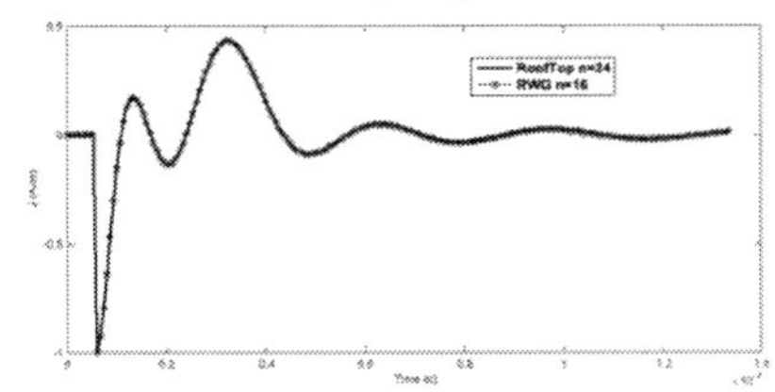

Fig.3. The validation of the obtained result with the Rooftop functions.

IV. CONCLUSION

In this paper, we have applied the MoM to solve the integral equation in time domain (TD-IE) in order to treat the scattering transient problem. In fact, we applied Galerkin's in the Methods of Moments context. Indeed, to obtain an optimal meshing we express the RWG function with polar coordination to simplify the 2-D formulation. The accurate and stable results are obtained. This developed 2-D formulation can be applied to study many complex structures.

REFERENCE

[1] B. H. Jung, Y.-S. Chung, T. K. Sarkar." Time-Domain EFIE, MFIE, AND CFIE formulationusing Laguerre Polynomialsas temporal basisfunctionsfor the analaysis of transient scattering from arbitrary shaped conducting structures ."Progress In Electromagnetics Research, PIER 39, 1–45, 2003.

[2] S. M.Rao, Donald R. Wilton, and Allen W. Glisson. "Electromagnetic scattering by surfaces of arbitrary shape." *Antennas and Propagation*, IEEE Transactions on antennas and propagation, vol. 30, no 3, p. 409-418, 1982.

[3] D. Omri, M. Aidi, and T. Aguili. "Transient response of coupled wire antennas using the electric field integral equation with Laguerre polynomials as temporal basis functions." *Ultra-WideBand (ICUWB), 2014 IEEE International Conference on*. IEEE, 2014.

2D BEM for Processing Magnetic Field Maps of Accelerator Magnets

Alberto Cosmai[1,2], Luca Di Rienzo [1]
[1] Politecnico di Milano,
Dipartimento di Elettronica, Informazione e Bioingegneria
Milano, Italy
luca.dirienzo@polimi.it

Stephan Russenschuck [2]
[2]CERN
Technology Department
Genève, Switzerland
stephan.russenschuck@cern.ch

***Abstract*— The rotating-coil magnetometer is a standard device for measuring integrated magnetic fields of accelerator magnets. The coil intercepts the magnetic flux at a radius given by the dimensions of the measurement shaft that comprises a set of induction coils. For magnets of a rectangular aperture with large aspect ratio (> 3:1) the cylindrical domain covers only a portion of the magnet bore and therefore a sampling technique is required, using the single-stretched wire or a moving fluxmeter. The method presented in this paper concerns the extraction of multipoles in the rectangular problem domain by using boundary data.**

Keywords*— *Accelerator magnets, magnetic measurements, boundary element method.

I. Introduction

Magnetic field measurements are of fundamental importance in every accelerator project. Knowing the generated magnetic field allows to verify the magnet design (modeling errors), the magnet manufacture (magnet to magnet reproducibility) and yields input for beam physics simulations and machine operation. Furthermore, magnetic measurements are essential to study dynamic effects, such as combinations of iron hysteresis and 3D eddy-currents, which are still a challenge in magnetic field simulations in the required accuracy of 1 unit in 10^4 to 10^6.

The magnetic field of accelerator magnets is commonly described by its main field component and the higher-order field errors. In a mathematical sense, this representation is an analytic function in a simply-connected domain developed into eigenfunctions with so-called multipole coefficients. This representation is therefore strictly two-dimensional and the magnetic field is an integrated quantity by the surface of the search coil that covers the magnet bore, its extremities, as well as the fringe-field regions [1].

Being the most precise tool to measure magnetic field errors in accelerator magnets, the rotating-coil magnetometer nevertheless lacks in versatility, because for the highest precision the shaft must be as large as possible. This is a problem for magnets with rectangular apertures of large aspect ratio. However, beam simulations require a complete representation of the field in the full domain.

For rectangular apertures large, stationary fluxmeters are often used for fast ramped magnets. For static operation the stretched wire method can be used, and both methods measure only the normal component of the field with respect to the traced surface [1].

In this paper, we apply 2D boundary element method for the field reconstruction in a rectangular domain from the measured boundary data. In [2] we investigated a 3D magnetostatic field formulation where boundary data are magnetic field point data. Here the boundary data are the normal components of the magnetic field integrated along the length of the magnet.

II. BEM Formulation

The scalar potential in the magnet aperture, free of magnetic material and current sources, satisfies the Laplace equation, $\nabla^2 \phi_m(x,y,z) = 0$. We define

$$\bar{\phi}_m(x,y) = \int_{-z_0}^{+z_0} \phi_m(x,y,z)\, dz \tag{1}$$

as the integrated potential on the interval $[-z_0, z_0]$ that covers the magnet bore and the fringe field regions at the magnet's extremities. It can then be easily proven that $\bar{\phi}_m(x,y)$ obeys the Laplace equation, $\nabla^2 \bar{\phi}_m(x,y) = 0$ [1]. Hence we can apply the representation formula

$$c\bar{\phi}_m = \oint_{\mathcal{L}} \left(\bar{\phi}_m \frac{\partial G}{\partial n} - G \frac{\partial \bar{\phi}_m}{\partial n} \right), \tag{2}$$

with $\mathcal{L} = \mathcal{L}_1 \cup \mathcal{L}_2 \cup \mathcal{L}_3 \cup \mathcal{L}_4$ according to Fig. 1.

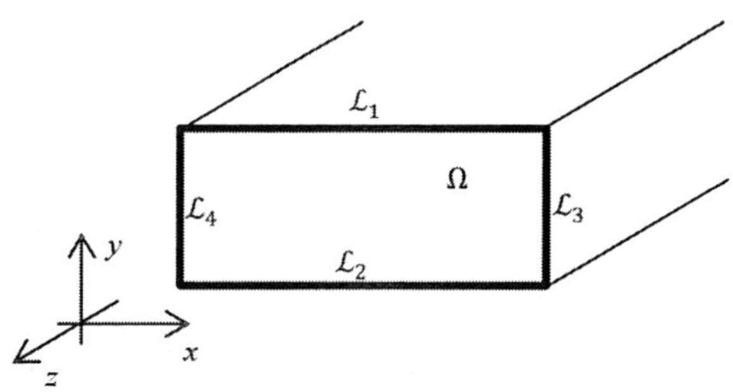

Fig. 1 – Domain of interest in the magnet aperture, typically a parallelepiped for a magnet with rectangular aperture.

We know $\frac{\partial \bar{\phi}_m}{\partial n}$ from magnetic measurements over the rectangular contour, for example over $\mathcal{L}_1$:

$$\left.\frac{\partial \bar{\phi}_m(x,y)}{\partial y}\right|_{\mathcal{L}_1} = \bar{B}_y(x,y) = \int_{-z_0}^{+z_0} B_y(x,y,z)\,dz. \tag{3}$$

We solve Eq. (2) with $c = 1/2$ over the discretized contour in order to obtain $\bar{\phi}_m$ from $\frac{\partial \bar{\phi}_m}{\partial n}$ on $\mathcal{L}$ (Neumann to Dirichlet map). We can then obtain $\bar{\phi}_m$ (up to a constant term) everywhere inside Ω from the representation formula with $c = 1$. Of course, this method is not limited to strictly rectangular domains. It is possible to perform these computations on deformed contours able to represent the actual path of a measurement system.

III. A Real-World Test Case

Fig. 2 shows a calibration dipole that has an aperture width of 320 mm and an aperture height of 80 mm. We consider a rectangle, with one side of 100 mm and the other one of 70 mm, centered in the magnet aperture (Fig. 3). The rectangle is discretized with N=2160 boundary elements. The main component of the magnetic flux density reconstructed by BEM is compared with that computed by the BEM-FEM package ROXIE [1] (Fig. 4-6).

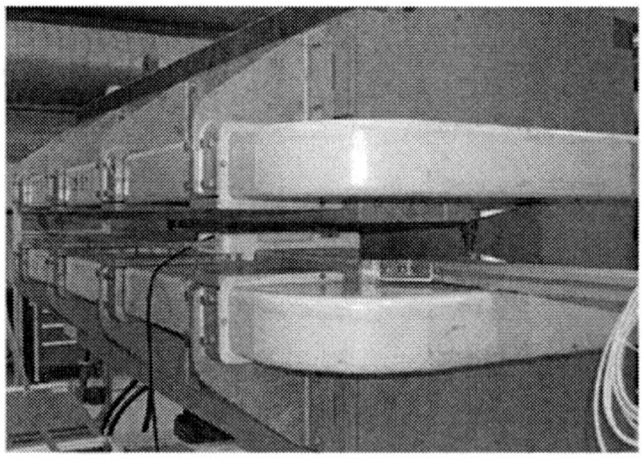

Fig. 2 – A calibration dipole at CERN.

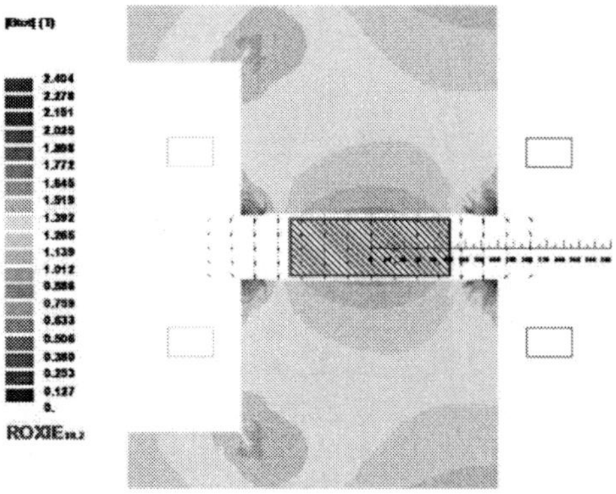

Fig. 3 – Cross section of the calibration dipole and magnetic field simulated by the BEM-FEM package ROXIE [1].

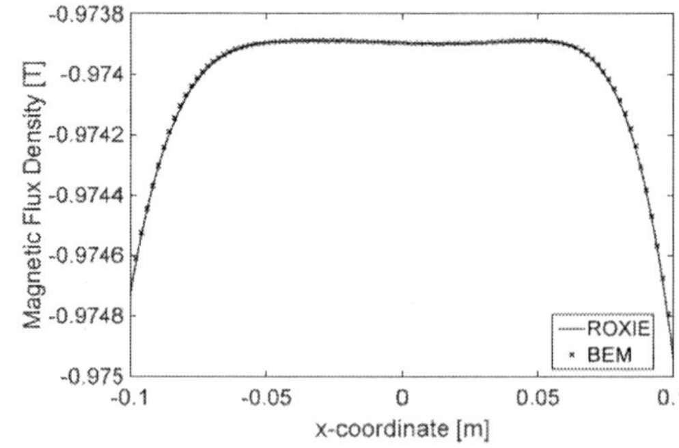

Fig. 4 – Main component of the magnetic flux density computed along the x-axis of the reference dipole using ROXIE and reconstructed by BEM.

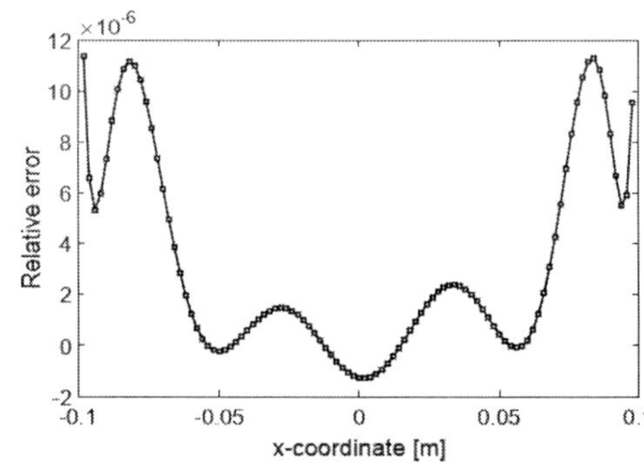

Fig. 5 – Relative error corresponding to Fig. 4.

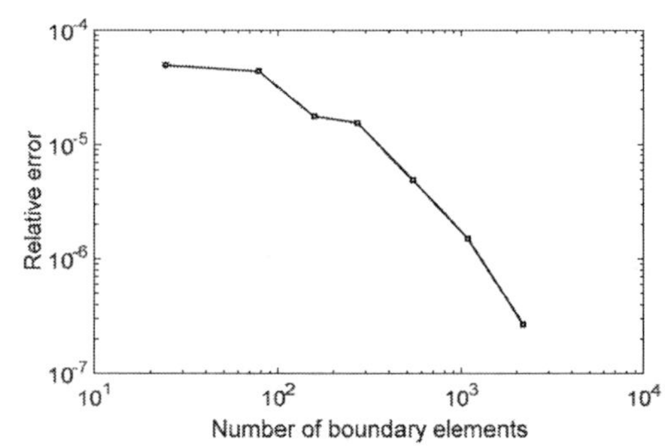

Fig. 6 – Relative error in the computation of B_y in the origin as a function of the number of boundary elements.

In the full paper the noise in the magnetic measurements will be simulated and its impact on the field reconstruction will be analyzed. Furthermore, measurement systematic errors will be compensated with the help of the proposed BEM approach.

IV. References

[1] S. Russenschuck, Field computation for accelerator magnets, Wiley-VCH, 2010.

[2] A. Cosmai, L. Di Rienzo, and S. Russenschuck, "Post processing magnetic-field maps of accelerator magnets by the boundary element method," accepted for presentation at the 17th *Biennial Conference on Electromagnetic Field Computation (CEFC 2016)*, Miami, FL, USA, 13-16 November, 2016.

Reconstruction of PWM Signal Based on Double Fourier Transform and Minimum Phase System

Yaxiu Sun , Yida Lai, Junpeng Fang, Meng Lin
College of Information and Communications Engineering,
Harbin Engineering University, Harbin, China, 150001
sunyaxiu@hrbeu.edu.cn laiyida@hrbeu.edu.cn

Abstract— **Since PWM signal is hard to express with formulation in time domain while it is simple in the frequency domain and taking the frequency dependence of the system into consideration, this paper establishes a new way to the reconstruction of PWM signal from frequency domain to time domain. It uses double Fourier transform to decompose the PWM signal in frequency domain, then gets terminal waveforms by using the model of different frequency viewing from motor. Finally, it refactors phase information based on principle of minimum phase system to recovery time domain waveform and then to compare with the waveform of reality. The recovery of the signal is nearly consistent to the real waveform. It can be laid the theoretical foundation of long-line transmission systems of oil exploration in our country.**

Keywords— **PWM; frequency domain; time domain; double Fourier transform; minimum phase system**

I. INTRODUCTION

Pulse Width Modulation (PWM) technology is widely used in the projects [1-3], however, by the reasons of not only the cable with complex structure is overlength, but environment is peculiar as well, negative effects such as severe overvoltage, Electromagnetic Interference (EMI) and crosstalk are caused which will affect the normal operations of the underwater system. Therefore, accurate model should be built to analyze the negative effects. Hence a novel method by translating the PWM signal from time domain to frequency domain is proposed to solve the problem of modeling. It uses double Fourier transform to decompose the PWM signal in frequency domain, gets terminal waveforms by using the model of different frequency viewing from motor. Finally, it refactors phase information based on principle of minimum phase system to recovery time domain waveform. The new method is significant not only in theory but also in the project. Moreover, it can be laid the theoretical foundation of long-line transmission systems in our country.

II. FREQUENCY-DOMAIN ANALYSIS OF PWM SIGNAL

Since the frequency spectrum of PWM signal is discrete, it is hard to set up parameters as sampling interval and the number of sampling point legitimately at the same time by using FFT, therefore it is necessary to solve frequency function by mathematical method. PWM signal modulated by isosceles triangle wave can be analyzed in frequency domain using double Fourier transform because of the periodicity and independence of fundamental wave and carrier wave. The isosceles triangle wave can be expressed as $x(t)=\omega_c t+\theta_c$, while sine wave can be expressed as $y(t)=\omega_0 t+\theta_0$. Since the $x(t)$ and $y(t)$ are independent, PWM signal can be expressed as a two-dimensional function $f[x(t),y(t)]$, which frequency spectrum is described as

$$f(x,y)=\frac{A_{00}}{2}+\sum_{n=1}^{\infty}[A_{0n}\cos ny+B_{0n}\sin ny]+\sum_{m=1}^{\infty}[A_{m0}\cos mx+B_{m0}\sin mx] \quad (1)$$
$$+\sum_{m=1}^{\infty}\sum_{\substack{n=-\infty\\ n\neq 0}}^{\infty}[A_{mn}\cos(mx+ny)+B_{mn}\sin(mx+ny)]$$

where coefficient of double Fourier integral can be obtained by

$$A_{mn}+jB_{mn}=\frac{1}{2\pi^2}\int_{-\pi}^{\pi}\int_{-\pi}^{\pi}f(x,y)e^{j(mx+ny)}dxdy \quad (2)$$

To take the symmetry of integrating range into account, and In consideration of integration period, double integral interval of $f[x(t),y(t)]$ in the range of $x:[-\pi,\pi)$, $y:[-\pi,\pi)$, can be described as

$$f(x,y)=\begin{cases}2\mathrm{V}_{dc},-\pi<x<\pi\mathrm{M}\cos y,-\pi\leq x<\pi\\ 0,\pi\mathrm{M}\cos y<x<\pi\end{cases} \quad (3)$$

In mathematics, the Jacobi–Anger expansion is an expansion of exponentials of trigonometric functions in the basis of their harmonics which is used while the calculation of harmonic components. The most general identity is given by:

$$e^{j\xi\cos\theta}=\sum_{k=-\infty}^{\infty}j^k J_k(\xi)e^{jk\theta}=J_0(\xi)+\sum_{k=-\infty}^{-1}j^k J_k(\xi)e^{jk\theta}+\sum_{k=1}^{\infty}j^k J_k(\xi)e^{jk\theta} \quad (4)$$

where $J_k(\xi)$ is the k -th Bessel function of the first kind which are the standard integer solution functions in a general way of the ordinary differential equation which can be expressed as

$$x^2\frac{\mathrm{d}^2y}{\mathrm{d}x^2}+x\frac{\mathrm{d}y}{\mathrm{d}x}+(x^2-v^2)y=0 \quad (5)$$

where v is the order of the Bessel functions. When $v=n$ is nonnegative integer, the corresponding solution is called n-Bessel function, whose Taylor series can be written as

$$J_n(x)=\sum_{k=0}^{\infty}(-1)^k\frac{1}{k!\Gamma(n+k+1)}(\frac{x}{2})^{n+2k} \quad (6)$$

Integrating on $e^{\pm j\xi\cos\theta}\cos n\theta$ from $-\pi$ to π :

$$\int_{-\pi}^{\pi}e^{+j\xi\cos\theta}\cos n\theta d\theta=\int_{-\pi}^{\pi}J_0(\xi)\cos n\theta d\theta+\int_{-\pi}^{\pi}2\sum_{k=1}^{\infty}j^{\pm k}J_k(\xi)\cos k\theta\cos n\theta d\theta \quad (7)$$

to further simplify the equality:

$$\int_{-\pi}^{\pi} e^{\pm j\xi\cos\theta}\cos n\theta d\theta = 2\pi j^{\pm n} J_n(\xi) \quad (8)$$

Thus harmonic components can be obtained.

(1) DC component: $A_{00} + jB_{00} = 2V_{dc}$

(2) Fundamental component: $A_{01} + jB_{01} = V_{dc}M$

(3) Carrier component: $A_{m0} + jB_{m0} = \frac{4V_{dc}}{m\pi} J_0(m\frac{\pi}{2}M)\sin m\frac{\pi}{2}$

(4) Sideband harmonics component:

$$A_{mn} + jB_{mn} = \frac{4V_{dc}}{m\pi} J_n(m\frac{\pi}{2}M)\sin([m+n]\frac{\pi}{2})$$

III. Reconstitution of Minimum Phase Signal

A signal in frequency domain which is lack of phase information can be reconstituted if it meets the condition of minimum phase system. The logarithm of magnitude spectra of a minimum phase signal and its phase function Hilbert transform pairs. A real signal $x[n]$ can be expressed as the sum of an odd signal and an even signal. Particularly when the signal is particularly when the signal is causal, $x[n]$ can be recovered by $x_o[n]$ ($n \neq 0$):

$$x[n] = 2x_o[n]u[n] - x_o[n]\delta[n] \quad (9)$$

The definition of complex cepstrum $\hat{x}[n]$ is the inverse Fourier transform of the logarithm to the Fourier transform of $x[n]$, which can be described as:

$$\hat{x}[n] = \frac{1}{2\pi}\int_{-\pi}^{\pi}\{\ln|X(e^{j\omega n})| + j\arg[X(e^{j\omega n})]\}e^{j\omega n}d\omega \quad (10)$$

Define real cepstrum $c_x[n]$ as the real part of $\hat{x}[n]$ which can be written as

$$c_x[n] = \frac{1}{2\pi}\int_{-\pi}^{\pi}|\ln[X(e^{j\omega n})]|e^{j\omega n}d\omega \quad (11)$$

To complex two equations, $c_x[n]$ is the oven signal decomposed by $\hat{x}[n]$ which can be also written as

$$c_x[n] = (\hat{x}[n] + \hat{x}[-n])/2 \quad (12)$$

As what shows in Fig.1, $x[n]$ will be reconstituted from $c_x[n]$ if $\hat{x}[n]$ is causal by Hilbert transform.

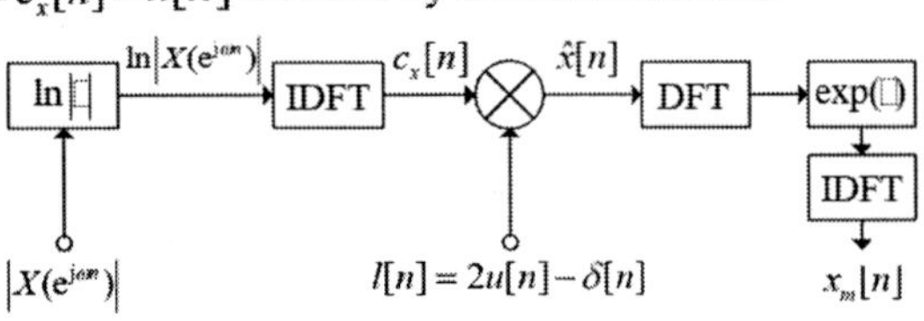

Fig. 1 The block diagram of signal restoration

IV. Numerical Results and Discussions

Fig. 2 contains the magnitude spectra of SPWM signal. f_0=50Hz, fs=1kHz. To get terminal waveforms by using the model based on Matlab Simulink of different frequency viewing from motor, the reconstructed signal based on minimum phase system and the original signal are shown in Fig.3. Not only the area of energy concentration, but the sensitivity of the system of different frequency is read in Fig.3.The recovery of the signal is nearly complete while it still has some problems about delay. What's more, the peak value is almost the same.

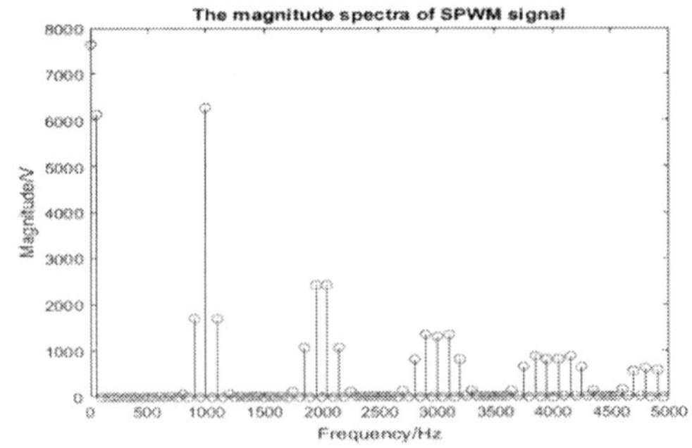

Fig.2 The magnitude spectra of SPWM signal

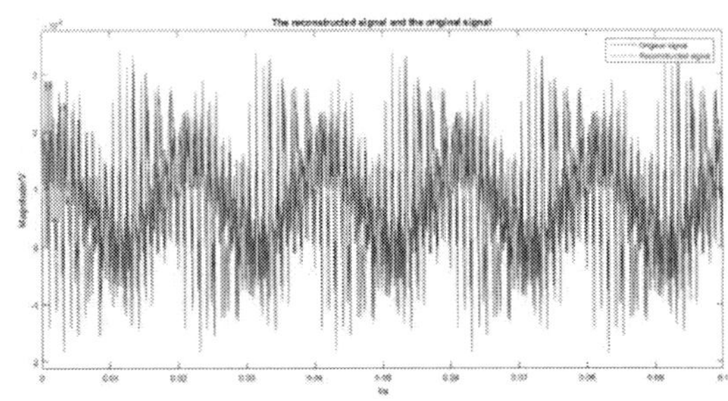

Fig.3 The reconstructed signal and the original signal

V. Conclusion

This paper has established a new way to the signal reconstruction of PWM from frequency domain time domain. Experimental result indicates the recovery of the signal based on minimum phase system is nearly the same to the real time domain waveform. It offers a new way to the reconstruction of PWM signal in frequency domain and can be laid the theoretical foundation of long-line systems. Moreover, it has a great significance to the submarine oil exploration.

Acknowledgment

This paper was supported by the National Natural Science Foundation of China (Grant No. 51209055), the China Postdoctoral Special Foundation (Grant No. 2015T80324), and the Natural Science Foundation of Heilongjiang, China (Grant No. F2015028).

References

[1] Shi L F, Shi Z B, Chen S, et al. Output Voltage Sampling Circuit for Discontinuous Conduction Mode Flyback Pulse-Width Modulation Controller[J]. Journal of Circuits System & Computers, 2016.

[2] Shayestehfard A, Mekhilef S, Mokhlis H. Modified scalar discontinuous pulse-width modulation method for two-level three-wire voltage source inverters under unbalanced and distorted conditions[J]. Iet Power Electronics, 2015, 8(8):1339-1348.

[3] Deng Y, Harley R G. Space-Vector Versus Nearest-Level Pulse Width Modulation for Multilevel Converters[J]. IEEE Transactions on Power Electronics, 2015, 30(6):2962-2974.

EM-AI Model of Microgrids in Islanding Mode

A.A. Arkadan
Colorado School of Mines, Dept. of Electrical Engineering and Computer Science
Golden, CO 80401, USA
aaarkadan@mines.edu

***Abstract*— An Electromagnetic-Artificial Intelligence (EM-AI) based model, for the characterization of microgrids in normal or islanding modes of operation, is presented. This EM-Data Mining based model is used to characterize microgrids with high-speed ac synchronous generators during normal and out of phase operation. The model could form the basis of a framework for online characterization of microgrids during normal or islanding modes of operation.**

Keywords—High-Speed AC Generators; Electromagnetic Field Analysis; Data Mining based models

I. INTRODUCTION

High-speed AC generators are used in distributed generation and microgrids, which can be operated in islanding mode. In contrary to integrated power systems that have virtually constant voltage and frequency, the addition or loss of one machine in a microgrid could have a large impact on the system [1]. Further, the addition of an out of phase ac generator during islanding mode could disturb the system and result in high currents in the machine windings and possibly high transients in the microgrid-load system. Accordingly, accurate characterization of such systems is paramount if it is to be used for the design of protection systems and for online characterization of microgrids during fault conditions.

Accurate performance characterization of an ac generator is critical if the machine is operated in dynamic modes. In such cases, computational electromagnetic models are usually used as it accounts for effects of saturation due to nonlinear magnetic material, space harmonics due to machine geometry, and time harmonics due to switching electronics [2]. Accurate models, however, require intensive computational resources and relatively long computational time. In recent years AI techniques performed well and were used efficiently in identification, characterization, and control problems.

II. THE MODELING APPROACH

The EM–Data Mining based model used in this work consists of two modules. The first utilizes an indirectly coupled Electromagnetic-State Space (EM-SS) approach used to accurately predict the performance characteristics of the two generators shown in Fig. 1 to generate the database needed to train the second AI based module. The electromagnetic module utilizes an indirectly coupled Finite Element-State Space (FE-SS) approach where a system of "n" AC generators in a microgrid is represented by the state space model of equation (1). The inductance matrices, L_{ij}, of this equation are computed, function of load and rotor position, from nonlinear Finite Element magnetic field solutions [2]. Sample mutual inductance waveforms are shown in Fig. 2. The inductance matrices are used in the state space model of an n-generator microgrid as follows:

$$\begin{bmatrix} V^1 \\ V^2 \\ \vdots \\ V^n \end{bmatrix} = \begin{bmatrix} (R_{ss}^1 + R_{eq}) & 0 & R_{eq} & 0 & \cdots & R_{eq} & 0 \\ 0 & R_{rr}^1 & 0 & 0 & \cdots & 0 & 0 \\ R_{eq} & 0 & (R_{ss}^2 + R_{eq}) & 0 & \cdots & R_{eq} & 0 \\ 0 & 0 & 0 & R_{rr}^2 & \cdots & 0 & 0 \\ \vdots & \vdots & \vdots & \vdots & \ddots & \vdots & \vdots \\ R_{eq} & 0 & R_{eq} & 0 & \cdots & (R_{ss}^n + R_{eq}) & 0 \\ 0 & 0 & 0 & 0 & \cdots & 0 & R_{rr}^n \end{bmatrix} \begin{bmatrix} I^1 \\ I^2 \\ \vdots \\ I^n \end{bmatrix}$$
$$+ \frac{d}{dt} \left\{ \begin{bmatrix} (L_{ss}^1 + L_{eq}) & L_{sr}^1 & L_{eq} & 0 & \cdots & L_{eq} & 0 \\ L_{rs}^1 & L_{rr}^1 & 0 & 0 & \cdots & 0 & 0 \\ L_{eq} & 0 & (L_{ss}^2 + L_{eq}) & L_{sr}^2 & \cdots & L_{eq} & 0 \\ 0 & 0 & L_{rs}^2 & L_{rr}^2 & \cdots & 0 & 0 \\ \vdots & \vdots & \vdots & \vdots & \ddots & 0 & \vdots \\ L_{eq} & 0 & L_{eq} & 0 & \cdots & (L_{ss}^n + L_{eq}) & L_{sr}^n \\ 0 & 0 & 0 & 0 & \cdots & L_{rs}^n & L_{rr}^n \end{bmatrix} \begin{bmatrix} I^1 \\ I^2 \\ \vdots \\ I^n \end{bmatrix} \right\} \quad (1)$$

where, s and r denote the generator stator and rotor quantities, V represents its voltage vector, I represents its current vector, and R and L represent its resistance and inductance matrices.

Fig. 1. Block Diagram of Microgrid

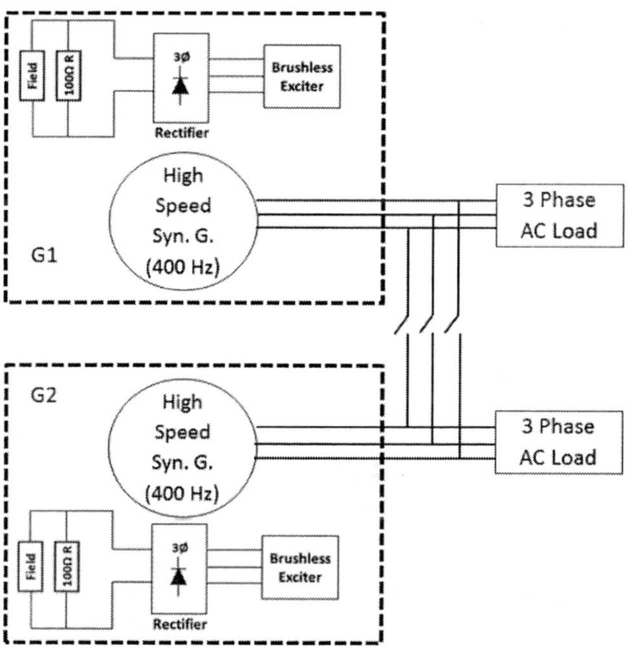

Fig. 2. AC Generator Sample Mutual Inductance Curves

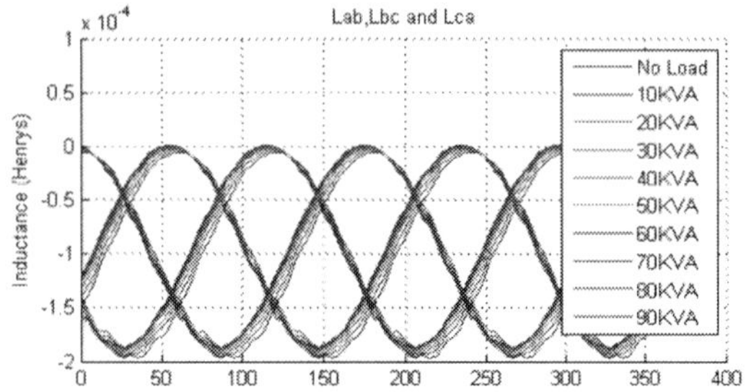

Fig. 3. Data Mining Process

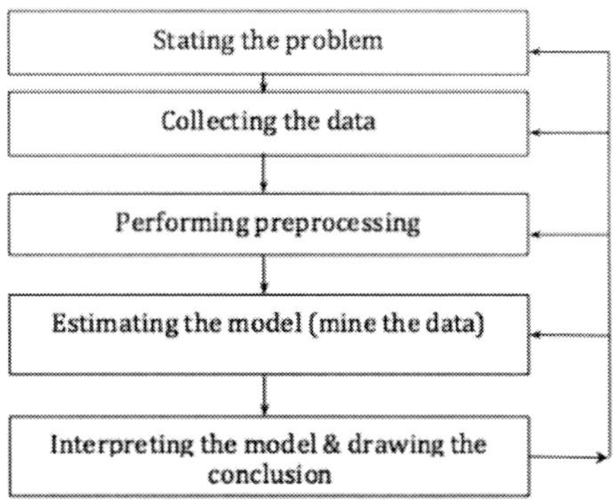

Table I Diode Peak Reverse Field Voltage for 10 KVA Load

Peak Field Reverse Voltage	EM-AI	Measured	% Difference
	750 V	760 V	1.3%

The Data Mining module is described in Fig. 3. The first step is to define the problem. Next, training data is used in the training process. Here, the EM or FE-SS module, described above was used to gather the training data. Then, the learning mechanism is executed to learn and predict the performance characteristics of the system. In the final step, the output of the Data Mining system is compared to the training output data. If the acceptable tolerance of the model is achieved, the data is processed and the iteration is stopped; otherwise the process is repeated [4]. In this work, ANNs with Radial Basis Functions, (RBF) as activation functions are used, [2,3]. In this case, the module has 12 networks connected in parallel. The inputs are the voltage phase shift α between the two generator units, the load condition in kVA, and time in seconds. The twelve outputs are the two generator units' winding currents.

III. EM-AI Model Results

The results of using the EM-Data Mining model to predict the dynamic performance due to the paralleling of two out of phase distributed generation units in an islanded microgrid, Fig. 1, are presented. The units are of the 3-phase, 400Hz, 208V, 4-pole, 90kVA high-speed synchronous generators type, feeding AC loads. It is assumed that after a temporary fault, and during breaker auto-reclose open time, Fig. 1, unit #1 accelerated and its terminal voltages led corresponding terminal voltages of unit #2 by an angle α. The application of the EM module resulted in the inductance family of curves as in Fig. 2. Further, the application of the EM-AI model resulted in the current values of both generators of Fig. 1. The value of the peak reverse field voltage in the brushless exciter, Fig. 1, are given in Table I, as obtained from measurement and the EM-AI module, for verification. In addition, the values of the peak reverse field voltage at different phase shift angles α and different load conditions ranging from 0 KVA to 90 KVA are shown in Fig. 4. These values are important as they are usually needed to rate the diodes of a generator brushless exciter rotating rectifier bridge, under dynamic operating conditions, including the out of phase paralleling of generators. The computation time needed to generate 720 data points of Fig. 4 are shown in Table II, as obtained using the EM module only, and the EM-AI Data Mining based method implemented in this work. As shown in Table II, the generation of the data in Fig. 4 could be done off-line when using the EM-Data Mining model. This is in contrast to the case where only the EM module is used. As such, it can be stated that the EM-AI based model is computationally accurate, Table I, and fast, Table II, so it could be used in the design of power system protection systems. Also, it could form the basis of a framework for online characterization of microgrids during normal or islanding modes of operation.

Table II Comparison of Computation Time

	EM	EM-AI
Off-Line Data Setup & Training	415 min	616 min
On-Line Data Generation	1,045 min	< 1 sec

Fig. 4. Data Mining Reverse Peak Field Voltage Values

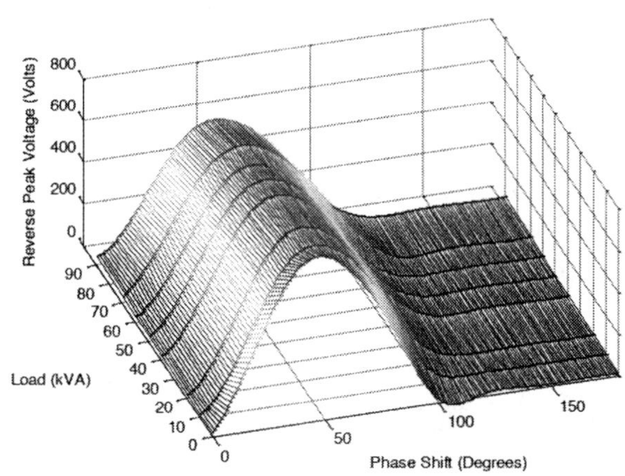

References

[1] X. Kong, F. Wang and Y. Sun, "Comparison of High Speed PM Generator with PM Doubly Fed Reluctance Generator for Distributed Power Generation System," 2nd IEEE Conference on Industrial Electronics and Applications, pp. 1193-1197, 2007

[2] A.A. Arkadan, Y. Abou-Samra, and N. Al-Aawar, "Characterization of Stand Alone AC Generators during No-Break Power Transfer using Radial Basis Networks," IEEE Trans. on Magnetics, Vol. 43, No. 12, pp. 1821-1824, April 2007.

[3] V. Kecman, V., Learning and Soft Computing: Support Vector Machines, Neural Networks and Fuzzy Logic Models (Complex Adaptive Systems), MIT Press, 2001.

[4] Groth, R., "Data Mining – Building Competitive Advantage," *Prentice Hall*, 1999, Upper Saddle River, NJ.

Electromechanical analysis of an electrodynamic bearing

Antonino Musolino, Rocco, Rizzo, Mauro Tucci,
Sami Barmada, Emanuele Crisostomi
DESTEC,
University of Pisa
Pisa, Italy

Fabrizio Impinna, Joaquim Girardello Detoni,
Nicola Amati, Andrea Tonoli
Department of Mechanical and Aerospace Engineering
Politecnico di Torino
Torino, Italy

***Abstract*— As known electrodynamic levitation occurs without active control due to motion induced eddy currents. There are two main drawbacks related to electromagnetic bearings: 1) the presence of losses caused by the eddy currents, and 2) the onset of instability in undamped supercritical rotor systems. Accurate analysis of these devices, especially when the axial symmetry cannot be assumed, can be performed by numerical methods only. This paper presents a comparison between the experimental data taken on a prototype of an electrodynamic bearing and the numerical simulations obtained by a research code. The good agreement envisages the use of this code for the reduction of losses and for a better characterization of the instability conditions.**

Keywords*— *Electrodynamic bearing, Rotordynamics, Stability, Eddy currents, Numerical modeling.

I. INTRODUCTION

Electrodynamic bearings (EDBs) are passive magnetic bearings that exploit Lorentz forces arising between a conductor and a magnetic field in relative motion to support a rotating shaft. Although promising in a variety of fields of application, rotors supported by EDBs are affected by rotordynamic instability problems. The literature on EDBs has studied these instabilities by means of simplified analytical models [1][2][3]. In order to improve the understanding of the instability issues affecting rotors on EDBs, the present paper presents a dynamic analysis of a rotor/EDB system based on a numerical modeling of the complete system. The model's results are compared to experimental results obtained from a dedicated test rig.

II. THE COUPLED ELECTROMECHANICAL CODE

The choice of the formulation to solve coupled electro-mechanical problem is still an open issue. A number of features makes the integral formulation attractive: they require the discretization of the active regions only, and the problem of coupling meshes with different speed is absent. Integral formulations automatically satisfy the far-field boundary conditions, and coarse discretization (with respect to those typically used in FEM) are able to provide good accuracy.

The details of the adopted formulation are reported in [4]. For the sake of simplicity, let us consider a system composed of two rigid bodies: one is attached to the coordinate system and the other is free to move without constraints (six DOFs). The active materials (conductors, Permanent Magnets (PMs), iron) are subdivided in elementary volumes characterized by uniformly distributed currents. By imposing the constitutive equations (Ohm law and the B-H characteristic) a set of equations governing an equivalent network, coupled with the rigid body equations, is obtained:

$$L(\xi)\frac{di}{dt}+\left[R(\xi)+K(\xi,\dot{\xi}\;\; i \quad e$$

$$F(\xi)=m\ddot{q}$$

$$M(\xi)=I_{\theta\theta}\dot{\omega}\quad \omega \quad I \quad \omega$$

where ξ is a vector including the set of positions and orientations of the elementary volume at the instant t, $L(\xi)$ is the inductance matrix; $R(\xi)$ is the resistance matrix and $K(\xi,\dot{\xi}$ takes into account the electromotive force due to the motional effects.

III. EXPERIMENTAL TESTING AND VALIDATION

The test rig developed at the Politecnico of Torino is shown in fig.1. Two aluminum plates (5) are rigidly connected between each other by four steel legs (15), and fixed to a seismic mass (14). A micrometric positioning stage (11) allows imposing a fixed, known, value of eccentricity between the two elements of the electrodynamic bearing, i.e., rotating conductor and static magnetic field. The electrodynamic bearing's stator is composed of two permanent magnet rings magnetized in attraction, and glued to an iron yoke that encloses the magnetic field (fig. 2 and table I). This element is bolted to an aluminum plate (13). which is connected to the test rig's structure through four compliant steel beams (6). The rotating part contains an aluminum shaft, coupled to the electric motor (1) through a flexible coupling (3). The rotating element of the electrodynamic bearing consists of a copper disc connected to the lower end of the shaft. The rotor spin speed is measured using an encoder (12), and the forces exchanged between rotor and stator can be measured using a load cell (10). An accelerometer is placed on plate (13).

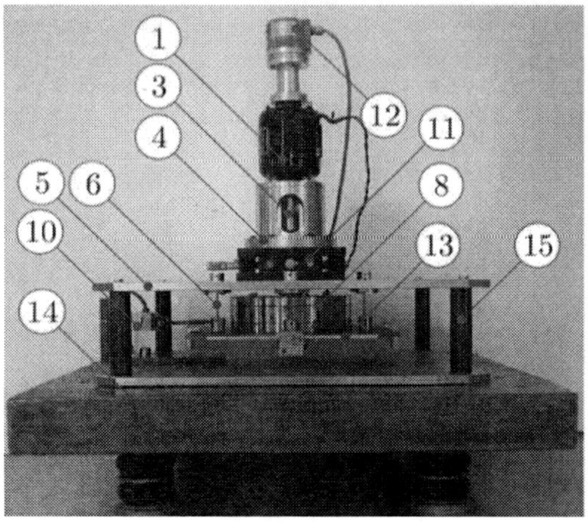

Fig. 1. Picture of the test rig used for quasi-static and dynamic studies of electrodynamic bearings

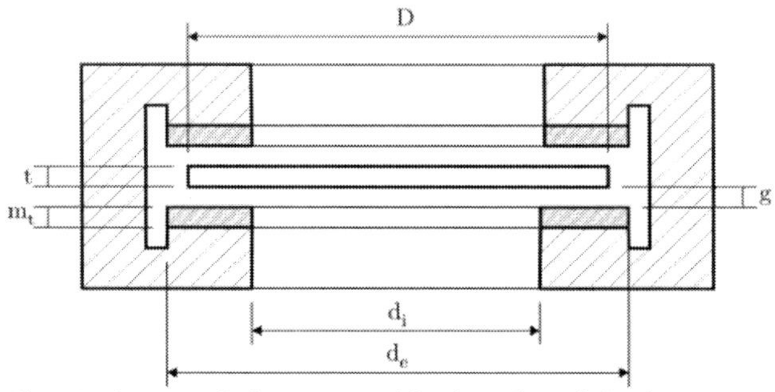

Fig. 2. Main geometrical parameters of the electrodynamic bearing.

Table 1 Main parameters of the test rig

Feature	Unit	Value
External diameter of each magnetic ring	mm	120
Internal diameter of the magnetic ring	mm	64
Thickness of each magnetic ring	mm	6
Residual magnetization of the PMs	T	1.09
External diameter of the disk	mm	100
Internal diameter of the disk	mm	15
Thickness of the conductor disk	mm	3
Conductivity of the conductor disk	S m-1	5.7e7
Air gap	mm	0.5
Mass of the nonrotating part	kg	7
Stiffness of the beams nominal value	N m-1	30300

We performed the comparison between the numerical analysis and the experimental measurements at different angular speeds. In the numerical analysis, we assumed a lateral initial displacement (eccentricity) of 0.34 mm, correspondent to a perturbation produced by an instrumented hammer used in the test rig.

Figures 3 and 4 show the comparison of the lateral accelerations in the direction of the eccentricity for the two angular speeds of 600 and 900 rpm. The agreement between the measured and the simulated quantities is excellent. Figure 3 illustrates a stable condition, while figure 4 refers to an unstable one, typical of an undamped supercritical rotor system on electrodynamic bearings.

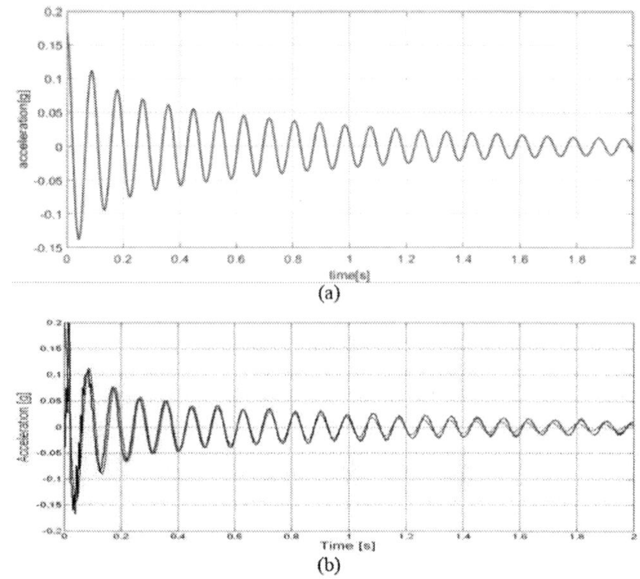

Fig. 3. Comparison between lateral acceleration (g) at 600 rpm: a) numerical, b) measured and analytical from [2].

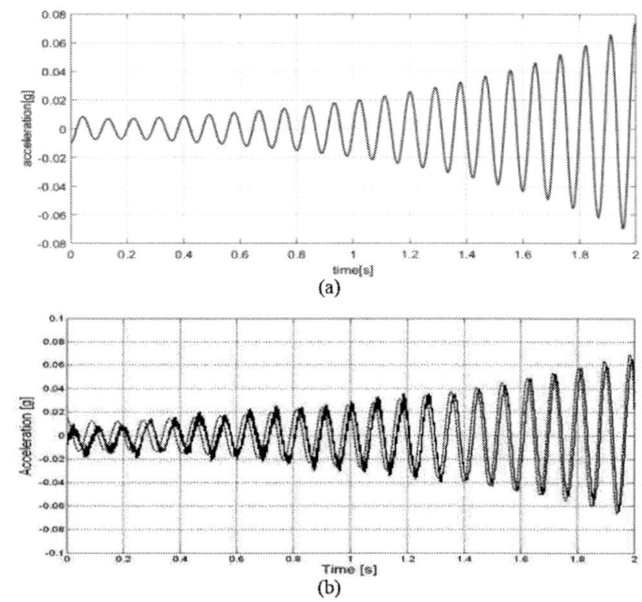

Fig. 4. Comparison between lateral acceleration (g) at 900 rpm: a) numerical, b) measured and analytical from [2].

REFERENCES

[1] C. Dumont, V. Kluyskens, B. Dehez, "Linear state-space representation of heteropolar electrodynamic bearings with radial magnetic field", *IEEE Trans. Magn.*, vol. 52, no. 1, pp. 1-9, 2016.

[2] A. Tonoli, N. Amati, F. Impinna, & J. G. Detoni. "A solution for the stabilization of electrodynamic bearings: Modeling and experimental validation" *Journal of Vibration and Acoustics*, vol. 133, n. 22, 2011.

[3]A. Filatov, E. H. Maslen, and G. T. Gillies. "Stability of an electrodynamic suspension." *J. of App. Phys.* vol. 92, no. 6, pp. 3345-3353, 2002.

[4] E. Tripodi, A. Musolino, M. Raugi and R. Rizzo," A new predictor-corrector approach for the numerical integration of coupled electromechanical equations" *Int, J. on Num Meth. Eng*,vol. 105, no. 4, pp. 261-285, 2016.

Breakdown Voltage Assessment of GaN HEMT Devices through Physics-Based Modeling

Christopher R. Lashway, Alberto Berzoy, Nour Elsayad, *Student Members, ACES & IEEE*
Osama Mohammed, *ACES, Fellow, IEEE*
Energy Systems Research Laboratory, 10555 West Flagler St, Engineering Center 3983, Miami, FL, 33174

Abstract— **An extensive study is conducted to evaluate breakdown mechanisms in gallium nitride (GaN) high electron mobility transistors (HEMT). A comprehensive physics-based model of a common HEMT provides the base comparison to conduct different material and geometric investigations. The variations are evaluated in a progression toward the optimal configuration: 1) varying the passivation material, 2) replacing the substrate material, 3) reducing the doping profile along the GaN and aluminum nitride (AlGaN) layers and 4) a field plate (FP) addition. The electric field distribution across the source, gate, and drain is analyzed for each case as well as their I-V curves until the breakdown voltage (BV). The best results are revealed under the FP case.**

Index Terms—**GaN, HEMTs, physics based modeling, finite element analysis, wide band gap devices.**

I. Introduction

GaN HEMTs have gained a great deal of attention within the power electronics industry as a result of their capability of operating at higher temperatures, higher switching frequencies, and increased voltage. Theoretical limits lines ($r_{on} - BV$) for lateral HEMT are better than vertical GaN devices as the mobility of the electrons in the two-dimensional electron gas (2DEG) is huge [1]. However, HEMTs are susceptible to surface breakdown and are not easily scalable to higher voltages and currents. Thus, there is a necessity to investigate how the BV of the HEMT can be increased. This question can be answered by delving deep into the physics of the HEMT operation. Physics-based models (PBM) can provide us with a specialized set of tools based on the geometry, materials, and physics of HEMT to evaluate mechanisms that can increase the BV [2], [3].

There are several BV mechanisms such as: source-drain breakdown (punch-through), gate-drain breakdown (leakage through the Schottky diode), vertical breakdown (poor compensation of the buffer layer) and impact ionization (an electron-hole pair generation close to the gate) [4]. In the last case, the BV depends on the material critical electric field (E_{crit}), or the field needed to initiate the impact ionization causing an avalanche breakdown [5]. Thus, there are 2 ways to avoid the BV: ensuring that the electric field (E_f) < E_{crit} at the operating point of the HEMT or enlarging the drift distance. However, the drift distance is kept fixed as a constraint. Thus, the only solution available is to redistribute E_f. From the literature review, there are 3 solutions to improve the BV: varying passivation material, changing the substrate material, and applying a field plate structure.

This work was partially supported by grants for the Office of Naval Research. The authors are with the Energy Systems Research Laboratory, Department of Electrical and Computer Engineering, Florida International University, Miami, FL 33174 (e-mail: mohammed@fiu.edu).

TABLE I. GaN-FET Design Parameters and Cases of Study

Name	Value		Name	Value
Substrate	Thickness 13.98 μm		AlGaN Composit.	$x = 20\%$
Source/Drain	Width 1 μm			
Gate	Width 3 μm		**Case of Study**	**Fig. 1 - Passiv. – Subst.**
Active GaN Layer	Thickness 1 μm		Original	Fig. 1(a)-SiO_2 - Si
AlGaN	Thickness 0.02 μm		Passivation	Fig. 1 (a)-SiN – Si
Doping	**Original**	**Light**	GaN Substrate	Fig. 1 (a)-SiN - GaN
GaN Layer (Acceptor)	2×10^{17} cm^{-3}	2×10^{14} cm^{-3}	Light Doping	Fig. 1 (a)-SiN – GaN
GaN Layer (Donor)	2×10^{16} cm^{-3}	2×10^{13} cm^{-3}	Ge Substrate	Fig. 1 (a)-SiN – Ge
AlGaN Layer (Donor)	1×10^{17} cm^{-3}	1×10^{14} cm^{-3}	Field Plate	Fig. 1 (b)-SiN - GaN

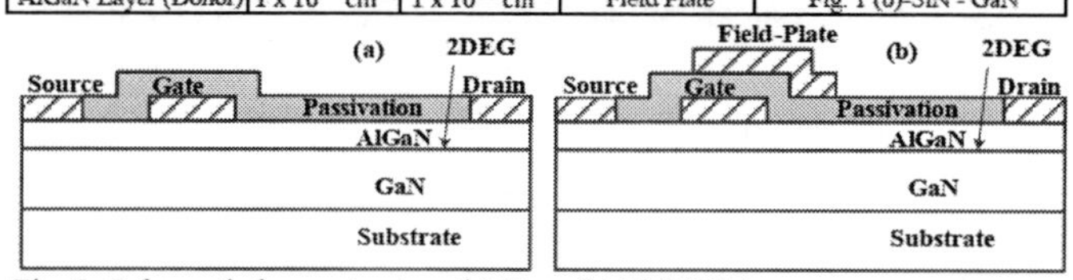

Fig. 1: Schematic layer structure (a) Base (b) Field Plate.

Different materials and geometric changes have been applied on a single HEMT. The passivation material, substrate, and doping level have been evaluated as well as the impacts of a FP inclusion. For each case, the BV progression and E_f distribution is discussed. A comparison of 6 different structures (Table I) is presented. The schematic layers of these cases are shown in Fig. 1 with the dimensions described in Table I. Table I indicates the structure for each case of study. For the final case shown in Fig. 1(b) [2], a FP is added to reshape the E_f distribution in the channel and reduce its peak at the point of interest [6].

II. Results Analysis of GaN HEMT

Results of the BV progression at $v_g = 0$ V and E_f distribution at 2 heights ($y_2 = 0.721\ \mu m$ and $y_4 = 1.02\ \mu m$) are shown in Fig. 2 and 3 where the BV is defined as the maximum slope of the I-V curve. Notice that changing the passivation from silicon dioxide (SiO_2) to silicon nitride (SiN) has a small positive effect on the BV and E_{fmax} (Fig. 2(a) and Table II), thus SiN is kept as the insulator. The next change is the removal of the Si substrate by etching. This results in a huge increase in the BV. This is an expected result as mentioned in [7]. The 4th case is the study of a doping variation as stated in Table I (Light doping). In this case, the variation is not favorable, presenting one of the smallest BV and largest E_{fmax} (Fig. 2(a) and Table II). Next, another change of the substrate from Si to germanium (Ge) in the base HEMT also was not positive. Finally, the addition of a FP to the current best case (Si substrate removal) yields the best results as it distributes the E_f (Fig. 3) in a way that does not allow an early BV. Fig. 2(b) demonstrates that the origin of the BV for the FP case is a drain-source sub-threshold leakage [4]. In Fig. 3 the E_f distribution along the x axis is presented at y_2 and y_4 which correspond to the surface of the device and the 2DEG channel, respectively, for all cases of study. Distance y_2 is the height where the E_{fmax} appears for the FP case and y_4 is where the E_{fmax} appears for the remaining cases. For a fair comparison, Fig. 3 is performed at the lowest BV for all structures which occurs in Ge substrate case (353.7 V). For each case, the drain voltage is as indicated in Table II which is approximately equal to the Ge BV. Thus, from Fig. 3(a) and Table II, it can be noted that as E_{fmax} decreases the BV increases in all the cases (as expected). However, E_{fmax} is the highest for the FP device which appears to be contradictory. This can be explained noticing that this E_{fmax} is located at $x = 0.5$ μm which is at the end of the FP contact and separated from the 2DEG by the passivation layer (SiN insulator) with very high dielectric strength of 10MV/cm. From Fig. 3(b), which corresponds to the cross section along the 2DEG, it is clear that the E_{fmax} of the FP is the minimum.

TABLE II. BV AND MAXIMUM E FIELD FOR ALL CASES AT 2 HEIGHTS

	Original	Passivation	Light Doping	Ge Substrate	GaN Substrate	Field Plate
$E_{fmax\, y_2}$ (MV/cm)	8.02	7.07	6.83	7.23	8.08	20.7
BV (V)	366.5	384.3	368.7	353.7	769.2	1092.1
V_{ds} (V)	354.6	351.9	354.4	353.7	354.3	350.5
$E_{fmax\, y_4}$ (MV/cm)	7.35	6.17	6.67	7.15	4.41	4.21

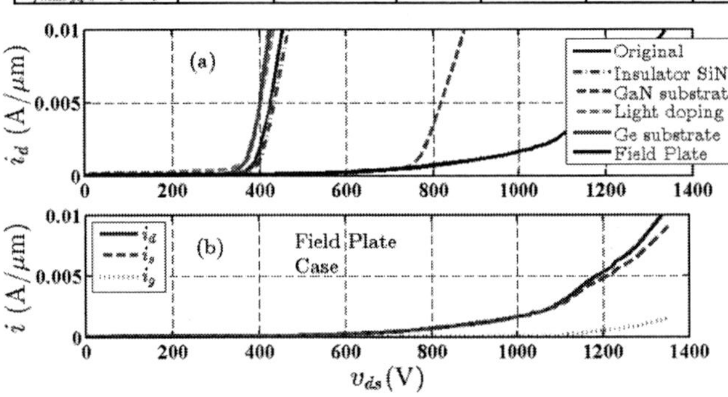

Fig. 2: (a) BV curves for all cases of study (b) Drain, source and gate currents for the FP case

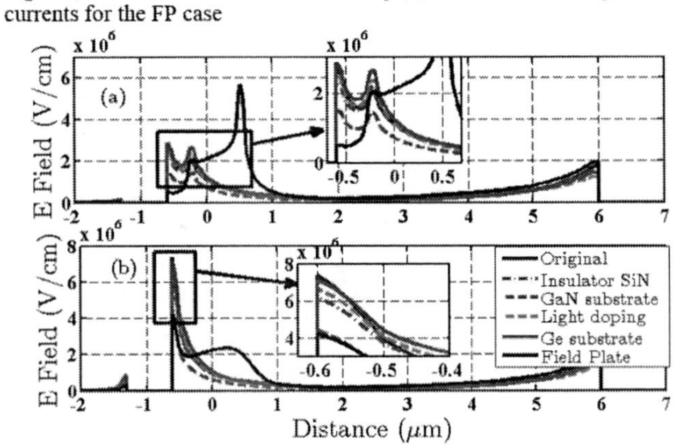

Fig. 3: E field distribution along x axis at (a) $y_2 = 0.721$ μm (b) $y_4 = 1.02$ μm

III. ANALYSIS OF THE FIELD PLATE CASE

For the final FP case, the E_f distribution along the x-direction at different heights (at $V_{ds} = BV = 1092.1$ V) is shown in Fig. 4 and also as a 2D map in Fig. 5. Fig. 4 shows the key advantage of the FP layout as it redistributes the field and relocates the peak electric field along the x and y plane keeping it below the critical value and hence increasing the BV. The same behavior is more clearly observed in Fig. 5 and 5(b). It is shown that the highest field strength is present right at the corner of the FP-SiN interface on the drain side of the gate, where a field of 20.7 MV/cm is experienced.

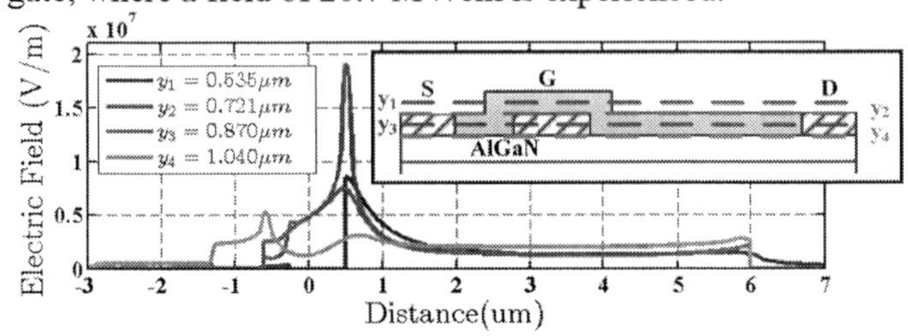

Fig. 4: E field distribution along the x axis at 4 y distances for the FP case.

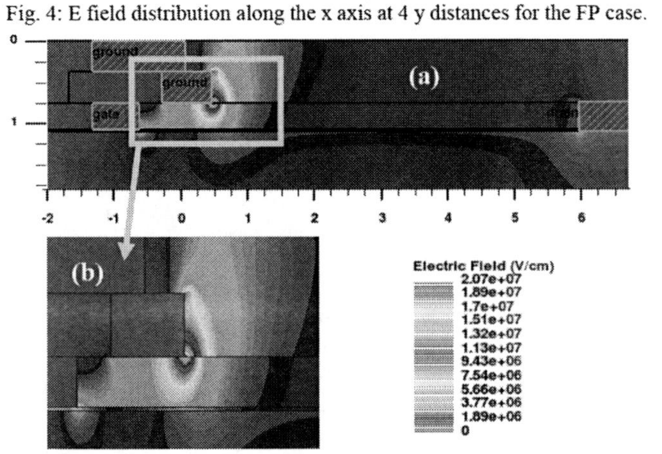

Fig. 5: 2D electric field distribution for the case of the FP.

IV. CONCLUSION

In order to increase the BV, it can be concluded that the best way is through a combination of the three well-known techniques: passivation, substrate removal, and a FP addition.

REFERENCES

[1] K. Shenai, "Switching Megawatts with Power Transistors," *Electrochem. Soc. Interface*, vol. 22, no. 1, pp. 47–53, Jan. 2013.

[2] S. Vitanov *et al.*, "Physics-Based Modeling of GaN HEMTs," *IEEE Trans. Electron Devices*, vol. 59, no. 3, pp. 685–693, Mar. 2012.

[3] F. Li, Q. H. Liu, and D. P. Klemer, "Numerical Simulation of high electron mobility transistors based on the spectral element Method," *Appl. Comp. Electromagn. Soc. J.*, vol. 31, no. 10, pp. 1144–1150, 2016.

[4] G. Meneghesso, M. Meneghini, and E. Zanoni, "Breakdown mechanisms in AlGaN/GaN HEMTs: An overview," *Jpn. J. Appl. Phys.*, vol. 53, no. 10, p. 100211, Sep. 2014.

[5] "Wiley: GaN Transistors for Efficient Power Conversion, 2nd Edition - Alex Lidow, Johan Strydom, Michael de Rooij, et al." [Online]. Available: http://www.wiley.com/ [Accessed: 19-Oct-2016].

[6] M. Kaddeche, A. Telia, and A. Soltani, "Study of field plate effects onAlGaN/GaN HEMTs," in *2009 International Conference on Microelectronics - ICM*, 2009, pp. 362–365.

[7] D. Visalli *et al.*, "Experimental and simulation study of breakdown voltage enhancement of AlGaN/GaN heterostructures by Si substrate removal," *Appl. Phys. Lett.*, vol. 97, no. 11, p. 113501, Sep. 2010.

Predictions of the Power Quality of AC Electric Arc Furnace Connected to Power grids

Hailong Zhang[1], Liang Wang[2], Gang Ma[1], Wei Yan[1], Enrong Wang[1]

[1]School of Electrical and Automation Engineering
Nanjing Normal University
Nanjing, Jiangsu, China, 210042
e-mail 61204@njnu.edu.cn

[2]Jiangsu Keneng Electric Power Engineering Consulting Co., Ltd.
Nanjing, Jiangsu, China, 210036

***Abstract*—A novel arc impedance model is proposed by separating resistance and inductance, as well as introducing the correction factor for inductance. Accordingly, the modified differential model of electric arc furnace (EAF) is established, and the method for estimating the model parameters is expounded. Furtherly, the model is revealed, and the conclusions are consistent with the reality.**

***Keywords*—EAF; correction factor for inductance; typical tonnage; grid intensity; power quality**

I. INTRODUCTION

AC electric arc furnace (EAF) exhibits excellent technological flexibility and economy. With the improvement of smelting technology, EAF has become the main equipment for steel production, more and more widely used in the metallurgical industry. Meanwhile, EAF is one of the largest load impact on the power grid in the power system, due to the nonlinear arc reactance, electrode furnace charge of contact with short circuit, burden collapses and sharp fluctuations in the molten steel surface. Its load impact change is caused by the voltage fluctuation, flicker and arc impedance. Power quality problems caused by EAF cannot allow to ignore [1-4].

A precise dynamic model is the core step to control the operating performance, electrode arc furnace system and power quality analysis. This paper puts forward a new kind of nonlinear time domain differential model of arc. Two typical of actual tonnage of EAF under different intensity of power grid are analyzed, including harmonics, reactive power and voltage fluctuation respectively.

II. MODEL OF AC EAF

A. Model Derivation and Parameters Estimation

Fig. 1 is AC EAF power supply system circuit diagram. Alternating current arc under steady state conditions shall meet the quasi-stationary electromagnetic field theory field. We assume that AC arc column does not exist space charge and electric field intensity is equally distributed. The nonlinear time domain differential model is derived according to the law of conservation of energy and the kinetic theory of gases as follow

$$\frac{dy}{dt} = \frac{k_2}{L} i^2 - k_1 k_2 y^{-\lambda} \tag{1}$$

where, y is arc admittance, L is length of arc, i is current of arc. k_1、k_2、λ denote power supply adjustment factor, temperature influence factor and the volt ampere relation adjustment factor, respectively, which are related to the actual parameters.

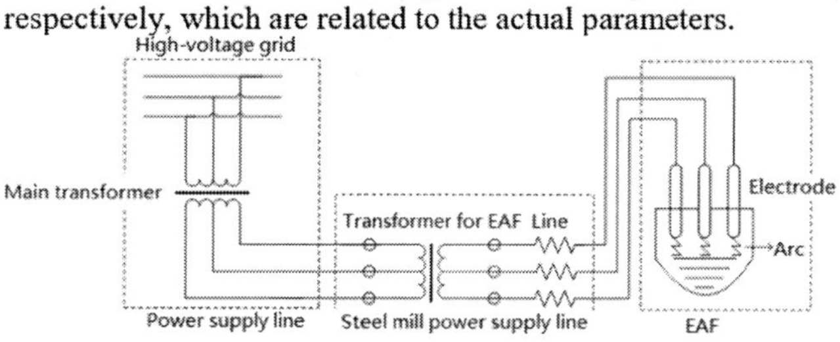

Fig. 1. Three-phase equivalent circuit diagram of the power supply system for AC EAF

At the same stage, smelting furnace transformer secondary side circuit is approximated for three-phase balance. k_1 is assumed as constant. Single-phase equivalent circuit diagram for the EAF and its impedance vector diagram is shown in Fig. 2, where U_p is EAF transformer with gear voltage corresponding phase voltage, r_d is short-net resistance, r_t is the internal resistance of the transformer, L_{dM} is short-net inductance, L_t is transformer internal inductance, Z_{arc} fixed voltage is the same stage of smelting arc gear under the average equivalent impedance, R_{arc} is corresponding to the arc resistance, L_{arc} is corresponding to arc inductance, and φ is corresponding to the power factor angle.

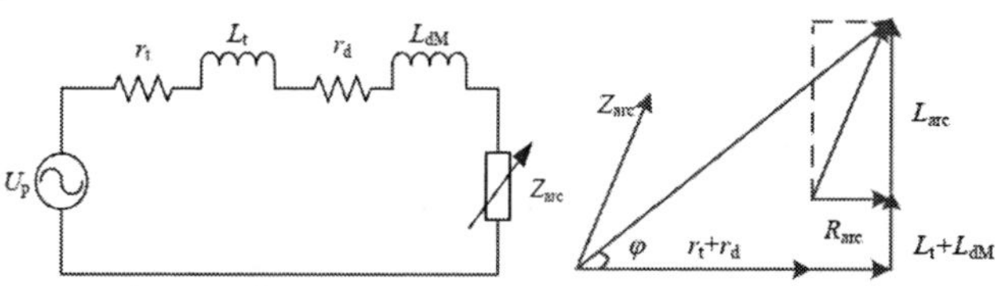

Fig. 2. Three-phase equivalent circuit diagram of the power supply system for AC EAF

According to the calculated impedance vector diagram

$$I_{\mathrm{RMSmean}} = \frac{U_{\mathrm{pRMS}} \sin\varphi}{\omega L_{\mathrm{arc}} + X} \tag{2}$$

where, $X = \omega L_t + \omega L_{dM}$, $I_{RMSmean}$ is average root mean square (RMS) value of the fixed voltage gear in the same stage of smelting the current. U_{pRMS} is the EAF transformer and gear corresponding phase voltage RMS voltage.

Actually, L_{arc} is time-varying. Then arc inductance correction coefficient h is put forward, equation (2) is deformed as

$$I_{\mathrm{RMSmean}} = \frac{U_{\mathrm{pRMS}} \sin\varphi}{X} h \tag{3}$$

RMS of arc voltage is expressed as

$$U_{\mathrm{arcRMS}} = \alpha + \beta_0 L \tag{4}$$

where, U_{arcRMS} denotes RMS of mean arc voltage. α is constant. β_0 denotes the gradient of arc column. L is the length of arc.

From circuit in Fig. 2, we get

$$U_{\mathrm{arcRMS}} = \sqrt{U^2_{\mathrm{pRMS}} - I^2_{\mathrm{RMSmean}} X^2} - I_{\mathrm{RMSmean}}(r_t + r_d) \tag{5}$$

Combined with Eqs. (3) (4) (5), mean length of the arc is calculated as

$$L = \{U_{\mathrm{pRMS}}[\sqrt{1 - h^2 \sin^2\varphi} X - h\sin\varphi(r_t + r_d)] - \alpha X\} / \beta_0 X \tag{6}$$

Under the same smelting stage fixed voltage gear, we get

$$I^2_{\mathrm{RMSmean}} Z_{\mathrm{arc}} = k_1 Z^{\lambda+1}_{\mathrm{arc}} L \tag{7}$$

Engineering estimation method of k_1 is got as

$$k_1 = \frac{U^2_{\mathrm{pRMS}} h^2 \sin^2\varphi}{X^2 Z^{\lambda}_{\mathrm{arcmean}} L} \tag{8}$$

In addition, the EAF system for sure, in the same stage of smelting under fixed voltage gear, λ range for [- 4-1].

$$R_{\mathrm{radius}} = \sqrt{I_{\mathrm{RMS0}} / J_c \pi} \tag{9}$$

where, R_{radius} is average arc radius, I_{RMS0} denotes the whole arc smelting cycle average current RMS. J_c is current density, general experience value. After identification of J_c value of 164.34 A/cm^2. k_2 was calculated as

$$k_2 = \frac{m}{0.354 p T_1 \pi R^2_{\mathrm{radius}}} \tag{10}$$

Eq. (10) includes constant m、 gas pressure p, EAF, furnace temperature T_1 and arc radius R_{radius}. There is just one time-varying parameter T_1, then k_2 describes the temperature influence on arc nonlinear impedance characteristics.

B. Veracity and Versatility of the Model

In this section, the modified differential time domain model of EAF are verified by observing the different characteristic parameters k1、k2、 λ.

As shown in Fig. 3, by fixing parameters k_1、 k_2 and varying λ at - 1.9, 2.0 and 2.1 respectively the arc voltage, current and volt-ampere characteristic curve are plotted. It can be seen that arc voltage changes from large to small with λ getting larger, while current changes from small to big. "zero time" is getting shorter, as well as arc impedance and conductivity are getting smaller.

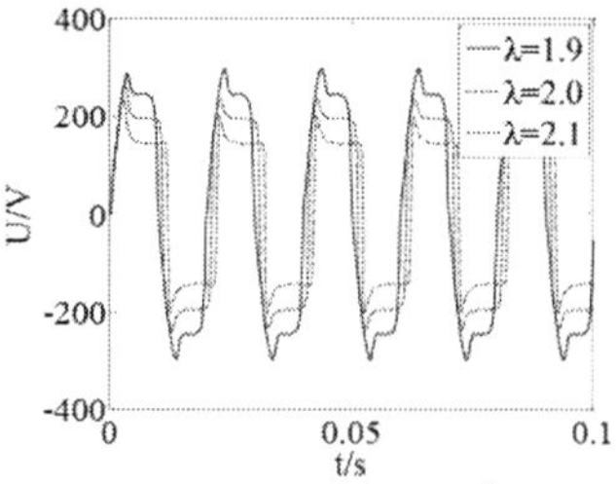

(a) arc voltage

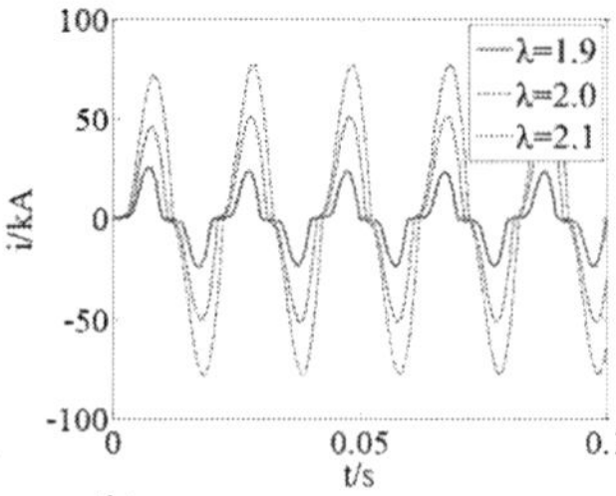

(b) arc current

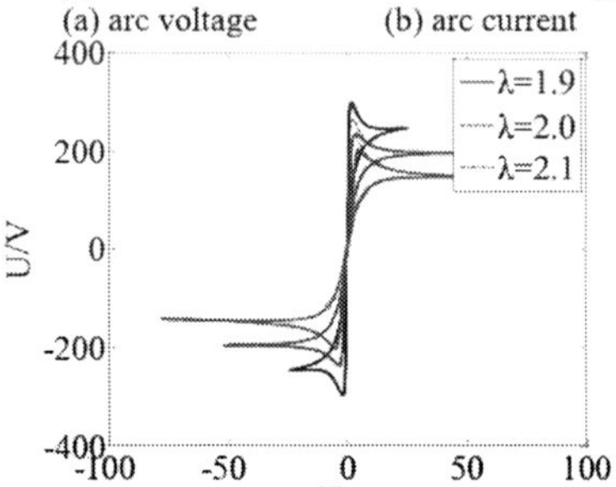

(c) volt-ampere characteristics of the arc of EAF

Fig. 3. Influence of λ on arc characteristic of EAF

Similarly, k_1 is related to the characteristics of the power supply circuit, smelting stage. k_2 is associated with the temperature of the EAF. This shows, the proposed model can be in the light of the condition of the EAF smelting and various phase simulation.

ACKNOWLEDGMENT

The research leading to these results has received funding from the National Science Foundation of China (Grant Nos. 51475246, 51075215), the National Science Foundation of Jiangsu Province (Grant Nos. BK20141452), the start-up funding scientific research projects of Nanjing Normal University. The engineering data are provided by Jiangsu Keneng Electric Power Engineering Consulting Co., Ltd.

REFERENCES

[1] Cano Plata E.A., Ustariz Farfan A.J., Soto Marin O.J.. Electric arc furnace model in distribution systems[C]. IEEE Industry Applications Society Annual Meeting, 2014, 1-7.

[2] QIN Ye, YIN Hui, DENG Ming, XU Zhi. The Research of Optimization of Coordinated Control in Submerged Arc Furnace Mixed Reactive Power Compensation System[J]. Journal of Electric Power, 2014, 06: 515-520.

[3] Zhang Feng, He Xin, Yang Lijun. The Simulation Models of Electric Arc Furnace For Analysis on Quality of Electric Power[J]. Electrical Engineering, 2013, 07: 34-38.

[4] Chang G.W., Min-Fu Shih, Yi-Ying Chen, Yi-Jie Liang. A Hybrid Wavelet Transform and Neural-Network-Based Approach for Modelling Dynamic Voltage-Current Characteristics of Electric Arc Furnace[J]. IEEE Transactions on Power Delivery, 2014, 29(2): 815-824.

Computation of Nonlinear Eigenvalues Related to Parameters of Microwave Structures by using Group Theory

Giovanni Angiulli
DIIES
Univ. Mediterranea
via Graziella - Loc. Feo di Vito
89122, Reggio Calabria, Italy
Email: giovanni.angiulli@unirc.it

Mario Versaci and Francesco Carlo Morabito
DICEAM
Univ. Mediterranea
via Graziella - Loc. Feo di Vito
89122, Reggio Calabria, Italy
Email: mario.versaci@unirc.it
morabito@unirc.it

***Abstract*—The evaluation of parameters of practical interest in microwave engineering is often related with the numerical solution of a suitable nonlinear eigenproblem defined on a symmetric domain D. In this work, we demonstrate as exploiting Group theory, it is possible to obtain a block diagonal matrix representation for this eigenproblem, which allows to accomplish a remarkable reduction of the computational requirement involved in its resolution.**

I. Introduction

Parameters having practical interest in microwave engineering (e.g., cutoff wavenumbers of waveguides, resonant frequencies of cavities, see for example [1]-[3]) are often computed by evaluating the nonlinear eigenvalues γ for which the related nonlinear eigenproblem

$$\mathbf{L}(\gamma)\mathbf{f} = 0 \tag{1}$$

admits a non trivial solution [1]. Singular Value Decomposition (SVD) is the procedure usually exploited to this purpose [1]. Although reliable, the SVD approach is very time consuming due to its high computational cost of order $\mathcal{O}(\frac{8}{3}N^3)$ [4]. In [1] a quicker numerical procedure than SVD has been developed. In the present work, we enhance that method by means of Group theory, exploiting the symmetries of the domain D on which (1) is defined. Collecting all the symmetry operations $g_i, i = 1, 2, 3\dots$ on D in a group $\mathcal{G}$, if the operator $L(\gamma)$ commutes with all the symmetry operation $g_i \in \mathcal{G}$, it is straightforward to demonstrate that its matrix representation $\mathbf{L}(\gamma)$ can be reduced in a block diagonal form $\mathbf{L}_{block}(\gamma)$. This allows to convert the eigenproblem (1) in a number of decoupled nonlinear eigenproblem having a smaller size, obtaining in this way a substantial computational saving when the method described in [1] is applied.

II. Basics on Group Theory

A set $\mathcal{G}$ of abstract elements $g_1, g_2, g_3\dots$ equipped with a dyadic composition law $\otimes$ which has the following properties:

1) closure property: for arbitrary $g_i, g_j \in \mathcal{G}$, $g_i \otimes g_j \in \mathcal{G}$
2) associative property: for arbitrary $g_i, g_j, g_k \in \mathcal{G}$ $(g_i \otimes g_j) \otimes g_k = g_i \otimes (g_j \otimes g_k)$
3) existence of the identity: there exists $g_e \in \mathcal{G}$ such that $g_e \otimes g_i = g_i \otimes g_e = g_i$
4) existence of inverse: for each $g_i \in \mathcal{G}$ there exists $g_i^{-1} \in \mathcal{G}$ such that $g_i \otimes g_i^{-1} = g_i^{-1} \otimes g_i = g_e$

is called *group* [5]. If $g_i \otimes g_j = g_j \otimes g_i, \forall i, j$ the group is called *abelian group*. The cardinality $|\mathcal{G}|$ of $\mathcal{G}$ represents the *order* of the group. A group having a finite order is a *finite group*. For any particular finite group $\mathcal{G}$ it is always possible to write a square table, the *Cayley table*, which summarizes all the possible results due by the action of $\otimes$ on pairs of group elements. Let $g_i, g_j \in \mathcal{G}$ [5]; the element g_i is said the *conjugate* of g_j if it can be written as $g_j = g_k g_i g_k^{-1}$ with $g_k \in \mathcal{G}$. The set C of all the elements that are conjugated to each other is called a *class* C. A group $\mathcal{G}$ always admits a number of classes $P \leq |\mathcal{G}|$. Two groups $\mathcal{G}$ and $\mathcal{G}'$ having the same order are said *isomorphic* if exists a one to one correspondence $g_i \leftrightarrow g_i', g_j \leftrightarrow g_j', g_k \leftrightarrow g_k', \cdots$ between the elements of $\mathcal{G}$ and $\mathcal{G}'$. If to $\mathcal{G}$ can be isomorphically associated the group $\mathcal{G}'$ of the square matrices $\mathbf{M}(g_i), \mathbf{M}(g_j), \mathbf{M}(g_k), \dots$ of order N, this set is called a *representation* of $\mathcal{G}$ having *dimension* N. The trace of each element of $\mathcal{G}'$ belonging to the class C_i' specifies the *character* for the class. If all the matrices $\mathbf{M}(g_i) \in \mathcal{G}'$ can be changed by a suitable equivalence transformation $\mathbf{S}$ to a block diagonal form

$$\mathbf{M}_{block}(g_i) = \mathbf{S}\mathbf{M}(g_i)\mathbf{S}^{-1} \quad i \in \{1 \cdots |\mathcal{G}|\} \tag{2}$$

the representation is said *reducible*, otherwise it is said *irreducible*. Any group $\mathcal{G}$ having finite order $|\mathcal{G}|$ is characterized by a finite number of irreducible representations $\mathbf{M}_{irr}^k(g_i) \quad k \in 1, \cdots, P$ equal to the number of classes P for $\mathcal{G}$ [5]. All the matrices $\mathbf{M}(g_i), i \in \{1, \dots |\mathcal{G}'|\}$ belonging to an arbitrary reducible representation $\mathcal{G}'$ can always be written as

$$\mathbf{M}_{block}(g_i) = \bigoplus_{k=1}^{P} m_k \mathbf{M}_{irr}^k(g_i) \tag{3}$$

where the symbol $\oplus$ represents the direct sum of matrices and the coefficients m_k are the number of times for which the irreducible matrix block $\mathbf{M}_{irr}^k(g_i)$ appears in $\mathbf{M}_{block}(g_i)$ [5]. The coefficients m_k are given by the following relation

$$m_k = \frac{1}{|\mathcal{G}|}\sum_{i=1}^{P} n_i \chi(\mathcal{C}_i')\chi(\mathcal{C}_{irr}^k)^* \quad (4)$$

where n_i is the cardinality of the class C_i belonging to $\mathcal{G}$, $\chi(\mathcal{C}_i')$ is the character for the class i belonging to the representation $\mathcal{G}'$ and $\chi(\mathcal{C}_{irr}^k)^*$ is complex conjugate of the character for the class i belonging to the irreducible representation $\mathcal{G}_{irr}^k$. Finally, if an operator L commute with all the element of the group $\mathcal{G}$, i.e. $Lg_i = g_iL$ for $i = \{1, \ldots, |\mathcal{G}|\}$ from (3) we can deduce that its matrix representation $\mathbf{L}$ of order N in order to commute with all the $\mathbf{M}_{block}(g_i)$ has to have the same diagonal block structure [5].

III. Symmetry and its Influence on Nonlinear Eigenproblem Computational Requirements

In order to demonstrate how Group theory can be usefully employed to enhance the computational performances of the numerical procedure described in [1] to solve the nonlinear eigenproblem (1), in what follows we take into account the classical problem of computing the cutoff wavenumbers in a metallic waveguide [1] characterized by a transverse section D having two symmetry axes (u_1, u_2) orthogonal to the direction of propagation z (i.e elliptic or rectangular transverse sections are included in this case). If we denote the operation of reflection across the symmetry axes (u_1, u_2) with σ, σ', the operation of rotation around the $\hat{z}$ axis by π radiants with C_2 and the identity operation with e, the set $\{e, C_2, \sigma, \sigma'\}$ makes up a group called the point symmetry group $C_{2\nu}$ [5]. Being $C_{2\nu}$ an abelian group, the number of classes P results to be equal to the cardinality of the group $|\mathcal{G}|$. For what concerns the class cardinality $n_i, i \in \{1, \ldots, 4\}$ it is the same for each class $C_i, i \in \{1, \ldots, 4\}$ and equal to 1. Accordingly $C_{2\nu}$ has four irreducible representations $\mathbf{M}_{irr}^1(e), \mathbf{M}_{irr}^1(C_2), \mathbf{M}_{irr}^1(\sigma), \mathbf{M}_{irr}^1(\sigma')$, all one dimensional [5]. Table I shows the character table related to $C_{2\nu}$. An N dimensional reducible matrix representation $\mathbf{M}(u), u \in \{e, C_2, \sigma, \sigma'\}$ for all the elements of the group $C_{2\nu}$ can be obtained by using the same basis function adopted to discretize the operator $L(\gamma)$ by Method of Moments. On the basis of the aforementioned results, we have that all the $\mathbf{M}(u)$ can be transformed to the matrix block form given by (3) in which $m_k = \frac{N}{4}$ for $k = 1, \ldots, 4$ [5]. To commute with all these block matrices, the discretized operator $\mathbf{L}(\gamma)$ has to have the same matrix block structure, i.e.

$$\begin{pmatrix} \mathbf{L}(\gamma)_{1,1} & & & 0 \\ & \mathbf{L}(\gamma)_{2,2} & & \\ & & \mathbf{L}(\gamma)_{3,3} & \\ 0 & & & \mathbf{L}(\gamma)_{4,4} \end{pmatrix} \quad (5)$$

where each diagonal matrix block $\mathbf{L}_{ii}, i \in \{1, 2, 3, 4\}$ has order $\frac{N}{4}$ [5]. Thus, the original eigenproblem (1) is now decoupled in four nonlinear eigenproblem of smaller order.

TABLE I
Character Table for C_2^ν.

	$\chi(e)$	$\chi(C_2)$	$\chi(\sigma)$	$\chi(\sigma')$
$\mathbf{M}_{irr}^1(e)$	1	1	1	1
$\mathbf{M}_{irr}^1(C_2)$	1	1	−1	−1
$\mathbf{M}_{irr}^1(\sigma)$	1	−1	1	−1
$\mathbf{M}_{irr}^1(\sigma')$	1	−1	−1	1

TABLE II
Normalized cutoff wavelengths of TM modes for a metallic elliptical waveguide.

Mode	This work	[6]
1	2.6062	2.6062
2	1.6377	1.6377
3	1.6336	1.6336
4	1.2204	1.2204

As can be easily verified the numerical resolution of these four decoupled eigenproblems by means of the algorithm described in [1] requires an overall computational complexity of $\mathcal{O}\left(\frac{n_0}{12}N^2 + 2n_0\right)$: If we compare this result with $\mathcal{O}\left(\frac{n_0 4}{3}N^2 + 2n_o\right)$ that is the required overall computational complexity for solving the original eigenproblem [1], it is evident as (for a large N) a computational speed-up of a factor of 16 is obtained. Concerning the memory requirements, an overall reduction of a factor of 4 is obtained (see [1],[4] for details about the evaluation of the computational complexity and memory requirements).

IV. Numerical Results

The aforementioned approach has been implemented in a computer code using Matlab. As a case of study, we have considered the computation of the cutoff wavelengths λ_c (normalized with respect to the semi-major axis) for a metallic elliptical waveguide having eccentricity $e = 0.1$ (see table I of [6]). All the numerical computations have been performed on an Intel Xeon DP E5405 Quad Core 2.0 based workstation, with 20 GB of main memory. Results reported in table II show as the use of Group theory do not cause any loss of numerical precision in the computation of these parameters.

References

[1] Angiulli G., "On the Computation of Nonlinear Eigenvalues in Electromagnetic Problems," Journal of Electromagnetic Waves and Applications, vol.21, no.4, pp.527-532, 2007.

[2] Angiulli G., "Design of Square Substrate Integrated Waveguide Cavity Resonators: Compensation of Modelling Errors by Support Vector Regression Machines," American Journal of Applied Science, vol.9, n.11, pp.1872-1875, 2012.

[3] Amendola G., G. Angiulli, E. Arnieri, L. Boccia," Computation of the Resonant Frequency and Quality Factor of Lossy Substrate Integrated Waveguide Resonators by Method of Moments," Progress in Electromagnetic Research Letters, vol.40, pp.107-117, 2013.

[4] Higham N. J., *Accuracy and Stability of Numerical Algorithms*, SIAM, 2002.

[5] Inui, T. Tanabe Y., Onodera, Y. *Group Theory and Its Applications in Physics*, Springer-Verlag, 1990.

[6] Zhang S., Y. Shen, "Eigenmode Sequence for an Elliptical Waveguide with Arbitrary Ellipticity," IEEE Trans. Microwave Theory and Tech., vol.41, n.11, pp.227-230, 1995.

Numerical study of a family of IMEX-DGTD methods for the 3D time-domain Maxwell's equations

Hao Wang, Li Xu, and Bin Li
School of Physical Electronics, UESTC, China
Stéphane Descombes and Stéphane Lanteri
Université Côte dAzur, Inria, CNRS, LJAD, France

***Abstract*—In this work, a new family of implicit-explicit (IMEX) schemes based on exponential time integration is developed for the 3D time-domain Maxwell's equations discretized by a high order discontinuous Galerkin (DG) scheme formulated on locally refined unstructured meshes. Numerical experiments demonstrate that the DGTD solver based on the proposed time integration scheme can be much faster than the one based on classical low-storage Runge-Kutta scheme, with the same accuracy and slight memory usage increase.**

Kewords—Explicit exponential time integration, IMEX-DGTD, Maxwell's equations

I. Introduction

For electromagnetic problems with heterogeneous media or complex geometries, adaptive mesh refinement is an attractive technique for the efficient numerical solution of Maxwell's equations. Local mesh refinement, however, also imposes a severe stability constraint on explicit time integration since the maximal time step is determined by the smallest elements in the mesh. A natural way to limit the impact of this problem is to adopt an unconditional implicit time integration. However, this approach is very expensive and even infeasible, especially in 3D, since a large global matrix system need to be solved in each time step. To overcome this resource consumption, various implicit-explicit (IMEX) schemes [1], [2] have been proposed, where implicit time stepping is used only for the small refined elements and efficient explicit time stepping is used for the remaining elements. On the other hand, the exponential time integration schemes seem to be especially well suited for locally refined problems. They combine excellent (unconditional) stability properties with ability to produce a very accurate solution even for relatively large time step sizes [3]. In this work, a new family of IMEX scheme based on exponential time integration is designed for the 3D time-domain Maxwell's equations discretized by a high order discontinuous Galerkin (DG) scheme formulated on locally refined unstructured meshes.

II. Novel IMEX scheme for DGTD

Unlike the traditional IMEX scheme which adopts implicit time stepping for the smallest elements, the Lawson time integration [4] is exploited in the proposed IMEX scheme. Consider a problem without source and the conduction is zero; the following ODEs with a single unknown vector is obtained by gathering the electric and magnetic unknowns in the global semi-discrete system from a DG discretization in space:

$$\partial_t \mathbf{U} = \mathbb{C}\mathbf{U}. \tag{1}$$

The entire mesh can be decomposed into two subsets, one consisting of the smallest elements, and the other one consisting of the remaining elements. The unknown vector can be split according to this decomposition. Thus system (1) becomes

$$\partial_t \mathbf{U} = \mathbb{C}_f\mathbf{U} + \mathbb{C}_c\mathbf{U}. \tag{2}$$

Then, a new unknown vector $\mathbf{V}(t) = e^{-t\mathbb{C}_f}\mathbf{U}(t)$ is introduced and used to replace the vector $\mathbf{U}$ in (2)

$$\partial_t \mathbf{V} = e^{-t\mathbb{C}_f}\mathbb{C}_c e^{t\mathbb{C}_f}\mathbf{V} = f(t, \mathbf{V}(t)). \tag{3}$$

In the transformed system (3), the term associated with the fine elements is completely eliminated; the remaining system can be time integrated by various high order accurate explicit time integration techniques. In this work, the fourth order five stage low-storage Runge-Kutta (LSRK(4,5)) [5] scheme is utilized. This makes it possible to design a solution strategy based on (3) which is much more efficient than the one obtained by applying an explicit time integration scheme to system (1).

III. Numerical results

We first validated the proposed combined Lawson and LSRK scheme by investigating its accuracy and numerical convergence order for a PEC cubic cavity, $\Omega = [0, 1m]^3$. The cavity is filled with vacuum and works on a standing wave mode of frequency $f = 260$ MHz. The simulation is performed on locally refined meshes; figure 1 gives the cross section view of a refined mesh, where the specified fine elements for the proposed scheme are marked in red. As shown in figure 2, the global L_2-norm error of fields for the combined Lawson and LSRK scheme agrees with the one obtained by LSRK(4,5) for both first order (P1) and second order (P2) interpolation. Sub-figure 3a shows that the numerical convergence rates of the combined Lawson and LSRK scheme are 1.2 and 2.3 for P1 and P2 respectively.

We then study the performance of the proposed scheme. Sub-figure 3b shows that the DGTD solver based on the proposed scheme can reach the same accuracy with much less CPU time than the one based on classical LSRK(4,5) scheme. The performance statistics of the proposed scheme versus fully explicit LSRK(4,5) scheme for a mesh with 40616 tetrahedrons and 7759 vertices are given in table I. With the proposed scheme, the time step size is around 32 times larger than that of LSRK(4,5) scheme which yields significant gain in total CPU time, the former is 18.33 and 10.86 times faster than the later for P1 and P2, respectively. As for the peak memory usage during the simulation, the required additional memory usage for the proposed scheme is less than 10%.

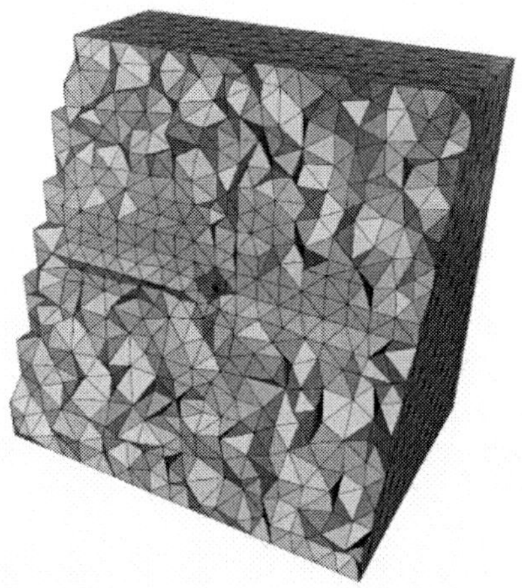

Fig. 1: Cross sections view of mesh

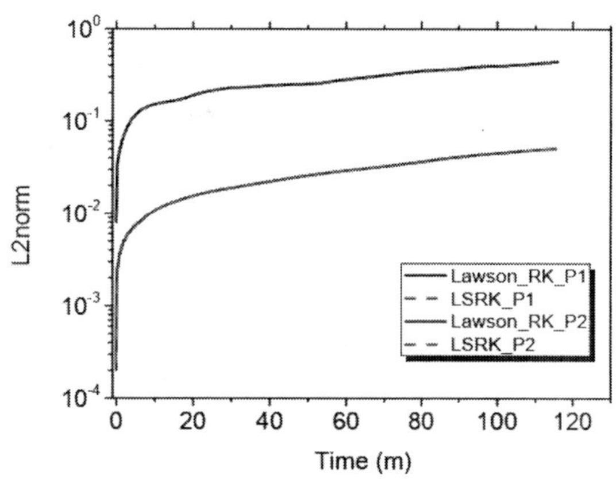

Fig. 2: The time evolution of L_2-norm error of fields for the combined Lawson and LSRK scheme versus LSRK(4,5) scheme within 100 periods

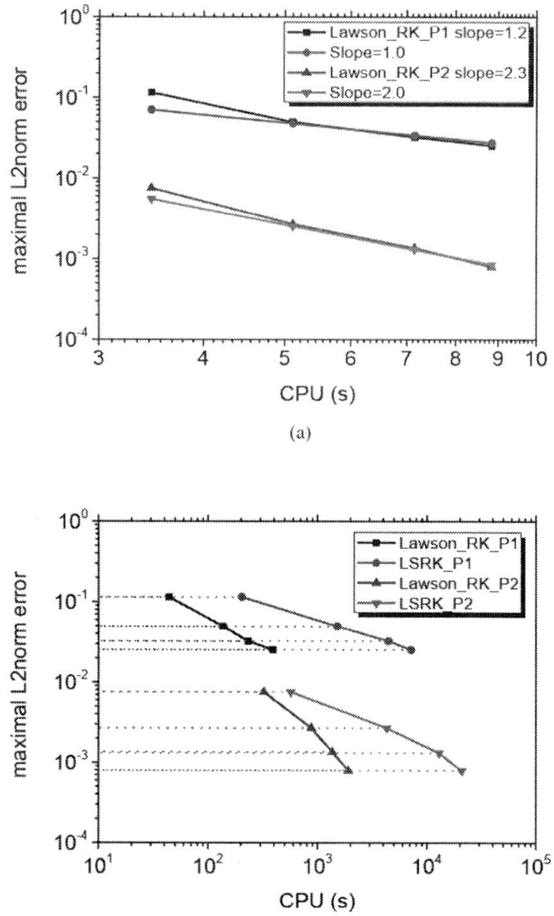

(a)

(b)

Fig. 3: The maximal L_2-norm error of fields in function of (a)the reciprocal of the largest edge length of the meshes, (b)total CPU time versus LSRK(4,5).

TABLE I: Performance of the combined Lawson and LSRK scheme versus LSRK(5,4) scheme

P_k	$\frac{\Delta t_{Lawson}}{\Delta t_{LSRK}}$	CPU (s)			Memory (Mb)	
		LSRK	Lawson	Gain	LSRK	Lawson
P1	32	7150	390	18.33	526	576
P2	32	20725	1909	10.86	1798	1947

REFERENCES

[1] S. Piperno, "Symplectic local time-stepping in non-dissipative dgtd methods applied to wave propagation problems," *ESAIM: Mathematical Modelling and Numerical Analysis*, vol. 40, no. 05, pp. 815–841, 2006.

[2] S. Descombes, S. Lanteri, and L. Moya, "Locally implicit time integration strategies in a discontinuous galerkin method for maxwells equations," *Journal of Scientific Computing*, vol. 56, no. 1, pp. 190–218, 2013.

[3] M. A. Botchev, "Krylov subspace exponential time domain solution of maxwells equations in photonic crystal modeling," *Journal of computational and applied mathematics*, vol. 293, pp. 20–34, 2016.

[4] J. D. Lawson, "Generalized runge-kutta processes for stable systems with large lipschitz constants," *SIAM Journal on Numerical Analysis*, vol. 4, no. 3, pp. 372–380, 1967.

[5] J. Williamson, "Low-storage runge-kutta schemes," *Journal of Computational Physics*, vol. 35, no. 1, pp. 48–56, 1980.

Analysis of Transmission-Line Equation Based on LOD-FDTD

Yaxiu Sun, Ming Zhang, Junzhu Qian, Jianli Wang
College of Information and Communications Engineering
Harbin Engineering University
Harbin, China
sunyaxiu@hrbeu.edu.cn zmeshocke@outlook.com

***Abstract*—The derivatives in the transmission-line equation can be approximated by difference formula which must satisfy CFL condition. LOD-FDTD provides an unconditional stability method to get the updating equation by alternately solving for the implicit and explicit equation, which improves the computational efficiency greatly, and saves computer resources and memory. In this paper, simulation results demonstrate the exactness and stability of the engineering LOD-FDTD in transmission-line equation.**

Keywords—LOD-FDTD; unconditional stability; transmission-line equation; exact solves

I. Introduction

In recent years, the application of the finite difference time domain (FDTD) method in computational electromagnetism has become more and more widely, because of its accuracy, clarity for physical meaning and easy to implement. But for the stability of the difference approximation, the discretization of position and time must satisfy the CFL condition, generally. There is a problem that computer resources will be greatly occupied when we want to run a simulation in a large size problem geometry with FDTD method, such as a long distance transmission line. LOD-FDTD method provided a new computing method for the deduction of updating equation of FDTD, and break the limits of discretization of time and space, so as to achieve the purpose of reducing the occupancy of computer resources. In this paper, the transmission line equations are discretized by LOD-FDTD method and the updating equations are obtained.

II. FDTD Updating Equation in the Transmission Line

The Finite-Difference Time-Domain method can be used in the analysis of transmission lines.

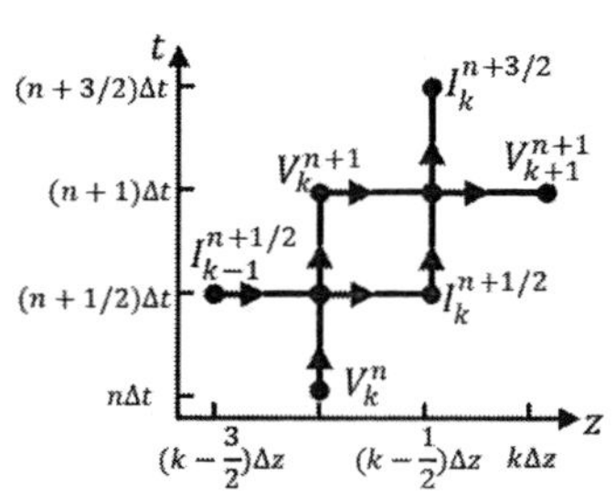

Fig. 1 Relationship of voltage point and current points

The derivatives in the transmission line equation can be approximated by using the central difference formula. Figure. 1 illustrates a relationship of computing. Each voltage point have a Δz distance with current points. The same as the time points.

Considering the transmission line equation, we get the updating equation

$$I_k^{n+\frac{3}{2}} = I_k^{n+\frac{1}{2}} - \frac{\Delta t}{\Delta z}\frac{1}{L}(V_{k+1}^{n+1} - V_k^{n+1}) \tag{1}$$

$$V_k^{n+1} = V_k^n - \frac{\Delta t}{\Delta z}\frac{1}{C}(I_k^{n+\frac{1}{2}} - I_{k-1}^{n+\frac{1}{2}}) \tag{2}$$

For the stability of the results, the discretization of position and time must satisfy the CFL condition.

$$\Delta t \leq \frac{\Delta z}{v} \tag{3}$$

Where v is speed of light in the medium of transmission line.

III. LOD-FDTD for the Transmission Line Equation

Due to the restriction of the Courant-Friedrich-Levy (CFL) condition, for the long distance transmission line model, the number of time steps was increased. The CFL condition limits the relationship between the number of time step (NDT) and distance step (NDZ) as follows.

$$NDT \geqq NDZ \times v \times (\mathrm{T/L}) \tag{4}$$

Consider again the transmission line equation as follows.

$$\begin{cases} \dfrac{\partial V(z,t)}{\partial z} = -RI(z,t) - L\dfrac{\partial I(z,t)}{\partial z} \\ \dfrac{\partial I(z,t)}{\partial z} = -GV(z,t) - C\dfrac{\partial V(z,t)}{\partial z} \end{cases}$$

We can manipulate it into a matrix form.

$$\frac{\partial}{\partial t}\boldsymbol{\Psi} = \boldsymbol{A\Psi} + \boldsymbol{B\Psi} \tag{5}$$

$$\boldsymbol{\Psi} = \begin{bmatrix} V(z,t) \\ I(z,t) \end{bmatrix}, \boldsymbol{A} = \begin{bmatrix} 0 & -\frac{1}{C}\partial_z \\ -\frac{1}{L}\partial_z & 0 \end{bmatrix}, \boldsymbol{B} = \begin{bmatrix} -\frac{G}{C} & 0 \\ 0 & -\frac{R}{L} \end{bmatrix}. \tag{6}$$

The solution of the equation can be expressed as follows.

$$\boldsymbol{\Psi}^{n+1} = \exp[(\boldsymbol{A}+\boldsymbol{B})\Delta t]\boldsymbol{\Psi}^n \tag{7}$$

$\Psi(t)|_{t=n\Delta t} = \Psi^n$, further rewritten as follows.

$$\psi^{n+1} = \frac{\exp\left[(A+B)\frac{\Delta t}{2}\right]}{\exp\left[-(A+B)\frac{\Delta t}{2}\right]}\psi^n = \frac{\exp\left[\frac{\Delta t}{2}A\right]\exp\left[\frac{\Delta t}{2}B\right]}{\exp\left[-\frac{\Delta t}{2}A\right]\exp\left[-\frac{\Delta t}{2}B\right]}\psi^n \quad (8)$$

Exponential term using Taylor series approximation.

$$\exp\left[\frac{\Delta t}{2}A\right] = \sum_{k=0}^{\infty}\frac{\left(\frac{\Delta t}{2}A\right)^k}{k!} \approx I + \frac{\Delta t}{2}A \quad (9)$$

Where the I is a unit matrix. Equation (8) can be approximated with Taylor series way as follows.

$$\psi^{n+1} \approx \frac{\left(I+\frac{\Delta t}{2}A\right)\left(I+\frac{\Delta t}{2}B\right)}{\left(I-\frac{\Delta t}{2}A\right)\left(I-\frac{\Delta t}{2}B\right)}\psi^n \quad (10)$$

The solution is divided into two sub time steps.

$$\begin{cases}\left(I-\frac{\Delta t}{2}A\right)\psi^{n+\frac{1}{2}} = \left(I+\frac{\Delta t}{2}A\right)\psi^n \\ \left(I-\frac{\Delta t}{2}B\right)\psi^{n+1} = \left(I+\frac{\Delta t}{2}B\right)\psi^{n+\frac{1}{2}}\end{cases} \quad (11)$$

The first sub time step from n to (n+1/2).

$$\begin{cases}V(z,t)^{n+\frac{1}{2}} + \frac{\Delta t}{2C}\frac{\partial I(z,t)^{n+\frac{1}{2}}}{\partial z} = V(z,t)^n - \frac{\Delta t}{2C}\frac{\partial I(z,t)^n}{\partial z} \\ I(z,t)^{n+\frac{1}{2}} + \frac{\Delta t}{2L}\frac{\partial V(z,t)^{n+\frac{1}{2}}}{\partial z} = I(z,t)^n - \frac{\Delta t}{2L}\frac{\partial V(z,t)^n}{\partial z}\end{cases} \quad (12)$$

The second sub time step from (n+1/2) to (n+1).

$$\begin{cases}V(z,t)^{n+1}\cdot\left(1+\frac{G\cdot\Delta t}{2C}\right) = V(z,t)^{n+\frac{1}{2}}\cdot\left(1-\frac{G\cdot\Delta t}{2C}\right) \\ I(z,t)^{n+1}\cdot\left(1+\frac{R\cdot\Delta t}{2L}\right) = I(z,t)^{n+\frac{1}{2}}\cdot\left(1-\frac{R\cdot\Delta t}{2L}\right)\end{cases} \quad (13)$$

Use the identity on the equation with

$$\begin{cases}\frac{\partial I(k)^{n+\frac{1}{2}}}{\partial z} = \frac{I(k)^{n+\frac{1}{2}} - I(k-1)^{n+\frac{1}{2}}}{\Delta z} \\ \frac{\partial V(k)^{n+\frac{1}{2}}}{\partial z} = \frac{V(k+1)^{n+\frac{1}{2}} - V(k)^{n+\frac{1}{2}}}{\Delta z}\end{cases} \quad (14)$$

We can obtain the LOD-FDTD updating equations for transmission line. From the updating equation, we can see each sub time step got the voltage component with solving the implicit equation first then use the explicit calculation to calculate the current component.

IV. Simulation Verification

To verify the validity of the new updating equation, the experiment of transmission line is simulated. Here the terminal voltage of two different conditions is compared. One is classical FDTD transmission line equation, the other is LOD-FDTD.

Figure. 2 describes the comparison between FDTD and LOD-FDTD in engineering computing. The transmission line is 100 meter and simulation time is 20 us. We can find the results of LOD-FDTD computing agree well with the FDTD computing results except some ringing effect. Obviously, the red line is a correct result in this simulation. The ringing effect in the blue line may be due to the longer time step. It needs to be discussed.

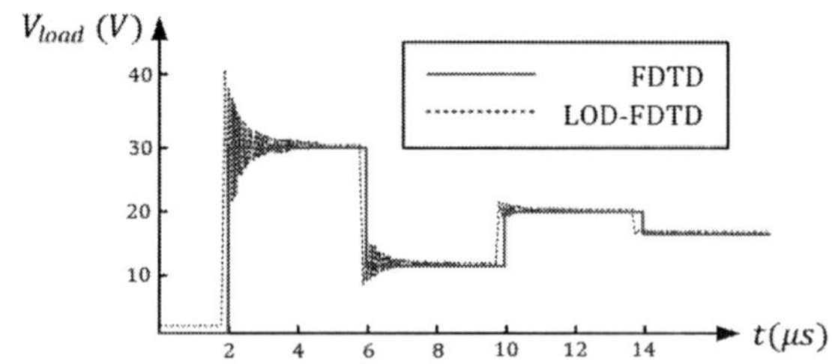

Fig. 2. Terminal voltage of FDTD and LOD-FDTD

TABLE I. Cost Time and CPU Memories of FDTD and LOD-FDTD

100 m transmission line, in 20 us		
	Cost time	***Memories***
LOD-FDTD	5 min	46 MB
FDTD	436 min	1.56 GB

And from TABLE I. we can come up LOD-FDTD cost less time and computer resources than FDTD in computing.

V. Conclusion

LOD-FDTD and transmission line equations were jointly analyzed in this paper, we obtained new updating equations. The feasibility of this method was demonstrated through application of simulated signals and comparison of FDTD and LOD-FDTD in transmission line problem solving. We can come to the conclusion that LOD-FDTD has the advantage of saving the computer resources and reducing the simulation time. LOD-FDTD has stronger adaptability than classical FDTD. It has important significance in computing of large size conductor.

Acknowledgment

This paper was supported by the National Natural Science Foundation of China (Grant No. 51209055), the China Postdoctoral Special Foundation (Grant No. 2015T80324), and the Natural Science Foundation of Heilongjiang, China (Grant No. F2015028).

References

[1] Iftikhar A, Chua E K, Li Erping. Numerical dispersion analysis of the unconditionally stable three-dimensional LOD-FDTD method[J]. IEEE Transactions on Antennas and Propagation, 2010, 58(12): 3983-3989.

[2] J Alok K, Kumar V. Stability and dispersion analysis of higher order unconditionally stable three-step locally onedimensional finite-difference time-domain method[J]. IET Microwaves, Antennas and Propagation, 2013, 7(12): 954-960.

[3] Liang F, Wang G, Lin H,et al. Numerical dispersion improved three-dimensional locally one-dimensional finite-difference time-domain method[J]. IET Microwaves, Antennas and Propagation, 2011, 5(10): 1256-1263.

[4] Kong Yongdan, Chu Qingxin. An unconditionally-stable FDTD method with low anisotropy in three-dimensional domains[C]//Progress in Electromagnetics Research Symposium, 2012: 1125-1130.

A General Model for Pattern Synthesis of Linear Antenna Arrays by Metaheuristic Algorithms

Suad Basbug
Department of Electrical and Electronics Engineering
Nevsehir Haci Bektas Veli University, Nevsehir, Turkey
suadbasbug@gmail.com

Abstract— **In this paper, a general model is proposed for the systems that optimize the linear antenna array parameters to synthesize a desired pattern by using metaheuristic algorithms. The model consists of a masking mechanism for the pattern shaping and a modular system for the whole optimization structure. To validate the skills of the proposed model, an antenna array synthesizer software is developed and tested with six different pattern examples. The results show that this implementation based on the proposed method can achieve the desired patterns successfully. The source code and compiled version of the software are shared on the Internet.**

Keywords— Linear antenna arrays, metaheuristic optimization, pattern synthesis, cost function, mask design

I. Introduction

Antenna array patterns can be shaped by three controllable parameters of the array elements: amplitude, phase, and position. For a pattern synthesis, the values of these parameters can be calculated individually or together. Metaheuristic algorithms provide acceptable solutions of the optimization problems of pattern synthesis in a reasonable time. In this paper, a general model for pattern synthesis of linear antenna arrays that uses metaheuristic algorithms is proposed. The model consists of two main parts, namely masking mechanism and modular system. Proposed masking mechanism is a very flexible method that can be used to generate many different types of masks with adjustable precisions. Likewise, the modular system in this paper offers an open structure that has replaceable modules to provide a general scheme for pattern synthesis works which employ metaheuristic algorithms.

II. Problem Formulation and Proposed Model

A. Array Factor

Consider a linear array having N isotropic antenna elements; the array pattern is given by

$$AF(\theta) = \sum_{n=1}^{N} a_n e^{j(k\lambda d_n \mathrm{Cos}\,\theta + \varphi_n)} \tag{1}$$

where n is the element number; $k = 2\pi/\lambda$ is the wave number; λ is the wavelength; a_n is the amplitude of the nth element, d_n is the distance of the nth element from the first element, φ_n is the phase of the nth element, θ is the scanning angle.

B. Masking Mechanism and Cost Function

A mask in the proposed model consists of mask segments. The cost function calculations highly depend on the mask segment definition. The cost function of an outer mask in our model is defined by

$$C = \sum_{g=1}^{G} \sum_{h=1}^{H_g} (\delta_{gh}) w_{gh} \tag{2}$$

where

$$\delta_{gh} = \begin{cases} AF_{dB}(\theta_{gh}) - M_{gh} & AF_{dB}(\theta_{gh}) > M_{gh} \\ 0 & else \end{cases} \tag{3}$$

where G is the number of mask segments; H_g is the maximum number of sample points of the gth segment. w_{gh} is the weight value of the hth sample point of gth segment. M_{gh} is the mask level value in dB of hth sample point of gth segment. Each point of a segment has individual M_{gh} level and w_{gh} weight values. All the five parameters of a mask segment, namely start angle, stop angle, number of points, level, and weight, are adjustable so that the inner and outer masks can be formed to meet design requirements. Where $h = 1$, θ_{gh} angle gets the lowest value which is the first point for the g_{th} segment. H_g is the last index value for the g_{th} segment, which means the highest angle value of θ_{gh}.

C. Modular Optimization System

Proposed technique divides the whole optimization mechanism into five sub modules. The main control module is the central unit of the model. The metaheuristic algorithm module carries out the optimization process iteratively. It uses the cost calculation module (CCM) to achieve the cost function value of each trial. In order to calculate the cost values, CCM engages the mask module (MM) for the mask calculations. MM contains and manages the outer and inner masks. CCM also uses the antenna array module (AAM) for the array factor calculations. AAM has the details of the antenna array parameters such as amplitude, phase, positions, and number of array elements.

D. Linear Antenna Array Synthesizer (LAAS)

LAAS is an implementation of the proposed method to synthesize linear antenna array patterns. Its user interface has been developed by using Java with Swing application programming interface. As a metaheuristic algorithm, classical version of differential evolution (DE) is used. LAAS is shared as an open-source software for further modification and developments at [7] and [8]. For the documentation, video tutorials and compiled version of LAAS, one can refer to [7].

III. Numerical Results

LAAS is used to validate the usability and flexibility of the proposed model. Six different examples taken from the literature are considered [1-6]. The examples have different characteristics in terms of optimization aims as well as usage of the optimization parameters, which are amplitude, phase and position values. For all examples, DE parameters are selected as follows: population number, maximum iteration number, scaling factor, and crossover rate are 70, 1000, 0.7, and 0.95, respectively. The number of array elements is 30 for the first example, 21 for the last example and 20 for the all other examples. For all examples, inter-element spacing is $\lambda/2$ except for the third and sixth examples in which position perturbation values are used as the optimization variables. The first example is a sidelobe suppression and main beam restriction simulation [1]. The maximum sidelobe level (SLL) obtained by LAAS, shown in Fig. 1(a), is -36.5 dB and half power beam width (BW) is 4.67°. In the second example, the main aim is to achieve multiple nulls at 57°, 80° and 110° angles of the pattern by controlling only phase values of the array elements [2]. The pattern in Fig. 1(b) has deeper null depth level (NDL) values than -100 dB for the all desired nulls and its maximum SLL is -23.35 dB. For the third example [3], LAAS has obtained the pattern shown in Fig. 1(c), which has -50 dB NDL and -28.4 dB maximum SLL values. For the fourth example, LAAS has succeeded to form a pattern whose main beam is steered to 70° [4] shown in Fig. 1(d) with a -30 dB maximum SLL and 7.93° BW. In the fifth example, a sector beam pattern is presented [5]. For the pattern attained by LAAS, the ripples of the sector beam are smaller than 0.45 dB and maximum SLL is -25 dB. The pattern is given in Fig. 1(e). For the sixth example, the desired pattern, presented in Fig. 1(f), has a pencil beam and asymmetric side lobes [6], with -30 dB left side and -20 dB right side maximum SLLs.

IV. Conclusion

A general model including a flexible masking mechanism and an overall modular structure for the systems that use the metaheuristic algorithms to synthesize linear antenna array patterns is presented. LAAS is a software developed by considering the proposed model. It is tested with six different examples from the literature. The results show that the proposed model can achieve the desired radiation patterns. It is also observed that LAAS based on the proposed model offers very flexible masking mechanism. Further information, source codes and compiled versions of LAAS software can be found at [7] and [8]

References

[1] K. K. Yan and Y. Lu, "Sidelobe reduction in array-pattern synthesis using genetic algorithm," IEEE Transactions on Antennas and Propagation, vol. 45, no. 7, pp. 1117–1122, Jul. 1997.

[2] K. Guney and S. Basbug, "Seeker optimization algorithm for interference suppression of linear antenna arrays by controlling position-only, phase-only, and amplitude-only," International Journal of RF and Microwave Computer-Aided Engineering, vol. 21, no. 5, pp. 505–518, Sep. 2011.

[3] K. Guney and S. Basbug, "Bacterial Foraging Algorithm for Null Synthesizing of Linear Antenna Arrays by Controlling Only the Element Positions," Journal of Optimization Theory and Applications, vol. 150, no. 3, pp. 635–656, Mar. 2011.

[4] A. Arce, M. Cardenas-Juarez, U. Pineda-Rico, D. H. Covarrubias, and E. Stevens-Navarro, "A Multiple Beamforming Network for Unequally Spaced Linear Array Based on CORPS," International Journal of Antennas and Propagation, vol. 2015, Article ID 757989, 7 pages, 2015.

[5] W. C. Weng, F. Yang, and A. Z. Elsherbeni, "Linear Antenna Array Synthesis Using Taguchi's Method: A Novel Optimization Technique in Electromagnetics," IEEE Transactions on Antennas and Propagation, vol. 55, no. 3, pp. 723–730, Mar. 2007.

[6] T. Isernia, F. J. A. Pena, O. M. Bucci, M. D'Urso, J. F. Gomez, and J. A. Rodriguez, "A hybrid approach for the optimal synthesis of pencil beams through array antennas," IEEE Transactions on Antennas and Propagation, vol. 52, no. 11, pp. 2912–2918, Nov. 2004.

[7] "Linear Antenna Array Synthesizer Web Site." [Online]. Available: http://www.silisyum.com/laas. [Accessed: 14-Nov-2016].

[8] "Linear Antenna Array Synthesizer." [Online]. Available: https://github.com/silisyum/laas. [Accessed: 14-Nov-2016].

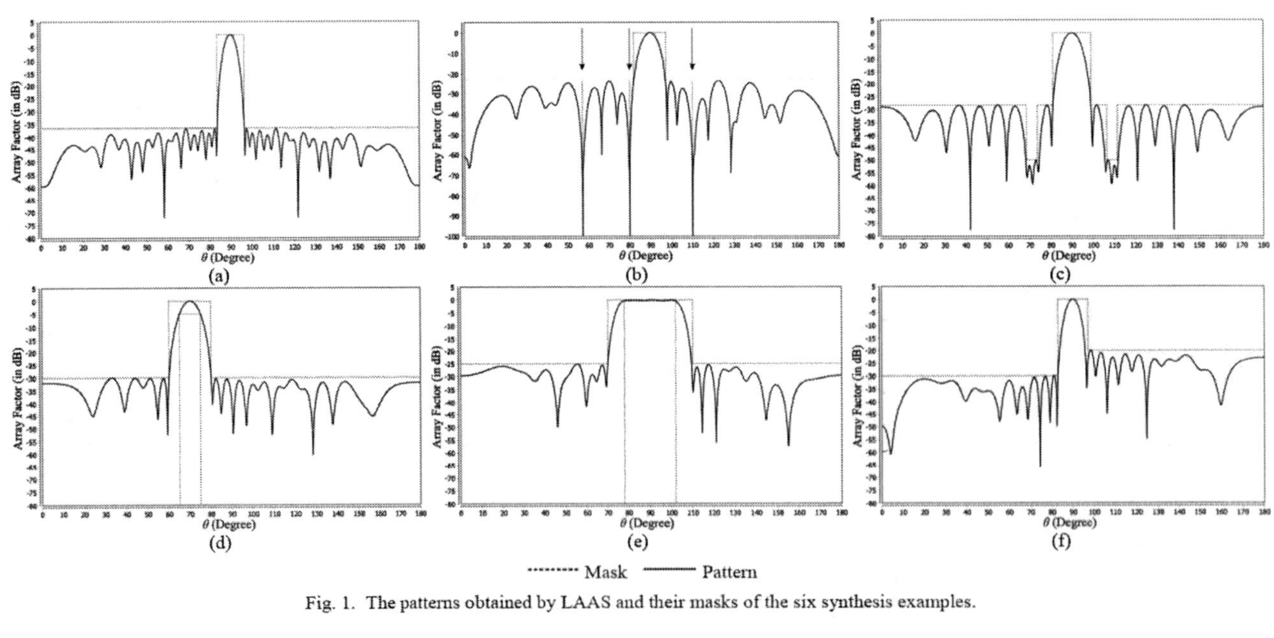

Fig. 1. The patterns obtained by LAAS and their masks of the six synthesis examples.

Discernibility of Metallic Sphere in Rectangular Waveguide

Kirill Zeyde
Ural Federal University,
Institute of radioelectronics and
information technologies
Ekaterinburg, Russia
Email: k.m.zeyde@urfu.ru

***Abstract*—This work describes the initial principles of microwave discernibility conditions for metallic sphere, placed at the center of waveguide cross section. Having previously obtained data for this position, low frequencies range for transmission line are in interest. For further clarification, recombination algorithm from free space to line reflection coefficient was developed. New obtained formulation describes in details the behavior of reflection in this diapason. Main interest in discernibility of sphere is the Reyleight region. Natural experiment for 7-12 GHz confirms the findings.**

***Index Terms*—waveguides measurements, reflection coefficients, transmission lines propagation, objects discernibility**

I. INTRODUCTION

In [1] empirically obtained reflectivity coefficient for the sphere, that touches the broad wall of waveguide was obtained. Single position case have the approximate solution, but in that formulation there are no frequency dependence. Work [2] specify this omission and also gives numerical and experimental results for central sphere position. In this form solution become closed, but low frequencies excluded from the analysis, however on certain electrical sizes of sphere, Mie resonance may be observed. Work [3] gives the detailed explanations, basically for Reyleight diapason, which is considered in this work.

Estimation of minimal displacement can be obtained in the terms of object tracking by setting the sensitivity of measurement instruments and observational error. This formulation may be examined in [4]. The discernibility of the object determines by using this provisions.

This work chases several aims. First is to confirm the recombination algorithm (this algorithm can be used in wide range of propagation problems). Second - determines the divergence between free space Mie formulation and corresponding situation in the waveguide (in closed space as well). This point leads to the main aim - general method of sphere discernibility prediction.

II. FORMULATION

Analytical representation for metallic sphere free space reflection obtained in a special approximation form in [5].

This research work was made in Ural Federal University. It was supported by grant N 14-19-01396 from the Russian Science Foundation.

Generalized complex sphere reflectivity, derived by propagation condition recombination is following (Reyleight diapason: $r/\lambda_w \leq 0.1$):

$$\dot{S} = 35cos(\theta)\left[\sqrt{\pi}r\left[1+3(k_w r)^2\right]e^{-j6(k_w r)^3} - 2\pi r\right], \quad (1)$$

where r - radius of the sphere, λ_w - wavelength in waveguide, k_w - wavenumber for transmission line and θ - incidence angle. This formulation allows to get the resonance Mie curve for perfect conducting sphere, placed at the center of rectangular waveguide cross section. Recombination algorithm for the case of broad or narrow wall touching not developed, due to new geometry accounting necessity (morphology reconstruction).

Propagation condition recombination affects three aspects: first - characteristic type of wave (fundamental mode only) introduce to (1) λ_w and k. Second - dephasing, due to wave dispersion, makes some corrections to exponent and optical formulation of sphere radar cross section. And, third - incidence at the certain angle (also due to dispersion), which explains the presence of trigonometric function in (1). At low frequencies the impact of this factor prevails.This formulation described by:

$$\theta = arccos\left[\sqrt{1-\left(\frac{c}{2af}\right)^2}\right], \quad (2)$$

where c - wave speed in free space, a - length of broad wall, f - frequency of incident wave. In this case work [6] gives the necessary explanations.

Detailed description of recombination method not included on this work. The basic idea is to replace the certain values from initial equation to recombinated with the saving of physical sense.

At the other hand, the reflection coefficient from [2] is following:

$$\Gamma = -j\left(\frac{2r}{b}\right)^3\left(\frac{\pi b}{2a}\right)^2 A\left[\frac{2}{\sqrt{1-A^{-2}}}+\sqrt{1-A^{-2}}\right], \quad (3)$$

where b - length of narrow wall and

$$A = \frac{a\sqrt{\left(\frac{\pi}{a}\right)^2+\left(\frac{2\pi}{\lambda_w}\right)^2}}{\pi}. \quad (4)$$

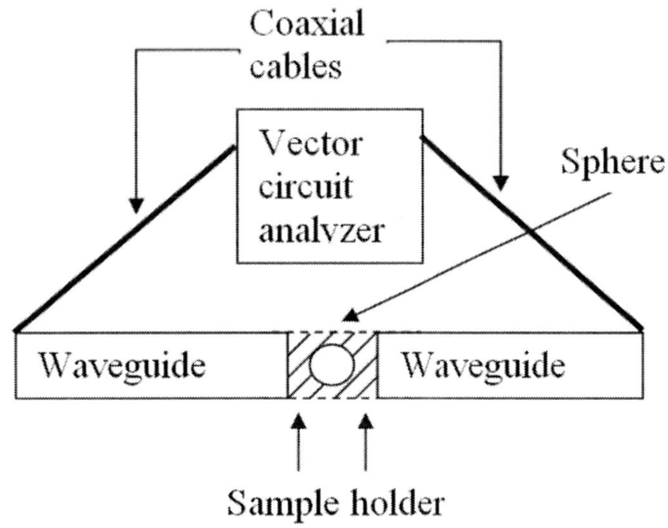

Fig. 1. Laboratory experimental stand.

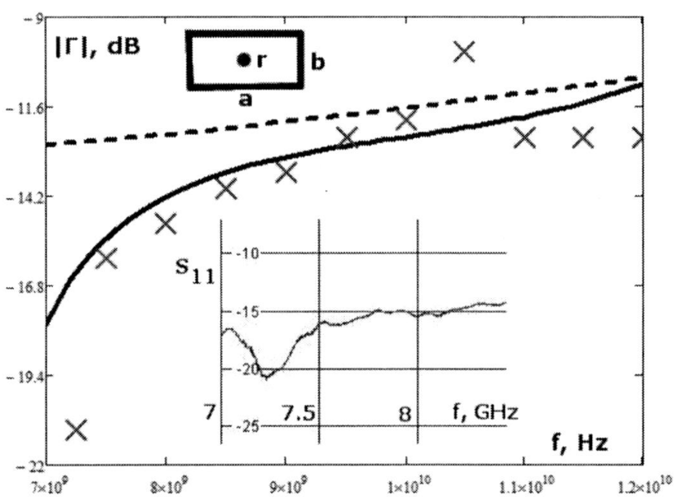

Fig. 2. Theoretical and experiment results for r=2.25mm: (solid line) - reflectivity (1); (dotted line) - reflectivity (3); (crosses) - experiment reflectivity.

Equations (1) and (3) will be compare for propagation recombination algorithm verification. At the same time natural experiment results reconciled with theoretical data.

III. Experiments setups

As the reference object sphere with r = 2.25 mm was used. Structure of the laboratory setup is common for waveguides measurements (fig. 1). Object placed at the center of the line cross section (fig. 2 on top), by using radio transparent holders. Waveguide transmission line for operating frequencies f = [7 - 12] GHz, determines by a = 23 mm and b = 10 mm. Electrical sizes ($k_w r$) in Reyleight region: [0.12 - 0.475]. Vector circuit analyzer - Rohde and Schwarz ZVA 24. Two port calibration method by TRM algorithm gives the observational error (the maximum deviation from the zero level for thought line) 0.03 dB.

Fig. 2 gives the complete findings of pointed formulation. Equations (1) and (3) were converted to dB for easy comparison with experimental data. Circuit reflection S_{11} as the output from analyzer also shown at fig. 2 in the low frequency range.

Estimation of center displacement was not made. In the case of sphere discernibility such a procedure is unnecessary. In more exact positioning situation this evaluation should be carried out [4].

IV. Results and conclusion

Analysis of fig. 2 gives following results. First, previously proposed method (3), excluding the initial operating frequencies of transmission line. Free space to line recombination equation (1) accurately describes the behavior of reflection process in all frequency band and most importantly gives the lost information about possible resonance decreasing. This formulation gives all necessary data to predict the discernibility of sphere in waveguides. Electrical radius 0.15 corresponding to minimum of reflectivity. Presents of this resonance processes lets to assume that Mie recombination algorithm may be saved in such a form for other closed spaces. The explanation of theory and experiment line significant deviation (2 dB) at point 10.5 GHz lies in arising coefficient oscillation at high frequencies (start from electrical radius equal to 0.3) due to multiple sphere-walls reflections. This point corresponding to maximum magnitude of this effect.

By virtue of (1) obtained from strict solution approximation with specific recombination, extremely small spheres in waveguides may be described by free space equation. But in this case dispersion and incident angle also will make the certain impact. Principled convergence of initial and recombination expression, determines by the limits: $k_w \to 0$ and $f \to \infty$. Obviously such condition, besides that not determines the possible discernibility of the sphere, as well as exceeds the waveguide frequency boundaries together with Reylight region approximation.

It should be noted that problem of invisibility of heterogeneous in transmission line may also be solved by the recombination equations. General algorithms causes also specified anisotropic medium.

References

[1] P. I. Somlo, D.L. Hollway, 'Conductive contacting spheres on the center of the broad wall of rectangular waveguides', Electron. Lett., vol. 8, no. 20, 1972.

[2] J.H. Hinken, 'Conducting spheres in rectangular waveguides', IEEE transaction on microwave theory and techniques, Vol. MTT-28, no. 7, 1980.

[3] Li Na NG, B. Eng 'Manipulation of particles on optical waveguides', Optoelectronics research center, University of Southhampton, United Kingdom, 2000.

[4] K.M. Zeyde, 'Estimation of optimal space-time sampling in the problems of tracking of rotating targets, using MDR provision', Electromagnetic waves and electronic systems, Radiotekhnika, 2016.

[5] A.I.Ladygin, A.A. Luchin, 'Approksimaciya tochnogo resheniya zadachi difrakcii na provodyashei sfere', Electromagnetic waves and Electronic systems, N 9, Vol. 8, Radiotechnica, 2003, pp. 20-25.

[6] A.M. Romanov, A.A. Belyaev, E.E. Bespalova 'Nedostatki volnovodnyh metodov izmereniya harakteristik radiopogloshaushih materialov', Works of VIAM, N 3, 2015.

An Efficient Numerical Method to Analyze Discontinuity of Coaxial Cable

Jingyi Wang, Junwu Tao
LAPLCE-ENSEEIHT
Toulouse, France
jywang@laplace.univ-tlse.fr

Fayçal Benmohamed
Laboratoire Hubert Curien
Saint-Etienne, France
faycal.benmohamed@univ-st-etienne.fr

***Abstract*—In this paper, we present a complex discontinuity in stratified structure by hybrid numerical methods. A rigorous analysis of the transverse operator formulations is carried on inhomogeneous coaxial cable filled with dielectric sample for propagation constants and the corresponding normalized field distributions. The new multimodal variational method is used to describe the dispersion characterization for cascaded uniaxial discontinuities, showing good agreement compared with the simulation results carried out by computer aided design software.**

Keywords—Scattering parameters; transverse operator method; new multimodal variation method

I. Introduction

Material characterization has become increasing important because of predicting accurate behaviors before manufacture. The currently available methods for use in dielectric properties calculation are elaborated, especially when there is a transition in the measurement [1-4]. In our study, we proposed a numerical method to solve dielectric properties problem of ceramic sample partially filling in coaxial cable including a conical transition, which is much more complex than these papers above because of its stratified structure in Fig.1. After fixed the cone calibration which takes into consideration the real loss, reflection and transmission parameters are related to the complex permittivity of the material which is under test, so discontinuity analysis in coaxial cable caused by the junction between different dielectric properties is encountered in our calculation.

Discontinuity analysis is significant for the microwave devices designs. The characterization analyses of the frequency dependent components are always encountered in the designs. Uniaxial waveguide discontinuity was delivered the detailed exposition for particular cases by TAO [5] which illustrates the scattering parameters compared with mode matching method. Similar to work of D. Lilonga et al [6], we applied the new multimodal approach to analyze interacting discontinuities caused by the filled dielectric simple with loss, which means the constituent waveguides are inhomogeneous. Transvers operator method is imperative to derive the propagating constants and field expansions which are described in [7]. The discontinuity analysis is carried out by new multimodal approach in which the tangential fields are expanded in series of total orthogonal eigenmodes between empty and filled with dielectric coaxial cable. The numerical results from the analytical methods are fairly accurate and quickly convergent, showing good agreements compared with that by simulation.

(a)

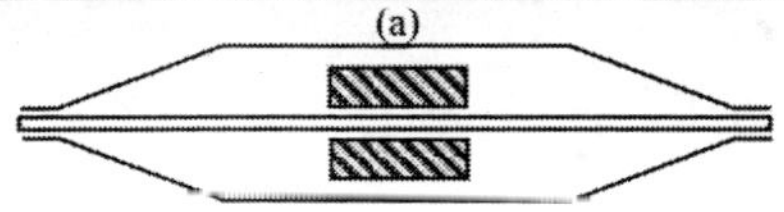

(b)

Fig.1 Photo (a) and section (b) of experimental structure

II. Analysis Theory

A discontinuity problem is shown in Fig. 2 between three uniaxial waveguides. For general cases, network expressions are described by the transverse electric and magnetic fields in a reciprocal waveguide.

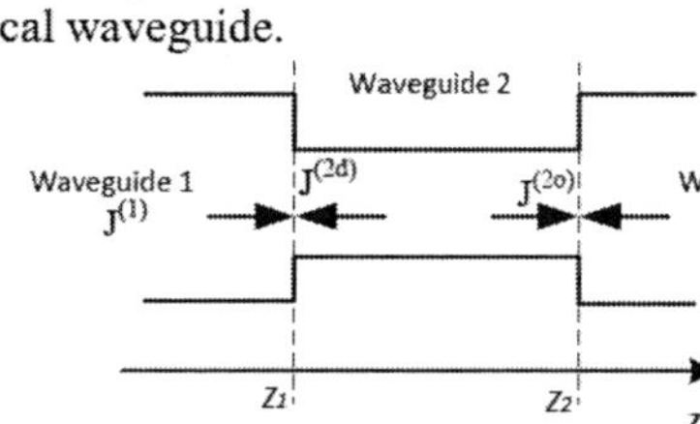

Fig. 2 double discontinuities structure

The surface current density vectors J is related to transverse magnetic field H_t at the discontinuity planes (z_i), which can be written in the integral equation:

$$\vec{J}(u,v,z_i) = \lim_{\delta \to 0} \vec{u}_z \times [\vec{H}_t(u,v,z_i+\delta) - \vec{H}_t(u,v,z_i-\delta)]$$

with $i = 1, 2$. By noting that $\vec{E}_t(u,v,z_i)$ is unknown tangential electric field at discontinuity plane between adjacent junctions, we can write the following coupled integral equations:

$$\vec{J}(u,v,z_1) = \hat{Y}_{11}\vec{E}_t(u_0,v_0,z_1) + \hat{Y}_{12}\vec{E}_t(u_0,v_0,z_2) \quad (1a)$$

$$\vec{J}(u,v,z_2) = \hat{Y}_{21}\vec{E}_t(u_0,v_0,z_1) + \hat{Y}_{22}\vec{E}_t(u_0,v_0,z_2) \quad (1b)$$

The integral type operator will be defined by:

$$\hat{Y}_{11} = \sum_{n=1}^{\infty} B_1^{(1)}\, g^{(1)} + \sum_{m=1}^{\infty} B^{(2d)}\, g^{(2)} \quad (2a)$$

$$\hat{Y}_{22} = \sum_{n=1}^{\infty} B_2^{(3)}\, g^{(3)} + \sum_{m=1}^{\infty} B^{(2d)} g^{(2)} \quad (2b)$$

$$\hat{Y}_{12} = \hat{Y}_{21} = \sum_{m=1}^{\infty} B^{(2o)} g^{(2)} \quad (2c)$$

with the defined parameters:

$$B_i^{(j)} = \frac{y_n^{(j)}(z_i)}{N_n^{(j)}} \vec{j}_n^{(j)}(u,v)$$

$$B^{(2d,o)} = \frac{y_m^{(2d,o)}(l)}{N_m^{(2)}} \vec{j}_m^{(2)}(u,v)$$

$$g^{(j)} = \iint_{S_j} \vec{j}_n^{(j)*}(u_0, v_0)du_0dv_0$$

$$g^{(2)} = \iint_{S_2} \vec{j}_m^{(2)*}(u_0, v_0)du_0dv_0$$

here $j = 1, 3$. The eigenmode set in each waveguide section is specified by its normalized electric and magnetic tangential part of field component, $\vec{e}_{tn}^{(k)}(u, v)$and $\vec{h}_{tn}^{(k)}(u, v)$ with z being propagating direction and k =1, 2 or 3.

$$N_n^{(k)} = \iint_{S_k} \vec{e}_{tn}^{(k)}(u, v)\vec{j}_n^{(k)*}(u, v)dudv \quad (3)$$

with $\vec{j}_n^{(k)}(u, v) = \vec{h}_{tn}^{(k)}(u, v) \times \vec{u}_z$, S_k being the cross section of kth waveguide. The impedance matrix for complete stratified structure can be characterized by:

$$Z = -jN^{-1}|N|^{+0.5}U^{T*}Q^{-1}U|N|^{-0.5} \quad (4)$$

The corresponding scattering matrix can be deduced

$$S = (Z + I)^{-1}(Z - I) \quad (5)$$

with I the unity matrix, Q, U, N are, respectively, matrice defined by the computational analysis above.

III. NUMERICAL RESULTS

In our reaeach, we analyzed a coaxial cable partially filled the multi-dielectric layers with loss including a conical transition, and a ceramic sample and Teflon are placed in the section of coaxial cable. Inner and outer radiuses are respectively, a and b, the length and thicknesses of Teflon and SiC sample are h, $h1$, $h2$. We assume relative permittivity for Teflon and SIC are ε_t and ε_r. To validate the new multimodal variational approach, we calculated scattering parameters of the coaxial cable with samples in comparison with that of simulation by simulation software, which show great agreements.

TABLE I. STRUCTURE PARAMETERS

parameters	*a*	*b*	*h*	*h1*	*h2*
dimensions	6mm	20mm	30mm	2mm	10mm

$\varepsilon_t = 2.1*(1 - 0.001*i)$; $\varepsilon_r = 16*(1 - \tan\sigma*i)$; $\tan\sigma = 0.01 - 0.4$;

Double discontinuity is an adaption section inserted by cascade connection of two simple discontinuities. The numerical and simulation results are compared in Fig. 3 of characteristic parameters.

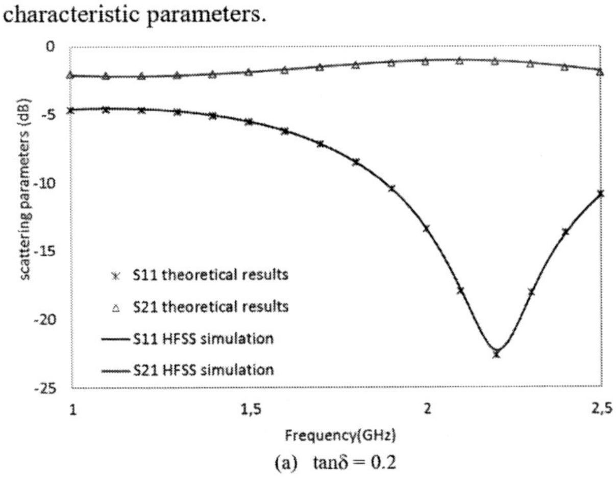

(a) tanδ = 0.2

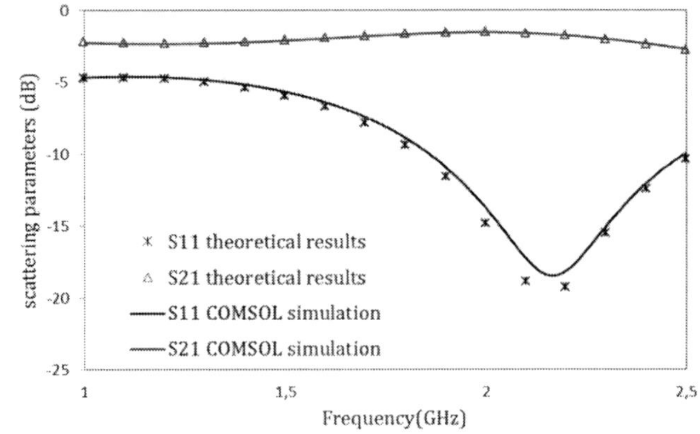

(b) tanδ = 0.3

Fig. 3 Reflection and transmission coefficients of double discontinuities

The proposed method gives quick convergence and favorable numerical results in comparison with the simulation results by HFSS when loss tangent is 0.2 and COMSOL when loss tangent is 0.3.

IV. CONCLUSION

A unified multimodal variational formulation is described for uniaxial coaxial cable discontinuities characterization. The numerical efficiency of this method allows the computation in coaxial cable structure, making it very suited to discontinuity analysis.

REFERENCES

[1] M.M. Eladendi, M. Tellache, J.W. Tao, B. Hadjadji, and M. Benmimoune, "Dielectric characterization using fem modeling and anns for coaxial waveguide with conical open ended radiation," International Journal of Microwave and Wireless Technologies, March 2016.

[2] I. Polaert, N. Benamara, J.W. Tao, T. Vuong, M.Ferrato, and L. Estel, "Dielctric properties measuement methods for solids of high permittivities under microwave frequency and between 20 and 250° c," AMPERE-15th International Conference on Microwave and High Frequency Heating, September 2015.

[3] J. Rammal, T. Vuong, J.W. Tao, Y.Huang, I.Polaert, L. Estel, and M. Ferrato, "comparison of different techniques of microwave characterization of high loss dielectric materials," AMPERE-15th International Conference on Microwave and High Frequency Heating, September 2015.

[4] L. Wu, J.W.Tao, and J. Lacout, "Estimating the salinity and effective permittivity of potato agata under radio frequency," AMPERE-15th International Conference on Microwave and High Frequency Heating, September 2015.

[5] J.W. Tao, and H. Baudrand, "Multimodal variational analysis of uniaxial waveguide discontinuities," IEEE Trans., vol. 39, no. 3, pp. 506-516, March 1991.

[6] D. Lilonga, J. W. Tao, and T. H. Vuong, "Uniaxial discontinuities analysis by a new multimodal variational method: application to filter design," International Journal of RF and Microwave Computer-Aided Engineering, vol. 17, no. 1, pp. 77-83. December 2006.

[7] J.Y. Wang, J.W. Tao, J. Rammal, F. Benmohamed, and L.Wu, "Analyse electromagnétique d'une ligne coaxiale partiellement remplie de diélectrique à fortes pertes," JCMM-14th Journées de Caractérisation Microondes et Matériaux, March 2016.

Radon Transform Interpretation of Retarded-Time Potentials for SWG Bases

Mahmut Akkuş, Fatih Dikmen, H. Arda Ülkü, A. Arif Ergin
Electronics Engineering Department
Gebze Technical University
Kocaeli, Turkey
makkus@gtu.edu.tr, dikmen@gtu.edu.tr, haulku@gtu.edu.tr, aergin@gtu.edu.tr

***Abstract*—The closed-form expression of the retarded-time potentials due to impulsively excited Schaubert-Wilton-Glisson (SWG) basis function is obtained using Radon transform interpretation and observation tetrahedron formulation. It has been shown that the closed-form expressions are yielding to geometric parameters, the solid angle and its gradient, formed during the intersection of the time dependent hyper-cone centered at the observation point and support of the SWG basis function. These geometric parameters are determined analytically using observation tetrahedron formulation. Numerical results that demonstrate the validity of the proposed method are presented.**

Keywords*—*Marching on-in-time (MOT) method, Schaubert-Wilton-Glisson (SWG) basis, time-domain analysis, volume integral equations (VIEs).

I. Introduction

Closed-form expressions to radiation integrals due to impulsively excited sources in time domain can be found using the Radon transform interpretation. For example, closed-form expressions to physical optics integrals for different observation cases has been developed in [1]-[3], and the closed-form expressions to retarded-time potentials for surface sources are developed in [4], [5] and successfully incorporated to marching on-in-time (MOT) scheme in [6], [7]. Besides it is possible to find closed-form expressions to retarded-time potentials due to impulsively excited Schaubert-Wilton-Glisson (SWG) basis function [8] using the Radon transform interpretation. In [9], it is shown that these potentials are related to the solid-angle and its gradient functions formed due to intersection of the tetrahedral supports of the SWG basis and the hyper-cone (a sphere in 3 dimensions inflating by time) centered at the observation point with radius ct where c is the speed of light.

In this work, analytical evaluation of these quantities, i.e. solid angle and its gradient, is presented using the observation tetrahedron formulation [10], [11]. Observation tetrahedron formulation, similar to closed-form expressions given in [5]-[7], takes into account of the contribution of artificial tetrahedrons formed for 4 faces for a tetrahedron, 3 edges for every face and 2 vertices for every edge, yielding 24 observation tetrahedrons. Four vertices of an observation tetrahedron are (i) observation point, (ii) vertex of the one of the tetrahedron for the SWG basis associated to a face and an edge, (iii) projection of the observation point to plane of the face, and (iv) projection of the observation point to the edge direction. Sum of the solid angle and gradient functions for 24 observation tetrahedrons properly yields the solid angle and gradient functions for the support of the SWG basis.

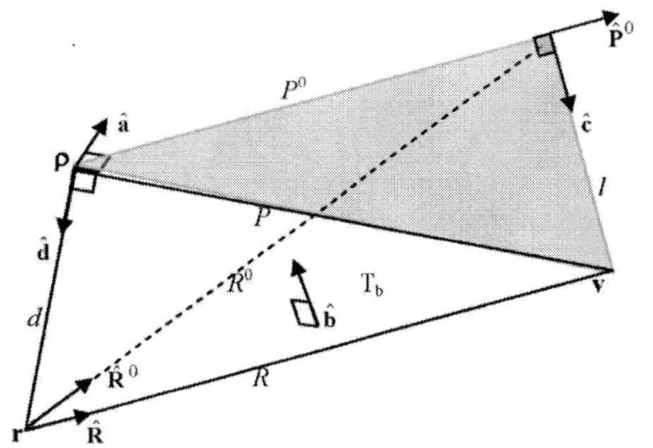

Fig.1. The observation tetrahedron and definition of associated parameters: vertex **v** belongs to the current tetrahedron; the gray right-triangle is on the plane of the current triangle.

The accuracy and validity of the proposed scheme are demonstrated via comparing the time samples of the retarded-time potentials obtained by the proposed method and those obtained by inverse Fourier transforming the frequency domain counterpart of retarded-time potentials.

II. Retarded-Time Potentials

The volumetric calculations regarding the retarded-time potentials on the tetrahedral support of the SWG basis involve two key geometric quantities [9]-[11]: The total solid-angle $\Omega(ct)$ and its gradient $\mathbf{m}(ct)$ emerging from the non-empty intersection of the hyper-cone inflating from the observation point $\mathbf{r}$ and the support of the tetrahedron. The retarded-time potentials can be determined by the auxiliary scalar and vector functions as defined in [10]:

$$\varphi_n(ct) = c^2 t\Omega(ct) \tag{1}$$

$$\Psi_2(ct) = c^3 t^2 \mathbf{m}(ct) \tag{2}$$

Except for $ct>R$ and $ct<d$ where the intersection is empty, the $\Omega(ct)$ and $\mathbf{m}(ct)$ are obtained by the triple sum:

$$\begin{bmatrix}\Omega(ct)\\ \mathbf{m}(ct)\end{bmatrix} = \sum_{k=1}^{4}\hat{\mathbf{d}}_k\cdot\hat{\mathbf{n}}_k\sum_{j=1}^{3}\hat{\mathbf{P}}_{kj}^{0}\cdot\hat{\mathbf{u}}_{kj}\sum_{i=1}^{2}\hat{\mathbf{c}}_{kji}\cdot\hat{\mathbf{l}}_{kji}\kappa_{kji}\begin{bmatrix}\Omega_{kji}(ct)\\ \mathbf{m}_{kji}(ct)\end{bmatrix} \qquad (3)$$

Here, parameters are defined as in Fig. 1 [12], subscripts k denotes the kth face, kj denotes the jth edge of the kth face, and kji denotes the ith vertex of the jth edge of the kth face of the SWG support. $\kappa_{kji}=(-1)^{i-1}$, where $i\in\{1,2\}$ and $\hat{\mathbf{c}}_{kji}\cdot\hat{\mathbf{l}}_{kji}>0$ always. The dot-products with single/double/triple superscripts account for the signs of the volumetric/areal/linear barycentric coordinates of the observation point $\mathbf{r}$.

Note that for each observation tetrahedron, solid angle (and its gradient) is the difference of the spherical and the conical (the center and apex of which are $\mathbf{r}$, respectively) intersection solid angles (and their gradients). Base of the cone is on the plane of the corresponding face, i.e. the gray triangle in Fig. 1.

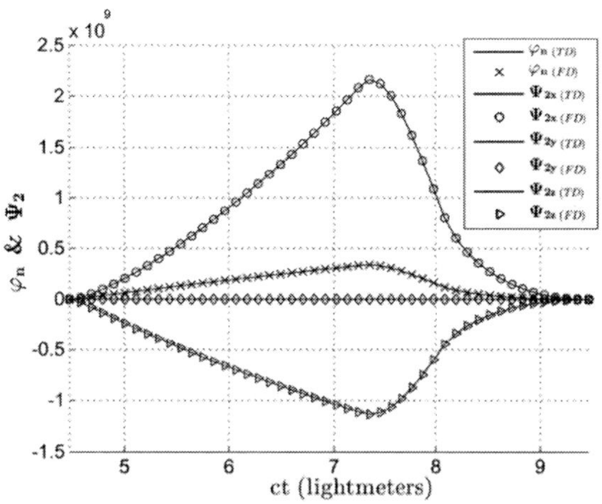

Fig.2. Time samples of $\varphi_n(ct)$, and x-, y-, z- components of $\Psi_2(ct)$ functions (*TD*: proposed method, *FD*: frequency domain evaluations).

III. Numerical Results

Time samples of the auxiliary scalar and vector functions, $\varphi_n(ct)$ and $\Psi_2(ct)$, are calculated for a tetrahedron with the vertices (10,0,1), (15,5,1), (15,-5,1), and (15,0,3). The observation point is located at (8,0,5) and time step size Δt=0.354 ns.

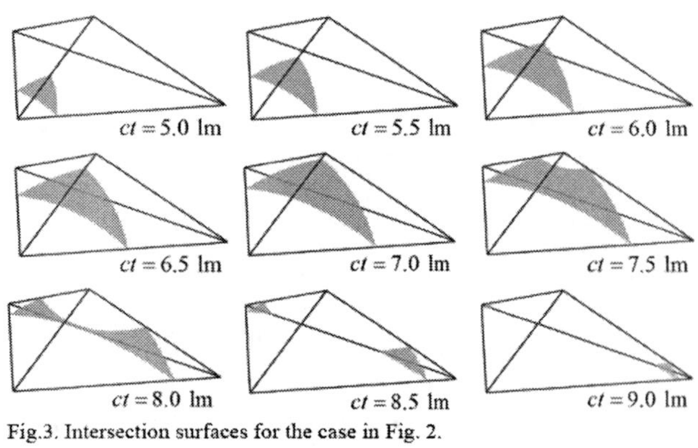

Fig.3. Intersection surfaces for the case in Fig. 2.

Fig. 2 plots the $\varphi_n(ct)$ and $\Psi_2(ct)$ obtained by the proposed method and inverse Fourier transforming the frequency domain counterpart of these auxiliary functions. All results show a perfect agreement. Note that $\varphi_n(ct)$ and $\Psi_2(ct)$ is zero for $ct>R$ and $ct<d$ since there is no intersection of hyper-cone and tetrahedron. Fig. 3 plots the intersection surfaces for different time steps. Fig. 4 shows the boundaries of 24 observation tetrahedra involved in the calculations at ct=7.5 lightmeters (lm). Note that the observation point is the common vertex of all 24 observation tetrahedra as seen in Fig. 4.

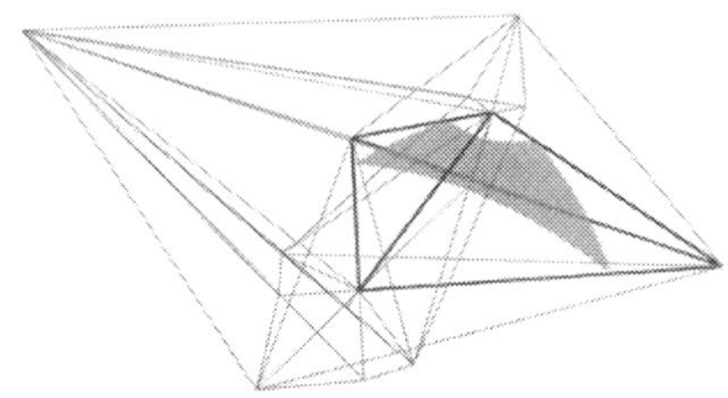

Fig.4. Illustration of the observation tetrahedra.

References

[1] D. Bolukbas and A. A. Ergin, "A Radon transformation interpretation of the physical optics integral," *Microw. Opt. Technol. Lett.*, vol. 44, pp. 284-288, Feb. 2005.

[2] S. Karaca and A. A. Ergin, "Closed-form time domain PO expressions of the electric field scattered from PEC objects illuminated by an electric dipole," *IEEE Trans. Antennas Propag.*, vol. 63, no. 10, pp. 4477-4485, Oct. 2015.

[3] H. A. Ülkü and A. A. Ergin, "Radon transform interpretation of the physical optics integral and application to near and far field acoustic scattering problems," in Proc. 2010, *IEEE AP-S Int. Symp.*, Toronto, ON, Canada, pp.1-4, 11-17 July 2010.

[4] A. C. Yücel and A. A. Ergin, "Exact evaluation of retarded-time potential integrals for the RWG bases," *IEEE Trans. Antennas Propag.*, vol. 54, no. 5, pp. 1496–1502, May 2006.

[5] H. A. Ülkü and A. A. Ergin, "Analytical evaluation of transient magnetic fields due to RWG current bases," *IEEE Trans. Antennas Propag.*, vol. 55, no. 12, pp. 3565–3575, Dec. 2007.

[6] H. A. Ülkü and A. A. Ergin, "Application of analytical retarded-time potential expressions to the solution of time domain integral equations," *IEEE Trans. Antennas Propag.*, vol. 59, no. 11, pp. 4123–4131, Nov. 2011.

[7] H. A. Ülkü, H. Bağcı, andE. Michielssen, "Marching on-in-time solution of the time domain magnetic field integral equation using a predictor-corrector scheme," *IEEE Trans. Antennas Propag.*, vol. 61, no. 8, pp. 4120–4131, Dec. 2013.

[8] D. H. Schaubert, D. R. Wilton, and A. W. Glisson, "A tetrahedral modeling method for electromagnetic scattering by arbitrarily shaped inhomogeneous dielectric bodies," *IEEE Trans. Antennas Propag.*, vol. 32, no. 1, pp. 77–85, Jan. 1984.

[9] H. A. Ülkü, A. A. Ergin, and F. Dikmen, "On the evaluation of retarded-time potential integrals for the SWG bases," *IEEE Antennas Wireless Propag. Lett.*, vol. 10, pp. 187–190, 2011.

[10] F. Dikmen, "On analytical evaluation of retarded-time potentials for SWG bases", *IEEE Trans. Antennas Propag.*, vol. 62, no.9, pp. 4860-4863, Sept. 2014.

[11] F. Dikmen, M. Akkuş, and H. A. Ülkü, "Correction to on analytical evaluation of retarded-time potentials for SWG bases," *IEEE Trans. Antennas Propag.*, vol. 64, no. 6, pp. 2587, June 2016.

[12] D. Wilton, S. Rao, A. Glisson, D. Schaubert, O. Al-Bundak, and C. Butler, "Potential integrals for uniform and linear source distributions on polygonal and polyhedral domains," *IEEE Trans. Antennas Propag.*,vol. AP-32, no. 3, pp. 276–281, Mar. 1984.

Integration Rules and Experimental Evidence for the Stability of Time Domain Integral Equations

Daniel S. Weile, Ismail Uluer, and Jielin Li
Department of Electrical and Computer Engineering
University of Delaware
Newark, DE 19711, USA
Email: weile@udel.edu

David A. Hopkins
RDRL-WMM-B
Army Research Laboratory, APG
Aberdeen, MD 21005, USA
Email: david.a.hopkins.civ@mail.mil

***Abstract*—Because the analysis of the time domain integral equations of electromagnetics is complicated and cannot easily take into account all sources of error in any given implementation, judgements of stability tend to rest on experience. While such an approach eliminates the worst methods immediately, subtle implementation issues may affect the stability of more promising approaches. In this work, we examine the effects of integration rules on stability. Numerical results demonstrate that increasing accuracy does not always increase stability.**

I. Introduction

Numerical methods based on the discretization of time-domain integral equations (TDIEs) have a history plagued by instabilities with causes that have been difficult to locate. Despite this, over the past two decades, several schemes have been introduced that seem to stabilize TDIE implementations, usually by ensuring that integrals over regions of complex shape encountered during the testing procedure are computed properly in some manner. Any analytical proof that these methods are stable must rely on an assumption that integrals are performed exactly, and while such a method does exist, its application is limited to flat patches [1].

Methods that do not rely on exact integration usually choose a temporal discretization technique that avoids the creation of a shadow region in one way or another. Several different methods have been proposed for this: One method uses a smooth bandlimited basis function and gives up causality for ease of integration [2], and another uses full domain basis functions [3]. A third method expands a conventional causal temporal Galerkin basis function into a series of functions that span the patch spatially [4], and a fourth method uses a Laplace domain to $\mathcal{Z}$ domain transform to effect a shadow region free integral computation [5]. All of these methods compute integrals numerically in some fashion (in [4], the numerical nature of the integral on flat patches can be hidden by a series expansion, but the truncation of the series is in essence a numerical approximation), and therefore their fealty to the physics and stability properties hinge on (among other things) the accuracy of the spatial overlap integral computations.

In this work, we examine the nature of this relationship in the context of the convolution quadrature (CQ) approach of [5]. In the course of this discussion, we will see that the stability of the method is not necessarily improved by increasing the order or accuracy of the integrals involved, and that in many cases stability hinges on using different orders of integration in the near field and the far field.

II. Convolution Quadrature

Consider a perfectly conducting surface S in free space (with permittivity μ_0 and permeability ϵ_0) excited by a Laplace domain electric field $\tilde{\mathbf{E}}^{\mathrm{inc}}(\mathbf{r},s)$. Ensuring that the tangential electric field vanishes on S leads to the Laplace domain electric field integral equation

$$s\tilde{\mathbf{E}}^{\mathrm{inc}}(\mathbf{r},s) = \frac{s^2\mu_0}{4\pi}\iint_S \tilde{\mathbf{J}}(\mathbf{r}',s)\frac{e^{-j\frac{s|\mathbf{r}-\mathbf{r}'|}{c}}}{|\mathbf{r}-\mathbf{r}'|}d\mathbf{r}' - \frac{1}{4\pi\epsilon_0}\iint_S \nabla'\cdot\tilde{\mathbf{J}}(\mathbf{r}',s)\frac{e^{-j\frac{s|\mathbf{r}-\mathbf{r}'|}{c}}}{|\mathbf{r}-\mathbf{r}'|}d\mathbf{r}'. \quad (1)$$

This equation can be discretized in space using the approximation

$$\tilde{\mathbf{J}}(\mathbf{r},s) = \sum_{n=0}^{N_s}\tilde{I}_n(s)\mathbf{S}_n(\mathbf{r}), \quad (2)$$

and then tested in space by multiplying it by the $\mathbf{S}_m(\mathbf{r})$ for $m=1,\ldots,N_s$ and integrating over S.

The resulting equation is discretized in time with time step Δt using CQ [5]. For exposition, we assume the second order backward difference formula is used. This amounts to substituting the finite difference approximation

$$s = \frac{3-4z^{-1}+z^{-2}}{2\Delta t} \quad (3)$$

in for the Laplace parameter s, and computing the inverse $\mathcal{Z}$ transform. This finally results in a set of equations for $\mathbf{I}_i$, the set of unknown currents at time $i\Delta t$, of the form

$$\mathbf{Z}_0\mathbf{I}_i = \mathbf{V}_i - \sum_{j=0}^{i-1}\mathbf{Z}_{i-j}\mathbf{I}_j, \quad (4)$$

which can be solved iteratively for the currents by marching on in time. The elements of the vectors $\mathbf{V}_i$ are given by

$$[\mathbf{V}_i]_n = \iint_S \dot{\mathbf{E}}^{\mathrm{inc}}(\mathbf{r},i\Delta t)\mathbf{S}_n(\mathbf{r})d\mathbf{r}, \quad (5)$$

where $\dot{\mathbf{E}}^{\rm inc}(\mathbf{r},t)$ is the derivative of the time domain incident field, and the elements of the matrices $\mathbf{Z}_k$ are given by

$$[\mathbf{Z}_k]_{mn} = \iint\limits_S \iint\limits_S \frac{\mu_0 \mathbf{S}_m(\mathbf{r}) \cdot \mathbf{S}_n(\mathbf{r}')}{4\pi |\mathbf{r}-\mathbf{r}'|} \beta_k (|\mathbf{r}-\mathbf{r}'|)\, d\mathbf{r}' d\mathbf{r} - \iint\limits_S \iint\limits_S \frac{\nabla \cdot \mathbf{S}_m(\mathbf{r}) \nabla' \cdot \mathbf{S}_n(\mathbf{r}')}{4\pi\epsilon_0 |\mathbf{r}-\mathbf{r}'|} \alpha_k (|\mathbf{r}-\mathbf{r}'|)\, d\mathbf{r}' d\mathbf{r}. \quad (6)$$

In this equation,

$$\alpha_k(t) = \frac{1}{k!}\left(\frac{t}{2}\right)^{\frac{k}{2}} e^{-\frac{3}{2}t} H_k\left(\sqrt{2t}\right) \quad (7)$$

for $k \geq 0$, $\alpha_k = 0$ for $k < 0$, $H_k(\cdot)$ is the $k^{\rm th}$ order Hermite polynomial, and

$$\beta_k(t) = \frac{\alpha_{k-4} - 8\alpha_{k-3} + 22\alpha_{k-2} - 24\alpha_{k-1} + 3\alpha_k}{4(\Delta t)^2}. \quad (8)$$

The primary question examined in this work is how the choice of integration rules used for the numerical approximation of (6) affect the stability of the algorithm. The discretization of other integral equations is similar.

III. Numerical Results

Thus, consider the excitation of a conducting NASA Almond, 25.8 cm long in its largest dimension (on the x-axis) and about 3.2 cm thick in its thinnest dimension (on the z axis). The almond is excited by an x-polarized incident field

$$E_x^{\rm inc}(\mathbf{r},t) = \exp\left[\frac{(t-t_0-z/c)^2}{2\sigma^2}\right]\cos(3\times10^9\pi t), \quad (9)$$

and discretized into 264 flat patches and a time step $\Delta t = 10$ ps. Here, $\sigma = \pi/3B$, with $B = 1$ GHz. The combined field integral equation is used with equal parts electric and magnetic field integral equation, and the simulation was run for 5000 time steps in each case.

Four types of spatial integration rules are used: a self rule, used whenever patches overlap; a close basis rule used whenever the centroids of two patches are 3 cm apart or less for basis function integration (the $\mathbf{r}'$ integration); a far basis rule used for basis integrations that are not close; and a testing rule used for all integrations in $\mathbf{r}$. Self integrations are based on the integration rules described in [6] using a six-triangle subdivision, Duffy quadrature, and $10^{\rm th}$ order Gaussian rules in both the radial and azimuthal dimensions. All of the other rules are based on the triangle integration rules in [7]. An experiment was done in which the order of the "close" integration rule was varied from 1 to 10, and the "testing" and "basis" (together the "far" rules) were also varied over the same range. Runs were considered stable if all currents were less than 1 fA/m^2 at the end of the run. (None of the runs settled to a constant value greater than this; that is, this choice was equivalent to ensuring there was no more growth in current values at the end of the run.)

Fig. 1 demonstrates the outcome of the experiment. While few general rules can be gleaned from this chart, some features

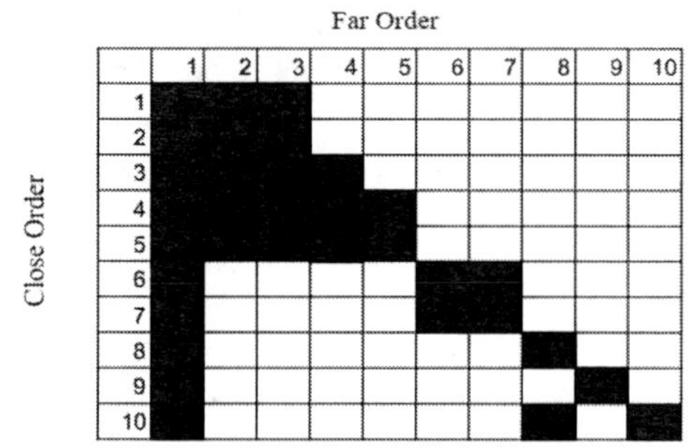

Fig. 1. Stability of the simulation versus integration rules; black squares mark unstable computations, white squares mark stable ones.

are evident. First, it is not clear that higher order rules are more important in the near field than the far field. This may be because high order is not high accuracy, and the higher order polynomial assumption underlying the high order rules are not especially good in the near field, and not especially needed in the far field. Second, for some reason, it seems important to distinguish near field from far field integrations. While it does not seem to matter much to accuracy, when the orders are equal, the simulation is always unstable.

IV. Conclusions

Details of TDIE implementations beyond temporal discretization strategy affect stability in complex and (currently) unpredictable ways. While the state of TDIE analysis may require experimental demonstrations of stability, care must be taken to ensure that all assumptions underlying the experiments are clear. Numerical results presented at the conference will further demonstrate the relationship between integration rules and stability.

References

[1] T. Ha-Duong, "On retarded potential boundary integral equations and their discretisation," in *Topics in Computational Wave Propagation: Direct and Inverse Problems*, Berlin: Springer-Verlag, 2003, pp. 301–336.

[2] D. S. Weile, G. Pisharody, N.-W. Chen, B. Shanker and E. Michielssen, "A novel scheme for the solution of the time-domain integral equations of electromagnetics," *IEEE Transactions on Antennas and Propagation*, vol. 51, no. 1, pp. 283–295, 2004.

[3] Y.-S. Chung, T. K. Sarkar, and B. H. Jung, "Solution of a time-domain magnetic-field integral equation for arbitrarily closed conducting bodies using an unconditionally stable methodology," *Microwave and Optical Technology Letters*, vol. 35, no. 6, pp. 493–499, 2002.

[4] A. J. Pray, N. V. Nair, and B. Shanker, "Stability properties of the time domain electric field integral equation using a separable approximation for the convolution with the retarded potential," *IEEE Transactions on Antennas and Propagation*, vol. 60, no. 8, pp. 3772–3781, 2012.

[5] X. B. Wang, R. A. Wildman, D. S. Weile, and P. Monk, "A finite difference delay modeling approach to the discretization of the time domain integral equations of electromagnetics," *IEEE Transactions on Antennas and Propagation*, vol. 56, no. 8, pp. 2442–2452, 2008.

[6] D. S. Weile and X. B. Wang, "Strong singularity reduction for curved patches for the integral equations of electromagnetics," *IEEE Antennas and Wireless Propagation Letters*, pp. 1370–1373, 2009

[7] D. A. Dunavant, "High degree efficient symmetrical Gaussian quadrature rules for the triangle," *International Journal for Numerical Methods in Engineering*, vol.21, pp. 1129–1148, 1985.

A novel preconditioner for the EFIE discretised with the H_{div} inner product

Kazuki Niino
Graduate School of Informatics
Kyoto University
Kyoto, Japan
Email: niino@acs.i.kyoto-u.ac.jp

Naoshi Nishimura
Graduate School of Informatics
Kyoto University
Kyoto, Japan
Email: nchml@i.kyoto-u.ac.jp

***Abstract*—A novel preconditioning for the electric field integral equation (EFIE) discretised with the H_{div} inner product is discussed. It is known that the EFIE suffers from bad accuracy in low-frequency problems. One of the remedies for this bad accuracy is the discretisation method using H_{div} inner product. The EFIE with this discretisation, however, shows slow convergence of iteration methods and, what is worse, a naive application of the Calderon preconditioning is not effective for accelerating the convergence. In this paper, we will propose a new preconditioning, which can efficiently reduce the computational time of the EFIE discretised with the H_{div} inner product.**

I. Introduction

It is known that the electric field integral equation (EFIE) suffers from bad accuracy when the frequencies are small [1]. This problem, called "low-frequency breakdown", is due to the ill-conditioning of the coefficient matrix obtained by discretising the EFIE. Widely used solutions to the low-frequency breakdown are the loop-tree decomposition [2] and the augmented integral equation [3]. Also, we have found that the low-frequency breakdown can be avoided as one uses the H_{div} inner product for the Galerkin method instead of the L^2 inner product [4]. The discretised EFIE with the H_{div} inner product, however, has the problem of slow convergence. Hence, in this paper, we propose a preconditioning for the EFIE discretised with the H_{div} inner product.

II. Formulation

We consider electromagnetic wave scattering problems with a single PEC. The domain of the PEC and outside the PEC are denoted by Ω^i and Ω^e. The PEC is enclosed by the smooth boundary Γ. The EFIE for this problem can be written as follows:

$$\mathrm{i}\omega\mu Q\boldsymbol{j} = \boldsymbol{E}^{\text{inc}} \times \boldsymbol{n},$$

where $\boldsymbol{j}$ is the unknown electric current on Γ,

$$Q\boldsymbol{j} = \boldsymbol{n} \times \int_\Gamma \left\{ G(\boldsymbol{x}-\boldsymbol{y}) + \frac{1}{k^2}\nabla\nabla G(\boldsymbol{x}-\boldsymbol{y}) \right\} \boldsymbol{j}(\boldsymbol{y})\mathrm{d}S_y,$$

$k = \omega\sqrt{\varepsilon\mu}$ and G is Green's function of the Helmholtz equation:

$$G(\boldsymbol{x}-\boldsymbol{y}) = \frac{\mathrm{e}^{\mathrm{i}k|\boldsymbol{x}-\boldsymbol{y}|}}{4\pi|\boldsymbol{x}-\boldsymbol{y}|}$$

The EFIE can be discretised into the following linear equation with the use of the H_{div} inner product [4]:

$$A_{H_{\text{div}}}\boldsymbol{x} = \boldsymbol{b}_{H_{\text{div}}} \tag{1}$$

where

$$(A_{H_{\text{div}}})_{ij} = \Bigg(\boldsymbol{s}_i, \boldsymbol{n} \times \int_\Gamma \Big\{ \mathrm{i}\omega\mu G(\boldsymbol{x}-\boldsymbol{y})\boldsymbol{t}_j(\boldsymbol{y}) + \frac{\mathrm{i}}{\omega\varepsilon}\nabla\nabla G(\boldsymbol{x}-\boldsymbol{y})\boldsymbol{t}_j(\boldsymbol{y}) \Big\} \mathrm{d}S_y \Bigg)_{H_{\text{div}}(\Gamma)}, \tag{2}$$

$$(\boldsymbol{b}_{H_{\text{div}}})_i = (\boldsymbol{s}_i, \boldsymbol{E}^{\text{inc}} \times \boldsymbol{n})_{H_{\text{div}}(\Gamma)},$$

$$(\boldsymbol{u}, \boldsymbol{v})_{H_{\text{div}}(\Gamma)} := (\boldsymbol{u}, \boldsymbol{v})_{L^2_T(\Gamma)} + \frac{1}{k^2}(\nabla_S \cdot \boldsymbol{u}, \nabla_S \cdot \boldsymbol{v})_{L^2(\Gamma)},$$

and $\boldsymbol{t}_i$ and $\boldsymbol{s}_i$ are the basis function and the dual basis function. For example, the Rao-Wilton-Glisson (RWG) basis function and the Buffa-Christiansen (BC) basis function can be used for $\boldsymbol{t}_i$ and $\boldsymbol{s}_i$, respectively.

III. Preconditioning

In this section, we discuss preconditioning for the discretised EFIE in (1). We first introduce a simple Calderon preconditioning which turns out not to be very effective in terms of the computational time. We obtain this preconditioning method by extending the multiplicative Calderon preconditioning [5] to the proposed method.

The well-known Calderon formulae for Maxwell's equations imply that the square of the operator Q is well-conditioned [6]. Actually, by discretising Q^2 with the H_{div} inner product, we find that the matrix $A_{H_{\text{div}}} T_{H_{\text{div}}}^{-1} A'_{H_{\text{div}}} T'^{-1}_{H_{\text{div}}}$ is expected to be well-conditioned where

$$(A'_{H_{\text{div}}})_{ij} = \Bigg(\boldsymbol{t}_i, \boldsymbol{n} \times \int_\Gamma \Big\{ \mathrm{i}\mu\omega G(\boldsymbol{x}-\boldsymbol{y})\boldsymbol{s}_j(\boldsymbol{y}) + \frac{\mathrm{i}}{\omega\varepsilon}\nabla\nabla G(\boldsymbol{x}-\boldsymbol{y})\boldsymbol{s}_j(\boldsymbol{y}) \Big\} \mathrm{d}S_y \Bigg)_{H_{\text{div}}(\Gamma)},$$

$$(T_{H_{\text{div}}})_{ij} = (\boldsymbol{t}_i, \boldsymbol{t}_j)_{H_{\text{div}}(\Gamma)}, \quad (T'_{H_{\text{div}}})_{ij} = (\boldsymbol{s}_i, \boldsymbol{s}_j)_{H_{\text{div}}(\Gamma)},$$

and $A_{H_{\text{div}}}$ is the matrix defined in (2). Hence the matrix $T_{H_{\text{div}}} A'^{-1}_{H_{\text{div}}} T'_{H_{\text{div}}}$ seems a good right preconditioner for equation (1). This preconditioning indeed decreases the iteration number of linear solvers for (1) but the computational time may not be reduced efficiently since the Gram matrices $T_{H_{\rm div}}$ and $T'_{H_{\rm div}}$ are ill-conditioned. In fact, the Gram matrix $T_{H_{\rm div}}$ is written as

$$(T_{H_{\rm div}})_{ij} = (\boldsymbol{t}_i, \boldsymbol{t}_j)_{L^2_T(\Gamma)} + \frac{1}{k^2}(\nabla_S \cdot \boldsymbol{t}_i, \nabla_S \cdot \boldsymbol{t}_j)_{L^2(\Gamma)}$$

with

$$(\boldsymbol{t}_i, \boldsymbol{t}_j)_{L^2_T(\Gamma)} \sim O(h^2), \quad \frac{1}{k^2}(\nabla_S \cdot \boldsymbol{t}_i, \nabla_S \cdot \boldsymbol{t}_j)_{L^2(\Gamma)} \sim O(\frac{1}{k^2}).$$

Thus,

$$(T_{H_{\rm div}})_{ij} \sim \frac{1}{k^2}(\nabla_S \cdot \boldsymbol{t}_i, \nabla_S \cdot \boldsymbol{t}_j)_{L^2(\Gamma)}$$

as $kh \to 0$, which is a singular matrix. The matrix $T'_{H_{\rm div}}$ also has the same ill-conditioning. Hence the Gram matrices $T_{H_{\rm div}}$ and $T'_{H_{\rm div}}$ are ill-conditioned in the low frequency region. This causes much computational time to invert these Gram matrices and, even worse, the failure of the preconditioning for smaller frequencies.

Now, we introduce a new preconditioning, which can reduce the computational time efficiently. We first define an operator:

$$\widetilde{Q} := \left(I - \frac{1}{k^2}\nabla_S \nabla_S\right) Q.$$

With this operator, the coefficient matrix $A_{H_{\rm div}}$ can be written as

$$A_{H_{\rm div}} = (\boldsymbol{s}_i, \mathrm{i}\omega\mu Q \boldsymbol{t}_j)_{H_{\rm div}} = (\boldsymbol{s}_i, \mathrm{i}\omega\mu \widetilde{Q} \boldsymbol{t}_j)_{L^2_T}.$$

Thus $A_{H_{\rm div}}$ can be regarded as a matrix obtained by discretising the operator $\widetilde{Q}$ with the L^2 inner product.

Now we construct a preconditioner for the operator $\widetilde{Q}$ with the help of principal symbols. We found that the principal symbol of $\widetilde{Q}$ is identical with that of the operator

$$\frac{1}{\mathrm{i}\omega\varepsilon}\widetilde{N} = \frac{1}{\mathrm{i}\omega\varepsilon}\boldsymbol{n} \times \int_\Gamma \frac{\partial^2}{\partial \boldsymbol{n} \partial \boldsymbol{n}} G \cdot \mathrm{d}S_y.$$

This means that the operator $\widetilde{Q} \cdot \mathrm{i}\omega\varepsilon\widetilde{S}$ is well-conditioned since Calderon's formulae for the integral operators of the Helmholtz equation show that $\widetilde{N}\widetilde{S}$ is well-conditioned [6]. The operator $\widetilde{Q} \cdot \mathrm{i}\omega\varepsilon\widetilde{S}$ is discretised into

$$A_{H_{\rm div}} T_{L^2}^{-1} \widetilde{S}_{L^2} T_{L^2}^{\prime\prime -1}$$

where

$$(\widetilde{S}_{L^2})_{ij} = (\boldsymbol{n} \times \boldsymbol{s}_i, \mathrm{i}\omega\varepsilon\widetilde{S}\boldsymbol{s}_j)_{L^2(\Gamma)},$$
$$(T_{L^2})_{ij} = (\boldsymbol{n} \times \boldsymbol{s}_i, \boldsymbol{t}_j)_{L^2_T(\Gamma)}, \quad (T''_{L^2})_{ij} = (\boldsymbol{s}_i, \boldsymbol{s}_j)_{L^2(\Gamma)}.$$

Consequently, the matrix

$$T_{L^2}^{-1} \widetilde{S}_{L^2} T_{L^2}^{\prime\prime -1}$$

is a good right preconditioner for solving equation (1).

IV. Numerical Examples

A spherical PEC with the radius of 0.25 illuminated by the plane incident wave given by $\boldsymbol{E}^{\rm inc}(\boldsymbol{x}) = \boldsymbol{E}_0^{\rm inc} \mathrm{e}^{\mathrm{i}\boldsymbol{k}\cdot\boldsymbol{x}}$ is considered where $\boldsymbol{k} = (0,0,k)^T$, $\boldsymbol{E}_0^{\rm inc} = (1,0,0)^T$. We set $\varepsilon = \mu = 1$ in the exterior domain Ω^e. The frequency is nondimensionalised such that the wavelength is equal to one when the frequency k is 2π. The surface of the spherical scatterer is divided with the meshes with 128000 triangular elements. The RWG and BC basis functions are used for $\boldsymbol{t}_i$ and $\boldsymbol{s}_i$, respectively. The GMRES with the error tolerance of 10^{-5} is used for both solving the discretised integral equation and calculating the inverse of the Gram matrices. The low-frequency FMM is used for accelerating the computation of the coefficient matrix. Fig. 1 shows the computational time of the proposed preconditioner, the Calderon preconditioner and no preconditioner. The proposed method is much faster than the other methods in all the frequencies we have tested.

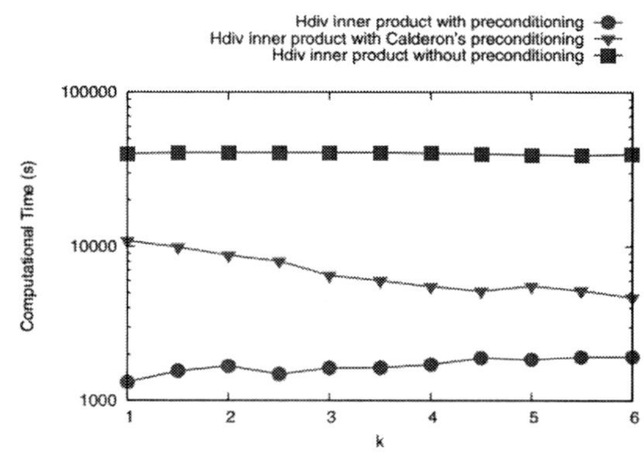

Fig. 1. The computational time of the GMRES with 128000 triangular elements.

V. Conclusion

We described two preconditioners for the EFIE discretised with the $H_{\rm div}$ inner product. We have verified that the preconditioning using the operator $\widetilde{S}$ is better in terms of the computational time than a naive application of the Calderon preconditioning.

References

[1] J. R. Mautz and R. F. Harrington, "An E-Field Solution for a Conducting Surface Small or Comparable to the Wavelength," *IEEE Transactions on Antennas and Propagation*, vol. 32, no. 4, pp. 330–339, 1984.
[2] W.-L. Wu, A. W. Glisson, and D. Kajfez, "A study of two numerical solution procedures for the electric field integral equation at low frequency," *Applied Computational Electromagnetics Society Journal*, vol. 10, no. 3, pp. 69–80, 1995.
[3] Z. G. Qian and W. C. Chew, "An augmented electric field integral equation for high-speed interconnect analysis," *Microwave and Optical Technology Letters*, vol. 50, no. 10, pp. 2658–2662, 2008.
[4] K. Niino and N. Nishimura, "A discretisation method with a h div scalar product for boudnary integra equation methods," in *2014 IEEE Antennas and Propagation Society International Symposium (APSURSI)*, 2014.
[5] F. Andriulli, K. Cools, H. Bagci, F. Olyslager, A. Buffa, S. Christiansen, and E. Michielssen, "A multiplicative Calderón preconditioner for the electric field integral equation," *IEEE Transactions on Antennas and Propagation*, vol. 56, no. 8, pp. 2398–2412, 2008.
[6] J. Nédélec, *Acoustic and Electromagnetic Equations: Integral Representations for Harmonic Problems*. Springer Verlag, 2001.

Modified Combined Tangential Formulation for Stable and Accurate Analysis of Plasmonic Structures

Barışcan Karaosmanoğlu and Özgür Ergül
Department of Electrical and Electronics Engineering
Middle East Technical University
Ankara, Turkey
ozgur.ergul@eee.metu.edu.tr

***Abstract*—We present a modified combined tangential formulation (MCTF) for stable solutions of plasmonic problems involving metallic objects that are modeled as penetrable structures. For a wide range of negative real permittivity values, corresponding to the varying characteristics of the metals at infrared and visible frequencies, MCTF provides both accurate and efficient solutions in comparison to the conventional formulations. We explain the stability of MCTF in terms of the discretized operators for the limit case and demonstrate its stability on canonical scattering problems involving plasmonic spheres.**

I. INTRODUCTION

Most metals at optical frequencies are known to possess plasmonic properties, which can be employed in diverse applications, such as sensing, energy harvesting, optical links, and super-resolution. In parallel with this, for numerical modeling of plasmonic structures involving arbitrary geometries, traditional solvers have been modified to handle negative permittivity values that can be used to represent metals at optical frequencies [1]. While volume formulations are mostly used in this area, plasmonic problems with increasing complexity and sizes often need more efficient solvers that are based on surface formulations [2]–[5]. In fact, if the structures can be represented as homogeneous or piecewise homogeneous objects, surface integral equations can provide the desired efficiency without sacrificing the accuracy. On the other hand, since most of the formulations have been developed for ordinary dielectric and magnetic objects [6], new numerical problems arise when the traditional solvers are employed to analyze plasmonic structures.

As a background of this study, we refer to [7] and [8], where we show that the conventional formulations may require very dense discretizations with respect to wavelength in order to obtain sufficient accuracy, while some formulations even break down as the negative permittivity increases. Therefore, we need more accurate and stable formulations that can be used in wide ranges of permittivity values, especially for increasingly large negative permittivities to close the gap towards perfectly conducting models. This study presents a modified combined tangential formulation (MCTF) that falls into this category.

In the following, time-harmonic problems and their formulations in the frequency domain are considered.

II. MODIFIED COMBINED TANGENTIAL FORMULATION

MCTF is a tangential formulation, similar to the combined tangential formulation (CTF) and the variants of the Poggio-Miller-Chang-Harrington-Wu-Tsai (PMCHWT) formulation. Hence, with the low-order discretizations employing the Rao-Wilton-Glisson functions and Galerkin scheme, it naturally provides more accurate solutions than the normal and mixed formulations [9], such as the electric and magnetic current combined-field integral equation (JMCFIE). For plasmonic problems, the advantages of MCTF are its higher efficiency in comparison to PMCHWTs and its better accuracy in comparison to CTF.

Matrix equations derived from MCTF can be written as

$$\bar{Z}^{\text{MCTF}} = \eta_o \begin{bmatrix} \bar{T}_o + \eta_p \eta_o^{-1} \bar{T}_p & \eta_o^{-1}(-\bar{K}_o - \bar{K}_p) \\ \eta_p(\bar{K}_o + \bar{K}_p) & \eta_p \eta_o^{-1} \bar{T}_o + \bar{T}_p \end{bmatrix}, \quad (1)$$

where $\bar{T}_{o,p}$ and $\bar{K}_{o,p}$ are the electric-field integral operator and the magnetic-field integral operator, respectively, which are tested tangentially ($\hat{a}_n \times \hat{a}_n \times$). In the above, η_o and η_p represent the intrinsic impedances of the outer (o) and inner (p) media (free space and plasmonic object). The limit term in the MFIE operator is extracted and $\bar{T}$ is scaled such that

$$\lim_{\epsilon_R \to -\infty} \bar{T}_p = -\bar{I}/2, \qquad \lim_{\epsilon_R \to -\infty} \bar{K}_p = 0, \quad (2)$$

where $\bar{I}$ is the Gram matrix, $\epsilon_R = \text{Re}\{\epsilon_r\}$, and ϵ_r is the relative permittivity of the object. Then, it can be shown that, in the limit of $\epsilon_R \to -\infty$ and $\eta_p \to 0$, MCTF turns into the tangential electric-field integral equation as

$$\lim_{\epsilon_R \to \infty} \bar{Z}^{\text{MCTF}} = \eta_o \begin{bmatrix} \bar{T}_o & 0 \\ 0 & \bar{I}/2 \end{bmatrix}, \quad (3)$$

where the second row makes the magnetic current zero (due to vanishing small right-hand side of this row). With an appropriate balance of the matrix blocks, this is achieved via a vanishing $\eta_p \bar{T}_p$, hence without a numerical problem.

III. NUMERICAL EXAMPLES

Fig. 1 presents the results of scattering problems involving plasmonic spheres of diameter $1.04\lambda_o$, where λ_o is the wavelength in the host medium (free space). For the relative permittivity, we consider different values $\epsilon_r = (\epsilon_R + i)$, where ϵ_R changes from -512 to 32. The spheres are illuminated by plane waves. For numerical solutions, the problems are discretized with $\lambda_o/10$ triangles, leading to matrix equations involving 2166 unknowns. In addition to different formulations, the problems are solved via Mie series to obtain reference values. In Fig. 1, the relative error in the far-zone electric field and the number of GMRES iterations (for 10^{-4} residual error, without preconditioning and restart) with respect to ϵ_R. For positive values of ϵ_R, it can be observed that the accuracy deteriorates as the contrast increases, as a result of increasing effective geometric deviation (discrete sphere vs. true sphere), integration problems (oscillatory interactions), formulation issues (unbalanced blocks, ill conditioning, etc.), or the combination of these problems. Focusing in the negative values as the purpose of this study, our observations are as follows.

- JMCFIE results have very large errors that become relatively smaller, but still significant, as the contrast increases. In the same direction (increasing contrast), the error of CTF increases dramatically up to around %20 when $\epsilon_R = -512$. Interestingly, the number of iterations for CTF drops, showing that the increasing error is not related to conditioning.
- MCTF has the same accuracy as PMCHWT and its scaled (balanced) version PMCHWT-S. All these formulations provide quite stable results in terms of the accuracy for all negative values of ϵ_R. On the other hand, MCTF requires less iterations than PMCHWT (especially for small values of negative ϵ_R) and PMCHWT-S (especially for large values of negative ϵ_R). Hence, in terms of the efficiency, MCTF is more reliable than PMCWHT and PMCHWT-S for plasmonic simulations.

While, in this paper, it is shown only for canonical objects of moderate sizes due to the lack of space, MCTF provides accurate and efficient solutions also for larger and more complicated structures in wide ranges of negative permittivity values.

IV. Conclusion

We present a new formulation, namely, MCTF, for stable formulations of plasmonic problems involving metallic objects with negative permittivity values. This type of formulations are needed, especially in the infrared spectrum where the negative permittivity is large, since the conventional formulations are unstable, inaccurate, and/or inefficient. Solutions with MCTF and similar formulations may close the gap between plasmonic and perfectly conducting simulations.

Acknowledgement

This work was supported by the Scientific and Technical Research Council of Turkey (TUBITAK) under the Research Grants 113E129 and 114E498, and by the Turkish Academy of Sciences (TUBA) in the framework of the Young Scientist Award Program.

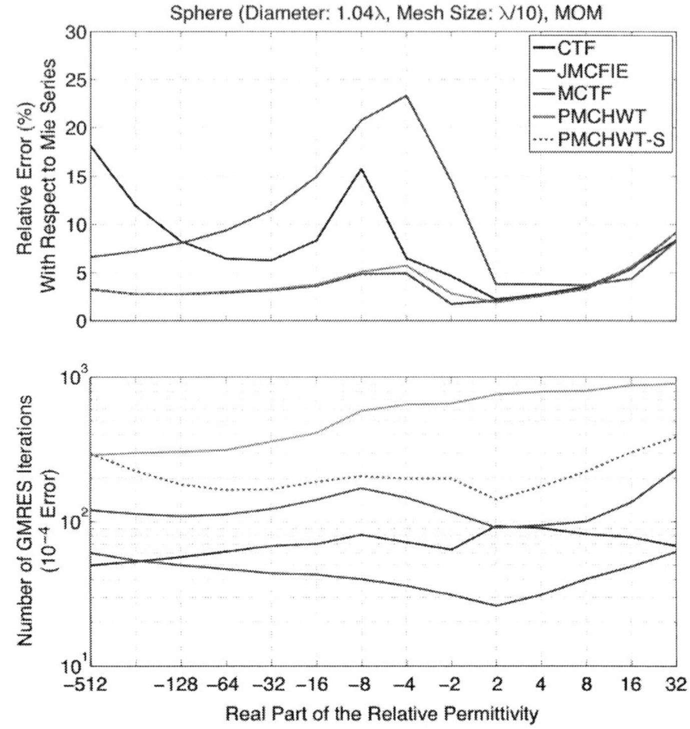

Fig. 1. Solutions of scattering problems involving spheres of diameter $1.04\lambda_o$. Far-zone relative errors and iteration counts are investigated with respect to the relative permittivity values $\epsilon_r = (\epsilon_R + i)$, where ϵ_R changes from -512 to 32.

References

[1] P. B. Johnson and R. W. Christy, "Optical constants of the noble metals," *Phys. Rev. B*, vol. 6, no. 12, pp. 4370–4379, Dec. 1972.

[2] M. G. Araujo, J. M. Taboada, D. M. Solis, J. Rivero, L. Landesa, and F. Obelleiro, "Comparison of surface integral equation formulations for electromagnetic analysis of plasmonic nanoscatterers," *Opt. Exp.*, vol. 20, no. 8, pp. 9161–9171, Apr. 2012.

[3] Ö. Ergül, "Analysis of composite nanoparticles with surface integral equations and the multilevel fast multipole algorithm," *J. Opt.*, vol. 14, no. 6, pp. 062701-1–4, Jun. 2012.

[4] D. M. Solis, J. M. Taboada, F. Obelleiro, "Surface integral equation method of moments with multiregion basis functions applied to plasmonics," *IEEE Trans. Antennas Propag.*, vol. 63, no. 5, pp. 2141–2152, May 2015.

[5] H. Gomez-Sousa, O. Rubinos-Lopez, and J. A. Martinez-Lorenzo, "Comparison of iterative solvers for electromagnetic analysis of plasmonic nanostructures using multiple surface integral equation formulations," *J. Electromagn. Waves Appl.*, vol. 30, no. 4, Feb. 2016.

[6] P. Ylä-Oijala, M. Taskinen, and S. Järvenpää, "Surface integral equation formulations for solving electromagnetic scattering problems with iterative methods," *Radio Sci.*, vol. 40, no. 6002, Dec. 2005.

[7] B. Karaosmanoğlu, A. Yılmaz, U. M. Gür, and Ö. Ergül, "Solutions of plasmonic structures using the multilevel fast multipole algorithm," *Special Issue on Challenges in RF and Microwave Defense Engineering, Int. J. RF Microwave Comput.-Aided. Eng.*, vol. 26, no. 4, pp. 335–341, May 2016.

[8] B. Karaosmanoğlu, A. Yılmaz, and Ö. Ergül, "On the accuracy and efficiency of surface formulations in fast analysis of plasmonic structures via MLFMA," in *Proc. Progress in Electromagnetics Research Symp. (PIERS)*, 2016.

[9] Ö. Ergül and L. Gürel, "Comparison of integral-equation formulations for the fast and accurate solution of scattering problems involving dielectric objects with the multilevel fast multipole algorithm," *IEEE Trans. Antennas Propag.*, vol. 57, no. 1, pp. 176–187, Jan. 2009.

Boundary Integral Equation Study of the Influence of Finite Conductivity on Antenna Radiation Using a 3-D Differential Surface Admittance Operator

Martijn Huynen, Daniël De Zutter, Dries Vande Ginste
Department of Information Technology
Ghent University, Belgium
Email: martijn.huynen@UGent.be

***Abstract*—A novel method to simulate scattering and radiation from arbitrary materials, including good conductors, in a boundary integral equation (BIE) framework, is described in this contribution. The utilized technique relies on the differential surface admittance operator, which introduces an equivalent surface current density, effectively changing the antenna's material to that of the background medium. Constructed out of the volume's eigenmodes, the operator is employed to assess the radiation properties of a lossy Yagi-Uda antenna.**

I. Introduction

The impact of the finite conductivity on scattering and antennas has been a research topic for over half a century. Initially, approximate current distributions were utilized to include the imperfect conductors' effect for thin-wire antennas [1]. This method has since been replaced by employing a surface impedance boundary condition, such as the Leontovich boundary condition, to couple the exterior electric and magnetic field without solving the interior problem [2]. This technique is, however, not applicable in all situations due to fundamental limitations and assumptions [3]. The differential surface admittance operator can circumvent these shortcomings [4]. This operator defines a fictitious surface current density that replaces the material by the background medium. Subsequently applying adequate numerical techniques such as the method of moments (MoM), yields the surface current density. This approach has been applied to 2-D scattering problems [5] and was recently proposed in 3-D for scattering at relatively simple geometries in [6]. In this contribution, the Dirichlet-to-Neumann operator [4] is applied in 3-D to assess the impact of conductivity on the characteristics of a realistic antenna structure. In Section II, the differential surface admittance operator concept is introduced for 3-D problems and an expression composed of the eigenvectors of the volume is presented. Section III features the validation of the novel method by means of a lossy Yagi-Uda antenna's analysis.

II. Theory

We study the geometries in Fig. 1 assuming time-harmonic ($e^{j\omega t}$ dependence) electromagnetic fields. In Fig. 1(a) a homogeneous, non-magnetic material with wavenumber k is confined to the volume $\mathcal{V}$ with boundary surface $\mathcal{S}$ while the remaining, surrounding space is denoted $\mathcal{V}_0$ and defined by the

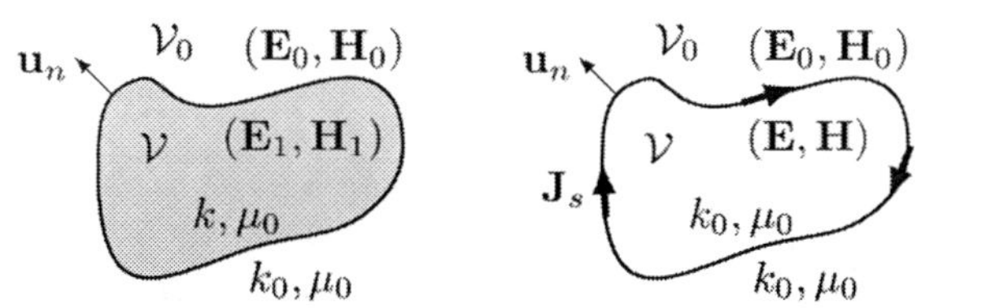

(a) Original situation. (b) Equivalent situation.

Fig. 1. (a) A homogeneous volume $\mathcal{V}$ with boundary $\mathcal{S}$ is embedded in another homogeneous volume $\mathcal{V}_0$. In (b), the inner material is replaced by the background medium and a surface current density $\mathbf{J}_s$ is introduced on $\mathcal{S}$.

wavenumber k_0. This outside region is governed by the fields $(\mathbf{E}_0, \mathbf{H}_0)$ while the inner region's fields are $(\mathbf{E}_1, \mathbf{H}_1)$. On $\mathcal{S}$, these quantities are related through the Dirichlet-to-Neumann (DtN) operator $\mathcal{D}_k$ as follows:

$$\mathbf{u}_n \times \mathbf{H}_1 = \mathcal{D}_k \mathbf{E}_1^t, \tag{1}$$

with $\mathbf{u}_n$ the outward pointing normal to $\mathcal{S}$ and the superscript t indicating the tangential component of a field. In the different, but similar case of Fig. 1(b), the inner material is replaced by the background material. The field quantities inside $\mathcal{V}$ are now given by $(\mathbf{E}, \mathbf{H})$. As before, a DtN operator on the boundary surface links these fields:

$$\mathbf{u}_n \times \mathbf{H} = \mathcal{D}_{k_0} \mathbf{E}^t. \tag{2}$$

In order to retain the same field distribution in $\mathcal{V}_0$, a surface current density $\mathbf{J}_s$ is introduced. Given the boundary condition

$$\mathbf{u}_n \times (\mathbf{H}_1 - \mathbf{H}) = \mathbf{u}_n \times (\mathbf{H}_0 - \mathbf{H}) = \mathbf{J}_s \tag{3}$$

and (1)–(2), we introduce the differential surface admittance operator $\mathcal{Y}$ in the following expression for the surface current density:

$$\mathbf{J}_s = \mathcal{Y}\mathbf{E}_1^t = (\mathcal{D}_k - \mathcal{D}_{k_0})\, \mathbf{E}_1^t, \tag{4}$$

where the tangential continuity of the electric field at $\mathcal{S}$ is exploited. An expression based on the eigenfunctions of the volume $\mathcal{V}$ is derived in [6] and is given by

$$\mathbf{J}_s = \mathcal{Y}\mathbf{E}_1^t = \eta \sum_l \left[\frac{|k_l|^2 \int_{\mathcal{S}} (\mathbf{u}_n \times \mathbf{E}_1^t) \cdot \mathbf{h}_l^* \, \mathrm{d}S}{(k_l^2 - k^2)(k_l^2 - k_0^2)\mathcal{N}_l^2} \right] (\mathbf{u}_n \times \mathbf{h}_l). \tag{5}$$

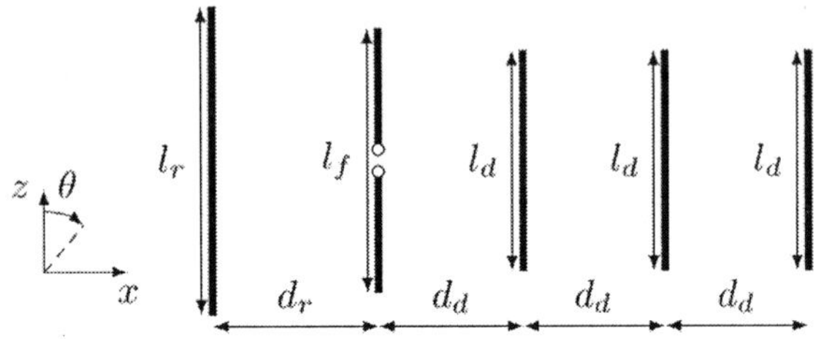

Fig. 2. Yagi-Uda wire antenna with dipole feed, one reflector and three directors. Dimensions for operation at 110 MHz can be found in Table I.

TABLE I
DIMENSIONS (IN m) OF THE ANTENNA IN FIG. 2.

Parameter	Value	Parameter	Value
l_f	1.332	r	0.001
l_r	1.348	d_r	0.8
l_d	1.12	d_d	0.637

The contrast parameter η is defined as $\left(k^2 - k_0^2\right)/j\omega\mu_0$, k_l is the wavenumber of the l-th eigenmode $\mathbf{h}_l$, the solenoidal magnetic eigenmodes of the volume $\mathcal{V}$ with normalization constant $\mathcal{N}_l^2$. These eigenvectors satisfy equations (10.13) and (10.14) in [7]. For general shapes, the eigenmodes have to be calculated numerically but for some simple, omnipresent shapes such as the cuboid or the circular cylinder, closed expressions can readily be found in literature. In order to solve for $\mathbf{J}_s$, the exterior problem has to be solved as well. A boundary integral equation method (BIE) such as MoM is ideally suited for this type of situation. Employing a standard discretization scheme to both the selected BIE and (5) results in a set of matrix equations that can be solved using regular techniques. A more detailed description of this procedure can be found in [6].

III. EXAMPLE

Consider the Yagi-Uda antenna displayed in Fig. 2. The driving component of this structure is a dipole antenna with length l_f. The remaining elements are of parasitic nature: one reflector with length l_r at a distance d_r behind the central dipole and three directors with length l_d which are placed in front with a spacing of d_d. All wires have the same radius r. Values for these parameters can be found in Table I for the Yagi-Uda operating at 110 MHz, i.e., the center frequency of the localizer in an instrument landing system (ILS). The gain of this configuration is calculated numerically by means of the differential surface admittance operator for circular cylinders for varying inclination angles θ in the vertical plane (xz-plane). This gain pattern is plotted in Fig. 3 for decreasing values of the skin depth $\delta = \sqrt{2/(\omega\mu\sigma)}$, i.e., for increasing conductivity σ. A reference solution for a perfectly electrically conducting (PEC) Yagi-Uda is obtained through 4nec2 [8], a free NEC based antenna modeler. Due to the inherent symmetry of the structure under study, only half the range of θ is shown. It is apparent that the antenna response evolves towards that of the PEC solution for decreasing skin

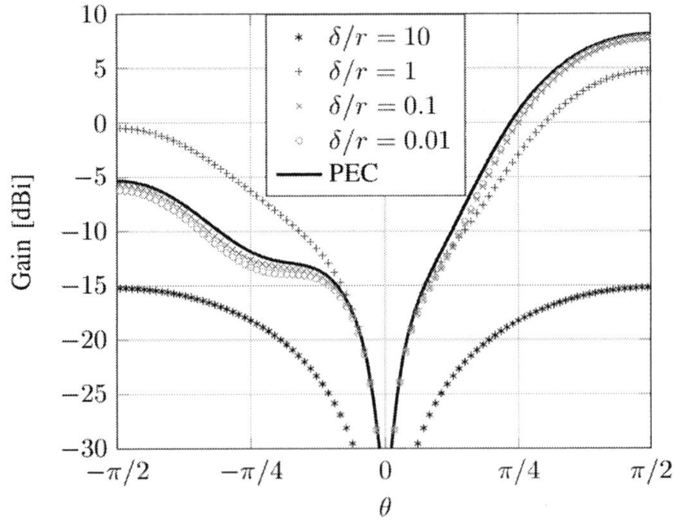

Fig. 3. Gain of the Yagi-Uda antenna at 110 MHz for various values of the skin depth. The reference PEC solution is obtained through 4nec2 [8].

depths. Moreover, it is shown that an insufficient conductivity detrimentally affects the antenna's characteristics. The remaining discrepancy between the solution for $\delta/r = 0.01$ and the PEC reference can be attributed to both the fundamental approximations of the reference solution, viz., thin-wire MoM, and the finite mesh of the employed method.

IV. CONCLUSION

In this paper, we have presented a 3-D differential surface admittance operator for the analysis of a realistic antenna configuration, i.e., a Yagi-Uda antenna used in ILS systems. Through incorporation into a BIE-MoM structure, the 3-D operator's appositeness to the assessment of material properties on antenna performance is demonstrated.

REFERENCES

[1] R. King and T. Wu, "The imperfectly conducting cylindrical transmitting antenna," *IEEE Trans. Antennas Propag.*, vol. 14, no. 5, pp. 524–534, Sep. 1966.

[2] L. Medgyesi-Mitschang and J. Putnam, "Integral equation formulations for imperfectly conducting scatterers," *IEEE Trans. Antennas Propag.*, vol. 33, no. 2, pp. 206–214, Feb. 1985.

[3] D.-S. Wang, "Limits and validity of the impedance boundary condition on penetrable surfaces," *IEEE Trans. Antennas Propag.*, vol. 35, no. 4, pp. 453–457, Apr. 1987.

[4] D. De Zutter and L. Knockaert, "Skin effect modeling based on a differential surface admittance operator," *IEEE Trans. Microw. Theory Techn.*, vol. 53, no. 8, pp. 2526–2538, Aug. 2005.

[5] H. Rogier, D. De Zutter, and L. Knockaert, "Two-dimensional transverse magnetic scattering using an exact surface admittance operator," *Radio Science*, vol. 42, no. 3, Jun. 2007.

[6] M. Huynen, M. Gossye, D. De Zutter, and D. Vande Ginste, "A 3-D differential surface admittance operator for lossy dipole antenna analysis," *IEEE Antennas Wireless Propag. Lett.*, 2016, Early Access. [Online]. Available: http://dx.doi.org/10.1109/LAWP.2016.2619558

[7] J. Van Bladel, *Electromagnetic Fields*. John Wiley & Sons, 2007.

[8] A. Voors, "4nec2: Antenna modeler," http://www.qsl.net/4nec2/, 2015.

On the Initial Condition Problem of the Time Domain PMCHWT Surface Integral Equation

Ismail E. Uysal and Hakan Bagci
Division of Computer, Electrical and Mathematical Sciences and Engineering
King Abdullah University of Science and Technology
Thuwal 23955-6900, Saudi Arabia
e-mails: {ismail.uysal, hakan.bagci}@kaust.edu.sa

A. Arif Ergin and H. Arda Ulku
Department of Electronics Engineering
Gebze Technical University
Gebze, Kocaeli, 41400, Turkey
e-mails: {aergin, haulku}@gtu.edu.tr

***Abstract*—Non-physical, linearly increasing and constant current components are induced in marching on-in-time solution of time domain surface integral equations when initial conditions on time derivatives of (unknown) equivalent currents are not enforced properly. This problem can be remedied by solving the time integral of the surface integral for auxiliary currents that are defined to be the time derivatives of the equivalent currents. Then the equivalent currents are obtained by numerically differentiating the auxiliary ones. In this work, this approach is applied to the marching on-in-time solution of the time domain Poggio-Miller-Chan-Harrington-Wu-Tsai surface integral equation enforced on dispersive/plasmonic scatterers. Accuracy of the proposed method is demonstrated by a numerical example.**

I. INTRODUCTION

Linearly increasing and constant current components are often observed in marching on-in-time (MOT) solution of time domain surface integral equations (TD-SIEs) [1]–[4]. The presence of these spurious components is attributed to the fact that initial conditions on time derivatives of unknown equivalent currents are not enforced properly [3], [4]. For example, the time domain electric field integral equation (TD-EFIE) expresses the time derivative of the scattered electric field in terms of the current and its second-order time derivative. Consequently, the MOT scheme used for solving the TD-EFIE has to enforce two initial conditions, one on the current and another one on its second-order derivative. However, traditional MOT schemes assume zero initial condition only on the current without considering the possibility of discontinuous/fast changes in the current's time derivatives.

In [5], [6], an MOT scheme, which solves the time domain Poggio-Miller-Chan-Harrington-Wu-Tsai surface integral equation (TD-PMCHWT-SIE), is developed for computing fields scattered from dispersive objects. Like the TD-EFIE, the linearly increasing and constant current components contaminates the MOT solution of this equation. As expected, these spurious components also affect the frequency response and might suppress physical resonance modes, especially when sensitive plasmonic interactions are considered.

In this work, the method developed in [3], is used for eliminating these spurious modes from the solution. This approach constructs the TD-PMCHWT-SIE in the time integral of the equivalent currents and uses the traditional MOT scheme to solve it for these auxiliary unknown variables. Differentiating these variables in time (during MOT steps) yields a solution that is free from spurious constant and/or linearly increasing components.

II. FORMULATION

Consider an object residing in an unbounded background medium. Let $\{\varepsilon_0, \mu_0\}$ and $\{\varepsilon_1(t), \mu_1\}$ represent the permittivity and permeability of the background medium and the object. Electromagnetic field $\{\mathbf{E}^{\text{inc}}(\mathbf{r}, t), \mathbf{H}^{\text{inc}}(\mathbf{r}, t)\}$ excites the object. Using the equivalence theorem and expressing the scattered field in terms of equivalent surface current densities $\mathbf{J}(\mathbf{r}, t)$ and $\mathbf{M}(\mathbf{r}, t)$ on the surface S of the object, one can construct the TD-PMCHWT-SIE:

$$\begin{aligned}
&\hat{\mathbf{n}}(\mathbf{r}) \times \partial_t \mathbf{E}^{\text{inc}}(\mathbf{r}, t) = -\hat{\mathbf{n}}(\mathbf{r}) \times [\mathcal{L}_0\{\mu_0 \mathbf{J}(\mathbf{r}, t)\} \\
&- \mathcal{Q}_0\{\varepsilon_0^{-1}\mathbf{J}(\mathbf{r}, t)\} + \mathcal{K}_0\{\mathbf{M}(\mathbf{r}, t)\} + \mathcal{L}_1\{\mu_1 \mathbf{J}(\mathbf{r}, t)\} \\
&- \mathcal{Q}_1\{\bar{\varepsilon}_1(t) * \mathbf{J}(\mathbf{r}, t)\} + \mathcal{K}_1\{\mathbf{M}(\mathbf{r}, t)\}] \qquad (1) \\
&\hat{\mathbf{n}}(\mathbf{r}) \times \partial_t \mathbf{H}^{\text{inc}}(\mathbf{r}, t) = -\hat{\mathbf{n}}(\mathbf{r}) \times \left[\mathcal{L}_0\{\varepsilon_0^{-1}\mathbf{M}(\mathbf{r}, t)\}\right. \\
&- \mathcal{Q}_0\{\mu_0^{-1}\mathbf{M}(\mathbf{r}, t)\} - \mathcal{K}_0\{\mathbf{J}(\mathbf{r}, t)\} + \mathcal{L}_1\{\varepsilon_1(t) * \mathbf{M}(\mathbf{r}, t)\} \\
&\left.- \mathcal{Q}_1\{\mu_1^{-1}\mathbf{M}(\mathbf{r}, t)\} - \mathcal{K}_1\{\mathbf{J}(\mathbf{r}, t)\}\right].
\end{aligned}$$

Here, $\hat{\mathbf{n}}(\mathbf{r})$ is the unit normal vector on S, $\bar{\varepsilon}_1(t)$ is the inverse permittivity function, and

$$\begin{aligned}
\mathcal{L}_m\{\mathbf{X}(\mathbf{r}, t)\} &= \int_S G_m(R, t) * \partial_t^2 \mathbf{X}(\mathbf{r}', t) ds' \\
\mathcal{Q}_m\{\mathbf{X}(\mathbf{r}, t)\} &= \nabla \int_S G_m(R, t) * \nabla' \cdot \mathbf{X}(\mathbf{r}', t) ds' \qquad (2) \\
\mathcal{K}_m\{\mathbf{X}(\mathbf{r}, t)\} &= \nabla \times \int_S G_m(R, t) * \partial_t \mathbf{X}(\mathbf{r}', t) ds'
\end{aligned}$$

for $m \in \{0, 1\}$. In (3), $R = |\mathbf{r} - \mathbf{r}'|$ and $G_m(R, t)$ is Green function of the unbounded medium with ε_m and μ_m. The MOT scheme developed in [5], [6] can be used to solve (1) for unknowns $\mathbf{J}(\mathbf{r}, t)$ and $\mathbf{M}(\mathbf{r}, t)$.

TD-PMCHWT-SIE in (1)-(2) involves the second-order time derivative of equivalent surface current densities due to $\mathcal{L}_m\{\cdot\}$ operator, which results in non-physical linearly increasing and constant components in the MOT solution as explained above. These components can be eliminated through the use of auxiliary surface current densities $\mathbf{P}(\mathbf{r}, t)$ and $\mathbf{Q}(\mathbf{r}, t)$ defined as

$$\partial_t^2 \mathbf{P}(\mathbf{r}, t) = \mathbf{J}(\mathbf{r}, t), \; \partial_t^2 \mathbf{Q}(\mathbf{r}, t) = \mathbf{M}(\mathbf{r}, t). \quad (3)$$

Inserting (3) into (1) and integrating the resulting equation in time twice yield the TD-PMCHWT-SIE in unknown $\mathbf{P}(\mathbf{r}, t)$ and $\mathbf{Q}(\mathbf{r}, t)$:

$$\begin{aligned}
&\hat{\mathbf{n}}(\mathbf{r}) \times \partial_t^{-1} \mathbf{E}^{\mathrm{inc}}(\mathbf{r}, t) = -\hat{\mathbf{n}}(\mathbf{r}) \times [\mathcal{L}_0\{\mu_0 \mathbf{P}(\mathbf{r}, t)\} \\
&- \mathcal{Q}_0\{\varepsilon_0^{-1} \mathbf{P}(\mathbf{r}, t)\} + \mathcal{K}_0\{\mathbf{Q}(\mathbf{r}, t)\} + \mathcal{L}_1\{\mu_1 \mathbf{P}(\mathbf{r}, t)\} \\
&- \mathcal{Q}_1\{\bar{\varepsilon}_1(t) * \mathbf{P}(\mathbf{r}, t)\} + \mathcal{K}_1\{\mathbf{Q}(\mathbf{r}, t)\}] \qquad (4) \\
&\hat{\mathbf{n}}(\mathbf{r}) \times \partial_t^{-1} \mathbf{H}^{\mathrm{inc}}(\mathbf{r}, t) = -\hat{\mathbf{n}}(\mathbf{r}) \times [\mathcal{L}_0\{\varepsilon_0(t) * \mathbf{Q}(\mathbf{r}, t)\} \\
&- \mathcal{Q}_0\{\mu_0^{-1} \mathbf{Q}(\mathbf{r}, t)\} - \mathcal{K}_0\{\mathbf{P}(\mathbf{r}, t)\} + \mathcal{L}_1\{\varepsilon_1(t) * \mathbf{Q}(\mathbf{r}, t)\} \\
&- \mathcal{Q}_1\{\mu_1^{-1} \mathbf{Q}(\mathbf{r}, t)\} - \mathcal{K}_1\{\mathbf{P}(\mathbf{r}, t)\}] .
\end{aligned}$$

Here, ∂_t^{-1} denotes integration in time. To numerically solve (4), first $\mathbf{P}(\mathbf{r}, t)$ and $\mathbf{Q}(\mathbf{r}, t)$ are approximated using Rao-Wilton-Glisson functions $\mathbf{f}_n(\mathbf{r})$ and Lagrange interpolation functions $T(t)$ as

$$\begin{aligned}
\mathbf{P}(\mathbf{r}, t) &= \sum_{j=1}^{N_t} \sum_{n=1}^{N_s} P_{jn} T(t - j\Delta t) \mathbf{f}_n(\mathbf{r}) \qquad (5) \\
\mathbf{Q}(\mathbf{r}, t) &= \sum_{j=1}^{N_t} \sum_{n=1}^{N_s} Q_{jn} T(t - j\Delta t) \mathbf{f}_n(\mathbf{r})
\end{aligned}$$

where Δt is time step size and P_{jn} and Q_{jn} are the unknown current coefficients. Inserting (5) into (4) and Galerkin testing the resulting equations at discrete times $i\Delta t$ yield the MOT matrix system:

$$\mathbf{Z}_0 \mathbf{I}_i = \mathbf{V}_i - \sum_{j=1}^{i-1} \mathbf{Z}_{i-j} \mathbf{I}_j, \; i = 1, .., N_t. \quad (6)$$

Here, $\mathbf{I}_i$ and $\mathbf{V}_i$ store the unknown coefficients and the tested incident fields, respectively, and $\mathbf{Z}_{i-j}$ are the MOT matrices. $\mathbf{I}_i, \; i = 1, .., N_t$ are obtained in an iterative fashion via time marching. Then, coefficients of $\mathbf{J}(\mathbf{r}, t)$ and $\mathbf{M}(\mathbf{r}, t)$ are computed from P_{jn} and Q_{jn} using numerical differentiation. It should be noted here that (i) $\mathbf{Z}_{i-j}$ are same as the matrices obtained from the MOT discretization of (1) and computed using the numerical scheme described in [5], [6], and (ii) $\mathbf{P}(\mathbf{r}, t)$ and $\mathbf{Q}(\mathbf{r}, t)$ obtained by solving (6) are contaminated by spurious components. However these are eliminated from $\mathbf{J}(\mathbf{r}, t)$ and $\mathbf{M}(\mathbf{r}, t)$ by the numerical differentiation applied to $\mathbf{P}(\mathbf{r}, t)$ and $\mathbf{Q}(\mathbf{r}, t)$ [see (3)]. The numerical differentiation is implemented using a finite difference scheme whose order is larger than or equal to the order of $T(t)$ not to introduce additional errors.

III. Numerical Results

Transient fields scattered from a gold sphere are computed by two MOT schemes solving (1) and (4). The sphere has a radius of 50 nm and is centered at the origin in free space. Time domain permittivity and Green function associated with gold are obtained using the method described in [6]. The electric field of the incident plane wave $\mathbf{E}^{\mathrm{inc}}(\mathbf{r}, t) = \hat{\mathbf{x}} \cos(2\pi f_0 \bar{t}) \exp(-\bar{t}^2/\sigma^2)$, where $\bar{t} = t - t_0 - \hat{\mathbf{z}} \cdot \mathbf{r}\sqrt{\varepsilon_0 \mu_0}$, $t_0 = 3.5\sigma$, $\sigma = 3/(2\pi f_{\mathrm{bw}})$, $f_{\mathrm{bw}} = 600$ THz, and $f_0 = 900$ THz. Unknowns are discretized using $N_s = 714$ RWG basis functions and simulations are carried out for $N_t = 600$ time steps with $\Delta t = 0.066$ fs.

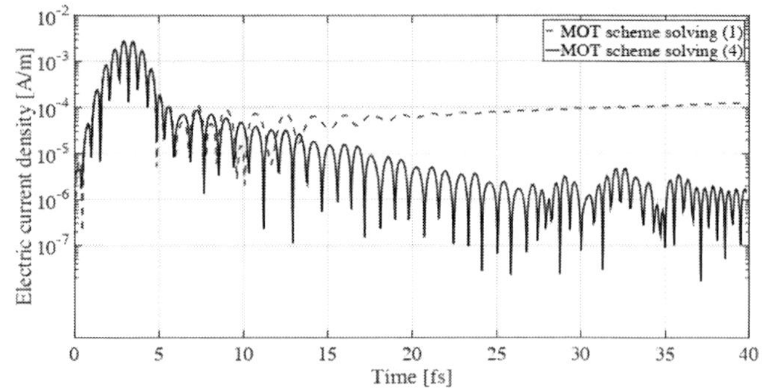

Fig. 1. One of the coefficients of the electric current density expansion computed by the two MOT schemes solving (1) and (4).

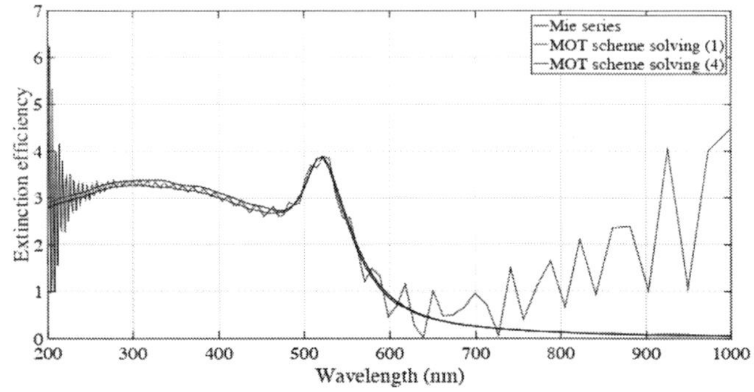

Fig. 2. Extinction cross sections obtained from Fourier transformed electric and magnetic surface current densities, which are computed by the two MOT schemes.

Fig. 1 compares one of the coefficients of the electric current density expansion computed by the MOT schemes by solving (1) and (4). It is clear the latter result is free from linearly increasing and constant components. Fig. 2 compares extinction cross sections which are obtained from Fourier transformed electric and magnetic surface current densities that are computed by the two MOT schemes. It is clearly shown that the solution free from spurious components produces more accurate frequency domain results.

References

[1] D. S. Weile, G. Pisharody, N.-W. Chen, B. Shanker, and E. Michielssen, "A novel scheme for the solution of the time-domain integral equations of electromagnetics," *IEEE Trans. Antennas Propag.*, vol. 52, pp. 283–295, 2004.

[2] Y. Shi, H. Bagci and M. Lu, "On the internal resonant modes in marching-on-in-time solution of the time domain electric field integral equation," *IEEE Trans. Antennas. Propag.*, vol. 61, no. 8, pp. 4389-4392, 2013.

[3] H. A. Ulku and A. A. Ergin, "Solution of the initial condition problem of the time-domain EFIE," *Proc. Comput. Electromagn. Workshop (CEM)*, pp. 17–18, 2013.

[4] Y. Shi, H. Bagci and M. Lu, "On the static loop modes in the marching-on-in-time solution of the time-domain electric field integral equation," *IEEE Antennas Wireless Propag. Lett.*, vol. 13, pp. 317–320, 2014.

[5] I. E. Uysal, H. A. Ulku, and H. Bagci, "MOT solution of the PMCHWT equation for analyzing transient scattering from conductive dielectrics," *IEEE Antennas Wireless Propag. Lett.*, vol. 14, pp. 507–510, 2015.

[6] I. E. Uysal, H. A. Ulku, and H. Bagci, "Transient analysis of electromagnetic wave interactions on plasmonic nanostructures using a surface integral equation solver," *J. Opt. Soc. Am. A*, vol. 33, no. 9, pp. 1747–1759, 2016.

Successes and frustrations in the solution of large electromagnetic problems in supercomputers

Luis Landesa, José M. Taboada, Juan Luis Campon, Alberto Serna
Dpt. Computers and Communication Technologies
University of Extremadura
Caceres, Spain
llandesa@unex.es

Fernando Obelleiro, Jose L. Rodríguez, Diego M. Solis, Marta Araujo
Dpt. Signal and Communications Theory
University of Vigo
Vigo, Spain

***Abstract*—The solution of very large electromagnetic problems might be obtained using large computer facilities as singular High Performance Computers or Supercomputers. In these solutions, suitable numerical methods for large structures should be used, as fast methods e.g. Multilevel Fast Multipole Algorithms. The implementation of this kind of methods in a Computer capable to deal with the large amount of data and calculations is not simple; depending on the nature of the computer (shared memory based, distributed memory based, multi-core, many-core, etc.) you can obtain different performances, you can solve different applications, you must adapt the method to the machine-type, or you should reconsider the implementation strategies to achieve success when you lead with bigdata issues.**

I. Introduction

High accuracy methods as Method of Moments (MoM) or Finite Element Method (FEM) are constrained by their huge growth in computer requirements when the length of the problem increases. However, fast solution methods in electromagnetics are capable of solving very large problems without excesive increment in computer resources. Among others, Multilevel Fast Multipole Algorithms (MLFMA) [1-8], are the best known method to solve the MoM in a efficient and fast manner with high control of the accuracy of the original MoM. If we denote by N the number of unknowns of the problem (proportional to the surface of the object for simple problems, and about 100-300 unknowns per square wavelength), a solution obtained by MoM requires a memory comsumption and time to solve in the order of $O(N^2)$. For example, the solution of the scattering of a sphere with radius r = 100□ would require almost 1,5 PBytes of memory (RAM) requirement and out of proportion time to solve it. Solving that with MLFMA may be possible with a 32GB PC in a reasonable amount of time (minutes) and with a high degree of accuracy.

Fast solutions in turn can use capabilities of High Performance Computers (HPC) as management of large amount of distributed memory resources and parallelism. This leads to the posibility of solve problems that could neves have imagineed two decades ago, consisting of hundreds millions of unknowns.

II. Solving in Parallel

The use of HPC systems, as parallel computers or even supercomputers, could help us to solve problems forbiden in PC computers. One significant point is the large amount of memory reources, but even more important is the possibility to use at the same time, teens, hundreds or several thousands of CPU's. In theory, this leads to divide the compsuption of time by the number of processors. But in practice the reality is very far from that; in addition, the use of large amount of memory is not as easy as in a single machine.

Among other possibilities, programming a method in a parallel HPC system can be performed by using MPI and OpenMP standards; in our lab we use these ones in a C++ platform. OpenMP is used only for shared memory computers (generally multicore computers), and MPI can be used for shared memory and mainly distributed memory computers (clusters of computers communicated by efficient and ussually wired networks). Given all our experience, combination of MPI and OpenMP programming techniques is the best way to obtain the better results.

III. Some Usual Handicaps in Parallelizing Electromagnetic Methods

In year 2006 we had been selected to participate in the release of the most reliable Supercomputer in Spain (in that date), *Finis Terrae*, of the Supercomputing Center of Galician (CESGA), using our implementation of the MLFMA algorithm. Only few weeks of work translating codes and compiling that, one important problem was emerging. In the cluster of our lab we obtain good speedup results when we use our codes parallelized with MPI/OpenMP. But, these speedup *good* behaviour was a not very good behaviour for the supercomputer technicians. For the first time, we bump into the importance of Amdahl Law. In our cluster we obtaind an almost 90% efficiency with 16 processes in parallel. Amdahl's law says that the program is only scalable to less than 64 processors, and we would never obtain an speedup more than 50x (the expected reduction of time for using hundreds of processors in that supercomputer was compromised). Amdahl law says that scalability of a parallel program is compromised by the serial fraction of the program in parallel (a portion of code common to all processors).

In the example above, only the 1% of the parallel code was the serial fraction, but this small fraction avoids the code to scale to more than 64 processors. This is a very compromised thing if the method need to use this repetitive operations in each processor. If not, as in our case, the serial fraction is dominated by programming issues; better programing and, by our experience, using efficiently cache memory in each processor can avoid these problems. In the challenge of the releasing of *Finis Terrae* supercomputer we analyse a problem with more that 30 million unknows using only a single level fast multipole method. In this first attempt we sacrified the speed of the MLFMA by the superscalability performance of a single level of MLFMA [7].

The best conclussion in our first incursion in programming electromagnetic problems in supercomputers is that *Scalability* is more important than *speed*, for a method. If method (a) is 10 times slower than (b) but (a) scales to thousands of processors and (b) scales only to a few tens of processors then method (a) is more suitable for supercomputing.

After this success in the use of a supercomputer for a large problem in electromagnetics we had improved the code to permit a good scalability for MLFMA. For that, we changed the memory and CPU distribution geometry based by a memory and CPU distribution mixing geometry and far-field directions as other authors [2-4]. The main difference is that we obtain better results in scalability not using a pure MLFMA scheme but a truncated MLFMA scheme. In our scheme only a few interpolation levels are used (geometrically distributed) and the translation operations are fast calculated by FFT (distributed in the far-field directions). Successive improvements of that technique allowed us to solve a problem modeled with more than one billion unknowns. We prove that MLFMA is faster but very difficult to scale for using hundreds or thousands of processors of a supercomputer. Sacrificing some of the performance of MLFMA with a truncated version and accelerating the translation operator with a FFT distributed by directions was a good option to take advantage of the supercomputer.

But a lot of problems appeared when we translate codes or when we run our code in a supercomputer when the problems are very large. Some of the problems are dependent of the supercomputer. For example, the use of large amount of data linked with extreme parallelization schemes caused estrange and unpredictable aborts in our code. In some supercomputers, the *Standard Library of C* is not thread-safe; this means that a lot of *malloc's* in parallel may fail. For us, a lot of important supercomputing resources were wasted while we didn't find the cause of this abort. This failure only appeared for very large simulation nor in the medium to large scale simulations.

We can collect a lot of problems that we have needed to solve for use large scale computing facilities. Some of the other not explained here we will explain at the conference. Some of these are related to 32-bits limitations even in 64-bits modern and cutting-edge technology supercomputers or very trivial but not immune to problems in the calculation of a norm of a very large vector. Certain problems are limiting, until now, the capability of the code to scale to problems bigger than more than two billion unknowns. Some of the new ideas, including new numerical techniques, to overcome that will be explained at the conference.

IV. New Improvements

In the last years we take advantadge in supercomputers for optimization. This includes not such very large problems but a lot of computation in medium and large size problems. This kind of problems includes new antennas for the optics regime or design of invisibility cloacks and potions.

Other improvements for medium and large scale problems includes the use of new processors as many core processors (GPU's) or Many Integrated Core Processors (MIC, Xeon Phi). Our experience is not as good as we expected. We didn't achieve good scalability results for fast methods like MLFMA. Nevertheless we obtained remarkable results when we use this processors to calculate the elements of the moment matrix of the MoM. Then we use these new mathematical co-processors as units that calculate MoM elements. This was very useful, for example for the in-core computation (without storing in memory) of the MoM matrices of near field interactions of the MLFMA or the aggregation matrices in each iteration. Our best results are obtained with the Xeon Phi processors.

ACKNOWLEDMENTS

This work was supported by the European Regional Development Fund (ERDF) and the Spanish Ministerio de Economia y Competitividad (Projects MAT2014-58201-C2-1-R, MAT2014-58201-C2-2-R, Project TACTICA), from the ERDF and the Extremadura Regional Government (Junta de Extremadura) (Project GR15052), from the ERDF and the Galician Regional Government under agreement for funding the Atlantic Research Center for Information and Communication Technologies (AtlantTIC)and from the Spanish Ministerio de Educación, Cultura y Deporte (Project FPU 00022/15).

[1] S. Velamparambil, W. C. Chew and J. M. Song, "10 million unknowns: Is it that big?", IEEE Antennas Propag. Mag., vol. 45, no. 3, pp. 43-58, Apr. 2003.

[2] O Ergul, L. Gurel, The Multilevel Fast Multipole Algorithm (MLFMA) for Solving Large-Scale Computational Electromagnetics Problems, Wiley, 2014.

[3] Ergul and L. Gurel, "Efficient parallelization of the multilevel fast multipole algorithm for the solution of large-scale scattering problems", IEEE Trans. Antennas Propag., vol. 56, no. 8, pp. 2335-2345, Aug. 2008

[4] Ergl and L. Grel, "Rigorous solutions of electromagnetic problems involving hundreds of millions of unknowns", IEEE Antennas Propag. Mag., vol. 53, no. 1, pp. 18-27, Feb. 2011.

[5] J. M. Taboada, L. Landesa, F. Obelleiro, J. L. Rodriguez, J. M. Bertolo, M. G. Araujo, et al., "High scalability FMM-FFT electromagnetic solver for supercomputer systems", IEEE Antennas Propag. Mag., vol. 51, no. 6, pp. 20-28, Dec. 2009.

[6] J. M. Taboada ; M. G. Araujo ; F. O. Basteiro ; J. L. Rodriguez ; L. Landesa, "MLFMA-FFT Parallel Algorithm for the Solution of Extremely Large Problems in Electromagnetics", Proceedings of the IEEE, vol. 101, no 2, 2013.

[7] L. Landesa, J. M. Taboada, F. Obelleiro, J. L. Rodriguez, C. Mourio and A. Gomez, "Solution of very large integral-equation problems with single-level FMM", *Microw. Opt. Technol. Lett.*, vol. 51, no. 6, pp. 20-28, Dec. 2009.

[8] J. M. Taboada, M. Arajo, J. M. Bertolo, L. Landesa, F. Obelleiro and J. L. Rodrguez, "MLFMA-FFT parallel algorithm for the solution of large-scale problems in electromagnetic (invited paper)", Progr. Electromagn. Res., vol. 105, pp. 15-30, 2010.

Electromagnetic optimization of MIMO channels using GPUs

Alfonso Breglia, Amedeo Capozzoli, Claudio Curcio, Salvatore Di Donna, and Angelo Liseno
Università di Napoli Federico II, Dipartimento di Ingegneria Elettrica e delle Tecnologie dell'Informazione, via Claudio 21, I 80125 Napoli (Italy)

Abstract— **We present an approach for the maximization of the MIMO channel capacity.**

The proposed scheme is based on the optimization of the singular values of the channel scattering matrix by properly facing the main computational key points of the problem. The approach is GPU-based, the propagation environment is described by an ultrafast Geometrical Optics (GO) approach, the singular values are computed by a very fast scheme and the required global optimization is performed by a differential evolutionary algorithm. The unknowns of the problem, namely the antenna locations, are given proper representations to reduce the overall number of optimization parameters.

Keywords—MIMO, Channel Optimization, SVD, GPU, CUDA, ray tracing

I. Introduction

Multiple Input - Multiple Output (MIMO) [1, 2] is a wireless communication technique using multiple antennas operating both, in transmission and reception modalities, aiming at increasing the channel capacity over a conventional SISO (Single Input - Single Output).

When designing a MIMO system, a relevant problem is determining the "most convenient" configuration of transmitting (TX) and receiving (RX) antennas, namely, the one maximizing the channel capacity for a given SNR (Signal to Noise Ratio) and propagation environment.

The electromagnetic environment is a critical aspect when determining the performance of a MIMO channel since it influences the properties of the channel matrix. Analyzing how propagation affects the channel and considering it when designing the most convenient MIMO configuration is a severely burdened computational problem.

We face how much accelerated analysis and optimization can make this goal viable. This entails understanding how to push the performance of employed algorithms and computational resources. In this sense, one should consider several computational key points:

1. properly choosing and accelerating a global optimizer, being local optimization typically not enough to find the best solutions;
2. properly choosing and accelerating the approach to compute the MIMO channel matrix;
3. being the channel capacity related to the singular values of the channel matrix, accelerating the computation of the singular values depending on the problem size (conventional - 4x4, 6x6 - MIMO vs. massive MIMO [3]);
4. properly representing the unknowns, to manage only the essential optimization parameters;
5. properly exploiting massively parallel computing platforms as Graphics Processing Units (GPUs) [4].

II. Optimization Approach and Unknowns Representation

The global optimization of the channel capacity approach should be chosen to exhibit good convergence properties and to profit of the massive parallelization, a particularly convenient feature to enable a satisfactory exploration of the objective functional landscape. In this sense, a less "complex", but massively parallelizable algorithm should be preferred to a more "involved", but "more sequential" scheme. From this point of view, the "genetic-like" differential evolutionary approach has been chosen as the global optimization scheme due to its main features matching both the above mentioned requirements [5].

Furthermore, since the dealt with problem concerns the optimization of the TX and RX antenna location for maximizing the MIMO channel capacity, to reduce the number of unknowns and improve efficiency, both the TX and RX antennas are assumed to be located on lines and their positions are searched for by properly representing them using Legendre polynomials [6-8].

Further details on the employed optimization approach can be found in [9].

III. Channel Matrix Calculation

The method exploited to calculate the channel matrix should properly trade off computational accuracy and speed to enable executions in an iterative optimization. Calculating at each generation the channel matrix for a large number of antenna configurations by a full wave method would be unfeasible, especially when large scenarios are involved. Opposite to that, Geometrical Optics (GO) is very appealing to quickly providing an approximate solution to Maxwell's equations.

Nevertheless, for electrically large scenarios, GO must be properly accelerated by adequate algorithmic structures capable to properly handle the intersections of the rays with the scene objects. Fortunately, the problem can be faced by tree-like structures, which, if properly setup, managed and explored, can significantly reduce the computational complexity. Data structures like spatial subdivision, or KD-tree, and object partitioning, or BVH (Bounding Volume Hierarchy), can be effectively applied to this purpose and may profit of a high degree of parallelization [10]. Split Bounding Volume Hierarchy (SBVH) scheme [10], mixing object partitioning and spatial subdivision has recently shown to have very appealing parallel computational features [10]. Accordingly, for this work, the Split BVH (SBVH) scheme has been exploited.

IV. GPU-based Singular Values Calculation

Computing the singular values of small or large matrices should be dealt with different approaches. Accordingly, the computational scheme to be employed differs if considering conventional or massive MIMOs. In this paper, we address the former case.

Furthermore, the number of involved matrices is related to the number of population members of the differential optimizer. Then, at each generation, the singular values of a large number of small sized matrices have to be computed. This task can be efficiently and effectively performed on a GPU as in [11].

V. Numerical Results

The optimizer, the ray tracer and the singular values calculation have been implemented in both parallel GPU (CUDA) and sequential CPU (C++) programming languages. For the CPU case, the singular values calculation has been achieved using the third party Eigen library.

The test case consists of a parallelepiped of size 25λ x 25λ x 25λ, centered at the origin of the *Oxyz* reference system and of a plate of size 50λ x 15λ, parallel to the *yz* plane and located at x=30λ. Both the objects are perfectly conducting. The scene has been discretized with 400 triangles.

Four TX antennas have been located on the line lying on the *xy* plane, parallel to the *x*-axis and passing by (15λ, -40λ, 0λ) while four RX antennas have been located on the line lying on the *xy* plane, parallel to the *x*-axis and passing by (15λ, 40λ, 0λ). The antenna positions have been represented using a number of 3 Legendre polynomials and minimum and maximum spacing of λ/4 and 2λ, respectively, have been enforced. The MIMO channel has been assumed noisy with SNR=20dB.

The code has been executed on a workstation equipped with two Intel Xeon E5-2650 2.00GHz, Eight core processors each and four NVIDIA Kepler K20c cards, but with multi-GPU disabled. Fig. 1 displays an OpenGL rendering of the MIMO channel with the optimized antenna locations. The Figure also depicts the GO rays connecting the transmitting antennas (the pink dots) with the receiving ones (not appearing in the image). As it can be seen, multiple interactions between the plane and the cylinder have been accounted for as well as diffraction from the plate border. Diffraction from the plate corners and the cylinder ends have been neglected for simplicity. The optimized antenna positions are reported in Table 1. The parallel GPU code has run in about 22mins, gaining a speedup of about 4 as compared to the sequential CPU execution. The optimized channel capacity has been 19.4bps/Hz, a value which well agrees with the statistical distribution of channel capacities for random channels with 4 transmitting and 4 receiving antennas reported in [2, Fig. 7].

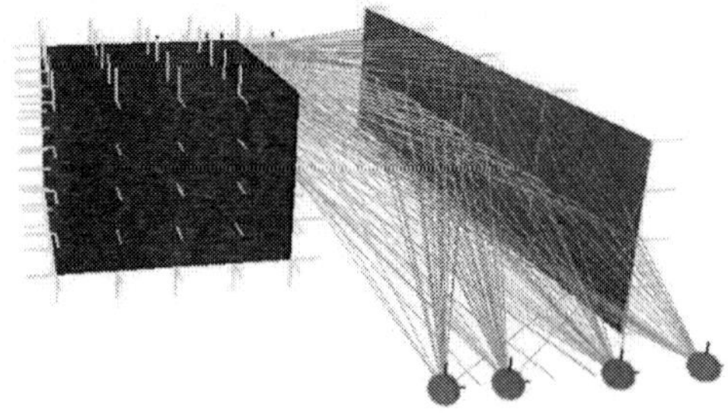

Fig. 1. MIMO channel with optimized antenna locations.

Table 1: Optimized TX and RX antenna positions

Antenna	*x*-coord.	Antenna	*x*-coord.
TX 1	8.16λ	RX 1	7.00λ
TX 2	11.7λ	RX 2	13.9λ
TX 3	17.9λ	RX 3	16.1λ
TX 4	23.0λ	RX 4	23.0λ

Acknowledgment

Work partially funded by the Italian Ministry of Education, University and Research (MIUR), project PON01_02425 "Services for wIreless netwoRk Infrastructure beyOnd 3G" (SIRIO).

References

[1] G.J. Foschini, M.J. Gans, "On limits of wireless communications in a fading environment when using multiple antennas," *Wireless Personal Commun.*, vol. 6, n. 3, pp. 311-335, Mar. 1998.

[2] J. Bach Andersen, "Array gain and capacity for known random channels with multiple element arrays at both ends," *IEEE J. Selected Areas Commun.*, vol. 18, n. 11, pp. 2172-2178, Nov. 2000.

[3] E. G. Larsson, *et al.*, "Massive MIMO for Next Generation Wireless Systems," *IEEE Commun. Mag.*, vol. 52, no. 2, pp. 186-195, Feb. 2014.

[4] A. Capozzoli, C. Curcio, A. Di Vico, A. Liseno, "NUFFT- & GPU-based fast imaging of vegetation", *IEICE Trans. Commun.*, vol. E94-B, n. 7, pp. 2092-2103, Jul. 2011.

[5] R. Storn, K. Price, "Differential evolution - a simple and efficient heuristic for global optimization over continuous spaces," *J. Global Opt.*, vol. 11, n. 4, pp. 341-359, Dec. 1997.

[6] A. Capozzoli, *et al.*, "Dielectric field probes for very-near-field and compact-near-field antenna characterization", *IEEE Antennas Prop. Mag.*, vol. 51, n. 5, pp. 118-125, Oct. 2009.

[7] A. Capozzoli, C. Curcio, A. Liseno, P. Vinetti, "Field sampling and field reconstruction: a new perspective," *Radio Sci.*, vol. 45, RS6004, 31 pp., 2010, doi:10.1029/2009RS004298.

[8] A. Capozzoli, *et al.*, "Photonic probes and advanced (also phaseless) near-field far-field techniques", *IEEE Antennas Prop. Mag.*, vol. 52, n. 5, pp. 232-241, Oct. 2010.

[9] A. Breglia, A. Capozzoli, C. Curcio, S. Di Donna, A. Liseno, "GPU-based electromagnetic optimization of MIMO channels", *ACES Express J.*, vol. 1, n. 4, pp. 1-4, Apr. 2016.

[10] A. Breglia, A. Capozzoli, C. Curcio, A. Liseno, "Comparison of acceleration data structures for electromagnetic ray tracing purposes on GPUs," *IEEE Antennas Prop. Mag.*, vol. 57, n. 5, pp. 159-176, Oct. 2015.

[11] A. Capozzoli, C. Curcio, S. Di Donna, A. Liseno, "Massive computation of singular values of small matrices on GPUs," *Proc. of the Int. Workshop on Comput. Electromagn.*, Izmir, Turkey, Jul. 1-4, 2015, pp. 36-37.

Accelerating Fast Marching for Geometrical Optics

Amedeo Capozzoli, Claudio Curcio, Angelo Liseno, Salvatore Savarese
Università degli Studi di Napoli Federico II, Dipartimento di Ingegneria Elettrica e delle Tecnologie dell'Informazione (DIETI), via Claudio 21, 80125 Napoli (Italy)

***Abstract*— We present an approach for a fast and accurate determination of the geometrical optics solutions to Maxwell's equations based on the determination of the eikonal function and devised to handle scenarios involving complex spatially varying refraction indices. The explicit solution of the eikonal equation allows to set up an inverse ray tracing scheme, which proves particularly convenient compared to direct ray tracing. The field amplitude and polarization are then found by solving the relative transport equations along each ray. The accuracy of the method is shown in the case of the scattering from a conducting sphere coated by a dielectric.**

Keywords*— *Geometrical Optics, Fast Marching Method, Ray Tracing.

I. Introduction

In applications of computational electromagnetics where the solution to Maxwell's equations is required for electrically large domains, an appealing approach is given by the geometrical optics (GO) approximation. While typical ray tracing techniques are particularly convenient when dealing with homogeneous media, they can be less favorable in complex scenarios with electromagnetically penetrable scatterers with cumbersome spatially varying refraction index. For these problems, approaches based on the direct solution of the eikonal equation are appealing, because they allow to easily work out inverse ray tracing schemes and to dismiss iterative procedures needed to the determination of the field on lines, surfaces or volumes with a prefixed step. Besides accuracy, approaches for these cases should also provide efficient numerical algorithms amenable also for parallel execution. Among different solutions, a convenient algorithm is given by the Fast Marching Method (FMM) [1]. Recently, an approach based on the FMM has been developed for a fast and accurate determination of the GO solutions to Maxwell's equations based on an explicit solution to the eikonal for 2D problems [2] and 3D problems involving metallic scatterers [3]. Aim of the paper is to spot on the main aspects of the approach and to show for the first time its extension to the non trivial case of a 3D scene in which penetrable scatterers are present, managed by the introduction of a tree data structure to handle the complexity of the computation and of an effective matching of eikonals at the scatterers boundaries. It is stressed that the *O(NlogN)* trend provided by the FMM allows to improve the computational burden for the evaluation of the GO solution, making the approach well suited for large problems involving non homogeneous media.

II. The Proposed Approach

In this Section, we give a brief overview of the main aspects of the proposed approach to the computation of the GO solution to the scattering by a set of objects in a 3D scene. As illustrated in Fig. 1, let us consider a source generating an incident field (depicted in green) which gives rise to a number of reflected and transmitted fields (first contribution, depicted in red). Each reflected/transmitted field is determined in three steps, namely by first solving the eikonal equation, then tracing the rays and finally computing the field intensity and polarization. Mutual interactions are taken in account by considering each contribution as a new source (second contribution, depicted in orange). The process can be iterated to include also the third contributions (depicted in yellow) or any higher order interaction, according to the desired accuracy.

- The solution of the eikonal equation is based on the FMM, which has been introduced as a convenient algorithm providing the $O(N \log N)$ computational complexity instead of the $O(N^2)$ one of "brute-force" approaches, N being the total number of grid points discretizing the computational domain [1].
- The correct implementation of FMM requires the matching of the incident/reflected/transmitted eikonals on the boundaries of the scattering objects [4], here addressed by a proper initialization procedure.
- To manage the arbitrary number of mutual interactions in a rational way, accelerating the computation and allowing the parallelization on GPU platforms, a tree data structure has been introduced. In particular, each node of the tree is associated to the field reflected/transmitted by one of the surfaces when illuminated by the field associated to its parent node. Using this data structure allows to easily trace the path of the rays across multiple reflections by traversing the tree from its leaf nodes back to the root.
- The explicit solution to the eikonal equation enables the setting up of an inverse ray tracing scheme. Accordingly, to avoid iterative schemes typical of direct tracing and save computational resources, only those rays hitting the points wherein the field must be calculated are traced backwards to the source. The tracing is based on an efficient implementation, profiting from a solution strategy exploited in the accurate and fast generation of textured images from vector fields, based on the fourth-order Runge-Kutta method with variable step-size [5].

- The field amplitude is found by solving the transport equations for the field intensity and polarization in their integral form [6].

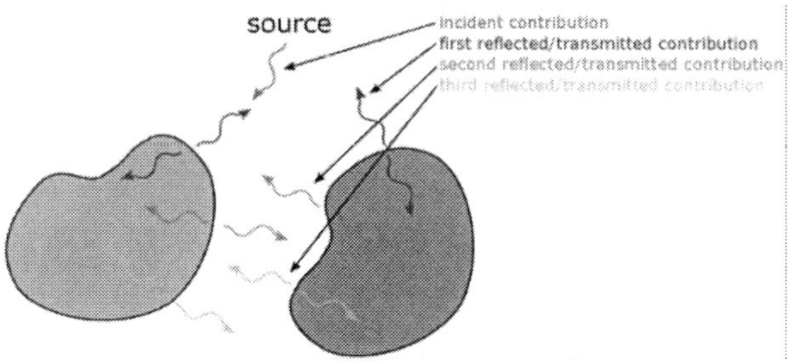

Fig. 1. Geometry of the problem. The incident field is depicted in green, the first contributions to the reflected/trasmitted field in red. The second and third contributions are depicted in orange and yellow, respectively.

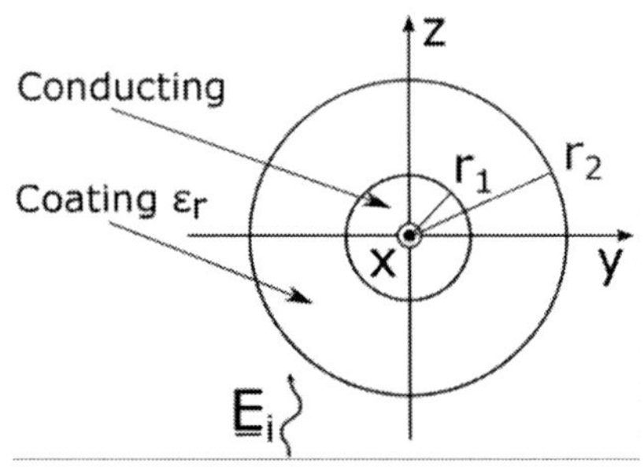

Fig. 2. Geometry of the scattering from a coated sphere.

III. Numerical Results

An application of the approach is shown for the scattering from a conducting sphere coated by a dielectric, and compared to a reference solution obtained by a full-wave approach. Fig. 2 shows the geometry of the problem. The sphere is illuminated by an x-polarized plane wave of unit amplitude and frequency equal to 1GHz (λ=30cm), propagating along the negative direction of the z-axis. The conducting sphere is centered at the origin of the reference system and has a radius r_1 equal to 3λ. The coating dielectric has a radius r_2 equal to 5λ and a relative permittivity ε_r equal to 1.2. A $16\lambda\times16\lambda\times16\lambda$ sized domain, discretized with a $\lambda/6$ step, is employed as the computational domain. The ray tracing for the calculation of the field amplitude has been performed in the x=0 plane and all the results shown are relative to this plane. The evaluated total field, shown in Fig. 3, is compared to that obtained by using the commercial software FEKO, shown in Fig. 4, and calculated using the Method of Moments solver. The solution obtained with the proposed algorithm shows a good agreement with the reference solution in the region in front of the sphere, as can be appreciated from Fig. 5, which shows a superposition of the two solutions for the total field on the segment x=0, y=0 and $z\in(-6.5\lambda,-3\lambda)$.

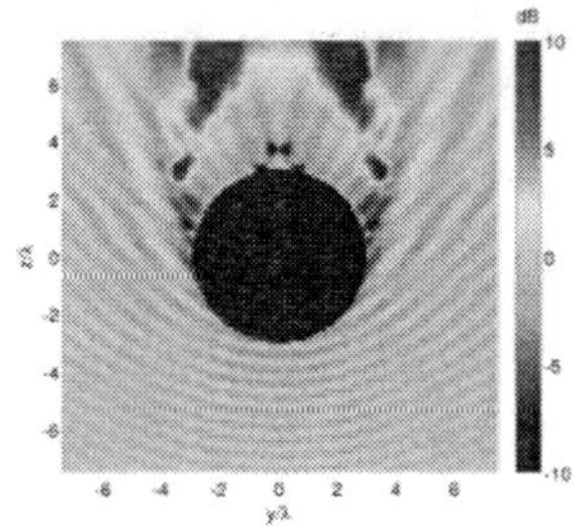

Fig. 3. Scattering from a coated sphere: Amplitude (in dB) of the total field obtained by the proposed algorithm.

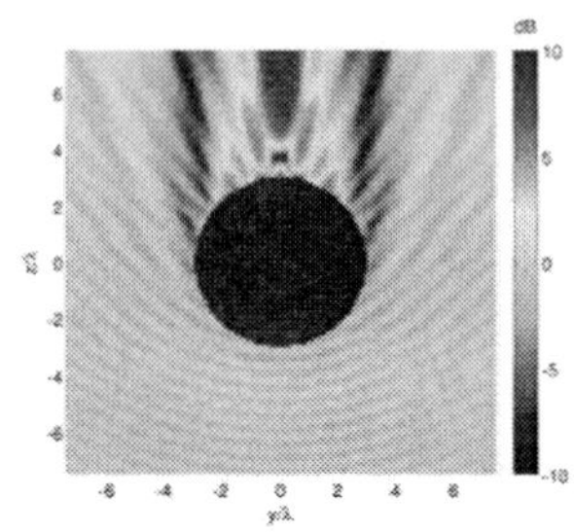

Fig. 4. Scattering from a coated sphere: Amplitude (in dB) of the total field obtained by FEKO.

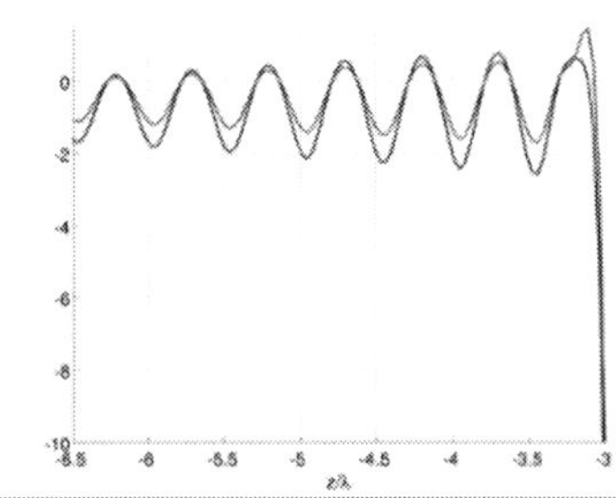

Fig. 5. Scattering from a coated sphere: Cuts of the amplitude (in dB) of the total field obtained by the proposed algorithm (blue line) and by FEKO red line) along a segment on the z-axis.

References

[1] J.A. Sethian, "Level Set Methods and Fast Marching Methods", (Cambridge University Press, 1999).

[2] A. Capozzoli, C. Curcio, A. Liseno, and S. Savarese, "Two-dimensional fast marching for geometrical optics", Opt. Express, vol. 22, n. 22, pp. 26680–26695, 2014.

[3] Capozzoli, A., C. Curcio, A. Liseno, and S. Savarese, "GO solutions with Fast Marching.", 2016 10th European Conference on Antennas and Propagation (EuCAP), pp. 1 5. IEEE, 2016.

[4] D. L. Chopp, "Some Improvements of the Fast Marching Method", SIAM J. Sci. Comput., vol. 23, n .1, pp. 230–244, 2001.

[5] D. Stalling, H.-C. Hege, "Fast and resolution independent line integral convolution", *Proc. of the 22nd Annual Conf. on Computer Graphics and Interactive Tech.*, Los Angeles, CA, Aug. 6-11, 1995.

[6] M. Born and E. Wolf, "Principles of Optics", (Pergamon Press, 1970)

Large Inverse-Scattering Solutions with DBIM on GPU-Enabled Supercomputers

Mert Hidayetoğlu, Carl Pearson, Weng Cho Chew, Levent Gürel, and Wen-Mei Hwu
Department of Electrical and Computer Engineering
University of Illinois at Urbana-Champaign, Urbana, Illinois 61801, U.S.A.

***Abstract*—We report inverse-scattering solutions on supercomputers involving large numbers of graphics processing units (GPUs). The distorted-Born iterative method (DBIM) is employed for the iterative inversions. In each iteration, the required forward problems are distributed among computing nodes equipped with GPUs, and solved with the multilevel fast multipole algorithm. A tomographic reconstruction of a synthetic object with a linear dimension of one hundred wavelengths is obtained on 256 GPUs. The results show that DBIM obtains images approximately four times faster on GPUs, compared to parallel executions on traditional CPU-only computing nodes.**

I. Introduction

Linear diffraction tomography techniques are inadequate for imaging when the multiple-scattering effects are strong. In that case, the scattered field is a nonlinear function of the unknown object, and therefore a nonlinear optimization is required for finding an object which minimizes the residual field at the receivers. The distorted-Born iterative method (DBIM) performs this optimization by solving

$$[\mu \overline{\boldsymbol{I}} + \overline{\boldsymbol{F}}^{\dagger} \cdot \overline{\boldsymbol{F}}] \cdot \delta \boldsymbol{O} = \overline{\boldsymbol{F}}^{\dagger} \cdot \boldsymbol{b} \tag{1}$$

in each iteration [1]. Here, $\overline{\boldsymbol{F}}$ is the functional derivative of the scattered field with respect to the object, and is formulated with the distorted-Born approximation. Each step is taken with the solution of (1), and then $\overline{\boldsymbol{F}}$ is updated with the new background object. Each multiplication involving $\overline{\boldsymbol{F}}$ implies forward-scattering solutions, where an object is known and the scattered field is found. Therefore these multiplications are expensive, especially when the size of the imaging window and the number of transceivers/receivers are large.

To decrease the computational cost, we employ the multilevel fast multipole algorithm (MLFMA) for the forward solutions [2]. It decreases the computational complexity of the dense matrix multiplications (representing free-space Green's function) from $\mathcal{O}(N^2)$ down to $\mathcal{O}(N)$, where N is the number of pixels (unknowns) in the imaging problem. Even with the reduced complexity, the computational cost of DBIM is humongous because many forward solutions are required for each iteration. As a remedy, the computational burden is distributed among message-passing (MPI) processes, where each process employs an MLFMA solver, each handling the corresponding forward problem(s) [3]. This strategy can parallelize DBIM among at most the number of nodes equal to the number of object illuminations. Further speedup is achieved with parallel MLFMA implementation employing multi-processing (OpenMP) threads inside the MPI processes.

TABLE I
NCSA Blue Waters Node Composition

	Socket 1	Socket 2
CPU Node	AMD Opteron 6276 (8 cores, 32 GB RAM)	AMD Opteron 6276 (8 cores, 32 GB RAM)
GPU Node	AMD Opteron 6276 (8 cores, 32 GB RAM)	NVIDIA Tesla K20x (14 SMX, 6 GB RAM)

The MLFMA multiplications are the main computational cost of DBIM and this paper introduces faster DBIM solutions with a GPU implementation of MLFMA. This proposal uses GPU-enabled computing nodes in a supercomputer and can provide more parallel speedup than a traditional CPU-only implementation does. We use the National Center for Supercomputing Applications (NCSA) Blue Waters supercomputer. There are two types of nodes available, as shown in Table I. The first type (noted as CPU node) has two CPUs and the second type (noted as GPU node) has a CPU and a GPU. The hardware specifications of these nodes are given. When CPU nodes are used, the DBIM solver can efficiently employ 16 threads per node. When GPU nodes are used, the DBIM solver uses a single GPU per node for MLFMA solutions, and eight threads for other computations. The GPU implementation is achieved with CUDA programming. This implementation requires a careful programming with MPI, OpenMP, and CUDA together.

II. GPU Implementation of MLFMA

MLFMA is efficiently implemented on GPUs for solving two-dimensional (2-D) volumetric (inhomogeneous) problems. A similar GPU implementation is previously reported for solving surface problems in [4]. Slightly different from that case, we formulate the MLFMA operations as matrix-matrix multiplications (which are performed by GPUs). The required data structures (matrices) are prepared in CPU and moved to GPU in the setup stage, prior to the iterative solution. We use certain symmetries found in volumetric problems to minimize memory allocations. Separate CUDA kernels are implemented for each MLFMA operation. These kernels are called for evaluation of samples in each level of the MLFMA tree structure. The costly memory fetches are minimized by exploiting caches on the GPU card.

Table II shows execution times (in miliseconds) of each MLFMA stage with sequential and parallel implementations. The parallel executions use either 16 CPU threads (third column), or a single GPU (fourth column). The corresponding

TABLE II
EXECUTION TIME (MS) OF A SINGLE MLFMA MULTIPLICATION

Stage	Sequent.	CPU Node	GPU Node	S/up
Aggregation	5,441.6	379.2 (14.35)	72.9 (74.60)	5.20
Translation	2,413.2	206.0 (11.71)	77.8 (31.01)	2.65
Disaggreg.	5,314.3	371.9 (14.29)	107.5 (49.44)	3.46
Farfield	**13,169.2**	**957.1 (13.76)**	**258.2 (50.99)**	**3.71**
Nearfield	**23,964.1**	**1,597.7 (15.00)**	**479.0 (50.03)**	**3.34**
Total	**37,193.8**	**2,595.5 (14.33)**	**737.7 (50.42)**	**3.52**

speedups over the sequential execution are shown in parentheses. The table shows that GPU can perform MLFMA multiplications approximately 50 times faster than a sequentially programmed CPU. This also demonstrates that a GPU node can perform MLFMA multiplications approximately 3.5 times faster than a CPU node. The demonstrated multiplication involves 10 levels and 16.8 million unknowns. The multiplication domain can include objects as large as 400λ, where λ is the wavelength in free space. Both CPU and GPU executions are highly optimized with careful in-house programming as well as standard compiler optimizations.

III. A LARGE INVERSION RESULT

To demonstrate the proposed parallelization strategy, a large logo of our institution is imaged on 256 computing nodes. The logo consists $1{,}024 \times 1{,}024$ (approximately one million) pixels. Each side of the imaging window has a length of 102.4λ. A relative permittivity of 1.02 or 1.0 is assigned to the pixels, depending on their positions. The object is illuminated with 256 plane waves from around the object and the scattered field is collected with 1,024 receivers placed in far-zone.

A conjugate-gradient solver is employed for the N-dimensional optimization problem. In each iteration, the negative-gradient direction is found via distorted-Born approximation involving a background object. The iterative solution is terminated after 50 iterations, where each of them requires solution of three forward problems (per illumination). This yields a total of 38,400 forward problems. The forward problems are distributed among the computing nodes where each node solves 150 forward problems, i.e., three problems per iteration. Each problem involves one million unknowns. The nodes are employed with BiCGS solvers for the MLFMA solutions. To prevent transferring data back-and-forth between the CPU and GPU in each BiCGS iteration, the solver is also implemented on GPU. The fields at the receivers are evaluated on-the-fly with MLFMA (on GPU) as well.

Table III shows the execution times of the inverse solution on 256 CPU (first row) and 256 GPU (second row) nodes in seconds. The CPU solution employs a total of 4,096 floating-point cores and the GPU solution employs 2,048 cores and 256 GPUs. The speedup of GPU nodes over CPU nodes is shown in the last row. The construction of the required data structures as well as solution of the known object (which is not available in real-life problems) are included in the setup part (second column). The iterative solution times of the imaging problem are shown in the third column. The last column shows the time spend in the MLFMA multiplications, which constitute the most of the computation. Table III shows that the GPU

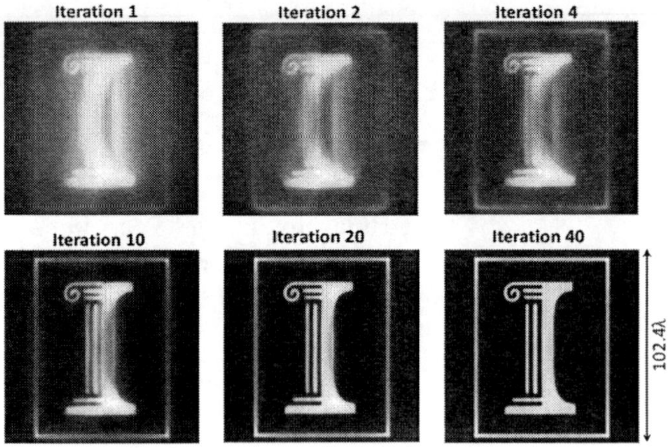

Fig. 1. Imaging of a 2-D logo larger than a hundred wavelengths. The object details can be clearly seen after 40 iterations. A total of 38,400 forward-scattering problems with one million unknowns are solved in 116 seconds on 256 computing nodes with GPUs. The same number of CPU nodes (refer to Table I for hardware details) solves the same problem in about 8.4 minutes.

nodes provide the final image approximately four times faster than the CPU nodes. Fig. 1 shows a few instances from the iterative solution of the inverse (imaging) problem.

TABLE III
EXECUTION TIMES (S) OF THE INVERSE SOLUTION

	Setup	Solution	Total	MLFMA
CPU Nodes	5.73	498.98	504.70	440.00
GPU Nodes	3.94	112.38	116.32	93.51
Speedup	1.45	4.44	4.34	4.71

IV. CONCLUSIONS

Supercomputer solutions of large inverse-scattering problems is demonstrated. The immense number of forward-scattering problems are distributed among GPU nodes and solved with MLFMA. For this purpose, MLFMA solver is efficiently implemented on GPUs. As a result, a very large object (with more than 100λ size and one million unknowns) is imaged on 256 GPU nodes in 116 seconds (near-real time). This is approximately four times faster than the same solution on an identical number of CPU nodes.

ACKNOWLEDGMENT

The authors would like to acknowledge allocation of computer time from NCSA Blue Waters (through NSF grants OCI-0725070 and ACI-1238993), NVIDIA GPU Center of Excellence grant, and NSF grant EECS-1609195.

REFERENCES

[1] W. C. Chew and Y.-M. Wang, "Reconstruction of two-dimensional permittivity distribution using the distorted Born iterative method," *IEEE Trans. Med. Imag.*, vol. 9, no. 2, pp. 218–225, 1990.

[2] A. J. Hesford and W. C. Chew, "Fast inverse scattering solutions using the distorted Born iterative method and the multilevel fast multipole algorithm," *J. Acoust. Soc. Am.*, vol. 128, pp. 679–690, Aug. 2010.

[3] M. Hidayetoğlu, C. Yang, L. Wang, A. Podkowa, M. L. Oelze, W.-M. Hwu, and W. C. Chew, "Parallel solutions of inverse multiple scattering problems with Born-type fast solvers," *PIERS Proc.*, Aug. 2016.

[4] J. Guan, S. Yan, and J.-M. Jin, "An OpenMP-CUDA implementation of multilevel fast multipole algorithm for electromagnetic simulation on multi-GPU computing systems," *IEEE Trans. Antennas Propag.*, vol. 61, no. 7, pp. 3607–3616, 2013.

Aircraft Electromagnetic Field Estimation for Wireless Avionics Intra-Communication Band Using Large-Scale FDTD Analysis

-Field Estimation of A320 Class Passenger Aircraft at 4 GHz Band-

Shunichi Futatsumori, Kazuyuki Morioka, Akiko Kohmura, Naruto Yonemoto
Surveillance and Communications Department, Electronic Navigation Research Institute
National Institute of Maritime, Port and Aviation Technology
Chofu, Tokyo, Japan
futatsumori@mpat.go.jp

Takashi Hikage, Kanji Yahagi, Masami Shirafune, Manabu Yamamoto, Toshio Nojima, Shoichi Narahashi
Graduate School of Information Science and Technology
Hokkaido University
Sapporo, Hokkaido, Japan
hikage@wtemc.ist.hokudai.ac.jp

***Abstract*—Electromagnetic compatibly (EMC) is required to be investigated for newly introduced on-board Wireless Avionics Intra-Communication (WAIC) systems. In this paper, the feasibility of the detailed electromagnetic field (EMF) estimation method for the Airbus A320 class passenger aircraft at 4 GHz band is discussed. Firstly, the three-dimensional analysis model based on Airbus A320-200 aircraft is developed for the EMF estimation using the large-scale finite-difference time-domain (FDTD) method. Then, the material constants and the FDTD analysis parameters are discussed. Finally, the analyzed EMF characteristics confirm the effectiveness of the EMC investigation at WAIC band using the numerical analysis.**

Keywords*—aircraft; avionics; electromagnetic compatibility; large scale finite-difference time-domain method; wireless avionics intra-commucation

I. INTRODUCTION

Assignment of the frequency band, which is allocated between 4,200 MHz and 4,400 MHz, for the Wireless Avionics Intra-Communication (WAIC) systems was carried out at the 2015 International Telecommunication Union world radiocommunication conference [1]. The WAIC systems are used for wireless communications around the avionics components [2]. The usage scenario and the standardization for the aircraft systems have been discussed in Radio Technical Commission for Aeronautics and European Organization for Civil Aviation Electronics. On the other hand, the electromagnetic compatibility (EMC) between WAIC devices and existing avionics systems is required to be investigated for further implementation.

For example, the radio altimeter, which antenna is shown in Fig. 1, utilizes the same frequency band as the WAIC systems. To investigate the EMC issues of the WAIC systems, the electromagnetic field (EMF) estimation method has been developed based on the large-scale finite-difference time-domain (FDTD) analysis [2], [3]. In this paper, the EMF distributions of Airbus A320 class passenger aircraft at 4 GHz band are analyzed and discussed to confirm the effectiveness of the EMC investigation using numerical analysis.

Fig. 1. Example of typical radio altimeter antenna equipped on the bottom of the Beechcraft B300 aircraft.

II. ANALYSIS MODEL

To investigate the feasibility of the numerical analysis method for the whole passenger aircraft at 4 GHz, the three-dimensional analysis model based on Airbus A320-200 is developed. Fig. 2 and Fig. 3 show the overview of the analysis model and cabin configurations. As shown in the figures, the outlines and internal structure are designed to have the dimensions of the actual aircraft. In addition, Table I shows the parameters of the aircraft model. The aircraft structures such as the body, the cabin partition, the lavatory, galley, and celling luggage rack consists of the perfect electric conductor (PEC). On the other hand, some structures such as the seats, cabin floor, inside panel wall, and windows have limited electric conductivity. This is because some materials used inside the aircraft cabin are non-flammable materials, which have

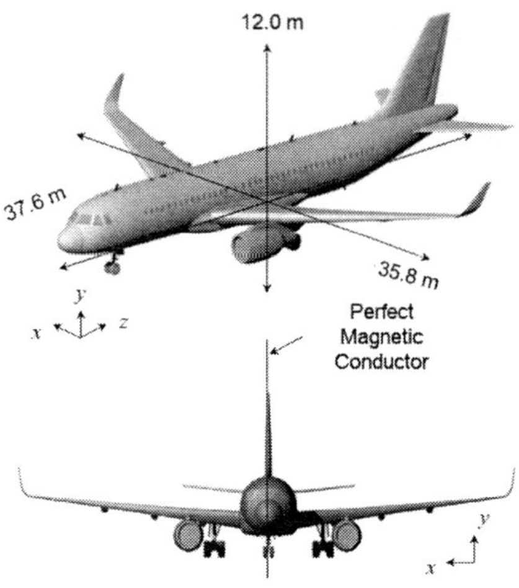

Fig. 2. Aircraft anaysis model based on Airbus A320-200.

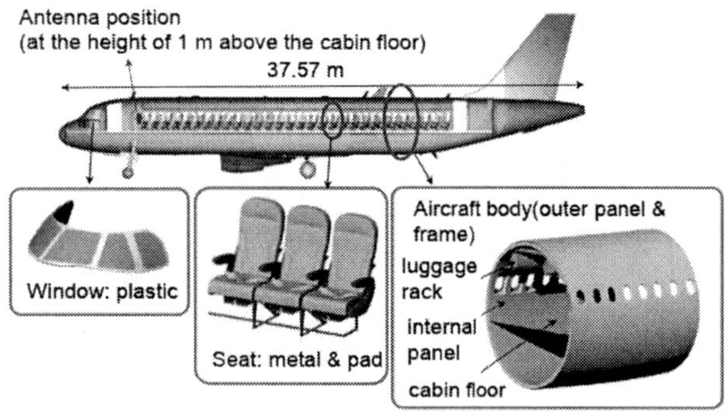

Fig. 3. Cabin configurations of the aircraft model.

electromagnetic lossy characteristics. No passengers are modeled to obtain the fundamental characteristics of the EMF propagation. The transmitting antenna is located at 1 m above the cabin floor as shown in Fig. 3.

III. Analyzed E-field Strength at 4 GHz

Table II shows the parameters of the FDTD analysis. The uniform 5 mm cubic cells are used for the analysis. In addition, to reduce the size of the required memory, the perfect magnetic conductor is modeled on the center of the aircraft. The number of cells including the 10-layer convolutional perfectly matched layer (CPML) absorbing boundary condition (A. B. C.) are 3,625×2,449×7,525. Assuming the WAIC device is operated at the 4 GHz band, the transmitting frequency is 4.4 GHz. The HITACHI SR16000 model M-1 supercomputer is employed for the analysis. The number of analysis nodes and required memory is 40 nodes and 6,400 GB, respectively.

Fig. 4 shows the typical analyzed two-dimensional E-field strength distributions along the *xz*-axis. As shown in this figure, the detailed EMF distributions are obtained both inside and outside the aircraft. In this case, the transmitting antenna is located inside the cabin, however, the interference pass loss values for the radio altimeter can be calculated when the radio altimeter antenna is used as the transmitting antenna.

TABLE I. Parameters of Aircraft Materials

Media	ε_r	σ (S/m)
Free space	1.0	0
Aircraft body, Seat (metal)	-	∞ (PEC)
Seat (pad)	2.0	3.02×10^{-3}
Cabin partition, Labatory, Galley, Celling luggage rack	-	∞ (PEC)
Cabin floor, Inside panel wall	3.5	1.51
Window	2.25	8.34×10^{-4}

TABLE II. Parameters of FDTD Analysis

Problem Space (mm^3)	18,125×12,245×37,625
Cell size (mm)	5
Number of cells	3,625×2,449×7,525
Frequency (GHz)	4.4
A. B. C.	CPML (10 layers)
Number of nodes	40
Required memory	6,400 GB
Antenna	1/2 dipole (0.1 W input power)

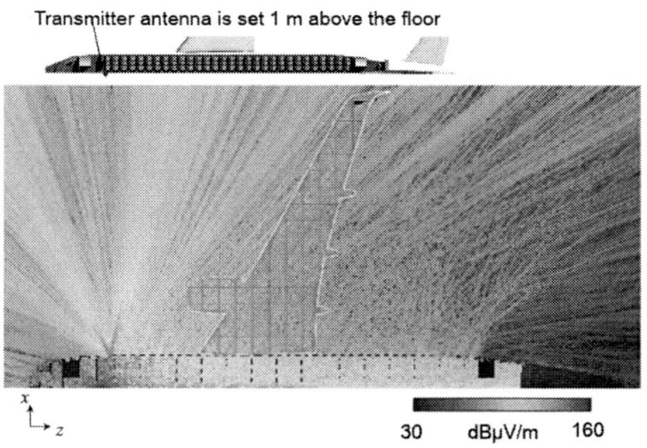

Fig. 4. Typical analyzed two-dimensional E-field strength distributions along the *xz*-axis.

IV. Conclusion

The EMF estimation method for the A320 class passenger aircraft at 4 GHz band was discussed for the EMC investigation of the future WAIC systems. The FDTD analysis, which used more than 6 TB analysis memory based on the supercomputer, successfully demonstrated the estimation of detailed EMF propagation at the WAIC frequency band.

References

[1] International Telecommunication Union, Resolution 424 of World Radiocommunication Conference 2015, "Use of wireless avionics intra-communications in the frequency band 4200-4400 MHz," Nov. 2015.

[2] International Telecommunication Union, "Technical characteristics and operational objectives for wireless avionics intra-communications (WAIC)," Report M.2197-0, Nov. 2011.

[3] T. Hikage, K. Yahagi, M. Shirafune, T. Nojima, S. Futatsumori, A. Kohmura and N. Yonemoto, "Numerical estimation of WAIC-band propagation characteristics in aircraft cabin using large-scale FDTD analysis," Proceedings of the 2016 IEEE International Symposium on Antennas and Propagation and USNC-URSI National Radio Science Meeting, TH-UB.5P.6, June 2016.

A Uniform Geometrical Theory of Diffraction Formulation for the Diffraction by a Perfect Electric Conductor and Impedance finite width strip

Mohammad Rashedi
Ghiaseddin Jamshid Kashani Higher Education Institute
Qazvin, Iran
mohammadrashedi10@gmail.com

Abdorreza Torabi
School of Engineering, Faculty of Engineering Science
University of Tehran
Tehran, Iran
ab.reza.torabi@ut.ac.ir

***Abstract*—In this paper, the total far-field pattern around a finite width strip in presence of an electric line source using perfect electric conductor (PEC) and impedance strip equations are presented. We used two dimensional uniform geometrical theory of diffraction (UTD) in both analysis for soft (TM) polarization. For finite PEC strip, we used PEC strip equations and for finite impedance strip we used impedance edge equations presented by Tiberio. These solutions are formatted in terms of diffraction coefficient in both PEC and impedance surfaces. Diffraction coefficient equations have Maliuzhinets terms which are replaced by equations presented by Tiberio for n=2 which refers to half plane.**

Keywords — diffraction, UTD, GTD, finite strip, impedance.

I. Introduction

Several authors have worked on UTD and GTD methods. UTD has been developed for many years and it widely and successfully employed in a variety applications involving edge diffraction in PEC and impedance surfaces. Objects with impedance surfaces have been interested in diverse applications. Diffraction by edge has been worked by [2] and several other authors [1], [3], [4]. Edges, cons, exterior and interior wedges and curve structures have an effective role in diffraction Phenomenon. So, these parts of obstacle have been interested in many basic problems such as diffraction by wedge, cylinder, sphere and pyramid. UTD is used for many applications nowadays.

II. Geometry Of Strip

An electric line source of infinite length is placed symmetrically a distance h above strip are shown in Fig. 1. Width of strip is $w=2\lambda$ and h is 0.5λ that λ refers to wavelength in 30 gigahertz. As shown in Fig. 1, incident shadow boundaries (ISB) and reflected shadow boundaries (RSB) segmented space around the strip to four regions. Total far-field in region I is obtained from sum of incident, reflected and diffracted terms of field. In region II and IV, incident and diffracted fields are present. In region III just diffracted field affects.

III. Perfect Electric Conductor Strip

To calculate the total far-field around PEC strip, we used the equations presented in [1]. Equations (1) and (2) show respectively the incident and reflected fields in this section.

$$E^i = E_0 \exp(+j\,\beta\, h\ sin\varphi)\frac{\exp(-j\beta\rho)}{\sqrt{\rho}} \quad (1)$$

$$E^r = -\,E_0 \exp(-j\,\beta\, h\ sin\varphi)\frac{\exp(-j\beta\rho)}{\sqrt{\rho}} \quad (2)$$

$$E_0 = -\frac{\beta^2 I_0}{4\omega\varepsilon}\sqrt{\frac{2j}{\pi\beta}} \quad (3)$$

$$\beta = \omega\sqrt{\varepsilon_0\,\mu_0} \quad (4)$$

Where μ_0 , ε_0 and ω respectively refer to vacuum permeability, vacuum permittivity and angular frequency. In (2), the reflect coefficient is assumed -1 for PEC strip. The diffracted field is obtained from (5) and (6) which refer to diffracted fields from edge 1 and 2.

$$E^{d1} = E_0\frac{\exp(-j\beta\rho)}{\sqrt{\rho}}\,D(\rho,\psi_1,\alpha,2)\exp(+j\,\beta\,\frac{w}{2}\cos\varphi)\,\frac{\exp(-j\beta\rho)}{\sqrt{\rho}} \quad (5)$$

$$E^{d2} = E_0\frac{\exp(-j\beta\rho)}{\sqrt{\rho}}\,D(\rho,\psi_2,\alpha,2)\exp(-j\,\beta\,\frac{w}{2}\cos\varphi)\,\frac{\exp(-j\beta\rho)}{\sqrt{\rho}} \quad (6)$$

$$\psi_1 = \begin{cases}\pi-\varphi & 0 \ll \varphi \ll \pi\\ 3\pi-\varphi & \pi \ll \varphi \ll 2\pi\end{cases} \quad (7)$$

$$\psi_2 = \varphi \quad 0 \ll \varphi \ll 2\pi \quad (8)$$

$$D(\rho,\psi,\alpha,n) = \frac{\exp\left(-j\frac{\pi}{4}\right)}{2n\sqrt{2\pi\beta}}\Big(\Big\{\cot\left[\frac{\pi+(\psi-\alpha)}{2n}\right]F[\beta\rho g^+(\psi-\alpha)] + \cot\left[\frac{\pi-(\psi-\alpha)}{2n}\right]F[\beta\rho g^-(\psi-\alpha)]\Big\} - \Big\{\cot\left[\frac{\pi+(\psi+\alpha)}{2n}\right]F[\beta\rho g^+(\psi+\alpha)] + \cot\left[\frac{\pi-(\psi+\alpha)}{2n}\right]F[\beta\rho g^-(\psi+\alpha)]\Big\}\Big) \quad (9)$$

Where α is shown in Fig. 1. D represents Diffract coefficient and F is transition function which is explained in (10). g is presented in (11) and (12) with N being a positive or negative integer or zero that satisfies (13) and (14).

$$F(X) = 2j\sqrt{X}\exp(jX)\int_{\sqrt{X}}^{\infty}\exp(-j\tau^2)\,d\tau \quad (10)$$

$$g^+ = 1+\cos[(\psi\pm\alpha)-2n\pi N^+] \quad (11)$$

$$g^- = 1+\cos[(\psi\pm\alpha)-2n\pi N^-] \quad (12)$$

$$2n\pi N^+ - (\psi\pm\alpha) = +\pi \quad \text{for } g^+ \quad (13)$$

$$2n\pi N^- - (\psi\pm\alpha) = -\pi \quad \text{for } g^- \quad (14)$$

2017 International Applied Computational, Electromagnetics Society (ACES) Symposium, March 26-30, 2017, Firenze,

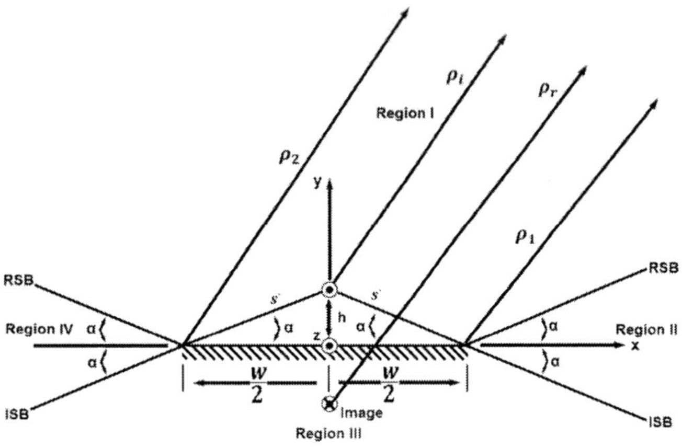

Fig. 1. Line source above a finite width strip.

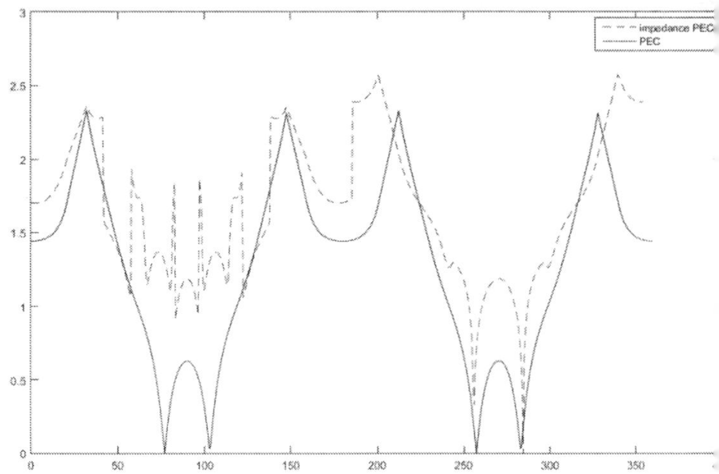

Fig. 2. pattern of diffracted field around a finite width strip in presence of a line source.

IV. Impedance Strip

For impedance strip, incident field is obtained from (1). Reflected coefficient for impedance surface comes from (15).

$$\Gamma_0(\varphi) = \frac{\sin\varphi - \sin\theta_0}{\sin\varphi + \sin\theta_0} \tag{15}$$

Diffraction coefficient is presented in (16).

$$D(\psi_1, \alpha, \theta_0, \theta_n; \beta\rho) = M_n(\psi_1, \alpha; \theta_0, \theta_n)$$

$$\{C_n(\psi_1, \alpha; \theta_0, \theta_n)[D^-(\beta^-: \beta\rho) + \Gamma_n(\alpha, \theta_0)D^-(\beta^+: \beta\rho)] +$$

$$C_n(n\pi - \psi_1, n\pi - \alpha; \theta_n, \theta_0)\ [D^+(\beta^-: \beta\rho) + \Gamma_n(\alpha, \theta_0)\ D^+(\beta^+: \beta\rho)]\} \tag{16}$$

The notations in (17) are explained in [2].

For PEC surface, sin θ is infinite. In this paper we used 1.36 – 36.94j for θ to approximate PEC strip. By using this θ, sin θ tends to a large number that is a good approximation.

V. Numerical Results

Smooth patterns of diffracted fields and total fields around PEC strip by applying two methods are shown respectively in Fig. 2 and Fig. 3. In Fig. 2 and Fig. 3, continuous line refers to the field around PEC strip and dashed lines refer to the field around impedance strip with very small impedance. In Fig. 3, we have one more pattern which refers to total fields around PEC strip by using HFSS software to simulate this problem. Fig. 3 shows that we have reached to a valid and accurate results. It should be noted that we used dB normalized format of field to plot the patterns in all results.

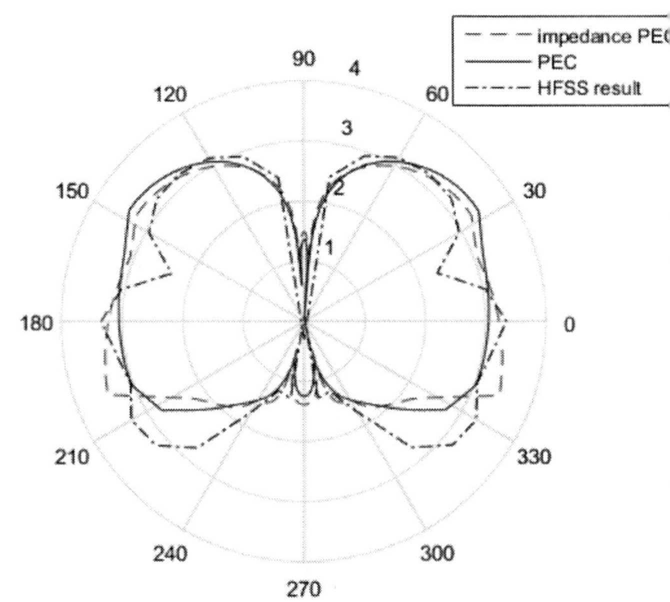

Fig. 3. Radiation amplitude pattern of electric line source above a finite width strip.

VI. Conclution

A high frequency solution to the diffraction by a finite width strip with two edges in presence of a line source for TM polarization has been presented in this paper. To show the pattern of diffracted fields and total fields of finite PEC strip and finite impedance strip in presence of an electric line source, we used two equations for diffraction coefficient and results of simulations are shown together in Fig. 2 and Fig. 3. It is clear that two results have a good agreement with each other and the approximation for impedance is a good approximation. In this article we presented a double edge structure which is one of the basic structures used in complex structures.

References

[1] Constantine A. Balanis, "Advance Engineer Electromagnetics," Arizona State University, 2nd ed, 2012.

[2] R. Tiberio, G. Pelosi and G. Manara, "A uniform GTD formulation for the diffraction by a wedge with impedance faces," IEEE Trans. Antennas Propagat., vol. AP-33, no. 8, pp. 867–873, Aug. 1985.

[3] J. J. Bowman, "High-frequency backscattering from an absorbing infinite strip with arbitrary face impedances," Canadian J. Physics, vol. 45, pp. 2409–2430, 1967.

[4] R. G. Kouyoumjian and P. H. Pathak, "A uniform geometrical theory of diffraction for an edge in a perfectly conducting surface," Proc. ZEEE, vol. 62, pp. 1448-1481, Nov. 1974

[5] G. D. Maliuzhinets, "Excitation, reflection and emission of surface waves from a wedge with a given face impedances,"Soviet Physics, Doklady, vol. 3, pp. 752–755, 1958.

Design of Rotatable Metasurface Microstrip Antenna with Reconfigurable Polarization

Felipe F. Araújo, Adaildo G. D'Assunção, Luis F. V. T. Costa, and William S. Alves
Department of Communication Engineering
Federal University of Rio Grande do Norte
Natal, Brazil
felipeffe@gmail.com, adaildo@ct.ufrn.br, luisfelipevcosta@gmail.com, william.gppcom@gmail.com,

***Abstract*—This paper presents the design of rotatable metasurface microstrip antennas with reconfigurable polarization. The structure consists of a circular metasurface placed on a circular microstrip antenna, both with diameters of 78 mm, to simplify the metasurface rotation enabling the reconfiguration from linear to circular polarization. A mechanically rotatable metasurface antenna structure is fabricated using a 3D printer and a very precise step motor, remotely controlled. The proposed antenna is designed to operate at 3.0 ~ 3.2 GHz, using Ansoft HFSS. A prototype of the proposed antenna geometry is fabricated and measured for comparison purpose. The antenna performance in terms of return loss and axial ratio is presented.**

Keywords—Metasurface microstrip antenna; rotatable antenna; reconfigurable antenna; polarization reconfiguration

I. INTRODUCTION

The exponential growth in the demand for wireless communication systems has required the evolution of the telecommunications technological apparatus. Thus, the integration of multiple wireless services on a single platform through reconfigurable antennas, for example, is attracting much attention of many researchers worldwide [1]-[4].

Lately, metasurface (MS) structures have been extensively investigated for improving microwave circuits, such as compact antennas, to provide frequency and polarization reconfiguration [5], [6], for example. For many applications in communications systems, metasurfaces can be used instead of metamaterials because they have the advantage of using smaller physical space than the tridimensional (3D) metamaterial structures, offering the possibility of reduced loss and lower cost of production [5], [6].

This paper main objective is to design and fabricate printed antennas coupled to metasurface structures in order to perform antenna polarization reconfiguration for application in wireless communications systems [5], [6].

II. PROPOSED ANTENNA STRUCTURE

The microstrip antenna structure is composed of a thin rectangular conducting patch printed on a dielectric surface placed on a ground plane with a thin rectangular slot. The dielectric substrate is fiber glass (FR-4). The antenna is fed by a 50 Ω coaxial cable using a SMA connector. The metasurface is a finite array of rectangular unit cells constituted by two parallel coupled rings with trapezoidal shapes (Fig. 1). To facilitate the antenna fabrication and rotation processes, the metasurface is printed on a circular dielectric layer with the same diameter of the microstrip antenna. The mechanically rotatable structure is fabricated using a 3D printer and a very precise step motor, remotely controlled, to get good rotation accuracy and also minimize friction between the laminates.

The proposed metasurface microstrip antenna is mounted by placing the side without copper of the metasurface (MS) laminate on top of the microstrip antenna dipole. This leads to a very good profile structure, with low thickness (Fig. 1). The microstrip dipole is oriented along y axis.

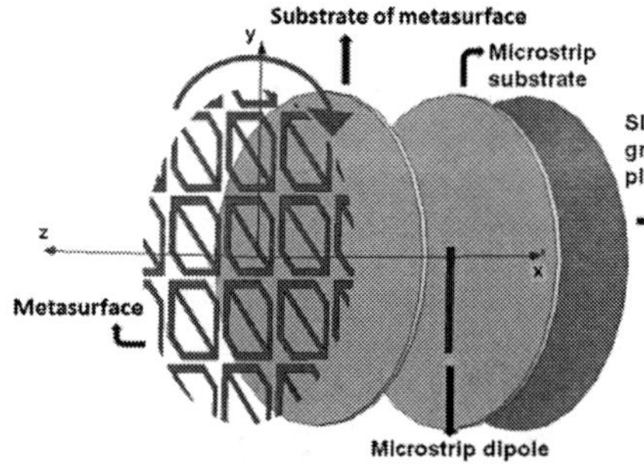

Fig. 1. Illustration of the antenna structure for reconfigurable polarization.

Fig. 2 indicates the structural parameters of the microstrip antenna dipole, slotted ground plane, and metasurface element. The antenna dimensions (in millimeters) are: D_1 = 98, D_2 = 78, W_{sg} = 20, L_{sg} = 3, W_p=2.5, L_p=24.5, L_{m1}=1.41, L_{m2}=18.7, and W_m=26.2 (mm). The unit cell overall dimensions are T_x=19.72 mm and T_y=20.46 mm.

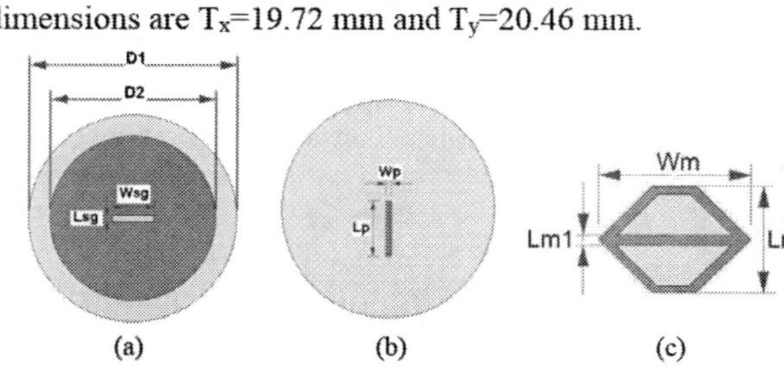

Fig. 2. Rotatable metasurface microstrip antenna parts. Microstrip antenna dipole (a), slotted ground plane (b), and metasurface element.

The reconfiguration of the antenna polarization can be reached rotating the MS structure around the center of the antenna. For example, it is possible to change the antenna polarization from linear to circular.

III. Simulated and Measured Results

The effect of placing a metasurface above a microstrip dipole is analyzed using Ansoft HFSS. Simulation results of the return loss and axial ratio of the metasurface antenna are presented. Prototypes are fabricated and measured for validation purpose. Simulation and measurements results are presented for the frequency range from 2.5 GHz to 3.5 GHz. Figs. 5 and 6 show return loss results for the metasurface antenna with rotation angles of 0° and 45°, respectively. Initially, the parallel sides of the unit cell ring elements are oriented along x axis, corresponding to an angle rotation of 0°. Then, the metasurface is rotated clockwise.

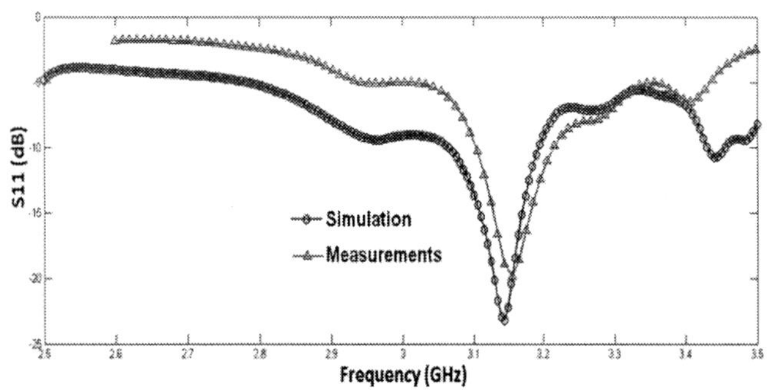

Fig. 5. Measurements and simulation results of the rotatable metasurface antenna return loss for an angle rotation of 0°.

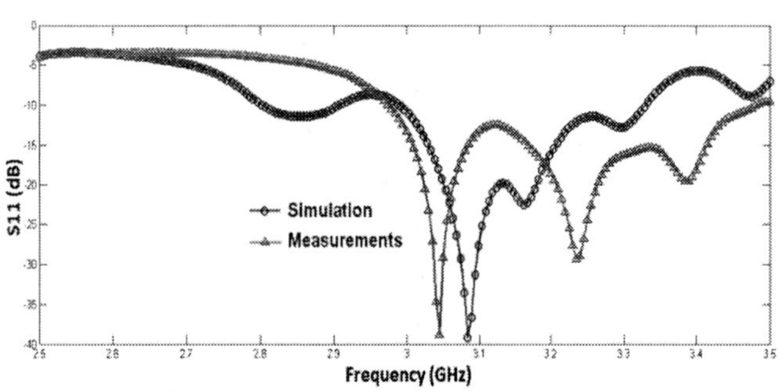

Fig. 6. Measurements and simulation results of the rotatable metasurface antenna return loss for an angle rotation of 45°.

For pure circular polarization, the axial ratio value is 1, or 0 dB. However, for axial ratio values lower than or equal to 3 dB, a circular polarization is considered. For axial ratio values higher than 3 dB the polarization deviates from circular to elliptical, and for very high values becomes linear. Fig. 7 shows that the axial ratio of the metasurface antenna with angle rotation of 0° is higher than 3 dB, at 3.15 GHz. Thus, the proposed antenna does not provide circular polarization. However, for an angle rotation of 45° the antenna axial ratio is lower than 3 dB, at 3.08 GHz, as shown in Fig. 8. Thus, the proposed antenna geometry provides circular polarization.

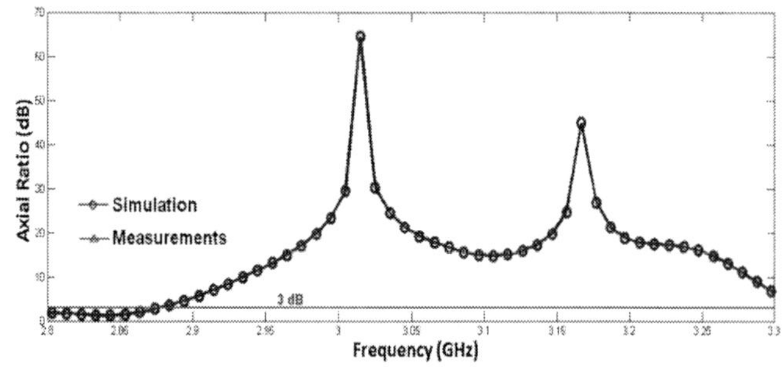

Fig. 7. Simulation results of the rotatable metasurface antenna axial ratio for an angle rotation of 0°.

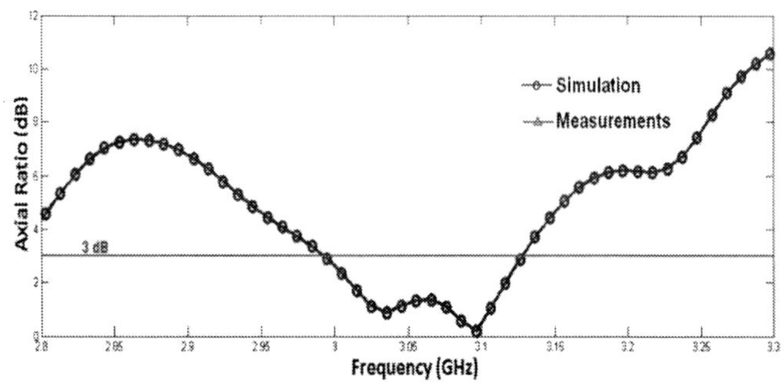

Fig. 8. Simulation results of the rotatable metasurface antenna axial ratio for an angle rotation of 45°.

IV. Conclusion

A rotatable metasurface microstrip antenna with reconfigurable polarization has been developed. The antenna geometry is composed of a microstrip dipole, with a slot on the ground plane, and a metasurface printed on a superstrate dielectric layer. The antenna polarization is reconfigurable through rotation of the metasurface structure. Results are shown for the antenna return loss and axial ratio, confirming the metasurface antenna polarization reconfiguration at about 3.0~3.2 GHz. Simulation and measurement results are in agreement.

References

[1] D. Peroulis, K. Sarabandi, and L.P.B. Katehi, "Design of reconfigurable slot antennas," IEEE Trans. Antennas Propag., vol. 53, pp. 645–654, 2005.

[2] R.L. Haupt and M. Lanagan, "Reconfigurable antennas," IEEE Antennas Propag. Mag., vol. 55, pp. 49–61, 2013.

[3] J. Costantine, Y. Tawk., S.E. Barbin, and C.G. Christodoulou, "Reconfigurable antennas: design and applications," Proc. IEEE, vol. 103, pp. 424-437, 2015.

[4] T.J. Jung, I.J. Hyeon, C.W. Baek, and S. Lim, "Circular/linear polarization reconfigurable antenna on simplified RF-MEMS packaging platform in K-band," IEEE Trans. Antennas Propag., vol. 60, pp. 5039-5045, 2012.

[5] H.L. Zhu, S. W. Cheung, X.H. Liu, and T.I. Yuk, "Design of polarization reconfigurable antenna using metasurface," IEEE Trans. Antennas Propag., vol. 62, pp. 2891-2898, 2014.

[6] H.L. Zhu, S.W. Cheung, K.L. Chung, and T.I. Yuk, "Linear-to-circular polarization conversion using metasurface," IEEE Trans. Antennas Propag., vol. 61, pp. 4615-4623, 2013.

A Speeding up Technique for Lossy Anisotropic Algorithm in FDTD Method

Fatih Kaburcuk
Electrical and Electronics Engineering Department
Erzurum Technical University
Erzurum, 25700, Turkey
fkaburcu@syr.edu

Atef Z. Elsherbeni
Electrical Engineering and Computer Science Department
Colorado School of Mines
Golden, CO 80401, USA
aelsherb@mines.edu

***Abstract*— In this paper, a speeding up technique is proposed to reduce the computation time of the lossy anisotropic (Lossy-ANI) algorithm integrated into the FDTD method. This algorithm is applied to a line-fed microstrip patch antenna (MPA) with anisotropic substrate and a Lossy-ANI scattering object. Numerical results show that the anisotropy effects the resonant frequencies of the MPA and the RCS of the scattering object.**

Keywords—FDTD; anisotropic medium

I. Introduction

A generalized 3D FDTD algorithm is formulated based on the Lossy-ANI algorithm to simulate an MPA with anisotropic substrate and a Lossy-ANI scattering object. The Lossy-ANI algorithm was proposed in [1] for the Lossy-ANI materials with permittivity and electric conductor tensors. This algorithm was extended in [2-3] for the Lossy-ANI materials with permittivity, permeability, magnetic, and electric conductor tensors.

The proposed speeding up technique provides remarkable reduction in the computation time of the Lossy-ANI algorithm. A line-fed MPA with anisotropic substrate, studied in [4] using the lossless anisotropic algorithm, and a Lossy-ANI scattering object are analyzed to investigate the simulation verification and its performance. Numerical results show that the scattering parameter of the MPA and the bistatic RCS of the scattering object are effected by the anisotropy.

II. Lossy-ANI Algorithm

A. Maxwell Equations for 3D Lossy-ANI Medium

The Maxwell equations for Lossy-ANI medium are

$$\nabla \times H = \bar{\bar{\varepsilon}}\frac{\partial E}{\partial t} + \bar{\bar{\sigma}}^e E \text{ and } \nabla \times E = -\bar{\bar{\mu}}\frac{\partial H}{\partial t} - \bar{\bar{\sigma}}^m H, \quad (1)$$

where $\bar{\bar{\varepsilon}}$, $\bar{\bar{\mu}}$, $\bar{\bar{\sigma}}^e$, and $\bar{\bar{\sigma}}^m$ are permittivity, permeability, electric and magnetic conductivity tensors, respectively. After some mathematical manipulation, one can obtain

$$E^{n+1} = \bar{\bar{p}}_e \cdot (\Delta \times H)^{n+\frac{1}{2}} + \bar{\bar{r}}_e \cdot E^n, \text{ and } H^{n+\frac{1}{2}} = \bar{\bar{p}}_m \cdot (\Delta \times E)^n + \bar{\bar{r}}_m \cdot H^{n-\frac{1}{2}}, \quad (2)$$

where

$$\bar{\bar{p}}_e = \left(\frac{\bar{\bar{\varepsilon}}}{\Delta t} + \frac{\bar{\bar{\sigma}}^e}{2}\right)^{-1}, \bar{\bar{r}}_e = \bar{\bar{p}}_e \cdot \left(\frac{\bar{\bar{\varepsilon}}}{\Delta t} - \frac{\bar{\bar{\sigma}}^e}{2}\right), \bar{\bar{p}}_m = \left(\frac{\bar{\bar{\mu}}}{\Delta t} + \frac{\bar{\bar{\sigma}}^m}{2}\right)^{-1}, \bar{\bar{r}}_m = p_m \cdot \left(\frac{\bar{\bar{\mu}}}{\Delta t} - \frac{\bar{\bar{\sigma}}^m}{2}\right), \quad (3)$$

The x component of the E- and H- fields in (2) are obtained after discretizing in space by the following equations:

$$E_x\Big|_{i-\frac{1}{2},j,k}^{n+1} = \begin{pmatrix} p_{e11}\left(\frac{\partial H_z}{\partial y}\Big|_{i-\frac{1}{2},j,k}^{n+\frac{1}{2}} - \frac{\partial H_y}{\partial z}\Big|_{i-\frac{1}{2},j,k}^{n+\frac{1}{2}}\right) + p_{e12}\left(\frac{\partial H_x}{\partial z}\Big|_{i-\frac{1}{2},j,k}^{n+\frac{1}{2}} - \frac{\partial H_z}{\partial x}\Big|_{i-\frac{1}{2},j,k}^{n+\frac{1}{2}}\right) \\ +p_{e13}\left(\frac{\partial H_y}{\partial x}\Big|_{i-\frac{1}{2},j,k}^{n+\frac{1}{2}} - \frac{\partial H_x}{\partial y}\Big|_{i-\frac{1}{2},j,k}^{n+\frac{1}{2}}\right) + r_{e11}E_x\Big|_{i-\frac{1}{2},j,k}^{n} + r_{e12}E_y\Big|_{i-\frac{1}{2},j,k}^{n} + r_{e13}E_z\Big|_{i-\frac{1}{2},j,k}^{n} \end{pmatrix}, \quad (4)$$

where the first subscript of the coefficients (p_{e11} and r_{e11}) refers to the type of the field and the second and third subscripts refer the element number of the matrix in (3).

Similarly, other components of E- and H- fields can be obtained. It is realized that i, j, and k indices used in equation (4) are not meant to give exact location where the fields are available. We must consider the exact location of the fields. Thus, linear interpolation is used to obtain the right location of fields in the Yee's cell. $E_y^n(i,j,k)$ and $E_z^n(i,j,k)$ in (4) are interpolated from neighboring quantities as follows:

$$E_y^n(i,j,k) = \frac{1}{4}\begin{pmatrix} E_y^n(i+1,j+1,k) + E_y^n(i,j+1,k) \\ +E_y^n(i+1,j,k) + E_y^n(i,j,k) \end{pmatrix}, \quad (5.a)$$

$$E_z^n(i,j,k) = \frac{1}{4}\begin{pmatrix} E_z^n(i+1,j,k+1) + E_z^n(i,j,k+1) \\ +E_z^n(i+1,j,k) + E_z^n(i,j,k) \end{pmatrix}. \quad (5.b)$$

The spatial derivatives of H- fields in (4) can be obtained using the following approximations

$$\frac{\partial H_z^{n+\frac{1}{2}}(i,j,k)}{\partial y} = \frac{1}{dy}\left(H_z^n(i,j+1,k) - H_z^n(i,j,k)\right), \quad (6.a)$$

$$\frac{\partial H_y^{n+\frac{1}{2}}(i,j,k)}{\partial z} = \frac{1}{dz}\left(H_y^n(i,j,k) - H_y^n(i,j,k-1)\right), \quad (6.b)$$

$$\frac{\partial H_x^{n+\frac{1}{2}}(i,j,k)}{\partial z} = \frac{0.25}{dz}\begin{pmatrix} H_x^n(i+1,j+1,k) + H_x^n(i,j+1,k) \\ +H_x^n(i+1,j,k) + H_x^n(i,j,k) \\ -H_x^n(i,j+1,k-1) - H_x^n(i+1,j,k-1) \\ -H_x^n(i+1,j+1,k-1) - H_x^n(i,j,k-1) \end{pmatrix}, \quad (6.c)$$

$$\frac{\partial H_x^{n+\frac{1}{2}}(i,j,k)}{\partial y} = \frac{0.25}{dy}\begin{pmatrix} H_x^n(i+1,j+1,k) + H_x^n(i,j+1,k) \\ +H_x^n(i+1,j,k-1) + H_x^n(i,j,k) \\ -H_x^n(i+1,j+1,k-1) - H_x^n(i,j+1,k-1) \\ -H_x^n(i+1,j,k-1) - H_x^n(i,j,k-1) \end{pmatrix}, \quad (6.d)$$

$$\frac{\partial H_z^{n+\frac{1}{2}}(i,j,k)}{\partial x} = \frac{0.25}{dx}\begin{pmatrix} H_x^n(i+2,j+1,k) + H_x^n(i+2,j,k) \\ -H_x^n(i,j+1,k) - H_x^n(i,j,k) \end{pmatrix}, \quad (6.e)$$

$$\frac{\partial H_y^{n+\frac{1}{2}}(i,j,k)}{\partial x} = \frac{0.25}{dx}\begin{pmatrix} H_y^n(i+2,j,k) + H_y^n(i+2,j,k-1) \\ -H_y^n(i,j,k) - H_y^n(i,j,k-1) \end{pmatrix}. \quad (6.f)$$

Now the x-component of the E- field in (4) can be updated using (5) and (6). Similarly, other component of the E- and H- fields can be updated.

B. A Speeding up Technique for Lossy-ANI Medium

With this Lossy-ANI algorithm, the E- and H- fields are produced by off-diagonal elements of anisotropic tensors are calculated in the entire computational domain as in [1-3]. It is realized that a considerable amount of computation time is spent for the calculation of these fields. Therefore, a speeding up technique is proposed here to reduce the computation time. In this technique, the fields produced by off-diagonal elements of anisotropic tensors are calculated in the region that contains anisotropic object whereas the fields produced by diagonal elements of anisotropic tensors are calculated in the entire computational domain. Then, the sum of these fields are considered as the total fields for the next time-step. This technique provides 70% reduction in the computation time.

III. Numerical Results

The program is based on [5] and is written and compiled in 64-bit MATLAB version 8.2.0.701 (R2013b).

A. A Line-Fed MPA with Anisotropic Substrate

A line-fed MPA with anisotropic substrate shown in Fig. 1 is analyzed to verify the efficiency of the Lossy-ANI algorithm. The discretization of the antenna in each direction are set to dx=0.3891 mm, dy=0.4 mm, and dz=0.1985 mm. The rectangular patch size is (31 dx)×(40 dy). The feeding line size is (6 dx)×(30 dy). A Gaussian pulse is chosen as a source for the MPA. The simulation is performed for 6000 time-steps.

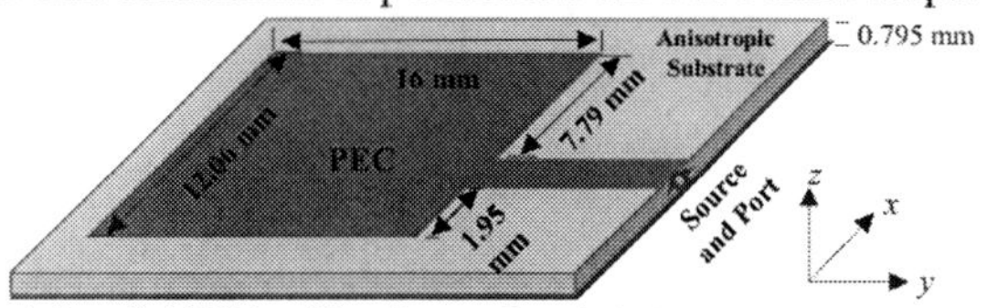

Fig. 1: A line-fed MPA with anisotropic substrate.

The elements of permittivity and permeability tensors for the anisotropic substrate are then given as follows:

$$\begin{aligned} &\varepsilon_{xx} = \varepsilon_1 \cos^2\theta + \varepsilon_2 \sin^2\theta, \varepsilon_{yy} = \varepsilon_1, \varepsilon_{zz} = \varepsilon_1 \sin^2\theta + \varepsilon_2 \cos^2\theta \\ &\varepsilon_{xz} = \varepsilon_{zx} = (\varepsilon_1 - \varepsilon_2) \sin\theta \cos\theta, \varepsilon_{xy} = \varepsilon_{yx} = \varepsilon_{yz} = \varepsilon_{zy} = 0 \\ &\mu_{xx} = \mu_1 \cos^2\theta + \mu_2 \sin^2\theta, \mu_{yy} = \mu_1, \mu_{zz} = \mu_1 \sin^2\theta + \mu_2 \cos^2\theta, \\ &\mu_{xz} = \mu_{zx} = (\mu_1 - \mu_2) \sin\theta \cos\theta, \mu_{xy} = \mu_{yx} = \mu_{yz} = \mu_{zy} = 0 \end{aligned} \quad (7)$$

where θ is the angle between the optical axis and the x-direction. The S_{11} as a function of θ obtained using the Lossy-ANI algorithm is shown in Fig. 2 when ε_1=2.35, ε_2=2.05, μ_1=1.15, and μ_2=0.85 in (7). It can be observed from Fig. 2 that the resonant frequencies of the MPA are effected by the anisotropic substrate. The computation time of the MPA with the speeding up technique is 13 min 55 s whereas those without the speeding up technique is 49 min 57 s. Therefore, the technique provides 72% reduction in the computation time.

B. Lossy-ANI Scattering Object

To further verify the efficiency of the Lossy-ANI algorithm with the speeding up technique, a lossy anisotropic sphere with radius of 0.4 m, is analyzed. The discretization of the sphere in each direction is 0.025 m. This sphere is excited by a θ-polarized plane wave with θ^{inc}=90° and ϕ^{inc}=90°. The simulation is performed for 2000 time steps.

Three different cases for the anisotropic sphere are considered in this simulation. In the first case, the material parameters of the anisotropic sphere are given as follows:

$$\bar{\bar{\varepsilon}} = \varepsilon_o \begin{bmatrix} 2.2 & 1.8 & 0 \\ 1.8 & 2.2 & 0 \\ 0 & 0 & 2.2 \end{bmatrix}, \bar{\bar{\mu}} = \mu_o \begin{bmatrix} 2 & 1.6 & 0 \\ 1.6 & 2 & 0 \\ 0 & 0 & 2 \end{bmatrix}, \bar{\bar{\sigma}}^e = \begin{bmatrix} 0.85 & 0.7 & 0 \\ 0.7 & 0.85 & 0 \\ 0 & 0 & 0.85 \end{bmatrix} \frac{s}{m}, \bar{\bar{\sigma}}^m = \begin{bmatrix} 0.65 & 0.5 & 0 \\ 0.5 & 0.65 & 0 \\ 0 & 0 & 0.65 \end{bmatrix} \frac{\Omega}{m}, \quad (8)$$

In the second case, the material parameters of the anisotropic sphere are given as follows:

$$\bar{\bar{\varepsilon}} = \varepsilon_o \begin{bmatrix} 2.2 & 0 & 1.8 \\ 0 & 2.2 & 0 \\ 1.8 & 0 & 2.2 \end{bmatrix}, \bar{\bar{\mu}} = \mu_o \begin{bmatrix} 2 & 0 & 1.6 \\ 0 & 2 & 0 \\ 1.6 & 0 & 2 \end{bmatrix}, \bar{\bar{\sigma}}^e = \begin{bmatrix} 0.85 & 0 & 0.7 \\ 0 & 0.85 & 0 \\ 0.7 & 0 & 0.85 \end{bmatrix} \frac{s}{m}, \bar{\bar{\sigma}}^m = \begin{bmatrix} 0.65 & 0 & 0.5 \\ 0 & 0.65 & 0 \\ 0.5 & 0 & 0.65 \end{bmatrix} \frac{\Omega}{m}, \quad (9)$$

In the third case, the material parameters of the anisotropic sphere are given as follows:

$$\bar{\bar{\varepsilon}} = \varepsilon_o \begin{bmatrix} 2.2 & 0 & 0 \\ 0 & 2.2 & 1.8 \\ 0 & 1.8 & 2.2 \end{bmatrix}, \bar{\bar{\mu}} = \mu_o \begin{bmatrix} 2 & 0 & 0 \\ 0 & 2 & 1.6 \\ 0 & 1.6 & 2 \end{bmatrix}, \bar{\bar{\sigma}}^e = \begin{bmatrix} 0.85 & 0 & 0 \\ 0 & 0.85 & 0.7 \\ 0 & 0.7 & 0.85 \end{bmatrix} \frac{s}{m}, \bar{\bar{\sigma}}^m = \begin{bmatrix} 0.65 & 0 & 0 \\ 0 & 0.65 & 0.5 \\ 0 & 0.5 & 0.65 \end{bmatrix} \frac{\Omega}{m}, \quad (10)$$

The bistatic RCS for the xy plane cut in Fig. 3 is computed at 300 MHz for the three cases with the material parameters in (8)-(10) and compared with that generated using the isotropic sphere when the material parameters are set to ε_r=2.2, μ_r=2, σ^e=0.85$\frac{s}{m}$, and σ^m=0.65$\frac{\Omega}{m}$. It can be seen from Fig. 3 that the anisotropy in the sphere effects the magnitude of the RCS. The computation time of the anisotropic sphere with the speeding up technique is 4 min 12 s whereas those without the speeding up technique 14 min 56 s. Therefore, the speeding up technique provides 72% reduction in the computation time.

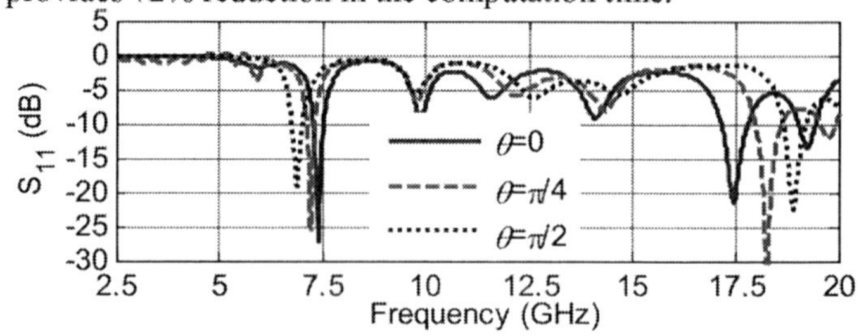

Fig. 2: S_{11} of the MPA as a function of θ obtained from Lossy-ANI algorithm.

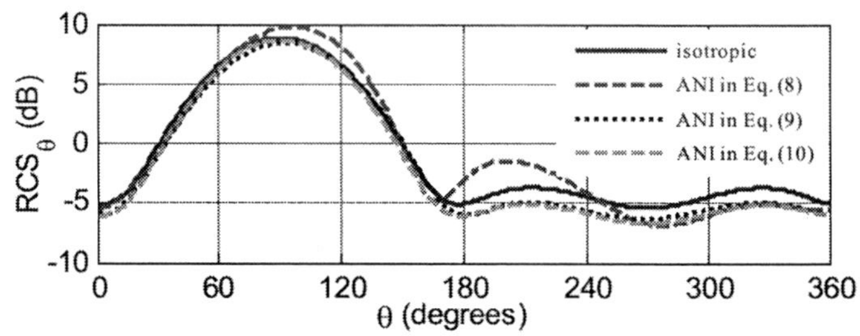

Fig. 3: Bistatic RCS for the xy plane cut.

IV. Conclusion

In this paper, the performance of a 3D FDTD algorithm based on the Lossy-ANI algorithm is presented in terms of computation time for solving the line-fed MPA with anisotropic substrate and the lossy anisotropic scattering object. The speeding up technique proposed here provides remarkable reduction in the computation time for configurations containing lossy anisotropic material. Numerical results show that the operating resonant frequencies of the MPA and magnitude of the bistatic RCS obtained from the scattering object are effected by the anisotropy of the material used.

References

[1] J. Schneider, S. Hudson, "The finite-difference time-domain method applied to anisotropic material", IEEE Trans. on Antennas and Propagat., vol. 41, pp. 994–999, July 1993.

[2] L. X. Yang, G. Wang, and S. Yan, "Parallel ANI-FDTD implementation for electromagnetic scattering by both electric and magnetic anisotropic medium", Microwave and Optical Technology Letters / Vol. 50, No. 5, May 2008.

[3] H. Zhang, Z. Li, Y. Wang, J. Wang, "Studying on the parallel FDTD algorithm for calculating the EM scattering from anisotropic ellipsoid", Cross Strait Quad-Regional Radio Science and Wireless Technology Conference (CSQRWC), 2011. Vol. 1. IEEE, 2011.

[4] A. P. Zhao, J. Juntunen, and A. V. Raisanen, "An efficient FDTD algortihm for the analysis of microstrip patch antennas printed on a general anisotropic substrate," *IEEE Trans. Microwave Theory Tech.*, vol. 47, pp. 1142–1146, 1999

[5] A. Z. Elsherbeni and V. Demir, *The Finite-Difference Time-Domain Method for Electromagnetics with MATLAB Simulations, second edition,* ACES Series on Computational Electromagnetics and Engineering, SciTech Publishing, an Imprint of IET, Edison, NJ, 2016.

Rapid Design Optimization of Compact Couplers Using Response Features and Adjoint Sensitivities

Slawomir Koziel[1,2] and Adrian Bekasiewicz[1,2]

[1] School of Science and Engineering
Reykjavik University, Reykjavik, Iceland
koziel@ru.is, bekasiewicz@ru.is

[2] Faculty of Electronics, Telecommunications and Informatics
Gdansk University of Technology
Gdansk, Poland

***Abstract*—A technique for rapid EM-driven design optimization of compact microwave couplers is presented. Our approach exploits response features and adjoint sensitivities and allows for low-cost design closure both in terms of performance enhancement and structure miniaturization. It is demonstrated using a compact rat-race coupler working at 1 GHz and compared to adjoint-based gradient optimization.**

Keywords—Design optimization, compact couplers, EM-driven design, response features, adjoint sensitivity.

I. INTRODUCTION

Reliable design of miniaturized microwave structures is a challenging task. Due to significant cross-coupling effects in tightly arrange layouts, equivalent circuit models lack accuracy so that design process has to involve full-wave EM analysis [1]. Furthermore, there are several figures of interest that have to be accounted for, e.g., operating frequency, bandwidth, power split, phase response, as well as the circuit size [2]. Interactive design approaches (e.g., parameter sweeping) are incapable of simultaneous handling of both the structure geometry and its electrical characteristics. Truly optimum design can only be found through rigorous numerical optimization [3]. Unfortunately, conventional optimization techniques (e.g., gradient-based optimization with numerical derivatives [4] or population-based metaheuristics [5]) are characterized by high, and often unacceptable, computational cost. Design speedup can be achieved by exploiting adjoint sensitivities [6] or surrogate-assisted techniques [3] such as space mapping [3], response correction methods [7], and, recently, feature-based optimization [8].

In this paper we demonstrate rapid design closure of compact microwave couplers using a combination of feature-based optimization (FBO) [8] with adjoint sensitivities [6]. FBO allows for cost reduction by appropriate reformulation of the design problem in terms of so-called response features, it can be further sped up by estimating feature point gradient using adjoints rather than finite differentiation [4]. Here, this approach is demonstrated using a 1-GHz compact rat-race coupler and compared to traditional adjoint-based optimization at the S-parameter response level.

II. FEATURE-BASED OPTIMIZATION WITH ADJOINTS

The problem at hand can be formulated as follows

$$x^* = \arg\min_x U(\boldsymbol{R}(x)) \quad (1)$$

where $\boldsymbol{R}(x)$ is an EM-simulated model of the structure of interest; U is an objective function that encodes performance specifications; $\boldsymbol{x}$ is a vector of design variables.

Responses of coupler structures are highly nonlinear and difficult to handle through optimization. Computational speedup can be obtained by reformulating the problem in terms of suitably-defined response features [9] as shown in Fig. 1. As we are interested in controlling the operating frequency, –20 dB bandwidth, and power split, the feature points correspond to minimum of matching and isolation characteristics, $|S_{21}|$ and $|S_{31}|$ at the required operating frequency, as well as the frequencies corresponding to –20 dB levels of $|S_{11}|$ and $|S_{41}|$ (necessary for bandwidth calculation). Feature-based optimization (FBO) benefits from the dependence of the feature point coordinates on geometry parameters of the structure being less nonlinear than for S-parameters vs. frequency. This leads to simplifying the functional landscape to be optimized.

We denote by $\boldsymbol{p}^j(\boldsymbol{x}) = [f^j(\boldsymbol{x})\ r^j(\boldsymbol{x})]^T$, $j = 1, \ldots, M$, the feature points of the response vector $\boldsymbol{R}(\boldsymbol{x})$ (f and r are the frequency and magnitude components). The original problem (1) is reformulated in the feature space as

$$x^* = \arg\min_x U_F(\boldsymbol{P}(x)) \quad (2)$$

Here, U_F is the objective function in the feature space (equivalent to U for the original response $\boldsymbol{R}(\boldsymbol{x})$); $\boldsymbol{P} = [(\boldsymbol{p}^1)^T \ldots (\boldsymbol{p}^M)^T]^T$ is the vector of aggregated feature points.

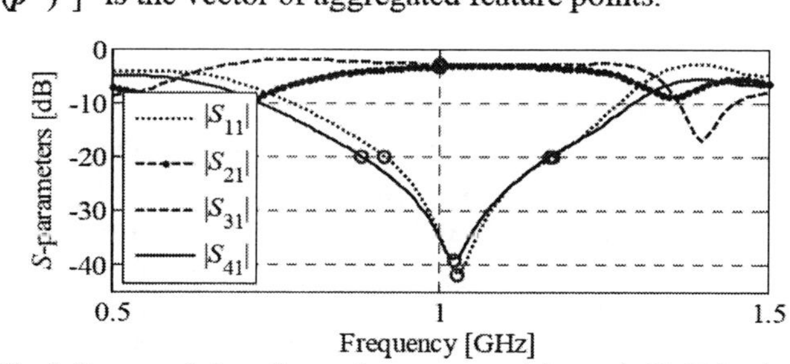

Fig. 1. Response features for coupler structures: minima and –20-dB-levels points of $|S_{11}|$ and $|S_{41}|$ as well as $|S_{21}|$ and $|S_{31}|$ values at the required operating frequency.

Our optimization technique produces a sequence of approximate solutions to (2), $x^{(j)}, j = 0, 1, \ldots$, by solving

$$x^{(i+1)} = \arg \min_{x:\|x-x^{(i)}\| \le \delta^{(i)}} U_F(H^{(i)}(x)) \quad (3)$$

Here, $H^{(i)}$ is the linear model of the feature vector P:

$$H^{(i)}(x) = P(x^{(i)}) + \nabla_P(x^{(i)}) \cdot (x - x^{(i)}) \quad (4)$$

where ∇_P is the gradient of P obtained using the adjoint sensitivity technique. The search radius $\delta^{(i)}$ is updated using the standard trust region rules [10]. The termination condition is $\|x^{(i)} - x^{(i-1)}\| < \varepsilon$, where ε is a user-defined constant (we use $\varepsilon = 10^{-2}$).

III. Case Study

For the sake of illustration, we consider a rectangular-shape, equal-split rat-race coupler (RRC) [11] shown in Fig. 2. The structure consists of two horizontal and four vertical compact microstrip resonant cells (CMRSs). The coupler is implemented on a Taconic RF-35 substrate ($\varepsilon_r = 3.5$, $\tan\delta = 0.0018$, $h = 0.762$ mm). The geometry parameters are $x = [w_1\ w_2\ w_3\ d_1\ d_2\ l_1]^T$, whereas $w_0 = 1.7$ mm is fixed. The computational model of the RRC is implemented in CST Microwave Studio (time domain solver, ~330,000 mesh cells, simulation time ~6 minutes).

We consider three requirements (S_{11}, S_{21}, S_{31} and S_{41} stands for matching, transmission, coupling and isolation, respectively):

- BW (bandwidth) defined as a symmetric (w.r.t. f_0) part of the frequency interval for which both $|S_{11}|$ and $|S_{41}|$ are below –20 dB is supposed to be maximized;
- $d_S = |S_{21.f}(x) - S_{31.f}(x)|$ is as low as possible (ideally 0 dB) at the operating frequency;
- the frequencies realizing minimum of $S_{11.f}(x)$ and $S_{41.f}(x)$, are as close to the operating frequency f_0 as possible.

Bandwidth maximization is a primary objective, other performance figures are controlled by means of suitably defined penalty functions [11].

The coupler has been optimized using the technique of Section II. The initial design is $x^0 = [4.0\ 0.3\ 2.0\ 0.3\ 0.2\ 1.0]^T$ mm. The final design, $x^* = [3.87\ 0.43\ 1.76\ 0.37\ 0.36\ 1.10]^T$ mm (see Fig. 3), has been obtained in 6 iterations of the FBO algorithm at the cost of only 8 EM simulations of the coupler. The circuit footprint is 440 mm^2, its –20 dB bandwidth is 343 MHz, whereas the power split error is only 0.15 dB.

For the sake of comparison, the coupler was optimized using adjoint gradient search (at the level of S-parameters, no FBO), which resulted in a very similar design (circuit size 441 mm^2, bandwidth 341 MHz, power split error 0.15 dB), however, the computational cost of the optimization process was considerably higher: 8 iterations and 13 EM simulations of the structure. In other words, combining adjoints with FBO results in almost 40% computational cost savings.

IV. Conclusion

In the paper, a technique for rapid design closure of compact microwave couplers has been presented. Our approach exploits feature-based optimization and adjoint sensitivities for fast feature point gradient evaluation. Numerical results obtained for an exemplary rat-race microstrip coupler indicate superiority of the proposed method (~40% savings) over conventional adjoint-based optimization.

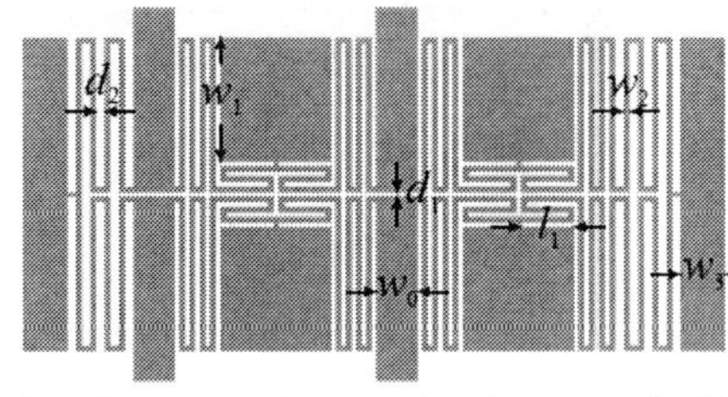

Fig. 2. Geometry of the compact microstrip rat-race coupler [11].

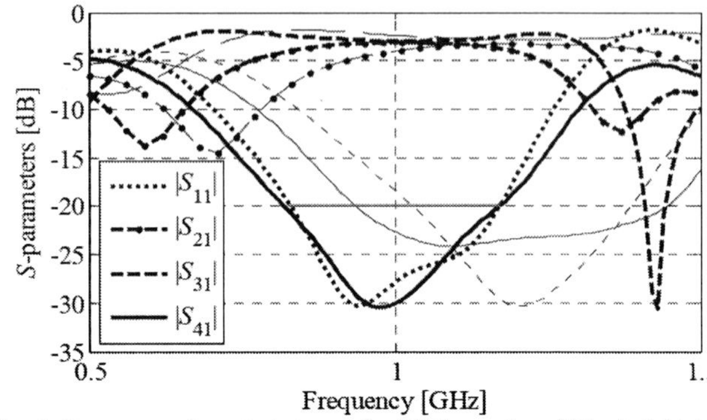

Fig. 3. Frequency characteristics of the RRC coupler of Fig. 1: initial design (thin lines), and FBO-optimized design (thick lines); –20 dB bandwidth marked with thick horizontal line.

Acknowledgment

This work is partially supported by the Icelandic Centre for Research (RANNIS) Grant 163299051 and by National Science Centre of Poland Grant 2014/15/B/ST7/04683.

References

[1] S. Koziel, A. Bekasiewicz, and P. Kurgan, "Size reduction of microwave couplers by EM-driven optimization," *Int. Microwave Symp.*, 2015.

[2] S. Koziel, P. Kurgan, and B. Pankiewicz, "Cost-efficient design methodology for compact rat-race couplers," *Int. J. RF and Microwave CAE*, vol. 25, no. 3, pp. 236-242, 2015.

[3] A. Bekasiewicz, P. Kurgan, and M. Kitlinski, "A new approach to a fast and accurate design of microwave circuits with complex topologies," *IET Microwaves, Ant. Prop.*, vol. 6, no. 14, pp. 1616-1622, 2012.

[4] J. Nocedal and S. Wright, *Numerical Optimization*, 2nd edition, Springer, New York, 2006.

[5] K. Deb, *Multi-Objective Optimization Using Evolutionary Algorithms*. New York, NY, USA: Wiley, 2001.

[6] S. Koziel, F. Mosler, S. Reitzinger, and P. Thoma, "Robust microwave design optimization using adjoint sensitivity and trust regions," *Int. J. RF and Microwave CAE*, vol. 22, no. 1, pp. 10-19, 2012.

[7] S. Koziel and S. Ogurtsov, "Design optimization of antennas using electromagnetic simulations and adaptive response correction technique," *IET Microwaves, Ant. Prop.*, vol. 8, no. 3, pp. 180-185, 2014.

[8] S. Koziel, and J.W. Bandler, "Rapid yield estimation and optimization of microwave structures exploiting feature-based statistical analysis," *IEEE Trans. Microwave Theory Tech.*, vol. 63, no. 1, pp. 107-114, 2015.

[9] A. Bekasiewicz and S. Koziel, "Response features and circuit decomposition for accelerated EM-driven design of compact impedance matching transformers," *Microwave Opt. Tech. Lett.*, vol. 58, no. 9, pp. 2130-2133, 2016.

[10] A. Conn, N.I.M. Gould, P.L. Toint, *Trust-region methods*, MPS-SIAM Series on Optimization, Philadelphia, 2000.

[11] S. Koziel and A. Bekasiewicz, "Novel structure and size-reduction-oriented design of microstrip compact rat-race coupler," *International Review of Progress in Applied Computational Electromagnetics*, pp. 1-2, Honolulu, HI, USA, 2016.

Multi-Objective EM-Driven Design of Integrated Spiral Inductors By Pareto Front Exploration

Slawomir Koziel and Piotr Kurgan

School of Science and Engineering, Reykjavik University, Reykjavik, Iceland
koziel@ru.is, kurgan@ru.is

***Abstract*—In this paper, multi-objective design of integrated spiral inductors is investigated. The method aims at finding the best possible trade-offs between inductor size and its quality factor. We adopt a penalty function approach to achieve a required inductance at a given operating frequency. The design process exploits a Pareto front exploration technique with trust-region-embedded gradient search as the optimization engine. Our considerations are illustrated using an example of a 3.5-nH 3.5-turn spiral inductor in a single-ended configuration.**

Keywords—Integrated inductors, electromagnetic simulation, EM-driven design, multi-objective optimization, size reduction.

I. Introduction

Spiral on-chip inductors are critical radio frequency (RF) components that tend to occupy large chip areas and have a huge impact on the performance of vital RF integrated circuits, such as voltage-controlled oscillators or mixers to name a few. Having this in mind, continuous efforts are made to obtain small-size and high-quality-factor coil implementations for silicon-based technologies. Inductor area minimization and quality factor maximization are conflicting design objectives that can be simultaneously handled only through multi-objective optimization [1]. This is an laborious process, aiming at identifying a Pareto-optimal set that represents the best possible trade-offs between non-commensurable goals. Traditionally, this is accomplished by means of population-based methods, such as genetic algorithms [1], [2]. In RF engineering, however, processing thousands of objective function calls is numerically prohibitive when done by using accurate, but computationally expensive electromagnetic (EM) simulations. On the other hand, the use of EM solvers is indispensable to satisfy design reliability requirements.

In this work, the best possible trade-off designs, describing the interrelations between inductor area and its quality factor, are obtained by solving a sequence of constrained single-objective optimization tasks. The discretized Pareto front is found point by point using EM-based gradient optimization routine in combination with a trust region technique.

II. Multi-Objective Optimization Approach

A. Multi-Objective Design Problem

Let $\boldsymbol{R}(\boldsymbol{x})$ be a response of a high-fidelity EM model of the inductor at hand; $\boldsymbol{x}$ is a vector of designable (geometry) parameters. Given N design objectives, $F_k(\boldsymbol{R}(\boldsymbol{x}))$, $k = 1, \ldots, N$, the goal is to find a representation of the Pareto front, i.e., a set of designs that are non-dominated in a Pareto sense. A dominance relation $\prec$ [2] is defined by saying that for the two designs $\boldsymbol{x}$ and $\boldsymbol{y}$, $\boldsymbol{x} \prec \boldsymbol{y}$ ($\boldsymbol{x}$ dominates $\boldsymbol{y}$) if $F_k(\boldsymbol{R}(\boldsymbol{x})) \leq F_k(\boldsymbol{R}(\boldsymbol{y}))$ for all $k = 1, \ldots, N$, and the inequality is strict for at least one k [2]. In this work, we consider two objectives $F_1(\boldsymbol{x}) = -Q(\boldsymbol{x})$, and $F_2(\boldsymbol{x}) = A(\boldsymbol{x})$, where Q and A are the inductor quality factor (at the operating frequency f_0) and the area occupied by the structure, respectively.

B. Multi-Objective Optimization by Pareto Front Exploration

For fast identification of the two-objective Pareto set, we use a Pareto front exploration method formulated in [3]. The algorithm produces a sequence of designs $\boldsymbol{x}^{(k)}$, $k = 1, 2, \ldots,$ where $\boldsymbol{x}^{(1)}$ is a solution to the single-objective optimization problem of the form

$$\boldsymbol{x}^{(1)} = \arg\min_{\boldsymbol{x}} F_1(\boldsymbol{R}(\boldsymbol{x})) \quad (1)$$

which produces the best possible solution pertaining to the first objective. We denote by $F_2^{(1)} = F_2(\boldsymbol{R}(\boldsymbol{x}^{(1)}))$ the corresponding value of the second objective. The subsequent designs are obtained by setting the thresholds $F_2^{(k)}$ and solving

$$\boldsymbol{x}^{(k)} = \arg\min_{\boldsymbol{x},\, F_2(\boldsymbol{R}(\boldsymbol{x}))\leq F_2^{(k)}} F_1(\boldsymbol{R}(\boldsymbol{x})) \quad (2)$$

Here, $\boldsymbol{x}^{(k)}$ is the kth element of the Pareto set. The process is continued until $F_1(\boldsymbol{R}(\boldsymbol{x}^{(k)}))$ is satisfactory from the point of view of the given design specifications.

C. Local Search Algorithm for Pareto Front Exploration

The problems (1) and (2) are solved here using a trust-region-embedded gradient search. Apart from the two aforementioned figures of merit (the quality factor Q and the inductor area A), we are also interested in the inductance $L(\boldsymbol{x})$ at the frequency of interest f_0. Because we aim at obtaining a required value of the inductance L_{target} at a given operating frequency f_0, the original formulation of the problem (2) is replaced by

$$\boldsymbol{x}^{(k)} = \arg\min_{\boldsymbol{x},\, F_2(\boldsymbol{R}(\boldsymbol{x}))\leq F_2^{(k)}} U(\boldsymbol{R}(\boldsymbol{x})) \quad (3)$$

where the objective function U is defined as

$$U(\boldsymbol{R}(\boldsymbol{x})) = U(Q(\boldsymbol{x}), L(\boldsymbol{x})) = -Q(\boldsymbol{x}) + \beta[(L(\boldsymbol{x}) - L_{target})/L_{target}]^2 \quad (4)$$

The penalty function forces L to get as close to L_{target} as possible (we set $\beta = 1000$). The area constraint $F_2(\boldsymbol{R}(\boldsymbol{x})) \le F_2^{(k)}$ is handled as an explicit constraint because $F_2(\boldsymbol{R}(\boldsymbol{x}))$ is calculated directly from $\boldsymbol{x}$.

The problem (3) is solved iteratively as ($\boldsymbol{x}^{(k.0)} = \boldsymbol{x}^{(k-1)}$)

$$\boldsymbol{x}^{(k.i+1)} = \arg \min_{\boldsymbol{x}^{(k.i)} - \boldsymbol{d}^{(k.i)} \le \boldsymbol{x} \le \boldsymbol{x}^{(k.i)} + \boldsymbol{d}^{(k.i)}} U\left(\boldsymbol{R}_L^{(k.i)}(\boldsymbol{x})\right) \quad (5)$$

$\boldsymbol{R}_L^{(k.i)}$ is a linear expansion model of $\boldsymbol{R}$ at $\boldsymbol{x}^{(k.i)}$ defined as

$$\boldsymbol{R}_S^{(k.i)}(\boldsymbol{x}) = \boldsymbol{R}(\boldsymbol{x}^{(k.i)}) + \begin{bmatrix} [\boldsymbol{R}(\boldsymbol{x}^{(k.i)} + \boldsymbol{h}_1) - \boldsymbol{R}(\boldsymbol{x}^{(k.i)})]^T / \delta_1 \\ \dots \\ [\boldsymbol{R}(\boldsymbol{x}^{(k.i)} + \boldsymbol{h}_n) - \boldsymbol{R}(\boldsymbol{x}^{(k.i)})]^T / \delta_n \end{bmatrix}^T \cdot (\boldsymbol{x} - \boldsymbol{x}^{(k.i)}) \quad (6)$$

The perturbation vectors $\boldsymbol{h}_k$ are $\boldsymbol{h}_k = [0 \ldots 0\ \delta_k\ 0 \ldots 0]^T$ with δ_k being finite differentiation steps. The new design $\boldsymbol{x}^{(k.i+1)}$ is only accepted if $U(\boldsymbol{R}(\boldsymbol{x}^{(k.i+1)})) < U(\boldsymbol{R}(\boldsymbol{x}^{(k.i)}))$. The search interval size $\boldsymbol{d}^{(i)}$ is adjusted using conventional trust-region rules [4]. The termination condition is $||\boldsymbol{d}^{(i)}|| < \varepsilon$, where ε is a user-defined value (here, 10^{-2}).

III. Case Study

Consider the structure of an on-chip spiral inductor shown in Fig. 1. The device is implemented in a standard CMOS technology that offers six thin copper sheets and a single thick aluminum layer placed on the top of the stack. Metal layers are embedded in silicon dioxide and reside on a conductive substrate. The presented coil is implemented in a single-ended configuration with a 3.5-turn aluminum winding and a copper undercrossing located beneath. The inductor is described by a vector of designable parameters $\boldsymbol{x} = [w\ g\ r]^T$.

We validate the multi-objective design methodology of Section II by executing process (3) using inductor EM model implemented in CST [5] (~120,000 mesh cells). The solution space is defined by the lower/upper bounds, $\boldsymbol{l} = [2\ 1\ 80]^T$, $\boldsymbol{u} = [20\ 10\ 160]^T$ (all dimensions in microns).

The goal is to accurately identify the trade-offs between inductor performance (here, the quality factor Q) and the area A occupied by the structure. Also, we search for inductors that operate at $f_0 = 3.25$ GHz and satisfy the target inductance condition, i.e., $L_{target} = 3.5$ nH. Solving the iterative process (3) results in a set of Pareto-optimal design solutions shown in Fig. 2. Detailed numerical data is listed in Table I. One can observe that the inductor layout area ranges from 14,000 μm^2 to 35,000 μm^2, which corresponds to Q values of ~13 and ~17, respectively. The example frequency characteristics of selected inductor Pareto-optimal design solutions are depicted in Fig. 3.

TABLE I. Numerical Results of Multi-Objective Optimization of Integrated Spiral Inductor

Designable parameters [μm]			Design objectives		
w	g	r	Q	A [μm^2]	L [nH]
9.58	3.83	89.61	16.5	35,820	3.50
7.95	2.73	93.23	16.3	30,000	3.50
6.27	2.17	94.92	15.6	25,000	3.49
4.32	1.80	96.11	15.3	20,000	3.49
3.80	1.34	95.69	14.4	18,000	3.48
3.26	1.19	93.26	13.5	16,000	3.48
2.57	1.00	91.78	12.7	14,000	3.48

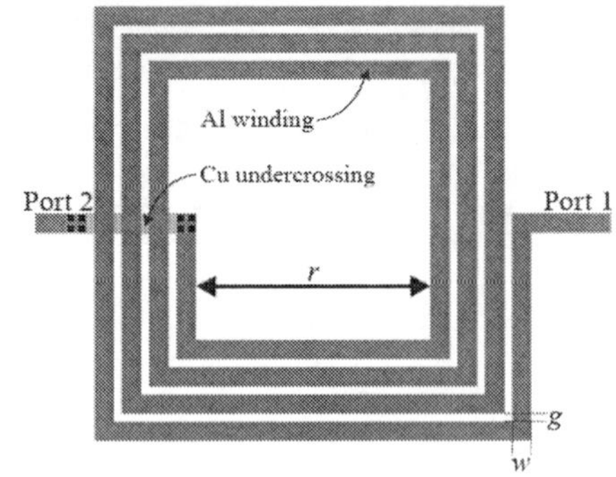

Fig. 1. Layout of 3.5-turn spiral on-chip inductor of single-ended type.

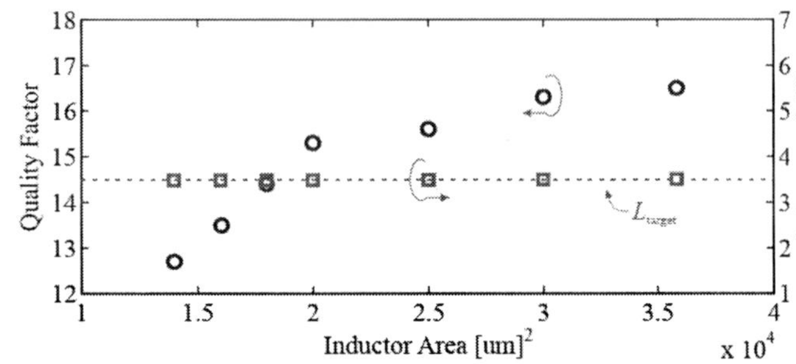

Fig. 2. Pareto-optimal set representing the best possible trade-offs between inductor area and the quality factor (○). The specific inductance value for each design solution is also included (□).

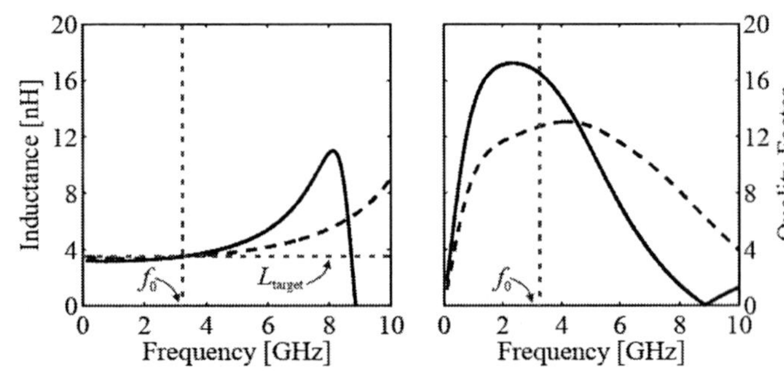

Fig. 3. EM-simulated frequency characteristics of 35,000-μm^2 (solid) and 14,000-μm^2 (dashed) Pareto-optimal inductors.

Acknowledgment

The authors thank Computer Simulation Technology AG, Darmstad Germany for making CST Microwave Studio available. This work is partially supported by the Icelandic Centre for Research (RANNIS) Grant 163299051.

References

[1] R. Gonzalez et al., "Automated generation of the optimal performance trade-offs of integrated inductors," *IEEE Transactions on Computer-Aided Design of Integrated Circuits and Systems*, vol. 33, no. 8, pp. 1269–1273, 2014.

[2] K. Deb, *Multi-objective optimization using evolutionary algorithms.* Wiley, New York, 2001.

[3] S. Koziel and A. Bekasiewicz, "Rapid multi-objective antenna design using point-by-point Pareto set identification and local surrogate models," *IEEE Trans. Antennas Prop.*, vol. 64, no. 6, pp. 2551-2556, 2016.

[4] A.R. Conn, N.I.M. Gould, and P.L. Toint, *Trust Region Methods*, MPS-SIAM Series on Optimization, 2000.

[5] CST Microwave Studio, ver. 2013. CST AG, Bad Nauheimer Str. 19, D-64289 Darmstadt, Germany, 2013.

Surrogate-assisted Transformation Optics Inspired GRIN Lens Design and Optimization

Sawyer D. Campbell, Jogender Nagar, John A. Easum, Douglas H. Werner, and Pingjuan L. Werner
Department of Electrical Engineering
The Pennsylvania State University
University Park, PA 16802, USA
sdc22@psu.edu, jun163@psu.edu, jae5377@psu.edu, dhw@psu.edu, plw7@psu.edu

Abstract—**It has been shown that Transformation Optics (TO)-derived gradient-index (GRIN) lenses often outperform more traditional GRIN designs. In order to better understand the origins of this performance improvement, such TO-derived solutions have previously been decomposed into a 2D-polynomial basis, which unveiled the presence of large radial-axial "cross-term" contributions to the index profile. While these terms are crucial in maximizing the performance of GRIN lenses, finding the optimal index profile becomes a more challenging problem due to the expanded number of input variables. However, this optimization process can be considerably accelerated through the introduction of surrogate models at several stages of the design process.**

Keywords—transformation optics; optimization; surrogate models

I. INTRODUCTION

The advent of Transformation Optics (TO) [1] and recent advancements in manufacturing techniques, such as 3D printing, have led to a renaissance in gradient-index (GRIN) optics [2]. By allowing the behavior of electromagnetic radiation in a given geometry (*i.e.* lens) to be replicated in an alternative, usually more desirable geometry, through an appropriate mapping of the constituent material parameters, TO has led to a number of exotic GRIN designs. Perhaps most notable are flattened TO-derived GRIN focusing lenses which typically possess better performance than traditional radial, axial, or spherical GRINs. These TO-derived lenses generally feature 3D index variations that have not been previously investigated and, consequently, their impact on optical performance were not well understood until recently. Through the decomposition of these solutions into a 2D-polynomial basis [3] and studying how individual terms in the basis govern specific wavefront aberrations, one can form a surrogate-model which acts as an empirically-derived analytical theory [4]. However, training the surrogate *a priori* to the optimization is undesirable as the training stage can require a considerable amount of time. A more advantageous procedure is to use a true analytical model as an *a priori* surrogate and train the empirically-derived model *in situ*. In this study, we present a simple analytical surrogate that provides rapid estimation of the design cost to screen out bad input parameter combinations for arbitrary GRIN lenses featuring 4th order radial contributions. Like any analytical model, the surrogate requires only a fraction of the time to evaluate and can be exploited to drastically reduce design optimization times. A discussion of extending the surrogate to more general GRIN lens optimizations and the inclusion of surrogates at other stages of the optimization procedure is provided.

II. SURROGATE MODEL SETUP

Consider a GRIN lens whose index variation is described by:

$$n(r,z) = n_0 + \alpha_0\left(\frac{z}{T}\right) + \left(\frac{r}{R}\right)^2 \sum_{i=0}^{1} \alpha_{2,i}\left(\frac{z}{T}\right)^i + \left(\frac{r}{R}\right)^4 \sum_{j=0}^{2} \alpha_{4,j}\left(\frac{z}{T}\right)^j \qquad (1)$$

where R, T are the lens radius and thickness and α_i are the index expansion coefficients, respectively. While this lens features axially-dependent cross-terms, it is limited to 4th order radial contributions. A candidate lens whose index profile is defined by (1) is shown in Fig. 1.

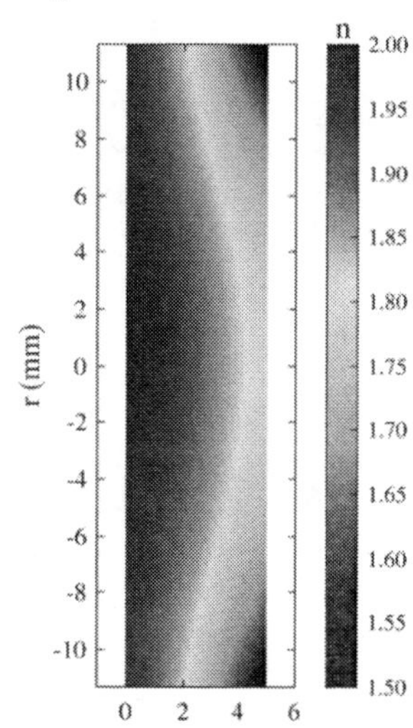

Fig. 1: Candidate GRIN lens whose index profile is defined by (1).

The *a priori* surrogate is applied in the form of a screening-test: if the chosen set of α's (*i.e.*, $\{\alpha_0, \alpha_{2,0}, \alpha_{2,1}, \alpha_{4,0}, \alpha_{4,1}, \alpha_{4,2}\}$) produce a lens with a focus that is outside a thresholded region around the focal plane, then the full-system ray-trace is bypassed and the evaluation is assigned a cost value according to the following conditional statement:

$$cost = \begin{cases} a\left(1 + \left|\frac{f_2 - f_T}{cf_T}\right| + \left|\frac{f_2}{f_4}\right|\right), & |f_G - f_T| > cf_T \\ \max\limits_{\theta,\lambda}\{SS_{rms}(\theta)\}, & otherwise \end{cases} \tag{2}$$

where f_2, f_4 are the focal lengths associated with the 2nd and 4th order radial contributions, f_G, f_T are the GRIN lens and target focal lengths, c is a threshold constant, and a is the cost scalar, respectively. If the candidate lens has a predicted focal length (f_G) that is within the threshold region, then the ray trace executes normally and the cost is the maximum rms spot size measured over all evaluation angles. Otherwise, the surrogate incentivizes the optimizer to minimize the 4th order power, which reduces the presence of higher order optical aberrations, and to match the target focal length with the 2nd order radial contribution. The focal lengths are inversely proportional to the optical powers and are related to the lens parameters by

$$\begin{aligned} \phi_2 &= -2\beta_2 T = f_2^{-1} \\ \phi_4 &= -2\beta_4 T R^2 = f_4^{-1} \\ \phi_G &= \phi_2 + \phi_4 = f_G^{-1} \end{aligned} \tag{3}$$

where $\beta_{2,4}$ are the averaged 2nd and 4th order power contribution coefficients. β_2 is calculated according to

$$\beta_2 = \frac{1}{R^2 T}\int_0^T \sum_{i=0}^{1} \alpha_{2,i}\left(\frac{z}{T}\right)^i dz \tag{4}$$

which finds the average contribution of the 2nd order radial variation over the entire lens volume. β_4 is calculated in a corresponding fashion.

III. Results

To test the cost savings of the surrogate model, the convergence behavior of a series of optimization trials were compared for both the full function evaluation and surrogate-assisted function evaluation cases. The goal is to minimize the cost (2) of an *f*/5 lens which performs over an 8 degree full field-of-view (FOV). For all cases, the index range is scaled to be within the range 1.5-2.0. The cost scalar a was chosen to be 1e6 so that there is a large disparity in costs between those outside the threshold region and those within. The threshold constant c was chosen to be 0.05 which screens out any candidate lens whose focal length is outside a range $\pm$5% from the target f_T. CMA-ES [5] was employed to optimize the index expansion coefficients over a range (-0.5, +0.5) and all optimization parameters were left to their default values with the exception that restarts were enabled. The optimization was stopped after 300 n^2 (10,800) function evaluations.

The results of the 10 trials were averaged and plotted against both number of function evaluations and time in Fig. 2. Interestingly, the surrogate-assisted evaluation is able to achieve a slightly-lower cost than the unassisted evaluation. The full function and surrogate evaluations take approximately 1.25 and 0.17 seconds, respectively. Approximately 21% of the total evaluations were screened by the surrogate model which reduces the potential optimization time by approximately the same percentage. However, it is noted that the surrogate-

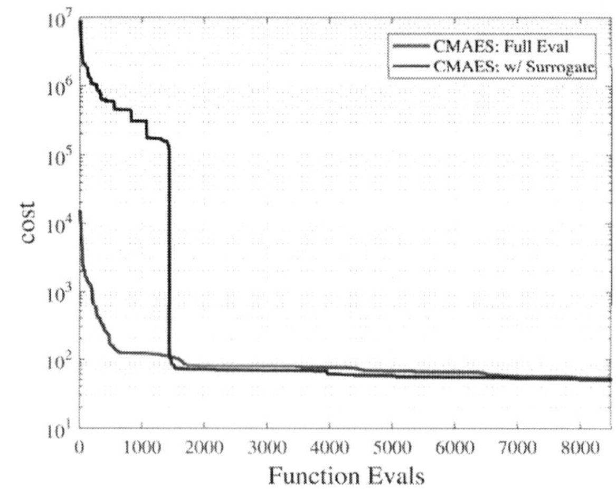

(a) Cost versus function evaluations.

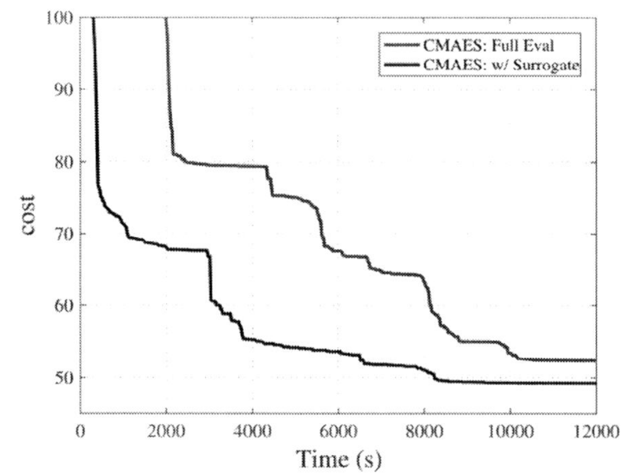

(b) Cost versus time.

Fig. 1: Convergence comparison of unassisted (red) and surrogate-assisted (blue) optimization procedures.

assisted optimization is able to achieve an intermediate cost value of 70 in ≈ 1,000 evaluations versus ≈ 5,600 for the unassisted optimization. Future studies include using the ray trace evaluated solutions within the "thresholded region" to train an *in situ* surrogate model which could lead to even further reduction in optimization time.

References

[1] J. B. Pendry, D. Schurig, and D. R. Smith, "Controlling Electromagnetic Fields," *Science*, vol. 312, Issue 5781, pp. 1780-1782, Jun. 2006.

[2] S. D. Campbell, D. E. Brocker, J. Nagar, J. A. Easum, D. H. Werner, and P. L. Werner, "Advancements in Transformation Optics-enabled Gradient-index Lens Design," *Proc. SPIE 9579, Novel Optical Systems Design and Optimization XVIII*, pp. 95790E/1-10, Sep. 2015.

[3] S. D. Campbell, J. Nagar, D. E. Brocker, and D. H. Werner, "On the Use of Surrogate Models in the Analytical Decompositions of Refractive Index Gradients Obtained Through Quasiconformal Transformation Optics," *J. Opt.*, vol. 18, no. 4, Apr. 2016.

[4] J. A. Easum, S. D. Campbell, J. Nagar, and D. H. Werner, "Analytical Surrogate Model for the Aberrations of an Arbitrary GRIN Lens," *Optics Express*, vol. 24, no. 16, pp. 17805-17818, 2016.

[5] M. D. Gregory, Z. Bayraktar, and D. H. Werner, "Fast Optimization of Electromagnetic Design Problems Using the Covariance Matrix Adaptation Evolutionary Strategy," *IEEE Trans. Antennas Propag.*, vol. 59, no. 4, pp. 1275-1285, Apr. 2011.

Research on EM Characteristics Modeling of Sea Surface by Ship EDF

Shuang Gao , Jiahe Mei , Lingfei Guo, Tao Jiang
College of Info. & Comm. Engineering
Harbin Engineering University
Harbin China 150001
{gaoshuang; meijiahe; guolingfei, jiangtao}@hrbeu.edu.cn

Yachen Zhang
School of Electrical Engineering
Heilongjiang University
Harbin, China
20151594@s.hlju.edu.cn

***Abstract*- In this paper, we firstly use the method of extending the sea surface area to get the effective electromagnetic calculation results by software of Ship EDF. Then, we estimate the optimal sample size for the two-dimensional ocean wave simulation model based on the theory of statistics. Finally, we obtain the radio wave propagation characteristics on the sea surface in different sea states, different wave incident angles and different incident frequencies.**

Keywords—electromagnetic simulation; extension of area; optimum sample size

I. INTRODUCTION

Due to the limited memory, when the number of facet of the effective scattering area is too much, EM simulation data will exceed the computing power of the computer [1]. In order to achieve the effective electromagnetic calculation results, the simulation area of the rough sea surface is needed to extend [2].

The result of each EM simulation is only a test sample to study the propagation characteristics of EM wave. If you want to get the EM waves propagation characteristics in different sea conditions, different wave incident angles and different incident frequencies. It is necessary to estimate the optimal sample size of the 2D wave simulation model according to statistics analysis.

II. EXTENSION OF SEA SURFACE SIMULATION AREAS

We assume to divide the effective scattering region sea surface into a plurality of small sea areas that calculation can be finished within the limited computer memory. This small area was simulated repeatedly, and then use the sea surface stitching method to get all the EM simulation results of the sea surface.

A. Electromagnetic simulation of effective scattering areas

For different incident angle and different incident frequency, the effective scattering region of EM waves shows different characteristics. The effective scattering region of sea EM simulation area is the union when presence of coherent signals. But when not presence of coherent signals the effective scattering region is the effective irradiation area [3-5].

Put the geometric model into EM simulation software Ship-EDF. Transmitter's height is 10km, the receiver height is 10m, sea states is three - level downwind non - linear sea surface, incident angle is 8°, the frequency of incident wave is 1GHz, sea region of computation is $32m \times 32m$, EM simulation graphics in and out the effective scattering area are shown respectively as Fig.1(a) and (b) .

Fig.1 (b) shows effective rays are all diffraction ray. The power ratio of non-direct paths to direct path is 0.00023, so we usually do not consider Fig.1 (b). In Fig.1 (a), it contains primary reflected ray and a large number of diffracted rays which have strong interference to the direct wave.

(a) Electromagnetic simulation of sea surface in effective scatter area (b) Electromagnetic simulation of sea surface out of effective scatter area

Fig. 1 electromagnetic simulation of sea surface

B. Extend the sea simulation areas

The EM simulation method is used to validate the feasibility of simulation area extension. EM simulation graphics of sea surface in effective scattering area as showed in Fig.2. The simulation conditions are the same as those in Fig.1 (a). The simulated sea surface area is $32m \times 16m$.

The first group of EM simulation sea surface model shown in Fig.1 (a); The second group of EM simulation sea surface model is $32m \times 16m$ rectangular sea surface, as shown in Fig.2 (a), for the upper half of the Fig.1 (a) simulation sea; The third is $32m \times 16m$ rectangular sea surface, as shown in Fig.2 (b), for the lower half of the Fig.1 (a) simulation sea. Consider primary reflected ray, primary reflected ray plus primary diffraction ray, primary diffraction ray, after EM simulation, the statistical results shown in Table 1, which is the average obtained by multiple EM simulation of different sea surface samples in the same sea state.

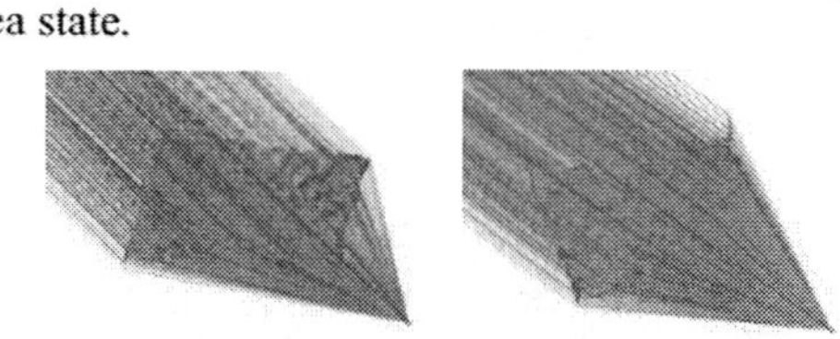

(a) Schematic diagram of EM simulation of second groups (b) Schematic diagram of EM simulation of third groups

Fig. 2. Electromagnetic simulation pattern of sea surface

TABLE I. THE AVERAGE NUMBER OF ELECTROMAGNETIC WAVE RADIATION

Simulation Group	the average number of electromagnetic wave radiation		
	Reflection	Diffraction	Reflection & Diffraction
1st	2	122	29
2nd	0	67	13
3rd	2	51	10

III. ESTIMATE THE NUMBER OF SAMPLES TO BE CALCULATED

The result of each EM simulation is just an experimental sample to study the propagation characteristics of EM waves. If we want to obtain the propagation characteristics more efficiently, we need to estimate the optimal sample size of simulation two-dimensional wave model according to statistics.

In accordance with the statistical formula [8], the sample size n can be expressed as:

$$n = Z^2\sigma^2 / E^2$$

E is the acceptable sample error, the smaller the allowable error is, the larger the need sample size is; z is the confidence level of the standard error, which indicates the reliability of the estimation result. The higher the confidence is, the larger the sample is, the general confidence is 95%, corresponding to z = 1.96; σ for the variance, denotes the sample dispersion degree.

When the incident angle is 45° and the sea level is 6. The number of primary reflection rays is the average of multiple EM simulation because of the small number of primary reflection rays. Considering the number of primary reflection plus primary diffraction and primary diffracted rays, the probability distribution of the number of rays is shown in Fig 3.

The fitting degree of the two curves is generally expressed by the correlation coefficient. The closer the correlation coefficient is 1, the better the correlation between the two curves. When the correlation coefficient is 0.8, it is called highly correlated. The correlation coefficient of the fitting degree of two curves is expressed as:

$$r = \sum_{i=1}^{n}(x_i - \bar{x})(y_i - \bar{y}) \Big/ \left(\sqrt{\sum_{i=1}^{n}(x_i - \bar{x})^2} \sqrt{\sum_{i=1}^{n}(y_i - \bar{y})^2} \right)$$

n is the number of samples; when the correlation of the number of rays and the normal distribution is calculated, x_i is the number of primary reflection plus primary diffraction or primary diffracted rays in the i-th EM simulation calculation, $\bar{x}$ is the average value, y_i is the sample value taken from the fitting of the normal distribution curve , take a total of n, $\bar{y}$ is the average value of the normal distribution curve.

Fig.3 (a) is the simulation 43 times fitting curve of the number rays of primary reflection plus primary diffraction and the normal distribution curve. The average of the normal distribution is 44 and the variance is 6.3. The correlation coefficient of the two curves is 93.324%. Fig.3 (b) shows the simulation 37 times fitting curves of the number of primary diffraction rays and the normal distribution curve. The average of the normal distribution is 302 and the variance is 4.7. The correlation coefficient of the two curves is 96.437%. The simulation results show that when the sample size is 45, the correlation coefficient between ray number distribution and its normal distribution curve is more than 0.9, so, the best sample size of the 2D wave model was 45.

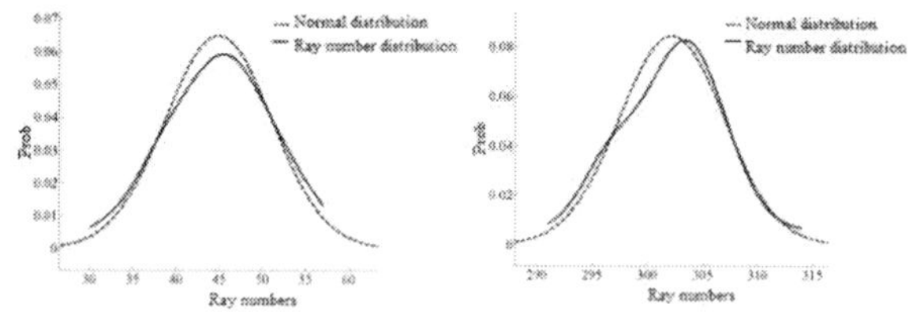

(a) The number of primary reflections plus primary diffraction rays (b) Number of primary diffracted rays

Fig. 3. The normal curve fitting of the number of EM radiation

IV. CONCLUSTION

In this paper, EM simulation method is used to verify the correctness of the simulation method of sea surface area extension. Simulation can be carried out by simulating the part of the sea surface in the effective scattering area first, then multiple simulating it by sea surface stitching, and then get the result of all effective scattering areas. The optimal sample size of EM simulation is analyzed in detail.

ACKNOWLEDGMENT

This paper is funded by the International Exchange Program of Harbin Engineering University for Innovation-oriented Talents Cultivation. This work was also partially supported by the Science and Technology innovative Talents Foundation of Harbin (2013RFXXJ083), the Foundational Research Funds for the Central Universities (HEUCF131602, HEUCFD1433).

REFERENCES

[1] L. X. Guo, L C Jiao, Z. S. Wu. "Electromagnetic Scattering from Two-Dimensional Rough Surface Using the Kirchhoff Approximation," Chinese Physics Letters, vol.18, pp.214-216, 2001.

[2] R. Q. Sun. "Research on Electromagnetic scattering from ship wakes," Xi'an Electronic and Science University .2013

[3] C. Y. Jiang, Y. Q. Li. "Formulae for the Active Scattering (Reflecting) Regions on a Plane," Chinese Journal of Radio Science, vol.02, pp. 70-75, 1996.

[4] J. H. Luo. "Study on electromagnetic scattering from random rough surface" ,Zhejiang University.2013

[5] B. M. Hannah. "Modelling and simulation of GPS multipath propagation," Global Positioning System, 2001.

[6] W. B. Gordon. "Far-field approximations to the Kirchoff-Helmholtz representations of scattered fields," Antennas & Propagation IEEE Transactions on, vol.23, pp.590-592, 1975.

[7] U. Kaatze. "Complex permittivity of water as a function of frequency and temperature," Journal of Chemical & Engineering Data, vol.34, pp.371-374, 2002.

[8] S. A. Wang. "Statistics," China Statistics Press.1994.

The Role of the Skin Modeling in LF Dosimetry

Valerio De Santis*, Tommaso Campi*, Silvano Cruciani*, Mauro Feliziani*

*Department of Industrial and Information Engineering and Economics, University of L'Aquila, L'Aquila, Italy
email: valerio.desantis@univaq.it, tommaso.campi@univaq.it, silvano.cruciani@univaq.it, mauro.feliziani@univaq.it

***Abstract*— The modeling of the skin plays a crucial role in low frequency numerical dosimetry. Current realistic anatomical models distinguish only a single-layer skin. While a previous work from the authors showed that for limb-non-touching postures a single-layer skin model could estimate the peak electric field in the skin, at least a two-layer model should be used for limb-touching exposure scenarios.**

I. Introduction

The appropriate modeling of the skin is very important in low frequency (LF) numerical dosimetry and bio-medical applications. In this work we focus on the validity of the skin layer currently implemented in up-to-date human-body anatomical models like the Virtual Population (ViP), from the IT'IS Foundation [1], or the Japanese models from the NICT Group [2]. Both families of anatomical models are indeed very sophisticated, including different tiers of population (age, sex, BMI), postures, and segmented tissues. However, for practical reasons, the several layers of the skin structure (stratum corneum, dermis, epidermis) are embedded into a unique fairly-thick (2-3 mm) layer encompassing all of them.

When dealing with LF magnetic field exposures, the following questions arouse: (1) from the numerical dosimetry point of view, is it accurate to model the skin using a single-layer structure? (2) what conductivity should be assigned to the single-layer? To answer these questions two different configurations should be considered: limb-non-touching postures (i.e., a normal standing position with the arms resting on the side) and limb-touching postures (i.e., skin-to-skin contacts at clasped hands or hand-to-limb touching).

A previous work from the first-author [3] showed that for limb-non-touching postures a single-layer skin model could conservatively estimate the peak induced E-field if the same conductivity of the dermis is chosen for the single skin layer. Instead, at least a two-layer skin model comprising of the stratum corneum (SC) and the remaining skin layers should be employed for limb-touching exposure scenarios. This implies notable computational efforts to discretize the tiny SC layer questioning the validity of current anatomical models [4].

II. Models and Methods

A. Limb-non-touching postures

For limb-non-touching posture, two different cases occur: 1) E-field tangentially oriented to the skin layers and 2) E-field perpendicularly oriented. The former is found all over the human body boundary, while the latter is exhibited only in the armpit and groin regions, i.e., at skin-to-skin overlapping [3]. When the E-field is tangentially oriented does not present any issue because the field is not affected by the contrast of tissue conductivities. E-field enhancements instead occurs in tissues with low conductivity (SC, SAT, bones) when the E-field is perpendicularly oriented to the tissue boundary.

B. Limb-touching postures

Another situation where the E-field is perpendicularly oriented to the several skin layers is at limb-touching postures, as shown in Fig. 1. The main question in this case is whether a single-layer skin model is appropriate or not due to the "isolating" or "reflecting" effect that the SC exert. Figure 1(e) shows how the E-field distribution in the bi-layer (SC + D) skin model is completely different from the case of using a single-layer skin model (figure 1(c)). The key issue is now how to discretize or account for the tiny SC layer without affecting the computational burden? To answer this question, a novel homogenization procedure has been proposed to eliminate the SC from the computational domain [4].

Considering for simplicity a 2D non-homogeneous square cell composed by two homogeneous material layers as shown in Fig. 2, where τ and v are local coordinates, d_D is the dermis layer thickness of conductivity σ_D and d_{SC} is the SC layer thickness of conductivity σ_{SC}. The homogenization procedure consists into model a multilayer medium as an anisotropic medium whose conductivity tensor in 2D is given by:

$$\sigma_{eff} = \begin{bmatrix} \sigma_{\tau\tau,eff} & 0 \\ 0 & \sigma_{vv,eff} \end{bmatrix} \tag{1}$$

where, after simple manipulations given in [4], the proper conductivities along the local axes are found to be:

$$\sigma_{\tau\tau,eff} = \frac{\sigma_d \sigma_{sc} \left(d_{sc} + d_d \right)}{\sigma_{sc} d_d + \sigma_d d_{sc}} \tag{2}$$

$$\sigma_{vv,eff} = \frac{\sigma_{sc} d_{sc} + \sigma_d d_d}{d_{sc} + d_d} \tag{3}$$

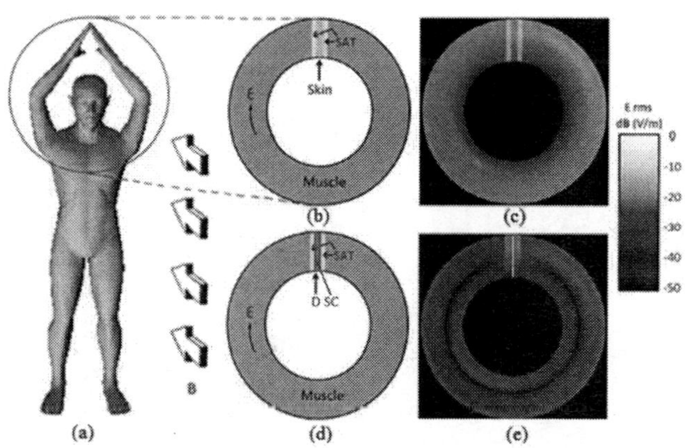

Fig. 1 Limb-touching configuration. (a) Realistic anatomical posture. (b) Canonical single-layer skin model and (c) obtained E-field distribution. (d) Canonical bi-layer (D+SC) skin model and (e) obtained E-field distribution.

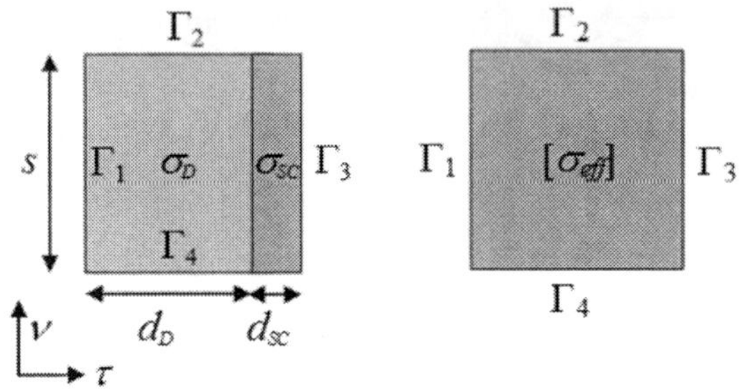

Fig. 2 Homogenization procedure. (a) Original medium with conductivities σ_D and σ_{SC}. (b) Homogenized media with effective conductivity tensor $[\sigma_{eff}]$.

III. RESULTS

A. Limb-non-touching postures

The work in [3] has demonstrated that the conductivity of the dermis (assumed to be 0.2 S/m) should be used as representative value for the single skin layer.

B. Limb-touching postures

To validate the proposed homogenization procedure, a canonical loop model exposed to a 50 Hz uniform B-field of 1 mT is considered, as shown in Fig. 3. Specifically, the field solution obtained with Sim4Life-v2.0 using the two-layer skin model (see Fig. 3(a)) is compared with the homogenized skin model (see Fig. 3(b)) having the effective conductivity tensor expressed by eq (1). The normalized E-field distribution along the x-direction in the center line of the tissue cross-section (see Fig. 3(a)) is reported in Fig. 4 showing a good agreement between the two different approaches.

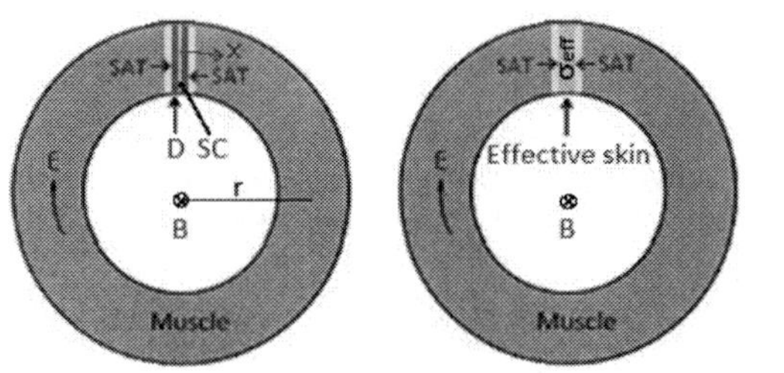

(a) (b)

Fig. 3 Canonical loop model exposed to a 50 Hz front-to-back uniform B-field of 1 mT. (a) Two-layer skin model. (b) Homogenized skin model with effective conductivity σ_{eff}.

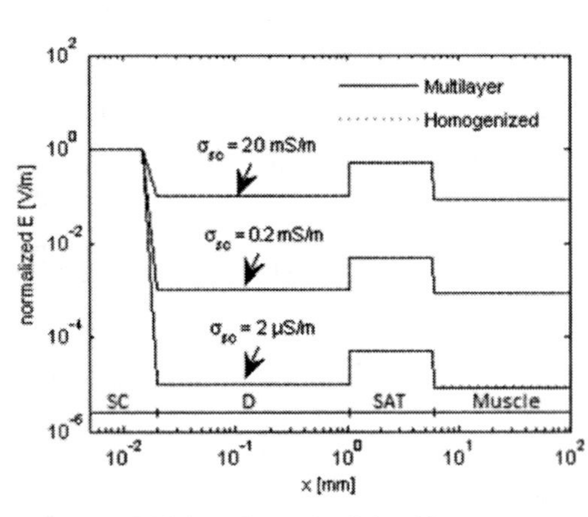

Fig. 4 Normalized E-field along the x-axis of Fig. 3(a).

IV. CONCLUSIONS AND DISCUSSION

This study addressed several open issues pertaining to the LF numerical dosimetry of magnetic induction with respect to the modeling of skin layers. While a previous work from the authors showed that for normal-standing postures a single-layer skin model could conservatively estimate the peak electric field induced in the skin, at least a two-layer skin model comprising of the SC and the remaining skin layers should be used for limb-touching exposure conditions. This is because the induced E-field distribution of a limb-touching posture is a function of the contact area, thickness and conductivity of the SC. In practice, only very thick (0.2 mm) or dry (2 μS/m) SC layers play an important role to the induced fields, exerting a reflection effect to the E-field lines. For instance, this occurs at dry or callous palm contacts.

Although the reflection effect is significant at thicker SC layers, discretizing the whole human body with a 0.1–0.2 mm grid resolution still yields to unaffordable computations. A homogenization procedure is therefore proposed in order to eliminate the tiny SC layer from the computational domain. This approach consists into model a multi-layer structure (SC and dermis) as an anisotropic single-layer medium having an effective conductivity tensor. In this way, the reflection effect of the SC is fully taken into account while maintaining the computational effort at an affordable level.

The proposed method has been validated comparing the obtained results with the solution of the bi-layer skin model derived by a commercial software tool. For the numerical results, a canonical loop model representing the arms upwards-standing with fingers touching each other has been investigated. This model is meant to represent a 'worst-case' configuration since an orthogonal E-field incidence on a flat-surface is a conservative assumption of more realistic rough skin contacts having oblique angles of incidence.

While considered for a 2D orthogonal test-case, the proposed approach can easily be extended to 3D configurations with a skin-to-skin contact having an arbitrary angle of incidence. It can be applied also for LF electric field sources, where the induced E-field is always orthogonal at the air-skin interface. Therefore, the skin model analysis presented in this study poses the basis for a more accurate LF numerical dosimetry assessment closing the gap even for contact-current or limb-touching body posture scenarios.

REFERENCES

[1] M. C. Gosselin, E. Neufeld, H. Moser, E. Huber, S. Farcito, L. Gerber M. Jedensjö, I. Hilber, F. Di Gennaro, B. Lloyd, E. Cherubini, D. Szczerba, W. Kainz, and N. Kuster, "Development of a new generation of high-resolution anatomical models for medical device evaluation: the Virtual Population 3.0," *Phys. Med. Biol.*, vol. 59, no. 18, pp. 5287-5303, Aug. 2014.

[2] T. Nagaoka, S. Watanabe, K. Sakurai, E. Kunieda, S. Watanabe, M. Taki, and Y. Yamanaka, "Development of realistic high-resolution whole-body voxel models of Japanese adult males and females of average height and weight, and application of models to radio-frequency electromagnetic-field dosimetry," *Phys. Med. Biol.*, vol. 49, no. 1, pp. 1–15, Jan. 2004.

[3] V. De Santis, X. L. Chen, I. Laakso, and A. Hirata, "An equivalent skin conductivity model for low-frequency magnetic field dosimetry," *Biomed. Phys. & Eng. Express*, vol. 1, no. 1, pp. 1–10, June 2015.

[4] V. De Santis, X. L. Chen, S. Cruciani, T. Campi, and M. Feliziani, "A novel homogenization procedure to model the skin layers in LF numerical dosimetry," Physics in Medicine and Biology, vol. 61, pp. 4402-4411, May 2016. *Special Section.*

Assessment of the uncertainty in 50 Hz foetal exposure due to tissues conductivity variation

Calculation of the uncertainty of electric field induced in the feotal tissues by means of stochastic dosimentry using polynomial chaos theory

Serena Fiocchi, Paolo Ravazzani, Marta Parazzini
CNR Consiglio Nazionale delle Ricerche
Istituto di Elettronica e di Ingegneria dell'Informazione e delle Telecomunicazioni IEIIT
Milan, Italy
serena.fiocchi@ieiit.cnr.it, paolo.ravazzani@ieiit.cnr.it, marta.parazzini@ieiit.cnr.it

***Abstract*—In this paper, the influence of conductivity values applied to the foetal tissues at 3, 7 and 9 months gestational age on the electric field distribution induced by a 50 Hz uniform magnetic field was explored by means of stochastic dosimetry performed by making use of polynomial chaos theory. The maximum variations of induced electric field peak can reach up to 12 % in foetal fat.**

Keywords—stochastic dosimetry; polynomial chaos: foetal exposure; ELF.

I. Introduction

Foetal exposure to extremely low frequency magnetic fields (ELF-MFs) at 50 Hz is a topic of high interest due to the possible correlation between this exposure and childhood leukaemia [1],[2]. At the purpose to explain a causal relationship between ELF-MF exposure and this kind of cancer, the exposure assessment studies need to explore all the possible realistic scenarios, taking into account their high degree of variability. Among the various factors of uncertainty, the change of tissues conductivity values plays a key role when we consider the foetal exposure: there is indeed a strong evidence that these values widely change with the age and also among subjects at the same age [3]-[4]. The few measurements of foetal tissues conductivities available [5]-[6] were all performed on the radiofrequency range, whereas data at 50 Hz are still not available.

In this study, starting from two empirical procedure for the assessment of foetal tissues conductivity variability at LF [7][8], we combined all the possible variation of dielectric properties within specific ranges and assessed the foetal exposure to ELF-MF at 50 Hz by means of a stochastic approach based on the polynomial chaos theory [9][10].

II. Materials and Methods

A. Polynomial Chaos Theory

The Polynomial Chaos (PC) is a spectral method and consists in the approximation of the system output in a suitable finite-dimensional basis $(\psi i(\mathbf{X}))_{0 \le i \le P-1}$, made of orthogonal polynomials. For computational purpose, the polynomial expansion is truncated after P terms:

$$Y = M(X) = \sum_0^{P-1} a_j \psi_j(X) + e \qquad (1)$$

where Y is the system output (i.e. E_{99th}: the 99th percentile value of root mean square of the fetal tissue-specific induced electric field averaged on a 2 mm side cube [11]), **X** is the random input vector (i.e. conductivity values of tissues), a_j are the coefficients of the PC expansion, estimated by the Least Angle Regression (LAR) algorithm [12][13], and *e* is the truncation error.

B. Foetal tissues conductivity range

The input vector **X** of the input parameters is made of the conductivity values of the foetal tissues that present a systematic variation of dielectric properties with age [4]: brain, bone, fat, skin and spinal cord.

Their ranges of variation were identified on the basis of the following approaches:

- 50% increase of the corresponding adult conductivity values
- As in [7], where the increased conductivity values are estimated based on the changes in water content. The ratio between foetal tissue conductivity σ_F and the adult tissue conductivity σ_A is estimated by:

$$\frac{\sigma_F}{\sigma_A} = \frac{(1-f_{vF})(2+f_{vA})}{(1-f_{vA})(2+f_{vF})} \qquad (2)$$

where f_{vF} and f_{vA} are the volume fractions of cells in the foetus and in the adult, respectively.

- As in [14] where the lower and upper bounds of foetal conductivity σ_F are expressed as a function of the adult conductivity σ_A:

$$\frac{\sigma_F}{\sigma_A} = \left(\frac{(1-f_{vF})}{(1-f_{vA})}\right)^s, \quad s = \frac{5}{3}, \frac{3}{2} \qquad (3).$$

C. Simulations

Three high-resolution pregnant woman models at 3, 7 and 9 months of Gestational Age (GA) (details provided in [15]) were used. Simulations were conducted using the Magneto Quasi-Static low frequency solver implemented in the simulation platform SEMCAD X [16]. The conductivities of the woman tissues were assigned according to the data available in literature [17]. The properties of the foetal tissues, whose conductivity values are not supposed to vary, were assigned as the adult ones. The pregnant models were exposed to a perfectly homogeneous **B**-field at 50 Hz of 1 μT amplitude. Based on the results already achieved by [17], the **B**-field orientation, which induced the highest E_{99th} in the foetal whole-body at each GA was chosen. In order to build the PC expansion of E_{99th} in each fetal tissue, N=20 observations were used for all GAs. Those PC models have been then used to randomly generate 1000 E_{99th} values, considering different exposure configurations by changing the conductivity values of foetal tissues in their range of variation, and a statistical analysis has been performed to estimate the trend of E_{99th}.

III. Results

Fig. 1 represent the trend as box-plot of E_{99th} in the 3 and 9 months GA foetal tissue that varies their conductivity values in the ranges defined by the approaches described above.

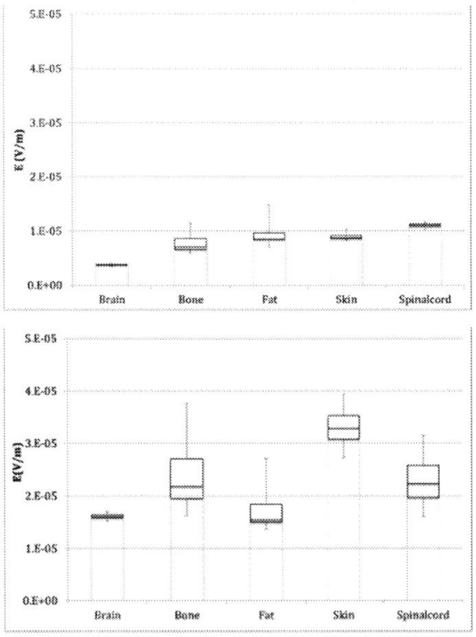

Fig.1: E_{99th} trend in foetal tissues at 3 and 9 months GA. The lower and upper bound of the box represent the 25th and the 75th percentiles, the line is the median value and the whiskers are the minimum and maximum value.

The variation of the exposure, calculated as quartile coefficient of dispersion, in the brain tissue is only of up to 3% for both GAs; the largest variations of E_{99th} was obtained in foetal bone and fat (up to 12%), whereas a variation of 13.2%, for the 9 months GA foetus, has been observed in the spinal cord.

IV. Conclusions

It was found that foetal fat presents the highest variation of dielectric properties with age, which determines also a variation of the induced electric field always higher than 7% across all gestational ages. On the contrary, foetal brain shows a variation of induced **E** of not more than 3% across all GAs. In the spinal cord, despite its limited conductivity range of variation, the induced electric fields are significantly variable. This is due to the close proximity to the bone whose conductivity varies in a broader range. The variation of the **E** in tissues across GAs could present differences due to the difference in anatomy of tissues and organs with GA and their position with respect to the surrounding organs.

Acknowledgment

The authors wish to thank Schmid & Partner Engineering AG (www.speag.com) for having provided the simulation software SIM4Life/SEMCAD X.

References

[1] A. Ahlbom, N. Day, and M. Feytching, "A pooled analysis of magnetic fields and childhood leukemia," *British Journal of Cancer*, vol. 83(5), pp. 692–698, 2000.

[2] L. Kheifets, A. Ahlbom, C.M. Crespi e al., "Pooled analysis on recent studies on magnetic fields and childhood leukemia," *British Journal of Cancer*, vol. 103(7), pp. 1128–1135, 2010

[3] C. Gabriel, "Dielectric properties of biological tissue: variation with age," *Bioelectromagnetics*, vol. supplement 7, pp. S12–18, 2005

[4] A. Peyman, "Dielectric properties of tissues; variation with age and their relevance in exposure of children to electromagnetic fields; state of knowledge." *Prog. Biophys Mol Biol.*, vol. 107, pp. 434–438, 2011.

[5] A. Peyman, C. Gabriel, H.R. Benedickter, and J. Fröhlich, "Dielectric properties of human placenta, umbilical cord and amniotic fluid," *Phys. Med. Biol.*, vol. 56, pp. N93–8, 2011

[6] A. Peyman, and C. Gabriel, "Dielectric properties of rat embryo and fetus as a function of gestation," *Phys. Med. Biol.*, vol. 57, pp. 2103–2116, 2012

[7] P. Dimbylow, "Development of pregnant female, hybrid voxel-mathematical models and their application to the dosimetry of applied magnetic and electric fields at 50 Hz," *Phys. Med. Biol.*, vol. 51, pp. 2383–2394, 2006

[8] R. Cech, N. Leitgeb, and M. Pediaditis, "Fetal exposure to low frequency electric and magnetic fields," *Phys. Med. Biol.*, vol. 52, pp. 879–888, 2007.

[9] N. Wiener, "The homogeneous chaos", *American Journal of Mathematics*, vol. 60(4), pp. 897–936,1938.

[10] C. Soize, and R. Ghanem. "Physical systems with random uncertainties: chaos representations with arbitrary probability measure," *SIAM Journal on Scientific Computing*, vol. 26(2), pp. 395–410, 2004

[11] ICNIRP, Guidelines for limiting exposure to time-varying electric and magnetic fields (1 Hz to 100 kHz). *Health Physics*, vol. 99(6), pp. 818–836, 2010

[12] B. Efron, T. Hastie, I. Johnstone, and R. Tibshirani, "Least angle regression," *The Annals of Statistics*, vol. 32(2), pp. 407–499, 2004

[13] G. Blatmannd, and B. Sudret, "Adaptive sparse polynomial chaos expansion based on least angle regression," *Journal of Computational Physics*, vol. 230, pp. 2345–2367, 2011

[14] M.J. Peters, M. Hendriks, and J. Stinstra, "The passive DC conductivity of human tissue described by cells in solution," *Bioelectroch.*, vol. 53, pp. 155–16, 2001

[15] A. Christ, R. Guldimann, B. Buehlmann et al., "Exposure of the human body to professional and domestic induction cooktops compared to the basic restrictions," *Bioelectromagnetics*, vol. 33(8), pp. 695–705, 2012

[16] SEMCAD X v14.8 by SPEAG, Schmid & Partner Engineering, AG, Zurich, Switzerland, www.speag.com.

[17] Liorni, M. Parazzini, S. Fiocchi, et al., "Dosimetric study of fetal exposure to uniform magnetic fields at 50 Hz," *Bioelectromagnetics*, vol. 35(8), pp. 580-597.

Assessment of fetal exposure to 4G LTE tablet in realistic scenarios using stochastic dosimetry

E. Chiaramello, M. Parazzini, P. Ravazzani
Istituto di Elettronica e di Ingegneria dell'Informazione e delle Telecomunicazioni
Consiglio Nazionale delle Ricerche (CNR)
Milano, Italy

J. Wiart
Télécom ParisTech, LTCI
University Paris Saclay, Chair C2M
Paris, France

Abstract— **Stochastic dosimetry is a promising approach that combines electromagnetic computational techniques and statistics to build surrogate models that can be used for the assessment of the EMF exposure accounting for variability and uncertainty intrinsic of real scenarios. In this study, we will use stochastic dosimetry to assess the exposure of a fetus at 9 months of gestational age to a 4G LTE tablet, analyzing how the exposure changes when moving the tablet in a range of positions representative of realistic exposure scenarios. Polynomial chaos theory, applied to build surrogate models of Specific Absorption Rate (SAR), will permit a fast estimation of the variability of the exposure due to the variation in the tablet position.**

Keywords*— *stochastic dosimetry, polynomial chaos theory, LTE exposure, Specific Absorption Rate

I. Introduction

The development of new devices and new infrastructure for the creation of smart environments based on wireless communications will lead, in the approaching era of the Internet of Things, to an always more pervasive use of Radio-Frequency devices [1]. This highlights the need of conducting appropriate health risk assessment in order to reveal possible health risks correlated to the exposure to these new sources of Radio-Frequency Electromagnetic Fields (RF-EMF) when used in daily realistic scenarios. This is especially true for fetuses who are early exposed to RF-EMF due to the indirect use of devices by adults [2].

The assessment of the exposure to EMF in real scenarios is a challenging task, due to the intrinsic uncertainty and variability of the parameters that influence the exposure (e.g., the source position, the morphology and posture of the subject exposed) [3]. Classical electromagnetic computational techniques typically involve highly time-consuming simulations, making almost impossible to characterize how the exposure changes in variable conditions. A promising approach to face this challenge is given by stochastic dosimetry [4], a method that combines electromagnetic computational techniques and statistics to build surrogate models able to replace the heavy numerical simulations by analytical equations. Among the statistical approaches that could be used to build surrogate models, the polynomial chaos (PC) theory [5], has already been used to study the exposure to low frequency (LF) and RF sources, resulting in an efficient tool to assess the exposure variability [6-7].

In this study, we will use stochastic dosimetry based on the PC theory to evaluate the exposure of a fetus at 9 months of gestational age to RF-EMF due to a 4G LTE tablet in realistic scenarios. The exposure will be characterized in terms of Specific Absorption Rate (SAR). A PC expansion will be built for the SAR induced in each specific tissue of the fetus, to assess the variability of the exposure with the change of the tablet position.

II. Materials and Methods

The Polynomial Chaos is a spectral method and consists in the approximation of the system output Y in a suitable basis Ψ(X) made of orthogonal polynomials [8]:

$$Y = M(X) = \sum_{0}^{P-1} \alpha_j \psi_j(X) + \varepsilon \,, \qquad (1)$$

where Y is the system output, X is the random input vector made of the input parameters x_i, ψ_j are the polynomials belonging to $\Psi(X)$, α_j are the coefficients to be estimated, ε is the error of truncation and P is the size of the polynomial basis Ψ(X).

In this study the random input vector X is composed by five independent input parameters, representing the spatial coordinates of the reciprocal position of the 4G LTE tablet and the exposed fetus (as shown in Fig. 1). All the input parameters x_i are supposed to be uniformly distributed, allowing using the Legendre polynomials as polynomial basis [9].

The coefficients α_j of the PC expansion have been estimated by the Least Angle Regression (LAR) algorithm [10-11] on the basis of a set of observations Y_0. The best solution among the ones generated by LAR has been chosen through a leave-one-out (LOO) cross-validation [12].

The system output Y we modelled by PC is the Specific Absorption Rate (SAR). More specifically, we estimated the SAR in each specific fetal tissue, analyzed in terms of both whole-tissue SAR (SAR_{WT}) and peak SAR averaged on 1 g of tissue ($pSAR_{1gT}$).

The set of observation Y_0 of the SAR have been estimated through deterministic dosimetry (Finite Time Domain Method, FDTD) applied to an input vector X_0 describing N possible position of the sources in the space. We used a high resolution pregnant woman model at 9 months of gestational age (GA), based on the model "Ella" of the Virtual Family [13]. The dielectric properties in each tissue have been assigned on the base of the data available in literature [14].

We used a numerical tablet model designed and validated within the Fp7 European LEXNET Project [15]. The simplified model was built respecting the physical characteristics of current commercial tablets and it is composed of the frame, the display, the battery, the printed circuit board (PCB) and four different antennas, all located on the upper side of the tablet. In this study we used the 4G LTE antenna working in the 800 MHz frequency band.

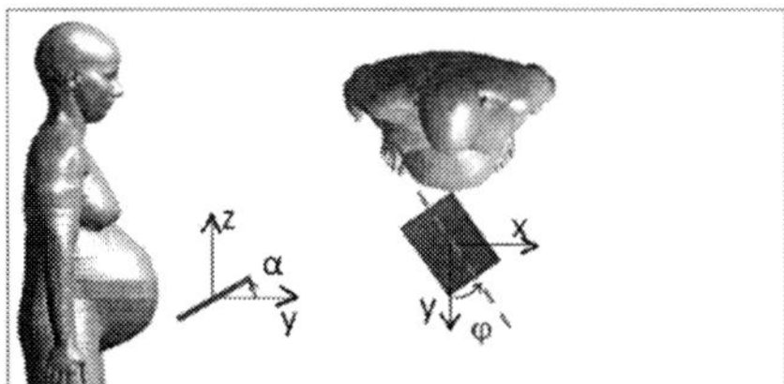

Input parameters	Range of variation
x	[-100, 100] mm
y	[0, 200] mm
z	[0, 200] mm
α	[0°, 45°]
φ	[0°; 90°; 180°; 270°]

Fig.1. Schematic view of the exposure scenarios of the pregnant woman to the 4G LTE tablet. The input parameters and their ranges of variation are reported.

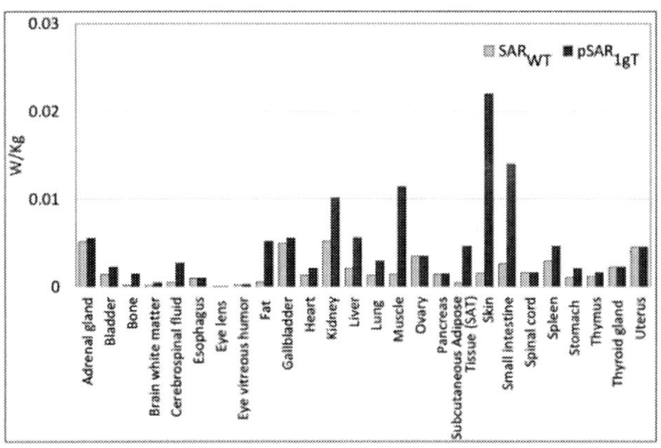

Fig.2. Preliminary results in terms of SAR_{WT} and $pSAR_{1gT}$ referred to the exposure 9-months GA fetus to the 4G LTE tablet in a generic position.

III. Expected Results

Fig.2 shows, as example, some preliminary results referred to the exposure of the 9-months GA fetus to the 4G LTE tablet in a generic position among those described in Fig.1. All the reported SAR values have been normalized to a radiated power equal to 1 W. In this specific position, among all fetal tissues, adrenal gland, gallbladder and kidney showed SAR_{WT} values slightly higher than 5 mW/kg. Considering the $pSAR_{1gT}$ values, among all tissues skin, small intestine, muscle and kidney showed values higher than 10 mW/kg (with maximum of 22 mW/kg in the skin tissue).

Using the PC expansion, we will use a set of these type of data to build a surrogate model that will allow us to evaluate the exposure variability due to realistic movement of the tablet in the range of positions described by Fig. 1. This will allow not only to understand if there are specific positions in which the exposure of fetal tissues is higher than in others, but also to obtain a robust tool for the estimation of the fetal exposure to the 4G tablet accounting for the uncertainty in the positioning of the tablet.

Acknowledgment

This research is supported by the European project FP7 EC Project GERONIMO "Generalized EMF research using novel methods. An integrated approach: from research to risk assessment and support to risk management" (1 Gen 2014 – 31 Dic 2018, AGREEMENT NUMBER 603794, 24/02/2014).

References

[1] G. Dürrenberger, J. Fröhlich, M. Röösli and M.O. Mattsson, "EMF Monitoring—Concepts, Activities, Gaps and Options," in Int. J. Environ. Res. Public Health, vol. 11(9), pp. 9460-9479, September 2014.

[2] CV. Bellieni, and I. Pinto, "Fetal and neonatal effects of EMF, " BioInitiative Working Group:" A Rationale for Biologically-Based Exposure Standards for Low-Intensity Electromagnetic Radiation" Section 19, 2012.

[3] J. Wiart, et al. "Handle variability in numerical exposure assessment: the challenge of the stochastic dosimetry," Antennas and Propagation (EuCAP), 7th European Conference on. IEEE, April 2013.

[4] J. Wiart, Radio-Frequency Human Exposure Assessment: From Deterministic to Stochastic Methods. John Wiley & Sons, 2016.

[5] N. Wiener, " The Homogeneous Chaos," American Journal of Mathematics, vol. 60(4), pp. 897-936, Oct., 1938.

[6] I. Liorni, M. Parazzini, S. Fiocchi, and P. Ravazzani, "Study of the Influence of the Orientation of a 50-Hz Magnetic Field on Fetal Exposure Using Polynomial Chaos Decomposition," International journal of environmental research and public health, vol. 12(6), pp. 5934-5953, May 2015.

[7] I. Liorni, M. Parazzini, N. Varsier, A. Hadjem, P. Ravazzani, and J. Wiart, "Exposure assessment of one-year-old child to 3G tablet in uplink mode and to 3G femtocell in downlink mode using polynomial chaos decomposition," Physics in medicine and biology, vol. 61(8), pp. 3237-3257, 2016.

[8] G. Blatman, "Adaptive sparse polynomial chaos expansions foruncertainty propagation and sensitivity analysis," Ph.D Thesis, Université Blaise Pascal, Clermont-Ferrand, 2009.

[9] D. Xiu, and G.E. Karniadakis, "The Wiener-Askey polynomial chaos for stochastic differential equations," SIAM Journal on Scientific Computing, vol. 24(2), pp. 619-644, 2002

[10] Efron et al., "Least angle regression", The Annals of Statistics, vol. 32(2), pp. 407-499, 2004.

[11] G. Blatman, and B. Sudret, "Adaptive sparse polynomial chaos expansion based on least angle regression", Journal of Computational Physics, vol. 230, pp. 2345-2367, 2011.

[12] M. Stone, "Cross-validatory choice and the assessment of statistical predictions (with discussion)," Journal of the Royal Statistical Society, vol. B36, pp. 111-33, 1974.

[13] A. Christ, et al. "The Virtual Family—development of surface-based anatomical models of two adults and two children for dosimetric simulations," Physics in medicine and biology, vol.55(2), N23, 2009.

[14] M. Tesanovic et al. "The LEXNET project: wireless networks and EMF: paving the way for Low- EMF networks of the future," IEEE Veh. Technol. Mag., vol. 9, pp. 20–8, 2014.

Exposure to electric and magnetic fields at intermediate frequencies of household appliances

Sam Aerts*, Günter Vermeeren*, Carolina Calderon†, Blaž Valič‡, Matthias Van den Bossche*, Leen Verloock*, Myron Maslanyj†, Darren Addison†, Peter Gajšek‡, Luc Martens*, Martin Röösli§, Elisabeth Cardis¶, and Wout Joseph*

*Ghent University / imec, Ghent, Belgium
Email: sam.aerts@intec.ugent.be
†Public Health England, Chilton, Didcot, Oxon OX11 0RQ, United Kingdom
‡Institute of Non-Ionizing Radiation (INIS), Ljubljana, Slovenia
§Swiss Tropical and Public Health Institute (Swiss TPH) and University of Basel, Basel, Switzerland
¶Barcelona Institute for Global Health (ISGlobal), Barcelona, Spain

***Abstract*—Human exposure to electric and magnetic fields has been amply investigated in the extremely-low frequency (ELF) and radiofrequency (RF) ranges. However, research on typical emissions in the intermediate-frequency (IF) range remains limited. In this study, an extensive measurement survey was performed on the levels of electric and magnetic fields at intermediate frequencies typically emitted by a wide range of household appliances. The emissions contained either harmonic signals, with fundamental frequencies between 6 kHz and 100 kHz, or much more capricious spectra, dominated by 50 Hz harmonics emanating far in the IF domain. Use of appliances at close distance (20 cm) of certain appliances may result in a relatively high exposure, but no appliance's IF emissions exceeded the ICNIRP2010 exposure summation rule (maximum electric- and magnetic-field exposure quotients were respectively 1.00, for a compact fluorescent lamp, and 0.13, for an induction cooker).**

I. Introduction

In the last decades, electric appliances have become indispensable in our households. Historically, the assessment of human exposure to electric and magnetic fields emitted by household appliances has focused on the extremely-low-frequency (ELF) [1] and radiofrequency (RF) ranges. However, the range of appliances with electrical components working in the intermediate-frequency (IF) range (300 Hz to 1 MHz) has grown significantly in recent years (e.g., induction cookers and compact fluorescent lighting) and there is still only limited information available on the typical strength of the IF fields emitted by household appliances [3]. In this study, the IF emissions in everyday circumstances were measured of 281 household appliances in residences across three European countries (Belgium, Slovenia, and the United Kingdom).

II. Materials & Methods

In each residence, a standardised measurement protocol was followed. Identification of IF-emitting household appliances was done by measuring the electric- or magnetic-field strength around the operational appliance in the 2 kHz to 1 MHz band with a compact handheld NFA-1000 meter (Gigahertz Solutions, Langenzenn, Germany). Then, the appliance's electric- and magnetic-field emissions in the 1 kHz to 100 kHz range were accurately characterized with a computer-operated narrowband EHP-50 probe (Narda Safety Test Solutions, Milan, Italy) at a measuring distance of 20 cm. During this measurement, the appliance was operated at settings typical for the residents and the probe was positioned in front of the face of the appliance closest to the user. Finally, to assess the total electric- (E) or magnetic-field (H) exposure of an IF-emitting household appliance, the Exposure Quotient (EQ_F, with $F = E$ or H) was calculated following the summation rule of the International Commission on Non-Ionizing Radiation Protection (ICNIRP) [4]:

$$EQ_F = \sum_{i=1}^{N} \frac{F_{peak,i}}{F_{R,i}}, \tag{1}$$

where only the peak field strengths $F_{peak,i}$ higher than 5% of the corresponding reference level $F_{R,i}$ at frequency i were considered in the EQ calculation (for i between 3 kHz and 150 kHz, $E_{R,i} = 83$ V/m and $H_{R,i} = 21$ A/m).

III. Results

In total, measurement data were collected for 281 household appliances. They were divided into 65 categories, of which, based on the 5% threshold of the exposure summation rule of Eq. (1), fourteen were considered exposure-relevant (Table I).

Of the exposure-relevant categories, *power tools* and *compact fluorescent lamps (CFLs)* were the most present in residences. Furthermore, three categories—fridges, laundry machines, and microwave ovens—had been split in two because of the presence of IF fields caused by the use of inverter technology (IT), which offers better control (speed or temperature) and a higher energy efficiency. The maximum wideband electric- and magnetic-field strengths (measured over the range 1–100 kHz) were 41.84 V/m and 3.71 A/m, both for *induction cookers*. For the appliances with IT, the higest field strengths were 13.03 V/m (refrigerator) and 1.43 A/m (microwave oven). When calculating the Exposure Quotients (Fig. 1), on the other hand, the highest EQ_E (1.00) was found for *CFLs*, while the maximum EQ_H (0.13) was again

TABLE I

IF EXPOSURE-RELEVANT HOUSEHOLD APPLIANCE CATEGORIES. n = THE TOTAL NUMBER OF SAMPLES, E_{max} AND H_{max} ARE THE CATEGORY'S HIGHEST ELECTRIC- AND MAGNETIC-FIELD STRENGTHS (WIDEBAND VALUES BETWEEN 1 AND 100 KHZ) MEASURED AT A DISTANCE OF 20 CM, AND f_{IF} SIGNIFIES THE FREQUENCY RANGE IN WHICH IF FUNDAMENTAL FREQUENCIES WERE FOUND.

category	n	E_{max} (V/m)	H_{max} (A/m)	f_{IF} (kHz)
battery charger	5	11.56	0.10	42–65
cold-cathode fluorescent lamp (CCFL)	1	10.75	0.08	39
compact fluorescent lamp (CFL)	28	37.27	0.11	25–65
cathode ray tube (CRT) display	11	22.81	0.40	15–31
electric toothbrush charger	6	4.26	0.17	21–45
fluorescent lamp	5	40.15	0.11	32–50
induction cooker	12	41.84	3.71	18–45
laundry machine IT	18	6.21	0.13	8–61
liquid crystal display (LCD)	5	42.70	0.72	45–90
microwave oven IT	5	2.47	1.43	—
power tool	48	19.78	2.28	—
refrigerator IT	1	13.03	0.10	6
spotlight transformer	5	6.91	1.51	15–60
welding machine	2	7.29	0.18	98

found for *induction cookers*. Furthermore, in most of these 14 categories, the appliance emissions had fundamental frequencies in the electric- and/or magnetic-field spectrum between 6 kHz (*refrigerator with IT*) and 98 kHz (*welding machine*) (Table I)—often accompanied by harmonics further down the spectrum—though in two cases (*power tools* and *IT microwave ovens*), the appliances' spectra were elevated throughout the examined frequency range.

IV. Discussion & Conclusions

Using a standardised protocol, a measurement survey spanning three countries resulted in a wealth of data on the typical emissions of electric and magnetic fields at intermediate frequencies by household appliances. IF exposure-relevant appliance categories identified in this study that were not yet described in the literature include liquid crystal displays (LCDs), electric toothbrush and battery chargers, power tools, and appliances with inverter technology (which could become increasingly important in the future). For previously assessed categories (in e.g., [5]), i.e., induction cookers, CFLs, and CRTs, the measurements were in line with the reported values. Overall, emissions in the IF range contained either harmonic signals, with fundamental frequencies between 6 and 100 kHz, or much more capricious spectra, possibly dominated by 50 Hz harmonics emanating far in the IF domain; and at a measuring distance of 20 cm, the maximum observed electric- (EQ_E) and magnetic-field Exposure Quotients (EQ_H) did not exceed the ICNIRP exposure summation rule. The information provided by this study fills a gap in knowledge on typical human exposures to electromagnetic fields, and, in combination with appliance usage data, can be valuable in future epidemiological studies assessing the impact of exposure to IF fields.

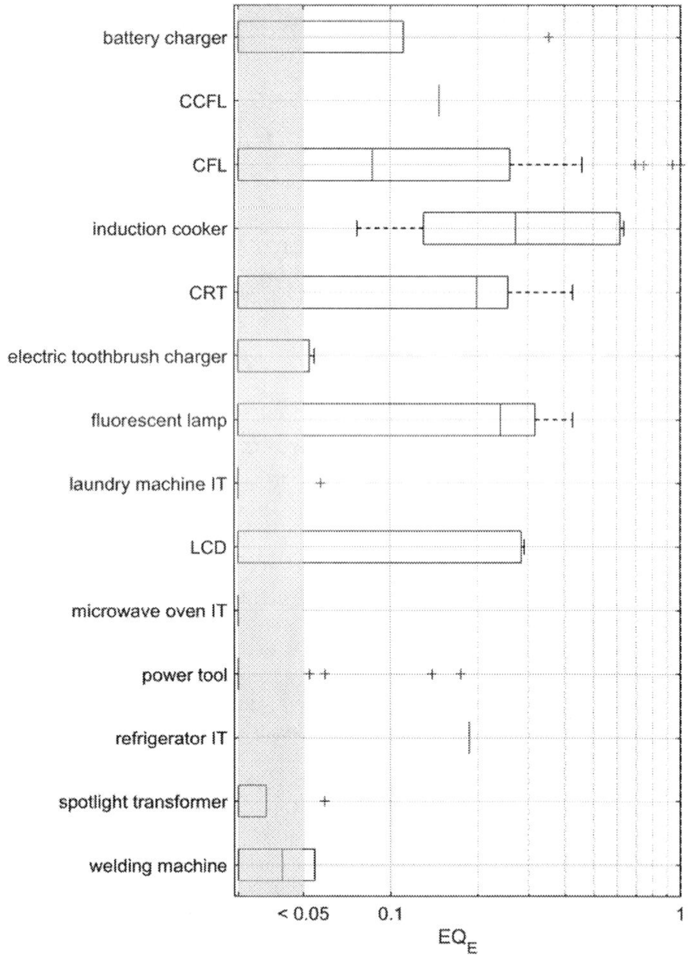

Fig. 1. Electric-field EQ boxplots at 20 cm calculated following guidelines in Ref. [4] for the exposure-relevant categories. All other categories only had EQs < 0.05. EQs in the gray area are < 0.05. Red crosses are outliers.

Acknowledgment

The research leading to these results has received funding from the European Community's Seventh Framework Programme (FP7/2007-2013) under grant agreement no 603794 – the GERONIMO project.

References

[1] N. Leitgeb, R. Cech, and J. Schröttner, "Electric emissions from electrical appliances," Radiat. Prot. Dosimetry, vol. 129, no. 4, pp. 446–455, 2008.

[2] G. Vermeeren, I. Markakis, F. Goeminne, T. Samaras, L. Martens, and W. Joseph, "Spatial and temporal RF electromagnetic field exposure of children and adults in indoor micro environments in Belgium and Greece," Prog. Biophys. Mol. Biol., vol. 113, no. 2, pp. 254–263, 2013.

[3] E. Litvak, K. R. Foster, and M. H. Repacholi, "Health and Safety Implications of Exposure to Electromagnetic Fields in the Frequency Range 300 Hz to 10 MHz," Bioelectromagnetics, vol. 23, no. 1, pp. 68–82, 2002.

[4] International Commission on Non-Ionizing Radiation Protection (ICNIRP), "Guidelines for limiting exposure to time-varying electric and magnetic fields (1 Hz to 100 kHz)," Health Phys., vol. 99, no. 6, pp. 818–836, 2010.

[5] E. D. Mantiply, K. R. Pohl, S. W. Poppell, and J. A. Murphy, "Summary of measured radiofrequency electric and magnetic fields (10 kHz to 30 GHz) in the general and work environment," Bioelectromagnetics, vol. 18, no. 8, pp. 563–577, 1997.

Phase-Only Synthesis of Convex Metallic Reflectarray Antennas for Multi-beam Radiations via Steepest Descent Method

Jen-Wei Liu and Hsi-Tseng Chou
Department of Electrical Engineering, National Taiwan University, Taipei 10617, Taiwan
b02901087@ntu.edu.tw

Abstract—**This paper presents the numerical analysis and synthesis of metallic reflectarray antennas to radiate multi-beams for the multi-sector coverage in wireless communications. The synthesis procedure is developed based on the concept of steepest descent method to optimize the phase variation of reflecting elements. In particular, closed-form formulations are obtained to update the phases in each iteration and completely avoid the cumbersome numerical summations of scattering fields. Numerical examples will be presented to demonstrate the concepts and validate the feasibility.**

Keywords—Reflectarray antenna, multi-beam radiation, steepest descent method, phase-only synthesis.

I. Introduction

Using a single set of antenna to radiate multiple beams for the multi-sector coverage of wireless communications attracts much attention in recent years. In particular, at millimeter waves (mmW), high-gain antenna radiation with subsequently resulting in narrow beamwidth is required to compensate the power loss of electromagnetic (EM) waves in propagation, which not only reduces the angular coverage area, but also significantly increases the cost as larger antennas need to be used. In addition, the high energy inside the PCB-based antenna structures is another bottleneck to worsen the situation of radio coverage at mmW.

This paper presents the design of metallic reflectarray antennas [1] for the multi-beam radiations, where the use of metallic reflecting elements consists of several advantages of high-energy efficiency, miniaturized sizes, compact structures, broad bandwidth of radiations, etc. In particular, this work develops a numerical model to fast analyze the radiation of reflectarray antennas and synthesize the phases of reflecting elements for the compromised multi-beam radiations. We have developed a procedure based on the concept of steepest decent method (SDM) [2], which results in closed-form formulations of phase variation for the reflecting elements along each synthesis iteration without the need to repeatedly compute the radiation patterns. In addition, the resulted phases can be directly mapped to find the profile of reflectarray based on the concept of geometrical optics (GO). As a result, the simulation tool is self-sufficient in the design of metallic multi-beam reflectarray antennas. Numerical examples will be presented to illustrate the design procedure. More details will be presented in the conference.

II. Design of The Multi-beam Reflectarray

A. Structure of Reflecting Elements

A convex metallic elemental structure is illustrated in Fig. 1, where the size is same as the array period, w_1. The phase variation of reflecting element is created by varying the height of the element, h_2. It can be shown by using the concept of GO that the relation of elemental phase to the height is described by

$$\Phi = kh_2(\cos\theta_i + \cos\theta), \quad (1)$$

where k is the wavenumber, θ_i is the angle of incidence by the feed's radiation with respect to the reflectarray boresight, and θ is the angle of scattering which is also measured from the array boresight. It is seen that the relative phase varies with respect to both the scattering and incident angles.

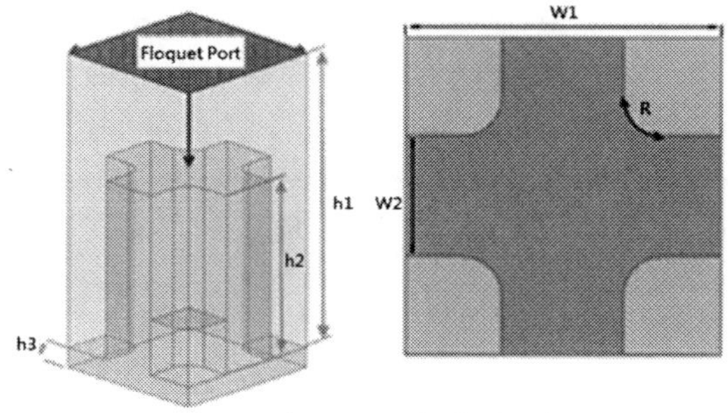

Fig. 1: Basic structure of reflecting elements

B. Formalism of the Reflectarray's Radiation

The radiation of reflectarray antenna can be modeled by [2]

$$E_{co}^{s}(\bar{r}) = \sum_{n=0}^{N-1} e^{j\Phi_n}\left[F(\hat{r}_{f\cdot n})\frac{e^{-jk\ell_n}}{\ell_n}\right]\left[G_n(\hat{r})e^{jk\hat{r}\cdot\bar{r}'_n}\right]\frac{e^{-jkr}}{r} \quad (2)$$

where N is the number of array elements with Φ_n being the required phase of the nth element. The reference element is denoted by $n = 0$. In (2), ℓ_n is the distance from the feed to the nth element with $\bar{r}'_n$ being the location. It is noted that the terms inside the first bracket of (2) denote the radiation of feed to illuminate the reflectarray while those inside the second bracket denote the scattering field of nth element. In particular, F and G are patterns of feed and reflecting element, respectively. For simplification, the feed's radiation pattern can be modelled by a cosine taper with a power q as [3]

$$F(\hat{r}_f) = Ae^{j\Phi_f}(\cos\theta_f)^q, \quad (3)$$

where the taper is matched to find the index, q. Similarly, the pattern function, G, is also modelled by another cosine taper function, whose pattern is found by matching it to the elemental radiation of an infinite array illuminated by a plane wave for simplification. Numerical experiments show that the patterns remain relatively staple regardless of the incident angles when the element is small. The phase term, Φ_n, in equation (2) is the relative phase of the nth reflecting element which is impressed to compensate the phase of scattering fields in the target zone for an optimum field distribution.

In the synthesis problem, the desired set of phases, Φ_n, is found by matching the radiation patterns of reflectarray fed by multiple feeding antennas, where each feed's radiation will result in a beam pointing to different directions at the same frequency. It is desired to make the overlapping of beams orthogonal or uniformly distributed for an optimum coverage. Thus, if M field points in the target area are selected, then the net scattered field at r_m (m=1~M) of each beam becomes

$$E^s_{co}(\bar{r}_m)=\sum_{n=0}^{N-1} e^{j\Phi_n}E_{nm}\approx E_d(\bar{r}_m) \quad (4)$$

where the co-polarized pattern is synthesized with E_d being the desired pattern. In (4), E_{nm} denotes the multiplication of the two bracket terms in (2) to denote the elemental contribution. In the multi-beam radiations, where the illumination of elements comes from various feeds when different beams are considered. In this case, Φ_n remains same for all beams while E_{nm} has different phases in excitation by different feeds. The initial guess of Φ_n is selected to make the radiation of the reflectarray focus toward a reference direction by a desired feed to resemble the characteristics of a parabolic reflector antenna. The phases are afterward adjusted to compromise the radiation gains for the various beams via the SDM based algorithm.

C. Phase-Only Synthesis Via SDM

The procedure starts with defining the cost function by

$$\Omega=\sum_{m=1}^{M}\sum_{p=1}^{P} f_{mp}\left|G_{mp}-G^d_{mp}\right|^2, \quad (5)$$

where M field points for each of P beams are considered, G_{mp} and G^d_{mp} are the computed and desired gains. As illustrated by SDM, the phases are found along the derivative of the cost function, which can be expressed as a closed form by [4]

$$\frac{\partial\Omega}{\partial\Phi_n}=2\sum_{m=1}^{M}\sum_{p=1}^{P}\left[f_{mp}\frac{\partial G_{mp}}{\partial\Phi_n}\left(G_{mp}-G^d_{mp}\right)\right]. \quad (6)$$

The advantage of this modelling is that the derivatives of G_{mp} can be found as a closed form, which will be shown in the conference presentation. In particular, in the procedure of simulation, the computation of gains in (6) does not need to repeat as each time of computation only an element's contribution is changed, which can be simply replaced in the gain computation without the need to re-compute the others.

III. Numerical Results

Numerical example considers a rectangular grid of reflecting element distribution (24 x 25 elements) at 38GHz. The parameters in Fig. 1 are selected as follows. The cell period, w_1, 4 mm, roughly a half wavelength, and w_2 is set as 1.5 mm. In this case, eight beams are considered to provide a coverage of ±30° coverage. The target is to have gains of larger 20dBi within the angular coverage area. The synthesized patterns of multi-beams are shown in Fig. 2, where the comparisons between the patterns of three cases that were obtained from the original non-optimized reflectarray resembling the parabolic reflector for the central feed, the optimized reflectarray, and the optimized reflectarray with additional feed location adjustment for proper beam overlapping, respectively. The comparison between the results of using the developed MATLAB codes and using the simulation tool FEKO are also shown to demonstrate the simulation accuracy for a single feed illumination. In particular, the green lines are the patterns obtained from the original reflectarray with the phase variations resembling a parabolic reflector for the directional beam radiation, where no optimization has been performed. This result serves as the reference solution to justify the effectiveness of multi-beam optimization. The blue lines show the patterns after the SDM based optimization is performed. The compromise to equalize the radiation gains has been observed. Here the gains of the central two beams drop by almost 3dB while the outer two beams increase by also 4dB. To assure a better beam overlapping, the feed locations are slightly adjusted after the optimization to make the beams orthogonal, which results are shown by the red lines. In this case, 23 iterations are used to obtain the converged results. Fig. 3 shows the reflectarray model done in FEKO, and the size of the reflectarray is also given.

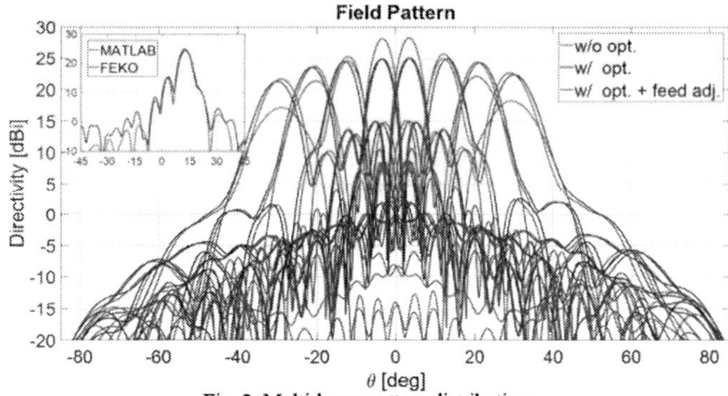

Fig. 2: Multi-beam pattern distribution

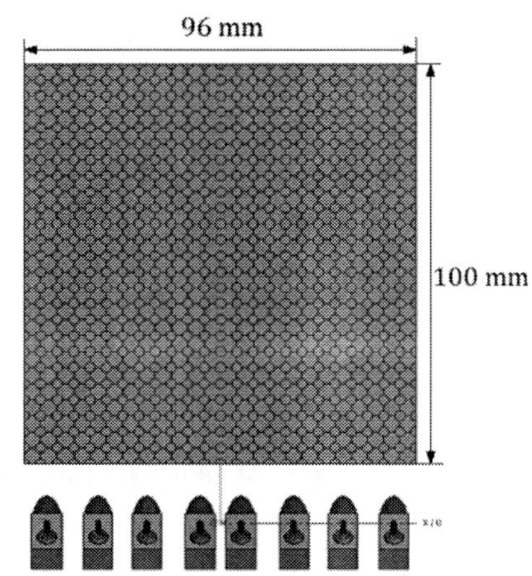

Fig. 3: The reflectarray model

IV. Conclusion

This paper presents a simple approach to design a metallic reflectarray antenna. Promising results have been obtained without the need of using sophisticated commercial codes. The comparison with full-wave simulation will be presented in the conference. In addition, the characteristics of convergence in iteration and phase variation will be also presented to demonstrate the validity.

References

[1] Huang, J., and J. A. Encinar (2007), Reflectarray Antennas, 216 pp., Wiley-IEEE Press,

[2] Chou, H.-T., Y.-X. Liu, X.-Y. Dong, B.-Q. You, and L.-R. Kuo (2015), "Design of reflectarray antennas to achieve an optimum near-field radiation for RFID applications via the implementation of SDM procedure", Radio Sci., 50, 283–293,

[3] Rahmat-Samii, Y., and S.-W. Lee (1983), Directivity of planar array feeds for satellite reflector applications, IEEE Trans. Antennas Propag., 31(3), 463–470,

[4] H. T Chou, T. M Hung, N. N Wang, H. H Chou, C Tung, and P. Nepa, " Design of a near-field focused reflectarray antenna for 2.4 GHz RFID reader applications," in IEEE Trans. Antennas and Propag. , vol. 59, no. 3, pp. 1013-1018, Mar. 2011

Energy Paradigms of Augmented Tags for the Internet of Things Deployment

Smail TEDJINI, Gianfranco ANDIA VERA
Grenoble-inp/LCIS
University Grenoble Alpes
Valence, France
smail.tedjini@grenoble-inp.fr

Yvan DUROC
Ampere Laboratory
University Lyon 1
Lyon, France
yvan.duroc@univ-lyon1.fr

Abstract—**This paper reviews and compares different techniques to collect more energy for passive UHF RFID Tags. The main objective is to allow the tags to embed new functions and provide more than identification. Such additional capture of energy transforms the simple tag into an augmented tag able to perform new functions such as sensing, channel diversity and much more.**

Keywords—RFID, UHF, Energy, Harvesting, Sensing, Channel diversity, Communication

I. Introduction

Todays, the majority of passive UHF (Ultra High Frequencies) RFID (Radio Frequency IDentification) tags is able to provide read-range of several meters and therefore is suitable to perform complex traceability applications. Remembering the birth and the development of RFID since the 1940s, it is interesting to notice that the first tag ever demonstrated was the device known as "the Thing" designed by Leon Theremin in 1945 and used as spying microphone for several years [1]. Nowadays, the technology allows the development of very sensitive tags exhibiting only -22 dBm as activation power and allowing a read range of more than 25 m [2]. In the same time, the concept of the Internet of Things (IoT) becomes more real and its effective implementation is highly expected. Indeed, IoT is not "science-fiction" or something that will happen in the future – it is real, and it is here now. Some players forecast that the number of connected devices outnumbers the number of men, women, and children on the planet about five years ago. It is expected that the number of connected objects will grow to about 50 billion over the next three years [3]. In the last few years, and in order to turn in reality the IoT, several evolutions of the RFID technology have been proposed and recently the idea of augmented tags appeared [4].

Adding new capabilities to RFID tags in order to provide more than ID is very effective in terms of applications in particular those involving networking. Indeed the use of the standardized RFID communication protocol will allow the designers to exploit the normalized RFID commands and to define new commands more compliant and specific to the implemented capability. In all these new scenarios the availability of additional amount of energy is mandatory. Indeed without energy nothing is possible. It is worth noting that adding batteries to tags is not a relevant solution that turns in more expensive and limited lifetime devices. The challenging is to consider either passive effects like antenna sensitivity to its immediate environment or to harvest more power from the one emitted by the interrogator. Indeed, the readers emit plenty of power (up to some watts) in comparison to the one collected by the conventional tag (less than milli-watt).

This paper discusses different options to collect power from the reader and to exploit this power to add new capabilities to the passive UHF Tags. In Section 2, we report the preliminary step RFID chip characterization, in particular the measurement of chip impedance states at different frequencies which will trigger proper design of multipurpose tag antennas. In Section 3, we demonstrate the capability of RFID tag to communicate at different frequencies in the same time, which turns in channel diversity. Section 4 focus on energy harvesting from ambient source and how this can improve the performance of RFID tags. The last section is dedicated to concluding remarks and perspectives for future developments.

II. RFID Chip Impedances

Any antenna design for RFID tag requires good knowledge of the impedance states at the communication frequency. In most cases the chip manufactory provides only the impedance of the absorbing state at certain frequency. However the knowledge of the two states allows the design of optimized tags in term of backscattered signal [5]. So, for purpose of effective tag design it is necessary to measure both impedance states at fundamental frequency [6] but also at harmonic frequencies [7]. An example of measured impedance is illustrated in Fig. 1.

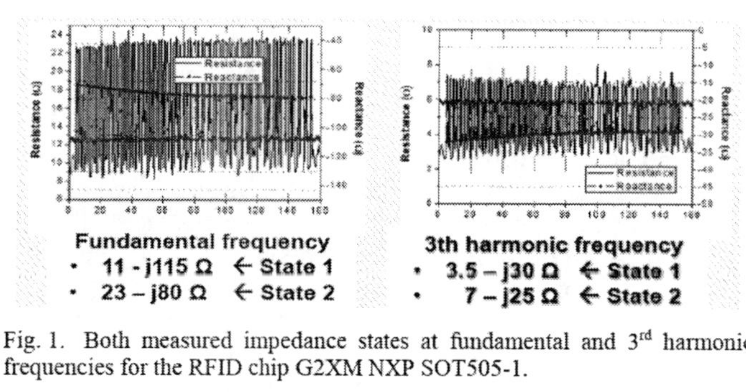

Fig. 1. Both measured impedance states at fundamental and 3rd harmonic frequencies for the RFID chip G2XM NXP SOT505-1.

III. CHANNEL DIVERSITY

It is worth noting that the first stage of any RFID chip is a rectifier circuit to harvest the energy that will empower the circuitry of the chip. Therefore nonlinear characteristics of the diode elements will generate harmonic signals. It has been demonstrated that the 3rd harmonic component has significant magnitude that allows its consideration in terms of applications. The pinpointed effective tag antenna design favors its response at the 3rd harmonic frequency will turn in channel diversity. The information backscattered at the 3rd harmonic is a replica of the one at fundamental frequency. A read range of several meters at the 3rd harmonic has been demonstrated as depicted in Fig. 2 that shows a comparison of the measured 3rd harmonic read-ranges for commercial tags and the so-called Harmonic Tag [8].

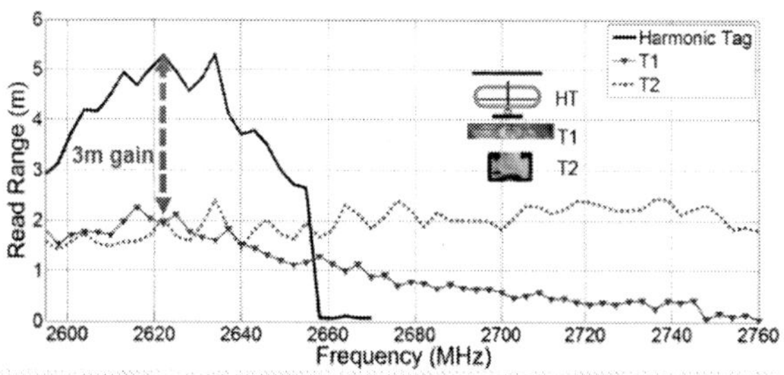

Fig. 2. Comparison of 3rd harmonic read-ranges of commercial tags (T1 & T2) and the Harmonic Tag (HT). The design of the HT tag antenna takes into account the impedance states at the 3rd harmonic frequency.

Redundant channel diversity is very relevant property that can be exploited in several applications, in particular in localization as it has been proposed in [9]. No additional source of energy is required: the 3rd harmonic is "naturally" generated due to the nonlinear behavior of the rectifier.

IV. ENERGY HARVESTING

Energy harvesting can be seen following several approaches. One challenging approach consists in harvesting the energy generated by nonlinear behavior of the rectifier that in non-optimized design, is lost on the harmonics. The measurement conducted in [8] demonstrated that the generated power in 2nd, 4th and 5th harmonic is quite low compare to one available in the 3rd harmonic. While the harvested power from the 3rd harmonic is certainly low, but it can be exploited to improve the read range of the tag or can be accumulated in a supercapacitance in order to feed another circuit such as sensor. A harvester circuit can be designed and integrated to the RFID chip. A typical arrangement for harvesting from the 3rd harmonic or external ambient source is depicted on Fig. 3. It is worth noting that the matching network for the rectifier circuit should be tuned at the frequency of the energy source (3rd harmonic or ambient source).

Another approach for energy harvesting consists in the control of the signal to be harvested in order to optimize the RF-to-dc conversion. It has been demonstrated that the temporal waveform of the harvested signal has large effect on the conversion efficiency. Larger is the PAPR (Peak to Average Ratio Power) better is the efficiency; in particular for low signal levels which is the case in RFID [10]. One way to exploit this fact is to mix the generated 3rd harmonic with another ambient signal that has a frequency close enough to the 3rd harmonic. An implementation of this approach that mixes the 3rd harmonic at 3×868 = 2.604 GHz and a Wi-Fi signal at 2.45 GHz provides the conversion efficiency depicted in Fig. 4. This figure demonstrates a significant improvement of the RF-to-dc conversion when Wi-Fi is combined to the 3rd harmonic.

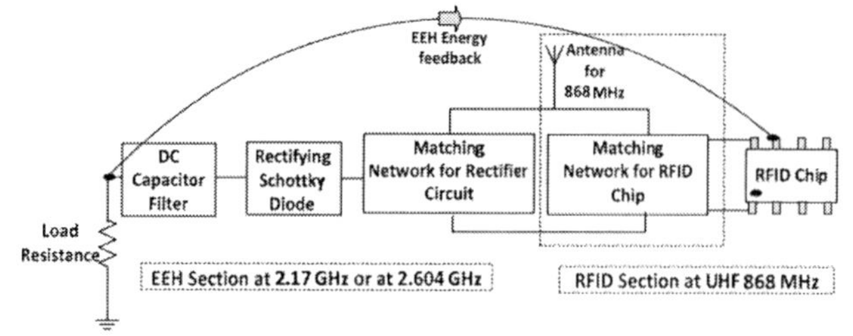

Fig. 3. Example of arrangement for harvesting the energy from the 3rd harmonic or other ambiant energy source.

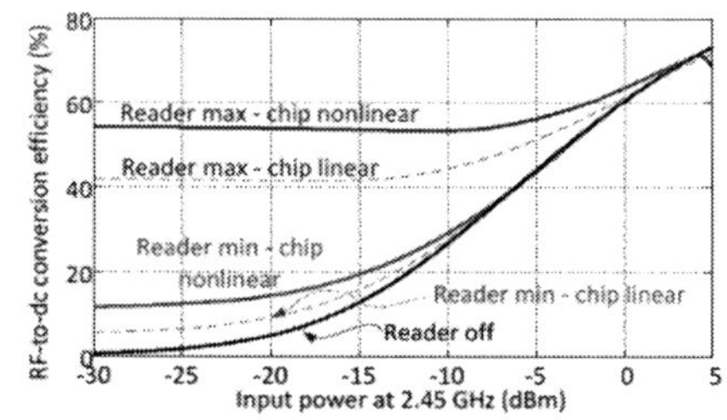

Fig. 4. Performance of harvesting a mixed signal combining the generated 3rd harmonic at 2.604 GHz and an ambient Wi-Fi signal at 2. 45 GHz.

V. CONCLUSION

This paper discusses different ways to transform the conventional RFID tags into augmented tags able to provide more than ID. New paradigms for harvesting, exploiting and management energy within the tag are carried out. These paradigms can extend the capabilities of RFID tags and turn them into a relevant option for the IoT implementation.

VI. REFERENCES

[1] P.V. Nikitin, "Leo Theremin (Lev Termen)," IEEE Antennas Propagation Magazine, vol. 54, no. 5, pp. 252-257, October 2012.

[2] http://www.impinj.com/products/tag-chips/

[3] https://www.cisco.com/c/dam/en_us/about/ac79/docs/innov/IoT_IBSG04 11FINAL.pdf

[4] S. Tedjini, G. Andia Vera, Z. Marcos, R.C.S Freire, Y. Duroc "Augmented RFID tags," in Proc. IEEE Radio and Wireless Week, Austin, TX, USA, January 23-27, 2016

[5] D. Hotte, R. Siragusa, Y. Duroc, S. Tedjini, "Optimization performance for the choice of impedances in the design of passive RFID tags," in Proc. Int. Conf. Electromag Adv. Appl, Turino, Italia, Sept 9-13, 2013.

[6] L. Mayer, A. Scholtz, "Sensitivity and impedance measurements on UHF RFID transponder chips," in Proc. EURASIP Workshop on RFID Technology, Budapest, Hungary, pp. 1- 10, 2007.

[7] G. Andia Vera, Y. Duroc, S. Tedjini, "RFID test platform: nonlinear characterization," IEEE Transactions on Instrumentation and Measurement, vol. 63, no. 9, pp. 2299-2305, September 2014.

[8] G. Andia Vera, Y. Duroc, S. Tedjini, "Tag-to-reader harmonic link in passive UHF RFID," in Proc. IEEE International Microwave Symposium, Tampa Bay, FL, USA, June 1-6, 2014.

[9] H.G. Gomes, N.B.C. Carvalho, "RFID for location proposes based on the intermodulation distortion," Sensors & Transducers Magazine, vol. 106, n.7, pp.85-96, July 2009.

[10] A. Collado, A. Georgiadis, "Optimal waveforms for efficient wireless power transmission, IEEE-MWCLvol.24, no.5, pp.354-356, May 2014.

Principal Component Analysis of CSI for the Robust Wireless Detection of Passive Targets

F. Viani[1], A. Polo[1], E. Giarola[1], M. Salucci[1], and A. Massa[1,2]
[1] ELEDIA Research Center (ELEDIA@UniTN - University of Trento)
Trento, Italy
[2] ELEDIA Research Center (ELEDIA@L2S - UMR 8506)
Gif-sur-Yvette, France
andrea.massa@eledia.org

Abstract— **Recent standards for wireless networks introduced spatial and frequency diversity to improve the quality and the bandwidth of the wireless communications. The arising channel state information has been exploited for the wireless localization of device-free targets. In this work, a principal component analysis has been applied to the channel state information in order to extract a target-dependent feature suitable to enable the robust detection of passive targets in large indoor areas. The experimental validation performed with commercial WiFi access points pointed out a failure rate lower than 3 [%] in a real indoor test field.**

Keywords—Device-free localization; channel state information; principal component analysis; MIMO systems.

I. Introduction

The passive wireless localization of device-free targets has attracted a lot of interest in the last years. The presence and the position of humans in indoor environments represent a fundamental information for many location-based services. The received signal strength indicator (RSSI) of the wireless links is usually measured by the nodes of a wireless sensor network (WSN) or by the access points of a WiFi local area network. The RSSI is affected by the targets' presence and its perturbations have been exploited by many localization algorithms [1]-[5]. The recent introduction of wireless standards based on the orthogonal frequency-division multiplexing (OFDM) and on multiple-input multiple-output (MIMO) architectures has made available the channel state information (CSI) [6], which is a powerful indicator of the electromagnetic (EM) propagation at multiple frequencies.

The spatial and frequency diversity of the CSI have been exploited in this work to identify a target-dependent feature of the CSI and to enable a truly robust detection of targets approaching the areas covered by the WiFi. The proposed method applies the principal component analysis (PCA) to isolate the signal components affected by the target presence. The CSI has been processed using a non-parametric Kruskal-Wallis (KW) test to estimate the similarity between the CSI distributions acquired in absence and in presence of the targets. The selected results of the experimental validation point out that a target-dependent component of the CSI exists and its separation from the remaining orthogonal components enables a robust detection of the target with failure rates lower than 3 [%]. The proposed method has been integrated on top of commercial WiFi access points and using a single wireless link in order to evaluate the detection performance when the simplest wireless architecture is adopted.

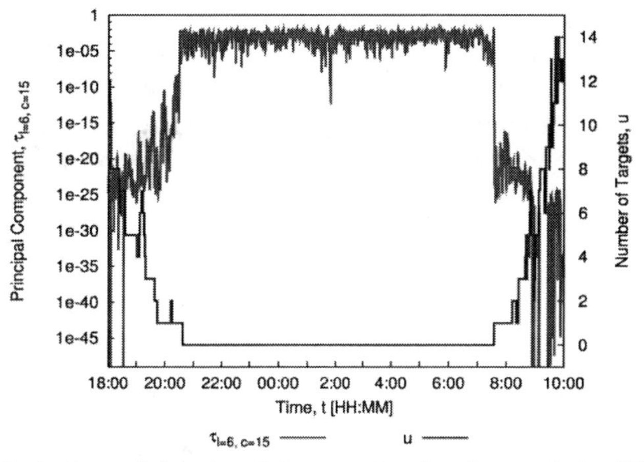

Fig. 1. Temporal behavior of the target-dependent feature of the CSI compared to the actual target presence.

II. Mathematical Formulation

Let us consider a single wireless link generated by a transmitter and a receiver placed in positions $\underline{r}_{TX}$ and $\underline{r}_{RX}$ separated by the distance $d = \|\underline{r}_{TX} - \underline{r}_{RX}\|$. The adopted MIMO configuration generates a set of $A = A_{TX} \times A_{RX}$ wireless links, where A_{TX} and A_{RX} are the number of transmitting receiving antennas, respectively. The CSI is measured at the $c = 1,...,C$ frequency carriers for all $l = 1,...,L$ wireless link.

The proposed strategy stores the CSI amplitudes in a sliding time window of size W with a sampling time interval Δt. The time windows are filled with samples collected both in absence (dataset $\underline{A}_{l,c}$, $l = 1,...,L$, $c = 1,...,C$) and in presence (dataset $\underline{P}_{l,c}$, $l=1,...,L$, $c=1,...,C$) of the targets. Successively, the absence correlation $\underline{\varsigma}_{l,c}^{A}=corr_{w}\left[\underline{R}_{l,c},\underline{A}_{l,c}\right]$ and the presence correlation $\underline{\varsigma}_{l,c}^{P}=corr_{w}\left[\underline{R}_{l,c},\underline{P}_{l,c}\right]$ are computed using the dataset $\underline{R}_{l,c}$ measured in a reference configuration without targets. The probability density functions (PDFs) $p\left(\underline{\varsigma}_{l,c}^{A}\right)$ and $p\left(\underline{\varsigma}_{l,c}^{P}\right)$ are then computed to evaluate the stability of the distributions in static environments and how they are perturbed in presence of targets. The well-known KW test is applied to the PDFs and the obtained p-values $\rho_{l,c}$ are used to determine the similarity level of the PDFs. The difference between two PDFs is statistically significant if the p-value is lower than a predefined threshold ($\rho \leq \varepsilon$), otherwise the PDFs belong to the same family of distributions. The *PCA* has been applied to the set of p-values ρ_{l}, $l=1,...,L$, and repeated for each carrier frequency $c=1,...,C$ in order to extract the uncorrelated components and to point out the subset of components mostly affected by the target presence. The obtained principal components $\underline{\tau}_{c}=\left[\tau_{l};l=1,...,L\right]_{c}$, $c=1,...,C$ given by the PCA method are directly analyzed to estimate the target presence exploiting the spatial relations among the multiple wireless links. Lower values of the principal components $\underline{\tau}_{c}$ are a consequence of lower CSI correlations, due to the perturbations caused by the target presence.

III. Experimental Validation

The performances of the proposed detection method have been assessed at the ELEDIA Research Center laboratories, at the University of Trento, Italy. The test field is an office area organized in rooms and corridors. The WiFi access point used as transmitter is a commercial device compliant to the standard IEEE 802.11n and equipped with $A_{TX}=2$ antennas. The receiver integrates the Intel IWL 5300 network interface card, which provides the CSI readings through a modified firmware and uses $A_{RX}=3$ antennas. The number of wireless links is $A=6$, the working frequency is set to $f_{C}=2.4\left[GHz\right]$ and the link length is $d=17\left[m\right]$. The receiver collects the CSI at $C=30$ frequency carriers, stored in sliding windows of length $W=40$, and with a sampling rate $\Delta t=1\left[\sec\right]$. The reference acquisition $\underline{R}_{l,c}$ has been measured when the indoor site was empty. The *absence/presence* configurations have been generated assuming a variable number of targets $u=0,...,U$, where $U=13$. The temporal evolution of the actual target number has been inferred from the recordings of a video-surveillance system. The KW test has been performed on the whole set of PDFs and the obtained p-values have been compared with the threshold $\varepsilon=0.05$. The principal components $\left[\tau_{l};l=1,...,L\right]_{c}$ have been computed for all the $C=30$ carriers. For the sake of brevity, the carrier $c=15$ has been selected as a representative example of the performance at the center frequency.

The first principal components are insensitive to the target presence. On the contrary, the last one (which is orthogonal to the previous ones) is strictly dependent by the target presence as clearly shown in Fig. 1. The actual number of targets $u=0,...,13$ is also reported in Fig. 1 to compare the results with the actual absence/presence status. The performances have been assessed computing the average percentage of the false positive and false negative detections assuming a simple thresholding operation (with threshold $\tau_{TH}=10^{-10}$) on the values of the principal components. The obtained failure rates range from $\delta=47.2\left[\%\right]$ for the first principal component τ_{1}, down to $\delta=10.3\left[\%\right]$ for τ_{5} and $\delta=2.6\left[\%\right]$ for τ_{6}.

IV. Conclusions

An innovative strategy for the detection of device-free targets has been proposed exploiting the spatial and the frequency diversity of the CSI. The PCA method has been exploited to identify a robust target-dependent feature starting from the distributions of the CSI correlations. The experimental validation pointed out an outstanding failure rate lower than *3*[%] when the smallest target-dependent principal component τ_{6} is considered.

References

[1] N. Patwari and J. Wilson, "RF sensor networks for device-free localization and tracking," *Proc. IEEE*, vol. 98, no. 11, pp. 1961-1973, 2010.

[2] F. Viani, F. Robol, A. Polo, P. Rocca, G. Oliveri, and A. Massa, "Wireless architectures for heterogeneous sensing in smart home applications – Concepts and real implementations," *Proc. IEEE*, vol. 101, no. 11, pp. 2381-2396, 2013.

[3] H. Ahmadi, A. Polo, T. Moriyama, M. Salucci, and F. Viani, "Semantic wireless localization of WiFi terminals in smart buildings," *Radio Sci.*, vol. 51, no. 6, pp. 876-892, Jun. 2016.

[4] B. Mrazovac, B. M. Todorović, M. Z. Bjelica, and D. Kukolj, "Device-free indoor human presence detection method based on the information entropy of RSSI variations," *Electron. Lett.*, vol. 49, no. 22, pp. 1386-1388, 2013.

[5] F. Viani, P. Rocca, M. Benedetti, G. Oliveri, and A. Massa, "Electromagnetic passive localization and tracking of moving targets in a WSN-infrastructured environment," *Inverse Probl.*, vol. 26, 074003, pp. 1-15, Mar. 2010.

[6] C. Wu, Z. Yang, Z. Zhou, X. Liu, Y. Liu, and J. Cao, "Non-invasive detection of moving and stationary human with wifi," *IEEE J. Sel. Areas Commun.*, vol. 33, no. 11, pp. 2329-2342, 2015.

Miniature Rectenna Design

Hubregt J. Visser
Department of Electrical Engineering
Eindhoven University of Technology
Eindhoven, The Netherlands
h.j.visser@tue.nl

***Abstract*—For powering small wireless IoT nodes, compact, efficient rectifying antennas have been realized. A first design for 868 and 915 MHz is described. Based on the lessons learned, a new design for 2.45 GHz is realized that is a factor 13 smaller in size.**

***Keywords*— antenna, rectenna, wireless power transfer**

I. Introduction

For the Internet of Things (IoT) we envisage the use of hundreds to maybe thousands of wireless sensors in a single building, monitoring people present, light, heating and other environmental conditions with a fine resolution. The gathered data can be used to adjust the (local) conditions to the presence or absence of people present, e.g. lowering or switching off light and heating. Powering all these sensors through cabling or primary batteries is expensive. Radiative Wireless Power Transfer (RWPT) offers a feasible powering alternative. One transmitter can power low-power, duty-cycled wireless sensor nodes within a radius of a few meters.

The sensor nodes therefore need to be equipped with compact, reliable and efficient *rec*tifying an*tennas* or *rectennas*. In the following we will describe the design of a 868-915 MHz rectenna and a 2.45 GHz rectenna. Both rectennas consist of an antenna, connected to a rectifier. The output of the rectifier is connected to a power management circuit that boost converts the rectified voltage and stores the energy in a capacitor.

II. 868 MHz Rectenna

The core of a rectenna is the rectifying circuit. For the rectifyer we use Schottky diodes in a cascade. For 915MHz we have found that a cascade of two diodes (voltage doubler) is the optimum choice with respect to RF-to-dc power conversion efficiency [1]. The input impedance of this rectifier is determined, at an RF input power level of -10dBm, for a load resistor representing the power management circuit. With our choice of the Texas Instruments power management IC BQ25570 [2] this load resistance was 10 kΩ. This value also happened to be close to the optimum load resistance. This led to an input impedance (at 868 MHz) of (7-j240) Ω.

This impedance opens up possibilities for designing an antenna that is directly – without using a matching network – complex conjugately matched to the rectifier. First of all, we see from the rectifier's input impedance that it is dominantly capacitive. Therefore the antenna needs to be inductive, so we choose for a printed loop structure. Next, we see that the real part of the antenna impedance needs to be small, so we need a small loop-like or folded-dipole-like antenna. As a means to control the input impedance we add additional arms to distribute the current through the structure, see Fig. 1 [3].

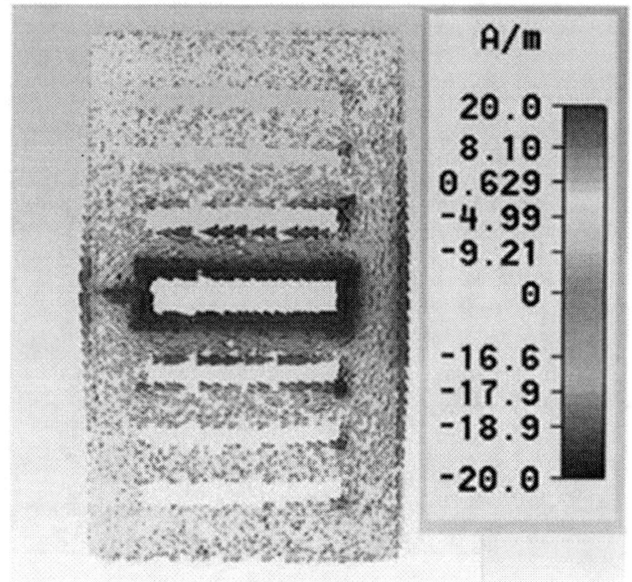

Fig. 1. Peak current density distribution for a printed rectangular loop antenna with additional arms. The feedpoint is on the left.

After testing the antenna with the rectifier and the antenna with the rectifier connected to a power management evaluation board [4], a single PCB demonstrator has been realized, operating at 915 MHz (North American ISM band), see Fig. 2.

Although the rectenna demonstrator is small compared to the wavelength (PCB: 60 mm x 105 mm. λ = 328 mm), the long dimension is dominated by the distance that is necessary to minimize the coupling between the electronics ground plane and the antenna.

Furthermore, the rectenna cannot be placed flush to a metal carrier since this would degrade the antenna performance too much. To overcome these drawbacks: size and environment dependency, we have designed a new rectenna.

Fig. 2. Prototype 915 MHz rectenna with power management circuitry on a single PCB board. The rectenna is powering a temperature sensor with display.

III. 2.45GHz Rectenna

As a first step in reducing the size of the rectenna we choose to use the worldwide available ISM frequency band around 2.45 GHz. To make the demonstrator less environment dependent we next opt for an antenna on a ground plane and finally we want to integrate the electronics for the power management in the antenna.

To cope with all these requirements we choose to use the PCB ground plane as an antenna [5].On top of the PCB we place a metal ring, connected to the ground plane with a via [6]. With this ring we tune the frequency of the antenna. A second, smaller ring is connected to this ring to tune the antenna to 50 Ω [7]. In contrast to our 868-915 MHz rectenna we have chosen to use a 50 Ω antenna and use a lumped-element impedance matching network between the antenna and rectifier. In this way, we will be able to replace the rectifier and matching circuit elements and investigate the maximum RF-to-dc power conversion efficiency for different diode types and different RF input power levels. The electronics is placed on the inside of the ring, sufficiently far away from the metalization to minimize the disturbance of the antenna.

Fig. 3a shows the lay-out of the antenna. Fig. 3b shows the simulated (CST Microwave Studio®) peak current density on the antenna and Fig. 3c shows the simulated radiation pattern.

The realized rectenna, (24 mm x 20 mm x 3 mm), powering a temperature sensor with display, is shown in Fig. 4.

IV. Conclusions

Through careful co-design of rectifier circuit, antenna and power management circuit it is possible to realize compact, efficient rectennas. Even though all sub-blocks may be sub-optimal, the total efficiency will be higher than for a design based on connecting optimized sub blocks.

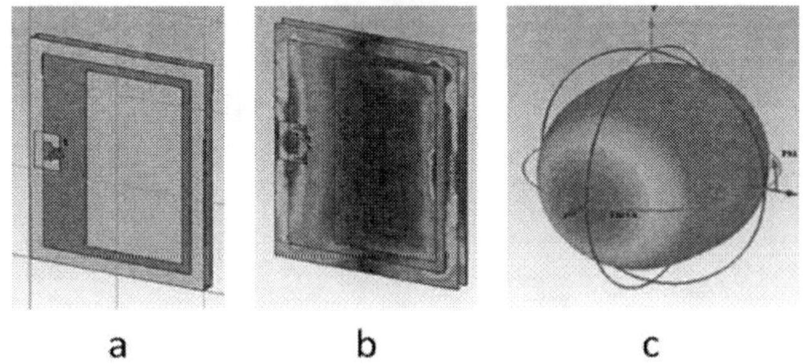

Fig. 3. a. Layout of the 2.45GHz rectenna. b. Peak current density distribution. c. Radiation pattern.

Fig. 4. 2.45 GHz rectenna powering a temperature sensor with display.

References

[1] S. Keyrouz, *Practical Rectennas, RF Power Harvesting and Transport*, PhD Thesis, Eindhoven University of Technology, 2014.

[2] Texas Instruments, *Ultra Low Power Harvester Power Management IC with Boost Charger and Nano-Powered Buck Converter, BQ25570*, Available: www.ti.com/product/bq25570.

[3] H.J. Visser, S. Keyrouz and A.B. Smolders, 'Optimized Rectenna Design', *Wireless Power Transfer*, Vol. 2, No. 1, pp. 44-50, March 2015.

[4] H.J. Visser, H.W. Pflug and S. Keyrouz, 'Rectenna Demonstrators at Holst Centre / imec and Eindhoven University of Technology', *European Conference on Antennas and Propagation, EuCAP*, 4pp., 2015.

[5] M. Vogel et al., 'Characteristic Mode Analysis: Putting Physics back into Simulation', *IEEE Antennas and Propagation Magazine*, Vol. 57, No. 2, pp. 307-317, 2015.

[6] Z. Miers, H. Li and B.K. Lau, 'Design of bezel Antennas for Multiband MIMO Terminals Using Characteristic Modes', *European Conference on Antennas and Propagation, EuCAP*, 5pp., 2014.

[7] J. Zhang and O. Breinbjerg, 'Self-Resonant Electrically Small Loop Antennas for Hearing-Aids Application', *European Conference on Antennas and Propagation, EuCAP*, 5pp., 2010.

A Portable RFID Reader Augmented with Tracking Capabilities for Indoor Monitoring of People

Giacomo Paolini, Diego Masotti, and Alessandra Costanzo
DEI "Guglielmo Marconi"
University of Bologna
Bologna, Italy

***Abstract* — With the accelerated ageing of the world population, progressively more people suffer from age-related illnesses and have the necessity to be monitored and assisted continually in the hospitals, in nursing homes or even better at home. It's demonstrated that the investigation of elderly patients' habits and movements can achieve an early detection of many disorders such as Alzheimer's disease or senile dementia. In this paper, we demonstrate the use of a 2.45 GHz microwave system, with the capabilities of an RFID reader exploited for an agile and accurate beam-steering to efficiently detect tagged people or objects, standing or moving in an harsh electromagnetic environment. This reader, called RID (acronym of Remotely Identify and Detect) has the ability to detect the angular position of the active tags in an indoor environment and gives an estimation of the distance from the reader with agreeable accuracy.**

***Index Terms* — RFID reader, indoor localization, tag detection, tracking old people, age-related illnesses, Alzheimer's disease.**

I. Introduction

In the last decades, the life expectancy of the world population has gone up by several years and that led the growth of the occurrence of age-related illnesses, such as Alzheimer's disease or other forms of dementia, that gradually invalidate individuals' physical and mental capabilities, in particular memory, reasoning and learning. In particular, Alzheimer's disease affects nearly thirty million people in the world and it has been appraised that one out of eighty-five people will have this illness in about 30 years' time.

It is demonstrated that an early detection of the signs of Alzheimer's disease is possible: these evidences are hard to be noticed by the family members or even by the doctors during a normal medical check-up, because they require lot of time to be identified and this can be done observing the movements and the behavior of the patients; as an example, going in the same room more often than usual could be an early sign of the disease [1].

Therefore a non-invasive continuous identification to locate patients at hospitals or rest homes can be practical to assist them in real-time: as an example, this could prevent their entrance in an unsafe zone, control if they fall and if they're lying in the bed for a long time and they need to go for a walk or to take drugs at specified times.

In this paper, we demonstrate how these operations could be achieved with an RFID reader working at microwave frequencies (i.e., 2.45 GHz), enhanced with Monopulse RADAR and electronic beam-steering capabilities. The hardware implementation adopted in [2] has demonstrated high-resolution proficiencies in detecting angular positions of hidden closely spaced objects, fixed or moving.

II. RID Working Principles

The operating principles of the RID are based on the combination of the RADAR-monopulse [3] and the array beam-steering [4] capabilities. Two flag-type dipole antennas were adopted to form a two-element array providing a radiation pattern strictly dependent on the phase shifts ($\Delta\varphi$) among antennas feedings. The block diagram of the prototype, with the Σ and Δ channels in connection with the two dipole antennas, is represented in Fig. 1.

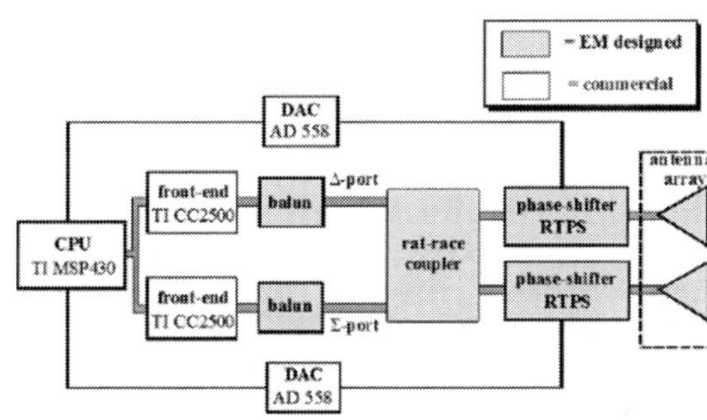

Fig. 1. Block diagram of the RID prototype working at 2.45 GHz [2].

The information flow between the reader and the tags foresees a discovery mode in which the IDs from the active tags are acquired in a time interval of about 200 ms. Later, an electronic beam-steering consisting of 40 scanning steps in a reading zone of ±45° is performed, taking 60 ms for the selection of each tag.

The Σ and Δ signals, received from the tags, are employed to evaluate the Maximum Power Ratio (MPR), that will be exploited to calculate the angular position of each tag:

$$MPR_i(\theta) = \Sigma^{db}(\theta) - \Delta^{db}(\theta) \;\; ; \;\; i = 1,\ldots,N_{tag} \qquad (1)$$

where N_{tag} is the total number of tags under evaluation, Σ^{dB} and Δ^{dB} are the RSSIs (Received Signal Strength Indicators) received at the reader Σ and Δ channels and θ is the steering angle. The MPR peak position determines the instantaneous angular position of the corresponding tag.

III. Real-Time Indoor Localization

With the purpose of tracking people movements in a bidimensional space in real-time and their room occupancy during certain moments of the daytime, an algorithm has been developed to estimate the tags' distance from the reader. These measurements are based on the RSSI (Received Signal Strength Indicator) of the acquired signals, under the assumption of static channel. In order to achieve this goal, a calibration of the room under evaluation has to be made: it consists in a preliminary detection of the maximum Σ RSSI received from the tags, placed in three different positions at a distance of 1 meter, sectorizing the room in three scanning zones (Zone #1: -45°÷-22.5°, Zone #2: -22.5°÷22.5°, Zone #3: 22.5°÷45°).

As an example, in Fig. 2, the picture of the room where this investigation took place, with the sectorization in the three calibration zones, is reported.

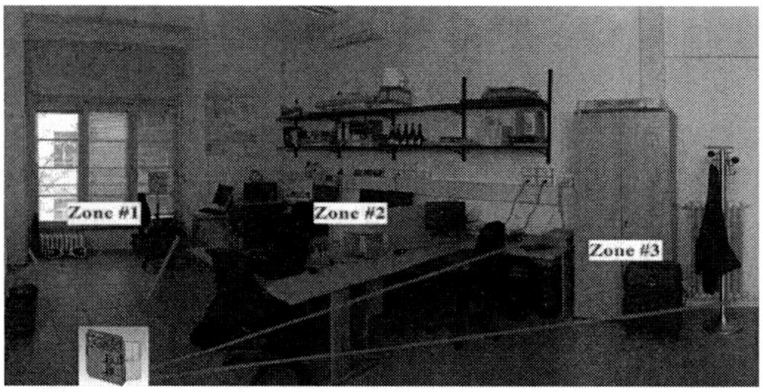

Fig. 2. Photo illustrating the laboratory where the measurements were held, the position of the RFID reader and the subdivision of the three zones [5].

In Fig. 3, the room map of the indoor scenario and the markers symbolizing the locations where the tag has been estimated in a walk test executed by a tagged person, are represented. These results have been obtained under the assumption of static channel, but a stochastic channel description could also be taken into account to represent a more realistic situation of everyday life.

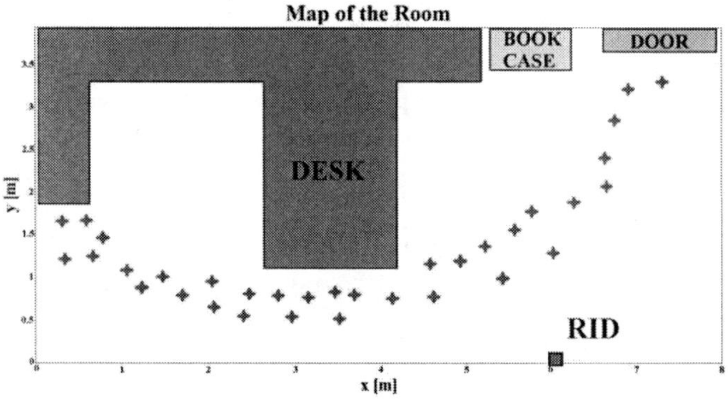

Fig. 3. Two-dimensional floor plan representing the considered room with the markers corresponding to the positions where the tag has been appraised in a thirty-seconds walk test [5].

IV. Conclusion

In this work, a portable, low-cost and low-power reader operating at the frequency of 2.45 GHz and realizing a real-time movement analysis, has been presented to identify the positions of people moving in an indoor environment considering a static channel. In order to calculate the reader-tag distance, an algorithm has been considered: it exploits calibration data in the room under evaluation within one meter's distance. The efficiency of the reader operations has been demonstrated by detecting the tags' position even in harsh electromagnetic areas, with the possibility to early diagnose specific age-related diseases strictly connected to the repetition of particular movements.

Acknowledgement

This work was partly funded by the European Union and partly by the Emilia-Romagna Region within the framework of the Operative Project HABITAT — Home Assistance Based on Internet of Things for the Autonomy of Everybody (http://www.habitatproject.info).

References

[1] H. T. Cheng and W. Zhuang, "Bluetooth-enabled in-home patient monitoring system: Early detection of Alzheimer's disease", in *IEEE Wireless Communications*, vol. 17, no. 1, pp. 74-79, Feb. 2010.

[2] M. Del Prete, D. Masotti, N. Arbizzani, and A. Costanzo, "Remotely Identify and Detect by a Compact Reader With Mono-Pulse Scanning Capabilities", in *IEEE Transactions on Microwave Theory and Techniques*, vol. 61, no. 1, pp. 641-650, Jan. 2013.

[3] J. C. Wu *et al.*, "Wireless indoor localization using dynamic monopulse receiver", *The 7th European Radar Conference*, Paris, 2010, pp. 69-72.

[4] M. Y. W. Chia *et al.*, "Electronic Beam-Steering IC for Multimode and Multiband RFID", in *IEEE Transactions on Microwave Theory and Techniques*, vol. 57, no. 5, pp. 1310-1319, May 2009.

[5] G. Paolini, M. Del Prete, F. Berra, D. Masotti, and A. Costanzo, "An Agile and Accurate Microwave System for Tracking Elderly People Occupancy at Home", *2016 IEEE MTT-S Latin America Microwave Conference (LAMC 2016)*, Puerto Vallarta, 12-14 Dec. 2016.

3D Antenna for Wireless Power Transmission

Aperture Coupled Microstrip Antenna with Dielectric Lens

Gonçalo Dias[1], Pedro Pinho[2], Ricardo Gonçalves[1], Nuno Carvalho[1]

[1]Instituto de Telecomunicações, Dep. de Eletrónica, Telecomunicações e Informática, Universidade de Aveiro, Portugal

[2]Instituto de Telecomunicações, ISEL, Portugal

Email: goncaloadias@ua.pt, ppinho@deetc.isel.pt, rgoncalves@av.it.pt, nbcarvalho@ua.pt

***Abstract*—Nowadays 3D printers are useful for the development and rapid prototyping of dielectric structures for radiation manipulation and support of antennas. This is possible since the materials used in this machines are essentially dielectric. These can be used as radiating elements (dielectric resonators), as radiation handlers (lenses) or as a supporting base for applying conductive material to radiation (substrates). In this paper we explore 3D printing technology to develop a lens antenna for wireless power transfer operating at 20 GHz. The design, simulation and measurement of an aperture coupled microstrip antenna with dielectric lens is presented and discussed. The lens is used to focus the beam of lower gain feed antenna to produce a highly directive pattern with low side lobe.**

Keywords—3D printing, Aperture coupled microstrip antenna, Dielectric lens antenna, Wireless power transmission.

I. Introduction

The great investment in research regarding the IoT is even pushing us to a greater dependency on self-sufficient electronic systems. The biggest disadvantage of current electronic devices comes from their dependence of external power connections or batteries in order to operate. It is thus necessary to make these devices able to be powered on a more effective and versatile way. The development of WPT (Wireless Power Transfer) systems gets us closer to a truly wireless world, as it was imagined by several brilliant minds before us (Nikola Tesla, William C. Brown ...). This will enable society a more comfortable use of electronics, be it from the integration of these mechanisms in implantable medical devices, the use of backscattering on sensors, easier charge of electronic devices, the power could be transmitted to the places where the wired transmission is not possible.

Additive manufacturing, namely 3D printing, has seen a very strong growth in the last five years, especially since the first 3D printers for regular consumer use, at lower prices, started to appear in the market.

It is possible to exploit the technology to create antennas with more complex shapes and in three dimensions quickly and less expensive, that until here was only accessible to development teams with high budget projects, such as military or space. The design freedom associated with the three-dimensional structures allows the creation of complex geometries that produce very specific characteristics of radiation for very demanding applications.

Given the typical dimensions of lens antennas, and in order to operate within a constrained size, we opted to design and antenna for operation in the sub-millimeter frequency bands, namely at 20 GHz, which are very attractive for various modern indoor and outdoor applications. Lens antennas consist of two main parts: the feeding antenna can be of several types (horns, dipoles, microstrip antennas, and even arrays of antenna elements) and lens that collimate incident divergent energy to prevent it from spreading in undesired directions. Integrated dielectric lens antennas (DLAs) [1], [2] are widely used in various communication, radar, and imaging systems in the millimeter (mm) and sub-mm wave bands. The key components of such antennas are dielectric lenses used for correction of radiation patterns of primary feeds, open waveguides or printed antennas.

This paper is organized as follows, in section I a brief introduction to the lens antennas is presented. Section II describes the structure of the aperture coupled microstrip antenna and the dielectric lens dimensions. A comparison between simulation and measured results is also presented. Finally in section III we present the main conclusions.

II. Aperture Coupled Microstrip Antenna with Dielectric Lens

Aperture-coupled feed was originally proposed by Pozar [3]. This feed structure eliminates the asymmetry problems present in the microstrip line and coaxial probe. This type of feed consists of two substrates separated by a ground plane. On the bottom side of the lower substrate, there is a microstrip feed line which has the form of an open-circuit stub while the top side of the upper substrate contains the microstrip patch element.

The main advantage of this configuration is that the feed network and the patch are well isolated from one another. In this way, no radiation from the feed network can interfere with the main radiation pattern since a ground plane separates the two mechanisms.

A. Design

In this paper is shown an aperture coupled microstrip antenna with a dielectric lens for WPT (Fig.1). The lens is used to focus the beam of lower gain feed antenna to produced highly directive pattern with low side lobe levels. The radiating microstrip patch element is etched on the top of the antenna substrate, and the microstrip feed line is etched on the bottom of the feed substrate.

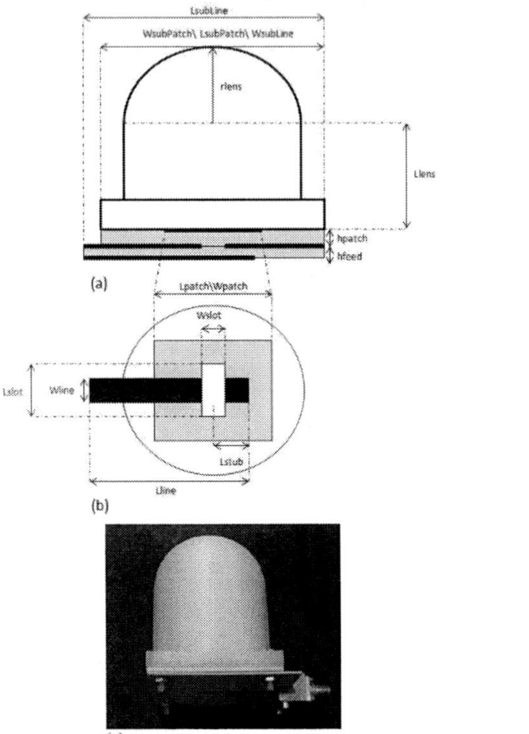

Fig. 1. Extended hemispherical lens fed by an aperture-coupled microstrip patch antenna (a) Cross-section view and (b) top view (c) photograph of the prototype.

The material used for both substrates was Isola Astra MT, which has a relative permittivity of 3.0 and a loss tangent of 0.0017. The lens is fabricated with PLA (Polyactic Acid) that has an estimated relative permittivity of 1.8 and a loss tangent of 0.01 [5]. The antenna has designed for 20 GHz.

B. Simulation

The antenna was modeled and optimized using the transient solver within CST MICROWAVE STUDIO®. The optimized physical parameters of the antenna are shown in Table 1.

TABLE I ANTENNA DESIGN PARAMETERS

Parameter	***Dimension (mm)***	***Parameter***	***Dimension (mm)***
Lpatch	3	Lens size	40x40x55
Wpatch	3	Lline	25
Lslot	3.5	Lstub	5.5
Wslot	1.7	Wline	1.93
LsubPatch	40	hpatch	1.52
WsubPatch	40	hfeed	0.76
LsubLine	45	Llens	35
WsubLine	40	rlens	20

C. Results

The simulated *versus* measured reflection coefficient obtained for the lens antenna is shown in Fig. 2. There is an observable shift in the measured resonant frequency that can be due to a misalignment of the line, slot and patch stacked structure, and also due to an erroneous definition of the PLA dielectric values used for simulation. The resulting farfield can be seen in Fig. 3 and 4. High directivity of 17 dBi at the main beam and 92.4% radiation efficiency can be achieved with this dielectric lens antenna configuration.

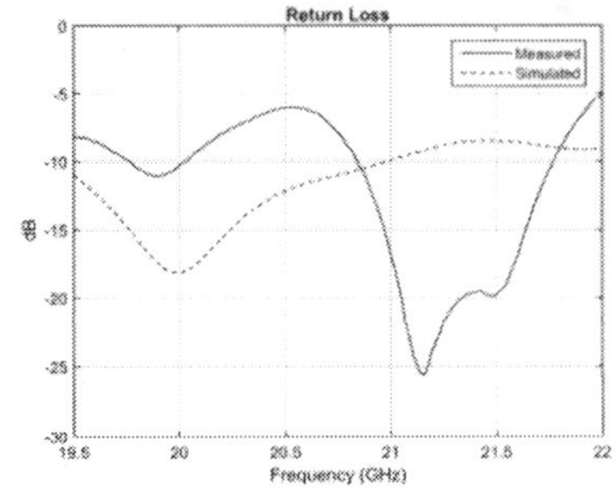

Fig. 2. Simulation and measurement of return loss

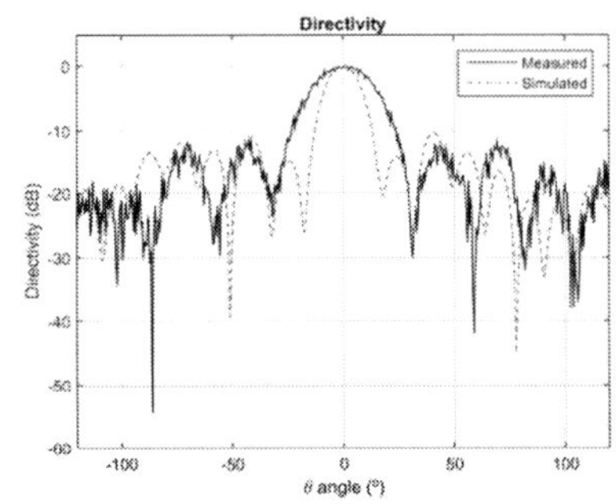

Fig. 3. Simulated and measured farfield directivity normalized

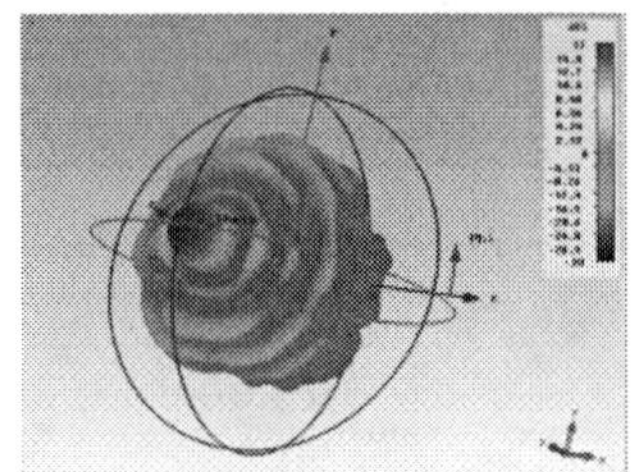

Fig. 4. Simulated 3D farfield directivity

III. CONCLUSION

A design, simulation and measurements of a 3D printed lens antenna has been presented with the intent of being used for wireless power transmission. The measurements match poorly to the simulation results and some improvements are required, namely in the correct definition of the lens material properties.

REFERENCES

[1] G. Eason, B. Noble, and I.N. Sneddon, "On certain integrals of Lipschitz-Hankel type involving products of Bessel functions," *Phil. Trans. Roy. Soc. London*, vol. A247, pp. 529-551, April 1955.

[2] J. Clerk Maxwell, A Treatise on Electricity and Magnetism, 3rd ed., vol. 2. *Oxford: Clarendon*, 1892, pp.68-73.

[3] D. M. Pozar. Microstrip antenna aperture-coupled to a microstrip line. *Electronics Letters*, 21(2):49–50, January 1985.

[4] G. Godi, R. Sauleau, and D. Thouroude. Performance of reduced size substrate lens antennas for millimeter-wave communications. *IEEE Transactions on Antennas and Propagation*, 53(4):1278–1286, April 2005

[5] R. Goncalves, R. Magueta, P. Pinho, N.B. Carvalho, Dissipation factor and permittivity estimation of dielectric substrates using a single microstrip line measurement, *Appl. Comput. Electromagn. Soc. J.* 31(2) (2016) 118–125.

RFID Sensing Breadboard for Industrial IoT

Cecilia Occhiuzzi, Sabina Manzari, Stefano Caizzone
RADIO6ENSE srl
Università di Roma Tor Vergata,
Via del Politecnico 1, 00118 Roma
occhiuzzi@radio6ense.com

Sara Amendola, Gaetano Marrocco
Pervasive Electromagnetics Lab
Università di Roma Tor Vergata,
Via del Politecnico 1, 00118 Roma
gaetano.marrocco@uniroma2.it

***Abstract*— A fully reconfigurable RFID Sensing breadboard for Industrial Internet of Things is here proposed. The board is completely tunable such to offer the best communication performances in different industrial operative scenario. Furthermore, thanks to the customizable expansion traces and the A/D frontend, the radio-board is capable to interface up to two external sensors and to work in both passive and BAP mode.**

Keywords—RFID sensors; antenna breadboard.

I. INTRODUCTION

The Internet of Things is recognized as one of the engines of the Fourth Industrial Revolution [1]. A key role in such perspective is played by the wireless sensor networks, and in particular by autonomous and reconfigurable monitoring infrastructures capable to sensibly improve the control of systems as well as to predict anomalous events, thus optimizing production, security and efficiency. In this scenario a promising technology is Radiofrequency Identification [2] (RFID, standard EPC C1G2), provided that the typical extreme variability of the antenna response to the specific hosting medium (metal, wall, cardboard, liquids) and the variety of application-specific requirements for the sensors can be easily and effectively managed.

This contribution introduces a fully configurable RFID sensing *bread-board* able to integrate different sensors and to operate in several modalities while making use of a same PCB core layout, thus speeding up the prototyping and customization of new products.

II. BOARD LAYOUT

The proposed RFID sensor bread-board (Fig.1) is logically composed of three parts: *i)* a radiating element made of a meander-line antenna (MLA); *ii)* a spiral impedance transformer connected to the RFID IC [3] and hosting a tuning inductor L_T; *iii)* additional expansion traces for battery and sensors interconnections. Both the MLA and the spiral traces are partly interrupted in several points, hereafter denoted as *trace gaps (M* in the MLA and *N* in the spiral), so that in overall, the device can be regarded as a multi-port antenna. Two further gaps (SW1 and SW2) split the transformer section from the MLA. The distribution of the surface current over the antenna, and hence its impedance and gain can be shaped, for a specific application, by a particular choice of the tuning inductor and by connecting a subset of the trace-gaps after the antenna manufacturing. For instance, acting onto the MLA, the size of the antenna is modified and hence also its gain and impedance, while by connecting some gaps, the spiral could be enlarged or reduced as needed for the specific microchip. Fig. 2 shows a parametric exploration of the simulated realized gain $G_T = G_T\tau$ of the radio-board in free space, along the broadside direction by acting either only on the trace gaps of the MLA (a) or only on the spiral transformer (b).

By acting of the inductor it is instead possible to adjust the residual antenna reactance and hence to maximize the peak of the realized gain. Finally, depending on the status of the SW1/2 ports, the board can be used either as a tunable standalone RFID sensor board (SW1 closed and SW2 open) for application onto low permittivity and low-losses materials, or as a basic module (SW1 open and SW2 closed) including the sensors, the chip and the spiral transformer to be electromagnetic coupled with an external antenna, like a patch booster, for application over metals, or concrete walls.

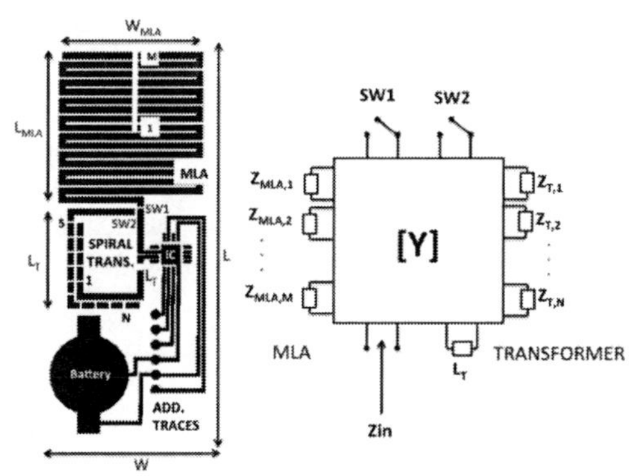

Fig. 1 Left) Schematics of the customizable sensing breadboard architecture (size in [mm]: W=28, L=66, W_{MLA}=24 , L_{MLA}=26, W_T=12.5, L_T=20 [mm]; traces width: 1 mm (MLA and spiral) and 0.25mm (sensor traces). Right) A Multi-port model.

III. DESIGN MECHANISM AND PROTOTYPES

The localized nature of the tuning parameters (inductor and open/closed trace-gaps) allows for a multi-port representation (Fig.1 right) that is suitable for computational cost reduction and automatic optimization. The admittance matrix of the system is referred to the N+M+1 ports of the antenna, excluded the SW1,2 ports which are fixed by the selected operative mode. The impedances $\{Z_{T,n}, n=1..N\}$ and $\{Z_{MLA,m}, m=1..M)$ may be only short circuits or open circuits.

The admittance matrix has to be computed for the specific configuration of the antenna, e.g. by including in the numerical simulation the hosting objects (for instance a ground plane or a concrete wall) and the eventual coupling with an external harvester. The radiated field of the specific combination of the port's impedances is derived by the method in [4] as weighted superposition of the fields corresponding to each port when the remainings are short-circuited. The above model is suitable to any automatic optimization tool aimed at defining the status of switch impedances and the value of tuning inductor.

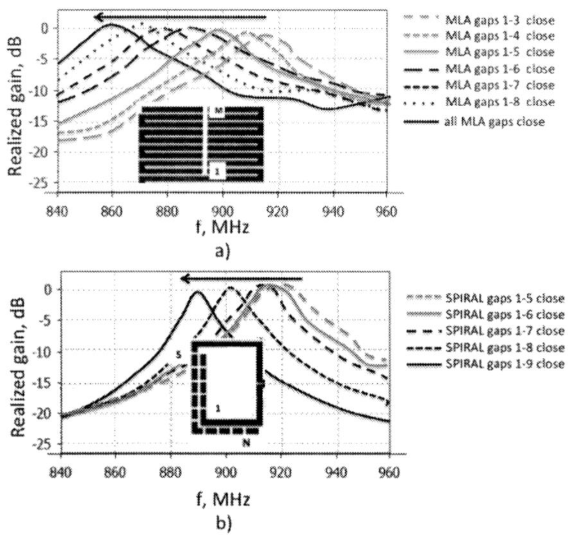

Fig. 2 Example of radio-board tuning. Simulated frequency shift of the realized gain by connecting an increasing number of the trace-gaps of (a) the MLA and (b) of the spiral transformer length.

The simulated and measured realized gains of the two extreme configurations (standalone and patch-boosted) are visible in Fig. 3. The experimented read-distances @ 868 MHz when the reader radiates 3.2 W EIRP in circular polarization, span from 2m to 7m depending on the operation mode (battery-less or BAP respectively).

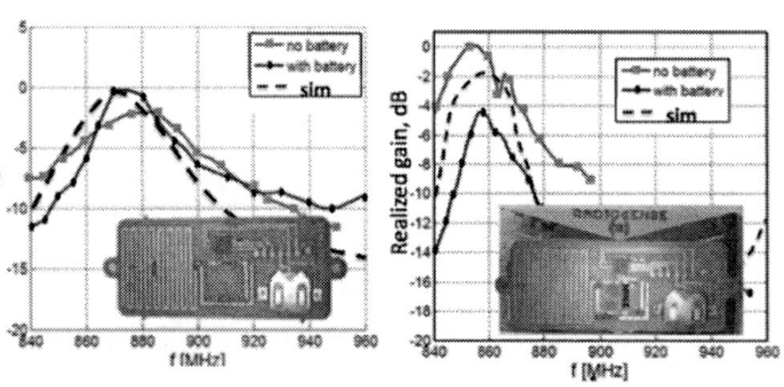

Fig. 3 Simulated and measured realized gais of two board configurations standalone in air (left) and patch-boosted on metal (right) .

IV. Sensing Capabilities

The radio-board is based on a new family of RFID chip transponders [3] providing a native integrated electronics for sensing activities beside the pure identification features. In particular the selected IC includes an Analog-to-Digital Converter (ADC) capable to control up to two low power external sensors, an integrated temperature sensor with programmable dynamic range in the interval -40/150°C and a power interface for integrating batteries and energy harvester. Several different applications of the board equipped with different resistive and capacitive sensors have been investigated. To provide an example, the board configured to log data from three sensors has been used to monitor the environmental condition into a public toilet (Fig.4). Other sensing applications in Industrial-IOT will be presented during the Conference.

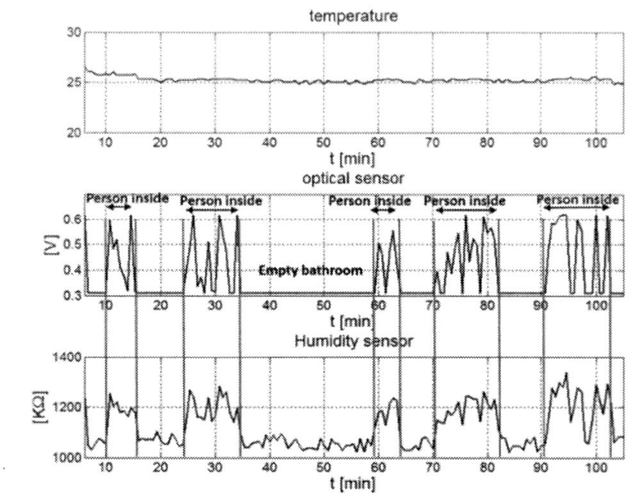

Fig. 4 Responses of the three sensors equipped radio-board (internal temperature sensor, S133-14 capacitive photodiode, HCZ-D5 RH% resistive sensor) during 110 minutes of datalogging inside the toilet of a public office.

V. Conclusion

The proposed antenna breadboard can be considered as a first attempt to master the high variability of possible applications of sensor-oriented RFID devices in the real world. The modular geometry provides enough degree of freedom for application in different scenarios and operative conditions with clear vantages respect to production, maintenance and installation costs.

Acknowledgments: The work was supported by the Horizon 2020 SCISSOR ICT project no. 644425. The authors whish to thank Nicola D'Uva for his valuable support in prototyping and test.

References

[1] "Industrial internet of things: Unleashing the potential of connected products and services," World Economic Forum, Tech. Rep., 2015.

[2] C. Occhiuzzi, S. Caizzone, and G. Marrocco, "Passive UHF RFID antennas for sensing applications: Principles, methods, and classifications," *Antennas and Propagation Magazine, IEEE*, vol. 55, no. 6, pp. 14–34, Dec 2013.

[3] AMS SL900A, available at http://ams.com/eng/Products/UHF-RFID/UHF-Interface-and-Sensor-Tag/SL900A

[4] A. Altman, R. Mitra, A. Boag, "New Designs of Ultra Wide-Band Communication Antennas Using a Genetic Algorithm", in *IEEE Transactions on Antennas and Propagation*, vol. 45, no. 10, pp. 1494-1501, Oct. 1997.

Numerical Simulation of Wave Propagation in Microstrip Line Containing Magnetic Layer

F. Benmohamed/ D. Vincent
Hubert Curien Laboratory
Saint-Etienne, France

J.Y. Wang / J.W. Tao
LAPLCE-ENSEEIHT
Toulouse, France

***Abstract*—A numerical full wave method has been applied to get the characteristic dispersion of microstrip line containing anisotropic magnetic layer. This method is based on the numerical formulation of the spectral dyadic Green's function by using the transverse operator method in the Fourier domain. Green's function obtained for the stratified multilayer structure is compared with previously published results and excellent agreement is achieved. The dispersion diagrams of microstrip line on magnetic substrate are computed numerically using method of moments and compared to previous work.**

Keywords— full wave method; anisotropic magnetic layer; transverse operator method; method of moments; microstrip.

I. Introduction

Anisotropic magnetic materials have played an important role in microwave technology while they have been successfully employed in the nonreciprocal planar structure [1]. In particular, ferrite materials are extensively used in microwave devices such as phase shifter and isolator [2]-[4]. A rigorous analysis of multilayer, arbitrarily biased ferrite structures can be carried out using the spectral domain method of moments. To get the integral equation, the Green's function must be formulated. For microstrip geometry consisting of an isotropic layer limited by a ground plane, the Green's function can be written in closed forms. However, for a stratified structure containing a multiple magnetic layers arbitrarily biased does not have a simple closed forms. During last decade, different methods have been used to formulate the spectral domain Green's function for a single bias direction for a single ferrite slab [5]-[6]. In addition, Green's functions for the planar stratified bianisotropic media [7] and the stratified structure containing left-handed medium [8] have been investigated. The aim of this work is to combine the Transverse Operator Method TOM [9] with the spectral domain approach in order to investigate the propagation diagrams of a multilayer planar structure via the application of the Galerkin moment method. The developed method makes it possible to study the convergence of characteristic propagation in microstrip line with a lossless anisotropic magnetic medium.

II. Method of Solution

In this section, the mono and multilayer structure are shown in Fig. 1. The transmission matrix using the transverse operator method is formulated in the spectral domain for a magnetic substrate with a thickness "h", arbitrarily biased by an external magnetic field (Fig. 1 a).

This work is founded by the Auvergne-Rhône-Alpes region.

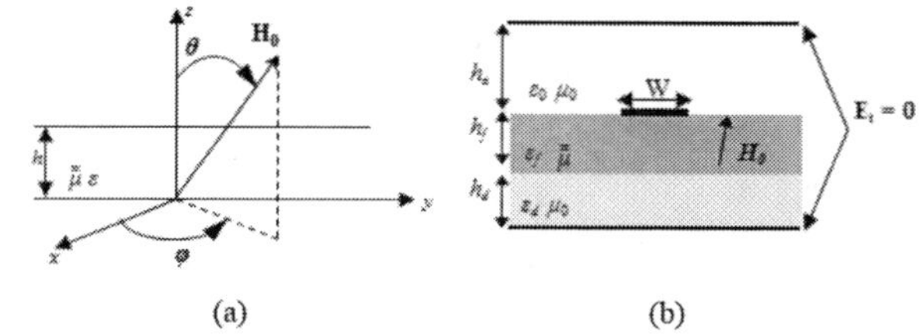

Fig. 1. (a) Geometry of single magnetic layer arbitrarily biased. (b) Geometry of microstrip multilayer Structure.

To find the SDGF, the transverse operator method [9] is employed to make use of a (4×4) matrix formulation to obtain the electromagnetic vector inside each layer.

A. Green's Function Formulation using TOM

A Green's function in the spectral domain is derived and relates the tangential electric field $\boldsymbol{E}_t$ on one surface to the electric surface currents $\boldsymbol{J}_s$ on the same surface as:

$$\tilde{\bar{\bar{J}}}_s(k_x,k_y)=\tilde{\bar{\bar{G}}}(k_x,k_y)\tilde{\bar{\bar{E}}}_s(k_x,k_y) \quad (1)$$

With $\tilde{\bar{\bar{G}}}(k_x,k_y)$ is the spectral domain Green's function.

By making use of the TOM, the total Green's function for the structure in Fig. 1(b) is given by:

$$\tilde{\bar{\bar{G}}}(k_x,k_y)=\frac{1}{Z_0}\bar{\bar{\eta}}_0\left(\tilde{\bar{\bar{Y}}}_{Bottom}-\tilde{\bar{\bar{Y}}}_{Top}\right) \quad (2)$$

With $\boldsymbol{Y}_{Bottom}$ and $\boldsymbol{Y}_{Top}$ are, respectively, the admittances operators in the layers below and above the metal strip.

The Galerkin's method is applied in the Fourier transform domain for solving the coupled equation (1). The unknown current components $\boldsymbol{J}_x$ and $\boldsymbol{J}_y$ are expanded in terms of known basis functions $\boldsymbol{J}_{xn}$ and $\boldsymbol{J}_{ym}$. The basis functions must be chosen such that their inverse Fourier transform are nonzero only on the strip. Once the eigenvalue problem has been posed, two main numerical problems arise: a) the numerical computation of the integrals and b) the calculation of the eigenvalues.

B. Numerical Results

The element of the computed spectral Green's function for fixed values of frequency and propagation constant of this structure is plotted in Fig. 2 with a normal magnetization ($\boldsymbol{H}_0 = H_0\boldsymbol{u}_z$). The solid lines represent our calculated data and the cross results represent the data of authors in [5].

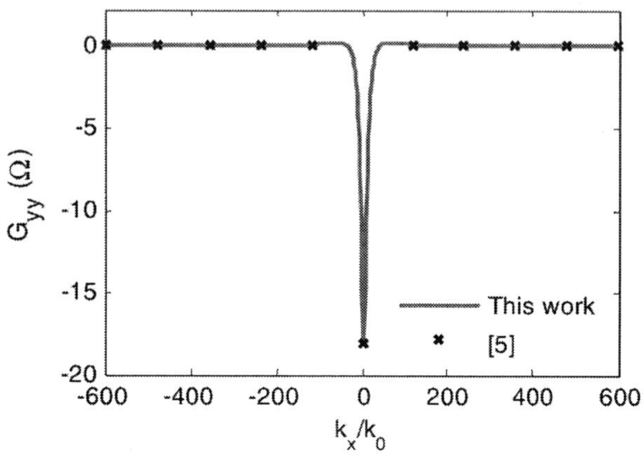

Fig. 2. Behavior of the computed Spectral Green's function as a function of k_x/k_0 compared with the method proposed in [5] with the following parameters [$\theta = \varphi = 0$, $h_d = 1$mm, $\varepsilon_d=30$, $h_f = 0.762$ mm, $\varepsilon_f=12$, $f=2$ GHz, $H_0=700$ Oe, $4\pi M_s= 2100$ Gs, $\Delta H = 0$ Oe, $k_y= 110$ rad.m^{-1}].

We compare the SDGF of the structure shown in Fig.1 (b) derived by our method with the Green's function derived by [8]. It can be seen from Fig. 2 that the behavior of the G_{yy} for large values of the normalized spectral variable is in a broad agreement with the published results.

Further validation for our theory is carried out by comparing the forward and backward propagation constant of the structure shown in Fig. 1 (b) with that [10]. This result is presents in Fig. 3.

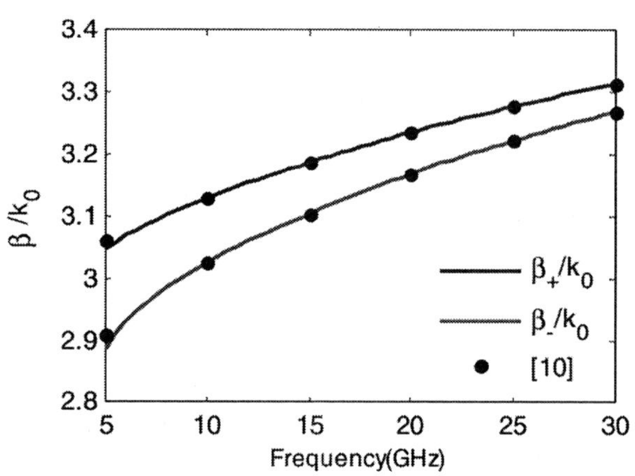

Fig. 3. Comparaison of the calculated propagation constant versus [10] for transversally biased magnetic layer ($\theta = \varphi = \pi/2$).

In this calculation, just five basis functions are adequate to achieve a definite convergence of the propagation constant and an excellent agreement is obtained as clear from Fig. 3.

III. Conclusion

This work presents an efficient numerical method for computing the SDGF using the TOM in the spectral domain. A good agreement between our results and published results is achieved. The Galerkin method in the spectral domain is applied for investigating the propagation constant as a function of frequency of a multilayer Microstrip line on a lossless magnetic substrate. The developed technique makes it possible to analyze a large o coplanar transmission lines including several strips on anisotropic magnetic layer for studying a passive device such as coplanar isolator.

References

[1] F. Mesa, R. Marques, and M. Horno, "An efficient numerical spectral domain method to analyze a large class of nonreciprocal planar transmission lines," IEEE Trans. Microwave Theory Tech., vol. 40, pp. 1630–1641, Aug. 1992.

[2] T. F. Elshafiey and J. T. Aberle, "Green's function for multilayer arbitrarily biased anisotropic structures application to phase shifters, transducers, and magnetization angle effect," IEEE Trans. MTT, Vol.54, No.2, pp. 513-521, Feb. 2006.

[3] J. W. Wang, A. L. Geilier, V. G. Harris and C. Vittoria, "Numerical simulation of wave propagation in y- and z-type hexaferrites for high frequency application," J. Appl. Phys, vol. 107, 09A515, 2010.

[4] S. Capraro, T. Rouiller, M. Le Berre, J. P. Chatelon, B. Bayard, D. Barbier, and J. J. Rousseau, "Feasibility of an integrated self biased coplanar isolator with barium ferrite films," IEEE Trans. MTT, Vol.30, No.3, pp. 513-521, Sept. 2007.

[5] T. F. Elshafiey and J. T. Aberle, E B. El-Sharawy, "Accurate and efficient evaluation of green's functions for multilayer normally biased ferrite structures," IEE Proceedings, Pt. H, vol. 144, No. 6, pp. 403-410, December 1997.

[6] H. How, X. Zuo, E. Hokanson, L. C. Kempel, and C. Vittoria, "Calculated and measured characteristics of a microstrip line fabricated on a Y-type hexaferrite substrate", IEEE Trans MTT, vol. 50, no. 5, pp. 1280–1288, Mai 2002.

[7] E. L. Tan and S. Y. Tan, "Unbounded and scattered field representations of the dyadic green's functions for planar statified bianisotropic media", IEEE Trans. Antennas Propag., vol. 49, no. 8, pp. 1218–1225, August. 2001.

[8] C. M. Krowne, "Electromagnetic-field theory and numerically generated results for propagation in left_handed guided-wave single-microstrip structures", IEEE Trans. MTT, vol. 51, no. 12, pp. 2269–2283, December 2003.

[9] F. Benmohamed. J. W. Tao, N. Ammar, D. Vincent and S. Youssef, "Modélisation electromagnetique d'une structure planaire à base du matériau magnétique anisotrope," JCMM, Calais, France march 2016.

[10] I. Y. Hsia, H. Yang, and N. G. Alexopoulos, "Basic properties of microstrip circuit elements on nonreciprocal substrate-superstrat structure," IEEE MTT-S Microwave Symp. Dig., pp. 665-668, 1990.

Wave Concept in MoM-GEC Formalism

Ahmed Nouainia *,1,2
[1]Department of Physics, Faculty of Sciences of Tunis
[2]Sys'Com Laboratory
National Engineering School of Tunis
Tunis El Manar university
B.P.37 Le Belvedere, Tunis 1002, Tunisia.
ahmed_nouainia@yahoo.fr

Mohamed Hajji
and Taoufik Aguili
Sys'Com Laboratory
National Engineering School of Tunis
Tunis El Manar university
B.P.37 Le Belvedere, Tunis 1002, Tunisia.
hadjimed88@yahoo.fr, taoufik.aguili@enit.rnu.tn

***Abstract*—The MoM-GEC method is an efficient tool used to study electronic circuits at high frequencies. The major problem with this method is that the required calculation time increases with the complexity of the circuit. In this article, we propose to accelerate the MoM-GEC process by using Wave concept to improve the convergence speed of this method. For validation purposes, the new developed MoM-GEC approach is applied to compute scattering in different in a rectangular waveguide. Numerical results are presented and show good agreement when compared to HFSS simulation and analytic formula of Marcuvitz.**

***Index Terms*—Inductive iris; MoM-GEC method; Waveguide; Wave concept.**

I. Introduction

The study of electromagnetic wave scattering has known considerable theoretical progress [1]. Numerical methods such as transmission-line matrix,[1] finite-difference time-domain (FDTD),[2] .. etc, were used to study the electromagnetic wave scattering of any given structure. However, when such methods are applied to large structures, important storage resources and processing time are required limiting then their range of applicability. Among these approaches, we are interested an integral equation (IE) method combined with the generalized equivalent circuit (GEC)[3]. The equivalent circuits have been introduced in the development of integral methods formula-tion. This constitutes the concept of MoM-GEC that consists of MoM method combined to the Generalized Equivalent Circuit (GEC). Our contribution is the application of wave concept in MoM-GEC method to improve the convergence speed of this method. Obtained results are discussed and possible interpretations are given in this work.

This paper is organized as follows: firstly we present the theoretical formulation of the MOM-GEC method. In fact, the wave concept of MoM-GEC is presented. The numerical results of convergence and computation time are given as well as a comparison of our results with HFSS simulation.

II. Theoretical Study

A. Description of the study method

The GEC consists in the conversion of electromagnetic problem represented by the Maxwell formalism to an equivalent circuit represented by Kirchhoff laws. It is based on the resolution of equation with (V, I) instead of (E,H). In fact, the modeling with GEC approach needs the presence of virtual sources, the impedance operator, and the excitation sources[3]. The virtual source describes the electromagnetic state in the discontinuity. It is decomposed in test functions to approximate the electric field E in the structure. The discontinuity environment is expressed by an impedance that represents boundary conditions on each side of discontinuity surface. The wave exciting the discontinuity surface is represented by a real field source because it delivers energy.

The wave concept [3] is introduced by expressing the electromagnetic quantities as a function of the incident and reflected waves :

$$\begin{aligned} A &= \frac{1}{2\sqrt{Z_0}}(E_T + Z_0 J), \\ B &= \frac{1}{2\sqrt{Z_0}}(E_T - Z_0 J). \end{aligned} \tag{1}$$

B. Model validation: application of the proposed approach

For validation purposes, we apply MoM-GEC method based on the wave concept for solving problem of electromagnetic diffraction in metallic waveguide depicted in Figure (1 A). The considered waveguide are infinite, lossless and symmetric through the discontinuity planes. The waveguide consists of four electric walls and associated to a modal basis f_{mn}.

The studied structure is invariant in y direction, and the waveguide excitations are assured by incident wave. The modeling of the study structure, is done by the GEC given by figure (1 B).

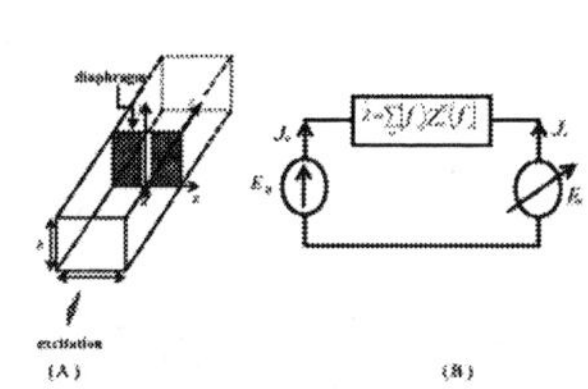

Fig. 1. Studied Structure: A) Inductive iris enclosed by EEEE waveguide.a = 11.45mm, b = 11.16mm and d = 2.5 mm. B) GEC of incident wave sources modeling the diffraction problem.

In this diagram, we have $E_0 = 2\sqrt{Z_0}A_0 f_0$ the excitation field source. Where f_0 represents the waveguide fundamental mode, A_0 the amplitude of the wave and Z_0 the impedance of the fundamental mode. The impedance operator $\widehat{Z}$ describes the environment of the discontinuity and E_e is the virtual source defined on the aperture domain. The resolution of the considered GEC follows the steps given as following:

Application of Ohm and Kirchhoff laws:

$$J_0 = \widehat{Z}^{-1}E_0 - \widehat{Z}^{-1}E_e, \quad J_e = -\widehat{Z}^{-1}E_0 + \widehat{Z}^{-1}E_e. \quad (2)$$

Galrekin method:

$$\begin{pmatrix} I_0 \\ 0 \end{pmatrix} = \begin{pmatrix} \langle f_0|\widehat{Z}^{-1}|f_0\rangle & -\langle f_0|\widehat{Z}^{-1}|g_p\rangle \\ -\langle g_q|\widehat{Z}^{-1}|f_0\rangle & \langle g_q|\widehat{Z}^{-1}|g_p\rangle \end{pmatrix} \begin{pmatrix} V_0 \\ v_p \end{pmatrix}, \quad (3)$$

$$\begin{pmatrix} I_0 \\ 0 \end{pmatrix} = \begin{pmatrix} D & -A \\ -A^T & B \end{pmatrix} \begin{pmatrix} V_0 \\ v_p \end{pmatrix}, \quad (4)$$

where $D = \langle f_0|\widehat{Z}^{-1}|f_0\rangle$, $A(1,p) = \langle f_0|\widehat{Z}^{-1}|g_p\rangle$, $B(p,q) = \sum_{m=0}^{\propto} \langle g_p|f_m\rangle Z_m^{-1}\langle f_m|g_q\rangle$, $\widehat{Z} = \sum_{m=0}^{\propto} f_m\rangle z_m \langle f_m|$ impedance operator, and $z_m = \frac{j\omega\mu_0}{\gamma_m}$ modal impedance.

From equation (4), we obtain the equations system:

$$I_0 = DV_0 - Av_p, \quad 0 = -A^T V_0 + Bv_p. \quad (5)$$

The resolution of this system allows to calculate the input impedance:

$$Z_{in} = \frac{1}{2}\left(\frac{1}{(D - A^T B^{-1} A)}\right). \quad (6)$$

It also permits to determine the current distribution J_0 and the diffracted field E_e in the discontinuity surface.

III. Numerical Results and Discussion

A. Variation of the input impedance with validation

Firstly, we start to draw the variation of the input impedance, where, the figure (2 A) shows it's behavior that computed for the frequencies range [13.5-39.3GHz]. In the case associated to the wave source excitation's example, we noticed that the input impedance is considred a complex number. This is explained by the effect of the source nature, where the fundamental propagative mode is included in the operator $\widehat{Z}$ with evanescent modes. This result conforms to literature [3]. As results, we plot the imaginary part of input impedance given by GEC configuration and we compare it with each given by other methods, depicted in figure (2 B). It is shown that our results are in agreement with those obtained by HFSS software. In addition, they show more precision than those obtained with Marcuvitz analytical formula [4].

Besides, we represent the field and current distributions in Figure (2 C). We note that all these distributions verify boundary conditions and the condition of continuity of the field. So, the electric field is null on metallic domains and it is defined in the dielectric aperture. However, the current is null on the aperture, maximum in the edges because of the charges density accumulation and it is defined on metallic domains. We compare the current and field distributions at the discontinuity surface with those obtained by HFSS Figure (2 C).

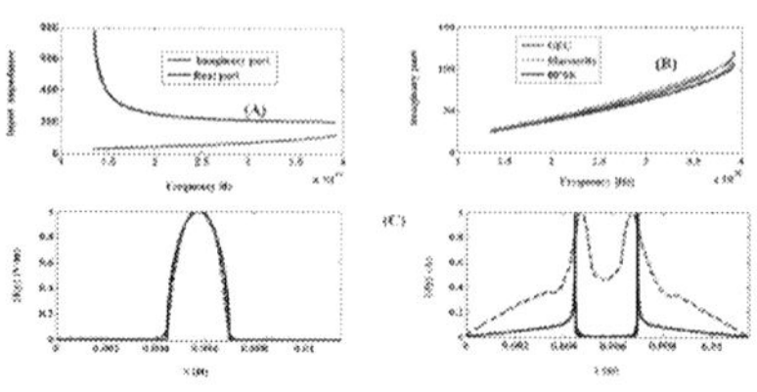

Fig. 2. A) Variation of input impedance against frequency B) Comparison with HFSS software and Marcuvitz analytical formula C) Comparison of current and field distributions with HFSS.

B. Computational time

To show the advantages of our study, we present a comparison between the GEC configurations in terms of computational time. Thus, Table 1 shows The required CPU time. The GEC (wave concept) converges faster than HFSS, this is due to used of the incident wave source as a source of excitation.

Table 1.Computational time consumed to reach Z_{in}

Method	CPU Time
GEC (wave concept)	38.43 seconds
HFSS	54.58 seconds

IV. Conclusion

In this work, we have proposed a wave concept to improve the speed of MoM-GEC method. This new approach shows good agreement when compared to HFSS simulation and demonstrates some new results especially the dependence of the input impedance on the excitation source. we note that when using the concept of wave, we can assume considerable gain in CPU time. The future scope of this idea consists on adapting this new method to more complex circuits in two dimensions 2D described by large matrices.

References

[1] R.E. Collin, Field Theory of Guided Waves, 2nd Edition, IEEE Press, New York, Mc Graw-Hill, 1991.

[2] T. Hiraoka, C. P. Chen, T. Anada, 1. P. Hsu, Z. W. Ma, and C. C. Christopoulos, "Electric field distributions in microwave planar circuits by small coaxial probe and comparison with FDTD method," in Microwave Conference, 2005 European, 2005, pp. 269-272.

[3] D. Bajon and H. Baudrand, "Equivalent circuit representation for integral formulation of electromagnetic problems," Int. journal of Num. Modeling, vol. 15, pp. 23-57, jan. 2002.

[4] N.Markuwitz, "Waveguide handbook", the institution of electrical engineering, 1986.

Determined Factor Parameter Analysis for System of Information Recovery from USB-Keyboard Compromising Emanations

Rostislav I. Sokolov, Renat R. Abdullin
Institute of Radioelectronics and Informational Technologies,
Ural Federal University named after the first President of Russia B.N.Yeltsin,
19 Mira str, Yekaterinburg, Russian Federation

***Abstract*—This paper is devoted to the development of calculation algorithm in order to determine the significance of different *a priori* information on the quality of USB-keyboard compromising emanation recovery. The system was investigated under condition of non-Gaussian interferences with Johnson distribution defining the industrial noise. As the calculation result according to developed algorithm based on elimination method it has been found the one of the most important factor is factor defining the noise parameters, and consequently, the achievement of maximal effective radio countermeasure is carried out at the choice of masking noise.**

Keywords—compromising emanations recovery; determined factor analysis; Gaussian noise; Johnson noise; masking effect.

I. Introduction

In present time the use of electronic devices in different communication systems has lead to the problem of protecting information against a leakage through the technical channels. Depending on the origin physical nature of the information signals, their propagation medium and interception methods technical leakage channels can be divided into electromagnetic, electrical, parametric and vibrational.

The source of compromising emanations is the elements of the technical device. The carrier of information is the electric current, whose parameters vary according to the pattern of information signal change. When the current is passing through the elements there are electric and magnetic fields around it. Therefore, the elements of technical device can be considered as emitters of information signal.

The quality of compromising emanation reception depends on not only the power, but on the kind of interference distribution. However, automated systems for special studies are universal and they are not calculated for each types of signal and noise.

Thus, in order to obtain a more complete and qualitative assessment of USB keyboard compromising emanations detection and restoration possibility and choose more adequate measures for the object protection it is necessary to undertake a study on evaluation of various factors impact in the system "emitting object – interceptor".

The quantity of *a priori* data on the signal and noise in the system of information detection and recovery from USB-keyboard compromising emanations influences on the choice of the most efficient signal processing method [1]-[3].

It should be divided into four general parameters in the interception system, a priori knowledge of which impacts on the received message processing quality at a given signal to noise ratio (SNR): the single pulse duration (the number of samples between adjacent leading edges); the arrival time of the intercept message first pulse; the noise type, and general signal parameters (the single pulse amplitude, the parcel duration, repetition interval). An addition of precise *a priori* knowledge about every parameter leads to the reception quality improvement. Thus, it is necessary to define the every parameter significance.

II. Algorithm Development

The determined factor analysis (DFA) has been used to solve this task: all factors except one (for independent factors) were eliminated [4], [5]. Investigated multiplicative model has the form:

$$SNR(p=0.1)=\sqrt[4]{K_1 K_2 K_3 K_4}, \qquad (1)$$

where SNR ($p = 0.1$) is signal to noise ratio for fixed error probability of correct recovery $p = 0.1$; K_1 is SNR for a certain value of the single pulse duration; K_2 is SNR for fixed values of signal parameters; K_3 is SNR for fixed value of signal arrival time; K_4 is SNR for fixed values of noise parameters.

The coefficients in the right side of (1) characterize the change in SNR for fixed correct recovery error probability $p = 0.1$ when changing the value of one of the four general factors. The purpose of this work is to assess the impact of i-th factor absolute change on the absolute change of a productive indicator.

Besides the general factors it is necessary to determine the degree of specific factors impact on the recovery quality: the variance σ^2; parameter γ; parameter η. In this case investigated model is also multiplicative:

The work was supported by Act 211 Government of the Russian Federation, contract № 02.A03.21.0006.

$$K_4 = \sqrt[3]{k_{\sigma^2} k_\gamma k_\eta}, \qquad (2)$$

where k_{σ^2} is SNR for certain value of variance σ^2; k_γ is SNR for fixed value of noise γ parameter; k_η is SNR for fixed value of noise η parameter.

The algorithm of isolated factor effect detection consists of the gradual definition of the following parameters (Table I):

1. The each factor mean value (MV) (Column 2 of Table I).
2. The each factor average deviation (AD) (Column 4 of Table I).
3. SNR MV for fixed correct recovery error probability.

$$[SNR] = \sqrt[4]{[K_1][K_2][K_3][K_4]}. \qquad (3)$$

4. The values of the absolute change in SNR when changing the i-th factor (ΔSNR (x_i)) by the product of all factors MV (except the i-th factor) and i-th factor AD (column 5 of Table I).
5. The overall value of the absolute change in SNR $\Delta SNR(\Sigma)$ as the sum of absolute changes when changing the each factor:

$$\Delta SNR(\Sigma) = \Delta SNR(K_1) + \Delta SNR(K_2) + \\ + \Delta SNR(K_3) + \Delta SNR(K_4) = 9.6. \qquad (4)$$

6. Values of the relative change in SNR when changing the i-th factor as the ratio of $\Delta SNR(x_i)$ to $\Delta SNR(\Sigma)$ (column 5 of Table I).
7. Similarly the points 3-6, it should be determined the relative change in the parameter K_4 when changing the i-th factor as the ratio of $\Delta K_4(x_i)$ to $\Delta K_4(\Sigma)$ in the study of different noise parameters impact in the model (2) (Column 5 of Table I).

III. Discussion of Numerical Experiment Results

1. *A priori* information on single pulse duration and initial sample arrival time is necessary condition for recovery of the informative signal obtained due to the channels of USB keyboards compromising emanations.
2. The determined factor analysis has shown that one of the most important factors is the general factor defining the noise parameters. Thus, the achievement of the most effective radio countermeasure is carried out with the choice of masking interference.
3. *A priori* information on signal amplitude, packet duration, and packets delay is the factor of smallest importance, affecting insignificantly on the possibility of qualitative data extraction from compromising emanations.
4. The determined factor analysis of noise parameters has shown the most important for masking properties are γ and η parameters of Johnson distribution. The masking effect is maximal when γ is equaled to 0, and η is maximal.

TABLE I

The Results of Isolated Factor Effect on SNR for Fixed Correct Recovery Error Probability $P = 0.1$.

Parameters of Multiplicative Model	Factor Turndown	MV, dB	AD, dB	Absolute Changes of ΔSNR(X_i), dB	Factor Influence ,%
K_1	-4-0	-2	2	2,4	25
K_2	-4--5	-4	1	1,7	18
K_3	-4-0	-2	2	2,4	25
K_4	-4-8	2	6	3,1	32
Parameters of Noise	Factor Turndown	MV, dB	AD, dB	Absolute Changes of K_4 (X_i), dB	Factor Influence ,%
k_{σ^2}	-4--2	-3	1	1,3	23
k_γ,	-4-0	-2	2	1,8	32
k_η	-4-2	-1	3	2,6	45

IV. Conclusion

The algorithm of determined factor analysis has been developed on the basis of elimination method. This algorithm allows evaluating the impact of various factors in conditions of Gaussian and non-Gaussian noises on the choice of optimal filtration way for PC unintentional emission. Analysis allows more completely and qualitatively evaluating USB keyboard compromising emanations detection and restoration possibility and choosing adequate measures for the object protection.

References

[1] M. Vuagnoux, S. Pasini. Compromising Electromagnetic Emanations of Wired and Wireless Keyboards, EPFL, Lausanne, Switzerland. https://www.usenix.org/legacy/events/sec09/tech/full_papers/vuagnoux.pdf

[2] V. Yu. Kobyakov, A. S. Luchinin, "Detection of unintentional electromagnetic emissions radiated by conductors and connectors of USB interface [Obnaruzheniye PEMI provodnikov i konnektorov pri peredache po interfeysu USB]". UrFO Newsletter. Security in the information sphere [Vestnik UrFO.Bezopasnost' v informatsionnoy sfere], no. 14, pp. 4-8, 2014.

[3] A. A. Horev, Technical protection of information: textbook for students [Tekhnicheskaya zashita informatsii: posobiye dlya studentov vuzov], vol. 1. Moscow, NPC Analitika 2008. 436 p.

[4] S. P. Vovk. Models of determined factor analysis in economics [Modeli determinirovannogo factornogo analiza v economike]. Taganrog, TRTU, 2004, 75 p.

[5] I. V. Sokolov, A. A. Smirnov, Yu. G. Antipin, R. I. Sokolov. "Influence of extraction parameters on the technology efficiency of underground mining of mineral deposits [Vliyaniye pokazateley izvlecheniya na effectivnost tekhnologii podzemnoy razrabotki rudnykh mestorozhdeniy]". News of Higher Schools. Mining Journal [Izvesyiya vishikh uchebnykh zavedeniy. Gorniy Zhurnal], no 3, pp. 4–11, 2012.

RADAR BIG DATA REDUCTION USING HARDWARE AND SOFTWARE SOLUTIONS

Sabikun Nahar, Lingyun Ren, Aly E. Fathy
Electrical Engineering and Computer Science Department
University of Tennessee
Knoxville, Tennessee, USA

Nghia Tran, Ozlem Kilic
Electrical Engineering and Computer Science Department
Catholic University of America
Washington, DC, USA

***Abstract*—Radars typically handle big data, and ways need to be developed to speed the data acquisition and processing. Here, we present methods to speed up step frequency continuous wave radar (SFCW) performance upon using multi-channels, compressive sensing algorithms, in addition to efficient OMP algorithms, and accelerated platforms for signal reconstruction based on FPGAs and GPUs.**

Keywords—SFCW, compressive sensing, fall detection

I. INTRODUCTION

There are different levels of accelerating platforms used for acquiring massive data in various radar applications. The acceleration could be in hardware, software or both. For example, using step frequency continuous wave (SFCW) radar has many great features like simplicity, no need for calibration, higher signal to noise ratio, simple ADC circuitry requirements, and the feasibility of operating over ultra wideband. However, it suffers from long acquisition time compared to UWB impulse radar, as it has to go through a large number of frequency steps. So, in order to speed up the process, we have designed a multi-channel radar system that simultaneously operates over different frequency bands. Additionally, we have utilized compressive sensing scheme to reduce these frequency steps significantly below Nyquist threshold.

II. RADAR OPERATION

A. FASTER HARDWARE

SFCW radar is an excellent candidate for fast data acquisition, as it can allow parallel data processing in the frequency domain. Moreover, SFCW radar can cover wide frequency range to improve imaging resolution. For the hardware implementation, the total bandwidth of the system is 2 GHz and the frequency step size is 20 MHz to provide a 7.5 cm resolution. In this case, the system has two channels where each channel has 50 distinct frequency points. Therefore the data processing time is reduced to almost half when compared with the single channel system. For even faster data acquisition, the number of SFCW radar channels can be increased from 2 to 4, 8 or even 16. Thus significantly reducing the processing time to cover wider band while utilizing low cost ADC circuitries. The challenge here is the synchronization and the effective combination of these channels. The direct digital synthesizer (DDS) board with two channels driven by one master clock can be used here to guarantee synchronization. The phase locked look (PLL) can be employed to generate the required stepped frequencies while allowing a frequency shift between the different channels.

The concept of the DDS board is comprised of four blocks: a phase accumulator (PA), a sine waveform lookup table (LUT), a digital-to-analog convertor (DAC) and a low pass filter (LPF), as shown in Figure 1. The DDS frequency step-up can be easily adjusted to be either a single frequency operation, a multi-step operation, or randomly selected. The frequency is given by

$$f_{out} = \frac{F}{2^I} f_{clk}, \qquad (1)$$

where F is the frequency control word with I-bit width, f_{clk} is the frequency of the DDS system clock. Typically, the control unit of the DDS reads this I-bit word from an algorithm that can be either sequential stepping, or randomly selected numbers.

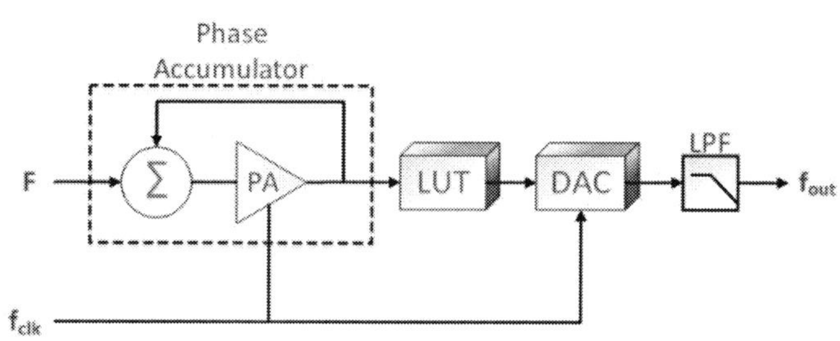

Fig. 1 Schematic of a DDS board

B. FASTER DATA PROCESSING

SFCW radar system is implemented using compressive sensing algorithms that are based on the orthogonal matching pursuit (OMP) algorithm to further speed up the data acquisition. Definitely, it is a challenging task to randomly select these frequencies and avoid the sequential stepping over all these frequency steps to effectively apply CS, while satisfying the sparseness condition of CS. The radar relates the received baseband signal to the range profile which is expressed as a Fourier transform as

$$s(f_n, m) = \sum_{l=0}^{N-1} x(r_l, m) \exp\left(-j2\pi f_n * 2r_l/c\right) \qquad (2)$$

where x is the received signal for a given frequency sample m, and can be rewritten in a matrix form as $s = \Phi_{DFT}x$, where s and x are the column vectors obtained by stacking $s(f_n)$ and $x(r_l)$, respectively. Φ_{DFT} is the measurement matrix of dimension $(N \times N)$, where each element is defined as $exp(-j \cdot 2\pi f_n \cdot 2r_l/c)$. In the CS-based approach, due to the sparseness of the target space, the baseband signals, s_{CS}, are measured at a random subset N_{CS} (< N) of frequencies of the total bandwidth. The reduced measurement matrix Φ_{DFT}^{CS} is constructed by randomly selecting N_{CS} rows of matrix Φ_{DFT}, i.e. corresponding to the selected frequencies.

Hence the reconstruction of the range profile is formulated as a convex optimization problem. Most CS algorithms are associated with intensive matrix operations, such as matrix-matrix multiplication, Cholesky decomposition, and matrix inversion. With the growth of the matrix size, computational costs will greatly increase, leading to unacceptably high execution time. This hampers applying the CS algorithm to time sensitive applications, such as real-time video pattern recognition, online model regression, and fast signal reconstruction. Therefore, our objective is to obtain acceleration of the CS computation by utilizing special purpose accelerators such as GPUs and FPGAs.

III. Examples

The SFCW radar was used to detect the range of a subject, and it was accurately identified with less than 20% compressive sensing ratio as compared to a complete set of frequency data as seen in Fig. 2. We plan to utilize this approach for human vital sign detection, and results will be presented at the conference. Our preliminary investigations anticipate that accurate results can be achieved with less than 30% compressive sensing ratio. More cases will be dissucesd in our presentation.

IV. Conclusion

Many radars handle big data in the range of terabits when dealing with high resolution, many freqency points, many directions, many objects detection and tracking that could have storage and slow data acquisition processing as well. SFCW radars have great features besides low cost but relatively slow in data acquisition, use of multi-channel SFCW radar, implementing CS, and utilization of OMP algortithm on FPGAs and GPUs can significantly speed up the imaging.

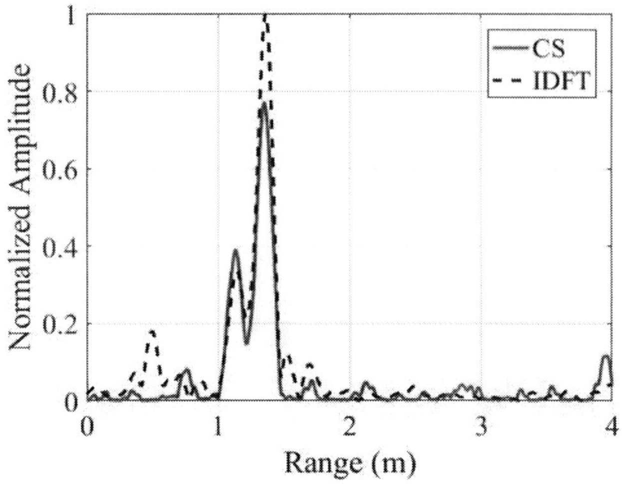

Fig. 2: SFCW results for Range Detection

References

[1] M. Mercuri, D. Schreurs, and P. Leroux, "SFCW microwave radar for in-door fall detection," in *Biomedical Wireless Technologies, Networks, and Sensing Systems (BioWireleSS), 2012 IEEE Topical Conference on*, 2012, pp. 53-56.

[2] H. Wang, L. Ren, E. Mao, and A. E. Fathy, "Phase based motion characteristics measurement for fall detection by using stepped-frequency continuous wave radar," in *2016 IEEE Topical Conference on Biomedical Wireless Technologies, Networks, and Sensing Systems (BioWireleSS)*, 2016, pp. 43-45.

[3] Zhang, Tong. "Sparse recovery with orthogonal matching pursuit under RIP."IEEE Transactions on Information Theory 57, no. 9 (2011): 6215-6221.

[4] Nghia Tran, Ozlem Kilic, Sabikun Nahar, Lingyun Ren, Haofei Wang, Aly E. Fathy,"Alternatives to BIG Data Acquisition for Health Monitoring Using Step Frequency Continuous Wave Radar and Compressive Sensing Algorithms," Submitted for publication.

[5] Haofei Wang, Lingyun Ren, Ozlem Kilic, Aly E. Fathy, "Fast and precise ranging based on Stepped-Frequency continuous wave radar measurements using compressive sensing algorithms", *Microwave Symposium (IMS) 2016 IEEE MTT-S Internatal.*

Complex Permittivity Measurements of Dielectrics for Space Antenna Radome and Substrates in X-band

Fahri Ozturk[1], Volkan Akan[1], Kagan Topalli[1], Ercan Kiraz[1], Lokman Kuzu[1], Mesut Gokten[1]

[1]TUBITAK Space Technologies Research Institute
Microwave and Antenna Systems Group
Ankara, TURKEY
fahri.ozturk@tubitak.gov.tr, volkan.akan@tubitak.gov.tr, kagan.topalli@tubitak.gov.tr, ercan.kiraz@tubitak.gov.tr, lokman.kuzu@tubitak.gov.tr, mesut.gokten@tubitak.gov.tr

Abstract— **A variety of material measurement systems based on transmission/reflection line method are available to characterize the dielectric properties of materials by extracting the S-parameters using a Vector Network Analyzer (VNA). A waveguide material measurement facility based on transmission/reflection line method has been developed in-house in order to accurately deduct relative dielectric permittivity and tangent loss values of dielectric materials used for manufacturing antenna radome and substrate. In this paper, the experimental measurements of VESPEL, PTFE (Teflon), and RO5880 have been realized in X-band (8-12 GHz) with a very low standard deviation.**

Keywords—waveguide transmission/reflection method dielectric characterization; X-band; VESPEL; TRL calibration

I. Introduction

In order to characterize the electrical properties of dielectric materials a test set-up has been developed by Microwave and Antenna Systems Group of TUBITAK UZAY. These materials are used to fabricate radome and substrate of antennas dedicated to space communication systems that we are developing for Low Earth Orbit (LEO) and Geosynchronous Earth Orbit (GEO) satellites. Commercially available materials, such as VESPEL SP-1 [1], are lack of material knowledge at the X-band frequencies. For the same material, the dielectric permittivity and tangent loss could vary from one supplier to another. The knowledge of variability of dielectric materials is crucial for EM simulation of space antennas. It is therefore of paramount importance that the test set-up gives very accurate measurements of materials. Depending on the frequencies and materials of interest, several measurement techniques exist to investigate the electrical properties of dielectric materials with one or two ports [2]. Since equipment cost is low and the method is convenient to use in hostile environment, the transmission/reflection line technique, also known as the waveguide method, is a very effective measurement tool among those techniques [2]. This paper reports accurate results for the relative dielectric permittivity and tangent loss values of VESPEL, PTFE (Teflon [1]) and RO5880 [3] by using the transmission/reflection line waveguide method in the frequency range between 8 to 12 GHz (X-band).

II. Method

Nicholson-Ross-Weir (NRW) algorithm is used to extract the dielectric parameters of materials [4]. In this method, the dielectric parameters can be deduced from the pair of S11 and S21 parameters. A set of equations relates the S parameters to the reflection and transmission coefficients, and finally complex dielectric permittivity is obtained [5]. The sample thickness is mostly chosen shorter than integer multiples of one half wavelength in order to avoid inaccurate peaks on the measurement data. Since the process of de-embedding can be performed using a computer code, the sample placed inside a rectangular waveguide does not need to fill completely the waveguide longitudinal axis. The calibration method to be performed during the measurements determine the measurement accuracy. A full two-port Through-Reflect-Line (TRL) calibration is appropriate for this waveguide based test setup [2]. Sample preparation is also critical. Measured results depend upon sensitive measures of sample thickness. Variations in sample measures are also included in the calculations of complex dielectric parameter. Hence, the measured data is given with error calculations obtained from the standard deviation calculations of successive measurements over different period of time.

III. EXPERIMENTAL MEASUREMENTS

Figure 1 shows the main parts of the waveguide test setup: VNA, two coax to waveguide adapters, two waveguide extensions and sample holder which are suitable for X-band. The test setup is positioned according to the longitudinal axis of the setup components clamped to a block guide profile to sustain the bench stability. This allows us linear translations of the test system during both TRL calibration and measurements. First, the TRL calibration is performed by setting the VNA for the X-band waveguide TRL calibration kit. Following this, the sample is inserted into the sample holder. Finally, the measured data is saved to an S2P format in order to calculate complex dielectric permittivity via a computer code.

Fig.1.: The main parts of the waveguide test setup.

The initial measurement was conducted for air to ensure that the system is working accurate enough. Random fluctuations in measured S parameters data can be reduced by careful stabilization of network cables. Relative permittivity and permeability results for air measurements are given in Figure 2. Next measurements were performed on VESPEL SP-1, PTFE and RO5880 samples with various thicknesses. The results of these measurements are summarized in Table 1 which gives relative permittivity and tangent loss for 1, 1.5 and 2 mm thick samples of each material.

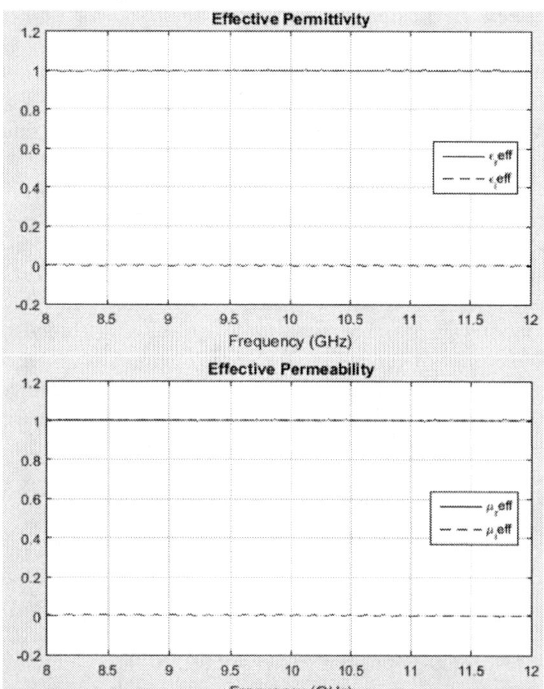

Fig.2. Permittivity and permeability plots for air measurements by using waveguide method.

TABLE I. MEASUREMENT RESULTS

Materials	Measurement Data @10 GHz	Literature Data @10 GHz
	Permittivity / Tangent Loss*10^{-3}	***Permittivity / Tangent Loss*10-3***
PTFE [6]	2,029±0,003 / 4,494±1,720	2,02 / 0,8
VESPEL [1]	3,119±0,043 / 20,893±4,042	3,55 / 3,4 @ 1 MHz
RO5880 [3]	2,228±0,002 / 1,993±0,401	2,20±0,02 / 0,9

Materials were fabricated by using a Computer Numerical Controlled machine (CNC). Table 1 also compares measured data with literature data. The calculations were done for a frequency of 10 GHz. RO 5880 was selected for comparison because its data sheet at 10 GHz is provided on the supplier website [3].

IV. RESULTS

In this paper, we have reported the measured results of the dielectric permittivity and tangent loss values for dielectric materials of PTFE, VESPEL SP-1 and RO5880 to third decimal places. The measured results of PTFE and RO5880 are in good agreement with the literature data. There is no measured complex permittivity value of VESPEL SP-1 in X-band so further attempts were made to measure this material. Further measurements with a variety of low loss dielectric materials used for space communication antennas are still being performed.

ACKNOWLEDGMENT

The authors would like to thank Ass. Prof. Evren Ekmekci for the help of writing computer code via using the mentioned method. We also acknowledge the support of Ministry of Development of Turkey for granting the project IMECE-7P130609.

REFERENCES

[1] Supplier website: http://www.dupont.com

[2] Rohde&Schwarz, Application Note, "Measurement of dielectric material properties".

[3] Supplier website: https://www.rogerscorp.com/

[4] A. M. Nicholson and G. F. Ross, "Measurement of the Intrinsic Properties of Materials by Time-Domain Techniques," IEEE Transactions on instrumentation and measurement, vol. IM-19, No.4, November 1970.

[5] American Society for Testing and Materials. ASTM D5568-08: Standard Test Method for measuring Relative Complex Permittivity and Relative Magnetic Permeability of Solid Materials at Microwave Frequencies. West Conshohoken, PA:ASTM, 2001.

[6] M. D. Belrhiti, et.al., "Complex permittivity of low loss materials in the X band", Int. Journal of Science and Advanced Tech., vol.1, August 2011.

Electron Beam Induced Terahertz Čerenkov Radiation from Multilayer Graphene Sandwiches

Konstantin Batrakov and Sergey Maksimenko
Institute for Nuclear Problems, Belorussian State University, Belarus
Email: kgbatrakov@gmail.com
Telephone: +3759126550

Abstract—**Terahertz lasing by electron beam propagating over a graphene/dielectric sandwich structure is considered. A dispersion equation for the surface electromagnetic modes propagating along graphene sheets is derived and Čerenkov synchronism between surface wave and electron beam is predicted at achievable parameters of the system. The generation frequency tuning is proposed by varying the graphene doping, the number of graphene sheets, the distance between sheets, etc.**

I. Introduction

Due to a variety of scientific and technical applications, there is a great need in the development of coherent terahertz radiation sources with tunable frequency. In particular, the tunability can be realized in the devices utilizing kinetic energy of moving electrons and transforming it into the energy of the emitted electromagnetic wave. Free electron laser, travelling wave tube (TWT) and backward wave oscillator, are the well-known devices of such a type.

In the case of Čerenkov-type emitter, the radiation frequency depends *also* on electrodynamic parameters of the medium providing the means of the resonant frequency tuning. Among different possibilities, graphene and carbon nanotubes (CNTs) are very promising materials from this point of view since there are well-known and rather facile methods of their constitutive parameters wide-range varying. In particular, well-developed methods of graphene doping inclusive of electrostatic doping allow smooth alteration of the surface conductivity. Besides, it has been shown that carbon nanotubes and graphene can considerably slow down surface electromagnetic wave [1], [2]. Čerenkov mechanism of generation of the coherent stimulated radiation in graphene and carbon nanotubes was theoretically investigated in Refs. [3], [4], [5], [6], [7] demonstrating realizability of the nanotube-based nano-TWT and nano-FEL at realistic parameters of CNTs and electron beams. In the present work we study excitation of surface waves propagating in graphene sandwich structures and resonantly interacting with an electron beam, aiming at the reveal of the generation conditions and methods of the smooth frequency tuning by variation of the system parameters.

II. Wave Slowing Down and Generation in Graphene Sandwiches

Consider an electron beam propagating parallel to a graphene sheet or multi-layer graphene sandwich structure comprising graphene sheets separated by dielectric layers. On its way over the sandwich the beam interacts with the surface electromagnetic wave supported by the graphene structure. For the coherent radiation generation, the beam should be synchronized with the electromagnetic wave on the beam propagation length over the structure. In particular, for the Čerenkov emission mechanism the electron beam velocity must coincide with the phase velocity v_{ph} of electromagnetic wave. Let us examine propagation of surface waves along the sandwich in free space, assuming the distances between graphene layers large on the atomic scale and, therefore, neglecting electron interlayer tunnelling in the sandwich. Further we follow the procedure developed in Refs. [8], [9]. Applying the procedure described to the sandwich structure consisting of n layers, we arrive at the homogeneous system of $2n$ linear equations for $2n$ coefficients. Dispersion equation of the system arises when we set the determinant of the system equal to zero and determines the frequency dependence of the surface wave wavevector. For single graphene layer the system comprises 2 equations for 2 coefficients that, assuming chemical potential considerably exceeding the temperature, leads to dispersion equation:

$$q^2c^2 = \omega^2 + \left[\frac{\hbar\omega\,(\omega + i\Gamma)}{2\mu\alpha}\right]^2 . \qquad (1)$$

q is tangential to graphene sheet component of the wave vector, μ is the chemical potential of electron subsystem, Γ is the broadening parameter (collision frequency), and α is the fine structure constant. In further calculations we assume $\Gamma \sim 10$ THz in accordance with our previous experiments on the electromagnetic radiation absorption in graphene sandwich structures [8], [9]. In the case of potential fields, when we can neglect the first term in the right-hand part of Eq. (1), we arrive at the dependence[10] $q \sim \omega^2$ or $\omega \sim \sqrt{q}$). Note that such a dependence drastically differs from the dependence inherent in the 3D case where eigenfrequency is proportional the Langmuir plasma frequency and does not depend on the wavevector [11]. Specific dispersion law admits strong slowing down of surface waves in 2D systems.

Substitution of the Čerenkov synchronism condition $q = \omega/v$ in (1) (v is electron beam velocity) gives dependence of the Čerenkov resonant frequency $\nu = \omega/(2\pi)$ on chemical potential which is depicted on Fig. 1 at different values of the electron beam energy. A double-layer graphene system

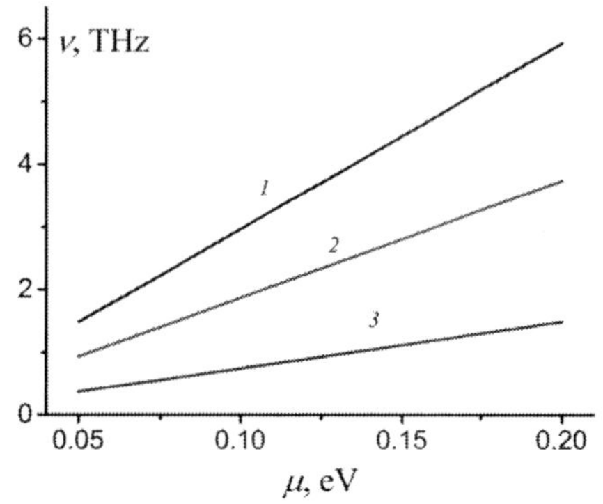

Fig. 1. Čerenkov resonant frequency *vs* chemical potential at the electron beam energy 4 KeV (1), 10 KeV (2) and 60 KeV (3).

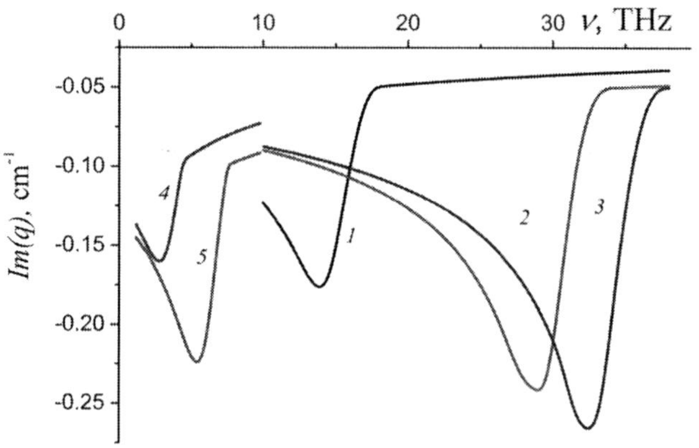

Fig. 2. Frequency dependence of the instability increment $Im(q)$ for 4 (1), 8 (2) and 9 (3) graphene layers with chemical potential of a single layer $\mu = 0.2$ eV. Electron beam energy $E = 10$ keV, $\Gamma = 10$ THz. For comparison, the same dependencies are given for a single graphene layer at the electron beam energy $E = 4$ keV, and chemical potential $\mu = 0.1$ eV (4) and $\mu = 0.2$ eV (5).

can be used for the generation of Čerenkov radiation by an electron beam [2]. The advantage being achieved by graphene doubling is the appearance of the acoustic mode among plasmon oscillations inherent in the system. This mode whose frequency is proportional to difference of frequencies of plasmonic oscillations in layers. As a result, the phase velocity of this wave appears to be much less than that achievable in monolayer and can be tuned by altering of interlayer distance. There is also optical mode in the double-layer. The dispersion equation of optical mode differs from the single-layer case in that only that the effective chemical potential (and sheet conductivity) is doubled as compared to the case of graphene monolayer. Analogous effect holds true for sandwich graphene structure with number of layers more then two. For this case, effective conductivity is equal to sum of layers conductivities. Such an additivity has been observed experimentally in studying of electromagnetic wave transmission through sandwich graphene structures[8], [9]. These frequencies appear to be in the THz range and significantly shift to short-wave side with the number of graphene layers. Simultaneously, the increment strongly growth in absolute value. Maximal absolute values of the instability increments presented in Figs. 2 show us that the strong amplification regime can already be realized at the interaction length of the order of several centimeters. At smaller lengthes, incorporation into the system of a feedback (for example, mirror) allows achieving generation in the low gain regime. Generation develops at frequencies near the points of maximum of increment negative value at corresponding choice of interaction length. Figs. 1 and 2 demonstrate the frequency tuning possibilities by variation of chemical potential and electron beam energy. Smooth frequency tuning can be achieved by electrostatic doping of graphene layers that changes μ smoothly, discrete tuning can be achieved by changing of the number of graphene layers in sandwich.

Acknowledgment

This publication is based on work supported by a grant from the U.S. Air Force under Agreement FA9550-15-D-0003, EU FP7 project FP7-612285 CANTOR and EU H2020 project 644076 CoExAN.

References

[1] G. Y. Slepyan, S. A. Maksimenko, A. Lakhtakia, O. Yevtushenko, and A. V. Gusakov, "Electrodynamics of carbon nanotubes: Dynamic conductivity, impedance boundary conditions, and surface wave propagation," *Phys. Rev. B*, vol. 60, p. 17136, 1999, DOI: 10.1103/PhysRevB.60.17136.

[2] K. Batrakov, V. Saroka, S. Maksimenko, and C. Thomsen, "Plasmon polariton deceleration in graphene structures," *J. Nanophotonics*, vol. 6, no. 1, p. 061719, 2012, DOI: 10.1117/1.JNP.6.061719.

[3] K. Batrakov, P. Kuzhir, and S. Maksimenko, "Radiative instability of electron beams in carbon nanotubes," in *Proceedings of SPIE - The International Society for Optical Engineering*, A. Lakhtakia and S. Maksimenko, Eds., vol. 6328. San Diego, California, USA: SPIE Digital Library, 2006, p. 63280Z, DOI: 10.1117/12.678029.

[4] ——, "Stimulated emission of electron beam in nanotube bundles," *Physica E*, vol. 40, no. 7, pp. 2370–2374, 2008, DOI: 10.1016/j.physe.2007.07.029.

[5] ——, "Toward the nano-fel: Undulator and cherenkov mechanisms of light emission in carbon nanotubes," *Physica E*, vol. 40, no. 5, pp. 1065–1068, 2008, DOI: 10.1016/j.physe.2007.08.003.

[6] K. G. Batrakov, S. A. Maksimenko, P. P. Kuzhir, and C. Thomsen, "Carbon nanotube as a cherenkov-type light emitter and free electron laser," *Phys. Rev. B*, vol. 79, no. 12, p. 125408, 2009, DOI: 10.1103/PhysRevB.79.125408.

[7] K. Batrakov, O. Kibis, P. Kuzhir, C. Rosenau, and M. Portnoi, "Terahertz processes in carbon nanotubes," *J. Nanophotonics*, vol. 4, no. 1, p. 041665, 2010, DOI: 10.1117/1.3436585.

[8] K. Batrakov, P. Kuzhir, S. Maksimenko, A. Paddubskaya, S. Voronovich, P. Lambin, T. Kaplas, and Y. Svirko, "Flexible transparent graphene/polymer multilayers for efficient electromagnetic field absorption," *Scientific Reports*, vol. 4, p. 7191, 2014, DOI: 10.1038/srep07191.

[9] K. Batrakov, P. Kuzhir, S. Maksimenko, A. Paddubskaya, S. Voronovich, G. Valusis, T. Kaplas, Y. Svirko, and P. Lambin, "Enhanced microwave-to-terahertz absorption in graphene," *Appl. Phys. Lett.*, vol. 108, p. 123101, 2016, DOI: 10.1063/1.4944531.

[10] S. DasSarma and E. H. Hwang, "Collective modes of the massless dirac plasma," *Phys. Rev. Lett.*, vol. 102, p. 206412, 2009, DOI: 10.1103/PhysRevLett.102.206412.

[11] E. M. Lifshitz and L. P. Pitaevskii, *Physical Kinetics*, 1st ed., ser. Course of Theoretical Physics. Oxford: Pergamon Press, 1981, vol. 10.

Tunable electromagnetic response of free-standing 3D carbon nanotube network in the Ka-band

M. V. Shuba, D. Yuko, P. P. Kuzhir,
S. A. Maksimenko
Institute for Nuclear Problems,
Belarus State University,
Minsk, Belarus,
mikhail.shuba@gmail.com

M. Scarselli
Dept. of Physics,
University of Rome Tor Vergata
Rome, Italy
manuela.scarselli@roma2.infn.it

Abstract—**The sponges made of multi-walled carbon nanotubes (CNT) demonstrate tunable electromagnetic response properties in the microwave range (27-36 GHz) governed by their mechanical deformation. The higher the applied stress, the denser the sponge, the more reflective it is in the Ka-band. The microwave effective conductivity of the CNT network macrostructure was proved to be linearly increased with its density.**

Keywords—carbon nanotube, network, Ka-band, conductivity

I. Introduction

Multi-walled carbon nanotubes (CNTs) are conductive elongated nanoparticles with very high aspect ratio (up to 10^4). They are under intensive study as inclusions for composite materials for electromagnetic shielding applications [1,2]. One of the problems of CNT-based composite fabrication is strong aggregation effect, which occurs in the host matrix during preparation process even at low volume fraction of the CNTs. This behavior hinders the effective interaction of the inclusions with electromagnetic field reducing electromagnetic response of the composite. Ultrasonic treatment and special functionalization of the CNTs are applied to get more homogeneous distribution of the CNTs in the samples. However, additional treatment usually leads to the reduction of nanotube lengths and intertube contact conductivity and, consequently, to a decrease of their electromagnetic efficiency [2].

Free-standing three-dimensional carbon nanotube network [3-5] could represent a great tool for studying electromagnetic wave interaction with CNTs. This network comprises homogeneously distributed curved and interconnected multi-walled CNTs; it has low density (≈ 40 mg/cm^3) and looks like a sponge. Scanning electron microscopy shows that the tubes form a random skeleton with open micrometre-size pores. Tube lengths are tenth and hundreds of microns. The statistical analysis gives a double distribution of the external CNT diameter centered at 91 ± 3 nm, and 418 ± 5 nm, respectively [3]. Such CNT network can be easily compressed giving a possibility to measure its dc- [4] and ac-conductivity at different nanotube densities. In the present report, we propose measurements of the microwave reflectance, transmittance and ac-conductivity of the sponges made of the CNT network of different densities changing smoothly via mechanical deformation in the Ka-band.

II. Materials and Measurements

The CNT-sponges network assembly was obtained following a chemical vapour deposition (CVD) process [2-5]. The synthesis was carried out in a stainless steel chamber hosting a horizontal hot-wall quartz furnace and operating under controlled pressure. Before starting the growth process argon gas was flushed into the chamber, to establish an ambient inert pressure (760 Torr) free from oxygen. Subsequently the furnace temperature was raised up to the selected value and then a solution containing the carbon and the catalyst was injected into the hot area. In particular, the solution contained ferrocene (2.3 wt %) dissolved in diclorobenzene to be used as catalyst and carbon precursor, respectively. A flux of argon and acetylene (500/200 sccm) helped to inject drops of solution from a 10 mL glass syringe through a stainless tube directly into the high temperature region of the quartz tube furnace. The CNT synthesis was carried out at a temperature of 900 °C, measured by an optical pyrometer and the growth time varied from 1-3 hours during which the solution was injected at a constant rate of 7 mL/h.

The microwave measurements of transmission/reflection coefficients in the Ka-band (27-36 GHz) were performed with a scalar network analyzer R2–408 (ELMIKA) after inserting the sample into a transmission line (waveguide of cross-section 7.2×3.4mm) perpendicular to wave propagation. Plate-form CNT sponge occupied all the space between the walls of waveguide and two parallel thin mica plates standing perpendicular to the waveguide axis. As the mica plates are very thin (a few micrometers), they were completely transparent for microwave radiation. Initially, the distance d between mica plates was 3.4 mm. Then it was reduced resulting in compression of the CNT network and, consequently, in an increase of its density ρ. The measurement of the reflectance and transmittance has been done for four different distances d. The effective permittivity and conductivity of the samples were found from the transmittance and reflectance. The values d and ρ for four different measurements are presented in Table I.

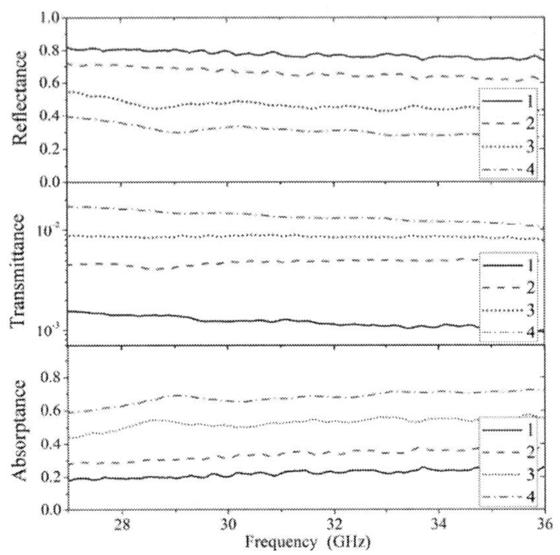

Fig. 1. Frequency dependence of (a) the reflectance R, (b) transmittance T, and (c) absorptance A ($A=1-R-T$) at different compressions extents (see Table 1).

TABLE I. MASS DENSITY ρ AND THICKNESS d OF THE CNT NETWORK AT DIFFERENT COMRESSION EXTENTS

	Number of Compression Extents			
	4	*3*	*2*	*1*
ρ, mg/cm^3	46	92	210	370
d, mm	32	1.6	0.7	0.4

III. EXPERIMENTAL RESULTS AND DISCUSSIONS

Fig. 1 shows the reflectance R, transmittance T and absorptance A ($A=1-T-R$) of the plate of the CNT-network at different compression extents presented in Table I. One can see from Fig. 1, that

(i) the screening effect is stronger for more dense plate at the same quantity of the CNTs in the sample; as all the samples are opaque, interference effect is not observed;

(ii) the reflectance increases and absorptance decreases as the CNT-network density increases; at minimal density 46 mg/ml the absorptance is high ($\approx 70\%$) and the reflectance is low ($\approx 30\%$), whereas opposite is true at maximal density 370 g/cm^3 – the absorptance is low ($\approx 20\%$) and the reflectance is high ($\approx 80\%$).

Fig. 2 shows effective conductivity of the CNT-network against its density. As shown in Fig. 2, the conductivity increases linearly with the CNT density in the range $\rho \in (46,370)$ mg/cm^3.

One can observe nonlinear dependence of the conductivity on the CNT density at $\rho = 370$ mg/cm^3. We suppose that at high density, the number of intertube contacts is high resulting in additional paths for the currents. This leads to an improvement of the effective conductivity of the CNT network.

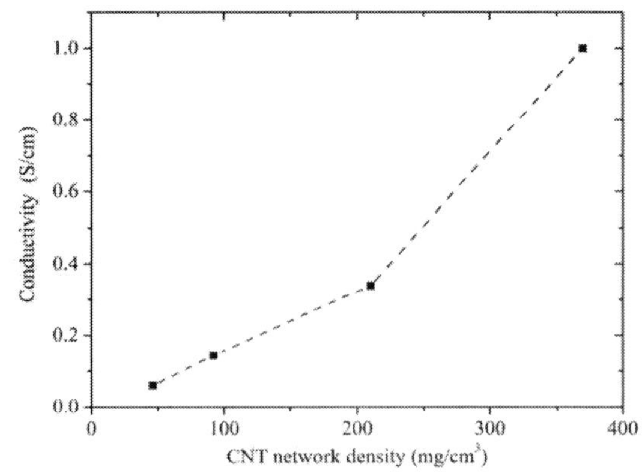

Fig. 2. Conductivity vs density of CNT-network at 30 GHz.

We propose simple and easy way to tune smoothly the electromagnetic response properties demonstrated by the CNT-sponges in the microwave range through applied mechanical stress to them, which changes the density of the samples and therefore changes the ac-conductivity and as the result the reflectance ability. Such a systems could be very interesting for different applications, where the tunability is the topical issue, e.g. for electromagnetic wave modulation in the cm-, mm-, and sub-mm frequency ranges.

ACKNOWLEDGMENT

This research was partially supported by H2020 RISE Project CoExAN GA644076.

REFERENCES

[1] P. Kuzhir, A. Paddubskaya, D. Bychanok, A. Nemilentsau, M. Shuba, A. Plusch, S. Maksimenko, S. Bellucci, L. Coderoni, F. Micciulla, I. Sacco, G. Rinaldi, J. Macutkevic, D. Seliuta, G. Valusis, J. Banys, "Microwave probing of nanocarbon based epoxy resin composite films: toward electromagnetic shielding," Thin Solid Films, vol. 519, pp. 4114-4118, 2011.

[2] M.V. Shuba, A.V. Melnikov, A.V. Paddubskaya, P.P. Kuzhir, S.A. Maksimenko, C. Thomsen, "The role of finite size effects in the microwave and sub-terahertz electromagnetic response of multiwall carbon nanotube based composite: theory and interpretation of experiment," Phys. Rev. B, vol. 88, p. 045436, 2013.

[3] L. Camilli, C. Pisani, E. Gautron, M. Scarselli, P. Castrucci, F. D'Orazio, M. Passacantando, D. Moscone, and M. De Crescenzi, "A three-dimensional carbon nanotube network for water treatment," Nanotechnology, vol. 25, pp. 065701, 2014.

[4] L. Camilli, C. Pisani, M. Passacantando, V. Grossi, M. Scarselli, P. Castrucci, and M. De Crescenzi, "Pressure-dependent electrical conductivity of freestanding three-dimensional carbon nanotube network," Appl. Phys. Lett., vol. 102, pp. 183117, 2013.

[5] M. Scarselli, P. Castrucci, F. De Nicola1, I. Cacciotti, F. Nanni, E. Gatto, M. Venanzi and M. De Crescenzi, "Applications of three-dimensional carbon nanotube networks" Beilstein J. Nanotechnol. vol. 6, pp. 792–798, 2015.

Carbon thin films as effective absorbers of microwave radiation: experiment and EMC applications

Polina Kuzhir, Alesia Padabskaya, Nadezhda Volynets, Konstantin Batrakov, Sergey Maksimenko
Institute for Nuclear Problems,
Belarusian State University
Minsk, Belarus
polina.kuzhir@gmail.com

Tommi Kaplas, Yuri Svirko
Institute of Photonics, University of Eastern Finland
Joensuu, Finland
yuri.svirko@uef.fi

Philippe Lambin
Namur University, Namur, Belgium
philippe.lambin@unamur.be

***Abstract*—The ability of graphene and other nm-thin carbon films including pyrolytic carbon (PyC) and pyrolyzed photoresist (PPF) to absorb microwave radiation is discussed. We show that being deposited on a properly chosen optically transparent dielectric substrate these films can provide more than 20 dB electromagnetic interference (EMI) shielding efficiency (SE).**

Keywords—graphene, glassy carbon, microwaves, absorption

I. Introduction

Recently we demonstrated [1,2] that 75 nm of PyC film and 4 CVD graphene monolayers separated by 100 nm thick polymer slabs can absorb up to 50% of the incident power at 30 GHz, being free standing in free space. Placing them onto appropriate dielectric substrate with anti-reflective properties (0-index, or quarter wavelength thick conventional dielectric) one may obtain almost perfect absorption of GHz-THz radiation [3]. In this presentation, we propose using for this purpose nm-thin PyC and PPF films as alternatives to graphene and perform comparative study of graphene, PyC and PPF in terms of EMI SE. We will also take into account other their physical properties (transparency in visible range, mechanical robustness, possibility to be grown up directly or easily transferred on the dielectric substrate of any shape) to specify how these films can be used to resolve the EM compatibility (EMC) problem at high frequencies.

II. Materials and Measurements

Graphene and PyC are fabricated by chemical vapor deposition (CVD) at ~1000 °C temperature regime using methane precursor. Graphene was grown on a copper foil, whereas PyC was grown directly on a silica substrate [4]. Changing slightly synthesis conditions, we may have different thickness (5-200 nm) of PyC and therefore different sheet resistance and optical density. Here we use 30 nm thick PyC film. A PPF was fabricated [5,6] by spin coating carbon based photoresist (nLOF-AZ2070 diluted with AZebr solvent with 1:4 ratio) on a substrate, baking it on a hot plate (110 °C/ 1 min) and then pyrolyzed in a CVD system. The PPF thickness can be vary by changing the thickness of the resist film. For this particular work we use 30 nm thick PPF.

The sandwich structure can be fabricated by using the Polymethyl methacrylate (PMMA) layer as a dielectric spacer between the carbon films. The sample fabrication process follows the conventional transfer process of graphene to the point where PMMA/graphene (PyC, PPF) film is deposited on a substrate. By repeating this procedure many times one may have 1…10 layers of carbon film (graphene, PyC, PPF) sandwiched between PMMA layers.

The microwave measurements were performed by using a scalar network analyzer R2-408R (ELMIKA, Vilnius, Lithuania) at room temperature and normal pressure. The EM response of the samples as ratios of transmitted/input (S_{21}) and reflected/input (S_{11}) signals has been measured in the 26–37 GHz frequency range (K_a-band). Reflectance (*R*), transmittance (*T*), and absorbance (*A*) values are obtained from the measured S-parameters in the following way: $R=S_{11}^2$, $T=S_{21}^2$, $A = 1 - R - T$.

III. Main Idea

It is known from classical electrodynamics that for every conductive material which thickness l is much thinner than skin depth, and permittivity ε and wavelength λ satisfy the following relations: $\mathrm{Im}\,\varepsilon \gg 1$, $l\sqrt{\varepsilon} \ll \lambda$, one may always find an optimal thickness l_σ, inversely proportional to film conductivity σ for which absorbance A, reflectance R and transmittance T are $A=50\%$, $R=25\%$, $T=25\%$ correspondently. When conductive film is in between two dielectric semi-infinite media with refractive indices n_1 and n_2, the absorbance $A = n_1/(n_1+n_2)$ can even exceed 50% if $n_1 > n_2$. Such a remarkably high absorbance of a few-atoms thin material can be achieved at $Im\ \sigma = 0$ and $Re\ \sigma = (n_1+n_2)\varepsilon_0 c$.

IV. Results and Discussion

The resistivities of PPF and PyC films are 110×10^{-5} Ωcm and 36×10^{-5} Ωcm respectively, being about 2 orders of magnitude higher than resistivity of CVD graphene 0.68×10^{-5} Ωcm. The difference in DC conductive properties will influence the thickness of film (number of layers in sandwich) necessary to reach maximal absorption.

As one can see from the Fig.1 one monolayer of CVD graphene, 30 nm thick PyC film and 30 nm thick PPF being deposited onto 0.5 mm silica substrate are highly absorptive in microwave range. With one graphene layer, one may absorb almost 20% of microwave radiation, slightly higher absorption could be achieved by PPF, and 30 nm thick PyC absorbs already 30% of EM power.

In order to absorb more than 50% of microwave radiation at normal incidence we need a sandwich structure consisting of 6-7 graphene layers, or 4 layers of PyC or 5 layers of PPF in case radiation comes from the substrate side (see TABLE I, data collected for 0.5 mm silica substrate). It is worth noting that if the substrate meets the radiation first, the overall EMI SE higher is because of absorption in carbon layers.

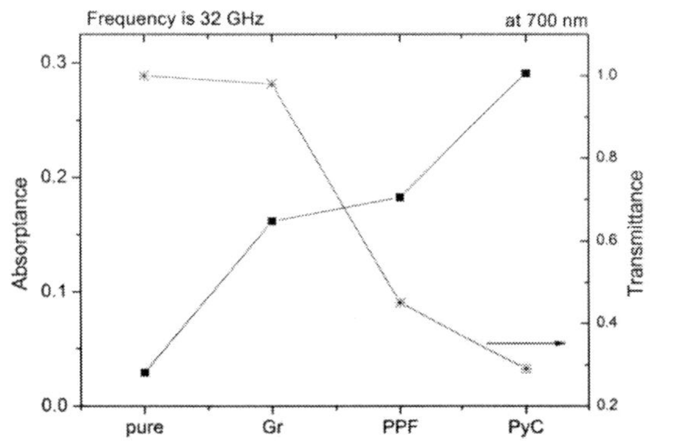

Fig. 1. Absorbance of graphene, PyC and PPF (both 30 nm thick) on the top of silica substrate vs their optical transmitance. Radiation comes from the side of carbon films.

TABLE I. EM RESPONSE PROPERTIES OF SANDWICH STRUCTURES COMPOSED OF 100NM PMMA AND GRAPHENE/CARBON FILMS

	EM response properties			
	0.5 mm silica substrate goes first EMI SE dB, absorbance, %		***Carbon goes first EMI SE dB, absorbance,%***	
graphene/PMMA 6 layers	6.9	0.53	6.9	0.39
graphene/PMMA 7 layers	7.7	0.52	7.7	0.39
PyC/PMMA 4 layers	6.62	0.53	6.62	0.39
PPF/PMMA 5 layers	6.95	0.53	6.95	0.39

Significant drawback of using PyC and PPF might be their limited transparency in visible range: 30 nm thick PPF and PyC absorb 50% and almost 70% of light respectively, whereas graphene absorbs 2.3% of incident light (see Fig.1).

However, the mechanical properties of PyC and PPF [7] are better than that of graphene/PMMA structures [8]. In addition PPF and PyC films can be deposited on a substrate with sophisticated geometry, allowing us to achieve perfect absorption in particular frequency ranges (see Fig.2: Absorbance is close to 90%, EMI SE = 19-21 dB).

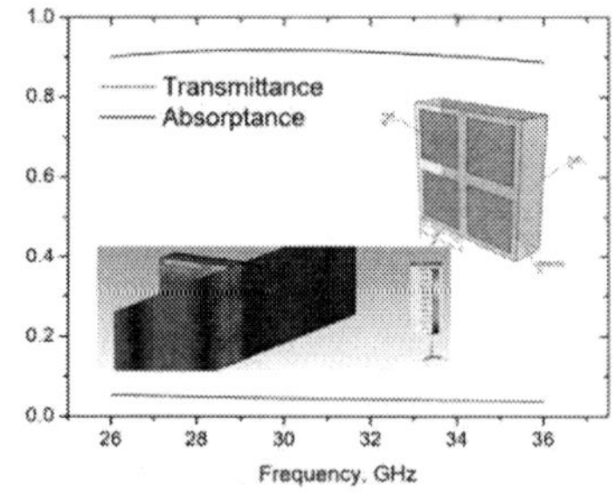

Fig. 2. Absorbance/Transmittance of PyC/polymer structure of sofisticated geometry (see inset) in microwaves and corresponding EM field distribution. Parameters of simulations (CST Studio): l_1=500 nm, l_2=1 mm, l_3=200 nm, a=2 mm, b=1.47mm, σ_{PyC}=36000 S/m, dielectric permittivity ε= 3.75.

V. CONCLUSIONS

The simplicity of PyC and PPF deposition on various surfaces (material, geometry) makes them a good competitor for graphene. Using dielectric substrate of proper geometry one may achieve with thin carbon films almost perfect absorption and EMI SE at the level of 20 dB. In case one does not need high transparency in visible range, PyC and PPF could offer important alternative to graphene opening an avenue towards development of a scalable protocol of cost-efficient production of ultra-light EM shields that can be transferred to commercial applications.

ACKNOWLEDGMENT

The work was carried out within the framework of H2020 project 696656 Graphene Core1 and H2020 project 644076 CoExAN.

REFERENCES

[1] K. Batrakov, P. Kuzhir, S. Maksimenko, A. Paddubskaya, et al., “Enhanced microwave shielding effectiveness of ultrathin pyrolytic carbon films”, Appl.Phys. Lett., vol. 103, pp. 073117, 2013.

[2] K. Batrakov, P. Kuzhir, S. Maksimenko, A. Paddubskaya, et al., “Flexible transparent graphene/polymer multilayers for efficient electromagnetic field absorption”, Scientific Reports, vol. 4, pp. 7191, 2014.

[3] K. Batrakov, P.Kuzhir, S. Maksimenko, N. Volynets, et al., “Enhanced microwave-to-terahertz absorption in Graphene”, Appl.Phys. Lett., vol. 108, pp. 123101, 2016.

[4] T. Kaplas, Y. Svirko, "Direct deposition of semitransparent conducting pyrolytic carbon films”, J. Nanophot., vol. 6, pp. 061703–6, 2012.

[5] R. Kostecki, B. Schnyder, D. Alliata, X Song, K Kinoshita, R Kötz, “Surface studies of carbon films from pyrolyzed photoresist”, Thin Solid Films, vol. 396, pp. 36–43, 2001.

[6] M. Schreiber, T. Lutz, G.P. Keeley, et al, “Transparent ultrathin conducting carbon films”, Appl. Surf. Sci., vol. 256, pp. 6186–6190, 2010.

[7] T. Kaplas, P. Kuzhir, “Pyrocarbon reinfoced graphene: synthesis and physical properties”, Nanoscale Research Letters, vol. 11:54, 2016.

[8] R. Kotsilkova, E. Ivanov, P. Todorov; et al, “Mechanical properties investigation of bilayer graphene/poly(methyl methacrylate) thin films at macro, micro and nanoscale”, Carbon, vol. 100, pp. 355-366, 2016.

Carbon Nanotube Interconnects with Negative Temperature Coefficient of the Resistance

A. Maffucci
Dep. of Electrical and Information Engineering
University of Cassino and Southern Lazio
Cassino, Italy
maffucci@unicas.it

G. Miano
Dep. of Electrical Engineering and Information Technology
University Federico II,
Naples, Italy
miano@unina.it

F. Micciulla, A. Cataldo, S. Bellucci
NEXT Nanotechnology Group
INFN-LNF, Frascati, Italy
federico.micciulla@lnf.infn.it
antonino.e.cataldo@gmail.com
bellucci@lnf.infn.it

***Abstract*—This paper demonstrates the possibility of obtaining interconnects with negative derivative of the electrical resistance with respect to temperature. The interconnect is made of multi-walled carbon nanotube, and is fabricated by self-assembly through a low-cost bottom-up technique. The results of an electro-thermal characterization demonstrate the possibility of obtaining a negative temperature coefficient of the electrical resistance and validate the theoretical model here adopted to justify such a behavior.**

Keywords— Carbon nanotube, Electro-thermal Analysis, Nano-interconnects, Temperature Coefficient of the Resistance.

I. Introduction

A major challenge for modern Integrated Circuits (ICs) is the correct heat management, aimed at limiting the operating temperature to affordable values. A major source of heat is given by the Joule effect in interconnects, whose number and lengths are expected to exponentially increase in the next technology nodes [1]. Conventional conductors exhibits an electrical resistance increasing with temperature, and thus the heat production via Joule effect increases for higher temperatures. The heat production also gives raise to major reliability issues due to electromigration, e.g., [2]. For the above reasons, the density of electrical current in conventional copper interconnects is expected to be limited to 10^7 A/cm^2, well below the values required for next generation ICs, [1].

Carbon Nanotubes (CNTs) have been proposed to replace conducting material for VLSI applications, given their outstanding physical properties, such as high current carrying capability (up to 10^8-10^9 A/cm^2, [3]), large electron mean free path (up to hundreds of μm, [4]) and excellent thermal conductivity (up to thousands of Wm^{-1}K^{-1}, [5]).

It has been proven that CNTs interconnects may exhibit, under certain conditions, a quasi-zero or even negative *Temperature Coefficient of the Resistance* (TCR), defined as:

$$TCR = \frac{1}{R}\frac{dR}{dT}, \tag{1}$$

being R the electrical resistance and T the absolute temperature. A negative TCR has been observed for isolated (*e.g.*, [6]) and for bundled (*e.g.*, [7]), multi-walled CNTs (MWCNTs). The theoretical explanation for such a behavior was given in [8] for CNTs and in [9] for all kind of carbon interconnects, including those based on graphene nanoribbons. The results suggested that TCR<0 cannot be obtained in single-walled carbon nanotubes (SWCNTs) but only in short MWCNTs (with lengths up to some μm). In addition, this favorable behavior may likely vanishes when grouping CNTs in bundles, as it usually is the case for interconnects of any practical use. These circumstances strongly limit the possibility to benefit from the negative TCR, for instance, at the global or at the chip-to-package levels

In this paper, we demonstrate the possibility of obtaining a negative TCR at a larger scale, i.e. with CNT interconnects of lengths and widths in the range of hundreds of μm. This is obtained by grouping CNTs of different lengths and diameters, through a bottom-up self-assembly technique, recently proposed by the Authors to realize graphene devices [10].

II. Theoretical Background

The electrical resistance of a single CNT of length l can be modeled by [9]:

$$R(T) = R_p(T) + \frac{R_0}{M(T)}\left(1 + \frac{l}{l_{mfp}(T)}\right), \tag{2}$$

being l_{mfp} the electron mean free path, M the number of conducting channels, $R_0 = 12.9\,\text{k}\Omega$ the *quantum resistance* and R_p a parasitic term related to the quality of the terminal CNT/metal contacts.

The resistance (2) depends on temperature trough the parameters M, R_p, and l_{mfp}. The number M depends on the CNT type, size, chirality and temperature (*e.g.*, [9]). For SWCNTs, it is almost constant with T: M=2 (M=0) for metallic (semiconducting) SWCNTs. Instead, for MWCNT, M is always an increasing function of T. As for any conductor, the mean free path l_{mfp} reduces as temperature increases. Finally, the parasitic resistance R_p increases with temperature, as shown in [7]. From (2) it is evident that there is the theoretical possibility that, for increasing T, the effect on M dominates over the effects on R_p, and l_{mfp}, so leading to a negative derivative of R with T.

III. MODELING AND CHARACTERIZATION OF THE TEST VEHICLE

To investigate the possibility of having a negative TCR for a large dimension CNT interconnect, we realized a test-vehicle consisting in a microstrip circuit, where two copper electrodes are lying on a FR4 dielectric, see Fig.1a. A 100 μm x 150 μm gap between such electrodes was completely filled by CNTs, by using a bottom-up technique that has been recently proposed by the Authors to realize a graphene interconnect [10]. The characteristics of the CNTs are reported in Table I.

Since the average CNT length l_{av} is shorter than the gap length, we model the CNT contact as the series of N_C groups of CNTs, where $N_c = L/l_{av}$. In addition, each group is formed by N_B CNTs carrying the electrical current in parallel. The overall resistance is then modeled by:

$$R_{tot} = 2R_{Cu} + \sum_{i=1}^{N_C} R_{CNT,N_B}, \qquad (12)$$

where R_{Cu} is the contribution of the single copper electrode, whereas the R_{CNT,N_B} is the resistance of each CNT group

(a)

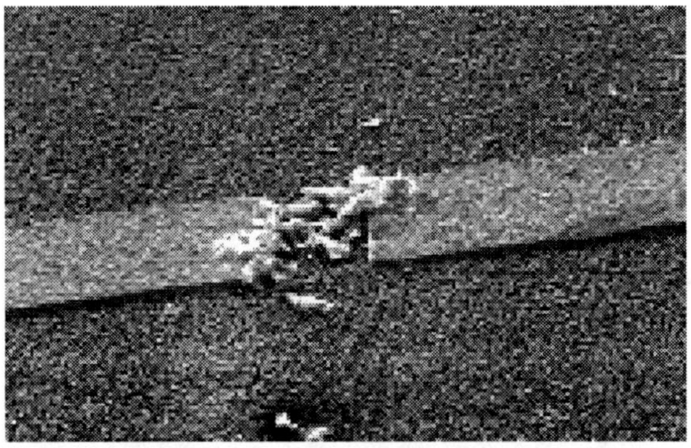

(b)

Fig. 1. Scanning Electron Microscope image of copper-CNT test vehicle: (a) overall view; (b) particular of the gap filled by CNTs.

TABLE I
CHARACTERISTICS OF THE CNTS

TYPE	Ext. Diameter [nm]	Int. Diameter [nm]	Length [μm]	Purity %
MWCNT	20-40	5-15	0.5-50	>99

According to our model, for the given diameters we could obtain TCR<0 at room temperature for CNT lengths of the order of tens of μm. In our experiment, we did not have the control on the effective CNT lengths, therefore we did not expect to obtain TCR<0 for all MWCNT. As a matter of fact, 2 out of realized 14 devices exhibited a negative derivative for the resistance, as shown in Fig.2. The modeling results are satisfactorily validated.

Further work will be devoted to refine the analysis, after a better characterization of the CNT interconnect, to assess those variables that can provide the full control of the resulting TCR.

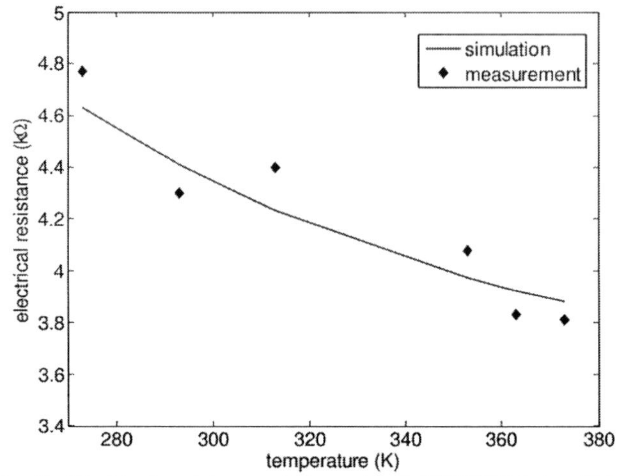

Fig. 2. Electrical resistance of the realized MWCNT test-vehicle: simulated vs measured data.

ACKNOWLEDGEMENTS

The work was partially supported by "GRAPHENE", Graphene-Based Revolutions in ICT and Beyond," project n.604391, FP7-ICT-2013-FET-F.

REFERENCES

[1] International Technology Roadmap for Semiconductors, 2013, http://public.itrs.net

[2] A. Christou and M. Peckerar, *Electromigration and Electronic Device Degradation*, Wiley and Sons, 1994.

[3] B. Q. Wei, R. Vajtai, P. M. Ajayan, "Reliability and current carrying capacity of carbon nanotubes," *Applied Phys. Lett.*, 79, 1172-1174, 2001.

[4] R. Saito, G. Dresselhaus, M. S. Dresselhaus, *Physical Properties of Carbon Nanotubes*, Imperial College Press, Singapore, 2004.

[5] E. Pop, D. Mann, Q. Wang, K. Goodson, H. Dai, "Thermal conductance of an individual single-wall carbon nanotube above room temperature". *Nano Letters*, Vol. 6, pp. 96–100, 2005.

[6] S.-B. Lee, et al., "Characteristics of multiwalled carbon nanotube nanobridges fabricated by poly(methylmethacrylate) suspended dispersion," *J. of Vacuum Sci. Technol.*, Vol. B 20, no.6, p.2773, 2002.

[7] S. Vollebregt, S. Banerjee, K. Beenakker, and R. Ishihara, "Size-dependent effects on the temperature coefficient of resistance of carbon nanotube vias," *IEEE Trans. Electron Dev.*, Vol. 60, pp. 4085-4089, 2013.

[8] A. Naeemi and J.D. Meindl, "Physical modeling of temperature coefficient of resistance for single- and multi-wall carbon nanotube interconnects," *IEEE Electron Dev, Lett.*, Vol. 28, pp.135-138, 2007.

[9] A.G. Chiariello, A. Maffucci, and G. Miano, "Circuit Models of Carbon-based Interconnects for Nanopackaging", *IEEE Trans. on Components, Packaging and Manufacturing*, Vol.3, pp.1926-1937, 2013.

[10] A.Maffucci, F. Micciulla, A. Cataldo, G. Miano, and S. Bellucci, "Bottom-up Realization and Electrical Characterization of a Graphene-Based Device," *Nanotechnology*, Vol.27, p.095204-1-9, 2016.

A System-by-Design Approach for Efficient Multiband Patch Antennas Design

M. Salucci[1], G. Oliveri[1,2], P. Rocca[1], A. Massa[1,2]
[1]ELEDIA Research Center (ELEDIA@UniTN - University of Trento)
Trento, Italy
[2]ELEDIA Research Center (ELEDIA@L2S - UMR 8506)
Gif-sur-Yvette, France
andrea.massa@eledia.org

***Abstract*—The design of multi-band patch antennas is addressed within the System-by-Design (*SbD*) paradigm. A fast optimization-driven strategy combining customized tools for the effective exploration of the solution space and the efficient evaluation of the antenna radiation performance is proposed. Toward this aim, an Ordinary Kriging (*OK*) predictor is used as a surrogate model of the cost function while the Differential Evolution (*DE*) algorithm is used to effectively minimize it. Some preliminary numerical results are reported to show the potentialities of the proposed design methodology.**

Keywords—multi-band antennas, system-by-design, antenna synthesis, fractals, optimization

I. INTRODUCTION

Modern wireless devices integrate many different communication (e.g., Wi-Fi, Bluetooth, *LTE*), localization (*GPS*), and identification (*NFC*) services. Multi-band antennas are thus needed to guarantee the functional operation of all services, while minimizing at the same time the dimension of the radio-frequency part [1]. However, the design of this kind of antennas, which must be low-profile, simple, and cheap is very challenging. In order to address these problems, several approaches have been proposed for the synthesis of multi-band antennas. In this framework, the use of microstrip patch antennas with perturbed fractal shapes has been proposed as a suitable solution [1]-[4]. However, the key issue of such designs is their extremely high computational burden. As a matter of fact, the proposed approaches are based on the integration of a global optimization algorithm [5],[6] and a full-wave solver to compute the antenna response.

To increase the efficiency of the design process, this work presents a new approach based on the System-by-Design (*SbD*) paradigm [7]-[9]. The *SbD* is a recently introduced concept and is defined as "*a functional ecosystem to handle complexity in the design of large systems*". It is based on the segmentation of the design problem into sub-problems, each solved by means of a customized and efficient tool. More specifically, the *SbD* paradigm is here applied to define a novel design procedure that integrates (*a*) an effective tool for the *solution space exploration* aimed at iteratively generating a sequence of trial solutions and (*b*) an efficient tool for the *physical response computation* of the performance of each trial antenna.

II. MATHEMATICAL FORMULATION

Let us consider a three-layer structure composed of two metallic layers separated by a dielectric substrate of thickness h and having relative permittivity ε_r and tangential loss $\tan\delta$. The bottom metallic layer acts as the ground-plane while the fractal antenna is designed on the top layer through metallic erosion (Fig. 1).

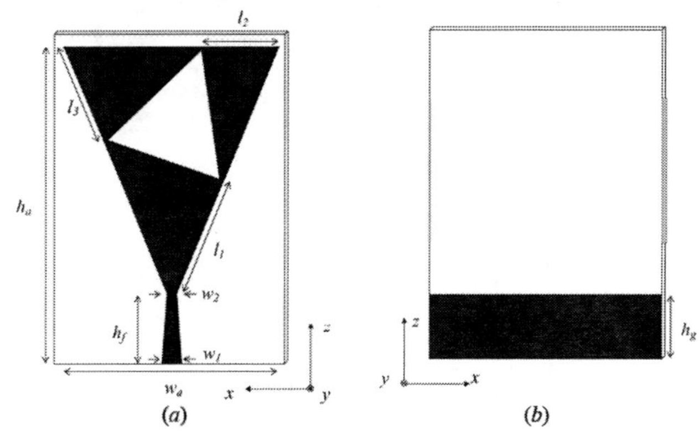

Fig. 1. (*a*) Front and (*b*) back of the Sierpinski fractal antenna geometry.

The objective of the design problem is the optimization of the degrees-of-freedom (*DoFs*) $\underline{s}$ describing the geometry of the patch antenna (i.e., fractal shape, feeder and ground plane height - Fig. 1) in order to satisfy the condition

$$\left|S_{11}(\underline{s}; f_n)\right| \le S_{11}(f_n)_{th}\,,\ f_n, n = 1,\dots,N \qquad (1)$$

where $\left|S_{11}(\underline{s}; f_n)\right|$ is the value of the reflection coefficient at frequency f_n and $S_{11}(f_n)_{th}$ is a user-defined threshold. In order to solve (1) by means of the *SbD*, the problem is re-formulated as an optimization one in which the objective is the retrieval of the optimal antenna geometry $\underline{s}^{opt}$ minimizing the following cost function

$$\Phi(\underline{s}) = \sum_{n=1}^{N} \alpha_n \Psi(\underline{s}; f_n) \qquad (2)$$

where

$$\Psi(\underline{s}; f_n) = \min\left\{0, \frac{|S_{11}(\underline{s}; f_n)| - S_{11}(f_n)_{th}}{S_{11}(f_n)_{th}}\right\} \quad (3)$$

α_n, $n = 1,...,N$ being a set of real weighs and $S_{11}(f_n)_{th}$ target values on the reflection coefficient. The following *SbD* functional blocks are exploited:

- *Solution Space Exploration*: the Differential Evolution (*DE*) algorithm is exploited, since it is particularly suitable for dealing with the optimization of real-valued parameters over continuous spaces [6];
- *Physical Response Computation*: the Ordinary Kriging (*OK*) [10] is used as a fast surrogate of (2). A set of T input-output pairs, $\{\underline{s}_t, \Phi(\underline{s}_t)\}$, $t = 1,...,T$ is used to train the predictor and the model is updated at each iteration by replacing the worst solution of the training set with the best of the current population, simulated through a full-wave solver.

III. Numerical Results

In order to validate the proposed *SbD* design method, the optimization of a dual-band ($N = 2$) Sierpinski Gasket fractal antenna operating in the *LTE*-1800 ($f_1 = 1795\ MHz$) and *LTE*-3500 ($f_2 = 3500\ MHz$) standards is addressed.

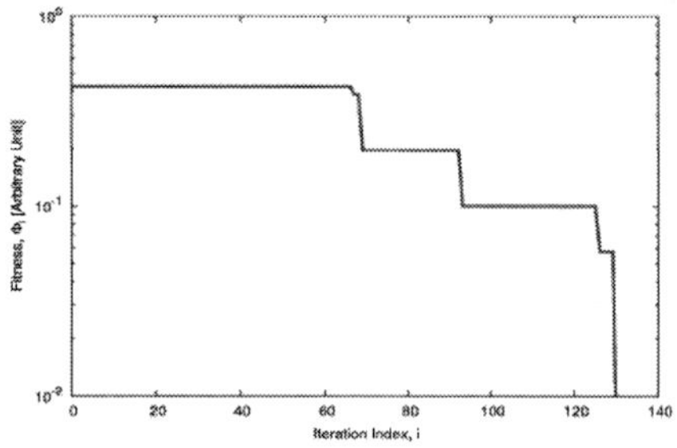

Fig. 2. Behaviour of the cost function vs. iteration index.

The vector of $K = 9$ design parameters is $\underline{s} = \{l_1, l_2, l_3, w_a, w_1, w_2, h_f, h_a, h_g\}$ (Fig. 1). An Arlon substrate ($\varepsilon_r = 3.38$, $\tan\delta = 0.0025$ and $h = 7.6\times10^{-4}[m]$) has been considered. As for the definition of the *OK* model, $T = 200$ training samples are selected according to a Latin hypercube sampling (*LHS*). The *DE* has been run with a population of $P = 50$ individuals, scaling factor $Q = 0.6$, crossover probability $p_c = 0.8$, maximum iterations $I_{\max} = 500$, and letting $\alpha_1 = \alpha_2 = 1$ and $S_{11}(f_n)_{th} = -20dB$. The behavior of the cost function versus the iteration index is reported in Fig. 2, showing that convergence is reached in $I_{tot} = 129$ iterations. It is worth remarking that the time required for the optimization, including the time for generating the training set and for building the *OK* model, amounts to 4.2 [h]. Figure 3 shows a plot of $|S_{11}(\underline{s}; f)|$ for the optimized antenna. It is simple to note the dual-band behavior, perfectly satisfying the design constraints at the desired operation bandwidths.

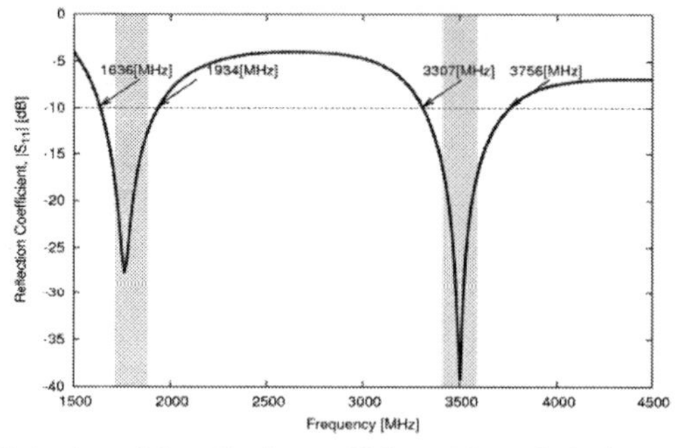

Fig. 3. Behaviour of the reflection coefficient of the optimized antenna.

IV. Conclusions

An efficient *SbD*-based method has been proposed for the design of multi-band fractal patch antennas. The integration of an efficient tool for the computation of the cost function based on a fast surrogate model and an effective global search algorithm have been exploited for designing novel antennas satisfying user-defined constraints. The reported result has demonstrated the efficiency and effectiveness of the proposed methodology. Future works will be devoted to the analysis of fabrication tolerances on the antenna geometry [11] and their impact on the radiation characteristics.

References

[1] C. Puente-Baliarda, J. Romeu, R. Pous, and A. Cardama, "On the behaviour of the Sierpinski multiband fractal antenna," *IEEE Trans. Antennas Propag.*, vol. 46, pp. 517-524, 1998.

[2] T. Moriyama, F. Viani, M. Salucci, F. Robol, and E. Giarola, "Planar multiband antenna for 3G/4G advanced wireless services," *IEICE Electronics Express*, vol. 11, no. 17, pp. 1-10, Sep. 2014.

[3] F. Viani, M. Salucci, F. Robol, and A. Massa, "Multiband fractal Zigbee/WLAN antenna for ubiquitous wireless environments," *J. Electromagn. Waves Appl.*, vol. 26, pp. 1554-1562 , 2012.

[4] F. Viani, M. Salucci, F. Robol, G. Oliveri, and A. Massa, "Design of a UHF RFID/GPS fractal antenna for logistics management," *J. Electromagn. Waves Appl.*, vol. 26, pp. 480-492, 2012.

[5] P. Rocca, M. Benedetti, M., Donelli, D. Franceschini, and A. Massa, "Evolutionary optimization as applied to inverse scattering problems," *Inverse Problems*, vol. 25, pp. 1-41, 2009.

[6] P. Rocca, G. Oliveri, and A. Massa, "Differential evolution as applied to electromagnetics," *IEEE Antennas Propag. Mag.*, vol. 53, pp. 38-49, 2011.

[7] A. Massa, G. Oliveri, P. Rocca, and F. Viani, "System-by-Design: a new paradigm for handling design complexity," EuCAP 2014, The Hague, The Netherlands, pp. 1180-1183, Apr. 6-11, 2014.

[8] G. Oliveri, F. Viani, N. Anselmi, and A. Massa, "Synthesis of multi-layer WAIM coatings for planar phased arrays within the system-by-design framework," *IEEE Trans. Antennas Propag.*, vol. 63, no. 6, pp. 2482-2496, 2015.

[9] G. Oliveri, E. T. Bekele, M. Salucci, and A. Massa, "Array miniaturization through QCTO-SI metamaterial radomes," *IEEE Trans. Antennas Propag.*, vol. 63, no. 8, pp. 3465-3476, Aug. 2015

[10] D. R. Jones, M. Schonlau and W.J. Welch, "Efficient global optimization of expensive black-box functions," *J. Global Opt.*, vol. 13, pp. 455-492, 1998.

[11] P. Rocca, L. Poli, N. Anselmi, M. Salucci, and A. Massa, "Predicting antenna pattern degradations in microstrip reflectarrays through interval arithmetic," *IET Microwaves Antennas Propag.*, vol. 10, no. 8, pp. 817-826, May 2016.

On the Comparison and Evaluation of Sparse Array Synthesis Methods

Daniele Pinchera, Marco Donald Migliore, Mario Lucido, Fulvio Schettino
DIEI - University of Cassino and Southern Lazio, Cassino, FR, Italy
pinchera@unicas.it, mdmiglio@unicas.it, lucido@unicas.it, schettino@unicas.it

***Abstract*—In this contribution we introduce a benchmarking procedure for sparse antenna arrays synthesis methods. The key point of our approach is the introduction, as reference, of an optimized equispaced linear array. The overall procedure is very easy to implement for the verification and comparison of synthesis algorithms.**

I. Introduction

The synthesis of sparse (or non uniform) arrays, i.e. the problem of finding the position and the excitations of the elements of an array in order to obtain a specific pattern, is one of the hottest topics in the antenna community. This popularity is due to two main reasons: the first is represented by the architectural advantages of sparse arrays, with respect to $\lambda/2$ equispaced arrays, like the reduction of the number of radiating elements, the achievement of a better excitation dynamic or the *possible* absence of grating lobes; the latter reason is relative to the fact that researchers are still searching for an optimal synthesis algorithm.

Actually, evolutionary algorithms are known to asymptotically provide the optimum solution to any problem, but the number of iterations needed to achieve the optimal solution is an exponential function of the number of unknowns [1] so, from a computational point of view, it could be very difficult to actually find the optimal solution when the number of antennas is large.

The non-linearity and non-convexity of the sparse array synthesis problem has been faced with a large number of approaches and methods, but it is not easy to distinguish among the best algorithms and methods. In particular, up to date, there are no benchmarking procedures widely accepted in our community to provide a researcher an useful tool to check the quality of its algorithm or to compare different algorithms.

In this short contribution we would like to propose a simple procedure to achieve this aim, at least for sparse linear arrays; our approach is based on the definition of a standard, well-known solution, that can be taken as a reference. This solution is the linear equispaced array with optimally chosen inter-element distance and number of elements, to which we will be referring as the "Benchmark Equispaced Array" (BEA).

The choice of this kind of array is due to its simplicity, since in an equispaced array there are only two parameters used to define its geometry, the aforementioned inter-element distance d and number of elements N. Once that this two values have been chosen, it is relatively easy to achieve the elements' excitation by means of smart techniques [2], [3].

Considering just linear arrays could be seen as a limitation of the benchmarking approach, but we have to underline that most of the researchers that have considered the synthesis of sparse arrays have faced first this "simpler" problem before considering conformal or planar arrays; furthermore, it is important that the reference solution to be used for a benchmark is as much "universal" as possible; finally, if a very sophisticated approach is not capable of "beating" the reference solution in a "simple case" it is unlikely that it could achieve significant solution on a tough problem.

II. Mathematical Formulation

We will now focus on the definition of the reference SEA solution; the pattern of the SEA, with N identical elements, is well known to be:

$$F(u) = g(u) \sum_{n=0}^{N-1} a(n) e^{j\beta d n} \quad (1)$$

where $u = sin(\theta)$ and θ is the angle with respect to the broadside direction, β is the free space wavenumber, $a(n)$ is the relative excitation of the $n-$th element, d is the constant inter-element distance and $g(u)$ is the element factor. An inessential multiplicative constant is understood and dropped.

The pattern specification are generally specified by means of a power pattern mask, as in Fig.1, and a maximum beam scanning range, usually in an angular range $(-u_s, u_s)$. The maximum allowed inter-element distance d to be used in the SEA, that allows to avoid the appearance of grating lobes when scanning the beam pattern in the assigned angular range is:

$$d_{MAX} = \lambda(1 + u_s + u_c)^{-1} \quad (2)$$

where λ is the free space wavelength, and $u_c = max(u_a, u_b)$, with $-u_a$ and u_b the angular directions for which the upper mask is greater than the prescribed side lobe level (SLL).

As stated in the introduction, for given values of d_{max} and N, the excitations can be found by means of [2], [4]. The presence of an element factor can be taken into account in the synthesis also using a modified power pattern mask, as in [5].

III. Benchmarking Procedure

Let us consider the benchmarking of some specific algorithms, taken from open literature. Let us first consider the $N_A = 24$ element pencil beam synthesized in [6]. This pattern is a pencil beam one, with a SLL lower than -14.45dB for $|u| \geq 0.04$ and $g(u) = 1$. If we calculate the maximum

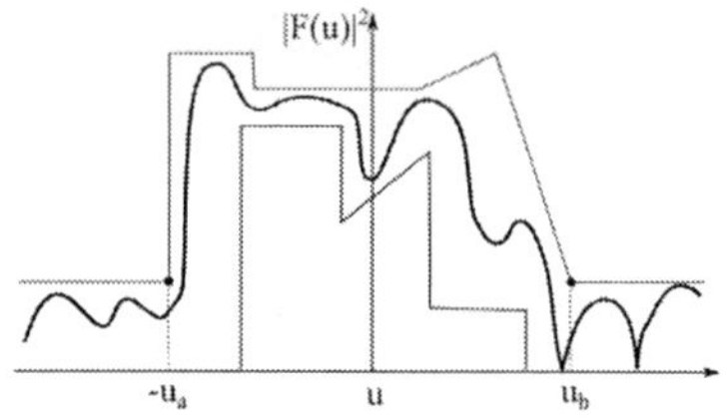

Fig. 1. Power pattern mask. The red curve is the upper mask, the blue curve is the lower mask, and the black curve, representing the power pattern, must lie between them.

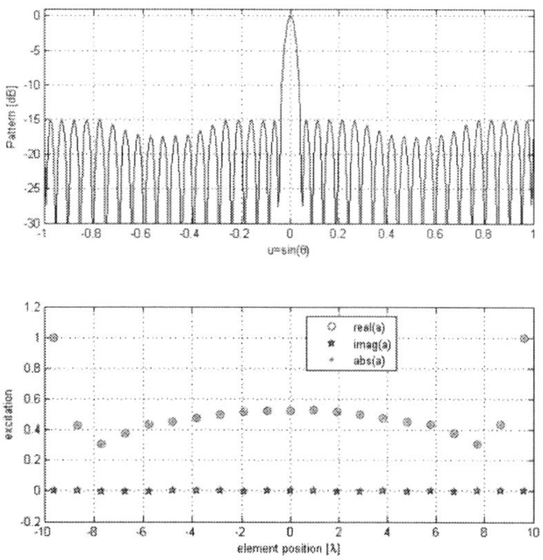

Fig. 2. The 21 element pencil beam SEA

inter element distance for this pattern with (2), we will find $d_{max} = 0.9615\lambda$. Now we can try finding a set of $N = N_A$ excitations to satisfy the same pattern mask:

- If we fail, we can try with a higher number of elements;
- if we succeed we can try with a lower number of elements.

In the aforementioned case we can see that it is possible to satisfy the power pattern mask with $N = 21$. Once we have found the minimum number of elements, we can try to see if it is possible to improve the solution, for instance lowering the SLL. In Fig.2 it is possible to see the excitations and the pattern for the achieved SEA, that achieves a better SLL (-15dB instead of -14.45dB) with respect to the algorithm under test with three elements less. This does not automatically imply that the considered algorithm is a bad one, but probably the authors should have chosen a better example to show the quality of their approach, or they should have considered some more "iterations" or a different tuning of the parameters.

Let us now consider the flat top pattern achieved with $N_A = 20$ elements with $g(u) = \sqrt{1-u^2}$ in [7]. By using (2) we obtain $d_{max} = 0.7029\lambda$, but if we use $N = N_A$ radiating elements it is not possible to fully satisfy the same pattern constraints of [7]. If we used one element more, we could instead satisfy the same power pattern mask (see Fig.3). In

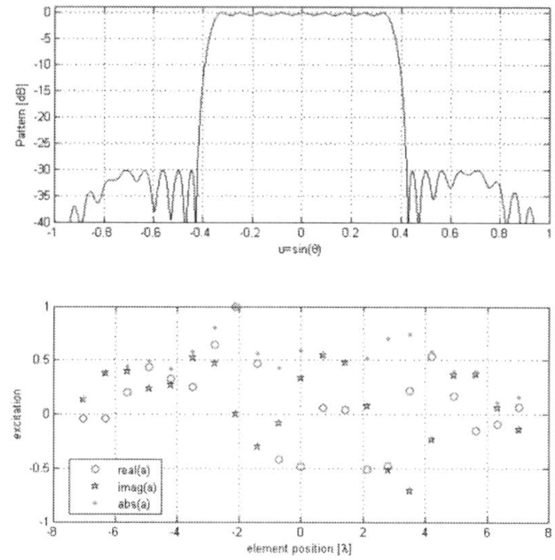

Fig. 3. The 21 element flat-top SEA

this case the algorithm under test outperforms the benchmark SEA.

IV. Conclusions

In the present contribution we have discussed a benchmarking procedure for sparse antenna array synthesis, based on the use of the Benchmark Equispaced Array (BEA).

For our best knowledge, this is the first time that someone has proposed a benchmarking technique for array synthesis methods: there are hundreds of different synthesis approaches and there are no methods to say if an approach and the solution obtained with it are significant or not.

The procedure proposed in not the best possible, but it can be simply implemented and is fast. The benchmark procedure presented has been applied to the results obtained by some algorithms published in open literature, as examples of its application. More cases will be discussed during the conference.

References

[1] A. Nemirovski, D.-B. Yudin, and E.-R. Dawson, "Problem complexity and method efficiency in optimization," 1982.

[2] T. Isernia, O. Bucci, and N. Fiorentino, "Shaped beam antenna synthesis problems: Feasibility criteria and new strategies," *Journal of Electromagnetic Waves and Applications*, vol. 12, no. 1, pp. 103–138, 1998.

[3] O. M. Bucci and D. Pinchera, "A generalized hybrid approach for the synthesis of uniform amplitude pencil beam ring-arrays," *Antennas and Propagation, IEEE Transactions on*, vol. 60, no. 1, pp. 174–183, 2012.

[4] D. Pinchera and M. D. Migliore, "Comparison guidelines and benchmark procedure for sparse array synthesis," *Progress In Electromagnetics Research M*, vol. 52, pp. 129–139, 2016.

[5] O. M. Bucci, T. Isernia, S. Perna, and D. Pinchera, "Isophoric sparse arrays ensuring global coverage in satellite communications," *IEEE Transactions on Antennas and Propagation*, vol. 62, no. 4, pp. 1607–1618, April 2014.

[6] A. Trucco and V. Murino, "Stochastic optimization of linear sparse arrays," *IEEE Journal of Oceanic Engineering*, vol. 24, no. 3, pp. 291–299, 1999.

[7] S. E. Nai, W. Ser, Z. L. Yu, and H. Chen, "Beampattern synthesis for linear and planar arrays with antenna selection by convex optimization," *IEEE Transactions on Antennas and Propagation*, vol. 58, no. 12, pp. 3923–3930, 2010.

Uniform Theory of Diffraction Approximation for Large Antenna Array Fields

Michael R. Johnson, Omar W. Ali
U. S. Air Force SEEK EAGLE Office
205 West D Ave Suite 348
Eglin AFB, FL 32542 USA
michael.johnson.10@us.af.mil, omar.ali@us.af.mil

Abstract—Knowing the electric fields that may be encountered in the proximity of large array antennas is critical for determining the compatibility of equipment near that antenna. Given a few parameters such as effective area, frequency and power, the electric field magnitudes at any given range can be approximated within easily determined boundaries using well-understood electromagnetic theory. This paper describes such a method and evaluates its results against simulated fields radiated from simple arrays with similar dimensions.

Keywords— Antenna Array, Field Approximation.

I. INTRODUCTION

The Air Force SEEK EAGLE Office is responsible for recommending the compatibility of stores in the electromagnetic environment (EME) of USAF aircraft. Many times it is not necessary to exactly quantify fields from an emitter in the course of our analysis. Understanding the bounds of a problem, such as an estimate of the maximum fields is often sufficient for example. Knowing these bounds allows us to solve very electrically-large problems using much simpler approximations. This is certainly the case for large array antennas that radiate energy in a narrow beam.

The premise of this paper is that, by making use of the principal of duality, the electric fields from a planar array antenna can be approximated by the reflection of Radio Frequency (RF) energy from a flat conductive plate with similar physical dimensions. In this paper the approximation is used to estimate the maximum expected antenna gain and the electric fields in the main beam of a large array in order to perform aircraft compatibility analysis of air vehicles in vicinity of the array. The flat plate approximation is particularly useful when little is known about a complex planar array, or simulation of the planar array is computationally prohibitive.

The approach is straight forward. An array can optimally be considered an aperture. An aperture can be replicated by the dual of the aperture; the reflection of incident waves from a plate. Thus we can replicate the behavior of a planar array by reflections from a plate with the same effective area. We will assume that the array is designed to make good use of the available surface area of the structure. Our effective area is therefore that surface area.

We will investigate how the flat plate approximation can be used to estimate the electric field along the main beam of a complex planar array antenna. The approximation will be verified for a specific test case by comparing the main lobe gain from a 1m x 1m flat plate reflection using Uniform Theory of Diffraction (UTD), to that of two simple dipole planar arrays using Method of Moments (MoM) wire basis functions. The results from both cases should be bounded by their ability to replicate a perfect aperture tuned at the transmitting frequency. The actual array gain in the main beam will never exceed the peak gain of the perfectly tuned aperture. This assumption is true regardless of the drive signal that may be used to optimize the array since diverting energy from some elements to others will negate the additive effect of those elements in the array. But for simplicity, in this work we will assume the array is linear, and the main beam is the area of interest.

In order to provide comparison data for flat plate approximations vs. actual arrays, two planar arrays were constructed of evenly spaced half wavelength (λ) dipoles oriented vertically in the YZ plane. The operating frequency was 1500 MHz. The first array spaced the elements one wavelength apart, making full use of the square meter of real estate, while the second spaced the elements a half wavelength apart, using a quarter of the available real estate.

II. FLAT PLATE REPRESENTATION OF AN ARRAY

The intent of this section is to show how the maximum gain of planar arrays is provided by calculating reflected RF energy from a plate with the same dimensions as the array. Electric or magnetic field strength can be calculated and compared with the susceptibility of a system at risk. The determination of compatibility with that array can then be made. We will limit ourselves to the understanding that we are interested only in the maximum field values, keeping with our planar assumption. In general, the maximum gain of an antenna [1], [2] is:

$$G_{max} = \frac{4\pi A_e}{\lambda^2} \quad (1)$$

where: A_e= affective area, λ = wavelength. The maximum gain of an array [1], [2] consisting of N elements each with element gain G_e is:

$$G_{maxArray} = \mathrm{N}G_\mathrm{e} \quad (2)$$

Using (2) we realize that we can simulate an array of elements with a single equivalent antenna, such as an aperture, as long as the effective area of N elements is less than or equal to the effective area of the aperture [3]. We can get a closed-form solution for the peak electric field at a range R from the main beam with transmitter power P_T of an arbitrary flat plate in free space ($Z_f = 120\pi$) by using:

$$|E(R)| = \frac{1}{R\lambda}\sqrt{2\, Z_f P_T A_e}\,. \quad (3)$$

III. Simulation Setup

A full wave frequency domain computational electromagnetic code, the General Electromagnetic Model for the Analysis of Complex Systems (GEMACS), was used to model and simulate the antennas. GEMACS also has a UTD capability that was used for thin-plate reflections.

For our reflection experiment using MoM, the reflected power is 1 W. For the UTD experiment, we used a normal-incident 1 V/m spherical wave at a distance of 10m. Fig. 1 shows the surface current distribution that is induced on the MoM plate from the incident plane wave. Lighter colors indicate areas with greater surface current densities, which appear to be spaced one wavelength apart. This figure is also an excellent examples of Huygens' Principle [4] in practice.

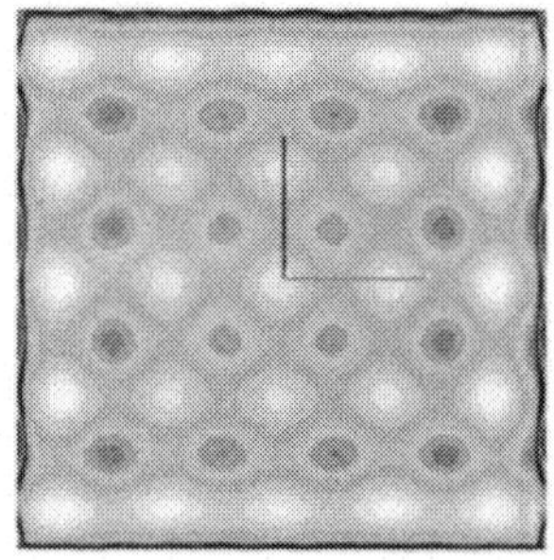

Fig. 1. Plane wave excitation of a 1m x 1m flat plate.

Construction of the dipole array was done in GEMACS exclusively with MoM. Twenty-five half wave dipoles, each with 11 wire segments 5 mm in diameter were place in a square 5 x 5 array of elements, driven in phase.

IV. Simulations and Results

Four antenna models were created and simulated in GEMACS. Two half-wave planar dipole arrays were simulated using MoM, with element spaced at 0.5λ and 1λ. Two plate reflections were simulated, one using UTD and the other MoM. All antennas were oriented in the YZ plane, centered at the origin. Dipole elements and Reflected waves were vertically polarized (parallel to Z axis).

Fig. 2 shows the portion of the all the corresponding antenna patterns radiating along the positive X-axis; φ= -90° to 90° and θ=90°, at 1500MHz. Each line represents the gain of the corresponding antenna in dBi. The black and green lines represent the plate reflections when using MoM and UTD respectively. The blue and red lines correspond to the 25 element planar dipole arrays, with 0.5λ and 1λ element spacing. As expected the plate reflections using the MoM and UTD are nearly identical, with the main beam gain and beamwidths overlapping and the nulls in approximately the same direction.

The theoretical maximum using (1) is 24.978 dBi. The table below summarizes the peak gain for each antenna.

TABLE I. Gains (Hemispherically Distributed Power Only)

Simulation	Peak Gain (dBi)
Dipole array, d = λ	15.779
Dipole array, d = λ/2	19.016
MoM Reflection	25.112
UTD Reflection	24.713

Data presented in Table 1 verifies the premise, at least anecdotally, that the main beam gain of the overmoded plate reflections will bound those of the dipole arrays, in this case by a significant margin. It is noted that the maximum gain from the finite-thickness plate modeled with MoM resulted in a peak gain slightly higher than the theoretical maximum; 0.134 dBi or about 3% in linear gain. This is due to the finite thickness of the plate used for the MoM simulation. The UTD plate is "infinitely" thin, and although the UTD implementation in GEMACS does consider edge effects, the finite plate in the MoM simulation influences the result by reflecting a small amount of energy back towards the main beam. We see that UTD simulations result in a maximum gain slightly lower than the theoretical maximum; 0.265 dBi, or about 6%. The mutual impedance losses in both dipole arrays account for the significant decrease in gain from the theoretical maximum.

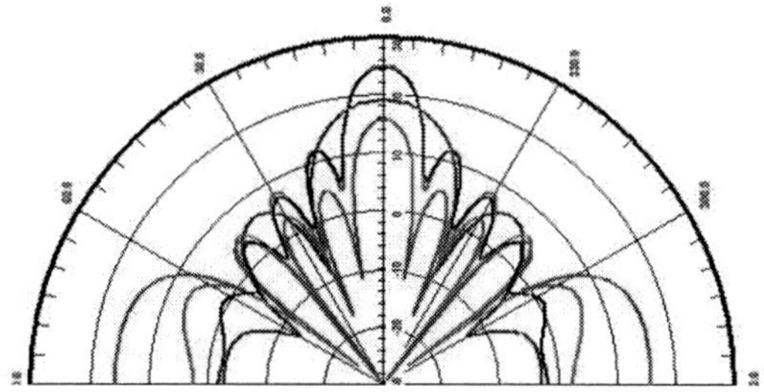

Fig. 2. UTD (black), MoM Patch Plate (green), d = λ (red) d = λ/2 (blue)

V. Uses of the Approach

The intent of this paper was to provide a method for approximating the electric fields that can be expected from planar array along the main beam. We have shown that given only a few simple specifications on an antenna it is possible to determine the upper limits of those fields. The simulation method should give valid e-field vectors in both the near and far field. Results are conservative in the context of EMC. We also note that the UTD thin plate model seems to give realistic approximations to the first few side lobes.

References

[1] S. J. Orfanidis, "Electromagnetics Waves and Antennas" Rutgers University, 1999-2000.

[2] C. A. Balanis, "Antenna Theory and Design," 3rd Edition, John Wiley and Sons, Inc., 2005.

[3] P. Hannan, "The Element-Gain Paradox for a Phased-Array Antenna," Antennas and Propagation, IEEE Transactions on, Vol 12, Issue 4, pp 423 – 433, Jul 1964

[4] Chr. Huygens, "Traitè de la Lumiere," completed in 1678, published in Leyden in 1690.

Optimal Synthesis of Monopulse Beamforming Weights for Airborne Radars through Convex Optimization

G. Gottardi[1], N. Ebrahimi[1], P. Rocca[1], A. Massa[1,2]
[1]ELEDIA Research Center (ELEDIA@UniTN - University of Trento)
Trento, Italy
[2]ELEDIA Research Center (ELEDIA@L2S - UMR 8506)
Gif-sur-Yvette, France
andrea.massa@eledia.org

***Abstract*—In this work, the optimal synthesis of monopulse beamforming weights for airborne radar systems is addressed by means of a custom convex programming procedure. The designed active electronically scanned array *(AESA)* is equipped with a single transceiver module (*TRM*) for each element, common to all patterns. The set of complex *TRM* coefficients is optimized in order to provide the maximum directivity and an asymmetric sidelobes envelope for the sum pattern along with the maximum slope for difference patterns. A representative application of the proposed method for monopulse radar system in side-looking configuration is discussed.**

Keywords—Monopulse Radar; Airborne Systes, Active Electronically Scanned Array, Optimal Beamforming, Convex Programming.

I. INTRODUCTION

Monopulse radar systems are used to track the position of a moving target through the comparison of signals coming from three patterns [1],[2]. One pattern is called "sum pattern" (Σ) and it is characterized by a single mainlobe in the boresight direction. Other two patterns, called "azimuth difference pattern" (*Δ-az*) and "elevation difference pattern" (*Δ-el*) are characterized by a null along the boresight direction, respectively in the horizontal and in the vertical planes. Monopulse tracking radars use a single *AESA*, which has to simultaneously generate sum and difference patterns through a suitable beam-forming network (*BFN*). The sets of *TRM* weights providing the best performance for each pattern can be so different, due to different requirements, that the optimal performances can be achieved only through a separate feeding network for each pattern [3]. However, such a solution requires a huge number of *TRMs*, that is unfeasible in practical applications [4]. Different approaches for the simplification of the *BFN* have been proposed in the literature [5]. Beside design methods based on the aggregation of elements in sub-arrays [6]-[11], the design of an innovative *BFN* architecture where elements are equipped with one *TRM* (except for a small subset of elements) is proposed in [12][13]. This work presents an advancement of the convex programming (*CP*) method proposed in [13]. The proposed approach introduces three main novelties with respect to [13] for the synthesis of sum and difference patterns: (*i*) the maximization of the sum pattern directivity, (*ii*) the use of a single *TRM*, common to all patterns, for each element and *(iii)* the optimization of both amplitude and phase of all *TRMs* for the generation of asymmetric patterns.

II. MATHEMATICAL FORMULATION

Let us consider a planar *AESA* with N_{tot} elements, placed on a regular triangular lattice on the *xy*-plane. The *n*-th element is located in (x_n ,y_n) and its *TRM* provides a complex weight $I_n = \alpha_n e^{j\beta_n}$. The array factor of the *AESA* is given by

$$AF(u,v) = \sum_{n=1}^{N_{tot}} I_n e^{j\{k[x_n(u-u_0)+y_n(v-v_0)]\}} \quad (1)$$

where $k = 2\pi/\lambda$ is the wave number, λ being the wavelength, $u = \sin\theta\cos\varphi$ and $v = \sin\theta\sin\varphi$ are the direction cosines and (u_0, v_0) is the boresight direction. The *AESA* layout is divided into four quadrants and the sum pattern is computed from the in-phase summation of all quadrants while a phase shift of π is applied to the two left or top quadrants for the azimuth or elevation difference patterns. The synthesis of the set of weights $\mathbf{I} = \{I_n : n = 1,\dots,N_{tot}\}$ is formulated as the following minimization problem

$$\min_{\mathrm{Re}\{\mathbf{I}\},\mathrm{Im}\{\mathbf{I}\}} \left\{ \int_0^{2\pi}\int_0^{\pi} \left|AF_\Sigma(\theta,\varphi)\right|^2 \sin\theta \, d\theta \, d\varphi \right\} \quad (2)$$

subject to

$$|AF_\Sigma(u_0,v_0)|^2 = 1 \quad (3)$$

$$|AF_\Sigma(u_0,v_0)|^2 \le M(u_a,v_a), \quad a = 1,\dots,A \quad (4)$$

$$-\left.\frac{\delta\{AF_{\Delta-az/el}(u,v)\}}{\delta w}\right|_{(u,v)=(u_0,v_0)} \ge \eta_{\Delta-az/el} \quad (5)$$

where Re{.} and Im{.} stand for the real and the imaginary part and $M(u_a, v_a)$ is a non-negative mask function for the power pattern while $\eta_{\Delta-az}$ and $\eta_{\Delta-el}$ are two lower bounds on difference patterns slopes. The condition (2) with the requirements (3) implies the maximization of the sum pattern directivity along the boresight direction. Since (2) is a quadratic function of the unknown sets $\text{Re}\{\mathbf{I}\}$ and $\text{Im}\{\mathbf{I}\}$ and the constraints (3)(5) are linear or quadratic (4) with respect the same unknowns, the problem is convex in both functional and constraints. As a consequence, a standard *CP*-based resolution method [14] can be applied and the retrieval of the optimal solution is guaranteed, if a feasible solution exists. Moreover, the asymmetric mask function is defined as follows

$$M(u_a, v_a) = \begin{cases} M_\Sigma, \text{ if } a \in \Theta_{boresigh} \\ M_\Sigma + \delta_u, \text{ if } a \in \Theta_{up} \\ M_\Sigma - \delta_d, \text{ if } a \in \Theta_{down} \end{cases} \quad (6)$$

in order to fit specific requirements for side-lobe looking airborne radars. In the Θ_{down} region the sidelobe level of the sum pattern (SLL_Σ) is required to be very low in order to suppress noise effects while in $\Theta_{boresight}$ and Θ_{up} regions the requirement can be relaxed due to the presence of lower noise.

III. Numerical Results

In this section the numerical assessment of the proposed method is carried out for a real scenario. An *AESA* of $N_{tot} = 640$ elements placed on a regular triangular lattice with inter-element distances $d_x = d_y = 0.5\lambda$ is considered.

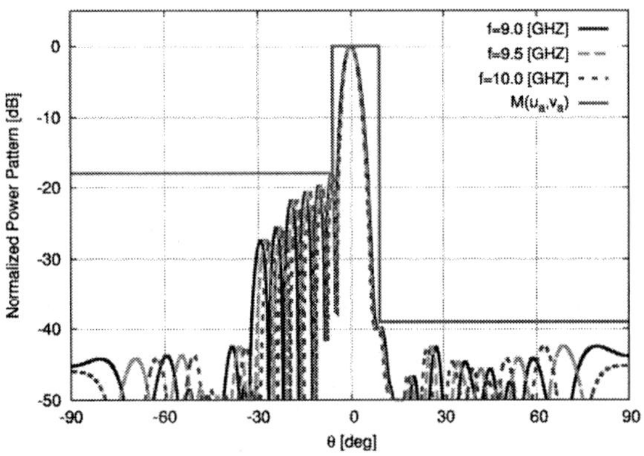

Fig. 1. Sum power pattern along the horizontal cut at minimum, central and maximum frequencies, with the mask requirements.

Mask parameters are defined as $M_\Sigma = -29[dB]$ and $\delta_d = \delta_u = 10[dB]$. The synthesis is performed at $f = 9.5[GHz]$ and patterns are evaluated for $f \in [9.0, 10.0]\,[GHz]$ in order to analyze the effects of real *TRM* (weights amplitude and phase quantized to 6 bits) on the monopulse performances. Figure 1 shows the sum power pattern along the horizontal cut ($\varphi = 0^\circ$) at the minimum, central and maximum frequencies of the analysis range. The mask is reported as well in order to confirm the requirements matching. The detailed analysis of monopulse patterns, for 42 scan angles ($\theta \in [-50^\circ, 50^\circ]$ and $\varphi \in [0^\circ, 90^\circ]$) and for 11 frequency samples, shows that the computed solution always meets the requirements. In particular, this solution is able to reach an average SLL_Σ value of -41.65 [dB] in the Θ_{down} region, while keeping good monopulse tracking performances (i.e., $\eta_{\Delta-az} \geq 5124$ and $\eta_{\Delta-el} \geq 3304$).

IV. Conclusions

In this work a new *CP*-based approach for the optimal synthesis of airborne monopulse radar systems is presented. The proposed approach allows to maximize the directivity of the sum pattern jointly with the monopulse tracking performance, when each *AESA* element is provided with a shared single *TRM*. The numerical assessment shows the effectiveness of the provided solution in a real application, over a large frequency band and a large scan angle range. Future works will be devoted at introducing tolerances on the optimized excitations within the synthesis process [15].

References

[1] M. I. Skolnik, *Radar Handbook*, 3rd Ed. New York, NY: McGraw-Hill, 2008.

[2] S. M. Sherman and D. K. Barton, *Monopulse Principles and Techniques*, 2nd Ed. Norwood, MA: Artech House, 2011.

[3] R. S. Elliott, *Antenna Theory and Design*. Hoboken, NJ: Wiley & Sons., 2003.

[4] J. S. Herd and M. D. Conwey, "The evolution to modern phased array architectures," *Proc. IEEE*, vol. 104, no.3, pp. 519-529, Mar. 2016.

[5] P. Rocca, G. Oliveri, R. J. Mailloux, and A. Massa, "Unconventional phased array architectures and design methodologies - A review", *Proc. IEEE*, vol 104, no. 3, pp. 544-560, Mar. 2016.

[6] P. Rocca, L. Manica, and A. Massa, "Hybrid approach for sub-arrayed monopulse antenna synthesis," *Electron. Lett.*, vol. 44, no. 2, pp. 75-76, Jan. 2008.

[7] G. Oliveri, M. Salucci, and A. Massa, "Synthesis of modular contiguously clustered linear arrays through a sparseness-regularized solver," *IEEE Trans. Antennas Propag.*, vol. 64, no. 10, pp. 4277-4287, Oct. 2016.

[8] M. D'Urso, T. Isernia and E. F. Meliado', "An effective hybrid approach for the optimal synthesis of monopulse antennas," *IEEE Trans. Antennas Propag.*, vol. 55, no. 4, pp. 1059-1066, Apr. 2007.

[9] L. Manica, P. Rocca, A. Martini and A. Massa, "An innovative approach based on a tree-searching algorithm for the optimal matching of independently optimum sum and difference excitations," *IEEE Trans. Antennas Propag.*, vol. 56, no. 1, pp. 58-66, 2008.

[10] Y. Chen, S. Yang, and Z. Nie, "The application of a modified differential evolution strategy to some array pattern synthesis problems," *IEEE Trans. Antennas Propag.*, vol. 56, no. 7, pp. 1919-1927, Jul. 2008.

[11] L. Manica, P. Rocca, M. Benedetti and A. Massa, "A fast graph-searching algorithm enabling the efficient synthesis of sub-arrayed planar monopulse antennas," *IEEE Trans. Antennas Propag.*, vol. 57, no. 3, pp. 652-663, Mar. 2009.

[12] M. Alvarez-Folgueiras, J. Rodriguez-Gonzales, and F. Ares-Pena, "Optimal compromise among sum and difference patterns in monopulse antennas: Use of subarrays and distributions with common aperture tail," *J. Electromagn. Waves Appl.*, vol. 23, pp. 2301-2311, 2009.

[13] P. Rocca and A. F. Morabito, "Optimal synthesis of reconfigurable planar arrays with simplified architectures for monopulse radar applications," *IEEE Trans. Antennas Propag.*, vol. 63, no. 3, pp. 1048-1058, Mar. 2015.

[14] S. Boyd and L. Vandenberghe, *Convex Optimization*. Cambridge, U.K.: Univ. Press, 2004.

[15] N. Anselmi, P. Rocca, M. Salucci, and A. Massa, "Optimization of excitation tolerances for robust beamforming in linear arrays," *IET Microwaves Antennas Propag.*, vol. 10, no. 2, pp. 208-214, 2016.

Optimization-based Design of Innovative Grating-lobe Free Radar UWB Architectures

L. Tenuti[1], P. Rocca[1], and A. Massa[1,2]
[1]ELEDIA Research Center (ELEDIA@UniTN - University of Trento)
Trento, Italy
[2]ELEDIA Research Center (ELEDIA@L2S - UMR 8506)
Gif-sur-Yvette, France
andrea.massa@eledia.org

***Abstract*—An innovative approach for reducing grating lobes appearing when the inter-element spacing of an *UWB* linear array is greater than half-wavelength is presented. The main innovation of the proposed new design methodology is related to the fact that the positions of the array elements are left unchanged in the direction of the axis of the array (thus not affecting the gain of the pattern), while they are optimized along broadside direction. Selected numerical results validate the proposed methodology.**

Keywords—Phased arrays, grating lobes, PSO.

I. INTRODUCTION

The necessity of increasing phased array performances in terms of bandwidth, directivity or polarization makes the cost of phased arrays growing [1]-[3]. A common approach in order to reduce this cost is that of reducing the number of elements starting from the fully populated half-wavelength array [4],[5]. However, the inter-element spacing may increase, allowing undesired grating lobes to appear in the visible pattern during scanning. Many approaches aimed at reducing these lobes rely on randomly distributing elements on a line (for a linear array) thus creating a-periodic layouts [6]. Other possible solutions involve the use of optimization algorithms in order to properly remove elements while keeping low the level of undesired lobes [3],[7] or the exploitation of sub-array techniques [8],[9].

In this paper an innovative technique which independently optimizes (considering appropriate geometric constraints) the position of the elements of an ultra-wideband (*UWB*) linear array is proposed. The innovation of the presented methodology relies in optimizing the positions of the elements in the boresight direction, without moving them along the array direction (thus not affecting the antenna gain at low frequencies). The particle swarm optimization (*PSO*) algorithm [10],[11] has been chosen because it allows to deal with real-valued unknowns (i.e., the position of the elements). In order to assess the effectiveness of the proposed methodology, a *UWB* linear array with inter-element spacing greater than half-wavelength is optimized in order to reduce the grating lobes appearing when steering the beam. The pattern radiated by the "flat" solution (i.e., the array with all the elements lying on a line) and the pattern radiated by the optimized array are compared.

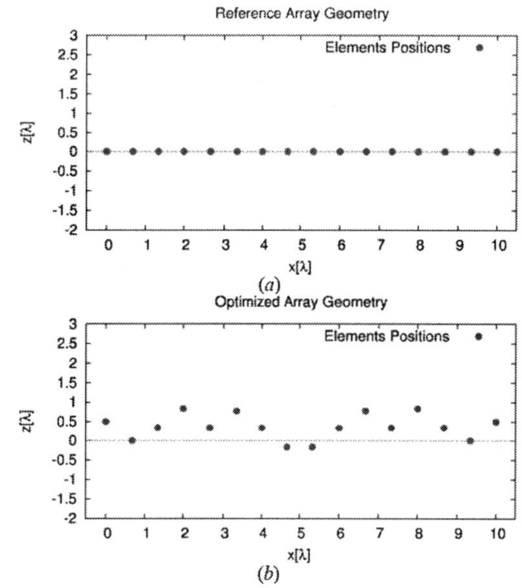

Fig. 1. *Numerical Assessment* - (*a*) Reference array and (*b*) optimized array with optimal positions along the z-axis.

II. MATHEMATICAL FORMULATION

Let us consider a *UWB* linear array of N ideal elements lying on the x-axis [Fig. 1(*a*)]. Let us indicate with $x_n, n = 1,...,N$ the x-coordinate and with $z_n, n = 1,...,N$ the z-coordinate of the elements of the array. Moreover, $[f_{min} : f_{max}]$ indicates the operational bandwidth of the array. The inter-element spacing along the x-direction, d_x, is assumed to be larger than $\lambda_{min}/2$, λ_{min} being the wavelength in free space at frequency f_{max}. Under these assumptions, grating lobes appear in the radiation pattern when steering the main lobe, as it is shown in Fig. 2. Such a result is in agreement with the following equation, defining the maximum allowed element spacing for avoiding grating lobes [12]

$$d_{max} = \frac{\lambda_{min}}{1 + \sin \vartheta}, \quad (1)$$

where ϑ is the steering angle.

In order to reduce these undesired lobes, the *PSO* algorithm is used for the optimization of the positions of the array elements along the z-axis, without changing the positions in the x-direction. Accordingly, the degrees of freedom (*DoFs*) of the optimization problem are N (i.e., $\mathbf{z} = (z_n, n = 1, \ldots, N)$), while the cost function to be minimized is defined as follows

$$\Phi(\mathbf{z}) = GLA(\mathbf{z}). \quad (2)$$

In (2) *GLA* stands for *Grating Lobe Area* and indicates the area of the power pattern out of the main beam with value greater than the desired sidelobe level. As an example, in Fig. 2 the *GLA* is indicated by a blue segment and corresponds to the portion of power pattern out of the main beam and above the desired threshold, which has been set equal to -10 dB.

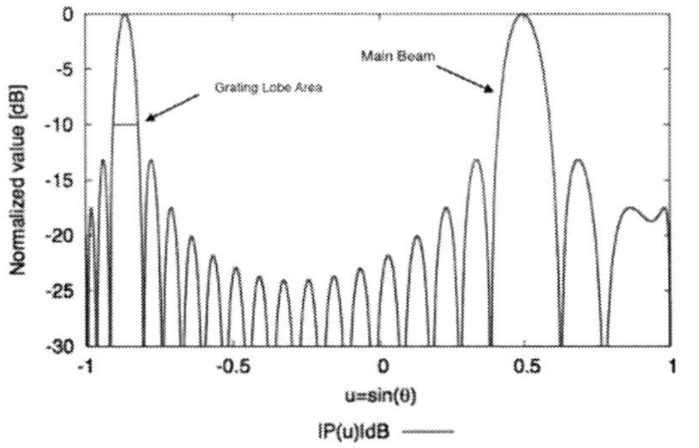

Fig. 2. *Illustrative Example* - Steered power pattern and GLA for a threshold equal to -10dB.

III. Preliminary Numerical Assessment

Let us consider a linear *UWB* array lying on the x-axis comprising $N = 16$ elements uniformly spaced and working in the frequency range $[f_{\min} : f_{\max}] = [6:18]$ GHz. The inter-element spacing is set equal to $d_x = 2/3\lambda_{\min}$ [Fig. 1(*a*)]. As it can be noticed, the condition (1) for having a pattern free from grating lobes for all steering angles and frequencies is not respected, since $d_x > \lambda_{\min}/2$. The power pattern radiated by such a reference layout is reported in Fig. 3 (green dashed line). The main beam is steered to the direction $\vartheta = 30$ [deg] and as it can be observed a grating lobe appears for $\vartheta = -90$ [deg]. The *PSO* algorithm has been applied in order to optimize the z-position of the array elements in order to reduce the *GLA*. For what concerns the setting of the *PSO* parameters, the following configuration values have been considered: the cognitive and social rates have been set equal to $C_{1,2} = 2.0$ [10]; the inertial weight has been set equal to $w = 0.4$ (constant during all optimization). Moreover, the swarm size has been set equal to $S = 10$ (i.e., lower than the total number of real valued unknowns), while the sidelobe level threshold has been set equal to -10 dB. Figure 1(*b*) shows the layout of the optimized array. As it can be noticed, the elements have been moved along the z-direction, making the linear array conformal. As a result, the randomness introduced in the arrangement allows to reduce the grating lobes, as it can be seen in Fig. 3 (where the red continuous line refers to the optimized power pattern). As a matter of fact, all the sidelobes are below the threshold of -10 dB, while the main lobe direction and beamwidth are preserved.

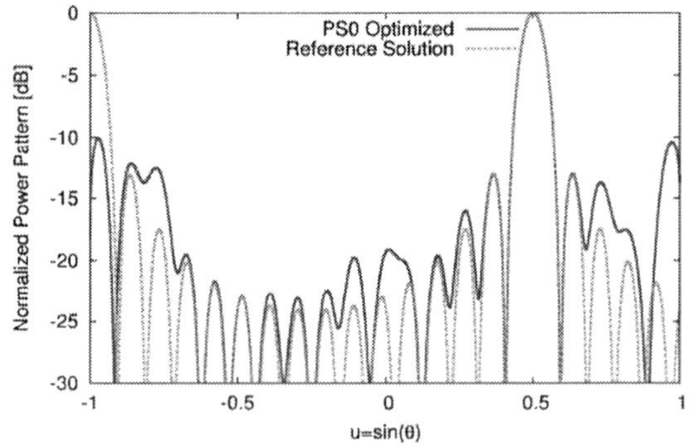

Fig. 3. *Numerical Assessment* - Reference and optimized power patterns.

IV. Conclusions

An innovative approach for reducing grating lobes appearing when the inter-element spacing of a *UWB* linear array is greater than half-wavelength has been presented. A preliminary numerical example has been shown to prove its effectiveness. Future works will be aimed at introducing the optimization of the excitation tolerances towards a more robust beamforming [13].

References

[1] L. Manica, *et al.*, "Design of subarrayed linear and planar array antennas with SLL control based on an excitation matching approach," *IEEE Trans. Antennas Propag.*, vol. 57, no. 6, pp. 1684-1691, Jun. 2009.

[2] L. Manica, *et al.*, "Synthesis of multi-beam sub-arrayed antennas through an excitation matching strategy," *IEEE Trans. Antennas Propag.*, vol. 59, no. 2, pp. 482-492, Feb. 2011.

[3] P. Rocca, *et al.*, "Unconventional phased array architectures and design methodologies - A review", *Proc. IEEE*, vol 104, no. 3, pp. 544-560, Mar. 2016.

[4] G. Oliveri, *et al.*, "Array miniaturization through QCTO-SI metamaterial radomes," *IEEE Trans. Antennas Propag.*, vol. 63, no. 8, pp. 3465-3476, Aug. 2015.

[5] G. Oliveri, *et al.*, "Sparsening conformal arrays through a versatile BCS-based method," *IEEE Trans. Antennas Propag.*, vol. 62, no. 4 (Part 1), pp. 1681-1689, Apr. 2014.

[6] B. Steinberg, "The peak sidelobe of the phased array having randomly located elements," *IEEE Trans. Antennas Propag.*, vol. 20, no. 2, pp. 129-136, Mar. 1972.

[7] R. L. Haupt, "Thinned arrays using genetic algorithms," *IEEE Trans. Antennas Propag.*, vol. 42, no. 7, pp. 993-999, Jul. 1994.

[8] P. Rocca, *et al.*, "Hybrid approach for sub-arrayed monopulse antenna synthesis," *Electron. Lett.*, vol. 44, no. 2, pp. 75-76, Jan. 2008.

[9] G. Oliveri, *et al.*, "Synthesis of modular contiguously clustered linear arrays through a sparseness-regularized solver," *IEEE Trans. Antennas Propag.*, vol. 64, no. 10, pp. 4277-4287, Oct. 2016

[10] P. Rocca, *et al.*, "Evolutionary Optimization as applied to inverse problems," *Inverse Problems*, vol. 25, pp. 1-41, Dec. 2009.

[11] P. Rocca, *et al.*, "Differential Evolution as applied to electromagnetics," *IEEE Antennas Propag. Mag.*, vol. 53, no. 1, pp. 38-49, Feb. 2011.

[12] C. A. Balanis, *Antenna Theory: Analysis and Design*, 3rd ed., Hoboken, NJ: John Wiley, 2005.

[13] N. Anselmi, *et al.*, "Optimization of excitation tolerances for robust beamforming in linear arrays," *IET Microw. Antennas Propag.*, vol. 10, no. 2, pp. 208-214, 2016.

Circular Slotted Reconfigurable Multiband patch Antenna for Wireless Applications

Rashid Saleem
Department of Telecommunication Engineering
University of Engineering and Technology (UET)
Taxila, Pakistan
rashid.saleem@uettaxila.edu.pk

Asim Quddus
Department of Electrical Engineering
University of Engineering and Technology (UET)
Taxila, Pakistan
asim.quddus@uettaxila.edu.pk

***Abstract*— A novel circular slotted multiband antenna for wireless communication application is presented in this paper. The antenna design is quite simple, a defected ground structure (DGS) is created by a circular slots of different radii, 50 ohm feeding line as a radiator, and rectangular shape slit connected to a circular slots at ground plane. Moreover, reconfigurable multiband resonances are achieved by an appropriate placement of PIN diodes at the circular slots of defected ground plane and switching (ON/OFF) them according to requirement. The suggested antenna exhibits three tunable resonant frequency bands which includes 2.5/3.5/5.7 GHz used in WLAN/WiMax/UWB applications. The antenna is designed on FR4 substrate. It is compact with dimensions of 28 × 16 × 0.8 mm³. The reconfigurable resonant frequency bands over a wide spectrum suggests that the proposed antenna design is appropriate candidate for different wireless communication applications.**

Keywords*— *Multiband; WLAN; WiMax; ultrawideband (UWB); reconfigurable; defected ground structure (DGS); PIN diodes

I. Introduction

Microstrip patch antenna (MPA) has long established its importance in the field of wireless communication systems such as WLAN, WiMAX, etc. [1-2]. In general, the focus of multiband microstrip patch antenna is on different wireless standards, which include but are not limited to WLAN, WiMAX as in IEEE 802.11 and 802.16 standards [3-5]. Therefore the researchers prefer to achieve these different communication standards within a single package. UWB antenna is one of the solutions but due to large band width i.e. 7.5 GHz, the interference with neighboring communicating devices is a major challenge. Another possible solutions to this problem is to design a reconfigurable multiband antenna. In the existing literature, many multiband designs have been reported to resonate at desired frequency bands [3-5].

In this paper, a miniaturized reconfigurable multiband antenna is proposed. The suggested antenna exhibits a tunable resonant frequencies having good matching ($S_{11} \leq -10dB$), at 2.5/3.5/5.7GHz. On rear side of substrate defected ground structure (DGS) is created by a circular slots of different radii. PIN diodes are used as a switch in circular slots of ground plane to achieve different resonant bands. The proposed antenna provides tunable band-pass characteristics at central frequency of 2.5 GHz (WLAN), 3.5 (WiMAX), 5.7 GHz (WLAN) and 6.5 GHz (C-band).

II. Antenna Design and Configuration

A. Design of Antenna Element

The geometric structure of proposed antenna design is demonstrated in Fig. 1. The antenna design is simulated on low cost FR4 substrate with relative permittivity ε_r = 4.4 and thickness 0.8 mm. The proposed antenna has a compact overall size of 28 × 16 mm². The upper side of laminate comprises of antenna feed line. The ground plane is designed on the rear side of substrate. The proposed radiating patch is 50 ohm fed microstrip antenna with dimensions 18.4 x 1.6 mm². It has rectangular profile to enhance the impedance match over wide band. The suggested design of an antenna element exhibits good match over band spectrum of 2 GHz – 7 GHz. The design parameters of antenna design are shown in Table I.

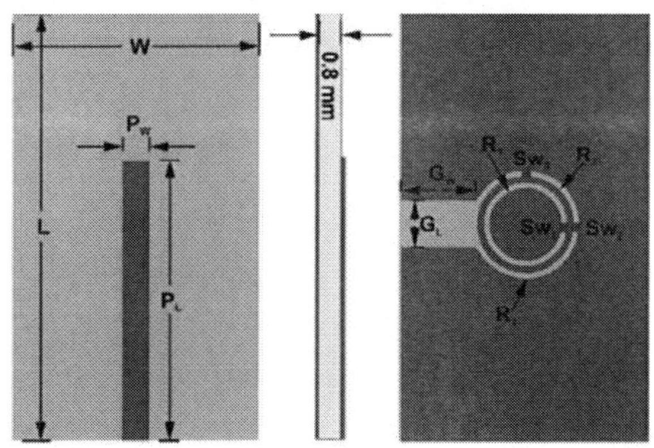

(a) (b) (c)

Fig. 1. Geometric configuration of proposed multiband antenna (a) Front view (b) Side view (c) Rear view

B. Design of Defected Ground Structure(DGS)

The design of ground structure for multiband antenna is demonstrated in Fig. 1(c). The resonance at multiple frequency bands is achieved by incorporating a defected ground plane on the rear side. The antenna element operating at wideband is adjusted to operate at multiple narrow and wide frequency bands through a circular slots of DGS. These slots have circular shape of radii R_1, R_2, and R_3. A rectangular shape slit is connected to a circular slots at ground plane. The overall defected ground plane provides triple-band operation with central frequency at 3.5/5.8/6.5 GHz.

III. Multiband Reconfigurability

The frequency band desired to be operated at is determined by the effective length and width of the resonant structure as well as the proper placement of the structure. From equation 1 and 2 the resonance parameters for desired frequency bands can be obtained.

$$W_{1,2,3}=\frac{c}{2f_o\sqrt{\frac{2}{\varepsilon_r+1}}} \tag{1}$$

$$L_{1,2,3}=\frac{c}{2f_o\sqrt{\varepsilon_r}} \tag{2}$$

Reconfigurability is achieved using three PIN diodes for switching purpose at the circular slots of ground plane. Three cases are given below:

Case I: When switches Sw_1 and Sw_2 are at 'OFF' state, and Sw_3 is at 'ON' state, the outer circular slot with radius R_3 in ground behaves like a capacitor and the radiating patch provides inductive effect, creating a band-pass filter for WLAN 2.5 GHz as shown in Fig. 2.

Case II: The dual band operation is achieved at WiMAX and C-band, as presented in Fig. 2. when both switches Sw_1 and Sw_3 are at 'OFF' state and switch Sw_2 at 'ON' state, as the capacitive effect of the slot is increased on both sides of the switch connection.

Case III: The triple-band operability is achieved by switching Sw_1 and Sw_2 to 'ON' state, and switching 'OFF' Sw_3. The bands of operations i.e. WiMAX/WLAN/C-band are demonstrated in the Fig. 2

TABLE I

Optimized values of proposed antenna					
Parameter	L	P_W	G_L	W	P_L
Value(mm)	28	1.6	3	16	18.4
Parameter	R_1	R_2	R_3	G_W	-
Value(mm)	2	3.1	2.7	4.8	-

IV. RESULTS AND DISCUSSIONS

A. S-parameter and VSWR

The proposed design is simulated on a FR4 laminate having thickness 0.8 mm, relative permittivity of 4.4 and a loss tangent of 0.02, as shown in Fig. 2. The results demonstrate that the antenna exhibits good return loss (S_{11} < -10 dB) at multiple resonant frequency bands. It includes 2.5/3.5/5.8 GHz used in WLAN/WiMAX/UWB applications. In Fig.4. Voltage standing wave ratio (VSWR) of proposed design is presented showing that proposed design is satisfying the required criteria (VSWR < 2) for resonating bands.

B. Radiation Patterns

The radiation characteristics in H-plane and E-plane of the suggested antenna are plotted in Fig. 3. The radiation patterns observed in E-plane are omnidirectional while in H-plane these patterns are somewhat directional within suitable limits.

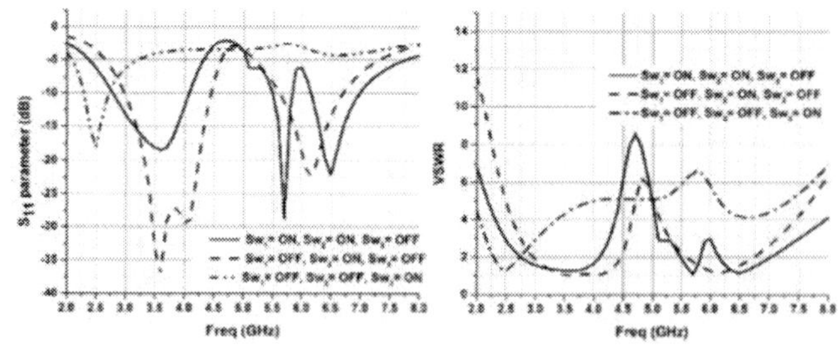

(a) (b)

Fig. 2. Simulated Results (a) S_{11} parameters of proposed antenna variations (b) VSWR of proposed antenna variations

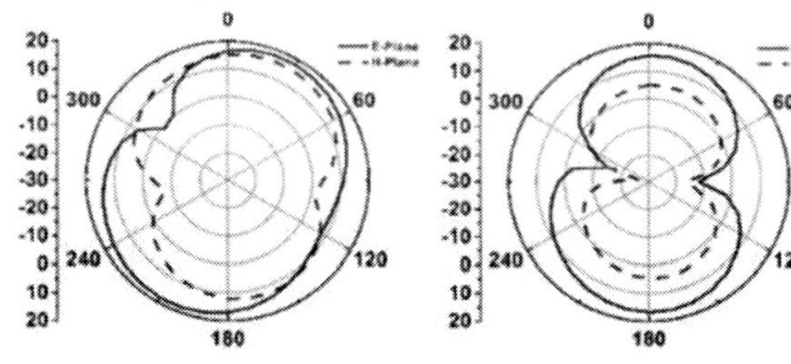

(a) (b)

Fig. 3. Radiation plots (a) at 2.5 GHz (b) at 6.5 GHz

V. CONCLUSION

A miniaturized multiband antenna capable of reconfigurable characteristics is presented in this paper for WLAN/WiMAX/UWB applications. Multiband operability is achieved by defected ground structure (DGS). Moreover, the tunability/reconfigurability characteristics for WLAN, WiMAX and C-band frequency spectrum is also achieved with central frequency of 2.5/5.7 GHz, 3.5 GHz and 6.5 GHz respectively. It indicates that the proposed antenna design is decent candidate for portable wireless communication application.

References

[1] Y. F. Cao, S. W. Cheung and T. I. Yuk, "A Multiband Slot Antenna for GPS/WiMAX/WLAN Systems," IEEE Transactions on Antennas and Propagation, vol. 63, pp. 952-958, March. 2015.

[2] Y. J. Chen; T. W. Liu; W. H. Tu, "CPW-Fed Penta-Band Slot Dipole Antenna Based on Comb-Like Metal Sheets," IEEE Antennas and Wireless Propagation Letters , vol. 99, pp.1-1, May. 2016.

[3] M. Cherian and D. Das, "Triple band reconfigurable dual patch antenna with multiband and wideband operation," International Conference on Control Communication & Computing India (ICCC), Trivandrum, pp. 437-441, Nov. 2015.

[4] S. Shoukat, S. Ullah, S. Rahim, B. Kamal and U. Ali, "Design of a dual band frequency reconfigurable patch antenna for GSM and Wi-Fi applications," 2016 International Conference on Computing, Electronic and Electrical Engineering (ICE Cube), Quetta, pp. 85-89, April. 2016.

[5] I. Ben Trad, I. Rouissi, J. M. Floc'h and H. Trabelsi, "Frequency reconfigurable multiband planar antenna with wide tuning frequency range," 10th European Conference on Antennas and Propagation (EuCAP), Davos, pp. 1-4, April. 2016.

Autonomous Wearable RFID-Based Sensing Platform for the Internet-of-Things

Sam Lemey, Sam Agneessens, Patrick Van Torre, Kristof Baes, and Hendrik Rogier
Ghent University/IMEC, IDLab
Department of Information Technology (INTEC)
B-9052 Ghent, Belgium
Email: Sam.Lemey@ugent.be

Jan Vanfleteren
Ghent University/IMEC
Centre for Microsystems Technology (CMST)
Department of Electronics and Information Systems (ELIS)
B-9052 Ghent, Belgium
Email: Jan.Vanfleteren@imec.be

***Abstract*—An autonomous wearable radio-frequency identification (RFID) tag with sensing, processing, and decision-taking capability is presented for operation in the 2.45-GHz RFID band. The tag relies on a dedicated textile shorted circular patch antenna with tailored radiation pattern for operation in a smart floor/ceiling environment. By means of an holistic design strategy, the textile antenna's functionality is augmented by reusing its surface as an integration platform for sensing, computing, transceiver, and light-energy-harvesting hardware. Special attention was paid to align the tag's power consumption profile with the power generation profile of the energy harvester. Measurements under free-space conditions and in a realistic indoor scenario demonstrate excellent wearability, very high read range, enhanced functionality, and extended system autonomy.**

I. Introduction

The Internet of Things (IoT) is currently the main force driving a massive change in industry and society. Fueled by the adaption of novel key-enabling technologies such as radio-frequency identification (RFID), wireless sensor networks (WSN) and energy-harvesting techniques, an ever-increasing number of everyday objects are augmented with sensing, processing, and wireless communication capabilities, enabling a far-reaching integration into the Internet.

However, to fully exploit the potential of the IoT, multiple, complementary key-enabling technologies should be combined. Incorporating WSN, energy-harvesting and RFID functionality within a single enhanced RFID tag that also enables unobtrusive integration within a garment will revolutionize many aspects of our daily lifes. Such a tag will leverage pervasive monitoring of the wearer's physiological parameters during his/her day-to-day activities, by wirelessly migrating gathered sensor data to the internet via a question-and-reply protocol, and this without the discomfort of frequent battery recharging or carrying additional, heavy equipment. The realization of such a autonomous wearable tag, however, imposes a challenging set of design requirements [1]. First, the tag must be flexible, low profile, and light weight in order not to affect the wearer's comfort. Second, a high and stable read range, even in the presence of the human body, is necessary. Finally, low-power and energy-efficient operation is requisite to allow self-powering from scavenged ambient energy.

In this work, we propose a wearable, enhanced RFID tag with integrated energy harvester that features an unprecedented combination of excellent wearability, very high read range, enhanced functionality, and extended system autonomy with respect to other similar tags in literature [2], [3]. Moreover, our tag is optimized for communication with a smart floor/ceiling in the 2.45-GHz RFID band. In this concept, the RFID reader(s) are integrated into the ceiling/floor of the building in which the wearer is located.

II. System Architecture and Implementation

Fig. 1, (a) and (b), depicts the architecture of our autonomous wearable RFID-based sensing platform and shows the holistic design approach. A textile circular patch antenna, designed for optimal performance in the 2.45-GHz RFID band, forms the base of the tag and serves as an integration platform for flexible light-energy-harvesting, sensing, processing and transceiver hardware. Such a design approach yields excellent results by relying on the textile antenna to obtain peak performance and by minimizing the amount of lossy and fragile interconnections between the diverse subsystems of a smart textile system by using the antenna as an integration platform.

The circular patch antenna consists of four shorting vias, connecting the patch to the ground plane, and a probe feed in the center to excite the TM22 mode. This particular mode gives the antenna a monopole-like radiation pattern, providing

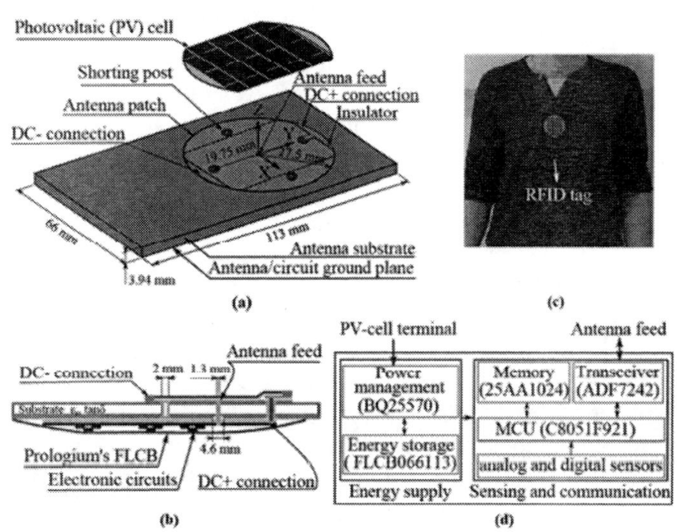

Fig. 1. Autonomous wearable RFID-based sensing platform. (a) Top 3D view. (b) Cross-sectional view. (c) Prototype worn on the chest of a test person. (d) Block diagram of the hardware integrated onto the antenna's backside.

reliable communication between a body-worn node (Fig. 1(c)) and an interrogator located in a smart floor/ceiling. A low-cost textile foam (ϵ_r = 1.42 and tanδ = 0.016 at 2.45 GHz [1]) is selected as antenna substrate to obtain a low-profile, flexible and light-weight antenna with sufficient bandwidth. Conductive textile with a surface resistivity R_s = 0.18 Ω/sq [1] is used to fabricate the antenna patch and ground plane. Both layers are laminated to the antenna substrate by means of thermally-activated glue, while hollow, brass eyelets are used to realize the shorting posts. The antenna is optimized in CST Microwave Studio for maximum -10 dB impedance bandwidth around the 2.45 GHz center frequency. The final dimensions are shown in Fig. 1 (a) and (b).

Next, a flexible and ultrathin (200 μm) Powerfilm SP3-37 a-Si:H photovoltaic (PV) module is fixed on top of the antenna patch, whereas dedicated power management (including energy storage), sensing, processing and transceiver hardware is integrated onto the antenna backside. Fig. 1(d) shows the block diagram of the hardware integrated on the antenna's feed plane and denotes the main component of each subsystem. These components are carefully selected for low power consumption and are implemented on a flexible polyimide circuit board (FCB) to maintain flexibility. In the integration process, the FCB's ground plane is bonded with the antenna ground plane (Fig. 1(a)), which allows using the antenna as a common DC ground and provides excellent shielding between the antenna patch and the active circuitry. Hence, the negative DC terminal of the PV module may now be directly connected to the antenna patch and only the positive DC terminal needs to be routed through one of the hollow eyelets (Fig. 1(b)). In a final step, Prologium's 066113 Flexible Lithium Ceramic Battery (FLCB) is integrated as depicted in Fig. 1(b). It allows the tag to remain fully operative in the absence of light.

Finally, our tag features flexible sensor interfacing via a I2C bus and via an embedded 10-bit analog to digital converter. This allows our tag to be used in diverse real-life applications by connecting the appropriate sensor(s).

III. System Performance

First, the antenna performance is validated by measuring its input reflection coefficient $|S_{11}|$ and radiation pattern under diverse operating conditions. First, these parameters are measured before and after the integration of the additional hardware. Afterwards, they are measured when the tag is worn on the human body. Measurements in an anechoic chamber demonstrate that the $|S_{11}|$ (with respect to 50 Ω) remains lower than -10 dB over more than 150 MHz around the 2.45 GHz center frequency, irrespective of the operating condition. Fig. 2 shows the simulated and measured radiation pattern in the XZ- and YZ-plane (Fig. 1(a)) at 2.45 GHz for the same operating conditions. It can be seen that the antenna exhibits a stable monopolar radiation pattern with most of the radiation directed towards the ceiling and the floor (YZ-plane), when worn as depicted in Fig. 1(c). In fact, the antenna exhibits a maximum gain of 2.7 dBi and a radiation efficiency of 65 % under any circumstance.

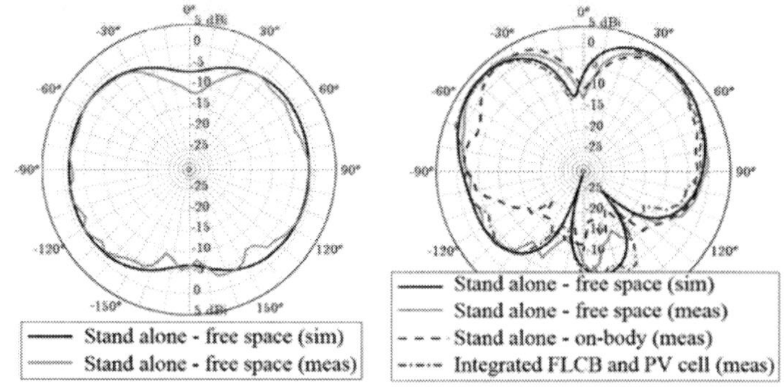

(a) (b)

Fig. 2. Radiation pattern at 2.45 GHz. (a) XZ-plane. (b) YZ-plane.

Furthermore, measurements in an indoor scenario show that our tag features a read range up to 23 m when three brick walls are in between both link ends. Moreover, it allows interrogation by a reader at an overhead floor, through a reinforced concrete floor. Hence, a very high read range is achieved by combining excellent antenna perfomance with a state-of-the-art transceiver.

Finally, our tag's system autonomy is analyzed. On the one hand, our node implements a low-power algorithm in which the system is primarily in sleep mode (consuming 48 μA) and only periodically (every wake-up period T_{sleep}) switches to its active state for 5 ms to perform sensing, processing and to listen if its interrogated by a RFID reader. In its active state, our tag's current consumption increases up to 35 mA. Hence, the average current consumption of the tag is determined by T_{sleep}. Measurements show that in case T_{sleep} is set to 60 s, our node only consumes 168 μW of power, guaranteeing a system autonomy of at least 138 days in complete absence of light (provided the battery was fully charged). For this setting, sensing and processing are performed every 60 s and the system will answer within maximally 60 seconds. On the other hand, measurements have shown that our node is capable of harvesting 50.1 mW under full sunlight (107 527 Lux) and approximately 250 μW under typical office lighting (330 Lux), thereby further extending system autonomy. In fact, measurements show that, under typical office lighting, T_{sleep} can be reduced to 20 s without using battery power.

IV. Conclusion

We have presented the design and realization of an autonomous wearable RFID-based sensing platform for operation in the 2.45-GHz RFID SHF band. The adopted holistic design approach yields a RFID tag that features excellent wearability, enhanced functionality, flexible sensor interfacing, very high read range and extended system autonomy.

References

[1] S. Lemey, S. Agneessens, P. Van Torre, K. Baes, J. Vanfleteren, and H. Rogier, "Wearable Flexible Lightweight Modular RFID Tag With Integrated Energy Harvester," *IEEE Trans. Microw. Theory Techn.*, vol. 64, no. 7, pp. 2304–2314, Jul 2016.

[2] R. Colella, L. Tarricone, and L. Catarinucci, "SPARTACUS: Self-Powered Augmented RFID Tag for Autonomous Computing and Ubiquitous Sensing," *IEEE Trans. Antennas Propag.*, vol. 63, pp. 2272–2281, 2015.

[3] T. Kaufmann, D. C. Ranasinghe, M. Zhou, and C. Fumeaux, "Wearable Quarter-Wave Folded Microstrip Antenna for Passive UHF RFID Applications," *Int J Antennas Propag*, vol. 2013, pp. 1–11, 2013.

Synthesis of Near Field Focused Arrays Including Far Field Constrains

Rafael G. Ayestarán, Marcos R. Pino
Dep. of Electrical Engineering
Universidad de Oviedo
33203 Gijón, Spain
Email: {rayestaran,mpino}@uniovi.es

Paolo Nepa
Dep. of Information Engineering
Università di Pisa
56122 Pisa, Italy
Email: paolo.nepa@unipi.it

***Abstract*—A scheme for the synthesis of antenna arrays accounting simultaneously for Near Field Focusing and Far Field specifications is proposed. The technique is based on the minimization of a proper cost function and the definition of a target Near Field distribution. This approach increases the flexibility of traditional focusing techniques to deal with different sets of specifications both in the near and far environments. Some illustrative examples are presented.**

I. INTRODUCTION

Near Field Focusing (NFF) [1], [2], [3] is a technique able to concentrate radiated field into a predefined position in the near environment of an antenna, the so-called focal spot. Among other applications, it is specially suitable for communication in close distances between devices with information about each other position, and avoiding interferences from other elements that might be placed in the same environment. However, most synthesis techniques for NFF only account for the relative position between the radiating elements and the focal spot. Other interferent elements might be distorting the communication from other positions in the near environment or from any direction in the far field. In this contribution we propose a scheme for synthesis of NFF able to take into account constrains both in the near and the far field radiation patterns. This allows designing both radiating systems able to concentrate the information into a focal spot without interfering on other devices, or able to read from a device placed in the focal spot without interference from other sources. The proposed technique is based on optimization of the weights applied to an antenna array, one of the most flexible methods to perform synthesis in NFF [4].

II. PROBLEM STATEMENT

The field radiated by the $N = N_x \times N_y$ elements of a planar, uniformly distributed array placed in the x-y plane, at any position $\vec{r}$ of the near environment is given by

$$E_{NF}(\vec{r}) = \sum_{n=1}^{N} \frac{w_n e^{-jk|\vec{r}-\vec{r'_n}|}}{|\vec{r}-\vec{r'_n}|} \quad (1)$$

where $\vec{r'_n}$ is the position vector corresponding to the n-th element of the array, $w_n \in \mathbb{C}$ is the weight applied to this n-th element, N_x is the number of elements in the x-axis, N_y is the number of elementos in the y-axis and $k = 2\pi/\lambda$.

In a similar way, the Far Field (FF) radiation pattern produced by the array can be expressed as

$$E_{FF}(\theta, \phi) = \sum_{n=1}^{N} w_n e^{j\vec{k}\cdot\vec{r'_n}} \quad (2)$$

where the direction of propagation is defined by the position vector, and hence by the angles θ and ϕ.

The goal in traditional Near Field focusing problems is to obtain a Near Field (NF) distribution focused in a predefined position of the near environment. However, in many applications it is also important that the FF radiation pattern is minimized, so that the power at each direction is minimized. Potentially, other applications might require additional constrains on the FF radiation pattern to be accounted for while the array is still focused on the NF target. A framework able to account for both NF and FF specifications at the same time is required.

The proposed technique is based on the minimization of a cost function able to account for both the NF and FF conditions at the same time. A target NF distribution is specified defining a vector $\mathbf{e}_{target}$ with null values except in the position corresponding to the desired focal point, where a value 1 is set. In this technique a matrix-version of eq. (1) will be used, so that

$$\mathbf{e}_{NF} = \mathbf{S}_{NF} \cdot \mathbf{w} \quad (3)$$

where $\mathbf{e}_{NF} = [E_{NF}(\vec{r_1}), E_{NF}(\vec{r_2}) \ldots E_{NF}(\vec{r_M})]^T$ is a column vector containing the values of the field radiated at the M considered positions of the near environment, $\mathbf{w} = [w_1, w_2, \ldots, w_N]^T$ is a vector with the weights applied to each element of the array, and $\mathbf{S}_{NF}$ is a matrix with elements $S_{n,m} = \frac{e^{-jk|\vec{r_m}-\vec{r'_n}|}}{|\vec{r_m}-\vec{r'_n}|}$. Similarly, FF vector and matrix $\mathbf{e}_{FF}$ and $\mathbf{S}_{FF}$ can also be defined so that

$$\mathbf{e}_{FF} = \mathbf{S}_{FF} \cdot \mathbf{w} \quad (4)$$

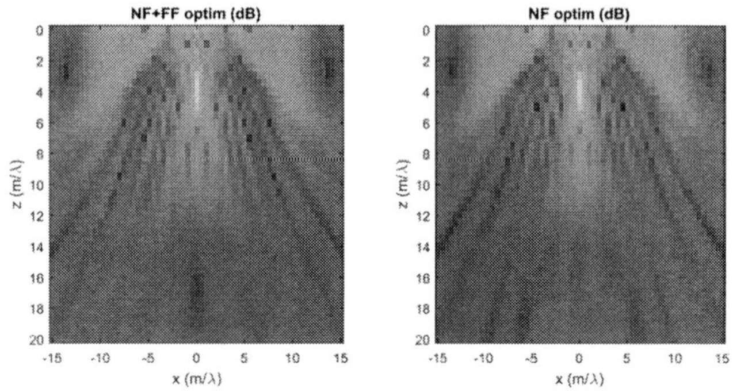

Fig. 1. Near field in the plane $y = 0$ obtained using both NF and FF optimization, and NF-only optimization.

A general cost function J to be minimized is then proposed as

$$J = \{||\mathbf{e}_{target} - \mathbf{S}_{NF} \cdot \mathbf{w}|| + \gamma \, f_{FF}(\mathbf{w})\} \quad (5)$$

where $||.||$ is the $l2$-norm, and $f_{FF}(\mathbf{w})$ is a generic function of the weights applied to the array, that should be defined according to the FF constrains for a specific application. The first term guarantees that the NF radiation is close to the desired pattern, with a maximum at the focal point and minimal values at any other position. The second term accounts for the specifications in the FF radiation pattern. The tradeoff parameter γ is used to determine the importance of each term in the cost function and hence in the obtained solution.

III. Example and Results

Let us consider the case aiming to guarantee a required field level at the focal spot and reducing the overall radiated power. For this problem, the proposed FF-specifications function might be defined according to:

$$f_{FF}(\mathbf{w}) = var\{\mathbf{S}_{FF} \cdot \mathbf{w}\} \quad (6)$$

where var stands for the variance, leading to the following optimization problem:

$$minimize \; \{||\mathbf{e}_{target} - \mathbf{S}_{NF} \cdot \mathbf{w}|| + \gamma \, var\{\mathbf{S}_{FF} \cdot \mathbf{w}\}\} \quad (7)$$

The second term minimizes the variance of the FF radiation, leading to a radiation pattern as omnidirectional as possible and with minimum power at the same time.

In the following example, the parameter γ has been set to 200 after previous tests. The focal spot has been defined at the position $\{0, 0, 4\lambda\}$. The results are depicted in figures 1, 2 and 3, where a comparison between the obtained results and a NF-only optimization is presented. It can be noticed that, for a same field level at the focal spot the FF level is reduced, and the field is properly focused on the defined target.

Other cases and definitions of the function $f_{FF}(\mathbf{w})$ will be presented. Cases such as $f_{FF}(\mathbf{w}) = ||\mathbf{w}||^2$,

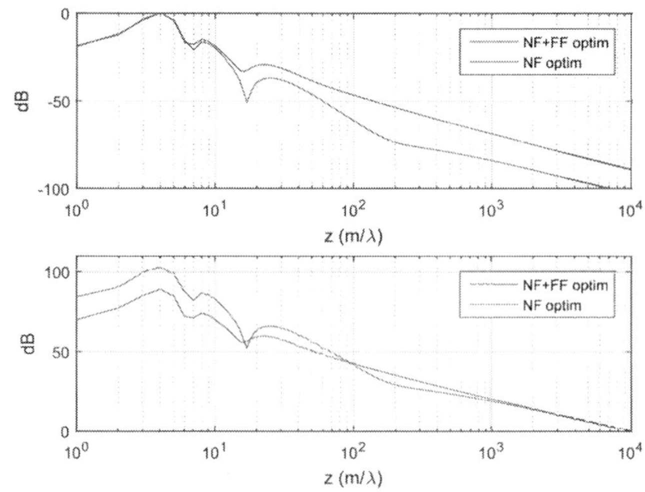

Fig. 2. Field level across the axis z. a) Normalized to the level at the focal spot. b) Normalized to FF level.

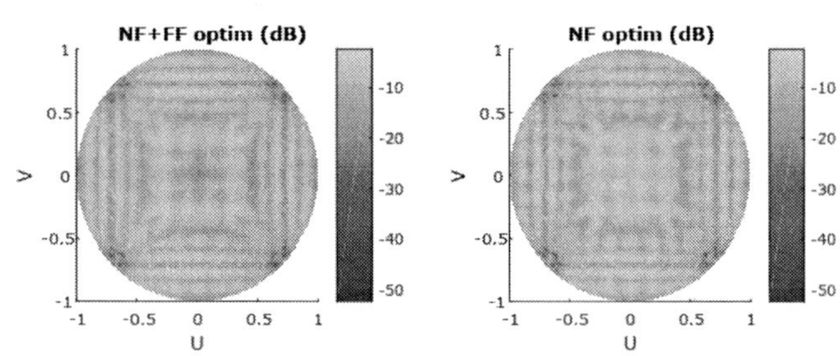

Fig. 3. UV representation of the FF level obtained using both NF and FF optimization, and NF-only optimization.

the use of constrained minimization or the definition of the function according to some typical figures of merit in NFF applications [2] will be explored, along with illustrative examples showing the flexibility of the proposed method.

Acknowledgment

This work has been supported by the Ministerio de Economía y Competitividad of Spain under project TEC2014-54005-P (MIRIIEM) and by the Gobierno del Principado de Asturias / FEDER under project GRUPIN14-114.

References

[1] J. Álvarez, R. G. Ayestarán, F. Las-Heras, "Design of antenna arrays for near-field focusing requirements using optimization", *Electronics Letters*, vol. 48, n0. 21, pp. 1323-1325, 2012.

[2] A. Buffi, P. Nepa, G. Manara, "Design criteria for near-field-focused planar arrays", *IEEE Antennas and Propagation Magazine*, vol. 54, no. 1, pp. 40-50, 2012.

[3] P. Nepa, A. Buffi, "Near-Field focused microwave antennas", to appear on *IEEE Antennas and Propagation Magazine*, 2016.

[4] J. Álvarez, R. G. Ayestarán, G. León, L. F. Herrán, J. A. López, F. Las-Heras, "Near field multifocusing on antenna arrays via non-convex optimization", *IET Microwaves, Antennas & Propagation*, vol. 8, n0. 10, pp. 754-764, 2014.

Resonant Inductive WPT Link Operating in a Coupling-independent Regime

Alessio De Angelis, Marco Dionigi, Paolo Carbone, and Mauro Mongiardo
DE
Univ. of Perugia
Perugia, Italy
alessio.deangelis@unipg.it

Qinghua Wang and Wenquan Che
DCE
Nanjing Univ. of Science and Technology
Nanjing, China

Franco Mastri and Alessandra Costanzo
DEI
Univ. of Bologna
Bologna, Italy
franco.mastri@unibo.it

Giuseppina Monti and Luciano Tarricone
DII
Univ. of Salento
Lecce, Italy
giuseppina.monti@unisalento.it

Abstract—**In this paper the feasibility of achieving a coupling-independent performance for a Wireless Power Transfer Link based on resonant inductive coupling is investigated. Theoretical and experimental results demonstrating that a coupling-independent regime can be realized by an appropriate selection of the operating frequency of a strongly-coupled synchronous WPT link are reported and discussed.**

I. Introduction

Wireless Power Transfer (WPT) based on near field magnetic coupling is receiving a growing interest [1].

In general, different applications impose different requirements in terms of distance to be covered, efficiency and power on the load. Accordingly, different architectures and operating regimes have been proposed and investigated in the literature. For instance, indirect schemes using additional resonators not directly connected to the generator and to the load have been investigated for extending the distance covered by the link [2]. As per the possibility of maximizing either the power on the load or the efficiency, the problem has been solved in [3]–[4] for the case of a resonant WPT link using a direct-scheme.

Another operating regime of interest is the *coupling–independent* which provides a power on the load and an efficiency independent of the magnetic coupling coefficient of the link ([5]). This operating regime is particularly attractive in applications, such as WPT links for energizing sensors for structural monitoring or implantable medical devices, where the secondary resonator is not accessible. In fact, as demonstrated in this paper, the coupling–independent regime requires to set the operating frequency so to nullify the reactive part of the input impedance seen at the primary side. Accordingly, this operating regime can be implemented by measuring the phase difference between voltage and current at the primary side and by modifying the operating frequency so as to realize zero phase difference. In the following part of the paper closed form analytical formulas will be presented and experimentally validated.

II. Theoretical Analysis

A schematic representation of the WPT link analyzed in this paper is illustrated in Fig. 1. It consists of two magnetically coupled resonators driven by a sinusoidal voltage generator $v_G(t) = \sqrt{2}V_G\cos(\omega t)$ with internal resistance R_G and connected to a resistive load R_L. The resonators losses are modeled by the equivalent series resistances R_1 and R_2 related to the quality factors Q_1 and Q_2 by the standard relationship: $Q_i = \omega_{0i}L_i/R_i$, $i = 1, 2$. The WPT is implemented by the coupled inductors L_1 and L_2, while the series capacitors C_1 and C_2 realize the resonance condition at the angular frequency $\omega_0 = 1/\sqrt{C_1L_1} = 1/\sqrt{C_2L_2}$. The coupling between L_1 and L_2 is expressed by the coupling coefficient k. Additionally, in order to simplify the analysis, the normalized parameters reported in Table I are introduced.

TABLE I
Parameter Definition

parameter	expression
normalized frequency	$u = \omega/\omega_0$
transform ratio	$n = \sqrt{L_1/L_2}$
normalized reactances	$X_{i0} = L_i\,\omega_0,\ i = 1, 2$
normalized resistances	$r_i = R_i/X_{i0} = 1/Q_i,\ i = 1, 2$ $r_G = R_G/X_{10} = 1/Q_G$ $r_L = R_L/(n^2X_{10}) = 1/Q_L$ $r_{iT} = r_i + r_G = 1/Q_{iT},\ i = 1, 2$

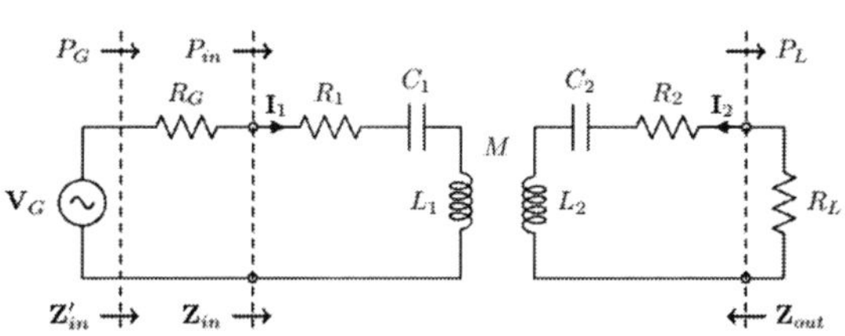

Fig. 1. Schematic of the WPT link.

By modeling the two coupled inductors as an impedance inverter with *transform ratio n*, it is possible to compute the input impedance $Z_{in} = R_{in} + jX_{in}$ which allows calculating the resonance frequencies of the WPT link defined as the frequencies where X_{in} vanishes. In particular, the following expressions can be obtained for the input resistance R_{in} and the input reactance X_{in}:

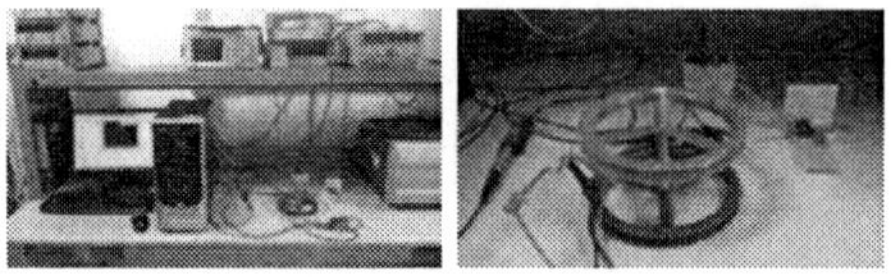

Fig. 2. Photos of the experiment analyzed in this paper.

$$R_{in} = X_{10}r_1 + X_{10}\frac{k^2u^4r_{2T}}{u^4-(2-r_{2T}^2)u^2+1}, \quad (1)$$

$$X_{in} = X_{10}\frac{(u^2-1)\left[(1-k^2)u^4-(2-r_{2T}^2)u^2+1\right]}{u\left[u^4-(2-r_{2T}^2)u^2+1\right]}. \quad (2)$$

It can be seen that, for any value of k, $X_{in} = 0$ at the frequency $u = u_0 = 1$, which will be referred to as the *main resonant frequency*. From (2) it can be also demonstrated that two further resonances, called *secondary resonances*, exist if the following two inequalities are simultaneously satisfied:

$$r_{2T} < \sqrt{2}, \quad (3)$$

$$k \geq k_b = r_{2T}\sqrt{1-\frac{r_{2T}^2}{4}}. \quad (4)$$

When (3) and (4) are satisfied, two secondary frequencies of resonance u_1 and u_2 appear, in addition to the main frequency of resonance u_0, (i.e., X_{in} vanishes at three different frequencies u_0, u_1 and u_2). These additional frequencies are given by:

$$u_1, u_2 = \sqrt{\frac{2-r_{2T}^2 \pm \sqrt{4k^2+r_{2T}^4-4r_{2T}^2}}{2(1-k^2)}} \quad (5)$$

As per the input resistance, from (1) it can be easily verified that at the secondary resonant frequencies R_{in} is independent of k, and the coupled resonators behave as an ideal transformer with transform ratio $n = \sqrt{L_1/L_2}$. Accordingly, a *coupling-independent regime* is achieved when the WPT link operates at the two secondary resonant frequencies. Here the term *coupling-independent regime* means that the efficiency and the power delivered to a given resistive load R_L are independent of the coupling coefficient k. Conversely, when the WPT link operates at u_0 both the efficiency and the power on the load depend on k.

III. Experimental results

To verify the analytical formulas reported in the section II, the experiment illustrated in Fig. 2 has been arranged. The inductors are 20-turns air-core copper wire coils of diameter 140 mm realizing an inductance of 128 μH. The capacitors are 330 nF nominal-value lumped capacitors realizing the resonance condition at $f_0 = 24.48\,\text{kHz}$. Referring to the equivalent circuit of Fig. 1, the measured values of the parameters of the WPT link are: $R_G = 0.98\,\Omega$, $R_1 = R_2 = 0.8\,\Omega$, $Q_1 = Q_2 = 20.8$, $r_{2T} = k_b = 0.11$. As per the coupling coefficient, measurements were performed for different values of the mutual distance between the two inductors corresponding to the following values of the mutual coupling: $k = 0.436$ (case *a*), $k = 0.266$ (case *b*), $k = 0.161$ (case *c*), $k = 0.104$ (case *d*). As a consequence, considering that for the analyzed system $r_{2T} = k_b = 0.11$, it can be concluded that the condition expressed in (3) is satisfied by all the analyzed cases, whereas the condition on the coupling coefficient (i.e., $k > k_b$) is satisfied only by the first three analyzed cases having a coupling coefficient larger than 0.11. Accordingly, it is expected that for cases a, *b* and *c* X_{in} vanishes at three different frequencies (i.e., at the main frequency of resonance ω_0 and at two secondary resonant frequencies). Conversely, only one resonant frequency is expected for case *d*.

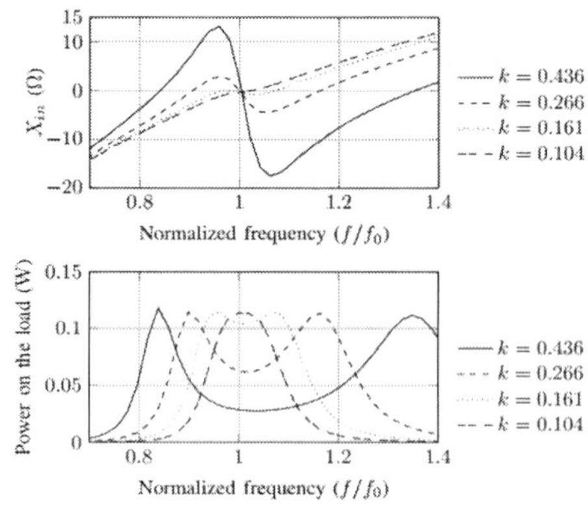

Fig. 3. Measured data achieved for different values of the coupling coefficient.

In order to verify the theory, the input impedance $Z_{in} = R_{in} + jX_{in}$, the active power on the load and the efficiency were measured. For the sake of brevity only the results referring to the input impedance and the power on the load are reported. From Fig. 3 it is evident that experimental data confirm the behaviour expected from the theory. In particular, it can be seen that two secondary resonances exist for the analyzed cases having a coupling coefficient larger than $k_b = 1.1$, see Fig. 3. Additionally, it can be seen that at the secondary resonances a power on the load independent of k has been obtained.

References

[1] A. Costanzo, M. Dionigi, M. Masotti, M. Mongiardo, G. Monti, L. Tarricone, and R. Sorrentino, "Electromagnetic energy harvesting and wireless power transmission: A unified approach," *Proceedings of the IEEE*, vol. 102, no. 11, pp. 1692–1711, Nov 2014.

[2] G. Monti, L. Tarricone, M. Dionigi, and M. Mongiardo, "Magnetically coupled resonant wireless power transmission: An artificial transmission line approach," in *Proc. of the Microwave Conf. (EuMC)*, Oct. 2012, pp. 233–236.

[3] M. Dionigi, M. Mongiardo, and R. Perfetti, "Rigorous network and full-wave electromagnetic modeling of wireless power transfer links," *IEEE Trans. on Microw. Theory and Techn.*, vol. 63, no. 1, pp. 65–75, Jan 2015.

[4] G. Monti, A. Costanzo, F. Mastri, M. Mongiardo, and L. Tarricone, "Rigorous design of matched wireless power transfer links based on inductive coupling," *Radio Science*, vol. 51, no. 6, pp. 858–867, June 2016.

[5] F. Mastri, A. Costanzo, and M. Mongiardo, "Coupling-Independent Wireless Power Transfer," *IEEE Microwave and Wireless Components letters*, vol. 26, no. 3, pp. 222–225, 2016.

The SARFID technique in handling systems applications

Alice Buffi, Paolo Nepa
Department of Information Engineering
University of Pisa
Pisa, Italy
alice.buffi@iet.unipi.it, p.nepa@iet.unipi.it

Marcos R. Pino
Department of Electrical Engineering
University of Oviedo
Gijon, Spain
mpino@tsc.uniovi.es

Abstract—**The application of the SARFID technique in handling systems applications is presented in this paper. The above phase-based localization method can be applied by moving the reader antenna along a known trajectory in front of several tagged items. Through an antenna scanning in a plane, a bi-dimensional localization with centimeter accuracy can be obtained.**

Keywords—UHF-RFID localization, Phase-based localization, Synthetic Array.

I. Introduction

The UHF-RFID technology represents a low-cost and easy-deployable solution to combine localization and tracking of tagged items with real-time inventory, in several scenarios such as warehouses, libraries, and hospitals. Thus, a large number of tagged items can be concurrently managed and the service processes can be faster.

Several techniques have been proposed to develop UHF-RFID localization system, exploiting both the amplitude and the phase of the tag backscattering signal measured at the output of the reader coherent receiver. The main goal is obtaining a spatial resolution comparable with the size of the tagged item. Good performance can be obtained with phase-based methods [1], which are more robust with respect to the multipath propagation phenomena typical of a crowded indoor scenario.

Recently, the authors of this paper proposed the SARFID technique, namely a phase-based localization method for tagged items moving along a conveyor belt, which exploits a synthetic-array radar approach [2]-[3]. It takes advantage of the fact that the tagged items move along a conveyor belt, whose speed and path are known, in front of a fixed reader antenna, so resembling the Inverse Synthetic Aperture Radar (ISAR) principle. It can be employed for a fully automatic management of tagged items moving on a conveyor belt of airport handling systems, parcel distribution centers, and assembly lines with a high automation level. The tagged items trajectory can be completely arbitrary. Actually, the SARFID technique can be employed in any scenario where a relative motion between the reader antenna and the tag exists or can be easily created with an handling system equipped with an antenna that moves in front of fixed tagged objects (Synthetic Aperture Radar – SAR – scenario) [4].

In this paper, the authors demonstrate the SARFID application in a scenario with an antenna moving with respect to fixed tagged items. In particular, a measurement campaign is carried out in a compact anechoic chamber by exploiting the antenna movement system, to verify the measured performance in a controlled environment.

II. Application Scenario

As already said, the SARFID technique requires the knowledge of the reader antenna instantaneous position to determine the tagged item location. This is easily guaranteed in such scenario already equipped with a handling system such as automatic warehouses (Fig. 1a) or overhead travelling crane warehouses (Fig. 1b). If the reader antenna can slide along two perpendicular directions, a bi-dimensional localization on the plane parallel to the antenna plane is possible. Preliminary simulated results have been recently presented in smart bookshelf scenario [4].

(a) (b)

Fig. 1. Examples of handling system in (a) automatic warehouses and (b) overhead travelling crane warehouses.

A. Measurement setup

A preliminary measurements campaign has been carried out at the Near-Field (NF) facility of the University of Oviedo (Fig. 2) were a small anechoic chamber ($1.5 \times 1.5 \times 0.4$ m^3) is available. In such ideal scenario, it is possible to evaluate the effect of the mutual coupling among tags.

The hardware consists of: Impinj Speedway R420 Revolution reader, a circularly-polarized WANTENNAX005 CAEN antenna, Smartrac-Dogbone tags equipped with Impinj-Monza4 chip. The reader antenna can move on the *xy*-plane at a speed of v=0.15 m/s. In particular, an L-shape trajectory, parallel to the upper border and left border, has been considered (each path is 1.4 m long) at a height of z_{ant}=1 m from the chamber floor. A square panel with 6×6 tags has been arranged on the floor of the NF chamber. The coordinate system is centered on the up-left corner tag (Fig. 2). The (m, n) tag is located in coordinates p_{tag}=[x_{tag}, y_{tag}, z_{tag}]=[(m-1)*d_{tag}, (n-1)*d_{tag}, 0], where d_{tag}=30 cm is the inter-tag distance. The operating frequency has been set at f_0=867.5 MHz (ETSI channel 13), and the reader sends query commands with an interval IRT=500 ms (IRT=Interrogation Repetition Time). It follows, that tag readings are collected with a spatial sampling interval of around Δx=Δy=7.5 cm.

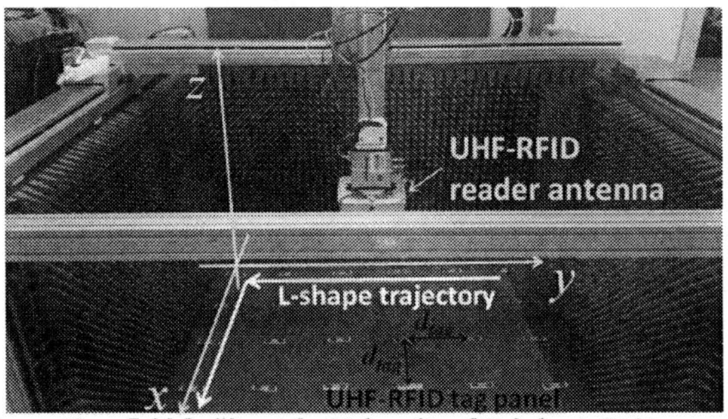

Fig. 2. Near-field facility at the University of Oviedo. A 6×6 tag panel has been placed on the camera floor. The reader antenna moves at a speed of v=0.15 m/s on the xy-plane.

III. Localization Performance

The relative phase history measured at the reader side is illustrated in Fig. 3, for the tag (1, 2) (circle marker) and the tag (6, 4) (square marker). By knowledge the reader antenna trajectory and the actual tag position, it is possible to calculate the theoretical phase history (empty-marker curves in Fig. 3). Due to the low-speed system, a large number of samples can be collected for each tag (207 for tag (1, 2) and 203 for tag (6, 4)), and a good agreement between the measured and the theoretical curves can be observed.

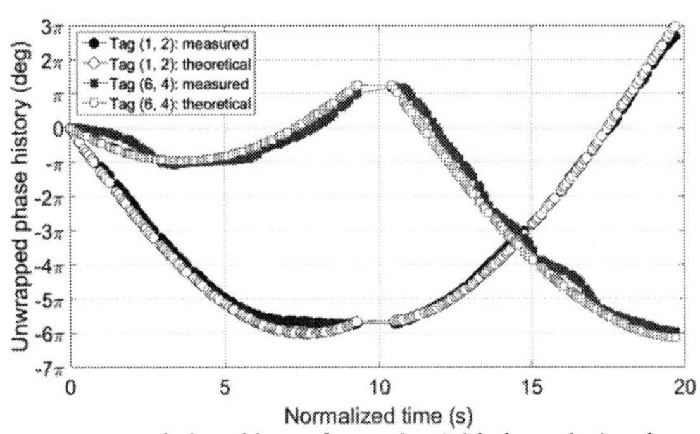

Fig. 3 Measured phase history for tag (1, 2) (circle marker) and tag (6, 4) (square marker) placed at [x_{tag}, y_{tag}, z_{tag}]=[0, 0.3, 0] m and [x_{tag}, y_{tag}, z_{tag}]=[1.5, 0.9, 0] m, respectively. The theoretical phase history is also added (empty-marker). The following system parameters have been considered: f_0=865.7 MHz, IRT=500 ms, v=0.15 m/s, z_{ant}=1 m.

By applying the SARFID technique to the measured phase histories of Fig. 3, the resulting bi-dimensional matching functions are represented in Fig. 4 with respect to the hypothetical tag coordinates in the xy plane, for the tag (1, 2) (Fig. 4a) and the tag (6, 4) (Fig. 4b). In both cases, a well distinct peak appears with a level of the secondary lobe less than 0.65. The estimated tag positions are [0.02, 0.3] m and [1.46, 0.9] m for tag (1, 2) and tag (6, 4), respectively. By considering all 36 tags in the scenario, a mean localization error less than 6 cm can be obtained for both coordinates (Fig. 5), confirming the good algorithm capability to locate a tagged item in a 2D plane. Work is in progress to evaluate the better reader antenna trajectory with respect to the tags population and to investigate the localization accuracy in dense scenario with tens of tags.

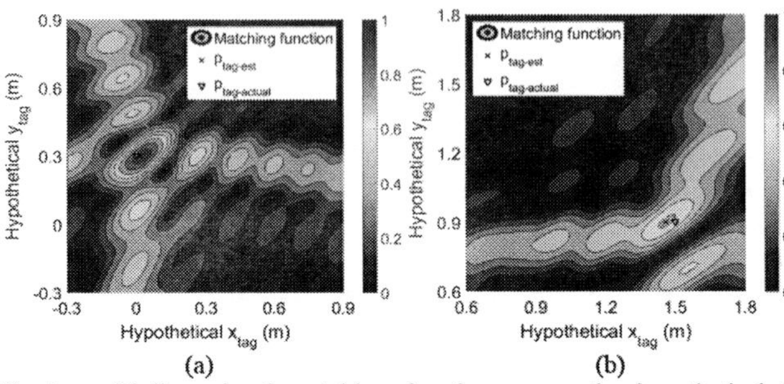

Fig. 4. Bi-dimensional matching function versus the hypothetical tag coordinates in the xy plane when considering 2 tags at the positions: (a) [0, 0.3, 0] m and (b) [1.5, 0.9, 0] m within a panel of 6×6 tags. Scanning and geometrical parameters are as in Fig. 3.

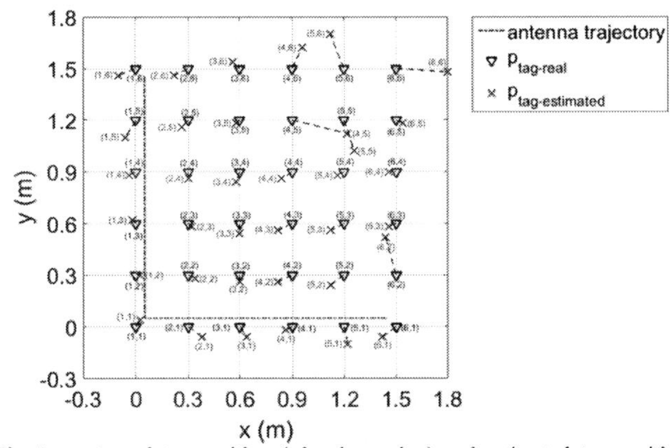

Fig. 5. Actual tag position (triangle marker) and estimated tag position (cross marker) for 6×6 tags at a distance of d_{tag}=30 cm each other's. Scanning and geometrical parameters are as in Fig. 3.

References

[1] P. V. Nikitin, R. Martinez, S. Ramamurthy, H. Leland, G. Spiess and K. V. S. Rao, "Phase based spatial identification of UHF RFID tags", *2010 IEEE International Conference on RFID (IEEE RFID 2010)*, Orlando, FL, 2010, pp. 102-109.

[2] P. Nepa, F. Lombardini, A. Buffi, "Method for determining the location of a moving RFID tag", EP2533173 (A1), IP: University of Pisa.

[3] A. Buffi, P. Nepa, F. Lombardini, "A Phase-Based Technique for Localization of UHF-RFID Tags Moving on a Conveyor Belt: Performance Analysis and Test-Case Measurements", *IEEE Sensors Journal*, vol. 15, no. 1, pp. 387-396, Jan. 2015.

[4] A. Buffi and P. Nepa, "Advanced SARFID: A localization technique for UHF RFID tags", *2016 URSI International Symposium on Electromagnetic Theory (EMTS)*, Espoo, 2016, pp. 322-325.

A Proximity Wireless Sensor Based on Backscatter Communication

Angel Servent
School of Engineering, Telecommunication and Aerospace of Castelldefels
Polytechnic University of Catalunya
Castelldels 08860, Bsrcelona, Spain

Spyros Daskalakis. Ana Collado, Apostolos Georgiadis
School of Engineering and Physical Sciences
Heriot-Watt University
Edinburgh EH14 4AS, Scotland, UK
a.georgiadis@hw.ac.uk

***Abstract*—A proximity sensor is designed as an antenna-based sensor, operating at 2.4 GHz. The operating principle relies on the fact that when an object approaches an antenna, it affects its radiation properties and its input impedance. A diode power detector is used to sense the antenna input impedance variation as a reflected wave at the input terminals of the antenna. The detector output analog dc voltage is read using an analog-to-digital (ADC) of a low power microcontroller and subsequently it is conveyed back to a reader using UHF backscatter communication based on the WISP architecture.**

Keywords—RFID, power decteor, antenna based sensor, proximity sensor, IoT

I. INTRODUCTION

The design of ultra-low power wireless sensor circuits is receiving significant interested as part of implementing the Internet-of-Things (IoT) [1]. RFID technology is considered one of the enabling technologies of IoT due to the simplicity of the tag circuit as well as the ability to operate with very low power based on backscatter communication.

Antenna based sensing has been introduced in RFID systems, to enhance their functionality by integrating sensing features in addition to identification in a simple manner [2]. Specifically, the circuit external to the tag IC is designed in such a way that a desired sensing parameter like the presence of a gas, temperature or humidity variation, object proximity results in a modification of the tag antenna radiation and impedance properties, or the impedance matching between the antenna and the tag IC, thus modifying the backscattered signal from the tag which can be detected by an RFID reader as a measure of the sensing parameter.

In this paper, the feasibility of a proximity sensor based on a 2.4 GHz patch antenna is investigated. First, the effect on the patch input impedance of a metallic rectangular sheet placed at a certain distance above the patch is investigated in simulation and measurements. Second, a diode detector circuit is designed and used to convert variations in the reflected signal at the patch input due to the presence of the metallic object in dc voltage. The patch antenna is excited using a continuous wave signal from a commercial signal generator. Third, a wireless sensor board is designed based on a MSP430 microcontroller, operating as a passive RFID backscatter node based on the WISP prototype [3] and one of its analog-to-digital (ADC) input pins is used to read the detector voltage and return this information in addition to its identification number when interrogated by a commercial RFID Impinj reader. Preliminary experiments utilizing a wired connection between the reader and the RFID enabled sensor tag are shown. Future work consists of implementing a low power high efficiency oscillator (similar to [4]) and integrating the oscillator and patch antenna with the RFID circuit in order to demonstrate wireless operation.

II. ANTENNA-BASED PROXIMITY SENSOR

The input s-parameters of a probe fed patch antenna designed on a 0.5 mm Duroid 5880 substrate, are measured while a metallic plate is placed on different distance values above the patch. The measurement and simulation setup is shown in Fig. 1.

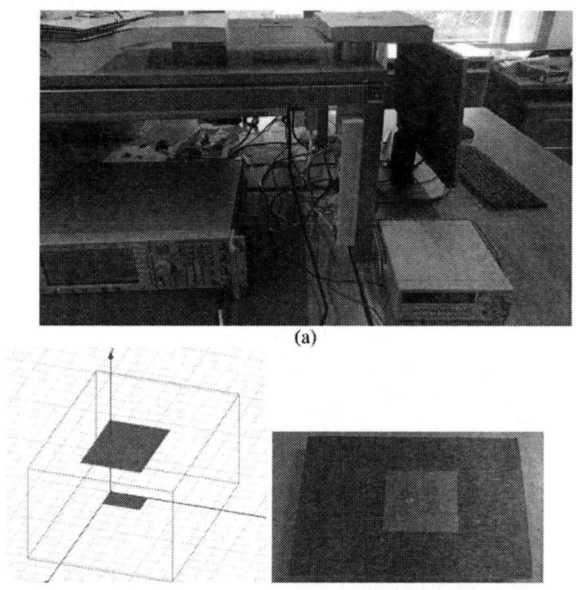

(a)

(b)

Fig. 1. Patch antenna with metallic object in placed in proximity, a) measurement setup, b) simulation setup.

A power detector using the SMS7630 Schottky diode connected in parallel to the antenna feed line was implemented (Fig. 2) in order to convert the antenna impedance variation due to the presence of the metallic object in dc voltage. Fig. 3 and Fig. 4 show the output voltage of the detector for different RF frequencies and object distance values respectively.

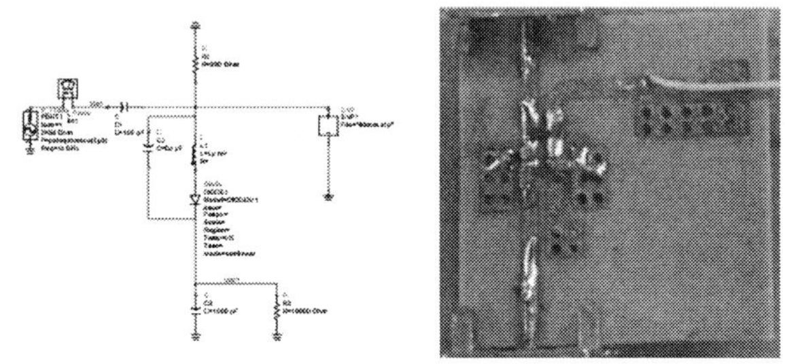

Fig. 2. Power detector circuit schematic (left) and prototype (right).

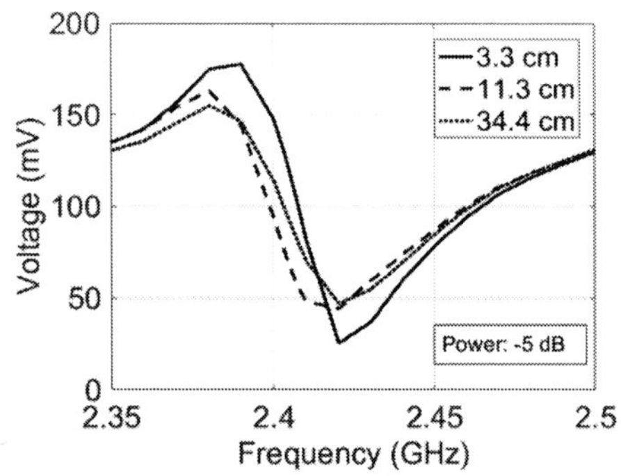

Fig. 3. Power detector output dc voltage versus the RF signal frequency for different distances of the metallic object from the patch. The transmit power is fixed at -5 dBm.

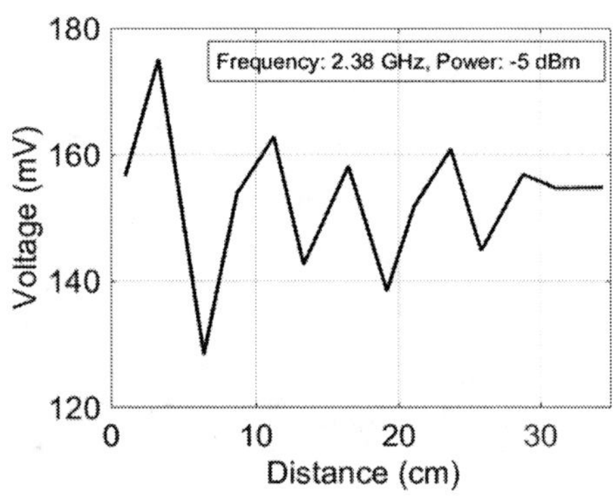

Fig. 4. Power detector output dc voltage versus distance at RF signal frequency of 2.38 GHz and transmit power of -5 dBm.

III. Communication

Finally, Fig. 5 shows the WISP type wireless sensor node operating as an RFID tag, and a screenshot of the read of the sensor node when interrogated by a commercial reader, where the jump in the reading is due to the presence of the metallic object.

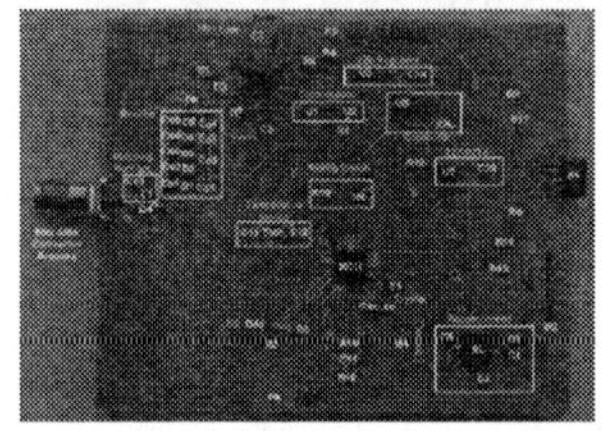

(a)

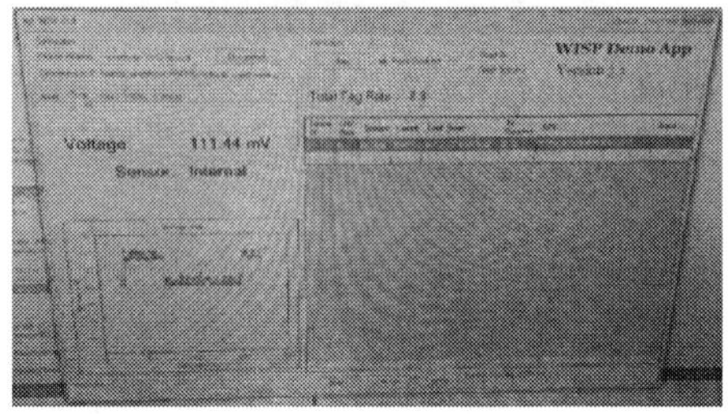

(b)

Fig.5. Wireless sensor node (a), and (b) demonstration of sensing operation.

IV. Conclusion

The feasibility of an antenna based proximity sensor is investigated. The sensing operation is performed at 2.4 GHz, while communication is based on a UHF Gen 2 RFID system similar to a WISP node. It is verified that the presence of metallic objects in close proximity of approximately 4-5 cm can be easily detected, while the presence of objects in larger distances of approximately 40 cm may require careful calibration, additional signal processing or multiple frequency detection.

Acknowledgment

The authors would like to acknowledge EU COST IC1301 Action on Wireless Power Transmission for Sustainable Electronics. The work of A. Georgiadis was supported under EU H2020 Marie Sklodowska-Curie Grant Agreement 661621.

References

[1] S. Kim, R. Vyas, J. Bito, K. Niotaki, A. Collado, A. Georgiadis, M.M. Tentzeris, "Ambient RF Energy-Harvesting Technologies for Self-Sustainable Standalone Wireless Sensor Platforms," in Proceedings of the IEEE , vol.102, no.11, pp.1649-1666, Nov. 2014.

[2] R. Bhattacharyya, C. Floerkemeier and S. Sarma, "Low-Cost, Ubiquitous RFID-Tag-Antenna-Based Sensing," in *Proceedings of the IEEE*, vol. 98, no. 9, pp. 1593-1600, Sept. 2010.

[3] A.P. Sample, D.J. Yeager, P.S. Powledge, A.V. Mamishev, J.R. Smith, "Design of an RFID-Based Battery-Free Programmable Sensing Platform," in Instrumentation and Measurement, IEEE Transactions on , vol.57, no.11, pp.2608-2615, Nov. 2008.

A. Georgiadis and A. Collado, "Solar powered Class-E active antenna oscillator for wireless power transmission," *2013 IEEE Radio and Wireless Symposium*, Austin, TX, 2013, pp. 40-42.

Experimental Assessment of a Design Criterion for RFID Wearable Antennas

P. Nepa, A. Michel, G. Manara
Dept. Information Engineering
University of Pisa
Pisa, Italy
p.nepa[a.michel,
g.manara]@iet.unipi.it

R. Colella, L. Catarinucci, L. Tarricone
Electromagnetic Lab Lecce (EML2)
University of Salento
Lecce, Italy
riccardo.colella[luca.catarinucci,
luciano.tarricone]@unisalento.it

G. A. Casula, G. Mazzarella, G. Montisci
Dip. Ing. Elettrica Elettronica
University of Cagliari
Cagliari, Italy
a.casula[mazzarella]@diee.unica.it,
giorgio.montisci@unica.it

***Abstract*—An experimental approach is proposed to validate the theoretical energy-based considerations for wearable UHF RFID antenna design. On the basis of numerical analysis, it has been shown that wearable antennas presenting an energy density peak far from the antenna border are more robust with respect to the distance from the human body. A flexible and cost-effective RFID tag characterization and performance evaluation platform is used here to validate the theoretical approach by considering a grounded UHF RFID tag.**

***Keywords*—wearable UHF RFID tag, Internet of Things, RFID Tag characterization system, body-antenna coupling**

I. Introduction

In the last few decades, hundreds of scientific papers on wearable wireless devices have been published for a large variety of applications related to the concept of Internet of Things [1], [2]. One of the challenges in the antenna design is making the antenna as robust as possible with respect to the random changes of the body-antenna coupling scenario (antenna-body distance changes randomly due to the wearer natural movements, and the dielectric and geometrical parameters of the human body tissues vary from person to person [3]-[6]). As a matter of fact, the strong coupling with the human body, which is a lossy and non-homogeneous material, can significantly degrade the antenna performance with respect to the case of free-space applications, modifying both the resonant frequency and the input impedance as well as degrading the radiation efficiency, due to the high absorption of the dispersive human tissues.

Recently, a design criterion to improve the antenna performance robustness has been presented [4]-[6]. On the basis of the numerical analysis of the electric and magnetic energy densities distributions around the antenna border, a proper ground plane and antenna shape and size can be chosen in order to make the antenna more robust to the antenna-body distance variation, without significantly increasing the antenna extent. Such an analysis has been presented for both grounded (PIFA) [4] and single-layer [5]-[6] antennas. In general, it has been demonstrated that a lower value of coupling between the antenna and the human body can be found if the maxima of the electric energy density are in the central part of the antenna. The maxima of the magnetic energy density should be therefore positioned close to the antenna borders, since they correspond, by duality, to the minima of the electric energy density, and vice-versa.

In this paper, a measurement setup is proposed to experimentally validate the effectiveness of such a theoretical approach for UHF RFID grounded tag antennas. Specifically, a flexible and cost-effective RFID tag characterization and performance evaluation platform is considered [7] for the calculation of the main metrics characterizing an RFID tag as a function of the tag activation power threshold when varying both interrogation frequency and tag orientation. By means of this platform, the main metrics used to assess the antenna performance (*i.e.* the power transfer efficiency, and the antenna radiation efficiency) can be estimated as a function of the distance between the tag and a human-body phantom.

II. Wearable RFID Tag Performance Evaluation

In [4]-[6], wearable antennas already presented in the scientific literature have been taken into account. In order to analyze the body-antenna coupling effect on the antenna performance, a numerical phantom has been added to the simulation scenario. Then, the radiation efficiency η and the power transmission coefficient τ have been numerically computed as a function of the antenna-body distance. The τ value has been calculated as

$$\tau = 1 - \left|\frac{Z_{IN} - Z_0^*}{Z_{IN} + Z_0}\right|^2 = \frac{4\,\mathrm{Re}(Z_0)\,\mathrm{Re}(Z_{IN})}{\left|Z_0 + Z_{IN}\right|^2} \qquad (1)$$

wherein Z_{IN} is the antenna input impedance, and Z_0 is a reference impedance. To analyze the robustness of the different antenna layouts with respect to the variations of the antenna-phantom model separation d, Z_0 has been assumed equal to the antenna input impedance at the resonant frequency and for d=0 mm (*i.e.*, the configuration with the antenna adherent to the body model). Then, the wearable antenna performance robustness has been estimated by means of two metrics, τ and $\tau \times \eta$, which are computed as a function of d. Therefore, for a given UHF RFID tag antenna layout such as the one presented in [4] and reported in Fig. 1 (ANT), two layout modifications can be taken into account [4]-[6]: ANT-H, in which the ground plane is extended toward the regions close to a magnetic energy density peak (Fig.1b), and ANT-E, in which the ground plane is extended toward the regions close to an electric energy density peak (Fig.1c);. In Fig.1d-e the variation against d of τ and $\tau \times \eta$ is shown for the three considered configurations. The robustness of the ANT-E configuration with respect to the body-antenna distance variation is apparent, whereas the ANT-H configuration presents only a negligible improvement with respect to the ANT configuration. This demonstrates that ground plane enlarging is more effective at those sections of the antenna border where the electric energy density exhibits a peak.

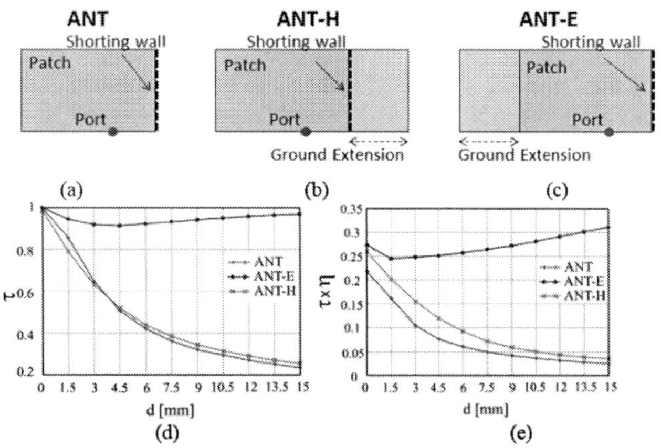

Fig.1. Layouts of the PIFA antenna considered in [4]: (a) ANT, (b) ANT-H, and (c) ANT-E configurations. Numerical results presented in [4] in terms of (d) τ and (e) $\tau \times \eta$ are also shown as a function of the antenna-body distance.

To experimentally validate the afore-described theoretical considerations, the two metrics, τ and $\tau \times \eta$, can be measured as a function of the distance d between a wearable UHF RFID tag antenna prototype and a human-body phantom, by considering different antenna layouts (*i.e.* ANT, ANT-E and ANT-H). Specifically, the antenna input impedance can be measured by means of a Vector Network Analyzer, for different antenna-body distances. Then, a commercial RFID chip can be soldered and the τ can be computed. Furthermore, in order to evaluate the term $\tau \times \eta$ when varying the distance d, an enhancement of the theoretical model proposed in [7] for the over-the-air evaluation of the whole tag sensitivity S_{tag} is proposed. In particular, the following formula was derived:

$$S_{tag} = \frac{S_{chip}}{\tau \cdot G_{tag}} = P_{tx,\mathrm{ON}} \cdot G_{tx} \cdot \left(\frac{\lambda}{4\pi d_{tag}} \right)^2 \eta_{plf} \cdot A_{cable} \qquad (2)$$

where the term $P_{tx,ON}$ denotes the minimum power value emitted by the RFID reader which turns on the chip (in correspondence of S_{chip}), G_{tx} and G_{tag} are the maximum gain of the reader and the tag antenna, respectively, λ is the wavelength in free space; d_{tag} is the distance between RFID tag and reader; η_{plf} is the polarization loss factor depending on the tag antenna structure; A_{cable} is the attenuation due to the cable connecting reader and antenna.

By rewriting (2) as a function of $\tau \times G_{tag}$ and by setting the directivity of the tag under test, the desired term $\tau \times \eta$ can be straightforwardly calculated when the distance d between tag and human tissue is varying. The architecture of the experimental setup for the evaluation of such a metric is shown in Fig. 2.

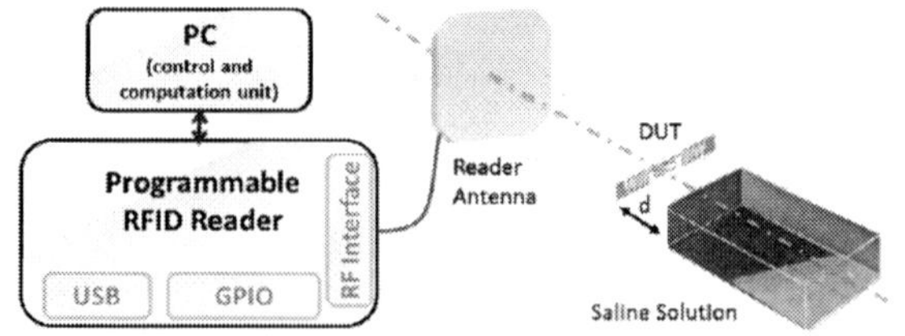

Fig.2. Architecture of the proposed RFID Tag characterization system.

The system is mainly composed of a special multi-programmable UHF RFID reader board, the ThingMagic Mercury 6e (M6e), having its RF interface connected to a patch antenna with known electromagnetic characteristics. This reader board allows to modify both the emitted power (in the range 5 – 31.5 dBm in steps of 0.5 dB) and the working frequency in the whole RFID bandwidth. It is worth highlighting that the wide power excursion along with the good power resolution of this reader are suitable features to allow the implementation of a measurement procedure based on the iterative research of the tag activation power threshold $P_{tx,ON}$, crucial in the calculation of the metric of interest. In the setup, the human tissue is simulated through a specific saline solution that allows to effectively simulate its dielectric properties [6].

REFERENCES

[1] P.S. Hall, Y. Hao, V.I. Nechayev, A. Alomainy, C.C. Constantinou, C. Parini, M.R. Kamarudin, T.Z. Salim, D.T.M. Heel, R. Dubrovka, A.S. Owadall, W. Song, A.A. Serra, P. Nepa, M. Gallo and M. Bozzetti, "Antennas and Propagation for On-Body Communication Systems", *IEEE Antennas and Propagation Magazine*, vol. 49(3), pp. 41–58, 2007.

[2] P. Nepa and H. Rogier, "Wearable antennas for off-body radio links at VHF and UHF bands (below 1 GHz): challenges, state-of-the-art and future trends," *IEEE Ant. Propag. Magaz.*, vol. 57, no. 5, 2015

[3] A. Michel, K. Karathanasis, P. Nepa and J.L. Volakis, "Accuracy of a Multi-probe Conformal Sensor in Estimating the Dielectric Constant in Deep Biological Tissues", *IEEE Sensors Journal*, vol. 15, no. 9, pp. 5217-5221, Sept. 2015.

[4] G.A. Casula, A. Michel, P. Nepa and G. Montisci, "Robustness of Wearable UHF-Band PIFAs to Human-Body Proximity", *IEEE Trans. Antennas Propag.*, vol. 64, no. 5, 2016.

[5] G. A. Casula, G. Montisci, A. Michel, and P. Nepa, "Analysis of Wearable Ungrounded Antennas for UHF RFIDs with respect to the coupling with Human-Body", IEEE International Conference on RFID Technology and Applications (RFID-TA), Shunde, Sept. 2016

[6] G.A. Casula, A. Michel, G. Montisci, P. Nepa, and G. Valente, "Energy-based Considerations for Ungrounded Wearable UHF Antenna Design", to appear on *IEEE Sensor Journal*

[7] R. Colella, L. Catarinucci, P. Coppola, and L. Tarricone, "Measurement Platform for Electromagnetic Characterization and Performance Evaluation of UHF RFID Tags," *IEEE Trans. on Instrumentation and Measurement*, vol. 65, no. 4, pp. 905-914, Apr 2016.

Sensor Selection via Convex Optimization in Remote Contact-free Measurement of Currents

Fatemeh Ghasemifard
School of Electrical Engineering
KTH Royal Institute of Technology
Stockholm, Sweden
Email: fatemehg@kth.se

Martin Norgren
School of Electrical Engineering
KTH Royal Institute of Technology
Stockholm, Sweden
Email: mnorgren@kth.se

***Abstract*—The sensor positions have substantial effect on the accuracy of remote contact-free reconstruction of currents in power transmission lines from magnetic field data, measured by a set of sensors located under the conductors. By maximizing a performance metric, based on the Fisher information matrix, $N_{\rm opt}$ sensors are selected from N candidate sensors. The main optimization problem is changed to a convex optimization problem using a relaxation of the integer constraints. The result for optimized sensor positions for a remote current reconstruction in power transmission lines using a planar sensor array is demonstrated.**

I. Introduction

Remote contact-free measurement of currents [1] and voltages [2] in power transmission lines could improve the reliability of the power system by providing more information about the transported power and the state of the grid [3], [4]. These techniques provide the possibility of measuring high-frequency voltages and currents, as well as, measuring voltages and currents at locations where measurement transformers cannot be installed. Hence, the contact-free technique could be a complement to the established technique of using measurement transformers.

Contact-free measurement of currents is a magnetic inverse source problems, where the currents are reconstructed using magnetic field data collected by a set of sensors located in the vicinity of the conductors [3], [5]. One significant difficulty is the influence of the magnetic field generated by other sources. In our recent work [3], the external magnetic field is modeled by an expansion into spherical harmonics, whose coefficients are determined together with the sought currents. This method can handle effectively the effect of disturbance fields, but in [3] we did not consider optimizing the sensor positions. Since the sensor positions have substantial effect on the accuracy of the current reconstruction, it is possible to reduce the effect of disturbance fields even further by finding the optimal positions of the sensors [5], [6].

In this paper, we extend our recent work [3] by sensor selection based on Convex Optimization [7]. Following the method presented in [7], we select $N_{\rm opt}$ sensors among N candidates by minimizing the negative of the determinant of the Fisher Information matrix [8]. By relaxing the integer constraints, we obtain a convex optimization problem, as explained in the next section.

II. Sensor Selection Optimization Problem

In the current reconstruction method proposed in [3], the x-, y-, and z-components of the magnetic field, measured by each sensor, are represented by linear combinations of the currents $\{I_i\}_{i=1}^3$ to be reconstructed and the unknown expansion coefficients, $\mathbf{A}_{\ell m}$, of the spherical harmonics. As a result, arranging all the parameters to be estimated in the vector $\mathbf{p} = \{\mathrm{Re}(I_i), \mathrm{Im}(I_i), \mathrm{Re}(\mathbf{A}_{\ell m}), \mathrm{Im}(\mathbf{A}_{\ell m})\}_{i=1}^3$, where the number of elements in $\mathbf{A}_{\ell m}$ depends on ℓ_{max}, the truncation number in spherical harmonic expansion [3], we have

$$B_{j,x} = \mathbf{a}_{j,x}^{\mathrm{T}}\mathbf{p} + n_{j,x}, \quad j = 1, ..., N, \tag{1}$$

$$B_{j,y} = \mathbf{a}_{j,y}^{\mathrm{T}}\mathbf{p} + n_{j,y}, \quad j = 1, ..., N, \tag{2}$$

$$B_{j,z} = \mathbf{a}_{j,z}^{\mathrm{T}}\mathbf{p} + n_{j,z}, \quad j = 1, ..., N, \tag{3}$$

where N is the number of measurement points, $\mathbf{B}_j = (B_{j,x}, B_{j,y}, B_{j,z})$ is the magnetic field data collected by the j-th sensor and $n_{j,x}$, $n_{j,y}$, $n_{j,z}$ are independent identically distributed Gaussian noise with mean zero and variance σ^2.

Note, if only the currents $\{I_i\}_{i=1}^3$ were to be reconstructed, we would have a biased reconstruction problem, with an unknown bias due to the disturbance field. Nevertheless, since both $\{I_i\}_{i=1}^3$ and $\mathbf{A}_{\ell m}$ are reconstructed, the reconstruction problem is unbiased. Thus, the Cramér-Rao lower bound (CRLB) theorem $\mathbf{C_p} \succeq \mathbf{I}^{-1}$, where $\mathbf{C_p}$ is the covariance matrix of the estimated parameters and $\mathbf{I}$ is the Fisher information matrix, is applicable. As a result, the Fisher information matrix could be a metric for the performance of the parameter estimation. In fact, the efficiency of the current reconstruction method is expected to improve by maximizing $\mathbf{I}$ in some sense. However, in general, it is not possible to find an optimal $\mathbf{I}$. Instead, a D-optimal solution [7] is sought, which means maximizing $\log\det(\mathbf{I})$ or minimizing $-\log\det(\mathbf{I})$.

The Fisher Information matrix, $\mathbf{I}$, is defined as [8], [9]

$$\mathbf{I} = \sum_{j=1}^{N} \mathbf{I}_j, \tag{4}$$

where $\mathbf{I}_j$, the Fisher information matrix corresponding to the j-th sensor, is defined as

$$\mathbf{I}_j = \frac{2}{\sigma^2}\mathrm{Re}\left\{(\nabla_{\mathbf{p}}\mathbf{B}_j)^{\mathrm{H}}\nabla_{\mathbf{p}}\mathbf{B}_j\right\}. \tag{5}$$

In (5), H denotes the conjugate transpose and $\nabla_{\mathbf{p}}\mathbf{B}_j = [\mathbf{a}_{j,x}\ \mathbf{a}_{j,y}\ \mathbf{a}_{j,z}]^{\mathrm{T}}$. Now, the sensor selection problem of finding N_{opt} D-optimal sensors from N candidates can be formulated as

$$\begin{aligned} \underset{w_j}{\text{minimize}} \quad & -\log\det\left(\frac{\sum_{j=1}^{N} w_j \mathbf{I}_j}{N_{\mathrm{opt}}}\right) \\ \text{subject to} \quad & w_j \in \{0,1\},\ j = 1, ..., N, \\ & \sum_{j=1}^{N} w_j = N_{\mathrm{opt}}. \end{aligned} \tag{6}$$

In (6), $w_j = 1$ means the j-th sensor should be used and $w_j = 0$ means the j-th sensor should be removed. There are $\binom{N}{N_{\mathrm{opt}}}$ combinations for selecting N_{opt} out of N sensors. Thus, (6) can be solved only for small N by an exhaustive search. However, when N is large, a relaxation of the integer constraints [7] turns (6) into a convex optimization problem, which can be readily solved using the CVX package [10]. In the relaxation, we assume that all N sensors are used to measure the magnetic field and that the weight on the j-th sensor is $\lambda_j = w_j/N_{\mathrm{opt}}$. Thus, the relaxed problem is formulated as

$$\begin{aligned} \underset{w_j}{\text{minimize}} \quad & -\log\det\left(\sum_{j=1}^{N} \lambda_j \mathbf{I}_j\right) \\ \text{subject to} \quad & 0 \le \lambda_j \le 1/N_{\mathrm{opt}},\ j = 1, ..., N, \\ & \sum_{j=1}^{N} \lambda_j = 1. \end{aligned} \tag{7}$$

The upper bound on λ_j ensures that at least N_{opt} weights are non-zero.

III. Result

Consider the example of reconstructing currents in three power transmission lines with a magnetic dipole and three line sources as external sources presented in [3]. The potential sensor positions are 21×21 measurement points (blue crosses in Fig. 1) distributed equidistantly with the separation 0.2 m in both x- and y-direction over a square measurement plane located at the height $z = 1.5$ m and with its boundaries at $x,\ y = \pm 2$ m. CVX package [10] is used to solve the relaxed convex optimization problem (7) with $N = 441$ and $N_{\mathrm{opt}} = 216$. It should be mentioned that calculating $\mathbf{I}_j$ was done by setting $\ell_{max} = 4$ for truncating the spherical harmonic expansion [3]. The result of sensor selection which is shown in Fig. 1 by red circles were 224 sensor positions with $\lambda_j > 10^{-3}$. It means the sensors with $\lambda_j < 10^{-3}$ can be removed. The currents were estimated using 224 sensors located at optimal sensor positions rather than using 441 sensors, but the variance of the estimated currents remained almost the same as the case when 441 sensors was used. However, the speed of the current estimation improved a lot.

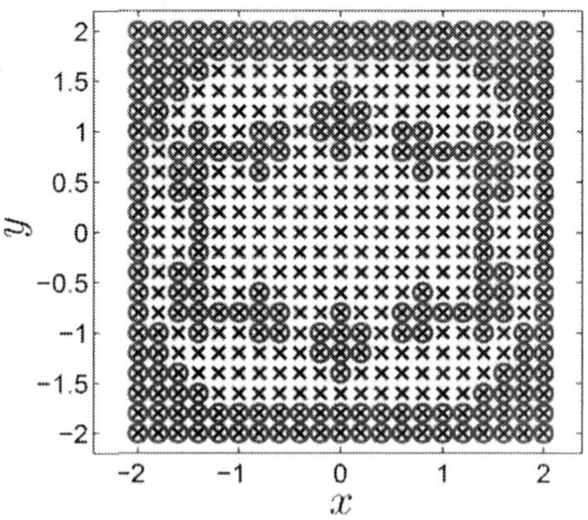

Fig. 1: The potential positions of the sensors (blue crosses) and the optimal positions of the sensors (red circles).

IV. Conclusions and Future Work

In this paper, a method for sensor selection based on convex optimization in remote contact-free reconstruction of currents in power transmission lines [3] was presented. The aim was to select N_{opt} sensors among N sensors with predetermined positions to maximize the performance of current estimation. For this purpose, the Fisher information matrix was used as a performance metric. This optimization problem could be solved only when the number of the potential sensors is small. To be able to find the solution for the large numbers of the potential sensors, the main optimization problem was altered into a convex problem by relaxing the integer constraint.

In future work, this method will be compared with other sensor selection methods, like the one in [6], and also tested with measurement data.

References

[1] Kruphalan Tamil Selvaa, et al., "Non-contact Current Measurement in Power Transmission Lines," *Procedia Technology: Smart Grid Technologies*, vol. 21, pp. 498–506, 2015.

[2] J. Törnqvist, Non-contact High Voltage Measurements: Modeling and On-site Evaluation, Umeå University, Umeå, Sweden, Tech. Rep., 2012.

[3] F. Ghasemifard, M. Johansson, and M. Norgren, "Current reconstruction from magnetic field using spherical harmonic expansion to reduce impact of disturbance fields," Submitted to *Inverse Problems in Sci. and Eng.*, pp. 1–15, 2016.

[4] F. Ghasemifard and M. Norgren, "Contact-free measurement of currents in two-dimensional parallel conductors using the Green identity approach," in *2016 URSI International Symposium on Electromagnetic Theory (EMTS)*, Aug. 2016, pp. 338–340.

[5] M. Norgren, "Explicit reconstruction of line-currents and their positions in a two-dimentional parallel conductor structure," *Inverse Problems in Sci. and Eng.*, vol. 22, no. 7, pp. 1196–1213, 2013.

[6] Z. Zhang Z, L. Di Rienzo, "Optimization of magnetic sensor arrays for current measurement based on swarm intelligence and D-optimality," *COMPEL - Int. J. Comput. Math. Electr. Electron. Eng.*, vol. 28, pp. 1179–1190, 2009.

[7] S. Joshi and S. Boyd, "Sensor Selection via Convex Optimization," *IEEE Trans. Signal Process.*, vol. 57, no. 2, pp. 451–462, 2009.

[8] Kay SM. Fundamentals of Statistical Signal Processing, Estimation Theory. NJ: Prentice-Hall; 1993.

[9] O. Talcoth and T. Rylander, "Sensor selection in magnetic tracking based on convex optimization," *Electronics Lett.*, vol. 49, no. 1, pp. 15–16, 2013.

[10] Grant, M., and Boyd, S.: "CVX: Matlab Software for Disciplined Convex Programming," version 2.1, October 2016, http://cvxr.com/cvx.

Magnetic Polarizability Tensors for Low Frequency Object Classification and Detection

P.D. Ledger
College of Engineering
Swansea University Bay Campus
SA1 8EN U.K.
Email: P.D.Ledger@swansea.ac.uk

W.R.B. Lionheart
School of Mathematics
The University of Manchester
M13 9PL U.K.
Email: Bill.Lionheart@manchester.ac.uk

***Abstract*—There is considerable interest in obtaining a low-cost mathematical description, which describes the interaction between a low frequency alternating magnetic field and a conducting object. Electrical engineers have proposed that the voltage perturbation in a coil placed in the field can be described in terms of a tensor that characterises its shape and material properties. In previous work [4], [6], we have obtained an explicit expression for the tensor's computation. This presentation extends on this to include a Bayesian inverse solution for the tensor coefficients of different objects. This has important applications in metal detectors for landmine clearance and airport security.**

I. Introduction

Metal detectors are widely used for locating hidden highly conducting objects in landmine clearance, for identifying threat items at airports and public events, locating buried treasure as well as finding items of archaeological significance. While metal detectors offer a low-cost portable means of detection, they are not able to distinguish between different shapes of conducting objects and there are challenges in differentiating between small objects concealed at small depths and larger objects, which might be buried deeper underground.

Location and discriminating between different objects requires the solution of an inverse problem. These are both mathematically and computationally challenging due to limited amounts of noisy measured data and the difficulty of inverting the system (the solution may not exist, be non–unique or not depend continuously on the data and hence is ill–posed). The forward, or direct, problem of determining the fields resulting from a known conducting object, is generally well–posed. In the context of metal detectors, the frequency of operation is low and the objects highly conducting so that eddy current approximation of Maxwell's equations applies.

To help address the challenges of solving the eddy current inverse problem, a low-cost description, which can characterise the shape and material properties of a conducting object in terms of a small number of parameters is used. In the electrical engineering community, it has been proposed that the voltage perturbation due to the presence of a conducting object in a single excitation–measurement coil pair is approximately

$$\boldsymbol{H}_0^{Ms}(\boldsymbol{z}) \cdot (\mathcal{M}\boldsymbol{H}_0^{Ex}(\boldsymbol{z})) \qquad (1)$$

where $\boldsymbol{H}_0^{Ex}(\boldsymbol{z})$ is the background magnetic field of the exciting (Ex) coil evaluated at the position of the target, $\boldsymbol{H}_0^{Ms}(\boldsymbol{z})$ is the background field that would result if the measurement (Ms) coil acts as a source and $\mathcal{M}$ is a rank 2 polarizability tensor, which describes the shape and material properties of the object, independent of the background field. However, apart from a spherical object, where $\mathcal{M}$ is known explicitly, it was not clear when this approximation will hold or what the form of $\mathcal{M}$ will be.

II. Asymptotic Expansions

In the applied mathematics literature, asymptotic formulae are available that describe the perturbation in the magnetic field $(\boldsymbol{H}_\alpha - \boldsymbol{H}_0^{Ex})(\boldsymbol{x})$ due to the presence of an object $B_\alpha = \alpha B + \boldsymbol{z}$, which means a unit object B placed at the origin, scaled by the object size α and translated by $\boldsymbol{z}$. Using Einstein's summation convention for implied summation in repeated indices, the ith orthonormal coordinate is

$$\begin{aligned}((\boldsymbol{H}_\alpha - \boldsymbol{H}_0^{Ex})(\boldsymbol{x}))_i =& (\boldsymbol{D}_{\boldsymbol{x}}^2 G(\boldsymbol{x},\boldsymbol{z}))_{ij}\mathcal{A}_{jk}(\boldsymbol{H}_0^{Ex}(\boldsymbol{z}))_k \\ &+ (\boldsymbol{R}(\boldsymbol{x}))_i, \end{aligned} \qquad (2)$$

as some suitable limit is taken. In the above, $\boldsymbol{R}(\boldsymbol{x})$ is a residual vector, $G(\boldsymbol{x},\boldsymbol{z}) := 1/(4\pi|\boldsymbol{x}-\boldsymbol{z}|)$, $(\boldsymbol{D}_{\boldsymbol{x}}^2 G(\boldsymbol{x},\boldsymbol{z}))_{ij} = \frac{1}{4\pi r^3}\left(3(\hat{\boldsymbol{r}})_i(\hat{\boldsymbol{r}})_j - \delta_{ij}\right)$, with $\boldsymbol{r} := \boldsymbol{x}-\boldsymbol{z}$, $r = |\boldsymbol{r}|$, $\hat{\boldsymbol{r}} = \boldsymbol{r}/r$, and δ_{ij} the Kronecker delta.

For the magnetostatic response of a small object [3], [5] then (2) holds as $\alpha \to 0$ with $\mathcal{A} = \mathcal{T}(\mu_*/\mu_0)$ being the Poylá–Szegö tensor and $\boldsymbol{R}(\boldsymbol{x}) = O(\alpha^4)$. The 6 real components of the symmetric Poylá–Szegö rank 2 tensor can be computed by solving a transmission problem [2]. This tensor is parameterised by the constant in permeability (μ_*/μ_0) and describes the response of magnetic, but not highly conducting objects.

For the eddy current case, Ammari *et al.* [1], have obtained an asymptotic formula for $(\boldsymbol{H}_\alpha - \boldsymbol{H}_0^{Ex})(\boldsymbol{x})$, which shows the response for highly conducting objects, with conductivity σ_* and permeability μ_*, can be expressed in terms of a rank 4 tensor, as $\alpha \to 0$. This, at first sight, appears to disagree with (1) however, in [4] we have shown that, for the case of orthonormal coordinates, their asymptotic expansion reduces to the form stated in (2) with $\boldsymbol{R}(\boldsymbol{x}) = O(\alpha^4)$ as $\alpha \to 0$. We provide an explicit expression for the complex symmetric rank 2 tensor $\mathcal{A} = \widetilde{\widetilde{\mathcal{M}}}$, which is different to $\mathcal{T}(\mu_*/\mu_0)$, and, if (2) is multiplied by the ith component of the dipole moment of

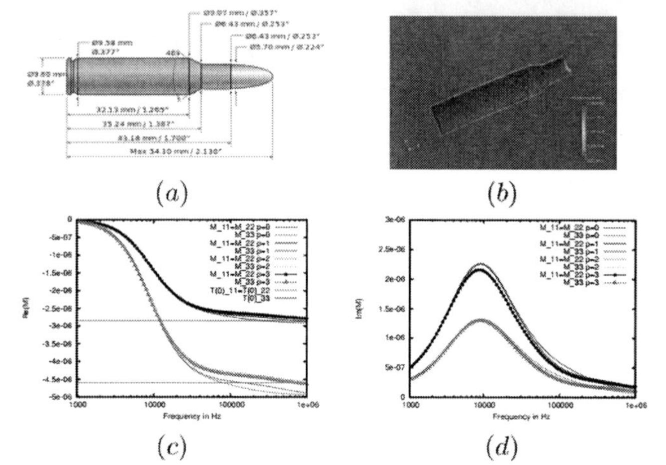

Fig. 1. Remington rifle shell casing showing: (a) geometry [7], (b) contours of $|\boldsymbol{\theta}_1|$, (c) frequency sweep of $\mathrm{Re}(\widetilde{\widetilde{\mathcal{M}}})$ and (d) frequency sweep of $\mathrm{Im}(\widetilde{\widetilde{\mathcal{M}}})$

the Ms coil, it reduces to the form in (1) thus providing a theoretical framework for the engineering prediction [4], [6].

III. Polarizability Tensor Computation

In [4], [6] we describe a numerical procedure for computing the coefficients of our $\widetilde{\widetilde{\mathcal{M}}} := \mathcal{N} - \check{\mathcal{C}}$ where

$$\check{\mathcal{C}}_{ij} := -\frac{\mathrm{i}\omega\sigma_*\mu_0\alpha^5}{4}\hat{\boldsymbol{e}}_i \cdot \int_B \boldsymbol{\xi} \times (\boldsymbol{\theta}_j + \hat{\boldsymbol{e}}_j \times \boldsymbol{\xi})\mathrm{d}\boldsymbol{\xi},$$

$$\mathcal{N}_{ij} := \alpha^3\left(1 - \frac{\mu_0}{\mu_*}\right)\int_B \left(\hat{\boldsymbol{e}}_i \cdot \hat{\boldsymbol{e}}_j + \frac{1}{2}\hat{\boldsymbol{e}}_i \cdot \nabla \times \boldsymbol{\theta}_j\right)\mathrm{d}\boldsymbol{\xi},$$

$\hat{\boldsymbol{e}}_i$ denotes the unit basis vector for the ith coordinate and $\boldsymbol{\theta}_i$ solves the vector valued transmission problem

$$\begin{aligned}
\nabla \times \mu_*^{-1}\nabla \times \boldsymbol{\theta}_i - \mathrm{i}\omega\sigma_*\alpha^2\boldsymbol{\theta}_i &= \mathrm{i}\omega\sigma_*\alpha^2\hat{\boldsymbol{e}}_i \times \boldsymbol{\xi} && \text{in } B,\\
\nabla \times \mu_0^{-1}\nabla \times \boldsymbol{\theta}_i = \mathbf{0},\ \nabla \cdot \boldsymbol{\theta}_i &= 0 && \text{in } B^c,\\
[\boldsymbol{\theta}_i \times \hat{\boldsymbol{n}}]_\Gamma &= \mathbf{0}, && \text{on } \Gamma,\\
\left[\mu^{-1}\nabla \times \boldsymbol{\theta}_i \times \hat{\boldsymbol{n}}\right]_\Gamma &= -2\left[\mu^{-1}\right]_\Gamma \hat{\boldsymbol{e}}_i \times \hat{\boldsymbol{n}} && \text{on } \Gamma,\\
\vec{\theta}_i(\boldsymbol{\xi}) &= O(|\boldsymbol{\xi}|^{-1}) \text{ as } |\boldsymbol{\xi}| \to \infty && .
\end{aligned}$$

Our approach is based on the application of high order edge-finite elements and we have previously applied it to a series of simply and multiply connected three dimensional objects. In Fig 1 we show illustrative results for a Remington rifle shell casing with $\mu_* = \mu_0$ and $\sigma_* = 1.5\times10^7$S/m with the truncated $B \cup B^c$ region discretised by 23 551 tetrahedra. The figure shows the geometry, the computed contours of a typical $|\boldsymbol{\theta}_1|$ and the convergence of $\mathrm{Re}(\widetilde{\widetilde{\mathcal{M}}})$ and $\mathrm{Im}(\widetilde{\widetilde{\mathcal{M}}})$ with polynomial refinement of the finite elements over a wide frequency range.

Depending on the symmetries of an object, we have shown that the number of independent coefficients of $\widetilde{\widetilde{\mathcal{M}}}$ can be fewer than 6 (it is 2 for the object in Fig. 1). We have obtained results for low frequency, high conductivity limiting cases of $\widetilde{\widetilde{\mathcal{M}}}$, which relate it to $\mathcal{T}(\mu_*/\mu_0)$ and $\mathcal{T}(0)$, respectively [4], [6]. We will summarise these results in our presentation.

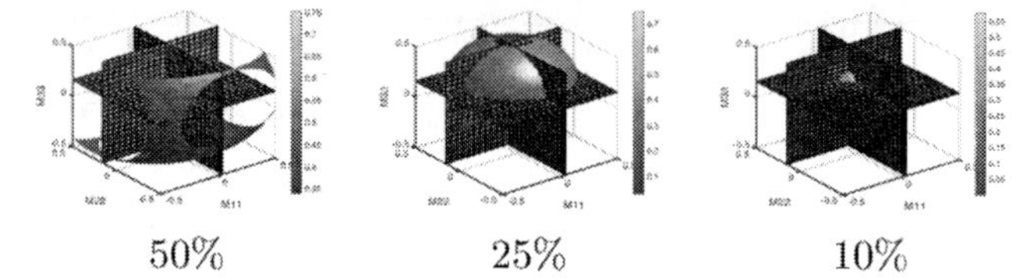

Fig. 2. Posterior probability density distribution $\pi(\boldsymbol{p}|\boldsymbol{V})$ interrogated by the MAP estimate when $\boldsymbol{p} = \{\widetilde{\widetilde{\mathcal{M}}}_{ii}, i = (1,2,3)\}$ for different noise levels

IV. Bayesian Inversion

Given a set of parameters used to describe the object, $\boldsymbol{p}$, an approach to describing the metal detection inverse problem is

$$\min_{\boldsymbol{p}} \|\boldsymbol{V} - \boldsymbol{F}(\boldsymbol{p})\|_P^2 + \lambda\|\boldsymbol{p}\|_Q^2 \qquad (3)$$

where $\boldsymbol{V}$ are the measured voltages and $\boldsymbol{F}(\boldsymbol{p})$ represents the direct problem and describes how the voltages depend on the parameters. To overcome measurement noise the regularisation term $\lambda\|\boldsymbol{p}\|_Q$ is added. For $\boldsymbol{F}(\boldsymbol{p})$ we have seen that we can use (1) and (2), which provides a rigorous way of describing objects in terms of $\widetilde{\widetilde{\mathcal{M}}}$ and its position $\boldsymbol{z}$. Typically P, Q are set as the 2-norm and Tikhonov regularisation is applied. However, there are difficulties in choosing λ as it can can dampen out or pollute the solution to (3).

In the Bayesian approach, the likelihood $\boldsymbol{V} - \boldsymbol{F}(\boldsymbol{p})$ and the previous knowledge about $\boldsymbol{p}$, known as the prior, are expressed as probability distributions, $\pi(\boldsymbol{V}|\boldsymbol{p})$ and π_{prior}, respectively. An application of Bayes' theorem leads to the result that the posterior distribution is $\pi(\boldsymbol{p}|\boldsymbol{V}) \sim \pi(\boldsymbol{V}|\boldsymbol{p})\pi_{prior}$ and, in the case of Gaussian distributions, as $\exp\{-\|\boldsymbol{V}-\boldsymbol{F}(\boldsymbol{p})\|_P^2 - \|\boldsymbol{p}\|_Q^2\}$ with P, Q being informed by the covariance of the likelihood and prior distributions, respectively. Then $\pi(\boldsymbol{p}|\boldsymbol{V})$ quantifies the uncertainty and can be interrogated to obtain different interpretations for the set of parameters $\boldsymbol{p}$ without the need to provide regularisation. Illustrative results are included in Fig. 2 and we will discuss this further in our presentation.

Acknowledgement

The authors gratefully acknowledge the support of EPSRC in the form of the grant EP/K039865/1.

References

[1] H. Ammari, J. Chen, Z. Chen, J Garnier, and D. Volkov. Target detection and characterization from electromagnetic induction data. *J. Math. Pures Appl.*, 201:54–75, 2014.

[2] H. Ammari and H. Kang. *Polarization and Moment Tensors: With Applications to Inverse Problems*. Springer, 2007.

[3] H. Ammari and D. Volkov. The leading-order term in the asymptotic expansion of the scattering amplitude of a collection of finite number dielectric inhomogeneities of small diameter. *International Journal for Multiscale Computational Engineering*, 3:149–160, 2005.

[4] P. D. Ledger and W. R. B. Lionheart. Characterising the shape and material properties of hidden targets from magnetic induction data. *IMA J. Appl. Math*, 80:1776–1798, 2015.

[5] P. D. Ledger and W. R. B. Lionheart. The perturbation of electromagnetic fields at distances that are large compared with the object's size. *IMA J. Appl. Math.*, 80:865–892, 2015.

[6] P. D. Ledger and W. R. B. Lionheart. Understanding the magnetic polarizability tensor. *IEEE Trans. Magn.*, 52:6201216, 2016.

[7] Wikipedia. https://en.wikipedia.org/wiki/.222_Remington.

Lorentz force evaluation with an extended area approach

E.-.M. Dölker[1], R. Schmidt[2], K. Weise[2], B. Petković[1], M. Ziolkowski[2], H. Brauer[2], J. Haueisen[1]
[1]Institute of Biomedical Engineering and Informatics, [2]Advanced Electromagnetics Group
Technische Universität Ilmenau
Ilmenau, Germany

***Abstract*— A goal function scan based on an extended area approach is applied to determine size and depth of a defect in Lorentz force evaluation (LFE). Four datasets of a laminated aluminium specimen with a cylindrical defect at depths of 2, 4, 8 and 14 mm are simulated with the finite element method. LFE yields the correct defect sizes and depths for all four defects with a root mean square error of 0.95, 1.21, 1.57 and 4.41 %, respectively.**

Keywords*— *Eddy current; Lorentz force evaluation; inverse problem; nondestructive evaluation

I. Introduction

The Lorentz force evaluation (LFE) deals with the reconstruction of defects from perturbations in the Lorentz force exerting on a permanent magnet that moves relative to a conductive specimen. Previous defect reconstructions, performed by truncated singular value decomposition [1], differential evolution method [2] and current density reconstruction [3] have shown a blurred depth estimation. These previous results are based on the approximate forward solution (AFS) for LFE [1]. Recently, a more accurate forward model, the extended area approach (EAA) has been proposed [4]. Thus, it is the aim to investigate the reconstruction performance in LFE using the EAA. For this task, a goal function scan is applied to four simulation data sets with different defect depths gained by finite element method (FEM).

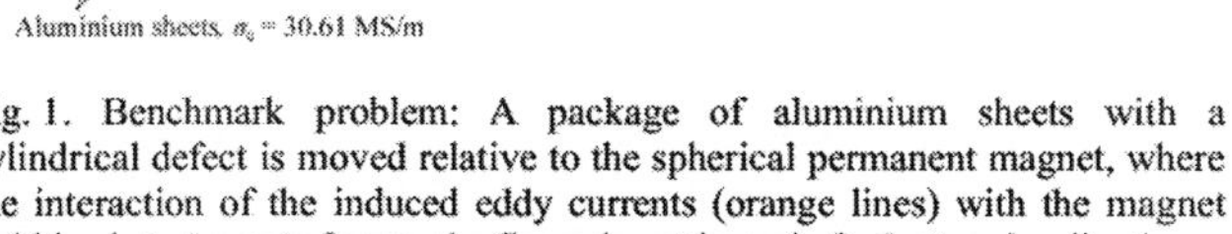

Fig. 1. Benchmark problem: A package of aluminium sheets with a cylindrical defect is moved relative to the spherical permanent magnet, where the interaction of the induced eddy currents (orange lines) with the magnet field leads to Lorentz forces; the figure is not in scale for better visualization.

This work has been supported by the Deutsche Forschungsgemeinschaft (DFG) in the framework of the Research Training Group "Lorentz force velocimetry and Lorentz force eddy current testing" (GRK 1567).

II. Methods

A. Benchmark problem

A package of stacked aluminium sheets with $L \times W \times H = 400\ \text{mm} \times 400\ \text{mm} \times 100\ \text{mm}$ and a conductivity $\sigma_0 = 30.61\ \text{MS/m}$ is moved with the velocity $v = 0.01\ \text{m/s}$ in the positive x – direction, Fig. 1. One single sheet possesses a thickness of $\Delta z = 2\ \text{mm}$. A spherical permanent magnet is located at the lift-off distance $\delta z = 1\ \text{mm}$ above the top surface of the specimen. It is characterized by the homogenous magnetization $\boldsymbol{M}$, including a remanence $B_r = 1.17\ \text{T}$, and a diameter $D_\text{m} = 15\ \text{mm}$. An ideal (conductivity $\sigma_\text{d} = 0\ \text{S/m}$) cylindrical defect with the diameter $D_\text{d} = 5\ \text{mm}$ and the height $h_\text{d} = 2\ \text{mm}$ is located at the $x-y-$ center of the specimen at the depth d. The four different defect depths $d = 2$, 4, 8 and 14 mm are analyzed.

B. Extended Area Approach

The permanent magnet is modelled as a magnetic dipole located at its center $\boldsymbol{r}_0$. The magnetic flux density at the point $\boldsymbol{r}$ can be calculated by

$$\boldsymbol{B}_\text{p} = \frac{\mu_0}{4\pi}\left(3\frac{[\boldsymbol{m}\cdot(\boldsymbol{r}-\boldsymbol{r}_0)]}{|\boldsymbol{r}-\boldsymbol{r}_0|^5}(\boldsymbol{r}-\boldsymbol{r}_0) - \frac{\boldsymbol{m}}{|\boldsymbol{r}-\boldsymbol{r}_0|^3}\right), \tag{1}$$

where $\boldsymbol{m}$ denotes the magnetic moment. Due to the small velocity $\boldsymbol{v}$, the secondary magnetic field from the induced eddy currents can be neglected. Thus, the weak reaction approach [5] can be applied.

The defect reconstruction in LFE considers only the defect response signal (DRS) $\Delta\boldsymbol{F}$. Using the EAA [4] it is defined by

$$\Delta\boldsymbol{F} = \underbrace{\int_{V-V_\text{d}} (\boldsymbol{j}-\boldsymbol{j}_0)\times \boldsymbol{B}_\text{p} dV - \underbrace{\int_{V_\text{d}} \boldsymbol{j}_0 \times \boldsymbol{B}_\text{p} dV}_{\text{AFS}}}_{\text{EAA}}, \tag{2}$$

where $\boldsymbol{j}$ and $\boldsymbol{j}_0$ represent the current density in the specimen with and without a defect, respectively. The volumes of the specimen and the defect are denoted by V and V_{d}. It can be seen, that the previously used AFS neglects the first term of (2), which means that only the defect as a fictitious conducting region is taken into account for the calculation of the DRS. The EAA approximates the first term by extending the region in the $x-$ and $y-$ direction around the defect. Discretizing the defect and the extended area into K and E cuboidal voxels, respectively, $\Delta \boldsymbol{F}$ can be approximated by [4]

$$\Delta \boldsymbol{F} \approx \sum_{e=1}^{E} \Delta \boldsymbol{j}_e \times \boldsymbol{B}_e + \sum_{k=1}^{K} \Delta \boldsymbol{j}_k \times \boldsymbol{B}_k \ . \tag{3}$$

The magnetic flux densities inside the voxels are accordingly denoted by $\boldsymbol{B}_k$ and $\boldsymbol{B}_e$. The distortion current density inside the defect $\Delta \boldsymbol{j}_k$ can be calculated by Ohm's law for moving conductors $\Delta \boldsymbol{j}_k = \sigma_0(-\nabla\varphi_k + \boldsymbol{v}\times\boldsymbol{B}_k)$ [1]. Thus, $\Delta \boldsymbol{j}_e$ can be determined by [4]

$$\Delta \boldsymbol{j}_e \cong C_{\mathrm{d}} \frac{V_{\mathrm{E}}}{2\pi \Delta z} \sum_{k=1}^{K} \left[2 \frac{\Delta \boldsymbol{j}_k \cdot (\boldsymbol{r}_e - \boldsymbol{r}_k)}{|\boldsymbol{r}_e - \boldsymbol{r}_k|^4} (\boldsymbol{r}_e - \boldsymbol{r}_k) - \frac{\Delta \boldsymbol{j}_k}{|\boldsymbol{r}_e - \boldsymbol{r}_k|^2} \right], \tag{4}$$

where V_{E} denotes the volume of one voxel. The dipolar correction factor $C_{\mathrm{d}} = 2$ holds for cylindrical defects [4]. The position vectors of the voxels' centroids in the defect and the extended region are denoted by $\boldsymbol{r}_k$ and $\boldsymbol{r}_e$.

In order to find an appropriate expansion size, $\Delta \boldsymbol{F}$ has been calculated for the benchmark problem with the defect in the 2nd layer. The squared expansion ranges from $ex = [\,0, 1, 2, \ldots, 16\,] \cdot R_{\mathrm{d}}$ in $\pm x-$ and $y-$direction, where R_{d} denotes the radius of the defect and 0 means the AFS without expansions is applied. The expansion has been chosen to $ex = 6 \cdot R_{\mathrm{d}}$ as the adapted normalized root mean square error (*aNRMSE*), (5), stopped improving. It means that for $R_{\mathrm{d}} = 2.5$ mm the used area for the whole calculation of $\Delta \boldsymbol{F}$ equals ± 15 mm in $x-$and $y-$direction.

C. Goal Function Scan

The DRS, is calculated according to (3) for different defect radii $R_{\mathrm{d}} = [\,0.5, 1.5, \ldots, 24.5\text{ mm}\,]$ from the 1st to the 11th layer. For each calculation the *aNRMSE* is determined as the goal function value by

$$aNRMSE = \frac{1}{3}\sum_{i=x,y,z}\left(\frac{\sqrt{\frac{1}{N}\sum_{n=1}^{N}\left(\Delta F_{n,i}-\Delta F_{n,i}^{\mathrm{FEM}}\right)^2}}{\min\left[\left(\max_{n=1\ldots N}\Delta F_i-\min_{n=1\ldots N}\Delta F_i\right),\left(\max_{n=1\ldots N}\Delta F_i^{\mathrm{FEM}}-\min_{n=1\ldots N}\Delta F_i^{\mathrm{FEM}}\right)\right]}\right), \tag{5}$$

where n indicates the current position of the magnetic dipole. The mean of $x-$, $y-$and $z-$error component and the adapted denominator is chosen to get a reliable value despite of large possible differences between force components and between EAA and FEM. For every aluminium layer, R_{d} with the lowest *aNRMSE* is determined. The layer with the lowest *aNRMSE* gives the result for the depth and the size of the defect produced by the goal function scan.

III. RESULTS AND DISCUSSION

Fig. 2 shows the *aNRMSE* and the corresponding defect radii (indices, Fig. 2) over the aluminium layer for the four different defect depths (color-coded, Fig. 2). It can be observed that the correct defect size and the correct depths have been found for all four cases.

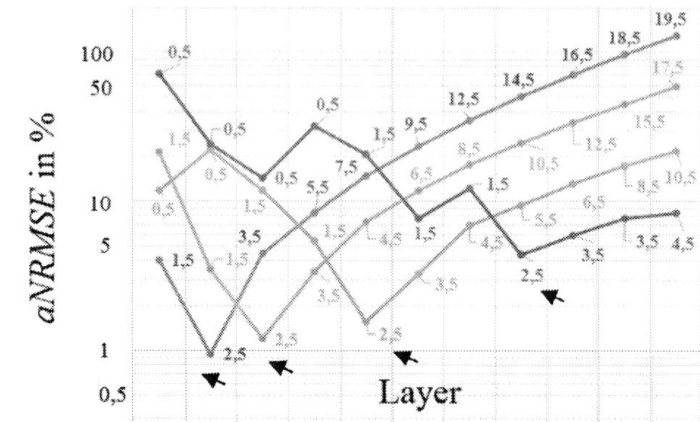

	1	2	3	4	5	6	7	8	9	10	11
2(d=2 mm)	4,06	0,95	4,51	8,46	14,99	23,75	35,43	50,50	70,10	95,89	129,37
3 (d=4 mm)	21,74	3,51	1,21	3,37	7,29	11,98	17,82	24,88	33,94	44,78	58,82
5 (d=8 mm)	12,00	22,16	11,85	5,42	1,57	3,26	6,94	9,57	13,31	17,41	21,92
8 (d=14 mm)	72,18	24,32	14,48	32,09	20,72	7,77	12,38	4,41	5,96	7,73	8,43

Fig. 2. Results of goal function scan with EAA for the four defect depths 2, 4, 8 and 14 mm: The minimal *aNRMSE* and its corresponding defect radius are shown for each layer. The correct defect sizes ($R_{\mathrm{d}} = 2.5$ mm) and depths have been found in all four cases (black arrows). The *aNRMSE* values are shown in the table.

IV. CONCLUSION

LFE based on a goal function scan with EAA yielded correct depth and size detection of a cylindrical defect at different depths. Current work focuses on investigations of different defect shapes and the application of the EAA for measurement data analysis.

REFERENCES

[1] B. Petković, J. Haueisen, M. Zec, R. P. Uhlig, H. Brauer and M. Ziolkowski. Lorentz force evaluation. NDT & E International, vol. 59, pp. 57–67, 2013.

[2] J. Mengelkamp, D. Lattner, J. Haueisen, M. Carlstedt, K. Weise, H. Brauer, M. Ziolkowski and R. Eichardt. Lorentz force evaluation with differential evolution. IEEE Transactions on Magnetics, vol. 52, no. 5, pp. 6201310 (1-10), 2016.

[3] J. Mengelkamp, M. Carlstedt, K. Weise, M. Ziolkowski, H. Brauer and J. Haueisen. Current density reconstructions for Lorentz force evaluation. Research in Nondestructive Evaluation, pp. 1-25, 2016.

[4] M. Ziolkowski, Modern methods for electromagnetic field problems. Szczecin, Poland: West Pomeranian University of Technology College Publisher, 2015.

[5] M. Zec, R. P. Uhlig, M. Ziolkowski, and H. Brauer, "Fast technique for Lorentz force calculations in nondestructive testing applications," IEEE Transactions on Magnetics, vol. 50, no. 2, pp. 7003104 (1-4), Feb. 2014.

Calculation of eddy currents in moving conductors using the meshfree charge simulation method

B. Petković, J. Haueisen
Institute of Biomedical Engineering and Informatics
Technische Universität Ilmenau
Ilmenau, Germany

***Abstract*—In this paper, the mesh free charge simulation method is used for determination of eddy currents inside a conductor translatory moving in a field of the permanent magnet. Using a reference finite element solution, we investigate the position of the inflated boundary surface where the fictitious sources are randomly located. The method can handle arbitrary shaped conductors and arbitrary oriented magnetization vectors. The proposed procedure is shown to be simple and computationally accurate.**

***Keywords*—Charge simulation method; eddy currents; moving conductor; permanent magnet**

I. INTRODUCTION

Lorentz force eddy current testing [1, 2] is a recently introduced nondestructive testing technique, based on the relative motion between a permanent magnet and conductive specimen under test. Due to this motion, eddy currents are induced into the specimen producing Lorentz forces acting with the same intensity and opposite direction on the specimen and the magnet. Presence of defects alters the eddy current flow and consequently the Lorentz force measured at the magnet. The measurements of force perturbations due to presence of a defect do not provide direct information about the distribution of eddy currents inside the conductor under test. In order to evaluate defect properties, an inverse problem has to be solved. Since an inverse problem requires a forward solution to be performed a lot of times, the forward solver needs to be simple and fast.

A standard numerical finite element model (FEM) requires full 3-D conductor volume meshing. Faster calculations and less storage requirements are enabled by a boundary element model (BEM), since it requires only surface discretization. However, mesh related artifacts can be avoided only by applying high quality meshes. Mesh generation is a time consuming preprocessing task. Furthermore, both FEM and BEM require numerical integration what results in complex and potentially not flexible codes.

The charge simulation method (CSM) [3] requires no integration. Moreover, when the source and collocation points are randomly placed, this method is meshfree. The basic idea is to represent the solution by means of a set of point sources randomly placed outside the region of a conductor. Satisfying the boundary condition for the normal component of the induced eddy currents at a selected number of points on the conductor surface, the charges are calculated. Finally, the eddy current density distribution can be determined inside the conductor.

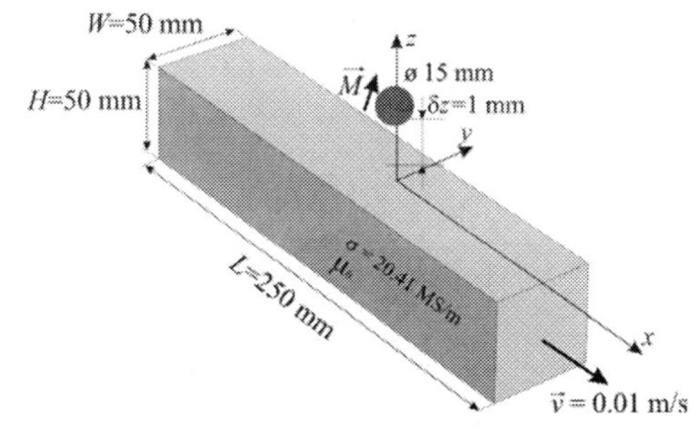

Fig. 1. Conducting bar moving with constant velocity below the spherical permanent magnet.

II. THEORY AND METHODS

A. Model Definition

We consider a parallelepipedical aluminium bar of dimensions $L \times H \times W = 250\,\text{mm} \times 50\,\text{mm} \times 50\,\text{mm}$ and isotropic conductivity $\sigma = 20.41\ \text{MS/m}$. The bar moves with a constant velocity $v = 0.01\ \text{m/s}$ in positive $x-$ direction, Fig. 1.

A spherical permanent magnet of diameter $15\,\text{mm}$ and homogeneous magnetization $\vec{M}$ is placed at the lift-off distance $\delta z = 1\,\text{mm}$ above the top surface of the bar.

B. CSM Solution

We model the permanent magnet by a single magnetic dipole with the magnetic moment $\vec{m}$ placed at the center of gravity of the magnet $\vec{r}_0$ and oriented as the magnetization vector $\vec{M}$. The magnetic flux density vector at the point $\vec{r}$ is calculated as [4]:

$$\vec{B}_{\text{p}} = \frac{\mu_0}{4\pi}\left(\frac{3\vec{m}\cdot(\vec{r}-\vec{r}_0)}{\left|\vec{r}-\vec{r}_0\right|^5}\cdot(\vec{r}-\vec{r}_0) - \frac{\vec{m}}{\left|\vec{r}-\vec{r}_0\right|^3}\right). \tag{1}$$

In the application of the CSM, we use the weak reaction approach [5]. This means that the magnetic field produced by the permanent magnet (1) is not influenced by the magnetic field produced by the induced eddy currents. Using Ohm's law for moving conductors, the induced eddy currents are calculated as $\vec{J}=\sigma(-\nabla\varphi+\vec{v}\times\vec{B}_{\mathrm{p}})$. According to the CSM, we use point fictitious charges placed randomly on a fictitious boundary obtained by inflating the real boundary. Determination of these charges is done satisfying the boundary condition on the conductor/air interface, $\vec{J}\cdot\hat{n}=0$, where $\hat{n}$ represents the unit normal vector on this interface. The matching points follow the random distribution of source points being the projections of source points at the surface of the conductor, Fig. 2. Since the only geometric quantities that are needed are the distances between source and matching points and normals to the faces of the conductor, which can be determined without constructing a mesh [6], the applied CSM is meshfree.

Superimposing the electric scalar potential from all the fictitious charges and satisfying the boundary condition of zero normal component at the walls of the conductor, we obtain a system of linear equations:

$$\sum_{i=1}^{N}\frac{q_j}{4\pi\varepsilon_0}\frac{\hat{n}_i\cdot(\vec{r}_i-\vec{r}_j)}{\left|\vec{r}_i-\vec{r}_j\right|^3}=-(\vec{v}\times\vec{B}_{\mathrm{p}})_i\cdot\hat{n}_i,\ j=1,\dots,N, \quad (2)$$

with q_j, $j=1,\dots,N$, as unknown charges. Since the number of unknowns is equal to the number of equations, the charges q_j can be uniquely determined, provided the system matrix is nonsingular. We can then calculate the induced eddy current density at any point inside the conductor.

III. Results and Discussion

We first investigate the influence of the distance of the inflated fictitious surface to the faces of the conductor. Box-Wiskers plots of the *NRMSD* [%] of J_x, J_y and J_z with respect to the reference FEM solution performing 100 runs per distance of the inflated surface are presented in the Fig. 3. The induced eddy currents J_x and J_y show satisfactory accuracy for all the investigated inflated surfaces. However, *NRMSD* of J_z depends on the position of the inflated surface. J_z shows minimal error for inflation of 7 mm where the maximal *NRMSD* is 0.85 % and the mean value 0.32 %. Visualization of the eddy current flow at the planes x=0, y=0, z=0 and $z=-0.005$ m, for the distance of inflated surface 7 mm from the bar, is presented in the Fig. 4.

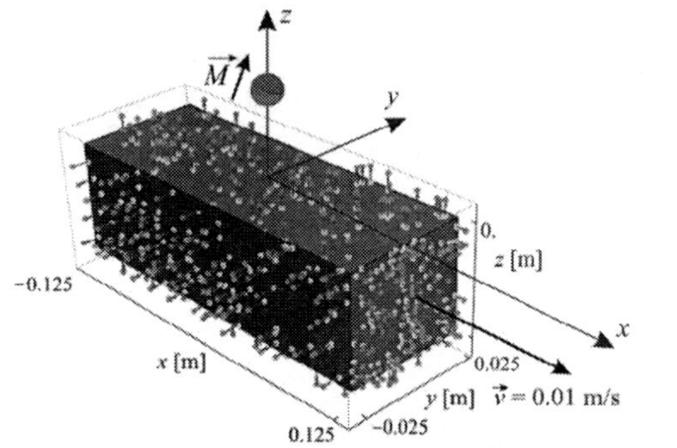

Fig. 2. Random placement of source points (green) on the inflated surface and collocation points (yellow) as projections of the source points at the faces of the conductor (brown).

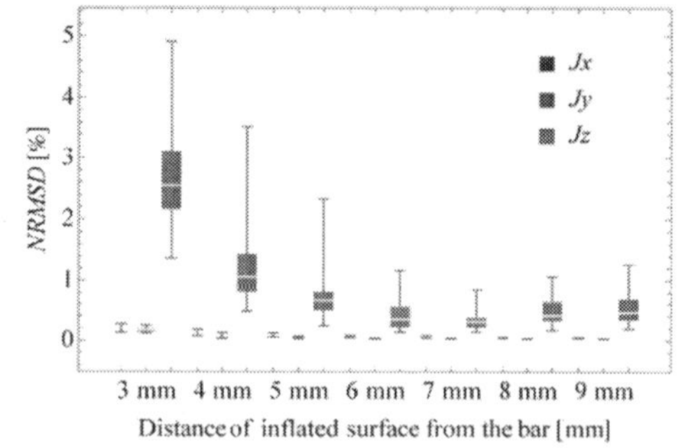

Fig. 3. Box-Wiskers plot of *NRMSD* [%] of eddy current density per distance of inflated fictitious boundary with respect to the bar (100 runs per distance).

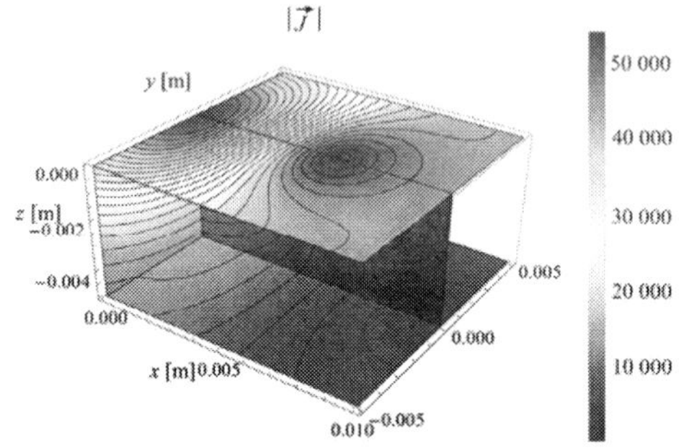

Fig. 4. Total eddy current profile at the planes x=0, y=0, z=0 and $z=-0.005$ m. The unit of the color bar is A/m².

IV. Conclusion

The mesh free charge simulation method is applied for calculation of induced eddy currents in a translatory moving conductor in the field of the permanent magnet. The distance of the inflated surface, where randomly arranged fictitious sources are positioned, is investigated with respect to the reference finite element solution. Future work will be focused on conductors containing defects of irregular geometry and an establishment of inverse reconstruction schemes for defects evaluation.

Acknowledgment

We thank Dr.-Ing. Konstantin Weise for proving the reference finite element solution.

References

[1] H. Brauer, K. Porzig, J. Mengelkamp, M. Carlstedt, M. Ziolkowski, and H. Toepfer, "Lorentz force eddy current testing: a novel NDE-technique," COMPEL, Int. J. Comput. Math. Electr. Electron. Eng., vol. 33, no. 6, pp. 1965–1977, 2014.

[2] B. Petković, J. Haueisen, M. Zec, R. P. Uhlig, H. Brauer, and M. Ziolkowski, "Lorentz force evaluation: a new approximation method for defect reconstruction," NDT&E Int., vol. 59, pp. 57–67, Oct. 2013.

[3] N. H. Malik, "A review of the charge simulation method and its applications," IEEE Trans. Dielectr. Electr. Insul., vol. 24, pp. 3–20, 1989.

[4] J. D. Jackson, „Magnetostatik, Faradaysches Induktionsgesetz, quasistationäre Felder," in Klassische Elektrodynamik, 3rd ed., de Gruyter, Berlin, 2002, pp. 217.

[5] M. Zec, R. P. Uhlig, M. Ziolkowski, and H. Brauer, "Fast technique for Lorentz force calculations in nondestructive testing applications," IEEE Trans. Magn., vol. 50, no. 2, Art. ID 7003104, Feb. 2014.

[6] G. E. Fasshauer. Meshfree approximation methods with MATLAB, World Scientific, River-Edge, NJ, 2007.

Spatial harmonic current density basis for faults identification in fuel cell stack from external magnetic field measurements

Lyes Ifrek[1, 2, 3, 4], Olivier Chadebec[1, 2], Gilles Cauffet[1, 2]
[1]Univ. Grenoble Alpes, G2Elab, F-38000 Grenoble, France
[2]CNRS, G2Elab, F-38000 Grenoble, France
[3]Univ. Grenoble Alpes, LEPMI, F-38000 Grenoble, France
[4]CNRS, LEPMI, F-38000 Grenoble, France

Yann Bultel[3, 4], Sébastien Rosini[5], Luc Rouveyre[6]
[5]Univ. Grenoble Alpes, CEA, LITEN, F-38054 Grenoble, France
[6]SymbioFCell, F-38600 Fontaine, France
lyes.ifrek@g2elab.grenoble-inp.fr

***Abstract*— An original approach used for the identification of faults in fuel cell stacks is presented. It is based on the 3D reconstruction of the current density from external magnetic field measurements which is an ill-posed magnetostatic linear inverse problem. Suitable current density and magnetic field basis are proposed in order to define both local and global faults on a fuel cell stack. In order to ensure the uniqueness of the solution, the inverse problem is regularized thanks to the truncated singular value decomposition (SVD).**

Keywords*— *Fuel cell stack, magnetostatic, inverse linear problems, non-invasive diagnosis, truncated SVD

I. Introduction

Environmental issues present the fuel cell stacks as an alternative to the combustion engines in vehicles. Until now the improvement of their lifetime presents a major objective. Many works have been done dealing with the faults identification in fuel cells. Our work focuses on a non-invasive technique based on the external magnetic field measurements and the inversion of the Biot and Savart law. A key point for this approach is the choice of the current distribution basis in order to efficiently solve the inverse problem. In this paper, an original harmonic decomposition for the current density is presented.

II. 3D Current Density Reconstruction Approach

A. Principle

In a first step, we consider the forward approach which consists in solving an electro-kinetic problem. From the electrical conductivities of each part of the fuel cell and by coupling the model with an external electrical circuit representation, we get the current density distribution inside the fuel cell. The key point being the current solenoidality, a Finite Element (FE) approach based on face shape function interpolation for the current distribution has been selected. In a second step, thanks to the Biot and Savart law (1) numerically integrated, we calculate the magnetic field on magnetic sensors located around the stack. The magnetic field generated by a healthy fuel cell has previously been studied with the purpose of defining suitable magnetic sensors positions optimizing the measurement ranges [2].

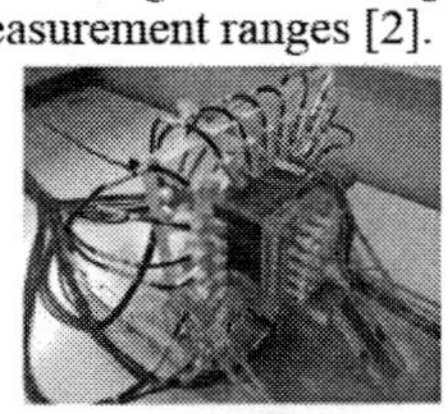

Fig. 1 Sensors around a stack simulator (left) and a real stack (right) [2]

$$\mathbf{B}(\mathbf{r})=\frac{\mu_0}{4\pi}\int_{\Omega_s}\frac{(\mathbf{r}_s-\mathbf{r})}{|\mathbf{r}_s-\mathbf{r}|^3}\times\mathbf{j}(\mathbf{r}_s)d\Omega_s \quad (1)$$

Let us suppose that the fuel cell is meshed into elements carrying uniform current density **J**. Equation (1) can be discretized and a linear relation between magnetic field on sensors and current density can be obtained.

$$\mathbf{B}=\mathbf{JS} \quad (2)$$

with **S** represents the discretized Biot and Savart operator, **B** the measurements vector and **J** the current density vector.

The forward model is used to simulate conductivity faults on fuel cell stacks and to obtain virtual measurements. In a second step, the measured radiated magnetic field **B** is used to reconstruct the current density distribution **J** by inversing the operator **S**. The problem being ill-posed [2], we can get the pseudo inverse $\mathbf{S}^+$ from classical singular value decomposition (SVD) which can be truncated in order to limit the influence of measurement noise.

$$\mathbf{J}=\mathbf{S}^+\mathbf{B} \quad (3)$$

B. Current density basis

A key point is the choice of a basis for **J** which has to be sufficiently compact in order to limit the number of degrees of freedom but also sufficiently large to cover the space of all possible faults configurations.

Different strategies have been tested to define the current density basis on the previous works. Reference [1] constructs a basis based on a lumped resistance equivalent circuit model. Each vector of the basis corresponds to the field generated by a current distribution flowing in the electric circuit with each resistant imposed to an infinite value successively. In [2], we have proposed a decomposition of the current distribution into a 2D spatial Fourier series completed by a 3D model in order to take into account the current flow in end plates. If this approach is suitable for 2D faults reconstruction (i.e homogenous current faults along the stack), it is not convenient for 3D local faults.

In this paper we propose to investigate another way to build the current density basis suitable for 3D current reconstruction. The vectors of the basis have to satisfy the free divergence of the current. Thus they are generated form an electrical vector potential **T** interpolated by edge shape functions and obtained by applying the curl operator.

In our configuration, the main current flow is along the **z** axis. In the case of faults, current loops on the **x**- plane and **y**- plane have to be added to a homogeneous current (Fig. 2).

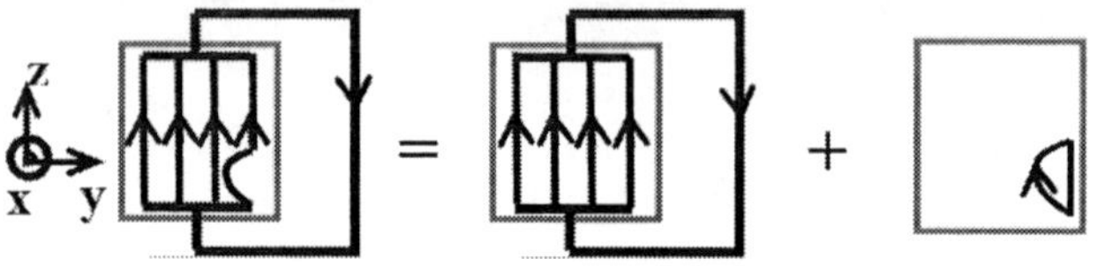

Fig. 2 Decomposition of a heterogeneous current into a sum of a homogeneous current and a faulty current loop

For a description of faults on the **x**-plane we have to decompose **T** along the **x** axis.

$$T=\sin(k_y \cdot y)\cdot\sin(k_z \cdot z)\cdot \mathbf{u_x} \qquad (4)$$

with $k_y=n\pi$ and $k_z=m\pi$ where n and m are the decomposition orders.

The current vectors in the x-plane are obtained by applying the curl operator to the vector potential **T** leading to different internal faulty loops configurations.

$$\mathbf{J}=\mathit{curl}\mathbf{T} \qquad (5)$$

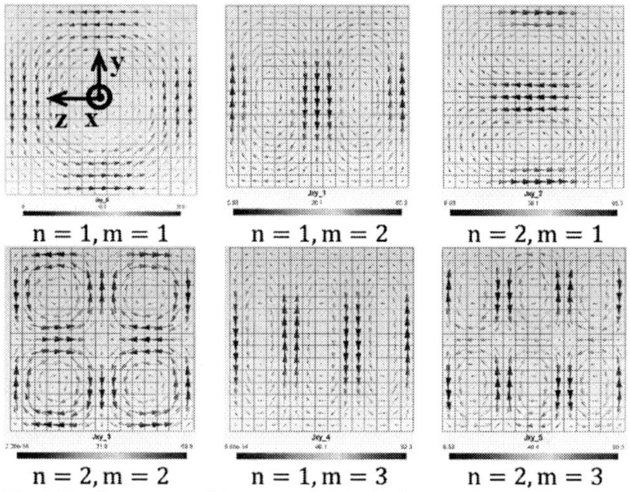

Fig. 3 The first vectors of the current density basis

The same process has to be applied in the **y**-plane in order to get the complete basis. The magnetic field basis is built by numerically integrating the Biot and Savart law (1) for each current distribution.

This spatial harmonic approach is very suitable for our problem. In theory the order of decomposition should tend to infinity but in practice it has to be truncated. Let us notice that a high expansion order corresponds to a large number of current loops (i.e a high order magnetic multipole) which creates a low field on sensors. In fact, order higher than 7 do not generate any significant signal on sensors enabling a proper truncation of the spatial decomposition.

C. Error criterion

The error of reconstruction is estimated by using the relative error defined as follows:

$$err=\sqrt{\frac{\int_{\Omega_s}(J_{real}-J_{idn})^T\cdot(J_{real}-J_{idn})d\Omega_s}{\int_{\Omega_s}(J_{real_{max}}^T\cdot J_{real_{max}})d\Omega_s}} \qquad (6)$$

with J_{real} is the real current, J_{idn} the identified current and $J_{real_{max}}$ the maximum value of the real current.

III. Numerical Results

A. Faulty fuel cell

A very low electrical conductivity is imposed on a part of the fuel cell (see Fig.4, left in blue). The electro-kinetic conduction problem is solved to get the total current distribution and the internal current loop caused by the fault. The faulty current is obtained by subtracting a homogeneous current (Healthy stack) to the current in the case of a fault.

The model to simulate the fault is presented in figure 4. 72 measurements points are placed around the fuel cell. The measurement vector contains the radial and the axial component of the magnetic field. The azimuthal component is not taken into account because it is mainly due to only the healthy current.

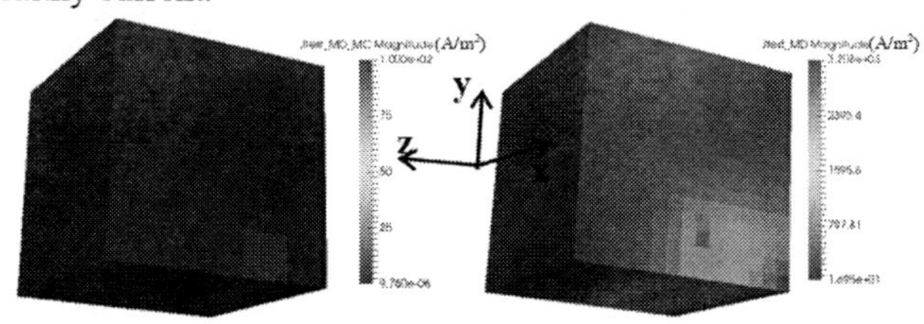

Fig. 4 Total current distribution (left) and faulty current (right)

B. Identification by external magnetic field

The radiated magnetic field created by the faulty current is inversed in order to identify the fault.

The equation system is composed of 98 unknowns and 144 equations which correspond to the number of measurements.

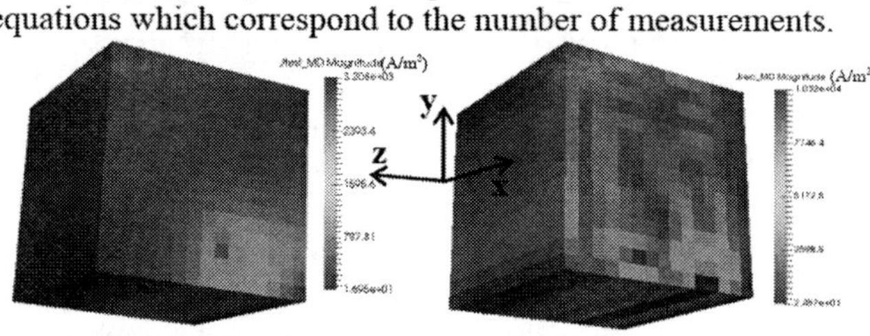

Fig. 5 Real current (left), Identified current (right)

After truncation of the matrix spectrum, the reconstruction error is calculated using (6) and an acceptable value of **11.35%** is obtained. The presented result shows a good match between the real current and the reconstructed one with a relatively small error.

Aknowledgment

Authors would like to thank the Auvergne-Rhône-Alps region for funding this project.

References

[1] K.H. Hauer, R. Potthast, and M. Wannert. "Algorithm for tomography – on the role of a priori knowledge and constraints", IOP Science, Inverse Problems 24, 2008.

[2] M. Le Ny et al. "Current Distribution Identification in Fuel Cell Stacks From External Magnetic Field Measurements", IEEE Trans. on Magnetics, Vol. 49, N°5, pp. 1925-1928, 2013.

Generalization of the Vector Hysteron Model through the dependence of moving functions on frequency

Antonino Laudani, Gabriele-Maria Lozito, Francesco Riganti-Fulginei and Alessandro Salvini
Department of Engineering
Roma Tre University
Rome, Italy

Ermanno Cardelli, Antonio Faba and Simone Quondam
Department of Engineering
University of Perugia
Perugia, Italy

***Abstract* — A generalization of the VHM (Vector Hysteron Model) is here described to reconstruct rotational magnetizations of electrical steels with weak anisotropy, like non oriented grain Silicon steel, in function of the frequency values. The VHM is a natural extension of the classical Preisach model where the scalar hysterons are changed with vector hysterons, defined as a closed curves, for 2-d magnetizations. By using different frequencies of the B field applied as a rotational excitation, the values of the moving functions characterizing VHM change. The aim of this paper is to provide a procedure to find the behavior of those moving functions as a dependency of frequency. Suitable simulations are reported within the final validations.**

Keywords—vector model; optimization; swarm intelligence; hysteresis; identification

I. INTRODUCTION

Several approaches have been investigated in literature to represent the behavior of magnetic materials, and among these, the most classical and often found is through the CPM (Classical Preisach Model). Although being useful for scalar behavior, this model lacks vector-hysteresis representation capabilities. Several solutions have been proposed in literature [1] [2] to represent this phenomenon. A modified Preisach model, the VHM (Vector Hysterion Model) [3-5], is able to represent correctly the rotational losses and is promisingly representative of the magnetization process. Unfortunately, this model exhibit the congruency property of minor loops for both scalar and rotational magnetizations. Several experiments showed the absence of this property for physical materials, and for this reason, it should be removed in the model behavior. In fact, due to this property, the VHM is not able to use the same hysterion density function to represent both scalar and rotational magnetization. A solution to this problem is found by considering a variable hysterion density distribution, which changes during the magnetization process. This is called the "moving" approach [6]. For the research proposed in this paper, the focus will be on an electrical steel with non-oriented grain. This kind of material is often used for electrical machines such as transformers, motors and generators. The VHM featuring a moving approach is characterized by a set of parameters that has to be found using an optimization technique. In this work, the parameters are found, at different frequencies, by using a powerful optimization algorithm, the Continuous Flock-Of-Starlings Optimization Cube (CFSO3) algorithm [7] [8]. The experimental dataset used for model identification comes from a set of measurements performed on a RSST (Rotational Single Sheet Tester) [9]. Then, a comparison between measured and computed data will be presented, along with a discussion on the accuracy of the proposed approach.

II. VECTOR HYSTERON MODEL

In the moving approach we postulated that the distribution function is:

$$P(\Omega,M,f)=\left(\frac{1}{\pi}\cdot\frac{\sigma(M,f)}{H_{Ix}^2+H_{Iy}^2+\sigma^2(M,f)}\right)\cdot \left(\frac{1}{\pi}\cdot\frac{\sigma_S(M,f)}{\left(H_S-H_C(M,f)\right)^2+\sigma_S^2(M,f)}\right)\cdot S_f(M,f) \quad (1)$$

where the model parameters are magnetization and frequency dependent, and the identification of the four moving functions $\sigma(M,f)$, $\sigma_S(M,f)$, $H_C(M,f)$ and $S_f(M,f)$ have to be performed (for an in depth analysis of VHM please see [6]). The moving functions $\sigma(M,f)$, $\sigma_S(M,f)$, $H_C(M,f)$ and $S_f(M,f)$ are computed using the magnetization state at the previous step M_{t-1} for a fixed frequency f. At the beginning, the magnetization state is zero. In [6] the frequency was 50 Hz, but in the present work, we aim to find how the moving functions change by varying f as well. In the next section, the procedure to identify that dependence is discussed.

III. CFSO^3 FOR MOVING FUNCTIONS IDENTIFICATION AT DIFFERENT FREQUENCIES

In this work, we focus on a non-oriented electrical steel. The characterization of the material was obtained by a RSST with a suitable feedback control to obtain sinusoidal magnetization.

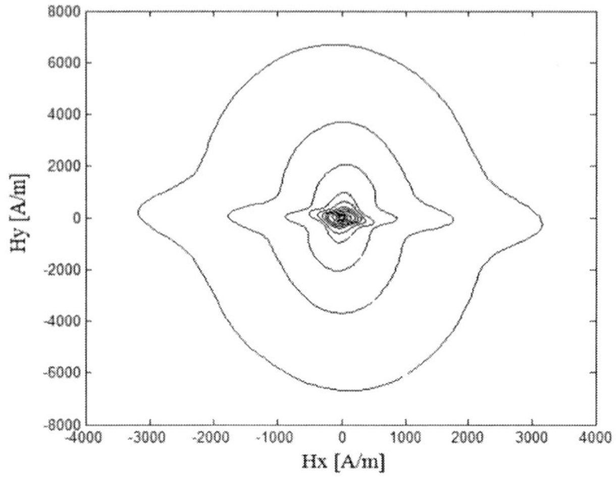

Fig. 1. Example of data set at f = 50Hz: magnetic field measured for rotational exitations (circular polarizations of B)

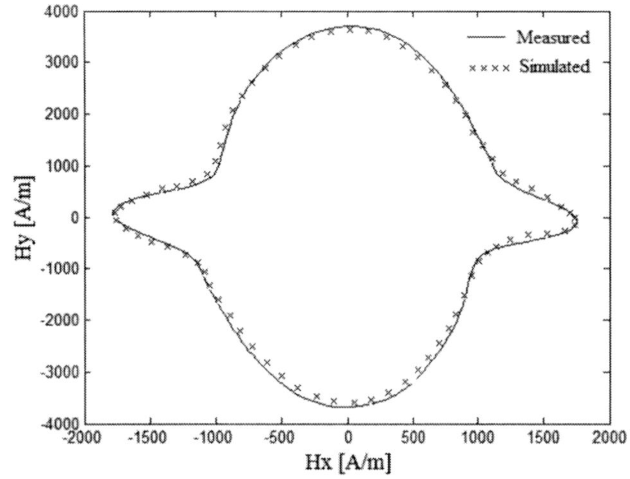

Fig. 2. Comparison between measured data and simulation performed by VHM at 400 Hz

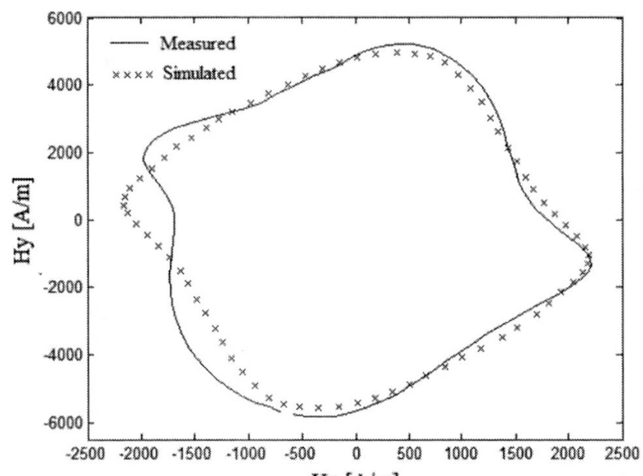

Fig. 3. Comparison between measured data and simulation performed by VHM at 700 Hz

The moving functions identification is performed in two steps using the CFSO^3 algorithm [7][8] and experimental data. We identified the moving functions for the representation of rotational magnetizations (i.e. circular polarizations of B) by using three sets of measured data (12 different loops for each data set) at different frequencies: 50 Hz, 400 Hz and 800 Hz. Fig. 1 shows the measured data-set of magnetic field H at 50Hz. Finally, a suitable accommodation procedure completes the formulation of the moving functions. When all the three cases have been identified (i.e. the related moving functions have been found), the cases with values of frequencies different from 50, 400 and 800 Hz can be obtained by simple interpolation.

IV. Results and Validations

In this section, a comparison between measured data and simulations is presented. Fig. 2 shows a comparison between measured data and simulation performed by VHM at 400 Hz by using the found moving functions. With the aim to validate the performances of the proposed approach also in the case in which the frequency value is different from those used to identify the moving functions, in Fig. 3 a comparison between measured data and simulation results is proposed for f = 700 Hz. The values of the moving functions have been obtained by performing an interpolation procedure among the three cases. In particular, the apparent error between the two curves on the left side of Fig. 3 is mainly due to the non-perfect symmetry of experimental data, due to the difficult measurement procedure. Indeed, it is very difficult to measure rotational excitations in function of frequency and some imprecision on experimental data may occur. However, Fig. 3 shows the worst among all results, where the mean of mean squared error on all simulation was about 0.2.

References

[1] A. A. Adly, I. D. Mayergoyz, A new vector Preisach-type model of hysteresis, J.Appl. Phys.73(1993) pp. 5824–5827.

[2] J K. Löschner, V. Rischmüller, M. Brokate, Natural vectorial extension of the Preisach operator, IEEE Trans.Magn.44(6) (2008) pp. 878–881

[3] E. Della Torre , E. Pinzaglia , E. Cardelli , Vector modeling - part II: ellipsoidal vector hysteresis model. Numerical application to a 2-D case , Physica B 372 (2006) pp. 115–119.

[4] E. Cardelli, E. Della Torre, A. Faba, A general vector hysteresis operator: extension to the 3-D case, IEEE Trans.Magn. 46(12)(2010) pp.3990–4000.

[5] E. Cardelli, A general hysteresis operator for the modeling of vector fields, IEEE Trans.Magn.47(8)(2011) pp. 2056–2067.

[6] E. Cardelli, A. Faba, A. Laudani, S. Quondam Antonio, F. Riganti Fulginei, A. Salvini, A moving approach for the Vector Hysteron Model, Physica B 486(2016) pp. 92–96.

[7] A. Laudani, F. Riganti Fulginei, A. Salvini, M. Schmid, S. Conforto, CFSO3: A new supervised swarm-based optimization algorithm, Mathematical Problems in Engineering, Volume 2013, 2013

[8] A. Laudani, F. Riganti Fulginei, G. M. Lozito, A. Salvini, Swarm/flock optimization algorithms as continuous dynamic systems, Applied Mathematics and Computation, Vol 243, 2014, pp.670-683

[9] E. Cardelli, A. Faba, Vector hysteresis measurements of not oriented grain SiFe steels by a biaxial hall sensors array, Phys.B: Condens. Matter435 (2014) pp. 34–39.

Power Pattern Sensitivity Analysis of Reflectarray Antennas to Substrate Uncertainties through the Minkowski Interval Analysis

N. Ebrahimi[1], P. Rocca[1], A. Massa[1,2]
[1] ELEDIA Research Center (ELEDIA@UniTN - University of Trento)
Trento, Italy
[2] ELEDIA Research Center (ELEDIA@L2S - UMR 8506)
Gif-sur-Yvette, France
andrea.massa@eledia.org

***Abstract*—In this work, the effect of the fabrication uncertainties on the substrate thickness on the radiation performance of the reflectarray antenna is addressed. An interval analysis (*IA*)-based method is used to compute the upper and lower bounds of the power pattern as a function of the deviations in the substrate thickness. The Minkowski Sum (*MS*) is exploited to combine interval phasors in order to mitigate the over-estimation of the power pattern bounds affecting standard Cartesian *IA* (*IA-CS*) techniques. A representative numerical example shows that the proposed *IA-MS* method provides narrower and more reliable bounds than the *IA-CS*.**

***Keywords*— reflectarray antennas; tolerance analysis; phase error; Minkowski sum; interval analysis**

I. Introduction

Thanks to their desirable features of low profile, low weight, low cost and high efficiency reflectarrays are one the most interesting and suitable antennas for space communications [1]-[5]. However, manufacturing errors can significantly deteriorate their radiation performances, requiring accurate fabrication processes to improve the robustness and reliability of the whole radiating system.

Within this context, tolerance analysis techniques can predict the power pattern degradation due to fabrication errors. Many of these methods are based on statistical approaches, requiring the a-priori knowledge of the error distribution and exploiting approximated formulas. As an example, a statistical method based on the knowledge of the root-mean-square error of the patch dimensions has been proposed in [2]. Recently, to overcome the current drawbacks of statistical approaches, a tolerance analysis tool based on the Interval Arithmetic [6]-[11] has been applied to microstrip reflectarray antennas to predict the pattern deviations due to the tolerances in etching the microstrip patches [3]. Such a Cartesian Interval Analysis (*IA-CS*) methodology provides inclusive and reliable bounds with respect to random errors in all considered geometrical parameters. However, the standard *IA-CS* is not applicable to large reflectarray antennas, for which the *redundancy* problem leads to a strong over-estimation of the power pattern bounds. To mitigate such an issue, the Minkowski Sum (*MS*) is introduced to sum complex interval phasors in this work. The proposed *IA-MS* approach is able to reduce the *redundancy* problem affecting the standard *IA-CS* when dealing with large reflectarray antennas, producing narrower but still inclusive bounds on the radiated power pattern due to fabrication errors in the substrate thickness. An illustrative example is presented to assess the validity of the proposed method, as well as to compare it to the standard *IA-CS*.

II. Mathematical Formulation

A. *Interval Power Pattern*

Let us consider a reflectarray antenna of $N = N_x \times N_y$ rectangular microstrip patches located on the top of an isotropic and homogeneous substrate having nominal thickness $\hat{d}$ and relative permittivity ε_r. We suppose that the substrate thickness is affected by unknown fabrication errors. To mathematically model such an uncertainty, the following interval is associated to the substrate thickness value:

$$[d] = \left[\hat{d} - \delta d, \hat{d} + \delta d\right] \quad (1)$$

where δd is the maximum fabrication deviation. Accordingly, the interval far field pattern can be presented by the following expression

$$\left[\underline{E}(\theta,\varphi)\right] = \frac{e^{-jkr} jk}{2\pi r}\left(\hat{\theta}cos\varphi - \hat{\varphi}sin\varphi cos\theta\right)\left[\tilde{E}^{Rx}(u,v;[d])\right] + \left(\hat{\theta}sin\varphi + \hat{\varphi}cos\varphi cos\theta\right)\left[\tilde{E}^{Ry}(u,v;[d])\right]\frac{e^{-jkr} jk}{2\pi r}, \quad (2)$$

where $k = \frac{2\pi}{\lambda}$ is the wave-number, λ being the wavelength, while $u = \sin(\theta)\cos(\varphi)$ and $v = \sin(\theta)\sin(\varphi)$ are the angular coordinates. Moreover, in (2) $\left[\tilde{E}^{Rx}(u,v;[d])\right]$ and $\left[\tilde{E}^{Ry}(u,v;[d])\right]$ are the Cartesian components of the interval Fourier transforms of the tangential electric field. According to [1], these Fourier transforms are computed from the summation of the complex coefficient of the reflected field in each reflectarray cell. A theoretical expression for the reflection coefficient is exploited to compute the crisp complex coefficient of each cell [5]. This reflection coefficient is the function of all physical parameters of each cell. By considering IA rules [6] the interval of the reflection coefficient, the complex coefficient of each cell and the Fourier transform of the electric filed can be properly computed. By substituting these interval values in (2), we can obtain the interval of the far field electric field, containing the upper and lower bounds due to the random errors on the substrate thickness.

B. Minkowski Interval Analysis Procedure (IA-MS)

Dependency and wrapping problems are the main problems associated with *IA* approaches, leading to an over-estimation of the power pattern bounds. To mitigate such issues, the Minkowski Sum (*MS*) [8] is applied. First, the minimum and maximum of the magnitude and phase of the complex coefficient in each cell are computed by dependency-free *IA*. Then, the phasors from these maximum and minimum amplitude and phase of each cell are considered. *MS* computes the summation among these phasors by a set of vertexes defined in the contour of the smallest convex hull encircling them. In *IA-MS*, the sum $[a_m] \oplus [a_{m'}]$ between the two interval phasors $[a_m]$ and $[a_{m'}]$ is defined as [7]:

$$[a_m] \oplus [a_{m'}] = \{a_m + a_{m'} : a_m \in [a_m], a_{m'} \in [a_{m'}]\} \qquad (3)$$

IA-MS reduces the redundancy of *IA-CS* by using a convex hull representation instead of the simplex rectangular representation of *IA-CS* in complex domain.

III. Numerical Results

To demonstrate the effectiveness of the proposed *IA-MS* procedure, a center-fed circular reflectarray antenna working at frequency $f = 32[GHz]$ with diameter of $15.5[\lambda]$ and consisting of $N = 749$ rectangular patch elements is selected as reference benchmark [5]. The feed antenna is a y-polarized horn antenna in working at $f = 32[GHz]$, whose pattern is modeled as $\cos(\theta)^q$ with q=1.5. The periodicity along x and y axes is set equal to 0.5λ. The maximum tolerance error in the fabrication of the reflectarray substrate thickness is set equal to $\Delta d = 1\mu m$. Therefore, the nominal substrate of $\hat{d} = 0.127[mm]$ is inside the interval $[d] = [0.126, 0.128][mm]$. Figure 1 shows the interval power pattern bounds computed by means of the proposed *IA-MS* methods and compares them to those obtainable by means of the standard *IA-CS*. As it can be easily observed, the *IA-MS* is able to provide much narrower bounds than the *IA-CS*. To prove that the computed bounds are still inclusive, a set of 10^4 Monte Carlo power patterns have been generated. All these patterns are included within the computed bounds (Fig. 1), thus verifying the reliability of the

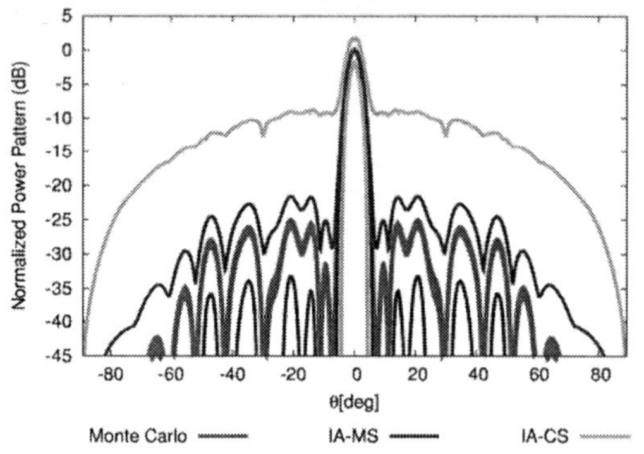

Fig. 1. *Illustrative Example* – Power pattern bounds computed by *IA-MS* and *IA-CS* techniques compared to 10^4 Monte Carlo simulations.

proposed method in predicting the pattern deviations due to fabrication errors on the substrate thickness.

IV. Conclusions

In this work, a novel *IA*-based approach exploiting the *MS* for the tolerance analysis of the reflectarray antenna has been presented. Random errors on the substrate thickness have been modeled as interval values and the *IA* rules have been exploited to compute the bounds on the power pattern. An illustrative numerical example proved that the *IA-MS* bounds are narrower compared to those computed by standard *IA-CS*, while still satisfying the inclusion property.

References

[1] J. Huang, J.A.Encinar, *Reflectarray Antennas*, Piscataway, NJ/New York: IEEE press/Wiley: Artech House, 2008.

[2] D. M. Pozar, *et al.*, "Design of millimeter wave microstrip reflectarrays," *IEEE Trans. Antennas Propag.*, vol. 45, no. 2, pp. 287-296, Feb 1997.

[3] P. Rocca, *et al.*, "Predicting antenna pattern degradations in microstrip reflectarrays through interval arithmetic," *IET Microw. Antennas Propag.*, vol. 10, no. 8, pp. 817-826, 2016.

[4] P. Nayeri, *et al.*, "Radiation analysis approaches for reflectarray antennas," *IEEE Trans. Antennas Propag. Mag.*, vol. 55, no. 1, pp. 127-134, Feb. 2013.

[5] K. K. Karnati, *et al.*, "Q factor analysis of reflectarray elements investigating the effects from angle of incidence using Floquet modes," *IEEE Trans. Antennas Propag.*, vol. 62, no. 10, pp. 5017-5028, Oct. 2014.

[6] N. Anselmi, *et al.*, "Tolerance analysis of antenna arrays through interval arithmetic," *IEEE Trans. Antennas Propag.*, vol. 61, no. 11, pp. 5496-5507, Nov. 2013.

[7] L. Poli, *et al.*, "Dealing with uncertainties on phase weighting of linear antenna arrays by means of interval-based tolerance analysis," *IEEE Trans. Antennas Propag.*, vol. 63, no. 7, pp. 3229-3234, July 2015.

[8] N. Anselmi, *et al.*, "A Minkowski-based interval analysis tool for pattern distortions in reflector antennas with localized surface deformations," *10th European Conf. Antennas Propag.* (EUCAP 2016), Davos, Switzerland, pp. 1-4, April 11-15, 2016.

[9] N. Anselmi, *et al.*, "Generalised interval-based analysis tool for pattern distortions in reflector antennas with bump-like surface deformations," *IET Microw. Antennas Propag.*, vol. 10, no. 9, pp. 909-916, June 2016.

[10] N. Anselmi, *et al.*, "Optimization of excitation tolerances for robust beamforming in linear arrays," *IET Microw. Antennas Propag.*, vol. 10, no. 2, pp. 208-214, 2016

[11] N. Anselmi, *et al.*, "Power pattern sensitivity to calibration errors and mutual coupling in linear arrays through circular interval arithmetics," *Sensors*, vol. 16, no. 6(791), pp. 1-14, 2016.

Equivalent Circuit Model of a Triple Frequency Rejection Band UWB Antenna

Yanyan Wang, Tao Jiang, Yingsong Li*
College of Information and Communications Engineering,
Harbin Engineering University,
Harbin, Heilongjiang 150001, China
Email: *liyingsong@ieee.org

***Abstract*—In this paper, an accurate equivalent circuit model is presented for a triple frequency rejection band UWB antenna that provides the desired frequency rejection function at center frequencies of 2.92 GHz, 4.06 GHz and 5.28 GHz. The extraction of the equivalent circuit model of the presented antenna mainly depends on the impedance characteristic of electromagnetic (EM) simulation. The equivalent circuit model consists of lumped elements which are optimized based on the ADS simulation. The equivalent circuit model simulation is compared with EM simulation, indicating that an excellent agreement is achieved.**

I. Introduction

In resent years, ultra-wide band (UWB) antenna with notched-band characteristic has attracted much attention and a great number of research achievements have been rendered for wireless communication applications. Novels of compact notched-band UWB antenna have been designed [1]–[3] for filtering out the unwanted potential narrow-band wireless communication signals, which overlap with the UWB wireless communication band. However, there are few researches on the equivalent circuit model of those notched-band UWB antennas. Furthermore, a directly optimum of an array antenna on the basis of the EM simulation is very time-consuming, particularly, when the geometry of the antenna is complex. In this case, the research and analysis of antenna equivalent circuit model is imperative. In [4], an equivalent circuit model has been reported for analyzing UWB patch antenna. However, it only gives a basic equivalent circuit model. As for multiple frequency rejection banded UWB antenna, accurate equivalent circuit model is required for practical application.

This paper presents an accurate equivalent circuit model of a triple frequency rejection band UWB antenna based on [5]. The configuration of the triple frequency rejection band UWB antenna [1], [6] is shown in Fig. 1. The antenna consists of a rectangular patch and a defected ground plane, which are printed on a substrate with a relative permittivity of 2.65 and a thickness of 1 mm. The optimal dimensions are: $X = 32$ mm, $H = 48$ mm, $x_0 = 18$ mm, $h_0 = 1$ mm, $x_1 = 19$ mm, $h_1 = 13$ mm, $x_2 = 8$ mm, $h_2 = 1.5$ mm, $x_3 = 4$ mm, $h_3 = 1.5$ mm, $g = 23.4$ mm, $g_0 = 3.5$ mm, $g_1 = 2.5$ mm, $g_2 = 2.6$ mm, $g_3 = 1$ mm, $s_0 = 7$ mm, $s_1 = 5$ mm, $s_2 = 0.1$ mm, $s_3 = 0.1$ mm, $s_4 = 0.5$ mm, $s_5 = 5$ mm, $s_6 = 4$ mm, $s_7 = 3.8$ mm, $s_8 = 3$ mm, $m = 0.3$ mm and $m_1 = 0.5$ mm. The desired triple frequency rejection

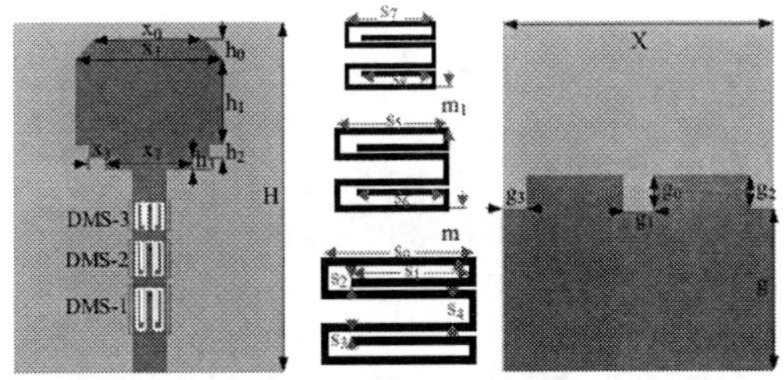

Fig. 1. Geometry of the triple frequency rejection band UWB antenna.

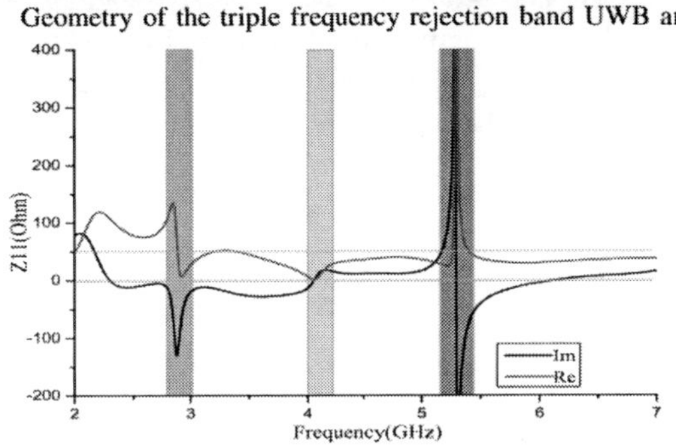

Fig. 2. Impedance of the triple frequency rejection band UWB antenna.

bands are obtained by etching defected microstrip structures (DMSs) on the microstrip feeding signal line. Herein, the center frequencies of these notch bands are located at 2.92 GHz, 4.06 GHz and 5.28 GHz, respectively. The equivalent circuit model extract process of the presented tri-band notched UWB antenna are followed as: 1) Extracted equivalent circuit model of the presented antenna depends on the impedance characteristic of the electromagnetic (EM) simulation. 2) The values of lumped elements are calculated by using formulas. 3) The proposed equivalent circuit model is simulated and optimized by using advance design system (ADS). 4) The simulation results of the equivalent circuit are compared with EM simulations, indicating that the proposed equivalent circuit model is excellent agreement with the EM simulation.

II. Proposed Equivalent Circuit Model

The proposed equivalent circuit model is obtained by taking the simulated impedance characteristic of the tri-band notched UWB antenna into consideration. Figure 2 shows the impedance characteristic of the presented antenna obtained from the HFSS simulation. It is known that the notch functions are generated by RLC elements. For the first two notch bands operating at 2.92 GHz and 4.06 GHz, the imaginary part

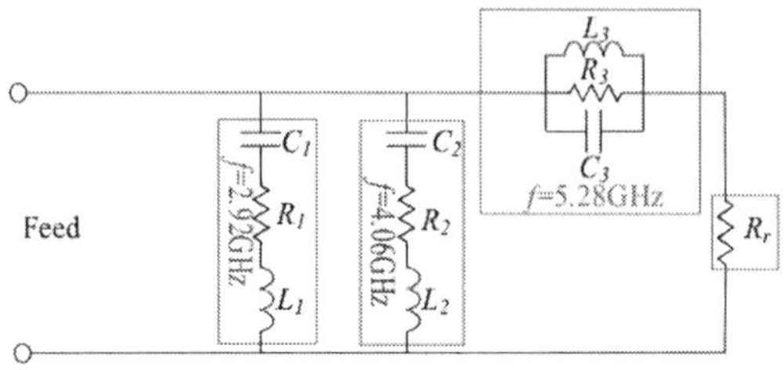

Fig. 3. Equivalent circuit model of the presented antenna.

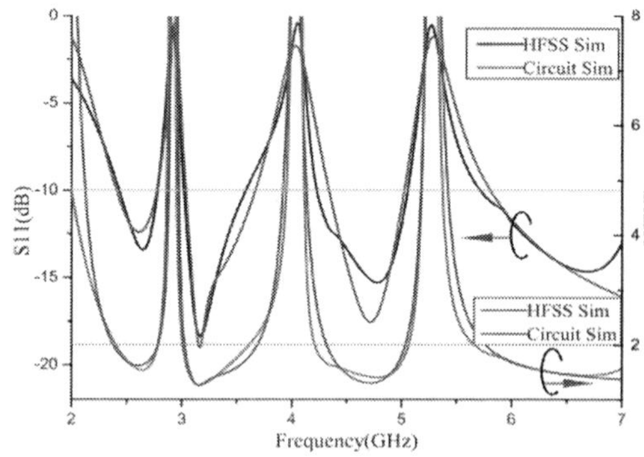

Fig. 4. Comparison of full-wave EM- and equivalent circuit model simulations.

shows a series resonance characteristic and the real part is almost close to zero. As for the notch band at 5.28 GHz, the imaginary part exhibits a parallel resonance characteristic, while the real part rushes to the peak of 400 Ohm. Therefore, we give the equivalent circuit model of the presented antenna, which is presented in Fig. 3. It can be seen that two series RLC are connected with a parallel RLC, and then it was connected to R_r in series, where R_r is the complex form of the input impedance of UWB antenna. R_i, L_i and C_i represent the values of the resisters, inductors and capacitors of the series and parallel equivalent circuit model, respectively. The series components R_1, L_1, C_1 and R_2, L_2, C_2 are operating for 2.92 GHz and 4.06 GHz, respectively, leading the input to be shorted. Additionally, the parallel components R_3, L_3, C_3 operating at 5.28 GHz create an open characteristics for the input. Thus, the presented antenna cannot radiate at the rejection frequency bands. For the series components, -3 dB bandwidth of RLC can be predicted based on the formula given in [5], [7]:

$$BW_i = \frac{R_i}{L_i}, i = 1, 2. \tag{1}$$

As for the parallel $\mathrm{R_3, L_3, C_3}$, the center resonance frequency and -3 dB bandwidth can be calculated by using the equations listed as follows:

$$w_3 = \frac{1}{\sqrt{L_3 C_3}}, \tag{2}$$

$$BW_3 = \frac{1}{R_3 C_3}. \tag{3}$$

III. The Results of Equivalent Circuit Model

The equivalent circuit model of the presented antenna is finalized in Fig. 3. The circuit parameters are extracted form the EM simulation and the optimized parameters are: $R_1 = 1.0$ Ohm, $L_1 = 58.804$ nH, $C_1 = 0.05$ pF, $R_2 = 59.0$ Ohm, $L_2 = 0.01$ nH, $C_2 = 1.509$ pF, $R_3 = 141.25$ Ohm, $L_3 = 0.5$ nH and $C_3 = 5.25$ pF. Then, the equivalent circuit model is created and simulated by using ADS. The equivalent circuit model and EM estimation results are compared and shown in Fig. 4. Figure 4 depicts that the comparison results of reflection coefficients and VSWR, which are obtained from both the equivalent circuit model and EM simulations. It is clear to see that the results of the circuit model agree well with EM simulation ones. The excellent agreement validates that the validity and correctness of the equivalent circuit model for the triple frequency rejection band UWB antenna.

IV. Conclusion

In this paper, an accurate equivalent circuit model of a triple frequency rejection band UWB antenna have been extracted and analyzed in detail. The equivalent circuit model is composed of series and parallel RLC for the desired rejection center frequency bands operating at 2.92 GHz, 4.06 GHz and 5.28 GHz. The validity of the equivalent circuit model have been extracted and investigated on the basis of the simulations which verify the effectiveness and correctness of the proposed equivalent circuit model.

Acknowledgments

This paper is funded by the International Exchange Program of Harbin Engineering University for Innovation-oriented Talents Cultivation. This work was also partially supported by the National Key Research and Development Program of China-Government Corporation Special Program (2016YFE0111100), the Science and Technology innovative Talents Foundation of Harbin (2016RAXXJ044), Projects for the Selected Returned Overseas Chinese Scholars of Heilongjiang Province and MOHRSS of China, and the Foundational Research Funds for the Central Universities (HEUCFD1433, HEUCF160815).

References

[1] Y. Li, W. Li, Q. Ye, "A reconfigurable triple-notch-band antenna integrated with defected microstrip structure band-stop filter for ultra-wideband cognitive radio applications," International Journal of Antennas Propagation, vol.2013, no.7, pp.721-724, 2013.

[2] A. N. Ghazali, S. Pal, "Planar UWB filter with multiple notched band and stopband with improved rejection level," Frequenz-Journal of RF-Engineering and Telecommunications, vol.69, no.5-6, pp.207-218, 2015.

[3] Y. Li, W. Li, W. Yu, "A switchable UWB slot antenna using SIS-HSIR and SIS-SIR for multi-mode wireless communications applications," Applied Computational Electromagnetics Society Journal, vol.27, no.4, pp.340-351, 2012.

[4] M. H. Badjian, C. K. Chakrabarty, S. Devkumar, "Circuit modeling of an UWB patch antenna," RF and Microwave Conference, IEEE International RFM (RFM'08), pp.139-149, 2008.

[5] F. Zhu, S. Gao, A. T. Ho, et al, "Multiple band-notched UWB antenna with band-rejected elements integrated in the feed line," IEEE Transactions on Antennas Propagation, vol.61, no.8, pp.3952-3960, 2013.

[6] Y. Wang, T. Jiang, Y. Li, "Development of a microstip-fed multi-band antenna by means of defected microstrip structures," Progress in Electromagnetics Research Symposium (PIERS'16), 8-11th Aug., 2016.

[7] Y. D. Dong, W. Hong, Z. Q. Kuai, "Analysis of planar ultra-wideband antennas with on-ground slot band-notched structures," IEEE Transactions on Antennas Propagation, vol.57, no.7, pp.1886-1893, 2009.

Innovative Simplified Array Design for Wireless Power Transmission

G. Oliveri[1], P. Rocca[1], L. Poli[1], A. Massa[1,2]
[1]ELEDIA Research Center (ELEDIA@UniTN - University of Trento)
Trento, Italy
[2]ELEDIA Research Center (ELEDIA@L2S - UMR 8506)
Gif-sur-Yvette, France
andrea.massa@eledia.org

***Abstract*—In this paper, the synthesis of arrays for long-distance wireless power transmission (WPT) based on unconventional architectures is addressed. A subarraying technique based on an enhanced version of the Contiguous Partition Method suitably customized in order to efficiently deal with a WPT scenario is presented, and a Compressive Sensing-based method developed in a multi-task Bayesian framework is proposed for designing sparse WPT arrays. Selected numerical results are reported to highlight the effectiveness of the proposed techniques.**

Keywords—Wireless power transmission, sub-arrayed antennas, sparse arrays, Contiguous Partition Method, Multi-Task Bayesian Compressive Sensing.

I. Introduction

Long-range Wireless Power Transmission is a technology devoted to the transfer of energy between remote locations without wired links, which requires the use of large arrays of antennas for a suitable delivering of the power via microwaves [1]. In the past years, the design of large WPT arrays has been only marginally addressed by the scientific community, whereas most of the efforts have been focused on the other issues still related to long-distance WPT systems such as the maximization of the receiving antenna efficiency or the RF-to-DC conversion efficiency [1]. Dealing with the synthesis of WPT arrays, solutions based on simple tapering approaches [2] and stochastic techniques have been presented [3]. Optimal methods for defining the tapered excitations that maximize the beam transmission efficiency (BTE) for both linear [4] and planar [5] arrangements of elements have been also proposed. However, although optimal from a theoretical point of view, the methods in [4, 5] deal with fully-populated arrays whose practical realization may be prohibitive due to high costs and beam forming network (BFN) complexity. This paper is aimed to propose two different approaches for the simplification of the array architecture, based on an enhanced version of the CPM [6] and the multi-task Bayesian Compressive Sensing (MT-BCS) method [7]. The former is a subarraying technique aimed to reduce the number of control points (namely, amplifies/attenuators and phase shifters) of the array, by means of an excitation matching method suitably adapted to the specific scenario in order to help the research of solutions providing higher BTE. The latter is a Compressive Sensing-based method used for designing a maximally sparse layout with minimum number of elements, implemented in a multi-task Bayesian framework in order to improve the matching of the radiation pattern with the optimal reference [5].

II. Mathematical Formulation

Let us consider a rectangular array composed by $M \times N$ elements displaced on a regular planar grid in the xy-plane and equally spaced by d along both the x and y axes. In the WPT framework, the synthesis of the element excitations $\mathbf{w}^{opt} = \{w_{mn}^{opt}; m = 1,...,M; n = 1,...,N\}$ is aimed to maximize the following ratio (namely, the BTE)

$$\eta = P_{INC}/P_{RAD} = \iint_{\Omega} |AF(u,v)|^2 \Big/ \iint_{4\pi} |AF(u,v)|^2 \tag{1}$$

being Ω the region where the received power has to be maximized, $AF(u,v) = \sum_{m=1}^{M} \sum_{n=1}^{N} w_{mn}^{opt} \exp[jkd(mu + nv)]$ the array factor term, $u = \sin\theta\cos\phi$, $v = \sin\theta\sin\phi$, $k = 2\pi/\lambda$ and λ the free-space wavelength. Starting from the reference excitations $\mathbf{w}^{opt}$ related to the fully-populated architecture and computed according to [5], the following approaches will be aimed to simplify the array structure by reducing (*i*) the number of control points by grouping the elements into sub-arrays or (*ii*) both the number of control points and elements by designing an arbitrary lattice for the element sparsification.

Dealing with the first approach, the optimal subarray configuration, described through a set of integer values $\mathbf{C} = \{c_{mn}; m = 1,...,M; m = 1,...,N\}$, as well as the subarray weighs are defined by means of an enhanced version of the contiguous partition method aimed to minimize the following cost function which combines two terms related to the excitation matching and to the BTE:

$$\Psi(\mathbf{C},\mathbf{I}) = \beta_1 \frac{1}{MN} \sum_{m=1}^{M} \sum_{n=1}^{N} \left| w_{mn}^{opt} - b_{mn}(\mathbf{C},\mathbf{I}) \right|^2 + \beta_2 \frac{\left| \eta^{opt} - \eta(\mathbf{C},\mathbf{I}) \right|^2}{\left| \eta^{opt} \right|^2} \tag{2}$$

where $\mathbf{B} = \{b_{mn}; m = 1,...,M; m = 1,...,N\}$ and $\mathbf{I} = \{i_q; q = 1,...,Q\}$ (being Q the number of clusters) are the vector of the element and subarray weights [6], respectively, and β_1 and β_2 are real weighting coefficients.

The design of a maximally sparse layout for minimizing the number of elements and for the definition of the corresponding excitations $\mathbf{G}=\{g_k;k=1,...,K\}$ (being $K>>MN$ the number of allowed positions (x_k,y_k) for the sparse array elements) are obtained through the solution of a pattern matching problem suitably formulated in a BCS framework. More in detail, the synthesis problem can be recast as that of maximizing the *a-posteriori* probability $P(\mathbf{G}|\mathbf{\Gamma}_{ref})$ subject to the sparsity of $\mathbf{G}$, where $\mathbf{\Gamma}^{ref}=\{\gamma_p^{ref};p=1,...,P\}$ is the vector of the reference array factor samples, calculated as $\gamma_p^{ref}=AF(u_p,v_p)$.The problem can be solved via maximization of the marginal likelihood [7] through a Relevance Vector Machine [7], by determining in a first step the auxiliary hyperparameter vector $\boldsymbol{\alpha}$ introduced for enabling the sparsity enforcement on the problem unknowns, and then by estimating the element excitations as follows

$$\mathbf{G}|_{MT-BCS}=\left[diag(\boldsymbol{\alpha})+\boldsymbol{\Phi}^H\boldsymbol{\Phi}\right]^{-1}\boldsymbol{\Phi}^H\mathbf{\Gamma}^{ref}, \quad (3)$$

being $\boldsymbol{\Phi}$ the matrix of the problem defined according to the guidelines of [7].

III. NUMERICAL ASSESSMENT

Let us consider a square planar array of $M\times N=20\times 20$ half-wavelength spaced semi-isotropic elements whose reference excitations, depicted in Fig. 1(*a*), have been defined through the optimal method proposed in [5] assuming a square region $\Psi=\{|u|,|v|\leq 1.63\times 10^{-1}\}$ corresponding to a beam collection efficiency value equal to $\eta^{opt}=99.9\%$. Such a high efficiency value clearly indicates that most of the power is focused in the desired region Ψ, as can be noticed from the radiation pattern shown in Fig. 1(*b*). Dealing with the subarraying strategy, a good trade-off solution with only $Q=9$ clusters per quadrant has been selected among the set of results generated by the CPM method. The quantization of the magnitudes of the compromise excitations [shown in Fig. 1(*c*)] does not affect significantly the radiation pattern depicted in Fig. 1(*d*), allowing to keep its features close to the optimal ones (in particular, $\eta^{CPM}=99.47\%$). An almost perfect matching with the optimal radiation pattern is obtained with the sparse array synthesized through the MT-BCS method [as shown in Fig. 1(*f*)], thanks to the introduction of an additional degree of freedom in the synthesis process (namely, the position of the array elements). The selected solution is an arrangement of N=175 elements whose sparse configuration is illustrated in Fig. 1(*e*). Such a solution guarantees a significant reduction on the number of both radiating elements and control points, affording a beam transmission efficiency very close to the optimal one, equal to $\eta^{MT-BCS}=99.77\%$.

IV. CONCLUSIONS

In this paper, an enhanced version of the CPM and a sparseness-regularized solver have been suitably employed in the synthesis of unconventional WPT arrays, enabling a significant reduction of the number of control points while keeping good performances in the terms of BTE. Future works will be devoted to the study of the impact of the tolerances of the electronic components on the performances of the WPT systems [8]-[11].

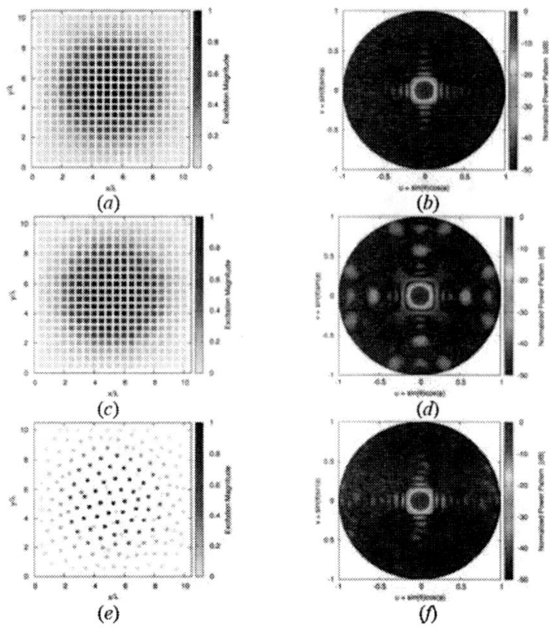

Fig. 1. *Optimal vs. Simplified Array Solutions* – (*a*)(*c*)(*e*) Excitation magnitudes and (*b*)(*d*)(*f*) radiation patterns synthesized through the (*a*)(*b*) optimal, (*c*)(*d*) CPM and (*e*)(*f*) MT-BCS methods.

REFERENCES

[1] A. Massa, G. Oliveri, F. Viani, and P. Rocca, "Array designs for long-distance wireless power transmission – State-of-the-art and innovative solutions," *Proc. IEEE*, vol. 101, no. 6, pp. 1464-1481, Jun. 2013.

[2] A. K. M Baki, *et al.*, "Isosceles-trapezoidal-distribution edge tapered array antenna with unequal element spacing for solar power satellite," *IEICE Trans. Commun.*, vol. E91-B, no. 2, pp. 527-535, Feb. 2008.

[3] N. Shinohara, *et al.*, "New stochastic algorithm for optimization of both side lobes and grating lobes in large antenna arrays for MPT," *IEICE Trans. Commun.*, vol. E91-B, no. 1, pp. 286-295, Jan. 2008.

[4] G. Oliveri, L. Poli, and A. Massa, "Maximum efficiency beam synthesis of radiating planar arrays for wireless power transmission," *IEEE Trans. Antennas Propag.*, pp. 2490-2499, vol. 61, no. 5, May 2013.

[5] S. Prasad, "On an index for array optimization and the discrete prolate spheroidal functions," *IEEE Trans. Antennas Propag.*, vol. 30, no. 5, pp. 1021-1023, Sep. 1982.

[6] L. Manica, *et al.*, "Design of subarrayed linear and planar array antennas with SLL control based on an excitation matching approach," *IEEE Trans. Antennas Propag.*, vol. 57, no. 6, pp. 1684-1691, Jun. 2009.

[7] G. Oliveri, *et al.*, "Synthesis of modular contiguously clustered linear arrays through a sparseness-regularized solver," *IEEE Trans. Antennas Propag.*, vol. 64, no. 10, pp. 4277-4287, Oct. 2016.

[8] N. Anselmi, *et al.*, "Power pattern sensitivity to calibration errors and mutual coupling in linear arrays through circular interval arithmetics," *Sensors*, vol. 16, no. 6(791), pp. 1-14, 2016.

[9] P. Rocca, *et al.*, "Predicting antenna pattern degradations in microstrip reflectarrays through interval arithmetic,", *IET Microw. Antennas Propag.*, vol. 10, no. 8, pp. 817–826, May 2016.

[10] N. Anselmi, *et al.*, "Generalized interval-based analysis tool for pattern distortions in reflector antennas with bump-like surface deformations," *IET Microw. Antennas Propag.*, vol. 10, no. 9, pp. 909–916, June 2016.

[11] N. Anselmi, P. Rocca, M. Salucci, and A. Massa, "Optimization of excitation tolerances for robust beamforming in linear arrays," *IET Microw. Antennas Propag.*, vol. 10, no. 2, pp. 208-214, 2016.

An Integer Genetic Algorithm for Optimal Clustering in Phased Array Antenna

L. Poli[1], G. Oliveri[1], A. Massa[1,2]
[1]ELEDIA Research Center (ELEDIA@UniTN - University of Trento)
Trento, Italy
[2]ELEDIA Research Center (ELEDIA@L2S - UMR 8506)
Gif-sur-Yvette, France
andrea.massa@eledia.org

***Abstract*—A subarraying technique based on a novel genetic algorithm (GA) whose operators have been suitably customized in order to deal with integer variables is presented in this paper. The method is aimed to prevent the generation of high-level quantization lobes in the scanned radiation pattern by properly combining a given number of clusters selected from an arbitrarily defined alphabet of tiles of various shapes. A representative numerical result is reported in order to show advantages and drawbacks of the proposed methodology.**

Keywords—Subarraying techniques, beam scanning, evolutionary optimization, integer genetic algorithm.

I. Introduction

The design of array antennas with simplified structure still represents a challenging task of interest to the antenna community [1, 2]. Since several years, many efforts have been devoting to the development of suitable techniques aimed to find solutions with reduced costs able to partially preserve the radiation performances of the array. In this framework, thinning and sparsening strategies have been widely investigated in the past decades. The former are aimed to fill the array aperture with uniformly excited elements placed on a regular lattice, according to some rules defined in a deterministic [3] or stochastic [4, 5] way. The latter are devoted to define sparse layouts in order to arbitrarily place the elements within the array aperture and to determine the non-uniform element excitations thus providing a better control on the pattern sidelobes due to the additional degrees of freedom (DoFs) exploited in the synthesis process [6]. Although both the approaches proved their good capability to efficiently design architectures with reduced number of elements, a lower aperture efficiency is unavoidably associated to such solutions and the use of non-regular layouts (for sparse arrays) increases the issues related to the array fabrication. Subarraying techniques [7]-[11] turn out to be attractive alternatives to the above approaches, as they allow to preserve the array aperture efficiency by reducing the complexity of the beamforming network (BFN). Dealing with planar arrangements, irregular subarraying strategies [7]-[11] have shown their good capability to avoid the formation of high-level quantization lobes, but without considering the effects on the radiation pattern caused by the use of a single phase control for each subarray. This paper is aimed to propose a novel and flexible strategy for both phase and amplitude subarraying aimed to mitigate the undesired sidelobes and to limit the degradation of the radiation pattern when acting on the phases at subarray-level for beam scanning purposes. Toward this aim, a novel integer genetic algorithm is applied to properly assemble within the array aperture a given number of subarrays with pre-defined shapes defined as desired through an alphabet of tiles.

II. Mathematical Formulation

Let us consider a square array of $N \times N$ elements displaced on the xy-plane and organized according to a regular rectangular lattice. From the feeding point of view, the architecture includes per-element magnitude control (real valued coefficients $\mathbf{A} = \{\alpha_q; q = 1,...,Q\}$) and per-cluster phase control ($\mathbf{B} = \{\beta_q; q = 1,...,Q\}$) being Q the number of clusters. Let us define also the vector $\mathbf{C} = \{c_{mn}; m,n = 1,...,N\} \in [1:Q]$, composed by a set of integer coefficients, namely the partition indexes, describing the sub-arrayed architecture (elements with the same index belong to the same sub-array). The far field pattern of the array can be expressed as

$$AF(\theta,\phi) = \sum_{q=1}^{Q}\sum_{m=1}^{M}\sum_{n=1}^{N}\delta_{c_{mn}q}\alpha_q e^{j\beta_q} e^{jk(x_{mn}\sin\theta\cos\phi + y_{mn}\sin\theta\sin\phi)}, \quad (1)$$

where $\delta_{c_{mn}q}$ is the Kronecker delta (equal to 1 if $c_{mn} = q$, equal to 0 otherwise) and (x_{mn}, y_{mn}) are the spatial coordinates of the mn-th array element. According to the simplified array architecture, the scanning of the beam toward a given direction (θ_0, ϕ_0) must be carried out by acting on the phases at the subarray level. Toward this aim, the set of coefficients $\mathbf{B}$ can be computed as

$$\beta_q = -\frac{2\pi}{\lambda}\left(\tilde{x}_q \sin\theta_0 \cos\phi_0 + \tilde{y}_q \sin\theta_0 \sin\phi_0\right), \quad q = 1,...,Q \quad (2)$$

where $(\tilde{x}_q, \tilde{y}_q)$ is the barycenter of the q-th cluster. The beam pattern of the broadside array will be unavoidably distorted in scanning due to the employment of the phase shifter at the subarray level, whose values, computed according to (2), are clearly dependent on the sub-array architecture. In order to properly define a simplified array structure by maximally reducing the number of clusters and thus of the phase shifters, a novel technique based on an integer genetic algorithm is then proposed. The method is aimed to determine the vector $\mathbf{C}$ via minimization of the following cost function

$$\Phi^{(i)}=\sum_{p=1}^{P}\sum_{\chi\in X}w_{\chi}\left[\left|\chi^{(i,p)}-\chi^{des}\right|^{2}/\left|\chi^{des}\right|^{2}\right]H\left(\chi^{(i,p)}-\chi^{des}\right)+w_{Q}Q^{(i)}, \quad (3)$$

where $H(\cdot)$ is the Heaviside function, w_χ and w_Q are real weighting coefficients, $X=\{SLL;-D_{\max};HPBW_{\phi_0}\}$, being SLL, $D_{\max}$ and $HPBW_{\phi_0^{(p)}}$ the sidelobe level, the directivity peak and the half power beamwidth along the $\phi_0^{(p)}$ cut, respectively, $p = 1,\ldots,P$, being P the number of considered cuts. Moreover, the subscripts $\cdot^{des}$ and $\cdot^{(i)}$ indicates the desired or the actual (at the i-th iteration) value of the descriptors, respectively. The genetic operators (i.e., selection, crossover and mutation [12]), suitably recast in order to deal with integer variables, are exploited to combine a given number of clusters picked up from an alphabet Λ of tiles of different shapes, whereas the excitation amplitudes at subarray-level are computed by means of the Contiguous Partition Method (CPM) [8, 9] starting from a set of reference weights.

III. Numerical Assessment

A square planar array of $N\times N=20\times 20$ semi-isotropic elements equi-spaced by $d=d_x=d_y=\lambda/2$ along both the x and y axes has been considered in the following numerical experiment. The performance of the array have been optimized at the scan angle $\theta_0=30°$, considering $P=9$ ϕ_0-cuts, equally distributed in the overall range $\phi\in[0:360]°$. The reference excitation amplitudes have been synthesized through an optimal Convex Programming (*CP*)-based method [11] aimed to maximize the directivity of the broadside array while keeping the sidelobe level below a given threshold set to $SLL^{ref}=-30dB$. The desired pattern features have been set according to the values obtained with the borderline case when $Q=N=400$, as follows: $SLL^{des}=-30dB$, $D_{\max}^{des}=29.12dB$, and $HPBW_{\phi_0}^{des}=7.3°$. Although such values will never be reached when $Q<400$, the aim of this experiment is the generation of an exhaustive set of trade-off solutions by properly varying w_Q and the selection of a representative example among such a set. In order to simulate a real-world design problem, the alphabet Λ has been created only with simple, modular, rectangular-shaped clusters (the realization of arbitrarily shaped tiles may be affected by several manufacturing issues) of size $R\times S$, being R and S the number of elements of the subarray along the x and y axes, assumed to be even numbers. A trade-off solution with $Q=180$ subarrays [combined within the array aperture as illustrated in Fig. 1(*a*)] has been selected for a detailed analysis. The excitation amplitudes of this result are given in Fig. 1(*b*) whereas Figs. 1(*c*) and 1(*d*) show the radiation pattern generated by the array in scanning toward $(\theta_0,\phi_0)=(30,0)°$ and $(\theta_0,\phi_0)=(30,90)°$, respectively. As expected, due to the significant reduction of the number of control points, the radiation pattern in steering is subject to degradation and consequently the pattern features worsen to $\max_{\phi_0}\left[SLL_{\phi_0}\right]=-16.1dB$, $\min_{\phi_0}\left[D_{\max}^{\phi_0}\right]=26.4dB$, and $\max_{\phi_0}\left[HPBW_{\phi_0}\right]=7.7°$. By properly varying w_Q, different trade-off solutions may be obtained (e.g., higher values of w_Q allow to find solutions having lower number of subarrays but providing a worse matching with the desired pattern features).

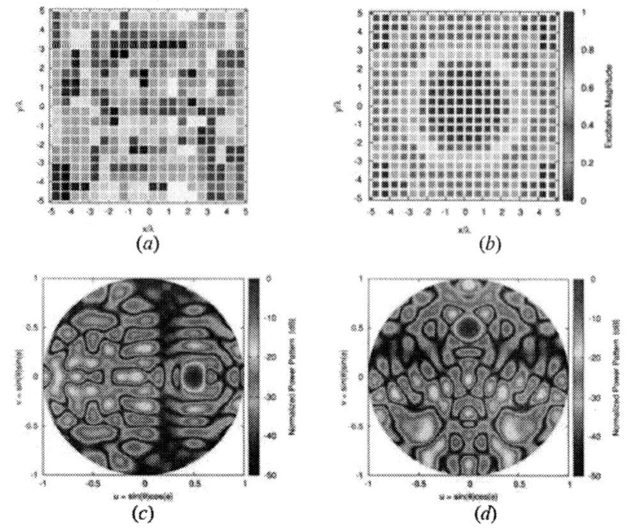

Fig. 1. *GA-optimized Solution, Q=180* - Excitation magnitudes (*a*), subarraying configuration (*b*), and normalized radiation pattern when steering the main lobe toward $(\theta_0,\varphi_0)=(30,0)°$ (*c*) and $(\theta_0,\varphi_0)=(30,90)°$ (*d*).

References

[1] R. L. Haupt, Antenna Arrays: A Computational Approach. Hoboken, NJ, USA: Wiley, 2010.

[2] P. Rocca, G. Oliveri, R. J. Mailloux, and A. Massa, "Unconventional phased array architectures and design methodologies - A Review," *Proc. IEEE*, vol. 104, no. 3, pp. 544-560, Mar. 2016.

[3] G. Oliveri and A. Massa, "Fully-interleaved linear arrays with predictable sidelobes based on almost difference sets," *IET Radar, Sonar & Navigation*, vol. 4, no. 5, pp. 649-661, 2010.

[4] M. I. Skolnik, *et al*, "Statistically designed density-tapered arrays," *IEEE Trans. Antennas Propag.*, vol. 12, no. 4, pp. 408-417, Jul, 1964.

[5] R. L. Haupt, "Thinned arrays using genetic algorithms," *IEEE Trans. Antennas Propag.*, vol. 42, no. 7, pp. 993-999, Jul. 1994.

[6] F. Viani, G. Oliveri, and A. Massa, "Compressive sensing pattern matching techniques for synthesizing planar sparse arrays," *IEEE Trans. Antennas Propag.*, vol. 61, no. 9, pp. 4577-4587, Sep. 2013.

[7] G. Oliveri, *et al.*, "Synthesis of modular contiguously clustered linear arrays through a sparseness-regularized solver," *IEEE Trans. Antennas Propag.*, vol. 64, no. 10, pp. 4277-4287, Oct. 2016.

[8] L. Manica, *et al.*, "Design of subarrayed linear and planar array antennas with SLL control based on an excitation matching approach," *IEEE Trans. Antennas Propag.*, vol. 57, no. 6, pp. 1684-1691, Jun. 2009.

[9] P. Rocca, L. Manica, and A. Massa, "An improved excitation matching method based on an ant colony optimization for suboptimal-free clustering in sum-difference compromise synthesis," *IEEE Trans. Antennas Propag.*, vol. 57, no. 8, pp. 2297-2306, Aug. 2009.

[10] P. Rocca, R. J. Mailloux, and G. Toso, "GA-based optimization of irregular sub-array layouts for wideband phased array design," *IEEE Antennas Wireless Propag.*, vol. 14, pp. 131-134, 2015.

[11] P. Rocca, L. Manica, R. Azaro, and A. Massa, "A hybrid approach for the synthesis of sub-arrayed monopulse linear arrays," *IEEE Trans. Antennas Propag.*, vol. 57, no. 1, pp. 280-283, Jan. 2009.

[12] P. Rocca, *et al.*, "Evolutionary optimization as applied to inverse problems," *Inverse Problems*, vol. 25, pp. 1-41, Dec. 2009.

Reconfigurable electrically small split ring resonator antenna

A.Bakhmutov, N.Knyazev, V.Chechetkin
Institute of Radioelectronics and Information Technologies
Ural Federal University
Yekaterinburg, Russia
v.a.chechetkin@urfu.ru

Abstract— **A reconfigurable electrically small microstrip-fed antenna composed of a broadside coupled split ring resonator with stubs connected through pin-diodes and an exciting arc-shaped monopole is presented. Numerical and experimental results are presented for an antenna configuration of 1/24.3 wavelength λ in diameter (antenna is inscribed in a sphere with radius a, k - wave number), ka = 0.13. The antenna size including the ground plane is 68 × 44 mm2 and it operates at 149 MHz with 7.15 MHz bandwidth (VSWR<2). Its resonant frequency can be tuned over a wide range of frequency without changing the antenna size. The antenna can be used with metamaterial cover, as a part of the antenna array or an active antenna.**

Keywords— Electrically small antenna, Split ring resonator antenna, Reconfigurable antenna

I. Introduction

In many electronic devices antenna covers the considerable part of the volume, sometimes it is fundamental part of the cost. The antennas with small size relative to the wavelength are particularly relevant for the modern miniature equipment. One of the promising trends of antenna technology is miniaturization of microstrip antennas. Methods of miniaturization microstrip antennas include the use of substrates with high permittivity, increasing of the electrical length of the antenna with a small area of the substrate (using meander, spiral and zigzag patterns), as well as use of resonators of special design, which will be considered in this paper. The main purpose of the work is to improve the split ring resonator antenna in order to extend its band-width.

II. Reconfigurable SRR antenna

The initial version of the antenna (Fig. 1) was designed on the basis of the geometry presented in [1]. Resonant frequency is 148 MHz, the substrate dimensions are 42 × 65 mm, the thickness h = 0.787 mm. Made of dielectric Rogers Duroid 5870 with relative permittivity εr = 2.33. ka ~ 0.119 (a = 0.0387 m, λ = 52.5 a).

The advantages of this antenna include a wide range of operating frequency setting. The strongest influences on the resonant frequency of the SRR have width t and the size of the gap between the resonator and monopole Sr. Effect of Sr is shown below in Fig. 2. The significant shift in resonant frequency is related to changes of antenna capacitance and inductance, which are related to Sr and t.

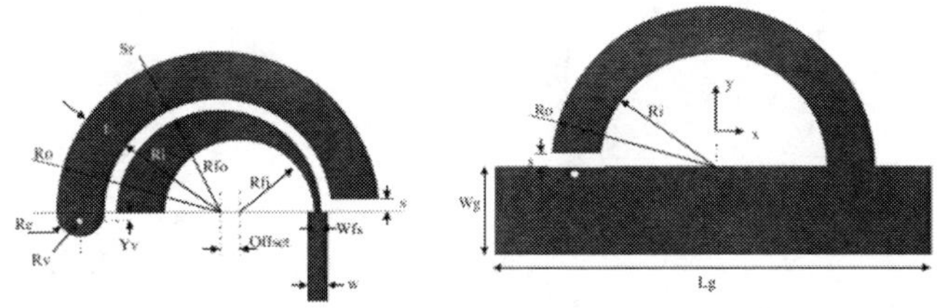

Fig. 1. Top and bottom layer of antenna [1]

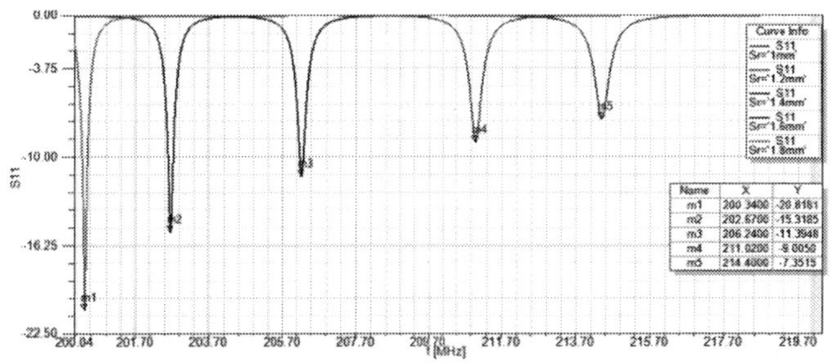

Fig. 2. Return loss with different Sr vs frequency

In order to extend the bandwidth, some changes in antenna design have been made. The substrate material was replaced by a FLAN-10-2 with the relative permittivity εr = 10.1 and the thickness h = 2 mm. By means of altering the gap between the SRR and a monopole Sr and width of rings t the antenna was set to resonant frequency 152 MHz. In the bottom layer of the resonator the cut-outs have been made. These cut-outs separate three stubs from the resonator. The stubs are connected with three pin-diodes to the antenna. The antenna is shown below on Fig. 3.

Computed S11 of the resulting antenna are given below in Fig. 4, for the convenience the diodes are numbered in order from the via.

The blocking inductors and the tracks to the edge of substrate were added to the model of the antenna/ The simulation showed that these changes did not affect the characteristics of the antenna, so further small conductors connected to the antenna through blocking inductors, were not included in the model, since they considerably increase the time of calculation.

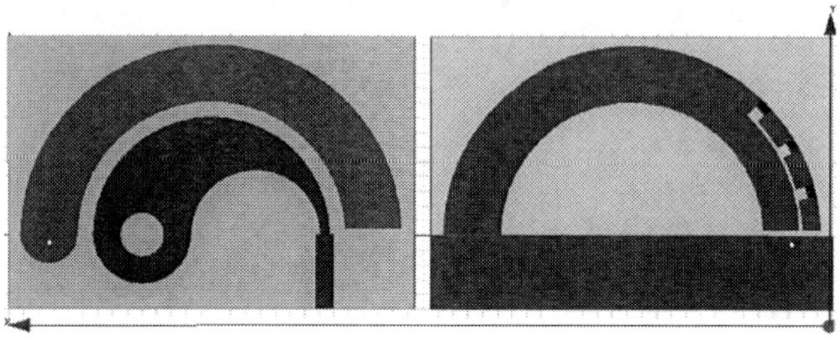

Fig. 3. Top and bottom view of reconfigurable antenna

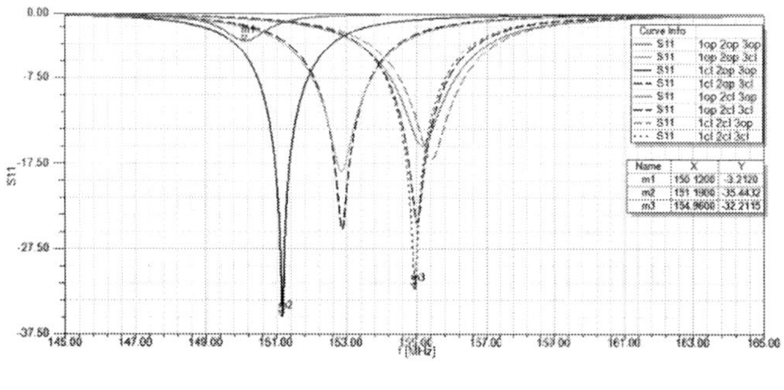

Fig. 4. Computed S11 of the antenna with 8 combinations of diodes states

III. EXPERIMENTAL RESURTS

The produced antenna is shown below in Fig. 5.

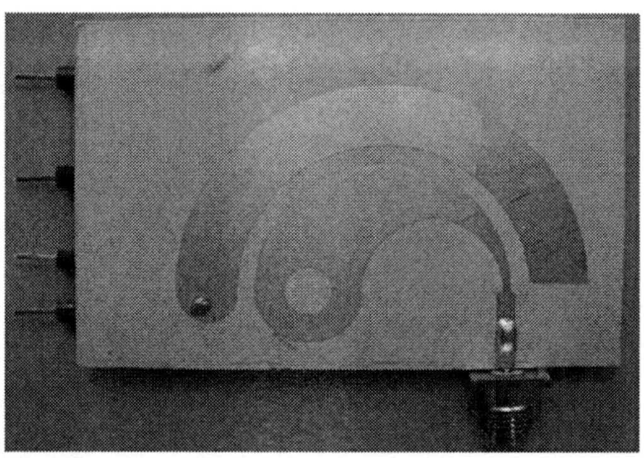

Fig. 5. Made antenna top view

The maximum linear dimension of the antenna (in the diagonal of the substrate) is 81 mm, which gives ka ~ 0.13 (f = 152 MHz, λ = 1.97 m, k = 3.2, a = 0.0405 m, λ = 48.6a). The antenna is fed by microstrip line, but for the convenience of the measurement to the edge of the board the SMA coaxial connector was soldered. With the device PLANAR OBZOR TR1300/1 frequency dependence of return loss to seven combinations of states of the diodes shown below in Fig. 6.

Fig. 6 shows that the central frequency of the antenna is offset by approximately 4 MHz downwards; it was caused by manufacturing inaccuracy.

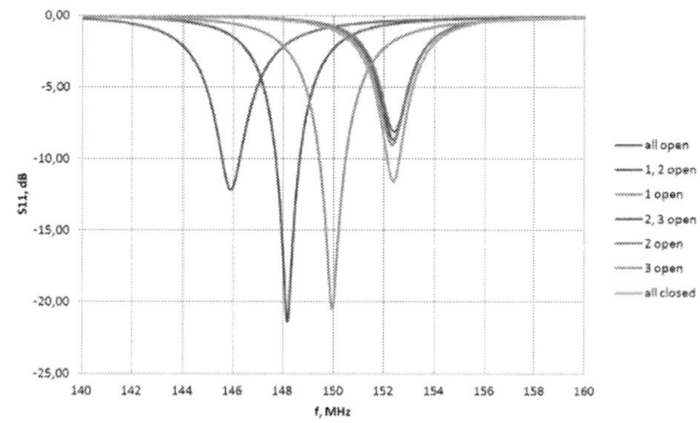

Fig. 6. Measured return loss of the antenna with 7 combinations of diodes states

The bandwidth of VSWR<2 is 7.15 MHz. This bandwidth is 132 times greater than in the initial version of the antenna. Figure 6 shows the dependence only for open and closed states of the diodes, so in the operating frequency band there are areas where the VSWR is greater than 2 or even 4, but with a smooth change of voltage on the diodes, you can get a standing wave ratio in the band of operating frequencies less than two. The measured antenna impedance with closed diodes at the resonant frequency (152.51 MHz) is 25 + j22 ohm. In anechoic chamber the radiation pattern of the antenna was measured. Co-polarization normalized gain of antenna (dB), in XOZ (left) and YOZ (right) planes is shown in Fig. 7

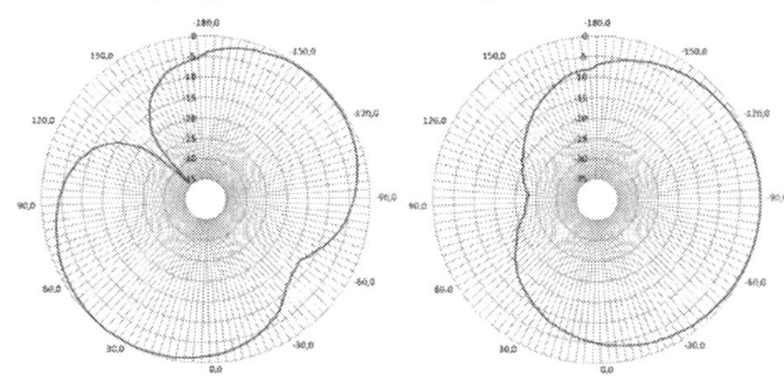

Fig. 7. Co-polarization normalized gain of antenna (dB), in XOZ (left) and YOZ (right) planes

CONCLUSION

Numerical and measured characteristics of reconfigurable electrically small microstrip-fed SRR antenna with stubs connected through pin-diodes were studied. The produced antenna has the maximum linear size 81 mm, which corresponds ka = 0.13. This antenna has omnidirectional radiation pattern with maximum gain of - 13.8 dB, but the use of the LNA (25 dB gain, 1.5 dB noise figure) increases the gain up to 9 dB. The bandwidth (VSWR<2) is 7.15 MHz (8.44 MHz: VSWR<4), which is 132 times greater than that of the original version of the antenna.

REFERENCES

[1] Eldek,A., Miniaturized microstrip-fed circular split ring resonator antenna. Progress In Electromagnetics Research, 17, pp. 219-227, 2010.

A square slot circularly polarized microstrip antenna with enhanced bandwidth

Obeng Kwakye Kingsford Sarkodie
School of Electronic Engineering
Univ. of Electronic Science and Technology of china
Chengdu, China

Kang Kai, Mujeeb Abdullah
School of Electronic Engineering
Univ. of Electronic Science and Technology of China
Chengdu, China

***Abstract*—A square slot circularly polarized (CP) microstrip antenna with enhanced bandwidth is presented. The proposed antenna consists of a C-shape patch and four rectangular strips around the four corners on the lower ground, and is excited by a microstrip feedline. A broadband CP antenna can be achieved by adjusting the size of the strips. The measured results of -10 db impedance bandwidth is 157.2% (2-16.7 GHz) and the measured 3 dB axial ratio(AR) bandwidth is 62.2% (8.2-15.7 GHz). Measured and simulated results show good agreement.**

Keywords*—*antenna, axial ratio, circular polarization, square slot.

I. INTRODUCTION

In recent modern communication systems such as global positioning system, radio-frequency identification and wireless local area network, particular attention has been given to printed slot antennas due to their low cost, light weight and wider bandwidth. In [1], a lot of printed slot antennas are analyzed to give broadband circularly polarized characteristics. More than 38.2% wide-band axial ratio bandwidth (ARBW) can be attained in [2], where two inverted L strips around two opposite corners is employed to achieve circular polarization radiation. In [3], a series microstrip-line-feed configuration coupling to two orthogonal sides of the square-ring slot is deployed to excite a circular polarization wave. The reported axial ratio bandwidth is more than 6%. A protruding T-shaped metallic strip from the ground plane is found to produce a circular polarization radiation in [4]. The axial-ratio bandwidths can reach as large as 18%. An inverted-L tuning stub protruded from the signal line of the CPW is employed by [5] to radiate a CP wave. Axial ratio bandwidth greater than 30% is reported. A CP wave is found to radiate in [6] by employing a branched microstrip feed line to excite the monopole and the slot in parallel, with a 46.8% axial ratio bandwidth.

In this letter, a new simple structure is proposed, where a microstrip-line-feed with a C-shape radiation patch square slot antenna radiates a circular polarization wave at 10.5 GHz. The measured -10 dB impedance bandwidth is 157.2% (2-16.7 GHz)and the 3 dB axial ratio bandwidth is 62.2% (8.2-15.7 GHz). With simplicity in the antenna structure, it is suitable for easy integration in a wide varieties of wireless systems.

A. Antenna Design

The structure of the proposed bandwidth enhancement CP antenna is shown in Fig. 1. The antenna consists of three parts, namely; an upper C-shape radiation patch, an FR4 substrate material where $(\varepsilon_r = 4.4, \tan\delta = 0.02)$ with dimensions $50\times50\times0.8\ mm^3$, and a lower ground. The C-shape radiation patch is fed by a $50\ \Omega$ microstrip line ($L_1\times W$) which is etched on the upper surface of the substrate. There

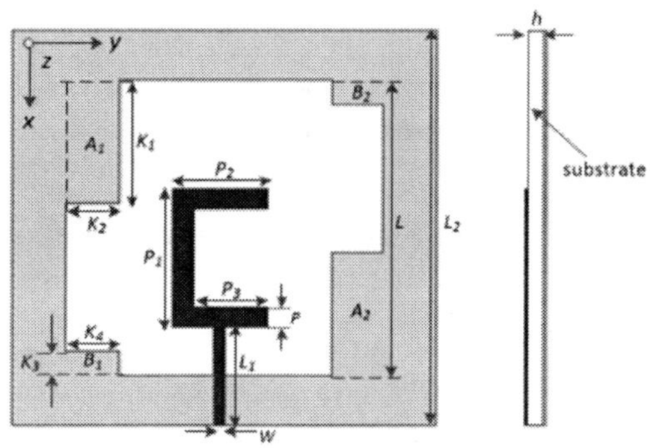

Fig. 1 Antenna structure
a. Top view
b. Side view

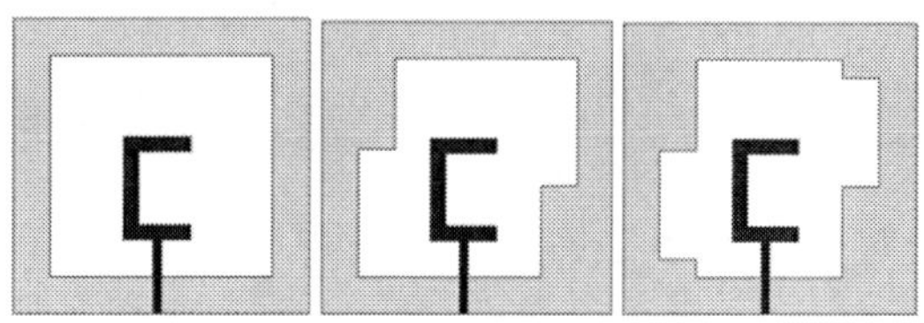

Fig. 2 Design steps to realize the proposed antenna (Ant. 1 - 3)

are four rectangular strips (A_1, A_2, B_1, B_2), where dimensions of $A_1 = A_2$, ($K_2\times K_1$) and $B_1 = B_2$, ($K_4\times K_3$), one at each corner of the lower ground. Fig. 2. depicts how the final structure of the proposed square slot CP antenna is achieved. Ant. 1 includes only the C-shape radiation patch. Ant. 2 includes two opposite but similar rectangle strips (A_1, A_2). Ant. 3 further includes two similar rectangular strips, (B_1, B_2) at the other opposite corners of the lower ground. Fig. 3 depicts the S_{11} and axial ratio bandwidths of the three antennas. All three antennas are circularly polarized. Ant. 1 has a poor S_{11}. After adding two opposite but equal rectangular strips (A_1, A_2), the impedance and axial ratio bandwidths are improved in Ant. 2. Two additional rectangular strips at the other opposite corners of the lower ground (B_1, B_2) greatly improves the impedance

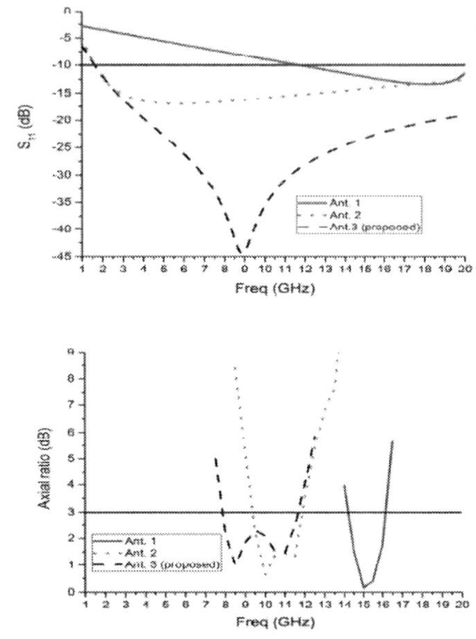

Fig. 3 S_{11} and axial ratio of the three antennas

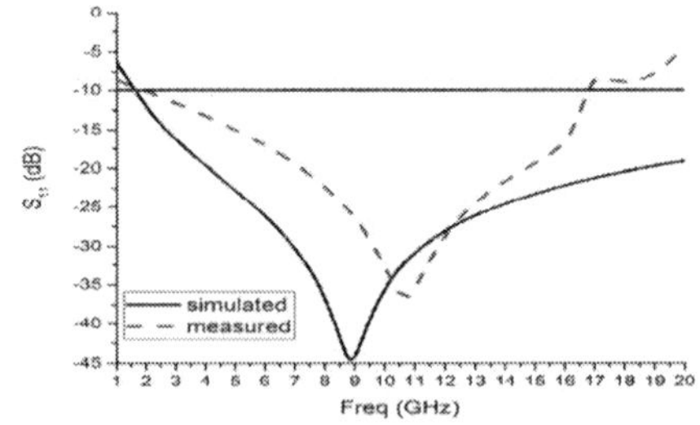

Fig. 4 Simulated and measured S_{11}

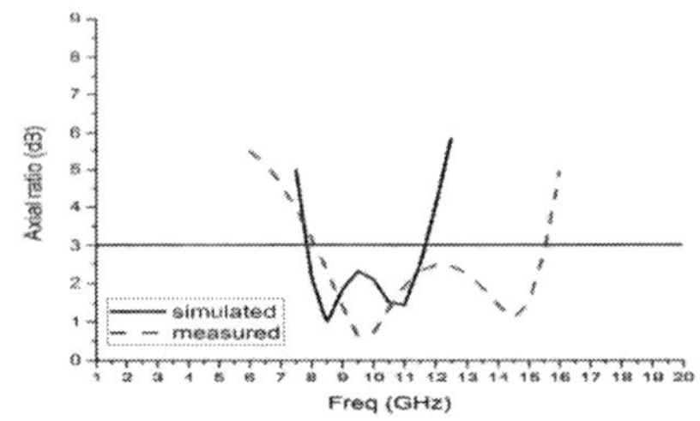

Fig. 5 Simulated and measured AR

and axial ratio bandwidths of Ant. 3.

B. Antenna Performance

The parameters of the proposed antenna are as follows: $L = 38$, $L_1 = 12.5$, $L_2 = 50$, $P = 3$, $P_1 = 18$, $P_2 = 11$, $P_3 = 8$, $K_1 = 15$, $K_2 = 6$, $K_3 = 3$, $K_4 = 6$, $W = 2, h = 0.8$; all units in mm. The performance comparison of simulated and measured return loss is shown in Fig. 4. The measured impedance bandwidth for $S_{11} < -10$ dB is 157.2% (2-16.7 GHz), whereas the simulated result is very wide, from 2 GHz to more than 40 GHz. Fig. 5 illustrates both the simulated and measured axial ratio bandwidth. The measured 3 dB AR bandwidth is 62.2% (8.2 - 15.7 GHz), whereas the simulated 3 dB AR bandwidth is 35.9% (8 - 11.5 GHz). Fig. 5 suggests that the measured 3 dB AR bandwidth is much greater than the simulated. The measured peak gain is 3.6 dBic at 10.5 GHz. The far-field pattern of the proposed antenna is shown in Fig. 6 (a) and (b). The figure depicts the normalized radiation patterns at 10.5 GHz in the *xoz*- and *yoz*-planes, which shows low side lobe levels and a -19 dB cross-polarization discrimination at beam peak. The simulated and measured results are in good agreement.

C. Conclusion

A square slot circularly polarized antenna with enhanced bandwidth is presented in this letter. Good agreements have been achieved between the measured and simulated results. The measured -10 dB impedance bandwidth is 157.2% (2 - 16.7 dB) and the 3 dB axial ratio bandwidth is 62.2% (8.2 - 15.7 GHz). Low side lobe levels and a -19 dB cross polarization levels at beam peak has been achieved. Due to the simple structure of the proposed antenna, it is suitable for easy integration in a wide varieties of wireless systems.

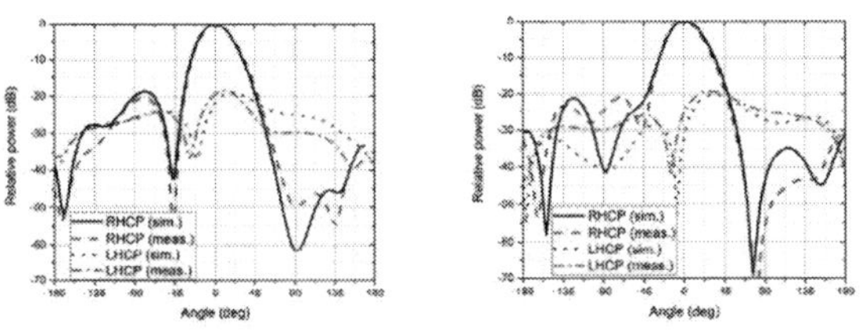

(a) *xz-plane* (b) *yz-plane*

Fig. 6 Measured and simulated radiation pattern of the proposed antenna at 10.5 GHz

REFERENCES

[1] Gao, S., Luo, Q., and Zhu, F.: "Antenna theory-analysis and design" (John Wiley & Sons, Ltd, 2014).

[2] Pourahmadazar, J., and Mohammadi, S.: "Compact circularly-polarized slot antenna for UWB applications," Electronics Lett., 2011, 47, (15), pp. 837-838.

[3] Row, J.-S.: "The design of a squarer-ring slot antenna for circular polarization," IEEE Trans. Antennas Propag., 2005, 53, (6), pp. 1967-1972.

[4] Sze, J.-Y., Wong, K.-L., and Huang, C.-C.: "Coplanar waveguide-fed square slot antenna for broadband circularly polarized radiation," IEEE Trans. Antennas Propag., 2003, 51, (8), pp. 2141-2144.

[5] Sze, J.-Y., Wang J.-C., and Chang C.-C.: "Axial ratio enhancement of asymmetric-CWP-fed circularly-polarized square slot antenna," Electronics Lett., 2008, 44, (18) pp. 1048-1049.

[6] Cai Yuan-Ming, Li Ke, Yin Ying-Zeng, Hu Wei, "Broadband circualrly polarized printed antenna with branched microstrip feed," Antenna and Wireless Propag., Lett., 2014, 13, pp. 674-677.

Wireless Power Transfer via Negative Permittivity Metamaterials as Resonating Elements

Antonios G. Pelekanidis, Antonios X. Lalas, Nikolaos V. Kantartzis
ECE Department, Aristotle University of Thessaloniki
Thessaloniki 54124, Greece
apelekan@ece.auth.gr; lalas@iti.gr; kant@auth.gr

Tadao Ohtani
1-17-134 Omachi
Asahikawa 070-0841, Japan
bytcg100@ybb.ne.jp

Yasushi Kanai
IEE Department
Niigata Institute of Technology
Kashiwazaki, 945-1195, Japan
kanai@iee.niit.ac.jp

***Abstract* — A negative permittivity type of split-ring resonator (SRR) is proposed as an efficient resonating component for wireless power transfer (WPT) systems, functioning via electromagnetic resonance. The principal properties of the SRR are firstly studied and introduced as a guide for the WPT system. The overall efficiency varies depending on the values of the system parameters and is proven to be very satisfactory, as successfully validated by an assortment of realistic applications.**

Keywords—Electric resonance; finite element method (FEM); metamaterials; negative permittivity; wireless power transfer.

I. Introduction

Although the concept of wireless power transfer (WPT) is known for several decades, there has been lately a growing interest in techniques able to achieve efficient systems. Among them, one technique is based on the magnetic coupling of two LC resonators, excited at/around their common resonance frequency; designated as electromagnetic resonance method [1]. The two resonators, i.e. the transmitter and receiver of the system, are inductively connected with a source and a load coil, respectively, and placed at a distance of a few centimeters. Lately, metamaterials have been incorporated as resonating elements in order to enhance the efficiency of a WPT structure at a satisfying level. Common metamaterials, utilized for this scenario, are various types of split-ring resonators (SRRs), which are proven to achieve their purpose [2, 3]. Such configurations exhibit a negative effective relative permeability within a spectrum above their resonance frequency, when excited by a suitably oriented external electric/magnetic field. In this manner, a magnetic resonance that increases the magnetic coupling between the SRRs is generated. However, a relatively confined research has been conducted on the impact of electrically resonant SRRs, like the one presented in [4]. These SRRs consist of an even number of loops, whose current creates opposite magnetic fields, hence the absence of a magnetic response.

Since WPT is achieved through the magnetic coupling of the equivalent coils of two resonators, elements with pure electric properties above their resonance frequency are not expected to improve dramatically the efficiency of the system. It is the aim of this paper to comprehensively investigate the changes in the efficiency, when electrically resonant SRRs are employed for diverse values of the system parameters. In particular, the distance between the two SRRs, the distances between each

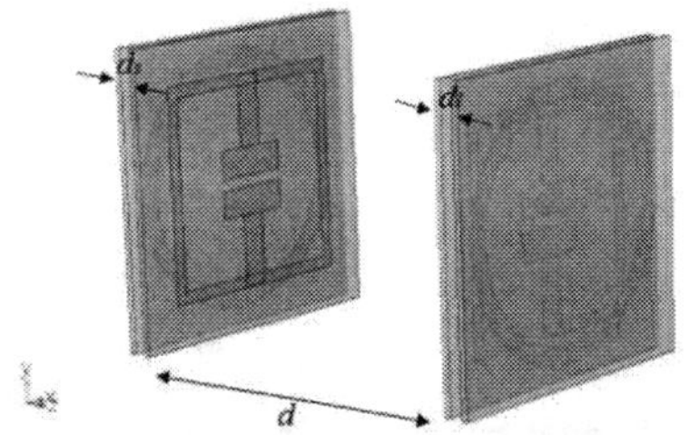

Fig. 1. Perspective view of a metamaterial-based WPT system including the source along with the load coils at the edges and the resonators in between.

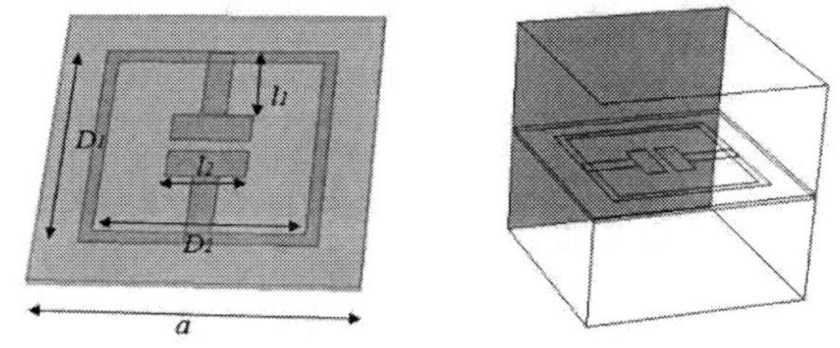

(a) (b)

Fig. 2. (a) Geometry and (b) unit cell of an electrically resonant SRR. The system is electrically excited from the shaded face (horizontal polarization), but it can also be excited from the neighbouring face (vertical polarization).

SRR and its inductively connected source or load loop, and the dimensions of the SRR metal parts are thoroughly examined and interpreted. Results, obtained via the finite element method (FEM) of the COMSOL Multiphysics® package [5] substantiate the merits of the analysis and support our concept for the effective use of electrically resonant SRRs in modern WPT systems.

II. Development of the Unit Cell

The primary concept of a WPT system, based on a general SRR type, is depicted in Fig. 1, while Fig. 2(a) shows the geometry of an electrically resonant component that will be incorporated in the proposed structure. The first step for measuring the efficiency of the novel WPT system determines the frequency region of optimal operation. According to [3], such a frequency is located in the spectrum of the SRR magnetic resonance. Herein, the electric resonances are alternatively obtained and compared to the optimal WPT frequency, enabling us to draw instructive conclusions for the system's total efficiency.

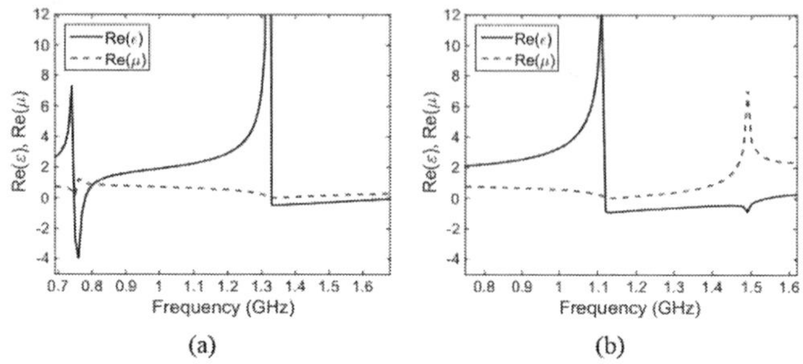

Fig. 3. Constitutive parameters of the electrically resonant SRR when excited with (a) horizontal and (b) vertical polarization.

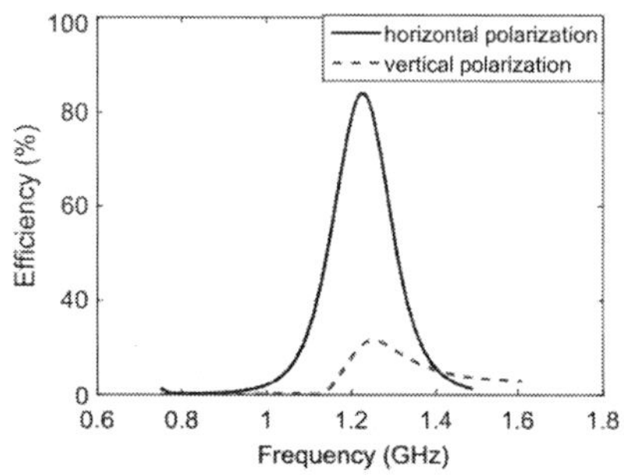

Fig. 4. Efficiency of the WPT system for both excitation polarizations.

The prior frequencies are calculated through a homogenization technique, which involves an infinite plane of periodically placed SRRs, excited by an external magnetic or electric field [6]. So, the S-parameters of the structure can be sufficiently measured. The unit cell of our system (for an SRR with D_1 = 57.6 mm, D_2 = 51.2 mm, l_1 = 19.2 mm, l_2 = 20 mm, and a = 8 mm) is presented in Fig. 2(b), along with the boundary conditions, which create an accurate model of the prior infinite plane. In this context, the effective permittivity and permeability of the selected SRRs are given in Fig. 3 for both polarizations. Note that there are frequency regions of negative equivalent permittivity that depend on the polarization, as stated in [4]. Specifically, two regions of electric resonance are resolved for the horizontal polarization, namely (a) from 0.75 GHz to 0.77 GHz and (b) from 1.33 GHz to approximately 1.7 GHz. On the other hand, there is only one region of electric resonance for the vertical polarization from 1.12 GHz to 1.53 GHz.

III. Validation of the Proposed WPT System

For the verification of our WPT system, the SRR of the previous section is used as a transmitter and receiver. The efficiency is calculated as $|S_{21}|^2$, with the S_{21}-parameter computed via the FEM implemented in the COMSOL Multiphysics® package [5]. The initial distance between the resonators is d = 5 cm and the distances of the source and load coil from the respective resonator are $d_s = d_l$ = 5 mm. Figure 4 shows the efficiency for each polarization, where it is stressed that the new WPT system functions optimally at around 1.2 GHz for both cases. Note the promising efficiency of the horizontal polarization case, which reaches the level of 85.76% at 1.226 GHz, as opposed to the much lower value of 20.43% of its vertical counterpart at 1.252 GHz. So, it is obvious that the two polarizations yield different electric responses, as discussed in [4].

A parametric analysis for various d for the horizontal polarization is presented in Fig. 5. In all simulations, the self inductance is 270 nH, while the mutual inductance varies between 12.5 μH to 18.7 μH and the coupling coefficient between 0.25 to 0.45, when d is between 10 cm to 3 cm. As expected, for smaller d, the efficiency is higher (up to 97.62%) due to the stronger coupling between the resonators. The optimal operation frequency remains relatively steady in the range of 1.223 GHz to 1.236 GHz. Finally, Fig. 6 illustrates the efficiency of our system for diverse distances between the source/load coil and the transmitter/receiver SRR, respectively, for a horizontal polarization, as well. The position of the coils is proven to be a crucial factor, since it can significantly affect the maximum efficiency and optimal frequency. For the distances of 2 mm, 5 mm, and 10 mm, the optimal frequency is 0.984 GHz, 1.226 GHz, and 1.342 GHz, while the maximum efficiency is 20.92%, 63.54%, and 91.78%, respectively. This implies that the coils position influences the performance and the overall losses of the system.

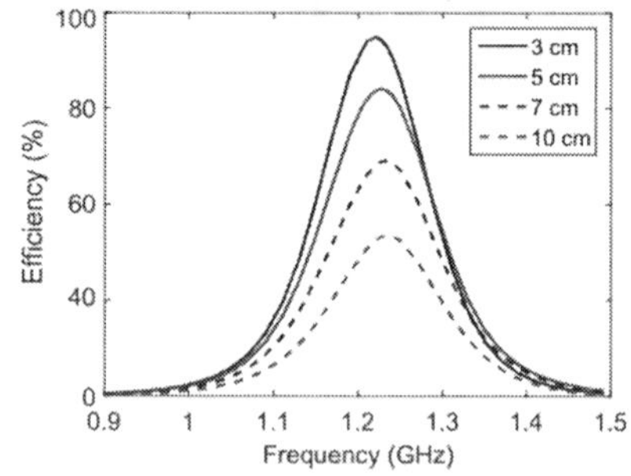

Fig. 5. System efficiency for various distances between the resonators.

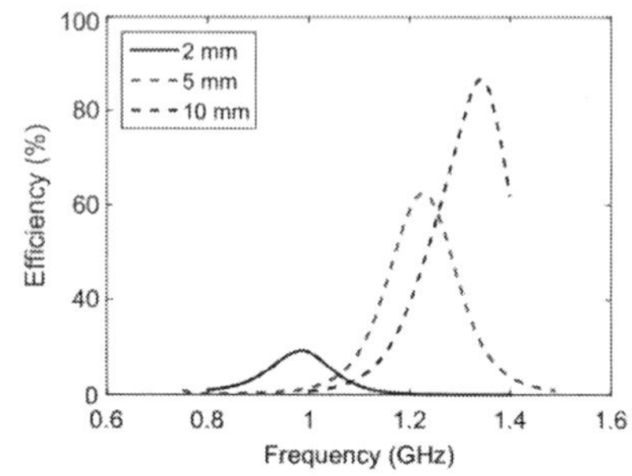

Fig. 6. System efficiency for various distances between the source/load coils and the transmitter/receiver resonators.

References

[1] H. Vázquez-Leal, A. Gallardo-Del-Angel, R. Castañeda-Sheissa, and F. J. González-Martinez, "The phenomenon of wireless energy transfer: Experiments and philosophy," in *Wireless Power Transfer – Principles and Engineering Explorations*, InTech Editions, 2012.

[2] H. Hu and S. V. Georgakopoulos, "Miniaturized strongly coupled magnetic resonance design based on dielectric split-ring resonator for wireless power transmission," in Proc. *29th ACES 2013*, pp. 940-944.

[3] A. X. Lalas, N. V. Kantartzis, and T. D. Tsiboukis, "Wireless energy transfer by means of metamaterial components," in Proc. *9th Metamaterials*, 2015, pp. 163-165.

[4] W. Padilla, M. Aronsson, C. Highstrete, M. Lee, A. Taylor and R. Averitt, "Electrically resonant THz metamaterials: Theoretical and experimental investigations," *Phys. Rev. B*, vol. 75, art. id. 041102(R), 2007.

[5] *COMSOL Multiphysics® Software*, COMSOL Inc., ver. 5.1, 2015.

[6] X. Chen, T. M. Grzegorczyk, B. Wu, J. Pacheco, and J. Kong, "Robust method to retrieve the constitutive effective parameters of metamaterials," *Phys. Rev. E*, vol. 70, art. id. 016608, 2004.

A Multiantenna Approach to Maximize Wireless Power Transfered to Implantable Devices

H. Dinis, I. Colmiais, P. M. Mendes
CMEMS, University of Minho, Guimarães, Portugal, hugodcdinis@gmail.com

***Abstract*—Power delivery from an external source to implanted devices through wireless links is hindered by SAR regulations, which limit the amount of power radiated by an external source that reaches an implant. In order to increase the power delivered to the implant, we studied a solution with two transmitters and compared results with the common single transmitter link. HFSS and COMSOL have been used to show that a power increase of around 40% inside a human head model was achieved while respecting SAR limits and keeping tissue temperature under control, stabilizing at around 37.4 °C.**

Keywords—Wireless power transfer, SAR, Implanted neurodevice

I. Introduction

Implantable medical devices are becoming smaller and more efficient, requiring less power to achieve their purpose. In order to allow further miniaturization, the cumbersome batteries that add to (and often limit) the device's final volume must be reduced in size or even completely removed. For this to be possible, the devices must be powered through an external source.

Currently, Wireless Power Transfer (WPT) links are developed resorting to two techniques: maximizing the receiver's efficiency and/or positioning the receiver with an orientation that favours energy transmission efficiency [2]. Solutions capable of delivering hundreds of mW to the implants have resulted from this approach, but the device's dimensions were in the order of the centimetre [3, 4]. When considering solutions in the millimetre scale, only a few devices that can deliver a couple of mW have been reported, with most of them operating in the µW region [5, 6]. There has been little work on the improvement of the delivered power through the manipulation of other parameters such as the number of transmitters, which is already done in other fields [7]. SAR levels are influenced by the tissue's dielectric properties, geometry, dimensions and orientation, and by the incident wave's frequency and modulation [8]. Therefore, we believe that instead of focusing on the optimization of the link between a receiver and a transmitter in a given position and with a set frequency and polarization, the possibility of using a multidimensional approach should be explored.

In this work, we implemented a solution with two transmission antennas which, when compared with the single transmitter solution, increased energy availability inside a simplified human head model, while maintaining the same SAR levels.

II. Problem setup

Fine and detailed electromagnetic simulation results related to brain structures are possible, but may require complex and time consuming simulation setups [9]. Moreover, simulation of interaction between electromagnetic waves and biological structures requires tools with multiphysics capabilities. In this work, simulations were done using low computational power, which led to the decision of using two simulation tools (HFSS and COMSOL) with a simplified head model. HFSS allows for the quick analysis of the electromagnetic problem and to quickly arrive to a preferred antenna configuration. COMSOL, on the other hand, allows the inclusion of head thermal regulation and quickly allows the study of temperature maps for the obtained antenna configurations.

Both simulation tools were used to simulate the same simplified head model's interaction with one and two dipole antennas radiating power at 1 GHz, with antennas being placed at 300 mm from the centre of the model, as demonstrated in Fig. 1. This step was implemented to validate both tools' results. The E-field inside the brain was calculated on both software, using a head model consisting of a 45 mm radius sphere, representing the brain, enveloped in two layers, corresponding to skin (1 mm thick) and skull (4.1 mm thick), all defined with the corresponding tissue's dielectric properties for 1 GHz. Fig. 2 presents slices from the results of both simulations across the XZ plane, where the E-field shapes match in both software. Furthermore, peak values, despite inherent software discretization, are very similar. HFSS presented a peak E-field of 92 V/m for one antenna and 114 V/m for the two antenna scenario, while COMSOL computed 100 V/m and 110 V/m for the same scenarios.

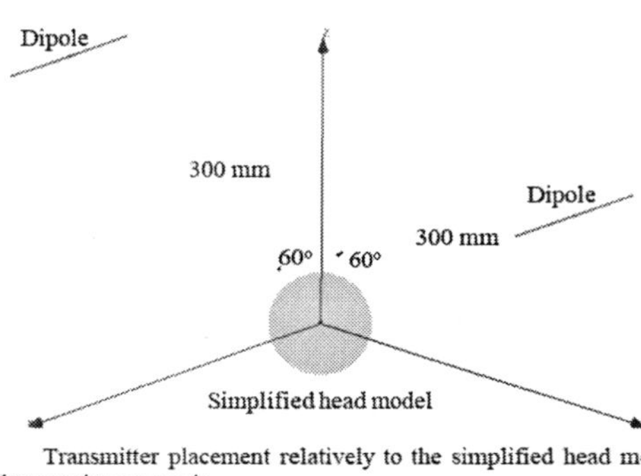

Fig. 1. Transmitter placement relatively to the simplified head model, for the dual transmitter scenario.

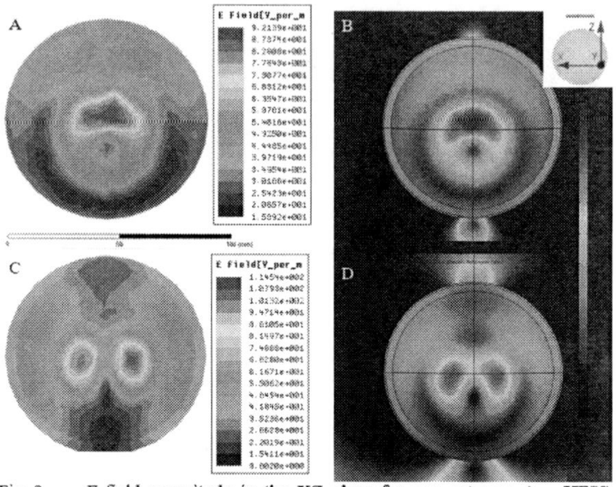

Fig. 2. E-field magnitude in the XZ plane for one antenna: A – HFSS, B - COMSOL; and two antennas: C – HFSS, D – COMSOL.

III. Results and Discussion

Simulations were used to trim a WPT solution based on two antenna solution, without surpassing SAR limits, and maintaining tissue temperature under control. In HFSS, the dipoles' positions, power input and phase were designed by simulation to maximize the Poynting vector's value inside the brain, while keeping the 10 g averaged SAR below the 2 W/kg established limit. When one dipole was used, SAR limits its power to 21 W. In the two dipole model, SAR limits each dipole power to 35.5 W, where the combination yielding the highest Poynting was with dipoles placed at 60° from the vertical axis, with phases set to 0° and 210°. Fig. 3 displays the Poynting vectors' magnitude for a slice that contained the hotspot. The usage of two antennas increased the available power from 55 W/m^2 to 76 W/m^2 in the hotspot, an increase of around 40%, which is also noticed in the surrounding areas.

With the previous parameters inserted into the COMSOL models, temperature values were obtained. The model was configured with the tissues' thermal properties, such as blood perfusion, metabolic heat generation rate, thermal capacity and thermal conductivity. Fig 4 contains the results from the one and two dipole cases. With no external radiation source, the model's temperature stabilizes at around 37.3 °C. When stimulated by one or two antennas, it increases to around 37.4 °C, a very small variation. Moreover, the maximum temperature in both scenarios is almost identical (37.42 °C and 37.46 °C, respectively), which was expected as SAR was the same for both cases.

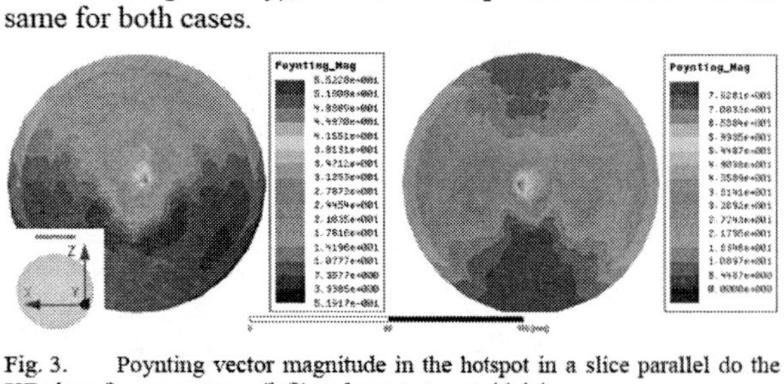

Fig. 3. Poynting vector magnitude in the hotspot in a slice parallel do the XZ plane for one antenna (left) and two antennas (right).

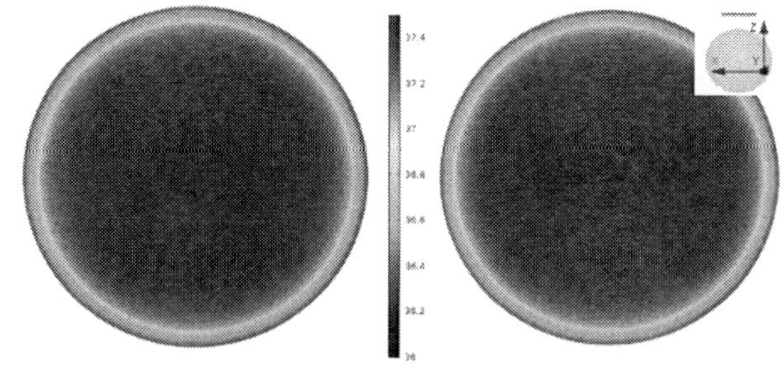

Fig. 4. Temperature plot resulting from the interaction of the head model with one (left) and two (right) antennas.

IV. Conclusion

With this work, it has been demonstrated that adopting a multidimensional approach to the design of WPT links might yield significant improvements over current methods. More specifically, it has been shown that using two transmission antennas instead of one, for the same SAR and temperature levels, the available power inside the head may increase by around 40%. As future work, more directive transmission antennas will be used, as we believe that higher Poynting vector values might be achieved and that it will allow us to accurately define the position of the hotspot inside the human head by adjusting the antennas' relative position and phase.

Acknowledgments

Work supported by FCT under project PTDC/EEI-TEL/5250/2014, by FEDER funds through Projeto 3599 – Promover a Produção Científica e Desenvolvimento Tecnológico e a Constituição de Redes Temáticas (3599-PPCDT).

References

[1] E. Katz, *Implantable Bioelectronics*. 2014.

[2] B. J. Walk, S. M. Ieee, J. Weber, S. M. Ieee, C. Soell, R. Weigel, F. Ieee, G. Fischer, S. M. Ieee, T. Ussmueller, and S. M. Ieee, "Implants for Telemonitoring," vol. 102, no. 11, pp. 1811–1832, 2014.

[3] D. Borton, M. Yin, J. Aceros, and A. Nurmikko, "An implantable wireless neural interface for recording cortical circuit dynamics in moving primates," *J. Neural Eng.*, vol. 10, no. 2, p. 26010, 2013.

[4] C. Mestais, G. Charvet, F. Sauter-starace, M. Foerster, and D. Ratel, "WIMAGINE : Wireless 64-Channel ECoG Recording Implant for Long Term Clinical Applications," vol. 23, no. 1, pp. 10–21, 2015.

[5] P. Troyk *et al*, "In-Vivo Tests of a 16-Channel Implantable Wireless Neural Stimulator *," vol. 4, pp. 22–24, 2015.

[6] R. Muller *et al*, "A Minimally Invasive 64-Channel Wireless ECoG Implant," vol. 50, no. 1, pp. 1–16, 2015.

[7] N. Pan, A. S. Boaventura, M. Rajabi, D. Schreurs, N. B. Carvalho, and S. Pollin, "Amplitude and Frequency Analysis of Multi-sine Wireless Power Transfer," *Integr. Nonlinear Microw. Millimetre-wave Circuits Work. (INMMiC), 2015*, no. 1, pp. 1–3, 2015.

[8] C. K. Chou *et al*, "Radio frequency electromagnetic exposure: tutorial review on experimental dosimetry", Bioelectromagnetics, vol. 17, no. 3, pp. 195–208, 1996.

[9] L. Zhao, Q. Ye, K. Wu, G. Chen, and W. Yu, "A New High-Resolution Electromagnetic Human Head Model," *IEEE Antennas and Propagation*, Vol 56 No. 5, October, 2016.

Coil Designs that Enable Wireless Powering by Cancelling Flux Leakage

Shishir Punjala, JSMN Inc, Charlotte, USA.
shesmesh9@gmail.com

***Abstract*—Wireless Power Transfer coil designs have been explored and two novel coil designs are presented in this paper. Controlling Specific Absorption Rate (SAR) and Leakage Electric Fields emanating from coils and antennas have been major issues. The two designs presented in this paper are applicable for the spiral as well as the solenoid coil designs. The self and mutual inductances, as well as the coupling coefficients obtained from HFSS, have been presented in this paper.**

***Keywords*—Coil, HFSS, Leakage Electric Field, Self Inductance, Mutual Inductance, coupling coefficient**

I. Introduction

The process of electromagnetic induction [2] involves a transmitter coil that upon excitation creates a magnetic field and induces current in a receiver coil situated at a short distance from the transmitter coil. As the distance [2] between the two coils increases the induction method becomes inefficient. This system [1] of wireless power transfer can be equated to the operation of a transformer. As the input current to the transmitter coil is increased, the leakage electric field and SAR in the surrounding area increases. In order to reduce the leakage electric field and SAR emanating from the coil, power factor correction [4] capacitances are used. Even though this is a good solution, coil designs that cancel outer fields and guide the magnetic flux to the receiver have to also be explored. This paper shows two coil designs and gives their self and mutual inductances as well as coupling coefficient results calculated from z-parameters obtained from HFSS.

II. Coil Layouts

The first coil layout in fig.1 has two spiral coils that have opposite windings to each other. Each spiral coil has 6 turns, so a combined number of 12 turns is used. Each coil has a ferrite core and an aluminum shield. The opposing leakage field generated by the other coil wound in the opposite direction will cancel the leakage field from the other coil. The dimensions of the transmitter and the receiver ferrite cores are 12.2cm×7.9cm×0.5cm & 6.2cm×10.6cm×0.5cm. The dimensions of the transmitter and the receiver aluminum shields are 9.9cm×14.2cm×0.2cm & 8cm×11.2cm×0.2cm.

The second coil layout in fig.2 has a spiral coil with the first turn wound in one direction, while the remaining 9 turns are wound in the opposite direction. The bottom side coil represents the transmitter coil while the top side coil represents the receiver. The dimensions of the transmitter and the receiver ferrite cores are 8.2cm×12.2cm×0.5cm & 6.2cm×10.6cm×0.5cm. The dimensions of the transmitter and the receiver aluminum shields are 9.2cm×13.2cm×0.2cm & 8cm×11.2cm×0.2cm. The third coil's layout is similar to the layout in figure 2 and has not been provided below, but it does not have an outer coil turn that is wound in the opposite direction.

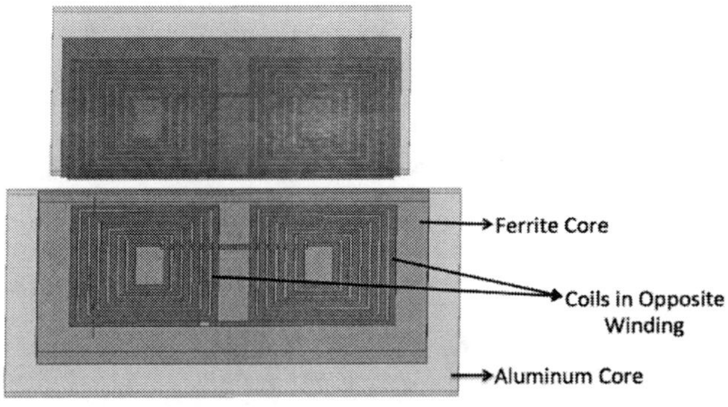

Fig.1 Case 1

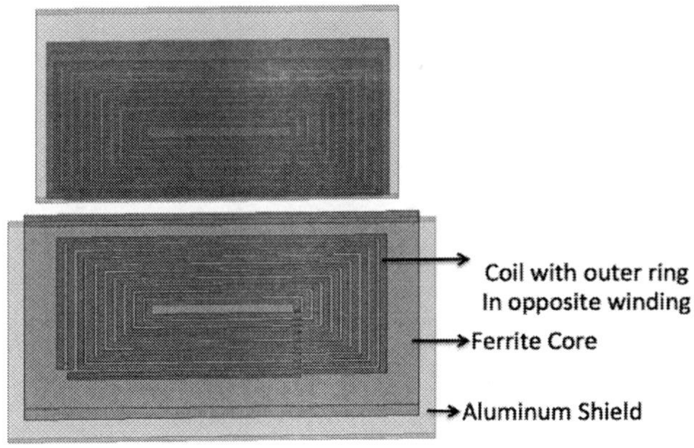

Fig.2

III. Calculations

The entire system was simulated in HFSS, and z-parameters were extracted. The self and mutual inductances and the coupling coefficients were calculated using the below formulas:

$$Self\ Inductance_{Transmitter} = \frac{Imaginary(Z_{11})}{\omega} \quad (1)$$

$$Self\ Inductance_{Receiver} = \frac{Imaginary(Z_{22})}{\omega} \quad (2)$$

$$Mutual\ Inductance = \frac{Imaginary(Z_{21})}{\omega} \quad (3)$$

$$Coupling\ Coefficient = \frac{(3)}{\sqrt{(1)\times(2)}}$$

IV. RESULTS

The self and mutual inductances in μH as well as the coupling coefficients (K) of the two cases obtained from HFSS have been provided in the table below:

	Frequency (MHz)	Self Ind (T)	Self Ind (R)	Mutual	K
Case 1	41.5	54.22	20.06	3.76	0.114
Case 2	22.85	48.72	44.33	5.74	0.123
Case 3	23.6	51.61	42.48	4.88	0.104

Below the vector electric field plots have been provided. A bowl depicting a human head with brain fluid was built in HFSS at a distance of 10cm from the coil model in the y-direction. The Peak Complex Magnitude of E-Field along a line inside the human head for all 3 cases has also been provided in a table.

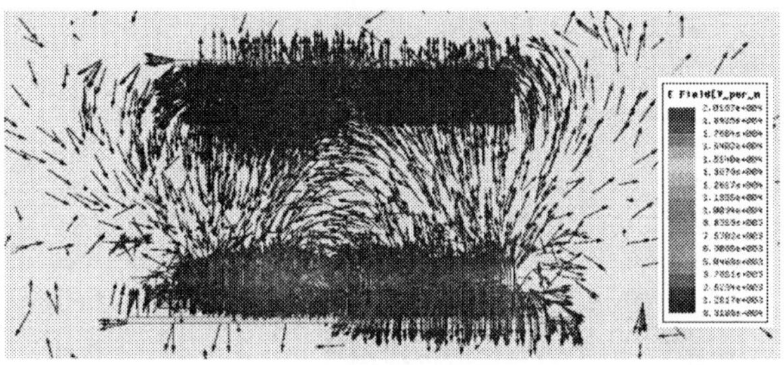

Fig. 3 E-Field for Case 1

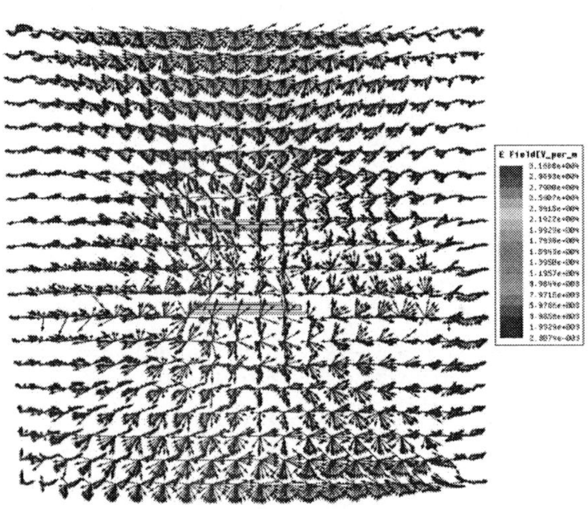

Fig. 4 E-Field for Case 2

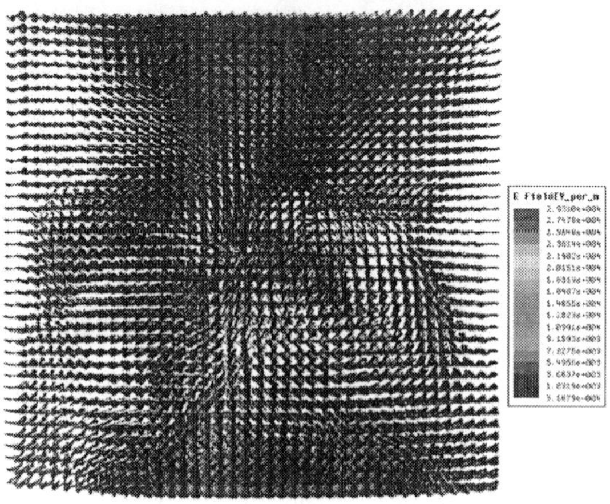

Fig. 5 E-Field for Case 3

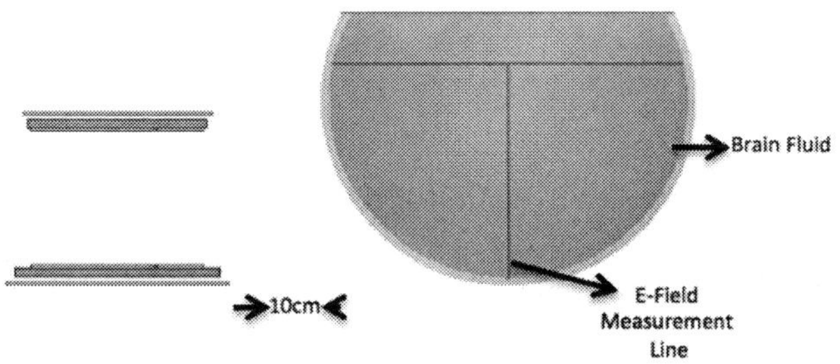

Fig. 6 E-Field Measurement Simulation Setup

	Peak Complex Magnitude E-Field (V/m)
Case 1	0.0369
Case 2	0.039
Case 3	0.0794

CONCLUSIONS

The layout of the new designs that can enable wireless powering for cell phones have been presented. The two designs have good coupling coefficient values. The E-fields of 3 cases have been provided for comparison. Clearly cases 1 and 2 display fields intersecting and cancelling each other and case 2 does not. The E-Field table also shows lesser peak E-Field values for cases 1 and 2.

REFERENCES

[1] Morris Kesler, "Highly Efficient Wireless Power Transfer: Sale, Efficient, and over Distance" Witricity Corporation, 2013.

[2] Mandip Jung Sibakoti; Joey Hambleton, "Wireless Power Transmission Using Magnetic Resonance", Cornell College PHY312, December 2011.

[3] S. S. Punjala, "Challenges in designing coils to enable wireless powering in electric vehicles and their EMC safety compliance," *2016 IEEE/ACES International Conference on Wireless Information Technology and Systems (ICWITS) and Applied Computational Electromagnetics (ACES)*, Honolulu, HI, 2016, pp. 1-4.

[4] Pickelsimer, Michael Christopher, "Wireless Power Transfer System with Power Factor Correction for Electric Vehicles. " Master's Thesis, University of Tennessee, 2012

Microwave Measurement Technique for Evaluating the Polarization of the Electromagnetic Field within a Reverberating Chamber

Antonio Sorrentino[1], José. J. Gil[2], Maurizio Migliaccio[1], Giuseppe Ferrara[1], Sergio Cappa[1],
[1] Dipartimento di Ingegneria, Università degli Studi di Napoli Parthenope,
Centro Direzionale Isola C 4, 80143 Napoli (Italy)
e-mail: asorrentino@uniparthenope.it
[2] Facultad de Educacion, Universidad de Zaragoza, Zaragoza 50009, Spain
ppgil@unizar.es

Abstract— **In this paper, a new measurement technique for estimating the polarization of the electromagnetic field within a reverberating chamber (RC) is proposed. The proposed technique also shows if the chamber is well-stirred. A comparison with previous methods is also achieved.**

***Index Terms*— electromagnetic field polarization, reverberating chamber.**

I. Introduction

Several studies and methodologies on the polarization of the electromagnetic field within a reverberating chamber (RC) have been proposed in these last years. Electromagnetic RCs are usually electrically large chambers employed as electromagnetic compatibility (EMC) test facilities in which the device under test (DUT) is exposed to a reference stochastic electromagnetic field representing the real world [1]. In wireless applications, the RC is a reference test-site for propagation measurements on every type of electromagnetic wireless device [2]. Without loss of generality, when a good randomization is accomplished, the electromagnetic field within an RC is generated in a manner that its structure is modelled by a Rayleigh distribution [3-4]. Obviously, randomisation affects all field components and therefore the polarisation nature of the field. This important fact has consequences both on the theoretical and practical characterization of the electromagnetic field polarization in the chamber. Only recently, some preliminary papers have been treated the special structure of the electromagnetic field within a RC by a polarimetric point of view [5]. Further, the polarization field properties are correctly suggested to be able to characterize effectiveness of the stirring process in a reverberating chamber [6]. The polarimetric characterization of the electromagnetic field is twofold: on one side, it is of interest in multiple scattering and free space propagation problems where the statistical nature bears the relevant information. On the other side, it is important to have a test-site able to properly manage the polarization characteristics of a desired electromagnetic field.

In this paper, a new technique for evaluating the polarization of the field within an RC is proposed. By employing the three dimensional coherence polarization matrix, R, the degree of linear polarization, P_l, and the degree of directionality, P_d, of the electromagnetic field, can be evaluated. Moreover, a comparison with the indicator presented in [7] is proposed. Measurements have been accomplished at the RC of the Università degli Studi di Napoli Parthenope.

II. Theoretical Facts

The field in a RC can be modelled as a superposition of several waves and these contributions comes from different directions, i.e. they are not at all paraxial and three-dimensional. The natural representation of such three-dimensional field is a 3x3 second-order field matrix known as a coherency or polarization matrix **R** [6]

$$\mathbf{R} = <\mathbf{E}\otimes\mathbf{E}^{\dagger}> = \begin{pmatrix} <E_1E_1^*> & <E_1E_2^*> & <E_1E_3^*> \\ <E_2E_1^*> & <E_2E_2^*> & <E_2E_3^*> \\ <E_3E_1^*> & <E_3E_2^*> & <E_3E_3^*> \end{pmatrix} \quad (1)$$

Thus, the three-dimensional description of polarization requires the use of quantities P_1 and P_2:

$$P_1 = \frac{\lambda_1 - \lambda_2}{\mathrm{Tr}\mathbf{R}} \quad P_2 = \frac{\lambda_1 + \lambda_2 - 2\lambda_3}{\mathrm{Tr}\mathbf{R}} \quad (2)$$

where λ_1, λ_2, λ_3 are the eigenvalues, real and non-negative.

In light of the physical interpretation of the intrinsic coherency matrix **R** and inspired by the definition of P_2 in terms of the eigenvalues of **R**, we find that a proper candidate for the desired degree of directionality P_d and the degree of linear polarization P_l are given by the non-dimensional quantities defined as [7]

$$P_d \equiv \frac{a_1 + a_2 - 2a_3}{a_1 + a_2 + a_3} \quad P_l \equiv \frac{a_1 - a_2}{a_1 + a_2 + a_3} \quad (3)$$

where the real non-negative quantities (a_1, a_2, a_3) are the eigenvalues of Re(**R**), with $0 \leq a_3 \leq a_2 \leq a_1$.

III. Experimental Results

In this section, we present and discuss a set of polarimetric measurements accomplished at the IUN mode-stirred RC: a cubic chamber of a 2 m side. The RC is all made of aluminium and the stirring is achieved by three large stirrers;

The S1 is on the left of the entrance door, the S2 is opposite to the entrance door and the S3 stirrer is on the roof. The three stirrers rotate at a speed of 190, 320, and 390 rpm, respectively. The stirring is accomplished in continuous mode. In Fig. 1 a picture of the employed RC is shown. Both antennas are dual-ridged horns certified to work in the 1 – 18 GHz frequency range. The operating frequency used in the experiments is 10 GHz. The comparison between two couples of indices (P_1, P_2) and (P_l, P_d) are obtained measuring the **R** matrix using 500 uncorrelated samples for each linear polarization. The antennas have been placed along the three orthogonal planes parallel to the walls of the RC in a way to obtain three independent estimations of the rectangular components of the RC field.

Fig.1: Photo of the IUN 2m x 2m x 2m mode-stirred RC used in the experiments

In Figg. 2-3-4 comparisons between the two couple of above mentioned index are shown. It must be noted that, in the case of RC measurements, the values of $P_l \leq P_d < 1$ witness that the electromagnetic field within the chamber has a not well-defined direction of propagation and no specific linear polarizations are defined, i.e. the RC stirring is well-accomplished.

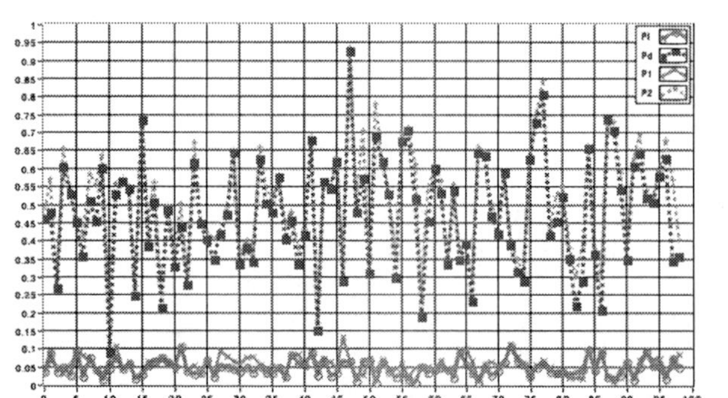

Fig.2: Comparison between indicators P_1 and P_l (green and grey lines) and P_2 and P_d (blue and red lines). The input frequency is 10 GHz and the transmitting antenna is x-polarized.

IV. CONCLUSIONS

In this paper, the stirring of an RC has been analyzed starting by the polarization analysis of the electromagnetic field received in the chamber. The generated states of polarization have the peculiarity that $P_1 = P_l$ and $P_2 = P_d$. That is, the degree of polarization is equal to the degree of linear polarization. P_2 (defined as the relative power of the component that is not 3D-unpolarized) is equal to P_d (defined as an objective measure of how close is the state to a 2D state). As expected, the proposed measurement technique shows that the stirring within the chamber is well-accomplished.

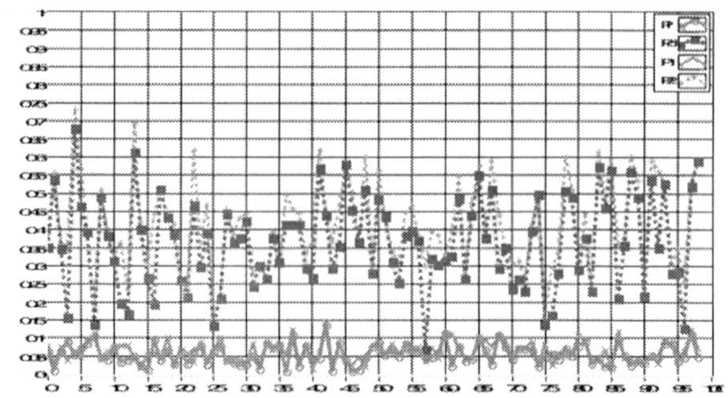

Fig.3: The same of Fig.2 with the transmitting antenna y-polarized.

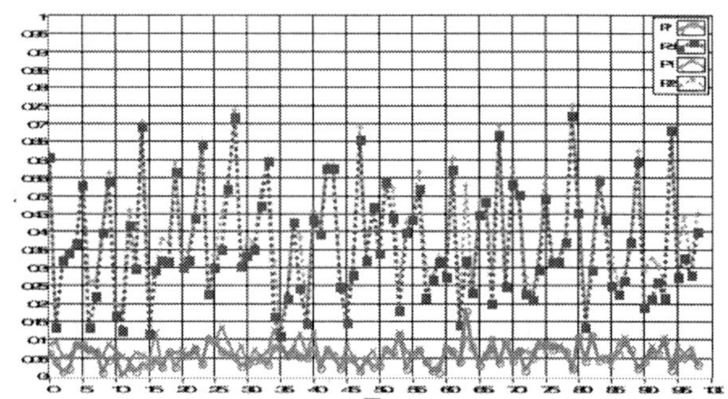

Fig.4: The same of Fig.2 with the transmitting antenna z-polarized.

REFERENCES

[1] IEC 61000-4-21, *Electromagnetic Compatibility (EMC)*, Part 4-21: Testing and measurement techniques – Reverberation chamber test-methods, International Electrotechnical Commission, Geneva, Switzerland, 2003.

[2] 3GPP - 3rd Generation Partnership Project RAN4 - R4-111690: TP for 37.976: LTE MIMO OTA Test Plan for Reverberation Chamber Based Methodologies, Azimuth Systems, Bluetest, CTTC, 2011.

[3] A.Sorrentino, F.Nunziata, G.Ferrara, M.Migliaccio, "Reverberating Chamber Profile Identification", *IET Microwaves, Antennas & Propagation*, vol.6, no.13, 1468-1472, 2012

[4] P. Corona, G. Ferrara, M. Migliaccio, "Polarimetric field characterization in reverberating chamber," *IEEE Trans, Electromagn. Compat.*, vol. 46, no.2, pp. 155-159, 2004.

[5] L. R. Arnaut, "Compound exponential distributions for undermoded reverberation chambers", *IEEE Trans. Electromagn. Compat.*, vol. 44, vol.3, pp. 442-457, 2002.

[6] M.Migliaccio, J.J.Gil, A.Sorrentino, F.Nunziata, G.Ferrara, "The polarization Purity of the Electromagnetic field in a Reverberating Chamber", *IEEE Trans, Electromagn. Compat.*, vol.58, no.3, pp.694-700, 2016.

[7] Josè J. Gill, "Interpretation of the coherency matrix for three-dimensional polarization states", *American Physical Society*, 90, pp.1-9, 2014.

Artificial Ionospheric Scintillation Effects on Communication Signals in the V and W Bands

David Smith, Peter Collins, James Fee, James C. Petrosky, Anderw Terzuoli, and Caglar Yardim

Institute of Electrical & Electronics Engineers (IEEE), USA

Abstract—**Secure communications are critical for many applications. While natural ionospheric effects will be negligible on frequencies above 30 GHz, amplitude scintillation caused by a high altitude nuclear event (HANE) could degrade communication links. Amplitude scintillation is modeled using the multiple phase screen method. The results show that after a HANE, amplitude scintillation will degrade signals at frequencies below 60 GHz but the duration of the effect is only for a few minutes after the event.**

Keywords—propagation; scintillation; artificial ionosphere; V band; W band; HANE

I. Introduction

Secure communication is of critical importance for many commercial and government applications. The increased reliance on global communications and real-time information has driven the need for continuous access to celestial communication. Currently, the radio frequency bands for celestial communication are cluttered with many commercial users making priority of use a concern. One solution is to take advantage of the unused V and W radio bands, 40 – 75 GHz and 75 – 110 GHz respectively. Currently, no commercial entities are using the V and W bands, leaving two entire bands free for exclusive use. Therefore, an investigation into the reliability of these bands during extreme conditions is warranted.

Under normal conditions the troposphere dominates celestial communication signal propagation with little to no effect from the ionosphere. However, the ionosphere can become an important factor for a period of time following a high altitude nuclear event (HANE); a nuclear event occurring is above 100 km [1]. Generally, a HANE is expected to occur between 100 – 300 km when the purpose of the detonation is to maximize EMP effects. Early time (E1-E2) EMP are phenomena that are related to the Compton current effect due to gamma propagation. Instead, this paper focuses on what is typically referred to as "other atmospheric effects" which includes EMP, but also includes Argus effect, Red Out and Blackout. After a HANE, a portion of the electrons and detonation debris, primarily in the form if ionized particles, travels downward into the Earth's denser atmosphere where it further ionizes the air molecules. The electrons and resultant ionized debris expand and rise along the earth's geomagnetic lines, Figure 1. As a result, the electron density in the ionosphere can rise to values of 10^9 electrons/cm^3. (The natural ionosphere is 10^6 electrons/cm^3 at its peak.) The elevated electron density can last for periods of 60 s or longer [1].

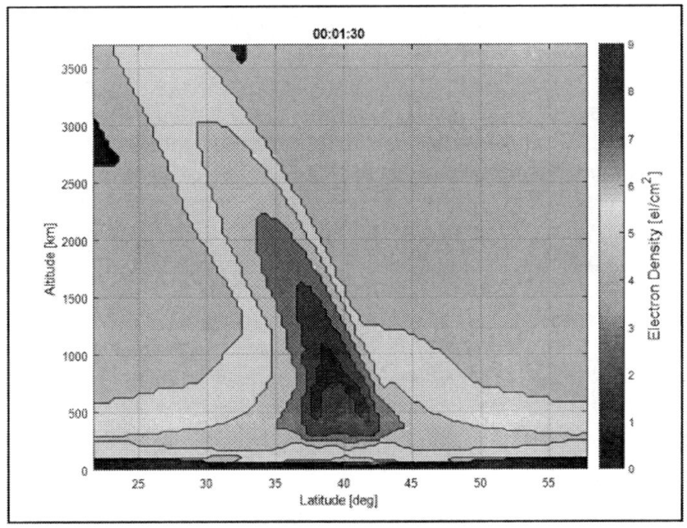

Fig. 1. Snapshot 90 s after a 5 MT detonation at 200 km. The electron structures rise in altitude along the Earth's geomagnetic lines. The numbers on the right of the bar graph represent powers of 10 (i.e. 10^4 through 10^9).

Based upon [2], a 1 MT HANE at an altitude of 600 km will increase the ion and electron density sufficient to interfere with SATCOM crosslinks up to 200 GHz. This paper will focus on the effects of a 5 MT detonation at 200 km, specifically examining the effects on an electromagnetic wave propagation from the ground to a location at 4,800 km above the earth's surface. The primary effect of interest is the amplitude scintillation caused by the increases in electron density. Ion debris absorption is not considered.

II. Propagation Effect

As an electromagnetic (EM) wave traverses through a plasma various effects can be observed. Some of these effects include Faraday rotation, group delay, phase advance, dispersion, and scintillation. Calculations can show that since frequency of the EM wave (40 – 110 GHz) is much greater that the resulting plasma frequency most of the effects will be negligible, with the exception of scintillation.[2]

Scintillation is defined as amplitude changes on an EM wave. Scintillation is caused by forward scattering of the propagating wave as it travels through the plasma. One approach to EM modeling of plane wave propagation through a plasma, naturally occurring (ionosphere), or artificial (e.g. HANE), is the multiple phase screen (MPS) method [3]. The MPS method is described by equations (1) and (2).

$$E(x,z,\omega)=U(x,z,\omega)e^{-jkz}$$
$$U(x,z_2,\omega)=e^{-jk\Delta z}\mathcal{F}^{-1}\left[\mathcal{F}[U(x,z_1,\omega)]e^{j(z_1-z_2)\sqrt{k^2K_x}-k}\right] \quad (1)$$

$$U(x,z_2,\omega)=U\left(x,-\frac{\Delta z}{2},\omega\right)e^{-jk\int_{-\Delta z/2}^{\Delta z/2}\Delta n(x,z',\omega)dz'} \quad (2)$$

Here $\mathcal{F}$ is a Fourier transform, z is the direction of propagation, x is transverse direction, K_x is the spatial wavenumber in the x direction, E is the electric field, U is the electric field in the parabolic approximation, ω is the radian frequency of the EM wave, k is the EM wavenumber, and n is the index of refraction. Equation (1) describes the wave propagation to the phase screen and equation (2) describes the wave propagation through the phase screen. Both equations (1) and (2) are used in an iterative manner until the wave has propagated through the entire plasma.

Phase screens are generated from the power-law phase power spectral density (PSD). The PSD method is useful as it represents many observations and allows control over inner and outer-scales of the ion turbulence. This PSD is defined in equation (3).

$$S_\phi(K_x)=\frac{\sigma_\phi^2\left(1/\sqrt{2\pi}\right)l_i\left(l_i/L_o\right)^{m-1/2}H_{m/2}\left(l_i\sqrt{K_x+1/L_o^2}\right)}{H_{m-1/2}\left(l_i/L_0\right)\left(l_i\sqrt{K_x+1/L_o^2}\right)^{m/2}} \quad (3)$$
$$\sigma_\phi^2=2(r_e\lambda)^2L_o\Delta z\sigma_{N_e}^2$$

Here H is a Bessel function of the third kind, L_o and l_i are outer and inner scales, m is the power law slope, r_e is the classic electron radius, λ is wavelength, and σ_{Ne}^2 is the plasma electron variance. The effect of plasma scintillation can be calculated with the MPS method. The S_4 scintillation index can then be determined from (4).

$$S_4=\sqrt{\frac{\left\langle\left(A-\langle A\rangle\right)^2\right\rangle}{\langle A^2\rangle}} \quad (4)$$

In (4) < > indicates averaging and A is the amplitude of the received wave. An S_4 index of 0.3 indicates signal fading with 0.6 indicating a strong scatter.

III. Results

Tables 1 and 2 list the scintillation effects and signal loss at the receiver for a given channel. The data in these tables show that the scintillation effects will only impact signals below frequencies of 60 GHz with the majority of the scintillation happening at 1 to 4 minutes after the HANE event. Significant signal loss can occur for frequencies between 40 and 50 GHz (up to 4 db). Comparably, an ionosphere naturally disturbed from solar radiation will produce scintillation loss up to 0.025 db at 40 GHz (determined using the MPS method).

The scintillation effects grow until they peak at about 1.5 minutes after the blast and then begin to drop off. After five minutes, the effects from the charged particle debris cloud dissipate as the electrons begin to spread along the magnetic field lines reducing the electron density. The resultant data suggest that the lower part of the V band will be unavailable for approximately 3 minutes after the HANE due to amplitude scintillation effects.

TABLE I. S_4 INDEX

Freq[a]	S4 Scintillation Index						
	0 sec	*3 sec*	*10 sec*	*1 min*	*1.25 min*	*1.5 min*	*5 min*
40	0.2	0.2	0.1	0.4	0.3	0.2	0.0
50	0.1	0.1	0.1	0.1	0.2	0.2	0.0
60	0.0	0.0	0.0	0.1	0.1	0.1	0.0
70	0.0	0.0	0.0	0.1	0.1	0.0	0.0
110	0.0	0.0	0.0	0.0	0.0	0.0	0.0

a. Frequency is in GHz

TABLE II. SIGNAL LOSS FROM HANE

Freq[b]	Signal Loss [db]						
	0 sec	*3 sec*	*10 sec*	*1 min*	*1.25 min*	*1.5 min*	*5min*
40	-1.52	-2.77	-1.20	-3.89	-3.64	-4.00	-0.06
50	-0.96	-1.52	-0.87	-2.23	-2.29	-2.70	-0.04
60	-0.63	-1.30	-0.55	-1.67	-1.76	-1.71	-0.03
70	-0.45	-0.89	-0.40	-1.23	-1.37	-1.37	-0.02
110	-0.20	-0.39	-0.16	-0.50	-0.52	-0.56	-0.01

b. Frequency is in GHz

IV. Conclusion

Although the natural ionosphere will have negligible effects on EM wave propagation from 40 – 110 GHz, an artificially disturbed ionosphere from a HANE will significantly reduce signals below 60 GHz. This research shows that the lower part of the V band will be limited for approximately 3 minutes after the HANE due to amplitude scintillation. Thus, the impact of amplitude scintillation is minimal, due to its short period after a HANE.

References

[1] S. Glasstone and P. J. Dolan, "The Effects of Nuclear Weapons," *United States Department of Defense*, 1977. [Online]. Available: https://www.fourmilab.ch/etexts/www/effects/. [Accessed: 15-Aug-2016].

[2] R. Middlestead, R. LeLevier, and M. Smith, "Satellite Crosslink Communications Vulnerability in a Nuclear Environment," *IEEE J. Sel. Areas Commun.*, vol. 5, no. 2, pp. 138–145, Feb. 1987.

[3] D. L. Knepp, "Multiple Phase-Screen Calculation of the Temporal Behavior of Stochastic Waves," *Proc. IEEE*, vol. 71, no. 6, pp. 722–737, 1983.

Variational Analysis of Substrate-Integrated Waveguides with Longitudinal Slot

Nghia Nguyen-Trong*, Leonard Thomas Hall† and Christophe Fumeaux*
*School of Electrical and Electronic Engineering, The University of Adelaide, Adelaide, SA, 5005, Australia
† Defence Science and Technology Group (DSTG), Adelaide, Australia
Email: nghia.nguyentrong@adelaide.edu.au

***Abstract*—The variational analysis to solve the propagation constant of substrate-integrated waveguides with a longitudinal slot is presented in this paper. A closed-form expression for the stationary equation is given, which is solved using a well-known root-searching Newton's process. Compared to the transverse resonance method, the present analysis does not require the values of the edge impedances and thus avoids any numerical simulation in the solution.**

***Index Terms*—Substrate-integrated waveguide (SIW), slot, analytical solution, variational method.**

I. Introduction

In the last decades, substrate-integrated waveguides (SIWs) [1] have attracted significant attention from many researchers as they provide excellent means to design and integrate various microwave components in planar technology. Inspired by this concept, many variations of SIWs have been proposed in literature [2]–[4]. Among these, the substrate-integrated waveguide with longitudinal slot (denoted in the following as slot SIW) has been proposed for leaky-wave antenna (LWA) applications [5] (Fig. 1). For the design and optimization of LWAs based on this structure, an analytical solution that can yield the propagation constant γ in a fast manner is desirable [6]. For this purpose, the transverse resonance method (TRM) has been utilized to analyze this structure [7], [8]. However, this method requires the values of the edge impedances at the slot position which are typically obtained through numerical simulations. To avoid this step, we present here the variational method to solve the slot SIW. This method has also been used successfully in solving folded SIWs [9] and a truncated half-mode SIW [10]. Closed-form formulas for the stationary equation are given in this paper. The results are validated with full-wave numerical simulations.

II. The Analysis of Slot Substrate-Integrated Waveguides

As initial step, the via walls of the SIW are converted into equivalent solid perfect electric conductor (PEC) walls using a well-known formula for the correction term of the SIW's width [11]

$$\Delta = \frac{d^2}{0.95s}, \tag{1}$$

where d is the via hole diameter and s is the spacing between two adjacent vias (Fig. 1a). Using this formula, the slot SIW is converted into a dielectric-filled slot rectangular waveguide as shown in Fig. 1c with

$$w = w' - \Delta, \quad a = a' - \Delta/2. \tag{2}$$

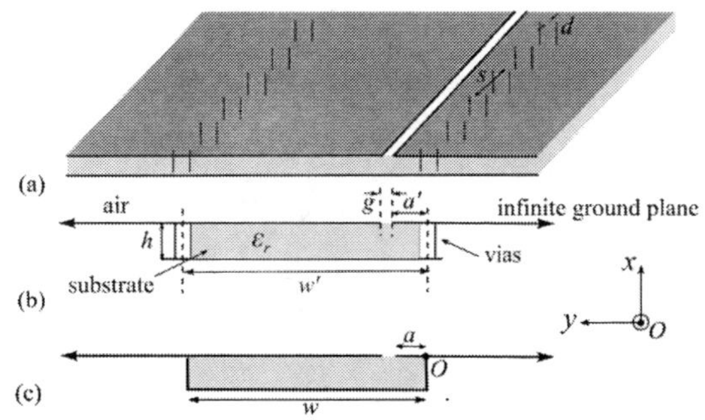

Fig. 1. (a) The 3D-view and (b) cross-section of the slot substrate-integrated waveguide; and (c) its equivalent slot rectangular waveguide.

To solve this slot rectangular waveguide, the analysis follows the variational procedure presented in [12]. It is noted that in [12], Rumsey solved the propagation constant for the case that the slot is placed on the side wall. In our case where a planar structure is considered, the slot is placed on the long side of the waveguide, thus the orientation of the dominant mode is different. Nevertheless, the stationary equation for the propagation constant γ is still the same as

$$\Phi(\gamma) = \int_a^{a+g} \left[E_y({}^iH_z - {}^eH_z) + E_z({}^iH_y - {}^eH_y)\right] dy = 0, \tag{3}$$

where ${}^iH$ and ${}^eH$, respectively, are the internal and external magnetic fields calculated from assumed tangential electric fields E_y and E_z within the slot (noting that the integral is evaluated across the slot in y-direction). In all solutions of (3), a first-order change in E_y and E_z only yields a second-order change in γ. Therefore, by applying a reasonable assumption for the tangential field distribution in the slot, the propagation constant can be calculated with a high accuracy. Since the slot is typically relatively narrow, a straightforward assumption that $E_z = 0$ and $E_y = 1$ allows us to significantly simplify the analysis while still yielding reasonably accurate results. With this assumption, equation (3) becomes

$$\Phi(\gamma) = \int_a^{a+g} ({}^iH_z - {}^eH_z) dy = 0. \tag{4}$$

To evaluate $\Phi(\gamma)$, the field equivalence principle is first applied to obtain the equivalent magnetic current in the slot. Orthogonal mode expansion inside the waveguide with appropriate boundary conditions is used to obtain ${}^iH_z$. Image theory with the formulation of cylindrical wave, assuming an infinite ground plane and infinite long uniform structure, are

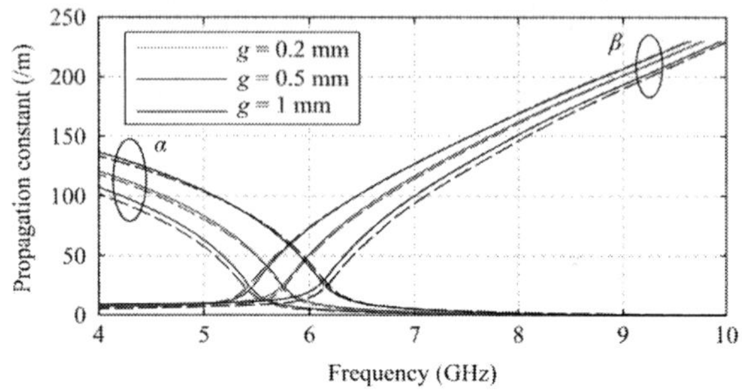

Fig. 2. Propagation constants for different values of g. The solid lines are analyzed results and the dashed lines are simulated results.

utilized to obtain ${}^eH_z$. The detailed derivation can be found in the Appendix of [12]. Here we only show a closed-form expression for the field integrals. For the internal field,

$$\int_a^{g+a} {}^iH_z(\gamma)dy = \frac{j}{\omega\mu}\left[\frac{g^2 l_0}{w}\cot l_0 h + 2\sum_{n=1}^{\infty} X_n \cot l_n h\left(\frac{\ln w}{(n\pi)^2}+\frac{1}{wl_n}\right)\right] \quad (5)$$

with

$$l_n = \sqrt{\epsilon_r k_0^2 + \gamma^2 - \left(\frac{n\pi}{w}\right)^2} \quad (6)$$

and

$$X_n = \left(\sin\frac{n\pi(g+a)}{w} - \sin\frac{n\pi a}{w}\right)^2, \quad (7)$$

where $k_0 = \omega/c$ and ϵ_r is the relative permittivity of the substrate. For the external field,

$$\int_a^{g+a} {}^eH_z dy = \frac{1}{\omega\mu}\left[g\kappa_e\left(\int_0^{\kappa_e g} H_0^{(2)}(u)du - H_1^{(2)}(\kappa_e b)\right) + \lim_{u\to 0} uH_1^{(2)}(u)\right], \quad (8)$$

with

$$\kappa_e = \sqrt{k_0^2 + \gamma^2} \quad (9)$$

and $H_i^{(2)}$ is the ith-order Hankel function of second kind. The stationary equation can be efficiently solved by an iterative Newton's process. The first guessed root of equation (4) can be chosen as

$$\gamma_0 = \sqrt{\left(\frac{\pi}{2(w-g-a)}\right)^2 - \epsilon_r k_0^2} \quad (10)$$

by approximating the slot SIW as the half-mode waveguide with a perfect magnetic conductor (PMC) wall at position $y = a + g$ (Fig. 1c).

III. Analysis and Simulation Results

To verify the above analysis, a geometry of slot SIW is chosen as an example with substrate relative permittivity $\epsilon_r = 2.2$, thickness $h = 0.787$ mm, via diameter $d = 0.6$ mm and spacing $s = 1$ mm, $w' = 10$ mm, $a' = 1.5$ mm (Fig. 1b). Figure 2 shows the analyzed and simulated results for different values of slot width g. For an accurate comparison, the multi-line method [13] is utilized for obtaining the propagation constant from full-field simulation results. It can be observed that the analysis shows a very good agreement with simulations, especially for small values of g. This is expected because when g is decreased, the assumed field distribution ($E_y = 1, E_z = 0$) in the slot becomes more accurate. It is noted that when g is increased, the structure approaches a half-mode SIW [14] or half-width microstrip line and the propagation can be calculated using the formulas provided in [15].

IV. Conclusion

The propagation constants of substrate-integrated waveguides with a longitudinal slot are solved using a variational approach. A closed-form expression is given for the stationary equation, which can be solved efficiently using an iterative Newton's process. The analysis is validated using full-wave numerical simulations. The provided results are useful for the design and optimization of LWAs based on slot SIWs.

References

[1] D. Deslandes and K. Wu, "Integrated microstrip and rectangular waveguide in planar form," *IEEE Microw. Wireless Compon. Lett.*, vol. 11, no. 2, pp. 68 –70, Feb. 2001.

[2] W. Che et al., "Analysis and experiments of compact folded substrate-integrated waveguide," *IEEE Trans. Microw. Theory Tech.*, vol. 56, no. 1, pp. 88–93, Jan 2008.

[3] G. H. Zhai et al., "Folded half mode substrate integrated waveguide 3 dB coupler," *IEEE Microw. Wireless Compon. Lett.*, vol. 18, no. 8, pp. 512–514, Aug 2008.

[4] Q. Lai et al., "Characterization of the propagation properties of the half-mode substrate integrated waveguide," *IEEE Trans. Microw. Theory Tech.*, vol. 57, no. 8, pp. 1996 –2004, Aug. 2009.

[5] Y. J. Cheng, W. Hong, K. Wu, and Y. Fan, "Millimeter-wave substrate integrated waveguide long slot leaky-wave antennas and two-dimensional multibeam applications," *IEEE Transactions on Antennas and Propagation*, vol. 59, no. 1, pp. 40–47, Jan 2011.

[6] N. Nguyen-Trong, L. Hall, and C. Fumeaux, "Transmission-line model of nonuniform leaky-wave antennas," *IEEE Transactions on Antennas and Propagation*, vol. 64, no. 3, pp. 883–893, March 2016.

[7] Z. Wang, X. Li, S. Zhou, B. Yan, R.-M. Xu, and W. Lin, "Half mode substrate integrated folded waveguide (HMSIFW) and partial H-plane bandpass filter," *Progress In Electromagnetics Research*, vol. 101, pp. 203–16, 2010.

[8] R. F. Xu, A. J. Farrall, and P. R. Young, "Analysis of loaded substrate integrated waveguides and attenuators," *IEEE Microwave and Wireless Components Letters*, vol. 24, no. 1, pp. 62–64, Jan 2014.

[9] N. Nguyen-Trong, T. Kaufmann, L. Hall, and C. Fumeaux, "Variational analysis of folded substrate-integrated waveguides," *IEEE Microwave and Wireless Components Letters*, vol. 25, no. 6, pp. 352–354, June 2015.

[10] N. Nguyen-Trong et al., "A semi-analytical solution of a tapered HMSIW with application to rapid antenna optimization," *IEEE Trans. Antennas Propag.*, vol. 62, no. 6, pp. 3189–3200, June 2014.

[11] Y. Cassivi et al., "Dispersion characteristics of substrate integrated rectangular waveguide," *IEEE Microw. Wireless Compon. Lett.*, vol. 12, no. 9, pp. 333–335, 2002.

[12] V. Rumsey, "Traveling wave slot antennas," *Journal of Applied Physics*, vol. 24, no. 11, pp. 1358–1365, 1953.

[13] R. B. Marks, "A multiline method of network analyzer calibration," *IEEE Trans. Microw. Theory Tech.*, vol. 39, no. 7, pp. 1205–1215, 1991.

[14] W. Hong, B. Liu, Y. Wang, Q. Lai, H. Tang, X. X. Yin, Y. D. Dong, Y. Zhang, and K. Wu, "Half mode substrate integrated waveguide: A new guided wave structure for microwave and millimeter wave application," in *Joint 31st International Infrared Millimeter Waves Conference/14th Int. Terahertz Electronic Conference, 2006. IRMMW-THz 2006.*, Sept. 2006, p. 219.

[15] E. F. Kuester, R. Johnk, and D. Chang, "The thin-substrate approximation for reflection from the end of a slab-loaded parallel-plate waveguide with application to microstrip patch antennas," *IEEE Transactions on Antennas and Propagation*, vol. 30, no. 5, pp. 910–917, 1982.

Proposal of EMTP Analysis Model for a Surge Phenomenon Arising on a Power Cable Assembled in a Transmission Tower

Ryoji Oshiro, Yuto Hachiman
Graduate School of Engineering and Science
University of the Ryukyus
1, Senbaru, Nishihara, Okinawa, 903-0213, Japan
k148655@eve.u-ryukyu.ac.jp

Taishi Shiozuka, Eiji Kaneko
Faculty of Engineering
University of the Ryukyus
1, Senbaru, Nishihara, Okinawa, 903-0213, Japan

EMTP (Electro-Magnetic Transient Program) is one of the best programs for surge analysis. However, the surge simulation model that corresponds to the power cable used in the transmission tower is not included in EMTP. In order to adequately treat the surge issue that arises on the electrical system, a more detailed simulation has been requested. Therefore, our research has focused on a new approach to the EMTP model. The best way to achieve this is to compare the analysis results between the proposed model and an experiment. The experiment was conducted with actual devices such as transformers, transmission towers, power cables, etc. Because executing such an experiment is very difficult, VSTL rev (Virtual Surge Test Lab rev), which is a surge analysis program based on the finite-difference time domain (FDTD) method, was utilized to confirm the accuracy of the proposed EMTP model. In this paper, the VSTL rev model, the EMTP models, and their comparison results are discussed.

***Keywords*—EMTP; FDTD method; power cable; surge phenomena; transmission tower**

I. Introduction

EMTP (Electro-Magnetic transient program) has been widely used to simulate of surge phenomena as it can easily analyze and treat issue arising in electrical power systems and their various components such as transformers, generators, and transmission systems. However, based on past research, it is well known that it is difficult to treat influence of 3-D construction in EMTP[1]-[4]. Therefore, in our research, the purpose is to model a co-axial cable assembled in a transmission tower by using EMTP. In this paper, the simulation of the co-axial model, and the comparison of these simulation results of the VSTL rev(Virtual Surge Test Lab rev) and EMTP models are discussed.

II. Analsys Model

A. Simulation model in VSTL rev.

The arrangement of the analysis model in VSTL rev is depicted in Fig. 1. This model consists of the current source, transmission line, voltage reference line (V.R.line), cable head, transmission tower, and power cable. Fig. 1(b) shows the cross section of the power cable in the radial direction. In this simulation, it is assumed that the power cable is composed of 4 layers (the inner and the outer conductors and the inner and the outer dielectrics, see Fig. 1(b)). This cable has the following parameters;

Dic: 10 mm, Dii: 38 mm, εii: 3.0, ρii: 1.0×10^{16} Ωm
Doc: 46 mm, Doi: 100 mm, εoi: 3.0, ρoi: 1.0×10^{16} Ωm
Characteristic impedance of the cable: 46.4 Ω

where D shows the diameter of each part, ε represents the relative permittivity of each insulator, and ρ is the resistivity of each insulator. The conductor parts consist of a perfectly conductive material model that has no resistivity. The characteristic impedance is calculated by using the capacitance and the inductance between the inner and the outer conductors.

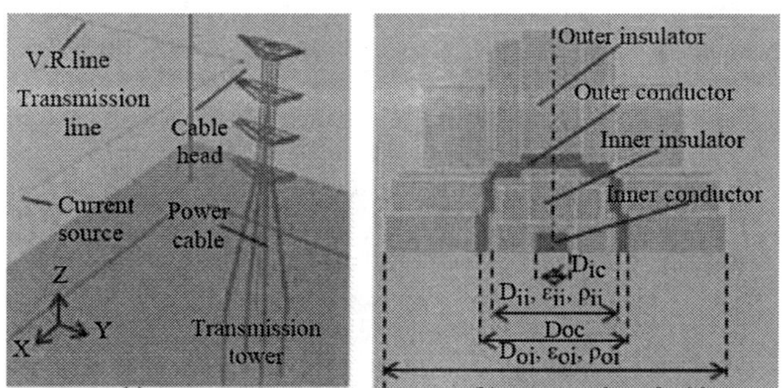

Fig.1 Simulation model displayed by VSTL rev

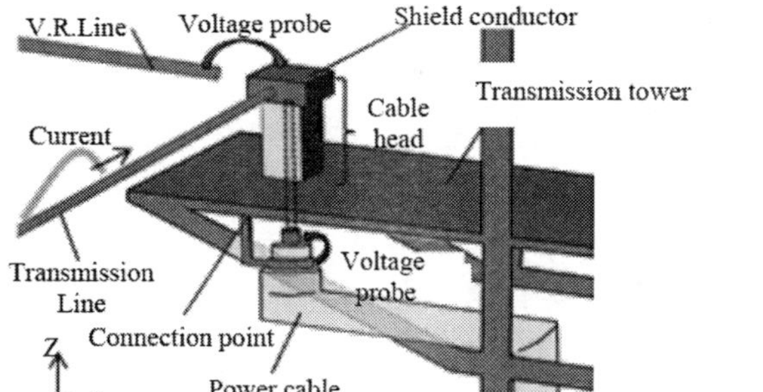

Fig.2 Arrangement in the vicinity of the cable head

Fig. 2 shows the arrangement in the vicinity of the cable head. The outer conductor of the cable is connected to the tower at the connection point. In this simulation, the voltage between the shield conductor and V.R.line (below, this voltage is called the gap voltage), and the voltage between the inner and the outer conductors at top of the cable are measured.

B. Simulation model in EMTP

Several methods for treatment of the surge phenomena have been proposed for the transmission [6]. IEEJ 4 story transmission tower model is one of these methods[3]. Figure 3 shows the EMPT analysis model. The upper diagram in Fig. 3 is the IEEJ 4 story model consists of the line model (Line 1 to Line 4), the decay resistances (R_{T1} to R_{T4}) ,and the inductances (L_{T1} to L_{T4}).

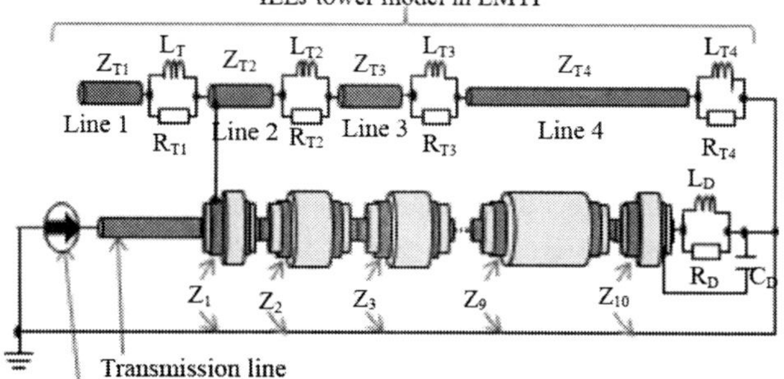

Fig.3 Assembled cable model in EMTP

The parameters of this 4 story model are as follows;

1) Lines 1,2, and 3

The length of three lines is 4 m, and it corresponds to the length between the arms of the tower. The surge impedances between the line and the earth (Z_{T1} - Z_{T3}) are 220 Ω. The voltage/current propagation velocity in the lines is the velocity of the light. R_{T1} - R_{T3} = 16.4 Ω, L_{T1} - L_{T3} = 3.0 μH.

2) Line 4

The length of this line is 17 m, and it corresponds to the length between the lowest arm and the ground. The surge impedance between the line and the earth(Z_{T4}) is 150 Ω. The voltage/current propagates at the velocity of the light on the lines. R_{T4} = 33.5 Ω, L_{T4} = 6.2 μH.

In the EMTP analysis model, the series connection cable is connected to the 4 story model. These cables have the same characteristic impedance of 46.5 Ω, different line lengths and different surge impedances. The total length of the series connection cable corresponds to the VSTL rev model shown in Fig. 1. In addition, the model where the power cable is simulated by one horizon cable is also analyzed for comparison. Fig. 4 shows the current waveform of the current source for each simulation. The peak value and the average rise time of this current are set to 1 kA and 1.0 μs, respectively.

III. ANALSYS RESULT

Fig. 5 shows the analysis results. The long and short dashed lines denote the analysis result of VSTL rev. The solid line represents the results of the one horizontal cable, and the dashed lines denote the series connection cable model results. From these results, our proposed EMTP model is a reasonable model for a power cable assembled in a transmission system.

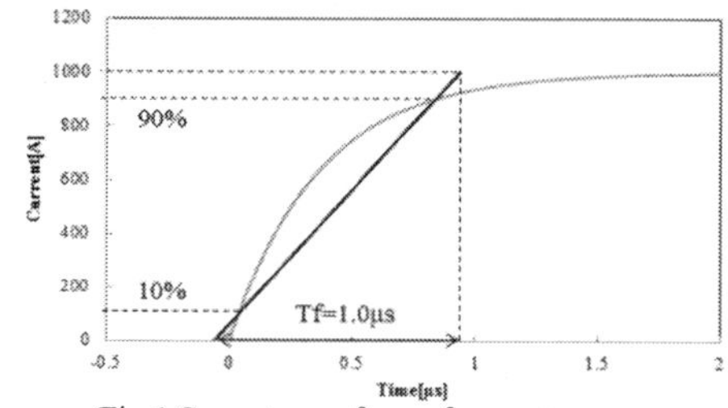

Fig.4 Current waveform of current source

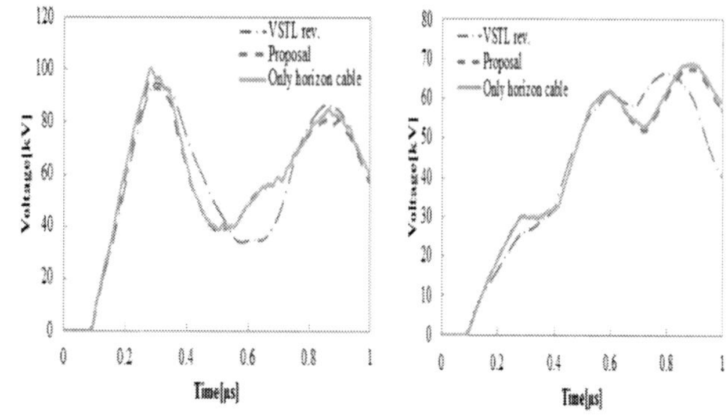

(a) Voltage across the gap

(b) Voltage between inner and outer conductors

Fig. 5 Analysis results

IV. CONCLUSION

In this paper, the EMTP model of the power cable assembled in the transmission tower was proposed. For the confirmation of analysis accuracy for the proposed model, the simulation results of the EMTP model are compared with the analysis results of the VSTL rev. By connecting the cable model and the IEEJ transmission tower model in EMTP, EMTP can treat the surge simulation for the power cable assembled in the transmission.

REFERENCES

[1] T. Hara, O. Yamamoto, M. Hayashi, C. Uenosono, "Emprical Formulas of Surge Impedance for Single and Multiple Vertical Cylinder " T. IEE Japan, Vol. 110-B, No. 2, pp. 129-137, '90

[2] N. Mori, Y. Yamashita, T. Yoshida, Y. Maruyama, T. Tanabe, " Surge Propagation characteristic of Cables Fixed to a Tower" T.IEE Japan, Vol. 111-B, No. 1, pp. 99-107, '91

[3] Y. Baba and M. Ishii, "Tower models for fast-front lightning currents" Trans. IEE Japan, Vol. 120-B, No. 1, pp. 18-23, 2000

[4] T. Noda, "A Tower Model for Lightning Overvoltage Studies Based on the Result of an FDTD Simulation" IEEJ Trans. PE, Vol. 127, No. 2, pp. 379-387, 2007

[5] T. Noda, H. Matsubara and S. Yokoyama "A New Tower Model for Lightning-Overvoltage Studies Using the Result of an FDTD Analysis" Electric Power Engineering Research Laboratory Rep. No. H04012, 2005

[6] Edited by Jaun A. Martinez-Velasco "Power System Transients - Prameter Determinations - " CRC press, pp. 50-66, 2010

Propagation Modelling and Channel Estimation: a Comparison among Different Channel Indicators in Severe Multipath Environments

Antonio Sorrentino, Giuseppe Ferrara, Maurizio Migliaccio, Sergio Cappa
Dipartimento di Ingegneria
Università degli Studi di Napoli Parthenope
Centro Direzionale Isola C 4, 80143 Napoli (Italy)
antonio.sorrentino@uniparthenope.it

Lorenzo Mucchi
Dipartimento di Ingegneria dell'Informazione
Università degli Studi di Firenze
via di Santa Marta 3, 50139, Firenze (Italy)
lorenzo.mucchi@unifi.it

***Abstract*— In this paper, different indicators are employed for modeling the propagation and estimating different wireless channel profiles. The measurements are accomplished in a modern laboratory/office building in which different line-of-sight (LOS) and non LOS (NLOS) are accomplished. The comparison between different wireless indicators is made in terms of standard error (*Se*). This analysis is focused on the enhancing of the channel estimation in order to decrease the latency of the communication time and to improve the quality of the transmission.**

***Index Terms*—wireless indicators, LOS-NLOS channels, standard error.**

I. Introduction

In this last years, studies on the propagation modeling and on the channel estimation have significantly increased. An accurate channel propagation model is particularly important above all in the design of new wireless communication systems. The first step toward this goal is to develop electromagnetic models whereas the quality service of the wireless communications is based on simple but efficient indicators able to assure high speed and reliable data transmission. Recently, increased efforts have been made to investigate the propagation mechanism characterizing the Ultra-Wideband (UWB) propagation channels since UWB systems offer several advantages over conventional narrowband systems [1-5].

In this paper, a comparison of different indicators employed for the UWB propagation channel is accomplished. Such a comparison is made on two different channel conditions: the line of sight (LOS) and the non-line of sight (NLOS)- conditions. In particular, the kurtosis k and the gamma-indicator γ are compared to establish which shows a greater sensibility to the presence of a direct link between the transmitting and the receiving antennas. Experiments have been accomplished within a modern laboratory/office building in which the two above mentioned channel profiles have been obtained. The accuracy of the two indicators is evaluated by computing the standard error of the indicators employed.

II. Review of the Theoretical Model

A. γ-indicator

The presence of the direct link within a generic UWB propagation channel, can be shown by analyzing the amplitude of the received electromagnetic field. The electromagnetic field within a wireless propagation channel is described by the Generalized K (GK) model. The GK embodies in a unitary formulation the statistic models used to characterize different propagation channel [4-5]. The GK model is a three parameter distribution. The three real and non-negative parameters, α, η and υ, dictate GK distribution behaviour. α parameter governs the shape of the GK probability density function (pdf), η is the slope parameter and υ takes into account the departure from the uniform phase distribution, e.g. the case in which a LOS component is present. When the coherent component, i.e. the LOS component is not present, the distribution degenerates in a Rayleigh distribution [4]. For the purpose of this study only η and υ (hereinafter termed as GK parameters) are accounted for, since they have been found to exhibit a pronounced sensitivity to the presence of a coherent component in the received field [4]. As a matter of fact, GK distribution is specialised to the Rician case by letting $\alpha \to \infty$, i.e.

$$p\left(E^2\right)=\frac{1}{\eta^2}\exp\left(-\frac{\upsilon^2}{4}\right)\exp\left(-\frac{E^2}{\eta^2}\right)I_0\left(\frac{\upsilon\sqrt{E^2}}{\eta}\right) \tag{1}$$

that depends only on η and υ values. The γ-indicator is based on the GK distribution of the electromagnetic field specialized to the Rice case. In particular, the γ-indicator is given by

$$\gamma=\left(\frac{\upsilon}{\eta}\right)^2 \tag{2}$$

The LOS condition is characterized by high values of υ, that means $\upsilon > 1$, and $\eta < \upsilon$. Accordingly, this calls for

$$\gamma > 1 \tag{3}$$

The NLOS condition is characterized by υ close to zero. In such a case, $\eta > \upsilon$ calls for

$$\gamma < 1 \tag{4}$$

B. kurtosis

The kurtosis is a statistical parameter that indicates the fourth order moment of the received signal amplitude. It is defined as

$$k = \frac{1}{\sigma^4} \frac{\sum_i (E_i - \mu)^4}{n} \qquad (5)$$

where σ is the standard deviation of the electromagnetic field E, μ is the mean value of E and n is the sample number. k is equal to 1.80 in the cases in which the phase pdf is flat about the mean as in the case of a rectangular phase pdf, that is, when the NLOS condition is in place. Such pdfs are called platykurtic pdfs [1]. In LOS conditions, when the coherent component increases, a Leptokurtic distribution is obtained [1].

III. KURTOSIS AND γ-INDEX STANDARD ERRORS

The standard error, *Se*, of the kurtosis index is defined as follows [6]

$$Se_k = 2\sqrt{\frac{6n(n-1)^2}{(n-2)(n+5)(n^2-9)}} \qquad (6)$$

where n represents the sample size. For n large (usually greater than 100), Se_k is equal to

$$Se_k \cong \sqrt{\frac{1}{n}} \qquad (7)$$

For the γ-index the standard error is defined as

$$Se_\gamma = \frac{1+n}{n^2} \qquad (8)$$

that become $1/n$ for n large. In Fig. 1 is reported the standard errors for k and γ.

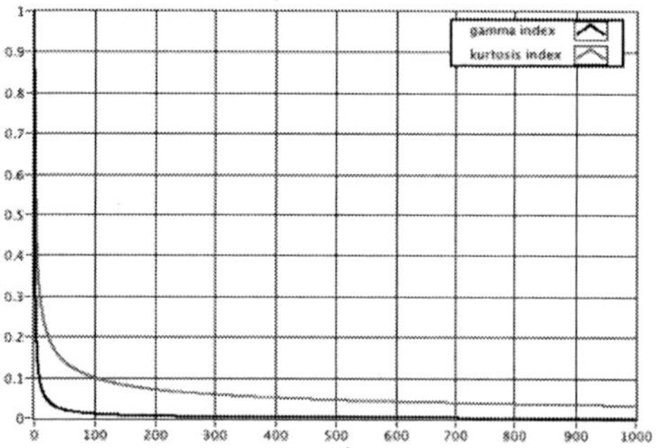

Fig. 1 Standard error (*Se*) comparison: the black line is relative to γ index. The red line is relative to the k index.

IV. EXPERIMENTAL RESULTS

In this section, some meaningful results are reported. The data are obtained from indoor UWB experiments. In the first set of data, a LOS scenarios are considered. The value of k and γ are reported in Table I. In the second set of experiments, real NLOS scenarios are considered. The value of k and γ are reported in Table II.

By a quantitative analysis on the comparison of the two indicators used for distinguishing LOS and NLOS scenarios, γ shows more granularity with respect to a k indicator. Moreover, in terms of standard errors, γ tends more quickly to zero with respect to k. Therefore, γ is more reliable than k in distinguish LOS and NLOS scenarios.

TABLE I: γ AND k VALUES FOR LOS SCENARIOS

	υ	η	γ	k
LOS1	9.78	0.03	84962.18	19.60
LOS2	7.72	0.04	28167.80	39.93

TABLE II: γ AND k VALUES FOR NLOS SCENARIOS

	υ	η	γ	k
NLOS1	0.08	0.24	0.27	6.95
NLOS2	0.06	0.28	0.12	4.85

V. CONCLUSIONS

In this paper, a comparison between γ and k indicators for defining UWB channel profiles, has been accomplished in terms of *Se*. Experiments have been done within a modern laboratory/office building in which the two above mentioned channel profiles have been obtained. A quantitative analysis shows that γ has a better granularity and a smaller error with respect to k indicator in distinguishing LOS and NLOS scenarios.

REFERENCES

[1] L. Mucchi, P. Marcocci, "A New Parameter for UWB Indoor Channel Profile Identification", *IEEE Trans. Wireless Communication*, vol.8, no.4, pp.1597-1602, 2009.

[2] T. Santos, F. Tufvesson, A. F. Molish, "Modeling the ultra-wideband outdoor channel: model specification and validation", *IEEE Trans. Wirel. Commun.*, vol.9, no.6, pp. 1987–1997, 2010.

[3] L. Mucchi, A. Sorrentino, A. Carpini, M. Migliaccio, G. Ferrara, "A Physically-Based Indicator for Identifying UWB Indoor Channel Condition", *IET Microwave, Antennas & Propagation*, 2014.

[4] A. Sorrentino, F. Nunziata, G. Ferrara, M. Migliaccio, "Reverberating Chamber Profile Identification", *IET Microwaves, Antennas & Propagation*, vol.6, no.13, 1468-1472, 2012.

[5] G. Ferrara, M. Migliaccio, F. Nunziata, A. Sorrentino, "GK-based observation of metallic objects at sea in full-resolution SAR data: a multi-polarization study", *IEEE Journal of Oceanic Engineering*, vol 36, no2. 2011.

[6] J. Kenney and E. S. Keeping, *Mathematics of Statistics*, van Nostrand, 1963.

Analysis of New Discrete-Rotary Crosstalk Model Based on FDTD

Yaxiu Sun, Meng Lin, Yida Lai, Junpeng Fang
College of Information and Communications Engineering,
Harbin Engineering University,
Harbin, China, 150001
sunyaxiu@hrbeu.edu.cn trtylm@outlook.com

***Abstract*—In this paper, a new model for calculating the crosstalk of wiring harness is established and this model is named discrete-rotary model. The results of the proposed model are confirmed by Finite-Difference Time-Domain (FDTD). The traditional model is imprecise and limitations because of the little sampling when to calculate the twisted-pair cable crosstalk. So the final update equations are build using more sampling, then according to simulation and verification, the results show that the more accurate can be obtained by the new model.**

Keywords—twisted-pair; crosstalk model; finite difference time domain (FDTD)

I. Introduction

Twisted-pair wire is a kind of common multi-conductor transmission line (MTL) mode. Due to its unique structure, it could reduce the space which be occupied by the transmission line and effectively restrains the crosstalk among the transmission lines. In order to calculate the crosstalk, C.R. Paul and J.W. McKnight [1] have proposed a calculation model of transmission crosstalk that the twisted pair is modeled as a cascade of loops consisting of uniform two-wire sections with abrupt interchanges of wire positions at the ends of each loop.[2] And then selecting two key nodes in the whole period for the simulation rather than the whole period, which causes the inaccuracy of calculation result.

So a discrete-rotation model, which needs to use the key points more than two, has been established in this paper. Then establishing the Finite-Difference Time-Domain (FDTD) equations and doing simulation based on this model to test the efficiency.

II. The Design of the Discrete-Rotation Model

As demonstrated in Fig.1, twisted-pair wire can be seen as two wires, with the increase of the transmission distance, use the center line of the two ends as the axis to rotate in uniform speed. The discrete-rotation model discretizes the continuous rotation process, a twist cycle is divided into several segments. Every segment is replaced by a uniform parallel wire. The chain parameter equation for each transmission line segment is soluble. Then the chain parameter matrix of the whole cycle can be solved with the method of cascade.

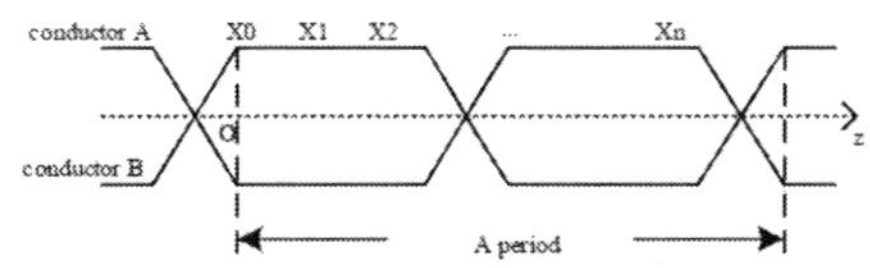

Fig.1 Twisted pair structure diagram

In each parallel wire, the relationship between the current and voltage can be expressed as follows:

$$\begin{bmatrix} V(z) \\ I(z) \end{bmatrix} = \begin{bmatrix} E\cos\beta z & -j\sin\beta z Z_c \\ -j\sin\beta z Z_c^{-1} & E\cos\beta z \end{bmatrix} \begin{bmatrix} V(0) \\ I(0) \end{bmatrix} \tag{1}$$

Where, E is an identity matrix, and Zc is the characteristic impedance matrix, define transport chain parameters as Φ.

$$\Phi = \begin{bmatrix} E\cos\beta z & -j\sin\beta z Z_c \\ -j\sin\beta z Z_c^{-1} & E\cos\beta z \end{bmatrix} \tag{2}$$

The transmission chain parameters of the whole cycle can be obtained by the product of the chain parameters of each segment, so the equation can be expressed as follows:

$$\Phi\left(s \cdot \frac{m}{k} + p\right) = \left[\prod_{i=1}^{m} \Phi_i\left(\frac{s}{k}\right)\right] \cdot \Phi_{m+1}(p) \tag{3}$$

Where, Φ is a chain parameter in the parallel line, p ($p<s/k$) is the incomplete cycle.

Meanwhile, the distribution parameter of this uniform parallel wire is a function of the rotation angle, which can be expressed by this angle. So assuming the initial deflection angle is θ_0, each fragment in the cycle with the same deflection angle. Then the deflection angle of the i segment is shown below

$$\theta_i = \theta_0 + \frac{(i-1/2)\cdot 2\pi}{k}, i = 1, 2, \ldots k \tag{4}$$

In particular, the result is same with the traditional model if we only select two points in one period. Thus, the result is more accurate because the model contains more fragments and could capture more accurate coupling crosstalk processes.

III. FDTD Algorithm of the Discrete-Rotation Model

The complex twisted-pair wire is generally calculated by the numerical method of transmission lines, such as FDTD, rather than the analytical method. Because the FDTD has a fixed space step size Δz, and using Δz as a fragment interval of the model can make the result more accurate.

Supposing the unit cycle length is still s and the number of fragments per unit length is k=s/Δz, so each Δz length is corresponding to the deflection angle of Δθ, If the source end deflection angle is θ_0, then

$$\theta_n = \theta_0 + (2\pi n \cdot \Delta z) / s \tag{5}$$

$$\theta_{n+1/2} = \theta_0 + \frac{2\pi(n+1/2) \cdot \Delta z}{s} \tag{6}$$

So in the discrete rotation model, the FDTD iterative equations of N moment and (1/2 N) moment are shown below:

$$\frac{V[(n+1)\Delta z, N\Delta t]}{\Delta z} = -L(\theta_{n+1/2}) \frac{I[(n+1/2)\Delta z, (N+1/2)\Delta t] - I[(n+1/2)\Delta z, (N-1/2)\Delta t]}{\Delta t}$$
$$-R(\theta_{n+1/2}) \frac{I[(n+1/2)\Delta z, (N+1/2)\Delta t] + I[(n+1/2)\Delta z, (N-1/2)\Delta t]}{2} \tag{7}$$

$$\frac{I[(n+1/2)\Delta z, (N+1/2)\Delta t] - I[(n-1/2)\Delta z, (N+1/2)\Delta t]}{\Delta z} = -C(\theta_n) \frac{V[n\Delta z, (N+1)\Delta t] - V[n\Delta z, N\Delta t]}{\Delta t}$$
$$-G(\theta_n) \frac{V[n\Delta z, (N+1)\Delta t] + V[n\Delta z, N\Delta t]}{2} \tag{8}$$

Where, distributed parameter L, C, R and G all are the functions of d, in other words all are the functions of deflection angle θ. As demonstrated in Fig.1, the set point is named $O(x_0,y_0)$ and the rotation radius is b. Then the point(x,y) to the A, B as follows.

$$d_A = \sqrt{(x_0 + b \cdot \cos\theta - x)^2 + (y_0 + b \cdot \sin\theta - y)^2}$$
$$d_B = \sqrt{(x_0 - b \cdot \cos\theta - x)^2 + (y_0 - b \cdot \sin\theta - y)^2} \tag{9}$$

Then according to the distance d and Maxwell equation, the distribution parameters. Finally the whole transmission chain parameter equation related to θ can be established.

IV. Simulation and Verification

Now I use the ground plane, single line and twisted-pair wire for numerical calculation. Lines' length is 4.705m, totally contain 255.5 half-twist cycles. Center height of a single line and twisted-pair wire of is 2cm, the lateral distance of them is 2cm. Radius of twisted-pair wire is 0.4064mm and spacing between two wires is 0.4191mm. Circuit diagram is as follows in Fig.2, R=50Ω, Us=1V (20MHz).

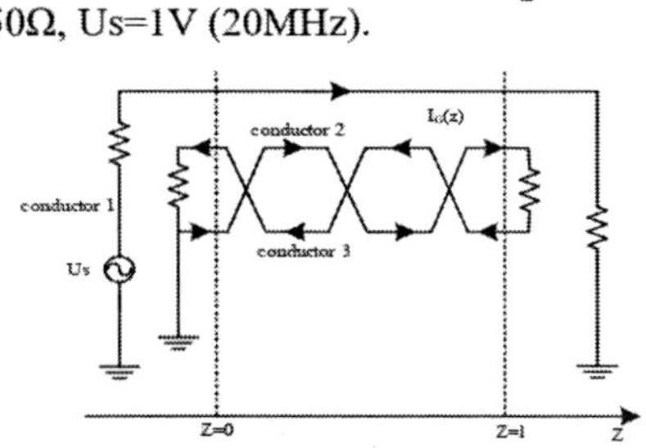

Fig.2 Twisted-pair wire circuit diagram

In order to illustrate the characteristics of twisted, using a model with the same parameters while the two lines are not kinked to do a comparison. The results are as follows.

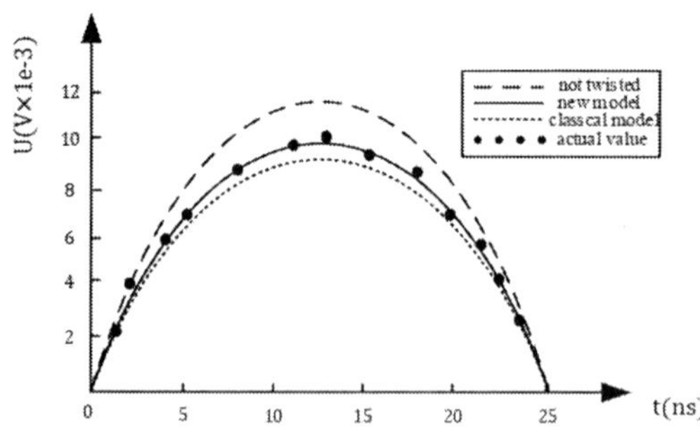

Fig.3 the near end crosstalk of twisted pair

The results show that the twist can effectively reduce the near end crosstalk. At the same time, the new FDTD model can be used to simulate the crosstalk of twisted pair cable effectively. And compared with the result of the traditional model, the result closes to actual value. And in order to get a more accurate result, usually requiring each half twist cycle contains 8 or more space steps, which have a strong limit in the selection of the space step and the time step value.

V. Conclusion

A new model has been established as mentioned before. Using the coordinate method to obtain the distance instead of the geometric logic of triangle. The calculation process is simpler. To solve the deficiency of the traditional model, the new discrete-rotary model has more sampling points, more accurate calculation results. This method is simple and general and not restricted by the shape of the model.

Acknowledgment

This paper was supported by the National Natural Science Foundation of China (Grant No. 51209055), the China Postdoctoral Special Foundation (Grant No. 2015T80324), and the Natural Science Foundation of Heilongjiang, China (Grant No. F2015028).

References

[1] Paul C R, Mcknight J W. Prediction of Crosstalk Involving Twisted Pairs of Wires-Part I: A Transmission-Line Model for Twisted-Wire Pairs[J]. IEEE Transactions on Electromagnetic Compatibility, 1979, EMC-21(2):92-105.

[2] Jullien C, Besnier P, Dunand M, et al. Advanced Modeling of Crosstalk Between an Unshielded Twisted Pair Cable and an Unshielded Wire Above a Ground Plane[J]. IEEE Transactions on Electromagnetic Compatibility, 2013, 55(1):183-194.

[3] Belkhelfa S, Lefouili M, El K D K. Frequency Domain Analysis of EM Crosstalk Problem in a Quad by the Equivalent Cable Bundle Method Among Twisted-Wire Pairs Cable Bundle[J]. IEEE Transactions on Magnetics, 2015, 51(11):1-1.

[4] Jullien C, Besnier P, Dunand M, et al. Crosstalk Inside a Bundle with Unshielded Twisted Pair Cables and a Single Wire[J]. Euroem, 2012.

[5] Wang Z Y, Chen S C, Hao W U. Method of crosstalk coupling noise of interconnects based on FDTD[J]. Journal of Chongqing University of Posts & Telecommunications, 2010.

Frequency Domain Analysis of New Differential-mode Twisted Wire Crosstalk Model

Yaxiu Sun , Jianli Wang, Junzhu Qian, Ming Zhang
College of Information and Communications Engineering,
Harbin Engineering University, Harbin, China, 150001
sunyaxiu@hrbeu.edu.cn S3I6080089@outlook.com

***Abstract*—In twisted wire crosstalk research, common-mode traditional alternative inverted model ignores cross section distance. A new differential-mode twist wire pair crosstalk model considering cross distance is established and the frequency domain of the model is analyzed in this paper with the method of establishing circuit model, mathematical model and solving the parameter matrix chain .The results show that it can accurately calculate the crosstalk and is of great significance to the EMC design of underwater vehicle.**

Keywords—crosstalk; twisted pair; cross section; differential mode excitation; new model.

I. Introduction

Research on the crosstalk between the lines begins with the MTL crosstalk model established by R. Paul C, the classical model to calculate the crosstalk is still in use [1]. Based on the typical MTL model, the alternative inverted twisted-pair model was established. But the transmission distance between the cross sections of the twisted-pair is regarded as zero [2], with great limitations. In the calculation of crosstalk, the traditional model usually only considers the common-mode crosstalk, ignoring the differential-mode crosstalk [3-4].

In order to accurately calculate the crosstalk between twisted pairs, the cross section distance of the twisted pair is not considered to be zero. The model can accurately calculate the crosstalk between the lines, which could guide EMC design.

II. Twisted Wire Pair Crosstalk Model in Differential Mode Excitation

When modeling, twisted-pair is connected to the differential mode excitation source Vs and the parallel transmission section and the cross section appear alternately. Each half reverse cycle consists of a parallel transmission section and cross section, the cross section includes non-parallel part and the intersection point. The new crosstalk circuit model of twisted-pair in differential mode excitation is shown in Fig 1.

Whether in the parallel section or in the non-parallel section, we can use the new equivalent circuit model of the infinitesimal section Δz in differential mode excitation to analyze and solve. The model is shown in Fig. 2.

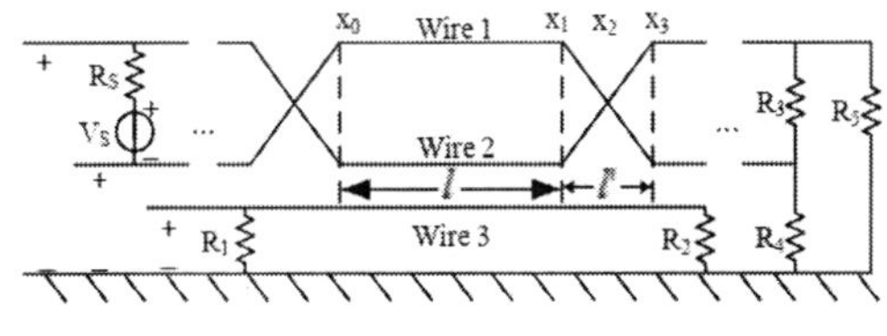

Fig. 1. New crosstalk circuit model of twisted-pair in differential mode excitation

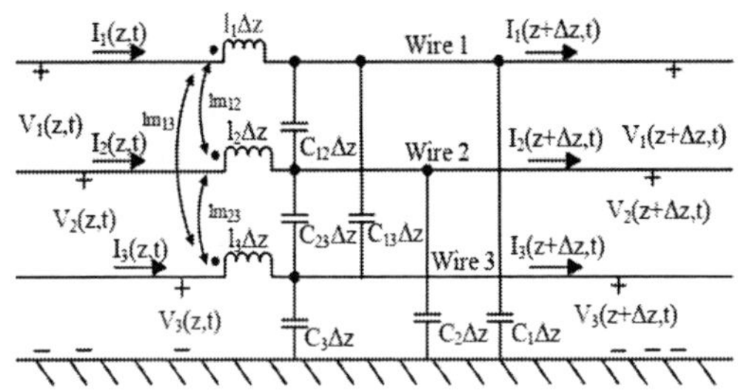

Fig. 2. The new equivalent circuit model of a transmission line infinitesimal section in differential mode excitation

The relationship of the transmission line voltages and currents can be determined as follows:

$$\begin{cases} \dfrac{\partial V_1(z,t)}{\partial z} = -l_1 \dfrac{\partial I_1(z,t)}{\partial t} - l_{m12} \dfrac{\partial I_2(z,t)}{\partial t} - l_{m13} \dfrac{\partial I_3(z,t)}{\partial t} \\ \dfrac{\partial V_2(z,t)}{\partial z} = -l_{m12} \dfrac{\partial I_1(z,t)}{\partial t} - l_2 \dfrac{\partial I_2(z,t)}{\partial t} - l_{m23} \dfrac{\partial I_3(z,t)}{\partial t} \\ \dfrac{\partial V_3(z,t)}{\partial z} = -l_{m13} \dfrac{\partial I_1(z,t)}{\partial t} - l_{m23} \dfrac{\partial I_2(z,t)}{\partial t} - l_3 \dfrac{\partial I_3(z,t)}{\partial t} \end{cases} \tag{1}$$

$$\begin{cases} \dfrac{\partial I_1(z,t)}{\partial z} = -(c_1 + c_{12} + c_{13}) \dfrac{\partial V_1(z,t)}{\partial t} + c_{12} \dfrac{\partial V_2(z,t)}{\partial t} + c_{13} \dfrac{\partial V_3(z,t)}{\partial t} \\ \dfrac{\partial I_2(z,t)}{\partial z} = c_{12} \dfrac{\partial V_1(z,t)}{\partial t} - (c_2 + c_{12} + c_{23}) \dfrac{\partial V_2(z,t)}{\partial t} + c_{23} \dfrac{\partial V_3(z,t)}{\partial t} \\ \dfrac{\partial I_3(z,t)}{\partial z} = c_{13} \dfrac{\partial V_1(z,t)}{\partial t} + c_{23} \dfrac{\partial V_2(z,t)}{\partial t} - (c_3 + c_{13} + c_{23}) \dfrac{\partial V_3(z,t)}{\partial t} \end{cases} \tag{2}$$

Use the mirror method to calculate the parasitic parameters, deriving the parasitic parameter matrix $\mathbf{L}$ and $\mathbf{C}$ .The line-line distance of cross section varies linearly with the infinitesimal section position, resulting in parasitic parameters is not uniform, and each parasitic parameters is a function of distance from the infinitesimal section position to the end of the adjacent parallel line.

III. RESEARCH OF FREQUENCY DOMAIN SOLUTION

In frequency domain, the crosstalk voltage needs to be solved by the two part of the chain parameter matrix and the initial end, the terminal boundary condition. The voltage and current of the beginning and the end of the terminal are linked through the chain parameter matrix.

Define chain parameter matrix of semi-periodic as $\mathbf{\Phi}_{sp}$ .Define chain parameter matrix of Parallel transmission section, non-parallel part of cross section and intersection point respectively as $\mathbf{\Phi}_s$, $\mathbf{\Phi}$, $\mathbf{P}$. Parallel line transmission distance is l , half of the cross section distance is l' .Take X_0, X_3 two points as the key point to carry out half cycle research.

The transmission chain parameter matrix of parallel lines is:

$$\mathbf{\Phi}_s(l) = \begin{bmatrix} \cos(\beta l)\cdot \mathbf{E} & -j\omega\left(\dfrac{\sin(\beta l)}{\beta l}\right)\mathbf{L} \\ -j\omega\left(\dfrac{\sin(\beta l)}{\beta l}\right)\mathbf{C} & \cos(\beta l)\cdot \mathbf{E} \end{bmatrix} \quad (3)$$

Divided the transmission distance of cross section into n parts, n is relatively large, each length is $\Delta l' = l'/n$, the transmission chain parameter matrix of section i is:

$$\mathbf{\Phi}(\Delta l', i) = \begin{bmatrix} \cos(\beta\Delta l')\cdot \mathbf{E} & -j\omega\left(\dfrac{\sin(\beta\Delta l')}{\beta\Delta l'}\right)\mathbf{L}(i\Delta l') \\ -j\omega\left(\dfrac{\sin(\beta\Delta l')}{\beta\Delta l'}\right)\mathbf{C}(i\Delta l') & \cos(\beta\Delta l')\cdot \mathbf{E} \end{bmatrix} \quad (4)$$

The transmission chain parameter matrix of entire cross section is:

$$\mathbf{\Phi}(l') = \prod_{i=1}^{n} \mathbf{\Phi}(\Delta l', i) \quad (5)$$

At the intersection, the voltage and the current on the different line of twisted-pair are exchanged, and the point also has the chain parameter matrix, it is:

$$\mathbf{P} = \begin{bmatrix} 0 & 1 & 0 & 0 & 0 & 0 \\ 1 & 0 & 0 & 0 & 0 & 0 \\ 0 & 0 & 1 & 0 & 0 & 0 \\ 0 & 0 & 0 & 0 & 1 & 0 \\ 0 & 0 & 0 & 1 & 0 & 0 \\ 0 & 0 & 0 & 0 & 0 & 1 \end{bmatrix} \quad (6)$$

Because the wire 1, 2 interchange at the intersection, that is, V1, V2 swaps, I1, I2 swaps, and so matrix P could be get by this method: For the 6 - order unit matrix, the first line and the second line swap, fourth line and fifth line swap. The Chain parameter matrix of Semi periodic X0-X3 is:

$$\mathbf{\Phi}_{sp}(l,\ l') = \mathbf{\Phi}_s(l)\mathbf{\Phi}(l')\mathbf{P}\mathbf{\Phi}(l') \quad (7)$$

FOR The twisted pair model whose number of half-twist twisted cycle is an integer, assuming that the model contains K full-twist cycles (K can be an integer, or an integer plus 1/2), the length of each period is $2(l'+l)$, N is an integer, then the transmission chain parameters of the whole model is:

$$\mathbf{\Phi}_T = \begin{cases} [\mathbf{\Phi}_{sp}(l,\ l')\cdot \mathbf{P}]\mathbf{P}^{2N}, k = N \\ [\mathbf{\Phi}_{sp}(l,\ l')\cdot \mathbf{P}]^{2N}\mathbf{\Phi}_{sp}(l,\ l'), k = N + 1/2 \end{cases} \quad (8)$$

IV. SIMULATION VERIFICATION

In order to show the effectiveness of the process, this paper use the new model and the traditional model to analyze crosstalk of the same twisted pair in frequency domain and compare the numerical results from 100MHz to 10MHz. Set wire radius r=0.405mm, the height of wire1 h_1=4.432 mm, the height of wire2 h_2=3.568 mm, the height of wire3 h_3=2 mm, the load of source and load end is 50 ohms in Fig. 1. The simulation result is shown in fig.3.

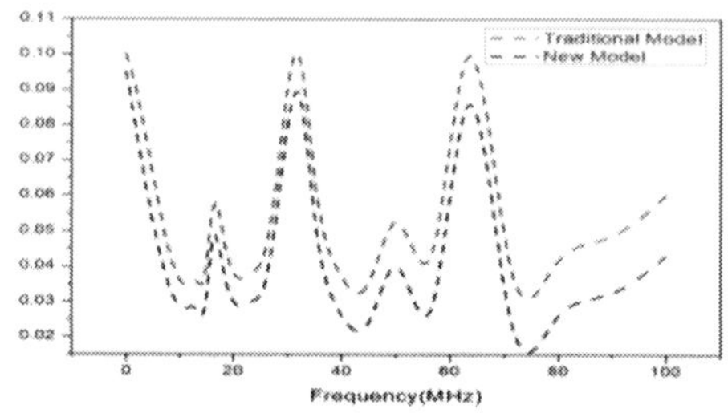

Fig. 3. The current value of the source end of the wire 3

V. CONLUSION

This paper has established a new model to calculate the twisted pair crosstalk in differential mode excitation, and simulated the twisted pair crosstalk of the new model and traditional model. For the same length twisted pair, the result shows that, the crosstalk voltage is lower when the cross distance is not zero. Therefore, in the actual engineering application, crosstalk cross section should not be ignored. In addition, the new model provides theoretical support for accurate predictions of the twisted pair differential-mode crosstalk.

ACKNOWLEDGE

This paper was supported by the National Natural Science Foundation of China (Grant No. 51209055), the China Postdoctoral Special Foundation (Grant No. 2015T80324), and the Natural Science Foundation of Heilongjiang, China (Grant No.F2015028).

REFERENCES

[1] C. R. Paul and J. A. McKnight, “Prediction of crosstalk involving twisted pairs of wires—Part I: A transmission line model for twisted wire pairs,” IEEE Trans. Electromagn. Compat, vol. EMC-21, no. 2, pp. 92–105, May 1979.

[2] Z. Li, L. Liu, J.Yan, A. Xu, Z. Niu, and C. Gu “An efficient simplification scheme for modeling crosstalk of complex cable bundles above an orthogonal ground plane,” IEEE Trans. Electroma-gn. Compat., vol. 55, no. 5, pp. 975-978, Oct. 2013

[3] L. Tang, Z. Ye, L. Chen, Z. Xiang, C. Liao, “The study on crosstalk of single wire and twisted-wire pair,” ISAP-2013 Int. Symp. vol. 02 pp. 1008-1011, Oct. 2013.

[4] S. A. Pignari and G. Spadacini, “Plane-wave coupling to a twisted-wire pair above ground,” *IEEE Trans. Electromagn. Compat.*, vol. 53, no. 2, pp. 508–523, May 2011.

Analysis and Evaluation of One-dimensional Sea Surface Features Based on FSV

Nan Bi, Xiaojun Wang, Tao Jiang*
College of Information and Communications Engineering
Harbin Engineering University
Harbin, China
{binan808, wangxiaojun, jiangtao }@hrbeu.edu.cn

Yachen Zhang
School of Electrical Engineering
Heilongjiang University
Harbin, China
20151594@s.hlju.edu.cn

***Abstract*—This paper presents a method of extracting and evaluating one-dimensional dynamic sea surface features based on the feature selective validation (FSV). The Monte Carlo method is used to model the one-dimensional dynamic sea surface. The influence of different wind speeds on sea surface height fluctuation is simulated and analyzed. At the same time, the distribution of gravity spectrum and tensor spectrum of one-dimensional rough sea surface under different wind speeds are analyzed based on FSV. The results show that this method can effectively extract the undulation feature of one-dimensional rough sea surface, and realize the quantitative and intuitionistic analysis and evaluation of data features.**

Keywords—sea surface; wind speed; FSV; Pierson-Moskowitz spectrum

I. INTRODUCTION

Rough sea surface modeling is based on linear wave theory, whose main method is linear filtering method. Linear filtering is the Monte Carlo method [1]. Its basic idea is to use the sea spectrum in the frequency domain to filter, and then to obtain the rough sea surface height fluctuation through the inverse fast fourier transform (IFFT). The method can construct the static sea surface at a certain moment, and then introduce time-dependent time factor based on the dispersion relation of sea wave, then the dynamic time-varying sea surface can be obtained [2]. Based on the Pierson-Moskowitz (PM) spectrum, the one-dimensional dynamic sea surface modeling is realized by the linear filtering method and the dispersion relation between the spatial wave number and frequency components. Because of the fast Fourier transform used in the linear filtering method, the computation time is greatly reduced, which will lay a foundation for large-scale sea surface modeling.

The purpose of rough sea modeling is to analyze the electromagnetic scattering characteristics of the sea surface. It is necessary to extract the basic feature information of the rough sea surface after modeling the sea surface. At present, the description of rough sea surface features is mainly based on waveform observation. Due to the randomness of the rough sea surface, it is difficult to form an intuitive impression. Based on the feature selective validation (FSV) thought and method [3,4], this paper presents an intuitive and quantitative method for characterizing the rough sea surface modeling.

II. ONE - DIMENSIONAL DYNAMIC SEA SURFACE MODELING

The linear ocean wave theory treats an infinite steady sea surface as a superposition of a large number of harmonics, and its amplitude is an independent Gaussian random variable. According to this theory, using the linear filtering method can be obtained dynamic sea surface height fluctuation expression. The basic idea is to do Gaussian Fourier transform, with the sea surface power spectrum of its filter in the frequency domain, and then the inverse of the Fourier transform to get the sea surface height of the expression, denoted as:

$$h(x_n,t)=\frac{1}{L}\sum_{j=-N/2+1}^{N/2} A(k_j)e^{ik_jx_n}e^{i\omega(k_j)t} \tag{1}$$

$$A(k_j)=\frac{2\pi}{\sqrt{2\Delta k}}\sqrt{S(k_j)}\cdot\begin{cases}[N(0,1)+iN(0,1)] & j=-N/2+1,\cdots,-1\\ N(0,1) & j=0,N/2\end{cases} \tag{2}$$

where $x_n=n\Delta x\ (n=-N/2+1,\dots N/2)$ represents the nth sampling point on the sea surface. L is the total sea surface length, $N(0,1)$ is to satisfy the standard normal distribution for the Gaussian random sequence. We define the discrete wavenumber as $k_j=2\pi j/L$, spatial wavenumber difference is Δk, the discrete wavenumber k_j and the propagation frequency $\omega(k_j)$ satisfy the dispersion relation:

$$\omega(k_j)=\sqrt{g_0k_j\left[1+\left(k_j/k_m\right)^2\right]} \tag{3}$$

where, the acceleration of gravity $g_0=9.81m/s^2$, k_m is related to sea surface tension T and water density ρ, and in this paper $k_m=\sqrt{\rho g/T}=363.2rad/m$.

In order to obtain the undulation function of sea surface height, we also need to determine the sea spectrum $S(k_j)$. In this paper, one-dimensional PM spectrum is used, and its expression is:

$$S(k)=\begin{cases}\dfrac{\alpha}{4|k|^3}\exp\left(-\dfrac{\beta g_0^2}{k^2U_{19.5}^4}\right), & k\ge 0\\ 0, & k<0\end{cases} \tag{4}$$

where, α and β are for the dimensionless empirical constant, $\alpha=8.10\times10^{-3}$, $\beta=0.74$, $U_{19.5}$ is the wind speed which is 19.5 meters high above the sea surface.

According to (1)-(4), we can calculate the sea surface height fluctuation. Fig. 1 shows a one-dimensional sea surface model based on PM sea spectrum generated by linear filtering at different wind speeds.

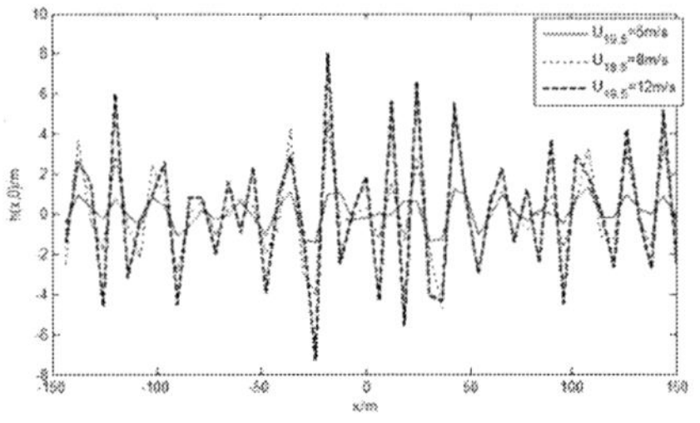

Fig.1 1-D sea surface model based on PM spectrum at different wind speeds

III. FSV DATA PROCESSING AND ANALYSIS

Based on the FSV thought and dynamic rough sea surface model's actual background, this paper puts forward a new data processing and analysis in view of the sea surface wind speed change on the influence of the surface wave. The basic idea is as follows:

a) To do the fast Fourier transform of sea surface height fluctuation data according to the one-dimensional dynamic sea surface at different wind speed generated above;

b) Select the appropriate cut-off point according to the wavelength of gravity wave and tension wave, and the frequency domain of the sea surface height fluctuation function is decomposed into two parts, namely, the high frequency component and the low frequency component, respectively;

c) Respectively calculate the proportion of the high frequency component and the low frequency component in the total spectrum value;

d) According to the high frequency component and the low frequency component, the influence of different wind speed on the sea surface waveform is analyzed.

The method is as follows: for the one-dimensional dynamic sea surface with length L, and the corresponding one-dimensional dynamic sea surface is generated under wind speed of 3m / s, 8m / s and 15m / s respectively. The Fourier transform of the height fluctuation function of the dynamic sea surface is performed by using the FFT method. Data processing and analysis process is as follows:

$$S=\sum_{i=1}^{N} TDWS(i) \tag{5}$$

$$Lf=\sum_{i=1}^{i_{25\%}} TDWS(i) \tag{6}$$

$$Hf=\sum_{i=i_{25\%}}^{N} TDWS(i) \tag{7}$$

where, TDWS(i) is the i-th frequency point's the spectrum value. S is the summation of the spectral values of all the frequency points, Lf is the sum of the spectral values of the low-frequency components, and Hf is the sum of the spectral values of the high-frequency components. According to the above data, we can get the proportion of the high-frequency and low-frequency components in the total spectrum value at different wind speeds, as shown in Fig. 2:

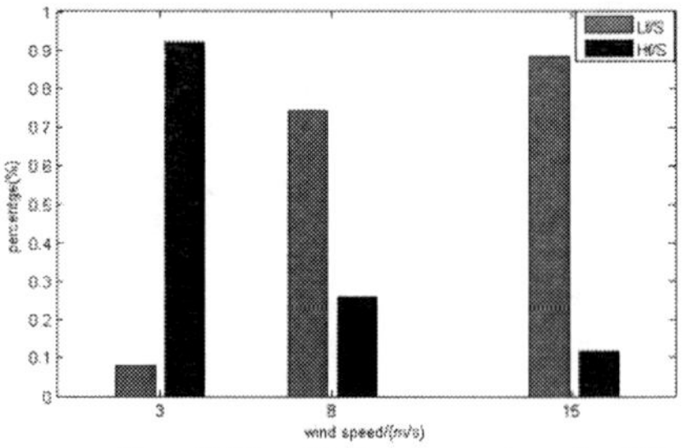

Fig.2 The proportion of Hf and Lf components under different wind speeds

As shown in Fig. 2, with the increasing of wind speed, the proportion of high-frequency components in the spectral components is significantly reduced, and the proportion of low-frequency components is significantly increased. When the wind speed is small, the local sea surface changes quickly, the overall ups and downs, the sea surface roughness mainly from the role of tension waves; and when the wind speed increases, the sea as a whole is ups and downs, local changes slow. At this point the surface roughness mainly comes from the effect of gravity wave, this change is consistent with the change of the actual surface.

IV. CONCLUSION

This paper presents a method of rough sea surface data processing and analysis based on FSV. The method can quantitatively and intuitively evaluate the influence of different wind speeds on the gravity spectrum and tension spectrum of 1D rough sea surface height fluctuation. The results obtained by this method are in agreement with the actual sea surface changes. It shows the effectiveness of the method, and shows that the constructed one-dimensional dynamic sea surface can truly reflect the fluctuation of sea surface under different conditions, which will lay the foundation for the study of rough sea surface electromagnetic scattering based on this method.

ACKNOWLEDGMENT

This paper is funded by the International Exchange Program of Harbin Engineering University for Innovation-oriented Talents Cultivation.

REFERENCES

[1] E. I. Thorsos, "The validity of the Kirchhoff approximation for rough surface scattering using a Gaussian roughness spectrum," *Journal of the Acoustical Society of America*, vol. 83, pp. 78-92, 1988.

[2] J. V. Toporkov and G. S. Brown, "Numerical simulations of scattering from time-varying, randomly rough surfaces," *IEEE Transactions on Geoscience and Remote Sensing*, vol. 38, pp. 1616-1625, 2000.

[3] A. P. Duffy, A. J. M. Martin, A. Orlandi, G. Antonini, T. M. Benson, and M. S. Woolfson, "Feature Selective Validation (FSV) for validation of computational electromagnetics (CEM). Part 1 - The FSV method," *IEEE Transactions on Electromagnetic Compatibility*, vol. 48, pp. 449-458, 2006.

[4] A. Orlandi, A. P. Duffy, B. Archambeault, G. Antonini, D. E. Coleby, and S. Connor, "Feature Selective Validation (FSV) for validation of computational electromagnetics (CEM). Part II - Assessment of FSV performance," *IEEE Transactions on Electromagnetic Compatibility*, vol. 48, pp. 460-467, 2006.

Groundwave Propagation in a Nonhomogeneous Atmosphere: Prediction Using 3D Parabolic Equation

Zeina El Ahdab[1,a] , Funda Akleman[2,b]
[1] Istanbul Technical University, ITU,
Istanbul, Turkey,
[a] elahdab@itu.edu.tr, [b]akleman@itu.edu.tr

Abstract— **The analysis of groundwave propagation over long distances in an atmosphere with non-homogeneous electromagnetic properties is conducted by using a three-dimensional parabolic equation method (3D-PE) based approach. The inhomogeneities in the atmosphere imply the formation of ducts which result in modifying the propagation direction and range of the waves. The signal is excited by a vertical line source, and the waves are marched in range by using the Fourier split-step algorithm. Multiple tests are conducted in which different types of ducts are considered in order to analyze and validate the results obtained by the 3D algorithm. These results are compared to those obtained from two-dimensional parabolic equation based algorithm (2D-PE).**

Keywords— **groundwave propagation, inhomogeneous atmophere, 3D Parabolic Equation.**

I. Introduction

The analysis of ground wave propagation is crucial for the design and implementation of efficient and robust land communication systems. The efficiency of the radio transmission depends directly on the characteristics of the lower layers of the atmosphere and the characteristics of the terrain over which the propagation takes place. One mechanism of wave in the atmosphere is ducting which consists of the bending of waves due to tropospheric refraction and can be strong enough to cause signals to propagate while following the surface of the Earth for both flat and curved earth models. This effect is mostly observed at high frequencies at VHF and UHF and thus the behavior of a signal in an atmosphere with ducts depends directly on the frequency of the propagating signal itself [1]. Ducting is more commonly observed in certain areas than others depending on parameters such as the temperature distribution of the atmosphere, its humidity, the concentration of certain atmospherical particles, etc.

In this paper, the wave is considered to propagate in an inhomogeneous atmosphere and over a regular terrain and analyzed by using a 3D-PE method based approach. The vector fields are expressed in terms of electric and magnetic vector potentials which are initiated at the source and then marched in range by applying the split-step Fourier algorithm. At each marching step, the variations of the index of refraction of the atmosphere are added to the propagator which marches the wave in range. Although this type of approach has been used in 2D tropospheric wave propagation problems [2-3], the formulation used in this paper differs in that it is based on a vector potential representation of the fields in a 3D space. This results in a possibility to simulate models in which 3-D variations of the atmospheric refraction index can be fully taken into consideration, a novelty previously not supported by 2-D models. In Section II, this formulation is explained in details, and the numerical simulations and results are presented in Section III where 3D PE results are compared to 2D results for different type of atmospherical ducts.

II. Formulation

The general formulation of the fields based on the vector potentials Π^e and Π^m can be derived from Maxwell's equations [4]. The potentials satisfy the inhomogeneous Helmholtz equations in an inhomogeneous atmosphere as

$$\nabla^2\Pi^e + k^2\Pi^e = J_z \tag{1}$$
$$\nabla^2\Pi^m + k^2\Pi^m = -M_z \tag{2}$$
$$k^2(x,y,z) = k_0^2(n^2(x,y,z) - 1) \tag{3}$$

where J_z and M_z represent electric and magnetic current sources respectively. Here k_0 and n(x,y,z) are the free space wavenumber and refractive index of atmosphere, respectively.

The addition of the variable index of refraction to the formulation implies a modification of the propagator we use in the SSPE algorithm. This modification impacts the x-component (direction of propagation) of the wave number in the following way

$$k_x \cong k_0 - \frac{{k_z}^2}{2k_0} - \frac{n^2 - 1}{2} \tag{4}$$

III. Numerical Results

The results of numerical implementations are presented in this section to demonstrate the performance of the 3-D Split Step PE (SSPE) algorithm for propagation in inhomogeneous atmosphere over a flat earth model. These results are compared to those obtained by the *SSPE-GUI* [5].

The fields in the examples below are excited by a vertically polarized current source with a Gaussian aperture distribution at a height of 20 meters above the surface. The frequency and beamwidth of the source are 100 MHz and 30°, respectively. The receiver is placed at a distance of 1km from the source. First, a "simple linearly increasing refractivity profile" is

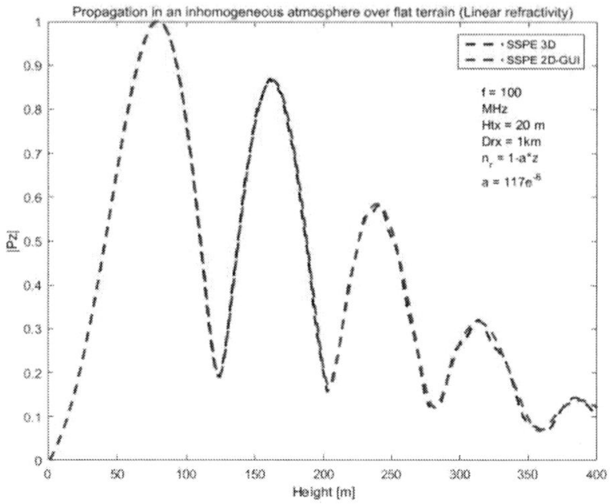

Fig. 1 Inhomogeneous atmosphere: Simple Refractivity Profile

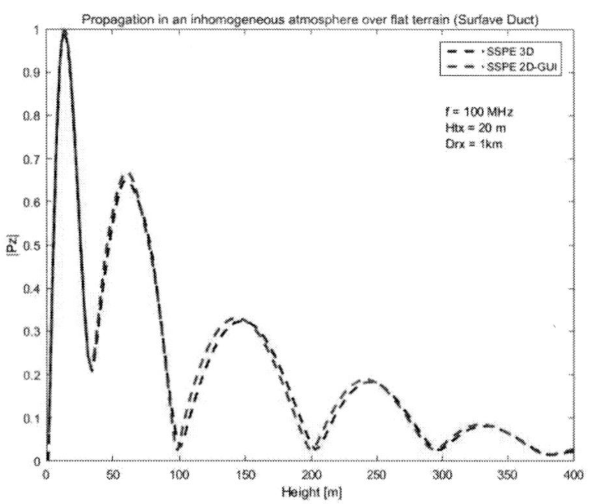

Fig. 2 Inhomogeneous atmosphere: Surface Duct, Tx at 20m heights

inserted and the results of the 3D-SSVPE and the 2- D *SSPE-GUI* are shown in Fig.1. |Pz| represents the absolute value of the z-oriented vector potential. In the case of a linearly increasing profile, a sliding of these maxima and minima positions to higher altitudes in the atmosphere is observed.

Secondly, propagation through a surface duct for two different transmitter heights 20m and 100m are considered and the variation with respect to height are plotted in Fig. 2 and Fig. 3, respectively. It can be observed that the wave shows larger oscillations in the second case, as observed in Fig.3 due to the fact that the wave immediately undergoes the change of refractivity at 100 meters.

It can be noticed that as the altitude increases, there is a slight shift between the curves of the 2D and 3D algorithms. This shift can be explained by the fact that the 3-D SSVPE is based on the wide-angle PE method whereas the 2-D *SSPE-GUI* is based on the narrow-angle PE method.

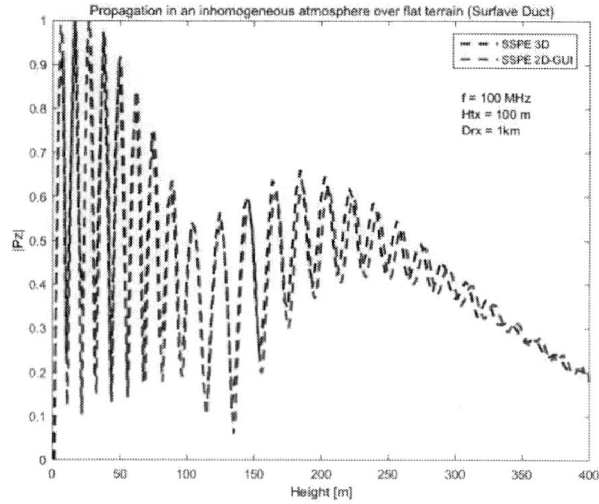

Fig. 3 Inhomogeneous atmosphere: Surface Duct, tx at 100m heights

IV. Conclusion

In this work, a 3D-PE based algorithm has been elaborated to include variable atmospherical index of refraction. Simulations of different types of refractivity profiles and source parameters were conducted in order to test the performance of the algorithm. The results of the tests have been compared to those obtained from a 2D-PE algorithm. The 3D algorithm provides results that are compatible with the 2D algorithm for simulations where the 3D space is modeled to represent the same 2D environment. The addition of the variable index of refraction to the 3D algorithm provides more information regarding 3D propagation of groundwaves over long distances. This increases the accuracy of the PE method in models where field prediction is necessary in regions where the electromagnetic properties of the atmosphere should be considered. This work can be generalized to include laterally variable refraction indexes as well as irregular terrain and electromagnetic obstacles.

References

[1] Curt A. Levis, Joel T. Johnson, Fernando L. Teixeira, Radiowave propagation: Physics and Applications. Hoboken, NJ: Wiley, 2010

[2] Janaswamy, R. "Path loss predictions in the presence of buildings on flat terrain: a 3-D vector parabolic equation approach". *IEEE Transactions on Antennas and Propagation,* 51(8), 1716–1728, 2003.

[3] L.Sevgi, F. Akleman, "A Novel MoM- and SSPE-based Groundwave-Propagation Field-Strength Prediction Simulator", *IEEE Antennas and Propagation Magazine*, vol. 49, no. 5, pp 69-82, Oct. 2007.

[4] O. Ozgun, "Recursive two-way parabolic equation approach for modeling terrain effects in tropospheric propagation", *IEEE transactions on Antennas and Propagation*, Vol. 57, no. 9, 2009

[5] L. Sevgi, C. Uluisik, F. Akleman, "A MATLAB-Based Two-Dimensional Parabolic Equation Radiowave Propagation Package", IEEE Antennas and Prop. Magazine, Vol. 47, no. 4, August 2005

The Calculation of Equivalent Electromagnetic Parameters in Multilayer Composite Materials

Yaxiu Sun , Junzhu Qian, Jianli Wang ,Ming Zhang
College of Information and Communications Engineering,
Harbin Engineering University, Harbin, China, 150001
sunyaxiu@hrbeu.edu.cn qianjunzhu@hrbeu.edu.cn

***Abstract*—Calculating the effective parameters (permittivity and permeability) in two-phase composite material is very important. In this paper, hierarchical computing method is used to study the equivalent permittivity and permeability of multilayer composite electromagnetic materials, and to obtain the electromagnetic shielding performance of the materials. Firstly, using of Helmholtz theorem gets electric field in space multilayer medium, then RVE models are established, and permittivity and permeability are obtained by the method of Volume weighted average algorithm in multilayer anisotropic medium.**

Keywords—A two-phase composite material; The equivalent electromagnetic constants; Volume weighted average algorithm

I. INTRODUCTION

The single homogeneous material is limited in engineering, the composite materials which are composed of variety of different dielectric properties are widely used in engineering [1]. The study of electromagnetic parameters of composite materials has become a hot topic [2].

Equivalent dielectric constant of composite materials is associated with the composition of the dielectric constant, volume fraction, spatial distribution and grain state. While the permeability and elastic modulus are dependent on the microstructure of the material and the shape and distribution of the internal particles. This article is studying the equivalent electromagnetic parameters and electromagnetic shielding effect of multilayer anisotropic composite materials [2-3].

II. THE CALCULATION OF ELECTROMAGNETIC FIELD

The problem of propagation of electromagnetic wave in medium can be extended to propagation of uniform plane waves in the medium with dielectric constant ε and permeability μ . If the media is homogeneous, Helmholtz equation is $\nabla^2 E_s = -k^2 E_s$, and wavenumber k is a function of dielectric constant ε and permeability μ : $k = w\sqrt{\mu\varepsilon} = k_0\sqrt{\mu_r \varepsilon_r}$ .Wave number k is a plural.

In a time-varying electric field, the form of the Helmholtz equation for the electric field vector is:

$$\nabla \times \left[\overline{\overline{\mu_r}}^{-1} \cdot \left(\nabla \times \vec{E} \right) \right] - k_0^2 \overline{\overline{\varepsilon_r}} \cdot \vec{E} = -jW \mu_0 \vec{J_S}$$

(1)

where $\vec{J_S}$ is Current source density.

To use the vector function $\vec{R}$ and $\vec{T}$ on the integral finite element solution domain, weak current form of the equation is obtained

$$\left\langle \vec{R}, \vec{T} \right\rangle = \iiint_\Omega \left\{ \left(\nabla \times \vec{T} \right) \cdot \left[\overline{\overline{\mu_r}}^{-1} \cdot \left(\nabla \times \vec{E} \right) \right] - k_0 \overline{\overline{\varepsilon_r}} \cdot \vec{E} \right\} d\Omega$$
$$+ j\omega\mu_0 \iiint_{\Omega_z} \vec{T} \cdot \vec{J_S} d\Omega_s - j\omega\mu_0 \iint_{\Gamma_0 + \Gamma_1} \vec{T} \cdot \left(\hat{n} \times \vec{H} \right) d\Gamma \quad (2)$$
$$+ j\omega\mu_0 \iint_{\Gamma_r} Y \cdot \left(\hat{n} \times \vec{T} \right) \cdot \left(\hat{n} \times \vec{E} \right) d\Gamma_r$$

$\hat{n}$ Is the surface normal unit vector, Y is the surface admittance.

If a electric field intensity $\vec{E}$ is approximate form: $\vec{E} = \sum_{i=1}^{N} W_i \vec{E_i}$,where E_i is the unit side. $\vec{W_i}$ is the vector basis functions, instead of test functions $\vec{T}$.

From inside the material structure, the electric field intensity is divided into horizontal component $\vec{E_t}$ and $\vec{E_z}$,and $\vec{E} = \vec{E_t} + \hat{z}\vec{E_z}$,so Helmholtz equation form of weak current is:

$$\left\langle \vec{R}, \vec{W} \right\rangle = \eta^2 \iint_\Omega \begin{bmatrix} \left(\nabla_t \vec{W_z} + \vec{W_t} \right) \times \hat{z} \cdot \overline{\overline{\mu_r}}^{-1} \cdot \left(\nabla_t e_z + \vec{e_t} \right) \times \hat{z} \\ -k_0^2 W_z \varepsilon_{r,zz} e_z \end{bmatrix} d\Omega$$
$$+ \iint_\Omega \left[\left(\nabla_t \times \vec{W_t} \right) \cdot \overline{\overline{\mu_r}}^{-1} \cdot \left(\nabla_t \times \vec{e_t} \right) - k_0^2 W_t \overline{\overline{\varepsilon_{r,t}}} \vec{e_t} \right] d\Omega \quad (6)$$

On the type of finite element for the matrix form

$$\begin{bmatrix} k_{\max}^2 [\bar{S}_z] & k_{\max}^2 [G_z] \\ k_{\max}^2 [G_t] & k_{\max}^2 [Q_t] + [\bar{S}_t] \end{bmatrix} \begin{Bmatrix} \{E_z\} \\ \{E_t\} \end{Bmatrix}$$
$$= \left(k_{\max}^2 - \eta^2 \right) \begin{bmatrix} [\bar{S}_z] & [G_z] \\ [G_t] & [Q_t] \end{bmatrix} \begin{Bmatrix} \{E_z\} \\ \{E_t\} \end{Bmatrix} \quad (7)$$

$k_{\max}$ is the material of a great number and $[\bar{S}_t] = [S_t] - k_0^2 [T_t]$, $[\bar{S}_z] = [S_z] - k_0^2 [T_z]$.

Matrix units are as follows:

$$S_{t,ij} = \iint_{\Omega} \left[\left(\nabla_t \times \overrightarrow{W}_{t,i}\right) \cdot \overline{\overline{\mu}}_r^{-1} \cdot \left(\nabla_t \times \overrightarrow{W}_{t,j}\right) \right] d\Omega \qquad (8)$$

$$Q_{t,ij} = \iint_{\Omega} \left[\left(\overrightarrow{W}_{t,i} \times \hat{z}\right) \cdot \overline{\overline{\mu}}_r^{-1} \cdot \left(\overrightarrow{W}_{t,j} \times \hat{z}\right) \right] d\Omega \qquad (9)$$

$$G_{t,ij} = \iint_{\Omega} \left[\left(\nabla \overrightarrow{W}_{z,i} \times \hat{z}\right) \cdot \overline{\overline{\mu}}_r^{-1} \cdot \left(\overrightarrow{W}_{z,j} \times \hat{z}\right) \right] d\Omega \qquad (10)$$

$$T_{t,ij} = \iint_{\Omega} \overrightarrow{W}_{t,i} \cdot \overline{\overline{\varepsilon}}_{r,t} \cdot \overrightarrow{W}_{t,j} d\Omega \qquad (11)$$

According to the solution of matrix equation can calculate electric field intensity of vertical component and horizontal component, thus to find the value of electromagnetic field.

III. The Establishment of RVE Model

Numerical solution of the electromagnetic effect of the composite first need to build RVE. According to the result of simulation, judge composite material under different working frequency electromagnetic shielding performance stability of unidirectional fiber number, the number is required for the corresponding obtained the stability of the composite material mesoscopic structure model RVE_1 and RVE_2.

Figure. 1. The numerical simulation model

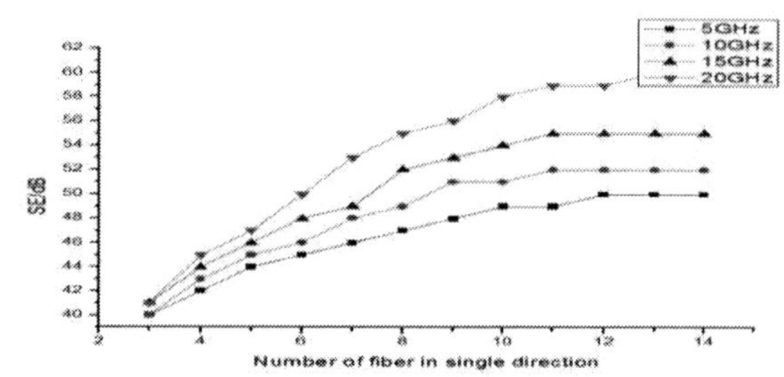

Figure. 2. The relationship of fiber numbers and electromagnetic shielding effectiveness

Results show that the higher the working frequency, the composite material of RVE is smaller, Fiber composite material structure of the electromagnetic shielding effectiveness is more than 38 dB in 5 ~ 20 GHZ working frequency range.

IV. Volumn Weighted Average Method

For simple dielectric anisotropy, the constitutive equation can be changed.

$$\begin{Bmatrix} D_x \\ D_y \\ D_z \end{Bmatrix} = \overline{\varepsilon E} = \varepsilon_0 \begin{bmatrix} \varepsilon_{rx} & 0 & 0 \\ 0 & \varepsilon_{ry} & 0 \\ 0 & 0 & \varepsilon_{rz} \end{bmatrix} \begin{Bmatrix} E_x \\ E_y \\ E_z \end{Bmatrix} \qquad (12)$$

$$\varepsilon_{rz} = \frac{1}{\varepsilon_0} \cdot \frac{\overline{D_z}}{\overline{E_z}} = \frac{1}{\varepsilon_0} \cdot \frac{\sum_{i=1}^{n} D_{zi} V_i}{\sum_{i=1}^{n} E_{zi} V_i} \qquad (13)$$

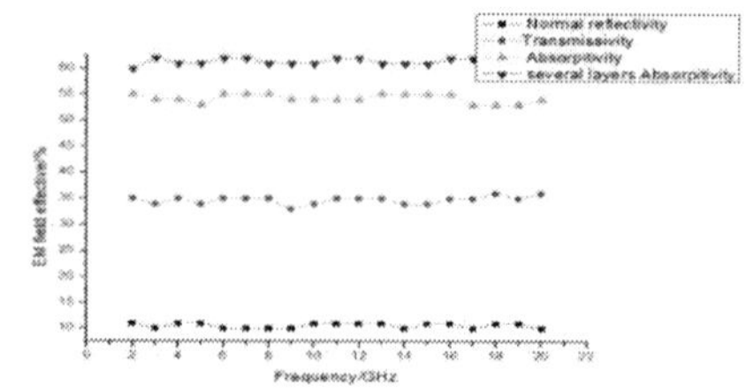

Figure.3. Reflectivity in different angle

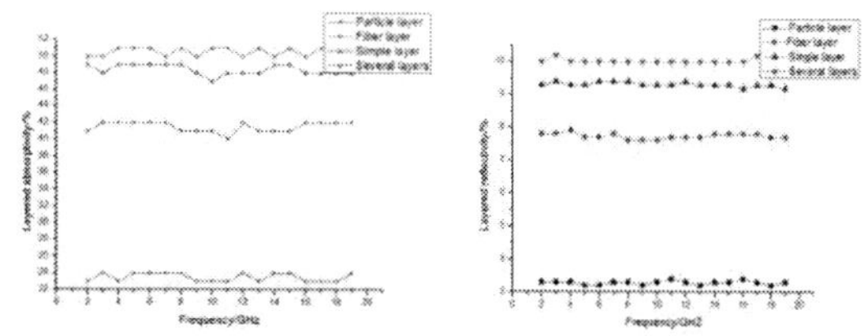

Figure.4. Layered absorptivity and reflectivity

V. Conclusion

Research method solves the problem of the computational complexity, and changes the difficult problems of multilayer composite materials. It can be used for two phase or multiphase composite material, and heterogeneous material. Using Volume weighted average algorithm can fill the vacancy of the calculation of the multi-layer heterogeneous anisotropic medium.

Acknowledgment

This paper was supported by the National Natural Science Foundation of China (Grant No. 51209055), the China Postdoctoral Special Foundation (Grant No. 2015T80324), and the Natural Science Foundation of Heilongjiang, China (Grant No. F2015028).

References

[1] Sainath K, Teixeira F L. Tensor Green's function evaluation in arbitrarily anisotropic, layered media using complex-plane Gauss-Laguerre quadrature. [J]. Physical Review E Statistical Nonlinear & Soft Matter Physics, 2014, 89(5):053303-053303.

[2] Mencagli M J, Martini E, Gonzalez-Ovejero D, et al. Efficient design of transformation optics devices based on anisotropic metasurfaces[C]// General Assembly and Scientific Symposium. IEEE, 2014:1-1.

[3] Yuan J, Gu C, Li Z. Electromagnetic scattering by arbitrarily shaped stratified anisotropic media using the equivalent dipole moment method[J]. International Journal of RF and Microwave Computer-Aided Engineering, 2010, 20(4):416-421.

Portable High-Performance Software Design Using Templated Meta-Programming for EM Calculations

Jamie Infantolino
Army Research Laboratory
Aberdeen Proving Grounds, MD
Jamie.K.Infantolino.civ@mail.mil

James Ross
Army Research Laboratory
Aberdeen Proving Ground, MD
james.a.ross176.civ@mail.mil

David Richie
Brown Deer Technology
Forest Hill, MD
drichie@browndeertechnology.com

***Abstract*—The Finite Difference Time Domain (FDTD) Method is used for full-wave electromagnetic (EM) simulations. FDTD is computationally intensive with performance depending critically on architecture-specific optimizations that have become more challenging given the rapidly changing architectures in modern high-performance computing platforms. We examine a templated meta-programming technique to implement the computational kernels in canonical form, without any architecture-specific optimizations, such that data layout and loop order optimizations can be applied through code transformations. These transformations are abstracted behind a simple yet flexible API for the application developer and require no special tools, relying only on a modern optimizing C++ compiler. Optimizations for data layout and loop order are selected at compile-time using C++ typedefs without the need to modify source code implementations of the algorithm.**

Keywords—FDTD, optimizations

I. INTRODUCTION

The Finite Difference Time Doman (FDTD) method is commonly used to solve a wide variety of electromagnetic (EM) problems. The FDTD method solves Maxwell's curl equations directly where the curls are separated into vector components and discretized over time and space [1]. In this work, we use a 2D formulation of the FDTD method for a transverse electric mode, whereby the electromagnetic field is describe by the components E_x, E_y, ande H_z.

The layout of the discretized problem space is prescribed by the Yee cell [2]. The solution is staggered in time by a half time step since the electric and magnetic fields are staggered spatially by half a cell edge. This allows the magnetic field to be held constant while the electric field is updated. Similarly, the electric field is held constant as the magnetic field is updated. This process is repeated in order to calculate the electromagnetic field propagation over time. The cell edges are each assigned a unique material based on the problem.

FDTD calculations are computationally intensive and implementations are generally optimized for each architecture. The nature of the optimizations that impact performance include choices for data layout in memory, impacting memory access patterns, and ordering of operations in the update kernels, including loop order, tiling, parallelization, and vectorization. The need for architecture-specific optimizations typically results in differing source code implementations found pervasively across the core components used to implement the calculations.

II. MOTIVATION

The motivation for this work stems from the recognition that, given the rapidly changing computer hardware architectures, supporting performance-efficient software becomes challenging as the source code base is fragmented into special implementations for a growing number of platforms. Today this includes multi-core CPUs of differing designs, GPGPU and MIC-based accelerators, and socketed MIC processors. The trend for greater heterogeneity, increased depth in multi-tiered parallelism, and complex memory architectures will likely continue and presents increasing challenges for application development and maintenance.

It would be ideal if algorithms could be implemented once, simply, and optimizing compilers were able to generate high-performance code fully optimized for target architectures without any modification to the source code. This proves to be impossible for even the most advanced optimizing compilers. Computational performance is critically impacted by the issues of data layout in memory and general loop ordering of computational operations, including parallelization and vectorization, which generally requires source-code modifications for specific target architectures. Advanced C++ techniques, such as code transformations through template meta-programming, offer a solution to this problem and the possibility of achieving performance-portable single-source implementations of computationally intensive code.

The proposition is not to introduce complex templated meta-programming techniques into application developer workflows, but rather implement algorithms once in a simple canonical form, shifting architecture-specific optimization into compile-time selected type specifications. We present the results from an investigation into techniques which rely on no special tools beyond a modern optimizing C++ compiler.

III. RELATED WORKS

ToyFDTD is a community-vetted open source FDTD code used as the basis for this work. It provides a good baseline to examine optimization techniques. Examining optimizations for the FDTD method is not a new research topic. Various optimizations of the FDTD method on a GPU were examined in [3] as well as optimization techniques utilizing MPI [4]. Our work differs from direct investigations of optimization techniques in that the approach is designed to enable a common source implementation and relies on templated meta-programming to generate the optimized implementation.

IV. METHOD

We extend the previous work employing templated meta-programming for data layout abstraction and apply it to loop order abstraction to enable a fully abstract implementation of the FDTD algorithm that may be optimized indirectly for different architectures without modification. Instead compile-time type selection is used to enable a C++ compiler to generate instructions optimized for a particular architecture based on concepts ordinarily requiring specialized software modifications. Thus, a single-source canonical implementation of the underlying algorithm may be optimized without special consideration of architecture-specific optimizations.

We provide a generalized array class for representing multi-dimensional fields and material parameters capable of instantiating arbitrary grouping of components within the data layout. This includes struct-of-arrays (SoA) and array-of-structs (AoS) data layouts as well as all possible hybrid variations without any modification to the generic array accessor used for each component in the algorithm implementation. In addition, the array class supports nested tiling, nested partitioning, arbitrary index order, memory type qualification, and alignment, padding and shuffling attributes.

Recognizing that performance optimization is not limited to issues of data layout, but also includes quite generally the distribution and order of parallel computation, we have developed a loop order abstraction using expression templates and the concept of plans for multi-dimensional parallel loop specification. As with the use of the generalized array class, algorithms implemented using this abstraction will require no direct modification for targeting different architecture for optimization. Instead, a unique plan is selected within an auxiliary header file allowing experimentation and tuning without modifying the single-source algorithm implementation. Thus, the goal of enabling single-source development without architecture-specific code is maintained.

Both data layout and loop order abstraction is described using a simple type selection. For convenience, a free-form type generator class can be used, eliminating the need for precise ordering of type parameters. In addition, very often the data layout in memory implies a preferred loop ordering for access in computation. Therefore, we introduce the optional capability of inferring loop order from data layout.

Expression templates are used for the construction of a loop order abstraction, the specification of loop range through intervals, and generalized constructs for applying lambda functions over multi-dimensional domains. In the case of an FDTD update, each update kernel for E_x, E_y, and H_z is written as a lambda function capturing the update equation for the respective field components. Then each of the update kernels are applied to the problem domain specified by intervals. The entire problem of ordering, decomposition, parallelization, and vectorization is handled through code transformations that allow the compiler to generate specialized, optimized instructions through type-selection.

V. RESULTS

For benchmarking, we used a 2D FDTD test problem comprised of a 6 centimeter metal cylindrical scatterer in free space. The problem is excited by a Gaussian pulse with a carrier frequency of 5 GHz. For each benchmark, the same source-code implementation is used with the only difference being typedef changes within a header file used for compile-time selection of all data layouts and loop order plans. Table 1 shows the total calculation time for an Intel multi-core CPU using different compile-time type-selected layouts.

Table 1: Execution times for compile-time selected data layouts employing AoS and SoA with IndexOrder<1,2> and IndexOrder<2,1>. The "Serial I,J" loop order plan was used for each benchmark.

Data Layout (convention)	Time (sec)
AoS IndexOrder<1,2> (C)	32.66
AoS IndexOrder<2,1> (FORTRAN)	14.20
SoA IndexOrder<1,2> (C)	7.01
SoA IndexOrder<2,1> (FORTRAN)	25.57

Table 2 shows the total calculation time for an Intel multi-core CPU using different loop ordering, including parallelization. The selection of an OpenMP model for loop parallelization required no changes to the FDTD source code and was selected from the templated plan specification.

Table 2: Execution times for different compile-time selected loop order plans using Serial and OpenMP parallel models, and with selecting the order of the loops to be I,J or J,I.

Loop Order Plan	Time (sec)
Serial I,J	6.97
Serial J,I	25.47
OpenMP(4 threads) I,J	5.77
OpenMP(4 threads) J,I	8.02

VI. CONCLUSIONS AND FURURE WORK

We demonstrate the performance impact of data layouts and employ compile-time type selection to enable compiler optimizations. The results indicate the importance of exploring data layout in order to improve performance. Future work will explore automating optimization steps to tune performance for a given architecture. The technique will also be extended to parallel decompositions and fine-grained parallel threading which are coupled to data layout optimization.

REFERENCES

[1] Kunz, Karl S. and Raymond J. Luebbers, The Finite Difference Time Domain Method for Electromagnetics, Boca Raton, CRC Press, 1993.

[2] Yee, Kane, "Numerical Solution of Initial Boundary Value Problems Involving Maxwell's Equations in Isotropic Media." IEEE Transactions on Antennas and Propagation, vol. AP-14, No. 3, pp. 802–807, May 1966.

[3] Livesey, M., Stack, J. F., Costen, F., Nanri, T. Fujino, S. and Nakashima, N. An alternative domain decomposition technique for CUDA-based 3D FDTD methods. In 2012 42nd European Microwave Conference. 2012.

[4] Su, M. F., El-Kady, I., Bader, D., & Lin, S. Y. (2004, August). A novel FDTD application featuring OpenMP-MPI hybrid parallelization. In Parallel Processing, 2004. ICPP 2004. International Conference on (pp. 373-379). IEEE.

Modeling of stability of electrostatic and magnetostatic systems

Analysis based on Gibbs methodology

Michael Grinfeld
The U.S. Army Research Laboratory
Aberdeen Proving Ground, USA
e-mail: michael.greenfield4.civ@mail.mil

Pavel Grinfeld
Department of Mathematics
Drexel University
Philadelphia, USA

Abstract—**Models, based on variational principles, provide for multiple features which of key importance for computational implementation. Based on this vision, we combine the Gibbsian thermodynamic (variational) method for heterogeneous systems with electrostatics. The substances under study are those which are able to accumulate free (i.e., not dipolar) electric charges. We announce several key formulas related to the first and second energy variations for these macroscopic heterogeneous systems.**

Keywords—electrostatics, magnetostatics, heterogeneous systems, variational methods, thermodynamics

I. Introduction

The systems carrying electric charges are widespread in nature and applications. Variational principles and methods play a key role in modeling these systems, and they have been developed for a couple of centuries (see very instructive publications [1–4]). The issues of stability and instability of electro- and magneto-static and quasi-static systems are extremely important in multiple electrostatic (remember the famous Earnshaw theorem or the Rayleigh surface instability) and in the multiple magnetostatic systems (for instance, the well-known surfacial patterning in ferrofluids.) Therefore, it is quite surprising that the key instruments in the analysis of stability (like, for instance, second energy variation) are still remain essentially underdeveloped. Also, various variational approaches, closely associated with the first and second energy variation. At the same time the variational approaches are of key importance in computational implementations of the models. It happens because of the a priori guaranteed mathematical self-consistency of these methods and open possibilities of using powerful numerical schemes based on minimization and optimization

Nonetheless, even a quick glance at the literature shows that the variational approach is definitely underdeveloped. In particular, in terms of calculus of variations, all the studies are based on the analysis of the first energy variations (i.e., analysis of ponderomotive forces and conditions of equilibriums.) The analysis of the second variation, the cornerstone of the stability investigation, is not even touched in those famous publications. Moreover, the very expressions of the second energy variations still remain unknown (the publications [5–10] and references therein are very rare exceptions from this rule.) In this paper, we present corresponding results relating to several systems: the systems accumulating and carrying free electric charges, pyroelectric crystals, growing on rigid substrates, patterns of ferromagnetic liquids, etc. To make the presentation as simple as possible we limit ourselves with incompressible substances and ignore polarization effects.

II. Formalization of the Gibbs Method

A. *Systems with distributed electric charges*

This is one of the simplest systems, which is not only useful in many applications but also convenient for illustration of the Gibbs method, as we interpret it in [11].

Consider a rigid substance with distributed electric charges that are able to move in it. Let the functions $\rho(z)$ and $\eta(z)$ be the densities per unit volume of the free distributed electric charges and entropy, respectively. We assume that these distributions can vary arbitrarily provided that their integral amounts remain fixed:

$$\int_\Omega d\Omega\,\rho(z)=Q,\ \int_\Omega d\Omega\,\eta(z)=H \tag{1}$$

We assume that the total energy of the system E_{tot} is comprised of the total internal energy internal E_{therm} and total electrostatic energy E_{elec} :

$$E_{tot}=\int_\Omega d\Omega U(\rho,\eta)+\frac{1}{2}\int_\Omega d\Omega\int_\Omega d\Omega^*\frac{\rho(z)\rho(z^*)}{|\vec{z}-\vec{z}^*|} \tag{2}$$

where $U(\rho,\eta)$ is the simplest model of the internal energy density. Using the standard method of the calculus of variations (see, for instance, [11] or any university textbook on calculus of variations), we arrive at the unconditional variational problem for the functional $\Phi=E_{tot}-\Lambda Q-\Gamma H$, where Λ and Γ are the Lagrange indefinite multipliers, associated with the constraints (1).

Separating the independent variations in the first variation, we arrive at the following conditions of the bulk equilibrium:

$$U_\eta = \Gamma,\ U_\rho + \int_\Omega d\Omega^* \frac{\rho(z^*)}{|\vec{z}-\vec{z}^*|} = \Lambda, \quad (3)$$

The first of the equilibrium equations (3) claim the absolute temperature should be constant throughout the body. The second one claims that the sum of enthalpy and electric potential of distributed charges should be constant across the body as well.

The energy-based analysis of electrostatic and magnetostatic systems, which can be interpreted as the first energy variations, have been discussed for different systems in a variety of monographs and textbooks, the authors of which arrived at different (sometimes incompatible) results. At the same time, the second variations have not been analyzed and the very expressions of the same variations remained unknown.

For the system at hand the second variation appears to be the integro-differential quadratic form of the variations of the charge density $\delta\rho$ and the specific entropy $\delta\eta$.

B. *Pyroelectric crystal growing on the rigid substrate*

When deriving (4) we assumed that the shape of the body is fixed. In many interesting problems though, the shape of the body can change significantly, and it should be treated as one more variable. One of those problems is the problem finding equilibrium shape of pyroelectric crystal growing on a substrate. This problem is of interest for technologies dealing with growth of thin solid films. In the model, analyzed in [9] it was assumed that the substance can change its shape due to surface diffusion or condensation from vapor. For simplicity we present here the second variation for the case of a rigid (non-deformable) crystal. We also assume that the polarization

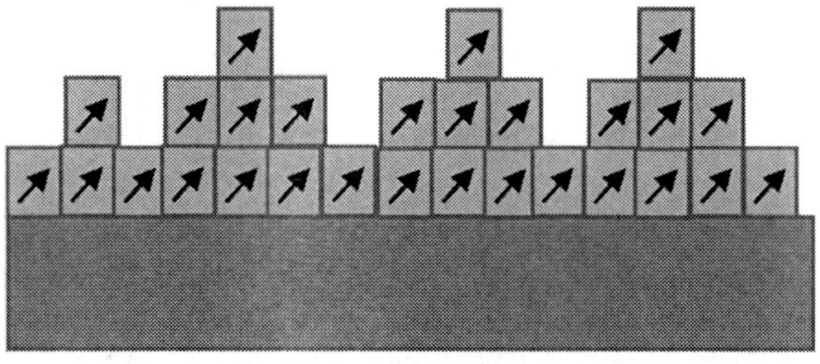

Figure. A cartoon picture of a pyroelectric dipole aggregate growing of a rigid substrate.

vector is fixed and the internal energy can be neglected. The total accumulated energy is just the total electrostatic energy. This energy, however, is sensitive to the shape of the crystal, and our analysis appears to be close to the problems of shape optimization. In vicinity of flat interface, parallel to the substrate, the small perturbations of the shape is characterized by the small displacements C in the normal direction. The second variation for this system was calculated in [10]. In terms of the Fourier components it reads (for the case of sufficiently thick film):

$$\delta^2 E = \iint_{all\ \boldsymbol{k}} d^2\boldsymbol{k}\,|C^*|^2\,|\boldsymbol{k}|\left\{\sigma|\boldsymbol{k}| + 2\pi\left(P_\parallel^2 - P_\perp^2\right)\right\} \quad (4)$$

where $C^*(\boldsymbol{k})$ is the Fourier component of the normal displacement function C, σ is the surface energy density of the film; $P_\parallel$ and $P_\perp$ are the components of the polarization vector that or parallel and orthogonal to the film, respectively.

The formula (4) leads to the important physical conclusion that the normal components $P_\perp$ of polarization destabilize the film, whereas the tangential components stabilize it $P_\parallel$.

In the full paper, we discuss various generalizations of the result (5), in particular, for surface instabilities in ferromagnetic liquids. Ferromagnetic liquids have already found multiple applications in the geological prospecting, ecology, medicine (tumors cure), various problems of mechanical engineering generalizations for this result for the electric double-layers.

III. CONCLUSION

The analysis of stability of equilibrium of electrostatic and magnetostatic systems can be included in the general Gibbs-like methodology based on the calculation of the first and second variations. Quite often, but not always, it confirms conclusions about instabilities that have been earlier explored with the help of different methods. In general, it shows that the tangential components of polarization vector stabilize the electrostatic and magnetostatic systems, whereas the normal components destabilize them.

REFERENCES

[1] J.W Gibbs., On the Equilibrium of Heterogeneous Substances, In: The Scientific Papers of J. Willard Gibbs, vol. 1, 1993.

[2] L.D. Landau, E.M. Lifshitz EM. Electrodynamics of continuous media. New York: Pergamon; 1963.

[3] M.C.H. Fiolhais et al. Prog Electromagn Res B 2011;27:187–212.

[4] J.A. Stratton, Electromagnetic Theory. McGraw-Hill; 1941.

[5] P. Grinfeld, "Morphological instability of liquid metallic nuclei condensing on charged inhomogeneities," Phys. Rev. Lett 2001; 87(9):095701.

[6] P. Grinfeld, M. Grinfeld, "Thermodynamic aspects of equilibrium shape and growth of crystalline films with electromechanical interaction," Ferroelectrics, vol. 342, pp. 89—100, 2006.

[7] P. Grinfeld, "Morphological instability of the dielectric Thomson nuclei," Phys Rev. B 2010;81(18):184110.

[8] M. Grinfeld, P. Grinfeld, Toward the Landau–Lifshitz version of the Thomson electrostatics theorem. Results Phys 2015;5:222–3.

[9] M. Grinfeld, P. Grinfeld, "A variational approach to electrostatics of polarizable heterogeneous substances," Adv. Math. Phys. 2015. Article ID 659127.

[10] M. Grinfeld, "Morphology, Stability, and Morphogenesis of Dipole Aggregates," Proc. Estonian Acad. Sci., 1999, 5/2, pp. 131—141.

[11] M. Grinfeld, Thermodynamic methods in the theory of heterogeneous systems. Longman; 1991.

Fast Wideband Solution Using MBPE with MOM

Fatih Kaburcuk
Electrical and Electronics Engineering Department
Erzurum Technical University
Erzurum, 25700, Turkey
fkaburcu@syr.edu

Mehmet Onur Kok
Electrical Engineering and Computer Science Department
Syracuse University
Syracuse, NY 13244, USA
mokok@syr.edu

***Abstract*—Integration of the Model Based Parameter Estimation (MBPE) technique into Method of Moments (MOM) provides fast solutions over a wide frequency band to solve radiation and scattering problems. The MBPE technique uses the Padé rational function to approximate solutions over a wide frequency band from a solution at a fixed frequency. In this paper, the technique is applied to a thin-wire antenna. Computed results show that solutions at a wider frequency band of interest are achieved with a remarkable saving in the computation time.**

Keywords*—*frequency derivative, MOM, parameter estimation

I. Introduction

A Model Based Parameter Estimation (MBPE) technique integrated into Method of Moments (MOM) can be used to obtain solutions at a wide frequency band from a solution at a fixed center frequency (f_0) [1-3]. The technique integrated into MOM has been studied to analyze two-dimensional scattering problems [4] and a thin-wire as a scatterer [5]. In this paper, a thin-wire antenna is analyzed using MBPE technique integrated into MOM to obtain solutions at any frequency of interest using the value of expansion coefficients and its frequency derivatives (FD) at f_0. The MBPE technique uses the values of expansion coefficients and their FD at f_0 to determine the model coefficients of the rational function. These model coefficients are used to obtain the expansion coefficients at any frequency of interest away from f_0. Using these expansion coefficients, the current distribution and input impedance for the thin wire antenna at any frequency of interest away from f_0 can be efficiently computed. The computation time of the MOM is more than that of MBPE technique because the MOM simulation is performed for each frequency of interest.

II. Procedure of MBPE with MOM

A. Model Based Parameter Estimation

In the MBPE technique, the ith expansion coefficient (I_i) can be expressed by a rational function of frequency. The rational function is defined as the ratio of two polynomials as follows:

$$I_i(s) = \frac{N_i(s)}{D_i(s)} = \frac{\sum_{j=0}^{n} N_{ij}s^j}{\sum_{j=0}^{d} D_{ij}s^j} = \frac{N_{i0}+N_{i1}s+N_{i2}s^2+\cdots+N_{in}s^n}{D_{i0}+D_{i1}s+D_{i2}s^2+\cdots+D_{id}s^d}, \tag{1}$$

where s is the variable of interest, N_{ij} and D_{ij} are the model coefficients in the numerator and denominator of the rational function, respectively. There are n+d+1 model coefficients in (1) to be determined ($D_{i0} = 1$). The high-order polynomials in both numerator and denominator are used to obtain more accurate results and solutions over a wider frequency band.

As an example, two expansion coefficients are expressed by rational functions of frequency as follows:

$$I(s) = \begin{bmatrix} I_1(s) \\ I_2(s) \end{bmatrix} = \begin{bmatrix} \frac{N_1(s)}{D_1(s)} \\ \frac{N_2(s)}{D_2(s)} \end{bmatrix} = \begin{bmatrix} \frac{\sum_{j=0}^{n} N_{1j}s^j}{\sum_{j=0}^{d} D_{1j}s^j} \\ \frac{\sum_{j=0}^{n} N_{2j}s^j}{\sum_{j=0}^{d} D_{2j}s^j} \end{bmatrix} = \begin{bmatrix} \frac{N_{10}+N_{11}s+N_{12}s^2+\cdots+N_{1n}s^n}{1+D_{11}s+D_{12}s^2+\cdots+D_{1d}s^d} \\ \frac{N_{20}+N_{21}s+N_{22}s^2+\cdots+N_{2n}s^n}{1+D_{21}s+D_{22}s^2+\cdots+D_{2d}s^d} \end{bmatrix}. \tag{2}$$

B. Computing Model Coefficents of the Rational Function

The model coefficients N_{ij} 's and D_{ij} 's in (1) can be determined using both frequency and FD samples. Starting with (1) and differentiating k times with respect to s gives

$$\begin{aligned} &I_i(s)D_i(s) = N_i(s) \\ &I_i'(s)D_i(s) + I_i(s)D_i'(s) = N_i'(s) \\ &\vdots \\ &I_i^{(k)}(s)D_i(s) + k\, I_i^{(k-1)}(s)D_i'(s) + \cdots + \binom{k}{k-m} I_i^{(m)}(s)D_i^{(k-m)}(s) \\ &\qquad + \cdots + k\, I_i'(s)D_i^{(k-1)}(s) + I_i(s)D_i^{(k)}(s) = N_i^{(k)}(s) \end{aligned} \tag{3}$$

where $\binom{k}{k-m}$ is the binomial coefficient and the superscripts represent the order of derivative. There are $k+1$ equations that can be used to determine the model unknown coefficients in (3).

When the frequency derivatives are known at only a single frequency s_0, Equation (3) can be simplified by replacing s by $s - s_0$, where $s - s_0$ represents the frequency shifting from s_0. The following linear equations are written for the model unknown coefficients after setting $k = n + d$ and $D_{i0} = 1$.

$$\begin{aligned} &N_{i0} = I_{i0} \\ &N_{i1} - I_{i0}D_{i1} = I_{i1} \\ &\vdots \\ &N_{in} - I_{i(n-1)}D_{i1} - I_{i(n-2)}D_{i2} - \cdots - I_{i(n-d)}D_{id} = I_{in} \\ &\quad -I_{in}D_{i1} - I_{i(n-1)}D_{i2} - \cdots - I_{i(n-d+1)}D_{id} = I_{i(n+1)} \\ &\quad \vdots \\ &\quad -I_{i(k-1)}D_{i1} - I_{i(k-2)}D_{i2} - \cdots - I_{i(k-d)}D_{id} = I_{ik}, \end{aligned} \tag{4}$$

where

$$I_{iP} = \frac{1}{P!} I_i^{(P)}(0) \qquad P = 0,1,\dots,k. \tag{5}$$

where I_i is a function of frequency $(s - s_0)$. Finally, the following matrix equation are obtained from the linear equations in (4) to determine the unknown coefficients in (1).

$$\begin{bmatrix} 1 & 0 & \cdots & \cdots & 0 & 0 & 0 & \cdots & 0 \\ 0 & 1 & \cdots & \cdots & 0 & -I_{i0} & 0 & \cdots & 0 \\ 0 & 0 & 1 & \cdots & 0 & -I_{i1} & -I_{i0} & \cdots & 0 \\ \vdots & \cdots & \cdots & \ddots & \vdots & \vdots & \vdots & \ddots & \vdots \\ 0 & 0 & \cdots & \cdots & 1 & -I_{i(n-1)} & -I_{i(n-2)} & \cdots & -I_{i(n-d)} \\ 0 & 0 & \cdots & \cdots & 0 & -I_{in} & -I_{i(n-1)} & \cdots & -I_{i(n-d+1)} \\ \vdots & \cdots & \cdots & \ddots & \vdots & \vdots & \vdots & \ddots & \vdots \\ 0 & 0 & \cdots & \cdots & 0 & -I_{i(k-1)} & -I_{i(k-2)} & \cdots & -I_{i(k-d)} \end{bmatrix} \begin{bmatrix} N_{i0} \\ N_{i1} \\ N_{i2} \\ \vdots \\ N_{in} \\ D_{i1} \\ \vdots \\ D_{id} \end{bmatrix} = \begin{bmatrix} I_{i0} \\ I_{i1} \\ I_{i2} \\ \vdots \\ I_{in} \\ I_{i(n+1)} \\ \vdots \\ I_{ik} \end{bmatrix}. \tag{6}$$

C. Integration MBPE into the MOM

The well-known MOM equation

$$\sum_{j=1}^{F} Z_{ij}I_j = V_i, \text{ for } i = 1, 2, \cdots, F, \tag{7}$$

where F is the order of the frequency dependent moment matrix Z. V and I are the voltage and expansion coefficient vector, respectively. The ith expansion coefficient (I_i) can be given by

$$I_i = \sum_{j=1}^{F} Y_{ij} V_j. \tag{8}$$

where Y is the inverse of the moment matrix Z.

In general, the kth frequency derivative of the ith expansion coefficient is given by

$$I_i^{(k)} = \sum_{j=1}^{F} Y_{ij} \left[V_j^{(k)} - \sum_{m=1}^{k} \binom{k}{m} \sum_{t=1}^{F} Z_{jt}^{(m)} I_t^{(k-m)} \right]. \tag{11}$$

where $\binom{k}{m}$ is the binomial coefficient, the superscript in parenthesis represents the order of frequency derivative. It can be seen from (11) that the derivatives and inverse of the moment matrix are required. Each successive derivative involves only the inverse of the moment matrix, and the derivative of the inverse matrix is not required.

The model unknown coefficients N_{ij}'s and D_{ij}'s in (1) can be determined after substituting the expansion coefficient I_i and its k derivatives at f_0 given in (11) into (5). Replacing the variable s by $f–f_0$ in (1), I_i can be written as

$$I_i(f-f_0) = \frac{N_{i0}+N_{i1}(f-f_0)+N_{i2}(f-f_0)^2+\cdots+N_{in}(f-f_0)^n}{1+D_{i1}(f-f_0)+D_{i2}(f-f_0)^2+\cdots+D_{id}(f-f_0)^d}. \tag{12}$$

III. Numerical Results

The proposed technique is applied to a thin-wire antenna of length L=1m and radius a=6.7mm which is fed by a delta-gap source. Piecewise sinusoidal expansion functions and 81 expansion coefficients are used for the simulation. The tangential component of the electric field produced by such functions is analytically given in [6]. The current distribution and input impedance of the thin-wire antenna calculated by MOM using a point-by-point approach are compared with the results obtained by MBPE technique with both frequency and different order FD samples at f_0=300 MHz.

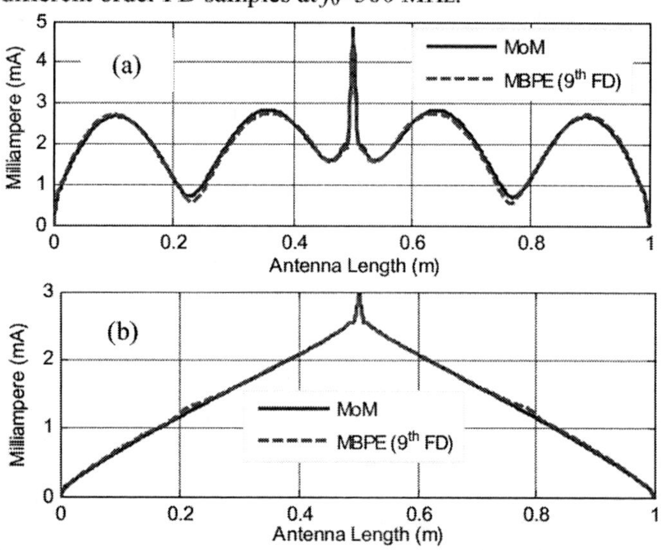

Fig. 1: Current distribution on the antenna at a) $f = 0.25f_o$ and b) $f = 2f_o$.

Fig.1 show the current distributions on the antenna computed using MOM and MBPE technique with 9 derivatives (n=5, d=4) at f=0.25f_0 and f=2f_0, respectively. The numerical comparison shows that result obtained using MOM is in a good agreement with that obtained using MBPE technique. It can be seen from the figure that MBPE technique can produce very accurate results over an 8:1 wide frequency band using the data obtained by MOM at f_0.

Fig. 2 shows the input impedance of the thin-wire antenna obtained by MOM and MBPE technique with 3, 5, and 9 derivatives. It is clear from Fig. 2 that increasing the number of derivatives gives more accurate results. The computation time of MBPE technique is 0.67 s whereas that of the conventional MOM is 32.55 s because the MOM simulation is performed for each frequency of interest. Therefore, the MBPE technique provides remarkable reduction in the computation time.

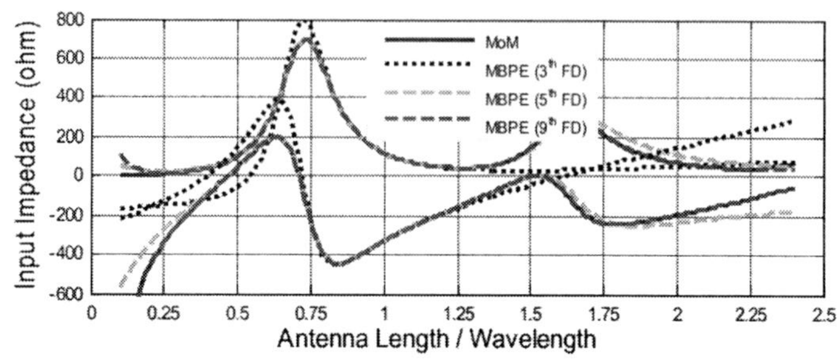

Fig. 2: Input impedance of the thin-wire antenna calculated conventional MOM and MBPE technique for 3th, 5th and 9th FD

IV. Conclusion

Integration of the MBPE technique into MOM can provide solutions over a wide frequency band. In this paper, this fact was once again proved by analyzing the thin-wire antenna. The current distribution and input impedance at any frequency away from the fixed center frequency f_0 obtained using MOM are in very good agreement with that obtained using MBPE technique. The computation time consumed by the conventional MOM is more than that consumed by MBPE technique. In general, it was observed that increasing the number of derivatives provides more accurate results over a wider frequency band.

References

[1] G. J. Burke, E. K. Miller, S. Chakrabarti, and K. Demarest, "Using Model-Based Parameter Estimation to Increase the Efficiency of Computing Electromagnetic Transfer functions," IEEE Transaction on Magnetics, Vol. 25, No. 4, pp. 2807–2809, July 1989.

[2] S. Chakrabarti, R. Ravichander, E. K. Miller, J. R. Auton, and G. J. Burke, "Applications of Model-Based Parameter Estimation in Electromagnetic Computations", Circuit and Systems, Proceeding of the 32nd Midwest Symp. on, Vol. 2, pp. 712–715, 1990.

[3] E. K. Miller, "Using Model-Based Parameter Estimation for Characterising Broadband Electromagnetic Transfer Functions", Asia-Pasific Microwave Conference, Vol. 1, pp. 451–454, Aug. 1992.

[4] H. Son, J.R.Mautz, and E. Arvas, "Use of Model-Based Parameter Estimation for Fast RCS Computation of a Conducting body of Revolution over a Frequency Band," Applied Computational Electromagnetics Society Journal, pp. 65–72, March 2004X. Yang and E. Arvas, "Use of frequency-derivative information in two- dimensional electromagnetic scattering problems," Proc. Inst. Elect. Eng., pt. H, vol. 138, no. 4, pp. 269–272, Aug. 1991.

[5] F. Kaburcuk, S. Arvas, E. Arvas, and J. K. Lee, "Wideband information in MOM obtained from narrowband data," Ultra-Wideband (ICUWB), 2012 IEEE International Conference on. IEEE, 2012.

[6] E.C. Jordan and K. G. Balmain, Electromagnetic Waves and Radiating Systems, 2nd ed. Englewood Cliffs, NJ: Prentice-Hall Inc., 1968, pp. 333.

Modelling of Electromagnetic Scattering from Large and General Intakes on Complex Platforms

A. Mori, S. Bertini, M. Bercigli, P. de Vita, S. Sensani
IDS Ingegneria dei Sistemi S.p.A.
Pisa, Italy
{a.mori,s.bertini,m.bercigli,p.devita,s.sensani}@idscorporation.com

***Abstract*—In the framework of the design of low observable aircraft, one of the most difficult problem is the numerical modelling of aeronautical air intakes with an – usually complex – arbitrary shape. Also the presence of radio absorbing material demands for accurate methods in evaluating the low level scattering for real life problems. In this contribution the use of a full wave approach, based on the Multilevel Fast Multipole Approach (MLFMA) is addressed, for a high fidelity modelling of the whole (real life) aircraft as well as the intake contribution, useful in the design and optimization stage of the intake itself.** (*Abstract*)

Keywords—Method of Moments (MoM); MLFMA; scattering; Radar Signature

I. Introduction

One of the most demanding problems in computational electromagnetics is given by the low observable design of modern aeronautical platform. This is due to the different scattering phenomena contributing to the global scattered field as well as to the electrical size of the platform at the typical impinging radar wave frequencies. The stealthness requirement in real life industrial problems requires computationally efficient and accurate electromagnetic computational tools able to assess low Radar Signatures.

In the nose on aspect angles, the jet intake is one of the major hot spots generating high level of radar signature for a large set of aspect angles. Particular design techniques are used to reduce the intakes' signature. For instance, line-of-sight blockage of the engine and usage of radar absorbing material / structure installation [1]. These techniques make usually intakes a complex – and electrically large – structure to be analyzed. In the design phase the capability to assess the scattering contribution of the only intake is a key point in order to optimize it in terms of shaping, materials, engine fan and air flow control structures. Other than the capability to aggregate the signature of the intake with the scattering contribution of the whole aeronautical platform it is also mandatory since the electrical size of the EM problem makes a brute force application of a full wave approach strongly inefficient.

Several works have been published for the solution of the intake scattering, resorting to asymptotic [2] and hybrid numerical techniques [3]-[5]. In this contribution, we address the use of a frequency domain full wave (MoM) method for a high fidelity modelling of intakes and aircraft structures, with MLFMA to allow the analysis of the electrically large problems arising in real life cases. The used formulation and the main characteristics of the numerical solver are summarized in Section II, while Section III describes the evaluation of the scattering contribution of a single intake to the overall radar signature. Some results are described in Section IV.

II. High Fidelity Aircraft Scattering Model

Real life aircrafts are very complicated structures. In order to accurately model their electromagnetic behavior, it is needed to accurately model their geometry and structures (high fidelity modelling). This leads to a multi-scale object, composed by different materials (conducting, dielectric, radio absorbing). The Method of Moments is able to give very accurate results on an arbitrary geometry at the expenses of a high numerical complexity. Acceleration method, like the MLFMA gives the possibility to analyze electrically large structures.

The used electromagnetic solver is a Frequency Domain Method of Moments with Galerkin's discretization on a triangular mesh. It implements the Poggio-Miller-Chang-Harrington-Wu-Tsai (PMCHWT) formulation [6], and any combination and arrangement of lossy and lossless materials can be considered. In particular, such formulation is applied on the dielectric interfaces separating homogeneous dielectric materials; while the Electric Field Integral Equation (EFIE) and the Combined Field Integral Equation (CFIE) are applied on open and closed conducting surfaces, respectively. The Multilevel Fast Multipole Approach (MLFMA) [7] is used to efficiently solve electrically large models. In such a case an iterative solver has to be employed (BiCGStab, GMRESR, etc.) and the MoM linear system has to be effectively preconditioned. Due to the multi-scale nature of the model (also determined by meshing the surface of dense materials), a MultiResolution (MR) preconditioning is adopted [8] to obtain a solver with high computational efficiency. By using such solver it is possible to consider real life structures (Fig. 1).

Particular materials can be characterized by means of a general anisotropic Impedance Boundary Condition (IBC) [9], relating the tangential electric and magnetic field through a local Surface Impedance $\underline{\underline{Z}}_s$ described by a 3×3 dyad:

$$\vec{E} - (\hat{n} \cdot \vec{E})\hat{n} = \underline{\underline{Z}}_s \, \hat{n} \times \vec{H} \Rightarrow \vec{M} = -\hat{n} \times \underline{\underline{Z}}_s \, \vec{J} \qquad (1)$$

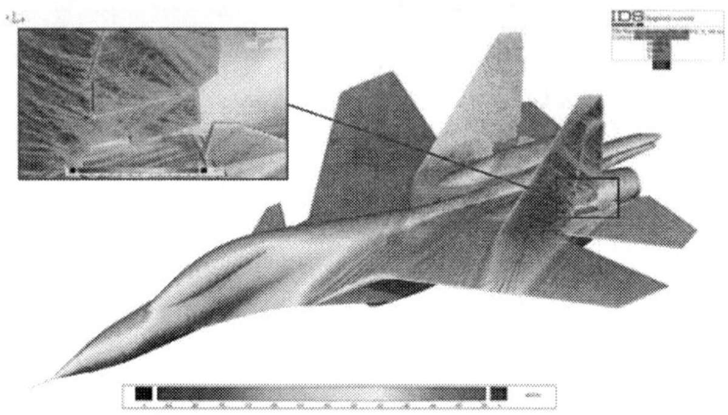

Fig. 1 – Equivalent electric current on a Sukhoi, induced by an impinging plane wave @ 10 GHz.

where $\hat{n}$ is the conducting surface normal. Equation (1) establishes a relation between the equivalent surface magnetic ($\vec{M}$) and electric ($\vec{J}$) currents on IBC surface (1, right). This allows to avoid magnetic unknowns on surface od IBC materials, but this has to be included carefully in the formulation, due to the fact that it defines a discontinuous distribution when RWG are used as basis functions.

Even if we can efficiently model whole aircrafts, it is important to consider the possibility of modelling the contribution of the single parts for design and optimization purposes. Next section considers the evaluation of the intakes contribution. All the results were obtained with the MoM-based IDSMMMP numerical code of IDS (IDS Method of Moment Multi-Port) [10].

III. Intake Contribution to Radar Signature

The problem of the evaluation of the contribution of an air intake is given by the fact some interaction are neglected (with the rest of the structure), and other interactions are added (with the outer surface of the intake, Fig. 2). We have three choices: to consider the isolated part as it is; place a fictitious dielectric interface on the intake's mouth, to solve the MoM equations and avoid the scattering of the outer skin of the intake in radiation; to place a fictitious dielectric interface on the mouth and avoid the creation of basis functions (MoM unknowns) on the outer skin (Fig. 2, bottom). The last way shows the better accuracy in reconstruction of the overall result. In every case, the inclusion of a small part of the aircraft structure near the mouth helps to increase the accuracy of the simulation.

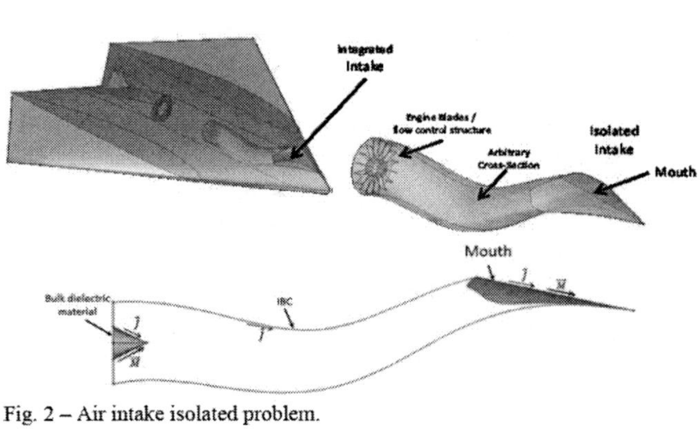

Fig. 2 – Air intake isolated problem.

IV. Example of Application

Figure 3 shows a comparison between the Radar Cross Section of an UCAV (30 × 31.4 λ @ 1 GHz) when evaluated by considering the whole structure and the composition of the intake and the body scattering. At higher frequencies, lower differences are observed. To the purpose of air intakes design, this result represents a good agreement.

References

[1] B. S. Haisty, "Lockeed Martin's - Affordable Stealth", *National Press Club*, Washington DC, 15 November 2000.

[2] P. H. Pathak, R. J. Burkholder, "Modal, ray, and beam techniques for analyzing the EM scattering by opne-ended waveguide cavities", *IEEE Trans. Antenna Propagat.*, vol. 37, pp. 635-647, May 1989.

[3] P. R. Rousseau, R. J. Burkholder, "A hybrid approach for calculating the scattering from obstacles within large open cavities", *IEEE Trans. Antenna Propagat.*, vol. 43, pp. 1068-1075, Oct. 1995.

[4] A. Barka, P. Soudais, D. Volpert, "Scattering from 3-D Cavities with a Plug and Play Numerical Scheme Combining IE, PDE, and Modal Techniques", *IEEE Trans. Antenna Propagat.*, vol. 48, pp. 704-712, May 2000.

[5] F. Hu, C. Wang, Y. Gan, "Efficient Calculation of Interior Scattering From Large Three-Dimensional PEC Cavities", *IEEE Trans. Antenna Propagat.*, vol. 55, pp. 167-177, January 2007.

[6] P. Yla-Oijala, M. Taskinen, and J. Sarvas, "Surface integral equation method for general composite metallic and dielectric structures with junctions," *Prog. Electromagn. Res.*, Vol. 52, 81-108, 2005.

[7] W. C. Chew, J.-M. Jin, E. Michielssen, and J. Song, *"Fast and Efficient Algorithms in Computational Electromagnetics"* Boston, MA: Artech House, 2001.

[8] Vipiana, F.; Vecchi, G.; Wilton, D.R., "A Multi-Resolution Moment Method for Wire-Surface Objects," *IEEE Trans. Antenna Propagat.* , vol.58, no.5, pp.1807-1813, May 2010.

[9] Glisson, Allen W., et al. "Electromagnetic scattering by an arbitrarily shaped surface with an anisotropic impedance boundary condition." *Applied Computational Electromagnetics Society Journal* 10.3 (1995): 93-106.

[10] https://www.idscorporation.com/

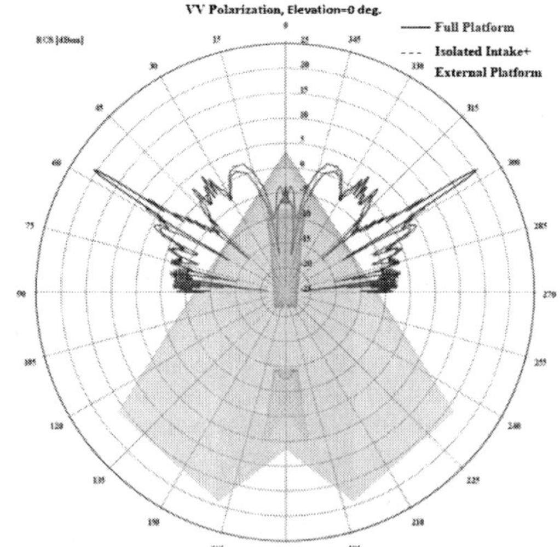

Fig. 3 – Radar Cross Section of a simulated UCAV @ 1GHz.

Electromagnetic Material Parameter Extraction of Ferrites up to the GHz Range via Measurements and Simulations

Christian Reinhold and Peter Scholz
PHOENIX CONTACT Electronics GmbH
Bad Pyrmont, Germany
Email: {creinhold,pscholz}@phoenixcontact.com

Ulrich Jumar
ifak - Institut f. Automation u. Kommunikation e.V.
Magdeburg, Germany
Email: ulrich.jumar@ifak.eu

Abstract—**A new methodology is presented for determination of electromagnetic material parameters $\underline{\mu}$ and $\underline{\varepsilon}$ for typical ferrite core geometries used in electronic and power electronic systems. The material parameters of a measurement sample are determined in such a way that measurements and simulations of the impedance have a maximum match in a broad frequency range. The extracted material parameters show that at high frequencies in the GHz range dielectric properties of the investigated MnZn ferrite core are significant. The simulated impedance parameters of a structure containing the ferrite are in good agreement with simulation showing the usability of the method.**

I. Introduction

Materials with a high permeability like ferrites are widely used in electronic systems. Power electronic systems components like inductive elements or transformers are typically operating in a low frequency range up to a few MHz. In order to design the system as well as forecast the electromagnetic behavior of electronic systems containing ferrites, the material parameters e.g. the complex permeability $\underline{\mu} = \mu_0(\mu_r' - j\mu_r'')$ need to be known in the operational frequency range. For some investigations like a combined wireless power and data transmission [1], [2], [3], the knowledge of the dielectric permittivity $\underline{\varepsilon} = \varepsilon_0(\varepsilon_r' - j\varepsilon_r'')$ in a broad frequency range is essential as well.

In this contribution a method is presented allowing for the extraction of material parameters via a coupling of measurement and simulation. In contrast to known techniques [4], [5], [6], [7] this method can be applied for typical core geometries used in electronic systems. This new approach does not require machining or preparation of the samples and it covers a wide frequency range extending from low frequencies in the kHz range up to the microwave region.

II. Material Parameter Extraction Technique

The proposed method is based on measurement of a transmission line containing the port $a-b$ and $c-d$ able of accepting a sample as presented in Fig. 1. The network parameters e.g. the impedance matrix $\underline{Z}$ of the transmission line can be measured. The network parameters of the transmission line change when a material sample is inserted.

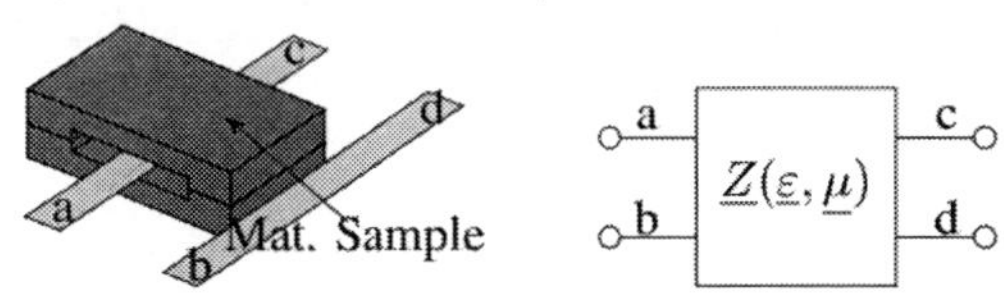

Fig. 1. Conceptual setup for determination of material parameters (a) and the network representation of the setup (b).

With the aid of EM-simulation techniques like the finite element method the network parameters can be calculated if the material parameters are known. However if the material parameters are sought based on the knowledge of the measured network parameters an inverse problem has to be solved. This is carried out via an iterative procedure sketched in Fig. 2.

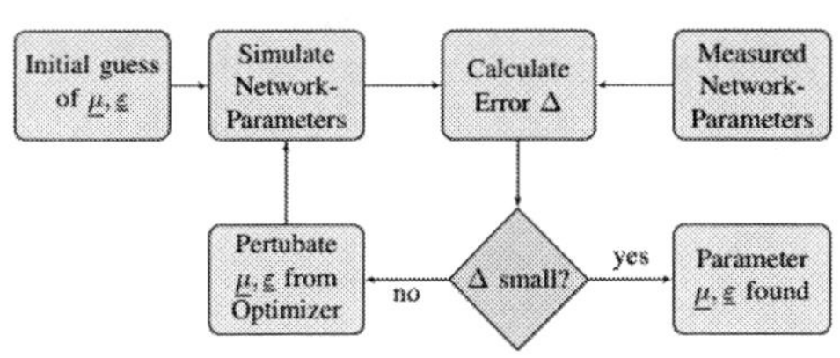

Fig. 2. Sketch of the iterative search procedure.

The iterative search procedure is carried out as follows: The network parameters are calculated with an initial guess of the material parameters. After this an error Δ is calculated quantifying the difference between the measured and calculated parameters. If the error is below a certain limit, the optimization is terminated, otherwise the material parameters are disturbed by means of an optimization algorithm and the new network parameters and the deviation from the measurement is calculated. The last steps are repeated until the desired accuracy is reached.

III. Measurement Results

A transformer core consisting of two U-shaped profiles as persented in Fig. 1 was used as the material under test. The core samples materials is a MnZn ferrite. An ungrounded coplanar line as presented in Fig. 3 was used as a transmission line allowing for guiding a wave in a broad frequency range. The two cores present a closed magnetic circuit enclosing the center conductor $a-c$ giving rise to a high sensitivity related to the magnetic material properties of the sample. In order to enhance the sensitivity of the structure with respect to dielectric properties, a metallic bridge was added in the center of the line.

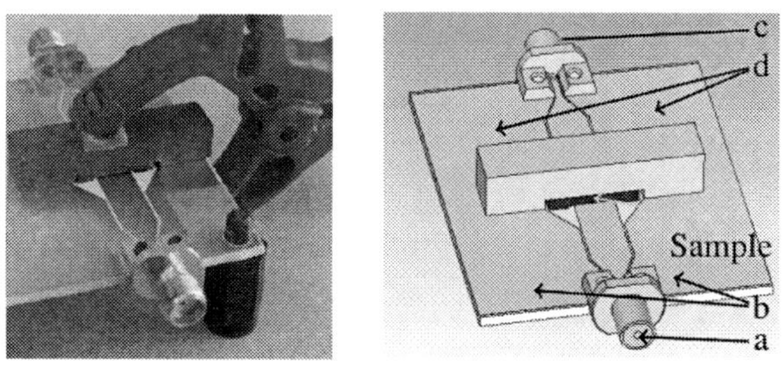

(a) Measurement setup (b) 3D Simulation Model

Fig. 3. Utilized measurement setup for the material parameter extraction.

Measurements were carried out with the aid of an impedance analyzer as well as a two-port vector network analyzer. All four material parameter $\mu_r', \mu_r'', \varepsilon_r', \varepsilon_r''$ are retrieved with a single optimization for discrete frequency samples. EM-Field simulations were carried out with CST® Microwave-Studio and the frequency domain solver. A Nelder-Mead simplex method was applied for optimization.

The relative permeability and relative permittivity as a function of frequency is shown in Fig. 4. A broadband fit allows for interpolation in the investigated frequency range. The real part of the relative permeability μ_r' approaches unity for frequencies above approximately 400 MHz. Magnetic losses represented by the imaginary part of the permeability μ_r'' are present in the entire investigated frequency band.

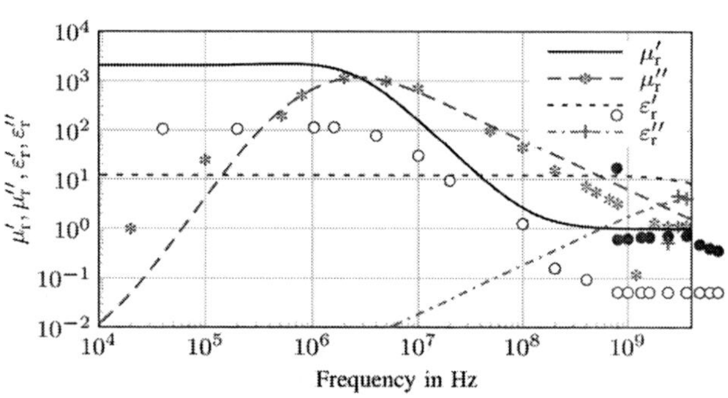

Fig. 4. The permittivity and permeability extracted from measurements. Markers: Gained data via the iterative scheme, solid lines: causal broadband material model fit fulfilling the Kramers-Kronig relations.

The dielectric parameters show a considerable value up to the microwave region. At 3 GHz a drop in the real part of the dielectric constant and an increase in the imaginary part seem to reveal an electronic relaxation.

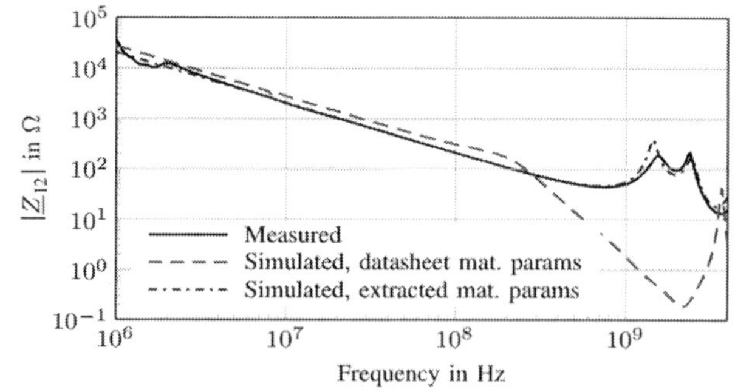

Fig. 5. Comparison between measurement and simulation of the impedance of a line with the investigated core.

In Fig. 5 a comparison between the measured and simulated magnitude of the impedance parameter $|\underline{Z}_{12}|$ is shown. If the material parameters given by the manufacturers data sheet are inserted into the simulation model i.e. only permeability data at low frequencies, a big deviation from the measured values is noticeable especially at high frequencies. However taking into account all material parameters from Fig. 4 strongly reduces the deviation proving the usability of the material model. Factors like the band limited causal fit and measurement imperfections give rise to slight deviations.

IV. Conclusion

The presented method allows for determination of the EM-material parameter for typical core geometries. The results show that the real part of the permeability of the investigated MnZn ferrite is significant in the low frequency range but at frequencies in the GHz range they can be neglected. However the dielectric parameters as well as magnetic losses cannot be neglected at high frequencies. Forecasting the impedance parameters via simulation shows good agreement if the deduced material parameters are included in the simulation model.

References

[1] R. Bosshard and J. Mhlethaler and J. W. Kolar and I. Stevanovi *Optimized magnetic design for inductive power transfer coils*, Applied Power Electronics Conference and Exposition (APEC), 2013 Twenty-Eighth Annual IEEE, 2013

[2] A. Abdolkhani *Fundamentals of Inductively Coupled Wireless Power Transfer Systems, Wireless Power Transfer - Fundamentals and Technologies*, InTech 2016

[3] R. Trevisan and A. Costanzo *A UHF Near-Field Link for Passive Sensing in Industrial Wireless Power Transfer Systems*, IEEE TRANSACTIONS ON MICROWAVE THEORY AND TECHNIQUES, VOL. 64, NO. 5, MAY 2016

[4] V. Radonić N. Blaž and Lj. Živanov *Measurement of Complex Permeability Using Short Coaxial Line Reection Method*, ACTA PHYSICA POLONICA A Vol. 117, No. 5, pp 820-824, 2010

[5] J. Xu and M. Y. Koledintseva and Y. He and R. E. DuBroff and J. L. Drewniak and B. Matlin and A. Orlando *Measurement of electromagnetic parameters and FDTD modeling of ferrite cores*, 2009 IEEE International Symposium on Electromagnetic Compatibility, pp 83-88, Aug 2009

[6] S. Takeda and T. Hotchi and S. Motomura and H. Suzuki *Permeability Measurements of Magnetic Thin Films using Shielded Short-Circuited Microstrip Lines* Journal of the Magnetics Society of Japan, 2015, Vol. 39, No. 6, pp 227-231

[7] C. Vollinger and F. Caspers and E. Jensen *Permittivity and permeability measurements methods for particle accelerator related materials*, Proceedings of IPAC2014, Dresden, Germany, 2014

Monotonicity Principle in Pulsed Eddy Current Testing and Its Application to Defect Sizing

Zhiyi Su and Lalita Udpa
Department of Electrical and Computer Engineering
Michigan State University, East Lansing,
Michigan 48824, USA
Email: suzhiyi@egr.msu.edu and udpal@egr.msu.edu

Gaspare Giovinco, Salvatore Ventre
and Antonello Tamburrino[1]
Department of Electrical and Information Engineering
Università di Cassino e del Lazio Meridionale, 03043
Cassino, Italy
Email: giovinco@unicas.it, salvatore.ventre@unicas.it
and tamburrino@unicas.it

***Abstract*—This article applies monotonicity principle to time constants in pulsed eddy current testing. This principle allows for a non-iterative imaging method for defects in conducting materials. The source free response in pulsed eddy current testing consists of linear combination of exponential decaying waveforms. A major challenge of this method is to accurately estimate the time constants from measurement of such responses. Preliminary results of estimating dominant time constants are presented. Potentially, this information can be used to predict the size of a volumetric defect regardless of its location, i.e. this method is robust in the case of both surface and buried defects.**

I. Introduction

Eddy current testing (ECT) is a widely used technique in detecting flaws in conducting materials. ECT is advantageous over other electromagnetic non-destructive evaluation (NDE) methods largely because it is low-cost, contactless and reliable [1]. The inverse problem of ECT is defined as the reconstruction of defect profile given the information of excitation system and measured signal. The solutions to inverse problem could generally be divided into two categories: iterative methods and non-iterative methods. Iterative methods update the estimation of defect profile by minimizing the error between the measured signal and the simulated signal for a given defect. Iterative methods are usually very time-consuming and suffer from the risk of being trapped in local minima. On the other hand, non-iterative methods determine if a voxel of the test specimen is part of the defect or not based on simple tests, and therefore, are computationally efficient and suitable for real-time imaging.

Monotonicity principle methods (MPM) belong to the class of non-iterative methods. MPM was first introduced in the field of electrical resistance tomography (elliptic PDEs) [2][3], and extended to parabolic PDEs such as those governing eddy current NDT in small skin depth regime [4] and large skin depth regime [5], with experimental validation provided in [6]. Its application to wave propagation and inverse scattering problems (hyperbolic PDEs) was presented in [7].

MPM was also introduced in pulsed eddy current testing (PECT) [8], [9], which is an emerging method with unique advantage of richness in frequency information. At this stage, a major challenge for MPM in PECT is the estimation of time constants from the transient waveform. This study applies the Padé-Laplace approach to this problem and demonstrates that the estimated time constants can be used in the problem of defect sizing.

[1]Antonello Tamburrino is also with the Department of Electrical and Computer Engineering, Michigan State University.

II. Monotonicity of Time Constants

In pulsed eddy current testing, the time constants characterizing the free response of test specimen depend monotonically upon the electrical conductivity.

In this study, the probe comprises an array of N_c coils and the measured signals consist of the voltages across these coils when known excitation currents are injected in the same coil array. More specifically, the source-free response, which is the transient response of the system when the excitation is switched-off, is measured. The responses can be expressed as follows:

$$v_k(t) = \sum_{i=1}^{+\infty} \beta_{k,i} \mathrm{e}^{-t/\tau_i}, \tag{1}$$

where $v_k(t)$ is the voltage across the k-th measurement coil, τ_i is the i-th time constant, with $\beta_{k,i}$ being the related linear coefficient.

Let Ω be a conducting domain and A and B be two possible defects with conductivity smaller than that of the background (see Fig. 1). The monotonicity of time constants is [8], [9]:

$$A \subseteq B \Rightarrow \tau_k^A \geq \tau_k^B, \forall k, \tag{2}$$

where τ_k^A (τ_k^B) is the k-th time constant related to defect A (defect B) assuming they are arranged in decreasing order.

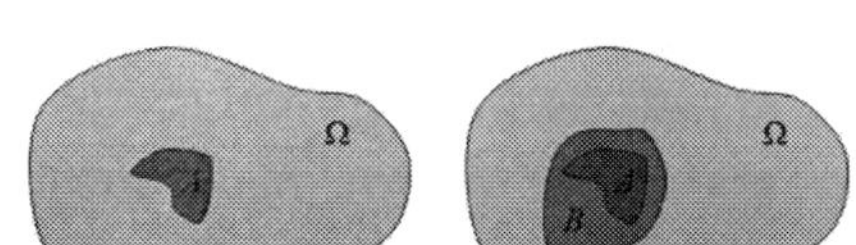

Fig. 1. Illustration of monotonicity of time constants. If defect A is completely contained in defect B, all the time constants related to defect A are larger than that of defect B.

Notice that the monotonicity of time constants has been applied to the problem of defect imaging, as presented in [9].

In the application of defect imaging, a large number of time constants are required. However, at the current stage only a few time constants can be readily estimated from the transient waveform. Thus, in this paper we focus on the problem of defect sizing rather than imaging.

III. MPM in Defect Sizing

This section presents the application of MPM to the practical case of defect detection and sizing. The probe comprises an array of 14 coils above an L-shape conductive block, which is the test specimen, as shown in Fig. 2. Defects of various sizes and locations are assumed buried in this specimen. More specifically the defects are considered to be cubes of size $2 \times 2 \times 2$ voxels (small, here after denoted as size S), $3 \times 3 \times 3$ voxels (medium, size M) and $4 \times 4 \times 4$ voxels (large, size L). The excitation coil is driven with current of 50% duty cycle square wave. The excitation coils are excited one at a time and the transient signal is measured at the same coil when the injected current is switch-off.

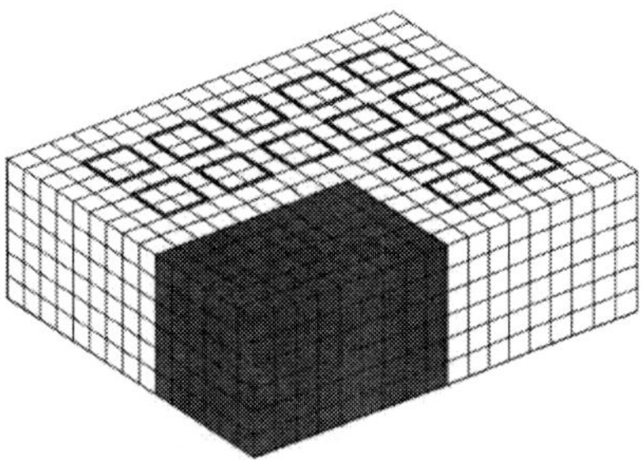

Fig. 2. Illustration of the numerical examples. The coil array is above the test specimen. The dark colored voxels represent the air domain.

The estimation of time constants from transient signal of (1) is very challenging. It is proved to be highly ill-posed when the number of time constants is large or when two consecutive time constants are close to each other [10]. In this study, a modified Padé-Laplace approach, as introduced in [11], is considered. This modified method has two advantages: (a) multiple waveforms which share the same time constants are simultaneously integrated in the solution to enhance the robustness w.r.t. noise, (b) it finds only real exponential components.

This algorithm is used to analyze the time domain waveform measured from the coil array. Different noise levels, as a portion to the magnitude of the measured signal, are assumed superimposed to the waveform. Two time constants can be estimated for each configuration associated with a specific defect profile. Each point in Fig. 3 represents a configuration in the time constant space. The defects of three different sizes natural group into three clusters and can be separated with straight lines. It is clearly illustrated in the figure that configurations associated with larger defects have smaller time constants. TABLE I summarize the probability of defects being correctly classified. For instance, the first row shows that in the case the signal has 0.1% noise, 94.81% of the small defects are correctly classified as small, 4.44% and 0.74% of them are classified as medium and large, respectively. This result is very encouraging as it shows the proposed method has a high probability ($\geq 90\%$) of correctly classifying defects of different sizes, even when the noise level is as high as 1%.

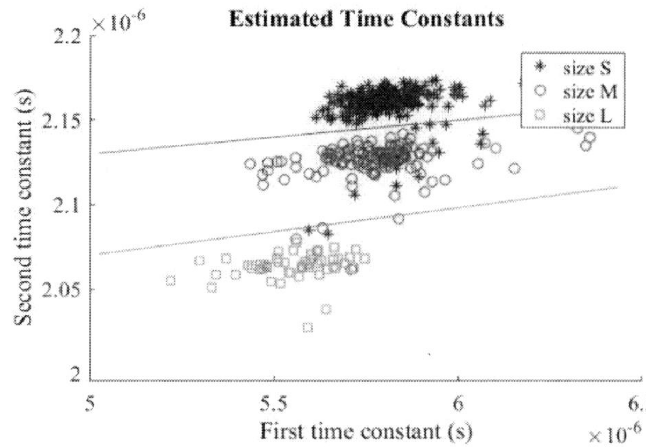

Fig. 3. The time constants associated with defect of different sizes group into three clusters. The measured signal has 0.1% noise.

TABLE I
Classification of Defects via Time Constants

real defect size	waveform has 0.1% noise identified as size			waveform with 1% noise identified as size		
	S	M	L	S	M	L
S	0.9481	0.0444	0.0074	0.9067	0.0896	0.0037
M	0	0.9643	0.0357	0.0786	0.8929	0.0286
L	0	0	1.0000	0	0.0577	0.9423

References

[1] S. S. Udpa and L. Udpa, "Eddy current nondestructive evaluation," 1999.
[2] A. Tamburrino and G. Rubinacci, *Inverse Problems*, vol. 18, no. 6, p. 1809, 2002.
[3] B. Harrach and M. Ullrich, *SIAM Journal on Mathematical Analysis*, vol. 45, no. 6, pp. 3382–3403, 2013.
[4] A. Tamburrino, S. Ventre, and G. Rubinacci, *Inverse Problems*, vol. 26, no. 7, p. 074016, 2010.
[5] A. Tamburrino and G. Rubinacci, *IEEE transactions on magnetics*, vol. 42, no. 8, pp. 2017–2028, 2006.
[6] A. Tamburrino, F. Calvano, S. Ventre, and G. Rubinacci, *NDT & E International*, vol. 47, pp. 26–34, 2012.
[7] A. Tamburrino, L. Barbato, D. Colton, and P. Monk, *Proc. of The 12th International Conference on Mathematical and Numerical Aspects of Wave Propagation*, 2015.
[8] A. Tamburrino, Z. SU, N. LEI, L. UDPA, and S. UDPA, *Electromagnetic Nondestructive Evaluation (XVIII)*, vol. 40, p. 159, 2015.
[9] Z. Su, A. Tamburrino, S. Ventre, L. Udpa, and S. Udpa, in *Applied Computational Electromagnetics (ACES), 2015 31st International Review of Progress in.* IEEE, 2015, pp. 1–2.
[10] A. A. Istratov and O. F. Vyvenko, *Review of Scientific Instruments*, vol. 70, no. 2, pp. 1233–1257, 1999.
[11] Z. Su, G. Giovinco, L. Udpa, S. Udpa, and A. Tamburrino, *21st International Workshop on Electromagnetic Nondestructive Evaluation*, 2016.

Concentric Substrate Geometry for a Multi-Mode and Dual-Band Rectangular Array

Gregory Mitchell and Amir Zaghloul
U.S. Army Research Laboratory
Adelphi, USA
gregory.a.mitchell1.civ@mail.mil / amir.i.zaghloul.civ@mail.mil

Abstract — **This paper presents a multi-mode, planar array made up of co-located elements. The array operates in dual-bands, S- and X-band, with dual-polarizations. The dual-band operation necessitates different electrical spacing between the S-band and X-band array elements. We optimize the electrical spacing by co-locating dual-band radiating elements with X-band only elements. The enabling technology for the co-located spacing is a concentric dual substrate that shrinks the size of the S-band element with respect to the X-band element. The results show 13.2 dB of realized gain for a 3x3 rectangular array at 2.9 GHz and 20.5 dB of realized gain for a 5x5 rectangular array at 9.4 GHz. The array achieves 4 distinct modes of operation by achieving either horizontal or vertical polarization at each of the two bands.**

Keywords— dual-band, dual-polarization, antenna array, concentric substrate

I. Introduction

The military has interest in combining the functionality of current S-band and X-band ground based radar systems into a single multi-mode radar system. Combining a multi-mode antenna front end with a digital common module back end would greatly simplify upgrading, maintaining, and networking radar capabilities for multi-mission applications.

We wish to investigate a dual-band and dual-polarization planar array as the antenna for such a multi-mode radar system. Both dual-polarization and dual-band antenna elements have been demonstrated in the past [1-5], where we use the concentric dual-band antenna of Dorsey and Zaghloul [2-4] as the initial template to realize multi-mode functionality. Incorporating such a dual-band element into an array presents challenges since we want a half free-space wavelength (λ_o) between elements at S- and X-band. We mitigate this problem using two concentric substrates to reduce the size of the S-band element with respect to the X-band element [6-9]. This allows us to co-locate an X-band element in between our dual-band elements retaining $0.45\lambda_o$ spacing between the S-band elements and $0.65\lambda_o$ spacing between the X-band elements. The full wave simulation of a subarray shows 13.2 dB of realized gain at 2.9 GHz (9 elements) and a 20.5 dB realized gain at 9.4 GHz (25 elements). All simulations are performed using the finite difference time domain (FDTD) electromagnetic solver CST Studio Suite 2016.

II. Antenna Designs

This section shows the designs of the concentric dual-band and dual-polarization antenna element as well as the fully populated multi-mode antenna array. All antenna elements are pin fed microstrip designs.

A. Dual-Band Radiating Element

We base the dual-band antenna element on that shown by Dorsey and Zaghloul [3-5]. Fig. 1 shows our geometry of the antenna on a dual substrate, where the S-band element is a square annular ring loaded with RO3006 (ε_{r1}=6.15, blue) while the X-band element is a concentric annular ring slot loaded with RO5880 (ε_{r2}=2.3, pink).

The concentric substrate shown on the right of Fig. 1 shrinks the footprint of the S-band element by 1.6 times with respect to the X-band element. The S-band element has two orthogonal pin feeds which provide vertical or horizontal polarization depending on which port is excited. The X-band element is a pin fed patch which couples to an annular ring slot also incorporating two orthogonal feeds. The slot is surrounded by shorting pins to suppress surface waves along the microstrip ground plane. The volume of this dual-band antenna is 1.6 x 1.6 x 0.2 in.^{3}.

This dual band element was investigated by the authors in a previous publication which showed a -14.0 dB return loss and 3.2 dB realized gain at 3.35 GHz. The design also shows a return loss of -10.0 dB and 6.4 dB realized gain at 9.0 GHz [9]. The lower gain at S-band is due to back radiation which will be mitigated by the incorporation into an array with a larger ground plane.

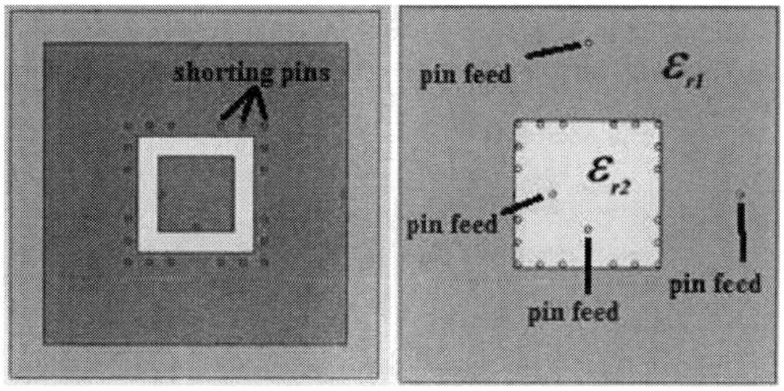

Fig. 1. Top view of concentric dual-band antenna (left) and substrate (right).

B. Antenna Array Geometries

This section details how the design of Fig. 1 lends itself to inclusion in a rectangular planar array. Ideal spacing between array elements is $D=0.5\lambda_o$. This spacing provides enough isolation to minimize the effects of mutual coupling and also mitigates the introduction of large sidelobes. Fig. 2 shows the simplest orientation of the elements into a 2x2 rectangular array. A spacing of $D=0.34\lambda_o$ at S-band will result in issues with isolation and mutual coupling. Furthermore, $D=0.9\lambda_o$ at X-band will result in large sidelobes.

We would like to see $D=0.5\lambda_o$ at both frequencies, or at least increase D between the S-band elements and decrease D between the X-band elements. Fig. 3 shows one solution to this problem. By shrinking the size of the S-band element using a higher dielectric constant, we create enough space between elements that when D approaches $0.5\lambda_o$ at S-band we can include an X-band element between them. This eliminates the S-band isolation problem of the layout in Fig. 2 while also reducing D between the X-band elements to $0.65\lambda_o$. The volume of the array in Fig. 3 is 5.2 x 5.2 x 0.2 in.^{3}. Note that we have minimized the dielectric border surrounding each dual-band element to minimize the footprint further.

Simulations show that for the layout of Fig. 3 at 2.9 GHz we have -20 dB or better isolation between elements. We also simulate a realized gain of 13.2 dB, a front-to-back ratio of -19.0 dB, and a sidelobe level ratio of -17 dB using uniform amplitude weighting. For X-band, simulations show that at 9.4 GHz we have realized gain of 20.5 dB, a front-to-back ratio of -25.0 dB, and a sidelobe level ratio of -12.5 dB using uniform amplitude weighting. The increase in sidelobe levels at X-band is due to D still being greater than $0.5\lambda_o$. We can suppress sidelobe levels further using a tapered amplitude weighting scheme at the expense of realized gain to the main beam. Additionally, it may be possible by using a higher dielectric constant for ε_{r1} to shrink the S-band annular ring to the point that we could include 2 X-band elements between each dual band element. This could result in $D=0.5\lambda_o$ in both band, but we have not investigated this possibility.

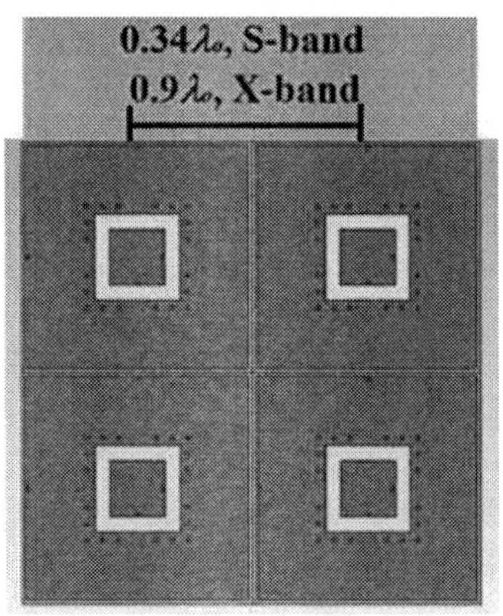

Fig. 2. Electrical spacing of a 2x2 rectangular array of dual-band elements.

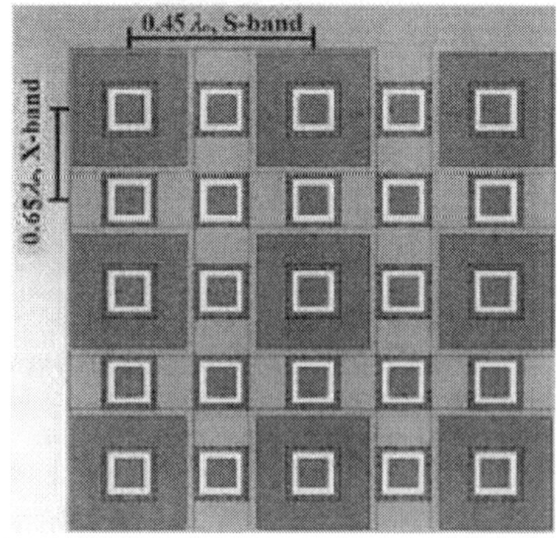

Fig. 3. Electrical spacing of a 5x5 rectangular array of co-located elements.

III. Conclusions

We present a multi-mode antenna array that comprises of two concentric radiating elements that operate at S- and X-band. The array achieves vertical or horizontal polarization utilizing a pair of orthogonal feeds at both bands. We populate a rectangular array with dual-band elements co-located with interspersed X-band elements to optimize electrical spacing at both frequencies. The S-band results show 13.2 dB of realized gain for a 3x3 rectangular array with a uniform amplitude distribution at 2.9 GHz. The X-band results show 20.5 dB of realized gain for a 5x5 rectangular array with a uniform amplitude distribution at 9.4 GHz.

References

[1] S.L.S Yang, K.M. Luk, H.W. Lai, A.A Kishk, and K.F. Lee, "A Dual-Polarized Antenna with Pattern Diversity', *IEEE Ant. Prop. Mag.*, vol. 50, pp. 71-79, 2008.

[2] W.M. Dorsey and A.I. Zaghloul, "Dual-Polarized Dual-Band Antenna Element for ISM Bands", *Proceedings of the IEEE APS International Symposium*, APS/URSI'09, June 2009.

[3] A.I. Zaghloul and W.M. Dorsey, "Evolutionary Development of a Dual-Band, Dual-Polarization, Low-Profile Printed Circuit Antenna", *Proc. of the Int. Conf. on Electromagnetics and Advanced Applications* (ICEAA), pp. 994-997, Sept. 2009.

[4] W.M. Dorsey and A. I. Zaghloul, "Dual-Band Dual-Circularly Polarized Antenna Element," *IET Micro. and Ant. Prop.*, vol. 7, pp. 283–290, 2013.

[5] M. Khan, Z. Yang, and K. Warnick, "Dual-Circular-Polarized High-Efficiency Antenna for Ku-Band Satellite Communication", *IEEE Ant. and Wireless Prop. Lett.*, vol. 13, pp. 1624-1627, 2014.

[6] G.A. Mitchell and A.I. Zaghloul, "Increased Bandwidth and Reduced Footprint of a Dual-band Microstrip Antenna", *Proc. of NRSM* (URSI 2015), Jan. 2015.

[7] G.A. Mitchell and A.I. Zaghloul, "Reduced Footprint of a Dual-Band Dual-Polarization Microstrip Antenna", *Proc. of Int. ACES Symposium*, March 2015.

[8] G.A. Mitchell and A.I. Zaghloul, "Design of a Multi-band, Dual Substrate Concentric Annular Ring Antenna", *Proceedings of the IEEE APS International Symposium*, APS/URSI'16, June 2016.

[9] G.A. Mitchell and A.I. Zaghloul, "Rectangular Array of Co-Located Elements with Dual Polarization at Dual Bands", *Proc. of the Allerton Ant. App. Symp.*, September 2016.

Suspended Plate Antenna Array for High Power

Seth A. McCormick
US. Army Research Lab
Adelphi, MD. USA
seth.a.mccormick.civ@mail.mil

William O. Coburn
US. Army Research Lab
Adelphi, MD. USA
william.o.coburn.civ@mail.mil

***Abstract*—A suspended plate antenna (SPA) array for a high power application is presented. The application required a compact and light weight antenna with at least 20 percent of impedance bandwidth and 14 dBi of gain as well as a low backlobe over a frequency range of 750 to 850 MHz. A single SPA has a little more than 36 percent impedance bandwidth and 8 to 9 dBi of gain. Forming a 2-dimensional array of four SPAs gives an additional 6 dB of gain within a four square foot aperture. The final design meets all design requirements with 37 percent impedance bandwidth from 708 to 964 MHz, 14 – 15 dBi of gain from 750 to 850 MHz, lightweight aluminum construction, and a compact size, as compared to alternatives, of 24 in. x 24 in x 1.4 in.**

Keywords—suspended plate antenna; two dimensional array; compact high gain array

I. Introduction

This paper presents the design, modeling, and measurement of a four element suspended plate antenna (SPA) array for a high power (400 W) application in which the back plane of the antenna would double as a heatsink for 4-100 W amplifiers and mounting plate for source connections and splitters. The design requirements were to build an antenna with an impedance bandwidth of at least 20 percent and 14 dBi of gain over the frequency band of 750 to 850 MHz. Additional design constraints required the antenna to be light and to minimize the aperture size so that it could be manageable when in use.

Three different antenna geometries were considered: the wire grid array, the bi-quad antenna, and the SPA. The wire grid array was able to meet the gain requirement and was simple to construct, but it could not meet the impedance bandwidth requirement and was very large. The bi-quad antenna could potentially meet the gain requirement in an array configuration and the impedance bandwidth, but was more difficult to build and was as large as the wire grid array. The SPA, however, was able to meet both the impedance bandwidth and gain bandwidth (when arraying four elements) while being 9 inches shorter in length and width compared to the wire grid and bi-quad arrays. The antenna down selection was for the SPA given its simplicity and the potential for ruggedness.

The next section details the background and design of the SPA and the array of SPA elements. The following section details the modeling and measurement comparisons for the reflection coefficient and gain. Modeling was performed using the Method of Moments (MoM) solver in the commercial computational electromagnetics (CEM) code FEKO (www.feko.info), and measurements were taken using a tapered anechoic chamber with dual ridged horns as calibration standards. The final section concludes the paper with final comments on results and additional information that will be included in the briefing.

II. Antenna Design

A. Suspended Plate Antenna

The SPA design can be initiated with the same theory as a typical microstrip patch antenna in the case where the substrate relative permittivity approaches unity and the thickness becomes large. Having smaller relative permittivity and larger ground separation than a patch antenna, gives the SPA the potential to have a much larger impedance bandwidth and radiation efficiency than a patch. Also, not needing a substrate can make the SPA simpler and cheaper to build [1].

There are several different ways to feed an SPA such as with a microstrip, vertical probe, and aperture coupled much like a patch [1]. The feeding method with the broadest impedance bandwidth is one using a non-connecting method like the aperture coupled, but a simpler method using an L-probe has been reported in the literature [1, 2]. The L-probe fed SPA can have a little more than 36 percent impedance bandwidth and 8 – 9 dBi of gain. Enlarging the bandwidth too much may impose other unintentional performance limitations such as pattern instability and poor cross-polarization isolation in the H-plane pattern. These problems are typically attributed to feed type and placement as well as induced higher order modes [3, 4].

The SPA in this paper is a scaled model from Antenna Magus (www.antennamagus.com). The antenna is L-probe fed with dimensions 6.25 in. x 5.21 in. (length x width) and is constructed from 6061 62 mil. thick aluminum. The L-probe is centered on a 24 in. x 24 in. sheet of 6061 62 mil aluminum, and is constructed from #10 bus wire. The L-probe is connected to an N-type panel mount connector that is also centered on the aluminum sheet. The height of the L-probe is 1.02 in. with a length after the bend of 2.35 in. The SPA is centered on the aluminum sheet length wise and the displacement from the center of the bulk head to the SPA bottom edge is 0.58 in. The SPA is vertically spaced exactly 1.4 in. from the sheet.

B. *Suspended Plate Antenna Array*

To achieve the desired gain using the SPA, required forming a 2-dimensional array with 4 elements. A 2-dimensional array was desired to produce equal E- and H-plane 3 dB beamwidths. The element center-to-center spacing was initially a one half wavelength at 800 MHz (4.25 in.) per antenna array theory for best performance. However, simulations showed that the desired 6 dB gain plus up was not achieved with that spacing. Spacing the elements width edge-to-width edge did give the desired gain increase. The center-to-center element spacing is 7.37 in. Each element is positioned such that there is equal distance from the center of the ground to the center of an SPA. All other dimensions are the same as the single SPA case.

III. Simulation and Measurement Results

The simulated and measured reflection coefficient comparisons is shown in Fig. 1. There is very good agreement between simulation and measurement for both the single SPA and the array. The noisy oscillations are due to reflections in the lab bay where the measurements were taken. The two dips at 750 and 925 MHz are attributed to a double resonance produced by the bottom and side edges (750 MHz) and the side edges only (925 MHz) respectively. The measured impedance bandwidth for the array is 264 MHz (37 percent) over the frequency band of 708 – 964 MHz.

The simulated realized gain (Fig. 2) shows the desired increase of about 6 dB across all frequencies. The oscillations in the gain measurement are due to chamber interactions, but the results are good to within 0.5 dB. The 1 dB realized gain bandwidth is about 221 MHz for the array which is about 43 MHz less than the impedance bandwidth. However, the realized gain still meets the 14 dBi requirement from 750 – 850 MHz.

The radiation patterns are not shown here, but will be shown in the conference briefing. There was found to be excellent agreement between simulation and measurement. The array produces a larger backlobe and sidelobes in both principal cuts which were not present for a single SPA. The sidelobes are about 15 dB less than peak, and the back lobe is about 20 dB down from peak.

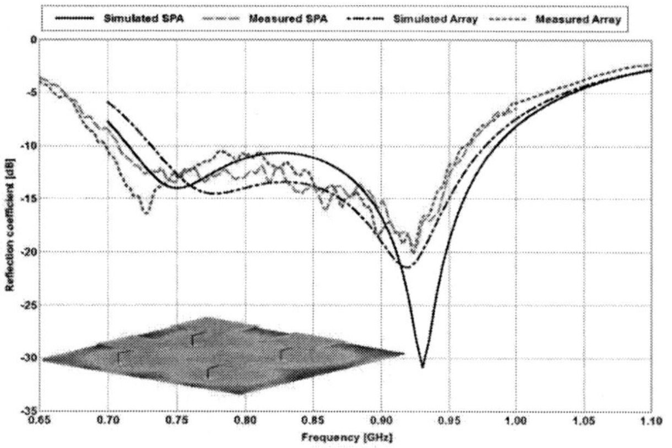

Fig. 1. Simulated and measured reflection coefficient for the SPA and 4 element array.

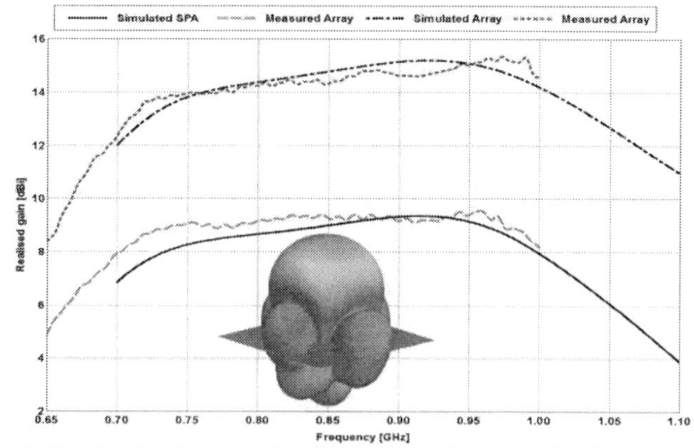

Fig. 2. Simulated and measured realized gain for the SPA and 4 element array.

I. Conclusion

The suspended plate antenna is a simple, lightweight antenna with high gain (8 – 9 dBi) and good impedance bandwidth (36 percent). It is an excellent antenna that outperforms most other low profile high gain antennas with the potential to also be cost effective. In applications where greater gain is necessary over a 36 percent bandwidth, a group of SPAs can be successfully arrayed together to improve the gain performance without losing bandwidth.

Although not shown in this paper, additional simulations with a perforated ground (for additional weight reduction) will be shown in the conference briefing. The results of such simulations showed that 1 in. diameter holes had no adverse impact on the antenna performance provided that the holes were not placed beneath the SPA elements or too close to the feed. The same can be said for 1 in. x 2 in. slots.

Arraying 4 SPA elements together into a 2-dimensional array with a 7.37 in. center-to-center spacing gives the intended 6 dB gain increase across the frequency band of 750 – 850 MHz. The final array has 37 percent impedance bandwidth (708 – 964 MHz), at least 14 dBi of gain (750 – 850 MHz), a 20 dB front-to-back ratio, a simple lightweight aluminum construction, and has a volume of 24 in. x 24 in x 1.4 in. All of these metrics meet the desired design goals.

Acknowledgment

The authors would like to acknowledge Arthur C. Harrison of ARL for constructing both the single SPA and array.

References

[1] J. L. Volakis, Antenna Engineering Handbook, 4th ed., New York: McGraw-Hill, 2007, pp. 37.2-37.10.

[2] C. L. Mak, K. M. Luk, K. F. Lee, and Y. L. Chow, "Experimental Study of a Microstrip Patch Antenna with an L-Shaped Probe," IEEE Trans. On Ant. and Prop., vol. 48, no. 5, May 2000.

[3] Z. N. Chen and M. Y. W. Chia, "Experimental Study on Radiation Performance of Probe-Fed Suspended Plate Antennas," IEEE Trans. On Ant. and Prop., vol. 51, no. 8, Aug. 2003.

[4] Z. N. Chen and M. Y. W. Chia, "Design of Broadband Probe-Fed Plate Antenna with Stub," IEEE Proc. Microw. Ant. Prop. Vol. 148, no. 4, Aug. 2001.

A one-dimensional randomly rough interface that produces a specified angular distribution of the intensity of the light transmitted through it

Ingve Simonsen*† and Alexei A. Maradudin‡

*Surface du Verre et Interfaces, UMR 125 CNRS/Saint-Gobain, F-93303 Aubervilliers, France

†Department of Physics, NTNU Norwegian University of Science and Technology, NO-7491 Trondheim, Norway

‡Department of Physics and Astronomy, University of California, Irvine, CA 92697, U.S.A.

***Abstract*—We use phase perturbation theory to design a one-dimensional randomly rough interface between two dielectric media that produces a specified mean differential transmission coefficient for light transmitted through it.**

I. Introduction

There have been few theoretical studies of how to design randomly rough interfaces between dielectric media that transmit light through them to produce a field with a specified angular dependence of the mean differential transmission coefficient [1]. In this paper we present an approach to the design of a one-dimensional randomly rough interface between two dielectric media that transmits light, incident on it from either medium, with a specified mean differential transmission coefficient. It is the simplest version of this design problem, but one that has not been treated until now.

II. Scattering Theory

We consider a system that consists of a dielectric medium whose dielectric constant is ϵ_1 in the region $x_3 > \zeta(x_1)$, and a dielectric medium whose dielectric constant is ϵ_2 in the region $x_3 < \zeta(x_1)$. Both ϵ_1 and ϵ_2 are assumed to be real, positive, and frequency independent. The interface profile function $\zeta(x_1)$ is assumed to be a single-valued function of x_1 that is differentiable and constitutes a random process.

The interface $x_3 = \zeta(x_1)$ is illuminated from the region $x_3 > \zeta(x_1)$ by a p- or s-polarized plane wave of frequency ω, whose plane of incidence is the x_1x_3 plane. The single nonzero component of the electromagnetic field in the region $x_3 > \zeta(x_1)$ can then be written as

$$F_\nu^{(1)}(x_1, x_3|\omega) = \exp[ikx_1 - i\alpha_1(k)x_3] + \int_{-\infty}^{\infty} \frac{dq}{2\pi} R_\nu(q|k) \exp[iqx_1 + i\alpha_1(q)x_3], \quad (1)$$

where $F_\nu^{(1)}(x_1, x_3|\omega)$ is $H_2^{(1)}(x_1, x_3|\omega)$ when $\nu = p$, and $E_2^{(1)}(x_1, x_3|\omega)$ when $\nu = s$. The single nonzero component of the electromagnetic field in the region $x_3 < \zeta(x_1)$ is given by

$$F_\nu^{(2)}(x_1, x_3|\omega) = \int_{-\infty}^{\infty} \frac{dq}{2\pi} T_\nu(q|k) \exp[iqx_1 - i\alpha_2(q)x_3], \quad (2)$$

where $F_\nu^{(2)}(x_1, x_3|\omega)$ is $H_2^{(2)}(x_1, x_3|\omega)$ when $\nu = p$, and $E_2^{(2)}(x_1, x_3|\omega)$ when $\nu = s$. The functions $\alpha_j(q) (j = 1, 2)$ are defined by $\alpha_j(q) = [\epsilon_j(\omega/c)^2 - q^2]^{\frac{1}{2}}$, with $\mathrm{Re}\,\alpha_j(q) > 0$, $\mathrm{Im}\,\alpha_j(q) > 0$.

The transmission amplitude $T_\nu(q|k)$ is given by first-order phase perturbation theory as [2]

$$T_\nu(q|k) = T_\nu(k) \int_{-\infty}^{\infty} dx_1 \exp[-i(q-k)x_1 + iF_\nu(q|k)\zeta(x_1)], \quad (3)$$

where

$$T_p(k) = \frac{2\epsilon_2\alpha_1(k)}{\epsilon_2\alpha_1(k) + \epsilon_1\alpha_2(k)}, \quad T_s(k) = \frac{2\alpha_1(k)}{\alpha_1(k) + \alpha_2(k)}, \quad (4)$$

while

$$F_p(q|k) = (\epsilon_2 - \epsilon_1)\frac{qk + \alpha_1(q)\alpha_2(k)}{\epsilon_2\alpha_1(q) + \epsilon_1\alpha_2(q)} \quad (5a)$$

$$F_s(q|k) = \alpha_2(q) - \alpha_1(q). \quad (5b)$$

The differential transmission coefficient $(\partial T_\nu/\partial\theta_t)$ is defined such that $(\partial T_\nu/\partial\theta_t)d\theta_t$ is the fraction of the total time-averaged flux incident on the interface that is transmitted into the angular interval $(\theta_t, \theta_t + d\theta_t)$, where the angle of transmission θ_t is measured counterclockwise from the negative x_3 axis. In the present case its average over the realizations of $\zeta(x_1)$ is given by [2]

$$\left\langle \frac{\partial T_\nu}{\partial \theta_t} \right\rangle (\theta_t, \theta_0) = \frac{1}{L_1} \frac{\epsilon_2}{\sqrt{\epsilon_1}} \frac{\kappa_\nu}{\lambda_\nu} \frac{\omega}{2\pi c} \frac{\cos^2\theta_t}{\cos\theta_0} \langle |T_\nu(q|k)|^2 \rangle, \quad (6)$$

where $\theta_0 = \sin^{-1}(ck/\sqrt{\epsilon_1}\omega)$ is the polar angle of incidence, L_1 is the length of the x_1 axis covered by the random interface, $\kappa_p = \epsilon_1, \kappa_s = 1$, and $\lambda_p = \epsilon_2$, $\lambda_s = 1$. For illumination at normal incidence $(k = 0)$, and in the geometrical optics limit of phase perturbation theory, the use of Eq. (3) yields the result

$$\left\langle \frac{\partial T_\nu}{\partial \theta_t} \right\rangle (\theta_t, 0) = \frac{1}{L_1} \frac{\epsilon_2}{\sqrt{\epsilon_1}} \frac{\kappa_\nu}{\lambda_\nu} \frac{\omega}{2\pi c} \cos^2\theta_t |T_\nu(0)|^2 \times \int_{-\infty}^{\infty} dx_1 \int_{-\infty}^{\infty} du \exp(iqu) \langle \exp[-iF_\nu(q|0)u\zeta'(x_1)] \rangle. \quad (7)$$

Equation (7) is valid for the interval $|\theta_t| < \sin^{-1}(\sqrt{\epsilon_1/\epsilon_2})$, in which $F_\nu(q|0)$, with $q = \sqrt{\epsilon_2}(\omega/c)\sin\theta_t$, is real.

Our goal is to obtain the profile function $\zeta(x_1)$ that produces a specified form of $\langle \partial T_\nu/\partial\theta_t\rangle(\theta_t, 0)$. To accomplish this we represent $\zeta(x_1)$ in the form [3]

$$\zeta(x_1) = a_n x_1 + b_n, \qquad nb \leq x_1 \leq (n+1)b, \quad n \in \mathbb{Z}, \quad (8)$$

where the $\{a_n\}$ are independent identically distributed random deviates, and b is a characteristic length. The probability density function (pdf) of a_n, $f(\gamma) = \langle\delta(\gamma - a_n)\rangle$, is therefore independent of n. If we require the interface profile function to be continuous at $x_1 = (n+1)b$ ($n \in \mathbb{Z}$) the relation

$$b_{n+1} = b_n - (n+1)(a_{n+1} - a_n)b \quad (9)$$

must be satisfied. This equation serves as a recurrence relation for the $\{b_n\}$ once the $\{a_n\}$ are known. With no loss of generality we assume that $b_0 = 0$.

With the use of Eq. (8), Eq. (7) is evaluated, with the result that

$$\left\langle \frac{\partial T}{\partial\theta_t}\right\rangle(\theta_t^{(\nu)}(\gamma), 0) = \frac{4\sqrt{\epsilon_1\epsilon_2}}{(\sqrt{\epsilon_1}+\sqrt{\epsilon_2})^2}\frac{\cos^2\theta_t^{(\nu)}(\gamma)}{|\sin\theta_t^{(\nu)}(\gamma)|}|\gamma| f(\gamma), \quad (10)$$

where $\theta_t^{(\nu)}$ is the solution of the equation $\gamma = q/F_\nu(q|0)$, with $q = \sqrt{\epsilon_2}(\omega/c)\sin\theta_t$. This equation is

$$\gamma = \frac{\sin\theta_t^{(p)}[(\eta - \sin^2\theta_t^{(p)})^{\frac{1}{2}} + \eta\cos\theta_t^{(p)}]}{(1-\eta)(\eta - \sin^2\theta_t^{(p)})^{\frac{1}{2}}} \quad (11a)$$

in p-polarization, and

$$\gamma = \frac{\sin\theta_t^{(s)}}{\cos\theta_t^{(s)} - (\eta - \sin^2\theta_t^{(s)})^{\frac{1}{2}}} \quad (11b)$$

in s-polarization, where $\eta = \epsilon_1/\epsilon_2$. From Eq. (10) we obtain finally the result

$$f_\nu(\gamma) = \frac{(\sqrt{\epsilon_1}+\sqrt{\epsilon_2})^2}{4\sqrt{\epsilon_1\epsilon_2}}\frac{|\sin\theta_t^{(\nu)}(\gamma)|}{\cos^2\theta_t^{(\nu)}(\gamma)}\frac{1}{|\gamma|}\left\langle\frac{\partial T_\nu}{\partial\theta_t}\right\rangle(\theta_t^{(\nu)}(\gamma), 0). \quad (12)$$

When the pdf $f_\nu(\gamma)$ has been determined in this way, a long sequence of $\{a_n\}$ is generated, e.g. by the rejection method [4], and the corresponding sequence of $\{b_n\}$ is obtained from Eq. (9). A realization of the interface profile function $\zeta(x_1)$ is then constructed on the basis of Eq. (8). If an ensemble of N_p realizations of $\zeta(x_1)$ is required, this procedure is carried out N_p times.

III. Results

We illustrate the preceding results by applying them to the design of an interface that for s-polarized plane wave illumination produces a transmitted field whose mean differential transmission coefficient is constant within the angular interval $|\theta_t| < \theta_m < \sin^{-1}\sqrt{(\epsilon_1/\epsilon_2)}$, and vanishes outside it. Thus, the mean differential transmission coefficient we wish to produce is $\langle\partial T_s/\partial\theta_t\rangle(\theta_t, 0) = AH(\theta_m - |\theta_t|)$, where $H(z)$ is the Heaviside unit step function. The value of the coefficient A is obtained from the normalization to unity of the pdf $f_s(\gamma)$ that is obtained by substituting this expression into Eq. (12). In Fig. 1 we present the dependence on θ_t of the mean differential transmission coefficient obtained by a rigorous computer simulation approach [5]. The values of the experimental and roughness parameters defining the system are $\nu = s$, $\theta_0 = 0°$, $\theta_m = 7°$, the frequency of the incident light is $\omega = 2\pi c/\lambda$, with $\lambda = 612.7\,\text{nm}$, $\epsilon_1 = 1$, $\epsilon_2 = 2.69$, $b = 20\,\mu\text{m}$, the length of the surface is $L_1 = 250\,\mu\text{m}$, the sampling length is $\Delta x = \lambda/8$, and $N_p = 10\,000$. Also plotted is the input form of this coefficient (dashed lines). The result obtained from the computer simulations is nonzero only for $|\theta_t| < 7°$, and is reasonably uniform within this interval.

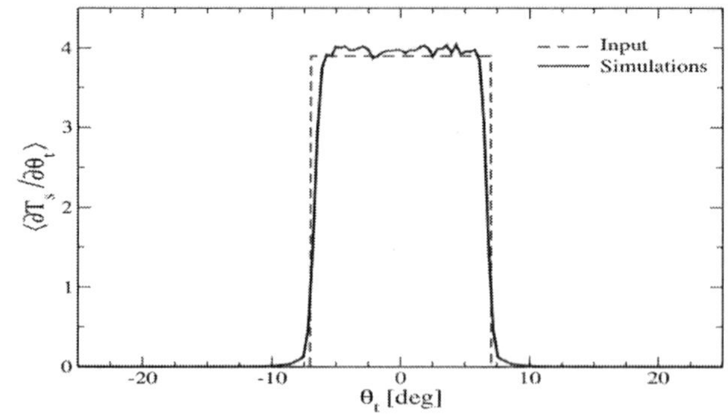

Fig. 1. Rigorous computer simulations results (solid line) and input (dashed line) for the dependence of the mean differential transmission coefficient, $\langle\partial T_s/\partial\theta_t\rangle$, on the transmission angle θ_t when the rough dielectric surface is illuminated at normal incidence by an s-polarized plane wave. The ensemble used in obtaining these results consisted on $N_p = 10\,000$ surface realizations. The values of the remaining experimental and roughness parameters assumed in obtaining these results are defined in the text.

IV. Conclusions

In this paper we have shown how to design a one dimensional randomly rough interface between two dielectric media that transmits p- or s-polarized light incident normally on it from either medium with a specified angular dependence of the mean differential transmission coefficient. This result could be useful in the design of illumination or display systems.

Acknowledgment

The research of I.S. was supported in part by The Research Council of Norway Contract No. 216699.

References

[1] A. A. Maradudin, E. R. Méndez, and T. A. Leskova, *Designer Surfaces*, Elsevier, Amsterdam, 2008.

[2] A. A. Maradudin and I. Simonsen (unpublished work, 2016).

[3] E.R. Méndez, E. E. García-Guerrero, T. A. Leskova, A. A. Maradudin, J. Muñoz-Lopez, and I. Simonsen, "The design of one-dimensional random surfaces with specified scattering properties," Appl. Phys. Lett. Vol. 81, pp. 798–800, 2002.

[4] W. H. Press, S. A. Teukolsky, W. T. Vetterling, and B. P. Flannery, *Numerical Recipes in Fortran*, 2nd ed., Cambridge University Press, New York, 1992, pp. 281–282.

[5] I. Simonsen, "Optics of surface disordered systems: A random walk through rough surface scattering phenomena," Eur. Phys. J. Special Topics Vol. 181, pp. 1–183, 2010.

Control of the coherence of light transmitted through a one-dimensional randomly rough interface that acts as a Schell-model source

Alexei A. Maradudin* and Ingve Simonsen†‡

*Department of Physics and Astronomy, University of California, Irvine, CA 92697, U.S.A.

†Surface du Verre et Interfaces, UMR 125 CNRS/Saint-Gobain, F-93303 Aubervilliers, France

‡Department of Physics, NTNU Norwegian University of Science and Technology, NO-7491 Trondheim, Norway

***Abstract*—We show how to design a one-dimensional randomly rough interface between two dielectric media that, when illuminated at normal incidence by a Gaussian beam, produces a transmitted beam whose spectral density in the mean interface has a Gaussian form, while its spectral degree of coherence in this plane has a nearly arbitrary form.**

I. Introduction

We consider the transmission of an s-polarized Gaussian beam, incident from a dielectric medium whose dielectric constant is ϵ_1, through a one-dimensional randomly rough interface with a dielectric medium whose dielectric constant is ϵ_2. Our aim is to design the interface so that it produces a transmitted beam whose special density [1] (intensity) in the mean interface also has a Gaussian form, and its spectral degree of coherence in this plane has a nearly arbitrary form. Such an interface can be regarded as a realization of a Schell-model source [2].

II. Scattering Theory

The physical system we consider consists of a dielectric medium whose dielectric constant is ϵ_1 in the region $x_3 > \zeta(x_1)$, and dielectric medium whose dielectric constant is ϵ_2 in the region $x_3 < \zeta(x_1)$. The dielectric constants ϵ_1 and ϵ_2 are assumed to be real, positive, and frequency independent. The interface profile function $\zeta(x_1)$ is assumed to be a single-valued function of x_1 that is differentiable and constitutes a random process.

The interface profile function $\zeta(x_1)$ is illuminated at normal incidence from the region $x_3 > \zeta(x_1)$ by an s-polarized Gaussian beam of frequency ω, whose plane of incidence is the x_1x_3 plane. The single nonzero component of its electric field can be written

$$E_2(x_1, x_3|\omega)_{inc} = \exp[-(x_1/w)^2 - i\sqrt{\epsilon_1}(\omega/c)x_3]. \quad (1)$$

The transmitted field in the region $x_3 < \zeta(x_1)$ can be written

$$E_2(x_1, x_3|\omega)_{tr} = \int_{-\infty}^{\infty} \frac{dq}{2\pi} T(q) \exp[iqx_1 - i\alpha_2(q)x_3], \quad (2)$$

where $\alpha_2(q) = [\epsilon_2(\omega/c)^2 - q^2]^{\frac{1}{2}}$, with $\mathrm{Re}\,\alpha_2(q) > 0, \mathrm{Im}\,\alpha_2(q) > 0$. We seek the interface profile function for which the transmitted field possesses a cross-spectral density function in the plane $x_3 = 0$ given by

$$\begin{aligned} W^{(0)}(x_1, x_1'|\omega) &= \langle E_2(x_1, 0|\omega)_{tr} E_2^*(x_1', 0|\omega)_{tr}\rangle \\ &= A^2 \exp(-x_1^2/4\sigma_s^2) g^{(0)}(|x_1 - x_1'|) \exp(-x_1'^2/4\sigma_s^2), \quad (3) \end{aligned}$$

where the angle brackets denote an average over the ensemble of realizations of $\zeta(x_1)$.

We reach this goal by evaluating the correlation function $\langle T(q)T^*(q')\rangle$ in two different ways. From Eqs. (2) and (3) we find that

$$\begin{aligned} \langle T(q)T^*(q')\rangle &= \sqrt{2\pi}\sigma_s A^2 \exp[-\frac{1}{2}\sigma_s^2(q - q')^2] \\ &\times \int_{-\infty}^{\infty} du\, g^{(0)}(|u|) \exp(-u^2/8\sigma_s^2) \exp[-i(q + q')u/2]. \quad (4) \end{aligned}$$

We next use the result that the simplest form of phase perturbation theory yields the result that [3]

$$\begin{aligned} \langle T(q)T^*(q')\rangle &= T^2(0) \int_{-\infty}^{\infty} dx_1 \int_{-\infty}^{\infty} dx_1' \\ &\times \exp[-i(qx_1 - q'x_1')] \exp[-(x_1/w)^2 - (x_1'/w)^2] \\ &\times \langle \exp[-ia(x_1 - x_1')\zeta'(x_1')]\rangle, \quad (5) \end{aligned}$$

where $T(0) = 2\sqrt{\epsilon_1}/(\sqrt{\epsilon_1}+\sqrt{\epsilon_2})$, and $a = (\sqrt{\epsilon_1}-\sqrt{\epsilon_2})(\omega/c)$.

To evaluate the double integral in Eq. (5) we express the interface profile function $\zeta(x_1)$ in the form [4]

$$\zeta(x_1) = a_n x_1 + b_n, nb \leq x_1 \leq (n+1)b, n = 0, \pm 1, \pm 2, \ldots \quad (6)$$

where the $\{a_n\}$ are independent identically distributed random deviates, and b is a characteristic length. The probability density function (pdf) of a_n, $f(\gamma) = \langle \delta(\gamma - a_n)\rangle$, is therefore independent of n. The $\{b_n\}$ are obtained recursively from [4]

$$b_{n+1} = b_n - (n+1)(a_{n+1} - a_n)b, \quad (7)$$

with $b_0 = 0$. With this representation of $\zeta(x_1)$ Eq. (5) becomes

$$\begin{aligned} \langle T(q)T^*(q')\rangle &= \pi w^2 T^2(0) \exp[-(w^2/8)(q - q')^2] \\ &\times \int_{-\infty}^{\infty} d\gamma f(\gamma) \exp\{-(w^2/2)[a\gamma + (q + q')/2]^2\}. \quad (8) \end{aligned}$$

On equating the right-hand sides of Eqs. (4) and (8) we are led to an integral relation between $g^{(0)}(|u|)$ and $f(\gamma)$ that can be solved by Fourier methods, with the result

$$f(\gamma) = \frac{1}{\pi}\int_0^\infty d\nu\, g^{(0)}\!\left(\frac{\nu}{|a|}\right)\cos(\nu\gamma), \quad (9)$$

provided that $\sigma_s = w/2$ and $A = T(0)$.

Once a form for $g^{(0)}(|u|)$ has been selected, the corresponding pdf $f(\gamma)$ is obtained from Eq. (9). A long sequence of $\{a_n\}$ is then generated, e.g. by the rejection method [5], and the corresponding sequence of $\{b_n\}$ is obtained from Eq. (7). A single realization of the interface profile function $\zeta(x_1)$ is then constructed on the use of Eq. (6). If an ensemble of N_p realizations of $\zeta(x_1)$ is required this procedure is repeated N_p times.

The propagation of the transmitted field in the region $x_3 < \zeta(x_1)$ can also be expressed in terms of $g^{(0)}(|u|)$, through the relation between the mean intensity of this field in the far zone, and its cross-spectral density function in the plane $x_3 = 0$, Eq. (3). In the parabolic approximation $\alpha_2(q) = \sqrt{\epsilon_2}(\omega/c) - (c/2\sqrt{\epsilon_2}\omega)q^2$, it is

$$\langle |E_2(x_1, x_3|\omega)_{tr}|^2\rangle = \left(\frac{2}{\pi}\right)^{\frac{1}{2}} A^2\sqrt{\epsilon_2}\frac{\omega}{c}\frac{\sigma_s}{|x_3|}\int_0^\infty du\, g^{(0)}(u)$$
$$\times \cos\left(\frac{\sqrt{\epsilon_2}\omega}{c}\frac{x_1 u}{|x_3|}\right)\exp\left[-\left(\frac{1}{8\sigma_s^2} + \frac{\epsilon_2\omega^2\sigma_s^2}{2c^2x_3^2}\right)u^2\right]. \quad (10)$$

A much simpler expression for the mean intensity of the transmitted field in the far zone can be obtained if the second term in the exponent in Eq. (10) is deleted, and $g^{(0)}(u)$ is replaced by the inverse of Eq. (9). In this way we obtain

$$\langle |E_2(x_1, x_3|\omega)_{tr}|^2\rangle = 2A^2\sqrt{\epsilon_2}\frac{\omega\sigma_s^2}{c|x_3|}$$
$$\times \int_{-\infty}^\infty d\gamma f(\gamma)\exp\left[-2\sigma_s^2a^2\left(\gamma - \frac{\sqrt{\epsilon_2}}{|a|}\frac{\omega}{c}\frac{x_1}{|x_3|}\right)^2\right]. \quad (11)$$

In the limit $2\sigma_s^2a^2 \gg 1$ we have the equivalence

$$\exp\left[-2\sigma_s^2a^2\left(\gamma - \frac{\sqrt{\epsilon_2}}{|a|}\frac{\omega}{c}\frac{x_1}{|x_3|}\right)^2\right]$$
$$= \left(\frac{\pi}{2}\right)^{\frac{1}{2}}\frac{1}{\sigma_s|a|}\delta\left(\gamma - \frac{\sqrt{\epsilon_2}}{|a|}\frac{\omega}{c}\frac{x_1}{|x_3|}\right). \quad (12)$$

With this result, Eq. (11) becomes

$$\langle |E_2(x_1, x_3|\omega)_{tr}|^2\rangle = \sqrt{2\pi}A^2\frac{\sqrt{\epsilon_2}}{|a|}\frac{\omega}{c}\frac{\sigma_s}{|x_3|}f\left(\frac{\sqrt{\epsilon_2}}{|a|}\frac{\omega}{c}\frac{x_1}{|x_3|}\right). \quad (13)$$

Thus, we have a simple way to design a one-dimensional randomly rough interface between two semi-infinite dielectric media which, when illuminated at normal incidence by an s-polarized Gaussian beam, produces a transmitted beam with a specified intensity profile in the far zone. One specifies the desired intensity profile as a function of x_1 for a large fixed value of $|x_3|$, and then uses Eq. (13) to obtain the pdf $f(\gamma)$ of the slopes $\{a_n\}$ from which realizations of the interface are generated by the use of Eqs. (6) and (7).

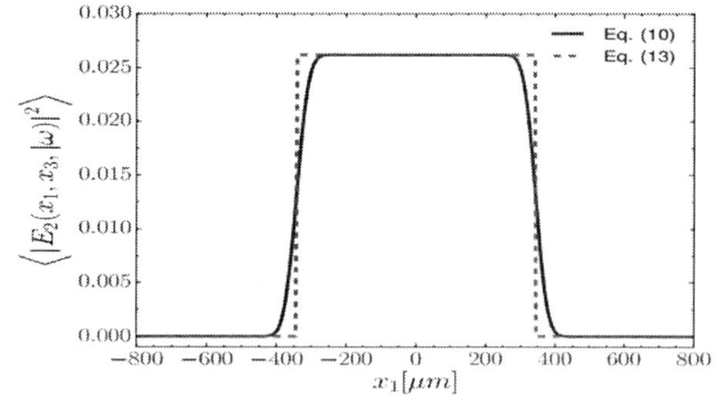

Fig. 1. The transmitted intensity profile $\langle |E_2(x_1, x_3|\omega)_{tr}|^2\rangle$ as a function of x_1 when calculated from Eqs. (10) and (13) for $x_3 = -10^4$ µm. The parameters assumed in obtaining these results are defined in the text.

III. Results

In Fig. 1 we present the mean intensity profile of the transmitted beam calculated from Eq. (10) (solid curve) when $g^{(0)}(|u|)$ is given by $g^{(0)}(|u|) = \mathrm{sinc}(\sqrt{3}u/\sigma_g)$ $[f(\gamma) = (|a|\sigma_g/2\sqrt{3})H(\sqrt{3}/(|a|\sigma_g) - |\gamma|)$, where $H(z)$ is the Heaviside unit step function]. The corresponding intensity profile, obtained from Eq. (13) together with the expression for $f(\gamma)$ given above, is plotted as a dashed curve. In these calculations $\omega = 2\pi c/\lambda$, $\lambda = 612.7\,\mathrm{nm}$, $\theta_0 = 0°$, $\epsilon_1 = 1$, $\epsilon_2 = 2.69$, $\sigma_s = 12.5\,\mu\mathrm{m}$, $\sigma_g = 3\,\mu\mathrm{m}$, $w = 25\,\mu\mathrm{m}$, $b = 20\,\mu\mathrm{m}$, and $x_3 = -10^4\,\mu\mathrm{m}$. The agreement between the results obtained from Eqs. (10) and (13) is very good.

IV. Conclusions

In this work we have shown how to design a one-dimensional randomly rough interface between two dielectric media that acts as a Schell-model source, when illuminated at normal incidence by an s-polarized Gaussian beam, that produces a transmitted beam with an arbitrary spectral degree of coherence. We have determined the evolution of the transmitted beam, and have shown how to design such a surface to shape the incident Gaussian beam into a transmitted beam with a specified intensity profile in the far zone.

Acknowledgment

The research of I.S. was supported in part by the Research Council of Norway Contract No. 216699.

References

[1] L. Mandel and E. Wolf, *Optical Coherence and Quantum Optics*, Cambridge University Press, New York, 1995, Section 4.3.2.

[2] A. C. Schell, *The Multiple Plate Antenna*, Ph.D. Dissertation, Massachusetts Institute of Technology, 1961, Section 7.5.

[3] A. A. Maradudin and I. Simonsen (unpublished work, 2016).

[4] E. R. Méndez, E. E. García-Guerrero, T. A. Leskova, A. A. Maradudin, J. Muñoz-Lopez, and I. Simonsen, "The design of one-dimensional random surfaces with specified scattering properties," Appl. Phys. Lett., Vol. 81, pp. 798–800 (2002).

[5] W. H. Press, S. A. Teukolsky, W. T. Vetterling, and B. P. Flannery, *Numerical Recipes in Fortran*, 2nd ed. Cambridge University Press, New York, 1992, pp. 281–282.

Complete families in inverse obstacle scattering

Giovanni Franco Crosta
Department of Earth- and Environmental Sciences
University of Milan Bicocca
Milan, Lombardy 20126, Italy
Email: Giovanni_Crosta@uml.edu

***Abstract*—After an outline of the properties of complete families, their application to an inverse obstacle problem in scalar electromagnetics is described. The approximate forward propagator is defined, which relates least-squares boundary coefficients to far zone scattering coefficients. A conjecture on the forward propagator is stated. Support to the conjecture comes from computational results, including the inversion of phaseless data.**

I. Complete Families

An inverse obstacle problem in electromagnetics, as well as in acoustics, is met when one aims at reconstructing some properties of the obstacle, such as size, shape and refractive index, from experimental data (incident and scattered waves) and *a priori* information. In spite of remarkable advances in the proper statement of the problem and in solution methods during the past three decades, inverse obstacle scattering in real-world situations still raises challenging questions. Geometrically, "the obstacle" is a bounded, open, simply connected and star-shaped domain $\Omega \subset I\!R^n$, $n = 2$ or 3, with sufficiently smooth boundary $\partial\Omega \equiv \Gamma$. Space outside $\bar{\Omega}$ is either empty (in electromagnetics) or filled by a homogeneous, uniform, compressible stationary fluid (in acoustics). Herewith the simplest form of the inverse problem is addressed, where incident waves are plane, have unit amplitude, the same frequency and different directions. Hence $\{\mathbf{k}_q | q \in Q\}$ is the set of Q incident wavevectors with $|\mathbf{k}_q| = k, \forall q \in Q$. Moreover, waves do not propagate through Ω: as a consequence Ω is characterised by its size, shape and boundary condition for the applicable wave equation. Although no relation shall in general be imposed between obstacle size, say diam$[\Omega]$, and wavelength, $2\pi/k$, discussion is limited herewith to the "resonance region": diam$[\Omega] \times k \approx 2\pi$. Another simplifying hypothesis pertains to wave functions, which are assumed herewith to be scalar-valued. The class of addressable problems is thus severely limited: however the results presented in the following provide guidelines for the vector-valued case as well. The purpose of this contribution is not to review all known methods and algorithms which address inverse obstacle problems: the focus is on methods which rely on complete families, the best known of which are **T**-matrix methods [1, 2].

Def. 1 (*complete family*) In a Banach space X a countable set of functions $\{v_\lambda | \lambda \in \Lambda\}$ which is linearly independent is said to be a complete family whenever, for a given approximation error $\epsilon > 0$ there are an approximation order $M[\epsilon] > 0$ and a set of coefficients $\{c_\lambda^{(M[\epsilon])} | \lambda \in \Lambda[M[\epsilon]]\}$, which depend on $M[\epsilon]$ and give rise to

$$||\phi - \sum_{\lambda \in \Lambda[M[\epsilon]]} c_\lambda^{(M[\epsilon])} v_\lambda||_X < \epsilon, \ \forall \phi \in X. \qquad (1)$$

If the function space is Hilbert, then closure of the function family can be defined. Closure is equivalent to completeness [3, p. 70 ff.]. A Hilbert space of interest herewith is $L^2(\Gamma)$, made of functions supported on the obstacle boundary.

Examples of complete families in $L^2(\Gamma)$ [2]. If the obstacle is a right cylinder of axis z and cross section Ω, then the scattering problem is set in two space dimensions: $n = 2$. Let λ stand for the index pair $\lambda \equiv \{p, m\}$ subject to $p = 0, 1; p \leq m$. The outgoing cylindrical wave functions, which depend on polar coordinates $\{r, \varphi\}$, are defined by

$$v_\lambda := \sqrt{\varepsilon_m} H_m^{(1)}[kr]((1-p)\cos[m\varphi] + p \sin[m\varphi], \qquad (2)$$

with ε_m the Neumann factor and $H_m^{(1)}[.]$ the Hankel functions of the first kind. The $\{v_\lambda\}$ are a complete family. Given the smoothness of Γ, the normal derivatives there, $\{\partial_N v_\lambda\}$, are a complete family as well. Let $\sigma(-\Delta_D)$ and $\sigma(-\Delta_N)$ stand for the spectra of the interior negative Dirichlet-Laplace and Neumann-Laplace operators. If $k^2 \notin \sigma(-\Delta_D)$ then real waves, $\{\Re[v_\lambda] \equiv u_\lambda\}$, form a complete family. Similarly for $\{\partial_N u_\lambda\}$ if $k^2 \notin \sigma(-\Delta_N)$.

II. Propagators

Let the incident electric fields be polarised along the z axis and be denoted by $E_{q,z}^{(\mathrm{inc})}, q \in Q$. If M is the approximation order, then $\Lambda[M] := \{\lambda | p = 0, 1, p \leq m \leq M\}$. The inner product in $L^2(\Gamma)$ is denoted by $\langle . | . \rangle$. Then one can define the following.

Def. 2 (*some vectors*). Let $\lambda \in \Lambda[M]$ and define

$$\mathbf{g}_q^{(M)} := [\langle v_\lambda | E_{q,z}^{(\mathrm{inc})} \rangle], \ \mathbf{b}_q^{(M)} := -\frac{\mathrm{i}}{4}[\langle u_\lambda | \partial_N E_{q,z}^{(\mathrm{inc})} \rangle]. \qquad (3)$$

Def. 3 (*some matrices*). Let $\lambda, \mu \in \Lambda[M]$ and

$$\mathbf{P}^{(M)} := [\langle v_\lambda | v_\mu \rangle], \ \Re\mathbf{L}^{(M)} := -\frac{\mathrm{i}}{4}[\langle u_\lambda | \partial_N v_\mu \rangle]. \qquad (4)$$

Prop. 1 (*the boundary coefficients*). The scattered electric field $E_{q,z}^{(\mathrm{sc})}$ which complies with the Dirichlet boundary condition $(E_{q,z}^{(\mathrm{inc})} + E_{q,z}^{(\mathrm{sc})})|_\Gamma = 0$ is approximated to order M on Γ by

$$E_{q,z}^{(\mathrm{sc},M)}[\mathbf{x}] = \sum_{\lambda \in \Lambda[M]} c_{q,\lambda}^{(M)} v_\lambda[\mathbf{x}], \ \mathbf{x} \in \Gamma, \qquad (5)$$

where the vector of coefficients $\{c_{q,\lambda}^{(M)}\} \equiv \mathbf{c}_q^{(M)}$ solves the algebraic system [2, 4, and references therein]

$$\mathbf{P}^{(M)} \cdot \mathbf{c}_q^{(M)} = -\mathbf{g}_q^{(M)}. \tag{6}$$

CONJECTURE 1 (*forward propagated boundary coefficients*). Let $\tilde{v}_\lambda$ denote the asymptotics of v_λ for $r \to \infty$; *ditto* for $\tilde{E}_{q,z}^{(\mathrm{sc})}$. Denote by S_1^1 the unit circle. If the far-zone scattering coefficients [1]

$$f_{q,\lambda} = -\frac{\mathrm{i}}{4}[\langle u_\lambda | \partial_N (E_{q,z}^{(\mathrm{inc})} + E_{q,z}^{(\mathrm{sc})})\rangle \tag{7}$$

are approximated by propagating $\mathbf{c}_q^{(M)}$ forward according to the affine transformation [4]

$$\mathbf{p}_q^{(M)} = \Re \mathbf{L}^{(M)} \cdot \mathbf{c}_q^{(M)} + \mathbf{b}_q^{(M)}, \tag{8}$$

then the following inequality holds

$$||\tilde{E}_{q,z}^{(\mathrm{sc})} - \sum_{\lambda \in \Lambda[M]} p_{q,\lambda}^{(M)} \tilde{v}_\lambda ||_{L^2(S_1^1)} <$$

$$< ||\tilde{E}_{q,z}^{(\mathrm{sc})} - \sum_{\lambda \in \Lambda[M]} c_{q,\lambda}^{(M)} \tilde{v}_\lambda ||_{L^2(S_1^1)}. \tag{9}$$

Forward propagation was suggested on a heuristic basis by JONES and MAO [5]. To the best of the author's knowledge, no proof of CONJECTURE 1 is available.

III. INVERSION OF PHASE-LESS SCATTERED DATA

The above CONJECTURE has been supported by numerical evidence, where complex valued data were inverted. More challenging is the application of the forward propagator of EQ. 8 to invert phaseless data. An aluminum triangular prism was illuminated by plane, z-polarised electromagnetic waves of frequency 10 GHz. For each of the $Q = 19$ incident directions (FIGURE 1), 34 scattered intensity values on the perigon were taken from the IPSWICH-009 data set [6]. The shape to be reconstructed from an initial guess (ellipse) was described by $I = 10$ parameters forming the vector $\vec{\psi} \in \Psi_{\mathrm{adm}} \subset I\!R^I$. The unknowns of the inverse problem were $\{M, \vec{\psi}\}$. The intensity far zone defect norm (to be inferred from EQ. 9) was minimised with respect to $\{M, \vec{\psi}\}$. The reconstructed shape at $M = 13$ is shown by FIGURE 2.

FIGURE 1. Wind-rose of $Q = 19$ incident wavevectors; $k = (2\pi/3)\ \mathrm{cm}^{-1}$.

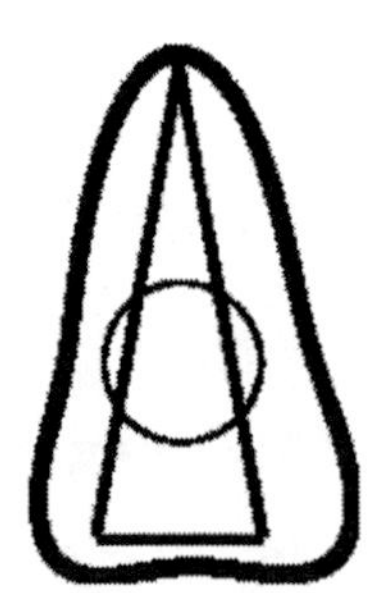

FIGURE 2. Triangle: exact shape; thick curve: reconstructed shape at $M = 13$. Circle has $r = 1$ cm.

IV. DISCUSSION

(*On estimation methods.*) Whereas estimates from above for the right side of INEQ. 9 are easily obtained in terms of the ϵ of INEQ. 1 [4], difficulties in the comparison with the left side arise because of the affine transformation in EQ. 8. This is a typical feature of **T**-matrix schemes, which offer no obvious way of comparing approximations of a given quantity according to different complete families. It remains to be seen whether generalised **T**-matrix schemes based e.g., on the method of discrete sources [7] lead to tractable estimates.

(*On extension to three space dimensions.*) A computer code implementing the forward propagation algorithm in the acoustic (scalar) case where $n = 3$, was applied to the reconstruction of axially symmetric, sound-soft obstacles from synthetic data [8]. The latter were scattering amplitudes computed by a standard **T**-matrix scheme [1], to which pseudo-random noise was added. If a proof of CONJECTURE 1 is found for $n = 2$, then it can be carried over to $n = 3$, or *vice versa*.

(*On capabilities and limitations of the method.*) Algorithms based on EQNS. 6 and 8 pertain to simply connected and star-shaped obstacles. Scattering data from limited apertures and multiple incident plane waves have been processed. Waves shall however not propagate inside the obstacle. Neither periodic arrays of scatterers nor dielectric obstacles are tractable. Shape reconstruction in $n = 2$ from horizontally polarised electric fields requires the translation of an available code [9]. The NEUMANN boundary condition can be addressed. Nothing has been done yet for impedance boundary conditions.

ACKNOWLEDGMENT

Support by *Fondo di Ateneo per la ricerca 2011-2015*, the *Digicom Co.* (Gallarate, IT) - *Research Grant* and the *US Army RDECOM ACQ CTR* contract *W911NF 11-1-0277 R&D 1449-BC-01*, is gratefully acknowledged. The Referees are warmly thanked for their constructive criticism: the issues they have raised have been addressed mainly in SECT. IV.

REFERENCES

[1] Waterman, P. C., "New formulation of acoustic scattering," *J. Acoust. Soc. Amer.*, Vol. 45, 1417-1429, 1969.
[2] Ramm, A. G., *Scattering by obstacles*, Dordrecht, NL: Reidel, 1986.
[3] Trenoguine, V. A., *Analyse fonctionnelle*, Moscou, RU: Éditions MIR, 1985.
[4] Crosta, G. F., "The forward propagation method applied to the inverse obstacle problem in electromagnetics," *Fields Institute Communications*, Vol. 25, 225-238, 2000.
[5] Jones, D. S. and Mao, X. Q., "A method for solving the inverse problem in soft acoustic scattering," *Inverse Problems*, Vol. 5, 731-748, 1989.
[6] Mc Gahan, R. V. and Kleinman, R. E., "Special session on image recostruction using real data," *IEEE Antenn. Propag. Magazine*, Vol. 38, No. 3, 39-40, 1996.
[7] Ерёмин, Ю. А., "Обоснование обобщенних схем метода **T**-матриц на основе интегральных преобразований," *Диффер-енц. уравнения*, Vol. 34, No. 9, 1254-1259, 1998.
[8] Crosta, G. F., "Obstacle reconstruction in acoustics: error analysis of an inversion algorithm set in the subspace of outgoing spherical wave functions," *Nonlinear analysis: Theory, methods and applications*, Vol. 30, No. 6, 3481-3492, 1997.
[9] Crosta, G. F., "Scalar and vector backpropagation applied to shape identification from experimental data: recent results and open problems," in *Inverse problems, tomography and image processing*, RAMM, A. G. Ed., Plenum: New York, 1998, pp. 9-31.

An Improved Subspace Projection Method of Underdetermined Direction of Arrival Estimation for Frequency Hopping Signals

Chaozhu Zhang and Yu Wang*
College of Information and Communication Engineering,
Harbin Engineering University ,
Harbin, 150001, China
*wangyu1256@hrbeu.edu.cn

Abstract—**In order to sort frequency hopping networks, the problem of estimating Direction of Arrival (DOA) of frequency hopping signals in underdetermined case is discussed in this paper. Inspired by the underdetermined blind source separation algorithm and product of hopping frequency and DOA in frequency hopping signals mixing matrix, a novel underdetermined DOA estimation method is proposed. Firstly, mixing matrix of frequency hopping signals is estimated, and secondly an improved subspace projection method based on Short Time Fourier transform (STFT) is exploited to recovery frequency hopping signals in order to achieve frequency information, and lastly DOAs estimations are obtained through mixing matrix and frequency information. Results of simulation demonstrate that the proposed algorithm can achieve superior performance than those got from previous algorithms.**

Keywords—Direction of arrival; Subspace projection; Short time fourier transform ; Frequency hopping signals.

I. INTRODUCTION

Frequency hopping (FH) signals are widely used in military and civilian communication due to their wide band, low probability of detection and interception, and anti-jamming. Meanwhile, sorting frequency hopping signals is of great importance. Estimating Direction of arrival (DOA) is an effective way to distinguish frequency hopping networks[1]. The algorithms in [1-3] regard frequency hopping signals as narrowband signals, these methods cannot deal with underdetermined case. In [4], DOA of frequency hopping signals is estimated via the particle filter with a temporal autoregressive moving average (ARMA) model, however, this method applies to over-determined case. In [5], the DOAs of FH signals are obtained by estimating underdetermined mixing matrix via k-means clustering algorithm in time frequency (TF) domain, but k-means algorithm cannot achieve satisfactory performance [6]. In this paper, a new DOAs estimation method is proposed which includes two steps .The first step is estimating mixing matrix and the second step is estimating hopping frequencies. Subspace projection is an effective method to recovery non-stationary source in time frequency domain[7, 8], however, the performance is not satisfactory. To accurately estimate multiple FH signals DOAs in underdetermined condition, an improved subspace projection algorithm is proposed by utilizing STFT and estimating mixing matrix. In this paper, mixing matrix is estimated by tensor decomposition algorithm in [6], and then an improved subspace projection method is exploited to estimate frequencies via recovery FH signals based on STFT. Finally, DOAs can be obtained with the mixing matrix and hopping frequencies.

II. PROBLEM FOMULATION

Suppose that there are N FH signals denoted by $\mathbf{s}(t)=[\mathbf{s}_1(t),\ldots,\mathbf{s}_N(t)]$ impinging onto a uniform linear array (ULA) with M elements, and the signals are segmented into several pure hops according to hop timing estimation. It is assumed that $\mathbf{y}(t)=[\mathbf{y}_1(t),\ldots,\mathbf{y}_M(t)]$ are M received signals. Then the underdetermined problem can be expressed as

$$\mathbf{y}_m(t)=\sum_{n=1}^{N}a_{m,n}\mathbf{s}_n(t)+\mathbf{v}_m(t) \tag{1}$$

where $\mathbf{v}_m(t)$ is an additive Gaussian white noise, $a_{m,n}$ is nth column of mth row element in mixing matrix. For ULA, $a_{m,n}$ is written as

$$a_{m,n}=e^{-j2\pi f_n(m-1)d\cos\theta_n/c} \tag{2}$$

where c is the speed of light, f_n and θ_n are nth FH signals hopping frequency and DOA respectively. The DOAs of FH signals can be successfully estimated by estimating mixing matrix and corresponding hopping frequencies. Mixing matrix can be estimated via tensor decomposition in [6]. However the column order of mixing matrix is indeterminate, so it is an effective way to recovery FH signals to estimate corresponding hopping frequencies.

III. PROPOSED WORK

The STFT of (1) is shown as follows

$$\mathbf{Y}(t,f)=\mathbf{A}\mathbf{S}(t,f)+\mathbf{V}(t,f) \tag{3}$$

where $\mathbf{Y}(t,f)$, $\mathbf{S}(t,f)$, and $\mathbf{V}(t,f)$ are STFT of $\mathbf{y}(t)$, $\mathbf{s}(t)$, and $\mathbf{v}(t)$ respectively. The method in [7] assumes that there are no more than M active sources at each TF point. However, it does not consider redundant signals' effect at each TF point. The number of active sources at each TF points are always estimated as M in [7] so the method in [7] causes additional error. In this paper, it is supposed that there are m ($m \le M$ is a variable number) active FH signals at each TF point, and corresponding mixing matrix column vectors are denoted by $[\mathbf{a}_{k_1},\dots,\mathbf{a}_{k_m}]$, where $\{k_1,\dots,k_m\} \in \{1,\dots,N\}$, $k_1 < k_2 < \cdots < k_m$. The m active FH signals at (t_a, f_a) can be detected by the following:

$$[\mathbf{a}_{k_1},\dots,\mathbf{a}_{k_m}] = \arg\min_{k_1,\dots,k_m}\left\{\|\mathbf{Q}_m\mathbf{Y}(t_a,f_a)\| < \varepsilon\|\mathbf{Y}(t_a,f_a)\|\right\}$$
$$\hat{\mathbf{S}}_m(t_a,f_a) = \left(\mathbf{A}_m^H\mathbf{A}_m\right)^{-1}\mathbf{A}_m\mathbf{Y}(t_a,f_a) \tag{4}$$

where $\mathbf{Q}_m = \mathbf{I} - \mathbf{A}_m\left(\mathbf{A}_m^H\mathbf{A}_m\right)^{-1}\mathbf{A}_m$, $\mathbf{A}_m = \left[\mathbf{a}_{k_1},\dots,\mathbf{a}_{k_m}\right]$ .is $M \times m$ sub-matrix of mixing matrix $\mathbf{A}$, ε is a small positive value relative to redundant weak signals. Corresponding Hopping frequencies of mixing matrix columns are estimated by

$$[f_1,\dots,f_N] = \arg\max_{f}\left\{\hat{\mathbf{S}}(t,f)\right\} \tag{5}$$

Then, θ_n can be estimated as follows:

$$\theta_n = \arg\cos\frac{\mathrm{Re}(a_{2,n}) \times c}{2\pi f_n} \tag{6}$$

The proposed algorithm can be summarized as follows:

Input: Mixing matrix $\mathbf{A}$ and received FH signals $\mathbf{y}$
Step1: Estimate each TH point active signals by (4)
Step2: Calculate corresponding hopping frequencies of mixing matrix columns by (5)
Step3: Calculate DOAs by (2) and (6)
Output : FH signals DOAs estimation $\theta_n, n = 1,\dots,N$

IV. SIMULATION RESULTS

In this section, numerical experiments are tested in underdetermined ($M < N$) case. Suppose that Six FH signals impinging on a four-element ULA from angles $\boldsymbol{\theta} = [20^\circ, 30^\circ, 44^\circ, 38^\circ, 56^\circ, 15^\circ]$ (in Fig.1), $\boldsymbol{\theta} = \left[20.17^\circ, 20.26^\circ, 20.34^\circ, 20.49^\circ, 20.58^\circ, 20.66^\circ\right]$ (in Fig.2). The proposed method correctly estimates DOAs as shown in Fig.1 and in Fig.2 under noiseless condition. The method in [7] under the same condition fails as shown in Fig.1, and when DOAs are similar, the method in [7] does not achieve satisfactory performance which is shown in Fig.2.

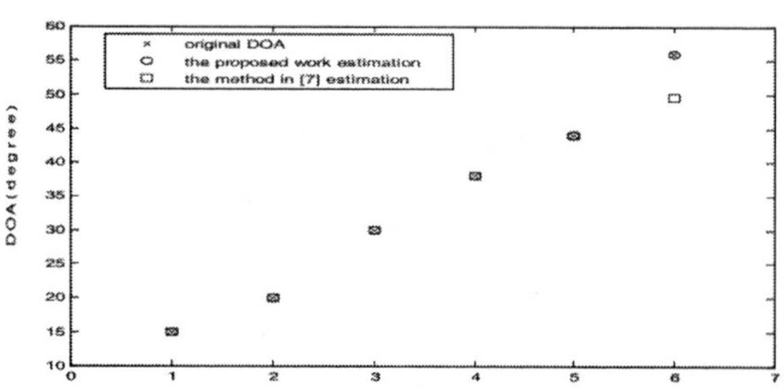

Fig 1. DOA estimation based on the proposed method and the method in [7]

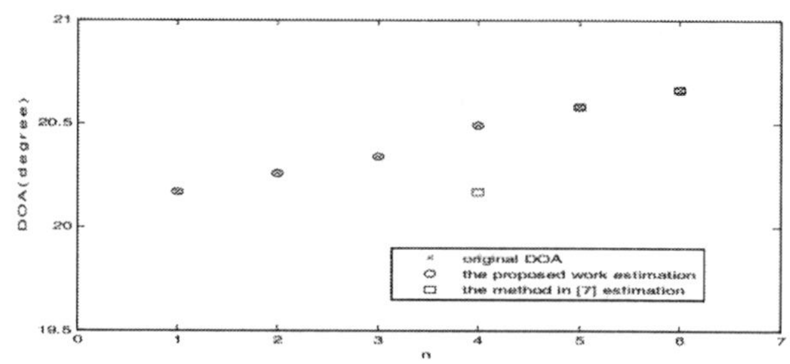

Fig 2. DOA accuracy of the proposed method and the method in [7]

V. CONCLUSION

An improved subspace projection method based STFT has been proposed to estimate FH signals DOAs in underdetermined condition in this paper. To enhance the estimation accuracy, active FH signals at each TF point is estimated. The simulations demonstrate that the proposed scheme can successfully estimate original FH signals DOAs with noiseless condition. In future work, the noise case DOAs estimation will be discussed.

ACKNOWLEDGMENT

This paper is funded by the International Exchange Program of Harbin Engineering University for Innovation-oriented Talents Cultivation. This work is also supported by the National Natural Science Foundation of China (Grant No.61172159) and the Fundamental Research Funds for the Central Universities (HEUCFT1101).

REFERENCES

[1] X. Liu, N. D. Sidiropoulos, and A. Swami, "Blind High-Resolution Localization and Tracking of Multiple Frequency Hopped Signals," *Signal Processing, IEEE Transactions on*, pp. 889-901, 2002.

[2] X. Liu, N. D. Sidiropoulos, and A. Swami, "Joint hop timing and DOA estimation for multiple noncoherent frequency hopped signals," in *Sensor Array and Multichannel Signal Processing Workshop Proceedings*, 2002, pp. 164-168.

[3] X. Liu, J. Li, and X. Ma, "An EM Algorithm for Blind Hop Timing Estimation of Multiple FH Signals Using an Array System With Bandwidth Mismatch," *IEEE Transactions on Vehicular Technology*, pp. 2545-2554, 2007.

[4] Z.-C. Sha, Z.-M. Liu, Z.-T. Huang, and Y.-Y. Zhou, "Online Hop Timing Detection and Frequency Estimation of Multiple FH Signals," *ETRI Journal*, pp. 748-756, 2013.

[5] W. Fu, Y. Hei, and X. Li, "UBSS and blind parameters estimation algorithms for synchronous or thogonal FH signals," *Systems Engineering & Electronics Journal of*, vol. 25, pp. 911-920, 2014.

[6] C. Zhang and Y. Wang, "Frequency hopping radar signals blind separation using tensor analysis in time domain," in *Ieee/aces International Conference on Wireless Information Technology and Systems*, 2016.

[7] F. B. Lu, Z. T. Huang, and W. L. Jiang, "Underdetermined blind separation of time-delayed non-stationary signal based on single source region in the time-frequency domain," *Acta Electronica Sinica*, vol. 39, pp. 854-858, 2011.

[8] A. Aissa-El-Bey, N. Linh-Trung, K. Abed-Meraim, A. Belouchrani, and Y. Grenier, "Underdetermined Blind Separation of Nondisjoint Sources in the Time-Frequency Domain," *IEEE Transactions on Signal Processing*, vol. 55, pp. 897-907, 2007.

A Hybrid LVD-HAF Method of Quadratic Frequency-Modulated Signals

Fulong Jing*, Weijian Si and Shuhong Jiao
College of Information and Communication Engineering,
Harbin Engineering University,
Harbin, 150001, China
*jing_fl@hrbeu.edu.cn

***Abstract*—This paper describes a novel algorithm for estimating the parameters of a quadratic frequency modulated (QFM) signal under low signal to noise ratio (SNR). The proposed method combines the frequency domain method called Lv's Distribution and the time domain method called high order ambiguity function (HAF) to improve the estimation performance. The algorithm is following two stage approaches. First, the phase differentiation is applied on the observed QFM signal to produce a linear frequency signal (LFM). Second, the parameters of LFM are estimated by the LVD, which is simple and can be easily implemented using the complex multiplication. The main significance of the LVD is to convert a 1-D LFM into a 2-D single-frequency signal. Through simulations and analyses, we verify the effectiveness of the Hybrid LVD-HAF algorithm.**

Keywords*—*quadratic frequency modulated (QFM) signal; high-order ambiguity function (HAF); Lv's Distribution (LVD); parameter estimation.

I. INTRODUCTION

The QFM signals (also known as cubic phase signals) presented in this paper are represented as a form

$$s(t)=\sum_{i=1}^{K}A_i e^{j2\pi(a_{i,1}t+\frac{1}{2}a_{i,2}t^2+\frac{1}{6}a_{i,3}t^3)}+z(t) \tag{1}$$

where A is the constant amplitude , K is the number of signal components, $z(t)$ is the additive complex white Gaussian noise with a variance of σ^2 and a_1 、 a_2 、 a_3 denote the centroid frequency, the chirp rate, and the quadratic chirp rate, respectively.

Quadratic frequency modulated signal is an important nonlinear module which exists widely in nature. It is applied in communication, radar, and sonar fields. Three practical applications of the QFM signal are described in [1-3]. The first is passive intelligent radar surveillance. The second application is in the processing of echolocation signals from brown bats. The third is in the imaging of inverse synthetic aperture radar (ISAR) for moving targets.

In this paper, an improved method is proposed which is called Hybrid LVD-HAF. Phase differentiation (PD) [4] is widely used to reduce signal order. In the Hybrid LVD-HAF method, it is applied on the QFM signal to produce a LFM signal, and then we use a new frequency domain method which is called LVD [5] to estimate the LFM parameters. The LVD algorithm is simple and fast, it is only requires a two-dimensional (2-D) Fourier transform of a parametric scaled symmetric instantaneous autocorrelation function (PSIAF). It has been verified effective in noise environment and can be easily implemented by using the complex multiplications and fast Fourier transforms (FFT).

II. PRELIMINARY

A. Brief review of HAF

Suppose that the Q th-order polynomial-phase signals (PPS) $y(t)$, and the Q th-order PD is defined as

$$PD^Q[t;\tau_1,\tau_2,...,\tau_Q]=PD^{Q-1}[t+\tau_Q;\tau_1,\tau_2,...,\tau_{Q-1}]$$
$$\times[PD^{Q-1}[t-\tau_Q;\tau_1,\tau_2,...,\tau_{Q-1}]]^* \tag{2}$$

where $\tau_i(i=1,2,\cdots,Q)$ are lag parameters. After substituting $y(t)$ into (2), the PPS order is reduced, and PPS will result in a complex sinusoid. Then, a_p can be estimated by Fourier transform (FT), which is referred to as the HAF. All parameters are estimated by repeating the procedure and dechirped.

B. Brief review of LVD

Given a LFM signal $x(t)$, and its PSIAF is defined by:

$$R_x^C(t,\tau)=x(t+\frac{\tau+a}{2})x^*(t-\frac{\tau+a}{2})$$
$$=\sum_{i=0}^{K-1}A_i^2\exp(j2\pi f_i(\tau+a)+j2\pi\gamma_i(\tau+a)t)+R_{cross}^C \tag{3}$$

where * denotes complex conjugation, a denotes a constant time-delay, R_{cross}^C denotes cross terms, f_i and γ_i denote the centroid frequency, and the chirp rate, respectively. It is well known that time variable t is coupled with lag variable τ in (3). And the coupling is removed by introducing a so-called keystone operator. The scaling operator Γ is defined by:

$$\Gamma[G(t,\tau)]\rightarrow G(\frac{t_n}{h(\tau+a)},\tau) \tag{4}$$

where G is the phase function of (t,τ). By the performing 2-D Fourier transformation on (4), which is applying the scaling operator Γ to (3), with respect to t and τ ,the parameters is estimated in the centroid frequency and chirp rate (CFCR) domain. As $K=2$, it is easily seen that two sharp peaks which represent the two LFM components with small values of cross-terms exist in Fig. 1.

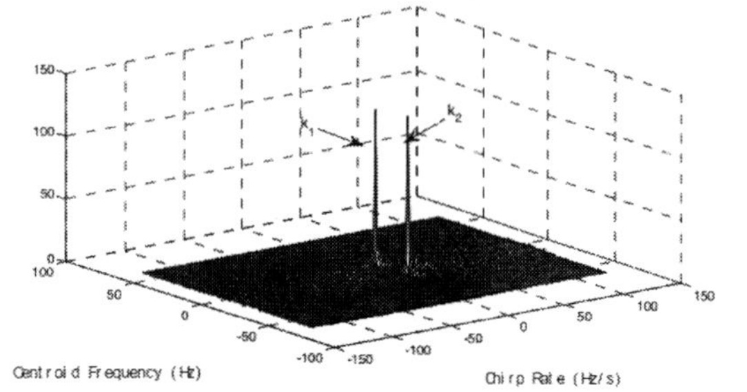

Fig.1. LVD of a signal containing two LFM components.

III. Hybrid LVD-HAF Method for Parameters Estimation

The Hybrid LVD-HAF algorithm is divided into two stage approach. First, we apply first-order PD on QFM to make a third order signal become a second order signal, it means that we obtain a LFM signal after that. And then we use the LVD method to estimate the parameters of LFM signal.

The first-order PD is representation as:

$$PD^1(t;\tau_1)=x(t+\tau_1)x^*(t-\tau_1) \tag{5}$$

Substituting (1) into (5), we obtain

$$PD^1(t;\tau_1)=\sum_i^K A_i^2 e^{j2\pi(2a_{i,1}\tau_1+2a_{i,3}\tau_1^3+4a_{i,2}\tau_1 t+6a_{i,3}\tau_1 t^2)} + PD^1_{cross}(t;\tau_1) \tag{6}$$

where $PD^1_{cross}(t;\tau_1)$ denotes the cross term. It is easily seen that (6) is a LFM signal as τ_1 being a constant. According to [4], the optimal τ_1 yields:

$$\tau_1^{opt}\approx\lceil(-0.006P+0.107)N\rceil \tag{7}$$

where P is the signal order, and N is the signal length. Hence the parameters a_3 and a_2 can be estimated by using the LVD method. The parameter a_1 can be estimated by the dechirp signal $y_1(t)=y(t)\times e^{-j2\pi(\frac{1}{2}a_2t^2+\frac{1}{6}a_3t^3)}$ and Fourier transform according to searching the maximum magnitude in the frequency domain.

IV. Simulation Results

In this section, the Hybrid LVD-HAF algorithm is applied to a QFM signal with additive, white Gaussian noise. Parameters of QFM are set as follow: $A=1$, $a_1=40$, $a_2=20$, $a_3=20$, $N=624$, and sampling rate is 256Hz. The signal is contaminated with the zero-mean white Gaussian noise. For each SNR value, 200 Monte Carlo experiments are performed, and the measured MSEs for the parameter estimations are shown in Fig. 2(a)-(b).

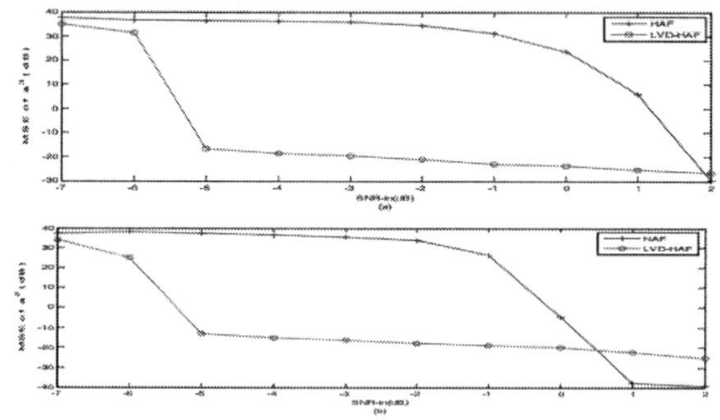

Fig.2. (a) MSE of a_2 estimation. (b) MSE of a_3 estimation.

It shows that if $SNRin\le 0.8dB$, the Hybrid LVD-HAF algorithm outperforms HAF algorithm in [6]. It means that the Hybrid LVD-HAF method is superior to the HAF method under low SNR. The parameter a_1 can be estimated by the dechirp technique and the Fourier transform.

V. Conclusion

A fast and precise algorithm for estimating the parameters of a QFM signal has been proposed in this paper. The proposed method combines the LVD and HAF, and it can not only improve antinoise performance, but also reduce the error propagation. Simulation results demonstrate that the proposed method can achieve better performance than the standard HAF approach.

Acknowledgment

This paper is funded by the International Exchange Program of Harbin Engineering University for Innovation-oriented Talents Cultivation. This work is also partially supported by the Aeronautical Science Foundation of China (Grant No. 201401P6001) and the Natural Science Foundation of Heilongjiang Province of China (No. QC2016085).

References

[1] S. Peleg and B. Porat, "Linear FM signal parameter estimation from discrete-time observations," *IEEE Transactions on Aerospace & Electronic Systems*, vol. 27, pp. 607-616, 1991.
[2] P. O'Shea, "A fast algorithm for estimating the parameters of a quadratic FM signal," *IEEE Transactions on Signal Processing*, vol. 52, pp. 385-393, 2004.
[3] Y. Wang and Y. Jiang, "Inverse Synthetic Aperture Radar Imaging of Maneuvering Target Based on the Product Generalized Cubic Phase Function," *Geoscience & Remote Sensing Letters IEEE*, vol. 8, pp. 958-962, 2011.
[4] Djurovic, I., Simeunovic, M., Djukanovic, S., *et al.*, "A Hybrid CPF-HAF Estimation of Polynomial-Phase Signals: Detailed Statistical Analysis," *Signal Processing IEEE Transactions on*, vol. 60, pp. 5010-5023, 2012.
[5] X. Lv, G. Bi, C. Wan, and M. Xing, "Lv's Distribution: Principle, Implementation, Properties, and Performance," *IEEE Transactions on Signal Processing*, vol. 59, pp. 3576-3591, 2011.
[6] S. Barbarossa and V. Petrone, "Analysis of polynomial-phase signals by the integrated generalized ambiguity function," *IEEE Transactions on Signal Processing*, vol. 45, pp. 316-327, 1997.

Equilibrium shape of ferrofluid in the uniform external field

Michael Grinfeld
The U.S. Army Research Laboratory
Aberdeen Proving Ground, USA
e-mail: michael.greenfield4.civ@mail.mil

Pavel Grinfeld
Department of Mathematics
Drexel University
Philadelphia, USA

***Abstract*—It is well-known that morphology of magnetic or electric ferrofluids is extremely sensitive to the applied external electromagnetic fields. Even in the static regimes, they demonstrate a variety of qualitative and quantitative transformations often mentioned as free surface instabilities. That makes their computational modeling rather challenging. Therefore, for the sake of validation and verification, there is a need for having exact solutions. Modelers noticed that quite often isolated ferrofluids take on the shape of a prolate spheroid. So, there were several claims that a consistent theory allows to prove that isolated drop of ferrofluid exposed to a uniform field, indeed, has a shape of a spheroid. In this paper we analyze this problem one more time using a special technique of the analysis of the equilibrium shape, which traces back to the papers of Eshelby.**

Keywords—ferrofluids; Maxwell stress tensor; ellipsoidal solutions; thermodynamics; equilibrium shapes

I. Introduction

Consider a finite chunk of ferrofluid exposed to a uniform magnetic field as shown in the Figure 1.

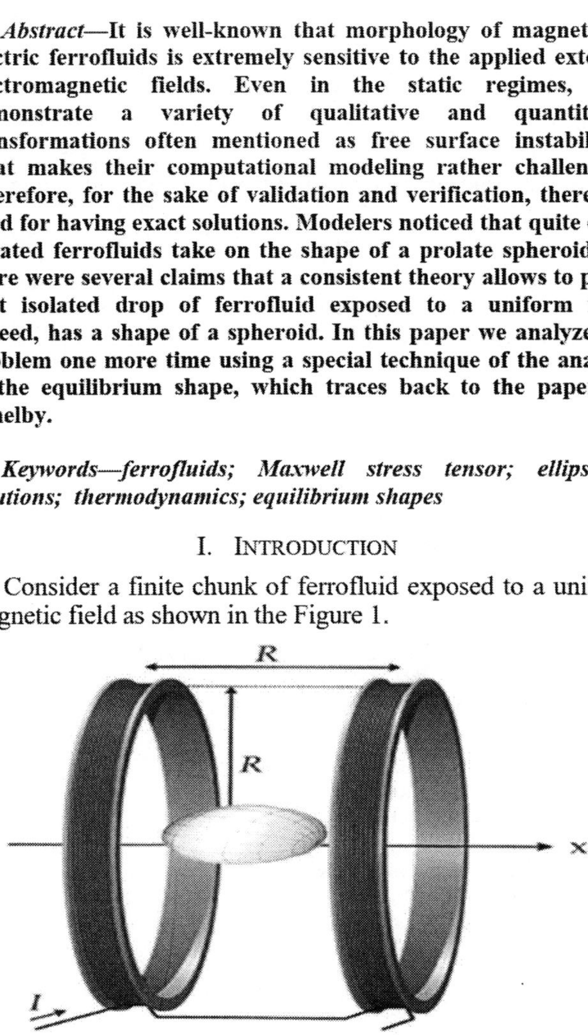

Figure. Equilibrium shape of a ferrofluid inside the Helmholtz coil takes on the shape of a prolate ellipsoid.

(image taken from a public domain of Wikipedia https://commons.wikimedia.org/w/index.php?curid=6648)

There is no doubt that the shape is, indeed, very close to the shape of a spheroid. Several authors claimed that this fact can be established on the basis of a rigorous theory, like it was done for the equilibrium shape of rotating self-gravitating uniform incompressible liquid (see the Chandrasekhar's classics [1] and multiple references therein.) In what concerns the magnetic ferrofluids in the uniform magnetic fields, the interested readers can find the approaches and further references in the monograph [2]. Other references, relating to ellipsoidal solutions in the problems of electromagnetism, can be found in the publications [3]-[5].

Despite all these remarkable efforts and progress, the problem of equilibrium shape of ferrofluid is far of being exhaustively explored. There are several reasons for the mandatory further improvements. For instance, the master systems, describing dynamics of ferrofluid, face various objections [6], [7]. Then, the problem of equations of state also needs further studies and for a long time remains to be the object of hot debates. From that standpoint it seems reasonable to limit ourselves with static (thermodynamic) approaches, especially when the problem under study is of a static (equilibrium) nature up-front. There are several sensitive problems, relating to the statics and thermodynamic aspects of the ponderomotive forces in substances with polar interaction: we recently discussed them in [8]-[12]. Nonetheless, overall, the *static* approaches are much older and face less objections that the *dynamics* of electromagnetic media. In this paper we will be analyzing the problem of equilibrium shape using directly the static approach (i.e. not deriving static system from the more questionable dynamic system of magnetohydrodynamics). Also, when considering the ellipsoidal configurations of ferrofluid, instead of the classical approaches of [1]-[5], we follow the method suggested in 1950s by Eshelby [13].

II. The Boundary Value Problem to be Solved

We assume that the ferrofluid is maintained at fixed temperature, and let ψ be the free energy density at this temperature. Because the fluid is assumed incompressible, the free energy density is the function of the polarization vector $\vec{P}$ only.

When there is no current of free charges, the system of electrostatic and magnetostatic equilibrium are the same [4]. Below we stick to the electrostatic terminology.

The boundary value problem, allowing to calculate the equilibrium shape of incompressible ferrofluid, includes the following equations and boundary conditions:

i) within the fluid

$$\vec{D} = \vec{E} + 4\pi\vec{P} \quad (1)$$

$$\nabla \cdot \vec{D} = 0 \quad (2)$$

$$\vec{E} = \psi_{\vec{P}} \quad (3)$$

ii) within vacuum

$$\nabla \cdot \vec{E} = 0 \quad (4)$$

iii) at the interface liquid vacuum

$$[\varphi]_-^+ = 0, \ \left[\vec{D}\right]_-^+ \cdot \vec{N} = 0 \quad (5)$$

$$\psi\left(\vec{P}\right) + \left[\frac{1}{8\pi}\left|\vec{E}\right|^2 - \frac{1}{4\pi}\vec{D}\cdot\vec{E}\right]_-^+ + \frac{1}{4\pi}\left[\left(\vec{D}\cdot\vec{N}\right)\left(\vec{E}\cdot\vec{N}\right)\right]_-^+ = -\Lambda \quad (6)$$

iv) at infinity

$$\vec{E} \to \vec{E}_\infty \quad (7)$$

In the combined system (1-7), φ is the scalar field potential; $\vec{E} = -\nabla\varphi$ is the electrostatic field; $\vec{D}$ is the displacement vector, respectively; $\vec{N}$ is the unit vector to the free external boundary; $\vec{E}_\infty$ is the external field, Λ is an unknown constant (the Lagrange multiplier, which can be determined from the condition of a given total mass of the ferrofluid).

Equations (1,3,5,7) comprise a standard problem of electrostatics; (2) is the thermodynamic identity implied by the Gibbs minimum principle or equivalent principle of total energy minimum (compare with [3-7]). The equation (6) is of the key importance: this is the additional equation allowing to determine equilibrium shape of the ferrofluid (compare with [8-12]).

Following [10, 13], and we will be looking for the fluid's boundary in the shape of ellipsoid; we will get the following presentation of the Cartesian component of the electrostatic field:

$$E_i = -A^k \nabla_i \nabla_k \omega + E_{i\infty} \quad (8)$$

where ω is the Newtonian potential of the field of the same ellipsoid having the mass density equal to 1, and A^k is a constant unknown vector. Both, the exact shape of the ellipsoid and the constant vector A^k have to be determined from the boundary conditions.

The Newtonian potential inside the ellipsoid is very simple

$$\omega = C_0 - \frac{1}{2}Y_{ij}z^i z^j \quad (9)$$

where C_0 and Y_{ij} are the constant scalar and symmetric tensor satisfying the condition

$$Y_{.i}^{i} = 4\pi \quad (10)$$

Using (9) we arrive at the following very simple relationship of the electrostatic field inside the ellipsoid:

$$E_i = A^k Y_{ik} + E_{i\infty}. \quad (11)$$

The field outside the ellipsoid is way more complex. Tensor Y_{ij} can be easily expressed in terms of the ellipsoid's semi-axes and orientation; and vice versa, when the tensor Y_{ij} is known we can determine the geometry of the ellipsoid.

In the full paper, we explore the conditions when all equations of the system (1-7) can be satisfied.

REFERENCES

1. S. Chandrasekhar, Ellipsoidal Figures of Equilibrium—an Historical Account. University of Chicago, 1969.
2. V.G Bashtovoy, B.M. Berkovsky, A.N. Vislovich, Introduction to Thermomechanics of Magnetic Fluids, Hemisphere Publishing Corporation: New York, 1988.
3. J.A. Stratton, Electromagnetic Theory. McGraw-Hill; 1941.
4. L.D. Landau, E.M. Lifshitz EM. Electrodynamics of Continuous Media. New York: Pergamon; 1963. A.I.
5. A.I. Akhiezer, V.G. Bar'yakhtar and S.V. Peletminsky, Spin Waves, Interscience, New York, 1967.
6. R.E. Rosenzweig, Introduction to Ferrohydrodynamics, Cambridge University Press, 1967.
7. A. Kovetz, The Principles of Electromagnetic Theory, Oxford University Press, 2000.
8. P. Grinfeld, "Morphological instability of liquid metallic nuclei condensing on charged inhomogeneities," Phys. Rev. Lett 2001; 87(9):095701.
9. P. Grinfeld, M. Grinfeld, "Thermodynamic aspects of equilibrium shape and growth of crystalline films with electromechanical interaction," Ferroelectrics, vol. 342, pp. 89—100, 2006.
10. P. Grinfeld, "Morphological instability of the dielectric Thomson nuclei," Phys Rev. B 2010;81(18):184110.
11. M. Grinfeld, P. Grinfeld, "A variational approach to electrostatics of polarizable heterogeneous substances," Adv. Math. Phys. 2015. Article ID 659127.
12. J.D. Eshelby, "The determination of the elastic field of an ellipsoidal inclusion, and related problems", Proceedings of the Royal Society A, **241** (1226): 376–396, 1957.
13. M.A. Grinfeld, Morphology, Stability, and Morphogenesis of Dipole Aggregates, Proc. Estonian Acad. Sci. Eng., vol. 5(2), 1999.

Scattering by a Chiral Elliptic Cylinder Placed in Another Infinite Chiral Medium

A-K. Hamid

Department of Electrical and Computer Engineering, University of Sharjah
P. O. Box 27272, Sharjah, United Arab Emirates
akhamid@sharjah.ac.ae

***Abstract* — Analytic solution is presented to the problem of scattering of a plane wave from a chiral elliptic cylinder placed in another infinite chiral medium, using the method of separation of variables. The incident, scattered as well as the transmitted electromagnetic fields are expressed in terms of appropriate angular and radial Mathieu functions with expansion coefficients. The scattered and transmitted field expansion coefficients are determined by imposing the boundary conditions at the surface of the chiral-chiral elliptic cylinder. Results are presented graphically for the normalized scattering widths for elliptic cylinders of different sizes and chiral materials to show the effects of these on scattering cross widths.**

Keywords — Scattering elliptic cylinder, chira-lchiral material, Mathieu functions, RSC.

I. INTRODUCTION

In a lossless chiral medium, a linearly polarized wave undergoes a rotation of its polarization as it propagates. For chiral cylinders, these properties result in a coupling of the TM and TE polarizations. Analytic and numerical solutions describing chiral media are given by [1-5]. Recent work on the scattering and radiation by elliptical structures is given for lossy and lossless dielectric material by [6-7].

The elliptic cylinder is a geometry that has been extensively analyzed in the literature due to its ability to produce cylindrical cross sections of different shapes by changing the axial ratio of the ellipse. Furthermore, since the elliptic cylindrical coordinate system is one of the coordinate systems in which the wave equation is separable, solutions to problems involving elliptic cylinders can be obtained in analytical form.

In this paper we present the solution to the scattering of a plane wave by chiral elliptic cylinder of arbitrary axial ratio and placed in a different infinite chiral medium while the earlier work in [7] the chiral cylinder was embedded in air. The present will require expanding the fields in two different chiral regions and the solution will provide more parameters to control the normalized bistatic scattering width compared to [7].

II. FORMULATION

Consider a uniform plane electromagnetic wave incident from chiral medium on an infinitely long elliptic cylinder with different chiral material of major axis length a and minor axis length b, at an angle φ_i with respect to the positive x axis of a Cartesian co-ordinate system located at the centre of the cylinder

For a TM polarized plane wave of amplitude E_0, the axial component of the incident electric field can be written as

$$E_z^i = E_0\, e^{jk_{R1}\rho\cos(\varphi-\varphi_i)} \tag{1}$$

where the right circularly polarized wave number is given by [7]

$$k_{R1} = \frac{\omega\sqrt{\mu_{c1}\varepsilon_{c1}}}{1+\gamma_1\omega\sqrt{\mu_{c1}\varepsilon_{c1}}} \tag{2}$$

γ_1 is the chiral admittance of the external chiral medium, μ_{c1} is the permeability and ε_{c1} is the permittivity of the external chiral medium and ρ, φ are the polar coordinates.

The incident Electric field may be expanded in terms of angular and radial Mathieu functions of the first type as

$$\mathbf{E}^i = \sum_m^{\infty} A_{\substack{em\\om}}\left[\mathbf{N}^{(1)}_{\substack{em\\om}}(k_{R1}) + \mathbf{M}^{(1)}_{\substack{em\\om}}(k_{R1})\right] \tag{3}$$

$$A_{\substack{em\\om}} = E_0 j^m \frac{\sqrt{8\pi}}{N_{\substack{em\\om}}(c_{R1})} S_{\substack{em\\om}}(c_{R1}, \cos\varphi_i) \tag{4}$$

$$N_{\substack{em\\om}}(c_{R1}) = \int_0^{2\pi} [S_{\substack{em\\om}}(c_{R1}, \eta)]^2 dv \tag{5}$$

where $c_{R1} = k_{R1}F$. The summation over m starts from 0 for even Mathieu functions while 1 for odd Mathieu functions.

Using Maxwell's equations, the magnetic field $\mathbf{H}^i$ can now be expanded in terms of angular and radial Mathieu functions as

As the elliptic cylinder is made up of chiral and surrounded by another chiral medium, the scattered ($\mathbf{E}^s, \mathbf{H}^s$) and transmitted ($\mathbf{E}^t, \mathbf{H}^t$) electromagnetic fields will have both cross-polarized and co-polarized components. The unknown expansion coefficients may be obtained by enforcing the tangential boundary conditions at the surface of the chiral-chiral elliptic cylinder, which may be expressed mathematically as

$$E_z^i + E_z^s = E_z^t \tag{6}$$

$$E_\eta^i + E_\eta^s = E_\eta^t \tag{7}$$

$$H_z^i + H_z^s = H_z^t \tag{8}$$

$$H_\eta^i + H_\eta^s = H_\eta^t \tag{9}$$

Substituting the appropriate expressions and applying the orthogonal property of the angular Mathieu, writing the system of equations in matrix form and solving for the unknown coefficients using matrix inversion.

III. NUMERICAL RESULTS

The obtained numerical results are presented as normalized echo pattern widths for chiral elliptic cylinder embedded in another infinite chiral material of different sizes, axial ratios, permittivities and permeabilities. We selected $ka = 0.5$, axial ratio 1.001, ε_{c1}=1.0, μ_{c1}=1.0, $k\gamma_1 = 0.0$ are the parameters of outside region, ε_{c2}=4.0, μ_{c2}=2.0, $k\gamma_2 = 0.15$ are the parameters of the cylinder, and $\varphi_i = 180^o$. To validate the analysis and the software used for calculating the results, we computed the normalized echo pattern widths for chiral circular cylinder. The results are in full agreement, verifying the accuracy of the analysis as well as the software used for obtaining the results [1,7].

Fig. 1 Normalized bistatic scattering width versus scattering angle for co (a) and cross polarized (b) chiral elliptic cylinder $ka=0.5$, $kb=0.25$, ε_{c1}=2.5, μ_{c1}=1.0, $k\gamma_1 = 0.1$, ε_{c2}=4.0, μ_{c2}=2.0, $k\gamma_2 = 0.15$ and $\varphi_i = 180^o$ The co and cross polarized patterns are close to each other compared when the cylinder is located in free space..

IV. CONCLUSION

An analytical solution to the problem of scattering of a plane electromagnetic wave by a chiral elliptic cylinder placed in another chiral material presented using the method of separation of variables. Results have been presented in the form of normalized bistatic chiral elliptic to show the effects of different parameters on scattering from elliptic cylinders. It was shown that the presence of two different chiral materials could significantly influence the co- and cross when it is compared where the cylinder is located in free space.

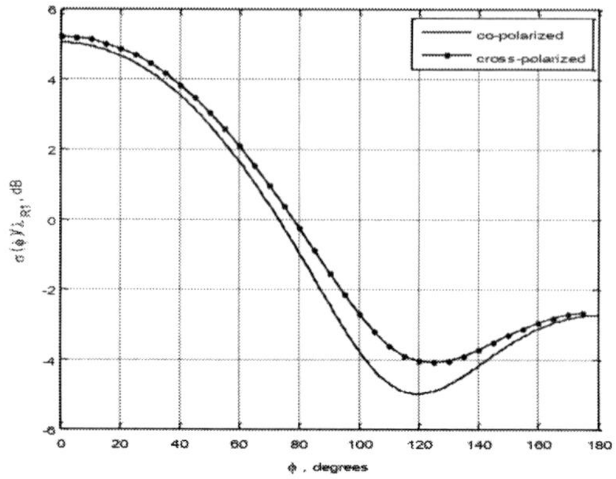

Fig. 1 Normalized bistatic scattering width versus scattering angle for co (a) and cross polarized (b) chiral elliptic cylinder $ka=0.5$, $kb=0.25$, ε_{c1}=2.5, μ_{c1}=1.0, $k\gamma_1 = 0.1$, ε_{c2}=4.0, μ_{c2}=2.0, $k\gamma_2 = 0.15$ and $\varphi_i = 180^o$.

ACKNOWLEDGMENT

Prof. A-K. Hamid wishes to acknowledge the support provided by the University of Sharjah, U.A.E.

REFERENCES

[1] M. S. Kluskens and E. H. Newman, "Scattering by a multilayer chiral cylinder", IEEE Trans. Antennas Propagat., vol. 39, pp.91 - 96 , 1991.
[2] R. Rojas, "Integral equations for EM scattering by homogeneous /inhomogeneous two-dimensional chiral bodies", Inst. Elect. Eng. Microw., Antennas Propag., vol. 141, pp.385-392 , 1994.
[3] M. A. Al-Kanhal and E. Arvas, "Electromagnetic scattering from a chiral cylinder of arbitrary cross section," IEEE Trans. Antennas Propag., vol. 44, no. 7, pp. 1041–1049, Jul. 1996.
[4] A. Semichaevsky, A. Akyurtlu, D. Kern, D. H. Werner, and M. G. Bray, Novel BI-FDTD approach for the analysis of chiral cylinders and spheres", IEEE Trans. Antennas Propagat., VOL. 54, NO. 3, pp. 925-932, 2006.
[5] S. Shoukat, S. Ahmed, M. Ashraf, A. Syed and Q. Naqvi, "Scattering of electromagnetic plane wave from a chiral cylinder placed in a chiral metamaterials". Journal of Electromagnetic Waves and Applications, Vol. 27, pp. 1127-1135, 2013.
[6] B. N. Khatir, M. Al-Kanhal, and A. Sebak, "Electromagnetic wave scattering by elliptic chiral cylinder," Journal of Electromagnetic Waves and Applications, vol. 20, no. 10, pp. 1377–1390, 2006.
[7] A-K. Hamid, "Scattering by Chiral Lossy Metamaterial Elliptic Cylinders" Applied Computational Electromagnetics Society Journal, vol. 27, pp. 603-609, 2012.

Frequency-Hopping GPR Prospecting of Sparse Scatterers Through Bayesian Compressive Sensing

M. Salucci[1], L. Tenuti[1], G. Oliveri[1,2], A. Massa[1,2]
[1] ELEDIA Research Center (ELEDIA@UniTN - University of Trento)
Trento, Italy
[2] ELEDIA Research Center (ELEDIA@L2S - UMR 8506)
Gif-sur-Yvette, France
andrea.massa@eledia.org

***Abstract*—An innovative ground penetrating radar (GPR) inverse scattering (IS) methodology for imaging *sparse* buried objects is proposed. The developed methodology integrates a customized Bayesian compressive sensing (BCS) solver within a frequency hopping (FH) strategy in order to (*i*) regularize the IS problem by enforcing *sparsity priors* on the unknown scatterers as well as to (*ii*) exploit the multi-chromatic informative content of GPR data. A preliminary numerical benchmark is shown to preliminarily assess the effectiveness of the proposed FH-BCS technique in providing robust and accurate subsurface images.**

***Keywords*—GPR microwave imaging, frequency-hopping, Bayesian compressive sensing**

I. Introduction

Ground penetrating radar (GPR) is widely used for performing non-invasive subsurface investigations in military operations, archaeological studies, as well as civil engineering [1]. However, the lack of accurate, robust and efficient techniques for processing the collected data and retrieving a tomographic image of the subsoil is pushing a lot of research towards the development of GPR inverse scattering (IS) techniques [1]-[3].

When dealing with the GPR-IS problem, a valid countermeasure to the *ill-posedness* and *non-linearity* issues is represented by the availability of wide-band measurements [2],[3]. As a matter of fact, such a frequency diversity allows to inject *additional information* into the inversion process in order to enhance the quality of the retrieved images. Such information can be exploited using both (*i*) multi-frequency (MF) approaches [2], which are based on the inversion of all the multi-chromatic data in a single step, and (*ii*) frequency-hopping (FH) strategies [3], which process each frequency in a cascaded manner, starting from the lowest one. Moreover, it is worth remarking that in many practical scenarios the sparsity of the unknown buried scatterers can be regarded as a *prior information* able to further regularize the GPR-IS problem [4]-[8]. In such a framework, Bayesian compressive sensing (BCS)-based approaches have been shown to be very effective in solving microwave imaging problems in which the unknowns can be represented by few non-null expansion coefficients, once a suitable basis is chosen [4]-[8]. Following this line of reasoning, an innovative FH-based strategy is proposed in this work to exploit the frequency diversity of GPR data, while enforcing *sparsity priors* on the sought unknowns through a customized BCS solver.

II. Mathematical Formulation

Let us consider a two-dimensional (2D) GPR imaging scenario, in which the upper half-space ($y > 0.0$ m) is free-space, while the permittivity and conductivity below the interface ($y < 0.0$ m) are equal to ε_{rb} and σ_b, respectively.

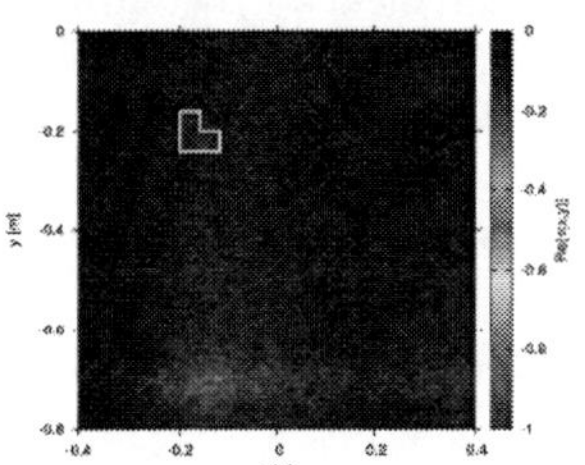

Fig. 1. *L-Shaped scatterer* - Actual contrast distribution.

The electromagnetic properties of a buried domain D are modeled by means of the contrast function, defined as [3]

$$\tau(\mathbf{r}, f) = \frac{\varepsilon_{eq}(\mathbf{r}, f) - \varepsilon_{eqb}}{\varepsilon_0}, \quad \mathbf{r} = (x, y) \in D \tag{1}$$

where $\varepsilon_{eq}(\mathbf{r}, f) = \varepsilon_0 \varepsilon_r(\mathbf{r}) - j\sigma(\mathbf{r})/2\pi f$ is the equivalent permittivity at position $\mathbf{r}$, while $\varepsilon_{eqb} = \varepsilon_0 \varepsilon_{rb} - j\sigma_b/2\pi f$. Under the hypothesis that D is illuminated by V sources radiating wide-band pulses, the time-domain electric field measured by M probes is Fourier-transformed to the frequency domain and H samples are extracted from the computed spectrum. Then, assuming a contrast source formulation and subdividing D into N square cells, the following *data equations* hold true

$$\widetilde{\mathbf{E}}_s^{(h,v)} = \mathbf{G}_{ext}^{(h)} \mathbf{J}^{(h,v)} + \mathbf{n}^{(h,v)}; \; v = 1, \ldots, V, \; h = 1, \ldots, H \tag{2}$$

where $\widetilde{\mathbf{E}}_s^{(h,v)} = \left\{ \Re\left[\widetilde{E}_s^{(h,v)}(\mathbf{r}_m)\right], \Im\left[\widetilde{E}_s^{(h,v)}(\mathbf{r}_m)\right]; m = 1, \ldots, M \right\}$ are scattered field samples, $\mathbf{G}_{ext}^{(h)}$ is the $M \times N$ external Green matrix for the half-space scenario,

$\mathbf{J}^{(h,v)} = \left\{\Re\left[J^{(h,v)}(\mathbf{r}_n)\right], \Im\left[J^{(h,v)}(\mathbf{r}_n)\right]; n = 1,...,N\right\}^T$ contains the unknown equivalent current, while $\mathbf{n}^{(h,v)}$ is an additive noise.

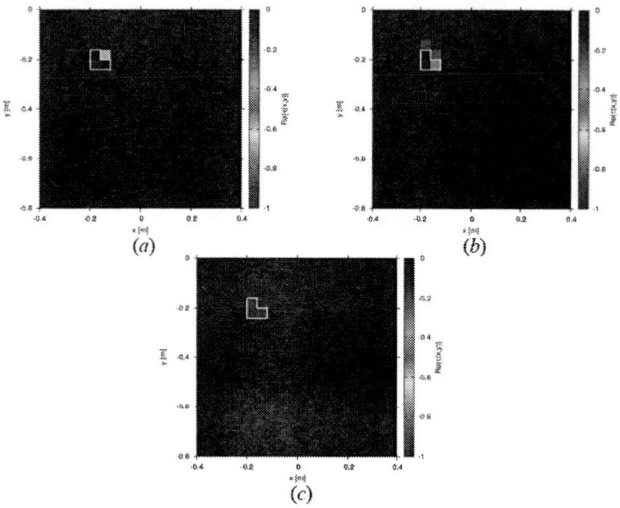

Fig. 2. *L-Shaped scatterer* - Intermediate reconstructions at (*a*) $f^{(1)} = 200$ MHz, (*b*) $f^{(2)} = 250$ MHz and (*c*) $f^{(3)} = 300$ MHz.

The inversion problem at the h-th frequency ($h = 1,...,H$) step is formulated within the BCS framework as [8]

$$\hat{\mathbf{J}}^{(h,v)} = \arg\left\{\max_{\mathbf{J}^{(h,v)}} P\left(\mathbf{J}^{(h,v)} \middle| \widetilde{\mathbf{E}}_s^{(h,v)}\right)\right\}, \; v = 1,...,V \quad (3)$$

subject to the condition that $\mathbf{J}^{(h,v)}$ are correlated over the different *views*, where P is the *posterior* probability. The solution of (3) is found for $v = 1,...,V$ as

$$\hat{\mathbf{J}}^{(h,v)} = \left[diag\left(\hat{\mathbf{a}}^{(h)}\right) + \left(\mathbf{G}_{ext}^{(h)}\right)^* \left(\mathbf{G}_{ext}^{(h)}\right)\right]^{-1} \left(\mathbf{G}_{ext}^{(h)}\right)^* \widetilde{\mathbf{E}}_s^{(h,v)} \quad (4)$$

$\hat{\mathbf{a}}^{(h)}$ being the vector of hyper-parameters estimated through a relevance vector machine (RVM) and $.^*$ the conjugate transpose operator. Following a FH strategy, the *acquired information* in $\hat{\mathbf{a}}^{(h)}$ is exploited to *guide* the solution at the $(h+1)$-th frequency stage (for $h \geq 2$). This is done by (*i*) identifying the region of interest (RoI) $D^{(h)}$ in which the object has been detected and (*ii*) limiting the RVM search space at frequency $f^{(h+1)}$ to just those entries of $\mathbf{a}^{(h+1)}$ corresponding to the $N^{(h)}$ cells belonging to $D^{(h)}$. Once the contrast sources have been retrieved ($h = 1,...,H$), the final reconstruction of (1) is obtained by exploiting the GPR-IS *state equation* and averaging over the different views ($v = 1,...,V$).

III. Preliminary Numerical Assessment

Let us consider a *L-shaped* scatterer ($\varepsilon_r = 3.0$, $\sigma = 10^{-3}$ S/m – Fig. 1) in a square investigation domain (side $L_D = 8.0$ m, $\varepsilon_{rb} = 4.0$ and $\sigma_b = 10^{-3}$ S/m). By simulating the GPR scenario through the *GprMax2D* simulator [9], a set of $V = 20$ transmitters above the interface is used to image D, while $M = 19$ probes co-located with the sources are used to collect the scattered data. Figure 2 shows the retrieved profiles of the contrast function at three successive frequency steps [i.e., $f^{(1)} = 200$ MHz – Fig. 2(*a*), $f^{(2)} = 250$ MHz – Fig. 2(*b*) and $f^{(3)} = 300$ MHz – Fig. 2(*c*)], when considering an additive white Gaussian noise on the collected time-domain total field characterized by a signal-to-noise ratio equal to $SNR = 50$ dB. As it can be observed, the quality of the reconstruction significantly improves from the lowest frequency until convergence, verifying the effectiveness of the proposed FH strategy to gradually improve the estimation capabilities of the BCS solver.

IV. Conclusions

In this work, an innovative frequency-hopping (FH) BCS-based method has been introduced to deal with the GPR-IS problem. A preliminary numerical example has been shown to prove the effectiveness of the proposed approach.

Acknowledgment

This work benefited from the networking activities carried out within the EU funded COST Action TU1208 "Civil Engineering Applications of Ground Penetrating Radar" and within the SIRENA project (2014-2017) funded by DIGITEO (France) under the "Call for Chairs 2014".

References

[1] A. Benedetto and L. Pajewski, Eds., *Civil Engineering Applications of Ground Penetrating Radar*, Springer Transactions in Civil and Environmental Engineering, 2015.

[2] M. Salucci, L. Poli, and A. Massa, "Advanced multi-frequency GPR data processing for non-linear deterministic imaging," *Signal Processing – Special Issue on 'Advanced Ground-Penetrating Radar Signal Processing Techniques,'* vol. 132, pp. 306-318, Mar. 2017.

[3] M. Salucci, G. Oliveri, and A. Massa, "GPR prospecting through an inverse scattering frequency-hopping multi-focusing approach," *IEEE Trans. Geosci. Remote Sens.*, vol. 53, no. 12, pp. 6573-6592, Dec. 2015.

[4] A. Massa, P. Rocca, and G. Oliveri, "Compressive sensing in electromagnetics - a review," *IEEE Antennas Propag. Mag.*, vol. 57, no. 1, pp. 224-238, Feb. 2015.

[5] G. Oliveri, P. Rocca, and A. Massa, "A Bayesian compressive sampling-based inversion for imaging sparse scatterers," *IEEE Trans. Geosci. Remote Sens.*, vol. 49, no. 10, pp. 3993-4006, Oct. 2011.

[6] L. Poli, G. Oliveri, F. Viani, and A. Massa, "MT-BCS-based microwave imaging approach through minimum-norm current expansion," *IEEE Trans. Antennas Propag.*, vol. 61, no. 9, pp. 4722-4732, Sep. 2013.

[7] G. Oliveri, N. Anselmi, and A. Massa, "Compressive sensing imaging of non-sparse 2D scatterers by a total-variation approach within the Born approximation," *IEEE Trans. Antennas. Propag.*, vol. 62, no. 10, pp. 5157-5170, Oct. 2014.

[8] N. Anselmi, G. Oliveri, M. Salucci, and A. Massa, "Wavelet-based compressive imaging of sparse targets," *IEEE Trans. Antennas Propag.*, vol. 63, no. 11, pp. 4889-4900, Nov. 2015.

[9] A. Giannopoulos, "Modelling ground penetrating radar by GprMax," *Constr. Build. Mater.*, vol. 19, no. 10, pp. 755-762, Dec. 2005.

Pros and cons of microwave imaging techniques for the reconstruction of velocity profiles of cylindrical targets in axial motion

Massimo Brignone #, Matteo Pastorino #, Mirco Raffetto #, Andrea Randazzo #

#Dept. of Electrical, Electronic, Telecommunication Engineering, and Naval Architecture (DITEN), University of Genoa, Via Opera Pia 11a, 16145, Genoa, Italy

Abstract—**In this contribution the strengths and the weaknesses of microwave imaging techniques for the reconstruction of dielectric and velocity profiles of inhomogeneous cylinders in non-uniform axial motion are presented. Some numerical results are presented to support the main conclusions.**

I. Introduction

The reconstruction of the dielectric and velocity profiles in pipelines is a topic of great practical interest. Pneumatic or oil pipelines are just a few examples [1], [2]. Such a reconstruction can be based on acoustic or electromagnetic waves. Acoustic sensors could be in trouble when they are exploited to recover the velocity profile of media in motion in pipelines [1]. For this reason, most of the techniques developed in the last decades are based on electromagnetic phenomena in different frequency bands, ranging from low [2] to optical frequencies [1].

Recently, our research group has proposed additional electromagnetic approaches [3], based on microwave inverse scattering techniques [4]. Such techniques have been proved to possess excellent properties in traditional inverse scattering problems [4], but to the best of authors knowledge, they have never been used before to solve inverse scattering problems involving the reconstruction of velocity profiles.

The most trivial application of inverse scattering techniques can provide satisfactory results when the motion is characterized by huge axial velocities [3], [5], [6]. For non-relativistic velocities a two-step algorithm provides much better performances than the traditional one-step extension of any microwave inverse scattering approach [3].

In this contribution, the strengths and the weaknesses of the proposed microwave inverse scattering techniques are investigated and some comparisons are performed.

II. The proposed approaches in short

In microwave inverse scattering techniques, information about dielectric and velocity profiles of cylindrical targets in axial motion can be recovered from the measurements of the axial components of the electromagnetic scattered field, E^s and H^s. In fact, such components depend on ε_r, μ_r and $\beta = \frac{v}{c_0}$ (here v is the velocity along the axis of the pipeline and c_0 is the speed of light in vacuum, as usual), on the position of the transmitting antenna x_s and on the position of the receiving sensor x_m. Therefore we can use the notation $E^s(x_s, x_m; \mu_r, \varepsilon_r, \beta)$ and $H^s(x_s, x_m; \mu_r, \varepsilon_r, \beta)$.

The most trivial application of a microwave inverse scattering technique tries to recover the fields of the constitutive parameters and the velocity profile by solving an optimization problem. More precisely, in the presence of S transmitting antennas and M receiving sensors, if the measured axial components of the electromagnetic field are denoted by $E^s_m(x_s, x_m; \mu_r, \varepsilon_r, \beta)$ and $H^s_m(x_s, x_m; \mu_r, \varepsilon_r, \beta)$, $s = 1, \dots, S$, $m = 1, \dots, M$, then one has to find μ_r^t, ε_r^t and β^t that minimize the cost function

$$f(\mu_r^t, \varepsilon_r^t, \beta^t) = g(\mu_r^t, \varepsilon_r^t, \beta^t) + h(\mu_r^t, \varepsilon_r^t, \beta^t), \qquad (1)$$

where

$$g(\mu_r^t, \varepsilon_r^t, \beta^t) = \frac{\sum_{s,m} |E^s(x_s, x_m; \mu_r^t, \varepsilon_r^t, \beta^t) - E^s_m(x_s, x_m; \mu_r, \varepsilon_r, \beta)|^2}{\sum_{s,m} |E^s_m(x_s, x_m; \mu_r, \varepsilon_r, \beta)|^2} \qquad (2)$$

and $h(\mu_r^t, \varepsilon_r^t, \beta^t)$ is the same as $g(\mu_r^t, \varepsilon_r^t, \beta^t)$ but with H in place of E. Another possible approach is based on a two-step procedure. In the first step one has to find $\mu_{r,0}^t$ and $\varepsilon_{r,0}^t$ that minimize $g(\mu_{r,0}^t, \varepsilon_{r,0}^t, 0)$ (respectively, $h(\mu_{r,0}^t, \varepsilon_{r,0}^t, 0)$), when a TM (respectively, TE) illuminating field is considered. In the second step, the recovered $\mu_{r,0}^t$ and $\varepsilon_{r,0}^t$ are exploited in order to find β^t that minimizes $h(\mu_{r,0}^t, \varepsilon_{r,0}^t, \beta_t)$ (respectively, $g(\mu_{r,0}^t, \varepsilon_{r,0}^t, \beta_t)$). The main idea behind this approach is that the reconstruction of the constitutive parameters could be retained to be almost independent of the axial velocity.

III. Pros and cons of the proposed approaches

Inverse scattering approaches have some very well known features, which are retained for the applications here considered. In particular, among the good qualities of such approaches, one can observe that they do not require any change in the pipeline. For example, there is no need for entry and exit windows, which are required by other microwave or optical techniques [1]. Another good feature of the proposed approaches is related to the fact that they do not require to place sensors all around the pipe [7]. The illuminating and the receiving antennas can be placed on a single side, when the pipelines are not directly accessible. Finally, the approaches are potentially able to provide a complete description of the profiles of interest.

Among the weaknesses of the proposed approaches, one has usually to consider the lack of real time reconstructions of the profiles of interest. Moreover, in the first of the considered approaches, the unknown profiles are treated without any reference to their physical meaning and in [3] it has been shown that good results can be achieved only for large values of β. On the contrary, when the values of β are known to be sufficiently small (i.e. $\max\beta < 0.01$, see [3]) the two-step procedure provides much better and satisfactory results [3]. However, for very low axial velocities, it has been shown that it is necessary to have an excellent polarization purity of the transmitting antennas and an extremely good cross-polarization isolation for the receiving ones [7]. For example, as a rough estimate, a flow with an average normalized axial velocity β of 10^{-r}, $r \in \mathbb{N}$, cannot be recovered if the sensors do not guarantee a cross-polarization isolation of at least $20r$ dB [7]. This kind of precision requirement on the instrumentation is not unusual, however. For example, in all techniques based on the Doppler-shift principle, the frequency shift (with respect to the signal frequency) to be appreciated is proportional to β.

IV. Numerical Results and Discussion

Some negative results on the capabilities of the two microwave inverse scattering approaches are easily obtained.

For example, the first approach, based on a single step, is in trouble when all cylinders involved in the problem of interest move with small normalized values of the axial velocity. This is related to the fact that all unknown fields are considered without any distinction while one of the two axial components of the scattered field could be related to one of the unknown fields in a really weak way. In particular, even in the presence of a single cylinder made up of a few layers, when $\max\beta < 10^{-4}$ (which, by the way, corresponds to a huge velocity of $\simeq 30$ kilometers per second), the errors on the reconstruction of β could be of the same order of β itself [3].

By its very definition, the two-step approach, which neglects the movement in the first of its two reconstruction processes, is in trouble in the presence of relativistic velocities [3]. This limitation is capable of affecting the performances of both the reconstructions, the one related to the constitutive parameters and that related to the axial speed.

More elusive is the limitation of the two-step approach in relation to the cross-polarization properties of the sensors adopted. This type of limitation was investigated in [7] and is in any case only related to the second step of the procedure, devoted to the reconstruction of the axial velocity profile. The first step is simply not affected by this type of considerations, the movement being a priori neglected in this stage of the procedure (devoted to the reconstruction of ε_r and μ_r).

Numerical simulations show that the reliable reconstruction of the β values even in the presence of a single homogeneous circular cylinder moving with a uniform axial speed cannot be achieved when β is smaller than the cross-polarization isolation of the sensors adopted.

Thus, the two-step approach, in the presence of a given set of sensors, is known in advance to have a well defined range of β values other which the reconstruction process of the axial velocity can provide reliable results. For example, for a cross-polarization isolation of 80 dB we get a range of β approximately given by $[10^{-4}, 10^{-2}]$ [7]. With these sensors, we have considered the reconstruction of a three layer circular cylinder. The relative permittivity of each layer was assumed to get a value equal to 2 or 4, for a set of 8 different dielectric configurations. All layers move with the same axial velocity $\beta \in \{10^{-8}, 10^{-7}, 10^{-6}, 10^{-5}, 10^{-4}, 10^{-3}, 10^{-2}\}$. By using ACO as an optimization technique [4], we get satisfactory results in terms of reconstructions of the relative permittivity values, with relative errors below 20% in all cases, for all considered values of β. The same optimization technique is not able to give the same quality of results in terms of reconstruction of (the constant) β. When β is equal to or smaller than 10^{-5} the errors are, on average, well above 100%. For higher β values the performances improve very quickly and are reliable when β is equal to or larger than 10^{-3}, with average errors of a few percent and a small standard deviation.

These additional results confirm the reliability of the two-step approach, when it is exploited taking account of the well known a-priori limitations and of the performances of the sensors adopted in terms of cross-polarization isolation.

V. Conclusion

Microwave inverse scattering techniques have recently been introduced as potential alternative approaches to the reconstruction of dielectric and velocity profiles of cylinders in axial motion. Their theoretical and practical advantages and disadvantages are discussed. Some numerical results are presented to point out the main features of these novel approaches.

References

[1] Y. Yan, "Mass flow measurement of bulk solids in pneumatic pipelines," *Measurement Science and Technology*, vol. 7, no. 12, p. 1687.

[2] W. Q. Yang, A. L. Stott, M. S. Beck, and C. G. Xie, "Development of capacitance tomographic imaging systems for oil pipeline measurements," *International Journal of Multiphase Flow*, vol. 22, no. 1001, pp. 144–145, 1996.

[3] M. Pastorino, M. Raffetto, and A. Randazzo, "Electromagnetic inverse scattering of axially moving cylindrical targets," *IEEE Transactions on Geoscience and Remote Sensing*, vol. 53, no. 3, pp. 1452–1462, March 2015.

[4] M. Pastorino, *Microwave Imaging*. New York: Wiley, 2010.

[5] M. Pastorino and M. Raffetto, "Scattering of electromagnetic waves from a multilayer elliptic cylinder moving in the axial direction," *IEEE Transactions on Antennas and Propagation*, vol. 61, no. 9, pp. 4741–4753, September 2013.

[6] M. Brignone and M. Raffetto, "Well posedness and finite element approximability of two-dimensional time-harmonic electromagnetic problems involving non-conducting moving objects with stationary boundaries," *ESAIM: Mathematical Modelling and Numerical Analysis*, vol. 49, no. 4, pp. 1157–1192, July-August 2015.

[7] M. Brignone, G. L. Gragnani, M. Pastorino, M. Raffetto, and A. Randazzo, "Noise limitations on the recovery of average values of velocity profiles in pipelines by simple imaging systems," *IEEE Geoscience and Remote Sensing Letters*, vol. 13, no. 9, pp. 1340–1344, 2016.

On Time-Domain Use of the Cylindrical Wave Approach

Cristina Ponti and Giuseppe Schettini
Department of Engineering
"Roma Tre" University
Rome, Italy
cristina.ponti@uniroma3.it, giuseppe.schettini@uniroma3.it

***Abstract*—Interaction of an un ultra-wideband source with buried cylinders is solved with a time-domain formulation of the Cylindrical Wave Approach. The pulsed excitation typical of remote sensing with the Ground Penetrating Radar can be implemented, i.e., the Gaussian monocycle or Gaussian doublet waveforms. The analysis is developed in the frequency domain, and spectra of the scattered field contributions are found. Time-domain waveforms are reconstructed with an inverse Fast Fourier Transform. Results are plotted as the typical A-scan or B-scan radargrams of the Ground Penetrating Radar technique.**

Keywords*— *Buried objects, electromagnetic scattering, radar applications.

I. INTRODUCTION

The ultra-wideband (UWB) remote sensing of buried objects has several applications within the Ground Penetrating Radar technique, for the sub-surface survey of buried targets [1]-[2]. Applications are also in the Through-the-Wall radar [3], for the detection of hidden targets beyond a wall, or in the breast cancer diagnosis through electromagnetic techniques [4].

A-scan or B-scan radargrams are the typical output of these radar techniques. The amplitude of the scattered field by the target and the background is recorded as a function of its time of arrival at one or more receiver points. Collected data are post-processed through imaging techniques that reconstruct position of the target, size, and its electrical properties, i.e., permittivity and conductivity [5]-[7]. A successful inversion often relies on the availability of accurate direct scattering solvers.

In this paper, we propose a method that solves the direct scattering by buried objects in the time domain, dealing with the typical pulsed UWB sources used with the Ground Penetrating Radar. The method is based on the Cylindrical Wave Approach (CWA), an analytical technique developed to solve the scattering by buried targets in the frequency domain [8]-[12]. A first application of the CWA to a pulsed wave was at first presented in [13], for a particular case of the spectrum. Now, the interaction with a pulsed source is obtained through a suitable iterative approach, where all the spectral components of the source field are dealt with as monochromatic excitations. A spectrum for the scattered field is found, and the final pulsed response from the target is reconstructed though an inverse Fast Fourier Transform.

II. THE TIME-DOMAIN CYLINDRICAL WAVE APPROACH

The geometry of the problem is given in Fig. 1. At the transmitter point (TX) a pulsed plane wave field is excited. Such a field is represented through its frequency-domain spectrum

$$V_i[\xi(f),\zeta(f)] = V_0^i(f)e^{i\{n_\perp[\xi(f)-\xi_0(f)]+n_\parallel[\zeta(f)-\zeta_0(f)]\}} \quad (1)$$

where $\xi=k_0x$, $\zeta=k_0z$ are the normalized coordinates at the observation point, with $k_0=2\pi f/c$ the vacuum wavenumber, and (ξ_0,ζ_0) the normalized coordinate for the reference point at the source.

In (1), $V_0^i(f)$ is the spectrum of the field. In particular, the typical spectra used in the Ground Penetrating Radar technique can be employed, as the Gaussian monocycle

$$V_i[\xi(f),\zeta(f)] = K_1\sigma\sqrt{\pi}(j2\pi f)e^{-(\pi\sigma f)^2}e^{j2\pi fT} \quad (2)$$

or the Gaussian doublet

$$V_i[\xi(f),\zeta(f)] = -K_2\sigma\sqrt{\pi}(j2\pi f)^2e^{-(\pi\sigma f)^2}e^{j2\pi fT} \quad (3)$$

with $\sigma=1/\sqrt{2}\pi f_0$, and $T=1/f_0$ the time delay.

A suitable sampling is applied on the source field, according to its frequency spectrum, and the interaction of each monochromatic component with the interface and the target is found applying the CWA [8]. The spectrum of the scattered-transmitted field in air is found, and the final time-domain scattered field can be reconstructed via an Inverse Fast Fourier Transform:

$$v_s(x,z;t) = 2\,\mathrm{Re}\{IFFT[V_s(f_k)]\cdot\Delta f\} \quad (4)$$

where Δf is the sampling step.

An example of B-scan is reported in Fig. 2. It is relevant to the simulation of a perfectly conducting rebar in a semi-infinite medium, under excitation from a Gaussian-doublet pulse with f_0 = 0.9 GHz. The radius of the cylinder is a = 2.5, depth 7.5, and ε_{r1} = 6. N = 41 receivers are aligned along a line x_0 = -2.5 cm. Frequency spectrum is sampled at 256 points, with a frequency step Δf = 30 MHz. A B-scan radargram is obtained, where the uppest part of the plot represents the source field and its interaction with the interface, that is usually removed through a 'gating' window. The hyperbolic response, typical of finite-size targets, is instead the scattering from the cylinder. Computation time of the central A-scan (z = 0) is 8 seconds on an Intel Xeon CPU E5420 @2.0 GHz, RAM 32 GB.

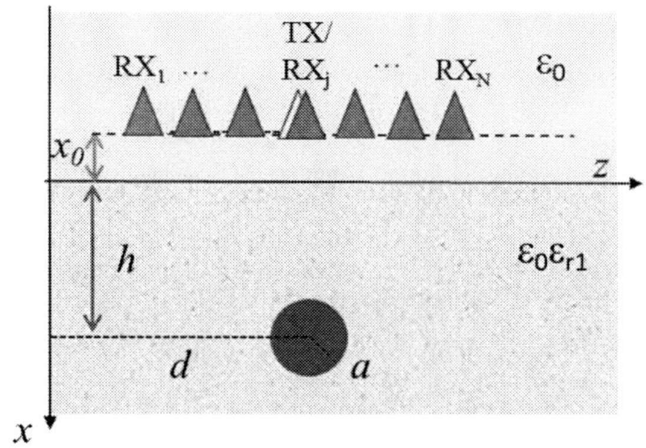

Figure 1. Geometry of the problem.

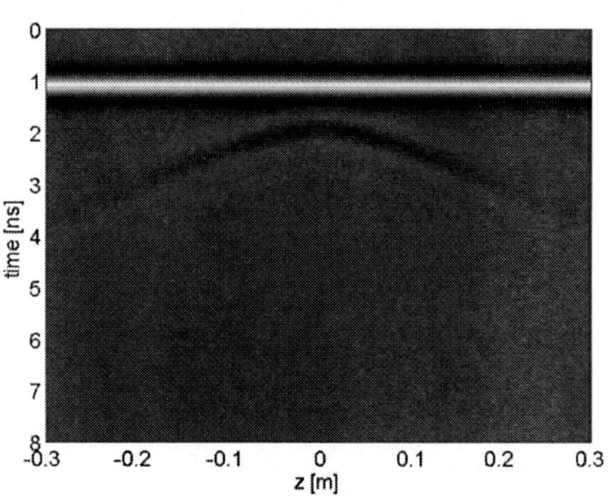

Figure 2. B-scan of a rebar in a semi-infinite medium.

III. CONCLUSIONS

An iterative technique to solve the time-domain scattering by buried cylinders from a pulsed source has been developed. Solution is found in the frequency domain, though a sampling of the source spectrum. The approach has an analytical basis, as the CWA formulation has been employed at each frequency of the spectrum. Therefore, in the numerical implementation the technique turns out to be accurate and efficient. Execution times are fast, compared to other techniques typically used in the simulation of GPR scenarios. In particular, the Finite-Difference Time-Domain (FDTD) method is commonly used, as, being developed directly in the time domain, results can be straightforwardly returned in the A-scan or B-scan radargrams. The FDTD is a purely numerical technique, and its application is based on a discretization of the investigation domain. With shallow scatterers, computational times with FDTD and CWA are almost comparable. The CWA, turns out to be faster than the FDTD, in the case of deeply buried cylinders. In larger domains, a denser mesh is needed with the FDTD, and computational time may become quite demanding.

REFERENCES

[1] D. J. Daniels, Surface Penetrating Radar, 2nd edition, London: IEE, 2004.

[2] H.M. Jol, Ground Penetrating Radar: Theory and Applications, Elsevier Science Ltd, 2008.

[3] M. G. Amin, Through-the-Wall Radar Imaging, CRC Press Taylor and Francis Group, 2011.

[4] E. Porter, M. Coates, and M. Popovic, "An Early Clinical Study of Time-Domain Microwave Radar for Breast Health Monitoring," IEEE Trans. Biomedical Eng.,Vol. 63, no 3, pp. 530 - 539, Mar. 2016.

[5] C. Estatico, A. Fedeli, M. Pastorino, and A. Randazzo, "A Multifrequency Inexact-NewtonMethod in Lp Banach Spaces for Buried Objects Detection," *IEEE Trans. Antennas Propag.*, vol. 63, no. 9, pp. 4198 -4204, Sept. 2015.

[6] M. Salucci, G. Oliveri, and A. Massa, "GPR Prospecting Through an Inverse-Scattering Frequency-Hopping Multifocusing Approach," *IEEE Trans. Geosci. Remote Sens.*, Vol. 53, no. 12, Dec. 2015.

[7] F. Soldovieri and R. Solimene, "Through-Wall Imaging via a Linear Inverse Scattering Algorithm," IEEE Trans. Geosci. Remote Sens. Letters, Vol. 4, no. 4, pp. 513-517, Oct. 2007.

[8] M. Di Vico, F. Frezza, L. Pajewski, and G. Schettini, "Scattering by a finite set of perfectly conducting cylinders buried in a dielectric halfspace: A spectral-domain solution," IEEE Trans. Antennas Propag., vol. 53, no. 2, pp. 719–727, Feb. 2005.

[9] F. Frezza, L. Pajewski, C. Ponti, and G. Schettini, "Electromagnetic scattering by perfectly-conducting cylinders buried in a dielectric slab through the cylindrical wave approach," IEEE Trans. Antennas Propag., vol. 57, pp. 1208–1217, 2009.

[10] C. Ponti, and S. Vellucci, "Scattering by conducting cylinders below a dielectric layer with a fast noniterative approach," *IEEE Transactions on Microwave Theory and Technique*, vol. 63, no.1, January 2015, pp. 30-39.

[11] M.A. Fiaz, F. Frezza, L. Pajewski, C. Ponti, and G. Schettini, "Scattering by a circular cylinder buried under a slightly rough surface: the Cylindrical-Wave Approach," IEEE Trans. Antennas Propag. Vol. 60, pp. 2834-2842, June 2012.

[12] M. A. Fiaz, F. Frezza, C. Ponti, and G. Schettini, "Electromagnetic scatterng by a conducting cylinder buried below a slightly rough Gaussian surface," J. Opt. Soc. Am. A, vol. 31, pp. 26-34, Jan. 2014.

[13] F. Frezza, P. Martinelli, L. Pajewski, and G. Schettini, "Short-pulse electromagnetic scattering by buried perfectly conducting cylinders," *Geosc. Remote Sens. Letters*, Vol. 4, No. 4, pp. 611-615, Oct. 2007.

[14] A. Giannopoulos, "Modelling ground penetrating radar with GprMax," *Constr. Build. Materials*, Vol. 1, pp. 755-762, Dec. 2005.

Development of electromagnetic simulators for Ground Penetrating Radar

Lara Pajewski
Sapienza University of Rome
Rome, Italy
lara.pajewski@uniroma1.it

Antonios Giannopoulos and Craig Warren
The University of Edinburgh
Edinburgh, United Kingdom
a.giannopoulos@ed.ac.uk, craig.warren@ed.ac.uk

Sinisa Antonijevic, Vicko Doric and Dragan Poljak
University of Split
Split, Croatia
sinisa.antonijevic@pmfst.hr, vicko.doric@fesb.hr, dpoljak@fesb.hr

Daniele Pirrone
Roma Tre University
Rome, Italy
e2gpr@gpradar.eu

***Abstract*—This paper presents two electromagnetic simulators based on the Finite-Difference Time Domain (FDTD) technique and Boundary Element Method (BEM), for Ground Penetrating Radar applications. The first simulator is the new open-source version of the software gprMax, which employs Yee's algorithm to solve Maxwell's equations by using the FDTD method and includes advanced features allowing the accurate analysis of realistic scenarios. Additionally, E^{2}GPR is a freeware package conceived to ease the use of gprMax: it assists in the creation, modification and analysis of two-dimensional models and can be used to plot results. The second simulator is TWiNS-II: this is free software for the analysis of multiple thin wires in the presence of two media, implementing the Galerkin-Bubnov Indirect BEM; calculations can be undertaken in the frequency or time domain. These tools have been developed by Members of the COST Action TU1208 "Civil Engineering Applications of Ground Penetrating Radar."**

Keywords*—*Ground-Penetrating Radar; Finite-Difference Time Domain; Boundary Element Method

I. Introduction

Founded in 1971, COST (European COoperation in Science and Technology) is the first and widest European framework for the transnational coordination of research activities. It operates through Actions, science and technology networks with a duration of four years.

The main objective of the COST Action TU1208 "Civil Engineering Applications of Ground Penetrating Radar" [1] is to exchange and increase knowledge and experience on Ground-Penetrating Radar (GPR) techniques in civil engineering, while promoting in Europe a wider use of this technique. Research activities carried out in TU1208 include all aspects of the GPR technology and methodology: design, realization and testing of radar systems and antennas; development and testing of surveying procedures for the monitoring and inspection of structures; integration of GPR with other non-destructive testing approaches; advancement of electromagnetic-modelling, inversion and data-processing techniques for radargram analysis and interpretation.

GPR radargrams often have no resemblance to the subsurface or structures over which the profiles were recorded. Various factors, including the innate design of the survey equipment and the complexity of electromagnetic propagation in composite scenarios, can disguise complex structures recorded on reflection profiles. Electromagnetic simulators can help to understand how target structures get translated into radargrams. They can show the limitations of GPR technique, highlight its capabilities, and support the user in understanding where and in what environment GPR can be effectively used. Furthermore, electromagnetic modelling can aid the choice of the most proper GPR equipment for a survey, facilitate the interpretation of complex datasets and be used for the design of new antennas. Electromagnetic simulators can be employed to produce synthetic radargrams with the purposes of testing new data-processing, imaging and inversion algorithms, or assess the effectiveness of existing ones. A fast and accurate forward solver can also be used as part of an inverse solver.

This paper presents two electromagnetic simulators, based on the Finite-Difference Time Domain (FDTD) technique and Boundary Element Method (BEM). In Section II, the new open-source version of the software gprMax is presented, which implements FDTD and includes advanced features for the analysis of realistic scenarios. E^{2}GPR is a freeware package conceived to ease the use of gprMax. In Section III, TWiNS-II is introduced: this is free software for the analysis of a thin-wire configuration in the presence of two media and implements the Galerkin-Bubnov Indirect BEM.

II. gprMax and E^{2}GPR

The open source software gprMax [2] employs Yee's algorithm to solve Maxwell's equations using the FDTD method. It was originally developed in 1996. Recently, the software has been rewritten in Python, with performance-critical parts implemented in Cython, and released under the GNU General Public License. In the process of rewriting the software, several changes have been made to improve its efficiency, speed, and usability. For instance, the Perfectly Matched Layer boundary conditions have been improved. Moreover, all geometrical and physical properties defining the scenario can now be parameterised.

New advanced features have been added to the simulator:

- A library of antennas that can be included in the models.

- It is possible to build heterogeneous media using fractals, as well as objects with rough surfaces.
- Anisotropic media can be defined. This allows materials such as wood and fibre-reinforced concrete, which are often inspected with GPR, to be accurately modelled.
- Media with arbitrary frequency-dispersive properties can be defined. This paves the way to the use of gprMax in new areas, such as the modelling of human tissues.
- Optimisation of parameters based on Taguchi's method can be performed. This feature can be useful to optimise material properties based on experimental data or to design new antennas.

E^2GPR [3] stands for 'Edit your geometry, Execute GprMax and Plot the Results!'. This freeware tool is conceived to ease the use of gprMax. The main purposes of E^2GPR are to:

- Assist in the creation, modification and analysis of two-dimensional (2D) gprMax models, through Computer-Aided Design.
- Facilitate parallel and/or distributed computing with gprMax, on multicore machines or networks of computers.
- Automatically plot radargrams generated by gprMax.

gprMax is command-line driven and does not feature a Graphical User Interface (GUI). This implies that, for complicated scenarios, creating or modifying a model can be a not straightforward work. Moreover, the geometry of a model cannot be checked in real time, while editing it. E^2GPR helps overcoming these limitations and assists the user in the creation of gprMax 2D models. It is written in HTML and JavaScript, hence it runs on any device. A new scenario can be created from scratch, or an existing input file can be loaded and modified. Electromagnetic properties of different media can be defined. Basic shapes are available and arbitrary shapes can be hand-drawn by using any pointing device. Objects can be copied and pasted, deleted, shifted and resized. It is possible to load a background picture and draw the model by tracing it. For the shift of transmitting and receiving antennas, a fixed step can be defined or an arbitrary path can be hand-drawn, to move the antennas on irregular curved and rough interfaces.

In the new gprMax, the FDTD loops (which are the most computationally intensive parts of the code) have been parallelised by using OpenMP: all CPU cores available on a machine can be exploited to perform calculations. A Message Passing Interface has been employed to implement a task farm, which can be utilised to distribute a series of models to different cores as independent tasks. This is very useful when a B-Scan is required: each A-Scan composing the B-Scan can be task-farmed as an independent model. E^2GPR facilitates the use of this feature (the user can set all parameters through an intuitive GUI) and allows monitoring how the calculation is advancing, through reader-friendly progress bars.

Finally, E^2GPR includes a plotter. This script automatically plots A- and B-Scans generated by gprMax, to offer a first and easy view of the results.

III. TWINS-II

TWiNS-II is free software for electromagnetic simulation of thin-wire configurations in the presence of two media. It is the improved version of the previously developed tool TWiNS [4] and implements the Galerkin-Bubnov Indirect Boundary Element Method. The package contains two applications called TD-TWiNS-II and FD-TWiNS-II, which can be used to undertake the analysis in the frequency or time domain, respectively. The software is focused primarily on calculation, but a rudimentary graphical representation is integrated in the package. A wide range of options exists, to export results for further processing with other tools, if specialized graphical representation or further calculation is required: the authors of the package feel that this approach simplifies its usage and allows a greater degree of flexibility for the final user.

The time-domain application TD-TWiNS-II is focused on the assessment of current distributions along thin wire structures. The configuration that can be analyzed is a set of parallel thin wires placed in free space above a perfect ground, or above a dielectric lossless half-space. The wire array resides in a plane parallel to the interface. The formulation is based on the space-time Hallen integral equation approach. Within this basic geometry, the user is allowed to arbitrarily change the number, size and position of wires, their excitation characteristics and the dielectric constant of the half-space.

The frequency-domain application FD-TWiNS-II is used for the frequency analysis of the same wire configuration as in the time domain counterpart. The formulation is based on the Pocklington integro-differential equation approach. In addition to features provided by TD-TWiNS-II, the FD-TWiNS-II accounts for the effects of losses in the ground.

IV. CONCLUSIONS

In this paper, two electromagnetic simulators based on the Finite-Difference Time Domain (FDTD) technique and on the Boundary Element Method (BEM) were presented: (i) the open source software gprMax, implementing FDTD, and the additional freeware tool E^2GPR; (ii) the TWiNS-II free package, implementing BEM, for the simulation of thin wires in the presence of two media.

ACKNOWLEDGMENT

The simulators presented in this paper are a contribution to COST Action TU1208 "Civil engineering applications of Ground Penetrating Radar."

REFERENCES

[1] L. Pajewski, A. Benedetto, X. Derobert, A. Giannopoulos, A. Loizos, G. Manacorda, M. Marciniak, C. Plati, G. Schettini, and I. Trinks, "Applications of Ground Penetrating Radar in civil engineering – COST Action TU1208," Proc. 7th International Workshop on Advanced Ground Penetrating Radar (IWAGPR), 2-5 July 2013, Nantes, France, pp. 1-6.

[2] C. Warren, A. Giannopoulos, and I. Giannakis, "gprMax: Open source software to simulate electromagnetic wave propagation for Ground Penetrating Radar," Computer Physics Communications, vol. 209, pp. 163-170, Dec. 2016.

[3] D. Pirrone and L. Pajewski, "E^2GPR – Edit your geometry, Execute GprMax2D and Plot the Results!," Proc. 2015 IEEE 15th Mediterranean Microwave Symposium, 30 November-2 December 2015, Lecce, Italy, pp. 1-4.

[4] D. Poljak, Advanced Modeling in Computational Electromagnetic Compatibility,. New Jersey: John Wiley & Sons, Inc., 2007.

Short-Term Scientific Missions on forward and inverse electromagnetic-scattering techniques for Ground Penetrating Radar

Lara Pajewski[1], Antonios Giannopoulos[2], Marian Marciniak[3], Simone Meschino[4], Alexei Popov[5], Igor Prokopovich[5], Alessio Ventura[6], Craig Warren[2]

[1] Sapienza University of Rome, Rome, Italy, lara.pajewski@uniroma1.it
[2] The University of Edinburgh, Edinburgh, United Kingdom, a.giannopoulos@ed.ac.uk, craig.warren@ed.ac.uk
[3] National Institute of Telecommunications, Warsaw, Poland, m.marciniak@itl.waw.pl
[4] Airbus Gmbh, Friedrichshafen, Germany, simone.meschino@gmail.com
[5] Pushkov Inst. of Terrestrial Magnetism, Ionosphere and Radio Wave Propagation, Moscow, Russia, prokop21@mail.ru, popov@izmiran.ru
[6] Roma Tre University, Rome, Italy, alessioventura@hotmail.com

***Abstract*—This work aims at offering an overview on the scientific results stemming from a selection of three Short-Term Scientific Missions (STSMs) carried out in 2016 and funded by the COST Action TU1208 "Civil Engineering Applications of Ground Penetrating Radar." The research activities focused on the development and use of electromagnetic modelling and inversion techniques for Ground Penetrating Radar applications. In a STSM, a scientist has the possibility to visit a colleague abroad, in order to undertake joint research and share experience, techniques, equipment and infrastructures that may not be available in the home institution. This is a powerful networking tool that allows developing linkages and scientific collaborations between institutions involved in a COST Action.**

Keywords*——*Ground Penetrating Radar; electromagnetic scattering; inversion techniques

I. Introduction

The main objective of COST (European Cooperation in Science and Technology) Action TU1208 "Civil Engineering Applications of Ground Penetrating Radar" [1] (April 2013 – October 2017) is to exchange and increase scientific and technical knowledge and experience on Ground-Penetrating Radar (GPR) techniques in civil engineering, while promoting a wider and more effective use of this safe and non-destructive technique. The Action involves participants from 28 COST Countries (Austria, Belgium, Croatia, Czech Republic, Denmark, Estonia, Finland, France, Macedonia, Germany, Greece, Ireland, Italy, Latvia, Malta, Netherlands, Norway, Poland, Portugal, Romania, Serbia, Slovakia, Slovenia, Spain, Sweden, Switzerland, Turkey, United Kingdom), 1 Cooperating State (Israel), 6 Near Neighbour Countries (Albania, Armenia, Egypt, Jordan, Russia, Ukraine), and 6 International Partner Countries (Australia, Colombia, Hong Kong, Philippines, Rwanda, United States of America). The scientific structure of the Action includes 4 Working Groups (WGs). WG1 focuses on the design of novel GPR equipment. WG2 deals with the development of guidelines for GPR surveying of transport infrastructures, buildings and construction materials, and for sensing of underground utilities and voids. WG3 develops forward and inverse electromagnetic techniques for the solution of near-field scattering problems, and data-processing techniques. WG4 studies the use of GPR outside from the civil engineering area and its integration with other non-destructive testing techniques.

Short-Term Scientific Missions (STSMs) are important means to develop collaborations between institutions involved in a COST Action. Scientists have the opportunity to visit colleagues abroad, in order to undertake joint research and share ideas, experience, techniques, equipment and other facilities. This paper aims at presenting scientific results stemming from a selection of TU1208 short missions carried out in 2016. The research activities dealt with the development and use of electromagnetic-modelling (Section II) and inversion (Section III) methods for GPR. Previous STSMs on these topics were presented in [2].

II. STSMs on Electromagnetic Modelling for GPR

In April 2016, Alessio Ventura (Italy) visited Antonis Giannopoulos and Craig Warren (United Kingdom). The activities focused on developing accurate models of GPR antennas with two different approaches, namely the Finite-Difference Time-Domain (FDTD) method and the Finite-Integration Technique (FIT). This study started in remote cooperation before the mission and involved also Lara Pajewski (Italy). High-frequency commercial GPR antennas were simulated in free space and over a lossy dielectric. The employed FDTD solver was gprMax, an open-source simulator [3], whereas the commercial software CST Microwave Studio was used for simulations with the FIT. Very good agreement between FDTD and FIT was observed. The comparisons highlighted the importance of understanding how features such as material dispersion and antenna feeding are modelled. This is especially relevant for GPR applications, where antennas operate in the near field and their interaction with the surveyed ground/structure and targets has important effects on the recorded radargrams. An example of cross-talk results obtained for a 1.5 GHz shielded bow-tie antenna is given in Fig. 1.

In April-May 2016, Alexei Popov (Russia) visited Marian Marciniak (Poland). They continued a study started by Igor Prokopovich (Russia) during a previous mission and involving Lara Pajewski (Italy) as well. A semi-analytical solution was developed, to solve the forward back-scattering problem of a pulsed field emitted by a dipole in the presence of a non-uniform dielectric half-space. A new coupled-wave version of the Wentzel–Kramers–Brillouin (WKB) approximation was proposed, obtained by extending the Bremmer-Brekhovskikh [4] approach to the time domain. Numerical results were obtained and compared with gprMax results, with very good agreement: see Fig. 2. To demonstrate the applicability of the approach to real scenarios, the technique was successfully employed for the post-processing and interpretation of GPR radargrams collected on the Lake Chebarkul, in Russia.

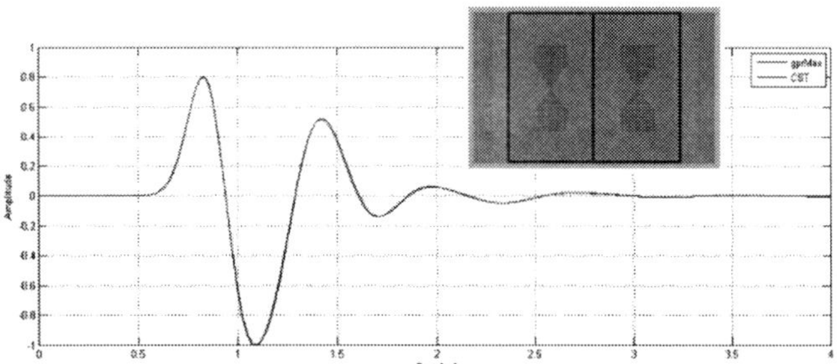

Fig. 1. Cross-talk results obtained for a 1.5 GHz antenna.

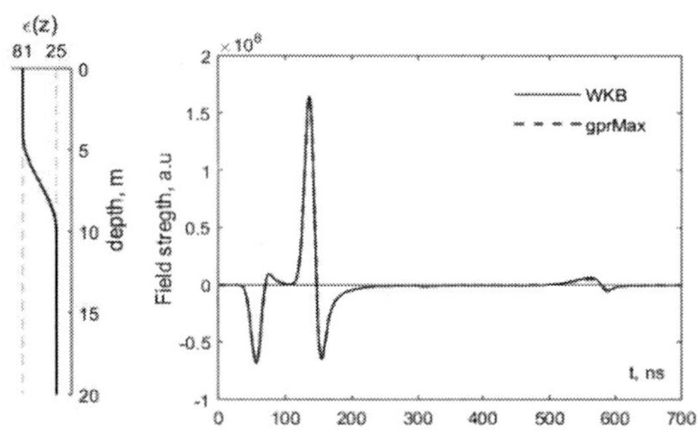

Fig. 2. Profile of half-space dielectric permittivity and simulated A-Scan.

III. STSMs on Inversion Techniques for GPR

In January 2016, Simone Meschino (Germany) visited Lara Pajewski (Italy). Aim of the mission was to continue a study started during a previous STSM, where a method based on Sub-Array Processing (SAP) and Direction of Arrival (DoA) algorithms was developed and applied to GPR data [5]. New tests were performed on synthetic radargrams calculated by using gprMax and involving concrete cells with circular-section steel rods of different radii and positions, dielectric rods, and other reinforcing elements. The SAP-DoA accuracy was compared to that of the standard time-domain hyperbola approach. As expected, both methods give better results when the distance between the sought reinforcing elements is longer. The hyperbolic interpolation method is more accurate than SAP-DoA for circular-section objects; nevertheless, in the case of targets with different shape, the hyperbola approach cannot be employed whereas the SAP-DOA method can still provide interesting results: see Fig. 3.

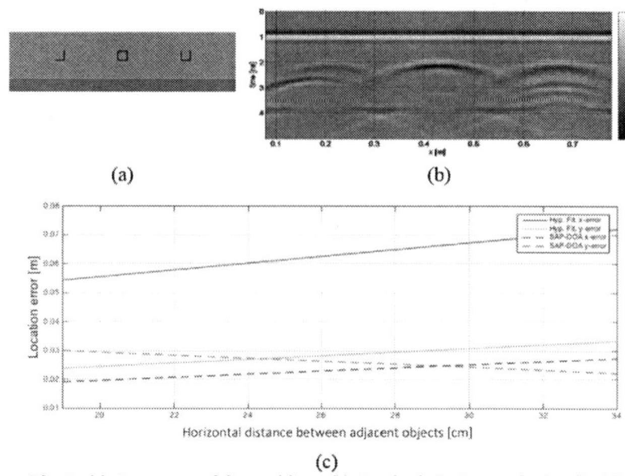

Fig. 3. (a) Geometry of the problem, (b) Synthetic B-Scan calculated with gprMax, (c) Results of SAP-DoA and hyperbola methods.

IV. Conclusions

This paper presents results obtained during three COST Short-Term Scientific Missions (STSM), dealing with the development of modelling and inversion techniques for Ground Penetrating Radar (GPR) applications. STSMs are flexible bottom-up networking tools, encouraging and supporting researchers to work together, start new international collaborations or strengthen existing ones. Most visits yield interesting scientific results in a short period of time.

Acknowledgment

The Authors thank COST (European COoperation in Science and Technology) for funding the Action TU1208 "Civil engineering applications of Ground Penetrating Radar."

References

[1] L. Pajewski, A. Benedetto, X. Derobert, A. Giannopoulos, A. Loizos, G. Manacorda, M. Marciniak, C. Plati, G. Schettini, and I. Trinks, "Applications of Ground Penetrating Radar in civil engineering – COST Action TU1208," Proc. 7th Internat. Workshop on Advanced Ground Penetrating Radar (IWAGPR), 2-5 July 2013, Nantes, France, pp. 1-6.

[2] L. Pajewski, A. Giannopoulos, S. Lambot, M. Marciniak, S. Meschino, N. Pinel, M. Sbartai, and C. Warren, "Short-Term Scientific Missions on electromagnetic modelling and inversion techniques for Ground Penetrating Radar – COST Action TU1208," Proc. 2016 IEEE European Conference on Antennas and Propagation (EuCAP), 11-15 April 2016, Davos, Switzerland, pp. 1-5.

[3] C. Warren, A. Giannopoulos, and I. Giannakis, "gprMax: Open source software to simulate electromagnetic wave propagation for Ground Penetrating Radar," Computer Physics Communications, vol. 209, pp. 163-170, Dec. 2016.

[4] L. M. Brekhovskikh, *Waves in Layered Media*. New York: Academic Press, 1980.

[5] S. Meschino and L. Pajewski, "Application of a SAP-DoA method to GPR data for the location of reinforcing elements in concrete," Microwave Mediterranean Symposium, Lecce, Italy, November 30-December 2, 2015, pp. 1-4.

Ground Penetrating Radar Data Imaging via Kirchhoff Migration Method

X. Liu, M. Serhir, A. Kameni, M. Lambert, L. Pichon

GeePs | Group of electrical engineering - Paris, UMR CNRS 8507, CentraleSupélec, Univ. Paris-Sud, Université Paris-Saclay, Sorbonne Universités, UPMC Univ Paris 06

3 & 11 rue Joliot-Curie, Plateau de Moulon 91192 Gif-sur-Yvette CEDEX, France, Xiang.liu@centralesupelec.fr

Abstract—**In this paper the imaging of Ground Penetrating Radar (GPR) scenario via Kirchhoff migration (KM) method is seen as a validation of the controlled experimental data and as a first step toward more elaborate imaging techniques. One of our goals is to have the possibility to acquire experimental data in a controlled laboratory environment. The bi-static GPR data is then acquired and validated by comparison with electromagnetic simulation. The imaging process is obtained using either the total field or the filtered one.**

***Index Terms*—GPR, imaging, Kirchhoff migration.**

I. Introduction

The use of Ground-Penetrating Radar (GPR) has been developed in an extended number of applications for many years. The GPR technique is used in geophysics and civil engineering to provide effective and accurate imaging of underground structures and for buried objects detection. It still needs development as shown by the recent COST Action TU1208 "Civil Engineering Application of Ground Penetrating Radar" [1], [2], [3]. Therefore, it is interesting to explore the GPR performance for estimating the target location.

The migration techniques are the traditional GPR imaging tools enabling to localize the targets with relatively high-resolution [4], [5], [6]. The Kirchhoff migration is applied onto the B-scan GPR data obtained either using the measurements in the CentraleSupélec anechoic chamber or the synthetic data computed by the electromagnetic simulation software CST MICROWAVE STUDIO (CST-MWS). The other migration techniques (Stolt, Stripmap, SAR) are equivalent to Kirchhoff one. We have chosen this technique because of its simplicity and reliability for GPR data analysis.

II. GPR Scenario

The front view scheme of GPR scenario is presented in Fig. 1(a), where E/R denote the transmission/reception Vivaldi antennas operating from 500 MHz to 3.5 GHz with 128 frequency-steps. The wooden box filled with dry sand ($\epsilon_r \simeq 2.53$) is placed over a metal plate in order to eliminate uncontrollable reflections below the box. Two metal bars of the same length and of square/circular cross-section are buried in the sand. The center of the sandbox is considered as the origin of the axis, the B-scan displacement range going from -200 mm to 200 mm with a step of 20 mm. More details of the GPR scenario parameters can be found in Fig. 1. The

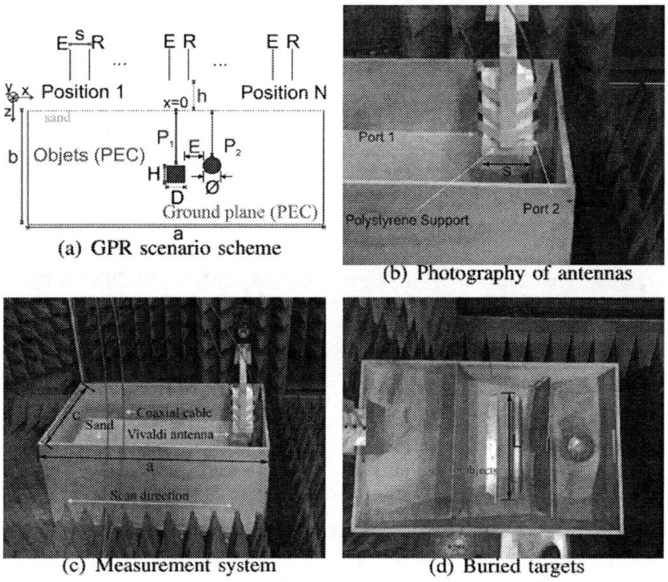

Fig. 1. GPR scenario scheme (a), the dimensions (in mm) being $a = 1000$, $b = 210$, $c = 600$, $H = 50$, $D = 50$, $L = 500$, $P_1 = 125$, $\varnothing = 50$, $P_2 = 95$, $E = 50$, $S = 100$, $h = 2$ and photos of the equipment (b) (c) (d).

same configuration is considered in the simulation procedure with CST-MWS in which both the antennas and sandbox are modeled (3D model). Comparison between experimental data and synthetic data (either computed using CST-MWS or using a laboratory-made software based on Discontinuous Galerkin Time-Domain method) are shown in [7].

The experimental and synthetic radargrams are presented in Fig. 2. The total field radargram (Fig 2(a)) includes the reflections due to the air/sand interface, the antennas coupling, then, the buried metallic objects and finally, the bottom metal plate placed under the sandbox. The reflections due to the air/sand interface and antennas coupling can be seen as a perturbation and should, when possible, be eliminated. One way to do it is to have access to the incident field defined as the electromagnetic field existing in the absence of the targets and to subtract it from the total field to be able to work with the scattered field. However, in the practical GPR case, the measurement of incident field is usually unavailable and could be replaced by the average of the total field on the receivers leading to the filtered field. The latter, shown in Fig 2(b),

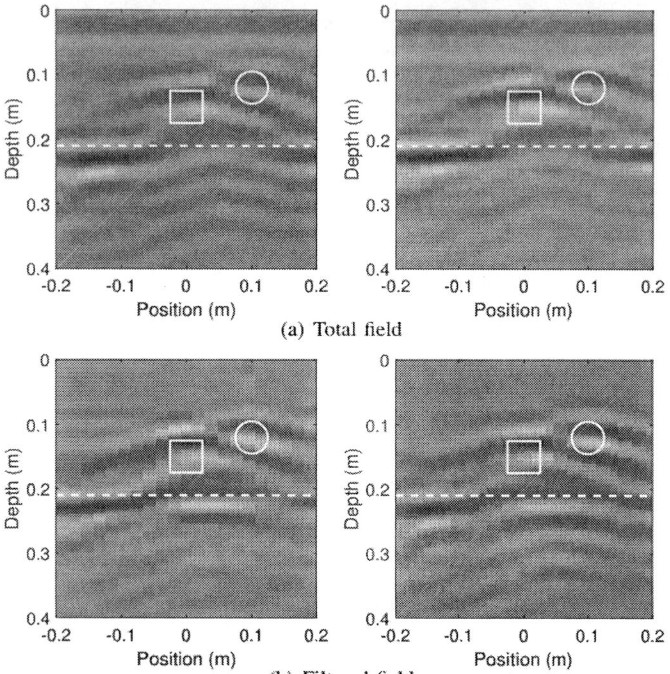

(a) Total field

(b) Filtered field

Fig. 2. Radargrams with two buried objects: CST-MWS (left) and measurement (right), the solid line contour present the exact position of buried objects, the dashed line is the bottom metal plate.

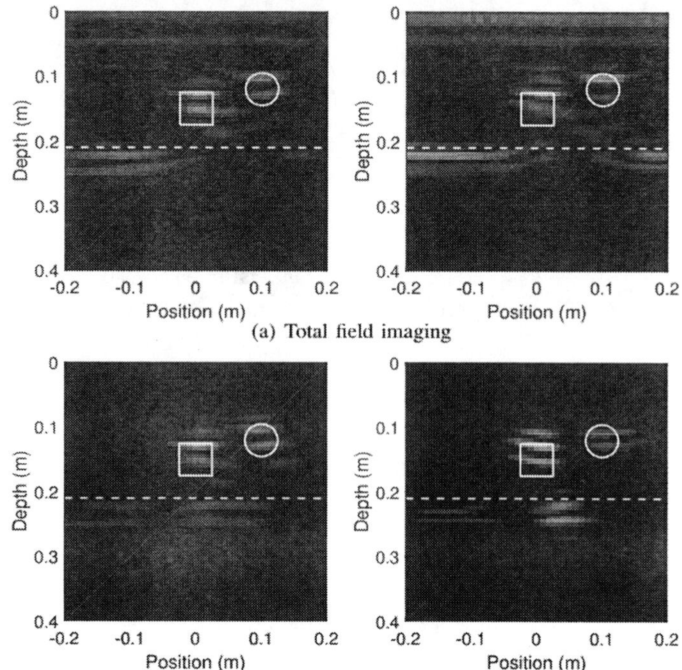

(a) Total field imaging

(b) Filtered field imaging

Fig. 3. KM imaging : CST-MWS (left) and measurement (right).

is similar to the scattered one. A good agreement between simulation and experimentation is obtained for all the fields.

III. GPR imaging results via Kirchhoff migration

As shown in the radargrams, the scatterers are delineated by hyperbola signatures. In this section, the KM imaging technique is applied to attempt to localize the targets with a higher resolution.

KM is based on an integral solution of the scalar wave equation. It is performed by using the Kirchhoff integral representation of a field at a given point as a superposition of waves propagating from adjacent points and times [8]. Our KM imaging results are displayed in Fig. 3. As expected the focusing onto the targets and the metal bottom plate locations is achieved by applying the KM either onto the measured data or the simulated one. The results using the filtered field (Fig. 3(b)) show an improvement of the localization by washing out the air/sand interface reflections and the antennas coupling.

IV. Conclusion

In this paper, the synthetic and measured B-scan GPR data are used for GPR imaging via Kirchhoff migration. Localization of two obstacles has been achieved. A filtering process is used to eliminate the environment influences while the incident field is absent. More detailed informations and results will be discussed during the conference.

As well-known the Kirchhoff migration does not provide any information about target shape and/or extension and should be seen as a first step toward more advanced imaging techniques such as an Enhanced Linear Sampling Method already developed by the authors in a free space configuration [9] and currently under extension for the GPR application.

Acknowledgment

This research was carried out within the framework of EU funded COST Action TU1208 Civil Engineering Applications of Ground Penetrating Radar.

References

[1] D. J. Daniels, *Ground Penetrating Radar*. Institution of Engineering and Technology (IET), 2004, vol. 1.

[2] L. Pajewski, A. Benedetto *et al.*, "Applications of ground penetrating radar in civil engineering–COST action TU1208," in *7th IEEE International Workshop on Advanced Ground Penetrating Radar (IWAGPR)*, 2013, pp. 1–6.

[3] A. Benedetto and L. Pajewski, *Civil Engineering Applications of Ground Penetrating Radar*. Springer, 2015.

[4] R. Stolt, "Migration by fourier transform," *Geophysics*, vol. 43, no. 1, pp. 23–48, 1978.

[5] C. G. Gilmore, "A comparison of imaging methods using GPR for landmine detection and a preliminary investigation into the sem for identification of buried objects," Master's thesis, University of Manitoba, 2004.

[6] F. Soldovieri, A. Brancaccio *et al.*, "A kirchhoff-based shape reconstruction algorithm for the multimonostatic configuration: The realistic case of buried pipes," *IEEE Transactions on Geoscience and Remote Sensing*, vol. 46, no. 10, pp. 3031–3038, Oct 2008.

[7] X. Liu, M. Serhir *et al.*, "3-d discontinuous galerkin time-domain antenna modelling and overall ground-penetration radar scenario," in *10th International Symposium on Electric and Magnetic Fields (EMF 2016)*, Lyon, France, pp. PC–1.

[8] J. Gazdag and P. Sguazzero, "Migration of seismic data," *Proceedings of the IEEE*, vol. 72, no. 10, pp. 1302–1315, 1984.

[9] X. Liu, M. Serhir *et al.*, "GPR imaging via multi-frequency linear sampling method," in *10th International Symposium on Electric and Magnetic Fields (EMF 2016)*, Lyon, France, pp. OA3–2.

Advanced Imaging for Down-Looking Contactless GPR Systems

Davide Comite[1], Alessandro Galli[1], Ilaria Catapano[2], and Francesco Soldovieri[2]
[1] Department of Information Engineering, Electronics and Telecommunications, Sapienza University of Rome, Via Eudossiana 18, 00184, Rome, Italy, email: davide.comite, alessandro.galli@uniroma1.it
[2] Institute for Electromagnetic Sensing of the Environment (IREA), National Research Council of Italy (CNR), Via Diocleziano 328, 80124, Naples, Italy, email: catapano.i, soldovieri.f@irea.cnr.it

***Abstract*—An advanced imaging procedure for Ground Penetrating Radar (GPR) operating in contactless configuration, i.e., when data are collected at a certain distance from the air-soil interface, is proposed in this contribution. The algorithm is based on an advanced implementation of a microwave tomographic approach recently proposed by the authors, which is capable of accounting for the near-field distribution generated by the transmitting antenna. Numerical data are obtained by means of a full-wave solution of the direct scattering problem, suitably implementing a realistic system on a commercial code. Both metallic and dielectric canonical objects can be considered to compare the performances of the proposed algorithm with respect to more conventional procedures based on simplifying hypotheses.**

***Index Terms*—Ground penetrating radar, inverse scattering, contactless configuration, microwave imaging.**

I. Introduction

Detection and reconstruction of shallow-buried targets by means of Ground Penetrating Radar (GPR) systems working both in ground-coupled or stand-off (i.e., contactless) configurations are highly desirable for several applications, such as demining and planetary exploration as well as for a wide class of non-destructing analyses [1], [2]. Several algorithms have been proposed in the last two decades for an effective representation of the raw data collected by GPR systems [2]. A large number of approaches are based on the linear Microwave Tomography (MT) [1], that has shown to be capable of providing effective 2D and 3D reconstructions in many real situations (e.g., archeology and structural diagnosis) and in different measurement configurations [1].

In standard implementations of the inversion and post-processing procedures, the source activating the scattering phenomenon is modeled as a filamentary electric current or even as an impinging plane wave, assuming, in this last case, the transmitter located in the far-field with respect to the illuminated object. In this context, some efforts have been already focused on the possibility of taking into the account the radiation pattern of the antenna that illuminates the considered object: in [3], a first insight into the role played by the antenna pattern for linear MT inversion algorithm has been provided, whereas in [4] an extension of a migration algorithm, capable to account for the radiation pattern of an ideal antenna for multicomponent GPR data, have been proposed. A diffraction tomography algorithm accounting for the incident near-field distribution has been also proposed in [5].

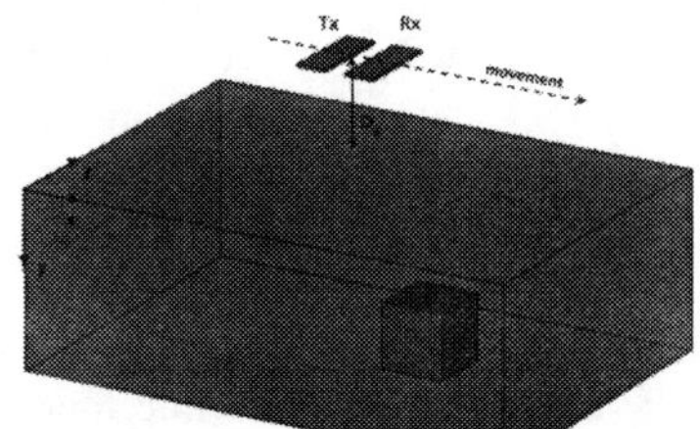

Fig. 1. 3D reference scenarios: a canonical object having dimension comparable with respect to the probing wavelength is buried in the shallow region made by a dielectric half-space. The GPR can operate in monostatic or bistatic configurations and is placed at a distance D_g from the air-soil interface.

For some applications, such as road prospecting [1] or planetary exploration [6], the capability to collect and elaborate data in contactless configuration, i.e., when the system is placed at a certain distance from the air-soil interface, is highly desirable. In this frame different theoretical solutions that consider the presence of the interface based on a spectral decomposition of the Green's function of the problem has been proposed (see e.g., [7] and references therein).

The present contribution aims at investigating the performance achievable through linear MT approaches when the radiative features of a realistic directional wide-band antenna are included in the algorithm. We focus our analysis on an antenna system as that proposed for the WISDOM rover, in the framework of the ongoing design of the ExoMars planetary mission [6], which requires a compact wide-band radiator to focus electromagnetic signals in the ground. A wide-band printed Vivaldi (0.5 - 3 GHz) antenna operating at a certain distance from the air-soil interface is thus considered as an effective and reliable solution to both Tx and Rx antennas [6]. We exploit here an efficient and reliable customized numerical implementation of CST Microwave Studio, widely tested by the authors to simulate actual GPR scenarios involving also commercial systems [8]. In this framework, the evaluation of the radiative features of the Vivaldi antenna working in ground-coupled configurations has been already developed by the authors e.g. in [9], where the near field distribution of the antenna has been included in the algorithm and the results are compared with those achieved when the inversion is performed by modeling the scattering phenomenon as occurring in a homogeneous medium. Here we propose some first new results for a more general implementation, which removes the assumption of homogeneous medium and allows us to account for the presence of the air-soil interface.

II. Theoretical Analysis and Discussion

We assume a 2D half-space model with a GPR working in monostatic configuration placed at a distance D_g from the interface between the air and a nonmagnetic dielectric medium with $\varepsilon_r = 3.2$ (see Fig. 1). As a simplifying hypothesis, but without loss of generality, we consider here the direct solution of the scattering problem on a 2D plane (i.e., the xy plane in Fig. 1 half-cutting the buried object). Thus, the dyadic nature of the wave/material interactions is neglected and the 2D scalar case is considered. Under the Born approximation (BA) [1] the imaging procedure is formulated as a linear inverse scattering problem in the frequency domain [1]. At each angular frequency ω and for each position of the antennas, the scattered field at the receiver can be modeled as follows

$$E_s(x_R,\omega) = k_b^2 \int_D G(x;\mathbf{r}';\omega)E_i(x_s;\mathbf{r}';\omega)\chi(\mathbf{r}')d\mathbf{r}' \quad (1)$$

where $E_s(x_R,\omega)$ denotes the complex scattered electric field at $f = \omega/(2\pi)$, probed at x when the source is located at x_s; k_b is the wavenumber in the lower half-spaces, G is the Green's function of the problem, χ the contrast function (unknown of the problem), and E_i is the incident electric field (i.e., radiated by the transmitting antenna) in the lower half-space (in absence of scatterers). To account for the presence of the air-soil interface we exploit the following spectral representation of the Green's function [1]:

$$G(x_R,\mathbf{r}') = \frac{-j}{2\pi}\int_{-\infty}^{\infty} \frac{e^{-jk_{y_b}y'}e^{jk_{y_0}D_g}}{k_{y_0}+k_{y_b}} e^{-jk_y(x_R-x')}dk_x \quad (2)$$

being $k_{y_0} = \sqrt{k_0^2 - k_x^2}$ and $k_{y_b} = \sqrt{k_s^2 - k_x^2}$. For the incident field we have $E_i(x_T, x', y') = -j\omega\mu_0 G(x_R, x', y')$ [1]. To solve for the unknown contrast function χ, equation (1) is discretized, inverted, and regularized through the truncated singular value decomposition (TSVD) approach [1], [3]. To account for the actual near-field distribution radiated by the antenna we have generalized the procedure outlined in [9]: the field radiated by a Vivaldi antenna and simulated on CST is exported and suitably inserted in equation (1), hence the TSVD regularization scheme is adopted [1], [2].

To assess and compare the capability of the advanced algorithm (accounting for the actual field radiated by the antenna [9]) we compare the imaging results with those provided by the MT approach as implemented in the standard way, i.e., modeling the incident field as radiated by a filamentary current through the spectral representation in (2). In Figs. 2(a) and (b) the reconstruction obtained for metallic cube (see caption for details) is reported for both the implementations. One can clearly recognize the signature relevant to the target. The upper

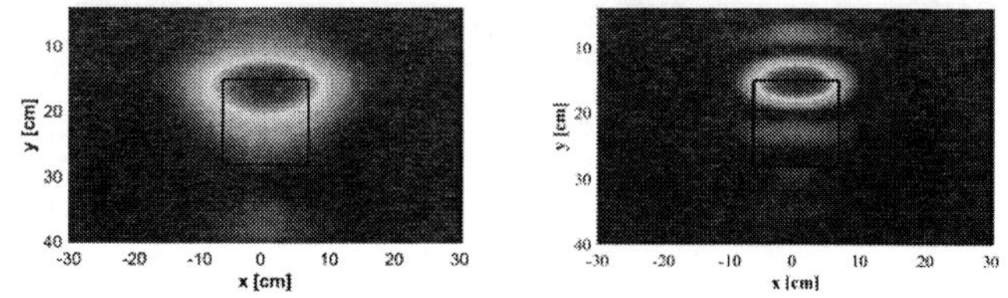

(a) (b)

Fig. 2. Tomographic reconstruction of a metallic cube (side 13 cm) buried at a distance $d = 15$ cm from the interface. a) Standard implementation od the algorithm based on the spectral representation of the Green's function. b) Advanced implementation taking into account the actual implementation of the near-field radiated by the Vivaldi antenna. $T^{\mathrm{tsvd}} = -20$ dB, the black square represents the xy section of the actual cube.

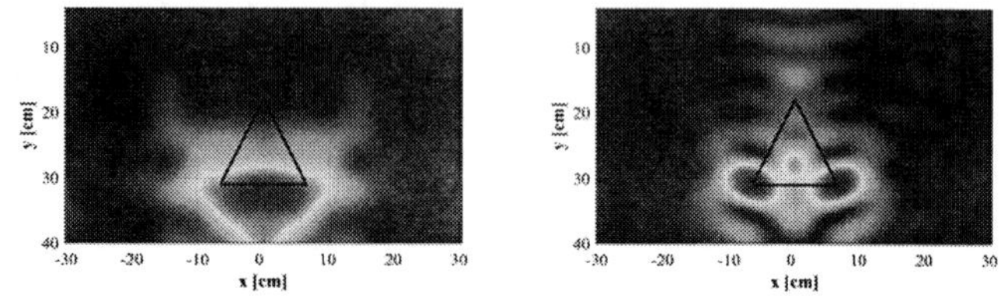

(a) (b)

Fig. 3. As in Fig. 2 for a metallic pyramid (base 13 cm, height 13 cm, depth 18 cm). a) Standard and b) Advanced algorithm, $T^{\mathrm{tsvd}} = -25$ dB.

side of the cube is better resolved by the advanced implementation, which provides also an improved focusing of the illuminated side of the object. In Fig. 3 the same comparison is presented for a pyramid scatterer. Also in this case the reconstruction capabilities of the advanced implementation are manifestly improved, since the two main edges at bottom of the pyramid are much better located and reconstructed. Extensions of the analysis to other targets are in progress and will be shown at the conference.

References

[1] R. Persico, *Ground Penetrating Radar: Inverse scattering and data processing*. John Wiley & Sons Inc, 2014.

[2] M. Pastorino, *Microwave Imaging*. John Wiley & Sons Inc, 2010.

[3] F. Soldovieri, R. Persico, and G. Leone, "Effect of source and receiver radiation characteristics in subsurface prospecting within the distorted Born approximation," *Radio Sci.*, vol. 40, pp. 1–13, Jun. 2005.

[4] R. Streich and J. van der Kruck, "Accurate imaging of multicomponent GPR data based on exact radiation patterns," *IEEE Trans. Geosci. Remote Sens.*, vol. 45, pp. 93-103, Jan. 2007.

[5] C. Dourthe, C. Pichot, J. Y. Dauvignac, and J. Cariou, "Inversion algorithm and measurement system for microwave tomography of buried object," *Radio Sci.*, vol. 35, pp. 1097–1108, Apr. 2000.

[6] V. Ciarletti et al., "WISDOM GPR designed for shallow and high-resolution sounding of the martian subsurface," *Proc. of IEEE*, vol. 99, pp. 825–836, May 2011.

[7] T. B. Hansen and P. M. Johansen, "Inversion scheme for ground penetrating radar that takes into account the planar air-soil interface," *IEEE Trans. Geosci. Remote Sens.*, vol. 38, pp. 496-506, Jan. 2000.

[8] D. Comite, A. Galli, I. Catapano, and F. Soldovieri, "The role of the antenna radiation pattern in the performance of a microwave tomographic approach for GPR imaging," *IEEE J. Sel. Topics Appl. Earth Observ. Remote Sens.*, doi 10.1109/JSTARS.2016.2636833, Jan. 2017.

[9] D. Comite, A. Galli, S. E. Lauro, E. Mattei, and E. Pettinelli, "Analysis of GPR early-time signal features for the evaluation of soil permittivity through numerical and experimental surveys," *IEEE J. Sel. Topics Appl. Earth Observ. Remote Sens.*, vol. 9, pp. 178–187, Jan. 2016.

Intersecting Silicon Nano-Walls With Planar Nano-Gold layers For Solar Energy Harvesting

Nihal F. F. Areed and Sami Zenad
Electronics and Electrical Communications Department
Faculty of Engineering, Mansoura University
Mansoura, Egypt
nfayez@zewailcity.edu.eg and sami9354@gmail.com

Salah S. A. Obayya
Centre for Photonics and Smart Material
Zewail City of Science and Technology,
Sheikh Zayed District, 6th of October City, Giza, Egypt,
sobayya@zewailcity.edu.eg

***Abstract*— In this paper, four designs for intersecting silicon Nano wall with planar nano-gold layers are proposed and simulated. Nano-gold layers are employed to create plasmonic modes at the Si/Gold interface. Adjusting the dimensions of the proposed hybrid Si-Gold structures shows 79.3% enhancement in the ultimate efficiency over the Si veins structure.**

Keywords— ***Energy harvesting; Silicon nano wires***

I. INTRODUCTION

Over the last five decades, silicon photovoltaics have been commercially developed to convert solar energy into electric energy with about 20% harvesting conversion efficiencies that relatively paved the way for replacing the nonrenewable energy sources. However, large-scale implementation is currently not economically feasible because the fabrication of the silicon photovoltaics depends on expensive silicon wafer, which requires extensive purification. Therefore, reducing the quantities of the silicon by using nanostructures solar cells will help drive large-scale implementation. Recently, SiNWs have been of particular interest in the solar harvesting research because of their highest ability for harvesting the solar energy [1-5]. In 2014, elliptical SiNW with broadband light absorption and 12.6% absorption enhancement as compared with circular has been reported by Ren *et al.* [4]. Additionally, Hussein *et. al.* has reported decagonal array of cylindrical SiNW with 39.95% ultimate showing improvement over the thin film solar cells of equal thickness with an efficiency of 13.83%. Plasmonic solar cells are considered as one of the most important topic among the scientific researchers in the last decade [6-7]. The combination of noble metallic nano particles that exhibit strong optical extinction and the silicon photovoltaic cells generates surface plasmonic polariton (SPP) modes at the Si/metal interface and hence the harvesting capabilities of such plasmonic photovoltaic cells can be enhanced. There are many designs for plasmonic solar cells which are differing in shapes, geometries and dimensions [6-7]. In [6], a design of decagonal array of SiNWs with hybrid Si/Au core is reported. The design of [6] shows broadband absorption with 32.62 % ultimate efficiency that is higher than that of decagonal array of SiNWs by 19.7%. It is worth noting that the previously reported highest efficiency nanostructured solar cells required complicated fabrication processing.

In contrast, in this paper, we propose and simulate four different square lattice hybrid Si-Gold veins structures that are relatively easy for fabrication and can be applied efficiently for solar energy harvesting. The optical simulation is carried out using 3D FDTD and mode solver implemented in Lumerical software [7]. The computational domain in FDTD comprises 3D unit cell surrounded by periodic boundary conditions (BCs) along x and y directions and perfect matched layers (PML) BCs along the z direction. X-polarized plane wave is used to illuminate the proposed structures to calculate the Si absorption. The ultimate efficiency is calculated based on the following relation [3]

$$\eta_{Si} = \frac{\int_{300\,nm}^{\lambda g} I(\lambda)A(\lambda)\frac{\lambda}{\lambda g}d\lambda}{\int_{300\,nm}^{4000\,nm} I(\lambda)d\lambda} \quad (1)$$

where λ is the wavelength, I (λ) is the solar spectral irradiance (AM1.5) of the direct normal and circumsolar spectrum, A (λ) is the absorption and λg is the wavelength corresponding to the bandgap of the Si and is equal to 1100 nm and the integral is evaluated using the trapezoid rule with 350 sampling points.

II. PROPOSED STRUCTURE AND RESULTS

Figure 1(a) shows the unit cell of proposed intersecting Si nano-walls structure shown in the inset of Fig.1 (b).

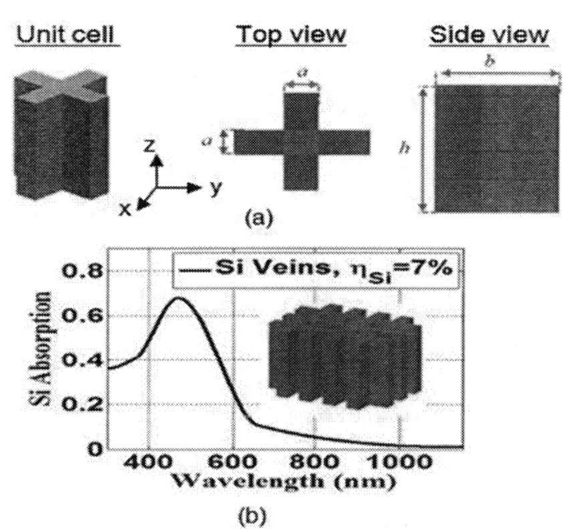

Fig.1 (a) Intersecting Si nano-wall structure, (b) absorption spectrum

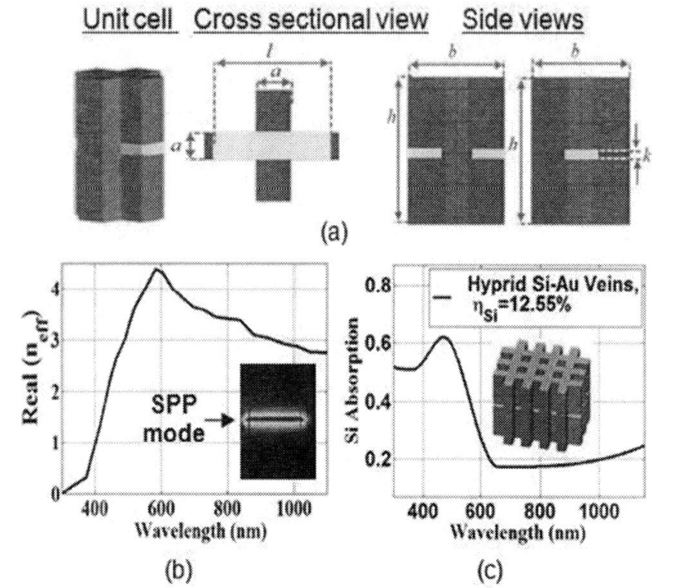

Fig. 2 (a) hybrid Si-Au structure unit cell, (b) SPP mode at the Si/Au interface, (c) Absorption spectrum

It is evident from the figure that Si wall has width a, length b and height h. Adjusting the dimensions of the intersecting Si nano-walls structure to a = 62 nm, b = 166 and h = 480 nm results in ultimate efficiency of about 7% as shown in Fig.1 (b). Figure 2(a) shows the unit cell of the proposed intersecting Si nano-walls structure with planar nano-gold layer. The insertion of the gold layer creates SPP modes at the Si/Gold interface as shown in the inset of Fig.2 (b). Figure 2(b) shows also the real part of effective index, n_{eff} of the estimated SPP mode that is calculated using FDM [3]. The figure illustrates that the values of the n_{eff} over the wavelength range extending from 650 nm up to 900 nm are approximately equal to the refractive index of the Si. Therefore, the generated SPP mode appears to enhance the energy harvesting capabilities of the Si layer as shown in Fig.2(c). The figure illustrates that at the tuned dimensions, a = 62 nm, b = 166, h = 490 nm, l = 166 nm and k =10 nm, the ultimate efficiency, reaches 12.55%.

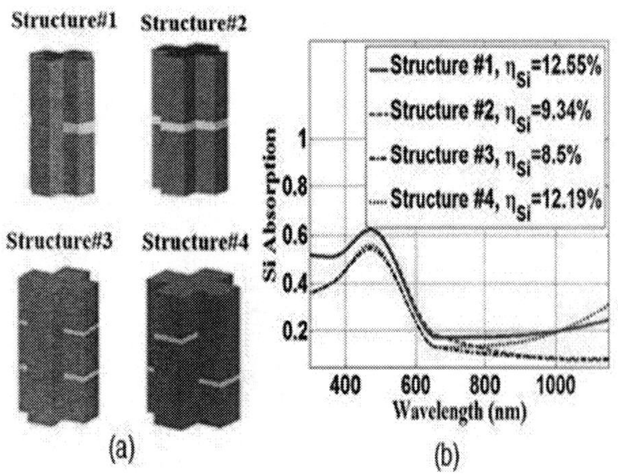

Fig.3 (a) proposed hybrid Si-Gold structures, (b) Absorption spectra.

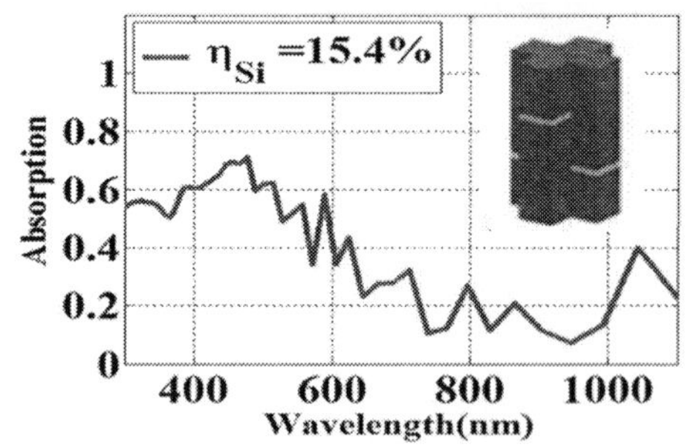

Fig.4 Proposed structure #4 with 1000 nm height

Figure 3(a) shows four unit cells for four proposed designs for intersecting Si nano-walls with planar Gold layers. Each structure differs than the other either in the positions or the numbers of the gold layers. Figure 3 (b) shows that 10 nm-thick gold layers should be added in the Si veins structure with 480 nm height as proposed either in structure#1 or structure#4, where the metal absorption loss is minimum and the ultimate efficiency is higher than 12%. Figure 4(a) shows the calculated absorption for the proposed structure#4 with 1000 nm height. It is evident from the figure that with increasing the height of the Si walls from 500 nm to 1000 nm increases the ultimate efficiency to 15.4%.

III. Conclusion

Four novel designs based on intersecting Si nano-walls and nano-gold layers have been proposed and simulated for harvesting solar energy. The tuned dimensions and the number of the gold layers that result in minimum metallic absorption losses and maximum harvesting efficiency have been investigated. The results reveal that combining the gold layers with the intersecting Si nano-walls approximately doubles the harvesting efficiency of the intersecting Si nano-walls.

References

[1] S. S. A. Obayya, Nihal F. F. Areed, Mohamed Farhat. O. Hameed and Mohamed Hussein, Optical Nano-antennas For Energy Harvesting, Innovative materials and systems for energy harvesting applications, Innovative materials and systems for energy harvesting applications, IGI Global, 2015.

[2] J. M. Kontio, H. Husu, J. Simonen, M. J. Huttunen, J. Tommila, M. Pessa, and M. Kauranen, "Nanoimprint fabrication of gold nanocones with ~10 nm tips for enhanced optical interactions," *Opt. Lett*, vol. 34, no. 13, pp. 1979-1981, 2009.

[3] Mohamed Hussen, M. F. O. Hameed, Nihal F. F. Areed, S.S.A. Obayya, "Ultra high efficient solar cell based on decagonal arrays of silicon nanowires", *Opt. Eng. J.*, vol. 5, no.11, pp. 117105, 2014.

[4] Rui Ren; Yong-Xin Guo; Ri-Hong Zhu, "Enhanced absorption in elliptical silicon nanowire arrays for solar energy harvesting," *Opt. Eng. J.*, vol. 53, no. 2, pp. 027102, 2014.

[5] Nihal. F. F. Areed, Mohamed Fouad, S. S. A.Obayya," Highly Efficient solid gear-shaped silicon nanowire for solar energy harvesting," *IEEE Photon. techno. Lett.*, DOI: 10.1109/LPT.2016.2636230, 2016.

[6] Mohamed Hussein, Nihal F. F. Areed, M. F. O. Hameed, S. S. A. Obayya, "Hybrid core semiconductor nanowires for solar cell applications" The 4th *International conference on Numerical Simulation of Optoelectronic Devices*, NUSOD 2014, 1-4 September, Palma de Mallorca, Spain, 2014.

[7] Nihal F. F. Areed, Sameh El Malt, and Salah S. A. Obayya, "Broadband omnidirectional nearly perfect plasmonic absorber for solar energy harvesting," IEEE Photonics Journal, vol. 41, no. 5, pp. 1010., 2016.

[8] https://www.lumerical.com

Padé Boundary Conditions for Finite Element Time Domain Beam Propagation Method

Khaled S. R. Atia, A. M. Heikal, S.S.A. Obayya*

Center for Photonics and Smart Materials,
Zewail City of Science and Technology
6th of October City, Giza, Egypt
sobayya@zewailcity.edu.eg*

Abstract— **In this paper, we present Padé approximation boundary conditions for domain truncation in time domain analysis using finite element (FEM) beam propagation method. The method removes the number of unknowns required for the conventional perfectly matched layer (PML). The line integral resulted from FEM discretization is treated by solving the one dimensional Helmholtz wave equation at domain ports. The square root resulted from the solution is handled using the conventional Padé approximation. A waveguide example is introduced to measure the Reflection of the proposed boundary condition. The comparison between our approach and the conventional PML shows that our method produces reflection far less than the conventional PML.**

Keywords— Finite element time domain; Padé boundary condition; perfectly matched layer.

I. Introduction

Perfectly matched layer (PML) is essential for suppressing the outgoing waves from the physical domain so that the outgoing waves do not reflect back into the physical domain and affect the physical data [1]. It is widely used in several time domain methods [2 - 5] and frequency domain methods [6]. However, the PML requires to be sufficiently discretized in order to effectively suppress the outgoing waves. This additional discretization is considered a computational burden as it increases the number of unknowns and hence increased the computational time.

In attempt to replace the PML and overcome the computational burden, Padé boundary conditions has been introduced in finite element (FEM) frequency domain analysis [6]. The idea is simple, the line integrals resulted from discretizing the frequency domain wave equation is approximated by solving the one dimensional wave equation at the domain ports. The solution includes computing the square root of the characteristic matrix where Padé method is utilized to compute the square root.

In this paper, we, to the best of our knowledge, use Padé boundary condition (BC) for time domain analysis in order to remove the number of unknowns that results from using conventional PML. The rest of this paper is organized as follows. In section II, the formulation of the proposed method is introduced. A simple waveguide example is used to assets the proposed method in section III. Finally, the conclusion is made in section IV.

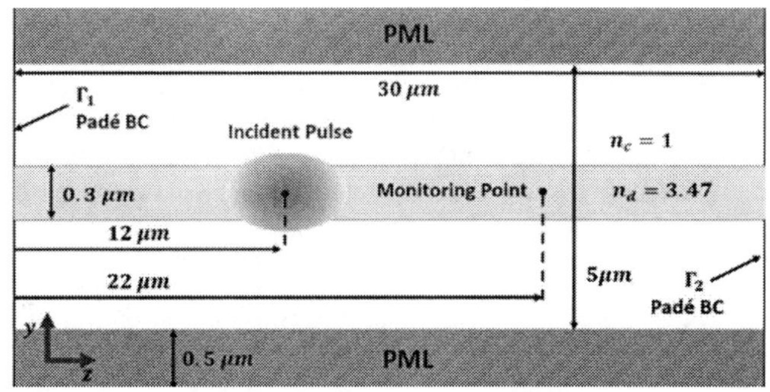

Fig. 1. Schematic diagram of the waveguide simulated.

II. Formulation

Consider the 2D structure shown in Fig. 1 where the propagation in yz plane and no variation in x direction. The Helmholtz wave equation in time domain under the slowly varying approximation can be written as

$$-s\frac{q}{c^2}\frac{\partial^2\phi}{\partial t^2} - 2js\frac{q\omega_o}{c^2}\frac{\partial\phi}{\partial t} + \frac{\partial}{\partial y}\left(p\frac{s_y}{s}\frac{\partial\phi}{\partial y}\right) + \frac{\partial}{\partial z}\left(p\frac{s_z}{s}\frac{\partial\phi}{\partial z}\right) + s\frac{\omega_o^2 q}{c^2}\phi = 0 \quad (1)$$

where for TE wave, $\phi = E_x$, $p = 1$, and $q = \varepsilon_r$. For TM wave, $\phi = H_x$, $p = 1/\varepsilon_r$, and $q = 1$. The PML parameters s, s_y, and s_z are described in [1, 2]. In addition, c is the speed of light and ω_o is the central angular frequency.

By dividing the spatial domain into triangular elements and apply the standard FEM procedure, we get the following equation,

$$\frac{-1}{c^2}[M]\frac{d^2\{\phi\}}{dt^2} - 2j\frac{\omega_o}{c^2}[M]\frac{d\{\phi\}}{dt} + \left([K] + \frac{\omega_o^2}{c^2}[M]\right)\{\phi\} + \sum_{i=1}^{ls}\int_{\Gamma_i}\psi\frac{\partial\phi}{\partial z_i}d\Gamma = 0 \quad (2)$$

where $[K]$ and $[M]$ are the standard FEM stiffness and mass matrices [1, 4]. Additionally, $\{\phi\}$ represents the global electric or magnetic field vector, ls is the number of boundaries to be replaced by Padé approximation, and ψ is FEM test function. It should be noted that Padé BC are used only in the direction of the propagation. Therefore, a PML is required at other boundaries. In order to compute the line integral in the previous equation, we solve the one dimensional wave propagation equation in frequency domain at the central frequency ω_o. Applying Padé approximation, we get the following expression for the derivative,

$$\frac{ps_z^2}{s}\frac{\partial}{\partial z_i}\phi\bigg|_m = \frac{1}{2j\beta_o}\frac{1}{\left(1-\frac{1}{2j\beta_o}\frac{\partial}{\partial z_i}\Big|_{m-1}\right)} \times\left\{k_o^2\left(qs - n_o^2\frac{ps_{zi}^2}{s}\right)\phi + s_y\frac{\partial}{\partial y}\left(p\frac{s_y}{s}\frac{\partial\phi}{\partial y}\right)\right\} - j\beta_o\frac{s_{zi}^2}{s}\phi \qquad (3)$$

where m corresponds to Padé order, β_o is the effective propagation constant, and n_o is the effective index. This equation is then discretized using FEM. The final formulation is obtained by plugging the discretized equation into Eq. 2. For simplicity, we may replace $[K]$ by $([K]+[C_i])$ where $[C_i]$ represents the discretized Eq. 3 which can be obtained from the algorithm introduced in [6]. We have to mention that $[C_i]$ is computed only once and integrated into $[K]$ so, we don't have to deal with it in each time step like conventional PML or convolutional PMLs. Finally, Padé approximation is utilized to reduce the modified Eq. 2 into first order differential equation and then Crank-Nicholson algorithm is applied [1, 4, 5].

III. Numerical Results

To show the performance of our method we consider the waveguide shown in Fig. 1. The central wavelength is $\lambda_o = 1.55\ \mu m$. The inputted Gaussian pulse is placed at $z_o = 12\ \mu m$ with a waist $W_o = 2\ \mu m$. Additionally, TE wave is considered here and 350 time steps are simulated with $\Delta t = 1\ fs$. In this example, Padé BCs are placed in y direction and a PML is placed in z direction. The computational domain is discretized into 29900 elements producing 15300 unknowns. The reflected wave is monitored at the monitoring point as in Fig. 1. The reflection characteristics are obtained by normalizing the Fourier transform of the reflected data to the input spectrum of the incident pulse.

We repeated the same calculations but using a PML layer instead of our boundary condition. The PML layer thickness is $1\ \mu m$ and is divided into 5 layers with a theoretical reflection $R = 10^{10}$. The PML added 1000 elements and the total number of unknowns are increased by 510 unknown. Figure 2 shows a comparison between our approach and the PML reported in [3 - 5]. It may be seen that our approach achieves lower reflection over a wide bandwidth while a high reflection can be noticed from the conventional PML. In addition, the normalized reflection of the presented method at the central wavelength is $\sim 1e-3$. It is worth noting that computing Padé approximation at the two ports is computed only once and it takes ~ 3 s. We should note that less reflections ($\sim 20\ dB$) can be obtained from the PML [2] but at the cost of adding more layers which increases the number of unknowns. An ultimate performance can be obtained by placing our boundary conditions behind a thin layer of PML where the reflection will be significantly reduced with less number of unknowns.

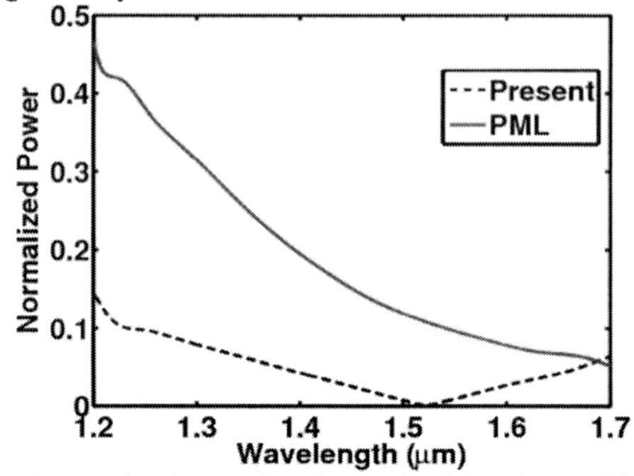

Fig. 1. A comparison between the reflection of Padé boundary conditions and the conventional PML.

IV. Conclusion

In this paper, padé boundary conditions is introduced to finite element time domain beam propagation method. The numerical results proved that our approach produces less reflection than a five layer PML. Moreover, our treatment significantly reduces the computational burden represented in additional number of unknowns used in the conventional PML.

References

[1] S. S. A. Obayya, Computational photonics, 1st ed. Chichester, West Sussex, U.K.: Wiley, 2011.

[2] M. Hussein, M. F. O. Hameed, N. F. F. Areed, A. Yahia, and S. S. A. Obayya, "Funnel-shaped silicon nanowire for highly efficient light trapping," Opt. Lett. 41, pp.1010-1013, 2016.

[3] K. S. R. Atia, and S. S. A. Obayya. "Novel Gradient Smoothing Method-Based Time Domain Beam Propagation Analysis of Optical Integrated Circuits." Signal Processing in Photonic Communications. Optical Society of America, 2015.

[4] K. S. R. Atia, A. M. Heikal, and S. S. A. Obayya. "Efficient smoothed finite element time domain analysis for photonic devices." Opt. Exp., vol. 23. no. 17, pp. 22199-22213, 2016.

[5] T. Fujisawa and M. Koshiba, "Time-Domain Beam Propagation Method for Nonlinear Optical Propagation Analysis and Its Application to Photonic Crystal Circuits", J. Lightwave Technol., vol. 22, no. 2, pp. 684-691, 2004.

[6] C. Rubio-Mercedes and H. Hernandez-Figueroa, "Padé Boundary Conditions for the Finite-Element Modeling of Arbitrary Planar Junctions", J. Lightwave Technol, vol. 22, no. 2, pp. 669-676, 2004.

Modified BPM for Plasmonic Modeling

Adel Shaaban, M.F.O. Hameed, S.S.A. Obayya*
Center for Photonics and Smart Materials,
Zewail City of Science and Technology
6th of October City, Giza, Egypt
sobayya@zewailcity.edu.eg*

Lotfi. R. Gomaa
Electrical Engineering Department,
Faculty of Engineering at Shoubra,
Banha University, Egypt

M. A. Swillam
Department of Physics,
The American University in Cairo,
New Cairo, Egypt

Abstract— **In this paper, we investigate the usefulness of the wide-angle Fast Fourier Transform-based Beam Propagation Method (FFT-BPM) in computational plasmonics. Major numerical difficulties associated with the singularity of the transverse derivative of the step-like refractive index at the interface plane, especially for the TM case, are circumvented using an equivalent-index formalism. A trigonometric function is used, for the first time to the authors' knowledge, to approximate the abrupt change of the refractive index at the interface. Accordingly, the TM problem is transformed to an equivalent TE one with no singular behavior.**

Keywords— ***Beam propagation method; plasmonics; computational electromagnetics.***

I. Introduction

Recently, the fast development of integrated electronic and photonic circuits has led to remarkable applications that permeate almost every facet of our daily lives. These devices scales with smaller dimensions have enabled faster, more efficient, and less expensive components a myriad of challenges. The plasmonics applications have attracted a lot of attention from the scientific community due to the interesting optical properties of metals in the presence of electromagnetic fields and this new plasmonic effects have many potential technological applications [1–4]. The plasmonics deal with the plasmons which are elementary excitations. The plasmon is created by the interacting of electromagnetic wave resonantly with collective electronic oscillations in a piece of metal, consequently produces a coupled hybrid state. One of the most common realizations of a plasmon wave is an optical mode propagating along an interface separating a dielectric medium and a metal. To study the propagation through plasmonic waveguide the beam propagation method (BPM) can be used [5-6]. The versatility of the BPM ranked it at the top of the numerical methods which are able to handle a broad class of applications in photonic integrated devices, nano-optical devices, near-field optical probing and sensors. The solution of wave equation allows only the TM mode to propagate inside such waveguide. The difficulties of using the BPM to model the TM field in plasmonic waveguide are obvious [7]. This is mainly due to the abrupt change in the refractive index at the interface.

In this paper, we seek to demonstrate the applicability of the BPM in studying the plasmonics waveguide, which were not studied before to the best of authors' knowledge by the FFT-BPM. We present also an extension of the BPM to investigate a severe case of the TM field at an abrupt discontinuity of the refractive index profile. It is shown that by a proper derivation of an "equivalent-index profile", the TM problem can be transformed to an equivalent TE one, where the usual BPM could be implemented very easily. As a demonstration, we present the results of the BPM to study plasmonics mode in metal insulator metal "MIM" and plasmonic directional coupler.

II. TM Beam Propagation Method

The scalar wave equation for the magnetic field $H_y(x,z)$ corresponding to the TM case takes the form:

$$\nabla^2 H_y(x,z) + k_0^2 n^2(x) H_y(x,z) - \frac{1}{n^2}\frac{\partial n^2}{\partial x}\frac{\partial H}{\partial x} \tag{1}$$

Obviously, the transverse derivative $\partial/\partial x$ of the square of the refractive index profile which is mixed with the transverse derivative of the field $\mathrm{H_y}(x,z)$ in the last term represents a major problem from the numerical point of view. However, Poladian et al. [8] have shown that the mixed term: $(\partial n^2/\partial x^2)(\partial H/\partial x)$ could be avoided by transforming the problem from the TM to an "equivalent" TE with an "equivalent" index given by:

$$n_{eq}^2(x) = n^2(x) - \frac{n(x)}{k_0}\frac{\partial^2}{\partial x^2}\frac{1}{n(x)} \tag{2}$$

Yamauchi et al. [9] have proposed a Sigmoid function to avoid this derivative singularity which takes the form:

$$n(a,x) = n_2 + \frac{\delta n}{1+e^{-(a/x)}} \tag{3}$$

Such sigmoid function has been tested to approximate the step-index profile at the interface for the TM case. Numerically, very large and sharp spikes (for $a \geq 500$) appear in the equivalent index when $n(x)$ is substituted with $n(a, x)$ from equation 3. Such spikes lead to a numerical diverging behavior, and hence the equivalent TE-BPM becomes impossible, unless "a" is reduced to much lower values than 10^4. However, this reduction in a degrades the accuracy of the equivalent TE-BPM. In this paper we proposed another function to solve the ambiguities associated with the sigmoid function. It is found that an "arctan" function is successful to approximate the abrupt change in the refractive index at x=0.

III. Numerical Results

Figure 1(a) shows a schematic diagram for the MIM plasmonics waveguide. In this study, the waveguide width is w=50 nm, the insulator material refractive index n_i=1.5 and the metal refractive index is taken as n_m=0.05+i4.27. The propagation distance is equal to 500 *nm*. Figure 1 (b) illustrates the propagated plasmonic mode inside the MIM waveguide. The results agree well with the theoretical expectations. Figure 2 (a) show the schematic diagram for two air grove (n=1.0) inside gold slab material. The gold refractive index is set to n_m =0.465+i10.34. The coupling between the two air waveguides after propagation distance of 1.5 μm is shown in Fig. 2 (b) approximate the abrupt change in the refractive index at x=0.

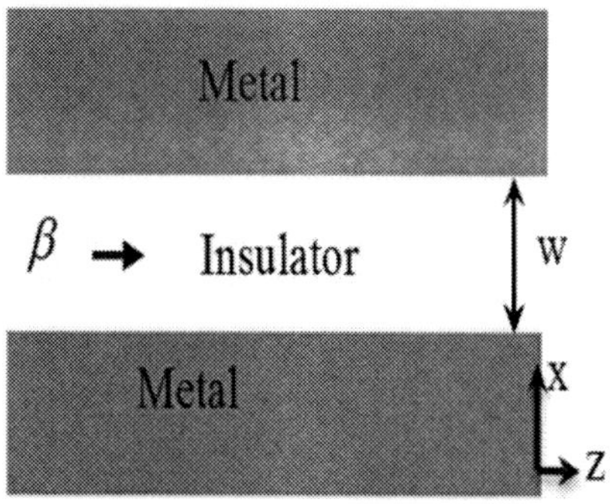

(a)

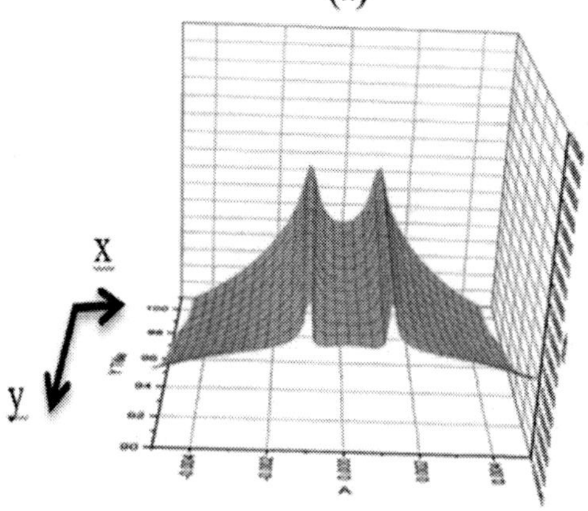

(b)

Fig. 1. (a) schematic diagram of the MIM plasmonic waveguide. (b) The plasmonics mode propagation through the MIM waveguide.

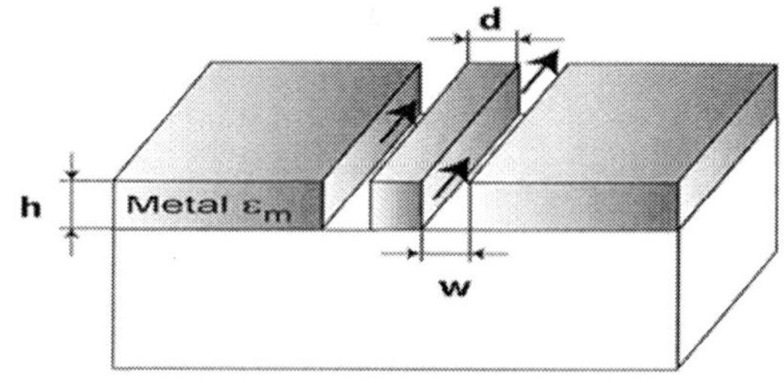

(a)

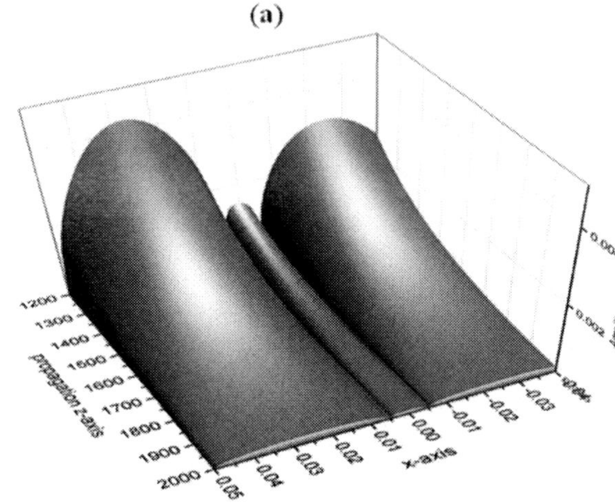

(b)

Fig. 2. (a) schematic diagram for the plasmonic directional coupler. (b) The coupled plasmonics mode propagation through the two air waveguides

IV. Conclusion

In this paper, the extreme usefulness of the BPM to study plasmonics waveguides is reported and analyzed. A new arctan function is used instead of sigmoid function to represent equivalent TM mode. Quite fair agreement between the theoretical results and the BPM results in MIM and plasmonics directional coupler applications.

References

[1] S.A. Maier, Plasmonics fundamentals and applications, Springer, New York, 2007.

[2] D. Sarid, W. Challener, Modern Introduction to Surface Plasmons, Cambridge University Press, Cambridge, 2010.

[3] Fillard, J., Near field optics and nanoscopy, World Scientific, 1996.

[4] F. F. K. Hussain, A. M. Heikal, M. F. O. Hameed, J. El-Azab,W. S. Abdelaziz, and S. S. A. Obayya, "Dispersion characteristics of asymmetric channel plasmon polariton waveguides," IEEE J. Quantum Electron., vol. 50, no. 6, pp. 474–482, Jun. 2014.

[5] A. Shaaban, M. B. El Mashade, L. R. Gomaa, M. Sayed, M. F. O. Hameed, S. S. A. Obayya, "Interaction Analysis of the Gaussian Beam On a Planar Dielectric Interface," International Conference on Renewable Energy (INCORE2016), Sharm El Sheikh, Egypt, 2016.

[6] Shaaban, L. R. Gomaa, M. F. O. Hameed, S. S. A. Obayya, "Study of Near and Far Fields of a Super-Gaussian Beam on a Step Discontinues Interface using FFT-BPM", The International Conference on Metamaterials, Photonic Crystals and Plasmonics (META) , Spain, 2016.

[7] Vassallo, C., "Difficulty with vectorial BPM," Electronics Letters, vol. 33. No. 1, pp. 61-62, 1997.

[8] Poladian L., F., Ladouceur, "Unification of TE and TM Beam Propagation Algorithms," IEEE Photonics technology letter, vol. 10, no. 1, pp. 105-107, 1998.

[9] J., Yamauchi, N. Shimada, Y. Nito, Hisamatsu N., "Transverse-Magnetic BPM Analysis of a Step-Index Slab Waveguide Expressed by a Sigmoid Function," IEEE Photonics technology letter., vol. 10, no. 1, 2009.

Light Absorption Enhancement in Thin Film Hydrgenated Amorphus Si Solar Cells

C. Mennucci, M.C. Giordano, C. Martella, D. Repetto, F. Buatier De Mongeot
Department of Physics,
University of Genova
Genova, Italy

M.H. Muhammad, A. H. K. Mahmoud, M.F.O. Hameed, S.S.A. Obayya*
Center for Photonics and Smart Materials,
Zewail City of Science and Technology
6th of October City, Giza, Egypt
sobayya@zewailcity.edu.eg*

***Abstract*—In this paper, light absorption enhancement in thin film solar cell (SC) is reported and analyzed. The suggested design is based on a nanostructured pattern that increases the diffuse scattered component of radiation and hence the absorption through the active layer. An ion beam sputtering (IBS) approach is used to texture large areas of the glass substrate with high aspect-ratio ripples in order to increase light scattering. Then, thin film SC supported on the textured glass is simulated and analyzed using 3D finite difference time domain (FDTD) method. The suggested SC can offer an ultimate efficiency of 19.26% with short circuit current of 15.76 mA/cm^2 with an enhancement of 31.435% over the SC without texturing surface.**

***Keywords*— thin film solar cell; finite difference time domain; textured glasses.**

I. Introduction

Recently, thin film solar cells (TF-SCs) have aroused great interest of researchers to minimize the cost of the photovoltaic devices. However, amorphous TF-SCs suffer from quite low carrier life time and short diffusion length. In order to increase light absorption in TF-SCs, light trapping techniques employing random textures or periodic grating structures can be used to increase the effective optical path length in a wide range of wavelengths. Photo-current enhancement in TF-SCs can be obtained using pseudo-periodic and random interface textures either at the front electrode or at the back reflector [1-2] since a large number of diffraction orders can be excited.

The aim of this paper is to demonstrate the feasibility of light trapping enhancement over a broad wavelength range employing nanofabrication methods based on self-organized approaches. Moreover, with the aim to meet large scale and cost effective production requirements, the potential of self-organized techniques based on ion beam sputtering (IBS) is explored.

II. AFM Analysis

Figure 1 shows the AFM topography of the nanostructured glass fabricated by defocused IBS at grazing incidence (θ=82°) through a self-organized sacrificial Au nanowire stencil mask. We stress that pseudo-periodic one-dimensional nanostructures (figure 1), elongated along the in-plane ion beam direction (red arrow), can be obtained over cm^2 area. AFM analysis allows to extract the relevant morphological parameters like root mean square roughness, in the range of 140 nm, and lateral periodicity distribution, which spans from about 200 nm to more than 1000 nm. Such a broadband distribution of surface features induces interesting behavior from the optical point of view. Optical investigation was carried out by measuring total and diffuse reflectance spectra in the VIS-NIR range by means of an integrating sphere. Textured glasses show broadband reduction of reflectance and enhanced scattering properties [3, 4]: Textured glass reflects 10% less light than a flat glass and shows that almost 60% of the light is scattered away from the specular angle of reflection indicating a Haze of 60% over the VIS-NIR spectrum.

Fig. 1. AFM topography of nanostructured glass. Red arrow indicates the in-plane ion-beam direction.

III. Simulation Methodology

Figure 2 shows cross section of a unit cell of the suggested TF-SC which is grown on a nano-patterned glass in a superstrate configuration. The transmission, reflection, and absorption of the proposed SC are calculated using 3D-FDTD method via Lumerical software package [5]. The incident plane wave has an electric field linearly polarized along the x-axis and propagates normal to the x-y plane as shown in Fig. 2 (a). In this study, a simple sinusoidal pattern with A=150 nm and D=800 nm is used to represent the textured geometry. Due to the symmetry of the structure, the suggested design with only one periodic texturing is simulated with periodic boundary

The authors would like to thank the "Science and Technology Development Fund" (STDF) at Egypt for the financial support under Italy/Egypt project number 25954.

condition (BC) in x and y- directions. Additionally, a perfect matched layer (PML) boundary condition is used in z-direction to eliminate unnecessary reflections at the top and bottom boundaries of the simulated unit cell. Two frequency domain monitors are used to calculate the total reflection R(λ) and the transmission T (λ), respectively as shown in Fig. 2 (a). In order to calculate the absorption through the hydrogenated amorphous Si active layer only, other two monitors are placed above and below the active layer.

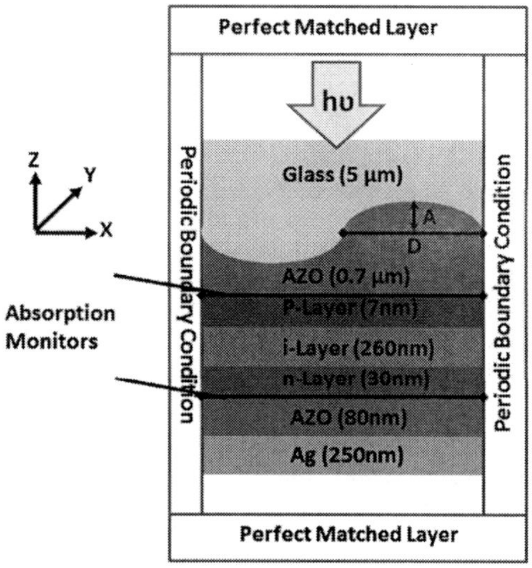

(a)

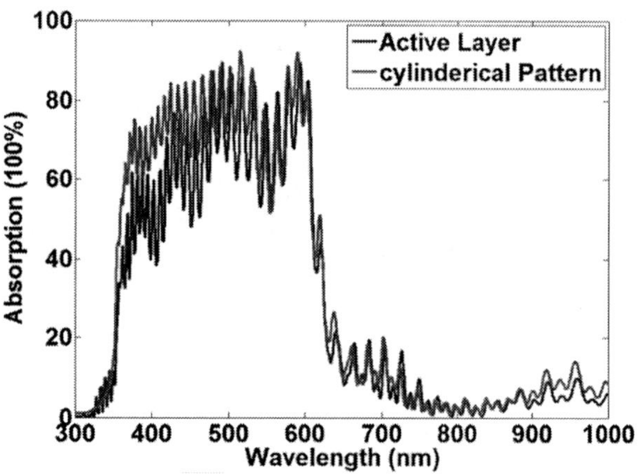

(b)

Fig. 2. (a) 2D side view of a unit cell of the proposed SC with periodic texturing, (b) Wavelength dependent absorption of the active layer of the thin film SC with and without surface texturing

The ultimate efficiency (η) can be used to evaluate the absorption capability of the proposed solar cell [6-9]. Figure 2(b) shows the wavelength dependent absorption of the active layer of the TF- SC with and without surface texturing. It may be observed from this figure that the absorption has been improved using the suggested texturing. Therefore, an ultimate efficiency of 19.26% with short circuit current of 15.76 mA/cm^2 has been achieved with an enhancement of 31.435% over the SC without textured surface. It is expected that the enhancement can be further improved when taking into account the randomness of the pseudo-periodic pattern. Additionally, the different geometrical parameters can be optimized to achieve broadband absorption enhancement using the texturing glass.

IV. Conclusion

High aspect ratio nanostructures formed by self-organized IBS process show high ability to enhance the effective optical path of photons into thin film PV devices and hence broadband absorption can be achieved. Further, the 3D-FDTD method shows that the TF-SC based on the textured glass offers an ultimate efficiency of 15.93% with short circuit current of 13 mA/cm^2 with an enhancement of 18% over the SC without textured surface. This improvement is due to light scattering at the corrugated interface which enhances the light absorption and hence the ultimate efficiency.

References

[1] C. Battaglia, et al., "Nanomoulding of transparent zinc oxide electrodes for efficient light trapping in solar cells," Nature, vol. 5, pp. 535-538, 2011

[2] C. V. Lare, F. Lenzmann, M. A. Verschuuren, A. Polman,"Dielectric Scattering Patterns for Efficient Light Trapping in Thin-Film Solar Cells," Nano letters, vol. 15(8), pp.4846-4852, 2015.

[3] C. Martella et al., "Self-organized broadband light trapping in thin film amorphous silicon solar cells", Nanotechnology , vol.24 (22), pp.225201, 2013.

[4] C. Martella et al., "Tailoring broadband light trapping of GaAs and Si substrates by self-organised nanopatterning," J. Appl. Phys. vol.115, pp.194308, 2014

[5] www.lumerical.com/tcad-products/fdtd/

[6] S. Obayya, N. F. Areed, M. F. O Hameed, M. Hussein, "Optical Nano-Antennas for Energy Harvesting", (IGI Global, 2015).

[7] M. Hussein, M. F. O. Hameed, N. F. F. Areed, A. Yahia, and S. S. A. Obayya, "Funnel-shaped silicon nanowire for highly efficient light trapping," Opt. Lett. 41, pp.1010-1013, 2016.

[8] M. H. Muhammad, M. F. O. Hameed, S. S. A. Obayya, "Broad band Absorption Enhancement in periodic structure solar cells" Optical Quantum Electronics, vol. 47, pp. 1487-1494, 2015.

[9] Doha. M. A. Rahman, M. F. O. Hameed, S. S. A. Obayya, "Light harvesting improvement of polymer solar cell through nanohole photoactive layer" Optical Quantum Electronics, vol. 47,pp. 1443–1449,2015.

[10] M. Hussen, M. F. O. Hameed, Nihal F. F. Areed, S.S.A. Obayya, "Ultra High Efficient Solar Cell Based on Decagonal Arrays of Silicon Nanowires," Optical Engineering Journal , Vol. 53(11), pp.117105, Nov 11, 2014.

Surface Plasmon Photonic Crystal Fiber Biosensor for Glucose Monitoring

Mohammad Y. Azab
Department Of Mathematics and Engineering Physics,
Mansoura University
Mansoura, Egypt

M.F.O. Hameed, A. M. Heikal, S.S.A. Obayya*
Center for Photonics and Smart Materials,
Zewail City of Science and Technology
6th of October City, Giza, Egypt
sobayya@zewailcity.edu.eg*

M. A. Swillam
Department of Physics,
The American University in Cairo,
New Cairo, Egypt

***Abstract*— In this paper, design consideration of a surface plasmon photonic crystal fiber (PCF) biosensor for Glucose monitoring is presented and analyzed. Based on a well-known large mode area (LMA) PCF, two different configurations have been studied to investigate the effect of the etching process. The numerical results show that the plasmonic D-shaped PCF after etching three rows of air holes can achieve sensitivity of 200 nm/RIU with corresponding resolution of 1.3×10^{-3} RIU^{-1}. The analysis is carried out using full vectorial finite element method (FVFEM) with perfect matched layer (PML) boundary conditions.**

Keywords*— Photonic Crystal Fiber; Surface Plasmon; Biosensor; Glucose Monitoring.

I. INTRODUCTION

Optical biosensors based on surface plasmon (SP) resonance have aroused great interest of researchers in the last decade. Photonic crystal fiber (PCF) [1] has also been the subject of intense research due to its uncommon properties and possible applications [2]. Qin et al. [3] have reported PCF biosensor selectively filled with the analyte with sensitivity of 4354.3 nm/RIU (refractive index unit) and 2280 nm/RIU for two resonance peaks. In addition, a highly sensitive SP temperature biosensor has been reported by Hameed et al. [4] with high sensitivity of 10 nm/°C. Moreover, a self-calibration biosensor based on SP PCF has been designed [5] with sensitivity of 6700 nm/RIU and 10000 nm/RIU with corresponding resolution of 1.49×10^{-5} RIU, and 1.0×10^{-5} RIU for the quasi transverse magnetic (TM) and quasi transverse electric (TE) modes, respectively. However, such configuration [5] depends on elliptical shape air holes, which will be difficult for fabrication. Azzam et al. [6] have also presented multichannel SP PCF biosensor with high sensitivities of 2200 nm/RIU, 2400 nm/RIU, 2200 nm/RIU, and 2400 nm/RIU according to the H_{11}^{x}, H_{11}^{y}, H_{12}^{x}, H_{12}^{y} modes, respectively. Further, photonic crystal biosensors have been recently implemented for glucose monitoring [7, 8].

In this paper, SP D-shaped PCF biosensor is presented and analyzed. The reported sensor is based on a well-known large mode area (LMA) PCF [9]. Then, the etching process is studied to achieve high sensitivity by the coupling between the core mode and the surface plasmon modes.

II. SYSTEM DESCRIPTION AND NUMERICAL RESULTS

A single mode LMA PCF shown in Fig.1 (a) is used for implementing the suggested SP D-shaped PCF biosensor. The PCF has three rings of air holes that are arranged in a triangular lattice in a silica background with a hole pitch Λ=3.3 μm, core radius R=2.5 μm and hole radius of r=0.7 μm. The LMA PCF has been etched to remove the outer two or three rows as shown in Fig. 1 (b) and (c), respectively. Further, a gold layer of thickness 50 nm is deposited on the silica surface after the horizontal etching process as presented in Fig.1 (b) and (c). An analyte of refractive index 1.33 is then added over the gold layer. The wavelength dependent refractive index of silica glass is taken from [5] while the gold has a wavelength dependent permittivity taken from [4].

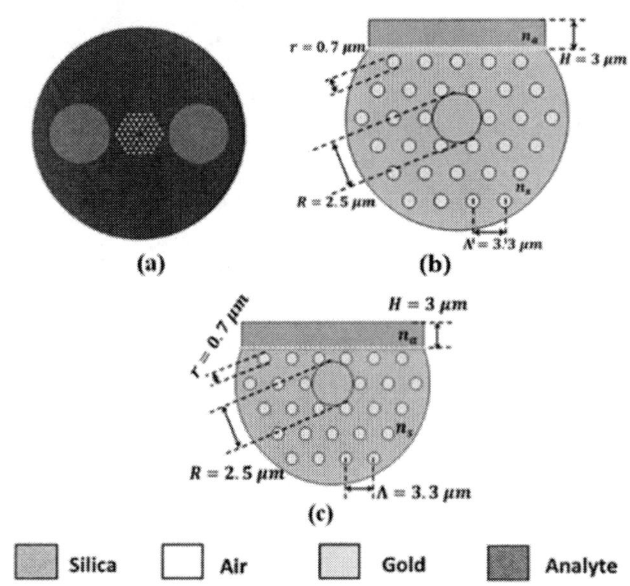

Fig. 1. (a) Cross section of PCF of type LMA-PM-5 [9], and the proposed D-shaped PCF design after etching (b) two and (c) three air holes rows, respectively.

The analysis is carried out using the Comsol Multiphysics software package [10] on a square computational domain of side 26.4 μm with a minimum element size of 0.000462 μm and degrees of freedom of 177517. Further, perfect matched layer (PML) boundary conditions are used to truncate the computational domain and calculate the confinement losses through the suggested designs. The proposed design shown in Fig. 1 (b) has been studied and it is found that the coupling between the core guided modes and SP modes is weak due to the long distance between the core and plasmonic material. Therefore, horizontal etching of three rows is required as shown in Fig. 1 (c).

It is worth noting that no coupling occurs between the quasi TE mode and SP mode. However, strong coupling occurs using the quasi TM mode as shown in Fig.2. Figure 2(a) shows the variation of the confinement losses and effective indices n_{eff} of the quasi TM mode and the SP mode of the suggested D-shaped biosensor shown in Fig. 1 (c). It may be seen from this figure that strong coupling occurs at λ=1663 nm between the quasi TM core mode and SP mode.

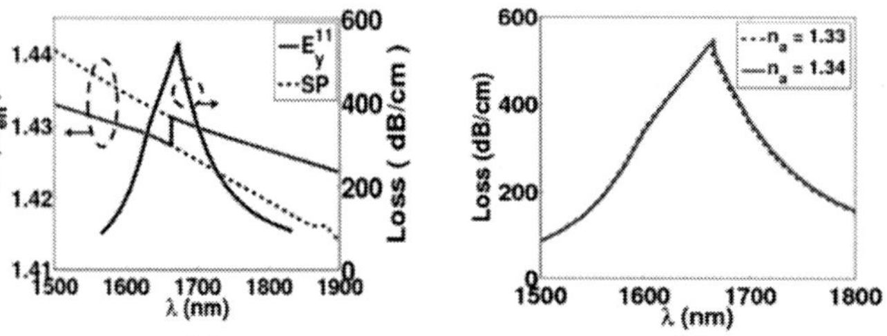

(a) (b)

Fig. 2. (a) Variation of the wavelength dependent confinement losses and effective indices of the quasi TM core mode, and n_{eff} of the SP modes. (b) Variation of the confinement losses of the quasi TM modes with the wavelength at different analyte refractive indices.

As the analyte refractive index changes from 1.33 to 1.34, the resonance wavelength of the quasi TM mode changes from 1663 to 1665 nm. The wavelength sensitivity is calculated from the following relation [5]:

$$S_\lambda(\lambda) = \frac{\partial \lambda_{peak}}{\partial n_a} \qquad \left(\frac{\text{nm}}{\text{RIU}}\right) \qquad (1)$$

where $\partial\lambda_{peak}$ and ∂n_a are the change in the resonance wavelength and analyte refractive index, respectively. Therefore, the proposed design has a sensitivity of 200 nm/RIU. Assuming that a change of 1% in the transmitted intensity can be detected reliably, sensor resolution of 1.3×10^{-3} RIU^{-1} can be detected. It may be noted that the achieved sensitivity is smaller than those reported in the literature [3, 5, 6] which are based on complicated designs. However, the suggested biosensor is based on commercially available PCF. Further, the sensitivity can be further enhanced by making radial etching or by infiltrating one of the holes by a gold material.

III. Conclusion

In this paper, a design consideration is applied on a commercial single mode LMA PCF to propose D-shaped sensitive biosensor for glucose monitoring. It is found that etching of 3 rows of air holes is essential to have a good coupling between core guided modes and surface plasmon modes. The suggested design has sensitivity of 200 nm/RIU with corresponding resolution of 1.3×10^{-3}.

IV. Acknowledgement

The authors would like to thank the "Science and Technology Development Fund" (STDF) at Egypt for the financial support under project number 10563.

References

[1] M.F.O. Hameed, S.S.A. Obayya, H.A. El-Mikati,"Highly nonlinear birefringent soft glass photonic crystal fiber with liquid crystal core", IEEE PTL, vol. 23, no.20, pp.1478-1480, 2011.

[2] M.F.O. Hameed, A.M. Heikal, S.S.A. Obayya, "Novel passive polarization rotator based on spiral photonic crystal fiber," IEEE Photonics Technology Letters, vol. 25, no.16, pp.1578-1581, 2013

[3] W. Qin, S. Li, Y. Yao, X. Xin, J. Xue, "Analyte-filled core self-calibration microstructured optical fiber based plasmonic sensor for detecting high refractive index aqueous analyte," Opt. Laser Eng., vol. 58, pp. 1–8, 2014.

[4] M.F.O. Hameed, M.Y. Azab, A.M. Heikal, S.M. El Hefnawy and S.S.A.Obayya, "Highly Sensitive Plasmonic Photonic Crystal Temperature Sensor Filled With Liquid Crystal", IEEE Photonics Technology Letters, vol. 28, pp.59-62, 2015.

[5] M.F.O. Hameed, Y.K.A. Alrayk and S.S.A. Obayya, "Self-Calibration Highly Sensitive Photonic Crystal Fiber Biosensor", IEEE photonics journal, vol. 8, no.3, pp. 1-12, 2016.

[6] S. I. Azzam, R. Eid A. Shehata, Mohamed Farhat O. Hameed, A. M. Heikal, Salah S. A. Obayya, "Multichannel Photonic Crystal Fiber Surface Plasmon Resonance Based Sensor," Journal of Optical Quantum Electronics, vol. 48(2), pp.142-1-11 (2016)

[7] Nihal F. F. Areed, Mohamed Farhat. O. Hameed, and S. S. A. Obayya, "Highly Sensitive Face-Shaped Label-Free Photonic Crystal Refractometer for Glucose Concentration Monitoring," Journal of Optical Quantum Electronics, vol.49 (5), pp.1-12. doi:10.1007/s11082-016-0847-9, 2016.

[8] M. S. Mohamed, Mohamed Farhat O. Hameed, Nihal F. F. Areed, M. M. El-Okr, and S. S. A. Obayya, "Analysis of Highly Sensitive Photonic Crystal Biosensor for Glucose Monitoring," Journal of Applied Computational Electromagnetics Society (ACES), vol. 31, No. 7, pp. 836- 842, 2016

[9] http://www.nktphotonics.com

[10] COMSOL Multiphysics, "http://www.comsol.com".

Electromagnetic Stimuli in Therapeutics and Resuscitation

Oana Mihaela DROSU
Department of Electrical Engineering
Politehnica University of Bucharest
Bucharest, Romania
oana.drosu@upb.ro

***Abstract* — Some of the most important applications of the electromagnetic field in medicine are the resuscitation and medical therapeutics. This paper presents a review on phenomena occurring in the application of stimuli with a future purpose of focusing on several models of external electromagnetic stimulation. Bi-dimensional models of the electro-conductive anatomy will be proposed, in order to investigate the fields and the currents generated by an electric field.**

Keywords—electromagnetic stimuli, resuscitation, stimulation function

I. INTRODUCTION

Some important applications of electromagnetic field in medicine are the cardiac stimulation and medical therapeutics such healing processes of bone (fractures, osteoporosis) and soft tissue (reduction of edema, healing burns, tissue and peripheral nerves regeneration), rheumatic and neurological disorders (Parkinson's, Alzheimer's, epilepsy etc., treatment of drug addiction etc.) [1-3].

The electromagnetic phenomena that occur in the biological tissues include: the behavior of excitable tissue (the sources), the electric currents and potentials in the conductive domain, the magnetic field inside and around the body, the response of excitable cells to electromagnetic field stimulation, the intrinsic electric and magnetic properties of the tissue.

This paper presents a review of fundamental phenomena occurring in the application of stimuli and a study case of cardiac stimulation with a future purpose of focusing on some other models of external electromagnetic stimulation. In order to validate the methods and the models, their specific characteristics can be computed and analyzed.

Within the stimulation for resuscitation, as well as in the case of therapeutic electromagnetic stimulation it is very important to generate a current density field with optimal distribution with respect to the stimulated tissues; this leads to a complicated problem of electromagnetic field that needs new models and computation procedures and testing a large number of direct problems, solved by specific numerical methods. The future target is even more complicated because we want to take into account both the electric stimulus (boundary conditions, sources) and the magnetic field lines.

II. STATE OF THE ART

The electric stimulation with an electric or magnetic field includes the effects of these fields applied to biological tissues, using different devices [4]. From biomedical application we mention: electrical or magnetic stimulation of the central nervous system, of muscles and motor nerves, the electrical stimulation of heart, electrotherapy, electro-surgery, electro-magneto-therapy, magneto-therapy, magnetization of the ferromagnetic contain of the tissues [5].

Within the biomedical sphere, the last years have brought a tremendous development of the studies and research at international level mainly within the field of electric stimulation, but lately within the magnetic one as well. Therefore, the optimization of the medical existent procedures is wanted, new techniques and models, laboratory experiments and computer simulations are proposed.

A research direction is represented by external electric stimulation. Within this domain, the models have in view the optimization of the external electrodes, regarding their number, position, shape or dimensions and the applied impulse [6]. The efficiency of the procedure considers the minimization of the side-effects on patients (pain, contact tissues injuries) and maximization of the beneficial effects in stimulated tissue. Another method is the magnetic cardiac stimulation, more precisely the stimulation with an electric field produced by a time-variable magnetic field. The modeling within this domain has in view the investigation of the induced currents in the body and the characteristics of the defibrillation coil (shape, number of turns, length) and the applied stimulus [6].

Within the majority of the studies a major aspect is the numerical modeling of the medical procedures. For this purpose, different models, more or less complex are proposed [7]. The main advantages are: saving time and resources, multiple possibilities of approaching a problem, direct transfer of the results in practice, the use of "virtual models" instead of real ones (human or animals), when in certain countries the testing is against the ethical rules. The numerical approach is done using different methods: Finite Element Method (FEM), Finite Difference Method (FDM), Boundary Element Method (BEM), considering stationary or dynamic models, simple or complicated anatomic domains, 2D or 3D cases, isotropic or non-isotropic.

III. Electric Stimulation of the Heart Tissue

A. *The Stimulation Function*

The stimulation function shows what electric quantity is active during the stimulation process. Assuming the coaxial cable model for the cylindrical fiber (the cell), under the action of an activation stimuli, its behavior is emphasized, resulting the space-time variation of the membrane voltage [6]:

$$\lambda^2 \frac{\partial^2 V_m'}{\partial' x^2} - \tau \frac{\partial V_m'}{\partial t} - V_m' = r_0 i_s \lambda^2 \qquad (1)$$

where $V_r' = V_m - V_r$ represents the trans-membrane voltage variation function of its steady-state value, $\lambda = r_{m/}(r_i + r_0)$ - is the space constant, $\tau = r_m c_m$ - represents the time constant and the free term represents the growth to be registered by the membrane voltage with respect to the steady-state, when subjected to a stimulus, to produce depolarization.

To highlight the stimulation function [6], the equation (1) can be written as:

$$\lambda^2 \frac{\partial^2 V_m'}{\partial' x^2} - \tau \frac{\partial V_m'}{\partial t} - V_m' = \lambda^2 f_s \qquad (2)$$

B. *Study Case – Electric Stimulation of the Cardiac Tissue*

The electric stimulation of the heart involves two electrodes applied on the thorax in order to defibrillate the cardiac tissue. The purpose is to have less side effects on the surrounding tissues, especially on the thorax wall which is in direct contact with the paddles. The heart caption and cardiac function restoring should be made in good conditions that suppose a minimization of the quality factor represented by the ratio R of the maximum current density in the thorax with respect to the maximum value in the myocardium.

Let's consider the 2D stationary FEM model (using the software MEGA), of a real cross-section of the human thorax a non-homogenous domain containing eight regions (tissues and organs), considered continuous, linear, time-invariant, homogenous, isotropic (excepting the muscles), with an average value of the conductivity assigned based on values found in the specialized literature. The electrodes have been considered as a superconductive media and the exterior as a perfect insulator. In order to simulate the anisotropy of the thoracic muscles and predicting the direction of the current density in the vicinity of the electrode, different values of the isotropic resistivity have been assigned as follows for the transverse muscles underneath the electrodes and the longitudinal muscles far apart from the electrodes.

The equation to be solved on each subdomain:

$$\Delta V = 0 \qquad (3)$$

This equation will be completed by the boundary conditions: Dirichlet (the positive electrode V_+=120V, the negative one V_- = 0V) and Neumann $\partial V/\partial n = 0$.

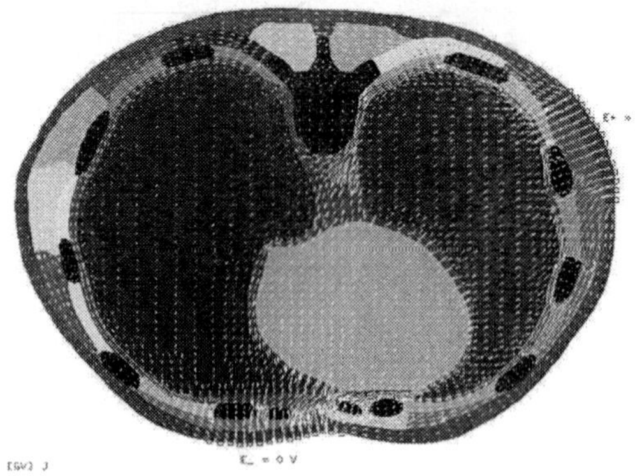

Fig. 1. 2D electrokinetic FEM model of the thorax(current density distribution)

The maximum values of the current density have been localized in the interstitial fluid (close to the cardiac apex and the back bone and all around the lungs) and the minimum values were inside the lungs and the bones.

IV. Conclusions

For the analyzed case, the efficacy of the medical procedure can be increased and the negative effects on the patient's thorax can be reduced at the same time with the descent of the trans-thorax level from the top to the bottom of the sternum. All the models can be improved, using better approximations of the real situation (geometry, electrical characteristics, regimes, optimization functions etc.). Techniques for determining the current density field will be further developed for mixed electric and magnetic stimulation.

Acknowledgment

This work has been funded by University Politehnica of Bucharest, through the "Excellence Research Grants" Program, UPB – GEX. Identifier: UPB–EXCELENȚĂ–2016, Research project title "Stimuli electromagnetici pentru tesuturile vii" (Electromagnetic Stimuli for alive tissues) Contract number 73.

References

[1] Wang S., Zhou X., Huang B., Wang Z., Zhou L., Wang L., Yu L, Jiang H., Noninvasive low-frequency electromagnetic stimulation of the left stellate ganglion reduces myocardial infarction-induced ventricular arrhythmia, Sci Rep. 2016; 6: 30783, doi: 10.1038/srep30783

[2] Chiba A., Inase M, Effects of pulsed magnetic stimulation on isolated crayfish heart, Journal Electromagnetic Biology and Medicine Vol. 35, 2016 - Issue 2 Pg 115-119 Published online: 29 Dec 2014 http://dx.doi.org/10.3109/15368378.2014.994067

[3] Kapeller B., Mueller J., Losert U., Podesser B.K., Macfelda K., Microcurrent stimulation promotes reverse remodelling in cardiomyocytes, http://onlinelibrary.wiley.com/doi/10.1002/ehf2.12080/

[4] Malmivuo J., Plonsey R., Bioelectromagnetism – Principles and Applications of Bioelectric and Biomagnetic Fields, Oxford University Press, New York, 1995.

[5] Rosch P. J., Markov M. S., Biolectromagnetism in medicine, Informa Health Care, 2004, ISBN 082474700.

[6] Drosu O., "Câmpul electromagnetic în bioingineria medicală", Ed. Electra, București 2004-ISBN 973-7728-03-3.

Sodium imaging of the human knee cartilage with Magnetic Resonance at Ultra High Field: development of a double frequency ($^{1}H/^{23}Na$) RF coil

Francesca Maggiorelli
Dip. di Scienze Fisiche della Terra e dell'Ambiente
Università degli Studi di Siena e INFN (Sez. Pisa)
Pisa, Italy

Joshua D. Kaggie, Martin J. Graves
Dep. of Radiology, University of Cambridge
Cambrige, UK

Guido Buonincontri, Alessandra Retico
Istituto Nazionale di Fisica Nucleare (INFN, Sez. Pisa)
Pisa, Italy

Laura Biagi, Gianluigi Tiberi, Michela Tosetti
IRCCS Stella Maris e Fondazione IMAGO7
Pisa, Italy

***Abstract*—Sodium Magnetic Resonance Imaging (MRI) is an attractive imaging technique for early detection of osteoarthritis, as sodium concentrations correlate with proteoglycan content. However sodium yields much less signal in human tissues compared to hydrogen: it has a very rapid transverse signal decay (T2) and rapid longitudinal relaxation (T1), low gyromagnetic ratio and much smaller concentration than hydrogen. Ultra High Field (UHF) 7T MRI systems play an essential role to enhance the SNR, to achieve sufficient spatial resolution and to obtain images with diagnostically relevant contrast. This work shows how to design, develop and test a dual-tuned proton/sodium surface radio-frequency coil for 7T UHF MRI systems.**

Keywords—Magnetic Resonance Imaging (MRI); ultra-high field MRI; dual tuned radio-frequency coils; sodium imaging

I. INTRODUCTION

A clinical application of Ultra High Field (UHF) 7T Magnetic Resonance Imaging (MRI) that could relevantly impact the daily life is in the early detection and assessment of osteoarthritis (OA). It is the most common chronic condition of the joints, affecting approximately 15% of the population. OA occurs when the cartilage between joints degrades leading to pain, stiffness and swelling. Negatively charged proteoglycans, which are significantly reduced in the cartilage affected by OA, attract positive sodium ions. Therefore, sodium MRI is an interesting technique for early detection of osteoarthritis (OA) [1]. MRI with nuclei different from ^{1}H, for which the available signal is limited, benefits from the improved SNR obtainable with ultra-high magnetic fields. However, imaging at high field comes with several limitations such as inhomogeneous RF fields, a higher Specific Absorption Rate (SAR), and a relative lack of specialized and commercially available RF coils compared to lower field systems. This research shows how to design, simulate, prototype and validate a dual-tuned ^{1}H-^{23}Na surface RF coil for knee MR imaging (see Fig. 1).

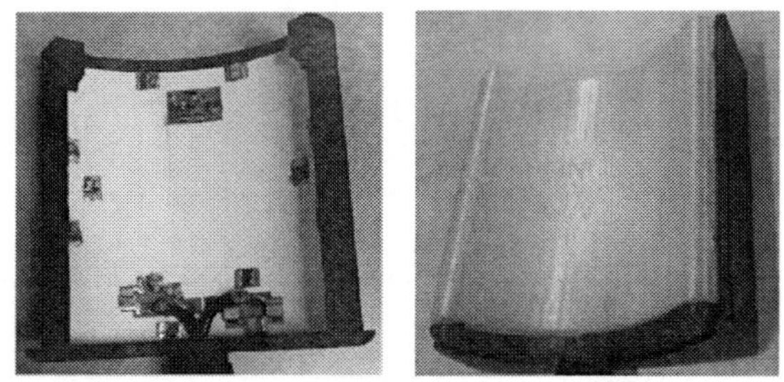

a) b)

Fig. 1. a) Double tuned $^{1}H/^{23}Na$ coil. b) Double tuned $^{1}H/^{23}Na$ coil showing holder & covers.

II. MATERIALS AND METHODS

The coil consists of two concentric loops: the inner is tuned to sodium Larmor frequency (78.89MHz @ 7T), the outer is tuned to proton Larmor frequency (298.03MHz @ 7T).

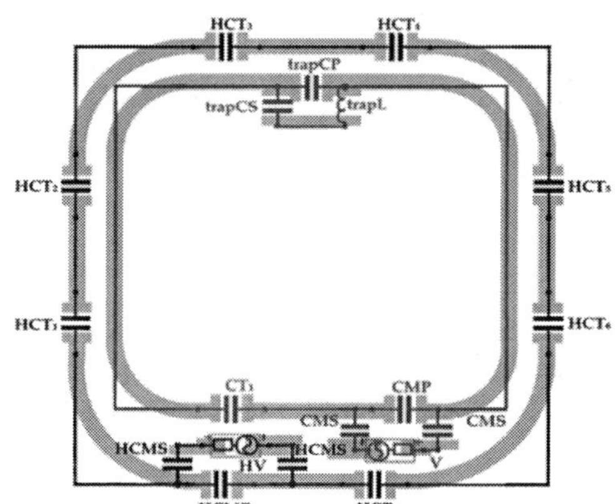

Fig. 2. Circuit of the dual-tuned ^{1}H and ^{23}Na RF coil. The trap circuit and the matching circuits are also visible.

The ^{1}H transmit and receive (Tx/Rx) loop is realized by etching an external square loop having side length of 110 mm. The ^{23}Na loop is realized by etching a rectangular loop of 95 mm × 85 mm (see Fig. 2). The corners of the coils are rounded: the curvature radius is 30 mm for the main loops and 2 mm for the end point of the strip. To minimize antenna effect the number of tuning capacitors is chosen so that the length of the conductors for both loop is less than λ/10, where λ is the wavelength at the two resonant frequencies (298.03MHz for proton and 78.89MHz for sodium). The matching for both loops is obtained with a series capacitive matching network and matching capacitors were determined by using a Smith Chart procedure [3]. The ^{23}Na channel is decoupled from the ^{1}H channel by the insertion in the ^{23}Na loop of a series second-order trap circuit [2]. The trap circuit is basically a parallel LC resonant circuit and acts as a high impedance (ideally an open circuit) at proton Larmor frequency at which coupling occurs [4]. The resonant circuits of the RF coil consist of a PCB in FR4 (board thickness 200 μm, copper thickness 35 μm). The other materials used in the design are Non-magnetic chip capacitors (100B, 800B, 800A from ATC ceramics), RG-58 cables (Micro-coax, Belden). The support holding, which is visible in Fig. 1, is designed in AutoCAD, and 3D printed, using a polylactide (PLA) thermoplastic as printing material.

Components' values are chosen in agreement with preliminary simulations. Referring to Fig. 2, the list of components used for assembling the coil is given in Table. 1.

Table 1. RF components of the dual-tuned coil.

$HCT_{1,4}$	8.2 pF	CMP	(33+10) pF
$HCT_{2,3,6}$	6.8 pF	CMS	22 pF
CT_{1}	33 pF	trapCP	(33+4.7) pF
HCMP	4.7 pF	trapCS	(33+2.1) pF
HCMS	33 pF	trapL	10 nH

Simulations performed with *CST Microwave Studio®*, are also used for evaluating B_1^+ - and E - fields maps.

The load used in the electromagnetic model is a cylinder equivalent to the human knee (radius 60 mm, height 200 mm, $\varepsilon_r = 80$ and $\sigma = 0.60$ S/m), placed 15 mm away from the coil circuit. The simulated B_1^+ - and E - fields maps obtained for unitary input power of 1 W for both the ^{1}H and the ^{23}Na channels are shown in Fig. 3. The ^{1}H and ^{23}Na B_1^+ field maps are in agreement with literature [5].

III. RESULTS

The workbench measurements for the ^{1}H and the ^{23}Na loops provided the performance values reported in Table 2.

Table 2. Workbench measurements for the dual-tuned coil.

	^{1}H loop	^{23}Na loop
Q unloaded	88	217
Q loaded (human knee)	23	37
Matching (S_{11}, S_{22})	-16dB	-20dB
Coupling (S_{12}, S_{21})	-19dB	-14dB

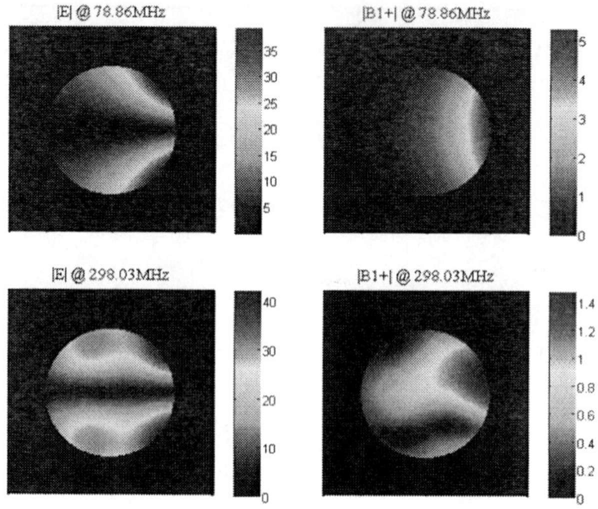

Fig. 3 Simulated B_1^+ (μT) and E (V/m) field maps for unitary input power of 1W for both the ^{1}H and the ^{23}Na channels of the dual-tuned surface RF coil.

Workbench measurements showed a satisfying agreement with simulated result (S_{11}=-23dB, S_{22}=-34dB, coupling <-14dB).

IV. CONCLUSIONS

We designed and developed dedicated RF surface coils for ^{1}H-^{23}Na imaging. Excellent agreement was obtained between workbench measurements and simulations. The RF coil prototype has been validated *in vivo* on healthy volunteers, showing that the knee cartilage imaging can take great advantage from the UHF MRI [6].

REFERENCES

[1] Schmitt B., Zbyn S., Stelzeneder D., et al, "Cartilage Quality Assessment by Using Glycosaminoglycan Chemical Exchange Saturation Transfer and 23Na RM Imaging at 7T", Radiology, Volume 260, No. 1, 2011.

[2] A. Retico, R. Stara, M. E. Fantacci, et al, "Non-Invasive Assessment of Neuromuscular Disorders by 7 Tesla Magnetic Resonance Imaging and Spectroscopy", IEEE-MeMeA 2015 CR 7145175, pp 74-78.

[3] J. Mispelter, M. Lupu and A. Briguet, "NMR Probeheads for Biophysical and Biomedical Experiments: Theorical Principles Pratical Guidilines," Imperial College Press, 2006.

[4] M. Alecci, S. Romanzetti, J. Kaffanke, et al "Practical design of a 4 Tesla double-tuned RF surface coil for interleaved 1H and 23Na MRI of rat brain," J. Magn. Reson., vol 181(2), pp. 203-211, Aug 2006.

[5] Tiberi, G., Fontana, N., Costagli, M., et al, "Investigation of maximum local specific absorption rate in 7 T magnetic resonance with respect to load size by use of electromagnetic simulations" Bioelectromagnetics, 36: 358–366, 2015.

[6] JD. Kaggie, F Maggiorelli, F Riemer et al, "7 T Sodium/Proton Knee Imaging: First Results", UHF ISMRM Symposium, 2016.

Robustness of Flexible 7T-MRI Coil Behaviour

Andrea Melis[1], Sergio Casu[1,2], Alessandro Fanti[1,2]*, Giuseppe Mazzarella[1,2]
[1]Department of Electrical and electronic Engineering, University of Cagliari
[2]INFN-Sezione Cagliari, Cagliari, Italy
Corresponding author*: alessandro.fanti@diee.unica.it

Claudio Puddu[a,b], Patrizia Boccacci[a]
[a]Department of Computer and Information Science, University of Genova
[b]INFN-Sezione di Genova, Genova,Italy

***Abstract*—In magnetic resonance imaging (MRI), the electrical performance of the RF coil is critical to achieve sufficient signal to noise ratio (SNR). In this work, the variation of performance of a plane and a flexible coil over a saline and a humanlike phantom is proposed. In order to evaluate the RF sensitivity of these flexible devices, we performed both an electrical characterization of the coil performances and a MRI simulation on a saline phantom.**

Keyword - High field; surface coil; flexible coil array; RF coil; RF coil sensitivity

I. Introduction

The main target for present-day MRI is to achieve the highest possible signal-to-noise ratio (SNR), which corresponds to the best quality achievable in the imaging process. The limitation is due to the extreme weakness of the MRI signal and to the thermal noise associated to the radiofrequency detection [1]. One of the most common strategies to increase the amount of detectable proton magnetization (and thus, increase the SNR) is to apply a higher static magnetic field [2]. This has motivated the development of human MRI systems at 7T and above. However, using such magnetic field intensities generates major challenges, one of which is the design of optimal RF coils and coil array for efficient MRI signal excitation and reception at ultrahigh frequencies. The design of RF coils for high fields is complicated by the fact that at higher RF frequencies there is a more complex interaction between the RF field and the subject that leads to excitation inhomogeneity due to wavelength effects and increased mutual coupling among coil elements [3]. Theoretical and experimental works suggested that to make the best use of an array coil is better to have a large number of coils that surround the imaging volume [4]. This is difficult to achieve in very variable anatomies in dimension and shape, leading to the develop of coil that are geometrically adjustable to the subject to analyze. A flexible receiver RF array is a device that offer several benefits for 7T because it allows the adjustment of the coil geometry to the subject and provide the better filling factors and improved SNR for different subjects while keeping a large field of view (FOV) of operation [5]. The major technical challenges of designing a flexible array coil is to develop geometry-independent decoupling for the coil elements. In fact, mutual inductance among coil elements varies with the coil size, thus the flexibility of the coil creates even more complicated decoupling issues [6]. Conventional decoupling techniques use either geometrical overlap (with the drawback of reduced FOV) or the application of LC-networks for non-adjacent loops.

II. Methods

A. Design and simulation

The basic layout of the loop considered here is a regular polygon of 8 equally long segments. The loop dimensions are determined by the body part the loop has to investigate. The ratio of the samples radius and the coils radius is approximately 1.3, the distance between the coil and the sample is variable and influences the coupling between them.

B. Coil charachterization

The coil has to resonate at the requested Larmor frequency. The coil itself is an inductor with inductance L. Tuning the coil is generally achived by placing a capacitor with capacitance C in parallel to the coil inductor. L and C are selected in a way that the circuits frequency ω_0 matches the Larmor frequency ωL. In making calculation for our circuit to resonate, we suppose the conditions of static inductance and static current, so that we can use the following equations [7]:

$$\omega_0 = \frac{1}{\sqrt{LC}}; I = \frac{V}{Z} = \frac{V}{R + j(\omega L - \frac{1}{\omega C})} \quad (1)$$

These equations can be used only under the condition that the individual segments of the coil have a length less than 1/10 of the wavelength at the Larmor frequency, to ensure a "static" behaviour of the current . The power transmitted to the sample depends on the impedance difference between coils input impedance and lines outer impedance, usually at 50 . Matching these impedances is therefore required task to have an efficient device. Among the various matching methods, the most common is the capacitive matching, adding a capacitor in series or parallel to the coil circuit. The value of the capacitance C, is found as [8]:

$$C_T\omega_s = \frac{1}{XC}; C_M = \frac{1}{Z} = \frac{1}{\omega_s Z_0 A}; XC_M = \sqrt{\frac{r}{Z_0 - r}} \quad (2)$$

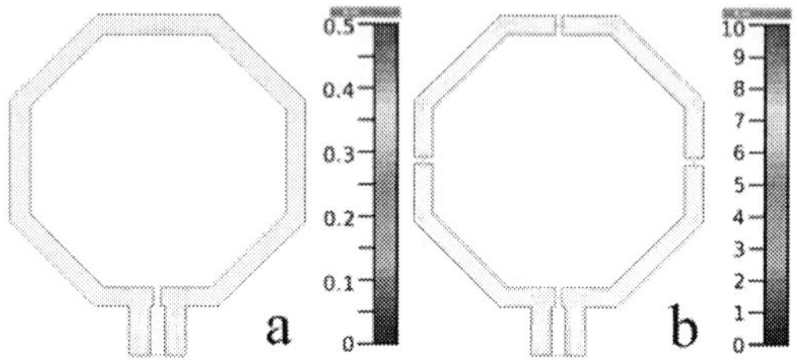

Fig. 1. Current distibution of a) a coil with one capacitor b) a coil with four capacitors of equal total capacity.

for a series and a parallel matching respectively, where: $A = \sqrt{(B/Z0) - 1}, B = r(1 + Q^2)$ and $Q = L\omega_s/r$.

III. Result and Conclusion

A single loop plane coil with one tuning capacitor was first simulated. As expected, using one capacitor entails that the length of the conductor has dimensions comparable to the wavelength at the Larmor frequency. In this case, the approximation of static current cant be used anymore, and the coil does not behave as a resonating LC circuit at that frequency. However, this issue can be easily overcome using four capacitors with the same total capacity, distribuited along the ring (fig.1). A phantom of saline solution was then added. The value of the tuning capacitors was chosen to obtain a resonance at 298 MHz, and a matching capacitor was added on the coil legs in parallel to the coil circuit. The resonance frequency was reached with four tuning capacitors of 5pF each, and a 4.9pF matching capacitor (fig.2).

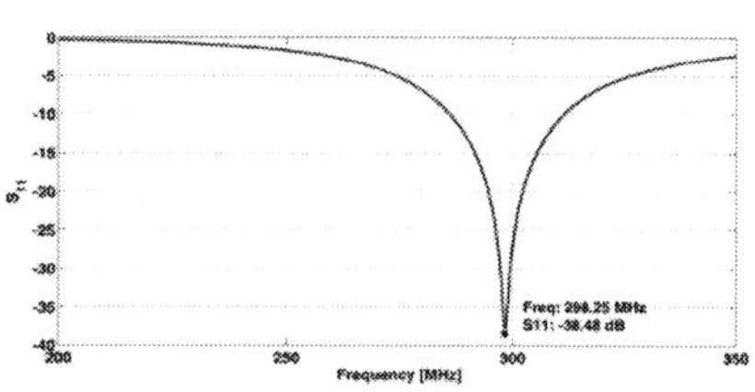

Fig. 2. Plot of plane coil obtained with four 5pF tuning capacitor and a 4.9 matching capacitor.

The model used to obtain the resonance for a plane coil, was then used for a flexible coil. First, a 90° bended coil was simulated, finding a coil response similar to the plane coil ones.

Then, a coil bended over the saline sample was simulated. As expected, the current distribution were similar to the distribution of the plane coil: the resonance was obtained using similar capacitor values, but the coupling between coil and sample was better overall, due to the better fitting and adaptability the flexible coil guarantees. In fact, to match the coil to the feed impedance, has been used a matching capacitor of 1.4pF, smaller than the capacitor used for the plane coil (fig.3). The difference in the (complex) dielectric constant leads to a different penetration of the magnetic field, differently from what happens in low-field MRI's.

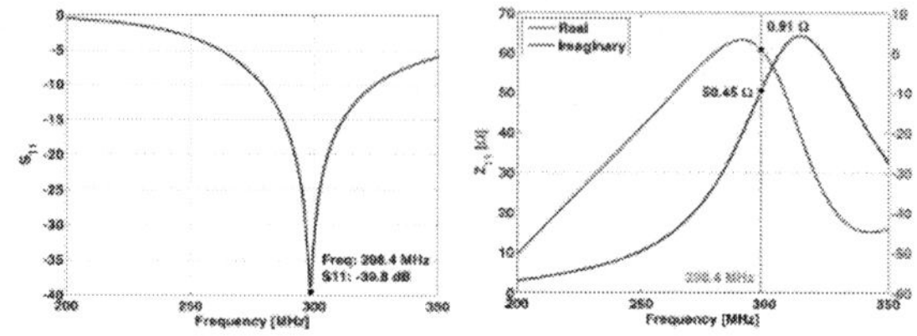

Fig. 3. S1,1, Z1,1 Real and Imaginary of a bended single loop coil with four 5pF tuning capacitors and 1.4pF matching capacitor.

Finally, the magnetic field penetration over the phantom was evaluated. A two-loops array coil was simulated over a saline solution phantom and a human arm-like phantom (fig.4).

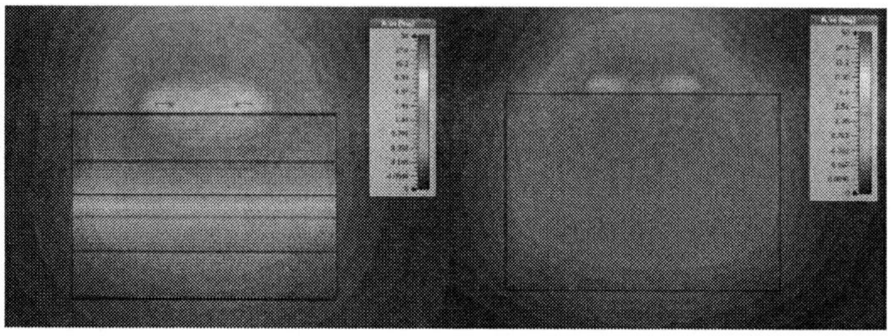

(a) (b)

Fig. 4. Magnetic field penetration for a) a body-like sample and b) a saline solution

In conclusion, the assumpion of static impedence can be exploited only for conductors with lenght approximatly under 1/10 of the wavelenght. Also it's clear that with a better-matching between coil and sample, the RF sensitivity of the coil is higher. In fact, flexibility gives a better coupling and depth penetration of the field. Impedence's value changes considerably with different sample and curvature radius, so a tailored matching and tuning has to be done.

References

[1] R. Kriegl, J.C. Ginefri, M. Poirier-Quinot, L. Darrasse, S. Goluch, A. Kuehne, E. Moser, E. Laistler, , *Novel inductive decoupling technique for flexible transceiver arrays of monolithic transmission line resonators*, Magn. Reson. Med. Epub (2014). doi:10.1002/mrm.25260

[2] Ernst R.R., Bodenhausen G., Wokaun A.*Principles of nuclear magneticresonance in one and two dimensions*, Oxford: Clarendon Press; 1987. p. 610.

[3] Vaughan J.T., Hetherington H.P., Otu J.O., Pan J.W., Pohost G.M.*Principles of nuclear magneticresonance in one and two dimensions*. [PubMed: 7968443]

[4] Boskamp E.B. *Improved surface coil imaging in MR: decoupling of the excitation and receiver coils*. Radiology 1985;157:449452

[5] Woytasik M., Ginefri J.C., Raynaud J.S., Poirier-Quinot M., Dufour-Gergam E., Grandchamp J.P., Girard O., Robert P., Gilles J.P., Martincic *Characterization of flexible RF microcoils dedicated to local MRI*. Microsyst Technol 2006;13:15751580

[6] Wang J. *A novel method to reduce the signal coupling of surface coil for MRI*. Proceedings of the 4th Annual Meeting of ISMRM, New York, New York, USA, 1996, p. 1434

[7] Frederick E.T.,*Radio Engineers'* ,1943;

[8] Robitaille P.M., Berliner L., *Ultra High Field Magnetic Resonance Imaging*, 2006

[9] Mispelter J., Lupu M., Briguet A., *NMR Probeheads for biophysical and biomedical experiments*, 2006.

Application of EMFs at Microwave Frequencies for Brain Stroke Detection: Preliminary Results

I. Bisio, A. Fedeli, F. Lavagetto, G. Luzzati, M. Pastorino, M. Raffetto, A. Randazzo, and E. Tavanti
Department of Electrical, Electronic, Telecommunications Engineering, and Naval Architecture (DITEN)
University of Genoa
Genoa, Italy
{igor.bisio; fabio.lavagetto; matteo.pastorino; mirco.raffetto; andrea.randazzo}@unige.it;
{alessandro.fedeli; giulio.luzzati; emanuele.tavanti}@edu.unige.it

***Abstract*—An approach for microwave imaging of brain strokes is presented. Numerical simulations show the potentialities of this technique in retrieving the dielectric properties of biological tissues inside the head. An efficient iterative two-loop method is used to face the ill-posedness of the considered inverse scattering problem, which is formulated in terms of integral equations.**

***Keywords*—Microwave imaging; brain stroke detection; inverse problems; imaging techniques.**

I. Introduction

In the last years, there has been a growing interest in studying biological effects of electromagnetic fields (EMFs) as well as their applications for diagnostics and therapies. Among the various proposals, EMFs at microwave frequencies have been considered for the development of diagnostic techniques in medical imaging, mainly for breast cancer detection [1]. Recently, microwave signals have also been proposed for inspecting the human head in order to evaluate the possible presence of ischemic or hemorrhagic brain strokes. As it is well known, a stroke occurs when the regular circulation of blood in the human brain is impeded [2]. We consider here the case of hemorrhagic strokes, for which the vessels rupture causes bleeding into the brain. Due to the capabilities of microwave signals in detecting the dielectric properties of a given medium, the use of this kind of radiation has been evaluated for diagnostic and imaging purposed by several research teams around the world. The reader must consider, for example, papers [3]–[8] and the references therein. In microwave imaging [9], the target under test (located in the so called investigation domain D_{inv}) is illuminated by a known incident electromagnetic wave, $E_i(\mathbf{r})$, and samples of the scattered electric field are collected in a proper observation domain, D_{obs}, which is the region of space where the receiving sensors are located. In the frequency domain, the scattering problem can be formulated by a set of two integral equations, which, under tomographic hypotheses, involve scalar two-dimensional quantities [9]. In order to solve this problem, several numerical techniques can be applied. In the scientific literature concerning the imaging of brain stroke several well-known solutions, previously proposed for other applications involving the use of inversion techniques, have been exploited (e.g., distorted-wave Born approximation, conjugate gradients, Gauss-Newton methods, etc.). It must be also mentioned that several interesting results have been obtained considering a classification approach to detect the presence of ictuses, without the ambition of retrieving the distributions of the dielectric parameters [8]. In this paper, following an approach previously developed by the authors [10], the application of a regularization approach based on two nested loop is proposed. The outline of the method is reported, together with some preliminary numerical results.

II. Outline of the Problem Formulation

The formulation of the problem is expressed in terms of the integral equations of the inverse scattering for two-dimensional configurations [1]. The data equation is given by

$$E_s(\mathbf{r}) = -k_b^2 \int_{D_{inv}} \Delta\chi(\mathbf{r}')E_t(\mathbf{r}')\tilde{g}(\mathbf{r},\mathbf{r}')d\mathbf{r}' = \tilde{\mathcal{G}}_{data}(\Delta\chi E_t)(\mathbf{r}), \qquad \mathbf{r} \in D_{obs} \tag{1}$$

where E_s denotes the measured axial component of the scattered electric field, E_t is the same component of the internal total electric field, k_b the wavenumber in the background medium, $\Delta\chi = \chi - \tilde{\chi}$ is the difference between the actual contrast function $\chi = (\epsilon - \epsilon_b)/\epsilon_b$ and the contrast function of the considered reference configuration $\tilde{\chi} = (\tilde{\epsilon} - \epsilon_b)/\epsilon_b$, $\tilde{\epsilon}$ being the reference profile of complex permittivity. Finally, $\tilde{g}$ represents the inhomogeneous Green's function for the dielectric distribution $\tilde{\chi}$. Following a well-known approach [9], a second equation, namely the state equation, is needed, i.e.,

$$E_t(\mathbf{r}) = \tilde{E}_t(\mathbf{r}) - k_b^2 \int_{D_{inv}} \Delta\chi(\mathbf{r}')E_t(\mathbf{r}')\tilde{g}(\mathbf{r},\mathbf{r}')d\mathbf{r}' = \tilde{E}_t(\mathbf{r}) + \tilde{\mathcal{G}}_{state}(\Delta\chi E_t)(\mathbf{r}), \qquad \mathbf{r} \in D_{inv} \tag{2}$$

where $\tilde{E}_t$ is the total field measured with the configuration $\tilde{\chi}$. If equations (1) and (2) are joined together, we obtain

$$E_s(\mathbf{r}) = F(\Delta\chi)(\mathbf{r}) = \tilde{\mathcal{G}}_{data}\Delta\chi\left(I - \tilde{\mathcal{G}}_{state}\Delta\chi\right)^{-1}\tilde{E}_t(\mathbf{r}) \tag{3}$$

in which I denotes the identity operator. Such equation, which describes the relationship between the scattered electric field and the dielectric properties of the investigated region, is solved by a two-loop Newton-based iterative regularization method [10]. In particular, the outer loop is composed by Newton linearizations, whereas in the inner loop a truncated conjugate gradient algorithm is used.

III. Preliminary Simulation Results

An example of the obtained results is reported in the following. We considered the model of the human head described in [11], and, in particular, we assumed the slice #40 corresponding to the head cross section at 54.6 mm from the top. The imaging configuration is composed by 36 antennas acting as both transmitters and receivers. They are located on a circumference of radius 0.11 m. The forward problem has been solved by using the moment method. The head cross section has been discretized into 6496 square cells of size 0.0022 m. The dielectric parameters of the various biological tissues have been deduced from [12]. In order to simulate a noisy environment, a white Gaussian noise with zero mean value and a signal-to-noise ratio equal to $SNR = 15$ dB has been added to the samples of the scattered electric field at the measurement points. The cross section of the human head has been assumed to be included in a circular investigation domain D_{inv} of radius 0.10 m and surrounded by a coupling medium with $\epsilon_b = 15\epsilon_0$. The simulated data ($f = 1\ GHz$) have been inverted by using the mentioned two-step algorithm. As shown in Fig. 1(a), a hemorrhagic brain stroke has been simulated with an elliptic inclusion centered at $(-0.02, -0.03)$ m, with a major axis of 0.04 m and a minor axis of 0.02 m (contrast function $\chi = 3.07 + j6.33$). 1626 square subdomains (size: 44 mm) have been used for the inverse problem. A maximum number of 10 outer steps and 50 inner steps have been considered. The inner loop is terminated when the normalized difference between the residuals in two subsequent iterations is less than 0.01 and the head without stroke has been considered as the reference configuration. One reconstruction example is shown in Fig. 1(b). in which the reconstructed differential contrast function allows a correct localization of the brain stroke.

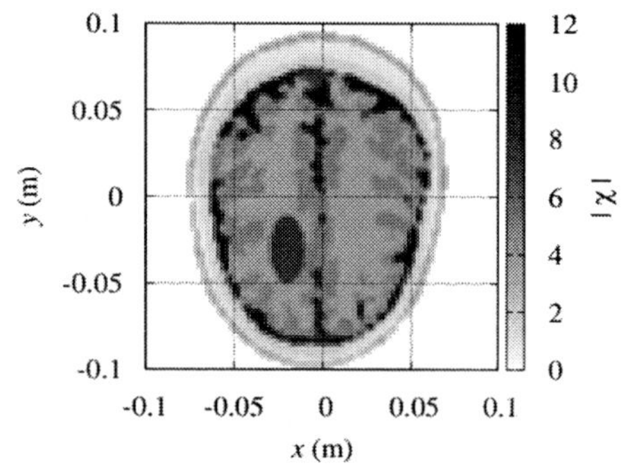

(a)

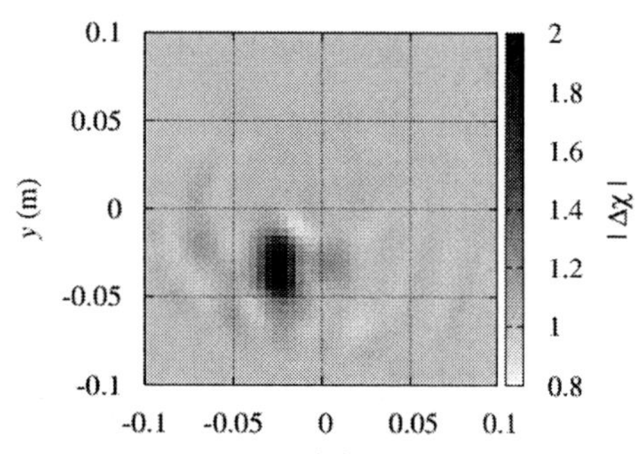

(b)

Fig. 1. (a) Absolute value of the actual contrast function of the considered head model with an elliptical hemorrhagic brain stroke. Model used for the solution of the forward electromagnetic problem. (b) Spatial distribution of the absolute value of the reconstructed differential contrast function. The dark region indicates the brain stroke location.

IV. Conclusions

In the framework of biomedical applications of EMFs, a microwave imaging approach has been proposed for hemorrhagic brain stroke detection. Based on a numerical solution of the integral equations of the inverse scattering problem under tomographic conditions, it has been proven to provide quite accurate maps of the dielectric properties of the human tissues from which one can deduce the presence of the stroke. Further developments will extend the present approach to a more realistic three-dimensional case.

Acknowledgment

The present work is partially supported by Compagnia di San Paolo, Italy.

References

[1] X. Li and S. C. Hagness, "A confocal microwave imaging algorithm for breast cancer detection," *IEEE Microw. Wirel. Compon. Lett.*, vol. 11, no. 3, pp. 130–132, Mar. 2001.

[2] T. G. Kwiatkowski *et al.*, "Effects of Tissue Plasminogen Activator for Acute Ischemic Stroke at One Year," *N. Engl. J. Med.*, vol. 340, no. 23, pp. 1781–1787, Jun. 1999.

[3] R. Scapaticci, O. M. Bucci, I. Catapano, and L. Crocco, "Differential Microwave Imaging for Brain Stroke Followup," *Int. J. Antennas Propag.*, vol. 2014, pp. 1–11, 2014.

[4] K. Bialkowski, D. Ireland, and A. Abbosh, "Microwave imaging for brain stroke detection using Born iterative method," *IET Microw. Antennas Propag.*, vol. 7, no. 11, pp. 909–915, Aug. 2013.

[5] S. Y. Semenov and D. R. Corfield, "Microwave tomography for brain imaging: feasibility assessment for stroke detection," *Int. J. Antennas Propag.*, vol. 2008, May 2008.

[6] N. Irishina and A. Torrente, "Brain Stroke Detection by Microwaves Using Prior Information from Clinical Databases," *Abstr. Appl. Anal.*, vol. 2013, pp. 1–8, 2013.

[7] I. Bisio *et al.*, "Brain stroke detection by microwave imaging systems: preliminary two-dimensional numerical simulations," in *2016 IEEE Int. Conf. on Imaging Systems and Techniques (IST)*, Crete, Greece, 2016.

[8] M. Persson *et al.*, "Microwave-Based Stroke Diagnosis Making Global Prehospital Thrombolytic Treatment Possible," *IEEE Trans. Biomed. Eng.*, vol. 61, no. 11, pp. 2806–2817, Nov. 2014.

[9] M. Pastorino, *Microwave imaging*. Hoboken N.J.: John Wiley, 2010.

[10] G. Bozza, C. Estatico, A. Massa, M. Pastorino, and A. Randazzo, "Short-range image-based method for the inspection of strong scatterers using microwaves," *IEEE Trans. Instrum. Meas.*, vol. 56, no. 4, pp. 1181–1188, Aug. 2007.

[11] I. G. Zubal, C. R. Harrell, E. O. Smith, Z. Rattner, G. Gindi, and P. B. Hoffer, "Computerized three-dimensional segmented human anatomy," *Med. Phys.*, vol. 21, no. 2, pp. 299–302, Feb. 1994.

[12] S. Gabriel, R. W. Lau, and C. Gabriel, "The dielectric properties of biological tissues: II. Measurements in the frequency range 10 Hz to 20 GHz," *Phys. Med. Biol.*, vol. 41, no. 11, p. 2251, 1996.

Antenna for contact microwave radiometers for monitoring of the brain microwave radiation

B.A. Panchenko, V.S. Kublanov, S.A. Baranov and V.I. Borisov
Ural Federal University
Yekaterinburg, Russian Federation
e-mail: kublanov@mail.ru

Y.E. Sedelnikov
Tupolev Kazan National Research Technical University
Kazan, Russian Federation

***Abstract*—In the paper, features of the brain microwave radiation measurements are considered. Influence of the contact pins addition on the antenna matching with head surface (changes of the reflection coefficient) is studied. Estimates of human head modelling with contact antenna-applicator are presented. Results of the investigations show that fluctuations of electromagnetic field in the near-field region is defined by magnetic component and depend on functional processes in the human brain.**

Keywords—microwave radiometer; antenna-applicator; near-field; brain microwave radiation; FEKO.

I. Introduction

Formation of emitted microwave radiation from any body is due to Brownian motion of charged particles when the temperature T of the body is different from absolute zero. The most commonly used methods for the registration of such radiation, imply placement of the antenna-applicator (AA) of the microwave radiometer on the body.

In general case the accuracy of the brightness temperature estimation for biological tissues, depends not only on the electro-physical properties of the AA and the antenna pattern, but also on the AA matching with the body. This problem is especially vital in case of long-term (at least more than 5 minutes) monitoring of the brain functional processes. For various structures of the AA body hair growth might cause issue during registration. Another issues are inhomogeneities: the skin "greenhouse" effect, changes in the microcirculation processes, gas exchange with the environment and so on.

The solution of the Ludeke K.M. [1], allows to decrease influence of the AA matching using the "noising" of the AA-body boundary. However, this solution has limited capabilities. The most perspective solution will imply either complete exclusion of the mentioned issues, or significant reduction of their influence of the brightness temperature estimation.

The goal of the present work, is to analyze features of the contact AA for the microwave radiometer. For this contact AA the best conditions for the brain radiation measurements during the long-term functional changes are implemented.

II. Modelling the Characteristics of the Electromagnetic Field AA

For the evaluation of the electromagnetic field (EMF) components impacts on the near-field region and selection of the best features for its configuration let as conduct model study.

Fig. 1 shows a flat version of bow-tie AA. One of the modelling tasks is to investigate influence of the parameters d, h, α and β on the characteristics of the AA.

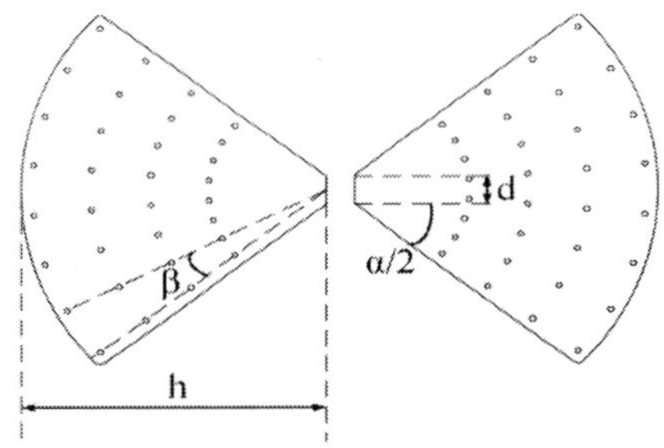

Fig. 1. Schematic of the AA.

Model calculations were carried out by a numerical hybrid method MOM / FEM (method of moments / finite element method) by a program of three-dimensional electromagnetic simulation FEKO (7.0) [2].

In this investigation, model of the head is represented by combination of plane-parallel dielectric structures. Electro-physical properties of these structures are defined by the corresponding characteristics of the scalp, cortical bone, cerebrospinal fluid, grey and white matter of the brain [3]. The simulation was performed in the frequency range 650–850 MHz.

III. Results

A. Modelling results

Modelling results allowed us to find the parameters of the optimized AA, at which intensity of EMF has maximal strength at a depth of 50 mm from body-AA border: $\alpha = 67.4^0$, $d = 3.8$ mm, $h = 26.0$ mm. For the estimation of the AA EMF distribution the spatial dependence of the normalized power flux density in the XZ cross-section is plotted, as shown on Fig. 2. Near the body-AA border, structure of the field is determined by presence of the longitudinal electric field component E_r. Therefore, the maximum amplitude of the vibrator is directed along the axis.

The modelling estimates have shown that distribution of the EMF in the reactive near-field zone for the direction along the AA axis is define by the sum of the Electric constituents $E_\theta + E_r$, that decreases in accordance with the cubic ratio

$$E_r = -\frac{il}{2\pi\varepsilon\varepsilon_0 w r^3}\cos\theta e^{iwt}, E_\theta = -\frac{il}{2\pi\varepsilon\varepsilon_0 w r^3}\sin\theta e^{iwt}. (1)$$

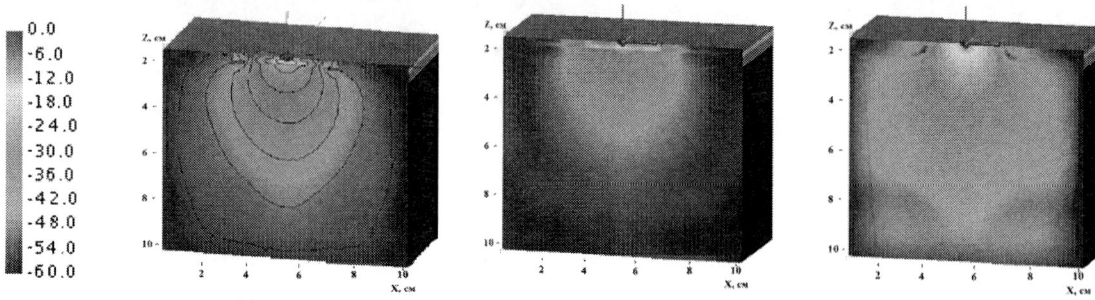

Fig 2. Normalized power flux density in the XZ cross-section, (a) EMF, dB W/m, (b) Electric field, dB V/m (c) Magnetic field, dB A/m.

Corresponding magnetic component H_φ in the near-field decreases proportionally to the square of the distance

$$H_\varphi = \frac{Il}{4\pi r^2} sin\theta e^{iwt}. \quad (2)$$

In the transition zone (for the head tissues at a depth from 0.9 to 5.6 cm for a frequency of 750 MHz) where electric component is insignificant (Fig. 2b); the EMF is mostly defined by the magnetic component (Fig. 2c). In turn, the magnetic component is formed by the mircocharges and microcurrents induced by fluctuations of the functional processes in the brain [4].

B. *Results of the laboratory tests*

In order to decrease influence of the mentioned inhomogeneities between the AA and head scalp we had developed prototype of the new AA. For this purpose, in each vibrator, we housed conductive pins that provide contact of the antenna to sculp. Schematic of such modified AA is proposed in [4] and general view is shown in Fig.3. Such AA allows one to provide good repeatability even considering hair on the head.

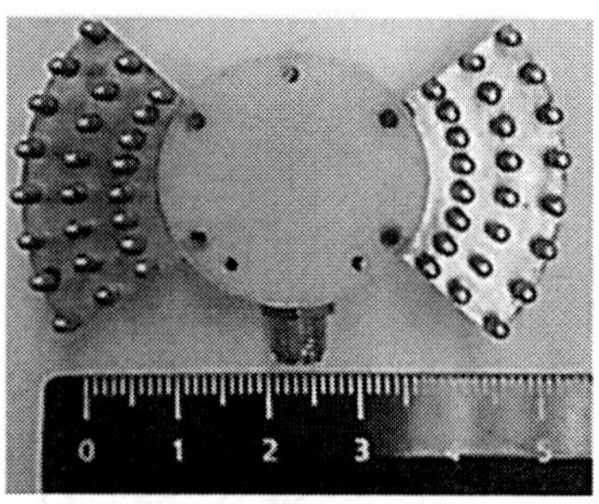

Fig. 3. The optimized AA prototype with contact pins.

Laboratory tests of the prototype AA with and without contact pins were conducted by the vector analyzer PXIe-5630 (National Instruments, USA). The AA was placed on head area with hair in the projection of the brain. Results of the tests are presented on Fig. 4.

Fig. 4 shows that highest reflection coefficient change during 30 minutes for the AA without contact pins is |0,12|. For the AA with contact pins the highest change of the reflection coefficient is no more than |0,06|.

IV. CONCLUSION

Results of the laboratory tests of the optimized AA with the contact pins confirms possibilities of its application for the long-term monitoring of the functional changes in the brain tissues (up to 30 minutes). The modelling had shown that these changes are mostly defined by the magnetic component changes. The influence of hair on the antenna pattern is almost nullified. The decrease of the reflection coefficient changes during the tests is the result of the addition of the contact pins.

REFERENCES

[1] K.M. Ludeke, J. Koehler, and J. Kanzenbach, "A new radiation balance microwave thermograph for simultaneous and independent temperature and emissivity measurements", J. Micr. Pow., 1979, vol. 14, pp. 117-121.

[2] D.B. Davidson, "Computational electromagnetics for RF and microwave engineering," Camb. Univ. Pr., 2005, p. 411.

[3] "Dielectric Properties of Body Tissues in the frequency range of 10 Hz - 100 GHz," [Electronic resource] http://niremf.ifac.cnr.it/tissprop/

[4] V.S Kublanov, "Microwave radiation as interface to the brain functional state," *Proc. of the Int. Conf. on Biom. Elec. and Dev. BIODEVICES*, Barcelona, pp. 318–322, 2013.

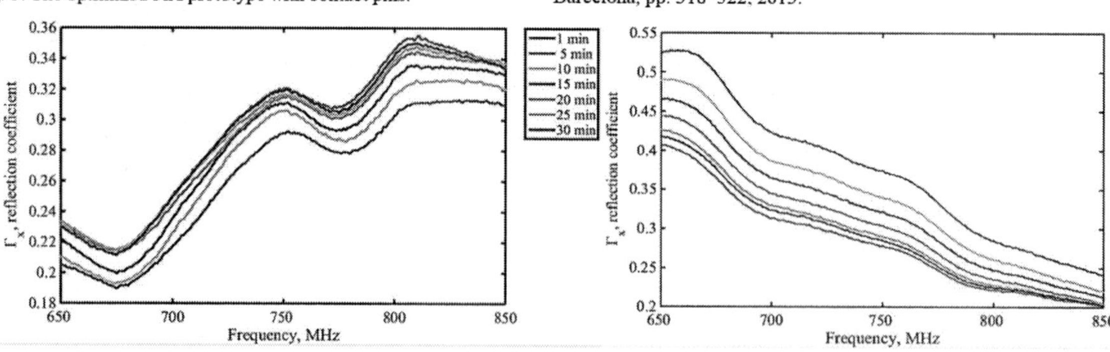

Fig. 4. Results of the laboratory tests during 30 minutes, (a) AA with pins, (b) AA without pins.

A Ku Band Circularly Polarized 2x2 Microstrip Antenna Array for Remote Sensing Applications

Roger Ferré, Fermín Mira, Guido Luzi, Jordi Mateu, Christos Kalialakis
Centre Tecnològic de Telecomunicacions de Catalunya (CTTC/CERCA)
Parc Mediterrani de la Tecnologia (PMT), Av. Carl Friedrich Gauss 7, 08860 – Castelldefels, Spain
christos.kalialakis@cttc.es

***Abstract*—This paper reports the development of a Circularly Polarized (CP) microstrip patch array working at Ku band and in particular between 16.9-17.2GHz for remote sensing applications. The design is based on a sequential rotation of four linearly polarized rectangular patches and appropriate phase shifts provided by a corporate feed network. The agreement between measurements and simulations carried out using HFSS is satisfactory.**

Keywords—Microstrip; antenna; circular polarization; antenna arrays; remote sensing.

I. Introduction

The use of circular polarization(CP) in telecommunications, both in terrestrial and space borne applications, is well consolidated owing to its capability to maximize the polarization efficiency component of the link budget and its lower sensitivity to multipath clutter with respect to the linear polarized radiation.

The antenna developed in this work is intended to be used in a recent ground based microwave remote sensing application, namely Ground Based radar interferometry using Synthetic Aperture Radar(GBSAR)[1]. Printed antennas offer the possibility of low cost, low weight and scalability to high gain version[2] compared to conventional horn antennas.

Usually CP antenna arrays are composed of individual CP elements. Alternatively, linearly polarized (LP) elements can be used [3] which are in general easier to design than CP elements. The technique is based on imposing appropriate phase differences on each element in order to produce a composite CP field [4]. A 2x2 microstrip antenna array is developed here following this method.

II. Antenna Design

A. Design requirements

The antenna array is intended as an antenna with a radar used for vibrations and deformations monitoring. The available in house radar device is a Continuous Stepped Frequency transceiver operating at Ku band. The apparatus is transportable and it is used in measurement campaigns in the field. Therefore lightweight components such as printed antennas are highly desirable. The frequency allocation for GBSAR[5] has a center frequency of f= 17.1 GHz and a total bandwidth of 300 MHz(16.9-17.2 GHz). The antenna gain requirements are related to the distance of operation. Typical values for the antenna gain range from 10dB to 20dB.

B. Geometry and design procedure

Exploiting the ideas in [3] and [4], four LP inset-fed half wavelength rectangular microstrip antennas are sequentially rotated(Fig.1a) and appropriate phase shift is applied on each branch of the feeding network (Fig.1b). The configuration for the case of Left Hand CP (LHCP) is shown in Fig.1. The design approach can be adjusted for Right Hand CP(RHCP) by employing rotations in the reverse sense.

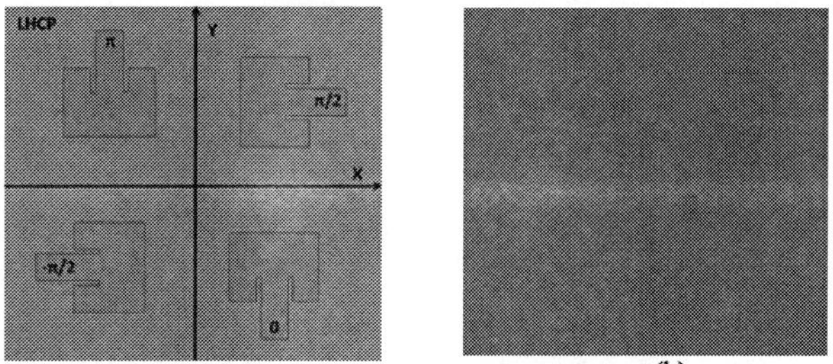

(a) (b)

Fig. 1. (a) Sequentially rotated patches (b) Feeding network

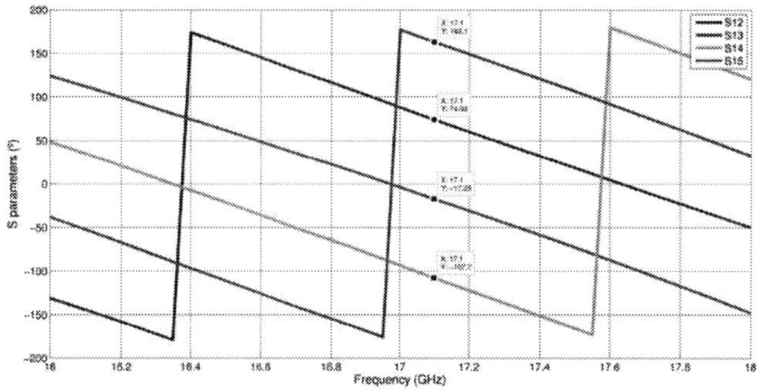

Fig. 2. Simulated S-parameters of the feeding network.

A critical point in the design procedure is the achievement of a proper 90° phase difference among the four branches of the feeding network. As a first step, the feeding network was designed as a circuit in Keysight's Advanced Design System (ADS) and then optimized in Momentum to account for electromagnetic effects. In Fig. 2, the phase of the simulated S-parameters is plotted. The relative phase difference is 90°±1° at the design frequency of 17.1 GHz.

Subsequently, the optimized feeding network along with the inset-fed antenna patches were simulated in HFSS. For the simulated antenna array, the calculated Axial Ratio(AR) remained below 2.5 dB in the frequency band of interest.

III. Antenna Measurements

A prototype array was fabricated on an Arlon 25N substrate (εr=3.38, h=0.762 mm) (Fig. 3) and measurements were carried out in an anechoic chamber.

Fig. 3. The LHCP Antenna array prototype for the Ku band.

The measured impedance matching of the array is shown in Fig. 4. The return loss is better than 10 dB over a much wider bandwidth.

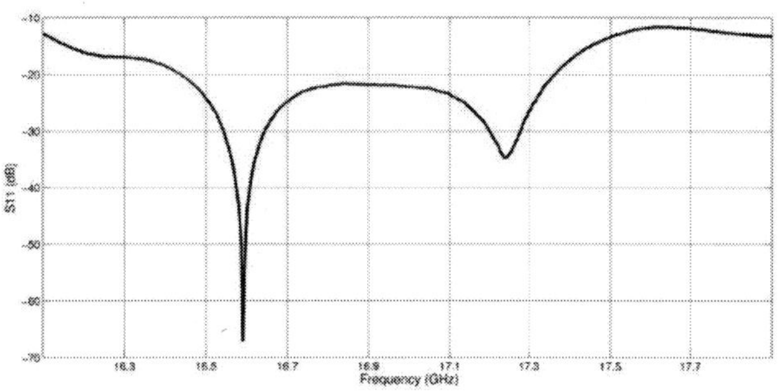

Fig. 4. Measured S11 of the LHCP antenna array.

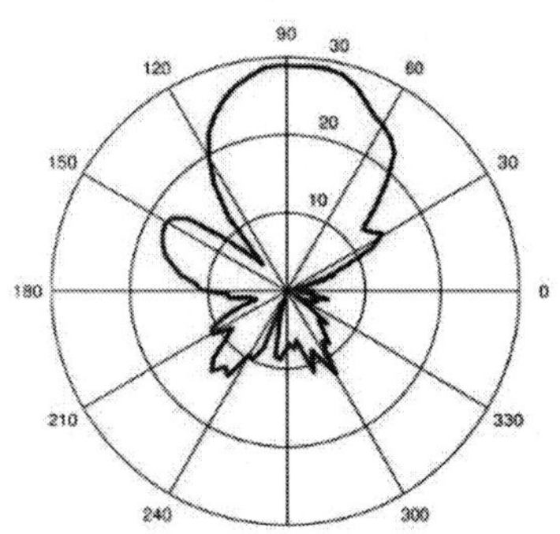

Fig. 5. Measured LHCP antenna pattern at 17.1 GHz

The measured antenna pattern at the center frequency is shown in Fig.5. If more gain is needed, the 2x2 antenna array can serve as a subarray for a larger array.

The most important metric for a CP antenna is its Axial Ratio. Measurements were carried out over frequency and angle (Fig. 6). As it can be seen, the measured broadside AR maintains values around 2.5 dB as predicted. The beamwidth is also stable.

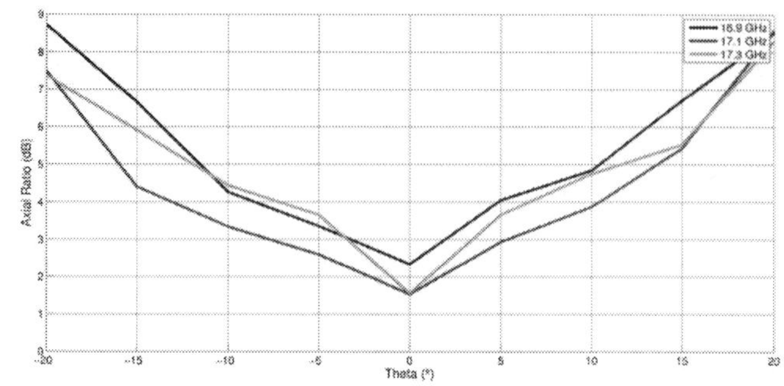

Fig. 6. Measured Axial Ratio over frequency and angle.

IV. Conclusions

An LHCP 2x2 antenna array has been implemented for the Ku band by appropriate phase combinations of linearly polarized microstrip patches. The antenna array presents good impedance matching and axial ratio over the band 16.9-17.2 GHz showing promise as a good antenna candidate (in itself or as a subarray) for GBSAR applications in this band. Furthermore, the method can be adjusted to produce RHCP by reversing the sense of sequential rotation.

Acknowledgments

The work has been supported by the Catalan Government under Grant 2014 SGR 1551. The work of C.Kalialakis was supported under EU H2020 Marie Sklodowska-Curie Grant Agreement 654734.

References

[1] G. Luzi, "Ground-based SAR interferometry:a novel tool for geoscience", in Geoscience and Remote Sensing,New Achievements, P. Imperatore and D. Riccio(eds), Vukopvar:InTechopen, 2010, pp. 1-26.

[2] N. Boskovic, B. Jokanovic, F. Olivieri, D. Tarchi, "High gain printed antenna array for FMCW radar at 17 GHz", 12th International Conference on Telecommunication in Modern Satellite, Cable and Broadcasting Services, 2015.

[3] J. Huang, "A technique for an array to generate circular polarization with linearly polarized elements," IEEE Transactions on Antennas and Propagation, vol. 34, pp.1113-1124,1986.

[4] M. A., Rahman, Q. D. Hossain, M. A Hossain, E Nishiyama, I. Toyoda, "Design and parametric analysis of a planar array antenna for circular polarization", International Journal of Microwave and Wireless Technologies, vol.8, pp. 921-929, 2016.

[5] European Communications Committee, "Compatibility studies between Ground Based Synthetic Aperture RADAR and existing services in the range 17.1 GHz to 17.3 GHz", Report 111, 2007. Online at http://www.erodocdb.dk/docs/doc98 /official/pdf/ECCRep111.pdf

Investigation of Efficient Simulation Methods for Finite Large X-Band Arrays in HFSS

Elicia Harper, Carolyn Reistad, and Alkim Akyurtlu
Electrical and Computer Engineering Department
Raytheon-University of Massachusetts Lowell Research Institute (RURI)
Printed Electronics Research Collaborative (PERC)
University of Massachusetts Lowell
Lowell, MA, USA
Elicia_Harper@student.uml.edu; Carolyn_Reistad@student.uml.edu; Alkim_Akyurtlu@uml.edu

***Abstract*— This paper investigates different simulation methods in HFSS for periodic arrays. Due to extensive computation times and memory requirements of explicitly simulating a large finite array, both HFSS's finite array domain decomposition method (DDM) and an infinite array simulation are studied as alternatives to reduce total simulation time. For these tests, a helix antenna operating between 8GHz and 8.4GHz is used as a unit cell. The single-element simulation is used to impedance-match the helix antenna before being used as the unit cell for the arrays. The time and accuracy of the explicit finite, finite DDM, and infinite array simulations are compared and the advantages and disadvantages of each method are studied.**

***Keywords*— Helix, HFSS, finite array, DDM, infinite array.**

I. Introduction

In the fast-paced world of technological research and development, designing and prototyping antenna arrays – particularly large arrays – quickly is essential. Although modern simulation software packages are powerful, as the number of elements in a simulation increases, the computational time and memory required grows exponentially [1]. Consequently, the ability to make adjustments, perform parameter sweeps, or detect model errors for rapid prototyping is severely hindered. Sub-array-based domain decomposition methods [2] and dual-primal finite element tearing and interconnecting (FETI-DP) [3] have been proven to reduce CPU time and RAM for large-array simulations. Several finite-difference time domain (FDTD) methods have also been developed to increase computation speed [4],[5]. However, many novel methods are inaccessible to most users. Therefore, until custom fast-simulation methods are made widely available, alternative simulation methods in commercial software packages must be thoroughly explored.

This paper studies three methods for simulating arrays in HFSS. A helix antenna operating between 8GHz and 8.4GHz is used as the unit cell. First the unit cell is designed. Next, the simulation methods are presented. Last, the array simulation times and accuracies are compared.

II. Unit Cell Design

The unit cell for the array analyses is an axial (end-fire) mode helix antenna consisting of a copper wire wrapped around a Teflon pole support (Figure 1). Using equations from [6], the helix antenna unit cell was designed. A combination of a quarter-wave transformer and a patch is used to impedance-match the helix antenna to 50Ω [7]. To minimize the time and RAM for the array simulations, optimization and impedance-matching were performed on the unit cell.

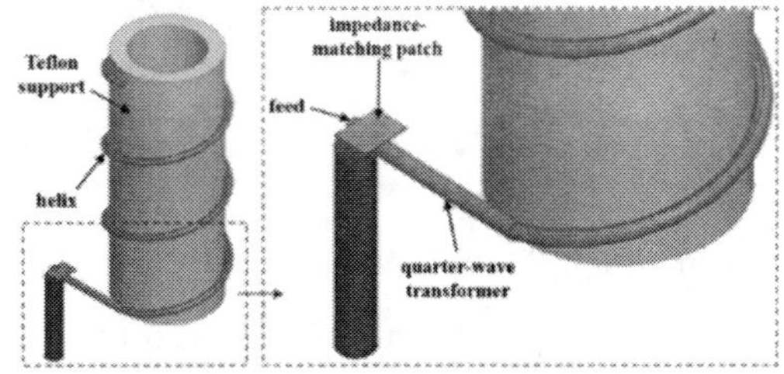

Fig. 1. HFSS helix antenna model; impedance-matching components for the helix antenna. Air box surrounding model is hidden from view.

III. Array Simulations

HFSS uses the finite element method to analyze models, breaking geometries into tetrahedra to form a mesh. The complexity of the calculations and mesh depend on the type of simulation used for the array: explicit finite method (EFM), finite array domain decomposition method (FA-DDM), or infinite array method (IAM). For all arrays in this study, the spacing between the array elements is 0.5λ, which prevents grating lobes from entering the real scan space [8]. Simulations were performed with an interpolating sweep, automatic meshing, and a Δδ of 0.02 required for convergence. The computers used for the simulations had a 64-bit operating system with 32GB of RAM and a 3.6GHz processor.

A. Finite Array Simulations

There are two primary methods of simulating finite arrays in HFSS. In the first method, EFM, all elements in the array are manually inserted and excited (Figure 2a). This method is advantageous because the results account for edge effects and the user has the most control over the simulation. However, EFM is demanding in terms of time and memory. The mesh required to perform the calculations contains numerous tetrahedra, making the mesh complicated [9].

The second method is FA-DDM. Rather than inserting the required number of elements, FA-DDM uses master/slave boundaries to create the array from a unit cell. The unit cell is repeated based on user-defined master/slave vectors, creating a purely periodic array in the XY plane. Unlike EFM, FA-DMM calculates the mesh for only the unit cell and adapts this mesh for the rest of the array. Overall, results obtained through FA-DDM do not differ from EFM analyses. It should be noted that FA-DDM simulations cannot be performed in HFSS with fewer than three cores [9]. Figure 2b shows a three-by-three helix array created using FA-DDM.

B. Infinite Helix Antenna Array Simulation

When finite arrays are not feasible to simulate, infinite arrays can be simulated instead. Like FA-DDM, IAM relies on master/slave boundaries. The infinite array is based on a unit cell upon which the user defines the master/slave vectors (Figures 2c and 2d). There are a few disadvantages to using IAM. First, results do not take into account array edge effects, sacrificing some simulation accuracy. Second, only a uniform magnitude excitation is assumed [9]. Furthermore, coupling parameters cannot be directly extracted from the simulation data, limiting available results.

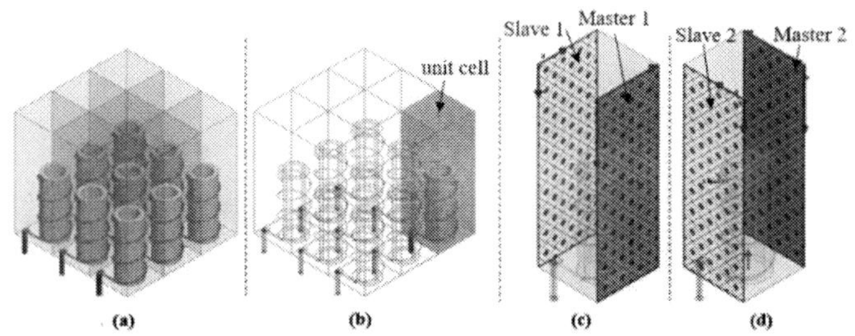

Fig. 2. Helix arrays in HFSS. (a) EFM model. (b) FA-DDM model. The blue outlines are the elements generated by FA-DDM. (c) IAM: 1st set of master/slave boundaries. (d) IAM: 2nd set of master/slave boundaries.

C. Comparison of Array Simulation Times and Accuracy

Table 1 compares the simulation methods and computational times (in real time) for the helix arrays.

TABLE 1: COMPARISON OF ARRAY SIMULATION TIMES

Array Size	Simulation Method; # of Cores	Total Simulation Time (hh:mm:ss)	% of Simulation Time for Meshing
1x1	EFM; 1	00:03:46	56.6%
2x2	EFM; 1	01:16:41	84.4%
2x2	EFM; 2	01:18:10	81%
2x2	FA-DDM; 4	00:31:13	33.9%
3x3	EFM; 1	03:20:51	84.9%
3x3	EFM; 2	02:55:23	88.9%
3x3	FA-DDM; 4	01:08:21	25.4%
8x8	FA-DDM; 4	17:00:19	29.3%
infinite	IAM; 1	00:02:09	57.4%
infinite	IAM; 2	00:02:23	61.5%

As can be seen in Table 1, the time to complete each simulation depends on the size of the array and the simulation method. For the same simulation method, larger arrays take longer to simulate. IAM has a significant time advantage over the finite simulation methods. In EFM simulations, the percentage of time required for meshing consumes the bulk of the simulation, indicating that mesh simplification is the primary driver for reducing overall simulation times. Compared to EFM, FA-DDM meshes faster due its use of a periodic mesh based on the unit cell rather than a mesh calculated for the entire array. Additionally, increasing the number of cores can help reduce the length of the simulation regardless of simulation method.

Table 2 shows the percent error of the S_{11} parameter for the corner element/unit cell of FA-DDM and IAM relative to EFM at 8GHz and 8.4GHz. Typically, the FA-DDM S_{11} values were higher than the EFM values while the IAM values were lower, demonstrating that IAM does not account for mutual coupling and edge effects. IAM became increasingly inaccurate as array size increased, indicating that IAM is a better approximation for small arrays than large arrays. Consequently, FA-DDM may be preferable for large arrays over IAM. Arrays with more than twenty-five elements could not be simulated using EFM, so FA-DDM and IAM may be the only options for large arrays when computer resources are limited.

TABLE 2: ACCURACY OF ARRAY ELEMENT S_{11} VALUE AT 8GHZ AND 8.4GHZ FOR FA-DDM AND IAM RELATIVE TO EFM

Array Size	% Error for FA-DDM vs. EFM at 8GHz	% Error for FA-DDM vs. EFM at 8.4GHz	% Error for IAM vs. EFM at 8GHz	% Error for IAM vs. EFM at 8.4GHz
2x2	7.5014%	20.3628%	15.8819%	5.6048%
3x3	9.9582%	17.5553%	14.8851%	7.1581%
4x4	12.0685%	16.0822%	11.9995%	8.7642%
5x5	0.4497%	16.6453%	20.6898%	33.6651%

IV. CONCLUSION

Finite and infinite helix antenna arrays were simulated in HFSS using three approaches. Simulation time and memory required are affected by array size and method used to simulate the array. FA-DDM is a viable alternative to EFM for large arrays. Additionally, FA-DDM allows for the simulation of array sizes that might not be possible with EFM. For small arrays, IAM's simulation time and small percent error make it ideal for rapid prototyping. However, when full array characterization is required, IAM will not suffice. Overall, when simulation time for an array must be minimized, FA-DMM or IAM must be considered. Ultimately, the simulation method used for arrays depends on array size, user accuracy and results needs, as well as computer and time constraints.

ACKNOWLEDGMENTS

The authors thank Tom Sikina of UMass Lowell/Raytheon, Jim DeLap of ANSYS, and the students and staff of RURI/PERC.

REFERENCES

[1] D. Chun and K. Sabet, "Full-wave moment method simulation of large-scale antenna arrays on high performance computing platforms," in *IEEE Antennas and Propag. Soc. Int. Symp.*, 2003 © IEEE. doi: 10.1109/APS.2003.1219276.

[2] X. Zhao *et al.*, "A sub-array-based DDM for full-wave EM simulation of large antenna arrays," in *IEEE Asia-Pacific Conf. on Antennas and Propag.*, 2015 © IEEE. doi: 10.1109/APCAP.2015.7374290.

[3] T. Wan *et al.*, "An efficient EM simulation method for the fast design and analysis of large antenna arrays," in *Int. Conf. on Inform. and Commun. Technologies*, 2015 © IET. doi: 10.1049/cp.2015.0234.

[4] W. Yu *et al.*, "A robust parallel conformal FDTD algorithm and its application to electrically large antenna array simulation," in *IEEE Antennas and Propag. Soc. Int. Symp.* 2004 © IEEE. doi: 10.1109/APS.2004.1329849.

[5] W. Simon *et al.*, "Efficient and accurate EM simulation of large array antennas and imaging systems," in *IEEE Int. Conf. on Electromagnetics in Advanced Applicat.*, 2012 © IEEE. doi: 10.1109/ICEAA.2012.6328636.

[6] C. A. Balanis, *Antenna Theory: Analysis and Design*, 3rd ed. Hoboken, NJ, John Wiley & Sons, Inc., 2005.

[7] J. D. Kraus, "A 50-Ohm input impedance for helical beam antennas," in *IEEE Trans. Antennas Propag.*, vol. AP-25, no. 6, p913, Nov 2005.

[8] R. J. Mailloux, *Phased Array Antenna Handbook*, 2nd ed. Norwood, MA: Artech House Inc., 2005.

[9] Ansys®, "Lecture 10: HPC for Finite Arrays," in *ANSYS HFSS for Antenna Design*, 2015 © ANSYS, Inc.

Genetic Algorithm Optimization of a Dual Polarized Concentric Ring Array

Pedro Mendes Ruiz, Israel D. Hinostroza Sáenz,
Régis Guinvarc'h
CentraleSupélec
Gif-sur-Yvette, France
pedro.mendesruiz@centralesupelec.fr

Randy L. Haupt
Electrical Engineering and Computer Science
Colorado School of Mines
Golden, CO

Abstract— **We use a genetic algorithm to minimize the Relative Sidelobe Level (RSLL) of a dual polarized concentric ring array. The optimization variables are the placement of uniformly weight spiral antennas in an aperture with a small area. We used isotropic sources for the optimization and the topology used is the concentric ring array. The computation of the Array Factor (AF) of the topology used is expensive and many function calls are required during the optimization, so we developed approaches to obtain a faster cost function and reduce the number of function calls.**

Keywords— wideband array, phased array, spiral antenna, genetic algorithms, optimization

I. Introduction

Dual circularly polarized wide band arrays find use in several applications, including weather forecast, Foliage PENetration and synthetic aperture radar. Two-arm center-fed spiral antennas are suitable elements, because they are very wide band, conformal and circularly polarized. Dual polarization is possible by interleaving spirals of opposite polarization [1] [2]. A dual polarized concentric ring array was developed using two-arm center-fed Archimedean spirals as the radiating element with each ring of spirals backed by a cavity. Non-uniformly spaced concentric rings mitigated the sidelobes [3]. In [4] we added a size constraint to the optimization to reduce the array's size.

The goal of the optimization described in this work is to find a smaller array than in [3] with a similar bandwidth by optimizing the rings positions using the size constraint in [4]. Section II presents the array geometry. Section III describes the genetic algorithm optimization. Section IV has results based on restricting the cost function to reduce run time.

II. Concentric Ring Array

A diagram of the concentric ring array appears in Fig. 1. Variables in the ring design include the ring spacing Δ_i and the ring rotation Φ_i. The array consists of Archimedean spirals of diameter of $D_{spi} = 10.5$ cm with a lower cut-frequency of 1 GHz [3]. The spacing between elements within a ring has a constant value of 24.34 cm [3]. There are 4 rings with a constraint of all radii being less than or equal to 1.2m [4]. Every other element in a ring is RH (right hand) polarized, while the others are LH (left hand) polarized. The array is modeled using isotropic point sources.

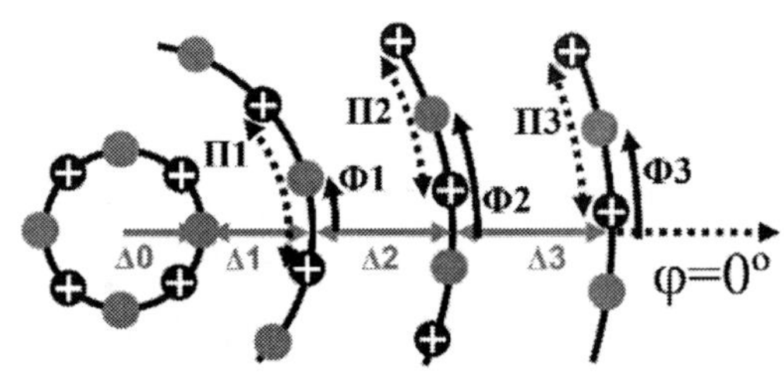

Fig. 1. Concentric ring array: filled and cross circles represent RH and LH polarized spirals, respectively.

III. Array Bandwitdh

The spirals used in this array have a reflection coefficient higher than -10 dB for frequencies below 1 GHz, so this is used as the lower limit of the bandwidth. In order to calculate the higher limit of the bandwidth of the array, we used a mean radiated element model to find the total radiated field, and then find the RSLL, that should be smaller than -10 dB [3].

The model used was single ring of 8 interleaved spirals of opposing polarization (4 per polarization) backed by a cavity [3, Fig. 4] with one being excited and the others loaded with 220Ω, simulated with FEKO.

IV. Genetic Algorithm Optimization

The goal of the optimization is to minimize the RSLL in the desired bandwidth (1-2 GHz), considering a maximal steering of θ_s=30°. In order to find the maximum sidelobe level in such a way to consider all steering directions up to θ_s, the array pattern was calculated, at 2 GHz, in the region

$$u^2 + v^2 \leq \left(1 + \sin\theta_s\right)^2 \qquad (1.1)$$

The cost function analizes that region and returns the highest RSLL in dB.

The genetic algorithm had a population size of 200 and ran for a maximum of 200 generations. A single function call for a concentric ring array of isotropic point sources took between 3.8 and 6.3 s. The whole optimization took 38 hours to finish using 4 cores, with a mean of 55 generations before reaching the stop criterion for each of the eight genetic algorithm iterations and a total of 88985 evaluations of the cost function.

The optimization results can be seen in Fig. 2. We plotted the u-cut of the absolute value of the normalized radiated field, showing a representative case of the highest sidelobes encountered. We can note that the RSLL is kept bellow -11dB for a steering up to 30° and a frequency up to 2 GHz with a maximum radius of 1.2m. We can also note that there are two distinguishable sidelobes. We called those closer to the main beam Inner Sidelobes (ISL) and those farther from the main beam, Outer Sidelobes (OSL). However, once considering the radiating pattern (see section III), the resulting array had a bandwidth from 1-1.3 GHz (27% of [3]).

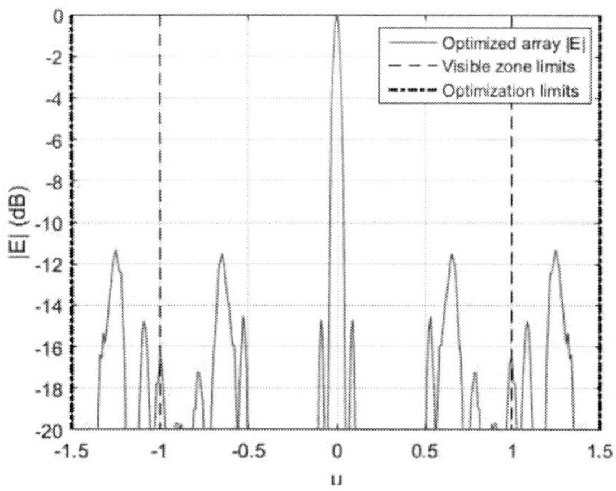

Fig. 2. Absolute radiated field (using isotropic sources) for the concentric ring array optimized using at the θ_s<30° zone, at 2 GHz.

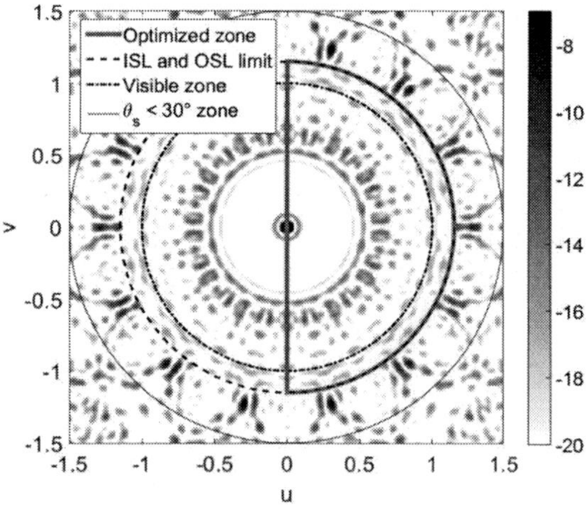

Fig. 3. Contour plot of the array factor of the optimized concentric ring array using half of the ISL at 2 GHz.

We noticed that we could restrict the optimization zone only to the ISL, as the OSL would be attenuated once the radiating pattern of the spiral antennas was taken into account. Prioritizing the ISL when optimizing the array's AF compensates their rise once the radiating pattern is considered. This way, the bandwidth was enhanced to 1-2 GHz (95% of [3]), as well as obtaining a faster optimization time (Table 1).

By comparing the arrays bandwidths (Table 1) we see that limiting the AF's optimized zone to the ISL is a good strategy.

By optimizing only half of the ISL there was no bandwidth reduction, proving it to be a reasonable way to accelerate the cost function evaluation. The resulting AF when evaluating only half of the ISL is shown in Fig. 3, highlighting the different zones described in this paper. Further reduction of the optimized region consistently caused a reduction in the bandwidth, so it was not considered in this paper.

As for the time reduction, there are two main factors. Firstly, by limiting the optimized zone in the AF there are less points to be computed in the u-v space, which results in a faster cost function. This is true for both the optimization with all the ISL and only half of them. Secondly, by reducing the optimized zone, the genetic algorithm started to converge faster. Having a smaller number of sidelobes being minimized there is probably a larger set of arrays that get close to optimal, which could explain this faster convergence. By comparing the first and last optimizations, the latter spent 22.3% of the time needed for the first one while enhancing the bandwidth from 27% to 95% (1-2 GHz) of [3].

Table 1. Comparison of results

Optimized zone	θ_s<30°	ISL only	Half ISL
Bandwidth (GHz)	1-1.3 (27%)	1-2 (95%)	1-2 (95%)
Cost Function call time (s)	3.8-6.3 (100%)	2.2-3.7 (59%)	1.1-1.9 (30%)
Cost Function Calls	88985 (100%)	77988 (88%)	59387 (67%)
Optimization time (h)	38 (100%)	21 (55%)	8 (22%)

V. Conclusions

By analyzing the concentric ring array topology with a size constraint [4] and redesigning its cost function, it was possible to find an array with 95% of the bandwidth in [3] and 32% of its surface, as well as an optimization 4.5 times faster than in [4]. For the bandwidth, the key factor was to identify the sidelobes to be optimized when considering the embedded element model. As for the time reduction, by reducing the optimized area we got a cost function 3.4 times faster. In addition, by considering less sidelobes, the genetic algorithm converges with 1.5 times less cost functions calls.

References

[1] Kaiser, J. A. (1960), The archimedean two-wire spiral antenna, IRE Trans. on Ant. & Prop., 8 (3), 312-323.

[2] Guinvarc'h, R. and Haupt, R. L., "Dual polarization interleaved spiral antenna phased array with an octave bandwidth," IEEE Trans. on Ant. & Prop., vol. 58, no. 2, pp. 397–403, 2010.

[3] Hinostroza Saenz, I. D.; Guinvarc'h, R; Haupt, R.L.; Louertani, K., "A Dual-Polarized Wideband Planar Phased Array With Spiral Antennas", IEEE Trans. on Ant. & Prop., vol. 62, no. 9, pp. 4547–4553, 2014.

[4] Mendes Ruiz, P.; Hinostroza, I; Guinvarc'h R.; Haupt, R.L., "Size constraint in design of concentric ring array", in IEEE Int. Symp. on Ant. & Prop. (APSURSI), 2015.

Mutual Coupling Reduction in Array Elements Using EBG Structures

Hassan Sajjad, Sana Khan, and Ercument Arvas
Istanbul Medipol University, Istanbul, Turkey
Email: hsajjad@st.medipol.edu.tr

***Abstract*—A 2D electromagnetic band gap (EBG) structure is designed on the ground plane of 1×2 rectangular patch antenna array to reduce the mutual coupling between the two elements and enhance the radiation pattern. An isolation of −41 dB has been achieved with the EBG structure relative to −20 dB without the EBG.**

Index Terms*—*Electromagnetic Band Gap, Patch Antenna Array, Mutual Coupling

I. Introduction

During the last decade tremendous advances have been made in the wireless technology. The use of high frequency bands result in miniaturization of the circuits. Antennas play a vital role in wireless communication. The radiation properties of antennas, when used in close proximity of other circuit elements, are highly affected by their presence. Microwave researchers are constantly in an effort to reduce these effects while designing the RF front ends to achieve the required results.

Mutual coupling between the elements in an array configuration has an adverse effect on the radiation pattern, return loss, and directivity of the antenna. Substrates of different permittivities, different thicknesses, negative permittivity, and negative permeability are being used [1]. Researchers are making use of defected ground structures (DGS), a simplified form of EBG, to enhance the radiation properties of microstrip patch antenna arrays [2]. EBG makes use of the periodic structures to create a frequency band gap. These periodic structures can suppress surface waves to reduce mutual coupling between array elements as suggested in [3], where a mushroom-like EBG structure is analyzed and an 8 dB reduction in mutual coupling is achieved. These structures can help in improving the operation bandwidth [4] of the microstrip antennas which are considered narrow band antennas.

This paper makes use of the surface wave suppression property of the EBG structure to reduce mutual coupling between a 1 × 2 rectangular microstrip patch antenna array (MPAA). COMSOL Multiphysics is used as simulation tool for this design.

II. Simulation Setup

A single patch antenna with length $L_p = 16$ [mm] and width $W_p = 12.45$ [mm] was designed on a lossless substrate of permittivity $\epsilon_r = 2.2$ and height 0.794 [mm] in COMSOL. The patch was fed with a coaxial feed of inner conductor radius 0.034 [mm] and outer conductor radius 0.114 [mm]. The patch resonated at 7.45 GHz.

Patch antennas are commonly used in array configuration to achieve high directivity and gain. In antenna arrays, mutual coupling has an adverse effect on the performance of the antenna elements. The main purpose of this paper is to reduce the mutual coupling between array elements. Therefore, the single rectangular patch was arranged in a 1×2 array configuration to take into account the mutual coupling between the two elements. The substrate dimensions were 30×60 [mm]^2 and the edge to edge separation between the patches was set to d = 6 [mm] which is $0.15\lambda_0$, where λ_0 is the free space wavelength at resonant frequency 7.45 GHz. EBG structure is used to increase the isolation between the two patches.

A unit cell of the EBG structure can have an I-shape, H-shape, circle, square etc. In this paper, a star shaped unit cell, shown in Fig. 1, has been optimized to reduce the mutual coupling between the antenna elements. A rectangle of width W=0.3 [mm] and length L=2 [mm] was rotated at $45°, 90°$, and $135°$ to generate the star shape.

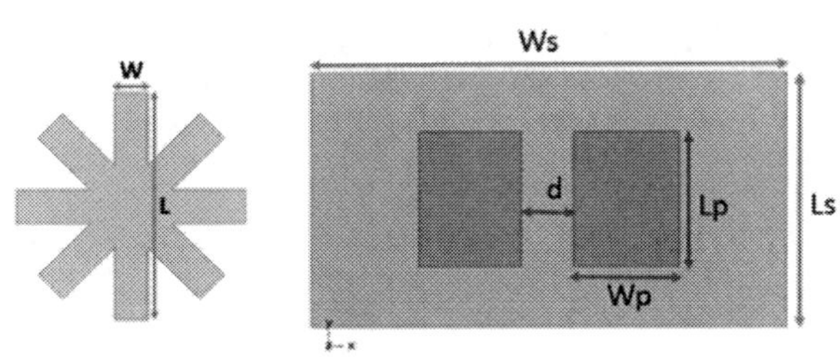

Fig. 1. Left: Unit cell of the EBG structure; Right: Top view of 1×2 patch antenna array on substrate.

The unit cell shown in Fig. 1 (left) was arranged in a 2D EBG structure. The first unit cell (top left) in Fig. 2 is offset, from the center, in x and y by −5 [mm] and 11.5 [mm], respectively. The horizontal and vertical edge to edge separation between any two unit cells is 0.5 [mm] and 1 [mm], respectively.

III. Simulation Results

The meshing used in COMSOL was set to normal with physics based meshing enabled, which means that there should be at least five mesh elements per wavelength. The patch array was simulated without the EBG structure to observe the S-parameters of the antenna. One patch was excited while the

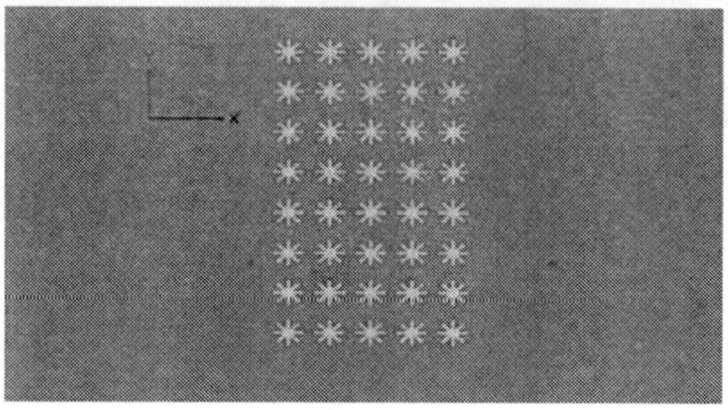

Fig. 2. 1×2 patch antenna array with the EBG structure between the patches.

other one was match terminated. Another simulation was run in the presence of the EBG structure to see its effect on the coupling. Figure 3 shows the S-parameters (S_{11} and S_{21}) for both the simulations.

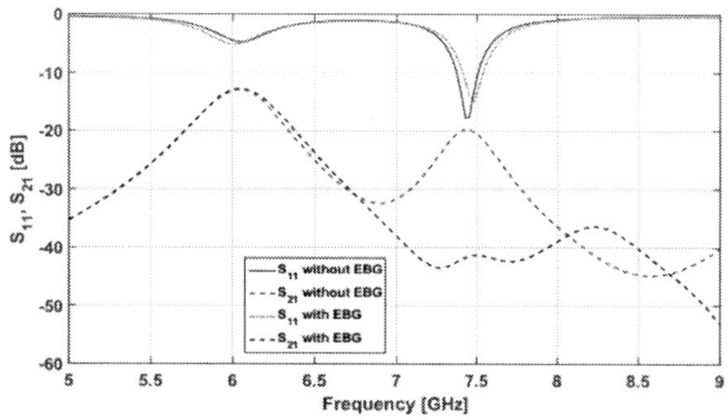

Fig. 3. S-parameters of the 1×2 patch array with and without the EBG structure.

Without the EBG, coupling (S_{21}) between the two elements is -20 dB at the resonant frequency. The second patch (right in Fig. 1) is not excited but radiations from the excited patch induces a current on it and disturbs the fields of the overall antenna.

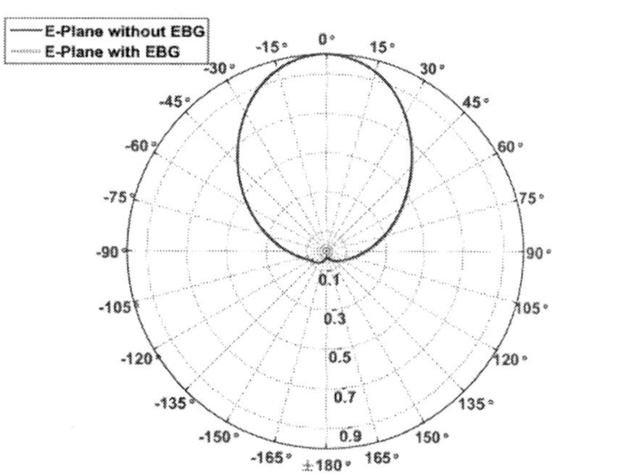

Fig. 4. Normalized E-plane far-field pattern [V/m] for a 1×2 patch array with and without the EBG structure.

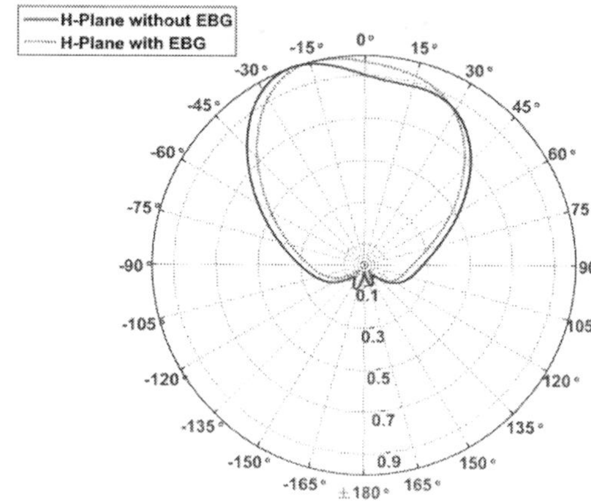

Fig. 5. Normalized H-plane far-field pattern [V/m] for a 1×2 patch array with and without the EBG structure.

With implementation of the EBG structure (S_{21}) dropped to -41 dB and the effect on the second patch is reduced to a higher degree. The second patch is placed perpendicular to the direction of current due to which the couping is more in the H-plane. The effect of coupling and decoupling on the normalized far-field [V/m] for both, E,H-planes, is presented in Figs. 4 and 5, respectively. The H-plane pattern in the presence of the EBG structure has recovered to the conventional pattern of a patch antenna.

IV. Conclusion

A star shaped DGS has has been arranged in a 2D EBG structure to improve the isolation between two patch antennas operating at the same frequency. The designed structure resulted in increased isolation from -20 dB to -41 dB. The EBG structure suppresses the surface waves and stops them from interfering with the adjacent patch.

References

[1] A. S. Chauhan, R. Ramesh and Usha Kiran K, "Efficient method of increase in isolation between patch antennas using metamaterial," Communications and Signal Processing (ICCSP), 2015 International Conference on, Melmaruvathur, 2015, pp. 0205-0208.

[2] F. Yang, and Y. R. Samii, "Electromagnetic band gap structures in antenna engineering," Cambridge University Press, 2008.

[3] Fan Yang and Y. Rahmat-Samii, "Microstrip antennas integrated with electromagnetic band-gap (EBG) structures: a low mutual coupling design for array applications," in IEEE Transactions on Antennas and Propagation, vol. 51, no. 10, pp. 2936-2946, Oct. 2003.

[4] R. Gupta and M. Kumar, "Bandwidth Enhancement of Microstrip Patch Antennas by Implementing Electromagnetic Bandgap (EBG) Structures," Computational Intelligence and Communication Networks (CICN), 2012 Fourth International Conference on, Mathura, 2012, pp. 15-18.

Design of Compact Dual-Element Antenna Array for LTE700 and WWAN Applications

Hari Shankar Singh
Department of Electronics and Communication Engineering
Thapar University
Patiala, India
harishankar.singh@thapar.edu

Manoj Kumar Meshram
Department of Electronics Engineering
Indian Institute of Technology (Banaras Hindu University)
Varanasi, India
mkmeshram.ece@iitbhu.ac.in

Abstract—**In this paper a multiband MIMO antenna suitable for long term evolution (LTE) and wireless wide area network (WWAN) application is presented. The MIMO antenna consists of two symmetric antenna elements, neutralization line and modified ground plane printed on a printed circuit board (PCB). The size of each radiators are 15 × 25 × 4 mm^3. To maintain the compactness, radiating elements are folded at the edge of substrate. The combination of neutralization line and modified ground plane are used to reduce the mutual coupling at single and wide frequency band. The proposed antenna operates over a frequency range of 747 MHz -787 MHz and 1750 MHz - 2570 MHz. It covers LTE700, GSM1800, GSM1900, UMTS, LTE2500, and Wi-Fi bands which is suitable for LTE and WWAN applications. The performances of the antenna in terms of *S*-parameters and radiation patterns are investigated. The measured result is found in close agreement with simulated one.**

Keywords—diversity antenna; isolation; LTE; neutralization line; WWAN

I. Introduction

The muliptle-input-multiple-output (MIMO) technology significantly enhances the performance of modern wireless communication standard, such as LTE, wireless LAN, and wireless interoperability for microwave access (WiMAX). The LTE is a new standard for four generation that can integrate MIMO technologies for reduced fading phenomenon, reliable high speed data transmission, and high channel capacity [1].

Recently, number of antennas have been proposed by several research group for MIMO terminals. Shoaib *et al.* [2] has been developed printed monopole antenna for MIMO terminals and decoupling achieved using modified ground plane. Unfortunately, the proposed antenna is not suitable for LTE handsets. In [3], a planar antenna array for WWAN/LTE smartphone applications with protruded ground plane for isolation improvement has been demonstrated. The chip inductor is used in the antenna design to minimize the physical length required for desired resonant modes, which produces losses as well as increase complexity in the fabrication process. Wang and Du in [4] has been developed a printed MIMO antenna for 2G/3G/4G mobile terminals, nevertheless the lower frequency (LTE700) is unable to cover. Recently few works [5], [6] draw their attention on this aspect. In [5], a quad-element MIMO antenna array in the smart phone has been developed for multi-wideband operations covering 750–960 MHz and 1700–3600 MHz but the larger form factor of the proposed antenna is appeared [5]. Reference [6] designed a 4 by 4 MIMO antenna system for LTE smart phones. But the proposed antenna covered area oriented frequency range of LTE i.e. 3.4-3.6 GHz which is used in Japan . In all the cases of different MIMO terminals either the antennas support a selective range of frequencies or having larger form factor.

In this paper, a dual-element antenna array is presented for LTE700 and WWAN applications. To make compact structure of single antenna elements folded technique is applied. The main radiating element is folded at the edge of substrate. Further, to reduce the mutual coupling between closely place MIMO antenna array over mobile circuit board, a combination of neutralization line and modified ground plane are used. The proposed antenna array operates over 747MHz to 787MHz and 1750MHz to 2570MHz based on -6 dB reflection coefficient. The detail dimensions and operation of the proposed MIMO antenna are given in the next sections.

II. Antenna Configuration

The configuration of the proposed dual-element diversity antenna array is shown in Fig. 1. The antenna is designed on 0.8 mm thick FR4 substrate of relative permittivity (ε_r = 4.4) and loss tangent (tan δ = 0.018). The size of PCB is chosen 100 mm × 60 mm. The zoomed and unfolded structure of single antenna element is shown in Fig. 1(a). The dual-element antenna array are placed on the top corner of mobile PCB. The dual elements are mirror image to each other. Each radiating elements are printed on the top of the substrate where no ground portion below to the elements. Each radiating elements are fed with coaxial probe at points A_1 and A_2 and shorting points of the antenna elements at B_1 and B_2. The feed point and shorting point of Element 1 is at (x_1, y_1 = 4.76mm, 84.5mm) and (x_3, y_1 = 6.43mm, 84.5mm), respectively with respect to origin. The front view and rear view (detail dimension of modified ground plane) of the proposed antenna are shown in Fig. 1(a) and detail dimensions of unfolded single antenna element is shown in Fig. 1(b). The proposed antenna consists of meandered and shorted radiating elements to make compact structure of the MIMO antenna system.

III. Results and Discussions

The design and optimization of the proposed antenna have been carried out in computer simulation technology (CST)

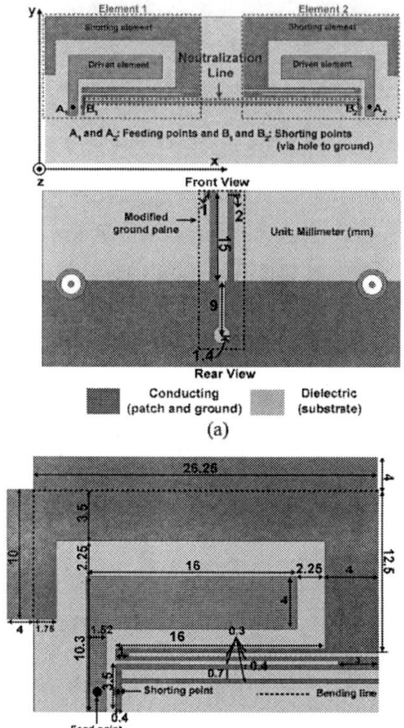

Fig. 1.(a) Front and rear view of the proposed antenna, and (b) Detail of single antenna element.

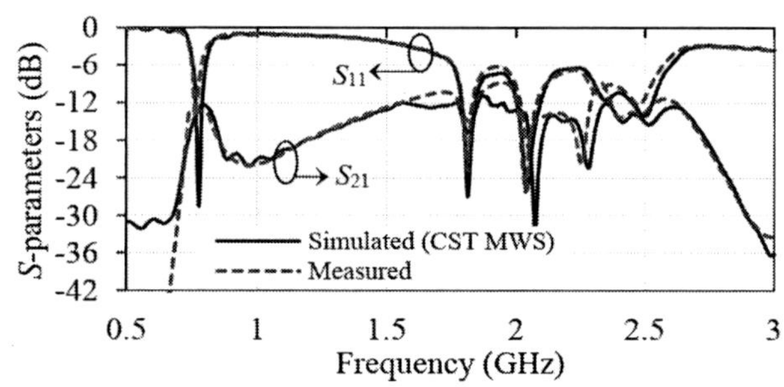

Fig. 2. Simulated and measured *S*-parameters of the proposed antenna.

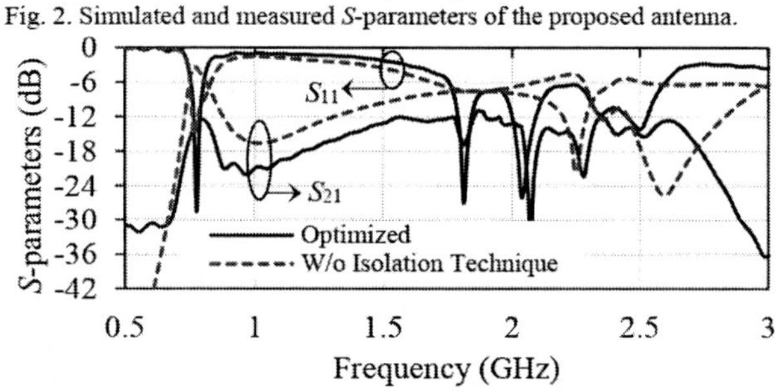

Fig. 3. Effect of isolation technique on *S*-parameters.

microwave studio (MWS) [7]. After optimization, antenna prototype is developed by T-Tech QC-5000 micro-milling machine. The fabricated prototype is measured by Anritsu VNA Master MS2038C (5 kHz–20 GHz). The simulated and measured *S*-parameters are shown in Fig. 2. Some discrepancies between simulated and measured results are observed, which are due to manufacturing tolerances. The effect of isolation technique can be observed from Fig. 3. It is observed that proposed isolation technique (combination of neutralization line and modified ground plane) not only increase isolation but also improves the impedance matching over desired operating bands.

The simulated 3D radiation patterns of the proposed antenna is shown in Fig. 4. The radiation patterns of the dual elements antenna array point to complimentary spatial region which shows pattern diversity of the proposed antenna, and this property can provide low correlation and good antenna diversity in free space. The calculated values of ECC using far field data are well below 0.02 over entire band of operation.

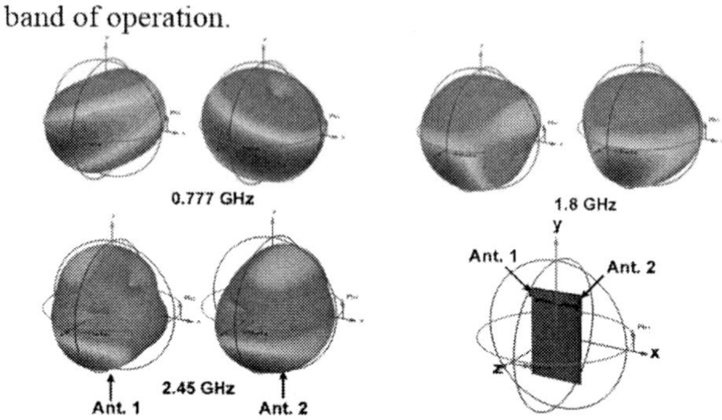

Fig. 4. Simulated 3D radiation patterns of the proposed antenna.

IV. Conclusion

In this paper a compact dual-element antenna array for MIMO terminal is proposed. To reduce the mutual coupling a combination of neutralization line and modified ground plane is utilized. The proposed antenna operates over a frequency range of 747 MHz -787 MHz and 1750 MHz - 2570 MHz which provide application platform of LTE700, GSM1800, GSM1900, UMTS, LTE2500, and Wi-Fi bands. The proposed antenna is potential candidate for modern mobile handset applications.

V. References

[1] G. J. Foschini, M. J. Gans, "On limits of wireless communications in a fading environment when using multiple antennas," Wireless Pers. Commun. vol. 6, no. 3 pp. 311-335, 1998.

[2] S. Shoaib, I. Shoaib, N. Shoaib, X. Chen, and C. G. Parini, "Desing and performance study of a dual-element multiband printed monopole antenna array for MIMO terminals," *IEEE Antenna and Wireless Propag. Lett.*, vol. 13, pp. 329-332, 2014.

[3] Y.-L. Ban, Z.-X. Chen, Z. Chen, K. Kang, and J. L.-W. Li, "Decoupled closely spaced heptaband antenna array for WWAN/LTE smartphone applications," *IEEE Antenna and Wireless Propag. Lett.*, vol. 13, pp. 31-34, 2014.

[4] Y. Wang and Z. Du, "A printed dual-antenna systems operating in the GSM1800/ GSM1900/ UMTS/ LTE2300/ LTE2500/ 2.4-GHz WLAN bands for mobile terminals," *IEEE Antenna and Wireless Propag. Lett.*, vol. 13, pp. 233-236, 2014.

[5] K. Li, Y. Shi, and C.-H. Liang, "Quad-element multi-band antenna array in the smart mobile phone for LTE MIMO operation," *Microwave Opt. Tech. Lett.*, vol 58, pp. 2619-2626, 2016.

[6] W.-W. Lee and B. Jang, "A smart 4 by 4 MIMO antenna systems for LTE smartphones," *Microwave Opt. Tech. Lett.*, vol 58, pp. 2668-2672, 2016.

[7] CST MWS, Online Available: http://www.cst.com.

A Modified CoSaMP Algorithm For Electromagnetic Imaging of Two Dimensional Domains

Ali Imran Sandhu and Hakan Bagci

Division of Computer, Electrical, and Mathematical, Sciences and Engineering
King Abdullah University of Science and Technology (KAUST)
Thuwal 23955-6900, Saudi Arabia
{aliimran.sandhu, hakan.bagci}@kaust.edu.sa

***Abstract*— The compressive sampling matching pursuit (CoSaMP) algorithm is used for solving the electromagnetic inverse scattering problem on two-dimensional sparse domains. Since the scattering matrix, which is computed by sampling the Green function, does not satisfy the restricted isometry property, a damping parameter is added to the diagonal entries of the matrix to make the CoSaMP work. The damping factor can be selected based on the level of noise in the measurements. Numerical experiments, which demonstrate the accuracy and applicability of the proposed algorithm, are presented.**

***Keywords*— Compressive sensing, inverse scattering, greedy pursuits, CoSaMP, microwave imaging**

I. INTRODUCTION

Various compressed sensing (CS) techniques [1-2], which have originally been developed for efficient reconstruction of sparse signals in image processing applications, have recently been applied to solving electromagnetic inverse scattering problems [3-6]. The resulting inversion algorithms have promising applications in nondestructive testing, crack detection and hydrocarbon reservoir exploration, which are naturally sparse domains.

Greedy heuristic algorithms including orthogonal matching pursuit (OMP) [7] and compressive sampling matching pursuit (CoSaMP) [8] have been developed as fast alternatives to techniques making use of convex relaxation. Even though they have gained popularity in signal and image processing communities, their application to solving inverse problems has been very limited [9-11]. This is simply due to the fact that scattering matrix, which is obtained by sampling the Green function between investigation domain and receiver locations, does not satisfy restricted isometry property [9].

In this work, for the first time, the CoSaMP algorithm is applied to solving the electromagnetic inverse scattering problem on two-dimensional (2D) domains where the dielectric permittivity profile is sparse. First, samples of the current induced in the investigation domain (under individual excitations from each transmitter) are recovered from the scattered field samples measured away from the investigation domain using the CoSaMP algorithm. The scattering matrix between the samples of the current and scattered field is "damped" by adding a constant parameter to its diagonal entries to make the CoSaMP work. Then, the recovered currents are used to estimate the total field samples in the investigation domain. At the final step, dielectric profile samples are obtained by solving a least squares problem involving the samples of the current and total field. Numerical results, which demonstrate the accuracy of the dielectric profile recovered using this approach, are provided.

II. FORMULATION

A. 2D Electromagnetic Scattering Equations

Let S represent the support of a 2D (z -invariant) investigation domain residing in an unbounded background medium. The permittivity and permeability on lossless S and in the lossless background medium are $\{\varepsilon(\mathbf{r}),\mu_0\}$ and $\{\varepsilon_0,\mu_0\}$. S is surrounded by N^T line-source transmitters. Let $E_i^{inc}(\mathbf{r})$ represent the transverse (to z direction) magnetic (TM^z) incident field generated by the ith transmitter. Upon excitation by $E_i^{inc}(\mathbf{r})$, electric current density $J_i(\mathbf{r})$ is induced on S and $J_i(\mathbf{r})$ generates the scattered field $E_i^{sca}(\mathbf{r})$:

$$E_i^{sca}(\mathbf{r}) = j\omega\mu_0 \int_S J_i(\mathbf{r}')G(\mathbf{r},\mathbf{r}')ds'. \tag{1}$$

where $G(\mathbf{r},\mathbf{r}') = H_0^{(2)}(k_0|\mathbf{r}-\mathbf{r}'|)/(4j)$ is the Green function in the background medium and $H_0^{(2)}(.)$ is the zeroth order Hankel function of the second kind. Additionally, $J_i(\mathbf{r})$ satisfies

$$J_i(\mathbf{r}) = j\omega\varepsilon_0\tau(\mathbf{r})E_i(\mathbf{r}) \tag{2}$$

$$E_i(\mathbf{r}) = E_i^{sca}(\mathbf{r}) + E_i^{inc}(\mathbf{r})\ . \tag{3}$$

Here, $\tau(\mathbf{r}) = \varepsilon(\mathbf{r})/\varepsilon_0 - 1$ is the contrast and $E_i(\mathbf{r})$ is total field. Investigation domain S is discretized by N square cells with dimension Δd. Let $p_k(\mathbf{r})$ denote a pulse basis function defined on cell k with support S_k and center $\mathbf{r}_k$. $J_i(\mathbf{r})$ is approximated using

$$J_i(\mathbf{r}) = \sum_{k=1}^{N} J_{i,k} p_k(\mathbf{r}) \tag{4}$$

where $J_{i,k} = J_i(\mathbf{r}_k)$. It is assumed that S is surrounded by N^R receivers located at $\mathbf{r}_m^R$, $m = 1,\ldots,N^R$. Inserting (4) into (1) and sampling the resulting equation at $\mathbf{r}_m^R$, $m = 1,\ldots,N^R$ yield

$$\bar{E}^{sca} = \bar{G}^s \bar{J} \tag{5}$$

where $\{\bar{E}^{sca}\}_{m,i} = E_i^{sca}(\mathbf{r}_m^R)$, $\{\bar{J}\}_{k,i} = J_{k,i}$, and $\{\bar{G}^s\}_{m,k} = j\omega\mu_0 \int_{S_k} G(\mathbf{r}_m^R,\mathbf{r}')ds'$.

B. Modified CoSaMP Algorithm

Since the support of $J_i(\mathbf{r})$ is assumed to be sparse, the electromagnetic inverse problem is constructed in the form

$$\bar{J} = \min_{\bar{J}} \left\| \bar{J} \right\|_0, \quad \text{s.t. } \bar{E}^{mea} = \bar{G}^s \bar{J} . \tag{6}$$

It is clear that (6) is a L_0 – minimization problem and it cannot be solved directly. One can use the CoSaMP algorithm directly on (6) to obtain the solution, however, it may not converge since $\bar{G}^s$ does not satisfy the restricted isometric property [9]. To address this problem and also to increase the robustness of the solution to noise in $\bar{E}^{mea}$, the minimization problem (6) is modified as

$$\bar{J} = \min_{\bar{J}} \left\| \bar{J} \right\|_0, \quad \text{s.t. } \bar{E}^{mea} = (\bar{G}^s + \lambda \bar{I})\bar{J} \tag{7}$$

where $\bar{I}$ is the identity matrix and λ is a damping factor which can be selected based on the priori knowledge of the noise level. Then the CoSaMP algorithm [8] is applied to (7).

C. Computation of Contrast Samples

Once $\bar{J}$ is computed using the modified CoSaMP algorithm described in Section II-B, samples of contrast $\tau_k = \tau(\mathbf{r}_k)$, $k = 1,...,N$ are obtained as explained next. Inserting (1) and (4) into (3) and sampling the resulting equation at $\mathbf{r}_k$, $k = 1,...,N$ yield

$$\bar{E} = \bar{E}^{inc} + \bar{G}\bar{J} \tag{8}$$

where $\{\bar{E}\}_{k,i} = E_i(\mathbf{r}_k)$, $\{\bar{E}^{inc}\}_{k,i} = E_i^{inc}(\mathbf{r}_k)$, and $\{\bar{G}\}_{k,k'} = j\omega\mu_0 \int_{S_{k'}} G(\mathbf{r}_k,\mathbf{r}')ds'$. Once $\bar{E}$ is estimated using (8), (2) is sampled at $k = 1,...,N$ and the resulting equations is solved using least squares to yield [11]

$$\tau(\mathbf{r}_k) = \tau_k = \sum_{i=1}^{N^T} \left(\{\bar{E}\}_{k,i}^{*} \{\bar{J}\}_{k,i} \right) \Big/ \sum_{i=1}^{N^T} \left| \{\bar{E}\}_{k,i} \right|^2 . \tag{9}$$

III. Numerical Results

The investigation domain includes four point-like targets [9]. The transmitter-receiver configuration is same as the one described in [9] with frequency 300 MHz, number of transmitter $N^T = 30$, and number of receivers $N^R = 50$. The domain is discretized with square cells of dimension $\Delta d = 0.1$m resulting in $N = 1369$ elements. Reconstruction of the dielectric profile is done using the modified CoSaMP proposed in this work and the flexible-tree-search based orthogonal matching pursuit (FTB-OMP) proposed in [9] for different levels of measurement noise changing between 5dB to 50dB. Damping parameter of the CoSaMP, $\lambda = 0.01$ for the first simulation with 5dB noise and $\lambda = 0.001$ for the rest. Relative error in the reconstructed dielectric profile is plotted against noise level in Fig. 1(a). Clearly, CoSaMP is more accurate for all noise levels. Fig. 1(b) plots the profile reconstructed by the CoSaMP under 30dB noise and demonstrates its accuracy.

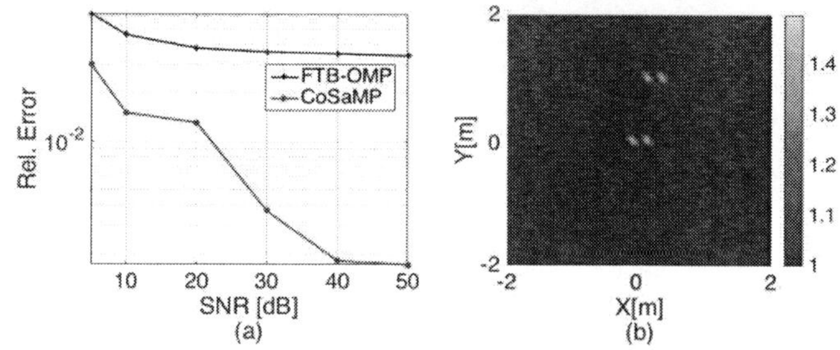

Fig. 1. (a) Relative mean square error in the dielectric profile reconstructed by the FTB-OMP and CoSaMP vs. the level of measurement noise. (b) The profile reconstructed by the CoSaMP under 30dB noise.

IV. Conclusions

The CoSaMP algorithm is used to solve the 2D electromagnetic inverse scattering problem on sparse domains. To make the CoSaMP work, a damping parameter is added to the diagonal entries of the scattering matrix. Numerical results demonstrate the potential of the proposed algorithm.

One limitation of the CoSaMP algorithm is that it requires the knowledge of the number of non-sparse samples in the domain (i.e., sparsity level). Integration of methods, which can adaptively estimate the sparsity level during the execution of the CoSaMP, is underway.

References

[1] E. J Candes, and M. B. Wakin, "An introduction to compressive sampling," *IEEE Signal Process. Mag*, vol. 25, no. 2, pp. 21-30, 2008.

[2] I. Daubechies, M. Defrise, and C. De Mol, "An iterative thresholding algorithm for linear inverse problems with a sparsity constraint," *Commun. Pure Appl. Math*., vol. 57, no. 11, pp. 1413–1457, 2004.

[3] A. Massa, P. Rocca, and G. Oliveri, "Compressive sensing in electromagnetics - A review." *IEEE Antennas Propag. Mag.*, vol. 57, no. 1, pp. 224-238, 2015.

[4] A. Desmal, and H. Bagci, "Shrinkage-thresholding enhanced Born iterative method for solving 2D inverse electromagnetic scattering problem," *IEEE Trans. Antennas Propag.*, vol. 62, no. 7, pp. 3878-3884, 2014.

[5] A. Desmal and H. Bagci, "A preconditioned inexact Newton method for nonlinear sparse electromagnetic imaging," *IEEE Geosci. Remote Sens. Lett.*, vol. 12, no. 3, pp. 532-536, 2015.

[6] A. Desmal, and H. Bagci, "Sparse electromagnetic imaging using nonlinear Landweber iterations," *Progress in Electromagnetics,* vol. 152, pp. 77-93, 2015.

[7] A. J. Tropp and A. C. Gilbert, "Signal recovery from random measurements via orthogonal matching pursuit," *IEEE Trans. Inf. Theory*, vol. 53, no. 12 ,pp. 4655-4666, 2007

[8] D. Needell and J. A. Tropp, "CoSaMP: Iterative signal recovery from incomplete and inaccurate samples," *Appl. Comput. Harmon. Anal.*, vol. 26, no. 3, pp. 301–321, May 2009.

[9] R. V. Senyuva, O. Ozdemir, G. K. Kurt, and E. Anarım,, "Electromagnetic imaging of closely spaced objects using matching pursuit based approaches," *IEEE Antennas Wireless Propag. Lett.*, vol. 15, pp.1179-1182, 2016.

[10] L. Pan, X. Chen and S. P. Yeo, "A compressive-sensing-based phaseless imaging method for point-like dielectric objects," *IEEE Trans. Antennas Propag*., vol. 60, no. 11, pp. 5472-5475, Nov. 2012.

[11] T. C. Ye, and S. Y. Lee, and S. Y. March, "Non-iterative exact inverse scattering using simultaneous orthogonal matching pursuit (S-OMP)," in Proc. *IEEE Int. Conf. Acoustics, Speech and Signal* Process., pp. 2457-2460, 2008.

Optimal Design of Closed Multilayer Magnetic Shields

Aldo Canova, Fabio Freschi, Luca Giaccone and Maurizio Repetto
Politecnico di Torino - Dipartimento Energia - DENERG
Corso Duca degli Abruzzi 24, 10129, Torino, Italy
aldo.canova@polito.it

Abstract—**The present paper deals with the optimisation of closed shield for the attenuation of magnetic fields produced by direct and alternating currents. A multilayer shield made of different concentric layers is proposed. The optimisation procedure defines the best thicknesses and the distances between layers. The shield performance is required in a wide range of frequencies and magnetic field strengths (from 50-100 nT to 10000-50000 nT). In a first step the optimisation procedure has been applied to a simplified structure as a 2D cylinder immersed in a uniform magnetic field. In a second step the procedure has been applied to a 3D case, with cubic shape, which simulates an actual situation that can be found in the so called Magnetically Shielded Rooms.**

I. Introduction

Shielding system are employed for reducing the magnetic flux density in a confined area in order to be compliant with acceptable maximum levels for persons [1], [2] or devices [3]. Shielding systems can be classified by different characteristics as the material, the working principle, the shapes, etc. One important classification regards open and closed shields. Open shields are mainly used for civil or industrial environment for shielding power lines or substations. The shield can be installed close to the area to be protected and the attenuation decays significantly far from the shield. This is acceptable because magnetic fields decay with the distance too [4], [5]. Open shields are often necessary for cost and architectural constraints. When a better performance is required these constraints can be relaxed and closed shields can be adopted. This is the case of a shielded room for electronic devices such as electronic microscopes or testing equipments. Some shielding solutions have been presented in the literature and the optimal configuration is influenced by the thicknesses and the distance between concentric layers [6]. Starting from a defined set of materials and a defined number of layers in the present paper an optimisation procedure for the best choice of the thickness and dimensions of the shield is presented.

II. Optimisation design

A. 2D closed shields

The 2D shield adopted for testing the optimisation procedure is a quite well known configuration constituted by a set of concentric cylindrical shields immersed inside a uniform magnetic field. The field solution of this problem has been also developed analytically in order to find a closed solution [7]. The limitation of such approach is the linearity of the ferromagnetic material which can be important for those having low saturation (e.g. mu-metal). Moreover, one of the goal of the paper is also to analyse concentric shields where an analytical solution is hard to find. For the above reason a numerical approach to the study of the magnetic field has bee adopted. Starting from the case of cylindrical shields, the optimisation parameters are the thickness of the different layers and the gaps among them. Fig. 1 represents a scheme of the multilayer shield made of three layers. Configuration, variables and parameters are summarized in Table I. The magnetic field is uniform and it is orthogonal to the axis of the cylinders. The two objectives are: the minimisation shield volume and the maximisation of the magnetic field attenuation. The last objective is expressed by the ratio between the magnetic flux density without and with the shield (shielding factor SF). A first parametric analysis based on the values reported in Table I have been carried out. The entire set of solutions is shown in Fig. 2 and the red points represent the pareto front. An automated optimisation procedure based on Virtual Immune System (VIS) [8] will be applied and the results will be reported in the final paper. Initial and optimised configuration will be experimentally tested by means of an Helmholtz coils system made according to the standard ASTM 698 (Fig. 3).

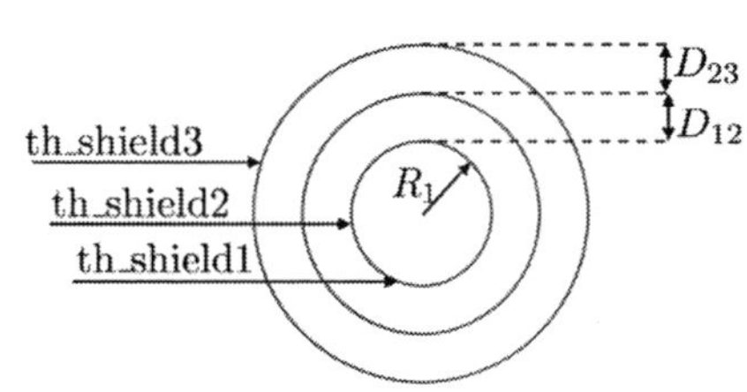

Fig. 1. Cylindrical shield scheme

TABLE I
OPTIMISATION VARIABLE AND PARAMETERS

Parameters	Values
internal radius R_1	100 mm
gap D_{12} and D_{23}	5 - 10 - 15 - 20 mm
th_shield1-2-3	0.35 - 0.5 - 0.65 mm

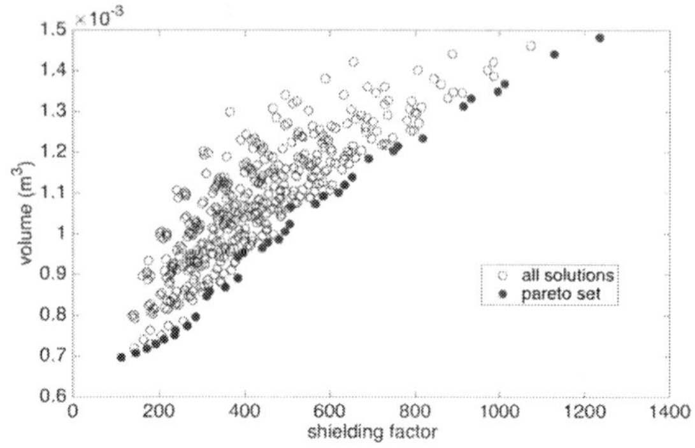

Fig. 2. Pareto front of the 2D configurations

Fig. 3. ASTM 698 Helmholtz configuration

B. 3D closed shields

The sensitivity analysis and the optimisation procedure applied to the 2D configuration provide useful general conclusions which can helps the design of a 3D shield. In this case the numerical modelling is more complicated and time expensive. In the case of ferromagnetic shields an integral formulation based on the reduced scalar potential is used [9], [10]. A multilayer shield made of 1, 2 or 3 cubic layers is analysed. The side of the external cube is 0.5 m and the gap between to consecutive cubes is 6 cm. The material ha relative magnetic permeability of 1000. Different configurations are tested by keeping constant the shield volume selecting the suitable thickness. In this paper the following configurations are presented: 1 layer of 3mm, 2 layers of 1.9 mm and 3 layers of 1.62 mm. The geometry of the three-layered shield is shown in Fig. 4. The first test is done applying a uniform magnetic flux density of 100 μT in the x direction. The performance of the shield is referred to the inspection line shown in Fig. 4. The results are the first three curves represented in in Fig. 5. It is observed that at the center of the shield the highest reduction is obtained by the three-layered shield. A second test is done considering an applied field of 100 μT aligned with the diagonal of the cubes. For brevity, only the performance of the three-layered shield under this applied field is shown by the fourth curves in Fig. 5. It is observed that the performance are constant at the center of the shied and much better on the outside of the external cube because the magnetic flux density is always lower than the applied field.

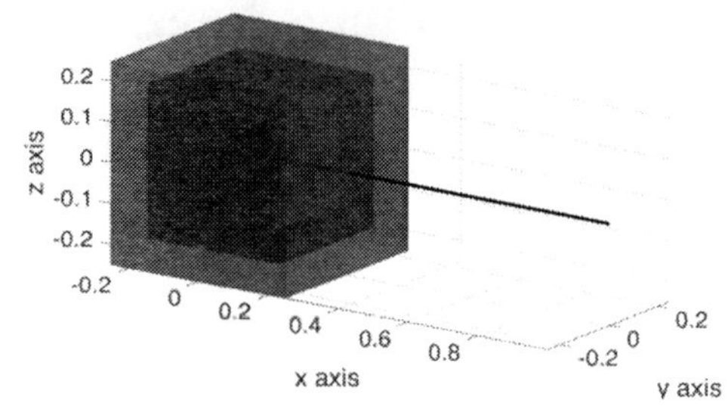

Fig. 4. 3D Shielding geometry

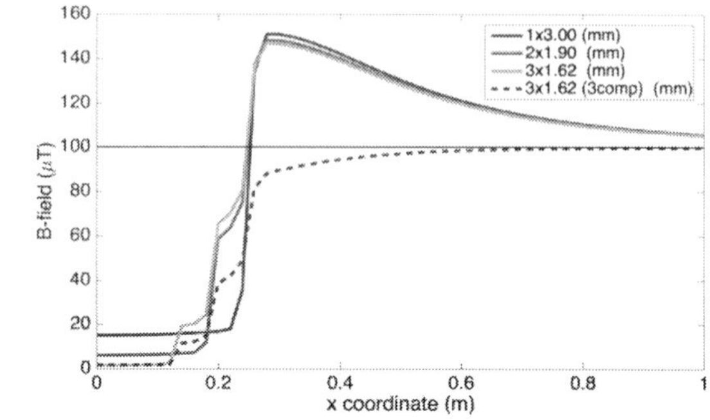

Fig. 5. Magnetic flux density along the inspection line

III. Conclusion

The full paper will give details on the optimisation procedure that will be applied to both 2D and 3D configurations. Experimental tests will be carried out to validated the design.

References

[1] ICNIRP, "Guidelines for limiting exposure to time-varying electric and magnetic fields (1 Hz - 100 kHz)," *Health Phys*, vol. 99, no. 6, pp. 818–836, 2010.

[2] D. Bavastro, A. Canova, F. Freschi, L. Giaccone, and M. Manca, "Magnetic field mitigation at power frequency: design principles and case studies," *IEEE Transactions on Industry Applications*, vol. 51, pp. 2009–2016, May 2014.

[3] D. A. Muller and J. Grazul, "Optimizing the environment for sub-0.2 nm scanning transmission electron microscopy," *Optimizing the environment for sub-0.2 nm scanning transmission electron microscopy*, vol. 50, no. 3, pp. 219–226, 2001.

[4] "Mitigation techniques of power frequency magnetic fields originated from electric power systems," Tech. Rep. Working group C4.204, International Council on Large Electric Systems (CIGRE'), 2009, ISBN: 978-2-85873-060-5.

[5] R. Olsen and P. Moreno, "Some observations about shielding extremely low-frequency magnetic fields by finite width shields," *Electromagnetic Compatibility, IEEE Transactions on*, vol. 38, no. 3, pp. 460–468, 1996.

[6] V. V. Yashchuk, S. K. Lee, and P. E., "Chapter 12 - magnetic shielding," in *Optical Magnetometry* (Derek F. Jackson Kimball, Dmitry Budker, ed.), Cambridge University Press, March 2013.

[7] C. P. Bidinosti and J. W. Martin, "Passive magnetic shielding in static gradient fields," *AIP Advances*, vol. 4, no. 4, 2014.

[8] F. Freschi and M. Repetto, "Vis: An artificial immune network for multi objective optimization," *Engineering Optimization*, vol. 38, no. 8, pp. 975–996, 2006.

[9] Y. Vuillermet, O. Chadebec, J. Coulomb, L.-L. Rouve, G. Cauffet, J. Bongiraud, and L. Demilier, "Scalar potential formulation and inverse problem applied to thin magnetic sheets," *IEEE Transaction on Magnetics*, vol. 44, pp. 1054–1057, June 2008.

[10] L. Giaccone, D. Ragusa, and M. Khan, O. Manca, "Fast magnetic field modeling for shielding systems," *IEEE Transaction on Magnetics*, vol. 49, pp. 4128 – 4131, July 2013.

Mitigation of Background Field Effects on Coils Characterization from Magnetic Measurements

Andrea Gaetano Chiariello, Alessandro Formisano, Francesco Ledda, Raffaele Martone, Francesco Pizzo
Dept. of Industrial and Information Engineering, Seconda Università di Napoli
Aversa (CE), Italy
Alessandro.Formisano@unina2.it

***Abstract*—In magnetic systems where small discrepancies of field map from the design value may strongly impact on the device performance, quality insurance procedures are foreseen to verify how each single coil meets the design criteria. External magnetic measurements can be used to estimate the possible deformations of conductors inside the magnet, but this implies inverse problem approaches. The measurement accuracy and the background field rejection are therefore critical; as a consequence, the measurement system must be carefully designed, taking into account several elements, including the probes characteristics, the characteristics of the windings and of the surrounding environment. In this paper, a possible numerical pre-processing of measured data to reduce the impact of background field is proposed. The method is based on a spectral decomposition of the gain matrix, and a filtering based on the projection of measurements on the matrix eigenvector basis.**

Keywords—Magnetic analysis, Filtering, Inverse Problems

I. INTRODUCTION

A number of quality check procedures are usually foreseen after manufacturing and before final assembly of high field magnets to try characterizing, and if possible correcting, discrepancies of the actual, manufactured magnet field map from the design one. The standard procedure is based on "optical" surveys, but deformations coming from insertion in the case and final assembly are not detectable with such approaches. Additional effective information can be gained using the "magnetic footprint" of the magnet, which is the actual flux density map outside the magnet. For the sake of exposition, in the following attention will be limited to large superconducting magnets, as for example those used in devices for Thermonuclear Fusion [1-2], but many of the exposed results can be easily extended to other type of problems [3-7]. During the magnetic testing, these coils are energized at room temperature, with a reduced current supply, most likely in the warehouse or in an assembly hall, where the presence of additional magnetic sources or external magnetic materials is to be expected. The difference between the nominal and the actual field map (the magnet "field error") is expected to be very small with respect to nominal field, since manufacturing and assembly tolerances are typically very tight. Therefore, in the case of high accuracy devices, the measurement procedure is quite demanding as it must appreciate small field variations with respect to the nominal field, in presence of noise, background field and other nuisances. The attention is here focused on the possible methods to reduce the effect of the background field and of possible magnetic parts on the quality of the estimation process. The mathematical formulation of the problem is firstly sketched (Sect. II), then it's application to a simple test case is presented (Sect. III).

II. INVERSE PROBLEM FORMULATION

During the actual measurement process, it is reasonable to expect several elements of disturbance in the warehouse where measurements are taken, including magnetic parts and additional field sources, giving rise to background field. In order to pursuit a problem formulation able to deal with such nuisances, it is profitable to start form the Biot-Savart law, providing the flux density from a current density map **J** in free space:

$$B(r_f) = \mu_0 \int_{\Omega_s} \frac{J(r_s) \times r_{fs}}{\|r_{fs}\|^3} d\Omega_s \tag{1}$$

where $\mathbf{r}_s \in \Omega_s$ is the source point vector, Ω_s the volume where current is flowing, $\mathbf{r}_f$ is the field point vector, and $\mathbf{r}_{fs} = \mathbf{r}_s - \mathbf{r}_f$.

As a further hypothesis, we will assume that magnetic parts, if present, are far enough from the magnet to be analyzed so that the relationship between field component due to the magnet itself and resulting flux density can be assumed linear, although the iron working point may depend non-linearly from other sources (e.g. iron shields near power lines in warehouse are nonlinearly magnetized by near sources, but their behavior with respect to far sources such as magnets under test can be assumed linear).

Under the exposed hypotheses, it is possible to define a linear "direct operator" $\mathfrak{F}_{fs}$, providing the flux density at point $\mathbf{r}_f$ once value of sources **J** in region Ω_s is given:

$$B(r_f) = \mathfrak{F}_{fs}(J_s; r_f, \Omega_s) \tag{2}$$

The operator is defined $\mathbf{r}_f$, Ω_s and by magnetostatic laws, in integral form if using (1). Eq. (2) does not provide the actual measured field, since the background field must be added:

$$B_{meas} = \mathfrak{F}_{fs}(J_s; r_f, \Omega_s) + B_{bcknd}(r_f) \tag{3}$$

Thanks to the linearity assumption, it is possible to define the $\mathfrak{F}_{fs}$ eigenfunctions, and project (3) onto the basis in the measurement space spanned by such eigenfunctions. Note that Eq. (2) can be discretized; this means considering a finite number of measurements and projecting **J** onto a finite dimensional basis (e.g. a set of filamentary currents); the operator $\mathfrak{F}_{fs}$ reduces to the multiplication times the "gain" matrix $\underline{\mathbf{E}}_{fs}$, and the $\mathfrak{F}_{fs}$ eigenfunctions to $\underline{\mathbf{E}}_{fs}$ eigenvectors. If we assume that the background field sources are far enough from Ω_s, their contribution to the measured field can be rejected by multiplying the measured field times the left eigenvectors $\underline{\mathbf{L}}_F$ of $\underline{\mathbf{E}}_{fs}$ and keeping only spectral components associated to local field. In the next section, a simple test case is presented.

III. Test Case

In order to demonstrate the relevant elements of the method, let's imagine an infinitely long "winding", composed by a square arrangement of 9 filamentary conductors in a jacket with 10 mm diameter (see Fig. 1, left). The nominal current distribution is uniform over all the conductors, but due to manufacturing errors, one of the conductors has a 10% higher current. This must be detected using an annular array of flux probes located around the conductor, and measuring the three flux density components.

In this simple example, the current representation base if given by the 9 filamentary currents at known positions (whose amplitudes represent the problem unknowns), the operator output are the measurements taken by 240 tangential and 240 normal field probes at a circumference 15 mm. away from the currents barycenter, and the operator $\mathfrak{F}_{fs}$ turns into a 480x9 matrix $\underline{\mathbf{E}}_{fs}$. By applying the formulation described in Sect. II, the left and right eigenvectors of the matrix $\underline{\mathbf{E}}_{fs}$ are obtained, using standard Matlab© SVD function (see Fig. 2 and Fig. 3).

The background noise is represented by an additional current filament 1 m from the coil, fed by 100 A. The dot product of the nominal field, of the field generated by unbalanced current and of the background field times the left eigenvectors of $\underline{\mathbf{E}}_f$ are reported in Fig.4. It can be easily observed that the spectral components for the three cases are well distinguished, and background can be rejected by suitable filtering.

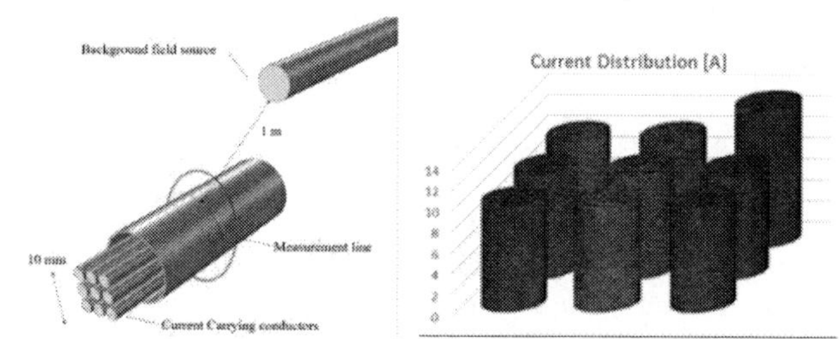

Fig. 1 – Schematic view of the simulated measurements, with background noise source (left) and current distribution among conductors (right).

IV. Conclusions

The magnet characterization problem from magnetic measurement suffers from adverse effects of background field and measurement noise. A possible approach to reduce the effect of such nuisances can be based on the spatial spectrum of the measured field around the coil. The method has been sketched, and a simple, demonstrative example reported.

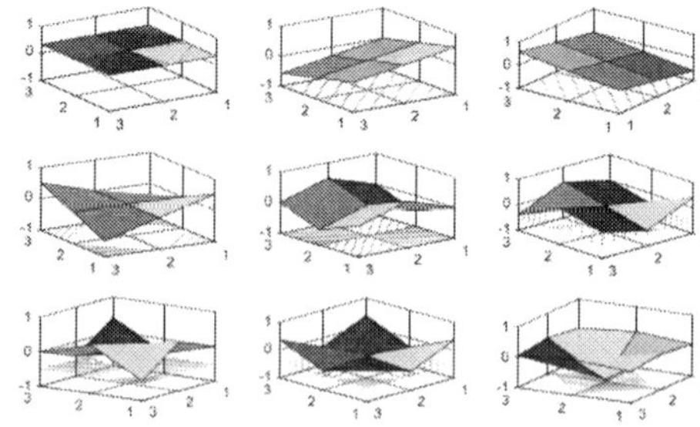

Fig. 2 – Right singular vectors of $\underline{\mathbf{E}}_{fs}$, that is modal current distributions.

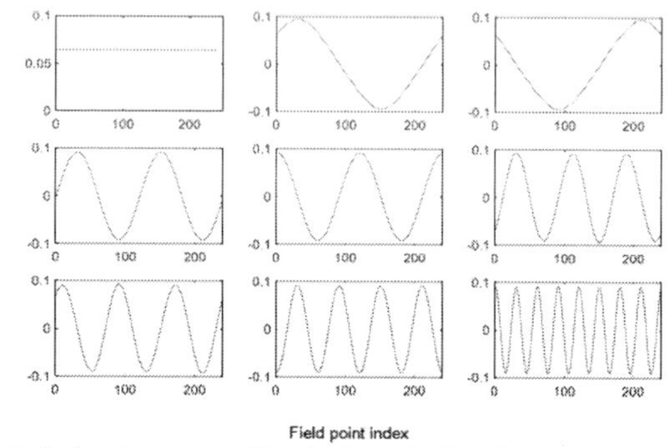

Fig. 3 – Left singular vectors of $\underline{\mathbf{E}}_{fs}$, that is modal field distributions. a.u. are used to ease comparison of different distributions.

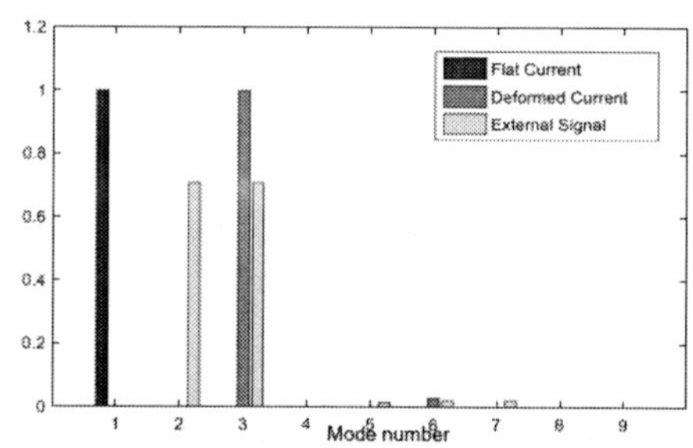

Fig. 4 – Spectra of field from nominal (uniform) distribution (blue), from background field (yellow) and from current unbalance (green). Spectra are in a.u., normalized to the highest harmonic present in each.

V. References

[1] A. Bonito Oliva et al, "Characterization of deformed magnets from external magnetic measurements", *IEEE Trans. on Magnetics*, Vol. 50 n° 2, DOI: 10.1109/TMAG.2013.2282315.

[2] A. Formisano, R. Martone, "Field-Map Characterization From Magnetic Survey in High-Field Magnets", *IEEE Trans. on Magnetics*, Vol. 52, n° 3, DOI: 10.1109/TMAG.2015.2478152

[3] L. Di Rienzo, R. Bazzocchi and A. Manara, "Circular arrays of magnetic sensors for current measurement", *IEEE Trans. Instrum. Meas.*, Vol. 50, n° 2, pp. 1093-1096, 2001.

[4] A. El Badia, T. Ha Duong, "Some remarks on the problem of source identification from boundary measurements", *Inverse Problems*, Vol. 14, n. 4, pp. 883-891, 1998.

[5] M. Norgren and S. He, "Exact and explicit solution to a class of degaussing problems", *IEEE Trans. Magnetics.*, Vol. 36, n° 1, pp. 308-312, 2000.

[6] A. Bonito Oliva et al, "Equivalent current models for magnets characterization", *Proc. of IGTE Symposium 2014*, Graz (Au), Sept. 2014.

ELF fields in agriculture: new techniques for a sustainable development

Bruno Bisceglia
Department of Industrial Engineering
University of Salerno
Fisciano (SA) - Italy
bbisceglia@unisa.it

Simona Valbonesi
Consorzio Elettra 2000
Pontecchio Marconi (BO) - Italy
svalbonesi@elettra2000.it

Abstract — **Lots of studies, some of them very recent, have demonstrated that a proper electromagnetic field exposure of seeds and sown can bring to an improvement of germination and growth indices. This phenomenon applied to agriculture can be extremely helpful in increasing raw materials productivity. The present work consist of an analysis of the scientific literature on the potential applications of ELF fields in agriculture.**

Keywords—electromagnetic fields, ELF fields, sustainable develompment, ELF fields applications

I. Introduction

Even today, in some parts of Africa and Asia the shortage of raw materials is a real problem which is expected to worsen over the years, given the projected increase in population. Therefore it becomes imperative to increase the productivity of fertile or infertile soils in those regions where, generally for climatic reasons, there is a quantity or quality shortage.

Electromagnetic fields, properly applied, can be excellent allies to sustainable agriculture, since they allow to carry out soil treatments for pests control and to improve plants germination and growth without producing water and air pollution and without using chemical substances harmful to final consumers health and environment.

Results from scientific research on the use of electromagnetic fields (EMF) to improve plants germination and growth indices are encouraging, efforts must be doubled to get from experimental phase to viable applications.

II. ELF Application in Agriculture

Germination is a key process in plant's phonological cycles. Accelerating this process could led to the improvement of the seedling growth as well as the cultivation efficiency.

Germination, growth and quality of crops are determined by the property of seed material, which can be improved by pre-sawing treatments involving physical agents such as electric field, magnetic field, laser and microwave radiation, included the use of magnetically treated water.

The idea of controlling and influencing plants biological cycles using electromagnetic fields was stated in early '60. It was the beginning of a scientific challenge still going on after more than 50 years.

Investigations do not concern only the effects but also the mechanism of interaction with the aim of finding waveforms, frequencies and signal modulations able to produce the better results.

A. *Results of recent studies*

In recent years an increasing number of scientific articles report biological effects on plants exposed to low-frequency magnetic fields. In particular, an Italian study published by Piacentini [1] in year 2001, indicates that ELF-EMF may have a stimulatory or inhibitory effect on plants tissues growth depending on the species involved.

The study was performed on mitotic cellular cycle and came to the conclusion that 10 minutes of ELF-EMF exposure affects the phosphoinositide signal triggering complex transductions influencing cellular mitosis and leading to an improvement of plant growth.

Namba et. Al in 1998 [2] studied the influence of 1-100 Hz (500 μT) magnetic fields on buckwheat, green shiso, radish and welsh onions, coming to the conclusion that for each vegetal species there is an ideal frequency range.

To provide an example radish germination increase by 30% as effect of 1 Hz magnetic field exposure; other plants don't present the same results if exposed to this specific frequency.

A study performed at Salerno University and published in 2016 [3], tested the effect of the exposure of Eruca sativa and Lactuga sativa seeds to a 75 Hz magnetic field.

E. sativa and L. sativa seeds were exposed for 15 minutes to a 75 Hz magnetic field (B= 1.5 and 15 mT) generated by a solenoid.

From this preliminary study emerged that the magnetic field increases significantly (25%) the germination of E. sativa but not influence the radicle elongation. After 50 days the pre sawing seeds treatment resulted in a more lush plant.

These results confirmed what emerged from a study focused on the effects of exposure of tomato seeds and young plants to a 50 Hz ELF field published in year 2015 by Slovak University of Agriculture [4].

Seeds and young plants were exposed to a 50 Hz electromagnetic field (20 mT, 40 mT, 60 mT) 20 minutes a day for 48 days; this resulted in a stimulatory effect on germination, growth characteristics and size of tomato fruit.

Some dated studies performed in '90 s reported a 10-20% growth increase in vegetables watered with magnetically treated water, giving rise to hopes for an eventual massive use of this technique to improve crop yields.

This hope has been neglected by the global results of one important study on sunflower seeds subjected to the influence of a 50 Hz magnetic field and magnetically treated water (one at time or in combination). [5]

Three series of measurements have been performed. Series I consisted of samples exposed to 50 Hz ELF magnetic field (B=30,60,100 mT – 1, 3, 10 repetitions - duration 4 to 30 sec). The influence of magnetically treated water was investigated in series II. Measurements in series III concerned the combination of both factors.

Application of 30 mT magnetic field (50 Hz) for 30 sec leads to the highest increase in growth rate.

The combination of magnetic field and treated water association presented also a positive effect.

For seeds only watered with magnetically treated water, a negative effect was obtained for most of the indicators characterizing sunflower seed germination and plants grow.

Theories attempting to explain the biological effects of the ELF magnetic fields are based on their possible impact on the permeability of ion channels in the membrane, which may affect the transport of ions into the cells and lead to biological changes in the organism. Magnetically treated water may enhance the magnetic field effect and cause an increase in permeability of cell membranes in the seed, acting on calcium ions and inhibiting the growth of harmful microorganisms during seed germination and plant growth processes.

B. Latest studies on static magnetic fields effects

During last five years many studies have been performed on the effects of static magnetic fields on plants growth parameters. In particular in a Spanish study [6], groups of 25 tomato seeds placed on a Petri dish, have been subjected to 125 and 250 mT static magnetic field for 1,10,20,60,1440 minutes corresponding to a daily dose calculated according to the formula:

$$B_{day} = \frac{B}{h_{day}} h_{\exp} \quad (1)$$

variable from 0.08 to 250 mT per day

In daily B dose formula h_{day} is the number of minutes composing a day and h_{exp} is the exposure duration

Results shows an improvement of germination rate and a significant reduction of mean germination time in treated seeds. In addiction magnetic field treatment increases the first stages of tomato plants growth.

This results found a confirmation in another study performed in Turkey [7] exposing seeds of stone pine to a 9.42 mT static magnetic fields for 15 – 30 - 45 minutes (calculated dose 0.08 – 0.29 mT/day).

III. Challenges for the Future

For what concerns sustainable agriculture and electromagnetic fields, two big challenges are open at the moment: the use of MW fields for soil disinfection and disinfestation as a viable alternative to the use of chemicals and the use of microwave and ELF magnetic field to improve plants germination and growth indices. At the present time these techniques have been tested in laboratory under controlled conditions, it is necessary to pass as soon as possible from the experimental phase to a test phase in uncontrolled conditions, followed by a commercial diffusion.

For what concerns scientific research is necessary to thoroughly study the physical mechanisms and biophysical interaction of electromagnetic fields on vegetal cells, seeds, plants embryos and plants in order to find the optimal conditions and make them become a standard in agriculture.

IV. Conclusions

The use of ELF fields as "clean technique" for improving the growth rate and germination of some plants for food use seems to be promising.

From a scientific point of view, revealing the relationship between EMF exposure and plant response is becoming more and more important to fully understand the mechanisms of interaction, to find the conditions giving repeatable results and make the use of ELF fields in agriculture a standard procedure.

From a social point of view the application of EMF to improve plants germination and growth opens new horizons not only in plant science, but also in economy, and could increase the chances for a Third World population dignified survival, without leading to an unsustainable environment deterioration

References

[1] M.P. Piacentini, D.Fraternale, E.Piatti, D.Ricci, F.Vetrano, M.Dachà, A. Accorsi, "Senescence delay and changes of antioxidant enzyme levels in Cucumis sativus L. etiolated seedlings by ELF magnetic fields", in *Plants Science*, 161, 1, 45-53, 2001

[2] K.Namba "Effect of electromagnetic field on plant germination", in *ASAE Annual International Meeting*, Orlando, 12-16 July, 1998

[3] L. Caputo, L. Souza, S. Greco, C. Severino, E. Caldarola, M.Polichetti, V.De Feo, B.Bisceglia, "Exposure of seeds to ELF MF. Effects on Germination and Growth. Preliminary results.", Proccedings del IV Convegno nazionale ICEmB, Milano 4-6 luglio, 2016

[4] J. Jedlika, O. Paulen, S. Ailer, "Research of effects of low frequency magnetic field on germination, growth and fruiting of field tomatoes.", *Acta Horticulturae et Regiotecturae*, 1/2015, 1-4, 2015

[5] A.Matwijczuk, K. Kornarzynski, S. Pietruszewski, "Effect of magnetic field on seed germination and seedling growth of sunflower", in *International Agrophysics*, 26(3), 271, 2012.

[6] E. Martinez, M.V. Carbonell, M. Florez, J.M. Amaya, R. Maqueda, "Germination of tomato seeds (Lycopersicon esculentum L.) under magnetic field", *Int. Agrophysics*, 23, 45-49, 2009

[7] E. Kirdan, C. Yucedag, B. Balaban, "The effects of magnetic fields on germination of seeds and seedling of stone pine", *Journal of forests*, 3(1), 1-6, 2016

Directive 2013/35/EU: a critical analysis

Bruno Bisceglia
Department of Industrial Engineering
University of Salerno
Fisciano (SA) - Italy
bbisceglia@unisa.it

Simona Valbonesi
Consorzio Elettra 2000
Pontecchio Marconi (BO) - Italy
svalbonesi@elettra2000.it

Claudia Carciofi
Fondazione Ugo Bordoni
Pontecchio Marconi (BO) - Italy
ccarciofi@fub.it

***Abstract* — The transposition of European Directive 2013/35/EU into National regulatory frameworks introduced a series of new obligations for employers. Aim of this paper is acritical analysis of the new regulatory text in particular for what concerns exposure limits, new obligations and operative procedures in general.**

Keywords—electromagnetic fields, regolamentary frameworks, exposure limits, safety at work

I. Introduction

Electromagnetic fields are generated and used in many work activities including manufacturing processes, research, communications, medical applications, power generation, energy transmission and distribution, broadcasting, aeronautical and marine navigation and security. Nevertheless, in the most part of the workplaces, the exposure levels are very low and will not represent a risk to workers.

July 2016 was the deadline for transposition of Directive 2013/35/UE – containing the minimum safety requirements regarding the professional exposures to electromagnetic fields - into National regulatory frameworks. This means a series of new stringent requirements for employers, a higher grade of protection for workers and new operative procedures.

Directive 2013/35/EU [1] comes from a review of the Directive 2004/40/CE [2] due to the need to adapt the framework to the new indications from International Commission on Non Ionizing Radiation Protection (ICNIRP) [3], [4] and to provide a guidance for the management of exposures of workers employed in magnetic resonance environment.

The two texts presents many differences, especially for what concerns exposure limits and the general approach to be followed in the risk assessment.

The aim of this work is to study and analyze the new regulatory text in particular for what concerns exposure limits, new obligations and operative procedures.

II. Old and New Directive: Main differences

The main difference between Directive 2013/35/EU and the old regulatory framework (Directive 2004/40/EC) lies in the fact that the new Directive limits maximum exposure by setting exposure limits values (ELVs) for sensory and health effects. These are defined in Annexes II (non thermal effects within the frequency range 0 Hz – 10 MHz) and III (thermal effects within 100 kHz – 300 GHz frequency range). The health effects ELVs must always be complaied with.

In most cases the ELVs are specified in terms of dosimetric quantities (internal E-Field, SAR) that cannot be directly measured or easily assessed. For these reason the Directive introduces action levels (ALs), which are set in terms of radiometric quantities (E, H or B field), directly measurable. Provided the ALs are not exceeded, then it can be assumed that exposures will comply with the ELVs and further assessment is not required.

Another relevant difference concerns static fields; Directive 2013/35/UE proposes limits and action levels for static or quasi-static fields (0 – 1 Hz) based on indications from ICNIRP Guidelines [5]

III. Risk Assessment: case studies

The first step in risk assessment is to gather information about specific woring procedures and the characteristics (frequency, intensity,,ecc..) of the fields present in the working area; this may be a really difficult step for a non-expert.

The Directive, in fact, requires employers to identify and assess EMF levels in the workplace. However, it allows employers to take account of general information from others (manufacturers, machinery data sheets, databases) and requires them to assess field levels only when is not possible to demonstrate compliance by any other means. So, in the most part of the cases, risk assessment can be performed only on a documental basis, saving time and money.

Typical exposure situations where it is possible to simply stop to the documental part are the WiFi devices. Very often technicians performing electromagnetic fields measurements are contacted to carry out measures on WiFi devices emissions

Proceed with these measures could be unnecessary, because WiFi devices have documented exposure levels far below the specific ELVs and ALs. In this case is enough to report in the risk assessment document data provided by the manufacturer. E-Field measurements performed by our technicians in numerous offices have confirmed the very low exposure levels produced by these devices [6].

Even when it is necessary to assess electromagnetic fields levels, the Directive permits to the employers to choose between measurements and calculations. This flexibility allows to select the simplest and less expensive approach for the particular situation.

Provided that ALs are not exceeded and other effects can be excluded, employers do not need to take any further action. In the case ALs are exceeded, the employer may wish to demonstrate compliance with the ELVs and the absence of other safety risks from EMF.

A typical case requiring measurements or numerical simulations are microwave ovens for industrial baking.

In this case the investigation should start from the identification of key points inside the working area on the basis of the position occupied by workers during standard working activity. Machine maintenance status must also be checked because it can affect electromagnetic fields emission. After this it is possible to proceed to EMF measurements and the comparison with the ALs and in caso of overrun it is necessary to proceed to the SAR numerical simulation which usually does not show any ELV exceedance [7].

IV. Impact of the new Directive on simulation studies

The new Directive imposes new dosimetric quantities to be evaluated and compared with the ELVs and the ALs; this may result in additional difficulties for what concerns numerical simulations. The most important innovations regard low frequency fields.

Prior to Directive 2013/35/EU the VLE for fields between 1 Hz and 10 MHz were expressed in terms of induced current density at trunk and head. The new Directive imposes limits for health effects and sensory effects based on the calculation of the internal electric field. This requires, from an operational point of view, to change the numerical evaluation criteria. Furthermore, the internal field calculation, especially at low frequencies is extremely difficult since the dielectric properties of the tissues heavily depend on their structural properties (cellular architectures, presence of membranes, response of large biomolecules to the electric field).

As regards the environmental impact simulations the variables to be simulated remain the intensity of the electric field (E) and the magnetic induction (B).

For what concerns radiofrequencies, no major changes have been introduced at the moment; the dosimetric parameter to be used in numerical simulation is SAR, evaluated by mediating on 10 g of contiguous tissue and 6 minutes temporal interval.

At the moment the ICNIRP activity is focused on a critical review of scientific literature, especially for what concerns RF dosimetry. From this review may emerge news regarding time interval to be used for local SAR numerical calculations, averaging mass and mass shape. New parameters and different VLE could also be proposed. This will lead to the need to introduce major changes to the numerical calculation procedures used in the SAR evaluation.

However it appears that substantial changes will not be introduced by the ICNIRP before 2018.

V. Conclusions

The new European Directive, based on the latest set of ICNIRP Guidelines, represents an high grade protection for workers exposed to electromagnetic fields and provides, indirectly, all the information needed to manage security.
The regulatory text provides information to employers on the new requirements and on how to perform risk assessment.

From an operative point of view, before carrying out measurement campaigns in workplaces is necessary to analyze in depth the electromagnetic fields sources present. Sometimes in fact an assessment on documental basis could be enough. Only in more complex situations it is necessary to proceed with measurements and numerical simulations.

Directive 2013/35/UE introduced news from the point of view of numerical simulations, especially for what concerns low frequency fields, where variations in basic dosimetric parameters to be compared with the ELVs, impose the need for changes in the programs used for numerical assessments. Other future changes could include procedures for RF exposures calculations, but this probably will not happen before the second part of year 2018.

References

[1] Directive 2013/35/UE on the minimum health and safety requirements regarding the exposure of workers to the risks arising from physical agents (electromagnetic fields), 2013

[2] Directive 2004/40/CE on the minimum health and safety requirements regarding the exposure of workers to the risks arising from physical agents (electromagnetic fields), 2004

[3] ICNIRP – "Guidelines for limiting the exposure to electric fields induced by movement of the human body in a static magnetic field and by time-varying magnetic fields below 1Hz. Health Phys. Apr;106(3):418-425, 2014

[4] ICNIRP – "Guidelines for limiting the exposure to time variyng electric and magnetic fields (1 Hz-100 kHz). Health Phys. Apr;99(6):818-836, 2010

[5] ICNIRP – "Guidelines for limiting the exposure to static magnetic fields. Health Phys. Apr 96(4):504-514, 2009

[6] M. Barbiroli, C. Carciofi, and D. Guiducci, "Assesment pf Population and Occupational Exposure to Wi-Fi Systems: Measurements and Simulations", IEEE Transactions on Electromagnetic Compatibility, 53, 219-228, 2011

[7] S.Valbonesi, L.Giordani, E.Papotti, S.Vaccari, A.Vanore, "Occupational exposure to industrial furnaces: radiometric and dosimetric considerations", Ital. J. Occup. Environ. Hyg., 4(2), 52- 59, 2011

Evaluation of temperature increase during Magnetic Resonance examinations by combining electromagnetic/thermal simulations and B1 maps

Nunzia Fontana
CNIT and Dip. di Ingegneria dell'Informazione, UNIPI
Pisa, Italy
nunzia.fontana@iet.unipi.it

Gianluigi Tiberi
IRCCS Stella Maris and Fondazione IMAGO7,
Pisa, Italy

Mauro Costagli
IRCCS Stella Maris and Fondazione IMAGO7,
Pisa, Italy

M. R. Symms
General Electric ASL Scientist (EMEA)
Pisa, Italy

Michela Tosetti
IRCCS Stella Maris and Fondazione IMAGO7,
Pisa, Italy

Agostino Monorchio
Dipartimento di Ingegneria dell'Informazione, UNIPI
Pisa, Italy

***Abstract*— The purpose of the present study is to evaluate the temperature increase due to radio-frequency (RF) exposure in Magnetic Resonance (MR) examinations, by combining electromagnetic/thermal simulations and B1 maps.**

Keywords*— *Magnetic resonance; temperature rise; SAR; multi-physics simulation; B_1 maps; measurements.

I. Introduction

This study aimed to evaluate the temperature increase (ΔT) due to radio-frequency (RF) exposure in magnetic resonance (MR) examinations, by combining electromagnetic/thermal simulations and B_1 maps. The study was validated by an experiment conducted on a phantom, and demonstrates that temperature increase in MR due to RF exposure can be accurately predicted by combining electromagnetic/thermal simulations and B_1^+ maps.

II. Methods

A. Electromagnetic/Thermal simulations

3D full wave numerical electromagnetic (EM) simulations using a Finite Integration Technique (FIT), employed in CST MW Suite (CST-Computer Simulation Technology AG, Darmstadt, Germany), were used to simulate a 7.0T 1H quadrature birdcage head coil manufactured by Nova Medical (Wilmington, MA, USA). The birdcage was loaded with an agar-agar cylindrical phantom with an height of12.5 cm and a radius of3 cm, with characteristics reported in TABLE I (taken from [1]), and positioned in the center of the coil with its axis parallel to the static magnetic field. The coil was tuned to the frequency of 298 MHz and matched to achieve Sxx < -10dB (more details can be found in [2]). B_1^+ was calculated in the axial slice crossing the center, while a map of SAR [W/kg] was calculated on the entire cylindrical phantom in order be used as input for the thermal simulation. Specifically, the time-average [3] SAR for a given sequence applied on a given slice can be determined by using a scaling factor which accounts for all the sequence-related parameters: time of repetition (TR), number and waveform of RF pulses, and the corresponding nominal flip angle (FA) averaged on the slice (which are related to the nominal B_1^+, i.e. $B_{1,\ nominal}^+$). In this context, the time-average SAR for the following sequence was determined: Axial "Zero" Time-of-Echo (ZTE) sequence [4] ("SILENT") centered on the slice crossing the center; 384 FA = 4° hard pulses of 12 μs length; 5 inversion and saturation pulses per TR (TR = 525 ms); time of echo (TE) = 16 μs; post-segment time of delay TD = 2 s; field of view (FOV) = 192 x 192 x 192 mm^3; voxel size = 1 x 1 x 1 mm^3. The EM simulation was combined with the transient thermal simulation of CST Suite through the multi-physics tool, to solve the thermal equation. The thermal equation for a thermally insulated and non-perfused material with an internal heat source (in our case, *SAR*) can be written as follows

$$c\frac{\Delta T}{\Delta t} = SAR \tag{1}$$

where *c* is the heat capacity, *Δt* is the scan duration, *ΔT* is the temperature change [3]. We simulated the temperature inside the phantom during SILENT execution (460 s), the initial temperature was set to 293.1 K (magnet room temperature).

B. B_1^+ maps and phantom experiment

The phantom was created by dissolving agar (7 g/L), NaCl (10 g/L) and $CuSO_4$ (1 g/L) in hot water and then allowing the solution to cool down and solidify in the cylindrical plastic frame [1]. The cylindrical phantom was placed in the center of the coil (Fig. 1).

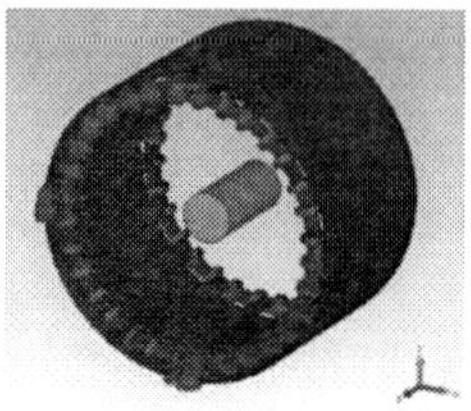

Fig. 1. Birdcage coil loaded with the cylindrical phantom.

We acquired $B_{1, map}^+$ with a Bloch-Siegert sequence [5] prescribed on the central axial slice corresponding to that used in simulations: parameters TR = 33 ms, TE = 15 ms, RBW = 15.6 kHz, thickness = 3.5 mm, matrix-size 64 x 64, square FOV = 22 cm, number of excitations (nex) = 2 (acquisition time: 9 s). A coefficient C, proportional to $avg(|B_{1, map}^+|)/B_{1, nominal}^+$ was calculated and used to appropriately scale the simulated temperature. Since C refers to B_1^+, temperature scaling must be performed multiplying by C [2]. ΔT generated by SILENT was measured with a fiber-optic temperature probe (Neoptix Canada LP, Quebec, Canada, resolution: 0.1 °C) with length of approximately 2 cm, placed at location of anticipated maximum SAR, near the surface of the phantom, on the central axial plane (white bar in Fig. 2). Before performing ΔT measurements, the phantom was equilibrated to room temperature; thermal insulation was achieved by inserting the phantom in an extruded polystyrene cavity and turning off the patient ventilation fan [6].

TABLE I. CHARACTERISTICS OF THE AGAR-AGAR CYLINDRICAL PHANTOM.

Quantity	Value
Heat capacity (c)	4.2 kJ/K/kg
Dielectric permittivity (ε_r)	77.52
Electric conductivity (σ)	1.886 S/m
Mass density (ρ)	1054 kg/m^3

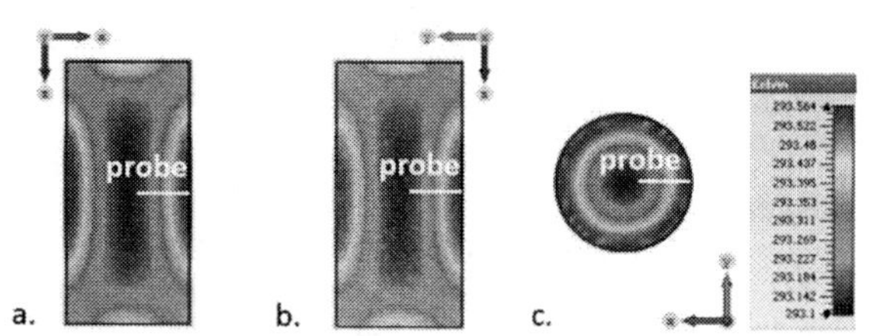

Fig. 2. Simulated temperature after B_1^+ map scaling obtained inside the phantom after SILENT execution (460 s) : a. sagittal plane; b. coronal plane; c. transverse plane. The white segment mimics length and position of the probe.

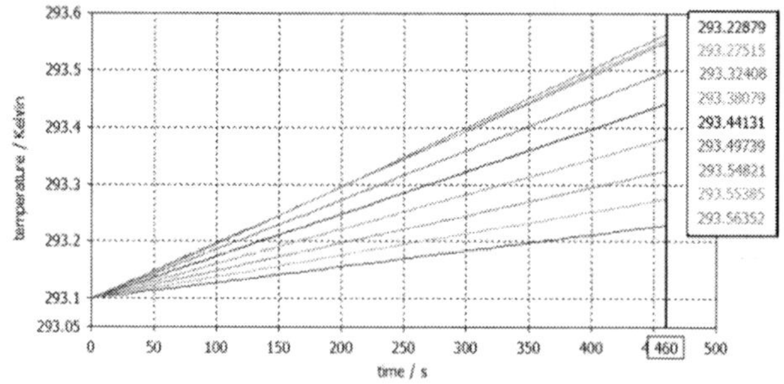

Fig. 3. Simulated temperature during 460 s for nine points evenly distributed along the white segment shown in Fig. 2.

III. RESULTS

Fig. 2 shows the simulated temperature after B_1^+ map scaling obtained inside the phantom after 460 s of SILENT scanning; the maximum temperature was 293.53 K. In order to compare the simulation and the measurements, we integrated the simulated temperature along a 2 cm segment mimicking the probe: we found that the simulated ΔT was 0.32 K, while the measure was 0.3 K. In Fig. 3 simulated temperature is shown during 460 s for nine points evenly distributed along the segment.

IV. DISCUSSIONS AND CONCLUSIONS

Simulated temperature behavior during time is consistent with literature [1], [3], [6]. There is a good agreement between the measured and the simulated ΔT due to the SILENT sequence at 7.0 T. Temperature increase in MR due RF exposure can be accurately predicted by combining electromagnetic/thermal simulations and B_1^+ maps.

REFERENCES

[1] Oh S., Webb A.G., Neuberger T., Park B., Collins C.M. , "Experimental and numerical assessment of MRI-induced temperature change and SAR distributions in phantoms and in vivo", Magn. Reson. Med. 2010, 63: 218–223.

[2] Tiberi G., Fontana N., Costagli M., Stara R., Biagi L., Symms M.R., Monorchio A., Retico A., Cosottini M., Tosetti M., "Investigation of maximum local specific absorption rate in 7 T magnetic resonance with respect to load size by use of electromagnetic simulations", Bioelectromagnetics 2015; 36: 358–366.

[3] Wang, Z. and Collins, C. M., "Effect of RF pulse sequence on temperature elevation for a given time-average SAR" Concepts Magn. Reson., 37B: 215–219.

[4] Costagli M., Symms M.R., Angeli L., Kelley D.A.C., Biagi L., Farnetani A., Rua C., Donatelli G., Tiberi G., Tosetti M., Cosottini M., "Assessment of Silent T1-weighted head imaging at 7T", European Radiology 2016, 26(6), 1879-1888.

[5] Sacolick L.I., Wiesinger F., Hancu I., Vogel M.W., "B1 mapping by Bloch-Siegert shift", Magn. Reson. in Med 2010, 63-5: 1315-1322.

[6] Sammet C.L., Yang X., Wassenaar P.A., Bourekas E.C., Yuh B.A., Shellock F., Sammet S., Knopp M.V., "RF-related heating assessment of extracranial neurosurgical implants at 7T", Magn Reson Imaging 2013; 31(6):1029-34.

Electromagnetic fields: scientific basis of regulatory frameworks

Bruno Bisceglia
Department of Industrial Engineering
University of Salerno
Fisciano (SA) - Italy
bbisceglia@unisa.it

Simona Valbonesi
Consorzio Elettra 2000
Pontecchio Marconi (BO) - Italy
svalbonesi@elettra2000.it

Abstract — **The World Health Organization (WHO) has always asserted the importance of uniformity of regulatory frameworks that need to be based on scientific evidences to be effective. Differing regulatory frameworks across different countries are confusing and may feed incorrect risk perception. This work consists of an analysis of the scientific basis of European and non-European regulatory frameworks with evaluation and study of non-standard cases.**

Keywords—electromagnetic fields, regolamentary frameworks, exposure limits, risk perception

I. Introduction

The use of electromagnetic fields in medicine, communication, transports and agriculture represents certainly a key element of global evolution.

The effects of electromagnetic fields on human health have been subjected to years of studies and investigations; the conclusions drawn from all the surveys are, for typical environmental levels, incontrovertibly reassuring [1] [2].

Nevertheless, in addressing the issue, both in everyday life and in the strategic evolution of regulatory frameworks, often prevails a cautious attitude due to many components: citizens concern, stakeholders interests, and lack of information from scientific world.

The legislative measures can be based on a purely scientific level or precautionary.

Precautionary measures, especially if not based on scientific evidence, can cause confusion, misperception of risk, and not allow the development of core technologies in the technical and economic growth of individual Countries.

The present work consists of an in-depth analysis of the European and non-European regulatory framework in order to identify the scientific basis and the variations locally introduced.

Lately it could be interesting to verify whether, regulatory frameworks without scientific basis lead to erroneous risk perception and to a distorted debate on the specific topic.

II. From Science to Regulatory Frameworks

A. A complex path

Studies and investigations on electromagnetic fields effects on human health started in the 50's, more than 30.000 articles have been published on peer reviewed journals.

Continuous revisions of the scientific literature are carried out by groups of experts, commissioned by the European Community or the World Health Organization.

The critical review of the scientific literature identifies data supporting a particular biological effect and the relative thresholds. To obtain limits and basic restrictions reduction factors are applied to increase security.

This activity lead to the publication of Guidelines based on the latest scientific knowledge, which can be used by lawmakers to implement an updated and consistent regulatory framework based on scientific foundations.

B. ICNIRP role and activities

ICNIRP (International Commission on Non-Ionizing Radiation) carries out periodic critical analysis of the available scientific literature on health effects of electromagnetic fields exposure, aimed at the continuous revision of the currently published Guidelines.

The guarantee of continuously updating the Guidelines with the progress of scientific knowledge, makes them extremely important tools in the definition of the individual countries regulatory frameworks.

According to WHO's opinion in fact, large disparities between single nations regulatory frameworks and limits reported in international official Guidelines, can promote misunderstanding and present a distorted risk perception as side effect. [3]

III. International Situation

The European regulatory framework is represented by the Reccomendation 1999/519/UE based on the ICNIRP Guidelines [4] published in 1998 for what concerns general public and by Directive 2013/35/UE for occupational exposures.

These Directives, in particular the 2013/35/EU are based on recent reviews of the scientific literature and do not address the possibility of long-term effects, since there is no scientific evidence of a causal relationship. The exposure limits and basic restrictions reported in the guidelines, have a scientific basis and are extremely protective with respect to all effects currently known. Most of European and non-European countries adopt, in their regulatory frameworks, what reported in the Guidelines.

IV. VARIATIONS

A. The" italian case" – a more cautelative framework

National frameworks [5] differs considerably from other European Countries regulatory frameworks, at least for what concerns general public exposures. The difference regards both the more conservative dimension of the adopted constraints and the laws architecture.

For what concerns general public exposure, since at the moment there is no quantitative correlation between exposure and increased cancer risk, scaling the 10% of the power density set as limit to obtain attention thresholds is to be considered completely arbitrary and not the result of a process based on scientific considerations. These considerations have made this specific part of the Italian regulatory framework one of the most cautelative in the world.

As for occupational exposures, the transposition of Directive 2013/35/EU into Legislative Decree 81/2008, leading to the introduction in Italy of limits and action values based on ICNIRP Guidelines, less precautionary.

This creates a disharmony between the limits for the general public and those for occupationally exposed that may be perceived as too high. This could feed a distorted debate that will be highly complex to be reported on the right terms.

B. Safety Code 6 in Canada – an example of selective limits reduction

The Canadian government has recently published an updated version of Safety Code 6 [6], the guidelines reporting the limits of exposure to electromagnetic fields in force in the Country.

In year 2014, a panel of scientists in charge of the Royal Society of Canada conducted an independent review of the scientific literature from which have emerged considerations that led the panel to propose limits selectively different from those indicated in the previous editions of the SC6 and not completely based on ICNIRP Guidelines.

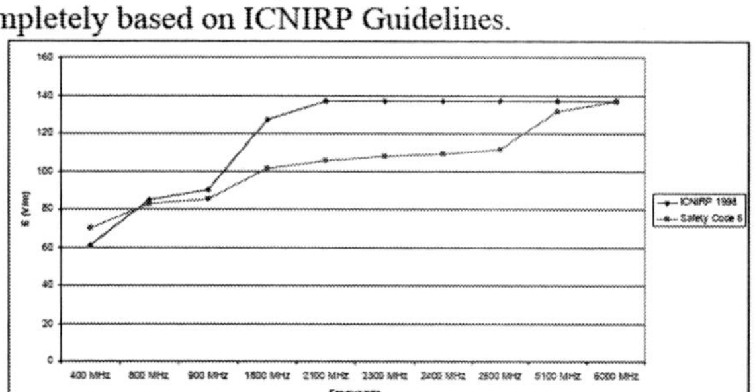

Fig. 1. E-field limits (400 MHz-6 GHz) – Safety Code 6 vs ICNIRP

The graph in Figure 1 shows a comparison between the E-field limits of exposure for general public reported in SC6 2015 and in ICNIRP Guidelines [4]. In the 400 MHz – 6 GHz range the new limits are lower up to a 30%. For all other frequency ranges limits are those set by ICNIRP.

It was therefore a selective limits lowering based on the facts that association studies between use of mobile phones and brain cancer present contrasting results and potential mechanism leading from the exposure to the pathology are currently unknown, but the scientific research progress could lead in short to their identification. In addiction there are no definite results on the effects of sub-thermal exposures and further investigations on effects on children, adolescents, fetuses and infants, are needed.

V. CONCLUSIONS

European and non-european regulatory frameworks for what concerns electromagnetic fields exposures presents, except for some particular situations, scientific foundation. In fact, they are derived directly from the Guidelines drawn up by ICNIRP on the basis of a continuous critical review of the scientific literature.

Regulatory framework without a scientific basis may present some contradictions, they may be confusing and locally origin a debate in which the scientific part presents a marginal role.

The continuous evolution of systems based on electromagnetic fields, make it easy to predict that in such countries where regulatory frameworks don't have a scientific basis, critical issues will represent periodically, unless the local Governments undertake a path of cultural growth and a regulatory frameworks audit.

REFERENCES

[1] European Commission SCENIHR, "Opinion on potential health effects of exposure to electromagnetic fields", 2015

[2] S.Lagorio, M.Roosli, "Mobile phone use and risk of intracranial tumors: a consistency analysis", DOI: 10.002/bem.21829, 2013

[3] IARC Monographs on the Evaluation of Carcinogenic Risks to Humans - " Non-Ionizing Radiation, Part 2: Radiofrequency Electromagnetic Fields" - Volume 102, 2013

[4] ICNIRP - "Guidelines for limiting exposure to time-varying electric, magnetic, and electromagnetic fields (up to 300 GHz). International Commission on Non-Ionizing Radiation Protection." - Health Phys. Apr;74(4):494-522, 1998

[5] Decreto Ministeriale 8 luglio 2003 e decreto legge 18 ottobre 2012 coordinato con legge di conversione 17 dicembre 2012, n.221, art. 14

[6] Health Canada – "Limits of human exposure to Radiofrequency Electromagnetic Energy in the frequency range from 3 kHz to 300 GHz – Safety Code 6", 2015

In Silico Analysis of Farmlands Disinfection using Microwave

Michele Spanu, Matteo Bruno Lodi
Department of Electronic and Electric Engineering
University of Cagliari
Italy
michele.spanu9200@gmail.com, matteobrunolodi94@gmail.com.

***Abstract*—This work deals with the heat transfer phenomena in agricultural soils exposed to microwave (MW) fields to disinfect them eliminating dangerous organisms without using pesticides. The soil, approximated to a transmission line model, is supposed to be subject to an incident plane wave coming from a horn antenna working at 2.45GHz. Assessing the dielectric constant as a function of the soil water content, with the present model, it was possible to evaluate the power absorption for the irradiated ground and, especially, the increase in temperature and its profile as a function of the exposure time. In this way, it is demonstrated the feasibility of the methodology here proposed to achieve difficult conditions for microbial and pathogens life, resulting in an effective disinfection of farmlands.**

Keywords— microwave disinfection, microbial, pathogens, bio-agriculture, soil dielectric constant, soil heat transfer

I. Introduction

Interest in biological and sustainable agriculture, nowadays, has widely spread. Actually, the term Bio-Agriculture indicates cultivation methods which allow solely the use of natural substances, without using chemical agents, such as herbicides and pesticides. Many different solutions were considered to avoid any invasive or harmfully methods, for both cultures and soil health. But the use of electromagnetic (EM) waves, in particular microwave (MW), for soil disinfection from pathogen agents (e.g. algae, fungi and fungine roots, but also viruses, nematodes, and, finally, protozoa) stands out as a reliable, selective and cheap technique. Microwaves are widely exploited in biotechnology since they lead to an increase in the rotational energy of water dipole. Therefore, as bacteria and microorganisms are mainly composed of water, the energy transfer, i.e. the temperature increase due to MW, can be exploited to inhibit or eliminate them simply creating an intolerable environment for their life. Such thermal effects of microwave on bacteria (but also MW non-thermal effects) have been already studied and described in the literature. In situ MW applications using driving structure or radiating devices should be addressed as a valuable enhancing factor in environmental remediation. The MW use seems to be promising since, contrary to synthetic chemical products, would not affect organic substances [1]-[5]. Therefore, in this work the feasibility of the use of high-power microwaves to disinfect the soil is assessed and a model to control and prevent overheating is presented.

II. Soil response to MW heating

Soil is defined as an inhomogeneous mixture of fragmented and eroded minerals, and of decomposing organic matter and a certain amount of water and air. This composition establish the texture of soil, which is an important characteristic identifying how the ground under analysis retains water or moisture, the amount of which is a relevant parameter influencing the dielectric constant. A pyramidal-base horn antenna coupled with a waveguide is supposed to irradiate the soil. The radiation system is fed with a constant power, P_{MW}, at the working frequency of 2.45 GHz. If the horn is placed at the distance of 0.95 m from the soil surface, a Poynting vector modulus S is associated with the MW field. In this configuration, soil behavior under MW exposition is necessarly described by the value of its relative dielectric constant, ε. But, from our previous discussion, it must be taken into account that such variable is a function of water content. Therefore, for humidity ranging from 0÷10 (dry soil) to 30÷40 % (wet soil), is it possible to quantify such physical parameter, both in term of the real, ε', and imaginary part, ε'', exploiting the empirical model derived by Hallikainen [6]:

$$\varepsilon = (a_0 + a_1 S + a_2 C) + (b_0 + b_1 S + b_2 C) m_v + (c_0 + c_1 S + c_2 C) m_v^2 \quad (2),$$

where a_i, b_i and c_i are fitting parameters and the index i refers to the component by the amount of which the parameter must be multiplied (0 for none, 1 for sand, 2 for clay). To evaluate electrical parameters when soil is irradiated, we modeled it with a lumped parameter model, approximating it to a transmission lines system, as shown in Fig. 1. Since soil is composed of several layers of different texture and moisture, but we are interested in the very first one, under the approximation of the antenna as a power source, this superficial layer can be considered as a line with impedance Z, length L and propagation constant k [7].

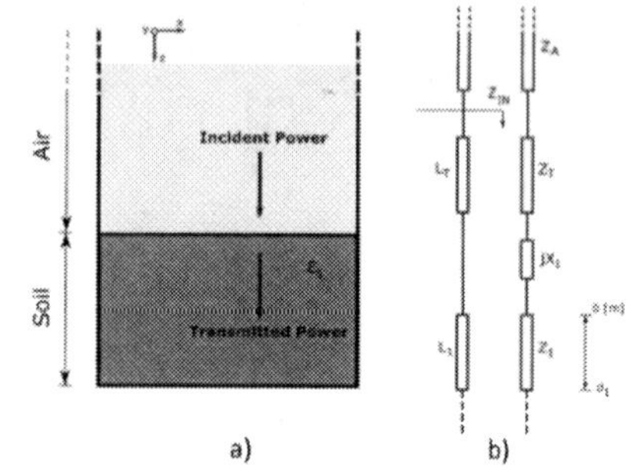

Fig. 1 Air-Soil interface (a) and its modeling as a transmission line system (b).

When the plane wave form the horn antenna impinges on soil surface, power is dissipated, due to the water present in it. This generated heat determines a temperature increase, which has to be accurately controlled and kept to the value of 65-75 °C in the whole layer. Therefore, to evaluate the actual heating of the soil, it is necessary to solve the following heat balance equation:

$$\rho C_p \frac{\partial T}{\partial t} = k\nabla^2 T + P \quad (2)$$

where ρ is the soil density (Kgm^{-3}), C_p is its specific heat, in the range ($JKg^{-1}K^{-1}$). Whereas k is the thermal conductivity ($Wm^{-1}K^{-1}$), T is the temperature (K), t is time (s), and P is the specific heat power ($W\ m^{-3}$) generated within soil. This last parameter can be calculated as:

$$P(z) = P(0)e^{-\alpha_E z} = 2\alpha_E S \cdot e^{-\alpha_E z} \quad (3)$$

where α_E is the imaginary part of the dielectric constant and is one of the main indicators of the feasibility of the technique here proposed. Since both the electromagnetic and the thermal properties of the soil are temperature-dependent, (2) is non-linear. However, to assess the feasibility of the proposed approach, we decided to solve a simplified linear and one dimensional model. We performed our analysis using moisture acquired from a measurement campaign performed on Sardinian farmland using TDR (Time Domain Reflectometry) probe and gravimetric measures [8]. The texture and characteristics of analyzed soils are summarized in Table 1.

III. Results

With a feeding power of 8 kW with Si=11 kWm^{-2} and an initial air and soil temperature of 20 °C, we found that, for a wet soil, α_E can be 15 m^{-1}, so that the EM power is dissipated quite uniformly in the layer of interest (4÷5 cm of depth from the surface). This results reflects the fact that heating is near independent from the thermal parameters of the soil, but only about 7-8 min would be necessary to reach the temperature of 65-75 °C in the whole layer (see Fig. 2). However, since the temperature field is almost uniform in the system, an increase of the MW power would reduce the heating time without overheating, which could damage the soil nutrients. requiring the lowest value of k. From this discussion the reader can infer that, using a proper horn power, we can reach the required temperatures for dry and slightly wet soils, preventing the surface overheating. However, for a given farmland soil, an optimization is needed to get the best water content and to reduce the overall disinfection time. The results here presented show that MW heating can be a viable method to disinfect the upper layer of agricultural soils.

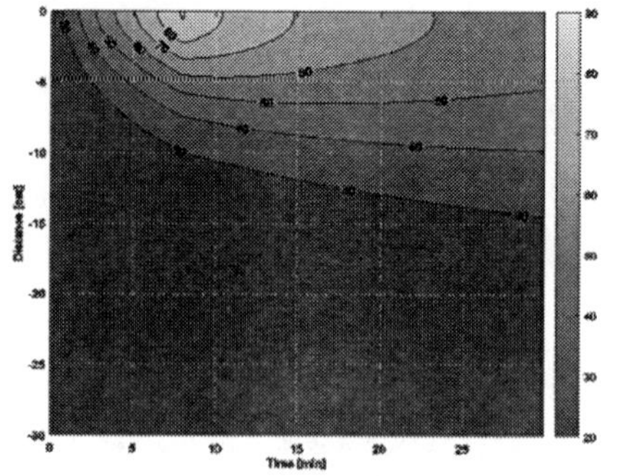

Fig. 2. Soil temperature as a function of depth and time of irradiation for a wet soil, A Field (ρ=1400 Kg m^{-3}; C=1200 J Kg^{-1} K^{-1}; k=2.47 W m^{-1} K^{-1}; h_c=2.0 W m^{-2} K^{-1}; S=11 kW m^{-2}; MW continuous irradiation; temperatures in °C)

TABLE I. Collected soil data of some Sardinian farmlands [8]

Fields	Coordinates (WGS84 GD)		Soil Texture (%)		
	Long.	Lat.	Sand	Silt	Clay
A	9.166919204	39.70296945	29	50.1	20.9

Acknowledgment

This work was supported in part by Regione Autonoma della Sardegna under contract "IDROSAR" CRP- 79793 (CUP F72I15000870002).

References

[1] S. O. Nelson, "A review and assessment of microwave energy for soil treatment to control pests," Transactions of the American Society of Agricultural Engineers, vol.39, pp. 281-289, 1996.

[2] J. Behari, "Physical Properties of Soils; Dielectric Behavoior of Soil," in "Microwave Dielectric Behavior of Wet Soils," New Delhi, India, Springer with Anamaya Publishers, pp. 1-38, 2005

[3] G.R. Vela, J.F. Wu, D. Smith, "Effect of 2450 MHz microwave radiation on some soil microorganisms in situ," Soil Science, vol.121

[4] A.S. Komarova, A.A. Likhacheva, D.G. Zvyagintsev, "Influence of microwave radiation on soil bacteria," Moscow University Soil Science Bulletin, vol.63, pp. 190-195, 2008.

[5] Cooper, Andrew, and Graham Brodie. "The Effect of Microwave Radiation and Soil Depth on Soil pH, N, P, K, SO {4} and Bacterial Colonies." *Plant Protection Quarterly* 24.2 (2009): 67.

[6] M.T. Hallikainen, et al. «Microwave Dielectric Behavior of Wet Soil-Part 1:Empirical Models and Experimental Observations,» IEEE T.Geosci.Remote Sensing, 1985.

[7] M. Spanu, et al. "Microwave disinfection of farmlands", Journal of Electromagnetic Waves and Applications, In press, http://dx.doi.org/10.1080/09205071.2016.1249802

[8] N. Montaldo, R. Corona, J.D. Albertson, "On the separate effects of soil and land cover on Mediterranean ecohydrology: two contrasting case studies in Sardinia, Italy," Water Resources Research, vol.49.

Analysis of Dielectric Coated Conducting Bodies Using Characteristic Mode Theory

Liwen Guo, Yikai Chen, Shiwen Yang

University of Electronic Science and Technology of China, Chengdu, China, 611731

ykchen@uestc.edu.cn

***Abstract*—The characteristic mode (CM) theory has been widely recognized as a powerful tool for radiation/scattering analysis and optimization designs. As a natural extension of PEC CM theory and dielectric material CM theory, we propose a novel CM formulation for the systematic analysis of dielectric coated conducting bodies. The newly developed CM formulation bases on the EFIE-PMCHWT equation. Numerical cases show the validity and accuracy of the proposed CM formulation in calculating characteristic currents and characteristic fields and predicting resonant frequencies.**

Keywords—Dielectric coated conducting bodies; characteristic modes

I. Introduction

The influence of dielectric coatings on radiation and scattering characteristics of the conducting bodies has been widely studied in past decades. However, regardless of analytical methods or numerical methods, they depend heavily on the exterior sources and provide little physical insight behind the radiation or scattering behavior. Fortunately, the characteristic mode (CM) theory, developed by [1] and refined by [2], offers a systematic approach for radiation and scattering characteristics analysis without considering any exterior excitations. Thus, this method can provide real and deep physical insight into the radiation or scattering mechanisms.

In this paper, we extend the well-developed PEC CM theory and newly-proposed dielectric material CM theory [3] to the CM theory for the dielectric coated conducting bodies based on the EFIE-PMCHWT surface integral formulation. By enforcing E-field continuity or H-field continuity, two types of generalized eigenvalue equations can be obtained to characterize the resonant characteristics of dielectric coated conducting bodies.

II. Characteristic Mode Formulation for Dielectric Coated Conducting Bodies

Apply moment of method (MoM), the EFIE-PMCHWT surface integral formulation can be written as the following matrix equation,

$$\begin{bmatrix} Z_c^{EJ_c} & Z_c^{EJ_d} & Z_c^{EM_d} \\ Z_d^{EJ_c} & Z_d^{EJ_d} & Z_d^{EM_d} \\ Z_d^{HJ_c} & Z_d^{HJ_d} & Z_d^{HM_d} \end{bmatrix} \begin{bmatrix} J_c \\ J_d \\ M_d \end{bmatrix} = \begin{bmatrix} 0 \\ V^E \\ V^H \end{bmatrix} \tag{1}$$

where the subscript 'c' and 'd' mean conductor and dielectric, respectively. Here it is worth noting that when tangential continuity of both electric and magnetic fields are enforced, the resultant resonance frequencies are complex numbers and modes obtained are equivalent to the modes as defined in [4] and [5]. It implies that, for the real working frequencies, the tangential continuity of EM fields may not be simultaneously satisfied. Therefore, by enforcing different field continuity conditions, two generalized eigenvalue equations are defined. In the presentation, we will detail two types of generalized eigenvalue equations and prove the resultant eigenvalues indicate the stored energy by invoking the Poynting's theorem.

Here only the generalized eigenvalue equation from the E-field continuity is given. We can replace the equivalent electric currents J_c over the conducting surface and equivalent electric currents J_d over the dielectric coating surface with M_d to form an equivalent system as $[Z^M][M_d]=[V^{H'}]$. Thus, a new matrix is obtained,

$$Z^M = Z_d^{HM_d} - Z_d^{HJ_d}\left(Z_d^{EJ_d}\right)^{-1} Z_d^{EM_d} - Z_d^{HJ_c} Z_{mul}^A Z_{mul}^B + Z_d^{HJ_d}\left(Z_d^{EJ_d}\right)^{-1} Z_d^{EJ_c} Z_{mul}^A Z_{mul}^B \tag{2}$$

where the two new matrices are defined for brevity as follow,

$$Z_{mul}^A = \left[Z_c^{EJ_c} - Z_c^{EJ_d}\left(Z_d^{EJ_d}\right)^{-1} Z_d^{EJ_c} \right]^{-1} \tag{3}$$

$$Z_{mul}^B = Z_c^{EM_d} - Z_c^{EJ_d}\left(Z_d^{EJ_d}\right)^{-1} Z_d^{EM_d}. \tag{4}$$

Apply the CM theory to (2), a generalized eigenvalue equation is formulated as,

$$X^M M_{dn} = \lambda_n R^M M_{dn} \tag{5}$$

where M_{dn} is the n order characteristic current, R^M and X^M are the Hermitian real and imaginary parts of Z^M, respectively. By solving (5), the resonant frequencies and characteristic fields can be readily obtained. It is of great help to understand the physical behavior behind the radiation/scattering of dielectric coated conducting bodies.

III. Numerical Validation and Discussion

Here the dielectric coated conducting cuboid with sizes of $h \times l \times w$ = 0.05×0.6×0.2 m^3 and coating thickness of 0.2h is taken as numerical case to validate the availability of the proposed formulation. Because there are little available modal analysis results in literatures for code validations, we compare the results of fictitious air coated conducting bodies solved from the proposed formulation and isolated conducting bodies solved from the PEC CM formulation. In the presentation, we will give more numerical cases and more detailed discussions for further validation.

The eigenvalues of the isolated conducting cuboid are presented in Fig. 1. As can be seen, there are two dominant modes within the frequency band of 0.1-0.7 GHz. The two modes resonate at 0.208 GHz and 0.484 GHz, respectively. Fig. 2 shows the characteristic currents and characteristic fields of the two modes at their own resonant frequencies. Fig. 3 shows the eigenvalues of the same cuboid with fictitious air coatings of thickness $0.2h$ solved from the proposed formulation. The two types of generalized eigenvalue equations show reasonable agreement and characterize the same resonant characteristics as the isolated conducting cuboid. The characteristic currents and characteristic fields of the dominant modes solved from $X^M\mathbf{M}_{dn}=\lambda_n R^M\mathbf{M}_{dn}$ at their own resonant frequencies are shown in Fig. 4. As compared with the isolated case shown in Fig. 2, the agreement is pretty good.

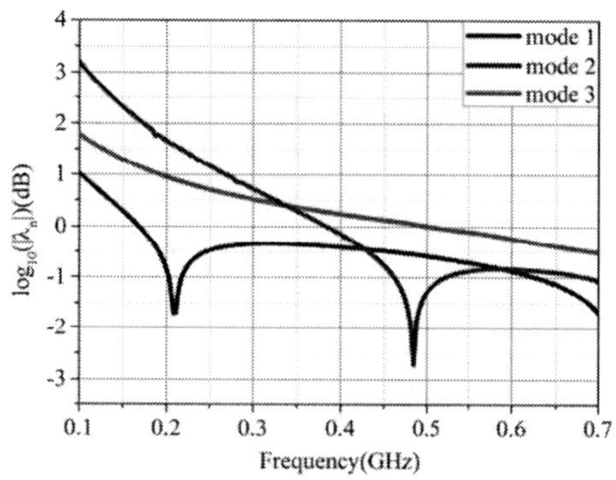

Fig. 1. Eigenvalues of the isolated conducting cuboid.

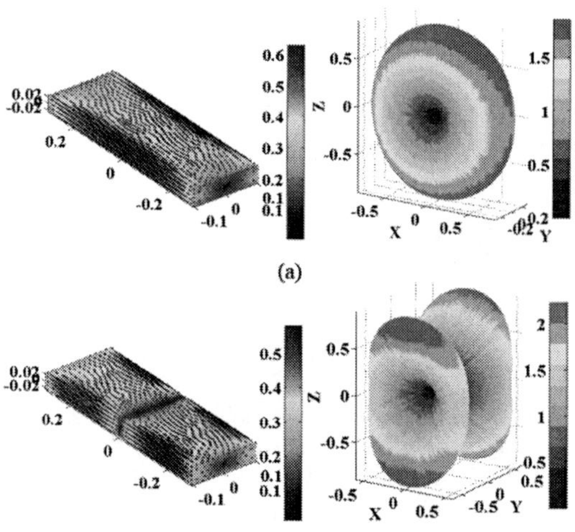

Fig. 2. Characteristic currents (left) and characteristic fields (right) of resonant modes of the isolated conducting cuboid at their own resonant frequencies. (a) Mode 1 resonates at 0.208 GHz; (b) mode 2 resonates at 0.484 GHz.

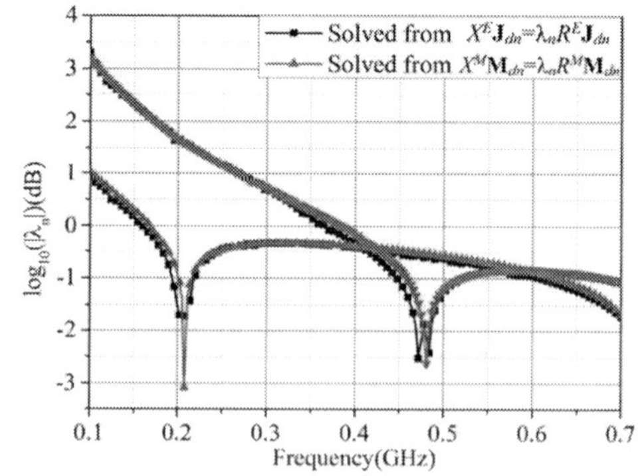

Fig. 3. Eigenvalues of the fictitious air coated conducting cuboid with a coatings thickness of $0.2h$.

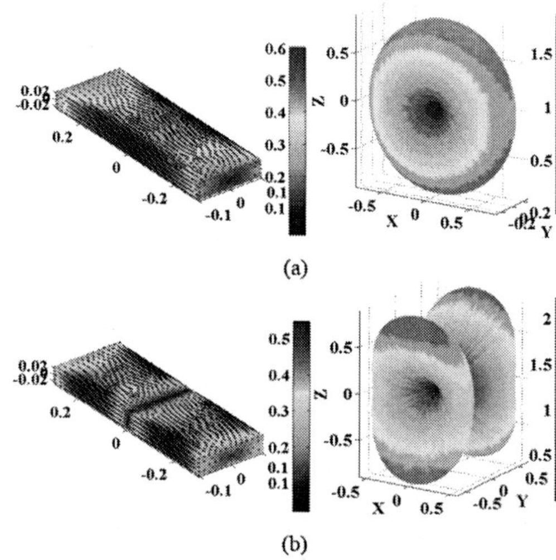

Fig. 4. Characteristic currents (left) and characteristic fields (right) of the resonant modes of the fictitious air coated conducting cuboid at their own resonant frequencies. The coatings thickness is $0.2h$. The fields are computed from $\mathbf{X}^M\mathbf{M}_{dn}=\lambda_n\mathbf{R}^M\mathbf{M}_{dn}$. (a) Mode 1 resonates at 0.208 GHz; (b) mode 2 resonates at 0.481 GHz.

REFERENCES

[1] R. J. Garbacz, "Modal expansions for resonance scattering phenomena," Proc. of the IEEE, vol. 53, pp. 856-864, Aug. 1965.

[2] R. F. Harrington and J. R. Mautz, "Theory of Characteristic Modes For conducting Bodies," IEEE Trans. Antennas Propag., vol. 19, pp.622-628, Sep. 1971.

[3] Y. Chen, "Alternative surface integral equation-based characteristic mode analysis of dielectric resonator antennas," IET Microw. Antennas Propag., vol. 10, pp. 193-201, Jan. 2016.

[4] D. Kajfez and A. W. Glisson, "Computed modal field distributions forisolated dielectric resonators," IEEE Trans. Microw. Theory Tech., vol. 32, pp. 1609-1616, Dec. 1984.

[5] Y. Liu, S. Safavi-Naeini, and S. K. Chaudhuri, "On the determination of resonant modes of dielectric objects using surface integral equations," IEEE Trans. Antennas Propag., vol. 52,pp. 1062-1069, Apr. 2004.

An Enhanced Algorithm in Tracking Characteristic Modes of Dielectric Objects.

H.Alroughani
Department of Electrical Engineering
Penn State University, University Park, PA, USA

Abstract — **Tracking PMCHWT-based characteristic modes (CMs) of dielectric or magnetic objects still remains a challenging task due to the presence of non-physical modes, but developing a robust tracking algorithm is essential to observe modal behavior over frequency. Thus, our efforts continue in enhancing an existing tracking algorithm which is based on eigencurrent correlation and far-zone eigenfield orthogonality for more reliability and efficient computational time. Also in this paper, some important findings about tracking are discussed.**

Keywords* — *electromagnetic characteristic modes; mode tracking algorithms; dielectric objects

I. Introduction

The interest of computing CMs of dielectric objects is on the rise due to the popularity of the analysis and its application on conducting objects found in the literature. The theory of CM was refined by Harrington and Mautz, and numerical experiments were performed [1-3]; however, there were still some unanswered questions remined until some research works emerged on the subject of analysing CMs of dielectric and magnetic objects. On the other hand, tracking CMs has been one of the hot topics in the field due to its necessity for a correct interpretation of the outcome, but some challenges encountered researchers in developing a reliable and efficient algorithm for tracking CMs of dielectric objects in particular still exist. Although several tracking algorithms exist in the literature [4-8], only few can reliably tackle the issue of tracking CMs of dielectric objects. The majority of those algorithms solely depend on modal current (eigencurrent) correlation, whereas far-zone modal fields (eigenfield) calculation becomes a complimentary parameter utilized in the tracking procedure [7,8]. A hybrid approach is used in [8] by relying on both eigencurrent correlation and eigenfield orthogonality relationship and the latter is essential in the tracking process to exclude non-physical modes as discussed in [9]. The appearance of non-physical modes is strictly as a result of using the PMCHWT surface integral equations (IEs) in CM calculation, and those can be detected by examining the field orthogonality, which is one of the most important properties of CMs. Therefore, eigenfield computation is an important step in tracking CMs calculated using PMCHWT. This paper focuses on further improvements brought to the algorithm introduced in [8] for more reliability and efficient computational time, and it also sheds the light on some important findings.

II. Description and Application of the Enhanced Tracking Algorithm

In this section, only those improvements applied to the proposed tracking algorithm in [8] will be discussed for brevity as the details are discussed in the reference. Though, the proposed algorithm can be applied for tracking CMs of PEC objects and lossless dielectric objects using volume IEs, tracking CMs of lossless dielectric objects using surface IEs is the main goal due to the issues discussed earlier. Accordingly, solving the generalized eigenvalue equation [3, Eq. (21)] results in finding the corresponding eigenvalues λ_n and eigencurrents $[F_n(f_q)] = [[J_n(f_q)]\,[jM_n(f_q)]]^T$ at frequency f_q, where q is the index of frequency iteration. FEKO [10] is utilized for modelling 3D geometries and exporting the moment method matrix to a MATLAB environment where the eigenvalue equation is solved, and tracking is performed. The far-zone eigenfields $(\bar{E}_n, \bar{H}_n)$ is computed by feeding the corresponding eigencurrents back to FEKO, and they must satisfy the condition [3]

$$\mathrm{P}_{mn}(f_q) = \frac{1}{\eta_0} \oint\!\!\!\oint_{S_\infty} \bar{E}_m(f_q) \cdot \bar{E}_n^*(f_q)\, dS = \delta_{mn} \qquad (1)$$

In the first iteration (q=1), $\mathrm{P}_{nn}(f_1)$ is computed for every mode based on the ascending order of λ_n magnitude up to the desired number of physical CMs. Declaring a mode to be physical is by specifying a threshold value ρ which P_{nn} must exceed. As a first improvement, ρ is increased from 0.2 to 0.5 to exclude non-physical modes in the selection process since P_{nn} of those modes cannot exceed 0.5 at any point [8]. It is recommended that first frequency step is chosen to be lower than the first expected resonance in order to avoid eliminating any physical mode whose P_{nn} drops below ρ in cases such as a crossing point with non-physical modes. In the subsequent iterations, correlating eigencurrents with those previously selected/tracked ones helps identifying which eigenfield to be calculated for the verification purposes; this step makes the computation more efficient by reducing the required number of eigenfield calculations. The mode whose $\mathrm{P}_{nn} > \rho$ with highest correlation value (greater than 1/3) is to be assigned; however, if no mode satisfies this condition, finding those modes whose $\mathrm{P}_{nn} < \rho$ may be assigned as long as the correlation value is greater than one third. This step is introduced to prevent assigning a non-physical mode to any tracked mode in order to eliminate an extra step for back tracking which was part of the developed algorithm. In addition, checking that eigenvalue is not discontinuous and no duplicate assignment is made ensures no discrepancies in the process and leads to smoother assignment.

The ideal correlation value between modal currents of those physical modes is unity (perfectly correlated), and the ideal value of P_{nn} is unity as well. However, this might not be the outcome due to mathematical discrepancies resulted from solving the eigenvalue equation of the moment method matrix. It is possible that either of those values dropped below the specified thresholds, 1/3 and 1/2 respectively, and if so, it would result in either an increase in computational time to search for more modes or a stoppage in tracking. The optimum solution for that is to increase the number of expansion functions used in the moment method solution, and that helps improving both the correlation and P_{nn} values. Unfortunately, this leads to higher computational time; nevertheless, more accurate and converged CM solution and smoother tracking process. As an example, Fig.1 shows the dominant mode's eigenvalues tracked for the object shown as a function of both frequency and number of unknowns, and Fig.2 depicts P_{nn} values for the same mode at every frequency iteration. It is evident that as the number of unknowns is increased, eigenvalues and their corresponding P_{nn} values (including the correlation values) are improved as well.

III. Conclusion

Several enhancements brought to the previously developed tracking algorithm are summarized as followed:
1) Modal correlation is used to determine which eigenfield(s) needs to be computed as a tracking parameter. This improves computational time significantly. 2) The threshold value is raised to 0.5 to avoid an extra step of back tracking. 3) Duplicate modal assignment is checked and corrected along with examining any discontinuity between eigenvalues. This improves the reliability of tracking and decrease any chance of confusion in the tracking process. Finally, it is found that refining moment-method solution mesh improves the CM solution, hence enhances the tracking parameters (both correlation and P_{nn} values) for a robust tracking process.

Acknowledgment

We want to thank Altair (FEKO) for contributing to our research by providing a copy of FEKO software and for sharing some results related to CM tracking.

References

[1] R.F.Harrington and J.R.Mautz, "Theory of characteristic modes for conducting bodies", *IEEE Trans. Antennas Propagat.*, Vol. 19, pp. 622–628, Sept.1971.

[2] R.F.Harrington, J.R.Mautz and Y.Chang, "Characteristic modes for dielectric and magnetic bodies", *IEEE Trans. Antennas Propagat.*, Vol. 20, pp.194-198, 1972.

[3] Y.Chang and R.F.Harrington, "A surface formulation for characteristic modes of material bodies", *IEEE Trans. Antennas Propagat.*, Vol. 25, pp.789-795, 1977.

[4] D.J.Ludick, J. van Tonder and U.Jakobus, "A hybrid tracking algorithm for characteristic mode analysis", in Proc. ICEAA, pp.455-458, Aruba, Aug. 2014.

[5] B. Raines and R.Rojas, "Wideband characteristic mode tracking", *IEEE Trans. Antennas Propagat.*, vol. 60, no. 7, pp.3537-3541, July 2012.

[6] M. Capek, P. Hazdra, and J. Eichler, "A method of tracking characteristic numbers and vectors", *Progress in Electromagnetics Research B*, vol. 33, pp. 115-134, 2011.

[7] Z.Miers and B.K.Lau, "Wideband characteristic mode tracking utilizing far-field patterns", *IEEE Antennas Wireless Propagat Letts.*, Vol. 14, pp. 1658-1661, 2015.

[8] H. Alroughani, J. L. T. Ethier and D. A. McNamara, "Numerical experiments in tracking the characteristic modes of dielectric objects," 2016 IEEE/ACES International Conference on Wireless Information Technology and Systems (ICWITS) and Applied Computational Electromagnetics (ACES), Honolulu, HI, 2016, pp. 1-2

[9] H.Alroughani, J.Ethier and D.A.McNamara, "Observations on computational outcomes for the characteristic modes of dielectric objects", *IEEE AP-S Int. Symp. Digest*, Tennessee, USA, July 2014.

[10] *FEKO*, Altair (www.altair.com)

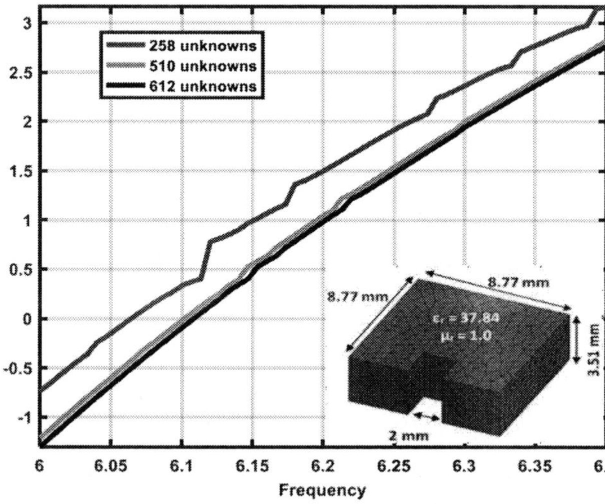

FIG.1 EIGENVALUES OF FIRST (PHYSICAL) CMS FOR THE 3D OBJECT SHOWN

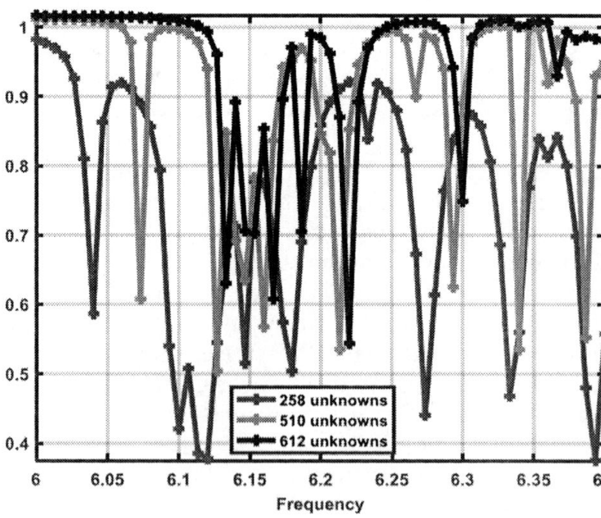

FIG.2 P_{NN} VALUES AT EVERY FREQUECNY ITERATION ASSOCIATED WITH FIG 1

Pattern Control for Portable Devices by Exploiting Phase-Shifted Characteristic Modes

Francesco Alessio Dicandia, Simone Genovesi, Agostino Monorchio
Dipartimento Ingegneria dell'Informazione, Università di Pisa
Consorzio Nazionale Interuniversitario delle Telecomunicazioni
Pisa, Italy
alessio.dicandia@for.unipi.it, simone.genovesi@iet.unipi.it, agostino.monorchio@unipi.it

***Abstract*—A pattern control for portable devices at 2.45 GHz is proposed by exploiting phase-shifted characteristic modes (CMs). Among all available orthogonal CMs, the pattern control of a rectangular conductive plane has been obtained by a weighted linear superposition of only two current modes (J_4 and J_8). A proper position of two capacitive coupling exciters (CCEs), hosted above the rectangular conductive plane, realize the selective excitation of the current modes, whereas the phase difference ($\Delta\theta$) between the CCEs allows obtaining the pattern control. The obtained results prove that the phase-shifted CM technique is reliable and can be applicable to other kind of structures.**

Keywords— characteristic modes; reconfigurable antennas; null-steering, pattern control.

I. Introduction

Reconfigurable antennas represent a very interesting topic in the field of antenna engineering for many applications [1]–[3]. In particular, the pattern reconfigurable feature allows increasing the reliability and coverage of the overall communication systems by varying the radiation propriety of the radiator element. Moreover, pattern reconfigurable antennas, can also act as spatial filtering with the consequence of reducing both the complexity and cost of the radio frequency (RF) front end [4]. In fact, by placing the null of the pattern in the direction of intentional or casual jammer, it is possible to eliminate or reduce the effect of the interference with the consequence enhance of the signal to interference ratio (SIR).

Over the past years, the characteristic modes theory (CMT) [5], [6] has received a meaningful interest in the field of the antenna design in several application. For instance, some antennas for multiple-input-multiple-output (MIMO) systems are proposed in [7]–[10]. In [11]–[13] the CMT has been exploited to design antenna on complex platform. Recently, the CMT has been successfully applied also for pattern reconfigurable antenna [14].

The aim of the paper is to propose a pattern control antenna for portable devices by exploiting the CMT. More in detail, two current modes (J_n) are asymmetrically stimulated over a rectangular ground plane by using two capacitive coupler exciters (CCEs) [15], [16]. The phase difference ($\Delta\theta$) between the two exciters allows obtaining a pattern control radiator.

II. Pattern Control Antenna Design

The proposed antenna is illustrated in Fig. 1 with all the geometrical dimensions. It consists of a rectangular conductive plane, which mimics a portable device of dimension 150 x 75 mm^2, placed above a substrate of a dielectric layer (FR4) with a thickness of 1.2 mm. Two CCEs are also located in the middle of shorter side. The rectangular exciters (5 x 32 mm^2) are located parallel to the short side of the conductive plane at a height of 4 mm. Two voltage sources are set between the ground plane and the centre of the CCEs.

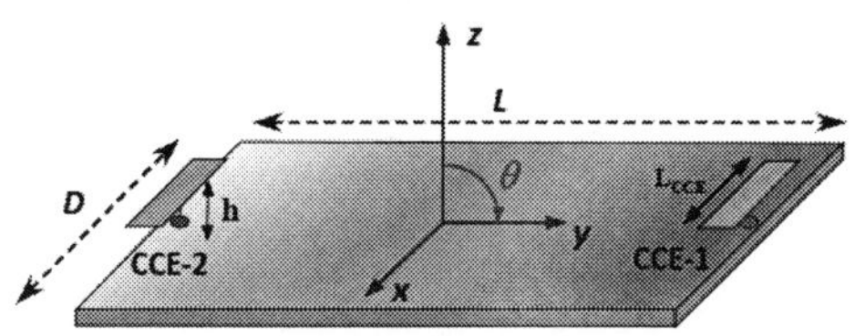

Fig. 1 Investigated antenna: L = 150 mm, D = 75 mm, L_{CCE} = 32 mm, h = 4mm.

In order to prove the orthogonality of the CM of the structure, the correlation between the first ten current modes (J_n) can be observed in Fig. 2. The correlation shown in Fig. 2 is calculated by taking into account the electric field associated to the current modes.

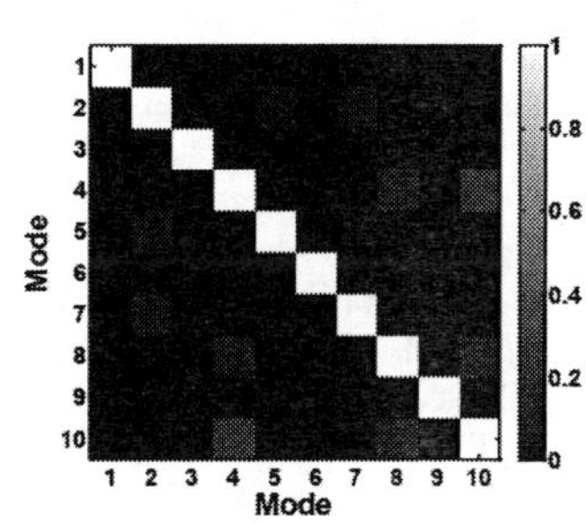

Fig. 2 Correlation of the first ten current modes (J_n) of the conductive rectangular plane.

The positioning and the kind of the applied sources play an important role in the selective excitation of the CM over the investigated structure [17]. In order to understand which current modes (J_n) are efficiently excited from the CCEs over the rectangular plane, the normalized Modal Weighting Coefficient (MWC) amplitude, evaluated when the CCEs are individually stimulated, is presented in Fig. 3*a*. From the same Fig. 3*a* it can be observed that Mode 4 and Mode 8 are both dominant when CCE-1 and CCE-2 are individually excited over the structure. Moreover, these current modes present a null of the radiation pattern at broadside direction (Mode 4) and at 30 ° off broadside direction (Mode 8), as shown in Fig. 3*b*.

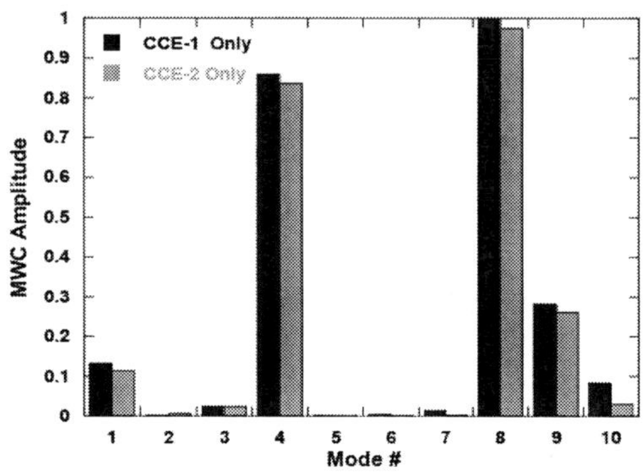

(a)

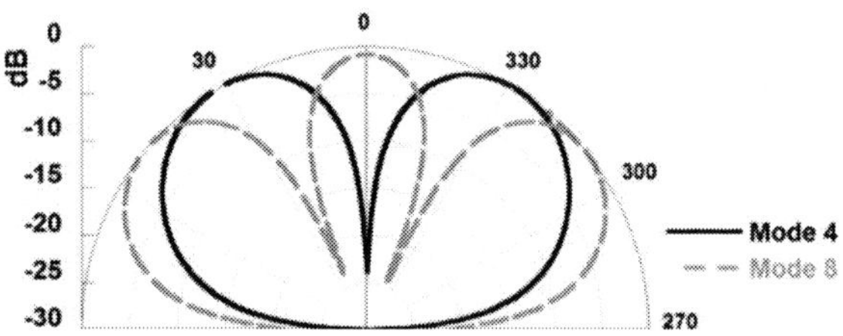

(b)

Fig. 3 *(a)* Normalized MWC amplitude when the probes are individually excited and *(b)* the normalized radiation pattern for the Mode 4 and Mode 8.

By exploiting the linear superposition of the Mode 4 and Mode 8 current, it is possible achieve a pattern-control antenna. More in detail, the excitation degree of the current distribution related to the Mode 4 and Mode 8 can be altered by modifying the phase difference ($\Delta\theta$) between the CCEs. This characteristic is well visible through Fig. 4 where the percentage power excitation related to the Mode 4 and Mode 8 are illustrated as a function of the phase difference between the CCEs. In particular, when the exciters are fed in phase, only Mode 4 will be efficiently stimulated over the antenna. On the contrary, if the CCEs are fed in out of phase, Mode 8 will be dominant over the antenna. In all the other configurations of the phase difference ($\Delta\theta$), there is a weighted linear superposition of the two excited modes. This variation of the modes excitation degree enables to obtain different radiation pattern useful to realize a pattern-control antenna.

Additional details regarding the feeding network and the total radiation pattern with respect to the phase difference will be presented at the conference.

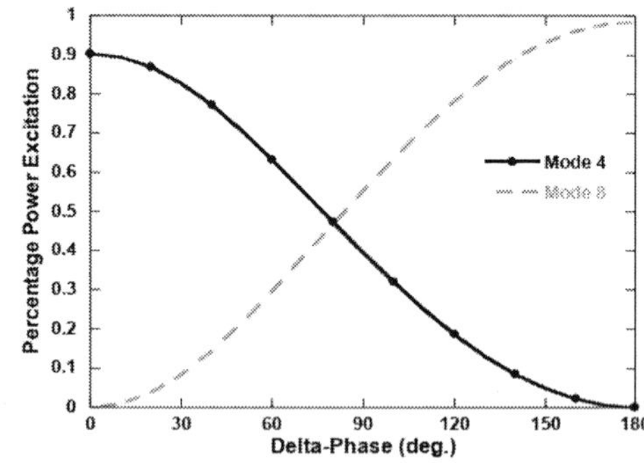

Fig. 4 Percentage of power excitation of the Mode 4 and Mode 8 as a function of the phase difference.

REFERENCES

[1] S. Genovesi, A. Di Candia, and A. Monorchio, "Compact and Low Profile Frequency Agile Antenna for Multistandard Wireless Communication Systems," *IEEE Trans. Antennas Propag.*, vol. 62, no. 3, pp. 1019–1026, Mar. 2014.

[2] S. Yang, C. Zhang, H. K. Pan, A. E. Fathy, and V. K. Nair, "Frequency-reconfigurable antennas for multiradio wireless platforms," *IEEE Microw. Mag.*, vol. 10, no. 1, pp. 66–83, Feb. 2009.

[3] S. Genovesi, A. Monorchio, M. B. Borgese, S. Pisu, and F. M. Valeri, "Frequency-Reconfigurable Microstrip Antenna With Biasing Network Driven by a PIC Microcontroller," *IEEE Antennas Wirel. Propag. Lett.*, vol. 11, pp. 156–159, 2012.

[4] C. G. Christodoulou, Y. Tawk, S. A. Lane, and S. R. Erwin, "Reconfigurable Antennas for Wireless and Space Applications," *Proc. IEEE*, vol. 100, no. 7, pp. 2250–2261, Jul. 2012.

[5] R. Harrington and J. Mautz, "Theory of characteristic modes for conducting bodies," *IEEE Trans. Antennas Propag.*, vol. 19, no. 5, pp. 622–628, Settembre 1971.

[6] R. Garbacz and R. Turpin, "A generalized expansion for radiated and scattered fields," *IEEE Trans. Antennas Propag.*, vol. 19, no. 3, pp. 348–358, Maggio 1971.

[7] D. Manteuffel and R. Martens, "Compact Multi Mode Multi Element Antenna for Indoor UWB Massive MIMO," *IEEE Trans. Antennas Propag.*, pp. 1–1, 2016.

[8] D. Manteuffel and R. Martens, "Systematic design method of a mobile multiple antenna system using the theory of characteristic modes," *IET Microw. Antennas Propag.*, vol. 8, no. 12, pp. 887–893, Sep. 2014.

[9] H. Li, Y. Tan, B. K. Lau, Z. Ying, and S. He, "Characteristic Mode Based Tradeoff Analysis of Antenna-Chassis Interactions for Multiple Antenna Terminals," *IEEE Trans. Antennas Propag.*, vol. 60, no. 2, pp. 490–502, Feb. 2012.

[10] H. Li, Z. T. Miers, and B. K. Lau, "Design of Orthogonal MIMO Handset Antennas Based on Characteristic Mode Manipulation at Frequency Bands Below 1 GHz," *IEEE Trans. Antennas Propag.*, vol. 62, no. 5, pp. 2756–2766, May 2014.

[11] T.-Y. Shih and N. Behdad, "Bandwidth Enhancement of Platform-Mounted HF Antennas Using the Characteristic Mode Theory," *IEEE Trans. Antennas Propag.*, pp. 1–1, 2016.

[12] Y. Chen and C.-F. Wang, "Electrically Small UAV Antenna Design Using Characteristic Modes," *IEEE Trans. Antennas Propag.*, vol. 62, no. 2, pp. 535–545, Feb. 2014.

[13] Y. Chen and C.-F. Wang, "HF Band Shipboard Antenna Design Using Characteristic Modes," *IEEE Trans. Antennas Propag.*, vol. 63, no. 3, pp. 1004–1013, Mar. 2015.

[14] F. Dicandia, S. Genovesi, and A. Monorchio, "Null-Steering Antenna Design by Using Phase-Shifted Characteristic Modes," *IEEE Trans. Antennas Propag.*, pp. 1–1, 2016.

[15] R. Martens, E. Safin, and D. Manteuffel, "Inductive and capacitive excitation of the characteristic modes of small terminals," in *Antennas and Propagation Conference (LAPC), 2011 Loughborough*, 2011, pp. 1–4.

[16] R. Valkonen, A. Lehtovuori, and D. Manteuffel, "Capacitive coupling elements—Changing the way of designing antennas," in *Antennas and Propagation (EuCAP), 2014 8th European Conference on*, 2014, pp. 229–233.

[17] R. Martens, E. Safin, and D. Manteuffel, "Selective excitation of characteristic modes on small terminals," in *Antennas and Propagation (EUCAP), Proceedings of the 5th European Conference on*, 2011, pp. 2492–2496.

Reverse Operation Self-consistent Evaluation Applied to IE-DDM with Phase Extracted Basis Function

Jun Hu, Ming Jiang, Lin Lei and Zaiping Nie
School of Electronic Engineering
University of Electronic Science and Technology of China,
Chengdu 611731
Email: hujun@uestc.edu.cn

***Abstract*—An integral equation with non-conformal and non-overlapping domain decomposition method has aroused wide interest in the engineering community. The contribution of this paper is twofold: (I) In the framework of IE-DDM, phase-extracted (PE) basis function is employed to reduce the required number of unknowns in the large and smooth sub-domain. (II) A reverse operation self-consistent evaluation (ROSE) presents a novel way to implement the Robin transmission condition, which is an attractive alternative to the traditional union mesh technique. We show that the benefit of the the application of ROSE is to redue the burden of Gaussian quadrature on the union mesh. Several numerical case studies will be presented to validate the efficacy and flexibility of the proposed technique.**

I. Introduction

The multi-scale simulation of reality electromagnetic problems is critical in practical engineering community. Surface integral equation (SIE) method enhanced by fast algorithms such as the multilevel fast multipole algorithm (MLFMA) has shown its great power for solving electromagnetic radiation or scattering problem. However, a computational bottleneck is that iterative method combined with fast algorithm deal poorly with the ill-conditioned matrix system which caused by complicated multi-scale structure. Domain decomposition method provides an effective way to solve these real applications. In the last few years, the surface integral equation based domain decomposition method (IE-DDM) [1] has been successfully applied to solve large, multi-scale electromagnetic problems. In fact, DDM provides a flexible and efficient framework for traditional integral equation methods, which decompose the original complicate problem into several smaller and more easily solved subproblems. Due to the decomposition into subproblems, IE-DDM is well suited for the coupling of a variety of IE solvers. In addition, DDM is often applied to construct efficient preconditioner for the finial matrix system. Applying these ideas, IE-DDM has been succesfully used to the lots of practical applications including arbitrarily shaped deep cavity, multilayer dielectric objects [2] , thin dielectric coating problems and general composite objects [3]. However, it is still thought to be a grand challenge when numerical simulation faces tremendous computational and memory cost. In order to reduce the number of knowns in EM simulation, lots of efforts focusing on new basis functions have been made in the last two decades. One of them called phase extracted (PE) basis functions is proposed. A theoretical derivation is given to show the travelling wave phase dependence of the induced current on the smooth surface of PEC targets as a physical explanation of such kind of basis functions. To further improve the computational efficiency, IE-DDM based on phase-extracted basis functions (IE-PE-DDM) is firstly proposed in this paper. PE basis functions [4] have the capability of describing the phase variation of the current in the definition domain, Because the traveling wave phase term is the dominant term of the induced current on the large, smooth PEC surface, the curvilinear Rao-Wilton-Glisson (CRWG) basis functions combined with the traveling wave phase factor can be defined on much larger patches than the traditional ones. When an electrically large system consists of the large platform and some tiny structures, DDM strategy is firstly employed to divide it into serval sub-domains. Then PE basis functions can be implemented to model the large and smooth sub-domain. This simple technique leads to obvious reduction of number of the basis functions. On the other hand, in this paper a novel reverse operation self-consistent evaluation (ROSE) is proposed to effectively deal with Robin transmission condition (TC) in our non-conformal IE-DDM. Different from traditional approach to address the issue of numerical integration over the non-conforming meshes on the interface, where the mortar matrix is implemented directly via a union mesh technique, the proposed method is constructed reversely from the mass matrix which can be achieved cheaply. And the accuracy of the recovered mortar matrix is similar to that of the direct method. The main advantage of this approach is to avoid dealing with non-conforming meshes on the curved interface.

II. Formulation

A. IE-DDM based on PE basis function

In the framework of IE-DDM, DDM strategy is firstly employed to divide complex structure into serval sub-domains according to the geometry feature of the structure. Then PE basis functions are employed to model the large and smooth subdomain to further reduce the number of unknowns required. For smooth and convex objects, it has been demonstrated that the phase dependence of the induced current on the PEC surface shows the same property of the traveling wave phase. The basis functions approximate the induced surface current can be expressed as the multiplication of two factors: the amplitude factor and the phase factor. Here, curvilinear RWG (CRWG) functions supposed by curvilinear triangular patches is chosen as the amplitude term of the PE basis functions, because of its quality of representing arbitrary curvilinear surfaces. So the phase extracted basis function can be defined as:

$$\boldsymbol{J}(\boldsymbol{r}) = \boldsymbol{j}(\boldsymbol{r})\, e^{i\boldsymbol{k}^{inc}\cdot\boldsymbol{r}} \tag{1}$$

Where, $\boldsymbol{j}(\boldsymbol{r})$ is the unknown amplitude factor, and $e^{i\boldsymbol{k}^{inc}\cdot\boldsymbol{r}}$ is the phase factor related to direction of the incident plane wave.

B. Reverse Operation Self-consistent Evaluation for TC in IE-DDM

Transmission condition plays an important role in the non-conformal domain decomposition method. In the IE-DDM, the Robin TC is used to enforce the continuity of electric current between adjoined subdomains. The corresponding discretization matrices are usually named mass matrix and mortar matrix respectively. Suppose the currents on the left and right mesh are expanded by and respectively,

$$\boldsymbol{j}_{12} = \sum_{i}^{m} \alpha_i x_i^L = \boldsymbol{\alpha}\cdot\boldsymbol{X}^L \tag{2}$$

$$-\boldsymbol{j}_{21} = \sum_{i}^{m} \beta_i x_i^R = \boldsymbol{\beta}\cdot\boldsymbol{X}^R \tag{3}$$

After using Galerkin test, we can get

$$\boldsymbol{B}\cdot\boldsymbol{X}^L = \boldsymbol{A}\cdot\boldsymbol{X}^R \tag{4}$$

Where $\boldsymbol{B} = \langle\boldsymbol{\beta},\boldsymbol{\alpha}\rangle$ and $\boldsymbol{A} = \langle\boldsymbol{\beta},\boldsymbol{\beta}\rangle$. Here, the inner product is defined as $\langle\boldsymbol{u},\boldsymbol{v}\rangle = \int \boldsymbol{u}\cdot\boldsymbol{v}\mathrm{dr}$. $\boldsymbol{A}$ is the mass matrix which can be easily calculated and $\boldsymbol{B}$ is mortar matrix. In ROSE, we reconstruct mortar matrix row by row from the mass matrix based on a set of chosen known samples of $\boldsymbol{X}^L$ and $\boldsymbol{X}^R$, which should satisfy the relation self-consistently.

III. Numerical results

A PEC sphere of radius $r = 16\lambda_0$ is considered. The geometry is averagely divided into two subdomains. The plane wave is incident from z axis with θ polarization. In the scheme of IE-DDM, ROSE is implemented in the Robin TC. PE basis function is used to model the induced current on the surface of sphere with a 0.5 mesh, which results in 65,422 unknowns. While traditional IE-DDM-MLFMA using RWG basis function with a 0.125 mesh, which results in 816,045 unknowns. The computational statistics comparison between traditional IE-DDM and the proposed method is shown in TABLEI. we can see that the proposed method can dramatically reduce the computational and memory cost. The bistatic RCS is presented in Fig.1. It shows the results of the proposed method agree well with those of Mie series and traditional IE-DDM-MLFMA.

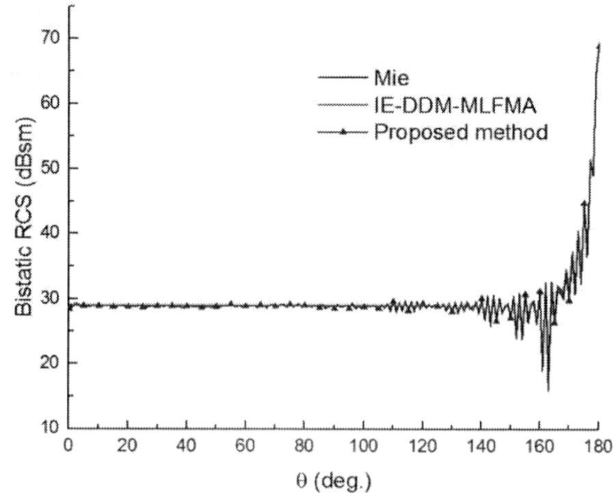

Fig. 1. The bistatic RCS for a PEC sphere ($16\lambda_0$) obtained from the Mie series, IE-DDM and the proposed method.

TABLE I
COMPUTATIONAL STATISTICS COMPARISON OF IE-DDM AND IE-DDM WITH PE BASIS FUNCTIONS

Methods	Unknowns	Memory(MB)	Iterations	CPU(h)
IE-DDM	816,045	12.5	7	6.2
IE-PE-DDM	65,422	1.2	5	1.2

IV. Conclusion

In this paper, IE-PE-DDM using ROSE is proposed to solve the electromagnetic scattering problems. Describing the phase variation of the induced current successfully, the PE basis functions can be used in the large and smooth subdomain, which results in the dramatic reduction of the number of unknowns. In the other hand, ROSE scheme provides great flexibilty and adantage for dealing with non-matching meshes on the touching face, especially for the curved surface.

Acknowledgment

The authors wish to acknowledge Professor Jin-fa Lee at Ohio State University for the valuable discussion on the ROSE. This work was partially supported by Chang Jiang Scholar Project of MOE.

References

[1] Z. Peng, K.H.Lim, and J. F. Lee "Computations of electromagnetic wave scattering from penetrable composite targets using a surface integral equation method with multiple traces," *IEEE Trans. Antennas Propag.*, vol. 61, no. 1, pp. 256–269,Jan. 2013

[2] J. Hu, R. Zhao, M. Tian, et al,"Domain Decomposition Method Based on Integral Equation for Solution of Scattering From Very Thin, Conducting Cavity," *IEEE Trans.Antennas Propag.* vol. 62, no.10 pp. 53445348, 2014.

[3] M. Jiang, J. Hu, M. Tian, R. Zhao, Z. Nie, "Solving Scattering by Multilayer Dielectric Objects Using JMCFIE-DDM-MLFMA," *IEEE Antennas and Wireless Propagation Letters,* vol. 13, pp. 11321135, Jun. 2014.

[4] Z. Nie, S.Yan, S. He and J. Hu "On the basis functions with traveling wave phase factor for efficient analysis of scattering from electrically large targets," *Progr. Electromagn. Res.*, vol.85, pp.83-114.2008.

Progress in Developing Custom Cubature Rules for Computational Electromagnetics

Malcolm M. Bibby and Andrew F. Peterson
School of Electrical Engineering
Georgia Institute of Technology
Atlanta, GA, 30332-0250, USA
mbibby@ece.gatech.edu, peterson@ece.gatech.edu

***Abstract*—Computational electromagnetics often requires the creation of quadrature and cubature rules beyond those found in the literature. In many situations rules are required for the accurate evaluation of integrals containing singularities; examples include 1/*R* singularities and singularities in the basis functions used to represent current or charge density at sharp edges and corners. Techniques for synthesizing quadrature rules involve the solution of nonlinear systems of equations. This presentation will describe recent progress as well as some of the challenges encountered by the authors in multidimensional quadrature rule synthesis.**

Keywords—cubature; nonlinear equations; optimization; quadrature

I. Introduction

Computational Electromagnetics often involves the evaluation of multidimensional integrals for which no analytical result is known. There is a need for quadrature rules, especially specialized rules that can accurately integrate non-polynomial functions that may contain edge singularities or Green's function singularities. At the present time, such rules are not generally available and must be synthesized by the user. This process requires the simultaneous solution of large systems of nonlinear equations. Algorithms such as Newton-Raphson iteration are quite useful for developing one-dimensional rules [1-2], but may not converge without a good initial estimate of the solution for multidimensional rules [3]. Furthermore, algorithms that use derivatives of the objective function require high precision due to the poorly-conditioned nature of the equations.

An alternative approach is to employ stochastic optimization algorithms to solve the nonlinear systems, or at least to use these algorithms to obtain a good initial estimate that can be used in a Newton-Raphson or other classical derivative-based optimizer. Simulated annealing was employed for this purpose in [4], while the MINPACK library was used in [5]. In the following, cuckoo search optimization [6-7] is investigated to obtain an approximate solution of the nonlinear system associated with two-dimensional quadrature. This approximate result is used as a starting point for Newton-Raphson iteration. During the cuckoo search optimization, the objective function evaluation involves a large number of repetitive computations and should be well-suited for implementation on a parallel architecture or a graphical processing unit (GPU). The authors' use of a GPU for these computations will be discussed in the presentation.

II. System of Equations for 1/R

As an example, consider a rule that will be used to integrate functions with a $1/R$ singularity on a rectangular domain, where

$$R = \sqrt{x^2 + y^2} . \tag{1}$$

Such a rule will exactly integrate certain terms. An order 0 rule should exactly integrate terms

$$1,\ 1/R \tag{2}$$

while a degree 1 rule will integrate those plus

$$x,\ y,\ x/R,\ y/R . \tag{3}$$

For functions with $1/R$, a rule of degree 2 will also integrate

$$x^2,\ xy,\ y^2,\ x^2/R,\ xy/R,\ y^2/R . \tag{4}$$

In the above, the term "degree" refers to the degree of the polynomial multiplying the $1/R$ factor. A system of equations imposing these constraints has entries

$$w_1 f(x_1, y_1) + \ldots + w_P f(x_P, y_P) = \iint f(x,y)\,dx\,dy \tag{5}$$

where f denotes any one of the terms appearing in (2)–(4) and P is the total number of sample points or nodes in the rule. The integral on the right side of (5) should be evaluated exactly if possible. While it is possible in principle to impose symmetry constraints of various types on the weights and nodes in these rules [5], we did not attempt to do that here. In the absence of those constraints, results are generally not unique.

To obtain a rule of degree p, we impose $k = (p+1)(p+2)$ constraints of the form (5); this is expected to produce a rule with a number of nodes

$$P > \frac{(p+1)(p+2)}{3}. \tag{6}$$

The actual value of P is determined by a trial and error process. Table I shows the number of quadrature nodes required to exactly integrate terms up to degree 8 for the $1/R$ rule.

TABLE I. PAARAMETERS FOR THE $1/R$ RULE

degree p	**# of eqns k**	**# of nodes P**	**error**
2	12	5	0.004
3	20	8	0.001
4	30	11	0.00002
5	42	15	0.00001
6	56	20	0.0000002
7	72	25	0.00000008
8	90	31	

III. CUCKOO SEARCH

The cuckoo search algorithm, which is loosely based on the behavior of cuckoo birds seeking other bird's nests in which to lay their eggs, involves the combination of a global random walk to avoid being trapped in a local minimum and a local random walk to provide systematic convergence to a solution [6-7]. For the quadrature application, the objective function to be minimized is a norm of the system residual. Unlike most optimization problems, it is known in advance that, if a solution exists, the "minimum" value of the objective function will be zero. In practice, the cuckoo algorithm may iterate for hundreds of millions of generations or more before a solution of acceptable accuracy is obtained. During each generation, the algorithm uses random variables to produce a large number of trial solutions for which the objective function must be evaluated. As mentioned above, these repetitive computations should be well-suited for implementation on a parallel architecture or a graphical processing unit (GPU).

The system of equations in (5) becomes increasingly ill-conditioned as k increases; evolutionary algorithms such as cuckoo search are relatively insensitive to this. In contrast, algorithms that compute derivatives (such as Newton-Raphson) require the use of precision higher than "double precision" to maintain accurate computations.

IV. PRELIMINARY RESULTS

The above procedure for $1/R$ was implemented and used to obtain the results in Table I. The number of required nodes P for a given degree up to 8 is reported. The fourth column in Table I reports the error in the test integral

$$\int_0^1 \int_0^1 \frac{\cos(\pi x/2)\cos(\pi y/2)}{R} dxdy \tag{5}$$

obtained using the quadrature rule for the indicated degree. As an example, Table II reports the 8 weights and nodes for a quadrature rule of degree 3.

TABLE II. WEIGHTS AND NODES FOR THE $1/R$ RULE OF DEGREE 3

w_i	x_i	y_i
0.070534423	0.1208076	0.079047263
0.064063936	0.5214616	0.016468737
0.093200885	0.058877312	0.3527261
0.063970089	0.9898745	0.1667722
0.079929873	0.1064754	0.9088678
0.084370360	0.9534074	0.9407588
0.2809690	0.6728699	0.3828864
0.2629614	0.4230915	0.7234123

V. CHALLENGES

The large computation times associated with cuckoo search in serial code motivated a GPU implementation. This was attempted in CUDA FORTRAN [8]. The transition from sequential to parallel code was not straightforward and involved a learning curve on both the semantics of CUDA and also on debugging tools suitable for use with the GPU. The implementation involved generating pseudo-random numbers on the GPU as a necessary part of the cuckoo search algorithm. Issues will be discussed in the presentation.

REFERENCES

[1] J. Ma, V. Rokhlin, and S. Wandzura, "Generalized Gaussian quadrature rules for systems of arbitrary functions," *SIAM J. Numerical Anal.*, vol. 33, pp. 971-976, 1996.

[2] A. F. Peterson and M. M. Bibby, *An Introduction to the Locally-Corrected Nyström Method*. San Rafael: Morgan & Claypool Synthesis Lectures, 2010.

[3] H. Xiao and Z. Gimbutas, "A numerical algorithm for the construction of efficient quadrature rules in two and higher dimensions," *Computers and Mathematics with Applications*, vol. 59, pp. 663-676, 2010.

[4] S. Wandzura and H. Xiao, "Symmetric quadrature rules on a triangle," *Computers and Mathematics with Applications*, vol. 45, pp. 1829-1840, 2003.

[5] L. Zhang, T. Cui, and H. Liu, "A set of symmetric quadrature rules on triangles and tetrahedra," *J. Comp. Math.*, vol. 27, pp. 89-96, 2009.

[6] X.-S. Yang and S. Deb, "Engineering optimisation by cuckoo search," *Int. J. Math. Modelling and Numerical Optimisation*, vol. 1, pp. 330-343, 2010.

[7] X.-S. Yang, ed. *Cuckoo Search and Firefly Algorithm*. Cham: Springer, 2014.

[8] CUDA FORTRAN, www.pgroup.com

Fast Monostatic Scattering Analysis Based on Bayesian Compressive Sensing

Huan Huan Zhang
The School of Electronic Engineering
Xidian University
Xi'an, China
Email: hhzhang@xidian.edu.cn

Wei E.I. Sha, Li Jun Jiang
Department of Electrical and Electronic Engineering
The University of Hong Kong
Hong Kong
Email: wsha@eee.hku.hk (Sha); jianglj@hku.hk (Jiang)

***Abstract*—In conjugation with the method of moments, the Bayesian compressive sensing algorithm is utilized to fast analyze the monostatic electromagnetic scattering problem. Different from the orthogonal matching pursuit based compressive sensing approach that cannot determine the required measurement times, the proposed method overcomes the difficulty by adopting the Bayesian framework to recover the underlying signal. Error bars of the signal can be obtained in the recovery procedure, which offers a way to adaptively determine the number of compressive-sensing measurements.**

Keywords—Monostatic scattering, method of moments, Bayesian compressive sensing.

I. INTRODUCTION

When utilizing method of moments (MoM) to acquire echo signals from a large amount of aspect angles, one has to run the simulation code multiple times depending on the number of aspect angles for obtaining all the echo signals. Actually, it takes a great amount of CPU times to analyze electrically-large objects per one simulation. Hence there is an urgent demand to accelerate the simulation process of monostatic scattering analysis.

Two kinds of efforts have been made to achieve this goal. One is to speed up the single simulation by using fast algorithms like fast multipole method. An alternative way is to reduce the total number of simulations by using algorithms including asymptotic waveform evaluation (AWE) [1], model-based parameter estimation (MBPE) [2], excitation matrix compression methods [3], etc. However, these algorithms show some shortcomings. For the AWE and MBPE, a multi-point expansion or interpolation is needed for wide-angle simulations. The major technical challenge is to adaptively choose the expansion points or interpolation points. The excitation matrix compression methods compress the excitation matrix and remove redundancies in the initial excitation assembly. The right-hand-side matrix has to be stored explicitly. Moreover, a SVD-based compression is limited to small-sized matrices due to the high computational complexity.

A compressive sensing (CS) based method is proposed in [4] for fast analysis of wide-angle monostatic scattering problems, which fall into the second category algorithm described above. This method employs CS to construct a new set of right-hand-side vectors for MoM, where the number of constructed right-hand-side vectors is much less than the original ones. Unfortunately, it has been found that for the orthogonal matching pursuit (OMP) algorithm [5] adopted to solve the optimization problem, the number of measurements cannot be determined adaptively, just like that the number of expansion or interpolation points is hard to be predefined in [1-2]. This sets up a limit for the practical applications of this technique. In this paper, we adopt the Bayesian compressive sensing (BCS) method [6] to remedy the limitation. Bayesian framework is utilized to recover the underlying signals. Error bars of the signal can be obtained in the recovery procedure, leading to an effective strategy for adaptively determining the number of compressive-sensing measurements.

II. PRINCIPLES AND FORMULATIONS

Considering a monostatic scattering problem with multiple incident angles $\theta_1, \theta_2, \cdots \theta_M$, then the following M matrix equations need to be solved

$$\mathbf{ZI}(\theta_i) = \mathbf{V}(\theta_i),\ i = 1, 2, \cdots, M. \tag{1}$$

Here, we assume that $\mathrm{I}_n(\theta_i)$ represents the current coefficients of the n-th element in $\mathbf{I}(\theta_i)$ and $n = 1, 2, \cdots, N$. Based on the CS theory, the measurement matrix $\phi = \left[c_{ij} \middle| i = 1, 2, \cdots, M';\ j = 1, 2, \cdots, M\right]$ can be constructed by independent and identically distributed Gaussian random variables. Then, the measurement values of $\{I_n(\theta_1),\ I_n(\theta_2), \cdots,\ I_n(\theta_M)\}$ can be written as

$$\begin{pmatrix} I_{n1}^{CS} \\ I_{n2}^{CS} \\ \vdots \\ I_{nM'}^{CS} \end{pmatrix} = \begin{pmatrix} c_{11} & c_{12} & c_{13} & \cdots & c_{1M} \\ c_{21} & c_{22} & c_{23} & \cdots & c_{2M} \\ \vdots & \vdots & \vdots & \ddots & \vdots \\ c_{M'1} & c_{M'2} & c_{M'3} & \cdots & c_{M'M} \end{pmatrix} \begin{pmatrix} I_n(\theta_1) \\ I_n(\theta_2) \\ \vdots \\ \vdots \\ I_n(\theta_M) \end{pmatrix}. \tag{2}$$

The m-th measurement can be expressed as

$$I_{nm}^{CS} = \sum_{i=1}^{M} c_{mi} I_n(\theta_i), \tag{3}$$

Let $\mathbf{I}_m^{CS} = \{I_{1m}^{CS}, I_{2m}^{CS}, \cdots, I_{Nm}^{CS}\}$, then we have

$$\mathbf{ZI}_m^{CS} = \mathbf{Z}\begin{pmatrix} \mathbf{I}_{1m}^{CS} \\ \mathbf{I}_{2m}^{CS} \\ \vdots \\ \mathbf{I}_{Nm}^{CS} \end{pmatrix} = \mathbf{Z}\begin{pmatrix} \sum_{i=1}^{M} c_{mi} I_1(\theta_i) \\ \sum_{i=1}^{M} c_{mi} I_2(\theta_i) \\ \vdots \\ \sum_{i=1}^{M} c_{mi} I_N(\theta_i) \end{pmatrix} = \sum_{i=1}^{M} c_{mi} \mathbf{ZI}(\theta_i) = \sum_{i=1}^{M} c_{mi} \mathbf{V}(\theta_i). \tag{4}$$

So the M' measurement values of each current coefficient can be obtained by changing the subscript m in (4) from 1 to M'. Since $M' < M$, the number of equations to be solved can be greatly reduced.

According to the theory of CS, if the unknown vector $\{I_n(\theta_1), I_n(\theta_2), \cdots, I_n(\theta_M)\}$ is compressible in terms of orthonormal bases Ψ, i.e.

$$\begin{pmatrix} I_n(\theta_1) \\ I_n(\theta_2) \\ \vdots \\ \vdots \\ I_n(\theta_M) \end{pmatrix} = \Psi\omega, \tag{5}$$

Substitute (5) into (2), ω can be obtained by solving the following matrix equation:

$$\begin{pmatrix} I_{n1}^{CS} \\ I_{n2}^{CS} \\ \vdots \\ I_{nM'}^{CS} \end{pmatrix} = \phi\Psi\omega = \Phi\omega \tag{6}$$

A reconstruction algorithm is required to recover ω from M' measurements. Here, we adopt the BCS algorithm [6]. Due to the nature of BCS, the proposed method can adaptively determine the number of measurement.

III. Numerical Results

A PEC missile model as shown in Fig. 1 is analyzed. The maximum size in the x, y and z directions are 1.4 m, 0.62 m and 0.25 m. It is discretized into 6792 unknowns at 1.5 GHz. The warhead is placed towards the positive direction of x-axis. The elevation angle of the incident wave is fixed to be 90°, while the aspect angle ranges from 0° to 180° with the increment of 0.5°. Both the proposed method (BCS) and the method in [4] (CS_OMP) are adopted to analyze the monostatic scattering problem and their results are compared to those of MLFMM as shown in Fig. 1. Table I lists the measurement number and CPU time for different methods. The number of measurements of the proposed method is determined to be 63 adaptively, and the result agrees well with

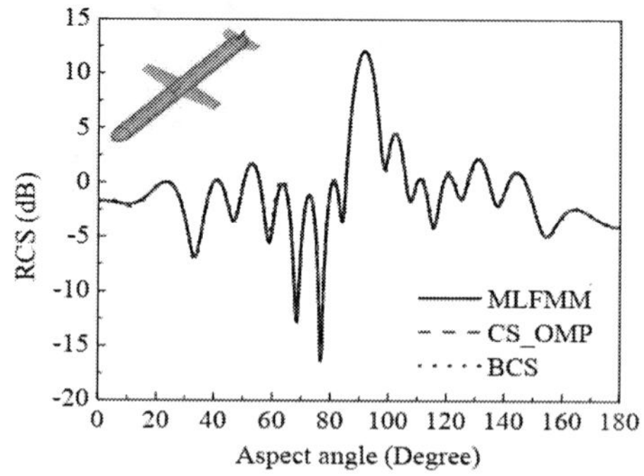

Fig. 1. Monostatic RCS of the missile model obtained by MLFMM, CS_OMP and BCS.

TABLE I. MEASUREMENT NUMBER AND CPU TIME OF THREE DIFFERENT METHODS FOR THE MISSILE MODEL

Method	Measurement Number	CPU Time (s)
MLFMM	360	5527
CS_OMP	71	1272
BCS	63	1295

that of MLFMM. Since the CS_OMP method cannot determine the number of measurement, we tried several different measurement number and selected the smallest one possessing a comparable level of accuracy with the proposed method. The measurement number determined in such a manner for the CS_OMP method is 71. Although the measurement time of the BCS method is less than the CS_OMP method, their CPU time are comparable because the computational complexity of the BCS algorithm is larger.

Acknowledgment

This work was supported in part by the Research Grants Council of GRF 17210815, GRF 17207114, GRF 716713E, NSFC 61271158, Hong Kong UGC AoE/P–04/08, Fundamental Research Funds for the Central Universities JB160218, XJS16048.

References

[1] M. S. Chen, X. L. Wu and W. Sha, "Asymptotic waveform evaluation technique based on fast lifting wavelet transform," *Appl. Comput. Electromagn. Soc. J.*, vol. 21, no. 1, pp. 99-104, 2006.

[2] E. K. Miller, "Model-based parameter estimation in electromagnetic III: Applications to EM integral equations," *IEEE Antennas Propag. Mag.*, vol. 40, no. 3, pp. 49–66, 1998.

[3] Arne Schröder, Heinz-D. Brüns, and Christian Schuster, "A hybrid approach for rapid computation of two-dimensional monostatic radar cross section problems with the multilevel fast multipole algorithm," *IEEE Trans. Antennas Propag.*, vol. 60, no. 12, pp. 6058–6061, 2012.

[4] M. S. Chen, F. L. Liu, H. M. Du, and X. L. Wu, "Compressive sensing for fast analysis of wide-angle monostatic scattering problems," *IEEE Antennas Wirel. Propag. Lett.*, vol. 10, pp. 1243-1246, 2011.

[5] J. A. Tropp and A. Gilbert, "Signal recovery from partial information by orthogonal matching pursuit," *IEEE Trans. Inf. Theory*, vol. 53, no. 12, pp. 4655–4667, 2007.

[6] S. H. Ji, Y. Xue, and Lawrence Carin, "Bayesian Compressive Sensing," *IEEE Trans. Signal Process.*, vol. 56, no. 6, pp. 2346-2356, 2008

Small Incident Angle Transient Scattering from Shallow Cavities in a Ground Plane

Richard Uber and Aihua Wood
Department of Mathematics and Statistics
Air Force Institute of Technology
Wright-Patterson AFB, OH 45419, USA
richard.uber@afit.edu

Abstract—**This work presents applications for modeling electromagnetic scattering from two-dimensional cavities embedded in a perfectly conducting ground plane. First, the problem is discretized in time with Newmark's method, then solved using finite-element boundary-integral technique. This approach computes solutions in both cavities at the same time to strictly enforce coupled boundary conditions. Numerical experiments are conducted on rectangular cavities of different depths spaced at different intervals using Gaussian fields incident at small angles, between 10 and 30 degrees.**

I. Introduction

Electromagnetic scattering from open cavities and cavity-backed apertures has been an active area of research with applications in aircraft design and radar cross-section (RCS) modeling. Past work on cavity scatterers has focused on single-cavity environments, as in [1], [2], and time-harmonic fields, as in [3], [4]. Previous work by the authors [5] looked primarily at normal incidence transient scattering from multiple cavities. This paper discusses interactions between cavities created by transient fields at near-grazing incidence, an issue that is seen in radar applications.

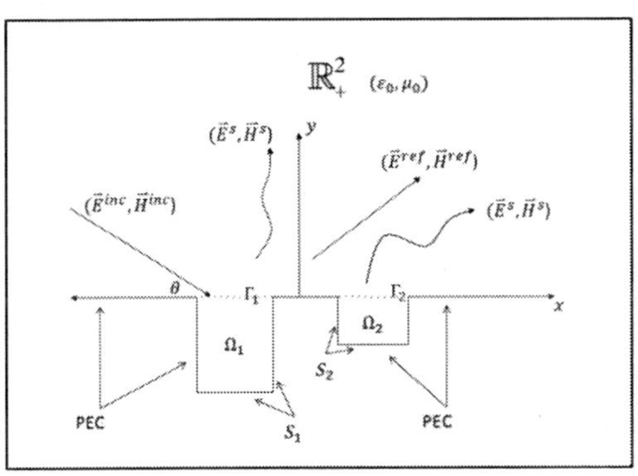

Fig. 1. Two cavity environment

II. Problem Statement

A. Problem Environment

This work considers an infinite perfectly-conducting ground plane (PEC) with two fully-embedded two-dimensional cavities. In three dimensions, these cavities are z-invariant infinite grooves, or channels. The TM^z orientation is considered here, admitting electric fields of the form $\vec{E} = [0, 0, u(x, y, t)]$. Above the ground plane is considered free space $\mathbb{R}^2_+ = \{x, y \in \mathbb{R}^2 : y \geq 0\}$ with permittivity and permeability ε_0, μ_0, respectively. The cavities, denoted Ω_1, Ω_2, may be filled with non-magnetic, non-dispersive, homogeneous, dielectric medium, with parameters μ_0, ε_j, $j = 1, 2$. $\varepsilon_j \in \mathbb{C}, \mathrm{Re}\{\varepsilon_j\} > 0, \mathrm{Im}\{\varepsilon_j\} \geq 0$. PEC cavity walls are denoted S_1, S_2 and transparent boundaries at cavity apertures are denoted Γ_1, Γ_2. This environment is illustrated in Fig. 1.

B. Transient Scattering Problem

The problem is posed as an initial value problem. Given an incident TM^z electric field $u^{inc}(x, y, t)$ defined in $\mathbb{R}^2_+ \times t \geq 0$, find the total field $u(x, y, T)$ for a given time $T > 0$ and $(x, y) \in \mathbb{R}^2_+$ subject to:

$$\begin{cases} -\Delta u + \varepsilon_r \dfrac{\partial^2 u}{\partial t^2} = 0 & \text{in } \mathbb{R}^2_+ \cup \Omega_1 \cup \Omega_2, \\ u = 0 & \text{on } \Gamma^c \cup S_1 \cup S_2, \\ \displaystyle\lim_{y\to 0+} \frac{\partial u}{\partial y} = \lim_{y \to 0-} \frac{\partial u}{\partial y} & \forall x : (x, 0) \in \Gamma_1 \cup \Gamma_2, \end{cases} \tag{1}$$

In the upper half plane, $u = u^{inc} + u^{ref} + u^s$, where u^{ref} is defined by a full reflection from a PEC ground plane. $u^s \in \mathbb{R}^2_+ \times [0, \infty)$ is purely outgoing, and subject to the standard radiation condition. Finally, we restrict the solution space to $\mathrm{H}^1(\mathbb{R}^2_+ \cup \Omega_1 \cup \Omega_2)$ so the differential form of Maxwell's equations are applicable. The numerical solution to this problem is found by first applying the Newmark method to discretize the time stepping, then using the finite-element boundary-integral (FE-BI) method at each time step to approximate the fields.

C. Newmark Method

The Newmark method, is applied as in [1], [5]. Using a fixed time step length h, the total steps to arrive at the final time T is $N = T/h$. The notation, $u^n(x, y)$ and $\dot{u}^n(x, y)$ are used to denote the approximations of $u(x, y, nh)$ and $u_t(x, y, nh)$, respectively. For the TM^z case, the generating equations are:

$$\tilde{u}^{n+1} = u^n + h\dot{u}^n + \left(\frac{1}{2} - \beta\right) h^2 \ddot{u}^n,$$

which is a prediction based on current time data, and

$$-\Delta u^{n+1} + \alpha^2 \varepsilon_r u^{n+1} = \alpha^2 \varepsilon_r \tilde{u}^{n+1}, \tag{2}$$

which is the screened Poisson equation. Equation (2) is solved numerically for u^{n+1}. Once a solution is obtained, the Newmark correction is applied:

$$\ddot{u}^{n+1} = \alpha^2(u^{n+1} - \tilde{u}^{n+1})$$
$$\dot{u}^{n+1} = \dot{u}^n + (1-\gamma)h\ddot{u}^n + \gamma h\ddot{u}^{n+1}$$

D. Exterior Solution

Given that u^{inc} is known for all time, then by applying image theory, u^{ref} is also known. Thus, u^s as the only unknown in the exterior field u in $\mathbb{R}^2_+$. Define g_0 as u^{n+1} on $\Gamma_1 \cup \Gamma_2$ and zero elsewhere on the ground plane. Given u^{inc} and g_0, the exterior fields can be solved analytically using the half-space Green's function, $G_\alpha(\vec{r}, \vec{r'})$, as demonstrated in [3], [1].

$$u^{ext}(\vec{r}) = u^{inc}(\vec{r}) - u^{inc}(\vec{r}_i) + u^s(\vec{r}).$$
$$u^s(\vec{r}) = \alpha^2 \int_{\mathbb{R}^2_+} G_\alpha \tilde{u}^s \, d\vec{r'} - \int_{\Gamma_1 \cup \Gamma_2} g_0 \frac{\partial G_\alpha}{\partial n} \, dx'.$$
$$G_\alpha(\vec{r}, \vec{r'}) = \frac{1}{2\pi}\left[K_0(\alpha|\vec{r} - \vec{r'}|) - K_0(\alpha|\vec{r} - \vec{r'_i}|)\right].$$

Where $\vec{r} = (x, y)$, $\vec{r_i} = (x, -y)$, and K_0 is the modified Bessel function of the second kind. Next, we define the Neumann boundary condition for the interior problem.

E. Interior Problem

The discretized interior problem is posed as a boundary value problem at each time step by combining information from equations (1) and (2). Thus, for each time step, in the manner presented in [1] and applied in [5]. We employ the finite element method to solve weakly the interior problem expressed by the variational formulation:

$$a(u^{n+1}, v) = b^{n+1}(v),$$

defined by:

$$a(u, v) = \langle \nabla u, \nabla v \rangle_\Omega + \alpha^2 \langle \varepsilon_r u, v \rangle_\Omega - \langle Tu, v \rangle_\Gamma,$$
$$b(v) = \alpha^2 \langle \varepsilon_r \tilde{u}, v \rangle_\Omega + \langle 2\frac{\partial u^{inc}}{\partial y} + \tilde{H}, v \rangle_\Gamma.$$
$$\tilde{H}^{n+1}(x) = \alpha^2 \int_{\mathbb{R}^2_+} \frac{\partial G_\alpha}{\partial y}((x, 0), \vec{r'}) \tilde{u}^{s,n+1}(\vec{r'}) d\vec{r'},$$
$$[T_\alpha g](x) = \frac{1}{\pi} \int_\Gamma \left[\frac{\partial^2}{\partial x^2} - \alpha^2\right] K_0(\alpha|x - x'|) g_0(x') dx'.$$

Here, Ω denotes $\Omega_1 \cup \Omega_2$ and Γ denotes $\Gamma_1 \cup \Gamma_2$.

III. Results

To demonstrate the effects of coupling between cavities, we model the multiple cavity response and compare that solution to the solutions generated from one cavity at a time. Numerical implementation of the transient FE-BI method models the aperture fields created by the incident wave. Fig. 2 shows the aperture fields from identical cavities of width 1 m and depth 0.25 m spaced 10 cm apart generated by a Gaussian incident wave

$$u^{inc} = \frac{2}{\sqrt{\pi}} e^{-\tau^2}, \quad \tau = 2(t - 3 + x\cos\theta + y\sin\theta),$$

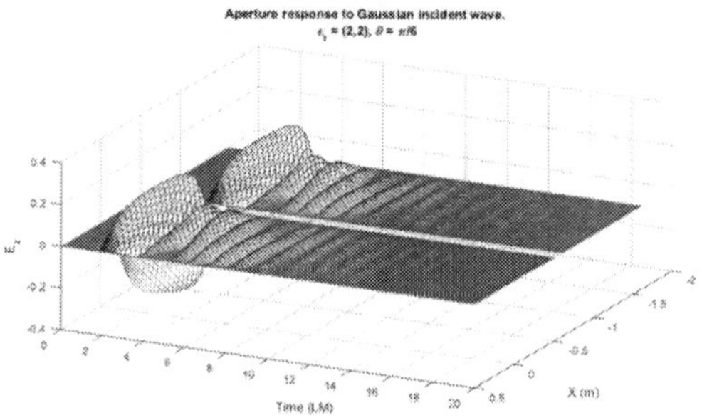

Fig. 2. Aperture fields over time with incident angle $\theta = \pi/6$

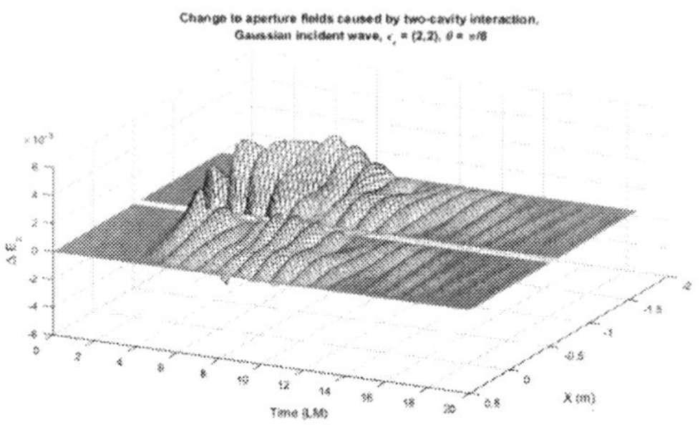

Fig. 3. Change in aperture fields due to interaction $\theta = \pi/6$

at $\theta = \pi/6$. Fig. 3 shows one example of the effect coupling has on the solution. For these cavities, spaced 10 cm apart, the relative strength of the coupling effect is about 1/500 peak response. This may be negligible at the peak, but as time progresses, the change due to interaction between cavities becomes a greater proportion of the total response.

IV. Conclusion

This work applies a computational model for transient scattering from multiple cavities to the small-incident angle environment. The novelty of this FE-BI approach is in computing solutions in both cavities at the same time to strictly enforce the coupled boundary conditions. Numerical tests were conducted on multiple cavities having different depths, spaced at different intervals, and with small incident angles ranging from 10 to 30 degrees. Expected effects from secondary reflections and interactions between the scattered fields were evident.

References

[1] T. Van and A. W. Wood, "A time-domain finite element method for Helmholtz equations", *J. Comp. Phys.*, vol. 183, pp. 486-507, 2002.

[2] P. Li, L.L. Wang, and A. W. Wood, "Analysis of transient electromagnetic scattering from a three-dimensional open cavity", *SIAM J. Appl. Math.*, vol. 75, no. 4, pp. 1675-1699, 2015.

[3] J. M. Jin, *The Finite Element Method in Electromagnetics, 3rd ed.*. Wiley: Hoboken, NJ, 2014, pp. 381-399.

[4] P. Li and A. W. Wood, "A two-dimensional Helmholtz equation solution for the multiple cavity scattering problem", *J. Comp. Phys.*, vol. 240, pp. 100-120, 2013.

[5] R. P. Uber, *Time Domain Analysis of Electromagnetic Scattering from Multiple Cavities in a Ground Plane*, PhD Dissertation, Air Force Inst. Tech., 2016.

Distributed macrobasis decomposition for the electromagnetic solution of large periodic structures

Alberto Serna, Luis Landesa
and José Manuel Taboada
Departamento de Tecnología de los
Computadores y Comunicaciones,
Escuela Politécnica, Universidad de Extremadura,
Avda. de la Universidad S/N, 10003 (Cáceres).
Correspondence to llandesa@unex.es

Mario F. Manzano
ADASA Sistemas,
Europe, Multilaterals and Africa Area,
Avda. de Sevilla, 11. 06400 Don Benito. Badajoz. And
Escuela Politécnica, Universidad de Extremadura,
Avda. de la Universidad S/N, 10003 (Cáceres).

***Abstract*—Large finite periodic problems are suitable for the application of methods to achieve high acceleration rates in the solution process. Applying distributed macrobasis decomposition to compress the method of moments impedance matrix combined to slotFFT algorithm allow to cover larger structures closer to real cases.**

Keywords*—Method of Moments, Periodic Structures, Plasmonic Materials, Surface Integral Equation, slotFFT, Macrobasis Decomposition.

I. Introduction

Periodic structures are present in many scopes of our days. The capability to analyze these structures depends on many factors: precision, mesh discretization, computing resources, etc.

To face this kind of problems in computational electromagnetics many methods have been developed. Most of them are focused on the acceleration of the matrix-vector product (MVP) in exchange of precision or the application of special conditions. Some examples are the precorrected fast Fourier transform (p-FFT)[1], the Floquet's harmony theory[2] or the multilevel fast multipole algorithm (MLFMA)[3-6].

The slotFFT algorithm[7] was developed as a proposal to face these problems, an algorithm capable of reducing the equivalent computing cost of the problem to $\mathcal{O}(N \log N)$ and applicable to finite periodic structures without precision lost. However, when nanoscale problems come under analysis the high discretization combined with the large number of elements give place to problems which still need unacceptable amounts of memory and time using the previous methods.

In order to approach these extremely large problems we combine the slotFFT algorithm with a matrix compression method based on distributed macrobasis decomposition. Through the application of this compression we can achieve great acceleration rates in the computation of the solution with a controlled precision lost.

II. slotFFT

The slotFFT algorithm takes advantage of the block patterns that appear in the impedance matrix when the structure under analysis is periodic. These patterns can be described based on the relative position between elements and the numbers of basis (N) which describe the periodic element, ie. the associated block to the coupling between adjacent elements $Z_{1,2}$ in a linear periodic structure will appear repeated in the impedance matrix with a stepped pattern, as shown in Fig. 1.

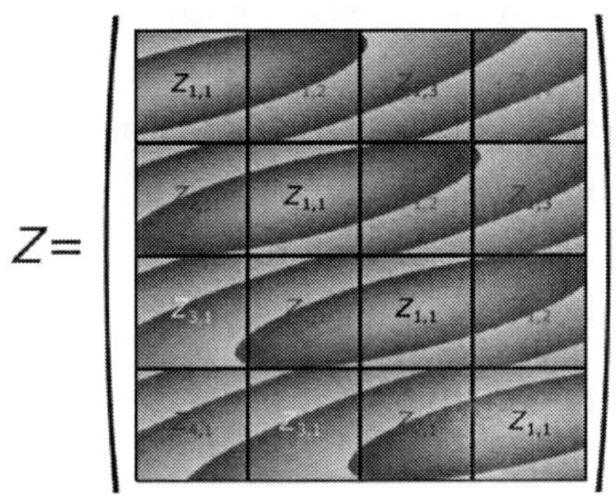

Fig. 1. Representation of a fictitious impedance matrix with periodic patterns.

Due to this patterns the impedance matrix can be posed only with the blocks contained in the first row and column of blocks ($Z_{i,1}$ and $Z_{1,i}$ blocks). This allows to apply signal theory concepts to perform the operations of the MVP in the transformed domain through fast Fourier transforms and inverse transforms, reducing the MVP cost from $\mathcal{O}(N^2)$ to an equivalent $\mathcal{O}(N \log N)$.

III. Distributed macrobasis decomposition

The aim of the distributed macrobasis decomposition is to allow the perform of matrix compression. The power radiated by the scattering of an object is related to the currents generated in that object(e.g. equivalent electric and magnetic currents in dielectric problems).

In general, a quadratic functional relates currents and the total radiated power by these currents. In a discretized solution of the currents, the total radiated power can be obtained as $P_r = x^H G x$, where x denotes the M coefficients describing the currents and G is a $M \times M$ positive definite matrix. In practice, G matrix is near to be rank deficient (only few eigenvalue are significative); this implies that only a small set of currents are radiating power in far-field. The remaining eigenvalues represents currents radiating only reactive modes in near field.

By picking only the first eigenvalues and eigenvectors it can be built a set of macrobasis functions for the currents which describes the far-field radiation. These macrobasis are not valid in the proximity of the object, since the reactive radiation is not well described by this macrobasis.

This method uses the first eigenvectors to build the macrobasis for far-field radiation combined with original basis for the near field interaction between objects. For the generation of the matrix G it has been demonstrated that G can be calculated using the original *kernel* integral operators of the method of moments. The eigenvalues and eigenvectors are calculated using the singular value decomposition method.

IV. Results

An example of the obtained results can be seen in Fig. 2. The scattering diagram shown belongs to a cube shaped array of gold spheres of $\lambda/2$ of diameter separated by 50nm analyzed for a wavelength of 785nm.

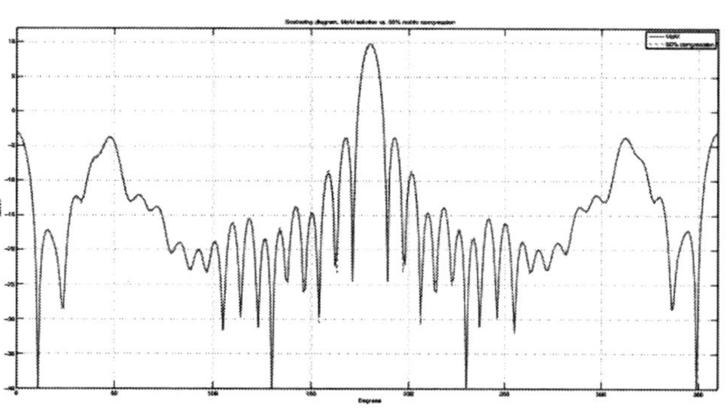

Fig. 2. Comparison of the scattering diagram obtained though method of moments and through application of the distributed macrobasis compression method.

The example needed over 37 hours of computing time to achieve a relative residual under 1e-6 using the generalized minimal residual method (GMRES), whereas the same example needed less than 12 hours applying a 50% compression.

V. Conclusion

The preliminary results show a high potential of application of the macrobasis decomposition method shown for extremely large periodic electromagnetic problems even in high coupling scenarios where the matrix compression tend to give poor results. More details about slotFFT and the macrobasis generation are going to be explained in the conference talk.

Acknowledgment

This work was supported by the European Regional Development Fund (ERDF) and the Spanish Ministerio de Economía y Competitividad (Projects MAT2014-58201-C2-1-R, MAT2014-58201-C2-2-R, Project TACTICA), from the ERDF and the Extremadura Regional Government (Junta de Extremadura) (Project GR15052) and from the Spanish Ministerio de Educación, Cultura y Deporte (Project FPU 00022/15).

References

[1] M. Veysoglu, R. Shin, and J. Kong, "A finite-difference time-domain analysis of wave scattering from periodic surfaces: Oblique incidence case," *Journal of Electromagnetic Waves and Applications*, vol. 7, no. 12, pp. 1595–1607, 1993.

[2] K. Yang, F. Wei, and A. Yilmaz, "Truncated multigrid versus pre-corrected fft/aim for bioelectromagnetics: When is o(n) better than o(nlogn)?," in *Computational Electromagnetics International Workshop (CEM), 2011*, pp. 153–158, Aug 2011.

[3] M. G. Araújo, J. M. Taboada, J. Rivero, D. M. Solís, and F. Obelleiro, "Solution of large-scale plasmonic problems with the multilevel fast multipole algorithm," *Opt. Lett.*, vol. 37, pp. 416–418, Feb 2012.

[4] Özgür Ergül and L. Gürel, "Fast and accurate analysis of large-scale composite structures with the parallel multilevel fast multipole algorithm," *J. Opt. Soc. Am. A*, vol. 30, pp. 509–517, Mar 2013.

[5] Özgür Ergül, "Analysis of composite nanoparticles with surface integral equations and the multilevel fast multipole algorithm," *Journal of Optics*, vol. 14, no. 6, p. 062701, 2012.

[6] Özgür Ergül and L. Gürel, "Accurate solutions of extremely large integral-equation problems in computational electromagnetics," *Proceedings of the IEEE*, vol. 101, no. 2, pp. 342–349, 2013.

[7] A. Serna, M. Manzano, L. Landesa, D. Solís, and J. Taboada, "Electromagnetic analysis of periodic structures with slotfft algorithm," in *2016 10th European Conference on Antennas and Propagation (EuCAP)*, April 2016.

Multi-trace boundary integral formulations with eddy current models

Xavier Claeys
Sorbonne Universités, UPMC Univ. Paris 6
Laboratoire Jacques-Louis Lions
INRIA EPC Alpines
4 place Jussieu, 75005 Paris, France
Email: claeys@ann.jussieu.fr

Edouard Demaldent
CEA LIST
Saclay, 91191 Gif-sur-Yvette, France
Email: edouard.demaldent@cea.fr

***Abstract*—We are interested in boundary integral formulations adapted to the solution of low frequency inductive electromagnetics in the case where the geometry is partitioned in (potentially irregular) subdomains. In the context of electromagnetics in piecewise homogeneous media, the multi-trace formalism (MTF) provides boundary integral formulations for Maxwell's equations posed at the interfaces between different media, with the unknowns associated to one medium a priori decoupled from the unknowns associated to other media. This makes MTF a comfortable paradigm for integral equation based domain decomposition.**

This formalism is recent and, so far, has been studied only for electromagnetics in time harmonic regime. In this contribution, we adapt the multi-trace approach to the case where the effective permittivity vanishes in certain subdomains. We study the theoretical properties of these new formulations, and discuss its numerical stability.

I. Motivations

Eddy current testing (ECT) is widely used by industrials for the inspection of conductive components, and simulation techniques are needed for the design of new testing procedures as well as for the evaluation of existing ones. Most often based on a finite element (FEM) calculation of the quasi-static fields, modelling a realistic inspection with thin air gap between the inspected part and the moving probe requires the introduction of specific discretization tools or the coupling to the boundary element method (FEM-BEM). The BEM can be used on both sides of the interface between the air and the conductive component as soon as the inspected workpiece is considered as an isotropic and homogeneous medium. For few years, the CEA LIST has been developping a BEM solution dedicated to low frequency electromagnetic testing [1], especially to model the ECT of steam generator tubes in nuclear pressurized water reactors [2]. This new contribution is the result of a recent collaboration with the JLL laboratory, and aims to extend this BEM solution to the modelling of piecewise homogeneous media with several components in contact, as illustrated in Figure 1.

II. A problem of low frequency electromagnetics

Consider a partition of free space $\mathbb{R}^3 = \cup_{j=0}^{n}\overline{\Omega}_j$ where $\Omega_j \cap \Omega_k = \emptyset$, each Ω_j being a potentially irregular subdomain that

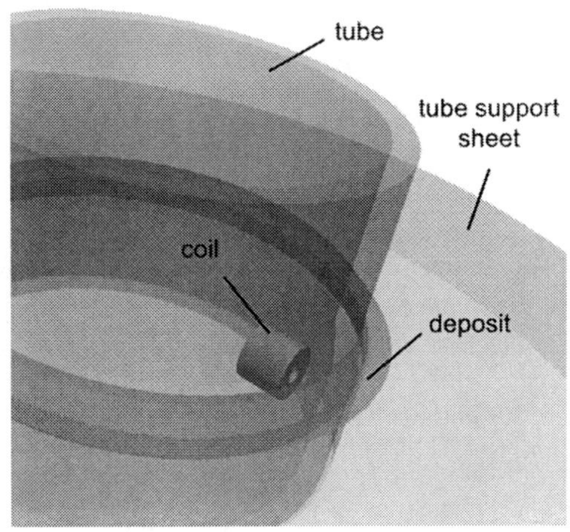

Fig. 1. Example of ECT involving several components in contact.

is bounded for $j \neq 0$. In this contribution, we are interested in solving the equations of time harmonic electromagnetics

$$\begin{array}{ll} \mathbf{curl}(\mathbf{E}) - \imath\omega\mu\mathbf{H} = 0 & \text{in } \mathbb{R}^3 \\ \mathbf{curl}(\mathbf{H}) + \imath\omega\epsilon\mathbf{E} = \mathbf{j} & \text{in } \mathbb{R}^3 \\ \text{+ Silver-Müller's radiation condition} & \end{array} \quad (1)$$

where $\mathrm{div}(\mathbf{j}) = 0$, and where ϵ (resp. μ) is the piecewise constant electric permittivity (resp. the magnetic permeability): $\mu(\mathbf{x}) = \mu_j > 0$ and $\epsilon(\mathbf{x}) = \epsilon_j$ with $\Re e\{\epsilon_j\}, \Im m\{\epsilon_j\} \geq 0$ for $\mathbf{x} \in \Omega_j$. Denoting

$$\kappa_j := \omega\sqrt{\mu_j \epsilon_j}$$

the effective wave number in the subdomain Ω_j, a particular feature of the present contribution is that $\kappa_j = 0$ in certain subdomains.

We propose a novel formulation of the above problem as a system of coupled boundary integral equations, by means of the multi-trace approach [3], [4]. We rely on the Hiptmair-Ostrowski eddy-current coupling scheme [5] to handle subdomains with vanishing ϵ. In what follows, we describe the bilinear form associated to our eddy-current multi-trace formulation.

III. Variationnal space and transmission operator

Our low-frequency multi-trace formulation is posed on the skeleton $\Sigma := \cup_{j=0}^{n}\Gamma_j$ where $\Gamma_j := \partial\Omega_j$ of the subdomain partition. Let $\mathcal{I}_* = \{j = 0\dots n \mid \kappa_j = 0\}$. The variational space takes the form

$$\begin{aligned}\mathbb{H}(\Sigma) := \{\ & \mathbf{u} = (\mathbf{u}_j)_{j=0}^{n}, \mathbf{u}_j = (\mathbf{u}_j^{\mathrm{E}}, \mathbf{u}_j^{\mathrm{H}}) \\ & \mathbf{u}_j^{\mathrm{E}}, \mathbf{u}_j^{\mathrm{H}} : \text{vector fields tangent to } \Gamma_j \\ & \mathrm{div}_{\Gamma_j}\mathbf{u}_j^{\mathrm{H}} = 0 \ \text{ for } j \in \mathcal{I}_*\}.\end{aligned}$$

In this variationnal setting, $\mathbf{u}_j^{\mathrm{E}}$ (resp. $\mathbf{u}_j^{\mathrm{H}}$) is related to the tangential trace of the electric (resp. magnetic) field at Γ_j. Next we introduce an operator that allows an enforcement of transmission conditions across interfaces between adjacent media. This is a local operator acting on pairs of tangent traces at the skeleton. For $\mathbf{u}, \mathbf{v} \in \mathbb{H}(\Sigma)$ it is given by

$$\begin{aligned}\Pi(\mathbf{u},\mathbf{v}) = \sum_{0\le j<k\le n} & \int_{\Gamma_j\cap\Gamma_k} \mathbf{u}_j^{\mathrm{E}} \times \mathbf{v}_k^{\mathrm{H}} + \mathbf{u}_k^{\mathrm{H}} \times \mathbf{v}_j^{\mathrm{E}} d\sigma \\ & + \int_{\Gamma_j\cap\Gamma_k} \mathbf{u}_k^{\mathrm{E}} \times \mathbf{v}_j^{\mathrm{H}} + \mathbf{u}_j^{\mathrm{H}} \times \mathbf{v}_k^{\mathrm{E}} d\sigma.\end{aligned} \tag{2}$$

IV. Integral operators

We also need to describe the integral operators coming into play in our formulation. Consider the outgoing Green kernel associated to Helmholtz equation $\mathcal{G}_\kappa(\mathbf{z}) := \exp(\imath\kappa|\mathbf{z}|)/(4\pi|\mathbf{z}|)$, as well as $\mathcal{B}(\mathbf{z}) := (\imath\kappa|\mathbf{z}| - 1)\,\mathbf{z}/|\mathbf{z}|^2$, and introduce the classical bilinear forms for EFIE and MFIE at each boundary

$$\begin{aligned}\mathfrak{a}_\kappa^\Gamma(\mathbf{p},\mathbf{q}) &:= \int_{\Gamma\times\Gamma} \mathcal{G}_\kappa(\mathbf{x}-\mathbf{y})[\mathbf{p}(\mathbf{x})\cdot\mathbf{q}(\mathbf{y}) \\ &\qquad -\kappa^{-2}\mathrm{div}_\Gamma\mathbf{p}(\mathbf{x})\mathrm{div}_\Gamma\mathbf{q}(\mathbf{y})]d\sigma(\mathbf{x},\mathbf{y}), \\ \mathfrak{b}_\kappa^\Gamma(\mathbf{p},\mathbf{q}) &:= \int_{\Gamma\times\Gamma} \mathcal{G}_\kappa(\mathbf{x}-\mathbf{y}) \\ &\qquad \mathcal{B}(\mathbf{x}-\mathbf{y})\cdot[\,\mathbf{p}(\mathbf{x})\times\mathbf{q}(\mathbf{y})\,]d\sigma(\mathbf{x},\mathbf{y}),\end{aligned}$$

where $\Gamma = \Gamma_j := \partial\Omega_j, j = 0\dots n$. Since we are interested in the low frequency regime, we shall also resort on bilinear forms related the behaviour of $\mathfrak{a}_\kappa^\Gamma$ as $\kappa \to 0$:

$$\begin{aligned}\mathfrak{a}_*^\Gamma(\mathbf{p},\mathbf{q}) &:= \int_{\Gamma\times\Gamma} \mathcal{G}_\kappa(\mathbf{x}-\mathbf{y})\mathbf{p}(\mathbf{x})\cdot\mathbf{q}(\mathbf{y})\,d\sigma(\mathbf{x},\mathbf{y}), \\ \mathfrak{a}_\sharp^\Gamma(\mathbf{p},\mathbf{q}) &:= -\int_{\Gamma\times\Gamma} \mathcal{G}_\kappa(\mathbf{x}-\mathbf{y})\mathrm{div}_\Gamma\mathbf{p}(\mathbf{x})\,\mathrm{div}_\Gamma\mathbf{q}(\mathbf{y})\,d\sigma(\mathbf{x},\mathbf{y}).\end{aligned}$$

Then, we associate to each subdomain a bilinear form A_{Γ_j} involving an integral operator. We have to distinguish two cases.

Case 1: $\kappa_j \neq 0$. In this case, A_{Γ_j} is the bilinear form associated to the classical Rumsey formulation. For $\mathbf{u}, \mathbf{v}$ two pairs of traces that are tangent to Γ_j, it is defined by

$$\begin{aligned}\mathrm{A}_{\Gamma_j}(\mathbf{u},\mathbf{v}) := \ & \kappa_j^2\,\mathfrak{a}_{\kappa_j}^{\Gamma_j}(\mathbf{u}^{\mathrm{E}},\mathbf{v}^{\mathrm{E}}) + \mathfrak{b}_{\kappa_j}^{\Gamma_j}(\mathbf{u}^{\mathrm{E}},\mathbf{v}^{\mathrm{H}}) \\ & + \mathfrak{b}_{\kappa_j}^{\Gamma_j}(\mathbf{u}^{\mathrm{H}},\mathbf{v}^{\mathrm{E}}) + \mathfrak{a}_{\kappa_j}^{\Gamma_j}(\mathbf{u}^{\mathrm{H}},\mathbf{v}^{\mathrm{H}}).\end{aligned} \tag{3}$$

Case 2: $\kappa_j = 0$. In this case, A_{Γ_j} is the bilinear form that is coming into play in Hiptmair-Ostrowski's eddy-current coupling. It is given by

$$\begin{aligned}\mathrm{A}_{\Gamma_j}(\mathbf{u},\mathbf{v}) := \ & \mathfrak{a}_*^{\Gamma_j}(\mathbf{u}^{\mathrm{E}},\mathbf{v}^{\mathrm{E}}) + \mathfrak{b}_0^{\Gamma_j}(\mathbf{u}^{\mathrm{E}},\mathbf{v}^{\mathrm{H}}) \\ & + \mathfrak{b}_0^{\Gamma_j}(\mathbf{u}^{\mathrm{H}},\mathbf{v}^{\mathrm{E}}) + \mathfrak{a}_\sharp^{\Gamma_j}(\mathbf{u}^{\mathrm{H}},\mathbf{v}^{\mathrm{H}}).\end{aligned} \tag{4}$$

V. Multi-trace formulation

The bilinear form associated to our multi-trace formulation can then be obtained simply by adding the transmission bilinear form with the bilinear form (3)-(4) associated to each subdomain. It takes the form

$$\left\{\begin{aligned} & \text{Find } \mathbf{u} = (\mathbf{u}_j) \in \mathbb{H}(\Sigma), \\ & \Pi(\mathbf{u},\mathbf{v}) + \textstyle\sum_{j=0}^{n} \mathrm{A}_{\Gamma_j}(\mathbf{u}_j,\mathbf{v}_j) = \mathfrak{f}(\mathbf{v}) \\ & \qquad\qquad \forall \mathbf{v} = (\mathbf{v}_j) \in \mathbb{H}(\Sigma).\end{aligned}\right. \tag{5}$$

where $\mathfrak{f}$ is a source term whose precise expression is related to the current $\mathbf{j}$ appearing in the right-hand side of (1).

VI. Conclusion

In this talk, we shall provide further details on the derivation of (5) and discuss its numerical stability in the low frequency regime. This will be illustrated by numerical experiments related to concrete applications in non-destructive testing considered at CEA.

Acknowledgment

This work has been supported by the CIVAMONT project, aiming at developing scientific collaborations around the NDT simulation platform CIVA developed at CEA LIST.

References

[1] A. Vigneron, E. Demaldent, and M. Bonnet, "A multi-step solution algorithm for maxwell boundary integral equations applied to low-frequency electromagnetic testing of conductive objects," *IEEE TM*, vol. 52, no. 10, 2016.

[2] E. Demaldent, C. Reboud, F. Nozais, J. Decitre, T. Sollier, and G. Cattiaux, "Modelling the ect of u-bend steam generator tubes by the boundary element method," in *Proceedings of the 19th World Conference on Non Destructive Testing*, 2016.

[3] X. Claeys and R. Hiptmair, "Electromagnetic scattering at composite objects: a novel multi-trace boundary integral formulation," *ESAIM Math. Model. Numer. Anal.*, vol. 46, no. 6, pp. 1421–1445, 2012.

[4] X. Claeys, R. Hiptmair, and C. Jerez-Hanckes, "Multitrace boundary integral equations," in *Direct and inverse problems in wave propagation and applications*, ser. Radon Ser. Comput. Appl. Math. De Gruyter, Berlin, 2013, vol. 14, pp. 51–100.

[5] R. Hiptmair and J. Ostrowski, "Coupled boundary-element scheme for eddy-current computation," *J. Engrg. Math.*, vol. 51, no. 3, pp. 231–250, 2005.

Tutorial Session

Advances in the Nonstandard Finite Difference Time Domain Methodology, the Devils in the Details

James B. Cole[1] and Saswatee Banerjee[2]
[1]US Army Research Laboratory and [2]UApple-Japan
[1]cole@cavelab.cs.tsukuba.ac, [2]saswateeb@gmail.com

ACES-2017
Florence, Italy

Reference:
Computing the Flow of Light,
Nonstandard FDTD for Photonics Design,
SPIE Press, 2017

Background and Motivation

Modeling and Simulation

Topics

- Introduction
  - Philosophy of modeling
  - Ordinary FDTD
- Nonstandard FDTD for high precision
- Example Problems
  - The scattered field
  - Structural color
  - Whispering gallery resonators
- Extensions to Dispersive Materials
  - Nanoparticles
  - Metallic gratings

Old Science

theory

experiment

Modern Science

theory

modeling
and
simulation

experiment

Simulation and Modeling

simulation ← similar

most things are too complicated to understand

so we make simple models that contain the most important features of the real system
and
use simulation to deduce the properties of the real system

what is a good model?

It captures the most important features,

but is

- **simple,**
- **with as few parameters as possible**

Occam's Razor*

The best model, is the simplest one that explains all the facts

***William of Okham (1285-1349), English philosopher and Franciscan Friar**

Examples of

Ugly, Bad,

and

Good Models

The Earth holds us up, but what holds up the Earth?

Atlas holds up the Earth

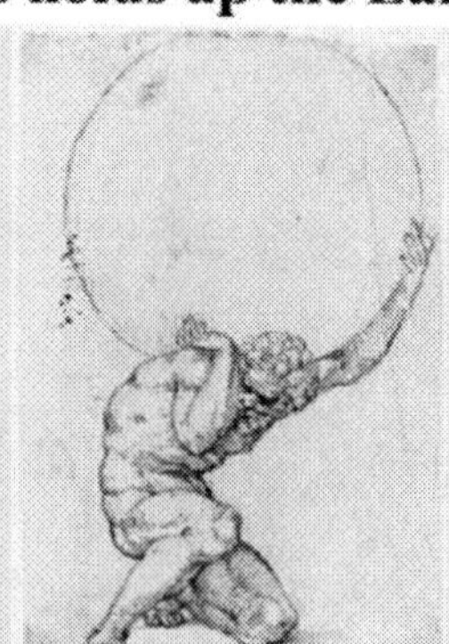

but what holds Atlas up?

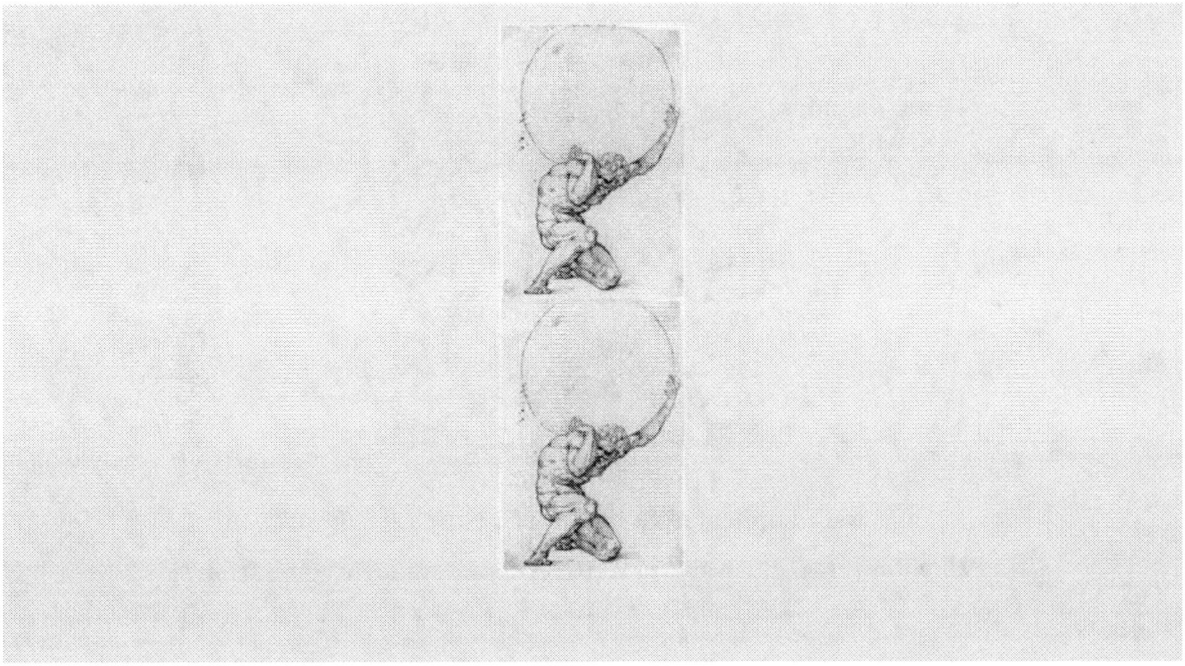

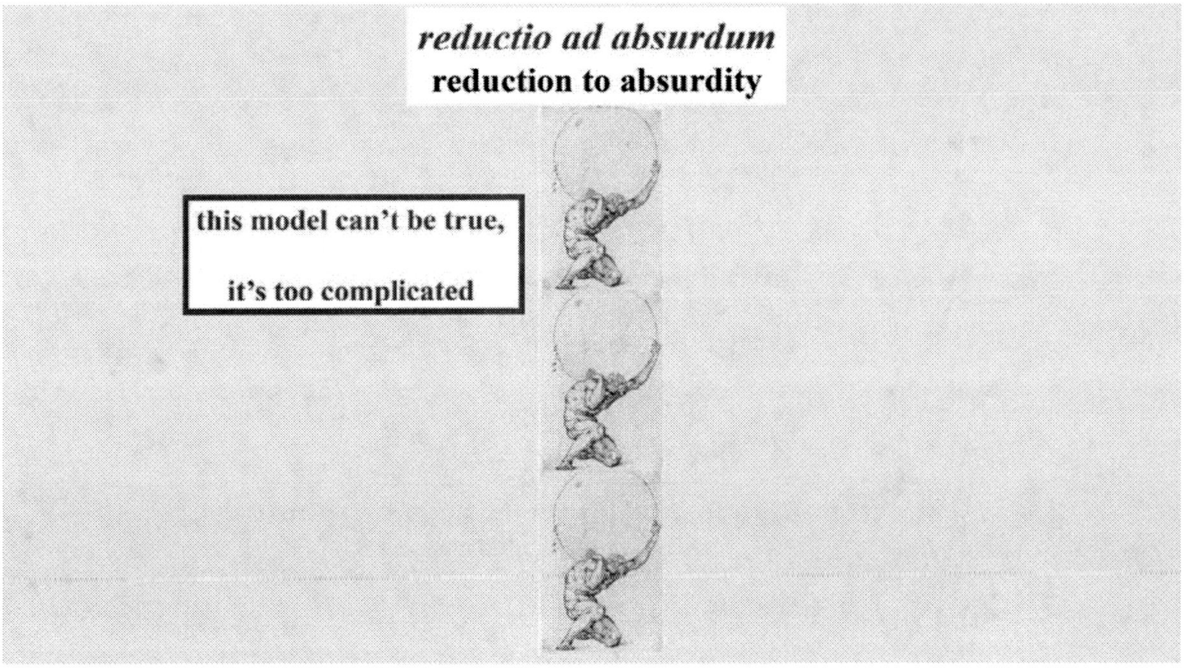
reductio ad absurdum
reduction to absurdity
this model can't be true,
it's too complicated

Earth floats freely in space, nothing holds it up

Anaximander of Miletus, 610-546 BC

"too complicated to be correct, simplest is best,"

Why does this idea work so well? Where does logic come from?

Ptolemy's Model of the Universe 90-168 AD

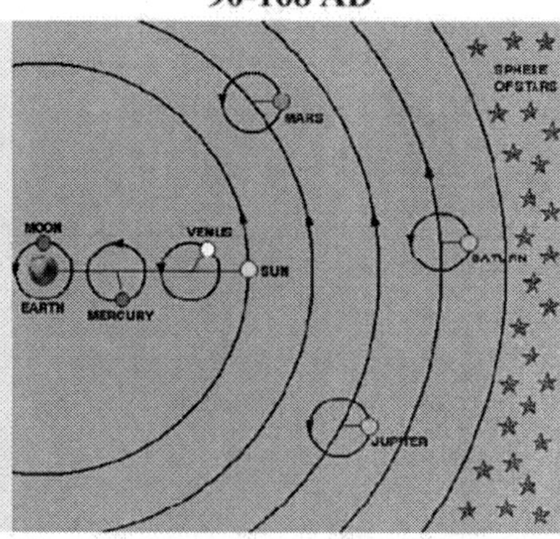

It's not really wrong, but it's not the simplest explanation and it's not predictive.

Introduction

Finite Differences

what they are and what they are not

The Basic Finite Difference Approximations to Derivatives

$$f'(x) \cong \frac{f(x+h/2)-f(x-h/2)}{h}$$ **central FD approximation**

$$f'(x) \cong \frac{f(x+h)-f(x)}{h}$$ **forward FD approximation**

$$f'(x) \cong \frac{f(x)-f(x-h)}{h}$$ **backward FD approximation**

The General Nonstandard Finite Difference Approximation

$$f'(x)\Big|_{x=y} \cong \frac{f(x+\Delta x)-a(\Delta x)f(x)}{s(\Delta x)}; \quad s(\Delta x),\ a(\Delta x) \text{ are functions}$$

$s(\Delta x)$ and $a(\Delta x)$ must satisfy $\lim_{\Delta x \to 0} \frac{f(x+\Delta x)-a(\Delta x)f(x)}{s(\Delta x)} = f'(x)\Big|_{x=y}$

sometimes **it is possible to construct**
exact nonstandard (NS) finite difference expressions
for non-infinitesimal Δx

all finite difference approximations are equal
(for *infinitesimal* Δx)
but
(for *non-infinitesimal* Δx)
some **approximations are *more equal* than others**
(to the derivative)

$f(x) = e^{ax}$

error ~ Δx — error = 0 for all Δx

$$f'(x) = \lim_{\Delta x \to 0} \frac{f(x+\Delta x)-f(x)}{\Delta x} = \lim_{\Delta x \to 0} \frac{f(x+\Delta x)-f(x)}{\left(e^{a\Delta x}-1\right)/a} =$$

error ~ Δx^2 — error = 0 for all Δx

$$\lim_{\Delta x \to 0} \frac{f\left(x+\Delta x/2\right)-f\left(x-\Delta x/2\right)}{\Delta x} = \lim_{\Delta x \to 0} \frac{f\left(x+\Delta x/2\right)-f\left(x-\Delta x/2\right)}{\sinh\left(a\Delta x/2\right)/a}$$

examples of exact NS-FD expressions for the derivative

$$f(x) = e^{ax}, \quad a \text{ is complex}$$

Exact forward finite difference expression

$$\frac{f(x+\Delta x) - f(x)}{\left(e^{a\,\Delta x} - 1\right)/a} = f'(x)$$

exact even when Δx *is not* infinitesimal

Exact central finite difference expression

$$\frac{f\left(x+\Delta x/2\right) - f\left(x-\Delta x/2\right)}{\sinh\left(a\,\Delta x/2\right)/a} = f'(x)$$

Finite Difference Models of Differential Equations

how to tweak them and make

High Precision (and *sometimes* exact) Models

wave equation $\left(\partial_t^2 - v^2\partial_x^2\right)\psi(x,t) = 0$

first difference $d_t f(t) = f(t + \Delta t/2) - f(t - \Delta t/2)$

second difference $d_t^2 f(t) = f(t+\Delta t) + f(t-\Delta t) - 2f(t)$

$$\partial_x^2 \to \frac{d_x^2}{\Delta x^2}, \quad \partial_t^2 \to \frac{d_t^2}{\Delta t^2}$$

Standard **finite difference model of the wave equation**

$$\left(d_t^2 - \frac{v^2\Delta t^2}{\Delta x^2} d_x^2\right)\psi(x,t) = 0$$

Finite Difference Time Domain (FDTD) Algorithm

rewrite the FD model of the wave equation

$$\left(d_t^2 - \frac{v^2\Delta t^2}{\Delta x^2} d_x^2\right)\psi(x,t) = 0 \to d_t^2\psi(x,t) = \frac{v^2\Delta t^2}{\Delta x^2} d_x^2\psi(x,t)$$

$$d_t^2 f(t) = f(t+\Delta t) + f(t-\Delta t) - 2f(t)$$

standard (S) FDTD algorithm

$$\psi(x,t+\Delta t) = -\psi(x,t-\Delta t) + 2\psi(x,t) + \frac{v^2\Delta t^2}{\Delta x^2} d_x^2\psi(x,t)$$

the Devil is in the Details

the accuracy of conventional (S) FDTD is low

fine grid → higher accuracy, but computational cost rises

monochromatic solution of the wave equation

$$\psi_0 = e^{i(kx-\omega t)}, \quad v = \omega/k$$

wave equation solution ≠ difference equation solution

$$\left(\partial_t^2 - v^2\partial_x^2\right)\psi_0 = 0, \quad \left(d_t^2 - \frac{v^2\Delta t^2}{\Delta x^2}d_x^2\right)\psi_0 = \varepsilon \neq 0$$

Error of S-FDTD

$$\varepsilon = 4\left[-\sin^2\left(\omega\Delta t/2\right) + \frac{v^2\Delta t^2}{\Delta x^2}\sin^2\left(k\Delta x/2\right)\right]\psi_0$$

Can we decrease the error by using a more accurate finite difference approximation for the derivative?

Yes we *could*!

but

NO! We Can't!

because the algorithm would be numerically unstable

Higher Order Finite Difference Approximations Don't Work

$f''(t) \cong$ **4th -order finite difference approximation**

$$\frac{1}{\Delta t^2}\left\{-\frac{1}{12}\left[f(t+2\Delta t)+f(t-2\Delta t)\right]+\frac{4}{3}\left[f(t+\Delta t)+f(t-\Delta t)\right]-\frac{5}{2}f(t)\right\}$$

A finite difference model of the wave equation based on 4th-order finite differences is very complicated

and

has solutions that are completely different from those of the wave equation

and

is numerically unstable.

What is Numerical Instability?

A numerical model of a differential equation is numerically unstable if

- **it has solutions that do not correspond to solutions of the original differential equation,**
- **and these solutions grow rapidly as the iteration proceeds.**

Why Doesn't a Higher Order FD Approximation Work?

decay equation

$$\partial_t \psi(t) = -\alpha \psi(t)$$

analytic solution

$$\psi(t) = \psi(0) e^{-\alpha t}$$

First Order FD Algorithm

backward FD approximation

$$\partial_t \psi(t) \to \frac{\psi(t) - \psi(t - \Delta t)}{\Delta t}$$

difference equation

$$\psi(t + \Delta t) = \frac{\psi(t)}{1 + \alpha \, \Delta t}$$

analytic solution

$$\psi(n\Delta t) = \frac{\psi(0)}{\left(1 + \alpha \, \Delta t\right)^n}$$

numerically stable

Why Doesn't a Higher Order FD Approximation Work?

decay equation

$$\partial_t \psi(t) = -\alpha \psi(t)$$

analytic solution

$$\psi(t) = \psi(0) e^{-\alpha t}$$

Second Order FD Algorithm

backward FD approximation

$$\partial_t \psi(t) \rightarrow \frac{\psi(t+\Delta t) - \psi(t-\Delta t)}{2\Delta t}$$

difference equation

$$\psi(t+\Delta t) = \psi(t-\Delta t) - 2\alpha \Delta t \psi(t)$$

analytic solution

$$\psi(n\Delta t) = a_+ \lambda_+^n + a_- \lambda_-^n$$

numerically unstable because $|\lambda_+| < 1, \quad |\lambda_-| > 1$ **and** $a_- \neq 0 \quad \text{for} \quad \Delta t > 0$

1 initial condition needed to solve the decay equation,
but
2 initial conditions needed to iterate the FD algorithm.
Weird, Unnatural

A nth order derivative must be modeled with n^{th} order FD approximations

There is a Smarter Way to increase accuracy without using higher order finite differences

*non*standard (NS) FDTD Model

$$\left(\partial_t^2 - v^2\partial_x^2\right)\psi(x,t) = 0 \rightarrow \left(d_t^2 - \frac{v^2\Delta t^2}{\Delta x^2} d_x^2\right)\psi(x,t) = 0$$

$$\frac{v^2\Delta t^2}{\Delta x^2} \rightarrow u^2 \qquad u = \frac{\sin(\omega\Delta t/2)}{\sin(k\Delta x/2)}$$

NS-FDTD Algorithm

$$\psi(x,t+\Delta t) = -\psi(x,t-\Delta t) + 2\psi(x,t) + u^2 d_x^2 \psi(x,t)$$

NS-FDTD is exact (in 1-D) for all ω and *k* that satisfy

$$u = \frac{\sin(\omega\Delta t/2)}{\sin(k\Delta x/2)}, \quad 0 < u \le 1$$

Prof. Kanai and Dr. Otani first pointed this out

in 2- and 3-D NS-FDTD is no longer exact, but still high precision

NS-FDTD is valid on a wide band, but the Nyquist limits must be satisfied

$$\frac{2\pi/\omega}{\Delta t} > 2, \quad \frac{2\pi/k}{\Delta x} > 2$$

What About Nonlinear Equations?

The Verhulst Equation

Verhulst equation

$$\partial_t \psi(t) = \alpha\left[1-\psi(t)\right]\psi(t)$$

analytic solution

$$\psi(t) = \frac{\psi_0 e^{\alpha t}}{1+\psi_0\left(e^{\alpha t}-1\right)}$$

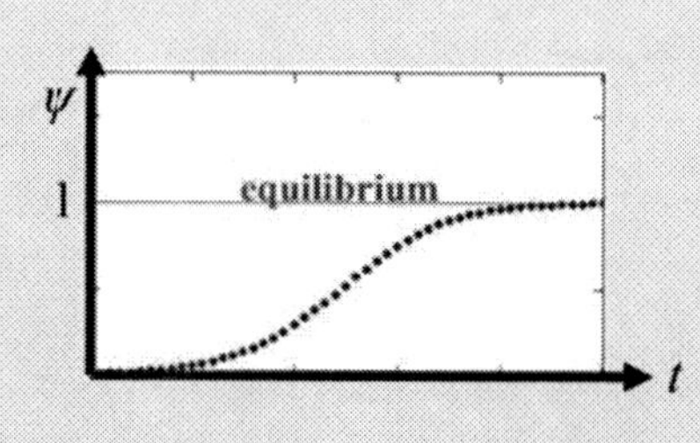

standard forward finite difference

$$\partial_t \psi(t) \cong \frac{\psi(t+\Delta t)-\psi(t)}{\Delta t}$$

standard finite difference algorithm

$$\psi\left(\left[n+1\right]\Delta t\right) = \psi(n\Delta t) + \alpha\Delta t\left[1-\psi(n\Delta t)\right]\psi(n\Delta t)$$

chaotic behavior

for $\alpha\Delta t = 2.667$

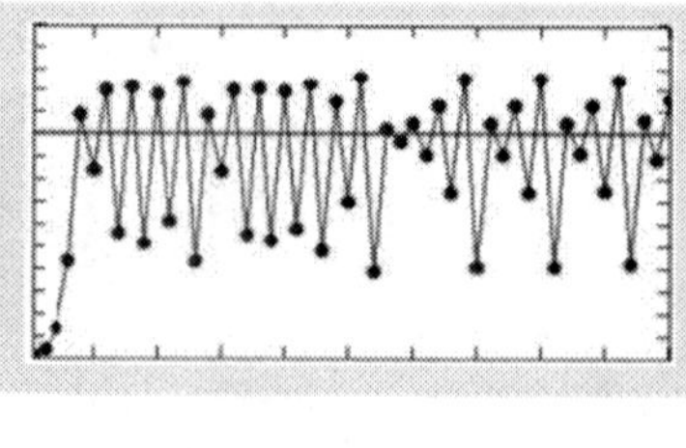

non-linear terms must be modeled non-locally

$$\psi(t)^2 \rightarrow \psi(t)\psi(t+\Delta t)$$

original differential equation

$$\partial_t \psi(t) = \alpha\left[1-\psi(t)\right]\psi(t) \rightarrow$$

standard finite difference (S-FD) model

$$\frac{\psi(t+\Delta t)-\psi(t)}{\Delta t} = \alpha\left[1-\psi(t)\right]\psi(t)$$

nonstandard finite difference (NS-FD) model

$$\frac{\psi(t+\Delta t)-\psi(t)}{\left(e^{\alpha\Delta t}-1\right)/\alpha} = \alpha\left[\psi(t)-\psi(t)\psi(t+\Delta t)\right]$$

for $f(x)=e^{ax}$

$$\frac{f\left(x+\Delta x\right)-f\left(x\right)}{\left(e^{a\Delta x}-1\right)/a} = f'(x)$$

where does this come from?

choose a NS-FD that is exact with respect to an important term in the solution

$$\left(e^{\alpha\Delta t}-1\right)/\alpha = \Delta t+\alpha\Delta t^2/2+\cdots$$

standard and nonstandard finite difference solutions of the logistic equation versus its analytic solution

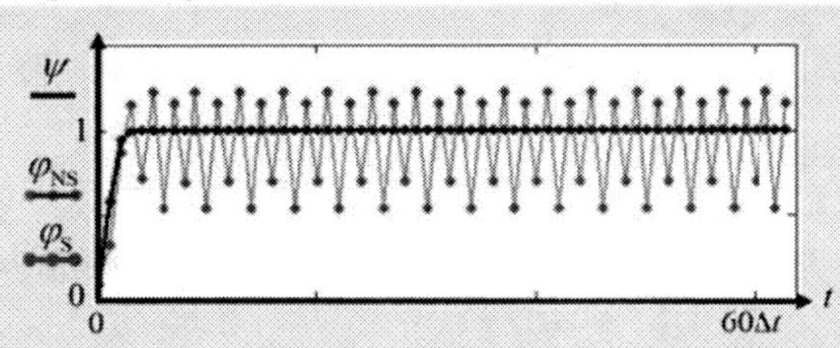

Analytic

$$\psi(t) = \frac{\psi_0 e^{\alpha t}}{1+\psi_0\left(e^{\alpha t}-1\right)}$$

S-FD

$$\varphi_{\tau+1} = \varphi_\tau + \alpha\Delta t\left[1-\varphi_\tau\right]\varphi_\tau$$

NS-FD

$$\varphi_{\tau+1} = \frac{e^{\alpha\Delta t}\varphi_\tau}{\left[1+\left(e^{\alpha\Delta t}-1\right)\varphi_\tau\right]}$$

$$\varphi_\tau = \varphi(\tau\,\Delta t), \quad \tau = 0,1,2,\cdots$$

Non-Linear Optics

$$\left(\partial_t^2 - v^2\partial_x^2\right)E(x,t) = -\chi E(x,t)^2$$

Using NS-methods we can solve problems like this in 2- and 3-D

NS-FDTD in 2- and 3-D

cannot make the error vanish in 2- and 3-D
but can bring it down to

$$\varepsilon \sim \frac{1}{h^8} \quad h = \Delta x = \Delta y = \Delta z$$

Standard FD Approximation for the Laplacian in 2-D

$$\nabla^2 f(x,y) \cong \frac{\mathbf{d}^2 f(x,y)}{h^2}, \quad \mathbf{d}^2 = d_x^2 + d_y^2$$

$$d_x^2 f(x,y) = f(x+h,y) + f(x-h,y) - 2f(x,y)$$

$$d_y^2 f(x,y) = f(x,y+h) + f(x,y-h) - 2f(x,y)$$

$$\mathbf{d}^2 f(x,y) = f(x+h,y) + f(x-h,y) + f(x,y+h) + f(x,y-h) - 4f(x,y)$$

standard computational molecule for the 2-D Laplacian

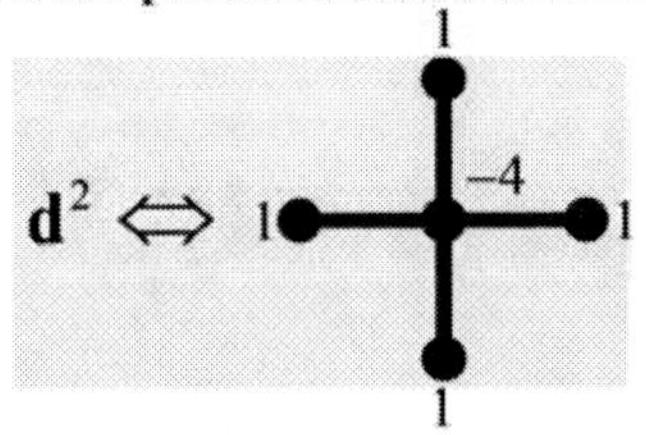

Another FD Approximation for the Laplacian in 2-D

$$\nabla^2 f(x,y) \cong \frac{\mathbf{d}'^2 f(x,y)}{h^2}$$

$$2\mathbf{d}'^2 f(x,y) = f(x+h,y+h) + f(x-h,y+h) + f(x+h,y-h) + f(x-h,y-h) - 4f(x,y)$$

you can prove that

$$\mathbf{d}'^2 = \mathbf{d}^2 + \frac{1}{2} d_x^2 d_y^2$$

Another Computational Molecule

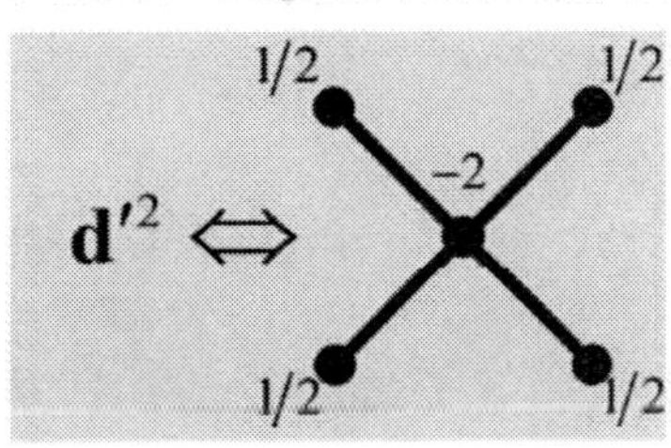

Most General Standard FD Approximation to the 2-D Laplacian

$$\mathbf{d}^2 = d_x^2 + d_y^2 \qquad \mathbf{d}'^2 = \mathbf{d}^2 + \frac{1}{2} d_x^2 d_y^2 \qquad \mathbf{d}_\gamma^2 = \mathbf{d}^2 + \gamma\, d_x^2 d_y^2 \;^{*}$$

$\mathbf{d}_\gamma^2 \Leftrightarrow$

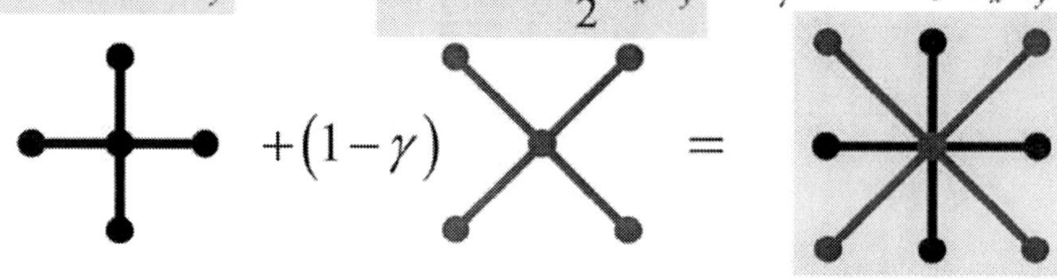

general computational molecule

*factor of 2 removed

$$\nabla^2 f(x,y) \cong \frac{\mathbf{d}_\gamma^2 f(x,y)}{h^2}$$

$\lim_{h\to 0}\left[\mathbf{d}_\gamma^2 f(\mathbf{x})/h^2\right] = \nabla^2 f(\mathbf{x})$ for all γ, so γ is a free parameter

Nonstandard FD Approximation to the 2-D Laplacian

exact nonstandard finite difference expression

1-D $$\frac{d_x^2 e^{ikx}}{e^{ikx}} = -4\sin^2(kh/2) \quad \text{and} \quad \partial_x^2 e^{ikx} = \frac{d_x^2 e^{ikx}}{4\sin^2(kh/2)/k^2}$$

with respect to plane waves $\varphi = e^{i\mathbf{k}\cdot\mathbf{x}}$ can we find γ such that

2-D $$\frac{\mathbf{d}_\gamma^2 e^{i\mathbf{k}\cdot\mathbf{x}}}{e^{i\mathbf{k}\cdot\mathbf{x}}} = -4\sin^2(kh/2) \quad \text{so that} \quad \nabla^2 e^{i\mathbf{k}\cdot\mathbf{x}} = \frac{\mathbf{d}_\gamma^2 e^{i\mathbf{k}\cdot\mathbf{x}}}{4\sin^2(kh/2)/k^2} \quad ?$$

No! We Can't!

but

Yes! We *Almost* Can!

Almost Exact Nonstandard FD Approximation to the 2-D Laplacian

choose $\gamma = \frac{1}{6} + \frac{(kh)^2}{180}$

Nonstandard FD for the 2-D Laplacian

$$\tilde{\mathbf{d}}^2 = \mathbf{d}^2 + \gamma d_x^2 d_y^2$$
$$= d_x^2 + d_y^2 + \left(\frac{1}{6} + \frac{(kh)^2}{180}\right) d_x^2 d_y^2$$

almost exactly

$$\frac{\tilde{\mathbf{d}}^2 e^{i\mathbf{k}\cdot\mathbf{x}}}{e^{i\mathbf{k}\cdot\mathbf{x}}} = -4\sin^2(kh/2) + O\left[\frac{(kh)^8}{2^8}\right]$$

$k = |\mathbf{k}|$

almost exactly

$$\nabla^2 e^{i\mathbf{k}\cdot\mathbf{x}} = \frac{\tilde{\mathbf{d}}^2 e^{i\mathbf{k}\cdot\mathbf{x}}}{4\sin^2(kh/2)/k^2}$$

error of the NS-FD Laplacian

$$\varepsilon_{\text{NS}} = \frac{1}{\nabla^2 e^{i\mathbf{k}\cdot\mathbf{x}}}\left[\frac{\tilde{\mathbf{d}}^2}{4\sin^2(kh/2)/k^2} - \nabla^2\right] e^{i\mathbf{k}\cdot\mathbf{x}}$$
$$= O\left[(kh)^6/256\right]$$

error of the S-FD Laplacian

$$\varepsilon_{\text{S}} = \frac{1}{\nabla^2 e^{i\mathbf{k}\cdot\mathbf{x}}}\left[\frac{\mathbf{d}^2}{h^2} - \nabla^2\right] e^{i\mathbf{k}\cdot\mathbf{x}}$$
$$= O\left[(kh)^2/16\right]$$

Almost Exact Nonstandard FD Approximation to the 3-D Laplacian

$$\tilde{\mathbf{d}}^2 = d_x^2 + d_y^2 + d_z^2 + \left(\frac{1}{6} + \frac{(kh)^2}{180}\right)\left[d_x^2 d_y^2 + d_x^2 d_z^2 + d_y^2 d_z^2\right] + \frac{1}{30} d_x^2 d_y^2 d_z^2$$

almost exactly

$$\nabla^2 e^{i\mathbf{k}\cdot\mathbf{x}} = \frac{\tilde{\mathbf{d}}^2 e^{i\mathbf{k}\cdot\mathbf{x}}}{4\sin^2(kh/2)/k^2}$$

Standard and Nonstandard FDTD in 2- and 3 Dimensions for the Wave Equation

standard (S) FDTD algorithm

$$\psi(\mathbf{x},t+\Delta t)=-\psi(\mathbf{x},t-\Delta t)+\left[2+\frac{v^2\Delta t^2}{h^2}\mathbf{d}^2\right]\psi(\mathbf{x},t)$$

nonstandard (NS) FDTD algorithm

$$\psi(\mathbf{x},t+\Delta t)=-\psi(\mathbf{x},t-\Delta t)+\left[2+u^2\tilde{\mathbf{d}}^2\right]\psi(\mathbf{x},t) \qquad u=\frac{\sin(\omega\Delta t/2)}{\sin(kh/2)}$$

error of S- and NS-FDTD with respect to plane waves

$$\varepsilon_{\text{S-FDTD}}=O\left[\frac{1}{3}\left(\frac{kh}{2}\right)^4\right] \qquad \varepsilon_{\text{NS-FDTD}}=O\left[\frac{1}{1890}\left(\frac{kh}{2}\right)^8\right]$$

S-FDTD versus NS-FDTD

infinite plane wave incident on an infinite dielectric cylinder

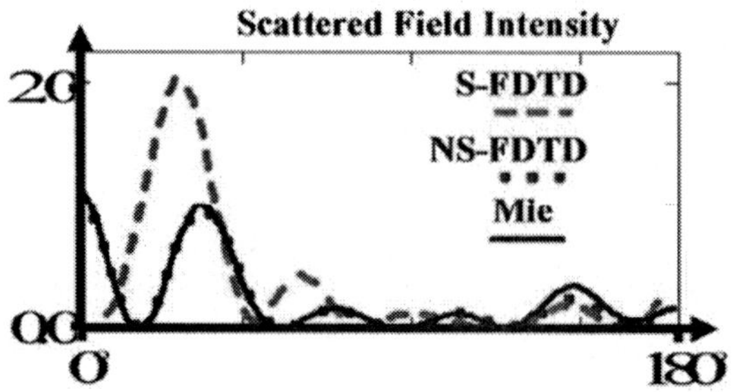

scattered field intensity

on contour of radius = $1.25\lambda_0$ about axis

refractive index =1.7 $\lambda_0/h=8$ radius $=0.75\lambda_0$

NS-FDTD for Maxwell's Equations

(Nonstandard Version of the Yee Algorithm)

from the NS-model of the wave equation we can construct an NS-model of Maxwell's equations, and obtain an NS version of the Yee algorithm

S-Yee Algorithm

substitute finite differences for derivatives

$\partial_t \to d_t/\Delta t \qquad \partial_{x,y,z} \to d_{x,y,z}/h$

vector difference operator

$\mathbf{d} = (d_x, d_y, d_z)$

Maxwell's Equations

$$\mu \partial_t \mathbf{H} = -\nabla \times \mathbf{E}$$

$$\varepsilon \partial_t \mathbf{E} = \nabla \times \mathbf{H}$$

Standard Finite Difference Model

$$\mu d_t \mathbf{H} = -\frac{\Delta t}{h} \mathbf{d} \times \mathbf{E}$$

$$\varepsilon d_t \mathbf{E} = \frac{\Delta t}{h} \mathbf{d} \times \mathbf{H}$$

The Standard S-Yee Algorithm

$$\mathbf{H}(\mathbf{x}_H, t + \Delta t/2) = \mathbf{H}(\mathbf{x}_H, t - \Delta t/2) - \frac{1}{\mu(\mathbf{x}_H)} \frac{\Delta t}{h} \mathbf{d} \times \mathbf{E}(\mathbf{x}_H, t)$$

$$\mathbf{E}(\mathbf{x}_E, t + \Delta t) = \mathbf{E}(\mathbf{x}_E, t) + \frac{1}{\varepsilon(\mathbf{x}_E)} \frac{\Delta t}{h} d \times \mathbf{H}(\mathbf{x}_E, t + \Delta t/2)$$

NS-finite difference expression for ∇

dot product of d with itself gives the S-FD operator for the Laplacian

$$\mathbf{d} = \left(d_x, d_y, d_z\right), \quad \mathbf{d}\bullet\mathbf{d} = \mathbf{d}^2 = d_x^2 + d_y^2 + d_z^2$$

but

we cannot define $\tilde{\mathbf{d}}$ such that $\tilde{\mathbf{d}}\bullet\tilde{\mathbf{d}} = \tilde{\mathbf{d}}^2$; $\tilde{\mathbf{d}}\bullet\tilde{\mathbf{d}} \neq \tilde{\mathbf{d}}^2$

cannot make the substitution $\nabla \to \tilde{\mathbf{d}}$

we can define

$\tilde{\mathbf{d}}$ such that $\tilde{\mathbf{d}}\bullet\mathbf{d} = \mathbf{d}\bullet\tilde{\mathbf{d}} = \tilde{\mathbf{d}}^2$

NS-finite difference expression for ∇

$$\tilde{\mathbf{d}}^2 = d_x^2 + d_y^2 + d_z^2 + \left(\frac{1}{6} + \frac{(kh)^2}{180}\right)\left[d_x^2 d_y^2 + d_x^2 d_z^2 + d_y^2 d_z^2\right] + \frac{1}{30} d_x^2 d_y^2 d_z^2$$

$$\tilde{\mathbf{d}} = \mathbf{d} + \left(\frac{1}{12} + \frac{(kh)^2}{360}\right)\begin{bmatrix} d_x\left(d_y^2 + d_z^2\right) \\ d_y\left(d_x^2 + d_z^2\right) \\ d_z\left(d_x^2 + d_y^2\right) \end{bmatrix} + \frac{1}{90}\begin{bmatrix} d_x\left(d_y^2 d_z^2\right) \\ d_y\left(d_x^2 d_z^2\right) \\ d_z\left(d_x^2 d_y^2\right) \end{bmatrix}, \quad \mathbf{d} = \begin{bmatrix} d_x \\ d_y \\ d_z \end{bmatrix}$$

$$\tilde{\mathbf{d}}\bullet\mathbf{d} = \mathbf{d}\bullet\tilde{\mathbf{d}} = \tilde{\mathbf{d}}^2$$

NS-Yee Algorithm

Maxwell's Equations

$$\mu \partial_t \mathbf{H} = -\nabla \times \mathbf{E}$$

$$\varepsilon \partial_t \mathbf{E} = \nabla \times \mathbf{H}$$

NS-FD Model

$$d_t \mathbf{B}' = -\mathbf{d} \times \mathbf{E}$$

$$d_t \mathbf{E} = \frac{\tilde{v}_0^2}{\tilde{\varepsilon}} \tilde{\mathbf{d}}' \times \mathbf{B}'$$

$$\tilde{v}_0 = \frac{\sin(\omega \Delta t/2)}{\sin(k_0 h/2)}, \quad \tilde{\varepsilon} = \frac{\sin^2[\sqrt{\varepsilon}\, k_0 h/2]}{\sin^2[k_0 h/2]}$$

assuming constant μ

The nonstandard S-Yee Algorithm

$$\mathbf{B}'(\mathbf{x}_H, t + \Delta t/2) = \mathbf{B}'(\mathbf{x}_H, t - \Delta t/2) - \mathbf{d} \times \mathbf{E}(\mathbf{x}_H, t)$$

$$\mathbf{E}(\mathbf{x}_E, t + \Delta t) = \mathbf{E}(\mathbf{x}_E, t) + \frac{\tilde{v}_0^2}{\tilde{\varepsilon}} \tilde{\mathbf{d}}' \times \mathbf{B}'(\mathbf{x}_E, t + \Delta t/2)$$

S-FDTD versus NS-FDTD

infinite plane wave incident on an infinite dielectric cylinder

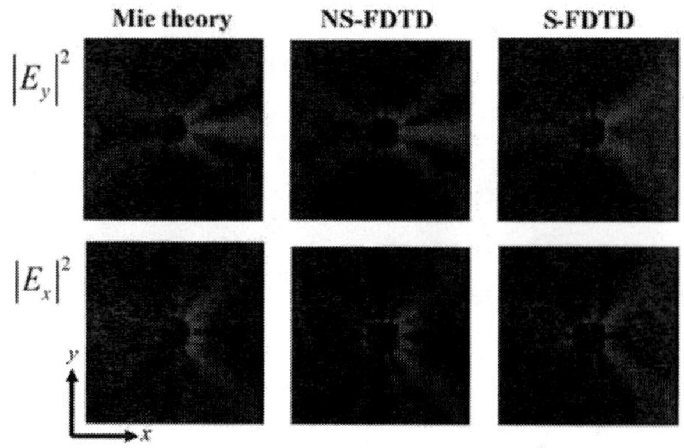

Infinite plane wave impinges from $-x$-direction onto infinite dielectric cylinder

vacuum wavelength = $\lambda_0 = 8h$, wave amplitude = 1,
cylinder radius $r = 0.75\lambda_0$, relative index of refraction $n_s = 1.7$,
E polarized in the y-direction, cylinder axis along z-axis,
TM mode ($H_x = H_y = E_z = 0$)

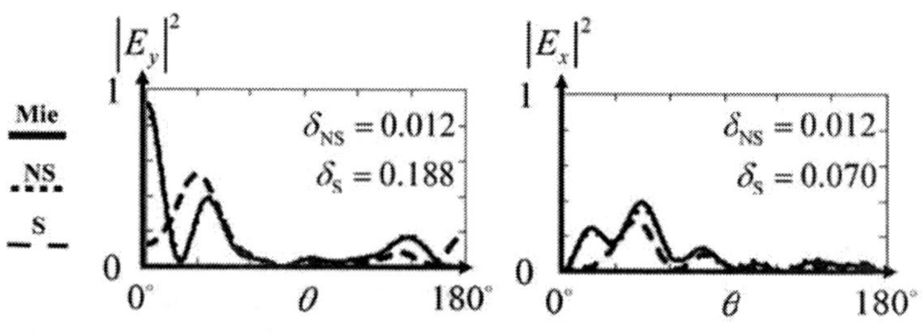

scattered fields on a circular contour
centered on the cylinder axis (outside the cylinder)

Whispering Gallery Modes in a Circular Dielectric Cylinder

the limitation on accuracy is not the FDTD algorithm, but the representation of objects on the numerical grid

Iridescence of the *Morpho Rhetenor* Butterfly

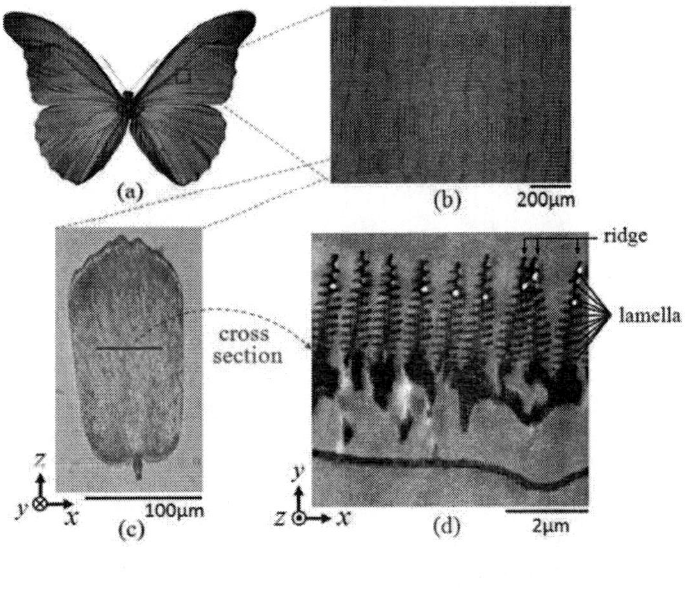

Model of the Butterfly Scales

ridges have random height, but one averaged ridge is approximately optically equivalent to an array of random ridges

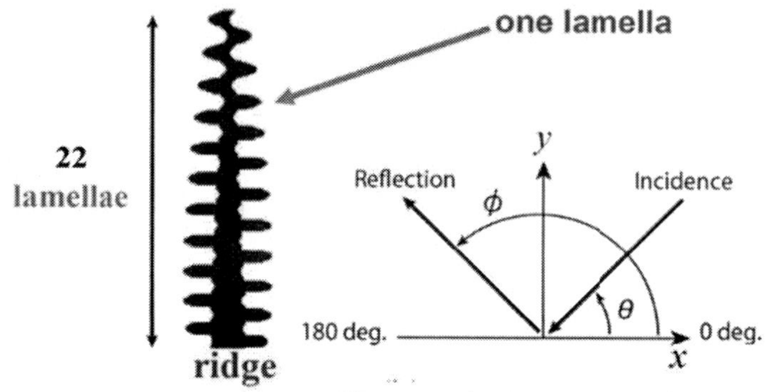

$\theta = \varphi$ is backscatter

FDTD Calculations for Silver Nanocylinders
(taking dispersion into account)

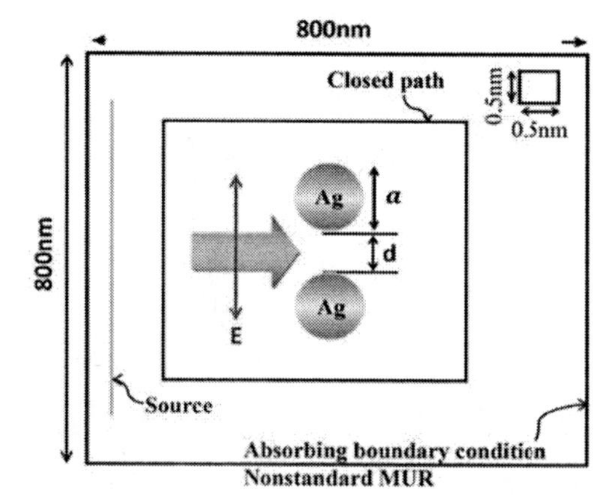

References

J. B. Cole,
"High Accuracy Yee Algorithm Based on Nonstandard Finite Differences: New Developments and Verifications,"
IEEE Trans. Antennas and Propagation, 50, 1185-1191 (2002)

J. B. Cole, N. Okada, S. Banerjee,
"Advances in Finite Difference Time Domain Methods," Chapter 4, pp. 115-175, *Light Scattering Reviews*, Volume 6, Springer, Berlin (2011)

further details in our forthcoming book

J. B. Cole and S. Banerjee,
"Computing the Flow of Light,
Nonstandard FDTD for Photonics design,"
SPIE Press (2017)

Higher-Order Hierarchical Vector Polynomial Bases for CEM

Roberto D. Graglia
Andrew F. Peterson

ACES 2017 Tutorial Notes
March 2017

Plan for Today

- Identify principles that have been used in the development of High-Order Hierarchical (Scalar and Vector) Bases
  - divergence conforming for EFIE
  - curl conforming for vector Helmholtz
- Illustrate few specific families
- Show and discuss numerical results

Some references…

INTERPOLATORY

– R.D. Graglia, D.R. Wilton and A.F. Peterson, "Higher order interpolatory vector bases for computational electromagnetics," invited paper, special issue on "Advanced Numerical Techniques in Electromagnetics" IEEE Trans. Antennas Propagat., vol. 45, no. 3, pp. 329-342, Mar. 1997.

– R.D. Graglia, D.R. Wilton, A.F. Peterson, and I.-L. Gheorma, "Higher order interpolatory vector bases on prism elements," IEEE Trans. Antennas Propagat., vol. 46, no. 3, pp. 442-450, Mar. 1998.

– R. D. Graglia, and I.-L. Gheorma, "Higher order interpolatory vector bases on pyramidal elements," IEEE Trans. Antennas Propagat., vol. 47, no. 5, May 1999.

HIERARCHICAL

– R. D. Graglia, A. F. Peterson, "Hierarchical Divergence-Conforming Nédélec Elements for Volumetric Cells," IEEE Trans. Antennas Propag., vol. 60, no. 11, pp. 5215-5227, Nov. 2012.

– R. D. Graglia, A. F. Peterson, "Hierarchical curl-conforming Nédélec elements for triangular-prism cells", IEEE Trans. Antennas Propag., vol. 60, no. 7, pp. 3314-3324, Jul. 2012.

– R. D. Graglia, A. F. Peterson, "Hierarchical curl-conforming Nédélec elements for quadrilateral and brick cells", IEEE Trans. Antennas Propag., vol. 59, no. 8, pp. 2766-2773, Aug. 2011.

– A. F. Peterson, R. D. Graglia, "Evaluation of hierarchical vector basis functions for quadrilateral cells", IEEE Trans. Magn., vol. 47, no. 5, pp. 1190-1193, May 2011.

– R. D. Graglia, A. F. Peterson, F. P. Andriulli, "Curl-conforming hierarchical vector bases for triangles and tetrahedra", IEEE Trans. Antennas Propag., vol. 59, no. 3, pp. 950-959, Mar. 2011.

– A. F. Peterson, R. D. Graglia, "Scale factors and matrix conditioning associated with triangular-cell hierarchical vector basis functions", IEEE Antennas Wireless Propag. Lett., vol. 9, pp. 40-43, 2010.

HIGHER ORDER TECHNIQUES IN COMPUTATIONAL ELECTROMAGNETICS

Roberto D. Graglia and Andrew F. Peterson

The Institution of Engineering and Technology

Year: 2015

Format: Hardback

Product Code: SBEW5070

ISBN: 978-1-61353-016-0

Pagination: 408pp

This talk will focus on the development of hierarchical bases

The following talk will focus on the development of singular hierarchical bases

Topics of current interest in CEM

- **Multiscale modeling** - some features that are much larger/smaller than others, need representations that can address both scales.
- **Accurate geometry** - be able to represent true curved surfaces, edges, etc.
- **Adaptive modeling** - need the flexibility to adjust the representation to produce the necessary accuracy but not more than we really need.

These lead to an approach based on:

- **hierarchical bases**
- **curvilinear cells**
- **singular bases** (or analogous nonsingular bases) for fine-scale features
- domain decomposition and a whole bunch of other things...

Higher-Order Models Require Curvilinear Cells (Few considerations in the optical limit)

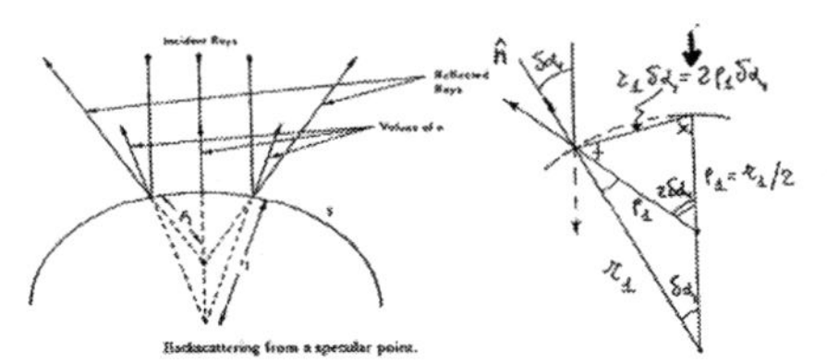

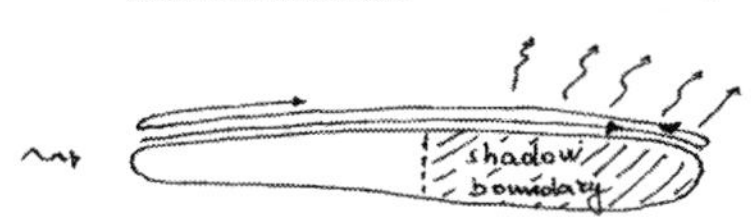

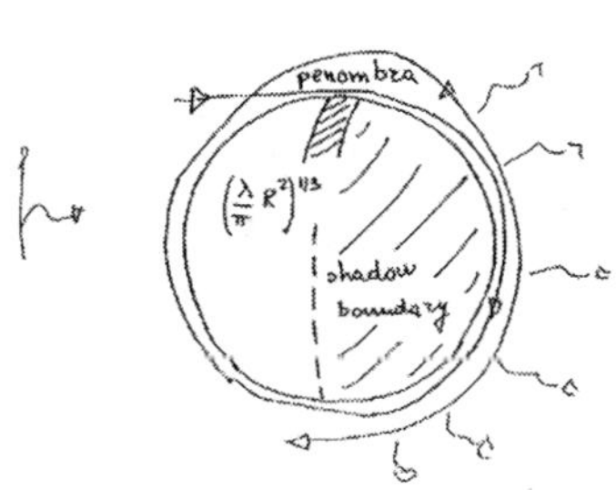

- **Contribution from specular points.** Angle of incidence = angle of reflection relative to the observation point.
- **Contribution from points with high curvature** (Travelling Waves).
- **Analysis in the shadow region** (Creeping Waves) the importance of the CW depends on the dimension in wavelength of the body.

V.A. Fock [1946], "The Distribution of Currents induced by a Plane Wave on the Surface of a Conductor," *J. Phys. USSR 10*, pp. 130-136.

Curvilinear Cells WITH High-Order Bases

- To better represent the geometry of the problem:
  - to better approximate the curvature of the geometry;
  - to better approximate small details in multiscale problems.
- To reduce the L_2 (*least squares*) norm of the solution error in regions of interest:
  - use subsectional bases thereby subdividing the geometry into simple (curved) elements.
  - use **vector** functions of higher polynomial order.
- To shorten the computation time.

❑ This usually improves the convergence of the results and/or reduces the size of the numerical matrices.

ALSO, Higher-Order Models Require Use of Singular bases

- To avoid heavy mesh refinement.
- To avoid the use of a high number of cells of small size.
- To improve the convergence of the results.

But, is there any problem?

- In FEM applications one has to use quadrature to evaluate the matrix entries, whereas for non-distorted cells there are often closed form results possible.
- For MoM applications people are already using quadrature, but the treatment of the Green's function singularity might be different with curved cells.
- The main "cost" of curved cells is
  - (1) the additional data structure necessary in the model,
  - (2) the additional computation arising from the quadrature.
- **Hierarchical Bases have the unhealthy trend to produce ill-conditioned system matrices.**

Bases must be as much **ORTHOGONAL** as possible, and well **NORMALIZED**

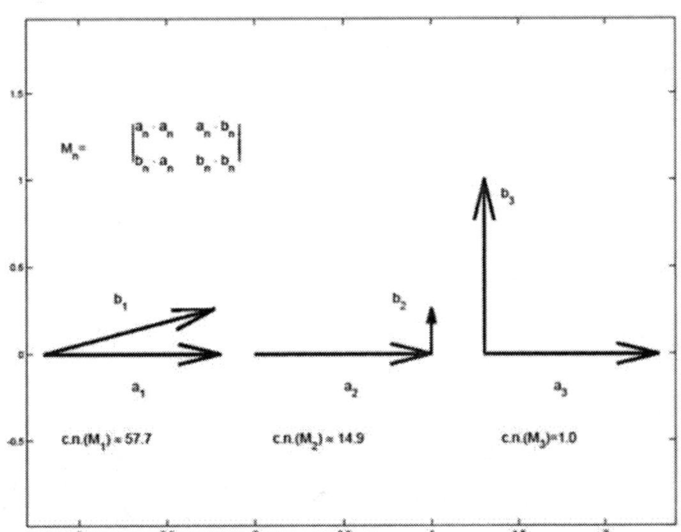

To get ***well-conditioned*** matrices, even for high order bases

What is a hierarchical basis?

The basis of order m is a subset of the basis of order (m+1). In FEM and MoM applications, these bases enable different expansion orders on different elements in the same mesh (***p***-adaptation)

Example → 2D-polynomial hierarchical bases:

0__ 1

1_↑ x _______ y

2__↑ x^2 ____ xy _____ y^2

3__↑ x^3 __ $x^2 y$ _____ $x y^2$ __ y^3

4__↑ x^4 __ $x^3 y$ __ $x^2 y^2$ ____ $x y^3$ __ y^4

This base produces ill-conditioned system matrices even for very low orders

ACES 2017: Hierarchical Bases 13

Hierarchical **non-orthogonal** bases produce ill-conditioned system matrices

Individual Element Mass-Matrix Condition Numbers for the Triangular Scalar Bases

Basis Order	p	G-matrix Order	CNI	CNH	CN for the bases of Ref. [*]
0.5	0	3	4	4	4
1.5	1	6	17.21	69.99	271
2.5	2	10	33.97	225.8	1.6×10^4
3.5	3	15	57.74	576.9	1.0×10^6
4.5	4	21	103.4	1,123	8.8×10^7
5.5	5	28	214.9	2,101	8.1×10^9
6.5	6	36	494.6	3,441	7.6×10^{11}
7.5	7	45	1,269	5,525	7.3×10^{13}
8.5	8	55	3,594	8,193	6.9×10^{15}
9.5	9	66	10,850	11,997	1.1×10^{18}
10.5	10	78	34,799	16,661	6.4×10^{19}

Individual element mass-matrix condition numbers for the hierarchical (CNH) and interpolatory (CNI) scalar polynomial bases up to order 10.5, for rectilinear triangular cells of any shape. The last column on the right-hand side of the Table reports the condition numbers obtained using the unscaled hierarchical bases given in [*] that do not employ orthogonal polynomials.

[*] Y. Zhu and A. Cangellaris, Multigrid Finite Element Methods for Electromagnetic Field Modeling. Piscataway, NJ, USA: Wiley-IEEE Press, 2006.

Higher order **vector** bases

- One can construct higher order vector bases complete to order p by forming the product of zeroth-order bases with complete polynomial factors of order p.
- The set of polynomial factors may take one of several different forms chosen for convenience (for sake of simplicity the expression at bottom considers a triangular cell and uses triangle area coordinates).

$$\textit{homogeneous}: \ \xi_1^r \xi_2^s \xi_3^t, \quad r+s+t=p$$

$$\textit{inhomogeneous}: \ \xi_i^r \xi_j^s, \quad 0 \le r+s \le p, \quad i \ne j$$

$$\textit{interpolatory}: \mathbf{R_r}(\mathbf{p},\xi_1)\mathbf{R_s}(\mathbf{p},\xi_2)\mathbf{R_t}(\mathbf{p},\xi_3), \quad r+s+t=p$$

$$\textit{hierarchical}: \ \mathbf{H_{ijk}}(\xi_1,\xi_2,\xi_3), \quad 0 \le i+j+k \le p$$

The polynomials at issue are functions of the element parent variables; keep in mind that:

- **Line element ⟶ 2 dependent parent variables;**
- **Triangular ⟶ 3 dependent parent variables;**
- **Quad. & Tetra. ⟶ 4 dependent parent variables;**
- **Prism ⟶ 5 dependent parent variables;**
- **Brick ⟶ 6 dependent parent variables.**

CONTINUITY OF THE NORMAL OR TANGENT COMPONET ACROSS BOUNDARIES OF ADJACENT CELL MUST BE GUARANTEED.

Higher order vector bases

- One can construct higher order vector bases complete to order *p* by forming the product of zeroth-order bases with complete polynomial factors of order *p*.

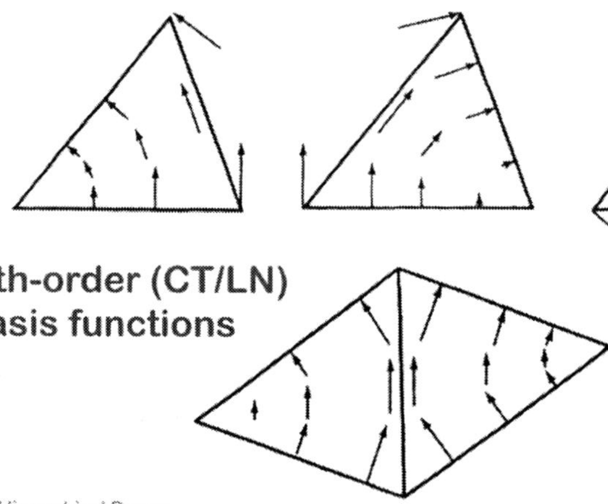

Zeroth-order (CT/LN) basis functions

Our idea

- ➢ Develop a set of **normalized,** hierarchical scalar **polynomials**;
- ➢ Define a redundant complete vector set by multiplying the zeroth-order vector functions (base vectors) with the hierarchical polynomials;
- ➢ and then eliminate redundancy to define the (unisolvent) hierarchical vector bases.
- **Same scheme used to define interpolatory vector bases on elements of different shape.**

Our idea

is equivalent to

linearly combining the terms of the existing HIGH-ORDER INTERPOLATORY VECTOR bases to form HIGH ORDER HIERARCHICAL VECTOR bases

R. D. Graglia, D. R. Wilton, and A. F. Peterson, “Higher order interpolatory vector bases for computational electromagnetics,” special issue on “Advanced Numerical Techniques in Electromagnetics,” IEEE Trans. Antennas Propagat., vol. 45, no. 3, pp. 329–342, Mar. 1997.

Two advantages of this approach:

- If the base vectors span the Nedelec spaces, their product with polynomials also spans the Nedelec spaces.
- Much easier to build a set of scalar polynomials with good linear independence than it is to subsequently orthogonalize a set of vector basis functions

One disadvantage:

- In the curl-conforming case, no basis functions of explicit gradient type are obtained

HIERARCHICAL VECTOR BASES

Curl /divergence-conforming vector bases of the **Nedelec** kind for 2D and 3D cells that:

•Allow one to mesh a structure with cells of ***different*** shapes

2D ➡ **Triangles & Quadrilaterals**

3D ➡ **Tetrahedrons & Bricks & Triangular Prisms**

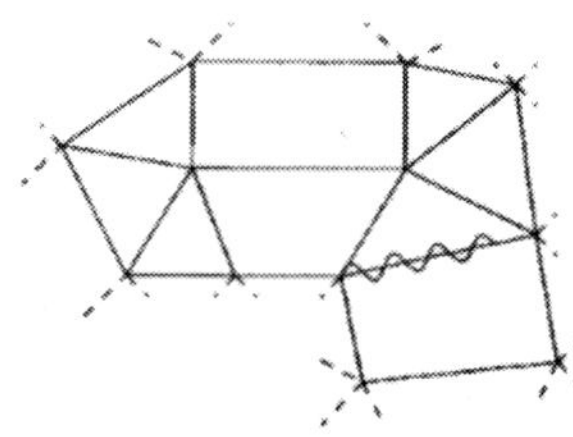

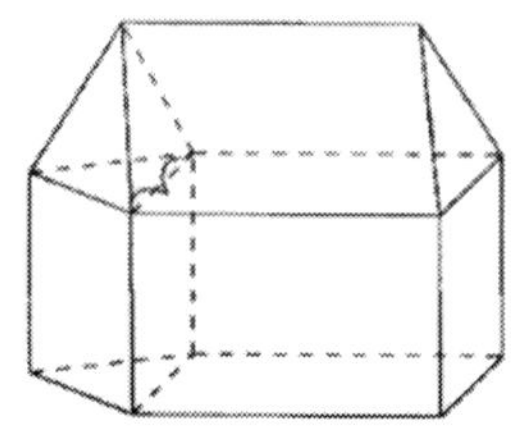

•Yield ***well-conditioned*** matrices, even for high order bases

• Are hierarchical

For the **curl-conforming** bases, the ***Generating Polynomials*** are subdivided from the outset into three different groups of **edge (E), face (F),** and **volume-based (V)** functions.

For each family, the number of the generating polynomials and their maximum polynomial order is the same as in the interpolatory family.

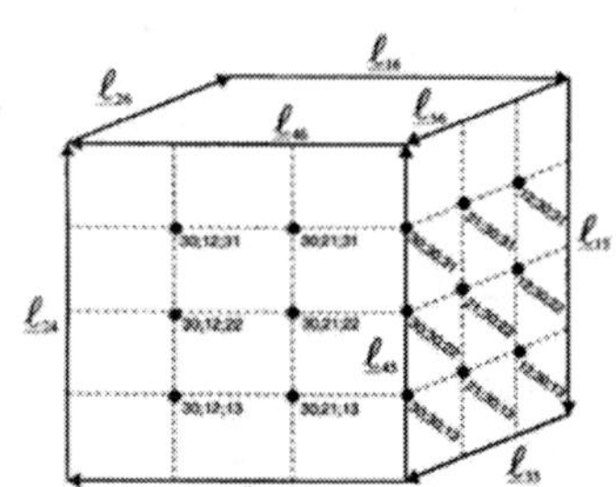

Fig. 9. Interpolation nodes for curl-conforming bases on brick elements. Only nodes in basis subset $\Omega^{43}_{ij;jm;kn}$ for $p = 2$ are shown (interior interpolation points omitted for clarity).

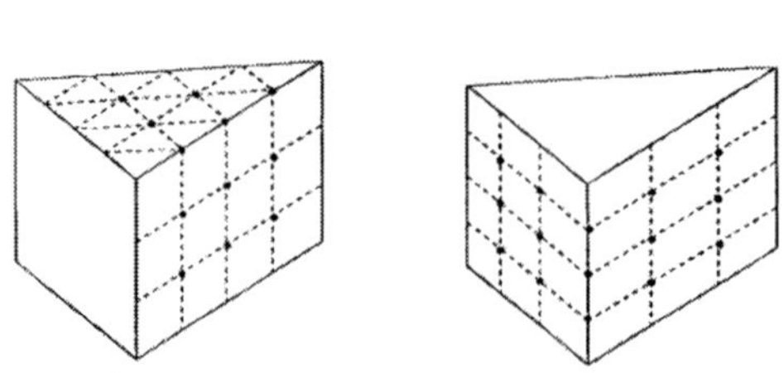

(a) (b)

Fig. 2. Interpolation points for curl-conforming bases of order $p = 2$ on prism elements (interior interpolation points omitted for clarity). (a) Nodes in basis subset $\Omega^{15}_{ijk:lm}$. (b) Nodes in basis subset $\Omega^{13}_{ijk:lm}$.

Curl-conforming bases

The definition process for the curl-conforming case is:

1) First define the volume-based polynomials;
2) Then the face-based ones;
3) Finally the edge-based ones.

Curl-conforming bases

Linear combinations of the volume-based polynomials are added to the face-based polynomials to make them orthogonal on the volume also.

Linear combinations of the volume-based polynomials AND of the face-based polynomials are added to the edge-based polynomials to make them orthogonal on the edge also.

Div-conforming bases

- In this case, the zeroth-order functions are not associated with edges but with each cell-face.
- Thus, there is the need to choose two reference parent variables on each cell-face to write the generating orthogonal polynomials in a way to easily ensure the continuity of the normal component of the vector functions across adjacent elements (i.e., by sign adjustment).
- The other face variables are obtained from the dependency relations.

Div-conforming bases

- The generating polynomials are subdivided from the outset into two different groups of face (F), and volume-based (V) functions.
- For each family, the number of the generating polynomials and their maximum polynomial order is the same as in the interpolatory family.
- The definition process for the divergence-conforming case is slightly simpler than the curl-conforming:
    1. First define the volume-based polynomials;
    2. Then the face-based ones.

Linear combinations of the volume-based polynomials are added to the face-based polynomials to make them orthogonal on the volume also.

The volume-based polynomials vanish on the bounding faces of each cell as well as on the snaked edge.

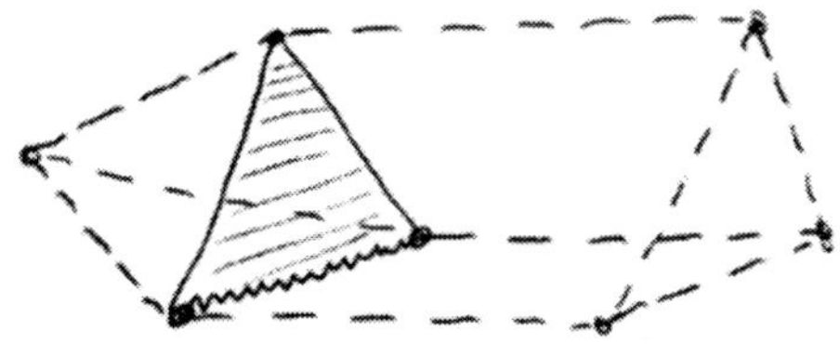

Some of the polynomial bases follow

Brick div-conforming bases

TABLE VI

FACE AND VOLUME-BASED HIERARCHICAL POLYNOMIALS FOR THE BRICK CELL.

It is understood that the first and second reference-edge of the $\xi_c = 0$ quadrilateral face of the brick are described by the variable ξ_a and ξ_b, respectively; for $\{0 \leq \xi_a, \xi_b \leq 1\}$, with $\xi_a + \xi_d = 1$, $\xi_b + \xi_e = 1$, and $\xi_c + \xi_f = 1$. For the $\xi_c = 0$ face, the reference zeroth-order vector function $\mathbf{\Lambda} = \pm \mathbf{\Lambda}_c = \pm \xi_f \nabla \xi_a \times \nabla \xi_b$ is obtained by adjusting the sign of the zeroth-order vector function $\mathbf{\Lambda}_c$ associated to the $\xi_c = 0$ face of the brick defined in [7]. At the p-th order, there are $(p+1)^2$ hierarchical face-based vector functions $F_{mn}(\boldsymbol{\xi})\, \mathbf{\Lambda}(\boldsymbol{r})$ associated to the $\xi_c = 0$ quadrilateral-face of the brick, and $p(p+1)^2$ hierarchical volume-based vector functions $V_{\ell mn}(\boldsymbol{\xi})\, \mathbf{\Lambda}(\boldsymbol{r})$ that vanish on the $\xi_c = 0$ quadrilateral-face of the brick. These vector functions are obtained by multiplying the zeroth order reference vector function $\mathbf{\Lambda}$ with the factors

$$\begin{aligned} F_{mn}(\boldsymbol{\xi}) &= E_m(\xi_{ad})\, E_n(\xi_{be}) \\ V_{\ell mn}(\boldsymbol{\xi}) &= \xi_c\, f_{\ell-1}(2\xi_c - 1)\, F_{mn}(\boldsymbol{\xi}) \\ & \quad \text{for } \ell = 1, 2, \ldots, p, \text{ and } m, n = 0, 1, \ldots, p \end{aligned}$$

with

$$E_k(z) = \sqrt{(2k+1)}\, P_k(z); \quad f_q(z) = (-1)^q f_q(-z) = \sqrt{\frac{(2q+5)(q+3)(q+4)}{3(q+1)(q+2)}}\, P_q^{(2,2)}(z)$$

and where $P_k(z)$ is the Legendre polynomial of order k while $f_q(z)$ is the q-th order re-scaled Jacobi polynomial [2], [3]. The factors $V_{\ell mn}$ are antisymmetric in (ξ_a, ξ_b) for odd value of n and symmetric otherwise, with $V_{\ell mn}(\xi_a, \xi_b) = (-1)^n V_{\ell mn}(\xi_b, \xi_a)$. These orthogonal polynomials are normalized as follows

$$\int_0^1 [\xi_c\, f_q(2\xi_c - 1)]^2\, d\xi_c = \frac{1}{3}; \quad \iint_Q F_{mn}^2\, dQ = 1, \quad \iiint_V \xi_f^2\, V_{\ell mn}^2\, dV = \frac{1}{3}$$

where V is the volume and Q the $(\xi_c = 0)$–face of the parent brick cell. To enhance the linear independency of the higher-order volume-based vector functions, the $V_{\ell mn}$ polynomials are normalized with the weight $w = \xi_f^2$ since $\sqrt{w}$ is a factor of $\mathbf{\Lambda}$. Notice that $\xi_f = 1$ on the $(\xi_c = 0)$–face of the brick.

The global order of each polynomial factor is equal to the sum of its subscripts.

Few polynomial bases follow

Quadrilateral & brick curl-conforming bases

$$\begin{cases} H_{00k} &= E_k &= \sqrt{2k+1}\, P_k(\xi_{cf}) \\ H_{i0k} &= F_{i0k} &= \xi_a\, f_{i-1}(\xi_{ad})\, E_k(\xi_{cf}) \\ H_{0jk} &= F_{0jk} &= \xi_b\, f_{j-1}(\xi_{be})\, E_k(\xi_{cf}) \\ H_{ijk} &= V_{ijk} & \\ &= \xi_a\, \xi_b\, f_{i-1}(\xi_{ad})\, f_{j-1}(\xi_{be})\, E_k(\xi_{cf}) & \end{cases} \quad (12)$$

for $i, j = 1, 2, \ldots, p$; $k = 0, 1, \ldots, p$; with ξ_{ad}, ξ_{be}, ξ_{cf} given in (7), and where

$$f_n(z) = \sqrt{\frac{(2n+5)(n+3)(n+4)}{3(n+1)(n+2)}}\, P_n^{(2,2)}(z) \quad (13)$$

$$i = p;\;\; j = 0, 1, \ldots, p;\;\; k = 0, 1, \ldots, p-1 \quad (4)$$

$$j = p;\;\; i, k = 0, 1, \ldots, p-1 \quad (5)$$

$$k = p;\;\; i, j = 0, 1, \ldots, p \quad (6)$$

Some numerical results

J error: pt-matched EFIE

EFIE w/ 4 different orders of div-conforming basis functions, point-matching

- sphere, *ka* = pi
- quadratic curved cells

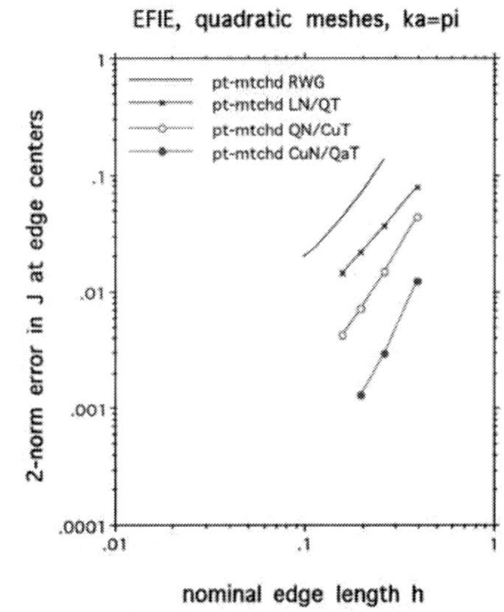

SCS error: pt-matched EFIE

EFIE w/ 4 different orders of div-conforming basis functions, point-matched testing

- sphere, *ka* = pi
- quadratic curved cells

Point tested SCS gives slopes that are O(h), O(h^2) , etc.

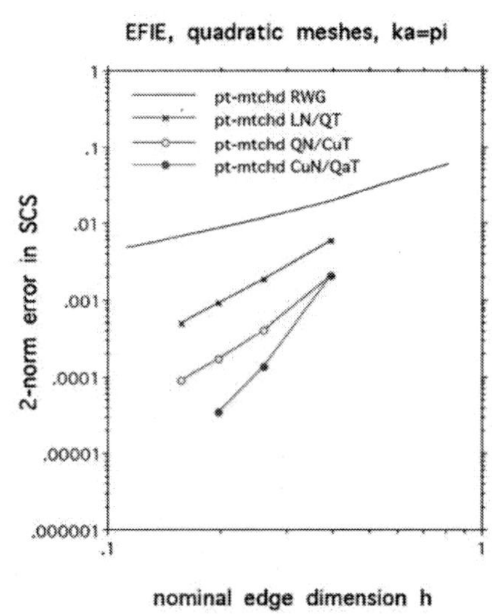

SCS error: Galerkin tested EFIE
Sphere *ka* = 2pi, with curved cells & div-conf functions

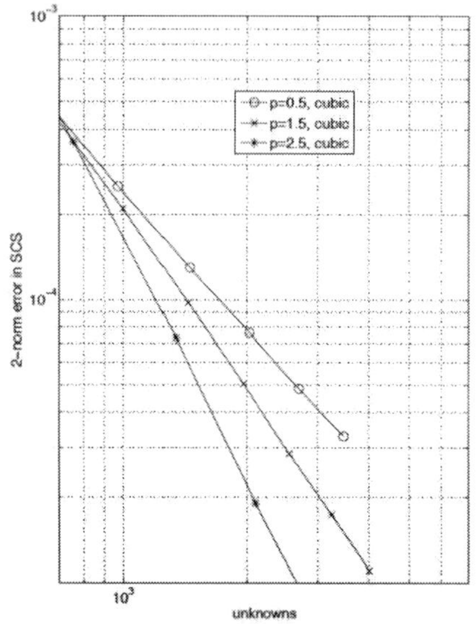

3. Error in the SCS versus number of unknowns for a sphere with $ka = 2\pi$, produce by the EFIE. Results are reported for p=0.5, p=1.5, and p=2.5 mixed-order divergence-conforming basis and test functions, in conjunction with cubic curve patch models.

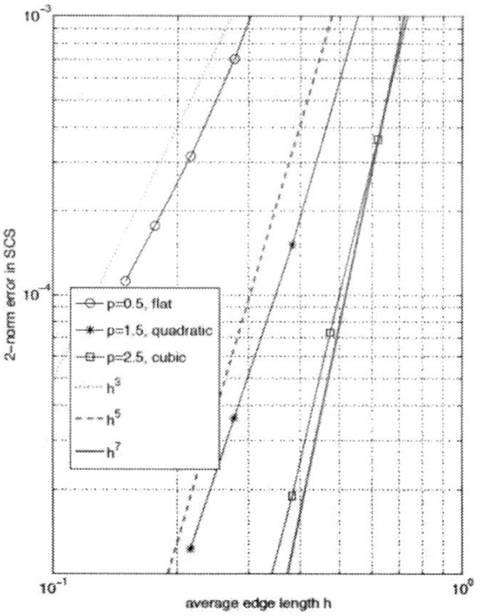

Error in the SCS versus the average edge lengths in the models, for a sphere with $ka = 2\pi$. EFIE results are reported for flat-faceted models used in conjunction with p=0.5 basis and test functions, quadratic-curved models used with p=1.5 functions, and cubic-curved models used with p=2.5 functions. Ideal asymptotic rates of $O(h^3)$, $O(h^5)$, and $O(h^7)$ are shown for comparison.

Volumetric Elements

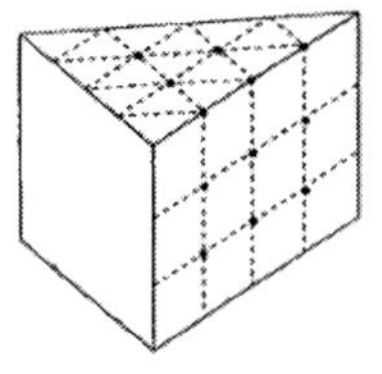

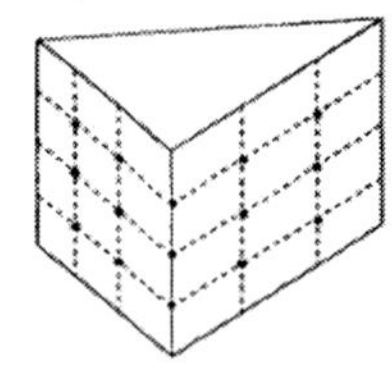

TABLE II
EIGENVALUES OF THE EQUILATERAL PRISM CAVITY OF FIG. 4(a)
COMPUTED WITH TENTH-ORDER COMPLETE FUNCTIONS

modal order number	mode;	degeneracy	kd exact	kd numerical	% error
1 2	$TE_{0,1,(-1),1}$	2	$\frac{5}{3}\pi$	5.2359877666 5.2359878015	2.0×10^{-7} 8.7×10^{-7}
3	$TM_{1,1,(-2),0}$		$\frac{4}{\sqrt{3}}\pi$	7.2551974558	-1.6×10^{-8}
4 5	$TE_{0,1,(-1),2}$	2	$\frac{2\sqrt{13}}{3}\pi$	7.5514489320 7.5514489354	-1.0×10^{-8} 3.6×10^{-8}
6 7	$TM_{1,1,(-2),1}$ $TE_{1,1,(-2),1}$		$\sqrt{\frac{19}{3}}\pi$	7.9061681227 7.9061681346	-1.2×10^{-7} 2.6×10^{-8}
8 9	$TE_{0,2,(-2),1}$	2	$\frac{\sqrt{73}}{3}\pi$	8.9472598127 8.9472698179	1.5×10^{-7} 2.1×10^{-7}
10 11	$TM_{1,1,(-2),2}$ $TE_{1,1,(-2),2}$		$\frac{2\sqrt{21}}{3}\pi$	9.5977240908 9.5977241043	-1.2×10^{-8} 1.3×10^{-7}
12 13	$TE_{0,1,(-1),3}$	2	$\frac{\sqrt{97}}{3}\pi$	10.313700246 10.313700250	4.6×10^{-6} 4.6×10^{-6}

TABLE II
EIGENVALUES OF THE EQUILATERAL PRISM CAVITY OF FIG. 4(a)
COMPUTED WITH TENTH-ORDER COMPLETE FUNCTIONS

modal order number	mode;	degeneracy	kd exact	kd numerical	% error
14 15	$TE_{0,2,(-2),2}$	2	$\frac{10}{3}\pi$	10.471975510 10.471975518	-2.3×10^{-8} 5.5×10^{-8}
16 17	$TM_{1,2,(-3),0}$	2	$\frac{4\sqrt{7}}{3}\pi$	11.08249777 11.08249781	5.4×10^{-6} 5.7×10^{-6}
18 19 20 21	$TM_{1,2,(-3),1}$ $TE_{1,2,(-3),1}$	2 2	$\frac{11}{3}\pi$	11.51917367 11.51917367 11.51917370 11.51917373	5.3×10^{-6} 5.3×10^{-6} 5.5×10^{-6} 5.7×10^{-6}
⋮	⋮		⋮	⋮	⋮
55 56	$TM_{2,2,(-4),2}$ $TE_{2,2,(-4),2}$		$2\sqrt{\frac{19}{3}}\pi$	15.812333 15.812351	-2.1×10^{-5} 9.3×10^{-5}
57 58	$TE_{0,1,(-1),5}$	2	$\frac{\sqrt{241}}{3}\pi$	16.266 16.266	5.7×10^{-2} 5.7×10^{-2}
59 60 61 62	$TM_{1,3,(-4),2}$ $TE_{1,3,(-4),2}$	2 2	$\frac{2\sqrt{61}}{3}\pi$	16.3579 16.3579 16.3581 16.3581	9.3×10^{-4} 9.3×10^{-4} 1.9×10^{-3} 1.9×10^{-3}

Volumetric Elements

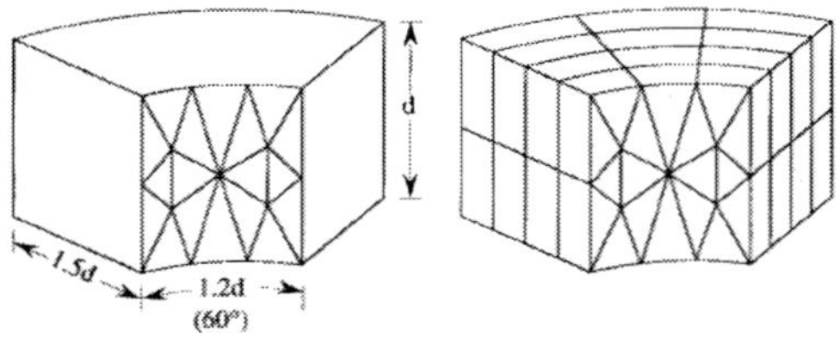

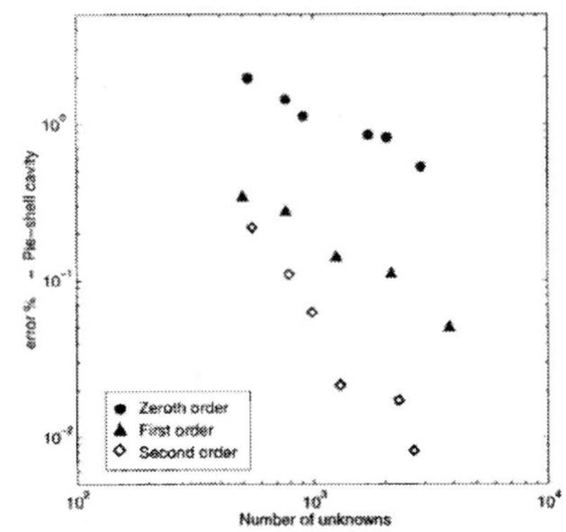

Volumetric Elements

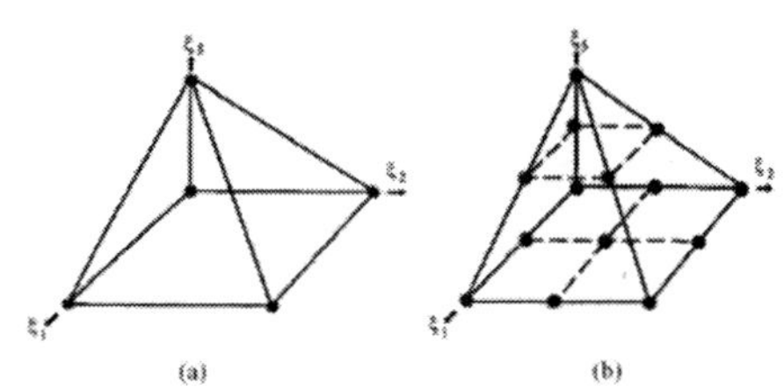

Fig. 3. Parent domain parametrization for a curvilinear pyramid. The pyramid shape functions interpolate 5 and 14 nodes for (a) first- and (b) second-order parametrization, respectively.

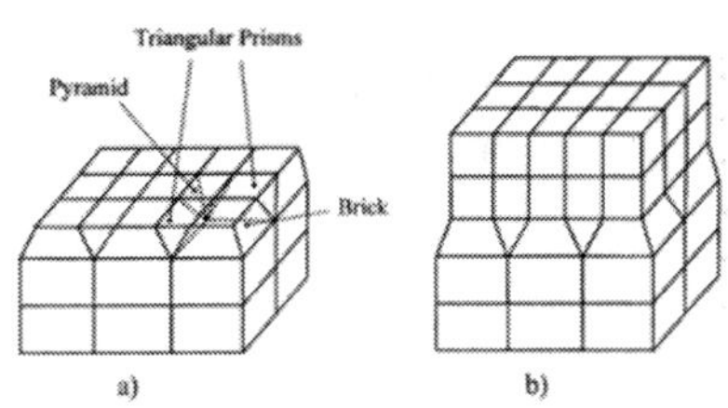

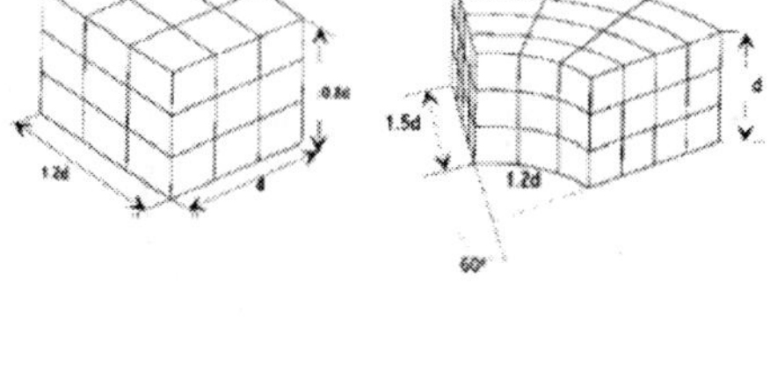

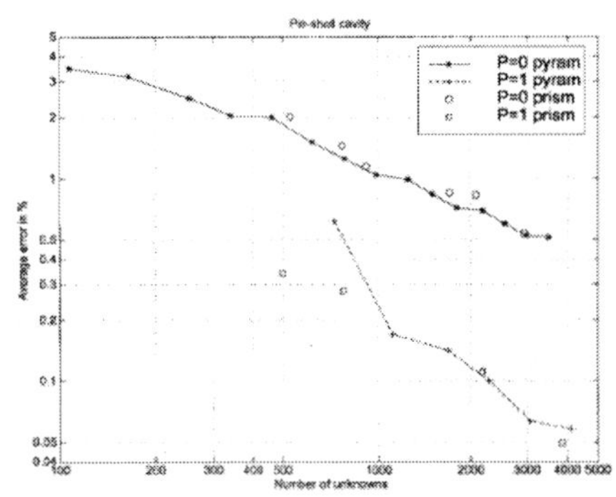

INHOM. FILLED WG - RELATIVE ERROR

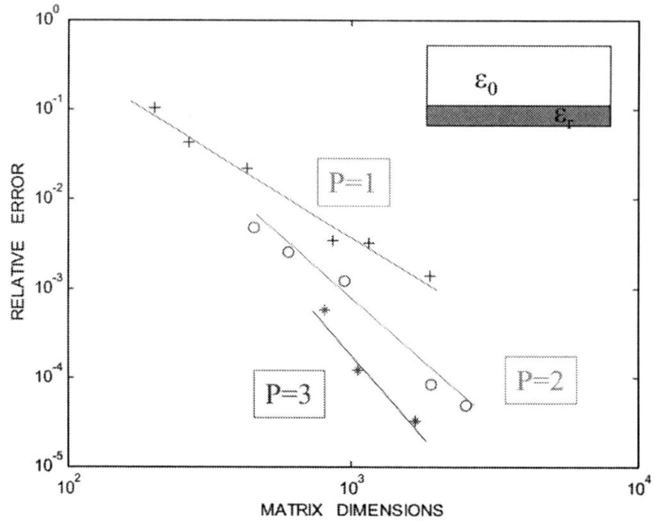

Normal field component at the air-dielectric interface.

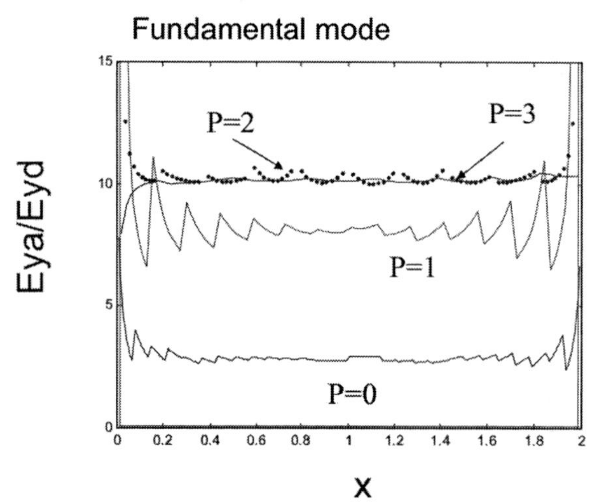

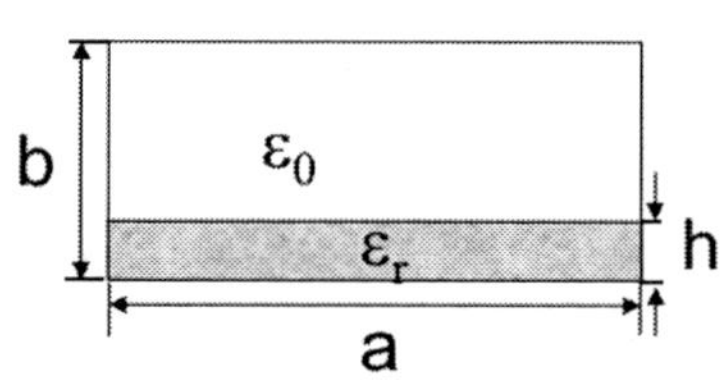

a =2b, h =0.2 b
ε_r =10, k_0a =7

~ 1800 UNKNOWNS

P	N
0	1641
1	1873
2	1897
3	1681

CNs obtained by use of the **Triangular** family

TABLE III

CONDITION NUMBER COMPARISON FOR TRIANGULAR BASES OF ORDER 2.5

The matrix condition number of the global **T**-matrix in (19) obtained by taking the ratio of the largest singular value to the smallest, for five triangular-cell meshes of different quality. For each basis family, the 15 curl conforming basis functions making up the Nédélec reduced-gradient QT/CuN representation were used with optimal scale factors*.

Family	Mesh 12	Mesh 42	Mesh 40a	Mesh 40b	Mesh 34
Graglia, Wilton, and Peterson (GWP) [2]	528	352	597	6,075	3,319
Graglia* *et al.* [9, 10]	720	459	855	1,923	1,366
Ingleström [8]	1,040	510	1,085	5,022	3,284
Webb orthogonal [5]	1,095	517	1,121	4,345	3,120
Lee, Lee, and Lee [6]	1,456	1,791	4,612	21,883	12,994
Preissig and Peterson [7]	1,137	1,510	4,359	27,974	26,765
Andersen and Volakis [3]	2,920	2,084	5,965	31,100	49,956

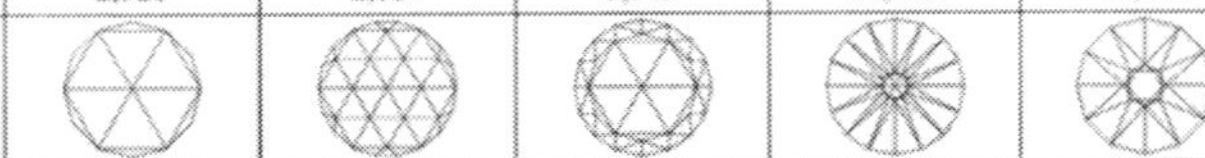

Number of cells:	12	42	40	40	34
Order of **T**:	114	468	444	444	384

*The "unscaled" Graglia *et al.* bases (using the original scaling from [9-10]) were used since those usually outperformed our "optimally" scaled Graglia bases. For the other families, the optimally scaled bases outperformed the original, unscaled bases for these meshes, and those results are reported.

CNs obtained by use of the **Triangular** family

TABLE IV

CONDITION NUMBER COMPARISON FOR TRIANGULAR BASES OF ORDER 3.5

The matrix condition number of the global **T**-matrix in (19) for five triangular-cell meshes of different quality. The Graglia *et al.* bases are in their original form; the Ingleström bases are scaled using the optimal factors.

Family	Mesh 12	Mesh 42	Mesh 40a	Mesh 40b	Mesh 34
GWP [2]	2,274	1,541	2,689	58,813	20,857
Graglia *et al.* [9-10]	2,298	1,502	3,160	6,449	5,093
Ingleström [8]	1,461	1,148	2,526	14,002	7,162
Order of **T**:	240	792	752	752	648

More recent numerical results

Cube cavity studied with curl-conforming **tetrahedral cells** of different orders

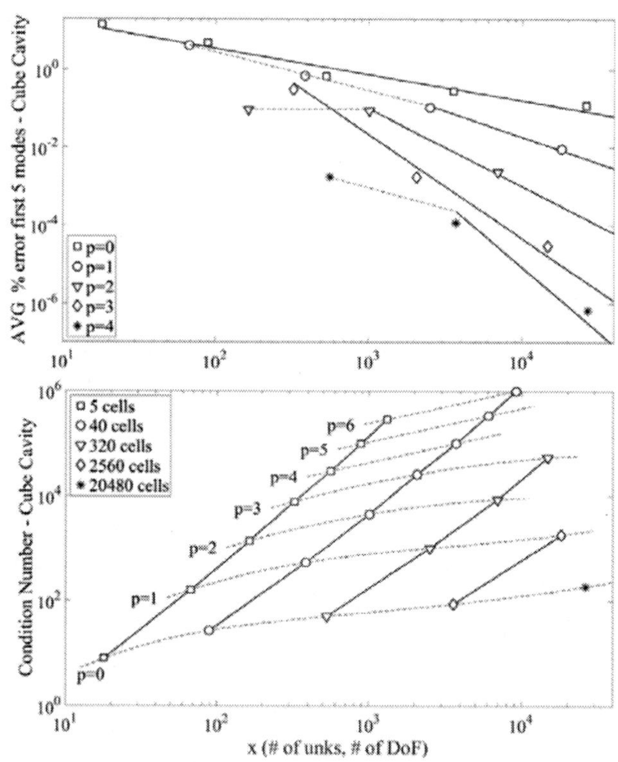

Prism cavity studied with curl-conforming **tetrahedral cells** of different orders

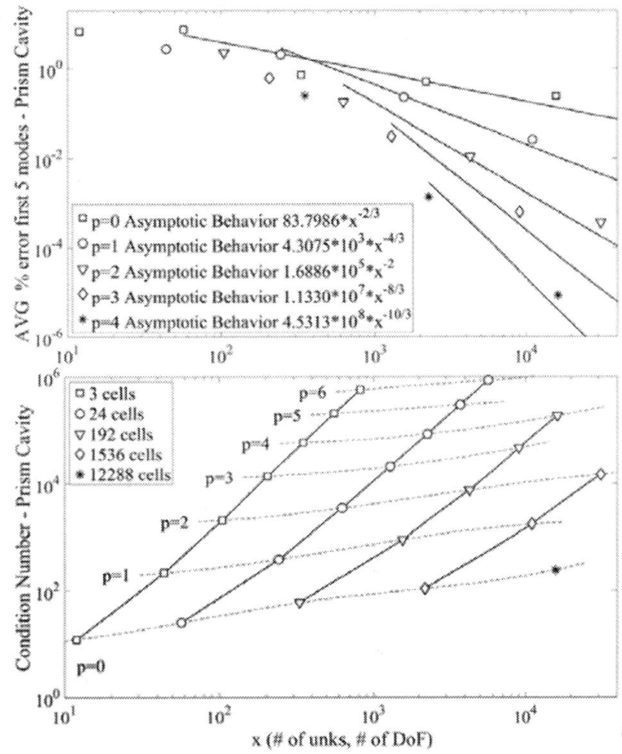

CUBE-CAVITY
Results with Tetra & Prism Elements

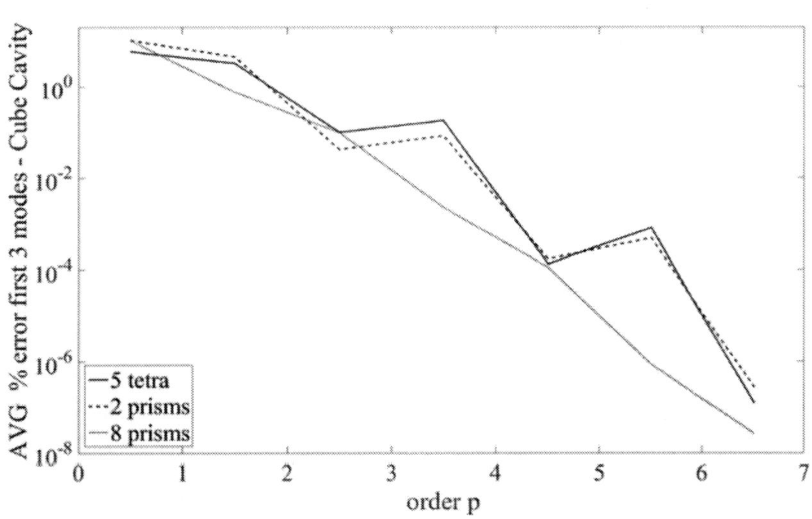

CUBE-CAVITY
Results with Tetra & Prism Elements

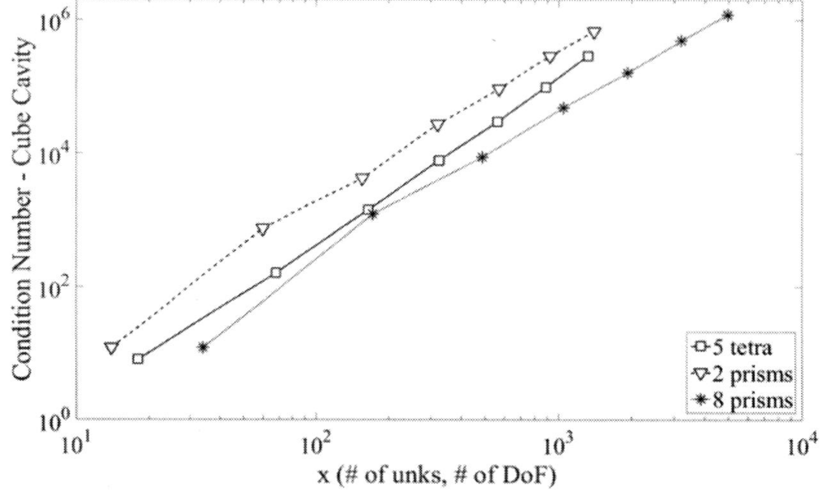

L-Shaped-CAVITY
Results with **8 Prism Elements**

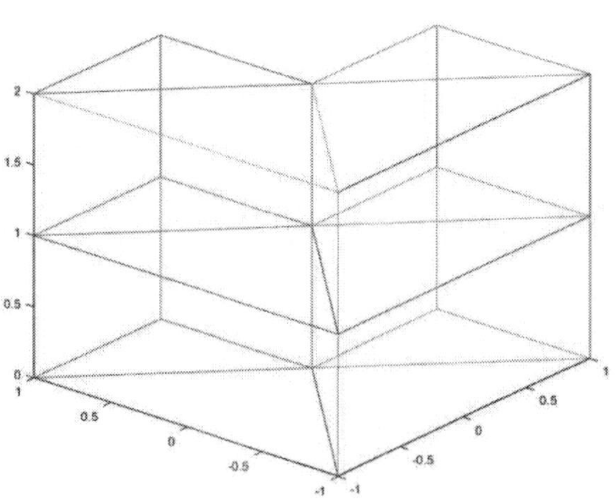

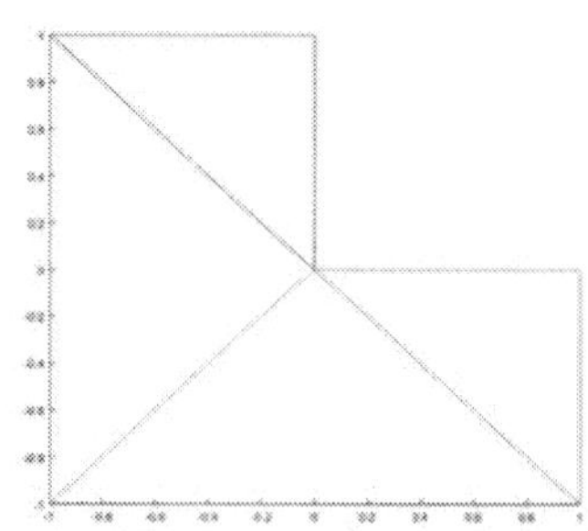

Percentage Error for Cavity Resonance

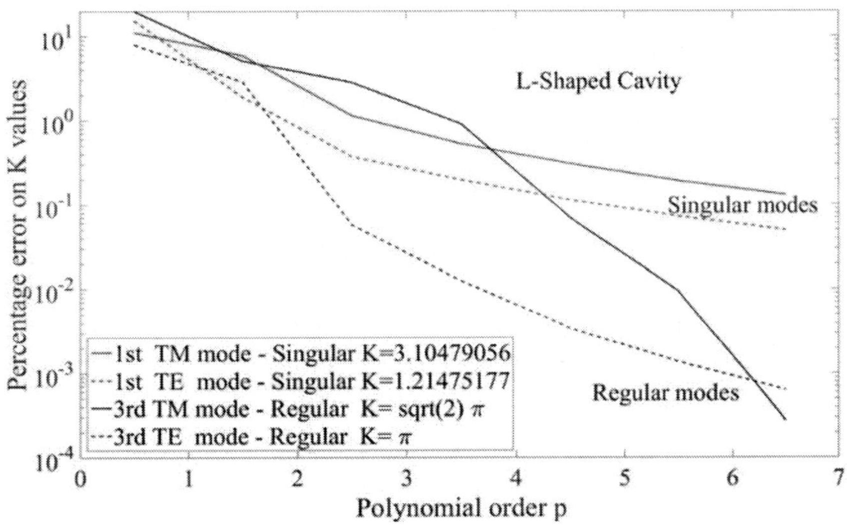

Condition Number (8 prisms)

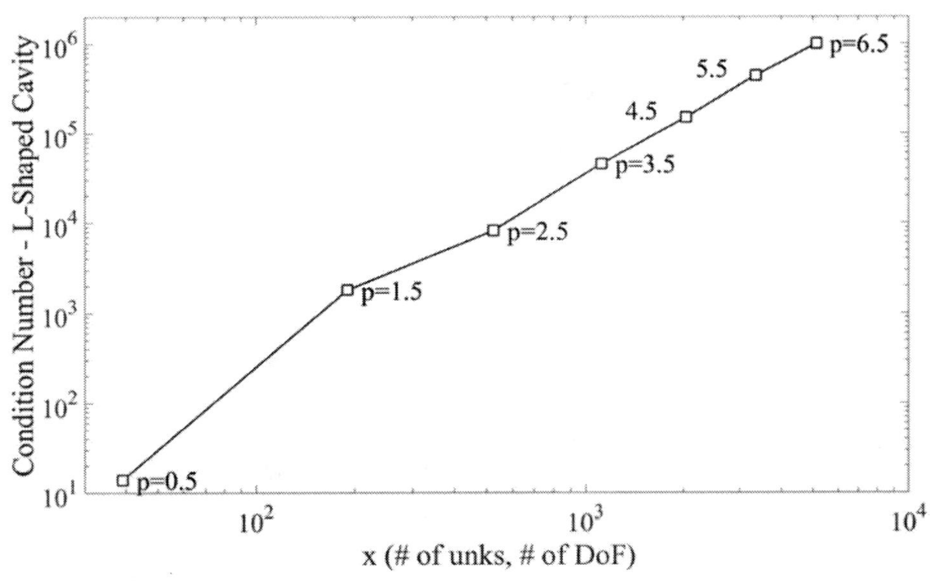

CONCLUSIONS

- With our construction scheme we obtain vector bases for
  - **triangular & quadrilateral cells**.
  - **curl-conforming** bases for tetrahedral, brick and prism cells.
  - **divergence-conforming** bases for 3D elements: tetrahedron, brick and prism.
- Our curl-conforming basis family produce well-conditioned matrices; the other basis families produce more ill-conditioned matrices, suggesting that their linear independence is not as good.
- The transitioning strategy for *p*-refinement is reported in: Peterson and Graglia, "Evaluation of hierarchical vector basis functions for quadrilateral cells," *IEEE Trans. Magnetics*, vol. 47, pp. 1190-1193, May 2011.
- Permits one to mesh a structure using cells of ***different*** shapes.

CONCLUSIONS

- **If the structure contains edges the results are not as good and singular bases must be used to obtain the expected accuracy at higher orders.**

Developing Singular Vector Bases for CEM

Andrew F. Peterson
Roberto D. Graglia

ACES 2017 Tutorial Notes
March 2017

Plan for Today

- Review the history of singular basis functions for EM problems
- Focus on low-order vector bases
  - divergence conforming for EFIE
  - curl conforming for vector Helmholtz
- Identify principles that have been used in their development
  - substitutive versus additive concept
  - use of gradients for curl conforming
  - triangular-polar coordinates for 2D
  - prism-cylindrical coordinates for 3D
- Illustrate with some specific examples

Some references...

- A. F. Peterson and R. D. Graglia, "Basis functions for vertex, edge, and corner singularities: A review," *IEEE J. Multiscale and Multiphysics Comp. Tech.*, vol. 1, pp. 161–175, December 2016.
- R. D. Graglia, A. F. Peterson, L. Matekovits, and P. Petrini, "Singular hierarchical curl-conforming vector basis functions for triangular cells," *IEEE Trans. Antennas Propagat.*, vol. 62, pp. 3632–3644, July 2014.
- R. D. Graglia, A. F. Peterson, L. Matekovits, and P. Petrini, "Hierarchical additive basis functions for the finite element treatment of corner singularities," *Electromagnetics*, vol. 34, pp. 171–198, 2014.
- R. D. Graglia, P. Petrini, A. F. Peterson, and L. Matekovits, "Full-wave analysis of inhomogeneous waveguiding structures containing corners with singular hierarchical curl-conforming vector bases," *IEEE Antennas and Wireless Propagation Letters*, vol. 13, pp. 1701–1704, 2014.

Why singular basis functions?

- Better accuracy in numerical results for problems with edges
  - dominant TM mode of cavity with septum

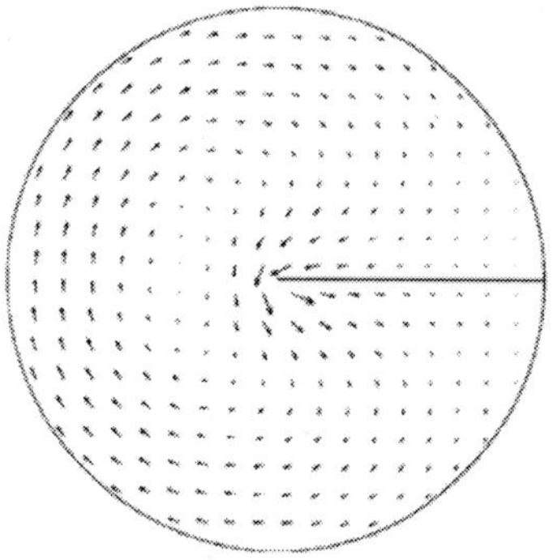

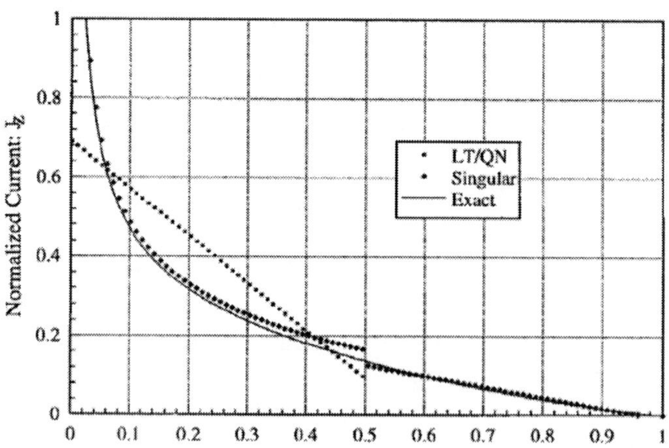

Why singular basis functions?

- Faster convergence of numerical results for problems with edges
  - tubular dipole input impedance, Richmond, *IEEE T-AP*, 1980
  - microstrip patch input impedance, Pinhas et al., *IEEE T-AP*, 1989

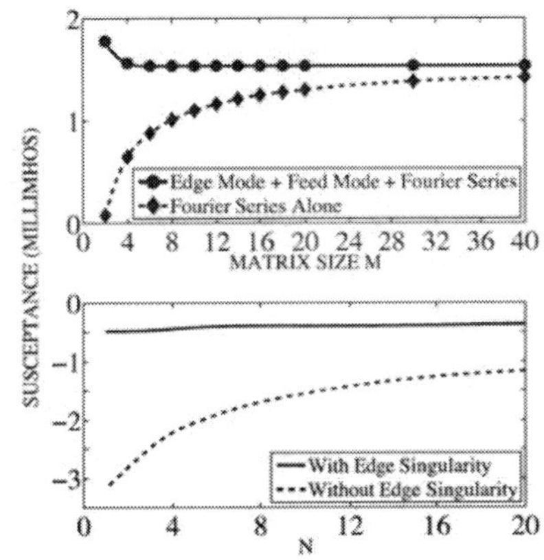

Why singular basis functions?

- Ability to extend to "higher order" as for smooth targets
  - TM PEC triangular cylinder, 7 wavelengths/side, plane wave incident on one corner, MFIE

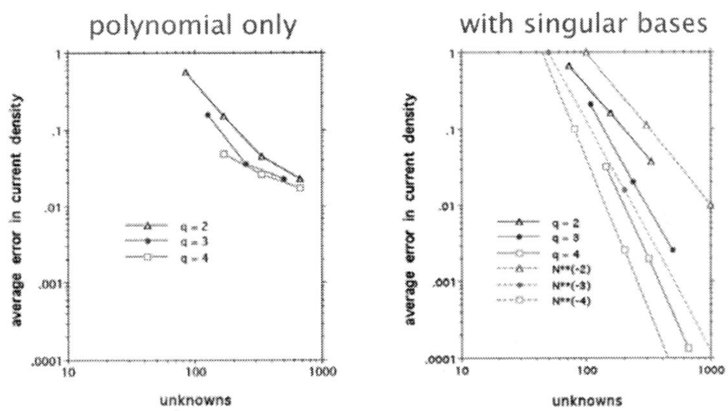

Early Applications in EM

- Papers began appearing in the EM literature circa 1971
- Mostly integral equation or spectral domain formulations
- typically a 1D entire domain expansion or Fourier series with an entire-domain singular function added
  - R. Mittra, and S. W. Lee, *Analytical Techniques in the Theory of Guided Waves.* New York: Macmillan, 1971.
  - J. C. Minor and D. M. Bolle, "Modes in the shielded microstrip on a ferrite substrate transversely magnetized in the plane of the substrate, *IEEE Trans. MTT*, vol. 19, pp. 570-577, July 1971.
  - L. Shafai, "Current induced on a conducting strip," *Canadian J. Phys.*, vol. 49, pp. 495-498, 1971.
  - etc...

Early Applications in EM

- First 1D subsectional basis functions for EM integral equation formulation
  - D. R. Wilton and S. Govind, "Incorporation of edge condition in moment method solutions," *IEEE Trans. AP*, vol. 25, pp. 845-850, Nov. 1977.

one wavelength strip

pulses (xxx), pulses with singular edge terms (ooo)

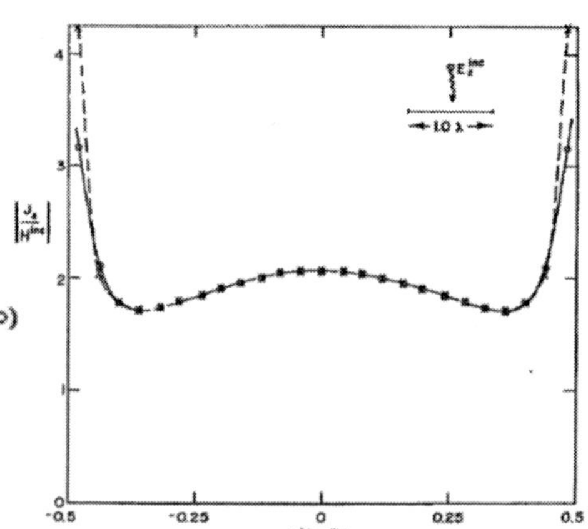

Early Applications, 2D FEM

- Papers began appearing in the ME & applied math literature in early 1970s
- Scalar differential equation formulations
- 2D vertex singularities, mostly for potentials of the form $r^{1/2}$ with an unbounded derivative (gradient) of $r^{-1/2}$
  - E. Byskov, *Int. J. Fracture Mech.*, 1970.
  - D. M. Tracey, *Eng. Fracture Mech.*, 1971.
  - R. Wait and A. R. Mitchell, *J. Comp. Physics*, 1971.
  - G. J. Fix, S. Gulati, and G. I. Wakoff, *J. Comp. Physics*, 1973.
  - G. Strang and G. J. Fix, *An Analysis of the FEM*, 1973.
  - J. E. Akin, *Int. J. Num. Methods Eng.*, 1976
  - R. Wait, *IMA J. Appl. Math.*, 1977
  - D. M. Tracey and T. S. Cook, *Int. J. Num. Methods Eng.*, 1977.
  - M. Stern and E. B. Becker, *Int. J. Num. Methods Eng.*, 1978.

Canonical problem: PEC wedge

TABLE I
EXPONENTS FOR PERFECTLY CONDUCTING WEDGE WITH INTERIOR ANGLE α

Transverse Magnetic (TM) to z case:

$$E_z \sim A\rho^{\nu} f(\phi)$$

$$\bar{H}_t \sim \frac{A\rho^{\nu-1}}{-j\omega\mu}\{\hat{\rho}\, f'(\phi) - \hat{\phi}\, \nu f(\phi)\}.$$

TE to z case:

$$H_z \sim B\rho^{\nu} g(\phi) + C$$

$$\bar{E}_t \sim \frac{B\rho^{\nu-1}}{j\omega\varepsilon}\{\hat{\rho}\, g'(\phi) - \hat{\phi}\, \nu g(\phi)\}.$$

Exponents (TM and TE):

$$\nu_{mn} = 2m + \frac{n\pi}{2\pi - \alpha}, \quad m = 0,\ 1,\ 2, \ldots,\ n = 1,\ 2, \ldots.$$

Canonical problem: PEC wedge

$$J_z \sim \sum_{m=0}^{\infty}\sum_{n=1}^{\infty} c_{mn}\rho^{2m+\upsilon_n-1}$$

$$J_\rho \sim \sum_{m=0}^{\infty}\sum_{n=0}^{\infty} d_{mn}\rho^{2m+\upsilon_n}$$

$$\upsilon_n = \frac{n\pi}{(2\pi-\alpha)}$$

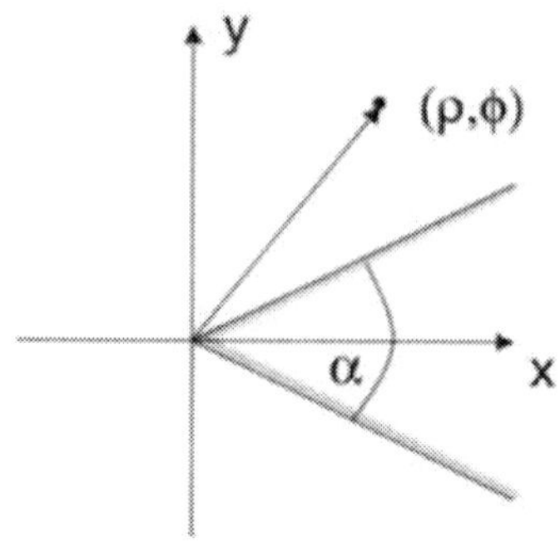

→ May consider *multiple* terms from the wedge solution

Canonical problem: Dielectric wedge

TABLE II
EXPONENTS FOR DIELECTRIC OR MAGNETIC WEDGE WITH INTERIOR ANGLE α

(Same field components as in Table I*)*

TE to z case: Exponents depend on ε_r and are solutions of

$$\varepsilon_r \tan\left(\frac{\nu\alpha}{2}\right) = -\tan\left(\nu\,\frac{2\pi-\alpha}{2}\right)$$

$$\frac{1}{\varepsilon_r}\tan\left(\frac{\nu\alpha}{2}\right) = -\tan\left(\nu\,\frac{2\pi-\alpha}{2}\right)$$

TM to z case: Exponents depend on μ_r and are solutions of

$$\mu_r \tan\left(\frac{\nu\alpha}{2}\right) = -\tan\left(\nu\,\frac{2\pi-\alpha}{2}\right)$$

$$\frac{1}{\mu_r}\tan\left(\frac{\nu\alpha}{2}\right) = -\tan\left(\nu\,\frac{2\pi-\alpha}{2}\right)$$

Canonical problem: Dielectric wedge

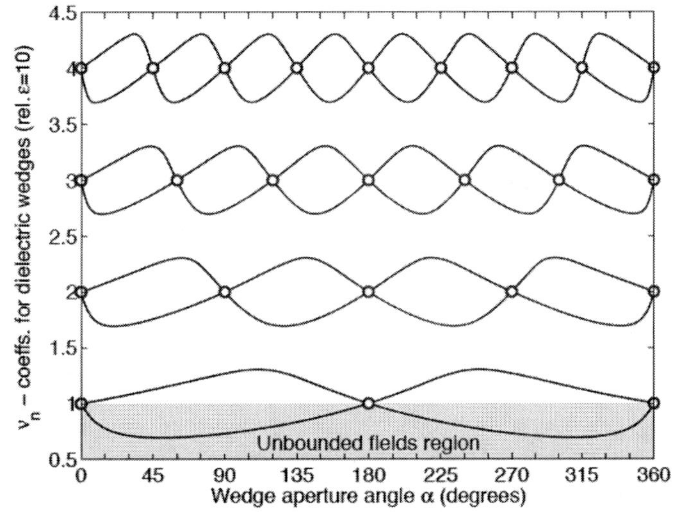

Canonical problem: Plane angular sector

TABLE III

CURRENT DENSITY FOR A PLANE ANGULAR SECTOR, IN SPHEROCONAL COORDINATES, WITH EXPONENTS FOR A 90° CORNER

$$J_r \sim \frac{1}{\sin\phi}\sum\left\{\begin{array}{l} A_{-1}(\phi)r^{\nu_{oi}-1} + A_0(\phi)r^{\nu_{ei}} \\ +A_1(\phi)r^{\nu_{oi}+1} + A_2(\phi)r^{\nu_{ei}+2} + \cdots \end{array}\right\}$$

$$J_\phi \sim \sin\phi\sum\left\{\begin{array}{l} B_{-1}(\phi)r^{\nu_{oi}-1} + B_1(\phi)r^{\nu_{oi}+1} \\ +B_3(\phi)r^{\nu_{oi}+3} + \cdots \end{array}\right\}$$

$$\nabla_S \bullet \bar{J} \sim \frac{1}{\sin\phi}\sum\left\{\begin{array}{l} C_{-1}(\phi)r^{\nu_{ei}-1} + C_0(\phi)r^{\nu_{oi}} \\ +C_1(\phi)r^{\nu_{ei}+1} + C_2(\phi)r^{\nu_{oi}+2} \\ +\cdots \end{array}\right\}$$

Exponents (90° corner)

Index	ν_{oi}	ν_{ei}
1	0.81 466	0.29 658
2	1.59 713	1.13 125
3	1.95 533	1.42 651

Today's focus

- 2D expansions
- triangular cells
- vertex singularities due to wedge apex in domain
- edge singularities such as those along plate boundaries

2D FEM: Triangular–Polar Coordinates

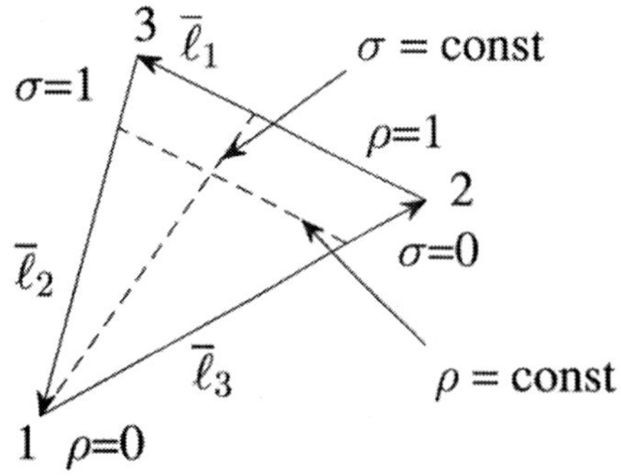

$$\xi_1 = 1 - \rho$$

$$\xi_2 = \rho(1 - \sigma)$$

$$\xi_3 = \rho\sigma$$

$$\rho = 1 - \xi_1$$

$$\sigma = \frac{\xi_3}{1 - \xi_1} = \frac{1 - \xi_1 - \xi_2}{1 - \xi_1}$$

Singular Scalar Basis

- The three linear polynomial basis functions are replaced by *substitutive* singular functions (they "substitute" for them) to provide singular behavior at rho = 0
  - polynomial basis functions:

$$B_1 = \xi_1,\ B_2 = \xi_2,\ B_3 = \xi_3$$

  - singular basis functions that replace them:

$$\begin{aligned} S_1 &= 1 - \rho^\nu \\ S_2 &= \rho^\nu (1 - \sigma) \\ S_3 &= \rho^\nu \sigma. \end{aligned}$$

2D Triangles: Singular Scalar Basis

- within a triangle, replace linear basis functions used to represent a bounded potential with the "singular" bases

$$\begin{aligned} S_1 &= 1 - \rho^\nu \\ S_2 &= \rho^\nu (1 - \sigma) \\ S_3 &= \rho^\nu \sigma. \end{aligned}$$

- these have gradients that are unbounded for nu < 1

$$\begin{aligned} \nabla S_1 &= \rho^{\nu-1} \nu \nabla \xi_1 \\ \nabla S_2 &= \rho^{\nu-1} \left\{ (1-\sigma)(1-\nu)\nabla\xi_1 + \nabla\xi_2 \right\} \\ \nabla S_3 &= \rho^{\nu-1} \left\{ \sigma(1-\nu)\nabla\xi_1 + \nabla\xi_3 \right\} \end{aligned}$$

(Pantic & Mittra, *IEEE Trans. MTT*, 1986; also early ME papers)

Gradients of Singular Scalar Bases

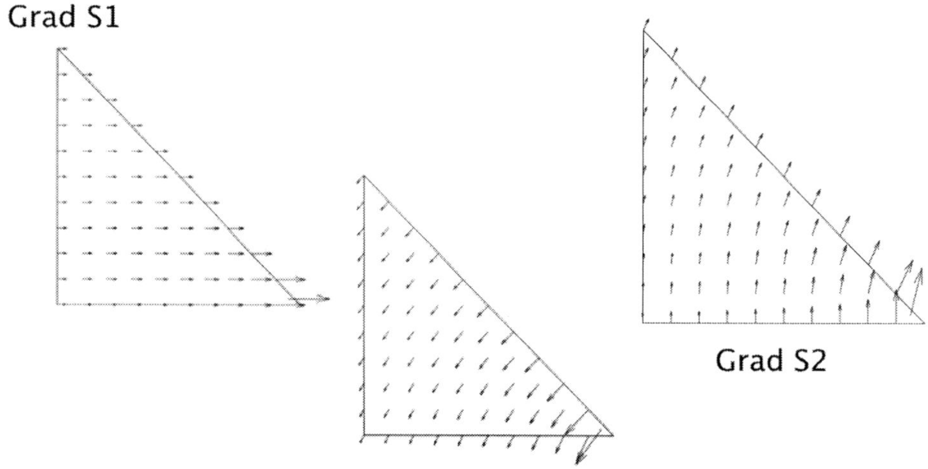

Substitutive basis functions

- Substitutive basis functions are the simplest way to incorporate leading-order singularities
  - 1:1 replacement of original functions
  - no additional unknowns introduced
  - often leads to accuracy/ convergence improvement
- Possible drawbacks
  - Singularity is present whether it is excited by the source or not
  - Polynomial degrees of freedom are removed

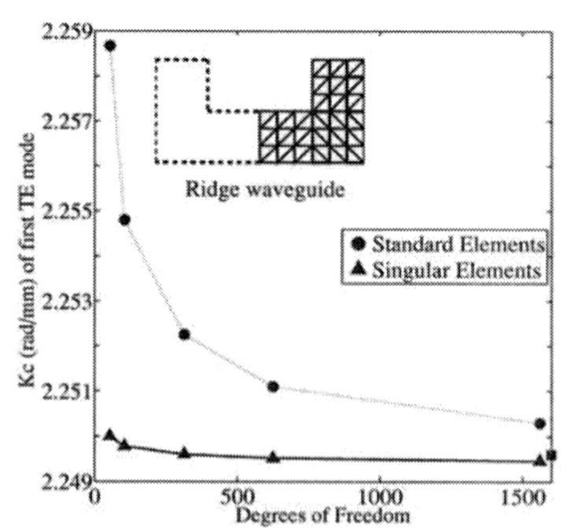

(Gil & Zapata, *IEEE Trans. MTT*, 1994)

Additive basis functions

- Alternative approach: additive singular basis functions
  - idea is to add some singular basis functions to the existing set of polynomial basis functions without removing any
  - demonstrates better accuracy when singularity not excited
  - often implemented in a hierarchical manner
  - needed to obtain "high order" behavior for problems with edge singularities
  - matrix conditioning suffers unless bases are orthogonalized

Polynomial vector basis, p=0.5

- Divergence conforming (p=0.5, RWG):

$$\bar{\Lambda}_1 = \xi_2\,\bar{\ell}_3 - \xi_3\,\bar{\ell}_2$$
$$\bar{\Lambda}_2 = \xi_3\,\bar{\ell}_1 - \xi_1\,\bar{\ell}_3$$
$$\bar{\Lambda}_3 = \xi_1\,\bar{\ell}_2 - \xi_2\,\bar{\ell}_1$$

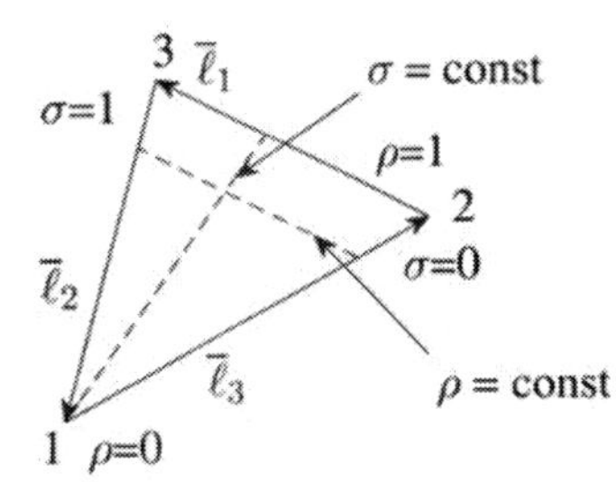

- Curl conforming (p=0.5):

$$\bar{\Omega}_1 = -\xi_2\nabla\xi_1 + (\xi_1 - 1)\nabla\xi_2$$
$$\bar{\Omega}_2 = -(\xi_2 - 1)\nabla\xi_1 + \xi_1\nabla\xi_2$$
$$\bar{\Omega}_3 = -\xi_2\nabla\xi_1 + \xi_1\nabla\xi_2.$$

(These are related by a 90 degree rotation)

Singular vector basis functions

- Divergence conforming
  - Used for representing current density and charge density when solving integral equations such as the EFIE
  - Typical application: singularity at an edge of a conducting plate
  - Tangential component of current and the charge density are unbounded at plate edge
  - Independent singularity at plate corner
  - Challenge: plate edge and certain triangle nodes not necessarily aligned

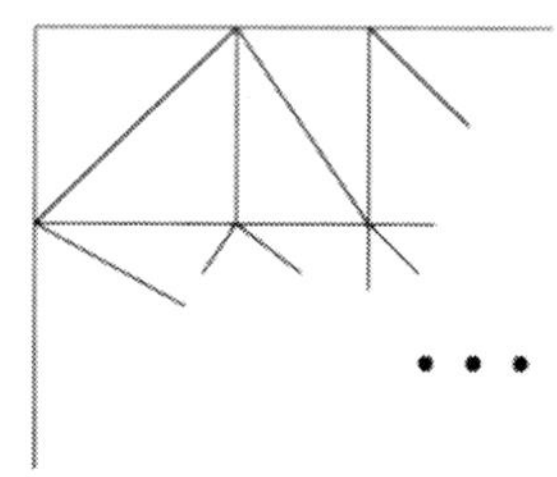

Singular vector basis functions

- Curl conforming in 2D
  - Used for representing fields when solving 2D vector Helmholtz differential equation
  - Typical application: wedge tip protruding into the domain
  - Transverse component of primary field (electric?) is unbounded at wedge apex
  - Other field (magnetic) bounded there; but is usually obtained from the curl; in some cases (dielectric wedge) may have behavior in 2nd field that is not directly related to the leading singularity of primary field

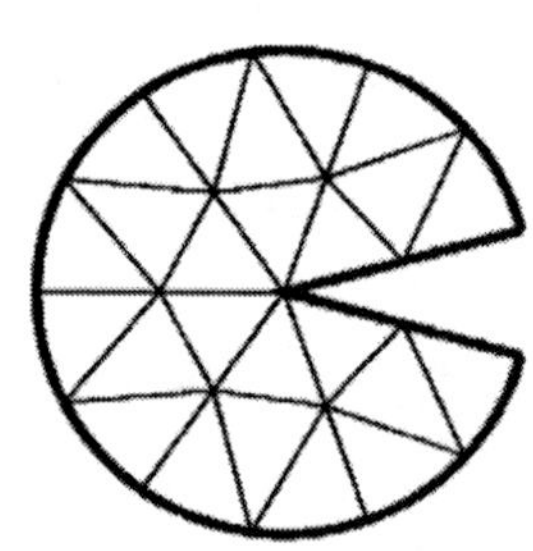

Singular vector basis functions

- Divergence-conforming (substitutive for p=0.5)
  - W. J. Brown and D. R. Wilton, "Singular basis functions and curvilinear triangles in the solution of the electric field integral equation," *IEEE Trans. AP*, vol. 47, pp. 347-353, February 1999
  - R. D. Graglia and G. Lombardi, "Vector functions for singular fields on curved triangular elements, truly defined in the parent space," *IEEE AP International Symposium Digest*, San Antonio, TX, pp. 62-65, 2002
- Divergence-conforming (additive)
  - R. D. Graglia, and G. Lombardi. "Singular higher order divergence-conforming bases of additive kind and moments method applications to 3D sharp-wedge structures," *IEEE Trans. AP*, vol. 56, pp. 3768-3788, December 2008

Singular vector basis functions

- Curl-conforming (substitutive for p=0.5)
  - R. D. Graglia and G. Lombardi, "Vector functions for singular fields on curved triangular elements, truly defined in the parent space," *IEEE AP International Symposium Digest*, San Antonio, TX, pp. 62-65, 2002
  - J. Masoni, G. Pelosi, and S. Selleri, "Substitutive divergent bases for FEM modeling of field singularities near a wedge," *Microwave and Optical Technology Letters*, vol. 44, no. 4, February 20, 2005
  - D.-J. Sun, L. Vardapetyan, and Z. Cendes, "Two-dimensional curl-conforming singular elements for FEM solutions of dielectric waveguiding structures," *IEEE Trans. MTT*, vol. 53, pp. 984-992, March 2005
- Curl-conforming (additive)
  - R. D. Graglia and G. Lombardi, "Singular higher order complete vector bases for finite methods," *IEEE Trans. Antennas Propagat.*, vol. 52, pp. 1672-1685, July 2004

Vector Bases for Vertex Singularities

- Can obtain a (rho)$^{nu-1}$ behavior in the primary unknown while obtaining
  - (rho)$^{nu-1}$ in the derivative (want this for div-conforming)
  - (rho)^{nu} in the derivative (want this for curl-conforming)
  - (rho)^{0} in the derivative (non-singular)
- Gradients are used to introduce singularities when one does not want more singular fields in the curl
  - Otherwise obtain (rho)$^{nu-2}$ in the derivative (not usually desired)
- May want to incorporate additional basis functions to give us an independent (rho)^{tau} behavior in the derivative
- Div-conf and Curl-conf are related by a 90 degree rotation

	Basis functions (all in curl-conforming format)	$\hat{n} \bullet \nabla \times \bar{S}_i$
Brown & Wilton	$\bar{S}_1 = \rho^{\nu-1}\,\bar{\Omega}_1$ $\bar{S}_2 = \rho^{\nu-1}\left\{\bar{\Omega}_2 + \frac{\nu-1}{\rho}\xi_3\nabla\xi_1\right\}$ $\bar{S}_3 = \rho^{\nu-1}\left\{\bar{\Omega}_3 - \frac{\nu-1}{\rho}\xi_2\nabla\xi_1\right\}$	$(\nu+1)\rho^{\nu-1}$, $i = 1,2,3$
Graglia & Lombardi	$\bar{S}_1 = \rho^{\nu-1}\,\bar{\Omega}_1$ $\bar{S}_2 = \rho^{\nu-1}\left\{\bar{\Omega}_2 + \frac{1-\nu}{\nu\rho}\xi_1\bar{\Omega}_1\right\}$ $\bar{S}_3 = \rho^{\nu-1}\left\{\bar{\Omega}_3 + \frac{1-\nu}{\nu\rho}\xi_1\bar{\Omega}_1\right\}$	$(\nu+1)\rho^{\nu-1}$, $i = 1$ $\frac{(\nu+1)}{\nu}\rho^{\nu-1}$, $i = 2,3$
	$\bar{S}_1 = \rho^{\nu}\,\bar{\Omega}_1$ $\bar{S}_2 = \rho^{\nu}\,\bar{\Omega}_1 - \rho^{\nu-1}\left\{\nabla\xi_3 + \frac{1-\nu}{\rho}\xi_3\nabla\xi_1\right\}$ $\bar{S}_3 = \rho^{\nu}\,\bar{\Omega}_1 + \rho^{\nu-1}\left\{\nabla\xi_2 + \frac{1-\nu}{\rho}\xi_2\nabla\xi_1\right\}$	$(\nu+2)\rho^{\nu}$, $i = 1,2,3$
Graglia & Lombardi	$\bar{S}_1 = [\rho^{\nu} + \nu\xi_1]\,\bar{\Omega}_1$ $\bar{S}_2 = \bar{\Omega}_1 - \rho^{\nu-1}\left\{\nabla\xi_3 + \frac{1-\nu}{\rho}\xi_3\nabla\xi_1\right\}$ $\bar{S}_3 = \bar{\Omega}_1 + \rho^{\nu-1}\left\{\nabla\xi_2 + \frac{1-\nu}{\rho}\xi_2\nabla\xi_1\right\}$	$(\nu+2)\rho^{\nu} + \nu(3\xi_1 - 1)$, $i = 1$ 2, $i = 2,3$
Masoni, Pelosi, Selleri	$\bar{S}_1 = [\rho^{\nu} + \nu\xi_1]\,\bar{\Omega}_1$ $\bar{S}_2 = [\rho^{\nu} + \nu\xi_1]\,\bar{\Omega}_1 - \rho^{\nu-1}\left\{\nabla\xi_3 + \frac{1-\nu}{\rho}\xi_3\nabla\xi_1\right\}$ $\bar{S}_3 = [\rho^{\nu} + \nu\xi_1]\,\bar{\Omega}_1 + \rho^{\nu-1}\left\{\nabla\xi_2 + \frac{1-\nu}{\rho}\xi_2\nabla\xi_1\right\}$	$(\nu+2)\rho^{\nu} + \nu(3\xi_1 - 1)$, $i = 1,2,3$
Sun et al.	$\bar{S}_1 = \bar{\Omega}_1$ $\bar{S}_2 = \rho^{\nu_1-1}\{\sigma(1-\nu)\nabla\xi_1 + \nabla\xi_3\}$ $\bar{S}_3 = \rho^{\nu_1-1}\{(1-\sigma)(1-\nu)\nabla\xi_1 + \nabla\xi_2\}$	2, $i = 1$ 0, $i = 2,3$

Vertex Singularities: Curl Conforming

Nonsingular Vector Basis (p = 0.5)

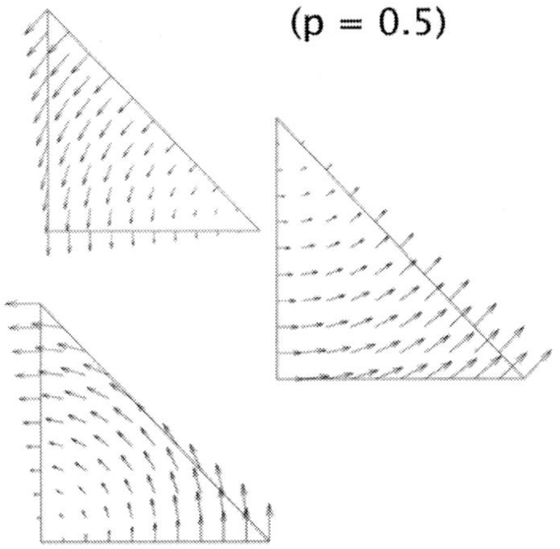

Brown & Wilton 1999

nu = 1/2

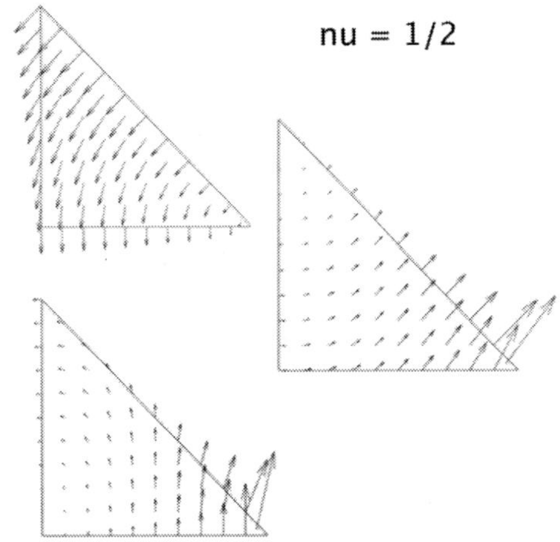

Vertex Singularities: Curl Conforming

- Nonsingular Vector Basis

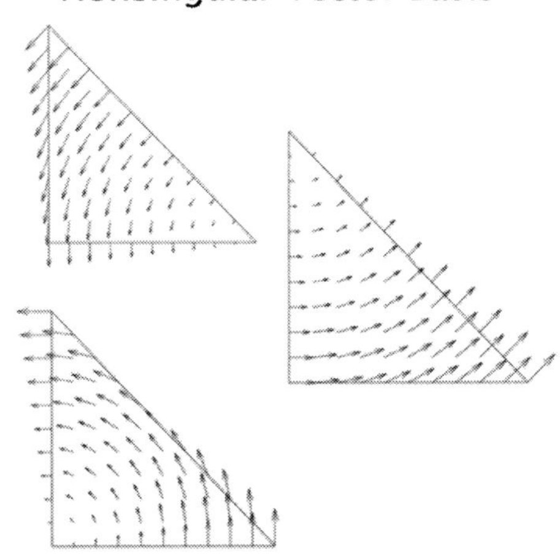

Graglia Lombardi 2002

nu = 1/2

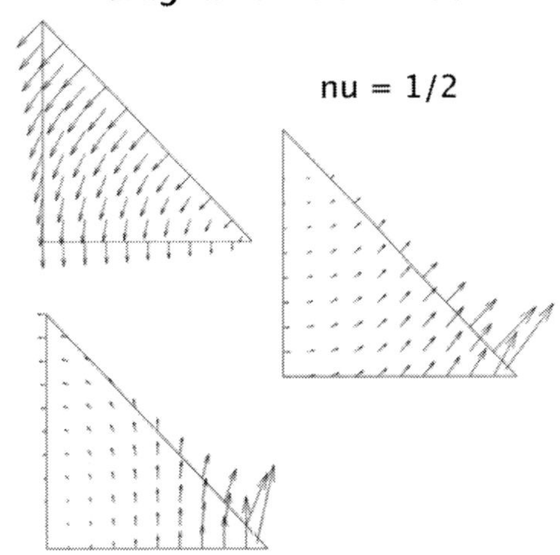

Vertex & Edge Singularities

- Vertex singularities
  - curl-conforming bases
  - 2D problems, vector Helmholtz eqn

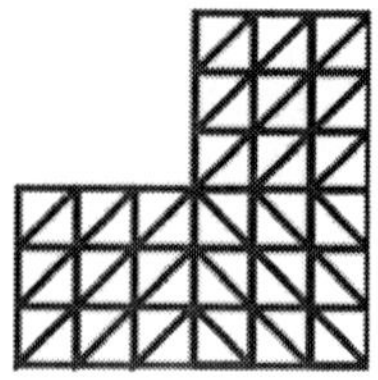

- Edge singularities
  - div-conforming bases
  - surface IE formulations
  - triangles: need combination of bases for singular edges and bases for vertex singularities

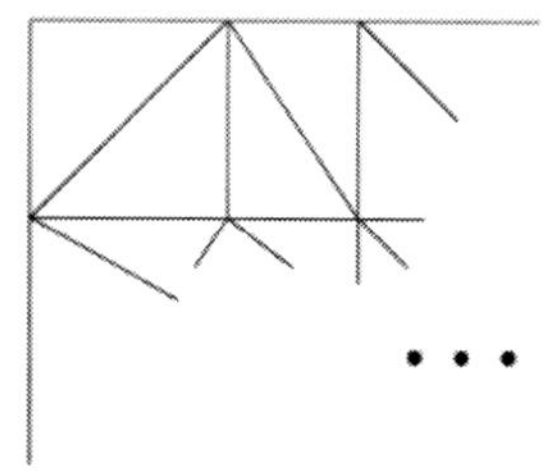

Vector Bases for Edge Singularities

- Typically divergence-conforming for use with current density
- Substitutive types for p=0.5:
  - Brown & Wilton, 1999

$$\bar{S}_1 = [(1-\xi_3)^\nu - \xi_1^\nu]\,\bar{\ell}_3 + [\xi_1^\nu - (1-\xi_2)^\nu]\,\bar{\ell}_2$$
$$\bar{S}_2 = \xi_1^{\nu-1}\xi_3\,\bar{\ell}_1 - \xi_1^\nu\,\bar{\ell}_3$$
$$\bar{S}_3 = \xi_1^\nu\,\bar{\ell}_2 - \xi_1^{\nu-1}\xi_2\,\bar{\ell}_1.$$

  - Graglia & Lombardi, 2002

$$\bar{\Lambda}_1 = \xi_2\,\bar{\ell}_3 - \xi_3\,\bar{\ell}_2$$
$$\bar{S}_2 = \xi_1^{\nu-1}\xi_3\,\bar{\ell}_1 - \xi_1^\nu\,\bar{\ell}_3$$
$$\bar{S}_3 = \xi_1^\nu\,\bar{\ell}_2 - \xi_1^{\nu-1}\xi_2\,\bar{\ell}_1.$$

Edge Singularities: Div-conforming

- Nonsingular RWG Basis

Brown & Wilton 1999

nu = 1/2

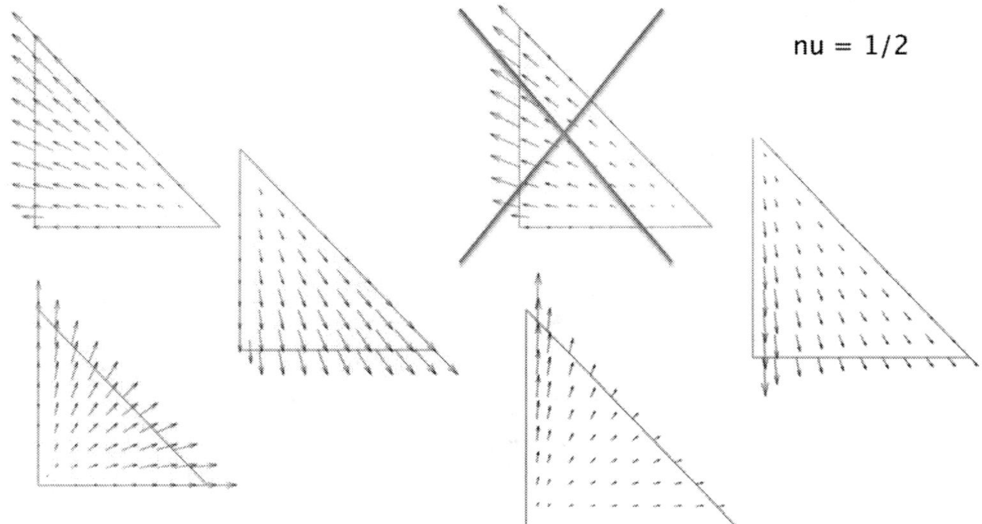

Example: Edge Singularity

The circular PEC-plate at normal incidence

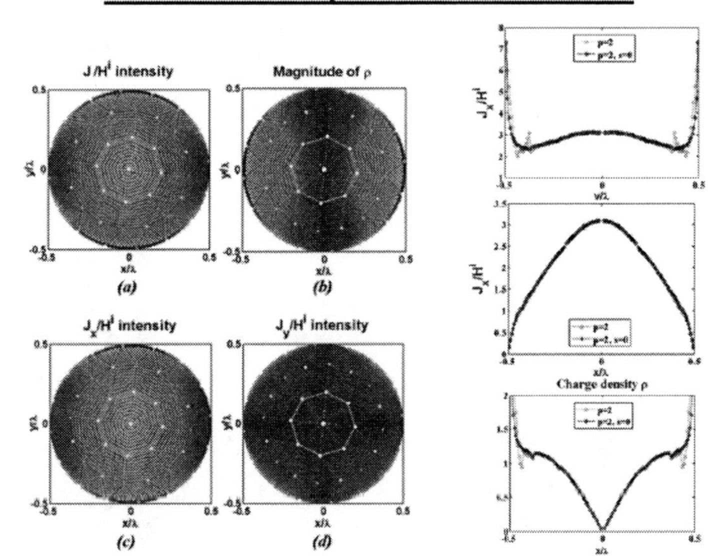

Example: Edge Singularity

The circular PEC-plate at normal incidence (d = λ/100)

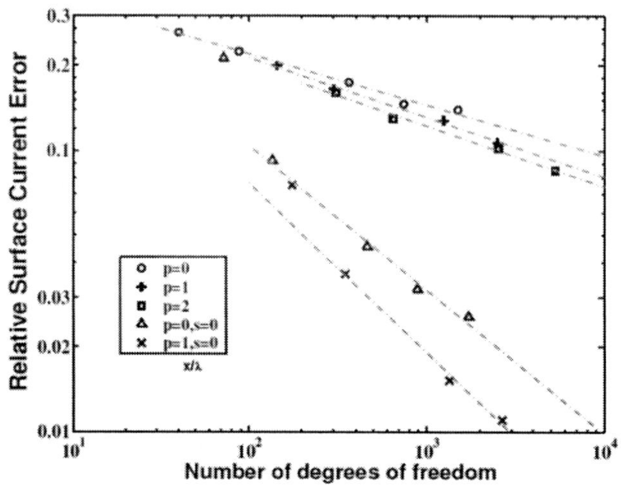

ACES 2017: Singular Bases

35

Example: Edge Singularity

(10 × 1) PEC-strip

Normal incidence Ex

Singualar bases p = 2, s = 0

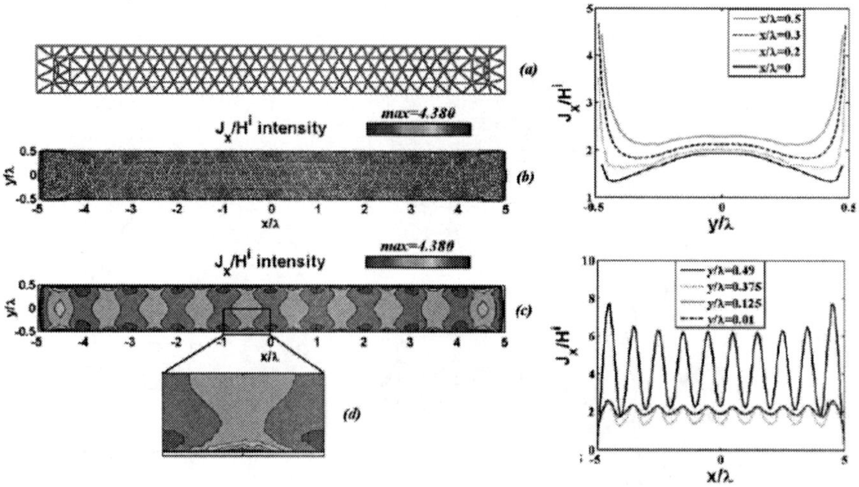

ACES 2017: Singular Bases

36

Summary

- Several existing families of *substitutive* singular basis functions for use with p=0.5 expansions
  - 6 families with $(rho)^{nu-1}$ behavior at vertex/edge
  - Curl conforming vertex bases for 2D vector Helmholtz eqn
  - Used to expand the transverse field
  - $(rho)^{nu}$ in the curl to represent the other (longitudinal) field
  - Div conforming vertex *and* edge bases for use with EFIE
  - Used to expand the current density
  - $(rho)^{nu-1}$ in the divergence to represent the charge density

Alternative: Additive Bases

- Additive bases offer more robustness, possibility of true high order expansions
  - develop additive bases for illustration
- Application:
  - vertex singularities
  - curl conforming

Additive for Vertex Singularity

- Additive functions
  - Lowest singular members of a hierarchical family
  - Builds upon triangular-cell hierarchical vector polynomial basis family (Graglia, Peterson, Andriulli, 2011).
  - Singularity incorporated using gradients of scalar bases

- Limitation of hierarchical bases: ill-conditioning
  - address by introducing partial orthogonality
  - need polynomial degrees of freedom to do so

Additive for Vertex Singularity

The key idea:

- Field component approximation:

$$F_z \approx F_{z-poly}(\xi) + \sum_{n=1}^{q} a_{zn}(\phi)\, \rho^{\nu_n}$$

$$F_t \approx F_{t-poly}(\xi) + \sum_{n=1}^{q} \left[a_{\phi n}(\phi)\, \hat{\phi} + a_{\rho n}(\phi)\, \hat{\rho} \right] \frac{d\,\rho^{\nu_n}}{d\,\rho}$$

$$\rho^{\nu_n} \Rightarrow b_0\, \rho^{\nu_n} + \sum_{\ell=1}^{n+k} b_\ell\, \rho^{\ell}$$

Additive for Vertex Singularity

- Incorporate polynomial degrees of freedom in the singular functions to enable orthogonalization
  - Means we must start with p=1.5 polynomial bases
- Triangle polynomial curl-conforming family:
  - (Graglia, Peterson, Andriulli, 2011).

$$\sqrt{3}(\xi_2 - \xi_3)\boldsymbol{\Omega}_1$$

$$\sqrt{3}(\xi_3 - \xi_1)\boldsymbol{\Omega}_2$$

$$\boldsymbol{\Omega}_1 = \xi_2 \nabla \xi_3 - \xi_3 \nabla \xi_2 \qquad \sqrt{3}(\xi_1 - \xi_2)\boldsymbol{\Omega}_3$$

$$\boldsymbol{\Omega}_2 = \xi_3 \nabla \xi_1 - \xi_1 \nabla \xi_3 \qquad 2\sqrt{3}\xi_1 \boldsymbol{\Omega}_1$$

$$\boldsymbol{\Omega}_3 = \xi_1 \nabla \xi_2 - \xi_2 \nabla \xi_1 \qquad 2\sqrt{3}\xi_2 \boldsymbol{\Omega}_2$$

Additive for Vertex Singularity

- p=1.5 polynomial bases

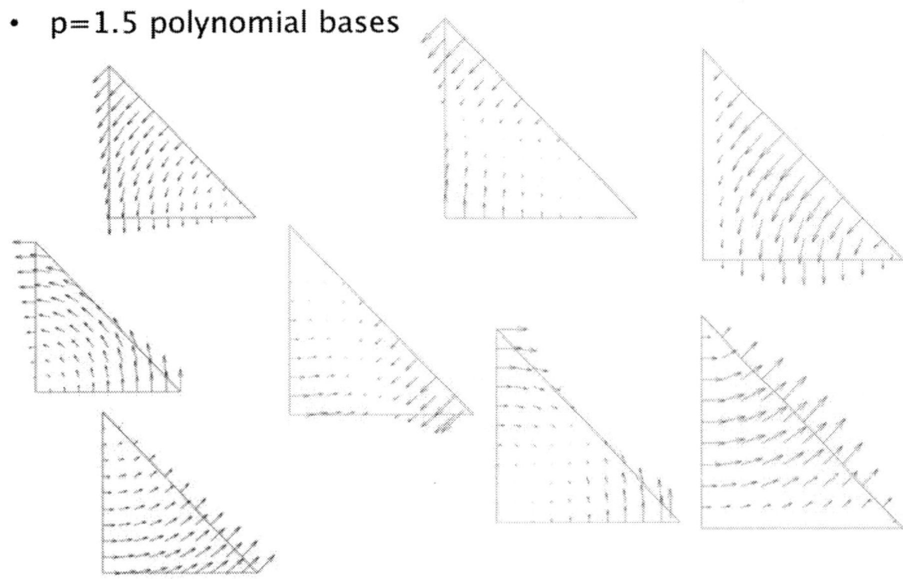

Additive for Vertex Singularity

- To introduce one fractional exponent, use the gradients of

$$S_{11}^{i-1} = (1-\sigma)\left\{a_{11}\rho^{\nu} - \left(b_{11}\rho + b_{12}\rho^{2}\right)\right\}$$

$$S_{11}^{i+1} = \sigma\left\{a_{11}\rho^{\nu} - \left(b_{11}\rho + b_{12}\rho^{2}\right)\right\}.$$

- To complete the expression to p=1.5, add the gradient of

$$S_{11} = \sigma(1-\sigma)\left\{a_{11}\rho^{\nu} - \left(b_{11}\rho + b_{12}\rho^{2}\right)\right\}$$

  - coefficients a_{11}, b_{11}, b_{12} are chosen to make the radial dependence orthogonal with the radial dependence of the nonsingular basis functions, these depend on nu
    - (expressions in Graglia, Peterson, Matekovits, *IEEE T-AP*, 2013 or Graglia & Peterson, *Higher-order Techniques in CEM*, 2016)

Additive for Vertex Singularity

- Singular bases obtained from the gradients:

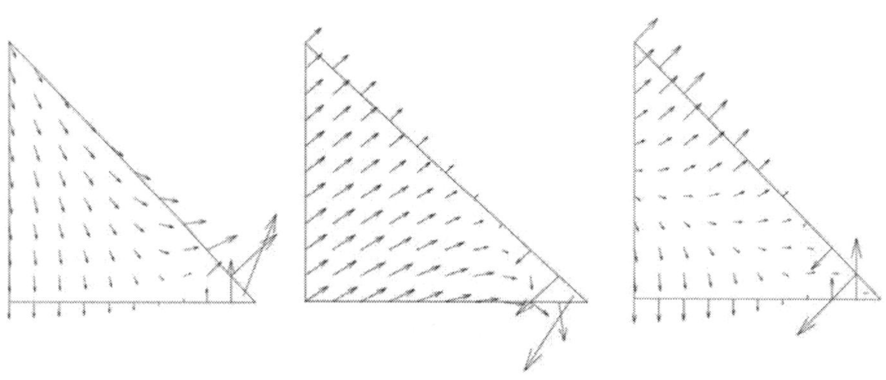

Additive for Vertex Singularity

- Start with 8 polynomial basis functions/cell
- Add minimum of 2 per singular cell (shared by neighbors)
- Add a third for best accuracy (recommended)
  - Set of 11 per singular cell
  - $(rho)^{nu-1}$ in transverse field
  - No singular behavior in the curl

Additive for Vertex Singularity

- To obtain singular behavior in the curl:
- Need to add 1-2 more functions
  - Obtain $(rho)^{nu}$ behavior or $(rho)^{tau}$ behavior in the curl
- However
  - Additional 1-2 bases may be needed to complete the transverse space and avoid spurious modes
  - May end up with 15 bases per singular cell

Additive for Vertex Singularity

- percent error in resonant frequency of cavity with 30 degree wedge

Order	$p=1.5$
Poly only (no singular)	2.20
Poly + $\nabla\phi_{11}$	0.15
Poly + $\nabla\phi_{11} + \nabla\phi_{12}$	0.11

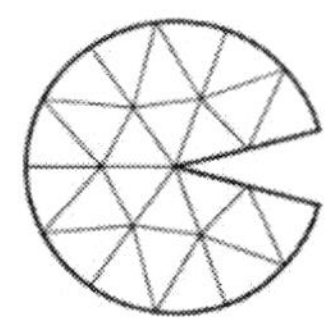

- matrix condition numbers

Order	$p=1.5$
Poly only (no singular)	42
Poly + $\nabla\phi_{11}$	53
Poly + $\nabla\phi_{11} + \nabla\phi_{12}$	53

Additive for Vertex Singularity

- Extensions possible:
  - higher order
  - curved cells
  - multiple fractional exponents
- Application to other problems

Modeling capability:
Multiple singular verteces and curvilinear singular elements

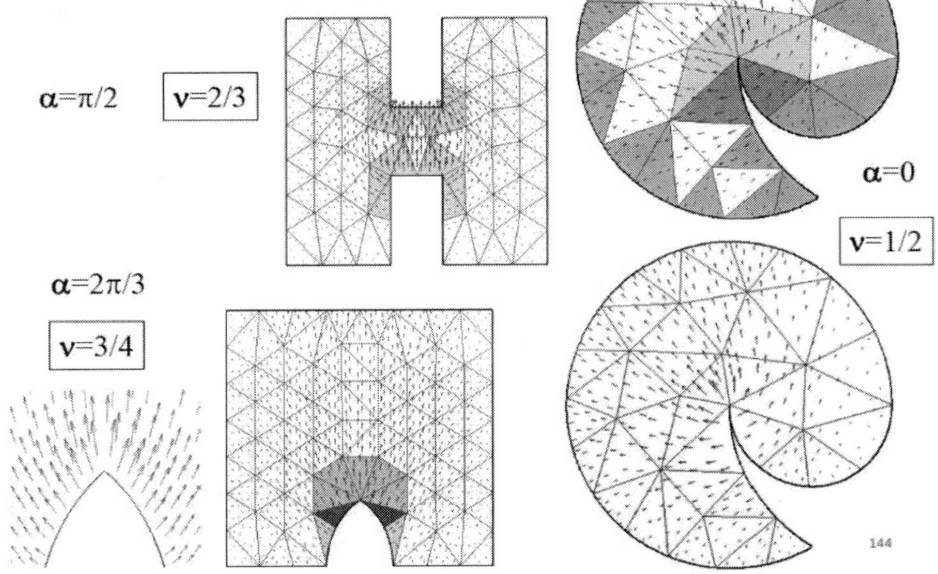

ACES 2017: Singular Bases 49

Conclusion

- Singular basis functions for EM problems
  - divergence conforming for EFIE
  - curl conforming for vector Helmholtz
- Substitutive type for p=0.5
  - vertex (6 examples)
  - edge (2 examples)
- Additive type for p=1.5
  - vertex (1 example)

ACES 2017: Singular Bases 50

Conclusion

- State of development
  - many papers on scalar bases for 2D vertex singularities
  - many papers on vector bases for 2D vertex singularities
  - some papers on vector bases for 2D edge singularities
  - a few papers on vertex and edge singularities in 3D
  - a couple of papers on corner singularities

  - Recent review:
    - A. F. Peterson and R. D. Graglia, "Basis functions for vertex, edge, and corner singularities: A review," *IEEE J. Multiscale and Multiphysics Comp. Tech.*, vol. 1, pp. 161-175, December 2016.

ELEDIA Research Center
ELEDIA@UniTN - University of Trento
Via Sommarive 9, I-38123 Trento, Italy
E-mail: paolo.rocca@eledia.org
Web: www.eledia.org/eledia-unitn

Tolerance Analysis and Robust Design in Engineering Electromagnetics
An Interval Analysis Perspective

Prof. Paolo ROCCA

ACES 2017 Tutorial Talk #4
March 30, 2017

2017 ACES Conference
(*March 26-30, 2017 – Firenze, Italy*)

Copyright Notice

Table of Contents (1/2)

 3

Table of Contents (2/2)

 4

Dealing with Uncertainty

GOAL "Measure the dimensions of a table"

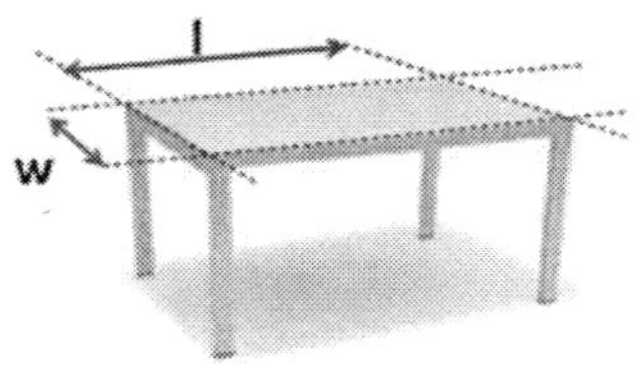

With a tailor meter...

l = 1.2 m +/- 0.1 m
w = 0.8 m +/- 0.1 m

... or with a more precise device

l = 1.20 m +/- 0.01 m
w = 0.80 m +/- 0.01 m

Whatever the measurement device, UNCERTAINTIES are ALWAYS PRESENT!

What's the Solution?

Also with the more precise measuring systems ...

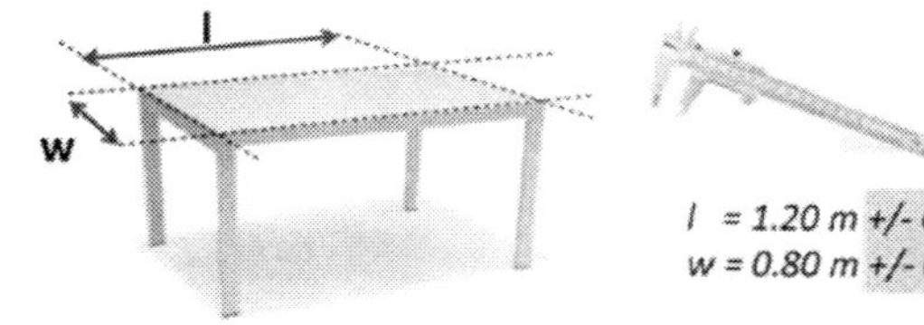

l = 1.20 m +/- 0.01 m
w = 0.80 m +/- 0.01 m

... the correct length/width lies within certain ***BOUNDS***

$1.19 \le l \le 1.21 \longrightarrow l \in [1.19, 1.21]$

$0.79 \le w \le 0.81 \longrightarrow w \in [0.79, 0.81]$

The length/width belongs to INTERVALs!

What's an Interval?

1. Real Intervals

Definition: Real Interval

A real interval [X] is a non-empty compact set of real numbers between and including the endpoints x_{inf} and x_{sup} [*]

$$[X] = \{x \in R : x_{inf} \le x \le x_{sup}\}$$

$$x_{\inf} \le x_{\sup}$$

Mandatory

Left Endpoint
$x_{\inf} = \min\{x \in [X]\}$

Infimum of [X]

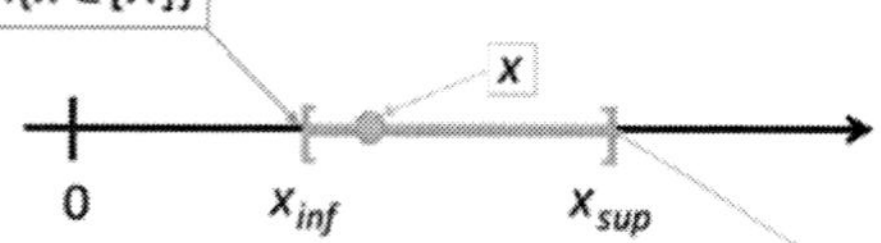

Supremum of [X]

Rigth Endpoint
$x_{\sup} = \max\{x \in [X]\}$

[*] R. E. Moore, Interval Analysis Prentice-Hall, Englewood Cliffs, New Jersey 1966.

1.a Real Intervals – Descriptions

Description #1 (Inf & Sup)

$$[X] = [x_{inf}, x_{sup}]$$

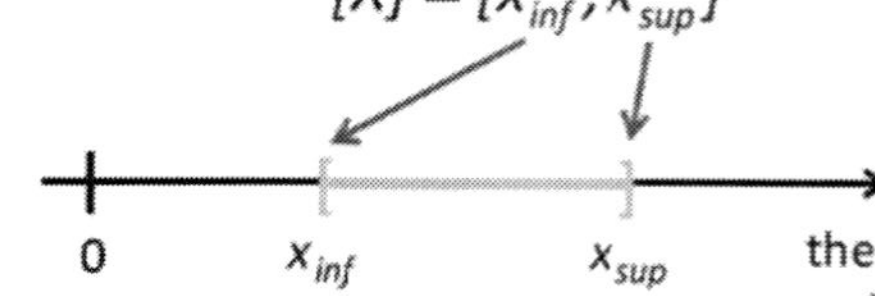

the symbol *[·]* identifies an interval

[X] is **UNIVOCALLY described** by x_{inf} and x_{sup}

1.a Real Intervals – Descriptions

Example: $[X] = [-1,3]$

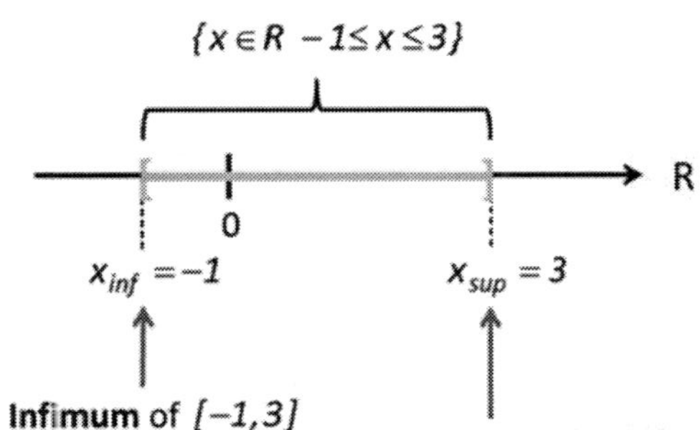

1.a Real Intervals – Descriptions

Description #2 (Midpoint & Width)

$$[X] = < m([X]), w([X]) >$$

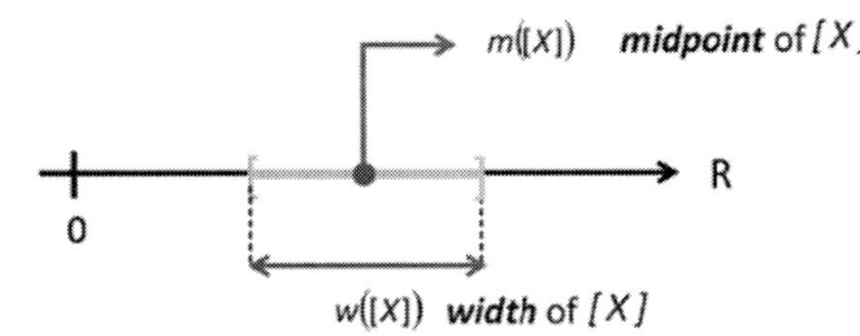

$[X]$ is **UNIVOCALLY described** by $w([X])$ and $m([X])$

1.a Real Intervals – Descriptions

Example: $[X] = < 1,4 >$

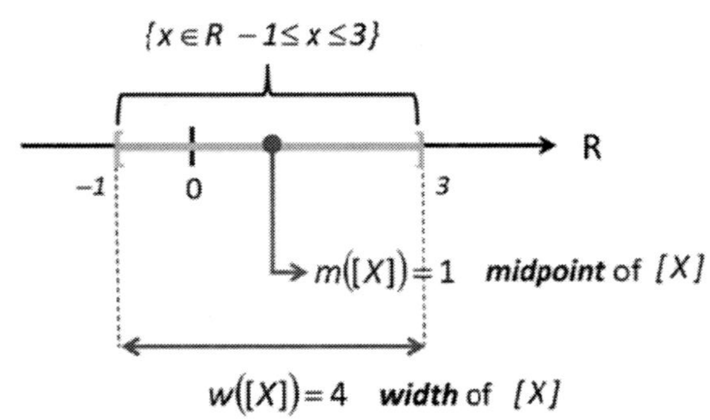

1.a Real Intervals – Descriptions

Description #1

$$[X] = [x_{inf}, x_{sup}]$$

Description #2

$$[X] = < m([X]), w([X]) >$$

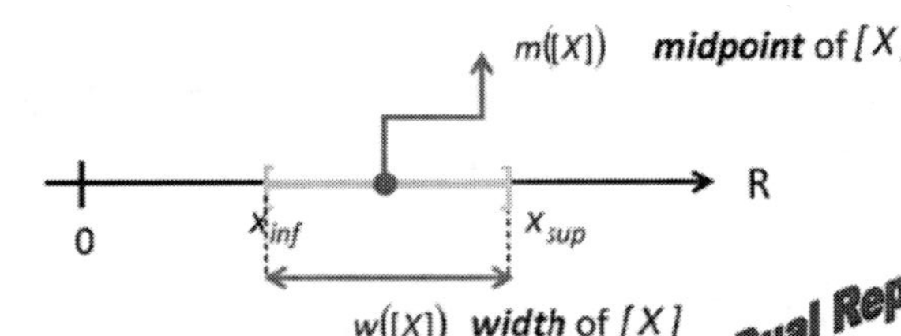

Dual Representation (1-2)

$$m([X]) = \frac{x_{sup} + x_{inf}}{2} \qquad w([X]) = x_{sup} - x_{inf}$$

1.a Real Intervals – Descriptions

Description #1

$[X] = [x_{inf}, x_{sup}]$

Description #2

$[X] = < m([X]), w([X]) >$

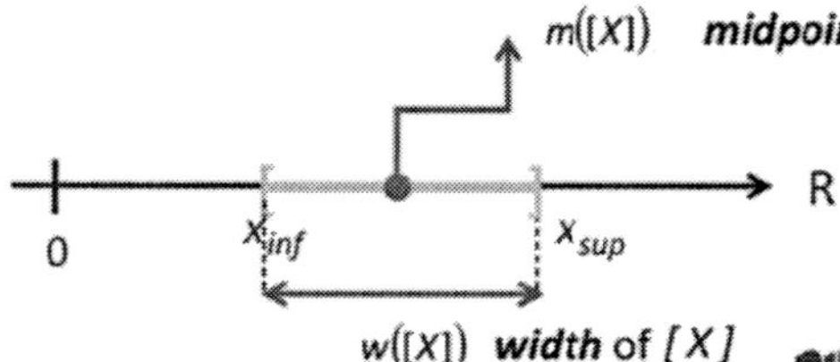

$m([X])$ ***midpoint*** of $[X]$

$w([X])$ ***width*** of $[X]$

Dual Representation (2-1)

$$x_{sup} = m([X]) + \frac{w([X])}{2} \qquad x_{inf} = m([X]) - \frac{w([X])}{2}$$

1. *Degenerate* Real Intervals (*Real Numbers*)

Definition: *Degenerate* Real Interval

A real number x is an interval whose endpoints coincide

$x_{inf} = x_{sup} = x$

$x = [x, x]$

$m([x,x]) = x$

$w([x,x]) = 0$

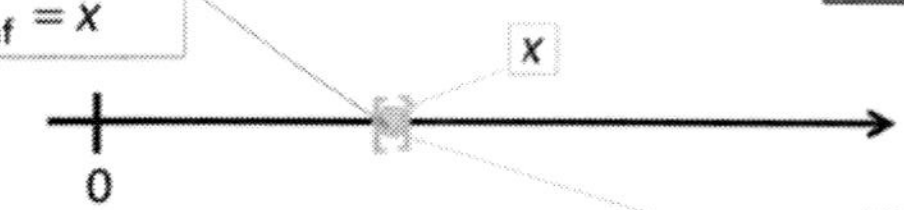

Left Endpoint $x_{inf} = x$

Rigth Endpoint $x_{sup} = x$

[*] R. E. Moore, Interval Analysis. Prentice-Hall, Englewood Cliffs, New Jersey 1966.

1.a.i Interval Elementary Operations

[L] and [W] are Intervals...

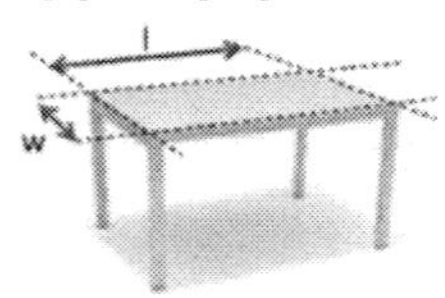

$[L] = [1.19, 1.21]$
$[W] = [0.79, 0.81]$

How to compute PERIMETER and AREA?

Traditional Arithmetic/Function	Interval Arithmetic/Function
Half perimeter $p = w + l$ →	$[P] = [W] + [L]$
Perimeter $2p = w + l + w + l$ →	$[2P] = [W] + [L] + [W] + [L]$
Area $a = w \cdot l$ →	$[A] = [W] \cdot [L]$

How to add intervals?
How to multiply intervals?

1.a.i Interval Elementary Operations

[L] and [W] are Intervals...

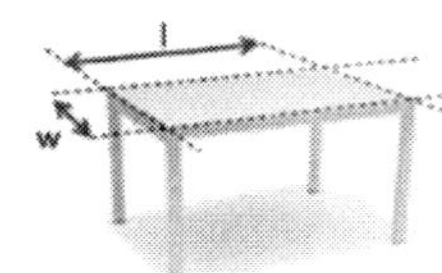

$[L] = [1.19, 1.21]$
$[W] = [0.79, 0.81]$

How to compute PERIMETER and AREA?

Traditional Arithmetic/Function	Interval Arithmetic/Function
Half perimeter $p = w + l$ →	$[P] = [W] + [L]$
Perimeter $2p = w + l + w + l$ →	$[2P] = [W] + [L] + [W] + [L]$
Area $a = w \cdot l$ →	$[A] = [W] \cdot [L]$

AN INTERVAL ARITHMETIC IS NEEDED!

1.a.i Interval Arithmetic

Definition: Interval Arithmetic

A *Set of Rules* for performing elementary arithmetic operations on INTERVALS

HOW ARE DEFINED?

1.a.i Towards an Interval Arithmetic

[L] and [W] are Intervals...

$[L]=[l_{inf}, l_{sup}]=[1.19, 1.21]=\{l \in R\ 1.19 \le l \le 1.21\}$

$[W]=[w_{inf}, w_{sup}]=[0.79, 0.81]=\{w \in R\ 0.79 \le l \le 0.81\}$

Intervals contain an **INFINITE** number of real values!

Infinite areas exist:

$A_{11}=l_{sup}\cdot w_{sup}=1.21\cdot 0.81=0.9801$

$A_{12}=l_{inf}\cdot w_{inf}=1.19\cdot 0.79=0.9401$

$A_{13}=m([L])\cdot m([W])=1.20\cdot 0.80=0.96$

$A_{14}=l_{inf}\cdot w_{sup}=1.197\cdot 0.805=0.963585$

... $A_{mn}=l_m\cdot w_n \quad \begin{cases} l_m \in [L] \Rightarrow m=1,\dots,\infty \\ w_n \in [W] \Rightarrow n=1,\dots,\infty \end{cases}$

ALL RELIABLE VALUES!

HOW TO CONSIDER THEM GLOBALLY?

1.a.i Interval Arithmetic

REQUIREMENT: WHAT DOES IT MEAN?

Interval arithmetic operations are defined such that the resulting interval ***encloses all possible*** solutions

Definition: Interval Arithmetic

Given $[X] = [x_{inf}, x_{sup}]$ and $[Y] = [y_{inf}, y_{sup}]$, the interval elementary operations are defined by:
$[X]\ \mathbf{op}\ [Y] = \{ x\ \mathbf{op}\ y \mid x \in [X] \text{ and } y \in [Y] \}$

op: + ; - ; · ; / (Sum – Subtraction – Product – Division)

1.a.i Interval Arithmetic – The Table

Area of the Table

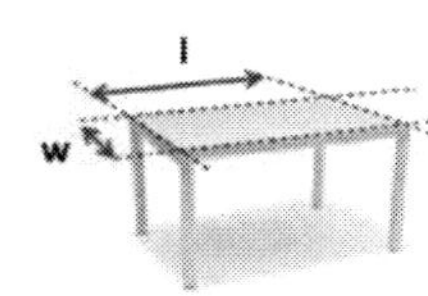

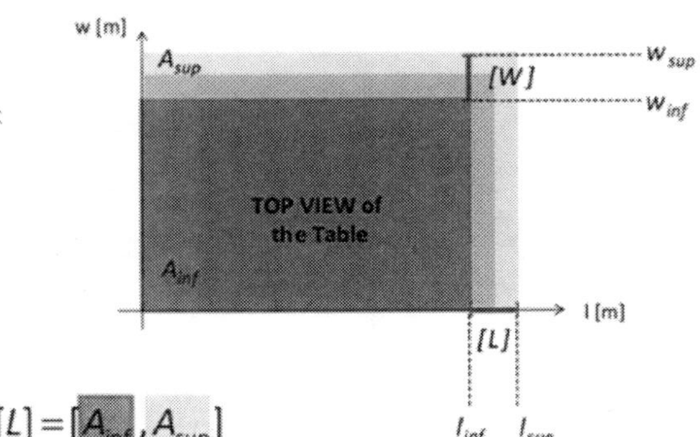

$[A]=[W]\cdot[L]=[A_{inf}, A_{sup}]$

Interval Area

1.a.i Interval Arithmetic – The Table

Perimeter of the Table

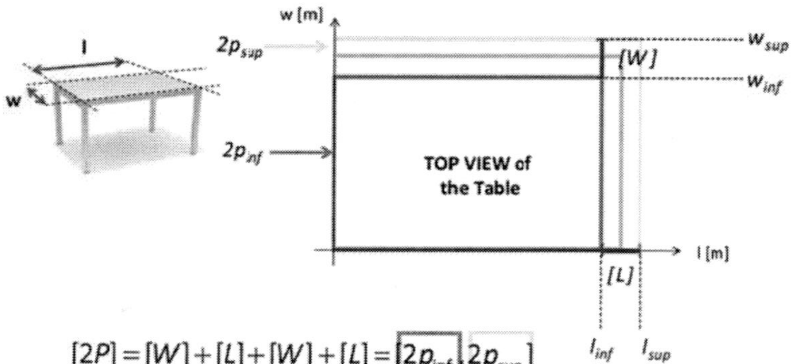

$[2P]=[W]+[L]+[W]+[L]=[2p_{inf},2p_{sup}]$

Interval Perimeter

1.a.i Interval Arithmetic – The Table

***Interval Perimeter/Area** of the Table*

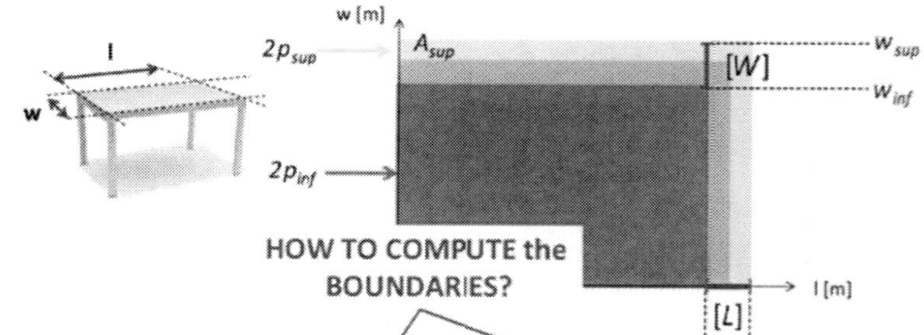

HOW TO COMPUTE the BOUNDARIES?

$[2P]=[W]+[L]+[W]+[L]=[2p_{inf},2p_{sup}]$

$[A]=[W]\cdot[L]=[A_{inf},A_{sup}]$

Needed INTERVAL ELEMENTARY OPERATIONS!!!

1.a.i Elementary Operations

Definition: Interval Sum

$[X]+[Y]=[x_{inf}+y_{inf},x_{sup}+y_{sup}]$

Sum of Intervals: $[X]+[Y]$

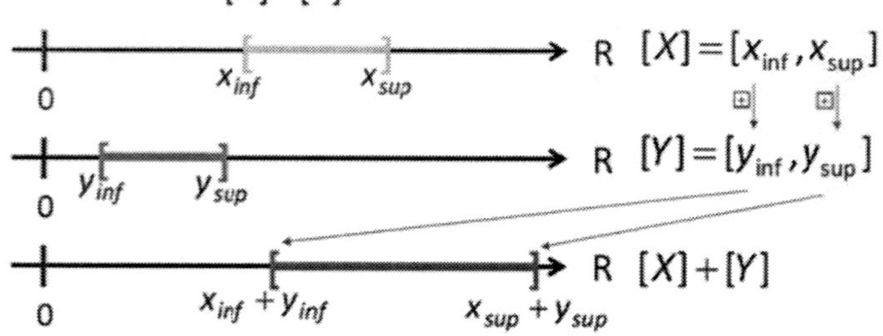

$[X]+[Y]=[x_{inf},x_{sup}]+[y_{inf},y_{sup}]=[x_{inf}+y_{inf},x_{sup}+y_{sup}]$

1.a.i Elementary Operations

$[X]+[Y]=[x_{inf}+y_{inf},x_{sup}+y_{sup}]$

Example: compute $[-2,3]+[1,2]$

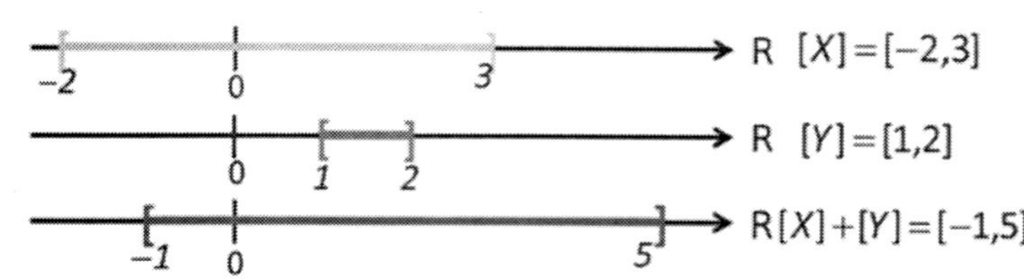

Sum of Intervals: [X] + [Y] = [-2, 3] + [1, 2] = [-2+1, 3+2] = [-1, 5]

ENCLOSE ALL THE POSSIBLE RESULTS?

1.a.i Elementary Operations

Verification 1: $x=2; y=\frac{3}{2} \Rightarrow x+y=2+\frac{3}{2}=\frac{7}{2}$

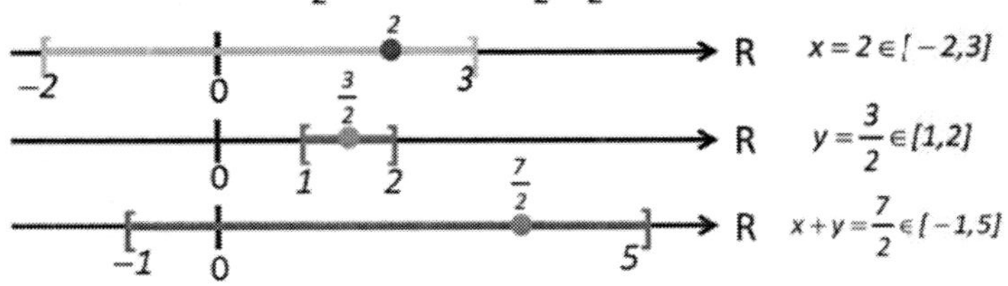

Verification 2: $x=-2; y=2 \Rightarrow x+y=-2+2$

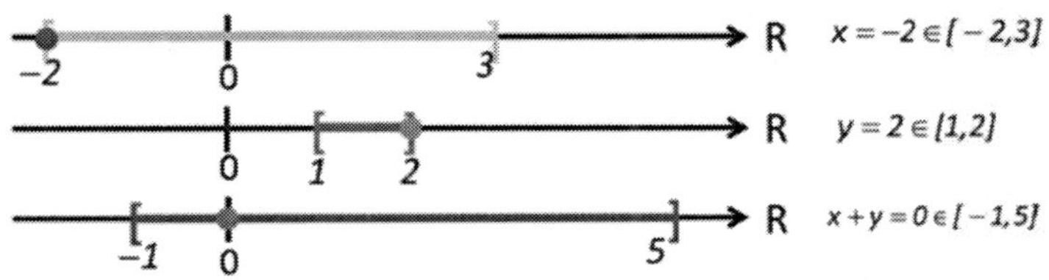

1.a.i Elementary Operations

Whatever $x \in [x_{inf}, x_{sup}]$ and $y \in [y_{inf}, y_{sup}]$, the sum lies within the interval sum $[x_{inf}+y_{inf}, x_{sup}+y_{sup}]$

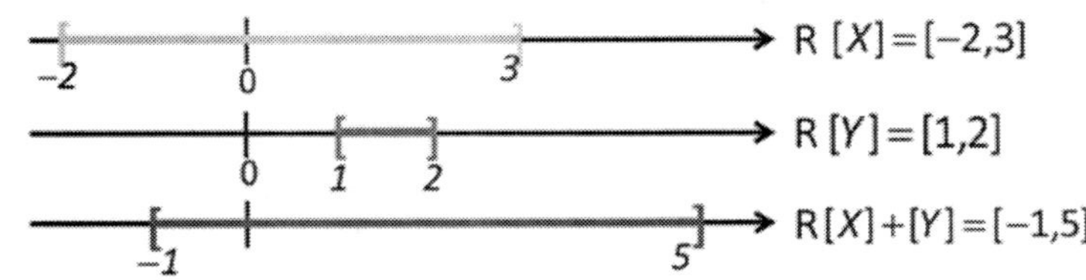

Whatever $x \in [-2, 3]$ and $y \in [1, 2]$,
It follows that $x+y \in [-1,5]$

1.a.i Interval Arithmetic – Property "Inclusion Property"

Remind:

Interval arithmetic operations are defined such that the resulting interval ***encloses all possible*** solutions

Inclusion Property

Definition: Inclusion Property

*Being $[F]=[f_{inf}, f_{sup}]=\{[X]$ **op** $[Y]\}$ the interval resulting from whatever operation between two intervals $[X]=[x_{inf}, x_{sup}]$ and $[Y]=[y_{inf}, y_{sup}]$, all values $f=\{x$ **op** $y\}$, with $x\in[X]$ and $y\in[Y]$, belongs to $[F]$ (i.e., $f\in[F]$)*

1.a.i Elementary Operations – Recipe

Sum: $[X]+[Y]=[x_{inf}+y_{inf}, x_{sup}+y_{sup}]$

Difference: $[X]-[Y]=[x_{inf}-y_{sup}, x_{sup}-y_{inf}]$

Product: $[X]\cdot[Y]=[\min(x_{inf}y_{inf}, x_{inf}y_{sup}, x_{sup}y_{inf}, x_{sup}y_{sup}), \max(x_{inf}y_{inf}, x_{inf}y_{sup}, x_{sup}y_{inf}, x_{sup}y_{sup})]$

Inverse: $1/[X]=[1/x_{sup}, 1/x_{inf}]$ $0\notin[X]$

Division: $[X]/[Y]=[\min(x_{inf}/y_{inf}, x_{inf}/y_{sup}, x_{sup}/y_{inf}, x_{sup}/y_{sup}), \max(x_{inf}/y_{inf}, x_{inf}/y_{sup}, x_{sup}/y_{inf}, x_{sup}/y_{sup})]$, $0\notin[Y]$

KEY FEATURES:

- Involve **just the boundaries** of the intervals: x_{inf} x_{sup} y_{inf} y_{sup}
- Include **all the possible results**

Coming back .... "The Table"

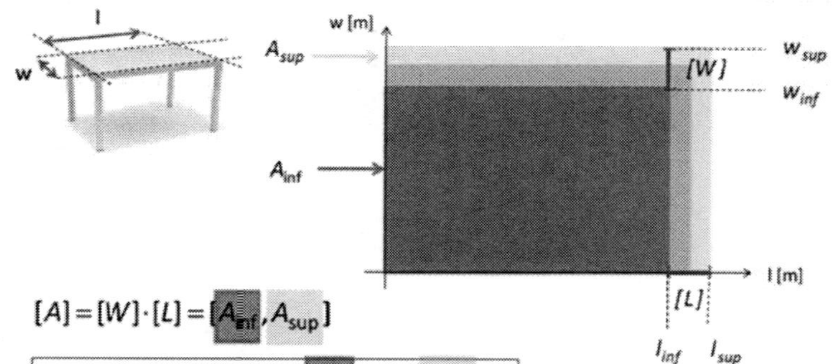

$[A]=[W]\cdot[L]=[A_{inf},A_{sup}]$

HOW TO DETERMINE A_{inf} AND A_{sup} ?

$$A_{inf}=\min_{mn}\{A_{mn}\} \quad A_{sup}=\max_{mn}\{A_{mn}\} \Rightarrow A_{mn}=l_m\cdot w_n \begin{cases} l_m\in[L]\Rightarrow m=1,\ldots,\infty \\ w_n\in[W]\Rightarrow n=1,\ldots,\infty \end{cases}$$

NO ! **(Infinite Evaluations)**

29

Coming back .... "The Table"

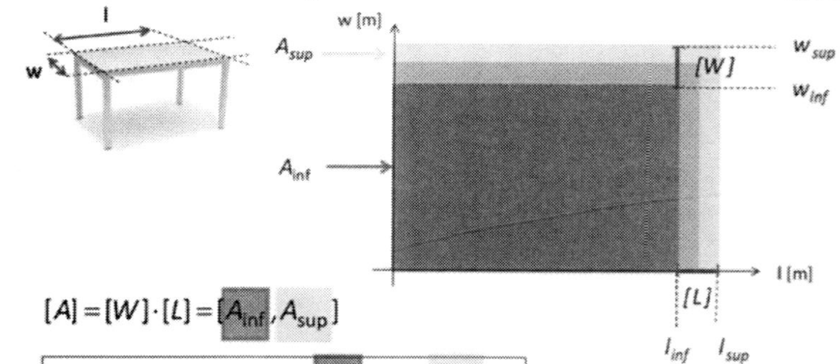

$[A]=[W]\cdot[L]=[A_{inf},A_{sup}]$

HOW TO DETERMINE A_{inf} AND A_{sup} ?

$$A_{inf}=\min\left(l_{inf}\cdot w_{inf}, l_{inf}\cdot w_{sup}, l_{sup}\cdot w_{inf}, l_{sup}\cdot w_{sup}\right)$$
$$A_{sup}=\max\left(l_{inf}\cdot w_{inf}, l_{inf}\cdot w_{sup}, l_{sup}\cdot w_{inf}, l_{sup}\cdot w_{sup}\right)$$

YES ! **(Finite Evaluations)**

30

Coming back .... "The Table"

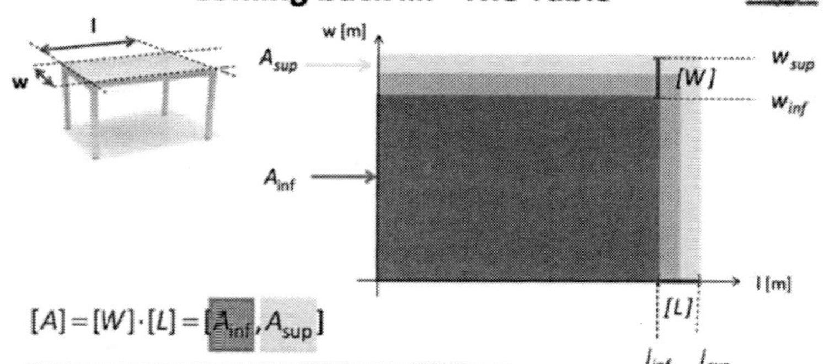

$[A]=[W]\cdot[L]=[A_{inf},A_{sup}]$

HOW TO DETERMINE A_{inf} AND A_{sup} ?

$$A_{inf}=\min\left(l_{inf}\cdot w_{inf}, l_{inf}\cdot w_{sup}, l_{sup}\cdot w_{inf}, l_{sup}\cdot w_{sup}\right)$$
$$A_{sup}=\max\left(l_{inf}\cdot w_{inf}, l_{inf}\cdot w_{sup}, l_{sup}\cdot w_{inf}, l_{sup}\cdot w_{sup}\right)$$

YES ! **(Need only Bounds [L] and [W])**

31

Elementary Operations – Properties Summary

	Standard Arithmetic	Interval Arithmetic
Addition		
Commutative	$a+b=b+a$	$[A]+[B]=[B]+[A]$
Associative	$(a+b)+c=a+(b+c)$	$([A]+[B])+[C]=[A]+([B]+[C])$
Neutral Element	$a+0=0+a=a$	$[A]+[0,0]=[0,0]+[A]=[A]$
Product		
Commutative	$a\cdot b=b\cdot a$	$[A]\cdot[B]=[B]\cdot[A]$
Associative	$(a\cdot b)\cdot c=a\cdot(b\cdot c)$	$([A]\cdot[B])\cdot[C]=[A]\cdot([B]\cdot[C])$
Neutral Element	$a\cdot 1=1\cdot a=a$	$[A]\cdot[1,1]=[1,1]\cdot[A]=[A]$
Distributive	$a\cdot(b+c)=a\cdot b+a\cdot c$	$[A]\cdot([B]+[C])\neq[A]\cdot[B]+[A]\cdot[C]$

"Sub-distributive" Property: $[A]\cdot([B]+[C])\subseteq([A]\cdot[B]+[A]\cdot[C])$

32

1.a.i Elementary Operations – The Table

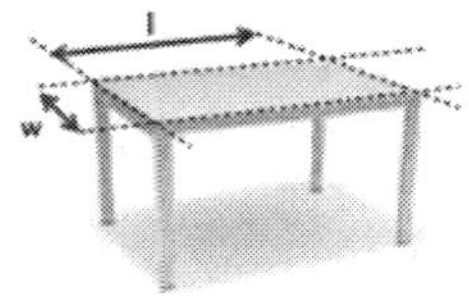

[L] = [1.19, 1.21] m
[W] = [0.79, 0.81] m

Exploiting IA rules:

$$[2P] = [1.19, 1.21] + [1.19, 1.21] + [0.79, 0.81] + [0.79, 0.81]$$
$$= [1.19 + 1.19 + 0.79 + 0.79,\ 1.21 + 1.21 + 0.81 + 0.81]$$
$$= [3.96,\ 4.04]\ m$$

$$[A] = [1.19, 1.21] \cdot [0.79, 0.81]$$
$$= [\min(1.19 \cdot 0.79, 1.19 \cdot 0.81, 1.21 \cdot 0.79, 1.21 \cdot 0.81),$$
$$\max(1.19 \cdot 0.79, 1.19 \cdot 0.81, 1.21 \cdot 0.79, 1.21 \cdot 0.81)]$$
$$= [0.94,\ 0.98]\ m^2$$

ARE INTERVAL RESULTS UNIQUE?

1.a.i Elementary Operations – The Table

ARE INTERVAL RESULTS UNIQUE?

Standard Arithmetic	Interval Arithmetic
$p_1 = w + l$ →	$[P_1] = [W] + [L]$
$p_2 = 2p - w - l$ →	$[P_2] = [2P] - [W] - [L]$
$p_1 = p_2\ \forall l, w$	$[P_1] = [P_2]$?

1.a.i Elementary Operations – The Table

GOAL: Compute the Half Interval Perimeter of the Table *[P]*

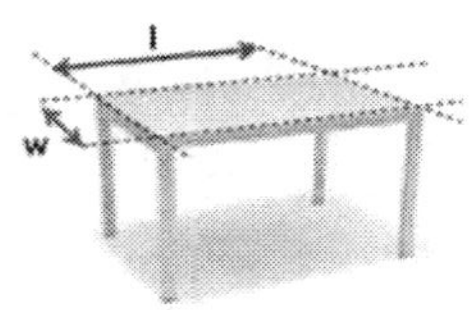

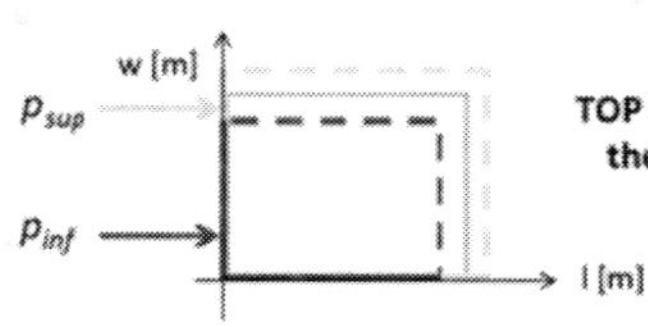

1. Adding *[W]* and *[L]*

$$[P] = [L] + [W]$$
$$= [l_{inf}, l_{sup}] + [w_{inf}, w_{sup}]$$
$$= [1.19, 1.21] + [0.79, 0.81]$$
$$= [1.19 + 0.79,\ 1.21 + 0.81]$$
$$= [1.98\ \ 2.02]\ m$$

Remember:

$$[X] + [Y] = [x_{inf} + y_{inf},\ x_{sup} + y_{sup}]$$

1.a.i Elementary Operations – The Table

GOAL: compute the half interval perimeter of the table *[P]*

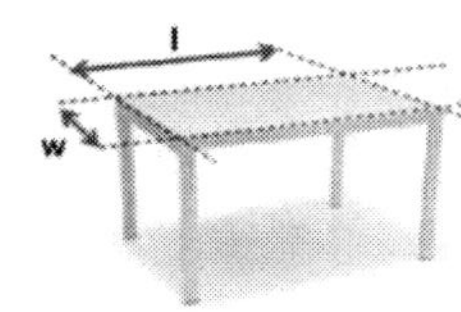

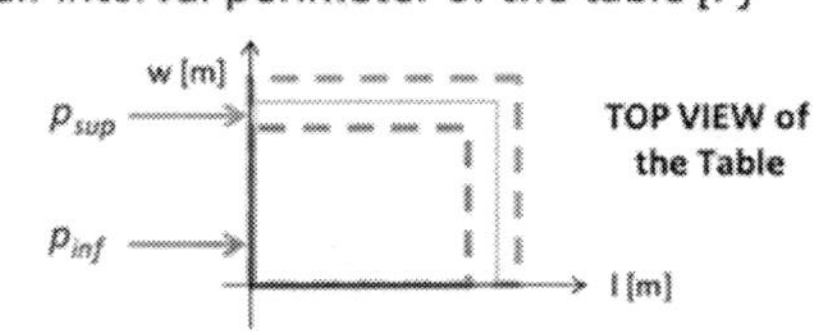

2. Subtracting *[W]* and *[L]* from *[2P]*

Remember:

$$[X] - [Y] = [x_{inf} - y_{sup},\ x_{sup} - y_{inf}]$$

$$[P] = [2P] - [L] - [W]$$
$$= [2P] - [l_{inf}, l_{sup}] - [w_{inf}, w_{sup}]$$
$$= [3.96, 4.04] - [1.19, 1.21] - [0.79, 0.81] = \{[3.96, 4.04] + (-[1.19, 1.21])\} - [0.79, 0.81]$$
$$= \{[3.96, 4.04] + [-1.21, -1.19]\} - [0.79, 0.81] = [2.75, 2.85] - [0.79, 0.81]$$
$$= [2.75, 2.85] + (-[0.79, 0.81]) = [2.75, 2.85] + [-0.81, -0.79] = [1.94, 2.06]\ m$$

1.a.i Elementary Operations – The Table

GOAL: compute the half interval perimeter of the table *[P]*

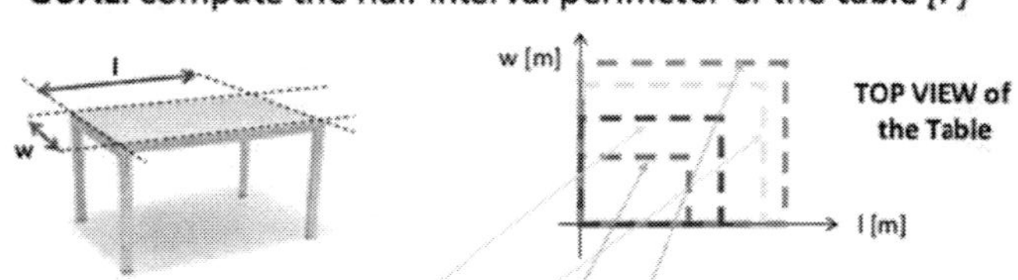

1. **Adding *[W]* and *[L]***

$[P]=[W]+[L]=[1.98,\ 2.02]\ m$

2. **Subtracting *[W]* and *[L]* from *[2P]***

$[P]=[2P]-[W]-[L]=[1.94,\ 2.06]\ m$

TWO DIFFERENT RESULTS for the same quantity!

WHAT IS WRONG?

© 2017 - ELEDIA Research Center 37

1.a.ii The Dependecy Problem

Definition: Dependency Problem

*In general, each occurrence of a given variable in an interval computation is treated as a **different variable***

*This causes **widening** of computed intervals and makes it difficult to compute sharp numerical bounds*

*This unwanted extra interval width is called the **dependency problem*** [*]

[*] E. Hansen and G. W. Walster. Global Optimization Using Interval Analysis. New York, NY: CRC Press, 2004.

© 2017 - ELEDIA Research Center 38

1.a.ii The Dependecy Problem – The Table

2. **Subtracting *[W]* and *[L]* from *[2P]***

$[P]=[2P]-[W]-[L]$

$=[W]+[W]+[L]+[L]-[W]-[L]$

$=[W]+[L]+([W]-[W])+([L]-[L])$ **IS ZERO?**

$=[0.79,0.81]+[1.19,1.21]+([0.79,0.81]-[0.79,0.81])+([1.19,1.21]-[1.19,1.21])$

Remember:

$[X]-[Y]=[x_{inf}-y_{sup},\ x_{sup}-y_{inf}]\quad if\ [X]=[Y]$

$[X]-[X]=[x_{inf}-x_{sup},\ x_{sup}-x_{inf}]$

$[W]-[W]=[0.79,0.81]-[0.79,0.81]=[0.79-0.81,0.81-0.79]=[-0.02,0.02]$

$[L]-[L]=[1.19,1.21]-[1.19,1.21]=[1.19-1.21,1.21-1.19]=[-0.02,0.02]$

NON ZERO!?

© 2017 - ELEDIA Research Center 39

1.a.ii The Dependecy Problem – The Table

2. **Subtracting *[W]* and *[L]* from *[2P]***

$[P]=[2P]-[W]-[L]$

$=[W]+[W]+[L]+[L]-[W]-[L]$

$=[W]+[L]+([W]-[W])+([L]-[L])$ **IS ZERO?**

$=[0.79,0.81]+[1.19,1.21]+([0.79,0.81]-[0.79,0.81])+([1.19,1.21]-[1.19,1.21])$

$=[1.98,2.02]+([-0.02,0.02]+[-0.02,0.02])$

$=[1.98,2.02]+[-0.04,0.04]$

$=[1.94,2.06]\ m$

$[W]-[W]\neq 0$ $\quad [L]-[L]\neq 0$

The Dependency Problem

Every occurrence of an interval variable is considered an independent variable

$[W]-[W]=[W_1]-[W_2]$ even if $[W]=[W_1]=[W_2]$ are the same interval!

© 2017 - ELEDIA Research Center 40

1.a.ii The Dependecy Problem – The Table

2. Subtracting *[W]* and *[L]* from *[2P]*

WHAT IS THE CONSEQUENCE?

$$[P]=[2P]-[W]-[L]$$
$$=[W]+[W]+[L]+[L]-[W]-[L]$$
$$=[W]+[L]+([W]-[W])+([L]-[L])$$
$$=[0.79,0.81]+[1.19,1.21]+([0.79,0.81]-[0.79,0.81])+([1.19,1.21]-[1.19,1.21])$$
$$=[1.98,2.02]+([-0.02,0.02]+[-0.02,0.02])$$
$$=[1.98,2.02]+[-0.04,0.04]$$
$$=[1.94,2.06]\ m$$

$[W]-[W]\neq 0$ $\quad$ $[L]-[L]\neq 0$

The Dependency Problem

Every occurrence of an interval variable is considered an independent variable

$[W]-[W]=[W_1]-[W_2]$ even if $[W]=[W_1]=[W_2]$ are the same interval!

1.a.ii The Dependecy Problem

1. Adding [*W*] and [*L*]

$[P]=[W]+[L]=[1.98,\ 2.02]\ m$

Optimal Solution
(Minimum width)
$w([P])=0.04\,m$

2. Subtracting [*W*] and [*L*] from [2*P*]

$[P]=[2P]-[W]-[L]=[1.94,\ 2.06]\ m$

Dependency Pb
(Larger width)
$w([P])=0.12\,m$

The dependency problem <u>increases the width</u> of the resulting interval → MORE UNCERTAINTY!

HOW TO AVOID?

1.a.ii The Dependecy Problem

<u>Rules to Avoid/Reduce the Dependency Problem</u>

1. Reduce the number of occurrences of each variable

From $[P]=[W]+[W]+[L]+[L]-[W]-[L]$ **to** $[P]=[W]+[L]$

2. Redefine Interval Operations / Functions

$[W]-[W]=0$ **instead of** $[w_{inf}-w_{sup},\ w_{sup}-w_{inf}]\neq 0$

1.a.ii Avoiding Dependecy Pb – The Table

2. Redefine Interval Operations / Functions

$[W]-[W]=0$ **instead of** $[w_{inf}-w_{sup},\ w_{sup}-w_{inf}]\neq 0$

$[L]-[L]=0$ $\quad$ $[l_{inf}-l_{sup},\ l_{sup}-l_{inf}]\neq 0$

$$[P]=[2P]-[W]-[L]$$
$$=[W]+[W]+[L]+[L]-[W]-[L]$$
$$=[W]+[L]+([W]-[W])+([L]-[L])$$
$$=[0.79,0.81]+[1.19,1.21]+([0.79,0.81]-[0.79,0.81])+([1.19,1.21]-[1.19,1.21])$$

Considering $[W]-[W]=0$ $\quad$ $[L]-[L]=0$

$$[P]=[0.79,0.81]+[1.19,1.21]$$
$$=[1.98,2.02]$$

$w([P])=2.02-1.98=0.04\,m$ $\quad$ Minimum Width

Proper INTERVAL FUNCTION definition allows to obtain <u>optimal interval solutions</u>!

1.b Interval Function – What is?

Definition: Interval Function

An interval-valued function of one or more intervals arguments [*]

Function → $f([X_1],[X_2],...,[X_N]) :\rightarrow [F]$ ← Interval function values

Interval arguments

Example:

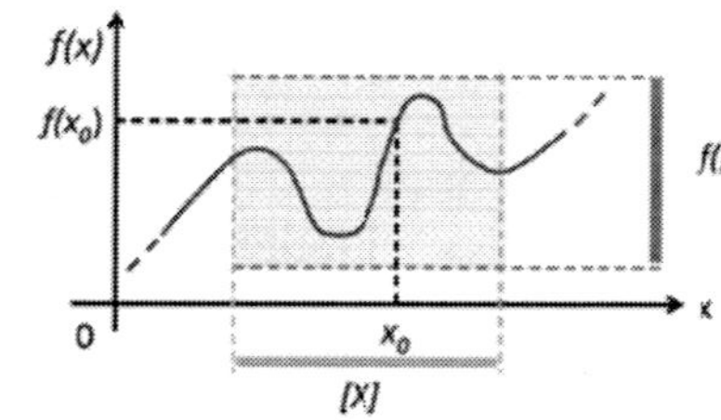

[*] R. E. Moore, Interval Analysis Prentice-Hall, Englewood Cliffs, New Jersey 1966.

1.b Interval Functions

$f([X_1],[X_2],...,[X_N]) :\rightarrow [F]$

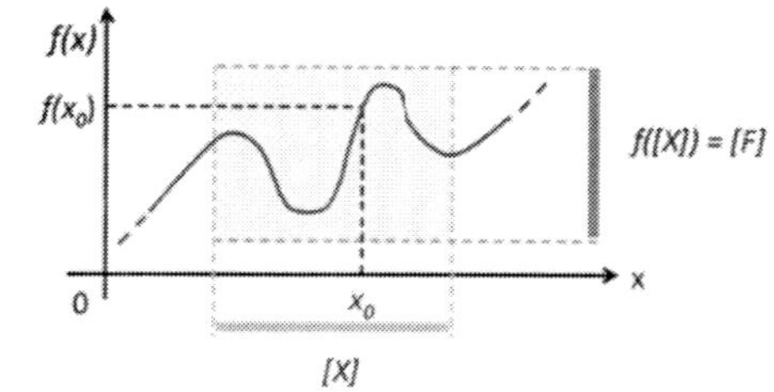

The interval function f([X])=[F] is an ***interval extension*** *of the function f(x)*

WHAT'S THE MEANING?

1.b.i Interval Functions – Property

If $[F] = f([X])$ is an interval extension of the function f then

The interval function *f*([X])=[F] must include all the values *f*(x) *for* x ϵ [X]

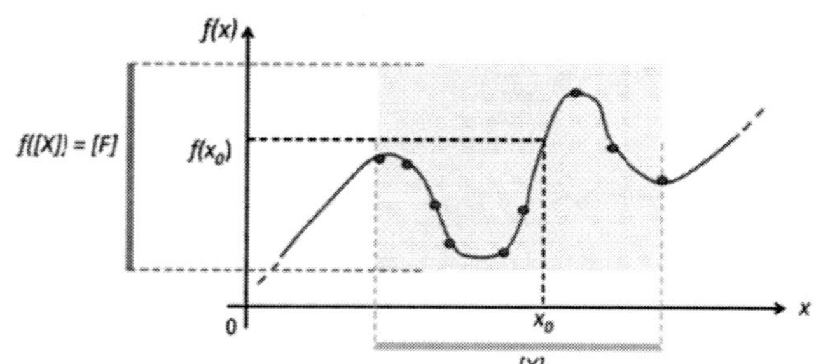

1.b.i Inclusion Monotonicity

Definition: Inclusion Monotonicity [*]

An ***interval function*** *$f([X_1], [X_2], ..., [X_N])$ is* ***inclusion monotonic*** *with respect to the function $f(x_1, x_2, ..., x_N)$ when $[F]=f([X_1], [X_2], ..., [X_N])$ contains the range of values of $f(x_1, x_2, ..., x_N)$ for all $x_n \in [X_n]$ $n=1,...,N$*

Key Observation:

WHAT'S THE RESULT?

"A single evaluation of a function over an interval give us information about the function values over all the (infinite) points of the interval" [**]

[*] R. E. Moore, Interval Analysis Prentice-Hall, Englewood Cliffs, New Jersey 1966.

[**] G.W. Walster, Interval arithmetic: The new floating-point arithmetic paradigm.

1.b.i Inclusion Theorem – Property

Consider: $f([X]) :\rightarrow [F]$ and $[X'] \subseteq [X]$

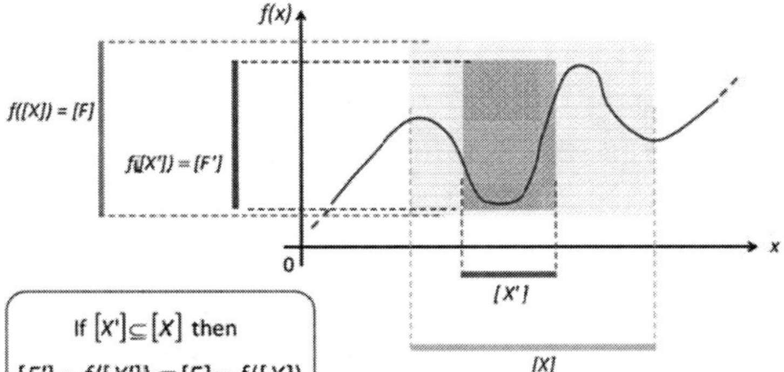

If $[X'] \subseteq [X]$ then

$[F'] = f([X']) \subseteq [F] = f([X])$

INCLUSION MONOTONICITY PROPERTY!

1.b.i Inclusion Theorem – Observation

Remind:

$f([X_1],[X_2],...,[X_N]) :\rightarrow [F]$

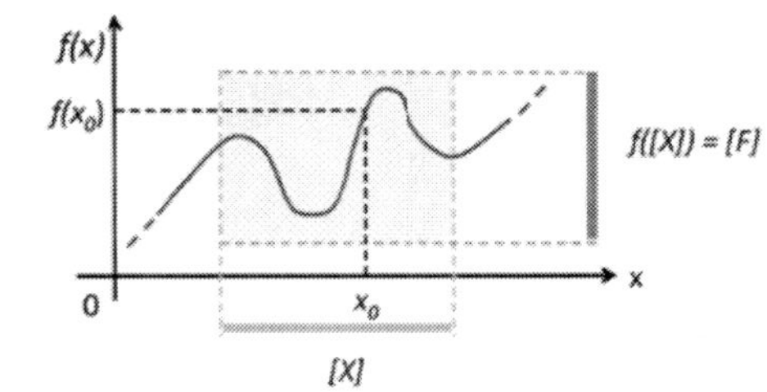

The interval function f([X])=[F] is ***AN*** *__interval extension__ of the function f*

Why AN? ... Is it UNIQUE?
What is the CONSEQUENCE?

1.b.ii Interval Functions – Dependency Pb.

Given: $f(x) = f_1(x) = f_2(x)$ evaluate: $f_1([X]) :\rightarrow [F_1]$, $f_2([X]) :\rightarrow [F_2]$

f_1([X]) and f_2([X]) are __two interval extensions__ of f

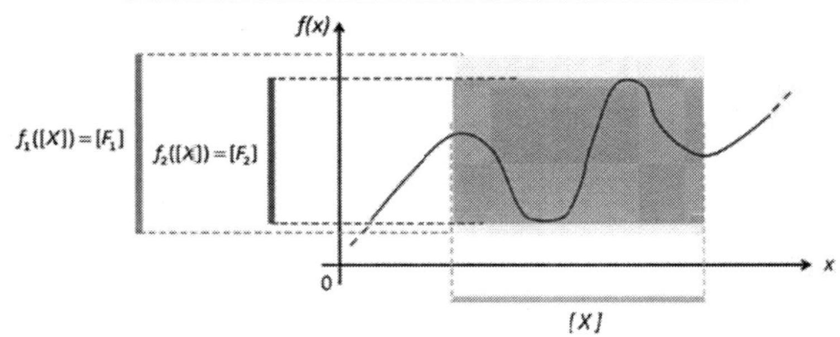

$[F_1]$ *and* $[F_2]$ include all values *f*(x) *for* x ∈ [X] *but...*

... w($[F_1]$) ***is larger than*** w($[F_2]$)

1.b.ii Interval Functions – Dependency Pb.

Remember... Half perimeter of the Table

Standard Arithmetic	Interval Arithmetic
$p_1 = w + l$ →	$[P_1] = [W] + [L]$
$p_2 = 2p - w - l$ →	$[P_2] = [2P] - [W] - [L]$
	BUT
$p_1 = p_2 \ \forall l,w$	$[P_1] \neq [P_2]$

Different resulting intervals even if the starting functions are equivalent in standard arithmetic

1.b.ii Interval Functions – Minimal Width

Given: $f(x) = f_1(x) = f_2(x)$ evaluate: $f_1([X]) :\rightarrow [F_1]$, $f_2([X]) :\rightarrow [F_2]$

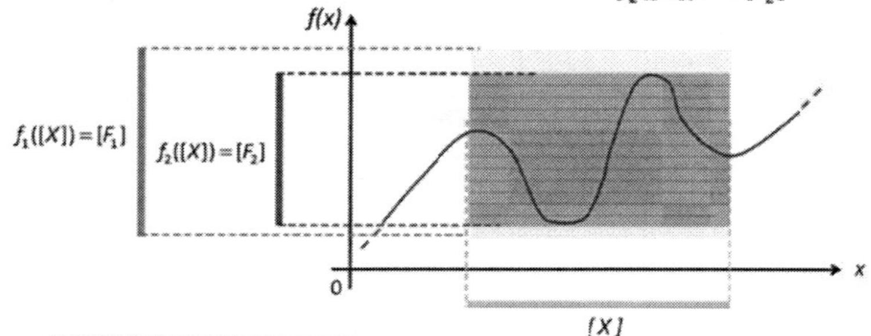

$f_1(x) = f_2(x)$, same $[X]$ but
$f_1([X]) \subset f_2([X])$

HOW TO OBTAIN
THE MINIMUM WIDTH?

1.b.ii Interval Functions – Minimal Width

Given: $f(x) = f_1(x) = f_2(x)$ evaluate: $f_1([X]) :\rightarrow [F_1]$, $f_2([X]) :\rightarrow [F_2]$

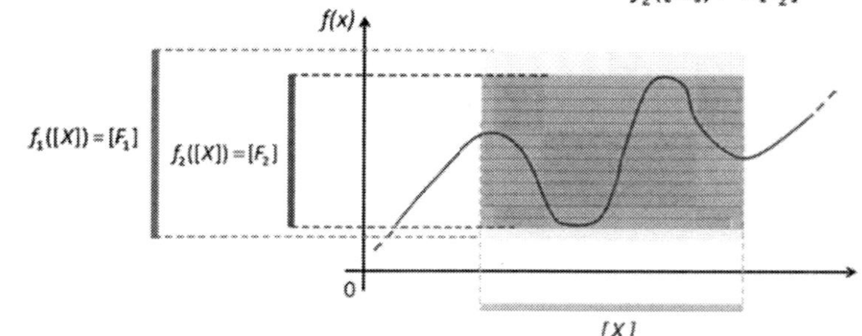

$f_1(x) = f_2(x)$, same $[X]$ but
$f_1([X]) \subset f_2([X])$

Interval functions must be defined in a suitable ("smart") way

1.a.ii Avoiding Dependecy Pb – The Table

2. Redefine Interval Operations / Functions

$[W]-[W]=0$, $[L]-[L]=0$ **instead of** $[w_{inf}-w_{sup}, w_{sup}-w_{inf}] \neq 0$, $[l_{inf}-l_{sup}, l_{sup}-l_{inf}] \neq 0$

$[P]=[2P]-[W]-[L]$
$=[W]+[W]+[L]+[L]-[W]-[L]$
$=[W]+[L]+([W]-[W])+([L]-[L])$
$=[0.79,0.81]+[1.19,1.21]+([0.79,0.81]-[0.79,0.81])+([1.19,1.21]-[1.19,1.21])$

Considering $[W]-[W]=0$ $[L]-[L]=0$

$[P]=[0.79,0.81]+[1.19,1.21]$
$=[1.98,2.02]$

$w([P]) = 2.02 - 1.98 = 0.04\,m$ **Minimum Width**

Proper INTERVAL FUNCTION definition allows to obtain <u>optimal interval solutions</u>!

1.b.ii The Dependecy Problem

Example: **Evaluation of** $f(x) = x^2 + 1$ **over the interval** $[X] = [x_{inf}, x_{sup}] = [-1, 2]$

$f([X]) = [X]^2 + [1,1] = [X]\cdot[X] - [1,1]$

f([-1,2]) = [-1,2]·[-1,2] + [1,1] =
= [min(1,-2,-2,4), max(1,-2,-2,4)]+ [2,2]
= [-2, 4] + [1,1] = [-2+1, 4+1] = [-1, 5]

Some questions arise from $f([-1,2])$...

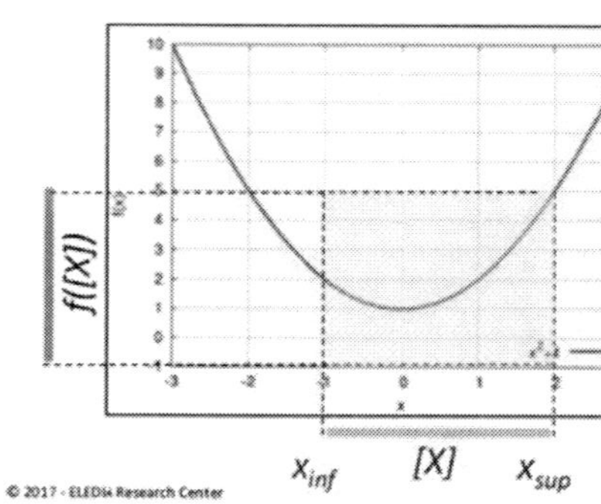

1.b.ii The Dependecy Problem

Example: Evaluation of $f(x) = x^2 + 1$ over the interval $[X] = [x_{inf}, x_{sup}] = [-1, 2]$

$f([-1,2]) = [-1,2]\cdot[-1,2] + [1,1] =$
$= [min(1,-2,-2,4), max(1,-2,-2,4)] + [2,2]$
$= [-2, 4] + [1,1] = [-2+1, 4+1] = [-1, 5]$

1. Can $[X]^2 + 1$ be negative?

2. Can we obtain a better bound?

PROPER DEFINITION of NON-ELEMENTARY FUNCTIONS!

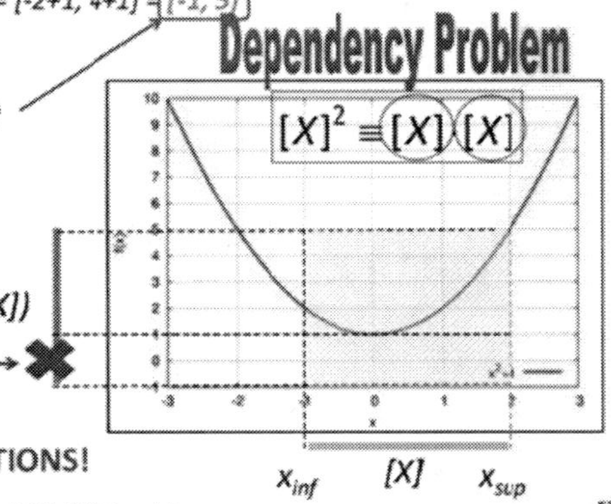

Interval Functions - Properties

a. ***Encloses all possible*** function values

The **Interval function** $f([X_1], ..., [X_N])$ **is inclusion monotonic** with respect to the real function $f(x_1, ..., x_N)$:
$x_1 \in [X_1], ..., x_N \in [X_N] \rightarrow f(x_1, ..., x_N) \in f([X_1], ..., [X_N])$

b. ***Has the minimal width*** (Avoid/Reduce Dependency Problem)

1.b.ii The Dependecy Problem

Example: Evaluation of $f(x) = x^2$ over the interval $[X] = [x_{inf}, x_{sup}]$

Hypothesis: $x_{inf} < 0$ and $x_{sup} > 0$

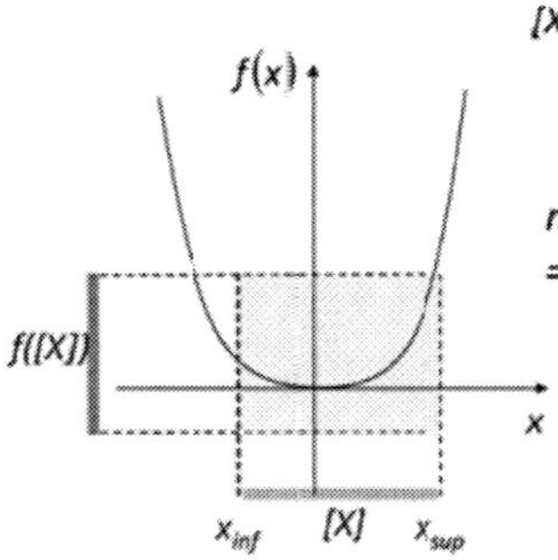

Remember:

$[X]\cdot[X] = [min(x_{inf}\cdot x_{inf}, x_{inf}\cdot x_{sup}, x_{sup}\cdot x_{inf}, x_{sup}\cdot x_{sup}), max(x_{inf}\cdot x_{inf}, x_{inf}\cdot x_{sup}, x_{sup}\cdot x_{inf}, x_{sup}\cdot x_{sup})]$

$min(x_{inf}\cdot x_{inf}, x_{inf}\cdot x_{sup}, x_{sup}\cdot x_{inf}, x_{sup}\cdot x_{sup})$
$= x_{inf}\cdot x_{sup} = x_{sup}\cdot x_{inf} < 0$

The square gives NEGATIVE values!

$$\inf\{[X]\cdot[X]\} = x_{inf}\cdot x_{sup} < 0$$

1.b.i Non-Elementary Functions (1/8)

Square of Intervals:

1. Compute $[X]^2 = [x_{inf}, x_{sup}]^2$ *if* $x_{inf} \geq 0$

Observation: *if* $x_{inf} \geq 0 \Rightarrow |x_{sup}| > |x_{inf}| \Rightarrow x_{sup}^2 > x_{inf}^2$

then: $[X]^2 = [x_{inf}^2, x_{sup}^2]$ *if* $x_{inf} \geq 0$

Example: compute $[X]^2 = [x_{inf}, x_{sup}]^2$ with $[X] = [1,2]$

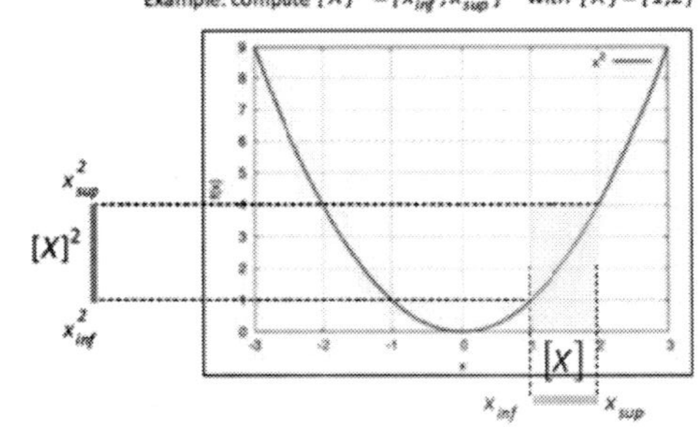

$[1,2]^2 = [1^2, 2^2] = [1,4]$

1.b.i Non-Elementary Functions (1/8)

Square of Intervals:

2. Compute $[X]^2=[x_{inf},x_{sup}]^2$ if $x_{sup}\le 0$

Observation: if $x_{sup}\le 0 \Rightarrow |x_{inf}|>|x_{sup}| \Rightarrow x_{inf}^2>x_{sup}^2$

then: $[X]^2=[x_{sup}^2,x_{inf}^2]$ if $x_{sup}\le 0$

Example: compute $[X]^2=[x_{inf},x_{sup}]^2$ with $[X]=[-3,-1]$

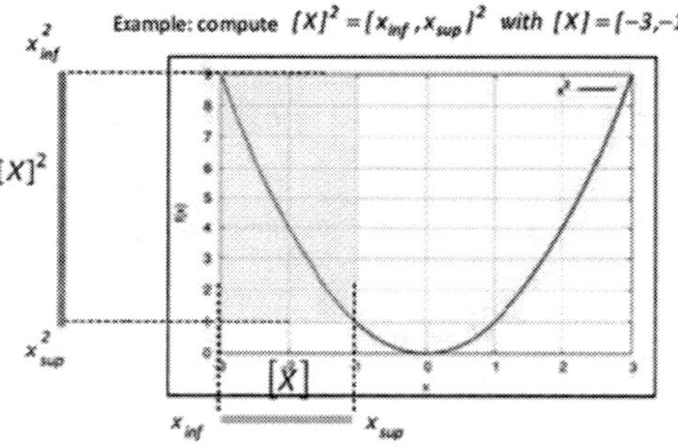

$[-3,-1]^2=[-1^2,-3^2]=[1,9]$

© 2017 - ELEDIA Research Center

61

1.b.i Non-Elementary Functions (1/8)

Square of Intervals:

3. Compute $[X]^2=[x_{inf},x_{sup}]^2$ if $x_{inf}\le 0\le x_{sup}$

Observation: if $x_{inf}\le 0\le x_{inf}$ $|x_{inf}|>|x_{sup}|$ OR $|x_{sup}|>|x_{inf}|$?

then: $[X]^2=[0,max(x_{inf}^2,x_{sup}^2)]$ if $x_{inf}\le 0\le x_{sup}$

Example: compute $[X]^2=[x_{inf},x_{sup}]^2$ with $[X]=[-2,1]$

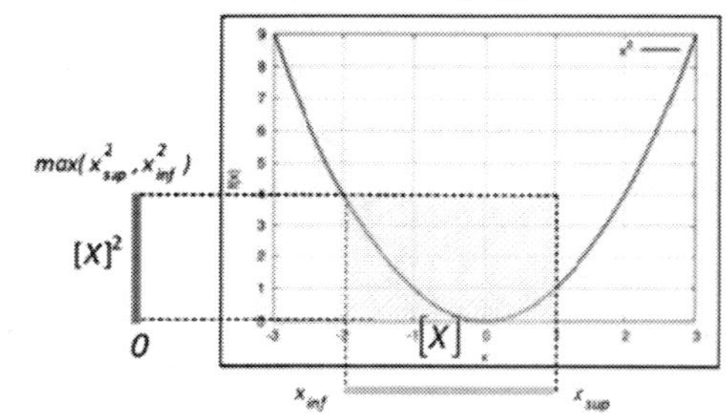

$[-2,1]^2=[0,max(-2^2,1^2)]$
$=[0,max(4,1)]=[0,4]$

© 2017 - ELEDIA Research Center

62

1.b.i Non-Elementary Functions (1/8)

Square of Intervals:

$[X]^2$ – A Summary

$$[X]^2=\begin{cases}[x_{inf}^2,x_{sup}^2] & if\ x_{inf}\ge 0\\ [x_{sup}^2,x_{inf}^2] & if\ x_{sup}\le 0\\ [0,max(x_{inf}^2,x_{sup}^2)] & if\ x_{inf}\le 0\le x_{sup}\end{cases}$$

Before ....

$[X]^2=\{x\cdot y: x\in[X], y\in[X]\}$

Dependency Problem

Now ....

$[X]^2=\{x^2: x\in[X]\}$

Suitable Definition Non-Elementary Function

... GO BACK TO $f(x)=x^2+1$ over $[-2,1]$

© 2017 - ELEDIA Research Center

63

1.b.i Non-Elementary Functions (1/8)

Example: evaluation of $f(x)=x^2+1$ over the interval $[X]=[x_{inf},x_{sup}]=[-1,2]$

before... $f_1([-1,2])=[-1,2][-1,2]+[1,1]=[-2,4]+[1,1]=[-2+1,4+1]=[-1,5]$

now... $f_2([-1,2])=[-1,2]^2+[2,2]=[0,4]+[1,1]=[0+1,4+1]=[1,5]$

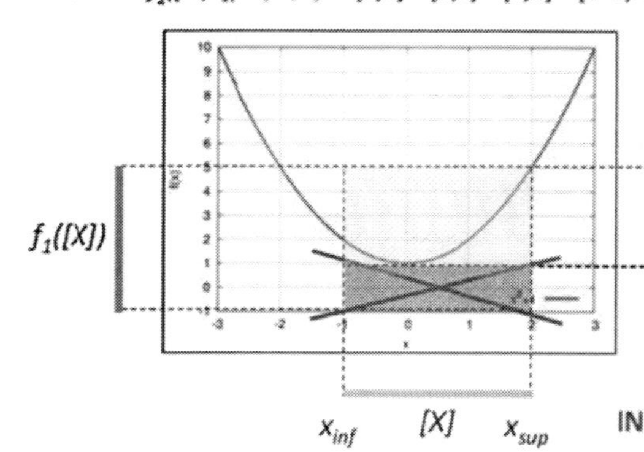

BETTER BOUNDS
and
INCLUSION PROPERTY!

© 2017 - ELEDIA Research Center

64

1.b.i Non-Elementary Functions

As $[X]^2$ other functions must be defined when using Intervals...

Cube of Intervals $\xrightarrow{?}$ $[X]^3$

Power of Intervals $\xrightarrow{?}$ $[X]^n$

Exponential of Intervals $\xrightarrow{?}$ $a^{[X]}$

Logarithm of Intervals $\xrightarrow{?}$ $log_a[X]$

Cosine of Intervals $\xrightarrow{?}$ $cos([X])$

Sine of Intervals $\xrightarrow{?}$ $sin([X])$

Tangent of Intervals $\xrightarrow{?}$ $tan([X])$

...

© 2017 - ELEDIA Research Center 65

Real Interval Functions – Key-Issues

Other **REAL INTERVAL FUNCTIONS**: $f([X]) \rightarrow [F]$,
[X], [F] REAL INTERVAL

- ❑ Apply the rules of Interval Arithmetic
- ❑ Exploit the function behavior to compute its boundaries

All REAL FUNCTIONS can be extended to REAL INTERVAL FUNCTIONS through IA

- **Bounds** of the INTERVAL FUNCTION S EXTENSIONS computed over an interval argument are **conservative** (i.e., inclusion monotonicity property)
- **Computational burden** for evaluating INTERVAL FUNCTION EXTENSION over an interval argument is **comparable** with the functional evaluation over a single point

© 2017 - ELEDIA Research Center 66

Real Intervals/Interval Functions - Summary

- ❑ What is a **Real Interval** ?
- ❑ How **Real Interval Arithmetic Operations** are defined ?
- ❑ What is the **Dependency Problem ?**
- ❑ How to solve the Dependency Problem ?
- ❑ What is a **Real Interval Function** ?
- ❑ The **Inclusion Theorem**
- ❑ How **Real Interval Function are defined ?**

but .... also Complex Intervals exist! How to deal with?

© 2017 - ELEDIA Research Center 67

2. Complex Intervals

Definition: Complex Interval

A complex interval [Z] is an ordered pair of intervals [Z]= [[X],[Y]] with [X] = [x_{inf} , x_{sup}] and [Y] = [y_{inf} , y_{sup}] real intervals. [*]

$$[Z] = \{z = (x+iy) \in C;\ x_{inf} \le x \le x_{sup};\ y_{inf} \le y \le y_{sup}\}$$

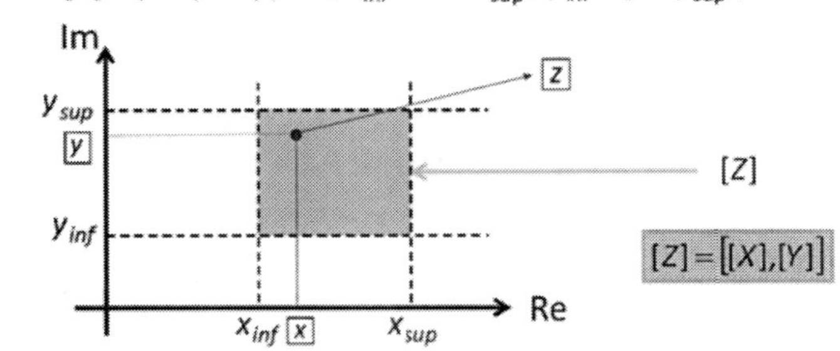

[*] R. Boche, "Complex Interval Arithmetic with some Applications," Lockheed Missile and Space Company, technical report, Feb. 1966.

© 2017 - ELEDIA Research Center 68

Complex Elementary Operations – Summary

Given: $[Z]=[X,Y]$ $[X]=[x_{inf}, x_{sup}]$ $[Y]=[y_{inf}, y_{sup}]$ $[X]$ $[Y]$ $[X']$ $[Y']$ **real intervals**

$[Z']=[X',Y']$ $[X']=[x'_{inf}, x'_{sup}]$ $[Y']=[y'_{inf}, y'_{sup}]$

Sum: $[Z]+[Z']=[X+X', Y+Y']$

Sum of Negative: $[Z]-[Z]=[0,0]$

Sum of Complex Conjugate: $[Z]+[Z]^*=[2X,0]$

Subtraction: $[Z]-[Z']=[X-X', Y-Y']$

Product: $[Z]\cdot[Z']=[XX'-YY', XY'+YX']$

Product of Complex Conjugate: $[Z]\cdot[Z^*]=[X^2+Y^2,0]$

Inverse : $1/[Z]=[X,-Y]/[X^2+Y^2,0]$

Division: $[Z]/[Z']=[(XX'+YY')/(X'^2+Y'^2),(YX'-XY')/(X'^2+Y'^2)]$

KEY FEATURE:

- Involve **just Real Intervals** $[X]$ $[Y]$ $[X']$ $[Y']$

Complex Interval Functions – Key-Issues

Observation:

Evaluation of Complex Interval Functions
recast as
Evaluation of Real Interval Functions

↓

- **Results** for **Real** hold true also for **Complex Interval Functions**
- **Dependency Problem** still remains
- **Inclusion Theorem** holds true also for Complex Interval Functions

3. Why use Interval Analysis?

At our disposal:

- A mathematical framework **to work with real/complex intervals**
- A reliable tool **to deal with uncertainty**
- A valid support to **analyze interval real/complex functions**

IA for Comms & Nets

IA at Work

Part C – IA for Comms & Nets

- Antenna Array Sensitivity Analysis
- Antenna Array Robust Design
- Inverse Scattering Problem

3.1 IA for Array Sensitivity Analysis

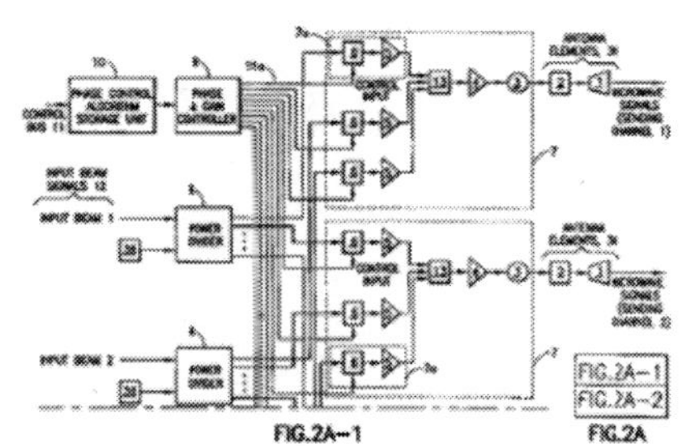

European Patent: EP 0 939 452 A2

Phased array beam-forming networks:

- Can be <u>very complex</u> (especially in case of multi-beam generation as required in modern systems)
- Contain several <u>heterogeneous control points</u>
- The control points are unavoidably characterized by <u>manufacturing tolerances</u>

What's the consequence?

Ideal vs. Real Phased Array Behavior

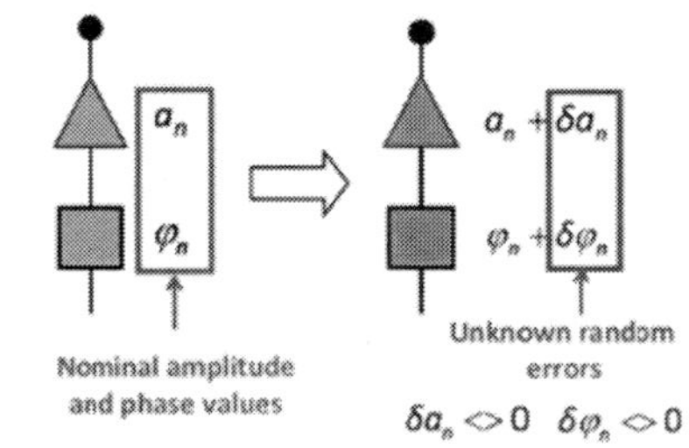

$\delta a_n <> 0 \quad \delta \varphi_n <> 0$

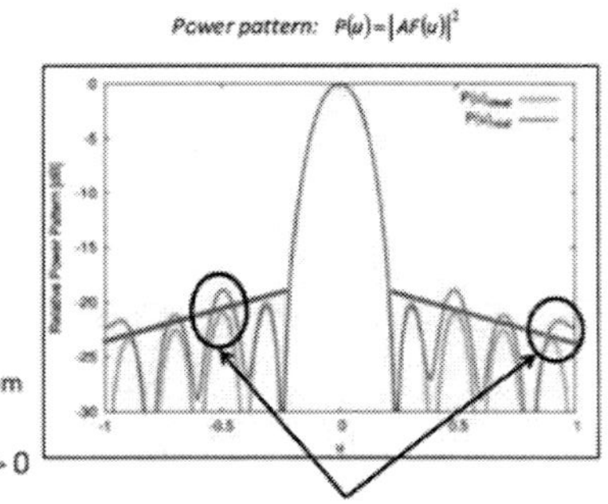

Pattern deviates from the nominal/expected one

<u>Ideal array factor</u>

$$AF(u) = \sum_{n=1}^{N} a_n e^{j(kd(n-1)u + \varphi_n)}$$

<u>Real array factor</u>

$$AF(u) = \sum_{n=1}^{N} (a_n + \delta a_n) e^{j(kd(n-1)u + (\varphi_n + \delta \varphi_n))}$$

How to predict the pattern behavior?

Phased Array Tolerance Analysis

- State-of-the-Art -

<u>Statistical</u> technique for pattern performance prediction

<u>Analytical Approaches</u>

J. Ruze, "The effect of aperture errors on the antenna radiation pattern," *Nuovo Cimento*, vol. 9, pp. 364-380, 1952.

R. E. Elliott, "Mechanical and electrical tolerances for two-dimensional scanning antenna arrays," *T-IRE Antennas Propag.*, vol. 6, pp. 114-120,1958.

M. I. Skolnik, "Nonuniform arrays," Ch. 6 in *Antenna Theory*, R. E. Collin and F. J. Zucker, New York, NY: McGraw-Hill, 1969, pp. 227-234.

J. K. Hsiao, "Design of error tolerance of a phased array," *Elect. Lett.*, vol. 21, no. 19, pp. 834-836, Sep. 1985.

P. D. Kaplan, "Predicting antenna sidelobe performance," *Microwave J.*, vol. 29, p. 201-204, Sep. 1986

<u>Computational Approaches</u>

M. Lanne, "Design aspects and pattern Prediction for Phased arrays with sub-array position errors," 2010 IEEE Int. Conf. Phased Array Systems and Technology, Boston, MA (USA), 12-15 Oct. 2010, pp. 440-446.

J. Lee, Y. Lee, and H. Kim, "Decision of error tolerance in array element by the Monte Carlo method," *IEEE Trans. Antennas Propag.*, vol. 53, no. 4, pp. 1325-1331, Apr. 2005.

Phased Array Tolerance Analysis

- State-of-the-Art -

<u>Statistical</u> technique for pattern performance prediction

<u>Analytical Approaches</u>

- ↑ Easy to implement
- ↓ Approximated formulation
- ↑ Fast computation
- ↓ **A-priori error distribution assumption** $\Pr(a_n)$ $\Pr(\varphi_n)$
- ↓ Not fully reliable/robust

<u>Computational Approaches</u>

- ↓ Enumerative (Monte Carlo) method
- ↑ Exact formulation
- ↓ High computational burden (ideally infinite number of error combinations)
- ↓ Not fully reliable/robust (analysis limited to a subset of combinations)

From Random to Interval Errors

Possible to easily (analytically) encompass an infinite number of random errors?

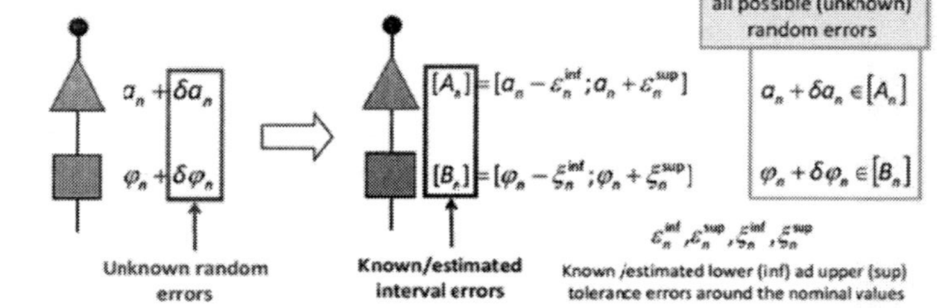

Real array factor

$$AF(u) = \sum_{n=1}^{N} (a_n + \delta a_n) e^{j(kd(n-1)u + \varphi_n + \delta\varphi_n)}$$

"Interval" array factor

$$[AF(u)] = \sum_{n=1}^{N} [A_n] e^{j(kd(n-1)u + [B_n])}$$

How to compute?

© 2017 - ELEDIA Research Center 77

Interval Analysis – Basic Arithmetic

Sum: $[X]+[Y] = [x_{inf} + y_{inf}, x_{sup} + y_{sup}]$

Difference: $[X]-[Y] = [x_{inf} - y_{sup}, x_{sup} - y_{inf}]$

Product: $[X]\cdot[Y] = [\min(x_{inf}y_{inf}, x_{inf}y_{sup}, x_{sup}y_{inf}, x_{sup}y_{sup}), \max(x_{inf}y_{inf}, x_{inf}y_{sup}, x_{sup}y_{inf}, x_{sup}y_{sup})]$

Inverse: $1/[X] = [1/x_{sup}, 1/x_{inf}]\quad 0 \notin [X]$

Division: $[X]/[Y] = [\min(x_{inf}/y_{inf}, x_{inf}/y_{sup}, x_{sup}/y_{inf}, x_{sup}/y_{sup}), \max(x_{inf}/y_{inf}, x_{inf}/y_{sup}, x_{sup}/y_{inf}, x_{sup}/y_{sup})]\quad 0 \notin [Y]$

KEY FEATURES:

- Involve **just the boundaries** of the intervals: x_{inf} x_{sup} y_{inf} y_{sup}
- Include **all the possible results**

Complex Elementary Operations – Summary

Given: $[Z] = [X, Y]$ $[X] = [x_{inf}, x_{sup}]$ $[Y] = [y_{inf}, y_{sup}]$ $[X]\ [Y]\ [X']\ [Y']$ **real intervals**
$[Z'] = [X', Y']$ $[X'] = [x'_{inf}, x'_{sup}]$ $[Y'] = [y'_{inf}, y'_{sup}]$

Sum: $[Z]+[Z'] = [X + X', Y + Y']$

Sum of Negative: $[Z]-[Z] = [0,0]$

Sum of Complex Conjugate: $[Z]+[Z]^* = [2X, 0]$

Subtraction: $[Z]-[Z'] = [X - X', Y - Y']$

Product: $[Z]\cdot[Z'] = [XX' - YY', XY' + YX']$

Product of Complex Conjugate: $[Z]\cdot[Z^*] = [X^2 + Y^2, 0]$

Inverse: $1/[Z] = [X, -Y]/[X^2 + Y^2, 0]$

Division: $[Z]/[Z'] = [(XX'+YY')/(X'^2+Y'^2), (YX'-XY')/(X'^2+Y'^2)]$

KEY FEATURE:

- Involve **just Real Intervals** $[X]\ [Y]\ [X']\ [Y']$

IA for Phased Array Analysis

Reference problem: uniform linear phased array with amplitude weighting errors and correct phase values

$[B_n] = \varphi_n \quad \xi_n^{inf} = \xi_n^{sup} = 0 \quad n = 1, \ldots, N$

$[A_n] = [a_n - \varepsilon_n^{inf}; a_n + \varepsilon_n^{sup}] \quad n = 1, \ldots, N$

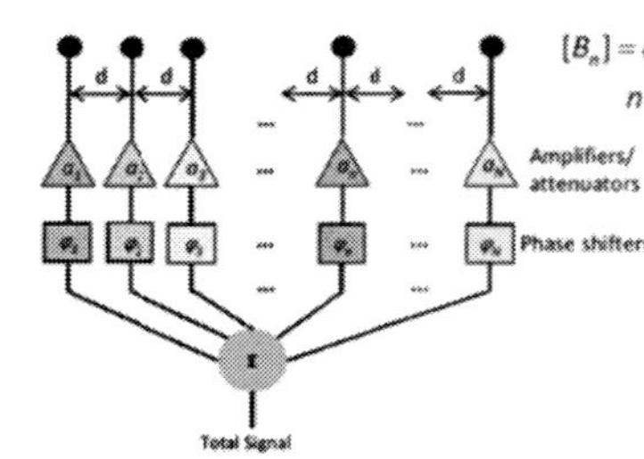

INTERVAL Array Factor:

$$[AF(u)] = \sum_{n=1}^{N} [A_n] e^{j(kd(n-1)u + \varphi_n)}$$

INTERVAL Power Pattern:

$$[P(u)] = |[AF(u)]|^2$$

GOAL

Compute the upper and lower bound of the interval power pattern

$\sup\{[P(u)]\}$ $\inf\{[P(u)]\}$

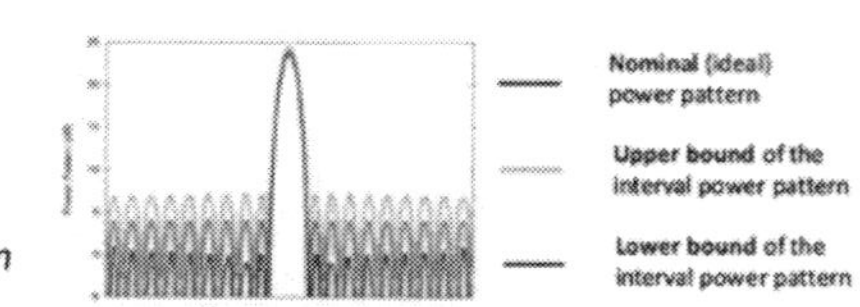

© 2017 - ELEDIA Research Center 80

Interval Array Factor

INTERVAL Array Factor:

$$[AF(u)] = \sum_{n=1}^{N} [A_n] e^{j(kd(n-1)u+\varphi_n)} \xrightarrow{\text{Complex interval}} [AF(u)] = \underbrace{\mathrm{Re}\{[AF(u)]\}}_{\text{Real part}} + j\underbrace{\mathrm{Im}\{[AF(u)]\}}_{\text{Imaginary part}}$$

$$[A_n] = [a_n - \varepsilon_n^{inf}, a_n + \varepsilon_n^{sup}]$$

Upper/lower bounds of AF:

$$\begin{matrix}\sup\\ \inf\end{matrix}[AF(u)] = \begin{matrix}\sup\\ \inf\end{matrix}\mathrm{Re}\{[AF(u)]\} + j\begin{matrix}\sup\\ \inf\end{matrix}\mathrm{Im}\{[AF(u)]\}$$

$$\begin{matrix}\sup\\ \inf\end{matrix}\mathrm{Re}\{[AF(u)]\} = \sum_{n=1}^{N}\left(a_n + \frac{\varepsilon_n^{sup} - \varepsilon_n^{inf}}{2}\right)\cos\Theta_n \pm \frac{1}{2}\sum_{n=1}^{N}\left(\varepsilon_n^{sup} + \varepsilon_n^{inf}\right)\left|\cos\Theta_n\right|$$

$$\begin{matrix}\sup\\ \inf\end{matrix}\mathrm{Im}\{[AF(u)]\} = \sum_{n=1}^{N}\left(a_n + \frac{\varepsilon_n^{sup} - \varepsilon_n^{inf}}{2}\right)\sin\Theta_n \pm \frac{1}{2}\sum_{n=0}^{N}\left(\varepsilon_n^{sup} + \varepsilon_n^{inf}\right)\left|\sin\Theta_n\right|$$

$$\Theta_n = kd(n-1)u + \varphi_n$$

Just needed the endpoints of $[A_n]$!

Interval Power Pattern (1/2)

INTERVAL Power Pattern:

$$[P(u)] = |[AF(u)]|^2 = [AF(u)][AF(u)]^* = \mathrm{Re}\{[AF(u)]\}^2 + \mathrm{Im}\{[AF(u)]\}^2$$

Complex interval arithmetic [*]

$$[Z][Z]^* = [X]^2 + [Y]^2$$

$$[Z] = [X] + j[Y]$$

Complex interval — Real interval

... after "some" interval-based mathematical steps: [**]

Upper Power Pattern bound:

$$\sup\{[P(u)]\} = \left(\left|\sum_{n=1}^{N}\left(a_n + \frac{\varepsilon_n^{sup} - \varepsilon_n^{inf}}{2}\right)\cos\Theta_n\right| + \frac{1}{2}\sum_{n=1}^{N}\left(\varepsilon_n^{sup} + \varepsilon_n^{inf}\right)\left|\cos\Theta_n\right|\right)^2 + \left(\left|\sum_{n=1}^{N}\left(a_n + \frac{\varepsilon_n^{sup} - \varepsilon_n^{inf}}{2}\right)\sin\Theta_n\right| + \frac{1}{2}\sum_{n=1}^{N}\left(\varepsilon_n^{sup} + \varepsilon_n^{inf}\right)\left|\sin\Theta_n\right|\right)^2$$

[*] R. Boche, "Complex interval arithmetic with some applications," Tech. Report Lockheed Missiles & Space Company, pp. 1-33, 1966.
[**] P. Rocca, L. Manica, N. Anselmi, and A. Massa, "Analysis of the pattern tolerances in linear arrays with arbitrary amplitude errors," *IEEE Antennas Wireless Propag. Lett.*, vol. 12, pp. 639-642, 2013.

Interval Power Pattern (2/2)

Lower Power Pattern bound: [**]

(1) $$\inf\{[P(u)]\} = \left(\left|\sum_{n=1}^{N}\left(a_n + \frac{\varepsilon_n^{sup} - \varepsilon_n^{inf}}{2}\right)\cos\Theta_n\right| - \frac{1}{2}\sum_{n=1}^{N}\left(\varepsilon_n^{sup} + \varepsilon_n^{inf}\right)\left|\cos\Theta_n\right|\right)^2 + \left(\left|\sum_{n=1}^{N}\left(a_n + \frac{\varepsilon_n^{sup} - \varepsilon_n^{inf}}{2}\right)\sin\Theta_n\right| - \frac{1}{2}\sum_{n=1}^{N}\left(\varepsilon_n^{sup} + \varepsilon_n^{inf}\right)\left|\sin\Theta_n\right|\right)^2$$

(2) $$\inf\{[P(u)]\} = \left(\left|\sum_{n=1}^{N}\left(a_n + \frac{\varepsilon_n^{sup} - \varepsilon_n^{inf}}{2}\right)\cos\Theta_n\right| - \frac{1}{2}\sum_{n=1}^{N}\left(\varepsilon_n^{sup} + \varepsilon_n^{inf}\right)\left|\cos\Theta_n\right|\right)^2$$

(3) $$\inf\{[P(u)]\} = \left(\left|\sum_{n=1}^{N}\left(a_n + \frac{\varepsilon_n^{sup} - \varepsilon_n^{inf}}{2}\right)\sin\Theta_n\right| - \frac{1}{2}\sum_{n=1}^{N}\left(\varepsilon_n^{sup} + \varepsilon_n^{inf}\right)\left|\sin\Theta_n\right|\right)^2$$

(4) $$\inf\{[P(u)]\} = 0$$

Depending on whether: [**]

$\sup\{\mathrm{Re}\{[AF(u)]\}\} <> 0$

$\inf\{\mathrm{Re}\{[AF(u)]\}\} <> 0$

$\sup\{\mathrm{Im}\{[AF(u)]\}\} <> 0$

$\inf\{\mathrm{Im}\{[AF(u)]\}\} <> 0$

Just needed the endpoints of $[A_n]$!

[**] P. Rocca, L. Manica, N. Anselmi, and A. Massa, "Analysis of the pattern tolerances in linear arrays with arbitrary amplitude errors," *IEEE Antennas Wireless Propag. Lett.*, vol. 12, pp. 639-642, 2013.

Interval Power Pattern

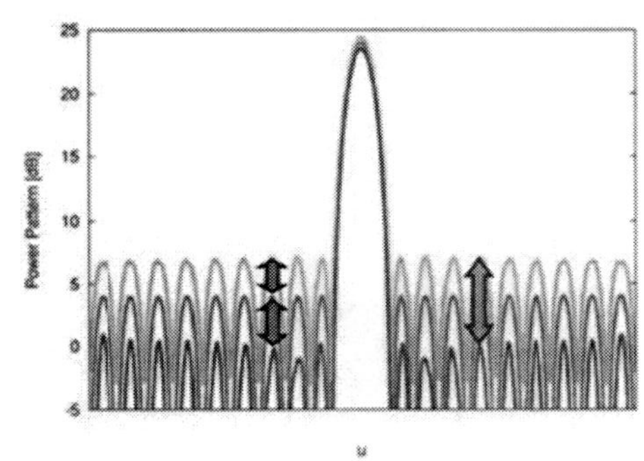

Nominal (expected) power pattern

Upper bound of the interval power pattern

Lower bound of the interval power pattern

For each angular direction, known the maximum tolerance of the power pattern or the deviation from the nominal beam

Results – The IA Inclusion

Test case description

- Uniform linear array: $N=10, d=\frac{\lambda}{2}$
- Taylor: $SLL=-25dB, \bar{n}=2$
- Amplitude tolerance: $\chi_n=5\%$, $n=1,...,N$

5% error on the amplitude weights wrt the nominal values

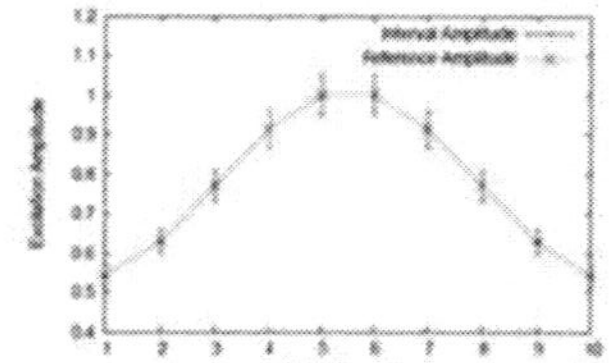

Nominal amplitudes and interval amplitudes

10^5 Monte Carlo error realizations are considered where

$$a_n+\delta a_n \in [A_n]$$

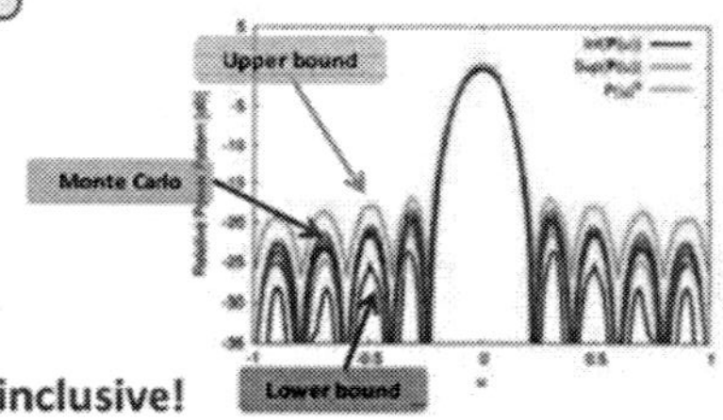

Interval power bounds and random patterns

The interval bounds are inclusive!

© 2017 - ELEDIA Research Center

85

Interval Power Pattern

Test Case – Increasing Amplitude Tolerance

- Linear Uniform Array: d=λ/2 – N=20
- Dolph Excitations – SLL=-30.0 [dB]
- Linear Symmetrical Tolerances: $\varepsilon_n^{sup}=\varepsilon_n^{inf}=a_n\delta a_n;\ n=1,...,N$
- δa_n = 1%, 5%, 10%

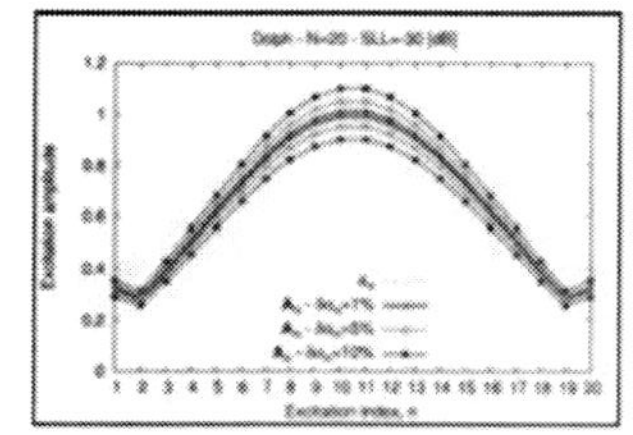

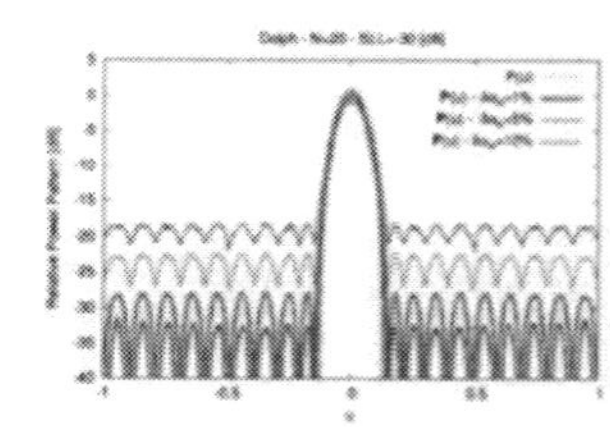

Higher Tolerances
Larger deviation from nominal pattern

δa_n %	HPBW [u]	SLL [dB]	Peak [dB]	D [dB]	Δ
0	1.12	-30.00	22.32	12.30	-
1	[1.08, 1.15]	[-31.69, -27.74]	[22.28, 22.46]	[12.22, 12.56]	0.4610
5	[1.02, 1.22]	[-45.73, -21.76]	[21.92, 22.72]	[11.53, 13.26]	2.4081
10	[0.73, 1.45]	[-∞, -14.85]	[21.46, 23.20]	[10.65, 14.13]	5.2499

© 2017 - ELEDIA Research Center

86

3.2 IA for Robust Array Design

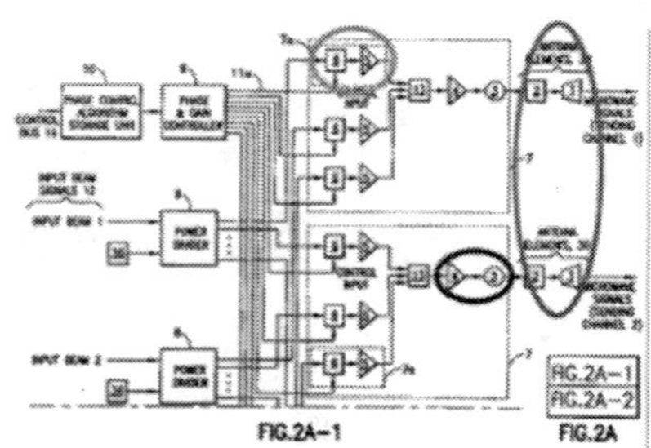

FIG.2A-1 FIG.2A

European Patent: EP 0 939 452 A2

Phased arrays:

- Can be very complex (especially in case of multi-beam generation as required in modern systems)
- Contain several control points and array elements
- Control points/elements are unavoidably characterized by manufacturing tolerances

Phased arrays DESIGN PROBLEM:

1) Suppose at disposal TOT $
2) Where to invest more/less $?
3) How "good" (robust) should be control points?

Control point at element level?
Control point at sub-array level?
Number of elements?
Else?

How to decide?

© 2017 - ELEDIA Research Center

87

Robust Array Synthesis Problem

Requirements

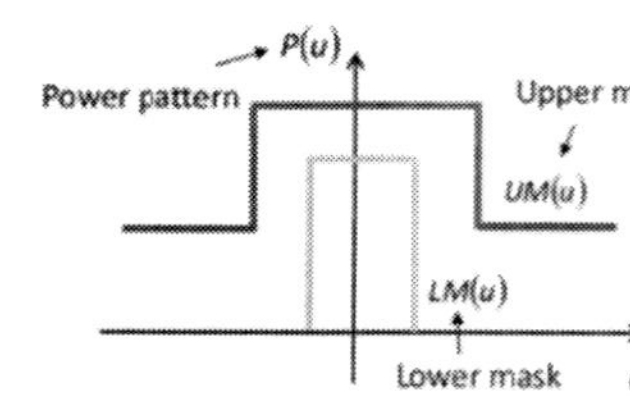

Parameters Setting

- Number of array elements and positions
- Amplitude values and expected errors
- Phase values and expected errors

Sensitivity Array Analysis

- Pattern generation
- Pattern features evaluation
- Tolerance analysis

Fitting?

© 2017 - ELEDIA Research Center

88

Robust Array Synthesis Problem

Requirements

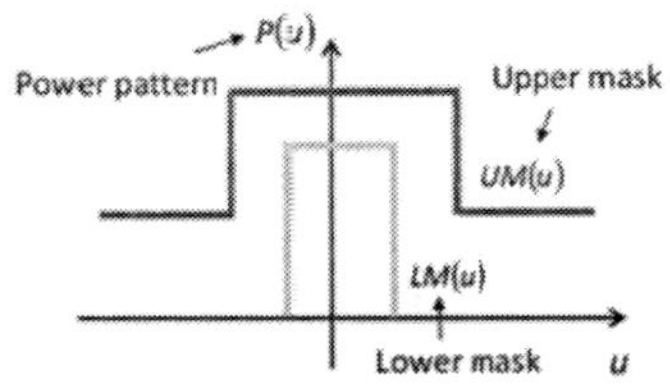

Parameters Setting

- Number of array elements and positions
- Amplitude values and expected errors
- Phase values and expected errors

Sensitivity Array Analysis

Interval Analysis

Fitting?

IA for Robust Array Synthesis

Requirements

Power pattern mask

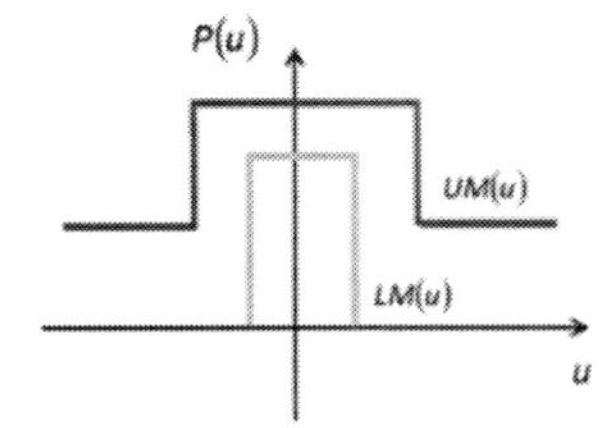

Control Point Tolerances

Amplifier response

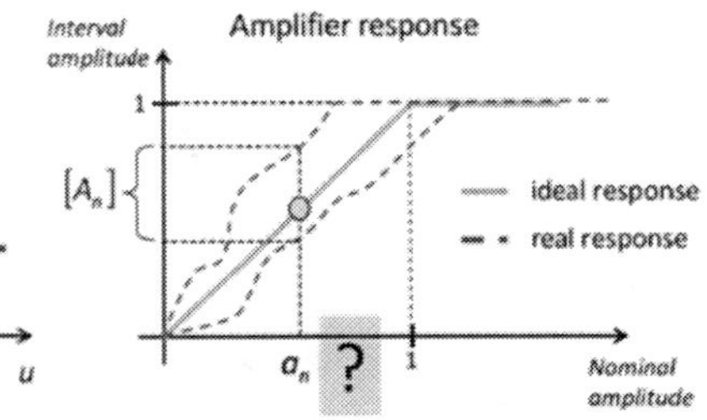

Objective

Given the control point tolerances, determine the values of the nominal amplitude coefficients a_n, $n=1,\ldots,N$ such that the interval power pattern computed with IA lays within the masks

IA for Robust Array Synthesis

Key advantage:

IA allows to **analytically** compute the **upper/lower bounds** of $[P(u)]$ for given $[A_n]$, $n=1,\ldots,N$

Enabled the use of optimization strategies to define the values of the nominal amplitude coefficients a_n, $n=1,\ldots,N$

Classical mask-constrained synthesis problem cast as:

INTERVAL Mask Constrained Power Synthesis

IA Mask Constrained Power Synthesis

Classical Approach

- Nominal excitations
- Nominal pattern must lay within the masks

IA-based Approach

- **Interval excitations**
- **Interval power pattern** must lay within the masks

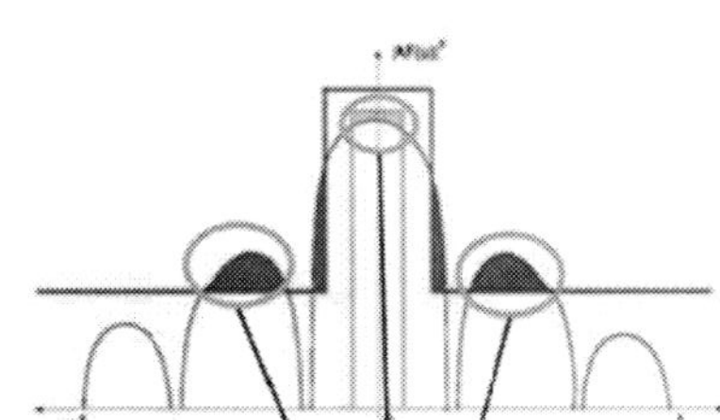

Nominal pattern above/below the upper/lower mask

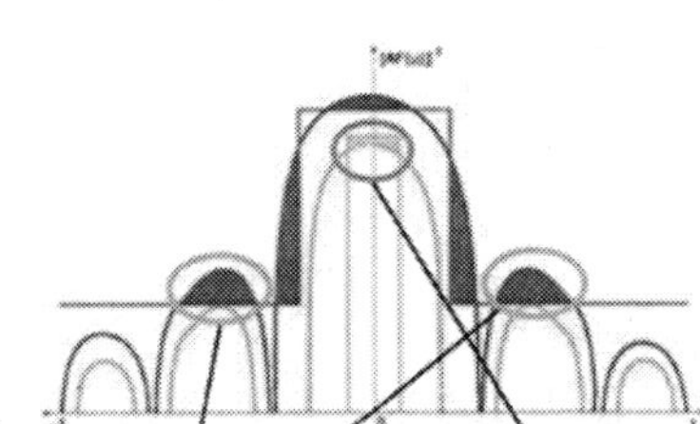

Upper pattern bound above the upper mask

Lower pattern bound below the lower mask

Problem Formulation

Cost Function

$$\Phi = \Phi_{inf} + \Phi_{sup}$$

$$\Phi_{inf} = \int_{-1}^{1} [LM(u) - \inf\{[P(u)]\}] H(LM(u) - \inf\{[P(u)]\})\, du$$

How much the lower pattern bound is below the lower mask

$$\Phi_{sup} = \int_{-1}^{1} [\sup\{[P(u)]\} - UM(u)] H(\sup\{[P(u)]\} - UM(u))\, du$$

How much the upper pattern bound is above the upper mask

Heaviside step function $H(x) = \begin{cases} 1 & if\ x \geq 0 \\ 0 & if\ x < 0 \end{cases}$ ← *constraint is satisfied!*

Observations:

- The cost function is multi-minima
- The unknown coefficient are real/continuous values
- The unknowns defines a high (N) dimensional space

→ Use of Particle Swam Optimization

Stochastic global optimizer

Numerical Results – Error Behavior

"Interval" excitations

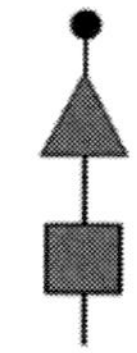

$[A_n] = [a_n - \varepsilon_n^{inf}; a_n + \varepsilon_n^{sup}]$

φ_n

$n = 1, \ldots, N$

Amplifier response

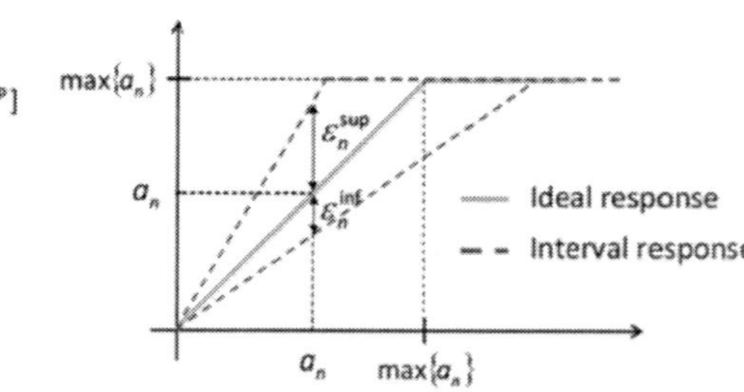

Amplitude errors are expressed as percentage of the nominal amplitude values

$$\varepsilon_n^{sup} = \begin{cases} a_n \chi_n & \varepsilon_n^{sup} < \max\{a_n\} \\ \max\{a_n\} & \varepsilon_n^{sup} \geq \max\{a_n\} \end{cases}$$ Saturation effect

$\varepsilon_n^{inf} = a_n \chi_n$

$n = 1, \ldots, N$

$\chi_n\%$ ← Percentage error

Numerical Results – PSO Behavior

Array Parameters

$N = 10$

$d = \lambda/2$

$\chi_n = 1\%$ $n = 1, \ldots, N$

Mask Parameters

$BW_{UM} = 0.46[u]$

$BW_{LM} = 0.23[u]$

$SLL_{UM} = -20[dB]$

$\Gamma = 5[dB]$

PSO Parameters [*]

$S = N$

$\omega = 0.4$

$C_1 = C_2 = 2.0$

$K_{max} = 400$

$\phi_{th} = 10^{-5}$

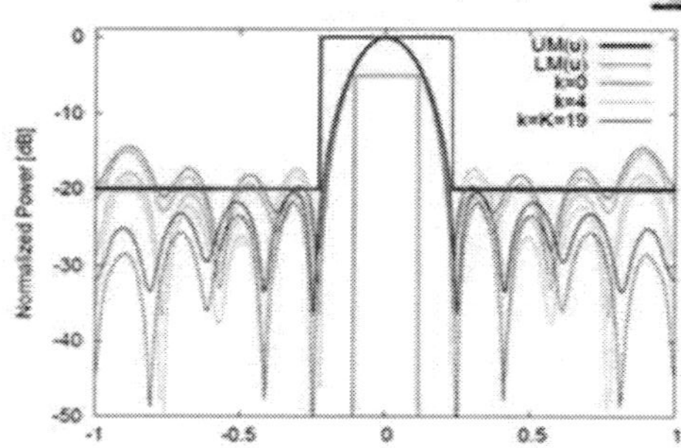

PSO iteratively converges to a solution satisfying the mask constraints

Φ	Φ_{inf}	Φ_{sup}	K_{end}
< 2x10^-20	< 10^-20	< 10^-20	19

Robust design!

[*] P. Rocca, M. Benedetti, M. Donelli, D. Franceschini, and A. Massa, "Evolutionary optimization as applied to inverse scattering problems," *Inverse Problems*, Invited Topical Review Paper, vol. 24, pp. 1-41, 2009.

Results – Robust Pencil-Beam Synthesis

Mask Parameters

$BW_{UM} = 0.22[u]$

$BW_{LM} = 0.10[u]$

$SLL_{UM} = -20[dB]$

$\Gamma = 5[dB]$

PSO Parameters [*]

$S = N$

$\omega = 0.4$

$C_1 = C_2 = 2.0$

$K_{max} = 400$

$\phi_{th} = 10^{-5}$

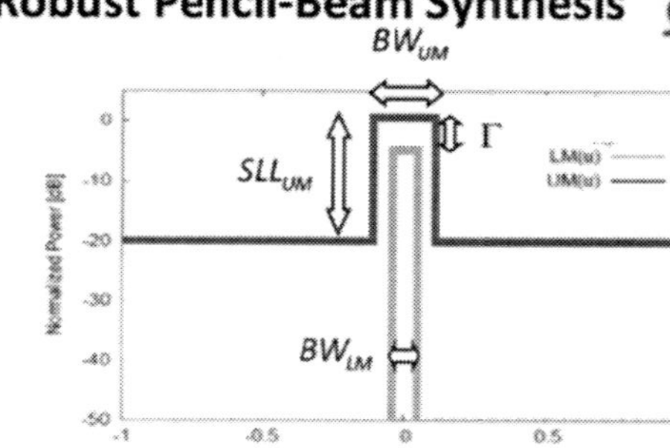

Objective

Design a robust uniform linear array with the most affordable architecture satisfying the mask constraints

Hypothesis

Three different kind of amplifiers:

- GOOD quality (χ_n=1%)
- MEDIUM quality (χ_n=5%)
- BAD quality (χ_n=8%)

COST

L. Manica, N. Anselmi, P. Rocca, and A. Massa, "Robust mask-constrained linear array synthesis through an interval-based Particle Swarm Optimization," *IET Microwaves, Antennas & Propagation*, vol. 7, no. 12, pp. 976-984, 2013.

Results – Robust Pencil-Beam Synthesis

(N=20, χ_n=5%)

Array Parameters

$N=20$

$d=\lambda/2$

$\chi_n=5\%$ $n=1,\ldots,N$

Mask Parameters

$BW_{UM}=0.22[u]$

$BW_{LM}=0.10[u]$

$SLL_{UM}=-20[dB]$

$\Gamma=5[dB]$

PSO Parameters

$S=20$

$\omega=0.4$

$C_1=C_2=2.0$

$K_{max}=400$

$\phi_{th}=10^{-5}$

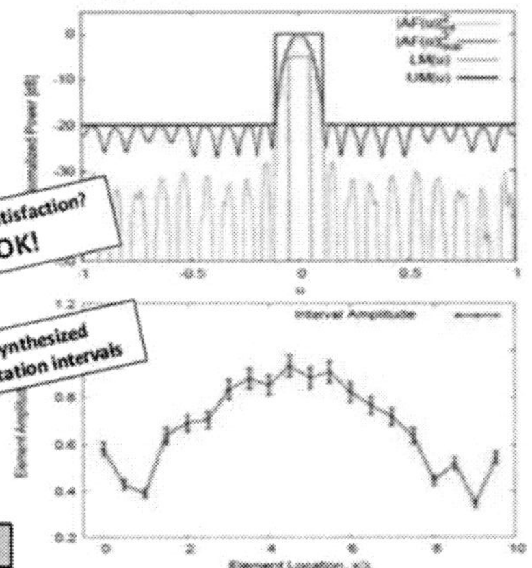

Φ	K_{end}
9.4x10^{-6}	320

Possible to simplify the antenna structure?

Results – Robust Pencil-Beam Synthesis

(N=18, χ_n=5%)

Array Parameters

$N=18$ ← 2 elements less

$d=\lambda/2$

$\chi_n=5\%$ $n=1,\ldots,N$

Mask Parameters

$BW_{UM}=0.22[u]$

$BW_{LM}=0.10[u]$

$SLL_{UM}=-20[dB]$

$\Gamma=5[dB]$

PSO Parameters

$S=18$

$\omega=0.4$

$C_1=C_2=2.0$

$K_{max}=400$

$\phi_{th}=10^{-5}$

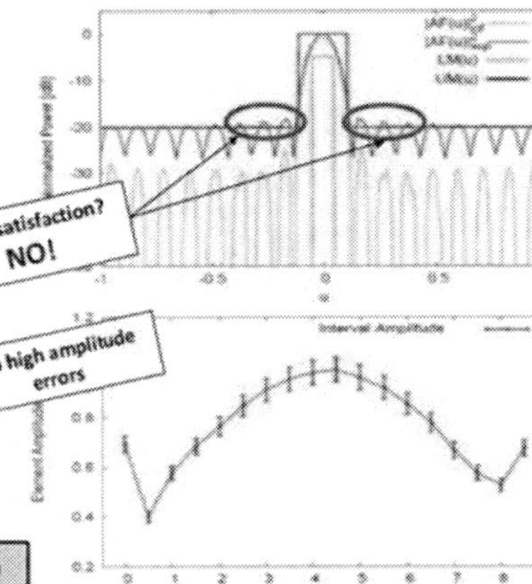

Φ	K_{end}
1.3x10^{-3}	400

With more robust amplifiers?

Results – Robust Pencil-Beam Synthesis

(N=18, χ_n=1%)

Array Parameters

$N=18$

$d=\lambda/2$

$\chi_n=1\%$ $n=1,\ldots,N$ ← Less errors

Mask Parameters

$BW_{UM}=0.22[u]$

$BW_{LM}=0.10[u]$

$SLL_{UM}=-20[dB]$

$\Gamma=5[dB]$

PSO Parameters

$S=18$

$\omega=0.4$

$C_1=C_2=2.0$

$K_{max}=400$

$\phi_{th}=10^{-5}$

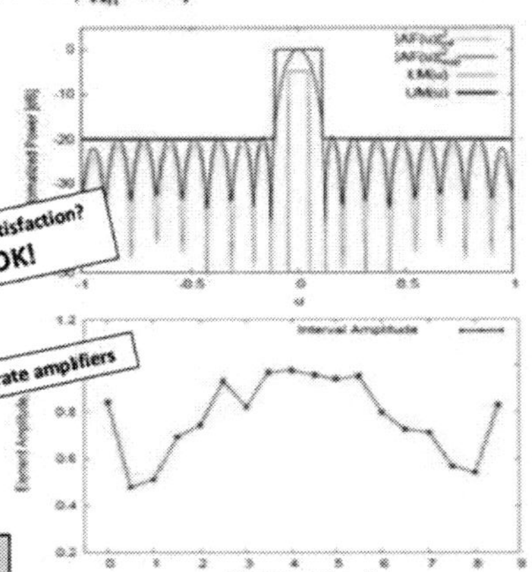

Φ	K_{end}
2.1x10^{-6}	275

Results – Trade-off Robust Designs

Array Parameters

$N=16,18,20,26$

$d=\lambda/2$

$\chi_n=1,5,8\%$ $n=1,\ldots,N$

Mask Parameters

$BW_{UM}=0.22[u]$

$BW_{LM}=0.10[u]$

$SLL_{UM}=-20[dB]$

$\Gamma=5[dB]$

PSO Parameters

$S=N$

$\omega=0.4$

$C_1=C_2=2.0$

$K_{max}=400$

$\phi_{th}=10^{-5}$

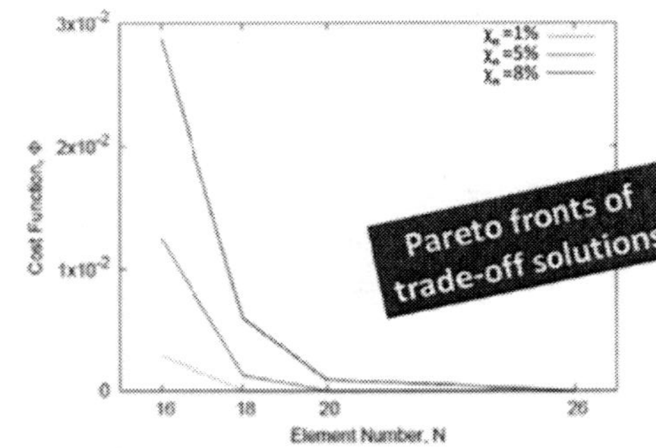

Values of at Φ convergence

χ_n	N=16	N=18	N=20	N=26
1%	2.8x10^{-3}	2.1x10^{-6}	< 10^{-20}	< 10^{-20}
5%	1.2x10^{-2}	1.3x10^{-3}	9.4x10^{-6}	9.9x10^{-19}
8%	2.8x10^{-2}	5.9x10^{-3}	8.9x10^{-4}	7.1x10^{-18}

3.3 Inverse Scattering Problem – What?

Objectives

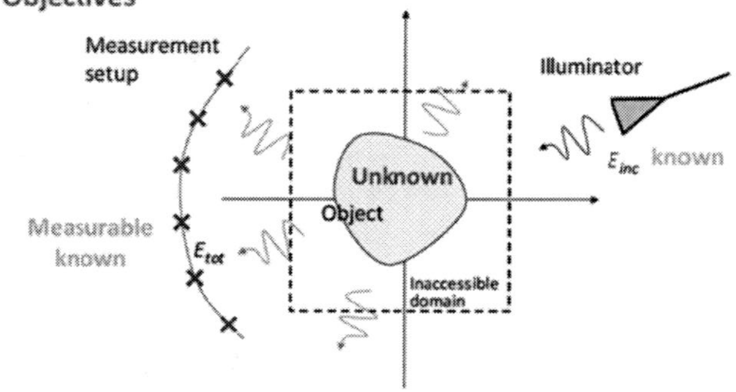

Inverse scattering problems are aimed at reconstructing the electrical properties of unknown objects embedded in an inaccessible domain probed by a known incident field from the measured field data

Inverse Scattering Problem – How?

In the real world, quantities are known within a certain degree of accuracy

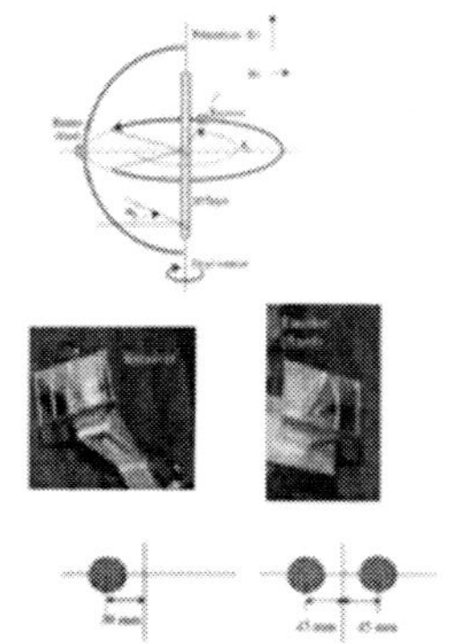

K. Belkebir and M. Saillard, "Special section: Testing inversion algorithms against experimental data," *Inverse Problems*, vol. 17, pp. 1565–1571, 2001

Sensors Locations:

$(x_{m(v)} \pm \delta x_{m(v)}, y_{m(v)} \pm \delta y_{m(v)})$

Possible position errors

Field Measurements:

$E^v_{scatt}(x_{m(v)}, y_{m(v)}) \pm \delta E^v_{scatt}(x_{m(v)}, y_{m(v)})$

Quantization errors, Frequency shifts, etc.

Actual Permittivity:

$\varepsilon_r \pm \delta \varepsilon_r$

Difficulty of knowing the exact contrast

Inverse Scattering Problem – How?

Classical IS Problem Goal:

Given the continuous data $E^v_{scatt}(x_{m(v)}, y_{m(v)})$

determine the actual contrast $\tau(x,y)$

Re-Defined IS Problem Goal:

Given the measured data $E^v_{scatt}(x_{m(v)}, y_{m(v)}) \pm \delta E^v_{scatt}(x_{m(v)}, y_{m(v)})$

determine the solution interval $[\tau(x,y)]$ containing the actual contrast $\tau(x,y) \in [\tau(x,y)]$

Inverse Scattering Problem – How?

REAL/ACTUAL world | MEASURABLE world

Data

REAL/ACTUAL world: $E^v_{scatt}(x_{m(v)}, y_{m(v)}) \quad (x_{m(v)}, y_{m(v)}) \in D_O \quad m(v) = 1, \ldots, M(v)$

MEASURABLE world: $[E^v_{scatt}(x_{m(v)}, y_{m(v)})] \quad (x_{m(v)}, y_{m(v)}) \in D_O \quad m(v) = 1, \ldots, M(v)$

Unknowns

REAL/ACTUAL world: $\tau(x,y) = \varepsilon_r(x,y) - 1 - j\frac{\sigma(x,y)}{2\pi f \varepsilon_0} \quad (x,y) \in D_I$; $E^v_{tot}(x,y) \quad (x,y) \in D_I$

MEASURABLE world: $[\tau(x,y)] \quad (x,y) \in D_I$; $[E^v_{tot}(x,y)] \quad (x,y) \in D_I$

Problem Formulation

REAL/ACTUAL world:

$$E^v_{scatt}(x_{m(v)}, y_{m(v)}) = \iint_{D_I} \tau(x',y') E^v_{tot}(x',y') G(x_{m(v)}, y_{m(v)} / x', y') dx' dy'$$

MEASURABLE world:

$$[E^v_{scatt}(x_{m(v)}, y_{m(v)})] = \iint_{D_I} [\tau(x',y')] [E^v_{tot}(x',y')] G(x_{m(v)}, y_{m(v)} / x', y') dx' dy'$$

Problem Solution

REAL/ACTUAL world:

$$\Phi(\underline{\tau}) = \frac{\sum_{v=1}^{V} \sum_{m=1}^{M} \left| E^{v,act}_{scatt,m} - E^{v,rec}_{scatt,m}(\underline{\tau}) \right|^2}{\sum_{v=1}^{V} \sum_{m=1}^{M} \left| E^{v,act}_{scatt,m} \right|^2}$$

MEASURABLE world:

$$\Phi(\underline{\tau}) = \frac{\sum_{v=1}^{V} \sum_{m=1}^{M} \left| [E^{v,act}_{scatt,m}] - [E^{v,rec}_{scatt,m}([\underline{\tau}])] \right|^2}{\sum_{v=1}^{V} \sum_{m=1}^{M} \left| [E^{v,act}_{scatt,m}] \right|^2}$$

How to minimize?

IA-based IS TM-2D Problem Solution

Cost function DATA TERM:

$$\Phi(\underline{\tau}) = \frac{\sum_{v=1}^{V}\sum_{m=1}^{M}\left|E_{scatt,m}^{v,act} - E_{scatt,m}^{v,rec}(\underline{\tau})\right|^2}{\sum_{v=1}^{V}\sum_{m=1}^{M}\left|E_{scatt,m}^{v,act}\right|^2}$$

Classical Approach

⇩

Reconstructed *INTERVAL* for the scattered field

$$[\Phi([\underline{\tau}])] = \frac{\sum_{v=1}^{V}\sum_{m=1}^{M}\left|[E_{scatt,m}^{v,act}] - [E_{scatt,m}^{v,rec}([\underline{\tau}])]\right|^2}{\sum_{v=1}^{V}\sum_{m=1}^{M}\left|[E_{scatt,m}^{v,act}]\right|^2}$$

IA-based Approach

Unknown *INTERVAL* object function

INTERVAL of the measured field data

How to minimize?

IA for Functional Minimization

The Branch and Bound Algorithm

Initialization (Iteration k=0): Set of the admissible values for the object function $[\underline{\tau}]^{(0)}$

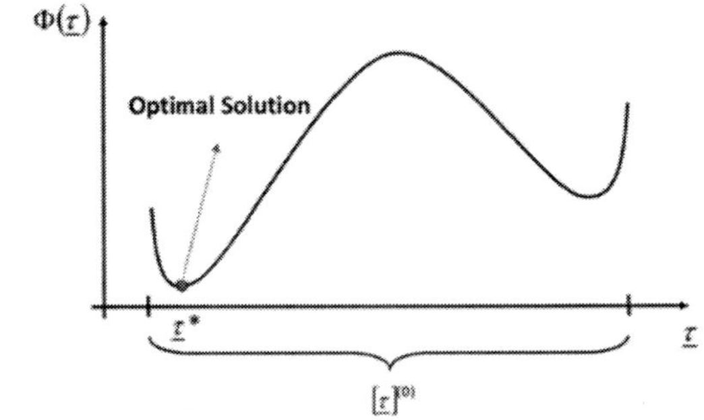

IA for Functional Minimization

The Branch and Bound Algorithm

First Iteration (k=1): Split the interval of the unknowns and check if possible to delete a sub-interval

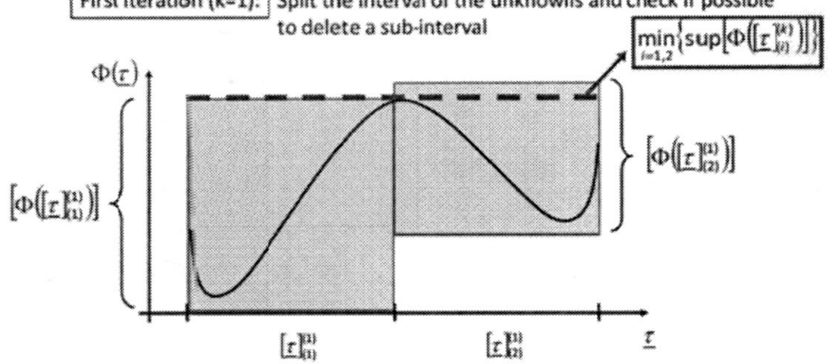

Interval Elimination Condition:

If $\inf[\Phi([\underline{\tau}]_{(i)}^{(k)})] > \min_{i=1,2}\{\sup[\Phi([\underline{\tau}]_{(i)}^{(k)})]\}$ ⟹ delete $[\Phi([\underline{\tau}]_{(i)}^{(k)})]$

IA for Functional Minimization

The Branch and Bound Algorithm

Iteration k=2

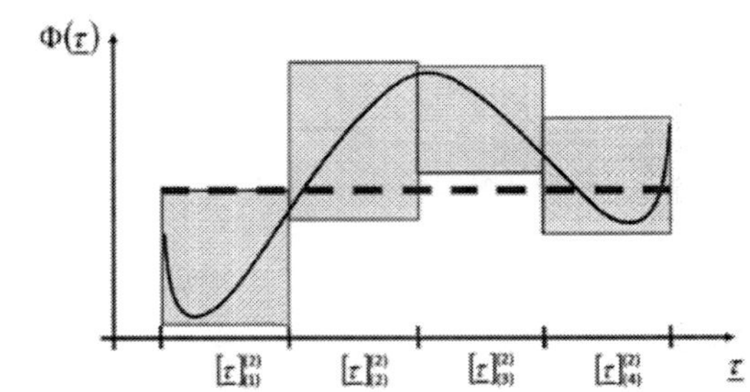

$$\inf[\Phi([\underline{\tau}]_{(3)}^{(2)})] > \min_{i=1,2,3,4}\{\sup[\Phi([\underline{\tau}]_{(i)}^{(2)})]\}$$

IA for Functional Minimization

The Branch and Bound Algorithm

Iteration k=2

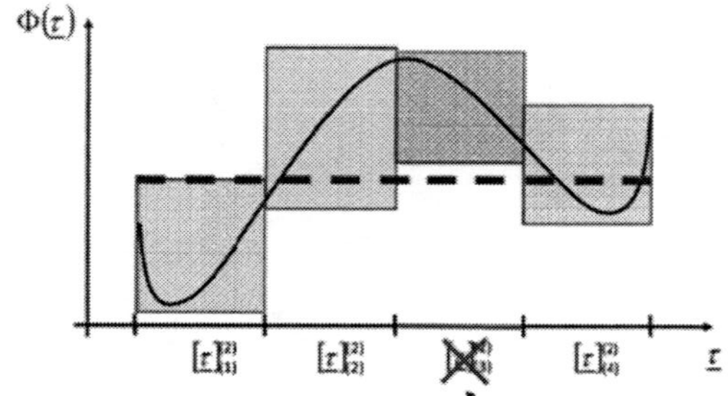

Convergence Criterion

The algorithm is stopped when a sufficient resolution for the intervals of the unknowns is achieved

Iteration k=K

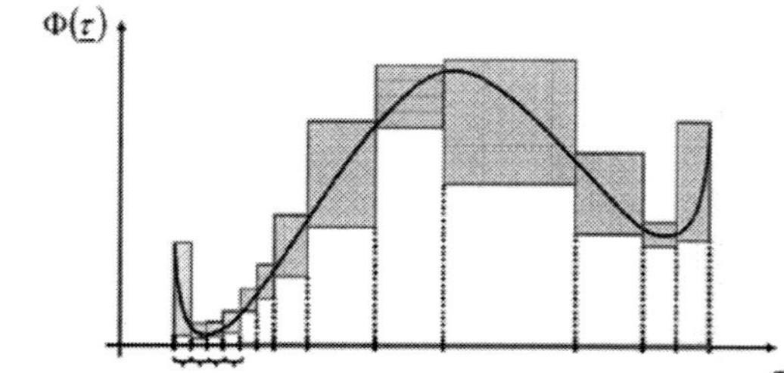

Optimal Interval Selection:

$$[\underline{\tau}]^{*} = \min_{i}\left\{\inf\left[\Phi\left([\underline{\tau}]_{(i)}^{(k=K)}\right)\right]\right\}$$

Interval Based Optimization

- Retrieval of the global optimum with **desired level of accuracy**
- Computational burden **grows exponentially** with the number of unknowns (2^N)

⇩

Almost **impracticable** for reconstruction of domain discretized with a limited number of cells/pixels (N)

HOW TO OVERCOME SUCH DRAWBACK?

Model Based Representation

Pixel Based Representation | Model Based Representation

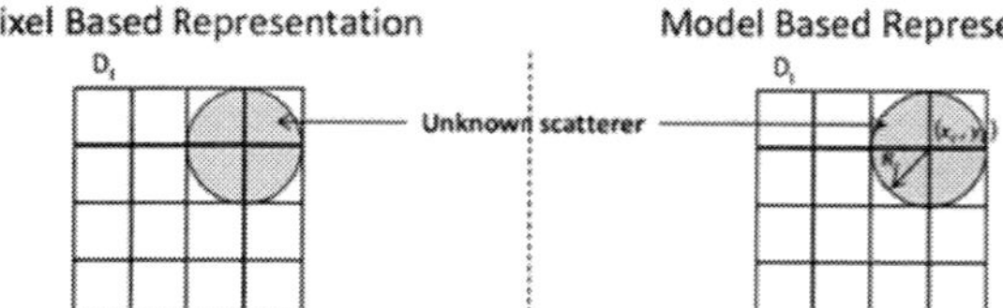

Scatterer Descriptors

Pixel Based: Value of τ_n defined for each of the N-cells

Model Based:

(x_c, y_c): center of the scatterer
R_c: radius of the scatterer
τ_c: object function of the scatterer

$$\tau_n = \begin{cases} \tau_c & if\ (x_c - x_n)^2 + (y_c - y_n)^2 \le R_c^2 \\ 0.0 & if\ (x_c - x_n)^2 + (y_c - y_n)^2 \le R_c^2 \end{cases}$$

Advantages and Drawbacks

Pixel Based: N unknowns ↓; No "a priori" knowledge needed ↑

Model Based: 4 unknowns ↑; "A priori" knowledge needed ↓

Numerical Example

Hypothesis: Unknown object is a homogeneous lossless circular cylinder

Unknown parameters (*Model-base representation*):

$$\underline{P}^* = \{x^*, y^*, R^*, \tau^*\}$$

Barycenter coordinates — Radius — Object function

$\underline{\tau}(\underline{P})$ ⟶ Single Solution ⟶

$\underline{P} = \{x, y, R, \tau\}$

Classical Approach

$[\underline{\tau}([\underline{P}])]$ ⟶ Interval of Solutions ⟶

$[\underline{P}] = \{[x],[y],[R],[\tau]\}$

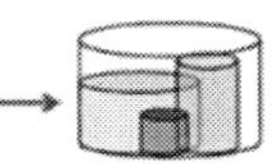

IA-based Approach

Solution Evolution

True Scatterer

Radius : $R_c^* = 0.25\lambda$

Center : $(x_c^*, y_c^*) = (-0.5, -0.5)\lambda$

Object Function : $\tau_c^* = 0.1$

$N = 1024$
$M = 7$
$V = 7$

Error Indexes

k	ξ_{tot}	ξ_{int}	ξ_{ext}
1	1.78×10^{-2}	4.55×10^{-2}	1.63×10^{-2}
3	3.38×10^{-3}	5.34×10^{-2}	7.29×10^{-4}
5	3.11×10^{-3}	6.18×10^{-2}	0.0
7	2.50×10^{-3}	2.27×10^{-2}	1.43×10^{-3}
19	4.41×10^{-4}	3.35×10^{-3}	2.77×10^{-4}

Mid-point of best Interval at Iteration k-th

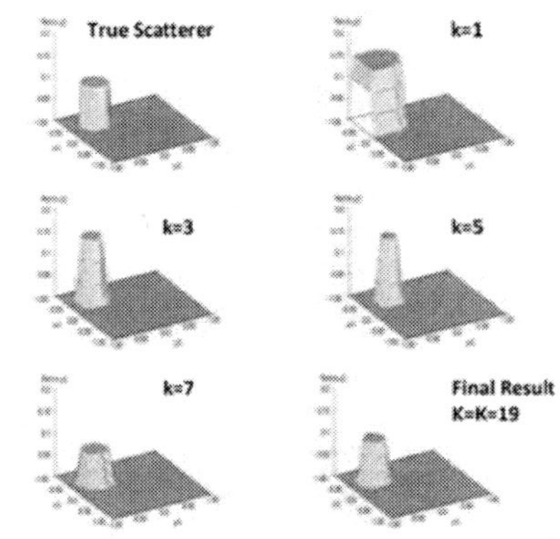

Barycenter Evolution

True Scatterer

Radius : $R_c^* = 0.25\lambda$

Center : $(x_c^*, y_c^*) = (-0.5, -0.5)\lambda$

Object Function : $\tau_c^* = 0.1$

$N = 1024$
$M = 7$
$V = 7$

$[\underline{P}] = \left([x_c]^{(k)}, [y_c]^{(k)}\right)$

Area covered by intervals

$\left([x_c]^{(k)}, [y_c]^{(k)}\right)$

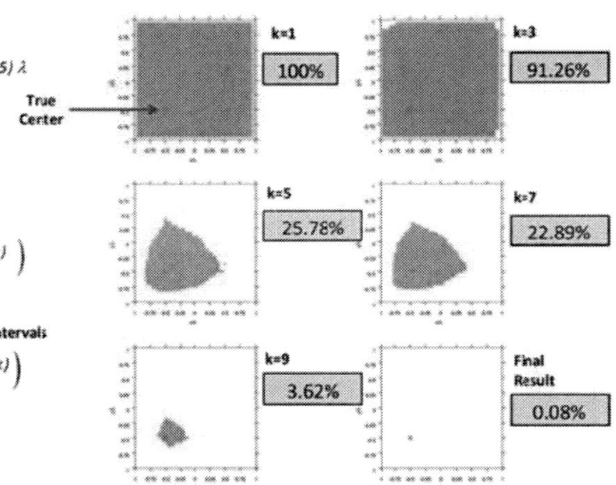

Support Evolution

True Scatterer

Radius : $R_c^* = 0.25\lambda$

Center : $(x_c^*, y_c^*) = (-0.5, -0.5)\lambda$

Object Function : $\tau_c^* = 0.1$

$N = 1024$
$M = 7$
$V = 7$

$[\underline{P}] = \left([x_c]^{(k)}, [y_c]^{(k)}, [R_c]^{(k)}\right)$

Area covered by intervals

$\left([x_c]^{(k)}, [y_c]^{(k)}, [R_c]^{(k)}\right)$

"True" value = 7.50%

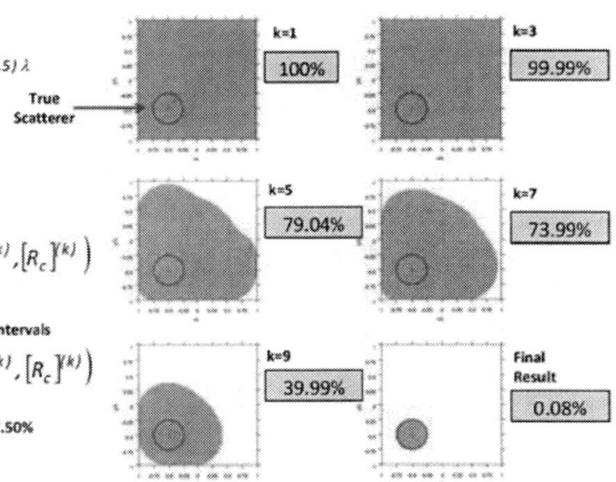

Object Function Evolution

True Scatterer

Radius : $R_c^* = 0.25\lambda$

Center : $(x_c^*, y_c^*) = (-0.5, -0.5)\lambda$

Object Function : $\tau_c^* = 0.1$

$N = 1024$

$M = 7$

$V = 7$

$$[\underline{P}] = \left([x_c]^{(k)}, [y_c]^{(k)}, [R_c]^{(k)}, [\tau_c]^{(k)} \right)$$

Minimum, Maximal and True value of

$\tau(x,y)\big|_{x=-0.5}$ $\tau(x,y)\big|_{y=-0.5}$

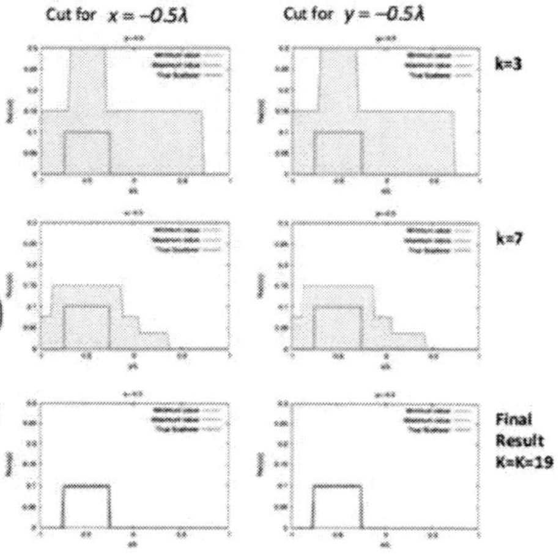

Analysis vs Noise

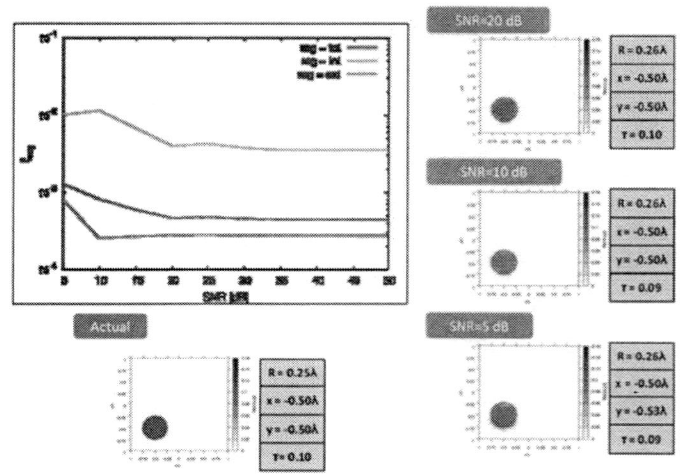

Robustness to Noise!

Conclusions

- IA Motivations (*Uncertainty*)
- IA in a Nutshell
- IA at Work
  - Sensitivity Analysis
  - Robust Design
  - Functional Optimization

Thank you for your attention!

ELEDIA Journal Publications on IA

1. P. Rocca, L. Manica, N. Anselmi, and A. Massa, "Analysis of the pattern tolerances in linear arrays with arbitrary amplitude errors," *IEEE Antennas and Wireless Propagation Letters*, vol. 12, pp. 639-642, 2013. doi: 10.1109/LAWP.2013.2261912
2. L. Manica, N. Anselmi, P. Rocca, and A. Massa, "Robust mask-constrained linear array synthesis through an interval-based Particle Swarm Optimization," *IET Microwaves, Antennas & Propagation*, vol. 7, no. 12, pp. 976-984, 2013. doi: 10.1049/iet-map.2013.0203
3. N. Anselmi, L. Manica, P. Rocca, and A. Massa, "Tolerance analysis of antenna arrays through interval arithmetic," *IEEE Transactions on Antennas and Propagation*, vol. 61, no. 11, pp. 5496-5507, November 2013. doi: 10.1109/TAP.2013.2276927
4. P. Rocca, M. Carlin, L. Manica, and A. Massa, "Microwave imaging within the interval analysis framework," *Progress in Electromagnetic Research*, vol. 143, pp. 675-708, 2013. doi: 10.2528/PIER13080304
5. P. Rocca, N. Anselmi, and A. Massa, "Optimal synthesis of robust beamformer weights exploiting interval analysis and convex optimization," *IEEE Transactions on Antennas and Propagation*, vol. 62, no. 7, pp. 3603-3612, July 2014. doi: 10.1109/TAP.2014.2318071
6. P. Rocca, L. Manica, and A. Massa, "Interval-based analysis of pattern distortions in reflector antennas with bump-like surface deformations," *IET Microwaves, Antennas & Propagation*, vol. 8, no. 15, pp. 1277-1285, 2014. doi: 10.1049/iet-map.2014.0162
7. P. Rocca, A. Anselmi, and A. Massa, "Interval arithmetic for pattern tolerance analysis of parabolic reflectors," *IEEE Transactions on Antennas and Propagation*, vol. 62, no. 10, pp. 4952-4960, October 2014. doi: 10.1109/TAP.2014.234275
8. L. Poli, P. Rocca, N. Anselmi, and A. Massa, "Dealing with uncertainties on phase weighting of linear antenna arrays by means of interval-based tolerance analysis," *IEEE Transactions on Antennas and Propagation*, vol. 63, no. 7, pp. 3229-3234, July 2015. doi: 10.1109/TAP.2015.2421952
9. N. Anselmi, P. Rocca, M. Salucci, and A. Massa, "Optimization of excitation tolerances for robust beamforming in linear arrays," *IET Microwaves, Antennas & Propagation*, vol. 10, no. 2, pp. 208-214, 2016. doi: 10.1049/iet-map.2015.0508
10. N. Anselmi, M. Salucci, P. Rocca, and A. Massa, "Generalized interval-based analysis tool for pattern distortions in reflector antennas with bump-like surface deformations," *IET Microwaves, Antennas & Propagation*, vol. 10, no. 9, pp. 909-916, 2016. doi: 10.1049/iet-map.2015.0583
11. P. Rocca, L. Poli, N. Anselmi, M. Salucci, and A. Massa, "Predicting antenna pattern degradations in microstrip reflectarrays through interval arithmetic," *IET Microwaves, Antennas & Propagation*, vol. 10, no. 8, pp. 817-826, 2016. doi: 10.1049/iet-map.2015.0837
12. N. Anselmi, P. Rocca, M. Salucci, and A. Massa, "Power pattern sensitivity to calibration errors and mutual coupling in linear arrays through circular interval arithmetics," *Sensors*, vol. 16, no. 6(791), pp. 1-14, 2016. doi: 10.3390/s16060791
13. L. Tenuti, N. Anselmi, P. Rocca, M. Salucci, and A. Massa, "Minkowski sum method for planar arrays sensitivity analysis with uncertain-but-bounded excitation tolerances," *IEEE Transactions on Antennas and Propagation*, vol. 65, no. 1, pp. 167-177, January 2017. doi: 10.1109/TAP.2016.2627548

The Applied Computational Electromagnetics Society (ACES)
www.aces-society.org

ISBN 978-1-5108-4285-4

9 781510 842854

CURRAN ASSOCIATES INC.
proceedings.com